The ETS Test Collection Catalog

Volume 1: Achievement Tests and Measurement Devices
Second Edition

Compiled by Test Collection,
Educational Testing Service

Table of Contents

ORYX PRESS
1993

The rare Arabian Oryx is believed to have inspired the myth of the unicorn. This desert antelope became virtually extinct in the early 1960s. At that time several groups of international conservationists arranged to have 9 animals sent to the Phoenix Zoo to be the nucleus of a captive breeding herd. Today the Oryx population is 800, and nearly 600 have been returned to reserves in the Middle East.

Copyright © 1993 by Educational Testing Service
Published by The Oryx Press
4041 North Central at Indian School Road
Phoenix, Arizona 85012-3397

Published simultaneously in Canada

Printed and Bound in the United States of America

∞ The paper used in this publication meets the minimum requirements of American National Standard for Information Science—Permanence of Paper for Printed Library Materials, ANSI Z39.48, 1984.

Library of Congress Cataloging-in-Publication Data
The ETS Test Collection catalog / compiled by Test Collection,
    Educational Testing Service. — 2nd ed.
        p.   cm.
    Includes indexes.
    Contents: v. 1. Achievement tests and measurement devices
    ISBN 0-89774-743-7 (v. 1: alk. paper)
    1. Educational tests and measurements—United States—Catalogs.
2. Achievement tests—United States—Catalogs.   3. Occupational
aptitude tests—United States—Catalogs.   4. Educational Testing
Service—Catalogs.   I. Educational Testing Service. Test
Collection.
LB3051.E79 1992   92-36992
016.3712'6—dc20   CIP

INTRODUCTION

The Test Collection, Educational Testing Service, is an extensive library of approximately 18,000 tests and other measurement devices. It was established to provide information on tests and assessment materials to those in research, advisory services, education, counseling, business, and other activities. As part of its function, the Test Collection acquires and disseminates information on hard-to-locate research instruments as well as on commercially available, standardized tests. Because the Test Collection deals only with tests and evaluation tools, it has been able to provide a reasonable amount of bibliographic control over what has historically been a scattering of information among many and diverse sources.

This catalog is a revision of *Volume 1: Achievement Tests and Measurement Devices*. Entries for tests that are no longer available have been removed, and descriptions of recently published achievement tests and research instruments have been added. There are approximately 2,000 test descriptions covering all age and grade levels. The information has been drawn from the Test Collection's computer-retrievable database and covers a variety of tests, including achievement, equivalency, screening, diagnostic, school readiness, reading readiness, and item banks. Certification tests, although assessing knowledge, are used in a vocational context and have therefore been omitted from this revised volume. A list of certification tests can be found in *The ETS Test Collection Catalog, Volume 2: Vocational Tests and Measurement Devices*. Other volumes in *The ETS Test Collection Catalog* series include *Volume 3: Tests for Special Populations; Volume 4: Cognitive Aptitude and Intelligence Tests; Volume 5: Attitude Tests;* and *Volume 6: Affective Measures and Personality Tests.*

Achievement tests are used to assess what an individual knows. They may be test batteries that cover the basic skills, end-of-course tests, or pre- and posttests used to assess individuals' gain in knowledge over a certain time span and/or as a result of taking a particular course.

Equivalency tests measure what an individual knows based on previous schooling, self-acquired knowledge, or experience. The tests may be used for such purposes as granting credit by examination or for granting advanced standing or placement in an educational program.

Screening tests are used to identify individuals who may have some difficulty in the area being assessed. These individuals can then be referred for further diagnosis and/or instruction.

Diagnostic tests pick up where screening tests leave off. Diagnostic tests are used to analyze the weaknesses indicated by the screening tests so that specific remedial steps can be taken to correct the individual's problems. The diagnostic tests described in this catalog deal with subject-oriented skills and knowledge and do not include tests for special populations, such as physically or mentally handicapped individuals.

School readiness and reading readiness tests are used with preschool and/or kindergarten children to assess those skills that are deemed necessary for a successful school experience.

Item banks are compilations of test items from which test administrators can select particular items to construct tests for their own purposes.

For each entry in the Main Entry Section of this directory, the following information is always present: test title, author, descriptors and/or identifiers (subject indexing terms), availability source, age or grade level, and an abstract. Other information, which is provided when available, includes publication or copyright date, subtests, number of test items, and the time required for an individual to complete the test. The test descriptions are arranged sequentially by the Test Collection's identification number in the Main Entry Section.

There are three indexes that provide access to the Main Entry Section: Subject, Author, and Title. The Subject Index uses Educational Resources Information Center (ERIC) descriptor terms from the *Thesaurus of ERIC Descriptors, 12th Edition*. Each test title and its unique identification number is listed under the major descriptors assigned to it, so that there are several subject access points. In addition, some tests may be indexed under major identifiers, which are uncontrolled subject indexing terms that help in describing the content of the tests. Identifiers are listed in the *ERIC Identifier Authority List (IAL) 1992*. In the Author Index, tests and their corresponding identification numbers are listed under the author's name. The Title Index is an alphabetical list of all tests included in the directory and their identification numbers.

Some of the tests referred to in the abstracts are listed in this volume. Check the Title Index to locate these tests. For information about tests not included in this catalog, contact Test Collection at Educational Testing Service.

At the time the test catalog was compiled, all the tests included were still available from the test distributors indicated in the availability source. However, distribution of certain tests may be discontinued by test publishers or distributors and new tests developed and published.

The staff of the Test Collection will be happy to answer any questions about this catalog or other products and services. Inquiries may be addressed to Test Collection, Educational Testing Service, Princeton, NJ 08541.

LIST OF TEST TITLE ACRONYMS

AAHPERD	American Alliance for Health, Physical Recreation, and Dance	**DANTES**	Defense Activity for Non-Traditional Education Support
AAPT/NSTA	American Association of Physics Teachers/National Science Teachers Association	**DIAL—R**	Development Indicators for the Assessment of Learning—Revised
ACER	Australian Council for Education Research	**EDS**	Educational Diagnostic Services
ACS	American Chemical Society	**ERB**	Educational Records Bureau
ACS/NSTA	American Chemical Society/National Science Teachers Association	**ESL**	English as a Second Language
		IEA	International Association for the Evaluation of Educational Achievement
ACT	American College Testing Program	**IER**	Institute for Educational Research
AGI/NSTA	American Geological Institute/National Science Teachers Association	**MAA**	Mathematical Association of America
		NABT/NSTA	National Association of Biology Teachers/National Science Teachers Association
AGS	American Guidance Service	**ORBIT**	Objectives Referenced Bank of Items and Tests
ATP	Admissions Testing Program		
BCD	Baltimore County Design		
CAT	California Achievement Tests	**PSB**	Psychological Services Bureau
CLEP	College-Level Examination Program	**R-B**	Roberts-Bloom
CTBS	Comprehensive Test of Basic Skills	**S-ESL**	Standard English as a Second Language
CUBE	Continuity and Unity in Basic Education	**SRA**	Science Research Associates
		STS	Scholastic Testing Services

SAMPLE ENTRY

ETS ACCESSION NO.

17209
Woodcock-Johnson Psycho-Educational Battery, Revised—Tests of Achievement, Standard Battery and Supplemental Battery. Woodcock Richard W.; Johnson, W. Bonner 1990

TEST TITLE

INSTITUTIONAL AND/OR PERSONAL AUTHOR(S)

TEST PUBLICATION DATE

SUBTESTS — *Subtests*: Standard: Letter Word Identification, Passage Comprehension, Calculation, Applied Problems, Dictation, Writing Samples, Science, Social Studies, Humanities; Supplemental: Word Attack, Reading Vocabulary, Quantitative Concepts, Proofing, Writing Fluency, Punctuation and Capitalization, Spelling, Usage, Handwriting

DESCRIPTORS (* = Indexed Subject Terms) — *Descriptors*: *Academic Achievement; *Achievement Tests; Adults; College Students; Elementary School Students; Elementary Secondary Education; High School Students; *Knowledge Level; *Mathematics Achievement; Older Adults; Postsecondary Education; Preschool Children; Preschool Education; *Reading Ability; *Standardized Tests; *Written Language

Identifiers: WJR

IDENTIFIERS (* = Indexed Subject Terms)

TEST AVAILABLE FROM — *Availability*: DLM Teaching Resources; One DLM Park, Allen, TX 75002-1302

Age Level: 2-90

GRADE LEVEL AND/OR AGE LEVEL

TIME TO TAKE TEST AND/OR NO. OF TEST ITEMS — *Notes*: Time, 50 min. approx.

ABSTRACT — Woodcock-Johnson-Revised is a battery of standardized tests measuring cognitive abilities, scholastic aptitudes, and achievement. Cognitive and achievement batteries are each organized in standard and supplemental test books. The standard batteries provide in-depth testing when more information is desired. Covers age range 2-90. Common norms are provided for cognitive and achievement batteries along with derived scores and profiles. With this revision, 10 new tests have been added to the cognitive abilities battery and 4 new ests to the achievement battery. The achievement battery now has alternate forms: A and B. The achievement standard battery consists of 9 tests. The supplemental battery also has 9 tests. Both batteries can be used to assess 4 curricular areas: reading, mathematics, written language, and knowledge.

MAIN ENTRY SECTION

19
Technical and Scholastic Test. Dailey, John T. 1964
Subtests: Technical; Scholastic
Descriptors: *Achievement Tests; *Adults; Career Guidance; Occupational Tests; Postsecondary Education; Secondary Education; *Secondary School Students; *Technical Occupations
Identifiers: *Dailey Vocational Tests; TST
Availability: The Riverside Publishing Co.; 8420 Bryn Mawr Ave., Chicago, IL 60631
Age Level: 13-64
Notes: Time, 65 min.; Items, 150

Designed to assess technical knowledge acquired through experience with electrical and mechanical equipment, academic knowledge of physical sciences, and general scholastic ability. Technical scale measures electricity, electronics, mechanical information, and physical sciences. Scholastic scale measures arithmetic reasoning, elementary algebra, and vocabulary.

20
Electrical Sophistication Test. Ciesla, Stanley 1963
Descriptors: *Achievement Tests; *Adults; *Career Counseling; Electrical Occupations; *Electricity; Higher Education; High Schools; *High School Students; Knowledge Level; Skilled Occupations; *Undergraduate Students; Vocational Aptitude
Availability: Psychometric Affiliates; P.O. Box 807, Murfreesboro, TN 37133
Grade Level: 9-16
Notes: Time, 10 min. approx.; Items, 14

Designed to discriminate between persons with substantial knowledge of electricity and those with very little or chance knowledge. Items emphasize practical electrical knowledge. May be used as a screening test or in vocational guidance.

69
Standardized Bible Content Tests. American Association of Bible Colleges, Fayetteville, AR 1980
Descriptors: *Achievement Tests; *Biblical Literature; *Church Related Colleges; Higher Education; Knowledge Level; Multiple Choice Tests; *Student Placement; *Undergraduate Students
Identifiers: SBCT
Availability: American Association of Bible Colleges; P.O. Box 1523, Fayetteville, AR 72702
Grade Level: 13-16
Notes: Time, 45 min.; Items, 150

Developed for use in Bible colleges to measure Bible knowledge of students. Forms A through F are available.

92
Brown-Carlsen Listening Comprehension Test. Brown, James I.; Carlsen, G. Robert 1955
Subtests: Immediate Recall; Following Directions; Recognizing Transitions; Recognizing Word Meanings; Lecture Comprehension
Descriptors: *College Freshmen; Higher Education; High Schools; *High School Students; Listening Comprehension; *Listening Comprehension Tests
Identifiers: Oral Testing
Availability: Communication Development, Inc.; 25 Robb Farm Rd., St. Paul, MN 55110
Grade Level: 9-13
Notes: Time, 50 min. approx.; Items, 76

Constructed to measure the ability of students to comprehend spoken language. There are 2 comparable forms. Test is administered orally, and students record their responses on answer sheets. Items are grouped into 5 parts, each measuring an important listening skill. The 2 forms can be used interchangeably or as pre- and posttests.

202
College Vocabulary Test. Gough, Harrison G.; Sampson, Harold 1954
Descriptors: *Achievement Tests; Higher Education; Multiple Choice Tests; *Undergraduate Students; *Verbal Ability; *Verbal Tests; *Vocabulary
Identifiers: CVT; Synonyms
Availability: Prof. Harrison G. Gough; Institute of Personality Assessment and Research, Dept. of Psychology, University of California, 2240 Piedmont Ave., Berkeley, CA 94720
Grade Level: 13-16
Notes: Time, 20 min. approx.; Items, 75

Designed as a brief and acceptable control measure for verbal ability. Developed to give a 6-sigma range for the 75 items, thus ensuring that the scores are widely dispersed and not clustered about the mean. Words taken from the moderate categories of use in the Thorndike-Logan tallies. Available in Form A and B. Also available in a 50-item version called General Vocabulary Test, Form A and B.

205
American Literacy Test. McCarty, John J. 1962
Descriptors: *Achievement Tests; Basic Vocabulary; *College Students; Language Tests; *Literacy; Multiple Choice Tests; Postsecondary Education; Secondary Education; *Secondary School Students; Timed Tests; *Verbal Ability
Availability: Psychometric Affiliates; P.O. Box 807, Murfreesboro, TN 37133
Grade Level: 8-19
Notes: Time, 4 min.; Items, 50

A vocabulary or word knowledge test, which the author feels may be used to determine the degree of literacy. Each question consists of one word; the respondent is to choose (among the words listed as possible answers) the one closest in meaning to the original word.

243
Watkins-Farnum Performance Scale. Watkins, John G.; Farnum, Stephen E. 1962
Descriptors: *Achievement Tests; *Bands (Music); Individual Testing; *Musical Instruments; Music Education; *Music Reading; Observation; *Performance Tests; Secondary Education; *Secondary School Students; Talent Development
Identifiers: Music Tests; Watkins Cornet Scale
Availability: Hal Leonard Publishing Corp.; 8112 W. Bluemound Rd., Milwaukee, WI 53213
Grade Level: 7-12
Notes: Items, 14

A standardized achievement test for measuring the performance and progress of students on band instruments. Testing done individually. Used for year-to-year progress, band tryouts, seating placement, and as a sight reading test. Covers 6 years of musical instrument study. All except those for the snare drum have 14 exercises; the snare drum has 12. An adaptation of Watkins Cornet Scale. Comes in 2 forms: Form A (copyrighted 1954) and Form B (copyrighted 1962).

700
Learning Methods Test, Revised Edition. Mills, Robert E.
Subtests: The Visual Method; The Phonic Method; The Kinesthetic Method; A Combination Method
Descriptors: Elementary Education; Individual Testing; Kinesthetic Perception; Phonics; *Reading Skills; *Reading Tests; *Remedial Reading; *Screening Tests; *Word Recognition
Identifiers: LMT; Oral Tests
Availability: Mills Center; Box 597, Black Mountain, NC 28711
Grade Level: 2-4

This instrument is a series of standardized teaching lessons with testing to determine the learning efficiency of various teaching methods most effective in teaching word recognition to various types of individuals. The teaching methods of concern in this study were the visual, the phonic, the kinesthetic, and a combination of the three others. Test designed to aid the remedial reading teacher in determining the student's ability to learn new words under different teaching procedures.

888
Test of English as a Foreign Language. Educational Testing Service, Princeton, NJ
Subtests: Listening Comprehension; Structure and Written Expression; Reading Comprehension and Vocabulary
Descriptors: Adults; College Admission; *English (Second Language); *Foreign Students; Graduate Students; Grammar; Higher Education; High School Students; *Language Proficiency; *Language Tests; Listening Comprehension Tests; Multiple Choice Tests; Reading Comprehension; Secondary Education; Sentence Structure; *Undergraduate Students; Vocabulary Skills; Writing Skills
Identifiers: Test of Written English; *TOEFL; TWE

Availability: TOEFL; P.O. Box 6155, Educational Testing Service, Princeton, NJ 08541
Grade Level: 11-18
Notes: Time, 120 min.; Items, 150

Designed to evaluate the English proficiency of nonnative speakers, primarily at the secondary level, who are preparing to study at North American colleges or universities. Administered worldwide at designated test centers. The Listening Comprehension section is administered with spoken material on reel-to-reel or cassette tapes. Multiple choice questions require test taker to answer questions based on spoken material, choose correct words and phrases, identify improper usage, answer questions based on reading passages, and choose correct word in context. Updated periodically. Beginning in 1986, the Test of Written English (TWE) was administered as part of TOEFL. The TWE provides candidates with opportunity to demonstrate their ability to compose in standard written English. The writing sample is scored on a 1 to 6 holistic scale, and the score is included in the official TOEFL score report.

1015
Curtis Verbal-Clerical Skills Tests. Curtis, James W. 1965
Subtests: Capacity Test; Computation Test; Checking Test; Comprehension Test
Descriptors: *Achievement Tests; Adults; *Clerical Workers; Computation; *Job Applicants; Logical Thinking; *Personnel Selection; Reading Comprehension; Timed Tests
Identifiers: Accuracy; Clerical Checking; Clerical Skills; Speededness (Tests)
Availability: Psychometric Affiliates; P.O. Box 807, Murfreesboro, TN 37133
Age Level: 16-61
Notes: Time, 8 min.; Items, 100

Designed to provide estimates of individual competence in basic areas of verbal skill usually associated with office and clerical work, as well as with potential for training at advanced or college level. May be administered to individuals or groups. Examinee may be given any one or all 4 subtests. Tests are independent of one another.

1016
National Achievement Tests: Vocabulary Test (for Grades 7 to 12 and College). Speer, Robert K.; Smith, Samuel 1954
Subtests: Vocabulary, or Word Meanings; Word Discrimination
Descriptors: *Achievement Tests; *College Students; Higher Education; Multiple Choice Tests; Reading Achievement; Secondary Education; *Secondary School Students; *Verbal Ability; Verbal Development; Verbal Tests; *Vocabulary; *Vocabulary Skills
Identifiers: Acorn Achievement Tests; National Achievement Series; *Synonyms; Vocabulary Test for Grades 7 to 12 and College
Availability: Psychometric Affiliates; P.O. Box 807, Murfreesboro, TN 37133
Grade Level: 7-16
Notes: Time, 15 min. approx.; Items, 80

Designed to measure the achievement level of one's vocabulary and the power of word discrimination. Untimed. Comes in 2 forms: Form A was copyrighted 1951; Form B, 1954. Earlier printings used the title: National Achievement Tests: Vocabulary Test (for Grades 7-12 Inclusive).

1142
National Achievement Tests: Social Studies Test (Grades 7-9). Speer, Robert K.; Smith, Samuel 1958
Subtests: Human Relations; Life Situations; Social Interpretations; Values of Products; Social Ideas; Miscellaneous Facts
Descriptors: *Achievement Tests; Human Relations; Junior High Schools; *Junior High School Students; *Social Studies
Availability: Psychometric Affiliates; P.O. Box 807, Murfreesboro, TN 37133-0807
Grade Level: 7-9
Notes: Time, 40 min.; Items, 70

Measures judgment and knowledge of life situations, human relations, social interpretations, product values, social ideas, and miscellaneous facts. Deals with community and international problems. Purpose of test is to measure students' basic knowledge of social studies, to indicate those areas in which remedial teaching may be necessary, to assist students in appreciating the value of social studies to themselves and their relationship with others; and to determine students' ability to apply their knowledge.

1143
National Achievement Tests: American History-Government Problems of Democracy. McGarrett, Vincent 1958
Subtests: Growth of a National Spirit; Growth of Democracy; The Constitution; Foreign Policy; Problems of American Democracy
Descriptors: *Achievement Tests; *College Students; Constitutional History; Democracy; Foreign Policy; Higher Education; High Schools; *High School Students; Postsecondary Education; United States Government (Course); *United States History
Availability: Psychometric Affiliates; P.O. Box 807, Murfreesboro, TN 37133-0807
Grade Level: 9-16
Notes: Time, 40 min.; Items, 100

There are 5 sections of this American history-government-problems of democracy test: (1) growth of a national spirit; (2) growth of democracy; (3) the Constitution; (4) foreign policy; and (5) problems of American democracy. The test is designed to measure the student's knowledge of American history, government, and politics; to indicate where reteaching may be used; to assess the student's knowledge of the democratic way of life in the U.S.; and to measure student's ability to make inferences between people and events.

1148
National Achievement Tests: History and Civics Test, Grades 6-8, Short Form. Speer, Robert K.; Smith, Samuel 1960
Subtests: Lessons of History; Miscellaneous Facts
Descriptors: *Achievement Tests; *Civics; *Grade 6; *History; Intermediate Grades; Junior High Schools; *Junior High School Students
Availability: Psychometric Affiliates; P.O. Box 807, Murfreesboro, TN 37133-0807
Grade Level: 6-8
Notes: Time, 15 min.; Items, 58

The test deals with lessons of history and miscellaneous facts.

1149
National Achievement Tests: History and Civics Test, Grades 3-6, Short Form. Speer, Robert K.; Smith, Samuel 1949
Subtests: Lessons of History; Historical Facts
Descriptors: *Achievement Tests; *Civics; Elementary Education; *Elementary School Students; *History
Availability: Psychometric Affiliates; P.O. Box 807, Murfreesboro, TN 37133-0807
Grade Level: 3-6
Notes: Time, 18 min.; Items, 70

Lessons of history and historical facts are covered.

1153
National Achievement Tests: Geography, Grades 6-8. Speer, Robert K.; Smith, Samuel 1958
Subtests: Geographical Ideas; Locating Products; Uses of Products and Instruments; Economic and Human Relations; Miscellaneous Problems
Descriptors: *Achievement Tests; *Geography; *Grade 6; Intermediate Grades; Junior High Schools; *Junior High School Students
Availability: Psychometric Affiliates; P.O. Box 807, Murfreesboro, TN 37133-0807
Grade Level: 6-8
Notes: Time, 35 min. approx.; Items, 125

This test covers an understanding of the concepts of geography; knowledge of products-geography (U.S. and world); an understanding of the values of products; knowledge of the uses of instruments and products; knowledge of important locations; appreciation of human relations and economics; and miscellaneous problems.

1202
National Achievement Tests: Geography, Grades 3-6, Short Form. Speer, Robert K.; Smith, Samuel 1949
Subtests: Geographical Ideas and Comparisons; Miscellaneous Facts
Descriptors: *Achievement Tests; Elementary Education; *Elementary School Students; *Geography
Availability: Psychometric Affiliates; P.O. Box 807, Murfreesboro, TN 37133-0807
Grade Level: 3-6
Notes: Time, 20 min.; Items, 40

This test covers geographic facts, ideas, and comparisons.

1203
National Achievement Tests: Geography, Grades 6-8, Short Form. Speer, Robert K.; Smith, Samuel 1961
Subtests: Geographical Ideas and Comparisons; Miscellaneous Facts
Descriptors: *Achievement Tests; *Geography; Grade 6; *Intermediate Grades; Junior High Schools; *Junior High School Students

Availability: Psychometric Affiliates; P.O. Box 807, Murfreesboro, TN 37133-0807
Grade Level: 6-8
Notes: Time, 20 min.; Items, 40

This test covers geographical ideas, comparisons, and facts.

1281
National Achievement Tests: American History, Grades 7-8. Speer, Robert K.; And Others 1961
Subtests: Lessons of History; Time Concepts; Historical Associations; Miscellaneous Problems
Descriptors: *Achievement Tests; Junior High Schools; *Junior High School Students; *United States History
Availability: Psychometric Affiliates; P.O. Box 807, Murfreesboro, TN 37133-0807
Grade Level: 7-8
Notes: Time, 40 min.; Items, 114

Included are questions on the lessons of history, time concepts, historical associations, and miscellaneous problems. The test was designed to test the ability to interpret major American history lessons, mastery of chronology, and recognition of important facts.

1333
Facts about Science Test. Educational Testing Service, Princeton, NJ 1958
Descriptors: *Achievement Tests; Adolescents; *High School Students; *Junior High School Students; *Knowledge Level; Multiple Choice Tests; *Sciences; Scientists; Secondary Education
Identifiers: FAS; TIM(B)
Availability: Tests in Microfiche; Test Collection, Educational Testing Service, Princeton, NJ 08541
Grade Level: 7-12
Notes: Time, 45 min.; Items, 80

Designed to measure students' knowledge of the general nature of science, the special characteristics of scientists, and the way science fits into our society.

1335
Test of Reasoning in Conservation. Conservation Foundation, New York, NY 1961
Descriptors: Adolescents; *Conservation (Environment); *Conservation Education; *Curriculum Development; High Schools; *High School Students; *Knowledge Level; Multiple Choice Tests
Identifiers: TIM(C)
Availability: Tests in Microfiche; Test Collection, Educational Testing Service, Princeton, NJ 08541
Grade Level: 9-12
Notes: Time, 40 min.; Items, 45

Measures students' knowledge of essential facts, concepts, and principles of conservation and their understanding of the implications of various aspects of conservation. The test is appropriate for students in grades 9-12. Forms A and B are available. Normative data for this instrument are based only on grades 9-12. It has been used, however, in colleges and may be used on an experimental basis in junior high schools.

1423
National Spanish Examination. American Association of Teachers of Spanish and Portuguese
Subtests: Listening Comprehension; Reading
Descriptors: *Achievement Tests; *Audiolingual Skills; Language Tests; Listening Comprehension Tests; Multiple Choice Tests; Reading Tests; Secondary Education; *Secondary School Students; *Second Language Learning; *Spanish; *Spanish Speaking; Timed Tests
Availability: National Spanish Examinations; University of Delaware, Newark, DE 19716
Grade Level: 7-12
Notes: Time, 60 min.; Items, 80

Measures aural comprehension, vocabulary mastery, grammatical control and reading skills for secondary school students studying Spanish. Requires the use of a tape recorder, cassette recorder, or a language laboratory. Comes in 4 levels: Level I, II, III and Advanced (which combined the previously known Levels IV and V). Each level consists of 30 oral comprehension and 50 reading items. May be used also for Spanish-speaking students, those born and/or reared in a Spanish-speaking environment. Restricted to students of teachers who are members of AATSP. Address changes frequently; check for latest address.

1506
National Achievement Tests: Social Studies Test, Grades 7-9. Crow, Lester D.; Augspurger, Everett F. 1950
Subtests: Human Relations and Life Situations; Products and Places; Social Ideas and Facts; Application of Knowledge

Descriptors: *Achievement Tests; Junior High Schools; *Junior High School Students; *Social Studies
Availability: Psychometric Affiliates; P.O. Box 807, Murfreesboro, TN 37133-0807
Grade Level: 7-9
Notes: Time, 40 min.; Items, 150

The test includes material about life situations and human relations; products and places; social ideas and facts; and application of knowledge. Its purpose is to measure basic knowledge of social studies. The test is a measure of social studies knowledge and ability to apply this knowledge.

1507
National Achievement Tests: Social Studies Test, Grades 4-6. Speer, Robert K.; Smith, Samuel 1955
Subtests: Human Relations; Life Situations; Social Problems; Products and Peoples; Meaning of Events
Descriptors: *Achievement Tests; *Elementary School Students; *Intermediate Grades; *Social Studies
Availability: Psychometric Affiliates; P.O. Box 807, Murfreesboro, TN 37133-0807
Grade Level: 4-6
Notes: Time, 35 min.; Items, 70

Measured in this test is knowledge of products and peoples; life situations; human relations; and meanings of events. Test deals with practical problems of the community and stresses the vital aspects of social life.

1512
Harvard-MLA Tests of Chinese Language Proficiency. Modern Language Association of America, New York, NY   Carroll, John B.; And Others 1965
Subtests: Pictorial Auditory Comprehension Test (75); Intermediate Reading Comprehension Test in Modern Chinese (126); Questionnaire on Training (11)
Descriptors: *Achievement Tests; Adults; *Chinese; Educational Background; Higher Education; Ideography; *Language Proficiency; Language Tests; Listening Comprehension; Modern Languages; Questionnaires; Reading Comprehension; *Second Language Learning; Sentence Structure; *Undergraduate Students; Vocabulary
Identifiers: TIM(A)
Availability: Tests in Microfiche; Test Collection, Educational Testing Service, Princeton, NJ 08541
Grade Level: 13-16
Notes: Time, 150 min.; Items, 212

Was administered in colleges, high schools, and government agencies. A measure of proficiency in modern Chinese. A student questionnaire is also included which elicits information on Chinese language background.

1534
Basketball Skills Test. Brace, David K. 1966
Subtests: Front Shot; Side Shot; Foul Shot; Under Basket Shot; Speed Pass; Jump and Reach; Overarm Pass; Push Pass; Dribble
Descriptors: Adolescents; *Athletics; *Basketball; Children; *Elementary School Students; Elementary Secondary Education; *Performance Tests; *Secondary School Students; *Skills
Availability: AAHPERD; 1900 Association Drive, Reston, VA 22901
Age Level: 10-18
Notes: Items, 9

Test of basketball skills for children in grades 5-12. Separate forms for boys and girls. May also be used to evaluate teacher's instruction in physical education.

1535
Football Skills Test. Brace, David K. 1966
Subtests: Forward Pass for Distance; 50-Yard Dash; Blocking; Forward Pass for Accuracy; Football Punt for Distance; Ball Changing Zig Zag Run; Catching the Forward Pass; Pull-Out; Kick-Off; Dodging Run
Descriptors: Adolescents; *Athletics; Children; *Elementary School Students; Elementary Secondary Education; *Football; *Performance Tests; *Secondary School Students; *Skills
Availability: AAHPERD; 1900 Association Drive, Reston, VA 22901
Age Level: 10-18
Notes: Items, 10

Designed to measure performance level in fundamental skills of football.

1536
Softball Skills Test. Brace, David K. 1966
Subtests: Throw for Distance; Overhand Throw for Accuracy; Underhand Pitching; Speed Throw; Fungo Hitting; Base Running; Fielding Ground Balls; Catching Fly Balls

Descriptors: Adolescents; Athletics; Children; *Elementary School Students; Elementary Secondary Education; *Performance Tests; *Secondary School Students; *Skills; *Softball
Availability: AAHPERD; 1900 Association Drive, Reston, VA 22901
Age Level: 10-18
Notes: Items, 8
Designed to measure performance level in fundamental skills of softball. Percentile score tables are included for boys and girls.

1769
Carrow Elicited Language Inventory. Carrow-Woolfolk, Elizabeth 1974
Descriptors: Articulation (Speech); *Audiotape Recorders; Audiotape Recordings; *Diagnostic Tests; Individual Testing; *Language Handicaps; Linguistic Performance; *Speech Skills; Young Children
Identifiers: CELI
Availability: DLM Teaching Resources; P.O. Box 4000, One DLM Park, Allen, TX 75002
Age Level: 3-7
Notes: Time, 5 min.; Items, 52
Designed to measure a child's productive control of grammar. Uses technique of eliciting imitations of a sequence of sentences systematically developed to include basic sentence construction types and specific grammatical morphemes. Used to identify children with language problems. May be administered by speech pathologists, or any trained examiner, with background in psycholinguistics and language disorders.

1810
School Readiness Test. Anderhalter, O. F. 1974
Subtests: Word Recognition; Identifying Letters; Visual Discrimination; Auditory Discrimination; Comprehension and Interpretation; Handwriting Readiness; Number Readiness
Descriptors: *Academic Ability; *Grade 1; *Kindergarten Children; *Learning Readiness; Primary Education; *School Readiness; *School Readiness Tests; Student Placement
Identifiers: Oral Testing; SRT
Availability: Scholastic Testing Service, Inc.; 480 Meyer Rd., P.O. Box 1056, Bensenville, IL 60106
Grade Level: K-1
Notes: Time, 60 min. approx.
Designed to measure learning readiness of students in late kindergarten or before the full third week of first grade. A Spanish manual of directions which translates all teacher's oral statements and directions to children into Spanish is available.

1841
STS High School Placement Test. Scholastic Testing Service, Bensenville, IL 1963
Subtests: Verbal; Quantitative; Reading; Mathematics; Language
Descriptors: Academic Ability; Academic Achievement; Achievement Rating; *Achievement Tests; *Admission (School); Cognitive Ability; *Cognitive Tests; *Grouping (Instructional Purposes); Intelligence Quotient; Junior High Schools; *Junior High School Students; Mental Age; Student Evaluation; *Student Placement; *Academic Aptitude
Identifiers: HSPT; Proficiency Tests; STS Closed High School Placement Test; STS HSPT; STS Open High School Placement Test
Availability: Scholastic Testing Service; 480 Meyer Rd., Bensenville, IL 60106
Grade Level: 8-9
Notes: Time, 150 min.; Items, 298
A testing program designed to aid in the selection and/or placement of high school students. May be used as a proficiency test or as part of a placement program. Comes in 2 forms. The Closed form (new each year) measures those abilities and skills basic to the high school curriculum. The Open form is a reprint of the recent Closed form. Optional tests—Mechanical Aptitude, Science, and Catholic Religion—are also available and take about 20 minutes each. Includes both cognitive skills (verbal and quantitative) and achievement in reading, math, and language arts.

2077
Doppelt Mathematical Reasoning Test. Psychological Corp., San Antonio, TX
Descriptors: *College Entrance Examinations; *Graduate Study; Higher Education; Logical Thinking; *Mathematical Concepts
Identifiers: DMRT
Availability: The Psychological Corp.; 555 Academic Ct., San Antonio, TX 78204-0952
Grade Level: 16-20
Notes: Items, 50
Designed primarily as an aid in selecting students for admissions to graduate study. May also be used in selecting applicants for positions in business and industry that require mathematical reasoning. Test measures ability to perceive mathematical relationships. Substantive content of items is derived from secondary school mathematics content.

2117
National Achievement Tests: High School Reading Test. Speer, Robert K.; Smith, Samuel 1962
Subtests: Vocabulary; Word Discrimination; Sentence Meaning; Noting Details; Interpreting Paragraphs
Descriptors: Academic Achievement; *Achievement Tests; Cloze Procedure; *College Students; Higher Education; Language Skills; Multiple Choice Tests; *Reading Ability; *Reading Achievement; *Reading Comprehension; *Reading Tests; Secondary Education; *Secondary School Students; Verbal Development; Word Study Skills
Identifiers: Acorn Achievement Tests; High School Reading Test; National Achievement Series; Reading (for Grades 7 to 12 and College); Synonyms
Availability: Psychometric Affiliates; P.O. Box 807, Murfreesboro, TN 37133
Grade Level: 7-16
Notes: Time, 40 min. approx.; Items, 134
Untimed test, designed to measure the level of reading achievement for secondary school and college students. Comes in 2 forms: Form A (copyrighted 1960) and Form B (copyrighted 1962). In later reprintings, title changed to National Achievement Tests: Reading (for Grades 7 to 12 and College).

2137
National Achievement Tests: First Year Algebra Test. Webb, Ray; Hlavaty, Julius H. 1962
Descriptors: *Achievement Tests; *Algebra; *High School Students; *Mathematical Applications; *Mathematical Concepts; *Mathematics Achievement; Mathematics Tests; Multiple Choice Tests; Secondary Education; Secondary School Mathematics; *Secondary School Students; Timed Tests
Identifiers: Acorn Achievement Tests; First Year Algebra Test; National Achievement Series; Number Operations
Availability: Psychometric Affiliates; P.O. Box 807, Murfreesboro, TN 37133
Grade Level: 7-12
Notes: Time, 40 min.; Items, 48
Designed to measure a student's achievement in first-year algebra and his or her ability to apply this knowledge. Comes in 2 forms: Form A is copyrighted 1962; Form B, 1959.

2138
Office Skills Achievement Test. Mellenbruch, Paul L. 1962
Subtests: Business Letter; Grammar; Checking; Filing; Arithmetic; Written Directions
Descriptors: *Achievement Tests; Adolescents; Adults; Business Correspondence; *Clerical Workers; Filing; High Schools; *High School Students; Timed Tests
Identifiers: Clerical Skills; English Usage
Availability: Psychometric Affiliates; P.O. Box 807, Murfreesboro, TN 37133
Age Level: 14-64
Notes: Time, 20 min.; Items, 99
Designed to measure achievement of office skills in areas of business letter writing, English usage, checking, filing, simple arithmetic, and following written instructions. Useful for high school guidance as well as a check on clerical training. May also be used for vocational placement and upgrading clerical personnel. Forms A and B are available.

2177
American Numerical Test. McCarty, John J. 1962
Descriptors: Adults; *Aptitude Tests; *Arithmetic; *Business Skills; Computation; Employees; Industrial Education; Mathematics Tests; Students; Timed Tests; *Vocational Aptitude; Vocational Education
Identifiers: *Clerical Skills; Number Operations; *Numerical Ability
Availability: Psychometric Affiliates; P.O. Box 807, Murfreesboro, TN 37133
Age Level: Adults
Notes: Time, 4 min.; Items, 60
Designed to measure numerical alertness and adaptability. The author's theory is that quantification of aspects of reality requires not only a readiness to count but also a flexibility in shifting from one type of arithmetical operation to another. He feels that this type of continuous numerical adaptation and flexibility presents the formation of a static mechanical set. The test contains 60 addi-

tion, subtraction, multiplication, and division problems; each problem requires a different numerical operation from the preceding and succeeding problem.

2179
National Achievement Tests: Arithmetic (Fundamentals and Reading), Grades 3-6. Speer, Robert K.; Smith, Samuel 1956
Subtests: Computation; Number Comparisons; Comparisons; Problem Analysis; Problems
Descriptors: *Achievement Tests; *Computation; Elementary Education; Elementary School Mathematics; *Elementary School Students; *Mathematical Applications; *Mathematical Concepts; Mathematics Achievement; Mathematics Tests; Multiple Choice Tests; *Problem Solving; Timed Tests
Identifiers: Arithmetic (Fundamentals and Reasoning); Arithmetic Test (Fundamentals and Reasoning); National Achievement Series; Number Operations; Reasoning; *Reasoning Ability
Availability: Psychometric Affiliates; P.O. Box 807, Murfreesboro, TN 37133
Grade Level: 3-6
Notes: Time, 60 min.; Items, 65
Measures fundamentals of arithmetic, number comparisons, mathematical judgments, problem reading, and problem solving. Each section is separately timed. Comes in 2 forms: Form A (copyrighted 1938) and Form B (copyrighted 1956).

2180
National Achievement Tests: Arithmetic (Fundamentals and Reading), Grades 6-8. Speer, Robert K.; Smith, Samuel 1938
Subtests: Computation; Number Comparisons; Comparisons; Problem Analysis; Problems
Descriptors: *Achievement Tests; *Computation; Elementary Education; Elementary School Mathematics; *Elementary School Students; *Mathematical Applications; *Mathematical Concepts; Mathematics Achievement; Mathematics Tests; Multiple Choice Tests; *Problem Solving; Timed Tests
Identifiers: Arithmetic (Fundamentals and Reasoning); Arithmetic Test (Fundamentals and Reasoning); National Achievement Series; Number Operations; Reasoning; *Reasoning Ability
Availability: Psychometric Affiliates; P.O. Box 807, Murfreesboro, TN 37133
Grade Level: 6-8
Notes: Time, 60 min.; Items, 67
Measures fundamentals of arithmetic, number comparisons, mathematical judgments, problem reading, and problem solving. Each section is separately timed.

2181
National Achievement Tests: Arithmetic Fundamentals. Speer, Robert K.; Smith, Samuel 1958
Subtests: Arithmetic Fundamentals—Timed Test; Number Comparisons—Timed Test; Arithmetic Fundamentals—Untimed Tests
Descriptors: *Achievement Tests; Computation; Elementary Education; Elementary School Mathematics; *Elementary School Students; *Mathematical Concepts; *Mathematics Achievement; Mathematics Tests; Multiple Choice Tests; Timed Tests
Identifiers: Acorn Achievement Tests; Arithmetic Fundamentals; Arithmetic Test (Fundamentals); National Achievement Series; *Number Operations
Availability: Psychometric Affiliates; P.O. Box 807, Murfreesboro, TN 37133
Grade Level: 3-8
Notes: Items, 100
Measures speed and accuracy in computation; judgment, speed, and accuracy in comparing computations; and skill and understanding without limiting these abilities by speed. Available in 2 forms: Form A (copyrighted 1955) and Form B (copyrighted 1958). The timed parts contains 30 questions and the untimed, 70.

2222
National Achievement Tests: General Mathematics. Eisner, Harry 1958
Subtests: Concepts; Problem Analysis; Problems
Descriptors: *Achievement Tests; Computation; Junior High Schools; *Junior High School Students; *Mathematical Applications; *Mathematical Concepts; Mathematics Achievement; Mathematics Tests; Multiple Choice Tests; *Problem Solving; Secondary School Mathematics; Timed Tests
Identifiers: Acorn Achievement Tests; *General Mathematics; General Mathematics (Eisner); Junior High School Mathematics Test; National Achievement Series; Number Operations
Availability: Psychometric Affiliates; P.O. Box 807, Murfreesboro, TN 37133

Grade Level: 7-9
Notes: Time, 52 min.; Items, 82
Designed to measure (1) the possession of correct concepts; (2) the ability to analyze a simple problem and indicate the method of solution; and (3) the ability to carry through a solution to a successful conclusion. It tests a junior high school student's achievement in arithmetic, algebraic and geometric concepts, applications, problem analysis, and reasoning. Comes in 2 forms: Form A (copyrighted 1952) and Form B (copyrighted 1958).

2287
National Achievement Tests; Solid Geometry.
Webb, Ray 1960
Descriptors: *Achievement Tests; High Schools; *High School Students; *Mathematical Applications; *Mathematical Concepts; Mathematics Achievement; Mathematics Tests; Multiple Choice Tests; *Problem Solving; Secondary School Mathematics; *Solid Geometry; Timed Tests
Identifiers: Acorn Achievement Tests; National Achievement Series; Number Operations; Solid Geometry (Webb)
Availability: Psychometric Affiliates; P.O. Box 807, Murfreesboro, TN 37133
Grade Level: 9-12
Notes: Time, 40 min.; Items, 48
To measure secondary school students' achievement level in solid geometry. Comes in 2 forms: Form A (copyrighted 1960); Form B (copyrighted 1959).

2288
National Achievement Tests; Plane Geometry Test.
Webb, Ray; Hlavaty, Julius H. 1960
Descriptors: *Achievement Tests; High Schools; *High School Students; *Mathematical Applications; *Mathematical Concepts; Mathematics Achievement; Mathematics Tests; Multiple Choice Tests; *Plane Geometry; *Problem Solving; Secondary School Mathematics; Timed Tests
Identifiers: Acorn Achievement Tests; National Achievement Series; Number Operations; Plane Geometry Test
Availability: Psychometric Affiliates; P.O. Box 807, Murfreesboro, TN 37133
Grade Level: 9-12
Notes: Time, 40 min.; Items, 48
Designed to measure students' knowledge of plane geometry and their ability to apply that knowledge.

2289
National Achievement Test: Plane Trigonometry.
Webb, Ray; Hlavaty, Julius H. 1960
Descriptors: *Achievement Tests; High Schools; *High School Students; *Mathematical Applications; *Mathematical Concepts; *Mathematics Achievement; Mathematics Tests; Multiple Choice Tests; Secondary School Mathematics; Timed Tests; *Trigonometry
Identifiers: Acorn Achievement Tests; National Achievement Series; Number Operations; Plane Trigonometry
Availability: Psychometric Affiliates; P.O. Box 807, Murfreesboro, TN 37133
Grade Level: 9-12
Notes: Time, 40 min.; Items, 48
Designed to measure students' basic knowledge of plane trigonometry and their ability to apply that knowledge. Comes in 2 forms: Form A (copyrighted 1960); Form B (copyrighted 1959).

2334
Belmont Measures of Athletic Performance: Basketball.   Wright, Logan; Wright, Patsy K. 1964
Descriptors: *Basketball; Females; *Forced Choice Technique; Higher Education; High Schools; *High School Students; *Performance Tests; *Undergraduate Students
Availability: Psychometric Affiliates; P.O. Box 807, Murfreesboro, TN 37133-0807
Grade Level: 9-16
Notes: Time, 3 min. approx.; Items, 10
A forced-choice rating scale that assesses playing skill in an actual game situation. Designed for grading purposes, but can also be used for general assessment. Useful for comparisons of players within the same group or class; less reliable for comparisons involving different groups. A minimum of 6 ratings should be acquired on each player. Team members are suitable raters. Psychometric data available.

2335
Belmont Measures of Athletic Performance: Field Hockey.   Wright, Logan; Wright, Patsy K. 1964
Descriptors: Females; *Field Hockey; *Forced Choice Technique; Higher Education; High Schools; *High School Students; *Performance Tests; *Undergraduate Students

Availability: Psychometric Affiliates; P.O. Box 807, Murfreesboro, TN 37133-0807
Grade Level: 9-16
Notes: Time, 3 min. approx.; Items, 26
A forced-choice rating scale that assesses playing skill in an actual game situation. Designed for grading purposes, but can also be used for general assessment. Useful for comparisons of players within the same group or class; less reliable for comparisons involving different groups. A minimum of 6 ratings should be acquired on each player. Team members are suitable raters. Psychometric data available.

2336
Belmont Measures of Athletic Performance: Softball.   Wright, Logan; Wright, Patsy K. 1964
Descriptors: Females; *Forced Choice Technique; Higher Education; High Schools; *High School Students; *Performance Tests; *Softball; *Undergraduate Students
Availability: Psychometric Affiliates; P.O. Box 807, Murfreesboro, TN 37133-0807
Grade Level: 9-16
Notes: Time, 3 min. approx.; Items, 12
A forced-choice rating scale that assesses playing skill in an actual game situation. Designed for grading purposes, but can also be used for general assessment. Useful for comparisons of players within the same class or group; less reliable for comparisons involving different groups. A minimum of 6 ratings should be acquired on each player. Team members are suitable raters. Psychometric data available.

2337
Belmont Measures of Athletic Performance: Volleyball.   Wright, Logan; Wright, Patsy K. 1964
Descriptors: Females; *Forced Choice Technique; Higher Education; High Schools; *High School Students; *Performance Tests; *Undergraduate Students; *Volleyball
Availability: Psychometric Affiliates; P.O. Box 807, Murfreesboro, TN 37133-0807
Grade Level: 9-16
Notes: Time, 3 min. approx.; Items, 12
A forced-choice rating scale that assesses playing skill in an actual game situation. Designed for grading purposes, but can also be used for general assessment. Useful for comparisons of players within the same group or class; less reliable for comparisons involving different groups. A minimum of 6 ratings should be acquired on each player. Team members are suitable raters. Psychometric data available.

2407
National Achievement Tests: Health Education Test: Knowledge and Application, Revised.   Shaw, John H; And Others 1964
Subtests: Basic Knowledge; Application of Knowledge
Descriptors: *Achievement Tests; Allied Health Occupations Education; *College Freshmen; *Health; Health Education; Higher Education; *Hygiene; Multiple Choice Tests; *Physical Education; Secondary Education; *Secondary School Students
Identifiers: Acorn Achievement Tests; Health Education Test; Knowledge and Application; National Achievement Series
Availability: Psychometric Affiliates; P.O. Box 807, Murfreesboro, TN 37133
Grade Level: 7-13
Notes: Time, 45 min. approx.; Items, 100
Measures students' basic knowledge of health and their ability to apply that knowledge. Includes the newer phases of health and many items on physical education. The basic-knowledge section uses multiple-choice type questions. The application-of-knowledge section presents 4 health problem situations; following each situation are a group of statements to which the respondent marks either true or false. Although not timed, the authors suggest having the respondents start on the second section after 25 minutes. Intended for secondary school students and students in the first-year college hygiene classes.

2408
National Achievement Tests: Health Knowledge for College Freshmen.   Bridges, A. Frank 1956
Descriptors: *Achievement Tests; *College Freshmen; *Health; Higher Education
Availability: Psychometric Affiliates; P.O. Box 807, Murfreesboro, TN 35133-0807
Grade Level: 13
Notes: Time, 40 min.; Items, 100
This test is constructed to measure the health knowledge of first-year college students. This test can be used for a pretest or a posttest or as a basis for assigning students to health education classes. The areas included were determined by a jury of 13 college health educators. Areas covered are nutrition, emotional health, exercise and rest, narcotics and stimulants, body functions, social health, community health, personal health, family living, sense organs, occupational health, and current health. Norms are

given. The test's reliability is 0.833. Statistical validity was secured by the use of the Votaw Curve. May also be used with high school seniors.

2410
National Achievement Tests: Health Test, Grades 3-8.   Speer, Robert K.; Smith, Samuel 1960
Subtests: Recognizing Best Habits; Health Comparisons; Causes and Effects; Health Facts
Descriptors: *Achievement Tests; Elementary Education; *Elementary School Students; *Health; Hygiene
Availability: Psychometric Affiliates; P.O. Box 807, Murfreesboro, TN 37133-0807
Grade Level: 3-8
Notes: Time, 40 min. approx.
This test has been designed to test the student's ability to select the best health habits, make comparative health judgments; understand health causes and effects; and knowledge of health facts.

2411
National Achievement Tests: General Science, Grades 7-9.   Speer, Robert K.; And Others 1958
Subtests: General Concepts; Identifications; *Important Men of Science*; Definitions; Uses of Objects; Miscellaneous Facts
Descriptors: *Achievement Tests; *General Science; Junior High Schools; *Junior High School Students
Availability: Psychometric Affiliates; P.O. Box 807, Murfreesboro, TN 37133-0807
Grade Level: 7-9
Notes: Time, 35 min. approx.
The test includes general concepts, identifications, important persons in science, definitions, uses of objects, and miscellaneous facts. The test deals with facts and judgment.

2412
National Achievement Tests: Elementary Science Test, Grades 4-6.   Crow, Lester D.; Shuman, W.L. 1960
Subtests: Practical Applications; Cause and Effect Relationships; Miscellaneous Facts; Simple Identifications; Evaluation of Statements
Descriptors: *Achievement Tests; *Elementary School Science; *Elementary School Students; *Intermediate Grades
Availability: Psychometric Affiliates; P.O. Box 807, Murfreesboro, TN 37133-0807
Grade Level: 4-6
Notes: Time, 35 min. approx.
The science test covers practical applications, cause and effect relationships, miscellaneous facts, simple identifications, and an evaluation of statements.

2414
National Achievement Tests: General Chemistry Test.   Crow, Lester D.; Cook, Roy S. 1958
Subtests: Uses, Processes, Results; Formulae and Valence; Miscellaneous Facts
Descriptors: *Achievement Tests; *Chemistry; *College Students; Higher Education; High Schools; *High School Students; Postsecondary Education
Availability: Psychometric Affiliates; P.O. Box 807, Murfreesboro, TN 37133-0807
Grade Level: 9-16
Notes: Time, 40 min. approx.; Items, 120
The test was designed to measure the student's basic knowledge of chemistry, and ability to apply that knowledge. The test measures uses, processes, results; formulae and valence; and miscellaneous facts.

2415
National Achievement Tests: General Physics Test.
Crow, Lester D.; Cook, Roy S. 1958
Subtests: Uses and Application of Principles; Miscellaneous Facts and Scientists
Descriptors: *Achievement Tests; *College Students; Higher Education; High Schools; *High School Students; *Physics; *Postsecondary Education
Availability: Psychometric Affiliates; P.O. Box 807, Murfreesboro, TN 37133-0807
Grade Level: 9-16
Notes: Time, 40 min. approx.; Items, 130
This was constructed to test the student's knowledge of physics, and ability to apply that knowledge. Uses and application of principles and miscellaneous facts and scientists are the 2 components of the test.

2477
How to Drive Tests.   American Automobile Association, Falls Church, VA, Traffic Engineering and Safety Dept. 1958
Descriptors: *Achievement Tests; Adolescents; Adults; *Driver Education; Multiple Choice Tests
Identifiers: *Driver Examinations; Drivers

Availability: American Automobile Association; 1712 G St., N.W., Washington, DC 20006
Age Level: 16-64
Notes: Items, 100
Designed to assess knowledge of driving and safety rules. Four tests based on the booklet "How to Drive." Each test consists of 25 questions covering 3 chapters of the booklet. Questions from each chapter are clearly marked.

2503
Group Diagnostic Reading Aptitude and Achievement Tests, Intermediate Form. Monroe, Marion; Sherman, Eva Edith 1966
Subtests: Paragraph Understanding; Speed; Word Discrimination; Arithmetic Computation; Spelling; Letter Memory; Form Memory; Discrimination and Orientation; Copying Text; Crossing Out Letters; Vocabulary
Descriptors: *Academic Aptitude; *Achievement Tests; *Aptitude Tests; *Computation; Elementary Education; *Elementary School Students; Junior High Schools; *Junior High School Students; *Reading Achievement; Spelling
Availability: CH Nevins Printing Co.; 311 Bryn Mawr Island, Bayshore Gardens, Bradenton, FL 33505
Grade Level: 3-9
Notes: Items, 390
Designed to measure achievement and aptitude of students in grades 3 through 9. Yields educational, word discrimination and aptitude data percentile scores.

2520
***Newsweek* News Quiz.** Newsweek Educational Div., Livingston, NJ
Descriptors: *Achievement Tests; *Current Events; High Schools; *High School Students; Humanities; Reading Comprehension; Sciences; *Social Sciences; *World Affairs
Identifiers: Monthly News Quiz; Newsmagazines; Newsweek Monthly News Quiz; Newsweek Monthly Objective Test; Newsweek Social Studies Program
Availability: Newsweek Educational Div.; The Newsweek Bldg., Box 414, Livingston, NJ 07039
Grade Level: 9-12
Notes: Time, 30 min. approx.; Items, 50
Part of the *Newsweek* Social Studies Program that measures the student's reading comprehension of the previous month's issues of *Newsweek*. In January and May, the *Newsweek* Current News Test (TC002521) is issued instead of the monthly *Newsweek* News Quiz. This teaching aid comes free with a minimum number of student subscriptions to *Newsweek*.

2521
***Newsweek* Current News Test.** Newsweek Educational Div., Livingston, NJ
Descriptors: *Achievement Tests; *Current Events; High Schools; *High School Students; Humanities; Reading Comprehension; Sciences; *Social Sciences; *World Affairs
Identifiers: Current News Test; Newsweek Social Studies Program
Availability: Newsweek Educational Div.; The Newsweek Bldg., Box 414, Livingston, NJ, 07039
Grade Level: 9-12
Notes: Time, 60 min. approx.; Items, 100
Part of the *Newsweek* Social Studies Program that measures the student's reading comprehension of the past three and one-half months' issues of *Newsweek*. Comes out in January and in May, and is issued in lieu of the monthly *Newsweek* News Quiz (TC002520). Includes multiple-choice, fill-in-the-blank and matching types of questions, and is used for review and retention of recent news items. This teaching aid comes free with a minimum number of student subscriptions to *Newsweek*.

2718
College-Level Examination Program: General Examination in English Composition. Educational Testing Service, Princeton, NJ
Descriptors: Achievement Tests; *Adults; *Equivalency Tests; *Expository Writing; Higher Education; Multiple Choice Tests; Undergraduate Students; Writing Skills
Identifiers: CLEP
Availability: College Board Publication Orders; Box 2815, Princeton, NJ 08541
Grade Level: 13-16
Age Level: Adults
Notes: Time, 90 min.; Items, 130
CLEP enables both traditional and nontraditional students to earn college credit by examination. Tests are updated periodically. Measures competency in writing expository essays that follow the conventions of standard written English. Concerned with skills that the first-year English student is expected to acquire, rather than with a technical vocabulary or with ability to do imaginative writing.

There are 2 editions of this test. Section 1 of both editions is multiple-choice. Section 2 is all multiple-choice in one edition and a 45-minute essay in the second edition.

2719
College-Level Examination Program: General Examination in the Humanities. Educational Testing Service, Princeton, NJ
Subtests: Literature; Fine Arts
Descriptors: Achievement Tests; *Adults; *Equivalency Tests; *Fine Arts; Higher Education; Humanities; *Literature; Undergraduate Students
Identifiers: CLEP
Availability: College Board Publication Orders; Box 2815, Princeton, NJ 08541
Grade Level: 13-16
Age Level: Adults
Notes: Time, 90 min.; Items, 150
CLEP enables both traditional and nontraditional students to earn college credit by examination. Items are evenly divided among the following periods of Western art and culture: Classical, Medieval and Renaissance, seventeenth through twentieth centuries. Designed to demonstrate understanding of humanities through recollection or recognition of specific information; comprehension and application of concepts; and analysis and interpretation of various works of art. Tests are updated periodically.

2720
College-Level Examination Program: General Examination in Mathematics. Educational Testing Service, Princeton, NJ 1981
Subtests: Skills and Concepts; Content
Descriptors: Achievement Tests; *Adults; Algebra; Arithmetic; *Equivalency Tests; Geometry; Higher Education; Logic; *Mathematics Achievement; Multiple Choice Tests; Probability; Statistics; Undergraduate Students
Identifiers: CLEP
Availability: College Board Publication Orders; Box 2815, Princeton, NJ 08541
Grade Level: 13-16
Age Level: Adults
Notes: Time, 90 min.; Items, 90
CLEP enables both traditional and nontraditional students to earn college credit by examination. Questions in Part B are more directly related to a college-level course than those in Part A. The score on Part B is counted twice in determining total score. Tests are updated periodically.

2721
College-Level Examination Program: General Examination in Natural Sciences. Educational Testing Service, Princeton, NJ 1981
Subtests: Biological Science; Physical Science
Descriptors: Achievement Tests; *Adults; *Biological Sciences; *Equivalency Tests; Higher Education; Multiple Choice Tests; *Physical Sciences; Undergraduate Students
Identifiers: CLEP
Availability: College Board Publication Orders; Box 2815, Princeton, NJ 08541
Grade Level: 13-16
Age Level: Adults
Notes: Time, 90 min.; Items, 120
CLEP enables both traditional and nontraditional students to earn college credit by examination. Designed to test knowledge and understanding of scientific concepts that should be attained by a well-educated adult. Tests are updated periodically.

2722
College-Level Examination Program: General Examination in Social Sciences and History. Educational Testing Service, Princeton, NJ 1981
Subtests: Social Sciences; History
Descriptors: Achievement Tests; *Adults; Economics; *Equivalency Tests; Higher Education; *Non Western Civilization; Political Science; *Social Psychology; *Sociology; Undergraduate Students; United States History; *Western Civilization
Identifiers: CLEP
Availability: College Board Publication Orders; Box 2815, Princeton, NJ 08541
Grade Level: 13-16
Age Level: 18-64
Notes: Time, 90 min.; Items, 125
CLEP enables both traditional and nontraditional students to earn college credit by examination. Measures knowledge of terminology and theories in a field, comprehension of meaning, ability to interpret or analyze graphic, pictorial or written material, and ability to select hypotheses and apply them to given data. Tests are updated periodically.

2723
College-Level Examination Program: Subject Examination in American Government. Educational Testing Service, Princeton, NJ 1981

Descriptors: Achievement Tests; *Adults; *Equivalency Tests; Essay Tests; Higher Education; Multiple Choice Tests; Undergraduate Students; *United States Government (Course)
Identifiers: CLEP
Availability: College Board Publication Orders; Box 2815, Princeton, NJ 08541
Grade Level: 13-16
Age Level: Adults
Notes: Time, 90 min.; Items, 100
CLEP enables both traditional and nontraditional students to earn college credit by examination. Tests are updated periodically. A 90-minute optional essay requires same knowledge and skills needed for multiple-choice examination but also measures ability to select material and present it in an organized and logical manner. A choice of writing on any 3 of 4 topics is offered. Examination measures knowledge of discrete facts about American government and politics, recognition of typical patterns of political processes and behavior, and understanding of data relevant to government.

2724
College-Level Examination Program: Subject Examination in Analysis and Interpretation of Literature. Educational Testing Service, Princeton, NJ
Descriptors: Achievement Tests; *Adults; *English Literature; *Equivalency Tests; Essay Tests; Higher Education; Multiple Choice Tests; Undergraduate Students; *United States Literature
Identifiers: CLEP
Availability: College Board Publication Orders; Box 2815, Princeton, NJ 08541
Grade Level: 13-16
Age Level: Adults
Notes: Time, 90 min.; Items, 100
CLEP enables both traditional and nontraditional students to earn college credit by examination. Tests are updated periodically. Measures ability to read prose and poetry with understanding. Student is expected to analyze elements of a literacy passage and respond to nuances of meaning, tone, mood, imagery, and style. An optional essay section enables student to demonstrate ability to write well-organized critical essays on given passages of poetry and on general literary questions.

2726
College-Level Examination Program: Subject Examination in General Chemistry. Educational Testing Service, Princeton, NJ
Descriptors: Achievement Tests; *Adults; Atomic Theory; Chemical Bonding; *Chemistry; *Equivalency Tests; Essay Tests; Higher Education; Kinetics; Multiple Choice Tests; Thermodynamics; Undergraduate Students
Identifiers: CLEP
Availability: College Board Publication Orders; Box 2815, Princeton, NJ 08541
Grade Level: 13-16
Age Level: Adults
Notes: Time, 90 min.; Items, 80
CLEP enables both traditional and nontraditional students to earn college credit by examination. Tests are updated periodically. Measures knowledge in several areas of chemistry, including structure of matter, states of matter, reaction types, equations and stoichiometry, equilibrium, kinetics, thermodynamics, descriptive chemistry, and experimental chemistry. Slide rules and calculators may be used during examination. There is an optional essay section, which includes quantitative problems and writing equations that predict formulas of the products of chemical reactions, as well as short essays that interpret chemical phenomena and illustrate chemical reasoning.

2727
College-Level Examination Program: Subject Examination in General Psychology. Educational Testing Service, Princeton, NJ
Descriptors: Achievement Tests; *Adults; Behavior Development; *Equivalency Tests; Essay Tests; Higher Education; Multiple Choice Tests; *Psychology; Social Psychology; Statistics; Undergraduate Students
Identifiers: CLEP
Availability: College Board Publication Orders; Box 2815, Princeton, NJ 08541
Grade Level: 13-16
Age Level: 18-64
Notes: Time, 90 min.; Items, 100
CLEP enables both traditional and nontraditional students to earn college credit by examination. Tests are updated periodically. Measures knowledge of terminology, principles, and theory, as well as ability to comprehend, evaluate or analyze problem situations and to apply knowledge to new situations. Areas covered include physiology and behavior perceptual and sensory experience, motivation and emotion, learning, cognition, life-span development, personality and adjustment, behavioral disorders, social psychology, measurements and statistics, history, and philosophy. An optional essay requires knowledge similar to those needed for multiple-choice.

2731
College-Level Examination Program: Subject Examination in Introductory Sociology. Educational Testing Service, Princeton, NJ
Descriptors: Achievement Tests; *Adults; *Equivalency Tests; Essay Tests; Higher Education; Multiple Choice Tests; Social Differences; Socialization; *Sociology; Undergraduate Students
Identifiers: CLEP
Availability: College Board Publication Orders; Box 2815, Princeton, NJ 08541
Grade Level: 13-16
Age Level: 18-64
Notes: Time, 90 min.; Items, 100

CLEP enables both traditional and nontraditional students to earn college credit by examination. Tests are updated periodically. This examination stresses basic facts and concepts and the general approach of sociologists in studying man and society. The optional essay section requires the application of both general principles of sociology and appropriate specific evidence. Student is required to answer 3 of 4 essay questions offered.

2753
Understanding Communication. Thurstone, Thelma Gwinn 1956
Descriptors: Achievement Tests; Adolescents; *Adults; Cognitive Processes; Communication Skills; Multiple Choice Tests; *Receptive Language; *Secondary School Students; Timed Tests; Verbal Ability; *Verbal Communication; *Verbal Learning; *Verbal Tests
Availability: London House Management Consultants; 1550 Northwest Hwy., Park Ridge, IL 60068
Age Level: 12-65
Notes: Time, 15 min.; Items, 40

Designed to measure comprehension of verbal material using the format of short sentences and phrases. Involves one's understanding of the sentences/phrases and their implications. The author feels that the test involves the solving of a problem presented in verbal form and not the recognition of the answer, nor memory, speed, or simply vocabulary.

2831
Advanced Placement Program: United States History. Educational Testing Service, Princeton, NJ
Descriptors: *Advanced Placement Programs; *Equivalency Tests; Essay Tests; High Schools; *High School Students; Multiple Choice Tests; *United States History
Identifiers: Advanced Placement Examinations (CEEB); APP
Availability: Advanced Placement Program; Box 977 PD, Princeton, NJ 08541
Grade Level: 10-12
Notes: Time, 180 min.; Items, 83

Based on a college full-year introduction to U.S. history from colonial times to the present. First 90 minutes of exam is objective questions; the remainder of exam is for essay questions, one of which is a document-based question. The number of test items will vary year to year. The Advanced Placement Program has been sponsored by the College Board since 1955.

2832
Advanced Placement Program: Biology. Educational Testing Service, Princeton, NJ 1981
Descriptors: *Advanced Placement Programs; *Biology; *Equivalency Tests; Essay Tests; High Schools; *High School Students; Multiple Choice Tests
Identifiers: Advanced Placement Examinations (CEEB); APP
Availability: Advanced Placement Program; Box 977 PD, Princeton, NJ 08541
Grade Level: 10-12
Notes: Time, 180 min.

Designed to test materials covered on a college full-year introduction to biology. Questions are evenly divided between selected essays and objective questions. The number of items will vary year to year. The Advanced Placement Program has been sponsored by the College Board since 1955.

2833
Advanced Placement Program: Chemistry. Educational Testing Service, Princeton, NJ
Descriptors: *Advanced Placement Programs; *Chemistry; *Equivalency Tests; Essay Tests; High Schools; *High School Students; Multiple Choice Tests
Identifiers: Advanced Placement Examinations (CEEB); APP
Availability: Advanced Placement Program; Box 977 PD, Princeton, NJ 08541
Grade Level: 10-12
Notes: Time, 180 min.

Designed to test contents of college full-year introduction to chemistry. Questions are divided into objective, selected reactions, problems, and short essays. The number of items will vary year to year. The Advanced Placement Program has been sponsored by the College Board since 1955.

2836
Advanced Placement Program: French Language. Educational Testing Service, Princeton, NJ
Subtests: Listening; Reading; Speaking; Writing
Descriptors: *Advanced Placement Programs; Audiotape Recordings; *Equivalency Tests; Essay Tests; *French; High Schools; *High School Students; *Language Proficiency; Language Tests; Multiple Choice Tests; Second Language Learning
Identifiers: Advanced Placement Examinations (CEEB)
Availability: Advanced Placement Program; CN6670, Princeton, NJ 08541-6670
Grade Level: 10-12
Notes: Time, 150 min.

Designed to assess achievement at the college third-year French level. Number of test items may vary from year to year. The Advanced Placement Program has been sponsored by the College Board since 1955. Listening skills are tested in 2 ways. First, candidates listen to a series of remarks or questions recorded on tape and answer written questions about those remarks. In the second portion of the listening section, students listen to recorded dialogues or monologues and answer written questions about them. Reading is tested through comprehension of sentences containing particular grammatical structures and comprehension of the content of prose passages. Writing is tested through sentence completions directed at measuring students' grammatical proficiency and through a free-response or essay question. Finally, speaking is assessed by students taping responses to a series of questions or directions and recounting the story that is suggested by a series of drawings.

2837
Advanced Placement Program: German Language. Educational Testing Service, Princeton, NJ
Descriptors: *Advanced Placement Programs; *Equivalency Tests; Essay Tests; *German; High Schools; *High School Students; *Language Proficiency; Language Tests; Multiple Choice Tests; Second Language Learning
Identifiers: Advanced Placement Examinations (CEEB); APP
Availability: Advanced Placement Program; Box 977 PD, Princeton, NJ 08541
Grade Level: 10-12
Notes: Time, 180 min.

Designed to assess achievement in college level third-year German course. Exam consists of objective questions on listening and reading and free response writing. The number of test items may vary from year to year. The Advanced Placement Program has been sponsored by the College Board since 1955. Candidates may take either or both German examinations.

2839
Advanced Placement Program: Mathematics—Calculus AB. Educational Testing Service, Princeton, NJ
Descriptors: *Advanced Placement Programs; *Calculus; *Equivalency Tests; High Schools; *High School Students; *Mathematics Tests
Identifiers: Advanced Placement Examinations (CEEB); APP
Availability: Advanced Placement Program; Box 977 PD, Princeton, NJ 08541
Grade Level: 10-12
Notes: Time, 180 min.; Items, 52

Designed to assess achievement in college-level full-year mathematics course. Calculus AB measures elementary functions and introductory calculus. The number of items may vary from year to year. The Advanced Placement Program has been sponsored by the College Board since 1955. Candidates take only 1 of 2 calculus examinations.

2840
Advanced Placement Program: Physics B. Educational Testing Service, Princeton, NJ 1981
Descriptors: *Advanced Placement Programs; Electricity; *Equivalency Tests; Essay Tests; High Schools; *High School Students; Kinetic Molecular Theory; Mechanics (Physics); Multiple Choice Tests; Optics; *Physics
Identifiers: Advanced Placement Examinations (CEEB); APP
Availability: Advanced Placement Program; Box 977 PD, Princeton, NJ 08541
Grade Level: 10-12
Notes: Time, 180 min.

Designed to assess achievement in a full-year college non-calculus course on general physics. The number of items may vary from year to year. The Advanced Placement

Program has been sponsored by the College Board since 1955. Candidates may take either Physics B or C examination.

2841
Advanced Placement Program: Spanish Language. Educational Testing Service, Princeton, NJ
Descriptors: *Advanced Placement Programs; Audiotape Recordings; *Equivalency Tests; Essay Tests; High Schools; *High School Students; *Language Proficiency; Language Tests; Multiple Choice Tests; Second Language Learning; *Spanish
Identifiers: Advanced Placement Examinations (CEEB); APP
Availability: Advanced Placement Program; Box 977 PD, Princeton, NJ 08541
Grade Level: 10-12
Notes: Time, 165 min.

Designed to assess achievement in college-level third-year Spanish. Objective questions on listening and reading, free response writing, and speaking. The number of test items may vary from year to year. The Advanced Placement Program has been sponsored by the College Board since 1955. Candidates may take either or both Spanish examinations.

3034
Screening Test of Academic Readiness. Ahr, A. Edward 1966
Subtests: Picture Vocabulary; Letters; Picture Completion; Copying; Picture Description; Human Figure Drawing; Relationships; Numbers
Descriptors: Academic Ability; *Cognitive Development; Cognitive Measurement; Diagnostic Tests; *Preschool Children; Preschool Education; *School Readiness; *School Readiness Tests; *Screening Tests
Identifiers: Oral Testing; STAR
Availability: Priority Innovations; P.O. Box 792, Skokie, IL 60067
Age Level: 2-5
Notes: Time, 60 min. approx.; Items, 50

Designed to assess readiness of preschool and kindergarten age children. STAR highlights strengths and weaknesses related to school readiness. Total score of 8 subtests may be converted to a deviation I.Q. score. Test should be administered in 2 sessions with a rest or activity period separating the sessions.

3045
National Achievement Tests: Algebra Test for Engineering and Science. Lonski, A.B. 1961
Subtests: Manipulation of Algebraic Symbols; Understanding of Algebraic Notation
Descriptors: *Achievement Tests; *Algebra; *College Students; Computation; *Engineering Education; Higher Education; High Schools; *High School Students; Mathematics Achievement; Mathematics Tests; Multiple Choice Tests; *Science Education; Secondary School Mathematics; Timed Tests
Identifiers: Algebra Test for Engineering and Science
Availability: Psychometric Affiliates; P.O. Box 807, Murfreesboro, TN 37133
Grade Level: 9-16
Notes: Time, 80 min.; Items, 65

Designed to represent the basic fundamentals of Intermediate Algebra in high school or college. Could be used for college entrants to engineering schools or colleges, technical schools, or high school students.

3083
Thompson Smoking and Tobacco Knowledge Test. Thompson, Clem W. 1967
Subtests: Personal and Psychological (18); Smoking and Tobacco Knowledge (25)
Descriptors: *Achievement Tests; *College Students; Diseases; Health Education; Higher Education; Knowledge Level; Questionnaires; Secondary Education; *Secondary School Students; *Smoking; *Tobacco
Identifiers: TIM(A)
Availability: Tests in Microfiche; Test Collection, Educational Testing Service, Princeton, NJ 08541
Grade Level: 7-16
Notes: Time, 30 min. approx.; Items, 43

Developed to measure the smoking and tobacco knowledge of high school and college students. The test is made up of 2 parts: Personal and Psychological, Smoking and Tobacco Knowledge.

3120
Information Test on Human Reproduction. Kilander, H. Frederick 1967

Descriptors: *Achievement Tests; *Adolescent Development; Adolescents; *Adults; *College Students; *High School Students; Multiple Choice Tests; *Reproduction (Biology); Sex Differences; *Sex Education; Sexuality
Availability: Dr. Glenn C. Leach, Publisher; 116 N. Pleasant Ave., Ridgewood, NJ 07450
Age Level: 14-64
Notes: Time, 20 min. approx.; Items, 33
General test of human reproduction for grades 9 through 16 and adults. Includes questions on fertilization, inherited characteristics and diseases, sex glands, physical changes during adolescence, and sterility.

3122
Information Test on Drugs and Drug Abuse.
Kilander, H. Frederick; Leach, Glenn C. 1974
Descriptors: *Achievement Tests; Adolescents; *Adults; *College Students; *Drug Education; Drug Use; *Health Education; *High School Students; Multiple Choice Tests; Stimulants
Identifiers: *Drugs; Information Test on Stimulants and Depressants; Stimulants and Depressants Test
Availability: Dr. Glenn C. Leach, Publisher; 116 N. Pleasant Ave., Ridgewood, NJ 07450
Age Level: 14-64
Notes: Time, 20 min. approx.; Items, 30
Designed to measure the knowledge of drugs and their effects. First 3 editions written by H. Frederick Kilander; 1974 revised by Glenn C. Leach. Test has used various titles such as Information Test on Stimulants and Depressants, and Stimulants and Depressants Test.

3123
Information Test on Smoking and Health. Kilander, H. Frederick 1964
Descriptors: Adolescents; *Multiple Choice Tests; *Physical Health; *Smoking
Availability: Glenn C. Leach, Publishers; 116 N. Pleasant Ave., Ridgewood, NJ 07450
Age Level: 13-17
Notes: Items, 25
Requests biographical data and information on smoking habits, also includes 25 multiple-choice questions regarding knowledge of smoking and health. Test questions based upon "Smoking and Health." A Report of the Advisory Committee to the Surgeon General of the Public Health Service, 1964. Public Health Service Publication No. 1103, 387p.

3148
ERB Modern Second Year Algebra Test. Bonan, Frederic; And Others 1968
Descriptors: *Achievement Tests; *Algebra; High Schools; *High School Students; Secondary Education
Availability: Educational Records Bureau; P.O. Box 6650, Princeton, NJ 08541
Grade Level: 9-12
Notes: Time, 80 min.; Items, 50
A measure of achievement in algebra. All questions are multiple-choice. Covers equations, word problems, logarithms, and simplifying. Available to suburban and independent schools who are members of the Educational Records Bureau.

3293
ATP Achievement Test in American History and Social Studies. Educational Testing Service, Princeton, NJ
Descriptors: *Achievement Tests; *College Bound Students; *College Entrance Examinations; High Schools; High School Seniors; *High School Students; Multiple Choice Tests; *Social Studies; *United States History
Identifiers: Admissions Testing Program Achievement Tests; MAPS; Multiple Assessment Programs and Services
Availability: The College Board; Box 2844, Princeton, NJ 08541
Grade Level: 9-12
Notes: Time, 60 min. approx.; Items, 100
Assesses knowledge of specific subject area. Designed as part of the Admissions Testing Program (ATP) administered by the College Board to high school juniors and seniors. Many colleges require the tests for admission, and some use the results for placement. Test specifications are revised periodically. Topics include political institutions, principles, issues, developments, and leaders; economic principles and developments, geographical factors and influences; foreign policy and foreign relations; and social, cultural, and intellectual developments. Covers history from pre-Columbian times to the present with emphasis on post-1763.

3294
ATP Achievement Test in Biology. Educational Testing Service, Princeton, NJ

Descriptors: *Achievement Tests; *Biology; *College Bound Students; *College Entrance Examinations; High Schools; High School Seniors; *High School Students; Multiple Choice Tests
Identifiers: Admissions Testing Program Achievement Tests; MAPS; Multiple Assessment Programs and Services
Availability: The College Board; Box 2844, Princeton, NJ 08541
Grade Level: 9-12
Notes: Time, 60 min. approx.; Items, 100
Assesses knowledge of specific subject area. Designed as part of the Admissions Testing Program (ATP) administered by the College Board to high school juniors and seniors. Many colleges require the tests for admission and some use the results for placement. Test specifications are revised periodically. Test is designed to measure what subject matter student knows and how effectively he or she can use this knowledge. Content areas include cellular and molecular biology, reproduction, growth and nutrition and development; ecology; genetics and evolution; organismal biology; systematics; behavior.

3295
ATP Achievement Test in Chemistry. Educational Testing Service, Princeton, NJ
Descriptors: *Achievement Tests; *Chemistry; *College Bound Students; *College Entrance Examinations; High Schools; High School Seniors; *High School Students; Multiple Choice Tests
Identifiers: Admissions Testing Program Achievement Tests; MAPS; Multiple Assessment Programs and Services
Availability: The College Board; Box 2844, Princeton, NJ 08541
Grade Level: 9-12
Notes: Time, 60 min. approx.; Items, 90
Assesses knowledge of specific subject area. Designed as part of the Admissions Testing Program (ATP) administered by the College Board to high school juniors and seniors. Many colleges require the tests for admission and some use the results for placement. Test specifications are revised periodically. Chemistry test is as appropriate for students of the Chemical Bond Approach course (CBA) and the Chemical Education Material Study Course (CHEMS) as for students of other courses. Test is designed to measure what subject matter student knows and how effectively he or she can use this knowledge.

3296
ATP Achievement Test in English Composition.
Educational Testing Service, Princeton, NJ
Descriptors: *Achievement Tests; *College Bound Students; *College Entrance Examinations; *College Freshmen; Essay Tests; *Grammar; Higher Education; High Schools; High School Seniors; *High School Students; Multiple Choice Tests; *Writing Skills
Identifiers: Admissions Testing Program Achievement Tests; MAPS; Multiple Assessment Programs and Services
Availability: The College Board; Box 2844, Princeton, NJ 08541
Grade Level: 9-13
Notes: Time, 60 min. approx.; Items, 90
Assesses knowledge of specific subject area. Designed as part of the Admissions Testing Program (ATP) administered by the College Board to high school juniors and seniors. Many colleges require the tests for admission and some use the results for placement. Test specifications are revised periodically. Used to evaluate ability to use standard written English, to express ideas correctly and effectively, and to use language with sensitivity to tone and meaning. Measures more sophisticated skills than do examinations in DTLS or CGP series or the Test of Standard Written English. Edition administered in December has 40 minutes of multiple-choice questions and a 20-minute essay question. This addition is identified as ES on score report. All multiple-choice test is identified as EN.

3297
ATP Achievement Test in European History and World Cultures. Educational Testing Service, Princeton, NJ
Descriptors: *Achievement Tests; *College Bound Students; *College Entrance Examinations; *European History; High Schools; High School Seniors; *High School Students; Multiple Choice Tests; *Non Western Civilization; *Western Civilization
Identifiers: Admissions Testing Program Achievement Tests; MAPS; Multiple Assessment Programs and Services
Availability: The College Board; Box 2844, Princeton, NJ 08541
Grade Level: 9-12
Notes: Time, 60 min. approx.; Items, 100
Assesses knowledge of specific subject area. Designed as part of the Admissions Testing Program (ATP) administered by the College Board to high school juniors and seniors. Many colleges require the tests for admission, and

some use the results for placement. Test specifications are revised periodically. Designed to measure student's understanding of the development of Western and non-Western cultures, comprehension of fundamental social science concepts, and ability to use basic historical techniques. Content areas include political and diplomatic history intellectual and cultural history, social and economic history, prehistory and ancient history, medieval history, early modern history, modern history, and cross periods. Major emphasis on period since midfifteenth century.

3298
ATP Achievement Test in French. Educational Testing Service, Princeton, NJ
Descriptors: *Achievement Tests; *College Bound Students; *College Entrance Examinations; College Students; *French; *Grammatical Acceptability; Higher Education; High Schools; *High School Students; Modern Languages; Multiple Choice Tests; *Reading Comprehension; Second Language Learning
Identifiers: Admissions Testing Program Achievement Tests; MAPS; Multiple Assessment Programs and Services
Availability: The College Board; CN 6200, Princeton, NJ 08541-6200
Grade Level: 9-14
Notes: Time, 60 min. approx.; Items, 85
Assesses knowledge of specific subject area. Designed as part of the Admissions Testing Program (ATP) administered by the College Board to high school juniors and seniors. Many colleges require the tests for admission, and some use the results for placement. Test specifications are revised periodically. Designed to measure ability and knowledge in areas including vocabulary in context, structure, and reading comprehension. Recommended for students who have completed a minimum of 2 years of secondary school French.

3299
ATP Achievement Test in German. Educational Testing Service, Princeton, NJ
Descriptors: *Achievement Tests; *College Bound Students; *College Entrance Examinations; College Students; *German; Grade 11; Grade 12; *Grammatical Acceptability; Higher Education; High Schools; *High School Students; Modern Languages; *Reading Comprehension; Second Language Learning; Vocabulary Skills
Identifiers: Admissions Testing Program Achievement Tests; MAPS; Multiple Assessment Programs and Services
Availability: The College Board; Box 2844, Princeton, NJ 08541
Grade Level: 11-14
Notes: Time, 60 min. approx.; Items, 90
Assesses knowledge of specific subject area. Designed as part of the Admissions Testing Program (ATP) administered by the College Board to high school juniors and seniors. Many colleges require the tests for admission, and some use the results for placement. Test specifications are revised periodically. Designed to measure ability and knowledge in vocabulary mastery, grammatical control, and reading comprehension.

3300
ATP Achievement Test in Hebrew. Educational Testing Service, Princeton, NJ
Subtests: Modern Conversational Vocabulary; Grammar; Text Comprehension; Common Word Combinations and Idioms
Descriptors: *Achievement Tests; *College Bound Students; *College Entrance Examinations; *Hebrew; High Schools; *High School Seniors; *High School Students; Language Proficiency; Multiple Choice Tests; Reading Comprehension; Second Language Learning
Identifiers: Admissions Testing Program Achievement Tests; MAPS; Multiple Assessment Programs and Services
Availability: The College Board; Box 2844, Princeton, NJ 08541
Grade Level: 9-12
Notes: Time, 60 min. approx.; Items, 90
Designed to measure student's language mastery skills with an emphasis on modern Hebrew. Areas assessed include modern conversational vocabulary, grammar, text comprehension, and common word combinations and idioms. Part of the Admissions Testing Program (ATP) administered by the College Board to high school juniors and seniors. Many colleges require the tests for admission, and some use the results for placement. Test specifications are revised periodically.

3301
ATP Achievement Test in Latin. Educational Testing Service, Princeton, NJ

Descriptors: *Achievement Tests; *College Bound Students; *College Entrance Examinations; Grade 11; Grade 12; Grammar; Higher Education; High Schools; *High School Students; *Latin; Reading Comprehension; Second Language Learning; *Undergraduate Students
Identifiers: Admissions Testing Program Achievement Tests; MAPS; Multiple Assessment Programs and Services
Availability: The College Board; Box 2844, Princeton, NJ 08541
Grade Level: 11-14
Notes: Time, 60 min. approx.; Items, 75

Assesses knowledge of specific subject area. Designed as part of the Admissions Testing Program (ATP) administered by the College Board to high school juniors and seniors. Many colleges require the tests for admission, and some use the results for placement. Test specifications are revised periodically. Measures ability to understand total meaning of a passage and points of detail, knowledge of grammar, vocabulary, scansion of hexameters, and rhetorical figures. Designed for students who have completed a minimum of 2 years of high school Latin or 2 semesters of college Latin.

3302
ATP Achievement Test in Mathematics, Level I (Standard).   Educational Testing Service, Princeton, NJ
Descriptors: *Achievement Tests; *Algebra; *College Bound Students; *College Entrance Examinations; College Preparation; Grade 11; Grade 12; High Schools; *High School Students; Multiple Choice Tests; *Plane Geometry; *Secondary School Mathematics
Identifiers: Admissions Testing Program Achievement Tests; MAPS; Multiple Assessment Programs and Services
Availability: The College Board; Box 2844, Princeton, NJ 08541
Grade Level: 11-12
Notes: Time, 60 min. approx.; Items, 50

Assesses knowledge of specific subject area. Designed as part of the Admissions Testing Program (ATP) administered by the College Board to high school juniors and seniors. Many colleges require the tests for admission, and some use the results for placement. Test specifications are revised periodically. Broad range cumulative test based on topics usually covered in a college preparatory mathematics sequence. Major emphasis is on algebra and plane Euclidean geometry. Other areas include coordinate geometry, trigonometry, functions and functional notation for composition and inverse, space perception of simple solids, mathematical reasoning, and the nature of proof.

3303
ATP Achievement Test in Mathematics, Level II (Intensive).   Educational Testing Service, Princeton, NJ
Descriptors: *Achievement Tests; *Algebra; *College Bound Students; *College Entrance Examinations; College Preparation; *Geometry; Grade 11; Grade 12; High Schools; *High School Students; Multiple Choice Tests; Secondary School Mathematics; Trigonometry
Identifiers: Admissions Testing Program Achievement Tests; MAPS; Multiple Assessment Programs and Services
Availability: The College Board; Box 2844, Princeton, NJ 08541
Grade Level: 11-12
Notes: Time, 60 min. approx.; Items, 50

Assesses knowledge of specific subject area. Designed as part of the Admissions Testing Program (ATP) administered by the College Board to high school juniors and seniors. Many colleges require the tests for admission, and some use the results for placement. Test specifications are revised periodically. Level II test overlaps that of Level I but is narrower in scope. Composed of algebra, geometry (including both coordinate and synthetic in 2 and 3 dimensions), trigonometry, functions, and a miscellaneous category. Stresses aspects of mathematics that are prerequisites for a course in calculus.

3304
ATP Achievement Test in Physics.   Educational Testing Service, Princeton, NJ
Descriptors: *Achievement Tests; *College Bound Students; *College Entrance Examinations; Electricity; High Schools; *High School Students; Mechanics (Physics); Multiple Choice Tests; *Physics
Identifiers: Admissions Testing Program Achievement Tests; MAPS; Multiple Assessment Programs and Services
Availability: The College Board; Box 2844, Princeton, NJ 08541
Grade Level: 9-12
Notes: Time, 60 min. approx.; Items, 75

Assesses knowledge of specific subject area. Designed as part of the Admissions Testing Program (ATP) administered by the College Board to high school juniors and

seniors. Many colleges require the tests for admission, and some use the results for placement. Test specifications are revised each year. Test is designed to measure what subject matter students know and how effectively they can use this knowledge. Content areas include classical mechanics, electricity and magnetism, heat and kinetic theory, and modern physics.

3306
ATP Achievement Test in Spanish, Levels 1 and 2.
Educational Testing Service, Princeton, NJ
Descriptors: *Achievement Tests; *College Bound Students; *College Entrance Examinations; College Students; Grade 11; Grade 12; Grammatical Acceptability; Higher Education; High Schools; *High School Students; Modern Languages; Reading Comprehension; Second Language Learning; *Spanish; Vocabulary Skills
Identifiers: Admissions Testing Program Achievement Tests; MAPS; Multiple Assessment Programs and Services
Availability: The College Board; Box 2844, Princeton, NJ 08541
Grade Level: 11-14
Notes: Time, 60 min. approx.; Items, 85

Assesses knowledge of specific subject area. Designed as part of the Admissions Testing Program (ATP) administered by the College Board to high school juniors and seniors. Many colleges require the tests for admission, and some use the results for placement. Test specifications are revised periodically. Designed to measure ability and knowledge in areas including vocabulary mastery, grammatical control, and reading comprehension.

3353
National Achievement Tests; World History.
McGarrett, Vincent; Merrill, Edward H. 1948
Descriptors: *Achievement Tests; *College Students; Higher Education; High Schools; *High School Students; Social Studies; World Affairs; World Geography; *World History
Identifiers: National Achievement Tests
Availability: Psychometric Affiliates; P.O. Box 807, Murfreesboro, TN 37133-0807
Grade Level: 9-16
Notes: Time, 40 min.; Items, 100

This test measures the student's knowledge and judgment of social studies terms; world geography; contribution of world peoples to civilization; political history; and economic, social, and cultural history. It is an accurate and reliable measure of the student's concept of world history and its application to present day world affairs. Reliability is 0.89.

3515
General Information Survey.   Gough, Harrison G. 1956
Descriptors: Adults; *Aptitude Tests; *Cognitive Ability; Cognitive Tests; *Intelligence; *Knowledge Level; *Leadership Qualities; Multiple Choice Tests; *Qualifications
Identifiers: GIS
Availability: Prof. Harrison G. Gough; Institute of Personality Assessment and Research, Dept. of Psychology, University of California, 2240 Piedmont Ave., Berkeley, CA 94720
Age Level: Adults
Notes: Time, 30 min. approx.; Items, 70

Designed to measure one's range and breadth of knowledge while avoiding the conventional instrument's emphasis upon formal, intellectual, academic-acquired knowledge. Emphasizes cultural lore, folk knowledge, music, athletics, recreation, etc. Based upon the theory that the breadth of interests and range of knowledge are among the important factors which seem to characterize individuals of exceptional leadership and executive talent. Available in Forms A and B. Distribution of tests restricted.

3567
National Achievement Tests: English Test, Grades 3-6 (Short Form).   Speer, Robert K.; Smith, Samuel 1955
Descriptors: *Achievement Tests; Capitalization (Alphabetic); Elementary Education; *Elementary School Students; *English; Intermediate Grades; Language Usage; Punctuation
Availability: Psychometric Affiliates; P.O. Box 807, Murfreesboro, TN 37133-0807
Grade Level: 3-6
Notes: Time, 30 min.

This test measures skill in language usage (words and sentences), including punctuation; capitalization; and expression of ideas. Reliability is 0.88.

3568
National Achievement Tests; English Test for Grades 3-8.   Speer, Robert K.; Smith, Samuel 1938
Subtests: Capitalization; Punctuation; Language Usage (Sentences); Language Usage (Words); Expressing Ideas; Letter Writing

Descriptors: *Achievement Tests; *Capitalization (Alphabetic); Elementary Education; *Elementary School Students; *Language Tests; Language Usage; *Letters (Correspondence); Punctuation
Availability: Psychometric Affiliates; P.O. Box 807, Murfreesboro, TN 37133-0807
Grade Level: 3-8
Notes: Time, 40 min. approx.

This test covers the essential elements and the important new practical phases of English instruction. Of special interest are the questions dealing with the pupils' ability to express their ideas.

3569
National Achievement Tests: English Tests, Grades 6-8 (Short Form).   Speer, Robert K.; Smith, Samuel 1938
Descriptors: *Achievement Tests; *Capitalization (Alphabetic); *Elementary School Students; *English; Intermediate Grades; Junior High Schools; *Junior High School Students; *Language Tests; *Language Usage; *Punctuation
Identifiers: National Achievement Tests
Availability: Psychometric Affiliates; P.O. Box 807, Murfreesboro, TN 37133-0807
Grade Level: 6-8
Notes: Time, 30 min.

This test measures skill in language usage (words), punctuation, and capitalization; and power to express ideas.

3570
National Achievement Tests: English.   Speer, Robert K.; Smith, Samuel 1960
Subtests: Word Usage; Punctuation; Vocabulary; Language Usage—Sentences; Expressing Ideas; Expressing Feeling
Descriptors: *Achievement Tests; *English; Grammar; Language; *Language Skills; Language Usage; Multiple Choice Tests; Punctuation; Secondary Education; *Secondary School Students; Semantics; *Verbal Ability; Verbal Development; Verbal Tests
Identifiers: Acorn Achievement Tests; English Test; National Achievement Series
Availability: Psychometric Affiliates; P.O. Box 807, Murfreesboro, TN 37133
Grade Level: 7-12
Notes: Time, 40 min. approx.; Items, 110

Measures both knowledge and skill of word usage; skill in the use of punctuation; vocabulary knowledge; ability to select correct, sensible sentences; ability to identify or express ideas; and ability to identify or express feeling. Includes multiple-choice type questions and items in which the respondent adds the punctuation. The emphasis is upon power of self-expression and judgment. Comes in 2 forms: A and B.

3571
National Achievement Tests: College English.
Jordon, A.C. 1958
Subtests: Punctuation; Capitalization; Language Usage; Sentence Structure; Modifiers; Miscellaneous Principles
Descriptors: *Achievement Tests; *College Freshmen; *English; Grammar; Higher Education; High Schools; *High School Seniors; Language; *Language Skills; Language Usage; Multiple Choice Tests; Punctuation; Semantics; Timed Tests; *Verbal Ability; Verbal Development; Verbal Tests
Identifiers: Acorn Achievement Tests; College English Test
Availability: Psychometric Affiliates; P.O. Box 807, Murfreesboro, TN 37133
Grade Level: 12-13
Notes: Time, 45 min.; Items, 120

Measures student's ability to use correct capitalization; ability to punctuate correctly; skill in the use of syntax; ability to determine the correct agreement of subject and verb; skill in sentence structure; ability to use modifiers correctly; and knowledge of miscellaneous principles. For high school seniors and first-year college students. Includes multiple-choice questions, underlining of appropriate words that should be capitalized, and adding punctuation.

3572
National Achievement Tests: Reading Test (Comprehension and Speed), Grades 6-8.   Speer, Robert K.; Smith, Samuel
Descriptors: *Achievement Tests; *Grade 6; Junior High Schools; *Junior High School Students; *Reading Comprehension; *Reading Rate; *Reading Tests
Availability: Psychometric Affiliates; P.O. Box 807, Murfreesboro, TN 37133-0807
Grade Level: 6-8
Notes: Time, 32 min.

This reading test combines the tests on comprehension and speed. Reliability is 0.91. Available in 2 forms, A and B.

3573
National Achievement Tests: Primary Reading Test for Grades 2-3. Stayton, W.E.; Ranson, F.C.; Beck, R.L.; Chinock, A.E. 1943
Descriptors: *Achievement Tests; *Grade 2; *Grade 3; Primary Education; Reading Comprehension; *Reading Tests; Vocabulary; Word Recognition; Young Children
Availability: Psychometric Affiliates; P.O. Box 807, Murfreesboro, TN 37133-0807
Grade Level: 2-3
Notes: Time, 31 min.

These tests measure word recognition, word meaning; and reading comprehension. Reading comprehension encompasses story, paragraph, and sentence meaning; a test for each is included in each division of the test. Although some reading tests measure word, sentence, and paragraph meaning in separate parts, none has combined them in one part or test. The ability to select the best title for a story is tested as a measure of story comprehension. Reliability is 0.95.

3574
National Achievement Tests: Reading Test, Grades 3-6. Speer, Robert K.; Smith, Samuel 1961
Descriptors: *Achievement Tests; Elementary Education; *Elementary School Students; Intermediate Grades; *Reading Comprehension; *Reading Rate; *Reading Tests
Availability: Psychometric Affiliates; P.O. Box 807, Murfreesboro, TN 37133-0807
Grade Level: 3-6
Notes: Time, 33 min.

The test includes following directions, sentence meaning, paragraph meaning, and reading speed. Reliability is 0.95.

3575
National Achievement Tests: Reading Comprehension Test, Grades 4-6. Speer, Robert K.; And Others 1953
Descriptors: *Achievement Tests; *Elementary School Students; *Intermediate Grades; *Reading Comprehension; *Reading Tests
Availability: Psychometric Affiliates; P.O. Box 807, Murfreesboro, TN 37133-0807
Grade Level: 4-6
Notes: Time, 30 min.

Measures word discrimination; sentence meaning; and paragraph indentation. The test is based upon the reading vocabulary of pupils in grades 4 to 6.

3576
National Achievement Tests: Reading Comprehension Test, Grades 3-8. Speer, Robert K.; Smith, Samuel 1957
Descriptors: *Achievement Tests; Elementary Education; *Elementary School Students; Intermediate Grades; Junior High Schools; *Junior High School Students; *Reading Comprehension; *Reading Tests
Availability: Psychometric Affiliates; P.O. Box 807, Murfreesboro, TN 37133-0807
Grade Level: 3-8
Notes: Time, 30 min.; Items, 16

The test covers following directions, sentence meaning, and paragraph meaning for grades 3 to 8 (inclusive). Reliability is 0.84.

3577
National Achievement Tests: Reading Comprehension, Grades 4-9. Crow, Lester D.; And Others 1961
Descriptors: *Achievement Tests; *Elementary School Students; Intermediate Grades; Junior High Schools; *Junior High School Students; *Reading Comprehension; *Reading Tests
Availability: Psychometric Affiliates; P.O. Box 807, Murfreesboro, TN 37133-0807
Grade Level: 4-9
Notes: Time, 30 min.; Items, 130

The test is designed to measure word discrimination, sentence meaning, and paragraph interpretation. The test is based upon the reading vocabulary of students in fourth to ninth grades. Reliability is 0.91. The questions for each reading selection should measure a student's ability to (1) understand the general meaning of the selection; (2) evaluate factual material in the selection; (3) interpret the author's feelings or attitudes; and (4) appreciate the literacy form of the selection.

3578
National Achievement Tests: Literature, Grades 7-12. Speer, Robert K.; Smith, Samuel 1954
Descriptors: *Achievement Tests; *Literature; Secondary Education; *Secondary School Students
Availability: Psychometric Affiliates; P.O. Box 807, Murfreesboro, TN 37133-0807
Grade Level: 7-12

Notes: Time, 40 min.
This test consists of 4 parts—recognizing effects, recognizing qualities, analyzing moods, and miscellaneous facts. This literature test covers 29 of 30 literature units most often used in secondary school (grades 7-12) English courses. Six passages deal with poetry; 9 with prose. Reliability is 0.93.

3579
National Achievement Tests: Vocabulary Test (for Grades 3-8). Speer, Robert K.; Smith, Samuel 1940
Descriptors: *Achievement Tests; Elementary Education; *Elementary School Students; Multiple Choice Tests; Reading Achievement; *Verbal Ability; Verbal Development; Verbal Tests; *Vocabulary; *Vocabulary Skills
Identifiers: Acorn Achievement Tests; National Achievement Series; *Synonyms; Vocabulary Test (for Grades 3 to 8)
Availability: Psychometric Affiliates; P.O. Box 807, Murfreesboro, TN 37133
Grade Level: 3-8
Notes: Time, 15 min. approx.; Items, 50
An untimed test designed to measure the achievement level of one's vocabulary and the power of word discrimination. Comes in 2 forms, A and B.

3580
National Achievement Tests: English Test, Grades 3-4. Speer, Robert K.; Smith, Samuel 1958
Descriptors: *Achievement Tests; Elementary Education; *Elementary School Students; *Grade 3; *Grade 4; *Spelling
Availability: Psychometric Affiliates; P.O. Box 807, Murfreesboro, TN 37133-0807
Grade Level: 3-4
Notes: Time, 25 min.; Items, 50
This spelling test, for grades 3 and 4, contains 50 spelling words to be written in blanks in printed sentences. The words were selected for frequency of use, practicality, social importance, and ease of substitution. The time is 25 minutes. Reliability is 0.92.

3581
National Achievement Tests: Spelling, Grades 5-8. Speer, Robert K.; Smith, Samuel 1957
Descriptors: *Achievement Tests; *Elementary School Students; Intermediate Grades; Junior High Schools; *Junior High School Students; *Spelling
Availability: Psychometric Affiliates; P.O. Box 807, Murfreesboro, TN 37133-0807
Grade Level: 5-8
Notes: Time, 25 min.; Items, 60
This spelling test, for grades 5-8, contains 60 words. Pupils write words in the blanks in printed sentences. Words are chosen for frequency of use, practicality, social importance, and ease of substitution. Reliability is 0.88.

3582
National Achievement Tests: Spelling, Grades 7-9. Speer, Robert K.; Smith, Samuel 1957
Descriptors: *Achievement Tests; Junior High Schools; *Junior High School Students; *Spelling
Availability: Psychometric Affiliates; P.O. Box 807, Murfreesboro, TN 37133-0807
Grade Level: 7-9
Notes: Time, 25 min.; Items, 60
This spelling test, for grades 7-9, consists of 60 words to be put into blank spaces in sentences. Words were selected on the basis of frequency of use, practicality, social importance, and ease of substitution. Reliability is 0.93.

3583
National Achievement Tests: Spelling, Grades 10-12. Speer, Robert K.; Smith, Samuel 1966
Descriptors: *Achievement Tests; High Schools; *High School Students; *Spelling
Availability: Psychometric Affiliates; P.O. Box 807, Murfreesboro, TN 37133-0807
Grade Level: 10-12
Notes: Time, 25 min.; Items, 60
This is a test of 60 spelling words to be inserted into blanks in preprinted sentences. Words are chosen for frequency of usage, practicality, social importance, and ease of substitution. Reliability is 0.94.

3625
College-Level Examination Program: Subject Examination in Education—Educational Psychology. Educational Testing Service, Princeton, NJ 1981
Descriptors: Achievement Tests; *Adults; *Educational Psychology; *Equivalency Tests; Essay Tests; Higher Education; Individual Development; Learning; Motivation; Multiple Choice Tests; Teaching Methods; Undergraduate Students
Identifiers: CLEP

Availability: College Board Publication Orders; Box 2815, Princeton, NJ 08541
Grade Level: 13-16
Age Level: 18-65
Notes: Time, 90 min.; Items, 100
CLEP enables both traditional and nontraditional students to earn college credit by examination. Tests are updated periodically. An optional essay selection requires knowledge similar to that needed for multiple-choice sections. Six major content areas include historical, philosophical, and theoretical foundations of educational psychology; teaching; evaluation; development; motivation; and learning.

3627
College Level Examination Program: Subject Examination in Introductory Marketing. Educational Testing Service, Princeton, NJ 1981
Descriptors: Achievement Tests; *Adults; Business Administration Education; *Equivalency Tests; Essay Tests; Higher Education; *Marketing; Multiple Choice Tests; Undergraduate Students
Identifiers: CLEP
Availability: College Board Publication Orders; Box 2815, Princeton, NJ 08541
Grade Level: 13-16
Age Level: Adults
Notes: Time, 90 min.; Items, 100
CLEP enables both traditional and nontraditional students to earn college credit by examination. Tests are updated periodically. The exam covers marketing in the economy, buyer behavior and consumption patterns, government-marketing interactions, marketing functions and institutions, and selected issues and policies. The 4 questions in the optional essay section are designed to test general understanding of marketing, including ability to apply understanding to basic problems.

3701
Graduate Record Examinations: Subject Tests—Biology. Educational Testing Service, Princeton, NJ 1982
Subtests: Cellular and Subcellular Biology; Organismal Biology; Population Biology
Descriptors: Academic Achievement; *Achievement Tests; *Biological Sciences; *Biology; College Admission; College Applicants; *College Entrance Examinations; College Science; *College Seniors; Degree Requirements; Doctoral Programs; Educational Counseling; Fellowships; *Graduate Students; Graduate Study; Higher Education; Majors (Students); Masters Programs; *National Competency Tests; *Predictive Measurement; Science Education; Science Tests; Student Evaluation; Timed Tests
Identifiers: GRE; Power Tests
Availability: Educational Testing Service; Princeton, NJ 08541
Grade Level: 16-18
Notes: Time, 170 min.; Items, 210
Designed to measure knowledge and understanding of biology basic to graduate study, and designed to be a power rather than speed test. For reasons of fairness, several editions are available each year. Large print answer sheets are available though the test itself is in regular sized print. In developing each new edition, special effort is made to survey the entire academic field and to include material from widely differing curricula. Used for selection of applicants for graduate school, selection of fellowship applicants, guidance and counseling, evaluation of the effectiveness of an undergraduate or master's program, requirement for conferral of a degree, senior comprehensive examination at the undergraduate level, and comprehensive examination for advancement to a master's or doctoral program. Known as Cooperative Graduate Testing Program until 1940.

3703
Graduate Record Examinations: Subject Tests—Chemistry. Educational Testing Service, Princeton, NJ 1982
Descriptors: Academic Achievement; *Achievement Tests; College Admission; College Applicants; *College Entrance Examinations; College Science; *College Seniors; Degree Requirements; Doctoral Programs; Educational Counseling; Fellowships; *Graduate Students; Graduate Study; Higher Education; Majors (Students); Masters Programs; *National Competency Tests; *Predictive Measurement; Science Education; Science Instruction; Science Tests; Student Evaluation; Timed Tests
Identifiers: GRE; Power Tests
Availability: Educational Testing Service; Princeton, NJ 08541
Grade Level: 16-18
Notes: Time, 170 min.; Items, 150
Designed to measure knowledge and understanding of chemistry basic to graduate study, and designed to be a power rather than speed test. For reasons of fairness, several editions are available each year. Large print answer sheets are available though the test itself is in regular

sized print. In developing each new edition, special effort is made to survey the entire academic field and to include material from widely differing curricula. Used for selection of applicants for graduate school, selection of fellowship applicants, guidance and counseling, evaluation of the effectiveness of an undergraduate or master's program, requirement for conferral of a degree, senior comprehensive examination at the undergraduate level, and comprehensive examination for advancement to a master's or doctoral program. Known as Cooperative Graduate Testing Program until 1940.

3704
Graduate Record Examinations: Subject Tests—Economics. Educational Testing Service, Princeton, NJ 1982
Descriptors: Academic Achievement; *Achievement Tests; College Admission; College Applicants; *College Entrance Examinations; *College Seniors; Degree Requirements; Doctoral Programs; *Economics; Economics Education; Educational Counseling; Fellowships; *Graduate Students; Graduate Study; Higher Education; Majors (Students); Masters Programs; *National Competency Tests; *Predictive Measurement; Student Evaluation; Timed Tests
Identifiers: GRE; Power Tests
Availability: Educational Testing Service; Princeton, NJ 08541
Grade Level: 16-18
Notes: Time, 170 min.; Items, 160

Designed to measure knowledge and understanding of economics basic to graduate study; designed to be a power rather than speed test. For reasons of fairness, several editions are available each year. Large print answer sheets are available though the test itself is in regular sized print. In developing each new edition, special effort is made to survey the entire academic field and to include materials from widely differing curricula. Used for selection of applicants for graduate school, selection of fellowship applicants, guidance and counseling, evaluation of the effectiveness of an undergraduate or master's program, requirement for conferral of a degree, senior comprehensive examination at the undergraduate level, and comprehensive examination for advancement to a master's or doctoral program. Known as Cooperative Graduate Testing Program until 1940.

3705
Graduate Record Examinations: Subject Tests—Education. Educational Testing Service, Princeton, NJ 1982
Descriptors: Academic Achievement; *Achievement Tests; College Admission; College Applicants; *College Entrance Examinations; *College Seniors; Degree Requirements; Doctoral Programs; Educational Counseling; *Education Majors; Fellowships; *Graduate Students; Graduate Study; Higher Education; Masters Programs; *National Competency Tests; *Postsecondary Education as a Field of Study; *Predictive Measurement; Schools of Education; Student Evaluation; Teacher Education Programs; Timed Tests
Identifiers: GRE; Power Tests
Availability: Educational Testing Service; Princeton, NJ 08541
Grade Level: 16-18
Notes: Time, 170 min.; Items, 200

Designed to measure knowledge and understanding of the education curricula basic to graduate study; designed to be a power rather than speed test. For reasons of fairness, several editions are available each year. Large print answer sheets are available though the test itself is in regular size print. In developing each new edition, special effort is made to survey the entire academic field and to include materials from widely differing curricula. Used for selection of applicants for graduate school, selection of fellowship applicants, guidance and counseling, evaluation of the effectiveness of an undergraduate or master's program, requirement for conferral of a degree, senior comprehensive examination at the undergraduate level, and comprehensive examination for advancement to a master's or doctoral program. Known as Cooperative Graduate Testing Program until 1940.

3706
Graduate Record Examinations: Subject Tests—Engineering. Educational Testing Service, Princeton, NJ 1982
Subtests: Engineering; Mathematics Usage
Descriptors: Academic Achievement; *Achievement Tests; College Admission; College Applicants; *College Entrance Examinations; College Science; *College Seniors; Degree Requirements; Doctoral Programs; Educational Counseling; *Engineering; Engineering Education; Fellowships; *Graduate Students; Graduate Study; Higher Education; Majors (Students); Masters Programs; Mathematical Applications; Mathematics Tests; *National Competency Tests; *Predictive Measurement; Science Tests; Student Evaluation; Timed Tests
Identifiers: GRE; Power Tests
Availability: Educational Testing Service; Princeton, NJ 08541
Grade Level: 16-18
Notes: Time, 170 min.; Items, 150

Designed to measure knowledge and understanding of the engineering field basic to graduate study; designed to be a power rather than speed test. For reasons of fairness, several editions are available each year. Large print answer sheets are available though the test itself is in regular sized print. In developing each new edition, special effort is made to survey the entire academic field and to include materials from widely differing curricula. Used for selection of applicants for graduate school, selection of fellowship applicants, guidance and counseling, evaluation of the effectiveness of an undergraduate or master's program, requirement for conferral of a degree, senior comprehensive examination at the undergraduate level, and comprehensive examination for advancement to a master's or doctoral program. Known as Cooperative Graduate Testing Program until 1940.

3709
Graduate Record Examinations: Subject Tests—Geology. Educational Testing Service, Princeton, NJ 1982
Subtests: Stratigraphy, Paleontology, and Geomorphology; Structural Geology and Geophysics; Mineralogy, Petrology, and Geochemistry
Descriptors: Academic Achievement; *Achievement Tests; College Admission; College Applicants; *College Entrance Examinations; College Science; *College Seniors; Degree Requirements; Doctoral Programs; *Earth Science; Educational Counseling; Fellowships; *Geology; *Graduate Students; Graduate Study; Higher Education; Majors (Students); Masters Programs; *National Competency Tests; *Predictive Measurement; Science Instruction; Science Tests; Student Evaluation; Timed Tests; Geophysics
Identifiers: Geochemistry; GRE; Power Tests
Availability: Educational Testing Service; Princeton, NJ 08541
Grade Level: 16-18
Notes: Time, 170 min.; Items, 200

Designed to measure knowledge and understanding of geology and related fields basic to graduate study; designed to be a power rather than speed test. For reasons of fairness, several editions are available each year. Large print answer sheets are available though the test itself is in regular sized print. In developing each new edition, special effort is made to survey the entire academic fields and to include materials from widely differing curricula. Used for selection of applicants for graduate school, selection of fellowship applicants, guidance and counseling, evaluation of the effectiveness of an undergraduate or master's program, requirement for conferral of a degree, senior comprehensive examination at the undergraduate level, and comprehensive examination for advancement to a master's or doctoral program. Known as Cooperation Graduate Testing Program until 1940.

3710
Graduate Record Examinations: Subject Tests—History. Educational Testing Service, Princeton, NJ 1982
Subtests: European History; American History
Descriptors: Academic Achievement; *Achievement Tests; College Admission; College Applicants; *College Entrance Examinations; *College Seniors; Degree Requirements; Doctoral Programs; Educational Counseling; *European History; Fellowships; *Graduate Students; Graduate Study; Higher Education; Majors (Students); Masters Programs; *National Competency Tests; *North American History; *Predictive Measurement; Student Evaluation; Timed Tests
Identifiers: GRE; Power Tests
Availability: Educational Testing Service; Princeton, NJ 08541
Grade Level: 16-18
Notes: Time, 170 min.; Items, 190

Designed to measure knowledge and understanding of U.S. and European history basic to graduate study; designed to be a power rather than speed test. For reasons of fairness, several editions are available each year. Large print answer sheets are available though the test itself is in regular sized print. In developing each new edition, special effort is made to survey the entire academic fields and to include materials from widely differing curricula. Used for selection of applicants for graduate school, selection of fellowship applicants, guidance and counseling, evaluation of the effectiveness of an undergraduate or master's program, requirement for conferral of a degree, senior comprehensive examination at the undergraduate level, and comprehensive examination for advancement to a master's or doctoral program. Known as Cooperative Graduate Testing Program until 1940.

3711
Graduate Record Examinations: Subject Tests—Literature in English. Educational Testing Service, Princeton, NJ 1982
Descriptors: Academic Achievement; *Achievement Tests; College Admission; College Applicants; *College Entrance Examinations; *College Seniors; Degree Requirements; Doctoral Programs; Educational Counseling; *English Literature; Fellowships; *Graduate Students; Graduate Study; Higher Education; Majors (Students); Masters Programs; *National Competency Tests; *Predictive Measurement; Student Evaluation; Timed Tests; *United States Literature
Identifiers: GRE; Power Tests
Availability: Educational Testing Service; Princeton, NJ 08541
Grade Level: 16-18
Notes: Time, 170 min.; Items, 230

Designed to measure knowledge and understanding of U.S. and English literature basic to graduate study; designed to be a power rather than speed test. For reasons of fairness, several editions are available each year. Large print answer sheets are available though the test itself is in regular sized print. In developing each new edition, special effort is made to survey the entire academic fields and to include materials from widely differing curricula. Used for selection of applicants for graduate school, selection of fellowship applicants, guidance and counseling, evaluation of the effectiveness of an undergraduate or master's program, requirement for conferral of a degree, senior comprehensive examination at the undergraduate level, and comprehensive examination for advancement to a master's or doctoral program. Known as Cooperative Graduate Testing Program until 1940.

3712
Graduate Record Examinations: Subject Tests—Mathematics. Educational Testing Service, Princeton, NJ 1982
Descriptors: Academic Achievement; *Achievement Tests; College Admission; College Applicants; *College Entrance Examinations; *College Mathematics; *College Seniors; Computation; Degree Requirements; Doctoral Programs; Educational Counseling; Fellowships; *Graduate Students; Graduate Study; Higher Education; Majors (Students); Masters Programs; *Mathematical Concepts; Mathematics Achievement; Mathematics Education; Mathematics Tests; *National Competency Tests; *Predictive Measurement; Student Evaluation; Timed Tests
Identifiers: GRE; Power Tests
Availability: Educational Testing Service; Princeton, NJ 08541
Grade Level: 16-18
Notes: Time, 170 min.; Items, 66

Designed to measure knowledge and understanding of mathematics basic to graduate study; designed to be a power rather than speed test. For reasons of fairness, several editions are available each year. Large print answer sheets are available though the test itself is in regular sized print. In developing each new edition, special effort is made to survey the entire academic field and to include materials from widely differing curricula. Used for selection of applicants for graduate school, selection of fellowship applicants, guidance and counseling, evaluation of the effectiveness of an undergraduate or master's program, requirement for conferral of a degree, senior comprehensive examination at the undergraduate level, and comprehensive examination for advancement to a master's or doctoral program. Known as Cooperative Graduate Testing Program until 1940.

3716
Graduate Record Examinations: Subject Tests—Physics. Educational Testing Service, Princeton, NJ 1982
Descriptors: Academic Achievement; *Achievement Tests; College Admission; College Applicants; *College Entrance Examinations; College Science; *College Seniors; Degree Requirements; Doctoral Programs; Educational Counseling; Fellowships; *Graduate Students; Graduate Study; Higher Education; Majors (Students); Masters Programs; *National Competency Tests; *Physics; *Predictive Measurement; Science Instruction; Science Tests; Student Evaluation; Timed Tests
Identifiers: GRE; Power Tests
Availability: Educational Testing Service; Princeton, NJ 08541
Grade Level: 16-18
Notes: Time, 170 min.; Items, 90

Designed to measure knowledge and understanding of physics basic to graduate study. Designed to be a power rather than speed test. For reasons of fairness, several editions are available each year. Large print answer sheets are available though the test itself is in regular sized print. In developing each new edition, special effort is made to survey the entire academic field and to include materials from widely differing curricula. Used for selection of applicants for graduate school, selection of fellowship applicants, guidance and counseling, evaluation of the effectiveness of an undergraduate or master's program, requirement for conferral of a degree, senior comprehensive examination at the undergraduate level, and comprehensive examination for advancement to a master's or doctoral program. Known as Cooperative Graduate Testing Program until 1940.

3717
Graduate Record Examinations: Subject Tests—Political Science. Educational Testing Service, Princeton, NJ 1982
Descriptors: Academic Achievement; *Achievement Tests; College Admission; College Applicants; *College Entrance Examinations; *College Seniors; Degree Requirements; Doctoral Programs; Educational Counseling; Fellowships; Governmental Structure; Government Role; *Graduate Students; Graduate Study; Higher Education; *International Relations; Majors (Students); Masters Programs; *National Competency Tests; *Political Science; *Predictive Measurement; Public Administration; Public Administration Education; Student Evaluation; Timed Tests
Identifiers: GRE; Power Tests
Availability: Educational Testing Service; Princeton, NJ 08541
Grade Level: 16-18
Notes: Time, 170 min.; Items, 170
Designed to measure knowledge and understanding of political science basic to graduate study. Designed to be a power rather than speed test. For reasons of fairness, several editions are available each year. Large print answer sheets are available though the test itself is in regular sized print. In developing each new edition, special effort is made to survey the entire academic field and to include materials from widely differing curricula. Used for selection of applicants for graduate school, selection of fellowship applicants, guidance and counseling, evaluation of the effectiveness of an undergraduate or master's program, requirement for conferral of a degree, senior comprehensive examination at the undergraduate level, and comprehensive examination for advancement to a master's or doctoral program. Known as Cooperative Graduate Testing Program until 1940.

3718
Graduate Record Examinations: Subject Tests—Psychology. Educational Testing Service, Princeton, NJ 1982
Subtests: Experimental Psychology; Social Psychology
Descriptors: Academic Achievement; *Achievement Tests; College Admission; College Applicants; *College Entrance Examinations; *College Seniors; Degree Requirements; Doctoral Programs; Educational Counseling; *Experimental Psychology; Fellowships; *Graduate Students; Graduate Study; Higher Education; Majors (Students); Masters Programs; *National Competency Tests; *Predictive Measurement; *Social Psychology; Student Evaluation; Timed Tests
Identifiers: GRE; Power Tests
Availability: Educational Testing Service; Princeton, NJ 08541
Grade Level: 16-18
Notes: Time, 170 min.; Items, 200
Designed to measure knowledge and understanding of social and experimental psychology basic to graduate study. Designed to be a power rather than speed test. For reasons of fairness, several editions are available each year. Large print answer sheets are available though the test itself is in regular sized print. In developing each new edition, special effort is made to survey the entire academic field and to include materials from widely differing curricula. Used for selection of applicants for graduate school, selection of fellowship applicants, guidance and counseling, evaluation of the effectiveness of an undergraduate or master's program, requirement for conferral of a degree, senior comprehensive examination at the undergraduate level, and comprehensive examination for advancement to a master's or doctoral program. Known as Cooperative Graduate Testing Program until 1940.

3720
Graduate Record Examinations: Subject Tests—Sociology. Educational Testing Service, Princeton, NJ 1982

Descriptors: Academic Achievement; *Achievement Tests; College Admission; College Applicants; *College Entrance Examinations; *College Seniors; Counseling; Degree Requirements; Doctoral Programs; Educational Counseling; Fellowships; *Graduate Students; Graduate Study; Higher Education; Majors (Students); Masters Programs; *Methods; *National Competency Tests; *Predictive Measurement; Sociology; Sociometric Techniques; *Statistics; Student Evaluation; Timed Tests
Identifiers: GRE; Power Tests
Availability: Educational Testing Service; Princeton, NJ 08541
Grade Level: 16-18
Notes: Time, 170 min.; Items, 200
Designed to measure knowledge and understanding of sociology basic to graduate study. Includes methodology and statistics, social psychology, race and ethnic relations, and general theory; family and sex roles, organizations, demography, stratification, social institutions, urban/rural sociology, deviance and social control and social change. Designed to be a power rather than speed test. For reasons of fairness, several editions are available each year. Large print answer sheets are available though the test itself is in regular sized print. In developing each new edition, special effort is made to survey the entire academic field and to include materials from widely differing curricula. Used for selection of applicants for graduate school, selection of fellowship applicants, guidance and counseling, evaluation of the effectiveness of an undergraduate or master's program, requirement for conferral of a degree, senior comprehensive examination at the undergraduate level, and comprehensive examination for advancement to a master's or doctoral program. Known as Cooperative Testing Program until 1940.

3822
Gilmore Oral Reading Test. Gilmore, John V.; Gilmore, Eunice C. 1968
Descriptors: *Achievement Tests; Braille; Elementary Education; *Elementary School Students; Individual Testing; Large Type Materials; *Oral Reading; Reading Achievement; *Reading Rate; *Reading Skills; Reading Tests; Visual Impairments
Availability: The Psychological Corp.; 555 Academic Ct., San Antonio, TX 78204-0952
Grade Level: 1-8
Notes: Time, 20 min. approx.; Items, 50
Designed to measure three aspects of oral reading ability—accuracy, comprehension, and rate. Equivalent forms C and D are available. Available in large-type print or Braille for visually impaired subjects from American Printing House for the Blind, 1839 Frankfort Ave., Louisville, KY 40206.

4032
Gillingham-Childs Phonics Proficiency Scales: Series I Basic Reading and Spelling. Gillingham, Anna; And Others 1970
Descriptors: *Achievement Tests; Basic Skills; *Elementary School Students; Elementary Secondary Education; Individual Testing; Oral Reading; *Phonics; Reading; *Secondary School Students; Spelling; *Student Improvement
Identifiers: *Proficiency Tests
Availability: Educators Publishing Service, Inc.; 75 Moulton St., Cambridge, MA 02238-9101
Grade Level: 1-12
Designed to check progress in mastery of sequential steps of the coding or phonic method of teaching initial skills of written language. After a particular point in phonics method is taught, the appropriate scale is used to determine whether new material has been sufficiently mastered.

4115
SRA Reading Index. Science Research Associates, Chicago, IL 1968
Subtests: Picture-Word Association; Word Decoding; Phrase Comprehension; Sentence Comprehension; Paragraph Comprehension
Descriptors: Achievement Tests; Adolescents; Adults; *Disadvantaged; *Entry Workers; Job Applicants; *Reading Achievement; Reading Tests; *Screening Tests; *Semiskilled Workers; *Unskilled Workers
Identifiers: RAI
Availability: London House, Inc.; 1550 Northwest Hwy., Park Ridge, IL 60068
Age Level: 14-64
Notes: Time, 25 min. approx.; Items, 50
Measures general reading achievement of adults and adolescents. Designed for use with applicants for entry-level jobs and special training programs, where the basic skills of applicants are too low to be reliably evaluated by typical selection tests.

4116
SRA Arithmetic Index. Science Research Associates, Chicago, IL 1968

Subtests: Addition and Subtraction of Whole Numbers; Multiplication and Division of Whole Numbers; Fractions; Decimals and Percentages
Descriptors: Achievement Tests; Adolescents; Adults; *Arithmetic; Computation; Decimal Fractions; *Disadvantaged; *Entry Workers; Fractions; Mathematics Tests; *Screening Tests; Semiskilled Workers; *Unskilled Workers
Identifiers: RAI
Availability: London House, Inc.; 1550 Northwest Hwy., Park Ridge, IL 60068
Age Level: 14-64
Notes: Time, 25 min. approx.
Measures computational achievement of adolescents and adults. Designed as a screening device for applicants for entry-level jobs and special training programs where the basic skills of applicants are too low to be reliably evaluated by typical selection tests.

4134
Farnum String Scale. Farnum, Stephen E. 1969
Descriptors: *Achievement Tests; *Individual Testing; Music Education; *Music Reading; Observation; *Performance Tests; Secondary Education; *Secondary School Students; Talent Development
Identifiers: *Music Tests; *Stringed Instruments
Availability: Hal Leonard Publishing Corp.; 8112 W. Bluemound Rd., Milwaukee, WI 53213
Grade Level: 7-12
Notes: Items, 14
An individually administered test for violin, viola, cello, and string bass players. To measure the sight-reading ability, auditions for seating placement and annual or semiannual testing to measure individual improvement. The types of errors brought out are pitch errors, time or rhythm errors, change of time errors, expression errors, bowing errors, rests, holds and pauses, and repeats. Students start with the first exercise and are told to stop when they have consecutively made too many errors in 2 different exercises.

4150
Volleyball Skills Test. Shay, Clayton 1969
Subtests: Volleying; Serving; Passing; Set-Up
Descriptors: Adolescents; *Athletics; Children; *Elementary School Students; Elementary Secondary Education; *Performance Tests; *Secondary School Students; *Skills; *Volleyball
Availability: AAPHERD; 1900 Association Drive, Reston, VA 22091
Age Level: 10-18
Notes: Items, 4
Designed primarily to help evaluate students' performance in the fundamental skills of volleyball and to provide an incentive for improvement. May also be used to evaluate teacher instruction and teaching programs. Separate forms for boys and girls.

4156
Parent Readiness Evaluation of Preschoolers. Ahr, A. Edward 1968
Subtests: General Information; Comprehension; Opposites; Identification; Verbal Associations; Verbal Description; Listening; Language; Concepts; Motor coordination; Visual-Motor Association; Visual Interpretation; Auditory; Visual Memory
Descriptors: *Individual Testing; *Kindergarten Children; *Parent Participation; Performance; *Preschool Children; *School Readiness Tests; *Screening Tests; Verbal Ability; Young Children
Identifiers: PREP
Availability: Priority Innovations; P.O. Box 792, Skokie, IL 60076
Age Level: 4-6
PREP is a parent-administered individual test for preschool and kindergarten children that assesses skills and abilities in 14 separate areas in addition to yielding verbal, performance, and total scores.

4209
Modern Photography Comprehension Test. Bruce, Martin M. 1969
Descriptors: Achievement Tests; Career Guidance; Higher Education; Knowledge Level; *Photography; *Undergraduate Students
Availability: Martin M. Bruce, Publishers; 50 Larchwood Rd., Box 248, Larchmont, NY 10538
Grade Level: 13-16
Notes: Items, 40
Designed to assess student's knowledge of modern photography. Useful in vocational guidance.

4242
Delaware County Silent Reading Tests. Newburg, Judson E.; Spennato, Nicholas A. 1965
Subtests: Interpretation of Ideas; Organization of Ideas; Vocabulary; Structural Analysis of Words

Descriptors: *Achievement Tests; Elementary Education; *Elementary School Students; *Reading Achievement; *Reading Tests; Vocabulary; Writing Skills
Availability: Nicholas A. Spennato, Language Arts Specialist; Delaware County Intermediate Unit, 6th and Olive Sts., Media, PA 19063
Grade Level: 1-8
Notes: Items, 20

Designed to measure specific strengths and weaknesses in 4 reading skill areas. Also measures ability to express ideas in sentences. Complete set of test materials at each level includes a reuseable story booklet, test booklet, answer key, and teacher's guide for administration. Assesses skill at levels 1.5, 2.0, 2.5, 3.0, 3.5, and levels 4-8. Test is untimed. It is suggested test be administered in 2 days—sections A and B on first day, sections C and D on second day.

4298
Goldman-Fristoe-Woodcock Auditory Memory Test. Goldman, Ronald; And Others 1974
Subtests: Recognition Memory; Memory for Content; Memory for Sequence
Descriptors: Adolescents; Adults; Audiotape Recordings; *Children; *Diagnostic Tests; Individual Testing; Learning Disabilities; *Memory; *Older Adults; Recall (Psychology); Recognition (Psychology)
Identifiers: *Auditory Memory; G F W Auditory Memory Tests; G F W Battery; Test Batteries
Availability: American Guidance Service; Publishers' Bldg., Circle Pines, MN 55014-1796
Age Level: 3-85
Notes: Items, 140

Goldman-Fristoe-Woodcock Auditory Skills Battery consists of a wide range of diagnostic instruments for identifying and describing deficiencies in auditory functioning. Designed for use by teachers of learning-disabled children, reading specialists, speech and hearing clinicians, and school psychologists. Useful with preschool through geriatric populations. Use of earphones is recommended to reduce distraction. Designed to assess aspects of short-term auditory memory performance including recognition memory, memory for content, and memory for sequence.

4299
Goldman-Fristoe-Woodcock Auditory Selective Attention Test. Goldman, Ronald; And Others 1974
Subtests: Quiet; Fanlike Noise; Cafeteria Noise; Voice
Descriptors: Adolescents; Adults; *Attention; Audiotape Recordings; *Auditory Perception; *Children; *Diagnostic Tests; Individual Testing; *Learning Disabilities; *Listening Comprehension; Listening Skills; *Older Adults
Identifiers: G F W Attention; G F W Battery; Test Batteries
Availability: American Guidance Service; Publishers' Bldg., Circle Pines, MN 55014-1796
Age Level: 3-85
Notes: Items, 110

Goldman-Fristoe-Woodcock Auditory Skills Battery consists of a wide range of diagnostic instruments for identifying and describing deficiencies in auditory functioning. Designed for use by teachers of learning-disabled students, reading specialists, speech and hearing clinicians, and school psychologists. Useful with preschool through geriatric populations. Use of earphones is recommended to reduce distraction. GFW attention is designed to assess ability to attend under increasingly difficulty listening conditions. Provides an index of individual's ability to listen to and to understand a message in the presence of competing sound that is varied in intensity and type.

4300
Goldman-Fristoe-Woodcock Diagnostic Auditory Discrimination Tests—Parts I, II, and III. Goldman, Ronald; And Others 1974
Descriptors: Adolescents; Adults; Audiotape Recordings; *Auditory Discrimination; Auditory Perception; *Children; *Diagnostic Tests; Individual Testing; *Learning Disabilities; *Older Adults
Identifiers: G F W Battery; G F W Diagnostic Discrim; Test Batteries
Availability: American Guidance Service; Publishers' Bldg., Circle Pines, MN 55014-1796
Age Level: 3-85
Notes: Items, 300

Goldman-Fristoe-Woodcock Auditory Skills Battery consists of a wide range of diagnostic instruments for identifying and describing deficiencies in auditory functioning. Designed for use by teachers of learning-disabled students, reading specialists, speech and hearing clinicians, and school psychologists. Useful with preschool through geriatric populations. Use of earphones is recommended to reduce distraction. Designed for diagnostic assessment of speech-sound discrimination problems. Used to determine individual's ability to discriminate speech sounds and provide a description of sound confusions. Parts II and III are separately bound from Part I and administered only to subjects who have experienced difficulty with speech sound discrimination in Part I. A Sound Confusion Inventory (SCI) shows the pattern of a subject's responses and is included for all parts. SCI simplifies identification and analysis of specific speech sound discrimination errors.

4326
Test on Understanding Science: Form EV. Klopfer, Leopold E.; And Others 1970
Descriptors: Elementary Education; *Elementary School Science; *Elementary School Students; Intermediate Grades; Multiple Choice Tests; *Science Tests; *Scientific Literacy
Identifiers: TOUS
Availability: Leopold Klopfer, Learning Research and Development Center; University of Pittsburgh, 3939 O'Hara St., Pittsburgh, PA 15260
Grade Level: 5-7
Notes: Time, 30 min. approx.; Items, 36

Designed to assess student understanding of nature of scientific inquiry, of science as an institution, and of scientists as people.

4327
Test on Understanding Science: Form JW. Klopfer, Leopold E.; Carrier, E.O. 1970
Descriptors: Junior High Schools; *Junior High School Students; *Science Tests; *Scientific Literacy; *Secondary School Science
Identifiers: TOUS
Availability: Leopold Klopfer, Learning Research and Development Center; University of Pittsburgh, 3939 O'Hara St., Pittsburgh, PA 15260
Grade Level: 7-9
Notes: Items, 45

Designed to assess student understanding of the nature of scientific inquiry, of science as an institution, and of scientists as people.

4337
Adston Mathematics Skills Series: Elementary School Mathematics: Whole Numbers. Adams, Sam; Ellis, Leslie 1971
Subtests: Survey Instrument; Addition Facts; Subtraction Facts; Multiplication Facts; Division Facts; Addition Operations; Subtraction Operations; Multiplication Operations; Division Operations
Descriptors: Achievement Tests; *Arithmetic; Computation; *Criterion Referenced Tests; *Diagnostic Tests; Elementary Education; *Elementary School Mathematics; *Elementary School Students; Junior High Schools; *Junior High School Students; *Mathematics Tests; *Whole Numbers
Identifiers: TIM(J)
Availability: Tests in Microfiche; Test Collection, Educational Testing Service, Princeton, NJ 08541
Grade Level: 3-8
Notes: Items, 52

Designed to help the teacher locate specific gaps in arithmetic skills that students may have in the 4 basic operations of whole numbers. The 52-item survey section is given first. Students who receive a perfect score do not take any other sections of the test. Students who answer at least half of the items correctly take the diagnostic instrument in that particular operation. Students who answer less than half of the items correctly take the diagnostic instrument for the facts in that operation. The teacher then analyzes the pattern of errors. A student may retake a particular section a short time later. There is no time limit. The number of items per section varies from 24 to 100.

4338
Adston Mathematics Skills Series—Elementary School Mathematics: Readiness for Operations. Adams, Sam; Sauls, Charles 1973
Descriptors: *Criterion Referenced Tests; *Diagnostic Tests; *Elementary School Mathematics; *Elementary School Students; *Learning Readiness; *Mathematics Tests; *Number Concepts; Primary Education; Whole Numbers
Identifiers: TIM(J)
Availability: Tests in Microfiche; Test Collection, Educational Testing Service, Princeton, NJ 08541
Grade Level: K-3
Notes: Items, 64

Diagnostic test designed to determine a student's readiness to work with arithmetic operations and to identify specific weaknesses in the student's background, which would cause the student failure in work with the operations. Most of the sections require no reading ability; those sections that do have some reading matter are read aloud by the tester. The total test may be administered in one session or broken up at any obvious point. The author points out that not all students will need to take the entire test and that others may take it several times. The test consists of 12 parts, each designed to give the teacher information regarding the student's conceptual background. The 12 sections are one-to-one correspondence, equality of groups, recognition of like numerals, verbal recognition of numerals, writing numerals, sequencing, recognition of cardinal numbers, writing numerals for sets, basic meaning of addition, basic meaning of subtraction, basic meaning of multiplication and division, structure of multidigit numbers.

4342
Harris Articulation Test. Harris, Gail S. 1973
Descriptors: *American Indians; *Articulation Impairments; *Children; *Diagnostic Tests; Individual Testing; *Pictorial Stimuli; *Speech Tests
Identifiers: Articulation Test; TIM(B)
Availability: Tests in Microfiche; Test Collection, Educational Testing Service, Princeton, NJ 08541
Age Level: Children
Notes: Items, 67

Designed for use with American Indians, the test identifies what sounds the child has difficulty producing and in what position those sounds are in words (beginning, middle, or end of word). The test consists of pictures of objects that are stimuli for testing sounds and requires that the tester go over the pictures with the entire class assembled as a group several days before conducting the individual tests. The Articulation Test Check Sheet is the Revised Edition, 1974.

4487
Newbery Medal Award Tests (1922-1974). Perfection Form Co., Logan, IA
Descriptors: *Achievement Tests; Book Reviews; Books; *Childrens Literature; Constructed Response; Critical Reading; Elementary Education; *Elementary School Students; *North American Literature; Reading Comprehension; *Reading Tests
Identifiers: *Book Reports; Newbery Award; *Newbery Medal Books; Test Book for Newbery Award Books
Availability: Perfection Form Co.; 1000 N. Second Ave., Logan, IA 51546
Grade Level: 4-8

A booklet of tests to measure knowledge of a selection of Newbery Medal Books. Also designed to encourage reading and to allow for a quick check of books read. Booklet includes 3 different tests for each selected title; each test contains 10 questions.

4710
Student Self-Appraisal Inventory of Interests and Estimated Knowledge in Major Health Education Areas. Gaines, Josephine 1961
Descriptors: Accidents; *College Students; Diseases; Drug Use; *Health Education; Health Needs; Health Occupations; Heredity; Higher Education; Knowledge Level; Marriage; *Mental Health; Nutrition; *Physical Health; Public Health; Recreation; Student Interests
Identifiers: TIM(A)
Availability: Tests in Microfiche; Test Collection, Educational Testing Service, Princeton, NJ 08541
Grade Level: 13-16
Notes: Items, 125

Designed to provide a functional instrument that could aid health educators in better assessing the current interests and previous knowledge backgrounds of their students in 18 major areas of health education: basic health concepts; health on the college campus; mental health; marriage and the family; heredity and the environment; care of the skin, teeth, eyes, and ears; fitness; posture and body mechanics; recreation and health; rest, sleep, and relaxation; nutrition and diet; consumer health; communicable diseases; chronic and degenerative diseases; stimulants and depressants; accidents and safety; community and international health; and health careers.

4713
Illinois Test of Psycholinguistic Abilities: Revised Edition. Kirk, Samuel A; And Others 1968
Subtests: Auditory Reception; Visual Reception; Visual Sequential Memory; Auditory Association; Auditory Sequential Memory; Visual Association; Visual Closure; Verbal Expression; Grammatic Closure; Manual Expression; Auditory Closure; Sound Blending
Descriptors: Auditory Perception; Children; Cognitive Processes; *Diagnostic Tests; Elementary Education; *Elementary School Students; Expressive Language; Individual Testing; *Intelligence; Intelligence Tests; Pictorial Stimuli; *Preschool Children; Preschool Education; *Psycholinguistics; Receptive Language; Visual Perception
Identifiers: ITPA; Sequential Memory
Availability: University of Illinois Press; 54 E. Gregory Drive, Champaign, IL 61820
Age Level: 2-10

Designed to assess abilities in psycholinguistic functions in children between the ages of 2 and 10. Different starting points are specified for children of differing ability levels. If child is suspected of being retarded or gifted, the estimated mental age should determine the starting point. In average children, the chronological age is used to determine the starting point.

4752
Portland Prognostic Test for Mathematics, Grade 7. Hayes, Ernest 1964
Subtests: Number Series; Arithmetic Comprehension
Descriptors: *Arithmetic; Diagnostic Tests; *Elementary School Mathematics; *Elementary School Students; *Grade 6; Grade 7; *Identification; Junior High Schools; *Mathematics Tests; *Prognostic Tests
Identifiers: Number Sequences
Availability: Hayes Educational Tests; 7040 N. Portsmouth Ave., Portland, OR 97203
Grade Level: 6-7
Notes: Time, 35 min. approx.; Items, 50
Designed to identify students capable of mastering mathematics content in accelerated grade 7 mathematics. A prognostic test to be administered at the end of grade 6.

4753
Portland Prognostic Test for Mathematics, Grades 7 and 8. Hayes, Ernest 1963
Subtests: Number Series; Arithmetic Comprehension
Descriptors: *Achievement Tests; Arithmetic; Diagnostic Tests; Junior High Schools; *Junior High School Students; *Mathematics Tests; *Prognostic Tests; *Secondary School Mathematics
Identifiers: Number Sequences
Availability: Hayes Educational Tests; 7040 N. Portsmouth Ave., Portland, OR 97203
Grade Level: 7-8
Notes: Time, 35 min. approx.; Items, 50
Designed to measure achievement in junior high school mathematics. May be used to predict success in junior high school mathematics courses.

4938
Atkins-McBride General Science Test. Atkins, Leona; McBride, R. 1969
Descriptors: *Achievement Tests; Biology; Chemistry; General Science; Multiple Choice Tests; Physics; *Science Tests; Secondary Education
Availability: Psychometric Affiliates; P.O. Box 807, Murfreesboro, TN 37133-0807
Grade Level: 8-12
Measures scientific knowledge of junior and senior high levels by means of specific multiple-choice questions concerning biology, chemistry, physics, and general science.

4948
Zip Test. Scott, Norval C.
Subtests: Language Facility Section; Word Recognition; Reading Comprehension; Word Opposites; Math Section; English Language Facility
Descriptors: Children; *Elementary School Students; English (Second Language); *Individual Testing; Language Fluency; Mathematics Achievement; *Mathematics Tests; *Migrant Children; Reading Achievement; Reading Tests; *School Readiness Tests; *Screening Tests; *Spanish Speaking; *Student Placement
Availability: ASIS/NAPS; c/o Microfiche Publications, P.O. Box 3513, Grand Central Station, New York, NY 10163-3513 (NAPS Document 0070)
Age Level: 5-12
Notes: Time, 30 min.
Determines grade placement of a migrant child in reading and math and assesses the child's English language facility. The test locates the instructional level at which a child can effectively use a mathematics book and a reader and should not be used for chronological grade placement.

4970
College English Placement Test. Haugh, Oscar M.; Brown, James I. 1969
Descriptors: *Achievement Tests; *College English; *College Freshmen; Essay Tests; Higher Education; Multiple Choice Tests; Placement
Identifiers: CEPT
Availability: The Riverside Publishing Co.; 8420 Bryn Mawr Ave., Chicago, IL 60631
Grade Level: 13
Notes: Time, 45 min.; Items, 106
Measures 4 areas of English-organization and paragraph structure, syntax and grammar, vocabulary development and diction, and usage and capitalization. Designed to assess student's ability to use language effectively, to provide accurate information for student placement in composition class, to indicate weaknesses in specific language areas, and to provide insights bearing on process of writ-

ten composition. Consists of mandatory objective section and optional essay section. Essay section consists of 2 topics. One essay topic requires 25 minutes and the other 35 minutes.

5004
Goldman-Fristoe-Woodcock Test of Auditory Discrimination. Goldman, Ronald 1970
Descriptors: Adolescents; *Adults; Audiotape Recordings; *Auditory Discrimination; *Children; Individual Testing; Older Adults; *Screening Tests
Identifiers: Goldman Fristoe Woodcock Test Auditory Discrim
Availability: American Guidance Service; Publishers' Bldg., Circle Pines, MN 55014-1796
Age Level: 4-85
Notes: Time, 15 min. approx.; Items, 125
Designed to measure auditory discrimination under ideal listening conditions and in the presence of controlled background noise. Training procedure precedes actual test administration. Use of earphones is suggested for test administration.

5147
Minorities Test. Aschenbrenner, Paul
Descriptors: *Achievement Tests; High Schools; *High School Students; *Minority Groups; *Racial Attitudes; *Social Bias; *Spanish Speaking
Identifiers: Pre Test (Spanish); Pre Test Minorities; Project Esperanza; Salinas Title VII Project
Availability: Paul Aschenbrenner; Instructor, Social Sciences, Hartnell College, 156 Homestead Ave., Salinas, CA 93901
Grade Level: 9-12
Notes: Time, 65 min. approx.; Items, 100
Measures a student's knowledge of minority groups. Originally developed for use by Project Esperanza, the Salinas Title VII Project. Available in both English and Spanish. Type of questions are multiple-choice and true-false.

5157
Cutrona Reading Inventory. Cutrona, Michael P. 1975
Descriptors: Elementary Education; *Elementary School Students; Individual Testing; *Informal Reading Inventories; *Kindergarten Children; Reading Achievement; *Sight Vocabulary
Availability: Dr. Michael P. Cutrona; 1298 Victory Blvd., Staten Island, NY 10301
Grade Level: K-6
Designed to determine approximate reading grade level using sight vocabularly for instructional purposes.

5163
Language Communication. Skills Task. Wang, Margaret C.; Rose, Suzanna; Maxwell, James 1973
Descriptors: Audiotape Recorders; *Elementary School Students; Language Acquisition; *Listening Comprehension; Primary Education; *Verbal Communication; Verbal Tests; *Young Children
Identifiers: LCST; TIM(C)
Availability: Tests in Microfiche; Test Collection, Educational Testing Service, Princeton, NJ 08541
Grade Level: K-2
Designed to assess the child's ability to get meanings and ideas from his or her sociolinguistic situations, transmit these meanings and ideas to others, respond to the language behavior of others, and adapt his or her communicative input to achieve effective language communication. It includes 2 parallel sets of tasks that were developed to measure the child's communication skills as both the speaker and the listener. The tasks are administered to one pair of children at a time, with one playing the message presenter role and the other playing the message receiver role. Untimed.

5194
ACS Cooperative Examination: Qualitative Analysis, Form 1969. American Chemical Society, Tampa, FL, Div. of Chemical Education 1969
Subtests: Recall of Information; Paper Unknowns; Problems and Equations
Descriptors: *Achievement Tests; *Chemistry; Higher Education; Multiple Choice Tests; Problem Solving; *Undergraduate Students
Identifiers: American Chemical Society Cooperative Examinations; Chemical Calculators; *Qualitative Analysis
Availability: American Chemical Society; Examinations Committee, University of South Florida, Tampa, FL 33620
Grade Level: 13-16
Notes: Time, 105 min.; Items, 64

Designed for use in separate qualitative analysis courses or general chemistry courses in which considerable emphasis is placed on the theory of ionic equilibria and on the qualitative chemistry of the common cations and anions. Test forms are updated periodically, and older forms may be retired from active use. Retired college-level forms may be released to high school teachers.

5328
Pre-Kindergarten Goal Card. Cincinnati Public Schools, OH Jacobs, James N. 1966
Subtests: Physical Coordination (6); Relationship of People and Things (45); Auditory Discrimination (4); Concepts of Size (4); Concepts of Color (3); Manipulation (1); Arithmetic (3); Location and Space (7); Listening (3); Mental Alertness (4); Language Ability (6); Social Awareness (13)
Descriptors: Arithmetic; Auditory Discrimination; Color; Coordination; *Diagnostic Tests; Individual Testing; Language Proficiency; Listening Skills; Object Manipulation; Observation; *Preschool Children; Preschool Education; *Preschool Tests; Social Adjustment; Spatial Ability
Identifiers: Cincinnati Public Schools OH; TIM(A)
Availability: Tests in Microfiche; Test Collection, Educational Testing Service, Princeton, NJ 08541
Age Level: 4-5
Notes: Items, 99
An individually administered evaluation of preschool-aged children based on observation of their performance of various tasks. Materials found in a classroom such as balls, blocks, tricycle, etc., are required.

5329
Pre-Grade One Goal Card. Cincinnati Public Schools, OH Jacobs, James N. 1966
Descriptors: Arithmetic; Color; Eye Hand Coordination; *Grade 1; Group Testing; Individual Testing; *Kindergarten Children; Language Proficiency; Primary Education; Tactual Perception; Vocabulary Skills
Identifiers: Cincinnati Public Schools OH; TIM(A)
Availability: Tests in Microfiche; Test Collection, Educational Testing Service, Princeton, NJ 08541
Age Level: 5-6
Notes: Items, 55
An evaluation of kindergarten children based on their performance of various tasks. The test is divided into 2 sections, group and individual. The individual section is based on the teachers' observation of the child's performance of certain activities. Props are required. Covers vocabulary, eye-hand coordination, rhyming words, counting, colors, sensory abilities.

5486
Optical and Mechanical Features of the Microscope. American-Optical Co., Buffalo, NY Instrument Div.
Descriptors: *Achievement Tests; *Microscopes; *Science Tests; Secondary Education; *Secondary School Students
Availability: American Optical; Instrument Div., Eggert and Sugar Rds., Buffalo, NY 14215
Grade Level: 7-12
Notes: Items, 41

Designed to measure knowledge of terms used in microscopy. Composed of 24 questions to identify the optical and mechanical features of the microscope and 17 completion questions on the microscope.

5575
Test of Science Comprehension. Nelson, Clarence H.; Mason, J.M.
Descriptors: *Achievement Tests; *Critical Thinking; *Elementary School Students; *General Science; Intermediate Grades; Pretests Posttests; Problem Solving; *Science Tests
Availability: Science Education; v47 n4 p320-30, Oct 1963
Grade Level: 4-6
Notes: Items, 60
Designed to assess critical thinking in science. To obtain the most meaningful results, arrangements should be made to give the test as a pretest early in the school year and again as a posttest near the end of the academic year.

5613
Walker Readiness Test for Disadvantaged Pre-School Children in the United States. Walker, Wanda 1969
Subtests: Similarities; Differences; Numerical Analogies; Missing Parts
Descriptors: *Concept Formation; Culture Fair Tests; *Disadvantaged Youth; English; French; *Individual Testing; Nonverbal Tests; Number Concepts; *Preschool Children; *Preschool Tests; *School Readiness Tests; Spanish Speaking; Young Children
Identifiers: Project Head Start

Availability: ERIC Document Reproduction Service; 7420 Fullerton Rd., Ste. 110, Springfield, VA 22153-2852 (ED037253, 147 p.)
Age Level: 4-6
Notes: Items, 50

An individually administered culture-fair, nonverbal readiness test, directions for which are available in English, Spanish, or French. (Included in ERIC Document ED037253, 147 pages). Test population is rural and urban disadvantaged preschool children.

5633
Tests of Achievement in Basic Skills: Mathematics—Level C.   Young, James C.; Knapp, Robert R. 1971
Subtests: Arithmetic Skills; Geometry-Measurement-Application; Modern Concepts
Descriptors: *Achievement Tests; Criterion Referenced Tests; Educational Objectives; Junior High Schools; *Junior High School Students; *Mathematics Achievement; Mathematics Tests; *Secondary School Mathematics
Identifiers: TABS; Test Batteries
Availability: Educational and Industrial Testing Service; P.O. Box 7234, San Diego, CA 92107
Grade Level: 7-9
Notes: Items, 64

Designed to assess individual students' achievement at their respective grade level and for evaluation of the effectiveness of instruction at these grade levels. Two parallel forms are available. Test is untimed. Test booklet may be used for Individualized Mathematics Program (IMP): Level C, (TC005632). IMP kit is available from Educational and Industrial Testing Service.

5717
A Test of Sentence Meaning. Revised Edition.
Marcus, Albert D. 1968
Descriptors: *Diagnostic Tests; *Elementary School Students; Intermediate Grades; Junior High Schools; *Junior High School Students; Multiple Choice Tests; Reading Achievement; *Reading Comprehension; *Sentences; *Syntax
Identifiers: ATSM; TIM(B)
Availability: Tests in Microfiche; Test Collection, Educational Testing Service, Princeton, NJ 08541
Grade Level: 5-8
Notes: Items, 102

A diagnostic instrument for use in determining a student's understanding of literal meaning through the use of syntactic clues within written standard English sentences. The test measures the ability to understand the syntactic structures of modification, prediction, complementation, and coordination.

5718
Kindergarten Goal Card.   Cincinnati Public Schools, OH 1969
Subtests: Group Test Part A. Vocabulary and Concepts (32); Ordinals Position (4); Concepts of Location and Space (6); Sequence (5); Part B. Visual Discrimination (12); Part C. Letter Recognition (8); Part D. Auditory Discrimination (22); Part E. Number Concepts (14); Part F. Copying (6); Individual Test (34)
Descriptors: Auditory Discrimination; *Classroom Observation Techniques; *Kindergarten Children; Number Concepts; Preschool Education; Visual Discrimination; Vocabulary Skills
Identifiers: TIM(C)
Availability: Tests in Microfiche; Test Collection, Educational Testing Service, Princeton, NJ 08541
Grade Level: K
Notes: Items, 119

An evaluation of kindergarten-aged children based on observation of their performance of various tasks. The instrument can be administered as an individual or group test. The group test covers vocabulary and concepts, visual discrimination, letter recognition, auditory discrimination, number concepts, copying.

5719
Pre-Kindergarten Goal Card: 1968 Revision.
Cincinnati Public Schools, OH 1968
Subtests: Tested Qualities (106); Observed Qualities (43)
Descriptors: Behavior Rating Scales; *Concept Formation; Creativity; *Language Skills; *Preschool Children; Preschool Education; Psychomotor Skills; *School Readiness Tests
Identifiers: TIM(A)
Availability: Tests in Microfiche; Test Collection, Educational Testing Service, Princeton, NJ 08541
Age Level: 2-5
Notes: Items, 149

This test is designed to measure various qualities in preschool-aged children. Variables assessed are physical coordination, relationship of people and things, auditory

discrimination, concepts of size, concepts of color, visual discrimination, concept of weight, manipulation of materials, arithmetic skills, concepts of location and space, and listening skills. The teacher observes the child's performance of certain activities: Mental Alertness; Language Ability; Social Awareness; Health Habits; Creative Abilities; Motor Coordination.

5795
Roswell-Chall Auditory Blending Test.   Roswell, Florence G.; Chall, Jeanne S. 1963
Descriptors: Elementary Education; *Elementary School Students; *Individual Testing; *Phonemes; *Phonics; *Reading Difficulties; *Reading Readiness; *Screening Tests; Verbal Tests
Identifiers: Auditory Blending Test; Oral Tests; Roswell Chall Tests
Availability: Dr. Jeanne Chall; Dept. of Education, Harvard University, Cambridge, MA 02138
Grade Level: 1-6
Notes: Time, 5 min. approx.; Items, 30

An individually administered test designed to measure a student's ability to blend sounds auditorily into words when the sounds are orally given. The student may or may not have learned to associate the given sounds with a corresponding letter. The authors feel that this instrument is useful for judging the ease or difficulty that students will experience in phonics instruction and may also be used in remedial reading.

5813
Arizona Articulation Proficiency Scale: Revised.
Fudala, Janet B. 1970
Subtests: Picture Test; Sentence Test
Descriptors: *Articulation (Speech); Children; *Individual Testing; Pictorial Stimuli; *Speech Evaluation; *Speech Tests
Identifiers: AAPS
Availability: Western Psychological Services; 12031 Wilshire Blvd., Los Angeles, CA 90025
Age Level: 3-11
Notes: Time, 15 min. approx.; Items, 75

A numerical scale of articulatory proficiency in which the numerical values for the sounds are related to their probable frequency in American English speech. Test must be individually administered. Picture cards are used with younger children; a sentence test is included for use with older children.

6049
Early Childhood Prekindergarten Assessment Instrument: Revised.   Schmaltz, Dwayne J.; And Others 1973
Descriptors: *Auditory Perception; Auditory Tests; Individual Testing; Language Acquisition; *Preschool Children; Preschool Education; *Preschool Tests; *Psychomotor Skills; School Readiness; Student Placement; Vision Tests; Visual Perception
Identifiers: Early Childhood Assessment Instrument
Availability: ERIC Document Reproduction Service; 7420 Fullerton Rd., Ste. 110, Springfield, VA 22153-2852 (ED086735, 52 p.)
Age Level: 3-5
Notes: Time, 5 min. approx.

Designed to locate prekindergarten children along a developmental curriculum sequence. Assesses development in areas of motor development, auditory perception, visual perception, and language development.

6050
Global Essay Test.   Veal, L. Ramon; Biesbrock, Edieann 1969
Descriptors: *Achievement Tests; Constructed Response; *Elementary School Students; *Essay Tests; *Primary Education; Timed Tests; *Writing (Composition); *Writing Skills
Availability: ASIS/NAPS; c/o Microfiche Publications, P.O. Box 3513, Grand Central Station, New York, NY 10163-3513 (Document No. 01235)
Grade Level: 2-3
Notes: Time, 30 min.

Designed to measure composition ability in young children in which the evaluation focuses upon the actual composition. The child is instructed to write on a certain theme, planning ahead before starting to write. Form A-E dictates the theme or topic. The obtained rating (score) represents a global or overall quality, not specific points. May be used to evaluate a specific composition, to measure the improvement of a class over a period of time, and to evaluate the teaching methods, materials, and programs upon composition performance.

6076
Cornell Critical Thinking Test, Level Z.   Ennis, Robert H.; Millman, Jason 1971
Descriptors: *Achievement Tests; Cognitive Processes; Cognitive Tests; *Critical Thinking; Higher Education; *Undergraduate Students

Identifiers: Cornell Critical Thinking Test; Self Administered Tests
Availability: Midwest Publications; P.O. Box 448, Pacific Grove, CA 93950
Grade Level: 13-16
Notes: Time, 50 min. approx.; Items, 52

Developed to assess ability in several aspects of critical thinking, the reasonable assessment of statements. Level Z is best adapted to students in higher education. However, some high ability secondary students would be able to cope with it.

6077
Cornell Critical Thinking Test, Level X.   Ennis, Robert H.; Millman, Jason 1971
Descriptors: Cognitive Processes; *Cognitive Tests; *Critical Thinking; Secondary Education; *Secondary School Students
Identifiers: Cornell Critical Thinking Test; Self Administered Tests
Availability: Midwest Publications; P.O. Box 448, Pacific Grove, CA 93950
Grade Level: 7-12
Notes: Time, 50 min. approx.; Items, 72

Developed to assess ability in several aspects of critical thinking, defined as the reasonable assessment of statements. Level X consists of 4 sections. The first section asks for bearing of information on a hypothesis. The second section assesses ability to judge reliability of information on the basis of its source. The third section assesses ability to judge whether statement follows from premises. The final section focuses on identification of assumptions.

6089
Informal Reading Inventory.   Grady, William E.; And Others 1956
Descriptors: Achievement Tests; *Diagnostic Tests; *Elementary School Students; Elementary Secondary Education; Individual Testing; Informal Reading Inventories; Kindergarten Children; Oral Reading; *Reading Achievement; *Reading Comprehension; Reading Readiness; *Secondary School Students; Silent Reading; *Word Recognition
Availability: The Reading Clinic; Temple University, Broad St. and Montgomery Ave., Philadelphia, PA 19122
Grade Level: K-9

Designed to identify learner needs in reading. Four levels of reading achievement are independent, instructional, frustration, and capacity (listening comprehension). Forms A, B, C, D, E, F, and G are available. May be administered to individuals or groups. Assesses reading levels from preprimer through ninth reader.

6092
Informal Evaluations of Thinking Ability.   Johnson, Marjorie Seddon 1957
Descriptors: *Cognitive Processes; *Diagnostic Tests; *Elementary School Students; Elementary Secondary Education; Informal Assessment; *Observation; *Reading Difficulties; *Secondary School Students
Availability: The Reading Clinic; Temple University, Broad St. and Montgomery Ave., Philadelphia, PA 19122
Grade Level: 1-12

Thinking Abilities can be evaluated by a classroom observer. This instrument suggests situations in which these evaluations can be made. Examples of the types of abilities that can be evaluated in this manner are cited. Instrument is used to diagnose reading disability caused by lack of adequate understanding of material in which all the words can be pronounced correctly.

6113
Oral English/Spanish Proficiency Placement Test.
Moreno, Steve 1974
Descriptors: Adolescents; Adults; Bilingualism; Children; *Diagnostic Tests; Elementary Education; *English (Second Language); *Individual Testing; *Language Proficiency; Pretests Posttests; *Spanish Speaking; *Student Placement
Identifiers: *Oral Tests
Availability: Moreno Educational Co.; 7050 Belle Glade Ln., San Diego, CA 92119
Age Level: 4-20
Notes: Time, 5 min. approx.; Items, 151

Test measures oral English proficiency as it relates to H200 Curriculum materials to identify the lesson on which the student should be started for instruction, to provide diagnostic information, and to provide achievement information. The test is based on the student's ability to produce basic linguistic structures in sentence patterns and measures oral English, oral Spanish, and bilingualism. The oral English test is administered in English. Only the initial directions are given in the student's native language. The test is useful for students of various language backgrounds. The test can be administered to children from ages 4 to 20. The test has also shown validity when used with adults.

6142
Body Parts Name Inventory. Dill, John R.; And Others
Subtests: Nonverbal Evaluative Task; Verbal Evaluative Task; Verbal Functions Taks
Descriptors: Achievement Tests; Body Image; *Human Body; Individual Testing; Knowledge Level; *Preschool Children; Preschool Education; *Self Concept
Identifiers: BPNI; COPKI; Curriculum Oriented Prekindergarten Inventories; Institute for Developmental Studies
Availability: Institute for Developmental Studies; Press Bldg., New York University, Washington Square, New York, NY 10003
Age Level: 2-5
Designed to evaluate the child's ability to identify and name 10 parts of his or her body. Child is also required to indicate some understanding of the functions of 5 other body parts—feet, head, nose, hand, and tongue. Body parts naming is believed to enhance child's self-awareness through greater differentiation of body parts. Instrument is also available from Alan R. Coller, 12 Burlington Ave., Vorhees, NJ 08043.

6144
Shape Name Inventory. Institute for Developmental Studies, New York, NY 1965
Subtests: Nonverbal Receptive; Verbal Expressive
Descriptors: Achievement Tests; *Concept Formation; Individual Testing; *Preschool Children; Preschool Education; Visual Perception
Identifiers: COPKI; Curriculum Oriented Prekindergarten Inventories; Institute for Developmental Studies; SNI
Availability: Institute for Developmental Studies; Press Bldg., New York University, Washington Square, New York, NY 10003
Age Level: 2-5
Notes: Items, 16
Designed to evaluate preschool child's ability to identify 8 common shapes. The nonverbal receptive task requires the child to point to specific shapes. In the verbal expressive task, the child is asked to name each shape as it is presented. Instrument is also available from Alan R. Coller, 12 Burlington Ave., Vorhees, NJ 08043.

6146
Color Name Inventory. Institute for Developmental Studies, New York, NY
Subtests: Non-verbal Receptive Task; Verbal Expressive Task
Descriptors: Achievement Tests; *Color; *Concept Formation; Individual Testing; *Preschool Children; Preschool Education
Identifiers: CNI; COPKI; Curriculum Oriented Prekindergarten Inventories; Institute for Developmental Studies
Availability: Institute for Developmental Studies; Press Bldg., New York University, Washington Square, New York, NY 10003
Age Level: 2-5
Notes: Items, 24
Designed to evaluate a child's ability to identify 12 common colors. An extensive color vocabulary is basic to learning more complex concepts. Instrument is also available from Alan R. Coller, 12 Burlington Ave., Vorhees, NJ 08043.

6147
Prepositions Inventory/Linguistic Concepts. Victor, Jack; Coller, Alan R. 1970
Descriptors: *Concept Formation; Early Childhood Education; *Elementary School Students; Individual Testing; *Language Acquisition; Language Tests; *Preschool Children; *Prepositions
Identifiers: Early Childhood Inventories; Institute for Developmental Studies; PILC
Availability: Institute for Developmental Studies; Press Bldg., New York University, Washington Square, New York, NY 10003
Age Level: 2-6
Notes: Items, 32
Designed to assess child's ability to comprehend linguistic concepts, especially prepositions. Examinee is asked to indicate picture described by administrator. Instrument is also available from Alan R. Coller, 12 Burlington Ave., Vorhees, NJ 08043.

6149
Numeral Name Inventory. Institute for Developmental Studies, New York, NY 1970
Subtests: Nonverbal Receptive Task; Verbal Expressive Task
Descriptors: Achievement Tests; Individual Testing; Knowledge Level; *Numbers; *Preschool Children; Preschool Education
Identifiers: COPKI; Curriculum Oriented Prekindergarten Inventories; Institute for Developmental Studies; NNI

Availability: Institute for Developmental Studies; Press Bldg., New York University, Washington Square, New York, NY 10003
Age Level: 2-5
Designed to evaluate the child's ability to identify 20 common numbers 0 to 19. Instrument is also available from Alan R. Coller, 12 Burlington Ave., Vorhees, NJ 08043.

6175
Bilingual Syntax Measure. Burt, Marina K.; And Others 1975
Descriptors: Bilingual Students; Culture Fair Tests; Elementary School Students; *English (Second Language); Language Dominance; *Language Proficiency; *Primary Education; Spanish; *Spanish Speaking; Visual Measures
Identifiers: BSM
Availability: The Psychological Corp.; 555 Academic Ct., San Antonio, TX 78204-0952
Grade Level: K-2
Designed to measure childrens' oral proficiency in English and/or Spanish grammatical structure by using natural speech as a basis for making judgments. The test is available in both English and Spanish.

6355
Language Development Inventory for Kindergarten or Preschool. Lamar Consolidated Independent School District 1976
Subtests: Object Recognition; Oral Comprehension; Form Discrimination and Categorizing; Picture Interpretation; Follow Simple Instructions
Descriptors: *Basic Skills; *Comprehension; *Interpretive Skills; *Language Acquisition; *Preschool Children; Reading Readiness; *Receptive Language; *Recognition (Psychology)
Identifiers: TIM(E)
Availability: Tests in Microfiche; Test Collection, Educational Testing Service, Princeton, NJ 08541
Age Level: Preschool Children
Notes: Items, 31
Designed to determine a pupil's eligibility for kindergarten or preschool resulting from inability to use and understand the common English language words that are necessary for normal progress in the first grade. The inventory consists of 5 areas: object recognition, oral comprehension, form discrimination and categorizing, picture interpretation, and following simple instructions.

6470
Africa South of the Sahara: An Objective Test for Secondary Schools. Carnegie-Mellon Univ., Pittsburgh, PA. Project Africa. 1967
Descriptors: *Achievement Tests; *African Culture; *African History; Cultural Awareness; Diagnostic Tests; Geographic Regions; *Knowledge Level; Secondary Education; *Secondary School Students; Social Studies
Identifiers: Africa (Sub Sahara); Project Africa
Availability: ERIC Document Reproduction Service; 7420 Fullerton Rd., Ste. 110, Springfield, VA 22153-2852 (ED030010, 16 p.)
Grade Level: 7-12
Notes: Time, 30 min.; Items, 60
Designed by Project Africa of Carnegie-Mellon University to determine what U.S. students know about Africa and other regions of the world.

6560
Test of Directional Skills. Sterritt, Graham M. 1973
Descriptors: *Preschool Children; Preschool Education; *Reading Readiness; Reading Readiness Tests; *Spatial Ability
Identifiers: TIM(D)
Availability: Tests in Microfiche; Test Collection, Educational Testing Service, Princeton, NJ 08541
Age Level: 2-5
Notes: Items, 12
Measures spatial orientation abilities prerequisite to learning to read: orienting to the beginning of a sentence or block of text, tracking words from left to right, and tracking lines of text from top to bottom. Consists of 12 cards bearing 1 to 4 lines of printing in primary size type.

6583
Inflection. Mehrabian, Albert 1969
Descriptors: Achievement Tests; *Grammatical Acceptability; *Individual Testing; *Language Acquisition; Language Proficiency; *Language Tests; *Language Usage; Pictorial Stimuli; *Preschool Children; Visual Measures
Identifiers: Measures of Vocabulary and Gramm Skills to Age 6; *Oral Tests
Availability: Developmental Psychology; v2 n3 p439-46, 1970.
Age Level: 2-5

Notes: Time, 5 min. approx.; Items, 11
One of 6 tests designed to measure a child's grammatical ability. This instrument requires a child to produce the correct inflection. Requires the use of a set of pictures. Individually administered. Based upon the theory that linguistic abilities are characterized through the interactive affects of 3 factors: (1) level of organization (representational); (2) psycholinguistic processes (decoding, encoding); and (3) channels of communications (auditory-vocal, and visual-motor).

6584
Judgment of the Grammaticalness of Sentences and Phrases. Mehrabian, Albert 1969
Descriptors: *Achievement Tests; *Grammatical Acceptability; *Individual Testing; *Language Acquisition; Language Proficiency; *Language Tests; Language Usage; *Preschool Children
Identifiers: Measures of Vocabulary and Gramm Skills to Age 6; *Oral Tests
Availability: Developmental Psychology; v2 n3 p439-46, 1970.
Age Level: 2-5
Notes: Time, 5 min. approx.; Items, 13
One of 6 tests designed to measure a child's grammatical ability. The child must distinguish correct from incorrect grammar when presented orally. Individually administered.

6612
Primary Economics Test. Larkins, A. Guy; Shaver, James P. 1967
Descriptors: *Achievement Tests; *Economics Education; *Grade 1; Primary Education
Identifiers: Matched Pair Scoring; TIM(A)
Availability: Tests in Microfiche; Test Collection, Educational Testing Service, Princeton, NJ 08541
Grade Level: 1
Notes: Items, 75
A verbally administered test of knowledge of economics that is written with reversals and scored using matched pairs. For every item for which the correct response is "Yes," there is a matching item for which the correct response is "No." The student is required to respond correctly to both the "Yes" and the "No" item in a matched-pair before receiving credit for either item.

6697
Questions and Problems in Science: Test Item Folio No. 1. Dressel, Paul L.; Nelson, Clarence H. 1956
Descriptors: Achievement Tests; *Biological Sciences; Educational Objectives; Higher Education; *Item Banks; *Physical Sciences; *Undergraduate Students
Availability: ERIC Document Reproduction Service; 7420 Fullerton Rd., Ste. 110, Springfield, VA 22153-2852 (ED054231, 850 p.)
Grade Level: 13-14
Designed to assist college instructors in preparing science examinations directly related to course work. The questions and problems are organized under 30 subject matter headings in each major subdivision: Biological Science and Physical Science. The major headings in the taxonomy of objectives are knowledge, comprehension, application, analysis, synthesis, and evaluation.

6708
Students Typewriting Tests: Typewriting I—First Semester. National Business Education Association, Reston, VA
Subtests: Timed Writing; Theme Writing; Centering; Letter Writing
Descriptors: *Achievement Tests; Adolescents; Adults; Business Education; Clerical Occupations; Educational Diagnosis; *Employment Potential; *Performance Tests; Student Evaluation; Students; Timed Tests; *Typewriting; Vocational High Schools
Identifiers: *Clerical Aptitude
Availability: National Business Education Association; 1906 Association Drive, Reston, VA 22091
Age Level: 13-64
Notes: Time, 35 min.; Items, 4
To be given to students who have completed their first semester of typing. Each part of the test is timed with 2 minutes of relaxation between each subtest. Requires typing paper and erasing materials if erasing is allowed. Measures the marketable productivity of the student and may be used for diagnostic purposes.

6709
Students Typewriting Tests: Typewriting II—Second Semester. National Business Education Association, Reston, VA
Subtests: Timed Writing; Business Letter with Corrections; Tabulation; Manuscript

Descriptors: *Achievement Tests; Adolescents; Adults; Business Education; Clerical Occupations; Educational Diagnosis; *Employment Potential; *Performance Tests; Student Evaluation; Students; Timed Tests; *Typewriting; Vocational High Schools
Identifiers: *Clerical Aptitude
Availability: National Business Education Association; 1906 Association Drive, Reston, VA 22091
Age Level: 13-64
Notes: Time, 35 min.; Items, 4

Given to students who have completed their second semester of typing. Requires typing paper, manifold paper, carbon paper, envelopes, and erasing materials. Each part of the test is timed with 2 minutes of relaxation between each subtest. Measures the marketable productivity of the student and may be used for diagnostic purposes.

6710
Students Typewriting Tests: Typewriting III—Third Semester. National Business Education Association, Reston, VA
Subtests: Timed Writing; Business Letter with Tabulation; Interoffice Memorandum; Business Form (Invoice)
Descriptors: *Achievement Tests; Adolescents; Adults; Business Education; Clerical Occupations; Educational Diagnosis; *Employment Potential; *Performance Tests; Student Evaluation; Students; Timed Tests; *Typewriting; Vocational High Schools
Identifiers: *Clerical Aptitude
Availability: National Business Education Association; 1906 Association Drive, Reston, VA 22091
Age Level: 13-64
Notes: Time, 28 min.; Items, 4

Given to students who are completing their third semester of typing. Requires typing paper, carbon paper, and erasing materials. Each part of the test is timed with 2 minutes of relaxation between each subtest. Measures the marketable productivity of the student and may be used for diagnostic purposes.

6711
Students Typewriting Tests: Typewriting IV—Fourth Semester. National Business Education Association, Reston, VA
Subtests: Timed Writing; Form letters; Rough-Draft Tabulation; Business Forms
Descriptors: *Achievement Tests; Adolescents; Adults; Business Education; Clerical Occupations; Educational Diagnosis; *Employment Potential; *Performance Tests; Students; Timed Tests; *Typewriting; Vocational High Schools
Identifiers: *Clerical Aptitude
Availability: National Business Education Association; 1906 Association Drive, Reston, VA 22091
Age Level: 13-64
Notes: Time, 35 min.; Items, 7

Given to students who are completing their fourth semester of typing. Requires typing, carbon, and manifold paper; envelopes; and erasing materials. Each part of the test is timed with 2 minutes of relaxation between each subtest. Measures the marketable productivity of the student and may be used for diagnostic purposes.

6730
Preschool and Kindergarten Performance Profile. DiNola, Alfred J.; And Others 1970
Subtests: Interpersonal Relations; Emotional Behavior; Safety; Communication; Basic Concepts; Perceptual Development; Imagination and Creative Expression; Self-Help; Gross Motor Skills; Fine Visual Motor Skills
Descriptors: Basic Skills; *Check Lists; *Interpersonal Competence; *Kindergarten Children; *Preschool Children; Psychomotor Skills; *School Readiness Tests; Young Children
Availability: Reporting Service for Children; 563 Westview Ave., Ridgefield, NJ 07657
Age Level: 4-6
Notes: Items, 50

Profile is an evaluative scale of a child's performance based upon the teacher's direct observation and indicates the levels of individual development that have been attained. Instrument points out areas and levels of development where the child shows deficiencies and/or readiness for new learning.

6822
Communicative Evaluation Chart from Infancy to Five Years. Anderson, Ruth M.; And Others 1963
Descriptors: Ability Identification; Child Development; *Communication Skills; Individual Testing; *Infants; *Language Skills; Perceptual Development; *Preschool Children; Psychomotor Skills; *Screening Tests

Availability: Educators Publishing Service; 75 Moulton St., Cambridge, MA 02238-9101
Age Level: 0-5

Designed for quick appraisal of child's overall abilities or disabilities in language and beginning visual-motor-perceptual skills. Contains language and performance levels for the child of 3 months, 6 months, 9 months, 12 months, 18 months, 24 months, 3 years, 4 years, and 5 years of age.

6823
Oliphant Auditory Discrimination Memory Test. Oliphant, Genevieve 1971
Descriptors: *Auditory Discrimination; Auditory Tests; Elementary Education; *Elementary School Students; Learning Disabilities; *Screening Tests
Availability: Educators Publishing Service; 75 Moulton St., Cambridge, MA 02238-9101
Grade Level: 1-6
Notes: Items, 20

Designed for use in screening the auditory discrimination ability of groups of children. Useful as an aid in identification of those children whose auditory perceptual abilities require more careful analysis.

6824
Oliphant Auditory Synthesizing Test. Oliphant, Genevieve 1971
Subtests: Two-Phoneme Words; Three-Phoneme Words; Four-Phoneme Words
Descriptors: *Auditory Perception; Auditory Tests; *Diagnostic Tests; Elementary Education; *Elementary School Students; Individual Testing; *Language Handicaps; Learning Disabilities; Screening Tests
Availability: Educators Publishing Service; 75 Moulton St., Cambridge, MA 02238-9101
Grade Level: 1-6
Notes: Items, 30

Designed to assess child's ability to listen to a word spoken in separate phonemes, retain them in memory in correct sequence, and blend these phonemes mentally and assign them a linguistic meaning. Especially useful in the establishment of a differential diagnosis of perceptual functioning in evaluation of specific language, or learning, disabilities.

6841
Aden-Crosthwait Adolescent Psychology Achievement Test. Aden, Robert C.; Crosthwait, C. 1963
Subtests: Physical; Mental; Emotional; Social
Descriptors: *Achievement Tests; *College Students; Educational Diagnosis; Higher Education; Pretests Posttests; *Psychology
Identifiers: *Adolescent Psychology
Availability: Psychometric Affiliates; P.O. Box 807, Murfreesboro, TN 37133-0807
Grade Level: 13-16
Notes: Time, 45 min.; Items, 112

The only standardized test in adolescent psychology, The Aden-Crosthwait Adolescent Psychology Achievement Test, is designed to measure knowledge in 4 areas: (1) physical; (2) mental; (3) emotional; and (4) social. Primarily measures achievement at the end of an undergraduate course, but can be used as a pre- and posttest and for diagnostic purposes.

6889
The Evaluation of Sounds: An Articulation Index for the Young Public School Child. Ham, Delta 1971
Descriptors: *Articulation (Speech); Diagnostic Tests; *Elementary School Students; Individual Testing; Pictorial Stimuli; Primary Education; Speech Tests; Speech Therapy
Availability: Charles C. Thomas Publisher; 2600 S. First St., Springfield, IL 62717
Grade Level: K-3

Designed to assess specific defective articulatory sounds in the speech of young elementary school children. Useful for speech clinicians.

6925
Motor-Free Visual Perception Test. Colarusso, Ronald P.; Hammill, Donald D. 1972
Subtests: Spatial Relationship; Visual Discrimination; Figure Ground; Visual Closure; Visual Memory
Descriptors: *Cerebral Palsy; Diagnostic Tests; Elementary School Students; Individual Testing; Learning Problems; Learning Readiness; Multiple Choice Tests; Perception Tests; *Primary Education; Reading Readiness; *Screening Tests; Visual Learning; Visual Measures; *Visual Perception; *Visual Stimuli; *Young Children
Identifiers: *Motor Impairment; MVPT; Oral Tests
Availability: Academic Therapy Publications; 20 Commercial Blvd., Novato, CA 94947-6191

Age Level: 4-8
Notes: Time, 10 min. approx.; Items, 36

Measures the overall visual perceptual processing ability in children without requiring a motor response. Used for identifying learning disabilities, as a screening, diagnostic and research instrument. Untimed, individually administered multiple-choice instrument. Used with nonhandicapped children and children with motor problems such as cerebral palsy, not with mentally retarded or sensorially handicapped children.

7006
Ott Test of Oral Language: English and Spanish. Ott, Elizabeth 1970
Subtests: Phonemic Analysis (33); Fluency (24)
Descriptors: *Language Fluency; Language Tests; *Oral Language; Second Language Learning; *Spanish Speaking; Speech Tests; *Visual Measures; Young Children
Identifiers: OTOLES; TIM(A)
Availability: Tests in Microfiche; Test Collection, Educational Testing Service, Princeton, NJ 08541
Age Level: 0-8
Notes: Items, 57

Designed to assess the level of proficiency in oral language production of young children from non-English-speaking backgrounds. Part I, Phonemic Analysis, covers common phonemic differentiations recognized as problems for Spanish speakers learning English. Part II, Fluency, assesses fluency including elaboration and intonation. Part II has been translated into Spanish. The test may be administered to small groups of no more than 4 children. Electronic equipment is needed to administer the test.

7061
Functional Grammar Test. Lackey, Joyce E. 1970
Descriptors: *Achievement Tests; *College Students; *Grammar; Higher Education; High Schools; *High School Students
Availability: Psychometric Affiliates; P.O. Box 807, Murfreesboro, TN 37133-0807
Grade Level: 9-16
Notes: Time, 15 min. approx.; Items, 41

The essentials of English grammar are tested here for the high school or college student. This includes parts of speech, their functions, identifications, phrases, active vs. passive tenses, etc. Pre- and posttesting are permitted because there are 2 matched forms of the test. The test is untimed. Students usually finish within 15 minutes. The forms are set up to measure what the student already knows at the beginning of the test. Preliminary norms are given.

7080
Children's English Proficiency Test. Webster, Sallye L. 1972
Descriptors: *Comprehension; *English (Second Language); Individual Testing; *Performance Tests; *Preschool Children; Preschool Education; Questionnaires; *School Readiness; Spanish; *Spanish Speaking
Identifiers: CEPT; TIM(A)
Availability: Tests in Microfiche; Test Collection, Educational Testing Service, Princeton, NJ 08541
Age Level: 2-5
Notes: Time, 7 min. approx.; Items, 37

Experimental instrument designed to assess the degree to which preschool Spanish-speaking children comprehend spoken English. Most of the questions require behavioral rather than verbal responses. The test is individually administered and requires props. Both English and Spanish versions are available. The translations are in the Spanish most frequently used by Mexican-Americans in the Houston, Texas, area.

7101
Oral Placement Test for Adults. Ferrel, Allen 1971
Descriptors: Achievement Tests; Adult Basic Education; Adults; Adult Students; Individual Testing; *Language Proficiency; *Listening Comprehension; *Oral Language
Availability: Southwestern Cooperative Educational Laboratory Publishers; 229 Truman, N.E., Albuquerque, NM 87108
Age Level: 18-64

Designed to determine ability to use English as a functional tool of communication. Proficiencies are measured in a structured individual interview of potential adult basic education learners. A videotape is available to use in training teachers to administer and score the test. Test may be recorded for later scoring or scored during administration. Proficiency levels are elementary, intermediate, advanced, and exempt.

7129
Science Vocabulary Inventory. Bethune, Paul 1969

Descriptors: *Achievement Tests; Adolescents; Objective Tests; *Readability; *Science Tests; Secondary Education; *Secondary School Students; *Word Lists; *Word Recognition
Identifiers: TIM(A)
Availability: Tests in Microfiche; Test Collection, Educational Testing Service, Princeton, NJ 08541
Grade Level: 7-12
Notes: Time, 30 min. approx.; Items, 48

Graded word list of science vocabulary words. The student matches each vocabulary word with the appropriate definition. The list facilitates determination of both the student's reading vocabulary in science and the level of readability of science materials. Six forms of test are available. Forms A-C, E, F have 48 items. Form D has 40 items.

7193
Analysis of Readiness Skills: Reading and Mathematics. Rodriques, Mary C.; And Others 1972
Subtests: Visual Perception of Letters; Letter Identification; Mathematics-Identification; Mathematics-Counting
Descriptors: *Elementary School Mathematics; Elementary School Students; English; English (Second Language); *Grade 1; *Kindergarten Children; *Learning Readiness; *Letters (Alphabet); Mathematical Concepts; Mathematics Tests; *Numbers; Pictorial Stimuli; Primary Education; *Reading Readiness; Reading Readiness Tests; Second Language Programs; *Spanish; Spanish Speaking; Visual Measures
Identifiers: Oral Tests
Availability: Riverside Publishing Co.; 3 O'Hare Towers, 8420 Bryn Mawr Ave., Chicago, IL 60631
Grade Level: K-1
Notes: Time, 40 min. approx.; Items, 35

To determine whether a child is ready to enter reading and mathematics programs by testing the child's knowledge of the alphabet and numbers. The test instructions are written in both English and Spanish; the results for Spanish-speaking children would determine their readiness for placement in an English-as-a-Second-Language program. The authors recommend administering to no more than 15 students at a time.

7194
Tests of Achievement in Basic Skills: Mathematics—Level B. Young, James C. 1972
Subtests: Arithmetic Skills; Geometry-Measurement-Application; Modern Concepts
Descriptors: *Achievement Tests; Criterion Referenced Tests; Educational Objectives; *Elementary School Mathematics; *Elementary School Students; Intermediate Grades; *Mathematics Achievement; Mathematics Tests
Identifiers: TABS; Test Batteries
Availability: Educational and Industrial Testing Service; P.O. Box 7234, San Diego, CA 92107
Grade Level: 4-6
Notes: Items, 69

Measures knowledge and understanding of basic mathematical skills. Designed to assess individual student achievement at his or her respective grade level. Two parallel forms are available. Test is untimed. Test booklet may be used for Individualized Mathematics Program (IMP): Level B (TC008070). IMP kit is available from Educational and Industrial Testing Service.

7195
Tests of Achievement in Basic Skills: Mathematics—Level D. Young, James C. 1972
Subtests: Arithmetic Skills; Arithmetic Application
Descriptors: *Achievement Tests; Criterion Referenced Tests; Educational Objectives; High Schools; *High School Students; *Mathematics Achievement; Mathematics Tests; *Secondary School Mathematics
Identifiers: TABS; Test Batteries
Availability: Educational and Industrial Testing Service; P.O. Box 7234, San Diego, CA 92107
Grade Level: 10-12
Notes: Items, 44

Designed to assess student's achievement in mathematics in terms of operationally defined and precisely stated educational objectives. Test is untimed. Two parallel forms are available. Test booklet may be used for Individualized Mathematics Program (IMP): Level D. IMP kit is available from Educational and Industrial Testing Service.

7228
Prereading Expectancy Screening Scale. Hartlage, Lawrence C.; Lucas, David G. 1973
Subtests: Sequencing Test; Spatial-Aural-Visual; Memory; Letter Identification
Descriptors: *Beginning Reading; *Diagnostic Tests; *Elementary School Students; *Grade 1; Primary Education; *Reading Difficulties; Reading Readiness

Identifiers: PRESS
Availability: Psychologists and Educators; P.O. Box 513, St. Louis, MO 63017
Age Level: 6-9
Notes: Time, 35 min. approx.

Group diagnostic battery used to predict reading problems in beginning readers. Developed to identify learning disabilities in early school years.

7256
Maintaining Reading Efficiency: Test Number 1— History of Brazil. Miller, Lyle L. 1970
Descriptors: *Achievement Tests; *Adults; Higher Education; Reading Achievement; *Reading Comprehension; *Reading Rate; Reading Tests; Secondary Education; *Secondary School Students; *Undergraduate Students
Identifiers: Brazil
Availability: Developmental Reading Distributors; 5879 Wyldewood Lakes Ct., Ft. Myers, FL 33919
Age Level: 13-64
Notes: Time, 10 min. approx.; Items, 50

Designed to measure ability to read effectively. Student is given 10 minutes to read a history selection. Questions are then answered on material read. Reading efficiency score is determined by multiplying reading rate by comprehension score.

7257
Maintaining Reading Efficiency: Test Number 2— History of Japan. 1970
Descriptors: *Achievement Tests; *Adults; Higher Education; Reading Achievement; *Reading Comprehension; *Reading Rate; Reading Tests; Secondary Education; *Secondary School Students; *Undergraduate Students
Identifiers: Japan
Availability: Developmental Reading Distributors; 5879 Wyldewood Lakes Ct., Ft. Myers, FL 33919
Age Level: 13-64
Notes: Time, 10 min. approx.; Items, 50

Designed to measure ability to read effectively. Student is allowed 10 minutes to read a history selection. Student then answers questions, based upon the reading. The reading efficiency score is determined by multiplying reading rate by comprehension score.

7258
Maintaining Reading Efficiency: Test Number 3— History of India. Miller, Lyle L. 1970
Descriptors: *Achievement Tests; *Adults; Higher Education; Reading Achievement; *Reading Comprehension; *Reading Rate; Reading Tests; Secondary Education; *Secondary School Students; *Undergraduate Students
Identifiers: India
Availability: Developmental Reading Distributors; 5879 Wyldewood Lakes Ct., Ft. Myers, FL 33919
Age Level: 13-64
Notes: Time, 10 min. approx.; Items, 50

Designed to measure ability to read effectively. Student is permitted 10 minutes to read a history selection. Student then answers questions, based upon the reading. The reading efficiency score is determined by multiplying reading rate by comprehension score.

7259
Maintaining Reading Efficiency: Test Number 4— History of New Zealand. Miller, Lyle L. 1970
Descriptors: *Achievement Tests; *Adults; Higher Education; Reading Achievement; *Reading Comprehension; *Reading Rate; Reading Tests; Secondary Education; *Secondary School Students; *Undergraduate Students
Identifiers: New Zealand
Availability: Developmental Reading Distributors; 5879 Wyldewood Lakes Ct., Ft. Myers, FL 33919
Age Level: 13-64
Notes: Time, 10 min. approx.; Items, 50

Designed to measure ability to read effectively. Student is permitted 10 minutes to read a history selection. Student then answers questions, based upon the reading. The reading efficiency score is determined by multiplying reading rate by comprehension score.

7260
Maintaining Reading Efficiency: Test Number 5— History of Switzerland. Miller, Lyle L. 1970
Descriptors: *Achievement Tests; *Adults; Higher Education; Reading Achievement; *Reading Comprehension; *Reading Rate; Reading Tests; Secondary Education; *Secondary School Students; *Undergraduate Students
Identifiers: Switzerland
Availability: Developmental Reading Distributors; 5879 Wyldewood Lakes Ct., Ft. Myers, FL 33919

Age Level: 13-64
Notes: Time, 10 min. approx.; Items, 50

Designed to measure ability to read effectively. Student is permitted 10 minutes to read a history selection. Student then answers questions, based upon the reading. The reading efficiency score is determined by multiplying reading rate by comprehension score.

7264
Iowa Tests of Basic Skills: Primary Battery, Forms 5 and 6, Levels 7 and 8. Hieronymus, A.N.; Lindquist, E.F. 1972
Subtests: Listening; Vocabulary; Word Analysis; Pictures; Sentences; Stories; Spelling; Capitalization; Punctuation; Usage; Maps; Graphs and Tables; References; Mathematics Concepts; Mathematics Problems
Descriptors: *Academic Achievement; *Achievement Tests; *Basic Skills; Elementary School Mathematics; *Elementary School Students; Language Skills; Listening Skills; Primary Education; Reading Comprehension
Identifiers: ITBS; Oral Testing
Availability: Riverside Publishing Co., 3 O'Hare Towers, 8420 Bryn Mawr Ave., Chicago, IL 60631
Grade Level: 1-3
Notes: Time, 203 min. approx.

Designed for comprehensive measurement of growth in the fundamental skills: listening, vocabulary, word analysis, reading, mechanics of writing, methods of study, and mathematics. Primary battery standard edition has 15 subtests. The basic edition has 8 subtests and does not include listening, capitalization, punctuation, usage, maps, graphs and tables, and references. It requires 113 minutes working time. Levels 7 and 8 refer to student's chronological age. Level 7 standard battery has 460 items; level 8 has 518 items. Level 7 basic battery has 227 items; level 8 has 250 items.

7271
Doren Diagnostic Reading Test of Word Recognition. Doren, Margaret 1973
Subtests: Letter Recognition; Beginning Sounds; Whole Word Recognition; Words within Words; Speech Consonants; Ending Sounds; Blending; Rhyming; Vowels; Discriminate Guessing; Spelling; Sight Words
Descriptors: *Achievement Tests; *Diagnostic Tests; Elementary Education; *Elementary School Students; Reading Achievement; *Reading Difficulties; Reading Skills; *Word Recognition
Availability: American Guidance Service; Publishers' Bldg., Circle Pines, MN 55014-1796
Grade Level: 1-4
Notes: Time, 180 min. approx.; Items, 395

Designed to provide an individual diagnosis through use of a group test. Measures degree to which student has mastered word recognition skills.

7281
The Knowledge about Psychology Test. Costin, Frank 1975
Descriptors: *Attitude Measures; *College Students; Higher Education; *Knowledge Level; Multiple Choice Tests; *Psychologists; Psychology; *Student Attitudes
Identifiers: KAP; TIM(A)
Availability: Tests in Microfiche; Test Collection, Educational Testing Service, Princeton, NJ 08541
Grade Level: 13-16
Notes: Time, 30 min. approx.; Items, 60

Test of general knowledge about psychology and psychologists is based on the Facts about Science Test (TC001333). It is intended for research purposes only. The test consists of 2 scales of 30 items each. Scale S measures students' understanding of scientific and professional characteristics of psychology. Scale P measures students' perception of personal characteristics of psychologists.

7333
English Phonemic Unit Production Test: Revised. Skoczylas, Rudolph V. 1972
Descriptors: Articulation (Speech); Audiotape Cassettes; Bilingual Students; *College Students; *Elementary School Students; Elementary Secondary Education; *English (Second Language); Higher Education; Individual Testing; *Phonemes; Pretests Posttests; *Secondary School Students; *Speech Skills
Availability: R.V. Skoczylas; 7649 Santa Inez Ct., Gilroy, CA 95020
Grade Level: K-16
Notes: Time, 8 min.; Items, 36

Measures student's ability to produce English sounds that have been identified as especially difficult ones that must be mastered to speak English well. The sounds are recorded by a native English speaker. Form A is used for pretest, Form B for posttest.

7334
Spanish Phonemic Unit Production Test: Revised.
Skoczylas, Rudolph V. 1972
Descriptors: Articulation (Speech); Audiotape Cassettes; Bilingual Students; *College Students; *Elementary School Students; Elementary Secondary Education; Higher Education; Individual Testing; *Phonemes; Pretests Posttests; *Secondary School Students; *Spanish; *Speech Skills
Availability: R.V. Skoczylas; 7649 Santa Inez Ct., Gilroy, CA 95020
Grade Level: K-16
Notes: Time, 5 min.; Items, 20
Designed to measure a student's ability to produce Spanish sounds considered as particularly difficult ones that must be mastered to speak Spanish well. The sounds are recorded by a native Spanish speaker. Form A is used as pretest, Form B for posttest.

7348
Kennedy Institute Phonics Test: Experimental Version.   Guthrie, John T. 1973
Subtests: Whole Word Production—Special Rules; Nonsense Word Production; Production of Words with Long Vowel Sounds; Production of Words with Short Vowel Sounds; Production of Vowel Consonant Combinations; Letter Sound Production; Letter Naming; Recognition of the Visual Form of Nonsense Words; Recognition of Vowel-Consonant Combinations; Recognition of Initial Letter Sounds
Descriptors: Children; *Criterion Referenced Tests; *Decoding (Reading); *Mastery Tests; *Phoneme Grapheme Correspondence; *Phonetic Analysis; *Phonics; Reading Readiness; *Reading Skills
Identifiers: KIPT; TIM(A)
Availability: Tests in Microfiche; Test Collection, Educational Testing Service, Princeton, NJ 08541
Age Level: Children
Notes: Time, 45 min. approx.; Items, 210
Designed to assess the subskills involved in single-word reading. KIPT has 4 alternate forms, each of which includes all the subtests.

7355
San Diego Quick Assessment.   Ross, Ramon
Descriptors: *Elementary School Students; Elementary Secondary Education; Individual Testing; Preschool Children; *Reading Achievement; *Reading Tests; *Screening Tests; *Secondary School Students
Identifiers: Oral Tests; Word Attack Skills
Availability: Dr. Ramon Ross; School of Education, San Diego State University, 5402 College Ave., San Diego, CA 92115
Grade Level: K-12
Notes: Time, 3 min. approx.; Items, 140
An oral screening device designed to quickly ascertain students' reading level and to provide some indication of their word attack skills.

7361
Wisconsin Tests of Reading Skill Development: Study Skills, Level A.   Otto, Wayne 1973
Subtests: Representation; Position of Objects; Measurement: Size
Descriptors: *Achievement Tests; Criterion Referenced Tests; *Elementary School Students; Grade 1; *Kindergarten Children; Performance Tests; Primary Education; *Reading Skills; *Study Skills
Identifiers: WTRSD
Availability: Learning Multi-Systems, Inc.; 340 Coyier Ln., Madison, WI 53713
Grade Level: K-1
Notes: Time, 25 min. approx.; Items, 27
Written tests designed to measure most skills in Word Attack Comprehension and Study Skills. A formal performance test or teacher observation is used for skills that cannot be adequately measured by brief written tests. More information may be obtained from WI Center for Educational Research 1025 W. Johnson St., Madison, WI 53706 (608) 263-4200.

7362
Wisconsin Tests of Reading Skill Development: Study Skills, Level B.   Otto, Wayne 1973
Subtests: Picture Symbols; Picture Grids; Measurement; Distance; Graphs: Relative Amounts
Descriptors: Achievement Tests; Criterion Referenced Tests; *Elementary School Students; Mastery Learning; Mastery Tests; Primary Education; Reading Skills; *Study Skills
Identifiers: Oral Testing; *Reference Skills; Test Batteries; WTRSD
Availability: Learning Multi-Systems, Inc.; 340 Coyier Ln., Madison, WI 53713
Grade Level: 1-2

Notes: Time, 65 min. approx.; Items, 51
Designed to assess skills necessary for locating, interpreting, and using varieties of printed material. Three subareas of Study Skills are maps, graphs and tables, and references. Two subtests should be administered at each testing session. Assessment component for the Study Skills area of the Wisconsin Design for Reading Skill Development.

7363
Wisconsin Tests of Reading Skill Development: Study Skills, Level C.   Otto, Wayne 1973
Subtests: Nonpictorial Symbols; Color Keys; Number-Letter Grids; Measurement: Size; Measurement: Distance; Graphs: Exact Amounts; Graphs: Differences; Tables: Relative Amounts; Tables: One Cell; Alphabetizing
Descriptors: *Achievement Tests; Criterion Referenced Tests; Elementary Education; *Elementary School Students; *Mastery Learning; Mastery Tests; Performance Tests; Reading Skills; *Study Skills
Identifiers: *Reference Skills; Test Batteries; WTRSD
Availability: Learning Multi-Systems, Inc.; 340 Coyier Ln., Madison, WI 53713
Grade Level: 2-4
Notes: Time, 130 min. approx.; Items, 141
Designed to assess skills necessary for locating, interpreting, and using varieties of printed material. Three subareas of Study Skills are maps, graphs and tables, and references. Two subtests should be administered at each testing session. Assessment component for the Study Skills area of the Wisconsin Design for reading Skill Development.

7364
Wisconsin Tests of Reading Skill Development: Study Skills, Level D.   Otto, Wayne 1973
Subtests: Point and Line Symbols; Scale: Whole Units; Graphs: Differences; Graphs: Approximate Amounts; Tables: Differences; Indexes; Tables of Contents; Alphabetizing; Guide Words; Headings and Subheadings; Selecting Sources; Facts or Opinions; Cardinal Directions; Dictionaries and Glossaries
Descriptors: *Achievement Tests; Criterion Referenced Tests; Elementary Education; *Elementary School Students; *Mastery Learning; Mastery Tests; Performance Tests; Reading Skills; *Study Skills
Identifiers: *Reference Skills; Test Batteries; WTRSD
Availability: Learning Multi-Systems, Inc.; 340 Coyier Ln., Madison, WI 53713
Grade Level: 3-5
Notes: Time, 160 min. approx.; Items, 177
Designed to assess skills necessary for locating, interpreting, and using varieties of printed material. Three subareas of study skills are maps, graphs and tables, and references. It is suggested test be administered in 4 sessions. Mastery for skills in Cardinal Directions and Dictionaries and Glossaries is assessed with formal performance tests. Parallel forms P and Q are available. Assessment component for the Study Skills area of the Wisconsin Design for Reading Skill Development.

7365
Wisconsin Tests of Reading Skill Development: Study Skills, Level E.   Otto, Wayne 1973
Subtests: Point, Line, and Area Symbols; Intermediate Directions; Scale: Multiple Whole Units; Graphs: Differences; Graphs: Purpose and Summary; Tables: Multiplicative Differences; Tables: Purpose and Summary; Indexes; Dictionary Meanings; Cross References; Guide Words; Guide Cards; Specialized References; Fact Checking
Descriptors: Achievement Tests; Criterion Referenced Tests; *Elementary School Students; Intermediate Grades; *Mastery Learning; Mastery Tests; Performance Tests; Reading Skills; *Study Skills
Identifiers: *Reference Skills; Test Batteries; WTRSD
Availability: Learning Multi-Systems, Inc.; 340 Coyier Ln., Madison, WI 53713
Grade Level: 4-5
Notes: Time, 190 min. approx.; Items, 213
Designed to assess skills necessary for locating, interpreting, and using varieties of printed material. Three subareas of study skills are maps, graphs and tables, and references. Test should be administered in 5 sessions. Performance tests are used to assess mastery in the following skills: use of varied sources, notetaking, and understanding special features of books. Parallel forms P and Q are available. Assessment component for the Study Skills area of the Wisconsin Design for Reading Skill Development.

7366
Wisconsin Tests of Reading Skill Development: Study Skills, Level F.   Otto, Wayne 1973
Subtests: Maps: Analysis; Map Projections; Inset Maps; Different Scales; Graphs: Differences; Schedules: Relationships; Subject Index; Dictionary Pronunciation; Card Filing Rules; Dewey Decimal System; Outlining; Catalog Cards
Descriptors: *Achievement Tests; Criterion Referenced Tests; Elementary Education; Elementary School Students; *Grade 5; *Grade 6; Library Skills; *Mastery Learning; Mastery Tests; Reading Skills; *Study Skills
Identifiers: *Reference Skills; Test Batteries; WTRSD
Availability: Learning Multi-Systems, Inc.; 340 Coyier Ln., Madison, WI 53713
Grade Level: 5-6
Notes: Time, 195 min. approx.; Items, 163
Designed to assess skills necessary for locating, interpreting, and using varieties of printed material. Three subareas of study skills are maps, graphs and tables, and references. Test should be administered in 5 sessions. Assessment component for the Study Skills area of the Wisconsin Design for Reading Skill Development.

7367
Wisconsin Tests of Reading Skill Development: Study Skills, Level G.   Otto, Wayne 1973
Subtests: Maps: Synthesis; Latitude and Longitude; Meridians and Parallels; Scale: Fractional Units; Graphs: Multiplicative Differences; Graphs: Projecting and Relating; Schedules: Problem Solving; Readers Guide; Card Catalogs; Outlining
Descriptors: *Achievement Tests; Criterion Referenced Tests; Elementary Education; *Elementary School Students; *Grade 6; *Grade 7; Library Skills; Mastery Learning; Mastery Tests; Reading Skills; *Study Skills
Identifiers: *Reference Skills; Test Batteries; WTRSD
Availability: Learning Multi-Systems, Inc.; 340 Coyier Ln., Madison, WI 53713
Grade Level: 6-7
Notes: Time, 180 min. approx.; Items, 151
Designed to assess skills necessary for locating, interpreting, and using varieties of printed material. Three subareas of study skills are maps, graphs and tables, and references. Test should be administered in 4 sessions. Assessment component for the Study Skills area of the Wisconsin Design for Reading Skill Development.

7493
Advanced Placement Program: Art History.   Educational Testing Service, Princeton, NJ 1981
Descriptors: *Advanced Placement Programs; *Art History; *Equivalency Tests; Essay Tests; High Schools; *High School Students; Multiple Choice Tests; Portfolios (Background Materials)
Identifiers: Advanced Placement Examinations (CEEB); APP
Availability: Advanced Placement Program; Box 977 PD, Princeton, NJ 08541
Grade Level: 10-12
Notes: Time, 180 min.
Designed to assess achievement in a college full-year introduction to Western art. The number of items will vary from year to year. Achievement in Studio Art is measured by evaluation of one portfolio, either General or Drawing, prepared and submitted according to specifications. The Advanced Placement Program has been sponsored by the College Board since 1955.

7494
Advanced Placement Program: Latin Vergil, Catullus-Horace.   Educational Testing Service, Princeton, NJ 1981
Subtests: Latin Sight Reading; Vergil; Catullus-Horace
Descriptors: *Advanced Placement Programs; *Equivalency Tests; Essay Tests; High Schools; *High School Students; *Latin; *Latin Literature; Multiple Choice Tests
Identifiers: Advanced Placement Examinations (CEEB); APP
Availability: Advanced Placement Program; Box 977 PD, Princeton, NJ 08541
Grade Level: 10-12
Notes: Time, 180 min.
Designed to measure achievement in 2 college middle level Latin courses (Vergil and Catullus-Horace). Candidate may take multiple-choice section and free response section on either Vergil or Catullus-Horace in which case exam would be 120 minutes. If candidate takes both free response sections, exam would last 180 minutes. The number of test items may vary from year to year. The Advanced Placement Program has been sponsored by the College Board since 1955.

7495
Advanced Placement Program: Music Theory.
Educational Testing Service, Princeton, NJ 1981
Subtests: Aural Perception; Music Theory
Descriptors: *Advanced Placement Programs;
*Equivalency Tests; Essay Tests; High Schools;
*High School Students; Multiple Choice Tests;
*Music Theory
Identifiers: Advanced Placement Examinations
(CEEB); APP
Availability: Advanced Placement Program; Box
977 PD, Princeton, NJ 08541
Grade Level: 10-12
Notes: Time, 110 min.

Designed to measure achievement in college full-year introductory music course. Forty minutes of objective questions on aural perception common to Music Listening and Literature and Music Theory Exams and 70 minutes of objective and essay questions on specified topic. Candidates take either or both examinations. The number of test items may vary from year to year. The Advanced Placement Program has been sponsored by the College Board since 1955.

7516
Northwestern Syntax Screening Test. Lee, Laura L. 1971
Subtests: Receptive; Expressive
Descriptors: Expressive Language; Individual Testing; *Language Acquisition; Receptive Language; *Screening Tests; *Speech Evaluation; Speech Therapy; *Syntax; *Therapists; *Young Children
Identifiers: NSST
Availability: Stoelting Co.; 620 Wheat Ln., Wood Dale, IL 60191
Age Level: 3-8
Notes: Items, 40

Screening instrument designed to identify children who are sufficiently deviant in syntactic development to warrant further study. May also be used to determine which children will benefit from a remedial language program.

7540
Word Preference Inventory. Dunn-Rankin, Peter 1972
Descriptors: Adults; *College Students; *Diagnostic Tests; *Elementary School Students; Elementary Secondary Education; Higher Education; *Reading Diagnosis; *Reading Difficulties; *Secondary School Students; *Word Recognition
Identifiers: TIM(B); WPI
Availability: Tests in Microfiche; Test Collection, Educational Testing Service, Princeton, NJ 08541
Grade Level: K-16
Notes: Time, 15 min. approx.; Items, 21

Designed to assess visual reading difficulties. Seven types of reading errors (reversal of the entire word, transposition of adjacent pairs of letters, movement of first letter to end of word, rotation of individual letter, change of individual letter to similarly appearing letter, repetition of letter, and deletion of letter) were developed into 5 factors. All 3 forms, A, B, and C, may be given as one test.

7545
Dos Amigos Verbal Language Scales. Critchlow, Donald E. 1974
Descriptors: *Bilingual Students; Elementary Education; *Elementary School Students; *English (Second Language); Individual Testing; Language Acquisition; *Language Dominance; Language Proficiency; *Language Tests; Second Language Learning; *Spanish
Identifiers: Oral Tests
Availability: United Educational Services; P.O. Box 1099, Buffalo, NY 14224
Grade Level: K-6
Age Level: 5-13
Notes: Time, 20 min. approx.; Items, 170

Designed to determine cognitive level of language functioning, in both English and Spanish, among individual students. Useful when mixed language proficiency exists to determine child's dominant language. Reveals comparative scores in Spanish and English development, and identifies functional language levels. Examiner must be fluent in both English and Spanish.

7570
The Kindergarten Questionnaire. Perlman, Evelyn; Berger, Susan 1976
Descriptors: Cognitive Development; Emotional Development; *Kindergarten Children; Language Acquisition; Learning Problems; *Maturity (Individuals); Physical Health; *Preschool Children; Preschool Education; Psychomotor Skills; *School Readiness; *Screening Tests
Availability: Evelyn Perlman; 10 Tyler Rd., Lexington, MA 02173

Age Level: 4-5
Notes: Time, 30 min.; Items, 65

Designed for use in identifying children who might have learning, emotional, behavioral, or language deficiencies. Used in the spring of the year prior to kindergarten entrance so that they may be deferred. Consists of a parent report of health and physical information and a series of drawing, copying, and gross motor tasks to be performed by the child.

7664
Minimal Reading Proficiency Assessment. Phoenix Union High School District, AZ 1972
Descriptors: *Achievement Tests; *Criterion Referenced Tests; *Critical Reading; *Functional Reading; High Schools; *High School Seniors; *Reading Comprehension; *Vocabulary Skills
Identifiers: MRPA; Phoenix Union High School District AZ; TIM(A)
Availability: Tests in Microfiche; Test Collection, Educational Testing Service, Princeton, NJ 08541
Grade Level: 12
Notes: Items, 48

Criterion-referenced test designed for the Phoenix Union High School District to assess various reading skills necessary to establish minimal reading proficiency for graduating seniors.

7726
Assessment by Behavior Rating. Sharp, Elizabeth Y.; Loumeau, Carol A. 1975
Subtests: Physical Skills; Self Help Skills; Language Skills; Social Skills
Descriptors: Child Development; Criterion Referenced Tests; *Language Acquisition; *Motor Development; *Preschool Children; Preschool Education; *Screening Tests; *Self Care Skills; *Socialization
Identifiers: ABR; Developmental Age; TIM(B)
Availability: Tests in Microfiche; Test Collection, Educational Testing Service, Princeton, NJ 08541
Age Level: 2-4
Notes: Items, 26

Developed for use by early childhood education programs. It indicates individual strengths and weaknesses in physical skills, self-help skills, language skills, and social skills and the child's developmental age in each of the 4 areas assessed.

7755
Preschool Disability Identification and Prevention. Metzger, H. Bruce 1973
Subtests: Language; Prereading and Reading Skills; Math; Perceptual-Motor
Descriptors: *Behavioral Objectives; Behavior Rating Scales; Developmental Tasks; *Identification; *Learning Disabilities; *Preschool Children; Preschool Education; Preschool Teachers; *Preschool Tests; Reading Readiness
Identifiers: TIM(C)
Availability: Tests in Microfiche; Test Collection, Educational Testing Service, Princeton, NJ 08541
Age Level: 2-5

Preschool curriculum, based on behavioral objectives, provides the teacher with a day-to-day evaluation tool that can facilitate decision making related to program planning for the child. Tasks are provided in 4 basic areas: language, prereading and reading skills, math, and perceptual-motor skills. As the child acquires a skill, the date is recorded so that the child's development is plotted on a continual basis.

7802
Essential Math and Language Skills. Sternberg, Les; And Others 1978
Subtests: Language Skills; Sets and Operations; Numbers and Operations; Part and Whole Relations; Spatial Relations; Measurement; Patterns
Descriptors: Academic Aptitude; Children; *Cognitive Ability; Cognitive Development; Cognitive Tests; *Concept Formation; *Diagnostic Tests; Disabilities; *Individual Testing; Language Skills; Learning Readiness; Mathematical Concepts; *Preschool Children; *Primary Education; *School Readiness; School Readiness Tests; Visual Measures; Visual Stimuli
Identifiers: EMLS Program; Numbers and Operations; Part Whole Relations; Pattern Recognition Skills Inventory; Sets and Operations; Spatial Relations
Availability: PRO-ED; 8700 Shoal Creek Blvd., Austin, TX 78758-6897
Age Level: 4-10

Individually administered instrument used to (1) assess a student's ability to recognize various pattern sequences and (2) measure the cognitive readiness of handicapped

(or nonhandicapped) students relating to mathematical and language concepts. Pattern Recognition Skills Inventory was incorporated into the Program.

7820
Assessment of Children's Language Comprehension, 1973 Revision. Foster, Rochana; And Others 1973
Subtests: Vocabulary; Two Critical Elements; Three Critical Elements; Four Critical Elements
Descriptors: Communication Skills; *Diagnostic Tests; Language Acquisition; *Language Handicaps; Language Processing; Listening Comprehension; Pictorial Stimuli; *Picture Books; *Receptive Language; *Visual Measures; *Young Children
Identifiers: ACLC; *Oral Tests
Availability: Consulting Psychologists Press; 3803 E. Bayshore Rd., Palo Alto, CA 94303
Age Level: 3-7
Notes: Time, 10 min. approx.; Items, 40

To determine the receptive language difficulties of children ages 3 to 7 and to indicate the guidelines for correction of language disorders. Subjects point to the correct picture as their response. Used for both nonhandicapped and handicapped children. Includes material for administering both to individuals and to groups. Group form is abstracted from individual form and has only 12 items.

7821
Porch Index of Communicative Ability in Children. Porch, Bruce E. 1974
Descriptors: Auditory Perception; Children; Cognitive Style; Communication Disorders; Elementary Education; *Elementary School Students; Individual Testing; Perception Tests; Perceptual Handicaps; *Performance Tests; *Preschool Children; Preschool Education; Verbal Communication
Identifiers: PICAC; Test Batteries
Availability: Consulting Psychologists Press; 3803 E. Bayshore Rd., Palo Alto, CA 94303
Age Level: 3-12
Notes: Time, 60 min. approx.

Clinical tool designed to assess and quantify verbal, gestural, and graphic abilities. Basic battery is for use with children ages 3 to 6 and has 15 subtests. The advanced battery is for students aged 6 to 12 and consists of 20 subtests. Advanced battery has more auditory and reading tasks.

7822
Readiness for Kindergarten: A Coloring Book for Parents. Massey, J.D. 1975
Descriptors: Emotional Development; Intellectual Development; *Parent Participation; Physical Development; *Preschool Children; *School Readiness Tests; *Screening Tests; Social Development
Availability: Consulting Psychologists Press; 3803 E. Bayshore Rd., Palo Alto, CA 94303
Age Level: 5
Notes: Items, 62

Using a coloring book format, this device enables parents to evaluate their preschool child's school readiness in the areas of intellectual, physical, and social-emotional development.

7827
Vocabulary Comprehension Scale. Bangs, Tina E. 1975
Subtests: Pronouns; Quality; Position; Size; Quantity
Descriptors: Achievement Tests; *Diagnostic Tests; Individual Testing; *Learning Disabilities; Performance Tests; Preschool Tests; *School Readiness; School Readiness Tests; *Verbal Development; Verbal Tests; *Vocabulary Development; *Young Children
Identifiers: Oral Tests
Availability: DLM Teaching Resources; P.O. Box 4000, One DLM Park, Allen, TX 75002
Age Level: 2-6

Orally and individually administered test to determine a child's comprehension of various words regarding size, position, number, etc. Used to give teachers of language- or learning-handicapped children baseline information needed to plan activities for helping these children develop vocabulary acquired for kindergarten or first grade. Requires the child to manipulate various materials upon spoken directions by the test administrator. Test packet includes the materials (tea set, trees, people, fence, ladder, cubes, buttons, etc.) to be manipulated.

7847
French Achievement Test: Language Arts, Kindergarten. Comeaux, Jane B. 1973
Subtests: Vocabulary-Oral Comprehension; Paragraph Meaning; Prereading Skills

Descriptors: *Achievement Tests; *Bilingual Education; *Criterion Referenced Tests; *French; *Kindergarten Children; *Language Skills; Preschool Education; Reading Readiness; *Visual Measures
Identifiers: TIM(C)
Availability: Tests in Microfiche; Test Collection, Educational Testing Service, Princeton, NJ 08541
Grade Level: K
Notes: Items, 21
One of a series of criterion-referenced tests based on Bilingual Education instructional objectives. Designed to assess language skills in French. Tests are available for kindergarten through grade 5. Directions for administration are in French.

7848
French Achievement Test: Language Arts, Grade 1.
Comeaux, Jane B.; And Others 1973
Subtests: Vocabulary-Oral Comprehension; Comprehension-Categories; Comprehension-Stories; Word Reading; Paragraph Meaning; Grammar-Syntax
Descriptors: *Achievement Tests; *Beginning Reading; *Bilingual Education; *Criterion Referenced Tests; Elementary School Students; *French; *Grade 1; Grammar; *Language Skills; Primary Education; Reading Comprehension; Vocabulary Skills; Young Children
Identifiers: TIM(C)
Availability: Tests in Microfiche; Test Collection, Educational Testing Service, Princeton, NJ 08541
Grade Level: K
Notes: Items, 53
One of a series of criterion-referenced tests based on Bilingual Education instructional objectives. Designed to assess language skills in French. Tests are available for kindergarten through grade 5. Directions for administration are in French.

7849
French Achievement Test: Language Arts, Grade 2.
Comeaux, Jane B.; And Others 1973
Subtests: Vocabulary-Oral Comprehension; Comprehension-Categories, Word Reading; Paragraph Meaning; Spelling; Language Analysis; Reading Comprehension
Descriptors: *Achievement Tests; *Bilingual Education; *Criterion Referenced Tests; Elementary School Students; *French; *Grade 2; *Language Skills; Primary Education; Reading Comprehension; Vocabulary Skills; Young Children
Identifiers: TIM(C)
Availability: Tests in Microfiche; Test Collection, Educational Testing Service, Princeton, NJ 08541
Grade Level: 2
Notes: Items, 85
One of a series of criterion-referenced tests based on Bilingual Education instructional objectives. Designed to assess language skills in French. Tests are available for kindergarten through grade 5. Directions for administration are in French.

7850
French Achievement Test: Language Arts, Grade 3.
Comeaux, Jane B.; And Others 1973
Subtests: Vocabulary; Spelling; Language Analysis; Reading Comprehension
Descriptors: *Achievement Tests; *Bilingual Education; *Criterion Referenced Tests; Elementary School Students; *French; *Grade 3; *Language Skills; Primary Education; Reading Comprehension; Vocabulary Skills; Young Children
Identifiers: TIM(C)
Availability: Tests in Microfiche; Test Collection, Educational Testing Service, Princeton, NJ 08541
Grade Level: 3
Notes: Items, 68
One of a series of criterion-referenced tests based on Bilingual Education instructional objectives. Designed to assess language skills in French. Tests are available for kindergarten through grade 5. Directions for administration are in French.

7851
French Achievement Test: Language Arts, Grade 4.
Comeaux, Jane B.; And Others 1974
Subtests: Vocabulary; Spelling; Language Analysis; Reading Comprehension
Descriptors: *Achievement Tests; *Bilingual Education; Children; *Criterion Referenced Tests; Elementary School Students; *French; *Grade 4; Intermediate Grades; *Language Skills; Reading Comprehension; Vocabulary Skills
Identifiers: TIM(C)

Availability: Tests in Microfiche; Test Collection, Educational Testing Service, Princeton, NJ 08541
Grade Level: 4
Notes: Items, 75
One of a series of criterion-referenced tests based on Bilingual Education instructional objectives. Designed to assess language skills in French. Tests are available for kindergarten through grade 5. Directions for administration are in French.

7852
French Achievement Test: Language Arts, Grade 5.
Guidry, Richard; Cluet, Jean Marc 1974
Subtests: Vocabulary; Spelling; Language Analysis; Reading Comprehension
Descriptors: *Achievement Tests; *Bilingual Education; Children; *Criterion Referenced Tests; Elementary School Students; *French; *Grade 5; Intermediate Grades; *Language Skills; Reading Comprehension; Vocabulary Skills
Identifiers: TIM(C)
Availability: Tests in Microfiche; Test Collection, Educational Testing Service, Princeton, NJ 08541
Grade Level: 5
Notes: Items, 80
One of a series of criterion-referenced tests based on Bilingual Education instructional objectives. Designed to assess language skills in French. Tests are available for kindergarten through grade 5. Directions for administration are in French.

7853
French Achievement Test: Mathematics, Kindergarten. Comeaux, Jane B.; And Others 1974
Descriptors: *Achievement Tests; *Bilingual Education; *Criterion Referenced Tests; *Elementary School Mathematics; *French; *Kindergarten Children; *Mathematics Tests; Number Concepts; Preschool Education
Identifiers: TIM(C)
Availability: Tests in Microfiche; Test Collection, Educational Testing Service, Princeton, NJ 08541
Grade Level: K
Notes: Items, 22
One of a series of criterion-referenced tests based on Bilingual Education instructional objectives. Designed to assess mathematical skills in French and emphasizes numerical concepts at the kindergarten level. Tests are available for grades K-5. Directions for administration are in French.

7854
French Achievement Test: Mathematics, Grade 1.
Comeaux, Jane B.; And Others 1974
Subtests: Numerical Concepts; Numerical Concepts and Fractions; Recognition of Numbers; Problem Solving
Descriptors: *Achievement Tests; *Bilingual Education; *Criterion Referenced Tests; *Elementary School Mathematics; Elementary School Students; *French; *Grade 1; *Mathematics Tests; Primary Education
Identifiers: TIM(C)
Availability: Tests in Microfiche; Test Collection, Educational Testing Service, Princeton, NJ 08541
Grade Level: 1
Notes: Items, 47
One of a series of criterion-referenced tests based on Bilingual Education instructional objectives. Designed to assess mathematical skills in French. Tests are available for kindergarten through grade 5. Directions for administration are in French.

7855
French Achievement Test: Mathematics, Grade 2.
Comeaux, Jane B.; And Others 1974
Subtests: Numerical Concepts; Problem Solving
Descriptors: *Achievement Tests; *Bilingual Education; *Criterion Referenced Tests; *Elementary School Mathematics; *French; *Grade 2; *Mathematics Tests; Primary Education
Identifiers: TIM(C)
Availability: Tests in Microfiche; Test Collection, Educational Testing Service, Princeton, NJ 08541
Grade Level: 2
Notes: Items, 52
One of a series of criterion-referenced tests based on Bilingual Education instructional objectives. Designed to assess mathematical skills in French. Tests are available for kindergarten through grade 5. Directions for administration are in French.

7856
French Achievement Test: Mathematics, Grade 3.
Comeaux, Jane B.; And Others 1974

Subtests: Numerical Concepts; Problem Solving
Descriptors: *Achievement Tests; *Bilingual Education; *Criterion Referenced Tests; *Elementary School Mathematics; *French; *Grade 3; *Mathematics Tests; Primary Education
Identifiers: TIM(C)
Availability: Tests in Microfiche; Test Collection, Educational Testing Service, Princeton, NJ 08541
Grade Level: 3
Notes: Items, 66
One of a series of criterion-referenced tests based on Bilingual Education instructional objectives. Designed to assess mathematical skills in French. Tests are available for kindergarten through grade 5. Directions for administration are in French.

7857
French Achievement Test: Mathematics, Grade 4.
Comeaux, Jane B.; And Others 1974
Subtests: Numerical Concepts; Problem Solving
Descriptors: *Achievement Tests; *Bilingual Education; *Criterion Referenced Tests; *Elementary School Mathematics; Elementary School Students; *French; *Grade 4; Intermediate Grades; *Mathematics Tests
Identifiers: TIM(C)
Availability: Tests in Microfiche; Test Collection, Educational Testing Service, Princeton, NJ 08541
Grade Level: 4
Notes: Items, 66
One of a series of criterion-referenced tests based on Bilingual Education instructional objectives. Designed to assess mathematical skills in French. Tests are available for kindergarten through grade 5. Directions for administration are in French.

7858
French Achievement Test: Mathematics, Grade 5.
Comeaux, Jane B.; And Others 1974
Subtests: Numerical Concepts; Problem Solving
Descriptors: *Achievement Tests; *Bilingual Education; *Criterion Referenced Tests; *Elementary School Mathematics; Elementary School Students; *French; *Grade 5; Intermediate Grades; *Mathematics Tests
Identifiers: TIM(C)
Availability: Tests in Microfiche; Test Collection, Educational Testing Service, Princeton, NJ 08541
Grade Level: 5
Notes: Items, 70
One of a series of criterion-referenced tests based on Bilingual Education instructional objectives. Designed to assess mathematical skills in French. Tests are available for kindergarten through grade 5. Directions for administration are in French.

7896
Short Tests of Linguistic Skills: Pilot Version Spanish-English. Frederickson, Charles 1975
Subtests: Listening; Reading; Writing; Speaking
Descriptors: *Bilingual Students; Culture Fair Tests; Elementary Education; *Elementary School Students; *English (Second Language); *Language Dominance; Language Proficiency; *Spanish; Spanish Speaking
Identifiers: STLS; TIM(C)
Availability: Tests in Microfiche; Test Collection, Educational Testing Service, Princeton, NJ 08541
Grade Level: 3-8
Notes: Time, 90 min. approx.; Items, 80
Measure has been developed in English and 10 other languages by teachers and language specialists. Tests in other languages are not translations from the English version. Parallel format is used throughout all the tests using the same linguistic areas, subtests, and parallel selection of items. Items are culturally specific and language specific. Tests are available in Arabic, Chinese, Greek, Italian, Japanese, Korean, Filipino, Polish, and Vietnamese as well as Spanish. Uses a contrastive linguistic approach to determine language dominance and proficiency of children bilingual in English and Spanish. Listening, reading, and writing subtests are administered in groups. Speaking subtest is individually administered and requires about 8 minutes.

7929
Wisconsin Test of Adult Basic Education. Wisconsin University, Madison, University Extension 1971
Subtests: Word Meaning, Reading; Arithmetic; Life Coping Skills; World around Me
Descriptors: Achievement Tests; Adult Basic Education; Adults; Cognitive Style; *Computation; *Daily Living Skills; *Functional Literacy; *Rural Population; *Verbal Ability

Identifiers: Rural Family Development Project; TIM(C); WITABE
Availability: Tests in Microfiche; Test Collection, Educational Testing Service, Princeton, NJ 08541
Age Level: Adults
Notes: Time, 90 min. approx.; Items, 68

Developed for use in monitoring the achievement of basic educational and coping skills by persons enrolled in the Rural Family Development Program. It consists of 3 subtests. Subtests 1 and 2 focus on basic reading and computational skills. Subtest 3 deals with the coping skills an adult normally needs in his or her daily life. It includes such tasks as using a road map, ordering by mail, filling out a tax return, using a phone book, and writing a letter of application.

8002
Ilyin Oral Interview. Ilyin, Donna 1976
Descriptors: Adult Education; Adults; *Adult Students; *English (Second Language); Individual Testing; Interviews; *Oral Language; Secondary Education; *Secondary School Students
Availability: Donna Ilyin; 1136 Clement St., San Francisco, CA 94118
Age Level: 14-64
Notes: Items, 50

Designed for use with standard English-as-a-Second-Language (ESL) programs. Designed to measure ability to use English orally in response to hearing it, in a controlled situation. Student is not required to do any reading or writing.

8004
Test of Grammatically Correct Spanish/English. Las Cruces School District No. 2, NM 1976
Descriptors: *Achievement Tests; Bilingual Education; *Bilingual Students; Elementary Education; *Elementary School Students; *Grammar; *Spanish Speaking; Verbal Tests; *Writing Skills
Identifiers: *Oral Tests; TIM(C)
Availability: Tests in Microfiche; Test Collection, Educational Testing Service, Princeton, NJ 08541
Grade Level: K-6
Notes: Time, 22 min. approx.

Consists of both oral and written tests assessing grammar skills in English and Spanish. Tests cover vocabulary, sentence patterns, grammar, and usage.

8012
Developmental Patterns in Elemental Reading Skills. Stennett, Richard G.; And Others
Subtests: Visual; Auditory; Auditory/Visual; Visual/Motor; Language Background Factors; Test Behavior and Attitude; Instructional Exposure; Mastery
Descriptors: Audiolingual Skills; Auditory Perception; Basic Skills; *Beginning Reading; Decoding (Reading); *Kindergarten Children; Language Acquisition; *Objective Tests; *Primary Education; Psychomotor Skills; *Reading Readiness; *Reading Readiness; Retention (Psychology); Student Attitudes; Student Behavior; Visual Discrimination
Identifiers: Canada; Test Batteries; TIM(C)
Availability: Tests in Microfiche; Test Collection, Educational Testing Service, Princeton, NJ 08541
Grade Level: K-3

Used to measure the normal development of several of the basic skills children must acquire if they are to become skilled readers.

8040
College Level Examination Program: Subject Examination in College French—Levels 1 and 2. Educational Testing Service, Princeton, NJ 1981
Subtests: Reading; Listening
Descriptors: Achievement Tests; *Adults; *Equivalency Tests; *French; Higher Education; *Second Language Learning; Undergraduate Students
Identifiers: CLEP
Availability: College Board Publication Orders; Box 2815, Princeton, NJ 08541
Grade Level: 14-16
Age Level: 18-65
Notes: Time, 90 min.

CLEP enables both traditional and nontraditional students to earn college credit by examination. Tests are updated periodically. Levels 1 and 2 designation indicates examination is focused on skills achieved from the end of first year through the second year of college study. Knowledge and ability in the following areas is assessed: vocabulary mastery, grammatical control, reading comprehension, and listening comprehension.

8041
College-Level Examination Program: Subject Examination in College German-Levels 1 and 2. Educational Testing Service, Princeton, NJ 1981
Subtests: Reading; Listening
Descriptors: Achievement Tests; *Adults; *Equivalency Tests; *German; Higher Education; *Second Language Learning; Undergraduate Students
Identifiers: CLEP
Availability: College Board Publication Orders; Box 2815, Princeton, NJ 08541
Grade Level: 14-16
Age Level: 18-65
Notes: Time, 90 min.

CLEP enables both traditional and nontraditional students to earn college credit by examination. Tests are updated periodically. Levels 1 and 2 designation indicates examination is focused on skills achieved from the end of first year through the second year of college study. Knowledge and ability in the following areas is assessed: vocabulary mastery, grammatical control, reading comprehension, and listening comprehension.

8042
College Level Examination Program: Subject Examination in College Spanish—Levels 1 and 2. Educational Testing Service, Princeton, NJ 1981
Subtests: Reading; Listening
Descriptors: Achievement Tests; *Adults; *Equivalency Tests; Higher Education; *Second Language Learning; *Spanish; Undergraduate Students
Availability: College Board Publication Orders; Box 2815, Princeton, NJ 08541
Grade Level: 14-16
Age Level: 18-65
Notes: Time, 90 min.

CLEP enables both traditional and nontraditional students to earn college credit by examination. Tests are updated periodically. Levels 1 and 2 designation indicates examination is focused on skills achieved from the end of first year through the second year of college study. Knowledge and ability in the following areas are assessed: vocabulary mastery, grammatical control, reading comprehension, and listening comprehension.

8046
Smith Alcohol Knowledge Test. Smith, Berneda C. 1967
Descriptors: *Alcohol Education; Alcoholism; Health Education; High Schools; *High School Students; *Knowledge Level; Multiple Choice Tests
Availability: ERIC Document Reproduction Service; 7420 Fullerton Rd., Ste. 110, Springfield, VA 22153-2852 (ED053220, 13 p.)
Grade Level: 9-12
Notes: Items, 76

Designed to assess knowledge of alcohol and its use.

8059
Tests of Achievement in Basic Skills: Mathematics—Level K. Young, James C. 1974
Subtests: Arithmetic Skills; Geometry-Measurement; Modern Concepts
Descriptors: *Achievement Tests; Criterion Referenced Tests; Educational Objectives; *Kindergarten Children; *Mathematics Achievement; Mathematics Tests; *Preschool Children; Preschool Education
Identifiers: TABS; Test Batteries
Availability: Educational and Industrial Testing Service; P.O. Box 7234, San Diego, CA 92107
Age Level: 2-5
Notes: Items, 18

Designed to determine how well each student has mastered specific academic objectives. This test is untimed. Forms 1 and 2 are parallel in content. This level is designed for use in preschool and kindergarten classes. Test booklet may be used for Individualized Mathematics Program (IMP): Level K (TC008066). IMP kit is available from Educational and Industrial Testing Service.

8060
Tests of Achievement in Basic Skills: Mathematics—Level 1. Young, James C. 1974
Subtests: Arithmetic Skills; Geometry-Measurement-Application; Modern Concepts
Descriptors: *Achievement Tests; Criterion Referenced Tests; Educational Objectives; *Elementary School Mathematics; Elementary School Students; *Grade 1; *Mathematics Achievement; Mathematics Tests; Primary Education; Screening Tests
Identifiers: TABS
Availability: Educational and Industrial Testing Service; P.O. Box 7234, San Diego, CA 92107
Grade Level: 1
Notes: Items, 36

Designed to assess mathematics achievement of grade 1 students. May also be used as a placement instrument. Two parallel forms are available. Test is untimed. Test booklet may be used for Individualized Mathematics Program (IMP): Level 1 (TC008067). IMP kit is available from Educational and Industrial Testing Service.

8061
Tests of Achievement in Basic Skills: Mathematics—Level 2. Young, James C. 1974
Subtests: Arithmetic Skills; Geometry-Measurement-Application; Modern Concepts
Descriptors: *Achievement Tests; Criterion Referenced Tests; Educational Objectives; *Elementary School Mathematics; Elementary School Students; *Grade 2; *Mathematics Achievement; Mathematics Tests; Primary Education; Screening Tests
Identifiers: TABS; Test Batteries
Availability: Educational and Industrial Testing Service; P.O. Box 7234, San Diego, CA 92107
Grade Level: 2
Notes: Items, 36

Designed to assess mathematic achievement of students in grade 2. Two parallel forms are available. The test is an untimed power instrument. Test booklet may be used for Individualized Mathematics Program (IMP): Level 2, (TC008068). IMP kit is available from Educational and Industrial Testing Service.

8062
Tests of Achievement in Basic Skills: Mathematics—Level A. Young, James C. 1973
Subtests: Arithmetic Skills-Combinations; Geometry-Measurement-Application; Modern Concepts
Descriptors: *Achievement Tests; Criterion Referenced Tests; Educational Objectives; Elementary Education; *Elementary School Mathematics; Elementary School Students; *Grade 3; *Grade 4; *Mathematics Achievement; Mathematics Tests
Identifiers: TABS; Test Batteries
Availability: Educational and Industrial Testing Service; P.O. Box 7234, San Diego, CA 92107
Grade Level: 3-4
Notes: Items, 49

Designed to assess mathematics achievement of students in grades 3 and 4. Two parallel forms are available. The test is an untimed power instrument. Test booklet may be used for Individualized Mathematics Program (IMP): Level A, (TC008069). IMP kit is available from Educational and Industrial Testing Service.

8063
Tests of Achievement in Basic Skills: Reading and Language—Level K. Educational and Industrial Testing Service, San Diego, CA 1974
Subtests: Word Analysis Skills; Oral Language Development; Comprehension; Study Skills
Descriptors: *Achievement Tests; Criterion Referenced Tests; Educational Objectives; Kindergarten; *Kindergarten Children; Language Acquisition; *Language Skills; Primary Education; *Reading Achievement
Identifiers: *Oral Testing; TABS
Availability: Educational and Industrial Testing Service; P.O. Box 7234, San Diego, CA 92107
Grade Level: K
Notes: Items, 38

Designed to assess skill competencies associated with students at preschool and kindergarten levels. Two parallel forms are available. The entire TABS survey should not be administered in one testing sessions. Each subtest should be given at separate sessions. Test booklet may be used for Teaching Essential Language and Reading (TELAR): Level K (TC008071). TELAR kit is available from Educational and Industrial Testing Service.

8064
Tests of Achievement in Basic Skills: Reading and Language—Level 1. Educational and Industrial Testing Service, San Diego, CA 1975
Subtests: Word Analysis; Oral Language Development; Comprehension; Study Skills
Descriptors: *Achievement Tests; *Basic Skills; Criterion Referenced Tests; Educational Objectives; Elementary School Students; *Grade 1; Language Acquisition; *Language Skills; Primary Education; *Reading Achievement
Identifiers: *Oral Testing; TABS
Availability: Educational and Industrial Testing Service; P.O. Box 7234, San Diego, CA 92107
Grade Level: 1
Notes: Items, 46

Designed to assess competencies in reading and language at first grade level. Two parallel forms are available. Test should be administered in 2 sessions. Reading booklet contains Word Analysis, Comprehension, and Study Skills. Language booklet contains Oral Language Development.

Test booklet may be used for Teaching Essential Language and Reading (TELAR): Level 1 (TC008072). TELAR kit is available from Educational and Industrial Testing Service.

8065
Tests of Achievement in Basic Skills: Reading and Language—Level 2. Educational and Industrial Testing Service, San Diego, CA 1975
Subtests: Word Analysis; Oral Language; Comprehension; Study Skills
Descriptors: *Achievement Tests; *Basic Skills; Criterion Referenced Tests; Educational Objectives; Elementary School Students; *Grade 2; Language Acquisition; *Language Skills; Primary Education; *Reading Achievement
Identifiers: *Oral Testing; TABS
Availability: Educational and Industrial Testing Service; P.O. Box 7234, San Diego, CA 92107
Grade Level: 2
Notes: Items, 49

Designed to assess reading and language skill competencies associated with second grade students. Two parallel forms are available. TABS Reading/Language should be administered in 2 testing sessions. The reading booklet contains Word Analysis, Comprehension, and Study Skills. The language booklet contains Oral Language Development. Test booklet may be used for Teaching Essential Language and Reading (TELAR): Level 2 (TC008065). TELAR kit is available from Educational and Industrial Testing Service.

8082
Simons Measurements of Music Listening Skills. Simons, Gene M. 1974
Subtests: Melodic Direction; Steps/Skips; Harmony: One Tone or More; Harmony: Chords; Meter; Tonal Patterns; Rhythm Patterns; Dynamics; Tempo
Descriptors: *Achievement Tests; Audiotape Cassettes; Criterion Referenced Tests; *Elementary School Students; Grade 1; Grade 2; Grade 3; *Listening Skills; *Music; Primary Education
Identifiers: SMMLS
Availability: Stoelting Co.; 620 Wheat Ln., Wood Dale, IL 60191
Grade Level: 1-3
Notes: Time, 75 min. approx.; Items, 45

Designed to measure achievement of young children in music listening skills through a listening test which does not require reading or writing ability. Useful in identification of musically talented children, as well as those who require improved instruction. Should be administered in 3 25-minute testing sessions.

8140
ACT Proficiency Examination Program: Educational Psychology. American College Testing Program, Iowa City, IA 1982
Descriptors: Adults; *Adult Students; *Educational Psychology; *Equivalency Tests; Objective Tests; Postsecondary Education; *Special Degree Programs; *Study Guides
Identifiers: American College Testing Program; New York; PEP; Regents External Degree
Availability: American College Testing Program; P.O. Box 168, Iowa City, IA 52240
Age Level: Adults
Notes: Time, 180 min. approx.

Developed as part of one of 2 New York programs, the College Proficiency Examination Program and the Regents External Degree Program. Designed to assist postsecondary institutions in granting credit by examination. Test covers terminology, concepts, theories, and principles in the following areas: individual growth and development; learning and instruction; the influence of social, cultural, and environmental factors and measurements. Tests are updated periodically. Administered by American College Testing Program in all states except New York.

8145
ACT Proficiency Examination Program: Fundamentals of Nursing. American College Testing Program, Iowa City, IA 1982
Subtests: The Nursing Process; Nursing Practice; Basic Needs; Nursing Intervention
Descriptors: Adults; *Adult Students; *Equivalency Tests; Nursing; Objective Tests; Postsecondary Education; *Special Degree Programs; *Study Guides
Identifiers: American College Testing Program; New York; PEP; Regents External Degree
Availability: American College Testing Program; P.O. Box 168, Iowa City, IA 52240
Age Level: Adults
Notes: Time, 180 min. approx.

Developed as part of one of 2 New York programs, the College Proficiency Examination Program and the Regents External Degree Program. Designed to assist postsecondary institutions in granting credit by examination. Areas covered include nursing process, nursing practice, basic human needs, and nursing intervention. Tests are updated periodically.

8157
ACT Proficiency Examination Program: Maternal and Child Nursing: Associate Degree. American College Testing Program, Iowa City, IA 1982
Subtests: Family; Antepartal Care; Intrapartal Care; Postpartal Care; Newborn; Expanding Family
Descriptors: Adults; *Adult Students; *Associate Degrees; *Equivalency Tests; *Nursing; Nursing Education; Objective Tests; Postsecondary Education; *Special Degree Programs; *Study Guides
Identifiers: American College Testing Program; New York; PEP; Regents External Degree
Availability: American College Testing Program; P.O. Box 168, Iowa City, IA 52240
Age Level: Adults
Notes: Time, 180 min. approx.

Developed as part of one of 2 New York programs, the College Proficiency Examination Program and the Regents External Degree Program. Designed to assist postsecondary institutions in granting credit by examination. Assesses knowledge of terminology, facts, principles, theories, and trends in areas of nutrition, pharmacology, familial interrelationships, pregnancy periods, and child care development. Tests are updated periodically. Administered by American College Testing Program in all states except New York.

8158
ACT Proficiency Examination Program: Maternal and Child Nursing: Baccalaureate Degree. American College Testing Program, Iowa City, IA 1982
Subtests: Individual; Family; Social Issues and Community Resources
Descriptors: Adults; *Adult Students; *Bachelors Degrees; *Equivalency Tests; *Nursing; Nursing Education; Objective Tests; Postsecondary Education; *Special Degree Programs; *Study Guides
Identifiers: American College Testing Program; New York; PEP; Regents External Degree
Availability: American College Testing Program; P.O. Box 168, Iowa City, IA 52240
Age Level: Adults
Notes: Time, 180 min. approx.

Developed as part of one of 2 New York programs, the College Proficiency Examination Program and the Regents External Degree Program. Designed to assist postsecondary institutions in granting credit by examination. Assesses knowledge in the area of physiology and pathophysiology of maternal and child nursing, the theoretical framework of family functioning, and the application of the nursing process to practical situations. Tests are updated periodically. Administered by American College Testing Program in all states except New York.

8160
ACT Proficiency Examination Program: Occupational Strategy, Nursing. American College Testing Program, Iowa City, IA 1982
Subtests: Influence of the Health Care System on Nursing; Legal Guidelines to Nursing Practice; Ethical Guidelines to Nursing Practice; Educational Guidelines to Nursing Practice; Organizations; Purposes, Membership Requirements, Reasons for Membership, Publications
Descriptors: Adults; *Adult Students; *Equivalency Tests; Legal Responsibility; *Nursing; Objective Tests; Postsecondary Education; *Special Degree Programs; *Study Guides
Identifiers: American College Testing Program; New York; PEP; Regents External Degree
Availability: American College Testing Program; P.O. Box 168, Iowa City, IA 52240
Age Level: Adults
Notes: Time, 180 min. approx.

Developed as part of one of 2 New York programs, the College Proficiency Examination Program and the Regents External Degree Program. Designed to assist postsecondary institutions in granting credit by examination. Covers the role and functions of the technical nurse within the legal limitations placed on the profession. Knowledge of how licensure, nursing organizations, and education influence the technical nurse's function, as well as ethical guidelines for nursing practice is assessed. Tests are updated periodically. Administered by American College Testing Program in all states except New York.

8165
ACT Proficiency Examination Program: Psychiatric/Mental Health Nursing. American College Testing Program, Iowa City, IA 1982
Subtests: Nursing Assessment; Nursing Evaluation; Nursing Planning and Intervention
Descriptors: Adults; *Adult Students; Bachelors Degrees; *Equivalency Tests; *Nursing; Objective Tests; Postsecondary Education; *Psychiatric Services; *Special Degree Programs; *Study Guides

Identifiers: American College Testing Program; New York; PEP; Regents External Degree
Availability: American College Testing Program; P.O. Box 168, Iowa City, IA 52240
Age Level: Adults
Notes: Time, 180 min. approx.

Developed as part of 1 of 2 New York programs, the College Proficiency Examination Program and the Regents External Degree Program. Designed to assist postsecondary institutions in granting credit by examination. Assesses knowledge of terminology, principles and dynamics in areas of personality development, family development, psychopathology, nursing intervention and nursing evaluation. Designed for and standardized at the baccalaureate degree level. Tests are updated periodically. Administered by American College Testing Program in all states except New York.

8166
ACT Proficiency Examination Program: Reading Instruction in the Elementary School. American College Testing Program, Iowa City, IA 1982
Subtests: Foundations of Reading; Program for Pupils; Working with Parents; Teacher and School Support Staff
Descriptors: Adults; *Adult Students; *Elementary School Curriculum; *Equivalency Tests; Objective Tests; Postsecondary Education; *Reading Instruction; *Special Degree Programs; *Study Guides
Identifiers: American College Testing Program; New York; PEP; Regents External Degree
Availability: American College Testing Program; P.O. Box 168, Iowa City, IA 52240
Age Level: Adults
Notes: Time, 180 min. approx.

Developed as part of one of 2 New York programs, the College Proficiency Examination Program and the Regents External Degree Program. Designed to assist postsecondary institutions in granting credit by examination. Areas covered include assessment, goal setting, materials and methodologies, instruction, evaluation, parental role, and school support staff. Tests are updated periodically. Administered by American College Testing Program in all states except New York.

8173
Criterion Test of Basic Skills. Lundell, Kerth; And Others 1976
Subtests: Letter Recognition; Letter Sounding; Blending and Sequencing; Special Sounds; Sight Words; Letter Writing; Correspondence; Numbers and Numerals; Addition; Subtraction; Multiplication; Division; Money Measurement; Telling Time; Symbols; Fractions; Decimals and Percents
Descriptors: Criterion Referenced Tests; *Diagnostic Tests; Elementary Education; *Elementary School Mathematics; *Elementary School Students; *Individual Testing; *Reading Skills
Availability: Academic Therapy Publications; 20 Commercial Blvd., Novato, CA 94947-6191
Age Level: 6-10
Notes: Time, 15 min. approx.

Designed to help educators identify individual skills that youngsters have learned and those that need to be learned so that instructional activities can be planned more precisely. A reading or arithmetic assessment should only take 10-15 minutes. Administration of the test is discontinued as the student experiences failure on 2 consecutive objectives.

8183
Multiple-Choice Marijuana Information Test. Colaiuta, Victoria; Breed, George 1976
Descriptors: *College Students; *Drug Use; Higher Education; *Marijuana; *Multiple Choice Tests; *Predictive Measurement
Identifiers: TIM(C)
Availability: Tests in Microfiche; Test Collection, Educational Testing Service, Princeton, NJ 08541
Grade Level: Higher Education
Notes: Items, 38

The authors feel that the test is a predictor of marijuana use among college students and that it discriminates between the user and the nonuser. The items cover 4 content areas: pharmacology, psychopharmacology, legal status, and history of marijuana. This form is a revision of the Form F (first form) and Form S (second form). The 12 items used in the final version were taken from this revised version of the test. These 12 items are doubled starred. Frequently there are 2 or more correct answers to an item.

8312
R-B Number Readiness Test. Roberts, Dorothy M.; Bloom, Irving 1974

Descriptors: *Kindergarten Children; *Mathematics Tests; *Number Concepts; Numbers; Pictorial Stimuli; Preschool Education; School Readiness; *School Readiness Tests
Identifiers: *Numerical Ability; Oral Testing; TIM(D)
Availability: Tests in Microfiche; Test Collection, Educational Testing Service, Princeton, NJ 08541
Grade Level: Kindergarten
Notes: Items, 19

Employs pictorial items to measure specific aspects of number readiness: counting, cardinality, ordinality, one-to-one correspondence, vocabulary, writing single numerals, recognition of shapes and patterns, and recognition and matching of numerals. It should be administered orally to small groups of children.

8317
Criteria for the Evaluation of Free-Response Interpretive Essays. Sanders, Peter L.
Descriptors: *Achievement Tests; Adolescents; *Adults; *Descriptive Writing; *Essays; Essay Tests; *Holistic Evaluation; *Literary Criticism; Literature; *Secondary School Students
Availability: Peter L. Sanders; Dept. of Teacher Education; Wayne State University, 5950 Cass Ave., Detroit, MI 48202
Age Level: 12-64

Measures a student's ability to understand and interpret various stories by having the student write an essay about the story. Using a 4-point scale, the scoring is based upon the reading of each essay holistically.

8330
Test of Grammatical Structure. Degler, Lois S. 1968
Descriptors: Elementary Education; *Elementary School Students; *Language Patterns; Language Skills; Sentence Structure; *Structural Grammar; *Syntax; Verbal Tests
Identifiers: TIM(D)
Availability: Tests in Microfiche; Test Collection, Educational Testing Service, Princeton, NJ 08541
Grade Level: 2-6
Notes: Items, 192

Designed to assess elementary grade pupils' knowledge of grammatical structure. The test consists of nonsense language sentences constructed to match 4 basic sentence patterns: noun-verb, noun-linking verb linking verb-complement, noun-verb-object, and noun-verb-indirect object-direct object or noun-verb-object-complement. The pupil must translate each sentence into English.

8359
Basic Inventory of Natural Language. Herbert, Charles H. 1979
Descriptors: Hmong; Arabic; Armenian; *Bilingual Students; Cambodian; Cantonese; *Criterion Referenced Tests; Dutch; *Elementary School Students; Elementary Secondary Education; English; English (Second Language); French; German; Greek; Hindi; *Language Dominance; *Language Fluency; *Language Proficiency; Mandarin Chinese; Navajo; Persian; Pictorial Stimuli; Polish; Portuguese; Russian; *Secondary School Students; Spanish; Tagalog; Ukrainian; Vietnamese
Identifiers: BINL; Creole; Farsi; Ilocano; Inupiag; Philipino; Taiwanese; Toishanese; Yugoslavian
Availability: CHECpoint Systems, Inc.; 1520 N. Waterman Ave., San Bernardino, CA 92404
Grade Level: K-12

A criterion-referenced language assessment system designed to measure language dominance, fluency, complexity of language, and language development or growth. Forms A and B are kits designed for grades K-6. Forms C and D are kits designed for grades 7-12. Computer scoring and analysis are available. Tests may be scored in 32 different languages. May be administered to groups or individuals. Found to be particularly useful in bilingual, English-as-a-Second-Language, and language development programs. Also used in speech and language remediation programs by therapists and language specialists.

8377
Nelson Reading Skills Test: Forms 3 and 4, Levels A, B, and C. Hanna, Gerald S.; And Others 1977
Subtests: Word Meaning; Comprehension
Descriptors: *Achievement Tests; Elementary Education; *Elementary School Students; Junior High Schools; *Junior High School Students; *Reading Achievement; *Reading Comprehension; Reading Skills; Reading Tests
Identifiers: RST
Availability: The Riverside Publishing Co.; 8420 Bryn Mawr Ave., Chicago, IL 60631
Grade Level: 3-9
Notes: Time, 33 min. approx.

Measures achievement in basic reading skills. Three levels in one booklet permit group-administered individualized testing. Level A is designed for grades 3.0 to 4.5. Level B covers grades 4.6 to 6.9. Level C designed for grades 7 to 9. All levels include word meaning and reading comprehension. Level A has 3 optional subtests: sound-symbol correspondence (9 minutes), root words (9 minutes), and syllabication (7 minutes). Levels B and C have an optional subtest in reading rate which requires 3 minutes.

8382
McCarthy Individualized Diagnostic Reading Inventory: Revised Edition. McCarthy, William G. 1976
Descriptors: Achievement Tests; *Diagnostic Teaching; *Diagnostic Tests; *Elementary School Students; Elementary Secondary Education; Individual Testing; *Reading Achievement; Reading Comprehension; *Reading Diagnosis; *Secondary School Students
Availability: Educators Publishing Service, Inc.; 75 Moulton St., Cambridge, MA 02138-9101
Grade Level: 2-12
Notes: Time, 90 min. approx.

Designed as an individualized placement and planning tool for teacher use. Items reveal student's reading level, comprehension skills, reading-thinking ability, and phonic knowledge.

8383
Quick Language Assessment Inventory. Moreno, Steve 1974
Descriptors: *Bilingual Education Programs; *Biographical Inventories; Children; Elementary Education; *Elementary School Students; English (Second Language); *Non English Speaking; *Preschool Children; Preschool Education; *Screening Tests; *Spanish Speaking
Availability: Moreno Educational Co.; 6837 Elaine Way, San Diego, CA 92120
Age Level: 2-11
Notes: Time, 1 min. approx.; Items, 11

Designed for use with children suspected of needing ESL instruction or those being screened for bilingual education. Provides information about a student's English and Spanish language background. Inventory may also be used with students whose native language is other than Spanish. Interviewer should substitute student's native language for Spanish in all questions.

8396
ACS Cooperative General Chemistry. American Chemical Society, Div. of Chemical Education, Stillwater, OK
Subtests: Stoichiometry of Reactions; Structure, Bonding; Periodicity and Geometry of Molecules; States of Matter; Acid Base Chemistry and Solution Stoichiometry; Equilibria Homogeneous and Heterogeneous; Electrochemistry, Oxidation, and Reduction; Thermochemistry, Thermodynamics and Kinetics of Reactions; Descriptive Chemistry; Carbon Chemistry; Laboratory
Descriptors: *Achievement Tests; *Chemistry; Higher Education; High Schools; High School Students; Multiple Choice Tests; *Undergraduate Students
Identifiers: *American Chemical Society Cooperative Examinations
Availability: ACS DivCHED Examinations Institute; Oklahoma State University, 107 Physical Sciences, Stillwater, OK 74078-0447
Grade Level: 9-16
Notes: Time, 115 min.; Items, 80

Designed to measure achievement in first-year college chemistry. Complete periodic table is in test booklet. Forms 1977, 1975, and 1975S have been redesigned in format with level of difficulty similar to 1973 form. Examination covers stoichiometry, states of matter, acid-base chemistry, equilibria including homogeneous and heterogeneous, electrochemistry, thermochemistry and thermodynamics, descriptive chemistry, carbon or covalent compound chemistry, and laboratory. Retired from college use. Now available to high schools. Test forms are updated periodically, and older forms may be retired from active use. Retired college-level forms may be released to high school teachers.

8397
ACS Cooperative Examination: Brief Qualitative Analysis. American Chemical Society, Div. of Chemical Education, Stillwater, OK
Subtests: Theory; Laboratory
Descriptors: *Achievement Tests; *Chemistry; Higher Education; Multiple Choice Tests; *Undergraduate Students
Identifiers: *American Chemical Society Cooperative Examinations; *Qualitative Analysis
Availability: ACS DivCHED Examinations Institute; Oklahoma State University, 107 Physical Sciences, Stillwater, OK 74078-0447
Grade Level: 13-16

Notes: Time, 50 min.; Items, 35

May be given as a semester test or as a supplemental test in combination with any of the general chemistry tests. Test forms are updated periodically, and older forms may be retired from active use. Retired college-level forms may be released to high school teachers.

8398
ACS Examination Brief Course in Organic Chemistry. American Chemical Society, Div. of Chemical Education, Stillwater, OK
Descriptors: *Achievement Tests; Higher Education; Multiple Choice Tests; *Organic Chemistry; *Undergraduate Students
Identifiers: *American Chemical Society Cooperative Examinations
Availability: ACS DivCHED Examinations Institute; Oklahoma State University, 107 Physical Sciences, Stillwater, OK 74078-0447
Grade Level: 13-16
Notes: Time, 90 min.; Items, 70

Items include bonding, isomerism, functional group recognition, IVPAC nomenclature, physical properties, acidity and basicity, characteristic reactions of major functional groups, reaction mechanisms, qualitative organic analysis, applications, lipids, carbohydrates, and proteins. Test forms are updated periodically, and older forms may be retired from active use. Retired college-level forms may be released to high school teachers.

8411
Reading and Following Directions Test. Calder, Clarence R.
Descriptors: *Achievement Tests; *Elementary School Students; Primary Education; *Reading Comprehension; Reading Tests
Availability: Clarence R. Calder, Jr.; School of Education, Dept. of Elementary Education, U-33, University of Connecticut, Storrs, CT 06268
Grade Level: 1-3
Notes: Items, 17

Designed to assess ability of young children to read and follow directions.

8416
Time Understanding Inventory. Forer, Ruth K.; Keogh, Barbara K. 1970
Subtests: Subjective Time; Objective Time; Historic Time; Time Estimation; Draw a Clock; Tell Time; Clock Matching; Fill in Time
Descriptors: *Achievement Tests; *Concept Formation; Elementary Education; *Elementary School Students; Individual Testing; *Time; *Time Perspective
Identifiers: Oral Tests; Perceptual Time Inventory
Availability: Barbara Keogh; UCLA Graduate School of Education; Los Angeles, CA 90024
Grade Level: 1-6
Notes: Time, 30 min. approx.; Items, 53

Evaluates a student's understanding of time and his or her ability to apply this knowledge. Individually administered and untimed. Type of answer varies from subtest to subtest: oral answer, multiple-choice, and drawing in clock hands.

8434
CTBS Readiness Test, Form S, Level A. CTB/Macmillan/McGraw-Hill, Monterey, CA 1977
Subtests: Letter Forms; Letter Names; Listening for Information; Letter Sounds; Visual Discrimination; Sound Matching; Language; Mathematics
Descriptors: Achievement Tests; *Grade 1; *Kindergarten Children; Primary Education; *Reading Readiness; *Reading Readiness Tests
Availability: CTB/MacMillan/McGraw Hill; Del Monte Research Park, 2500 Garden Rd., Monterey, CA 93940
Grade Level: K-1
Notes: Items, 168

Assesses many of the skills included in prereading programs. There are 8 subtests. Letter names measures students' ability to identify orally named letters of the alphabet. Letter forms test provides an estimate of the extent to which a student can distinguish forms of letters. Listening for information assesses students' ability to obtain information from the spoken word. Letter sounds subtest requires the student to select the letter sound heard at the beginning of a word. Visual discrimination measures students' ability to discern similarities and differences in words, shapes, and other visual stimuli. In the sound matching subtest, students must determine whether 2 orally presented words are the same or different. The language test assesses students' ability to recognize correct and incorrect grammar and syntax when presented orally. The mathematics section is not used to estimate readiness levels. Test is used for grades K-1.3.

8453
Language Assessment Battery: Level 1. New York City Board of Education, Brooklyn, Office of Educational Evaluation 1976

Subtests: Listening and Speaking; Reading; Writing

Descriptors: *Bilingual Students; *Diagnostic Tests; *Elementary School Students; English (Second Language); Individual Testing; *Kindergarten Children; *Language Proficiency; Language Tests; Primary Education; Spanish; *Spanish Speaking

Identifiers: LAB

Availability: Riverside Publishing Co.; 3 O'Hare Towers, 8420 Bryn Mawr Ave., Chicago, IL 60631

Grade Level: K-2

Notes: Time, 10 min. approx.; Items, 40

Designed for use in New York City Public Schools to determine student's effectiveness in English and Spanish. Student is assessed for English competencies and compared against a monolingual English-speaking norm group. A Spanish version is used to determine whether child is more effective in Spanish than in English. Main purpose of battery is student classification. Spanish language skills may be measured by using Spanish language battery.

8454

Language Assessment Battery: Level II. New York City Board of Education, Brooklyn, Office of Educational Evaluation 1976

Subtests: Listening; Reading; Writing; Speaking

Descriptors: *Bilingual Students; *Diagnostic Tests; Elementary Education; *Elementary School Students; English (Second Language); *Language Proficiency; Language Tests; Spanish; *Spanish Speaking

Identifiers: LAB

Availability: Riverside Publishing Co.; 3 O'Hare Towers, 8420 Bryn Mawr Ave., Chicago, IL 60631

Grade Level: 3-6

Notes: Time, 41 min. approx.; Items, 92

Designed to assess reading, writing, listening comprehension and speaking in English and Spanish. Used for classification of students to determine whether their learning is more effective in English or Spanish. Spanish language skills may be measured by use of the Spanish language battery. All subtests are group administered with the exception of Speaking which is individually administered.

8455

Language Assessment Battery: Level III. New York City Board of Education, Brooklyn, Office of Educational Evaluation 1976

Subtests: Listening; Reading; Writing; Speaking

Descriptors: *Bilingual Students; *Diagnostic Tests; English (Second Language); *Language Proficiency; Language Tests; Secondary Education; *Secondary School Students; *Spanish; *Spanish Speaking

Identifiers: LAB

Availability: Riverside Publishing Co.; 3 O'Hare Towers, 8420 Bryn Mawr Ave., Chicago, IL 60631

Grade Level: 7-12

Notes: Time, 41 min. approx.; Items, 92

Designed to assess reading, writing, listening comprehension, and speaking in English and Spanish. Used for classification of students to determine whether their learning is more effective in English or Spanish. Spanish language skills may be measured by use of the Spanish language battery. All subtests are group administered with the exception of Speaking which is individually administered.

8459

Critical Reading. Scandura, Alice M. 1973

Descriptors: Autoinstructional Aids; *Critical Reading; Deduction; Elementary Education; *Elementary School Students; *Gifted; Logical Thinking; Reading Comprehension; *Reading Tests; Workbooks

Identifiers: Self Administered Tests

Availability: Ann Arbor Publishers; P.O. Box 7249, Naples, FL 33941

Grade Level: 3-6

Series of workbooks designed primarily for upper elementary school students but may be used by anyone needing experience with application of logical rules to improve critical reading. Pretests help determine where each student should begin working in carefully graded material. Posttests used to test mastery of each concept. Materials measure ability to use basic logical inference rules.

8505

New York State Physical Fitness Screening Test. New York 1976

Descriptors: *Diagnostic Tests; *Elementary School Students; Intermediate Grades; Physical Education; *Physical Fitness; *Screening Tests; Secondary Education; *Secondary School Students

Availability: University of the State of New York; Div. of Educational Testing, State Education Dept., Albany, NY 12224

Grade Level: 4-12

Notes: Time, 30 min. approx.; Items, 4

Designed to evaluate student performance in agility, strength, speed, and endurance. Designed to identify physically underdeveloped pupils. A more thorough diagnostic appraisal is the individual performance-type test composed of 7 test items. This form is called New York State Physical Fitness Test. The components measured are posture, accuracy, strength, agility, speed, balance, and endurance.

8562

Dallas Pre-School Screening Test: Spanish Version. Percival, Robert R. 1972

Subtests: Auditory; Language; Motor; Visual; Psychological; Articulation

Descriptors: Auditory Perception; *Bilingual Teachers; *Handicap Identification; Individual Testing; Language Acquisition; *Learning Disabilities; Number Concepts; *Preschool Children; Preschool Education; Psychomotor Skills; *Screening Tests; *Spanish; Speech; Visual Perception; Vocabulary

Availability: Dallas Educational Services; P.O. Box 831254, Richardson, TX 75083-1254

Age Level: 3-6

Designed to identify learning disabilities in children 3 to 6 years of age. Primary learning areas screened are psychological, auditory, visual, motor, language, and articulation development. Spanish edition is identical to English except that pupil record form is in Spanish. Assumption is made that test administrators are bilingual.

8576

College Level Examination Program: Subject Examination in Business-Computers and Data Processing. Educational Testing Service, Princeton, NJ 1981

Descriptors: Achievement Tests; *Adults; *Computer Science; *Data Processing; *Equivalency Tests; Essay Tests; Higher Education; Multiple Choice Tests; Programing; Undergraduate Students

Identifiers: CLEP

Availability: College Board Publication Orders; Box 2815, Princeton, NJ 08541

Grade Level: 13-16

Age Level: 18-65

Notes: Time, 90 min.; Items, 100

CLEP enables both traditional and nontraditional students to earn college credit by examination. Tests are updated periodically. An optional essay section requires knowledge similar to that needed for multiple-choice sections. It contains 5 questions and is designed to evaluate candidate's ability to deal in depth with important topics. Examination is about equally divided between problems that test knowledge of terminology and basic concepts and those that require student to apply knowledge. Areas of emphasis include hardware, data, software, and systems concepts. The focus is on concepts and techniques applicable to a variety of languages.

8577

College-Level Examination Program: Subject Examination in Elementary Computer Programming—Fortran IV. Educational Testing Service, Princeton, NJ 1981

Descriptors: Achievement Tests; *Adults; *Computer Science; *Equivalency Tests; Essay Tests; Higher Education; Multiple Choice Tests; *Programing; Undergraduate Students

Identifiers: CLEP; *FORTRAN Programing Language

Availability: College Board Publication Orders; Box 2815, Princeton, NJ 08541

Grade Level: 13-16

Age Level: 18-65

Notes: Time, 90 min.; Items, 100

CLEP enables both traditional and nontraditional students to earn college credit by examination. Tests are updated periodically. An optional essay section requires knowledge similar to that needed for multiple-choice sections. It requires candidate to produce flow charts and write actual programs in Fortran IV. Because there are many variations of Fortran IV, the test attempts to measure only those elements of the language common to most users. Elements covered include constants, variables, arrays, subscripts, arithmetic expressions, logical and arithmetic IF, logical expressions, GO TO, DO, READ and WRITE, DATA, DIMENSION, explicit type, COMMON, EQUIVALENCE, statement functions, function subprograms, subroutine subprograms. No longer administered nationally. For institutional use only.

8578

College Level Examination Program: Subject Examination in Introduction to Management. Educational Testing Service, Princeton, NJ 1981

Descriptors: Achievement Tests; *Adults; *Business Administration; *Equivalency Tests; Essay Tests; Higher Education; Multiple Choice Tests; Undergraduate Students

Identifiers: CLEP

Availability: College Board Publication Orders; Box 2815, Princeton, NJ 08541

Grade Level: 13-16

Age Level: 18-65

Notes: Time, 90 min.; Items, 100

CLEP enables both traditional and nontraditional students to earn college credit by examination. Tests are updated periodically. An optional essay section is intended to test ability to relate the concepts of management to current issues and bring together in a coherent fashion material drawn from different parts of the subject. Material covered in the test includes humanpower and human resources, operational aspects of management, functional aspects of management, and miscellaneous aspects of management.

8579

College-Level Examination Program: Subject Examination in Introductory Accounting. Educational Testing Service, Princeton, NJ 1981

Descriptors: *Accounting; Achievement Tests; *Adults; *Equivalency Tests; Essay Tests; Higher Education; Multiple Choice Tests; Undergraduate Students

Identifiers: CLEP

Availability: College Board Publication Orders; Box 2815, Princeton, NJ 08541

Grade Level: 13-16

Age Level: 18-65

Notes: Time, 90 min.; Items, 80

CLEP enables both traditional and nontraditional students to earn college credit by examination. Tests are updated periodically. An optional essay section requires knowledge similar to that needed for multiple-choice sections. It contains 6 questions which test candidate's ability to apply generally accepted accounting concepts and procedures to a stated problem and combine coherently material from various areas of accounting. The examination deals with financial accounting topics and managerial accounting topics. Candidates are permitted to use silent hand calculators when taking this examination.

8580

College-Level Examination Program: Subject Examination in Introductory Business Law. Educational Testing Service, Princeton, NJ 1981

Descriptors: Achievement Tests; *Adults; *Business Administration Education; *Equivalency Tests; Essay Tests; Higher Education; *Legal Education (Professions); Multiple Choice Tests; Undergraduate Students

Identifiers: CLEP

Availability: College Board Publication Orders; Box 2815, Princeton, NJ 08541

Grade Level: 13-16

Age Level: 18-65

Notes: Time, 90 min.; Items, 100

CLEP enables both traditional and nontraditional students to earn college credit by examination. Tests are updated periodically. An optional essay section requires knowledge similar to that needed for multiple-choice sections. It contains 5 questions to be completed in 90 minutes which are based on case materials or require discussion of important concepts in business law. Six major content areas include history and sources of U.S. law, U.S. legal systems and procedures, agency and employment, sales and miscellaneous.

8581

College-Level Examination Program: Subject Examination in Human Growth and Development. Educational Testing Service, Princeton, NJ 1981

Descriptors: Achievement Tests; *Adults; *Child Development; Child Psychology; *Equivalency Tests; Essay Tests; Higher Education; Multiple Choice Tests; Undergraduate Students

Identifiers: CLEP

Availability: College Board Publication Orders; Box 2815, Princeton, NJ 08541

Grade Level: 13-16

Age Level: 18-65

Notes: Time, 90 min.; Items, 90

CLEP enables both traditional and nontraditional students to earn college credit by examination. Tests are updated periodically. An optional essay section requires knowledge similar to that needed for multiple-choice sections. Examination has 14 major content categories including theoretical foundations; research strategies and methodology; biological aspects of development; perceptual and sensorimotor development; cognitive, language, and emotional development; personality; intelligence testing; influences of schooling; social development; family relations and child-rearing practices; learning; and atypical behavior and development.

8582

College-Level Examination Program: Subject Examination in American Literature. Educational Testing Service, Princeton, NJ 1981

Descriptors: Achievement Tests; *Adults; *Equivalency Tests; Essay Tests; Multiple Choice Tests; Undergraduate Students; *United States Literature
Identifiers: CLEP
Availability: College Board Publication Orders; Box 2815, Princeton, NJ 08541
Grade Level: 13-16
Age Level: 18-65
Notes: Time, 90 min.; Items, 110

CLEP enables both traditional and nontraditional students to earn college credit by examination. Tests are updated periodically. An optional essay section requires knowledge similar to that needed for multiple-choice sections. It contains 3 questions of which candidate must answer 2. The purpose of this section is to test ability to make organized statements about American literature that are informed and pertinent. Designed to measure familiarity with prose and poetry written in the U.S. from colonial times to midtwentieth century. Primarily assesses knowledge of specific literary works.

8583
College Level Examination Program: Subject Examination in College Composition. Educational Testing Service, Princeton, NJ 1981
Descriptors: Achievement Tests; *Adults; *Equivalency Tests; Essay Tests; Grammar; Higher Education; Multiple Choice Tests; Undergraduate Students; *Writing (Composition); *Writing Skills
Identifiers: CLEP
Availability: College Board Publication Orders; Box 2815, Princeton, NJ 08541
Grade Level: 13-16
Age Level: 18-65
Notes: Time, 90 min.; Items, 100

CLEP enables both traditional and nontraditional students to earn college credit by examination. Tests are updated periodically. An optional essay section requires knowledge similar to that needed for multiple-choice sections. It is strongly recommended that every student take the optional essay section. Examination is designed to measure knowledge of theoretical aspects of writing and ability to put principles of standard written English into practice. Topics covered include the sentence, the paragraph and essay, style, logic in writing, the English language, library information, and manuscript format and documentation.

8584
College-Level Examination Program: Subject Examination in English Literature. Educational Testing Service, Princeton, NJ 1981
Descriptors: Achievement Tests; *Adults; *English Literature; *Equivalency Tests; Essay Tests; Higher Education; Multiple Choice Tests; Undergraduate Students
Identifiers: CLEP
Availability: College Board Publication Orders; Box 2815, Princeton, NJ 08541
Grade Level: 13-16
Age Level: 18-65
Notes: Time, 90 min.; Items, 100

CLEP enables both traditional and nontraditional students to earn college credit by examination. Tests are updated periodically. Primarily designed to assess knowledge of major authors and texts. Many questions are based on passages and poems supplied in test. Questions call for information related to literary background, content of major works, chronology, the identification of authors, metrical patterns, and literary references. Other questions require analysis of elements of form in a passage, perception of meanings, identification of tone and mood, and characteristics of style.

8585
College Level Examination Program: Subject Examination in Freshman English. Educational Testing Service, Princeton, NJ 1981
Descriptors: Achievement Tests; *Adults; *College English; *Equivalency Tests; Essay Tests; Higher Education; Multiple Choice Tests; Reading Comprehension; Undergraduate Students; Writing (Composition); Writing Skills
Identifiers: CLEP
Availability: College Board Publication Orders; Box 2815, Princeton, NJ 08541
Grade Level: 13-16
Age Level: 18-65
Notes: Time, 90 min.; Items, 100

CLEP enables both traditional and nontraditional students to earn college credit by examination. This test was completely revised. Designed to measure a candidate's ability to recognize and apply principles of good writing. The optional essay section allows a candidate to demonstrate writing skills in 3 sustained tasks. The topics present concrete problems that involve personal knowledge and require control and flexibility in the use of language.

8586
College-Level Examination Program: Subject Examination in Calculus with Elementary Functions. Educational Testing Service, Princeton, NJ 1981
Descriptors: Achievement Tests; *Adults; *Calculus; *Equivalency Tests; Higher Education; Mathematics Tests; Multiple Choice Tests; Undergraduate Students
Identifiers: CLEP
Availability: College Board Publication Orders; Box 2815, Princeton, NJ 08541
Age Level: 18-65
Notes: Time, 90 min.; Items, 45

CLEP enables both traditional and nontraditional students to earn college credit by examination. Tests are updated periodically. Primarily concerned with intuitive understanding of calculus and experience with its methods and application. The 3 major areas assessed are elementary functions (algebraic, trigonometric, exponential, and logarithmic), differential calculus and integral calculus.

8587
College Level Examination Program: Subject Examination in College Algebra. Educational Testing Service, Princeton, NJ 1981
Descriptors: Achievement Tests; *Adults; *Algebra; *College Mathematics; *Equivalency Tests; Higher Education; Mathematics Tests; Multiple Choice Tests; Undergraduate Students
Identifiers: CLEP
Availability: College Board Publication Orders; Box 2815, Princeton, NJ 08541
Grade Level: 13-16
Age Level: 18-65
Notes: Time, 90 min.; Items, 80

CLEP enables both traditional and nontraditional students to earn college credit by examination. Tests are updated periodically. Examination is about equally divided between questions that require solution of straightforward problems and those which require candidate to demonstrate the understanding of concepts or to apply concepts or skills to unfamiliar situations. Areas covered include basic algebraic operations, real number system, sets, equations, complex numbers, and mathematical induction.

8588
College-Level Examination Program: Subject Examination in College Algebra—Trigonometry. Educational Testing Service, Princeton, NJ 1981
Descriptors: Achievement Tests; *Adults; *Algebra; *College Mathematics; *Equivalency Tests; Higher Education; Mathematics Tests; Multiple Choice Tests; *Trigonometry; Undergraduate Students
Identifiers: CLEP
Availability: College Board Publication Orders; Box 2815, Princeton, NJ 08541
Grade Level: 13-16
Age Level: 18-65
Notes: Time, 90 min.; Items, 80

CLEP enables both traditional and nontraditional students to earn college credit by examination. Tests are updated periodically. The examination contains 2 sections, each consisting of 40 multiple-choice questions. One section is exclusively college algebra, the other trigonometry. A single score is based on the entire examination.

8589
College Level Examination Program: Subject Examination in Trigonometry. Educational Testing Service, Princeton, NJ 1981
Descriptors: Achievement Tests; *Adults; *Equivalency Tests; Higher Education; Mathematics Tests; Multiple Choice Tests; *Trigonometry; Undergraduate Students
Identifiers: CLEP
Availability: College Board Publication Orders; Box 2815, Princeton, NJ 08541
Grade Level: 13-16
Age Level: 18-65
Notes: Time, 90 min.; Items, 80

CLEP enables both traditional and nontraditional students to earn college credit by examination. Tests are updated periodically. Examination is about equally divided between questions that require solution of straightforward problems and those which require candidate to demonstrate the understanding of concepts. Candidate should be familiar with current trigonometric vocabulary and notation.

8590
College-Level Examination Program: Subject Examination in Clinical Chemistry. Educational Testing Service, Princeton, NJ 1981
Descriptors: Achievement Tests; *Adults; *Chemistry; *Equivalency Tests; Higher Education; *Medical Technologists; Multiple Choice Tests; Undergraduate Students
Identifiers: CLEP; *Clinical Laboratory Occupations
Availability: College Board Publication Orders; Box 2815, Princeton, NJ 08541
Grade Level: 13-16
Age Level: 18-64
Notes: Time, 90 min.; Items, 100

CLEP enables both traditional and nontraditional students to earn college credit by examination. Tests are updated periodically. This examination measures knowledge in areas of general chemical principles, general clinical chemistry principles, instrumentation for important techniques, specific analyses of biologic fluids, quality control, clinical pathology, biochemistry, physiology, genetics, and toxicology. No longer administered nationally. For institutional use only.

8594
College-Level Examination Program: Subject Examination in Anatomy, Physiology, Microbiology. Educational Testing Service, Princeton, NJ 1981
Descriptors: Achievement Tests; *Adults; *Anatomy; *Equivalency Tests; Higher Education; *Microbiology; Multiple Choice Tests; *Nurses; *Physiology; Practical Nursing; Undergraduate Students
Identifiers: CLEP; North Carolina
Availability: College Board Publication Orders; Box 2815, Princeton, NJ 08541
Grade Level: 13-16
Age Level: 18-64
Notes: Time, 90 min.; Items, 75

CLEP enables both traditional and nontraditional students to earn college credit by examination. Tests are updated periodically. Nursing series was developed by North Carolina Regional Medical Program in cooperation with the College Board to afford licensed practical nurses and other individuals an opportunity to earn credit toward first year's work in an Associate Degree Nursing (ADN) Program. No longer administered nationally. For institutional use only. This examination covers basic physiological and security (integrity of organism) subject areas.

8598
College-Level Examination Program: Subject Examination in Sciences—General Biology. Educational Testing Service, Princeton, NJ 1981
Descriptors: Achievement Tests; *Adults; *Biology; *Equivalency Tests; Higher Education; Multiple Choice Tests; Undergraduate Students
Identifiers: CLEP
Availability: College Board Publication Orders; Box 2815, Princeton, NJ 08541
Grade Level: 13-16
Age Level: 18-65
Notes: Time, 90 min.; Items, 120

CLEP enables both traditional and nontraditional students to earn college credit by examination. Tests are updated periodically. Examination is divided into 3 broad areas: molecular and cellular biology, organismal biology, and population biology.

8601
College Level Examination Program: Subject Examination in Introductory Macroeconomics. Educational Testing Service, Princeton, NJ 1981
Descriptors: Achievement Tests; *Adults; *Economics; *Equivalency Tests; Essay Tests; Higher Education; Multiple Choice Tests; Undergraduate Students
Identifiers: CLEP; *Macroeconomics
Availability: College Board Publication Orders; Box 2815, Princeton, NJ 08541
Grade Level: 13-16
Age Level: 18-65
Notes: Time, 90 min.; Items, 90

CLEP enables both traditional and nontraditional students to earn college credit by examination. Tests are updated periodically. Test places particular emphasis on the determinants of aggregate demand and on the monetary and/or fiscal policies that are appropriate to achieve particular policy objectives. Material covered includes basic or generic concepts and macroeconomic concepts. An optional 90-minute essay exam measures ability to select and organize material related to macroeconomic policy and present it articulately.

8602
College Level Examination Program: Subject Examination in Introductory Microeconomics. Educational Testing Service, Princeton, NJ 1981
Descriptors: Achievement Tests; *Adults; *Economics; *Equivalency Tests; Essay Tests; Higher Education; Multiple Choice Tests; Undergraduate Students
Identifiers: CLEP; *Microeconomics
Availability: College Board Publication Orders; Box 2815, Princeton, NJ 08541
Grade Level: 13-16
Age Level: 18-65
Notes: Time, 90 min.; Items, 90

CLEP enables both traditional and nontraditional students to earn college credit by examination. Tests are updated periodically. Material covered includes basic or generic concepts and microeconomic concepts. An optional 90-

minute essay section measures ability to select and organize materials related to microeconomic issues and present them articulately.

8676
Gallistel-Ellis Test of Coding Skills. Gallistel, Elizabeth; Ellis, Karalee 1974
Subtests: Giving Sounds for Letters; Reading; Spelling
Descriptors: Criterion Referenced Tests; Diagnostic Tests; Elementary Education; *Elementary School Students; *Handicap Identification; Individual Testing; *Learning Disabilities; Phonics; *Reading Skills; *Spelling
Availability: Montage Press, Inc.; P.O. Box 4322, Handen, CT 06514
Grade Level: 1-6
Notes: Time, 35 min. approx.
Designed to measure coding skills in reading and spelling. Assesses child's ability to give sounds for various letters and units. Student's ability to recognize and spell words made up of these sounds is also measured. Useful in identification of children with learning disabilities.

8679
Santa Clara Inventory of Developmental Tasks. Santa Clara Unified School District, CA 1974
Subtests: Social-Emotional; Motor Coordination; Visual Motor Performance; Visual Perception; Visual Memory; Auditory Perception; Auditory Memory; Language Development; Conceptual Development
Descriptors: Auditory Perception; *Child Development; *Classroom Observation Techniques; Concept Formation; *Developmental Tasks; Interpersonal Competence; Language Acquisition; Motor Development; Perceptual Motor Coordination; *Primary Education; Recall (Psychology); *Screening Tests; Visual Perception; *Young Children
Identifiers: Elementary Secondary Education Act Title I; IDT; TIM(N)
Availability: Tests in Microfiche; Test Collection, Educational Testing Service, Princeton, NJ 08541
Grade Level: K-2
Age Level: 5-7
Notes: Items, 72
Developed as an ESEA Title I project of the Santa Clara Unified School District. Consists of 72 tasks which represent milestones in children's development. Tasks are sequenced by chronological age and arranged into 9 skill areas. Inventory can be used as a screening device; as a basis for parent conferences; or as a record of a child's performance to facilitate correct placement by student's next teacher.

8692
Reading Management System: Elementary Reading Placement Test, Revised Edition, January 1976. Clark County School District, Las Vegas, NV 1976
Descriptors: Criterion Referenced Tests; *Diagnostic Tests; Elementary Education; *Elementary School Students; *Reading Achievement; Reading Diagnosis; *Reading Skills; *Student Placement
Availability: Clark County School District; 2832 E. Flamingo Rd., Las Vegas, NV 89121
Grade Level: 1-6
Designed to assess student competencies in reading skills. Breakdown clusters identified correspond to Diagnostic Step Clusters in Reading Management System. Placement test is one component in overall reading management system.

8693
Reading Management System: Elementary Diagnostic Step Tests. Clark County School District, Las Vegas, NV 1977
Descriptors: Criterion Referenced Tests; *Diagnostic Teaching; *Diagnostic Tests; Elementary Education; *Elementary School Students; *Reading Achievement; Reading Diagnosis; *Reading Skills
Availability: Clark County School District; 2832 E. Flamingo Rd., Las Vegas, NV 89121
Grade Level: 1-6
Diagnostic Step Cluster Tests are a series of 13 individual test booklets which are components of the Reading Management system. Reading skills are categorized into 8 levels, appropriate to instructional grade level, and further subdivided into clusters, A-M for steps 1-42. They are used to aid the classroom teacher in a diagnostic-prescriptive approach to reading skills.

8796
Test of Ability to Explain. Sawin, Enoch I. 1969
Subtests: Recognition of Events Connected by Causality; Recognition of Principles that Explain Events; Application of Principles that Explain Cause-and-Effect Relations
Descriptors: Deduction; Elementary School Students; Essay Tests; *Grade 6; Intermediate Grades; *Logical Thinking; Multiple Choice Tests; Social Studies
Identifiers: ABEX; Explanations; Reasoning
Availability: ERIC Document Reproduction Service; 7420 Fullerton Rd., Ste. 110, Springfield, VA 22153-2852 (ED040106, 374 p.)
Grade Level: 6
Notes: Time, 50 min. approx.; Items, 33
Designed to assess student's ability to explain ideas involving social studies content. Forms available as multiple-choice or essay. Essay test consists of 8 items which yield 3 part scores: ability to explain relationships, recognition of relevant facts, and recognition of relevant generalizations.

8877
Student Geometry Achievement Test. Backman, Carl Adolph 1969
Subtests: Recall of Factual Knowledge; Perform Mathematical Manipulations and Solve Routine Problems; Demonstrate Comprehension of Mathematical Ideas and Concepts
Descriptors: *Achievement Tests; *Elementary School Students; *Geometry; Intermediate Grades; Multiple Choice Tests
Identifiers: TIM(E)
Availability: Tests in Microfiche; Test Collection, Educational Testing Service, Princeton, NJ 08541
Grade Level: 4-5
Notes: Items, 21
A measure of student achievement in geometry. Designed to accompany the author's Survey Instrument: Geometry Test and Teaching Geometry Test.

8891
Pre-Academic Learning Inventory. Wood, M.H.; Layne, F.M. 1975
Subtests: Language Development; Speech Development; Concept Development; Body Concept; Auditory Channel Development; Visual Channel Development, Visual-Motor Integration; Eye-Hand Coordination; Gross Motor Coordination; Behavior
Descriptors: Auditory Perception; Concept Formation; *Diagnostic Tests; *Grade 1; Individual Testing; *Kindergarten Children; Language Acquisition; *Learning Problems; Motor Development; Primary Education; *School Readiness Tests; Screening Tests; Visual Perception; Vocabulary; Young Children
Identifiers: PAL
Availability: United Educational Services; P.O. Box 357, East Aurora, NY 14052
Grade Level: K-1
Notes: Time, 35 min. approx.
Inventory aids in providing appropriate education and intervention during kindergarten, prefirst or first grade.

8895
Prescriptive Reading Performance Test. Fudala, Janet B. 1978
Descriptors: Adults; *Diagnostic Tests; *Elementary School Students; Elementary Secondary Education; Individual Testing; *Reading Achievement; *Reading Diagnosis; *Reading Difficulties; *Secondary School Students; Spelling
Identifiers: PRPT
Availability: Western Psychological Services; 12031 Wilshire Blvd., Los Angeles, CA 90025
Grade Level: K-12
Designed to obtain quick assessment of reading level, determine grade level at which to begin testing for paragraph reading comprehension, and facilitate diagnosis of strengths and weaknesses in reading and word attack skills. Provides individual assessment of student reading and spelling performance and classifies patterns into normal and 3 atypical patterns suggestive of subtypes of developmental dyslexia. Graded word lists cover age and grade range from prereading readiness level through adult level.

8932
Science Reasoning Level Test. Duszynska, Anna
Descriptors: Academic Achievement; Achievement Tests; *Cross Cultural Studies; *Elementary School Students; Foreign Countries; Intermediate Grades; *Logical Thinking; *Science Tests; *Scientific Literacy; *Piagetian Theory
Identifiers: Poland; SRLT
Availability: ERIC Document Reproduction Service; 7420 Fullerton Rd., Ste. 110, Springfield, VA 22153-2852 (ED144988, 28 p.)
Grade Level: 4-6
Notes: Items, 16
Designed to determine whether a test based on Piaget model of development of thought processes could be used to study the development of scientific reasoning in ele-

mentary school students. Relationship between reasoning and academic achievement and patterns in development of thought processes were compared for students in Poland and U.S.

8945
Literacy Assessment Battery. Sticht, Thomas G.; Beck, Lawrence J. 1976
Subtests: Paragraphs: Auding; Paragraphs: Reading; Vocabulary: Auding and Reading; Vocabulary: Reading; Decoding
Descriptors: Achievement Tests; *Adult Literacy; Adults; Aptitude Tests; Decoding (Reading); *Listening Comprehension; Listening Comprehension Tests; *Reading Ability; Reading Achievement; *Reading Comprehension; *Reading Diagnosis; *Reading Difficulties; Timed Tests; Vocabulary
Identifiers: LAB; Synonyms
Availability: ERIC Document Reproduction Service; 7420 Fullerton Rd., Ste. 110, Springfield, VA 22153-2852 (ED129900, 166 p.)
Age Level: Adults
Notes: Time, 50 min. approx.; Items, 101
Designed for adults who have a reading problem. Experimental battery of tests to determine the relative efficiency with which adults can comprehend language by reading or listening and gives estimates of discrepancies between the ability to aud (listen to speech) and the ability to read. The authors feel that information concerning auding/reading discrepancies are useful in identifying the nature and extent of a reading problem, estimating reading potential, and revealing the type of needed remedial training. Requires the use of a stopwatch and cassette recorder. Types of answer are short answer (filling in information), multiple-choice, and encircling the spoken error.

8979
Productive Language Assessment Tasks. Bond, James T. 1975
Descriptors: *Achievement Tests; *Cognitive Processes; Elementary School Students; *Grade 2; *Grade 3; *Language Experience Approach; Language Tests; Primary Education; Program Evaluation; *Writing Skills
Identifiers: PLAT; Project Follow Through; *Writing Sample
Availability: ERIC Document Reproduction Service; 7420 Fullerton Rd., Ste. 110, Springfield, VA 22153-2852 (ED142560, 44 p.)
Grade Level: 2-3
Designed to assess impact of Project Follow Through. Task-oriented instrument is suitable for measuring nontraditional objectives. Writing samples produced as a result of test were reviewed for fluency, syntactic maturity, vocabulary diversity, descriptive quantity, diversity and scope, reporting quality, narrative organization, explanatory statements, and decodability. Positive effects of Follow Through program were evident by third grade.

8983
Bilingual Syntax Measure II. Psychological Corp., San Antonio, TX 1978
Descriptors: Bilingual Students; Culture Fair Tests; Elementary Secondary Education; *English (Second Language); *Language Dominance; Language Proficiency; Spanish Speaking; Visual Measures
Identifiers: BSM II
Availability: The Psychological Corp.; 555 Academic Ct., San Antonio, TX 78204-0952
Grade Level: 3-12
Notes: Time, 15 min. approx.; Items, 26
An extension of the Bilingual Syntax Measure. Measures language dominance (Spanish or English), structural proficiency in English as a Second Language, and the degree of maintenance or loss of basic Spanish structures.

8990
French FLES Test. Barry, Doris; And Others
Subtests: Oral Comprehension; Reading Comprehension
Descriptors: Audiotape Recordings; *Comprehension; *Elementary School Students; *FLES; *French; Intermediate Grades; Language Skills; Language Tests; *Reading Comprehension; *Second Language Learning
Identifiers: TIM(E)
Availability: Tests in Microfiche; Test Collection, Educational Testing Service, Princeton, NJ 08541
Grade Level: 4-6
Notes: Items, 100
Multiple-choice test of French language reading and aural comprehension for grades 4 to 6. The aural section includes the identification of pictures, numbers, time, and a listening comprehension exercise. The reading section includes the identification of category and completion exercises.

8991
Examen de Espanol Para Escuelas Elementales: Spanish FLES Test. West Hartford Public Schools, CT 1976
Descriptors: Audiotape Recordings; *Comprehension; *Elementary School Students; *FLES; Intermediate Grades; Language Skills; Language Tests; *Oral Language; *Reading Comprehension; *Second Language Learning; *Spanish
Identifiers: TIM(E)
Availability: Tests in Microfiche; Test Collection, Educational Testing Service, Princeton, NJ 08541
Grade Level: 4-6
Notes: Items, 70

Multiple-choice test of Spanish reading and oral comprehension for grades 4-6. For oral sections students respond to passages on a cassette tape. The reading comprehension section includes vocabulary and completion exercises.

9010
Comprehension Test for Literature. Weiss, Lucile 1976
Descriptors: *Adolescent Literature; *Cloze Procedure; *Literature; Reading Achievement; *Reading Comprehension; Reading Skills; *Reading Tests; Secondary Education; *Secondary School Students
Identifiers: TIM(E)
Availability: Tests in Microfiche; Test Collection, Educational Testing Service, Princeton, NJ 08541
Grade Level: 7-12
Notes: Time, 45 min. approx.; Items, 100

Cloze tests used to determine whether high school students have the reading skills to read a specific assignment. A representative passage is chosen, and every fifth word is deleted. Passages for use with Heinlein's *Stranger in a Strange Land* and Hawthorne's *The Great Stone Face* are included. Passages for use with other titles are also available.

9011
Reading Test for Vocational Education. Weiss, Lucile 1976
Subtests: Autosense; How to Change a Gasket; Communications; Television; Drill Press; Sources of Electrical Energy
Descriptors: Aptitude Tests; *Cloze Procedure; High Schools; *High School Students; *Reading Comprehension; *Screening Tests; *Vocational Aptitude; Vocational Education
Identifiers: TIM(E)
Availability: Tests in Microfiche; Test Collection, Educational Testing Service, Princeton, NJ 08541
Grade Level: 9-12
Notes: Items, 300

Designed to function as a screening procedure to identify students who lack academic skills but who, because of interest and knowledge in nonacademic areas, will succeed in vocational education programs. It was developed to serve as an alternative to academically oriented tests used for screening purposes.

9104
Steenburgen Quick Math Screening. Steenburgen-Gelb, F. 1978
Descriptors: Criterion Referenced Tests; Elementary Education; *Elementary School Mathematics; *Elementary School Students; Mathematical Concepts; *Mathematics Tests; Pretests Posttests; Remedial Mathematics; *Screening Tests
Availability: Academic Therapy Publications; 20 Commercial Blvd., Novato, CA 94947-6191
Grade Level: 1-6

This criterion-referenced, untimed screening test in basic math functions offers a remedial follow-up program to help children in grades 1 through 6 and older remedial students with math skills at elementary levels. Developed with the needs of distractible students in mind, the spacious presentation of problems does not overstimulate hyperactive or distractible children.

9119
College Outcome Measures Project. American College Testing Program, Iowa City, IA 1978
Subtests: Communicating; Solving Problems; Clarifying Values; Functioning within Social Institutions; Using Science and Technology; Using the Arts; Speaking; Writing
Descriptors: *Achievement Tests; Art; Communication Skills; Essay Tests; Higher Education; Interpersonal Competence; *Objective Tests; Problem Solving; Sciences; Speech Communication; Tape Recordings; Technology; *Undergraduate Students; Values Clarification; Writing Skills
Identifiers: COMP

Availability: American College Testing Program; P.O. Box 168, Iowa City, IA 52240
Grade Level: 13-16
Notes: Time, 90 min.; Items, 240

An integrated program that includes assessment instruments, an alumni survey, on-campus consultation, national conferences, and research reports. Each element is designed to help an institution to evaluate, improve, and build support for the general education curriculum. Institutions may choose to use all or any of the program components. The core of the program consists of a group of assessment instruments which provide detailed diagnostic information on the strengths and weaknesses of a general education program. The three primary instruments are the Composite Examination, the Objective Test, and the Activity Inventory. The Composite Examination takes approximately 4 hours and uses simulation activities that require application of general knowledge and skills to problems and issues generally met by adults. The Objective Test takes approximately 2 hours and is a quick, inexpensive, and valid way to estimate how college students would do on the Composite Examination. The Activity Inventory assesses student involvement in various out-of-class activities. It is untimed but generally takes 90 minutes. Outcome areas assessed in the program include communicating, solving problems, clarifying values, functioning within social institutions, using science and technology, and using the arts.

9129
Industrial Reading Test. Psychological Corp., San Antonio, TX 1977
Descriptors: *Achievement Tests; Adolescents; Adults; *Employees; *Employment Potential; *High School Students; Industrial Education; *Reading Ability; Reading Achievement; Reading Comprehension; Reading Tests; *Vocational Education; Vocational High Schools; Vocational Rehabilitation
Identifiers: IRT; Power Tests
Availability: The Psychological Corp.; 555 Academic Ct., San Antonio, TX 78204-0952
Age Level: 14-65
Notes: Time, 40 min.; Items, 38

Developed for use in industry and vocational schools. Designed to measure reading ability; and is a power rather than speed test. The test determines whether an individual with some high school education has the necessary reading ability to comprehend written technical materials. Used to determine whether an individual would make satisfactory progress in technical training. Comes in 2 forms: Form A is sold only to business and industry; Form B is sold both to businesses and to schools.

9131
Auditory Automotive Mechanics Diagnostic Achievement Test. Swanson, Richard Arthur 1968
Descriptors: *Achievement Tests; Adults; Audiotape Recordings; *Auditory Perception; Auditory Tests; *Auto Mechanics; Listening Skills; Occupational Tests; Postsecondary Education; Trade and Industrial Education
Identifiers: AAMDAT
Availability: ERIC Document Reproduction Service; 7420 Fullerton Rd., Ste. 110, Springfield, VA 22153-2852 (ED154034, 125 p.)
Age Level: 18-64
Notes: Items, 44

Designed to measure ability to diagnose malfunctions in automobiles using auditory clues.

9135
Kindergarten Screening Instrument. Houston Independent School District, TX 1975
Subtests: Vision; Hearing; Eye Hand Coordination; Language Learning; Gross Motor
Descriptors: Child Development; *Cognitive Development; *Individual Development; Individual Testing; *Kindergarten Children; Learning Readiness; *Performance Tests; Primary Education; *Psychomotor Skills; School Readiness; *Screening Tests; Spanish; *Spanish Speaking; Visual Measures; Visual Stimuli; Volunteers
Identifiers: HISD Kindergarten Screening Instrument; Oral Tests; Public Schools (Houston)
Availability: ERIC Document Reproduction Service; 7420 Fullerton Rd., Ste. 110, Springfield, VA 22153-2852 (ED153999, 84 p.)
Grade Level: K

Screening device developed by the Board of Education of the Houston Independent School District through the Volunteers in Public Schools. Used to detect possible difficulties in such areas as perception, discrimination, physical development, and cognitive development. Individually administered by the trained volunteers. Requires the use of numerous items, such as eye chart, cassette tape playback, various drawings and pictures, scissors, a 24-inch hoop, etc. Instructions that are to be given to the child are written in both Spanish and English.

9246
How Much Do You Know about Workers. Gordon, Michael E.; And Others
Descriptors: Adults; *Knowledge Level; *Lay People; Managerial Occupations; Objective Tests; *Psychology
Identifiers: TIM(E)
Availability: Tests in Microfiche; Test Collection, Educational Testing Service, Princeton, NJ 08541
Age Level: Adults
Notes: Items, 72

In a study of the degree to which industrial/organizational psychology is a reflection of common sense, this true-false test was prepared from recently published research results. The research results were rewritten in common, lay terminology. Nine items were added to collect demographic information.

9250
Leamos: Orientation and Placement Tests, Fundamental Stage: Primary, Steps 4-15. Los Angeles Unified School District, CA 1976
Descriptors: *Diagnostic Teaching; *Diagnostic Tests; *Elementary School Students; Functional Literacy; Orientation; Primary Education; Reading Tests; *Spanish; *Spanish Speaking; *Student Placement
Identifiers: Spanish Developmental Reading; Test Batteries
Availability: Paul S. Amidon and Associates; 1966 Benson Ave., St. Paul, MN 55116-9990
Grade Level: K-3

Designed to acquaint students with test format and determine appropriate learner entry level on skills continuum. Used as part of Leamos; Spanish Developmental Reading Program (DRP).

9251
Leamos: Diagnostic/Prescriptive Tests, Fundamental Stage: Primary, Steps 1-3. Los Angeles Unified School District, CA 1976
Descriptors: *Diagnostic Teaching; *Diagnostic Tests; *Elementary School Students; Functional Literacy; Pretests Posttests; Primary Education; *Reading Skills; Reading Tests; *Spanish; *Spanish Speaking
Identifiers: Spanish Developmental Reading; Test Batteries
Availability: Paul S. Amidon and Associates; 1966 Benson Ave., St. Paul, MN 55116-9990
Grade Level: K-3

Designed by Spanish Developmental Reading Task Force for use with primary grade children, who are Spanish speakers. The program is based upon the idea that, after literacy is achieved in Spanish, the transfer to the reading of English is accomplished with greater ease and assurance of learner success. Step I consists of 21 items. Step II also has 21 items, and Step III consists of 24 items. Contents are similar to English Developmental Reading.

9252
Leamos: Diagnostic/Prescriptive Tests, Fundamental Stage: Primary, Steps 4-6. Los Angeles Unified School District, CA 1976
Descriptors: *Diagnostic Teaching; *Diagnostic Tests; *Elementary School Students; Functional Literacy; Pretests Posttests; Primary Education; *Reading Skills; Reading Tests; *Spanish; *Spanish Speaking
Identifiers: Spanish Developmental Reading; Test Batteries
Availability: Paul S. Amidon and Associates; 1966 Benson Ave., St. Paul, MN 55116-9990
Grade Level: K-3

Designed for Spanish-speaking primary grade children by the Spanish-speaking reading consultants of the Developmental Reading Task Force. The program is based on the premise that, after literacy is achieved in Spanish, the transfer to the reading of English is accomplished with greater ease and assurance of learner success. It is the Spanish version of the Developmental Reading Program. Step 4 has 20 items, Step 5 has 29 items, and Step 6 has 36 items.

9253
Leamos: Diagnostic/Prescriptive Tests, Fundamental Stage: Primary, Steps 7-9. Los Angeles Unified School District, CA 1976
Descriptors: *Diagnostic Teaching; *Diagnostic Tests; *Elementary School Students; Functional Literacy; Pretests Posttests; Primary Education; *Reading Skills; Reading Tests; *Spanish; *Spanish Speaking
Identifiers: Spanish Developmental Reading; Test Batteries
Availability: Paul S. Amidon and Associates; 1966 Benson Ave., St. Paul, MN 55116-9990
Grade Level: K-3

Designed for Spanish-speaking primary grade children by the Spanish-speaking reading consultants of the Developmental Reading Task Force. The program is based on the premise that, after literacy is achieved in Spanish, the transfer to the reading of English is accomplished with greater ease and assurance of learner success. It is the Spanish edition of the Developmental Reading Program. Step 7 has 28 items, Step 8 has 27 items, and Step 9 has 36 items.

9254
Leamos: Diagnostic/Prescriptive Tests, Fundamental Stage: Primary, Steps 10-12. Los Angeles Unified School District, CA 1976
Descriptors: *Diagnostic Teaching; *Diagnostic Tests; *Elementary School Students; Functional Literacy; Pretests Posttests; Primary Education; *Reading Skills; Reading Tests; *Spanish; *Spanish Speaking
Identifiers: Spanish Developmental Reading; Test Batteries
Availability: Paul S. Amidon and Associates; 1966 Benson Ave., St. Paul, MN 55116-9990
Grade Level: K-3
Designed for Spanish-speaking students by the Spanish-speaking reading consultants of the Developmental Reading Task Force. The program is based on the premise that, after literacy is achieved in Spanish, the transfer to the reading of English is accomplished with greater ease and assurance of learner success. It is the Spanish edition of the Developmental Reading Program (DRP). Step 10 has 19 items, Step 11 has 29 items, and Step 12 has 20 items.

9255
Leamos: Diagnostic/Prescriptive Tests, Fundamental Stage: Primary, Steps 13-15. Los Angeles Unified School District, CA 1976
Descriptors: *Diagnostic Teaching; *Diagnostic Tests; *Elementary School Students; Functional Literacy; Pretests Posttests; Primary Education; *Reading Skills; Reading Tests; *Spanish; *Spanish Speaking
Identifiers: Spanish Developmental Reading; Test Batteries
Availability: Paul S. Amidon and Associates; 1966 Benson Ave., St. Paul, MN 55116-9990
Grade Level: K-3
Designed for Spanish-speaking students by the Spanish-speaking Reading Consultants of the Developmental Reading Task Force. The program is based on the premise that, after literacy is achieved in Spanish, the transfer to the reading of English is accomplished with greater ease and assurance of learner success. It is the Spanish edition of the Developmental Reading Program (DRP). Step 13 has 25 items, step 14 has 26 items, and step 15 has 20 items.

9282
Pennington-Passey Alcohol Knowledge Questionnaire. Pennington, Dempy F.; Passey, George E. 1959
Subtests: Etiology; Physiological Action; Treatment Procedures; Facilities; Effectiveness; Symptoms; Prevalence; Effects; Legal Control; Manufacture; Drinking Customs
Descriptors: *Adults; Alcohol Education; Alcoholism; *Drinking; Higher Education; *High Schools; *High School Students; *Knowledge Level; Rating Scales; *Undergraduate Students
Availability: CARRF; Center of Alcohol Studies, Rutgers University, Allison Rd., Piscataway, NJ 08854
Grade Level: 9-16
Age Level: 13-64
Notes: Items, 44
Designed to assess knowledge concerning alcohol and its use. Instrument is available as entry 1.8B.

9323
Developmental Reading: Orientation and Placement Tests, Fundamental Stage: Primary, Steps 4-30. Reading Task Force, Los Angeles Unified School District, CA 1975
Descriptors: Diagnostic Teaching; *Diagnostic Tests; *Elementary School Students; *Functional Literacy; Individual Testing; Orientation; *Preschool Children; Preschool Education; Primary Education; *Student Placement; Test Wiseness
Identifiers: Test Batteries
Availability: Paul S. Amidon and Associates; 1966 Benson Ave., St. Paul, MN 55116-9990
Age Level: 2-8
Designed to establish appropriate entry level or reading continuum for each learner. Brief orientation test familiarizes learners with placement test format. Steps 4-12 are designed for learners 5 years old and younger. Steps 7-30 are for learners 6 years old and above. May be group administered or individually administered to learners 5 years old and above. Preschoolers should be individually tested.

9324
Developmental Reading: Orientation and Placement Tests, Fundamental Stage: Advanced, Steps 7-30. Reading Task Force, Los Angeles Unified School District, CA 1975
Descriptors: Adolescents; *Adults; Children; *Diagnostic Tests; *Elementary School Students; Elementary Secondary Education; *Functional Literacy; Orientation; *Secondary School Students; *Student Placement; Test Wiseness
Identifiers: Test Batteries
Availability: Paul S. Amidon and Associates; 1966 Benson Ave., St. Paul, MN 55116-9990
Age Level: 9-64
Designed to determine which 3-step battery of Diagnostic/Prescriptive Pretests each learner should take. Determination is made by assessment of decoding ability. Orientation test introduces learners to test format. Fundamental Stage: Advanced tests are for use with learners 9 years of age through adulthood who have not attained functional literacy.

9325
Developmental Reading: Diagnostic/Prescriptive Tests, Fundamental Stage: Primary, Steps 1-3. Reading Task Force, Los Angeles Unified School District, CA 1975
Descriptors: *Diagnostic Teaching; *Diagnostic Tests; *Elementary School Students; *Functional Literacy; *Kindergarten Children; Letters (Alphabet); Phonics; Pretests Posttests; Primary Education; *Reading Readiness; Reading Tests; Spelling
Identifiers: Test Batteries
Availability: Paul S. Amidon and Associates; 1966 Benson Ave., St. Paul, MN 55116-9990
Age Level: 5-8
Designed to determine specific skill strengths and needs of each learner as a basis for differentiated instruction. A sequential reading program applicable for learners from prekindergarten through adult level. Designed to measure achievement of functional literacy. The major goals of the program include multisensory readiness skills, alphabetic mastery skills, regular spelling patterns, variant spelling patterns, and phonic generalizations. Step 1 measures visual discrimination; semantic labels and functions; and auditory discrimination of word pairs. Step 2 measures visual discrimination; semantic labels and functions; and auditory letter name pairs. Step 3 measures visual discrimination; semantic labels and functions; semantic labels for object position; and auditory discrimination.

9326
Developmental Reading: Diagnostic/Prescriptive Tests, Fundamental Stage: Primary, Steps 4-6. Reading Task Force, Los Angeles Unified School District, CA 1975
Descriptors: *Diagnostic Teaching; *Diagnostic Tests; *Elementary School Students; *Functional Literacy; *Kindergarten Children; Letters (Alphabet); Phonics; Pretests Posttests; Primary Education; *Reading Readiness; *Reading Skills; Reading Tests; Spelling; *Visual Discrimination
Identifiers: Test Batteries
Availability: Paul S. Amidon and Associates; 1966 Benson Ave., St. Paul, MN 55116-9990
Age Level: 5-8
Designed to determine specific skill strengths and weaknesses of each learner as a basis for differentiated instruction. A sequential reading program applicable for learners from prekindergarten through adult level. Designed to measure achievement of functional literacy. The major goals of the program include multisensory readiness skills, alphabetic mastery skills, regular spelling patterns, variant spelling patterns, and phonic generalizations. Step 4 measures visual discrimination; semantic labels and functions; and semantic labels for object position. Step 5 measures visual discrimination; auditory discrimination; and semantic labels for animals, action pictures, and object position. Step 6 measures visual discrimination; semantic labels for numerals, object position, and adjectives; and comprehension detail.

9327
Developmental Reading: Diagnostic/Prescriptive Tests, Fundamental Stage: Primary, Steps 7-9. Reading Task Force, Los Angeles Unified School District, CA 1975
Descriptors: *Auditory Discrimination; *Diagnostic Teaching; *Diagnostic Tests; *Elementary School Students; *Functional Literacy; *Kindergarten Children; Letters (Alphabet); Phonics; Pretests Posttests; Primary Education; *Reading Readiness; *Reading Skills; Reading Tests; Spelling
Identifiers: Test Batteries
Availability: Paul S. Amidon and Associates; 1966 Benson Ave., St. Paul, MN 55116-9990
Age Level: 5-8
Designed to determine specific skill strengths and weaknesses of each learner as a basis for differentiated instruction. A sequential reading program applicable for learners from prekindergarten through adult level. Designed to measure achievement of functional literacy. The major goals of the program include multisensory readiness skills, alphabetic mastery skills, regular spelling patterns, variant spelling patterns, and phonic generalizations. Step 7 measures skills in auditory discrimination; letter names, and beginning consonant sounds; label name for numerals, and main idea. Step 8 measures skills in auditory discrimination, letter names, and beginning consonant sounds; ordinal designations; and sight words. Step 9 tests auditory discrimination; semantic labels for comparative relationship; sight words; and classification.

9328
Developmental Reading: Diagnostic/Prescriptive Tests, Fundamental Stage: Primary, Steps 10-12. Reading Task Force, Los Angeles Unified School District, CA 1975
Descriptors: Auditory Discrimination; *Diagnostic Teaching; *Diagnostic Tests; *Elementary School Students; *Functional Literacy; *Kindergarten Children; Letters (Alphabet); Phonics; Pretests Posttests; Primary Education; *Reading Readiness; Reading Tests; Spelling
Identifiers: Test Batteries
Availability: Paul S. Amidon and Associates; 1966 Benson Ave., St. Paul, MN 55116-9990
Age Level: 5-8
Designed to determine specific skill strengths and weaknesses of each learner as a basis for differentiated instruction. A sequential reading program applicable for learners from prekindergarten through adult level. Designed to measure achievement of functional literacy. The major goals of the program include multisensory readiness skills, alphabetic mastery skills, regular spelling patterns, variant spelling patterns, and phonic generalizations. Step 10 measures visual discrimination of words; auditory discrimination of final consonant sounds and phonograms; sight words; and relationships. Step 11 measures auditory discrimination, letter names, and short vowel sounds; phonograms; sight words; and details. Step 12 measures CVC words and label name; plurals; sight words; main idea; and sequence.

9329
Developmental Reading: Diagnostic/Prescriptive Tests, Fundamental Stage: Primary, Steps 13-15. Reading Task Force, Los Angeles Unified School District, CA 1975
Descriptors: *Diagnostic Teaching; *Diagnostic Tests; *Elementary School Students; *Functional Literacy; *Kindergarten Children; Letters (Alphabet); Phonics; Pretests Posttests; Primary Education; *Reading Readiness; Reading Tests; Spelling
Identifiers: Test Batteries
Availability: Paul S. Amidon and Associates; 1966 Benson Ave., St. Paul, MN 55116-9990
Age Level: 5-8
Designed to determine specific skill strengths and weaknesses of each learner as a basis for differentiated instruction. A sequential reading program applicable for learners from prekindergarten through adult level. Designed to measure achievement of functional literacy. The major goals of the program include multisensory readiness skills, alphabetic mastery skills, regular spelling patterns, variant spelling patterns, and phonic generalizations. Step 13 measures knowledge of long vowel sounds; initial consonant clusters; VCe phonograms; decodable label names; sight words; context; main idea; classification; and relationships. Step 14 measures knowledge of final consonant clusters; regular vowel digraphs; VVC phonograms; S-form verbs; sight words; decodable word meanings; antonyms; details; relationships; and inferences. Step 15 measures knowledge of consonant digraphs; VVC phonograms; possessive; label names; sight words; decodable word meanings; main idea; punctuation marks; sequences; drawing conclusions.

9330
Developmental Reading: Diagnostic/Prescriptive Tests, Fundamental Stage: Primary, Steps 16-18. Reading Task Force, Los Angeles Unified School District, CA 1975
Descriptors: *Diagnostic Teaching; *Diagnostic Tests; *Elementary School Students; *Functional Literacy; *Kindergarten Children; Letters (Alphabet); Phonics; Pretests Posttests; Primary Education; *Reading Readiness; Reading Tests; Spelling
Identifiers: Test Batteries
Availability: Paul S. Amidon and Associates; 1966 Benson Ave., St. Paul, MN 55116-9990
Age Level: 5-8
Designed to determine specific skill strengths and weaknesses of each learner as a basis for differentiated instruction. A sequential reading program applicable for learners from prekindergarten through adult level. Designed to measure achievement of functional literacy. The major goals of the program include multisensory readiness skills, alphabetic mastery skills, regular spelling patterns, variant spelling patterns, and phonic generalizations. Step 16 measures skills in hard and soft sounds of [c] and [g]; finally sounds; or vowel controller; long or short sound of diph-

thong [oo]; syllabication; sight words; decodable word meanings; context; cause and effect; and inference. Step 17 measures skills in [or] or [ar] vowel controller; compound words; syllabication; concrete and abstract words; sight words; compound word meanings; main idea; sequence; simile; emotional reactions. Step 18 measures skills in vowel controllers [er], [ir], [ur]; diphthongs; plural possessive; sight words; decodable word meanings; synonyms and antonyms; details; relationships; conclusions; compare and contrast; and dictionary skills.

9331
Developmental Reading: Diagnostic/Prescriptive Tests, Fundamental Stage: Primary, Steps 19-21.
Reading Task Force, Los Angeles Unified School District, CA 1975
Descriptors: *Diagnostic Teaching; *Diagnostic Tests; *Elementary School Students; *Functional Literacy; *Kindergarten Children; Letters (Alphabet); Phonics; Pretests Posttests; Primary Education; *Reading Readiness; Reading Tests; Spelling
Identifiers: Test Batteries
Availability: Paul S. Amidon and Associates; 1966 Benson Ave., St. Paul, MN 55116-9990
Age Level: 5-8

Designed to determine specific skill strengths and weaknesses of each learner as a basis for differentiated instruction. A sequential reading program applicable for learners from prekindergarten through adult level. Designed to measure achievement of functional literacy. The major goals of the program include multisensory readiness skills, alphabetic mastery skills, regular spelling patterns, variant spelling patterns, and phonic generalizations. Step 19 measures skills in controlled vowels; 3-letter consonant clusters; silent letters; variant spelling patterns; syllabication for V/CV patterns; sight words; main idea; classification; emotional reactions; dictionary skill, first letter. Step 20 measures skills in consonant digraphs; variant vowel digraphs; contractions; syllabication; prefixes; sight words; decodable word meanings; details; sequence; similes; conclusions; dictionary skill; second letter. Step 21 measures skills in final y sounds; plurals; contractions; syllabication; analogies; sight words; main idea; cause and effect; inference; comparison or contrast; table of contexts; and following directions.

9332
Developmental Reading: Diagnostic/Prescriptive Tests, Fundamental Stage: Primary, Steps 22-24.
Reading Task Force, Los Angeles Unified School District, CA 1975
Descriptors: *Diagnostic Teaching; *Diagnostic Tests; *Elementary School Students; *Functional Literacy; *Kindergarten Children; Letters (Alphabet); Phonics; Pretests Posttests; Primary Education; *Reading Readiness; Reading Tests; Spelling
Identifiers: Test Batteries
Availability: Paul S. Amidon and Associates; 1966 Benson Ave., St. Paul, MN 55116-9990
Age Level: 5-8

Designed to determine specific skill strengths and weaknesses of each learner as a basis for differentiated instruction. A sequential reading program applicable for learners from prekindergarten through adult level. Designed to measure achievement of functional literacy. The major goals of the program include multisensory readiness skills, alphabetic mastery skills, regular spelling patterns, variant spelling patterns, and phonic generalizations. Step 22 measures skills in schwa sound; variant vowel digraphs; reflexive compounds; plurals; words with prefixes; sight words; meanings of prefixed words; paragraph details; conclusions; reliability and validity; and following directions. Step 23 measures skills in silent letters; irregular plurals; contraction of are; syllabication and accenting of affixed words; words with suffixes; decodable word meanings; synonyms; main idea; inference; comparison or contrast; and following directions. Step 24 measures skills in contractions of have; words with suffixes; spelling patterns; context; homonym meanings; cause and effect; emotional reactions; reliability and validity; and following directions.

9333
Developmental Reading: Diagnostic/Prescriptive Tests, Fundamental Stage: Primary, Steps 25-27.
Reading Task Force, Los Angeles Unified School District, CA 1975
Descriptors: *Diagnostic Teaching; *Diagnostic Tests; *Elementary School Students; *Functional Literacy; *Kindergarten Children; Letters (Alphabet); Phonics; Pretests Posttests; Primary Education; *Reading Readiness; Reading Tests; Spelling
Identifiers: Test Batteries
Availability: Paul S. Amidon and Associates; 1966 Benson Ave., St. Paul, MN 55116-9990
Age Level: 5-8

Designed to determine specific skill strengths and weaknesses of each learner as a basis for differentiated instruction. A sequential reading program applicable for learners from prekindergarten through adult level. Designed to measure achievement of functional literacy. The major goals of the program include multisensory readiness skills, alphabetic mastery skills, regular spelling patterns, variant spelling patterns, and phonic generalizations. Step 25 measures skills in phonic generalizations for consonant sound; inflectional ending ed; decodable word meanings; synonyms; main idea; sequence; similes; conclusions; and following directions. Step 26 measures skills in phonic generalizations for short vowels, long vowels, and controlled vowels; context; figurative phrase meanings; classification; emotional reactions; inference; dictionary skill; and guide words. Step 27 measures skills in phonic generalizations for consonant digraphs; possessive forms; decodable word meanings; homonyms; main idea; punctuation marks; cause and effect; conclusions; and organizing information from paragraph format.

9334
Developmental Reading: Diagnostic/Prescriptive Tests, Fundamental Stage: Primary, Steps 28-30.
Reading Task Force, Los Angeles Unified School District, CA 1975
Descriptors: *Diagnostic Teaching; *Diagnostic Tests; *Elementary School Students; *Functional Literacy; *Kindergarten Children; Letters (Alphabet); Phonics; Pretests Posttests; Primary Education; *Reading Readiness; Reading Tests; Spelling
Identifiers: Test Batteries
Availability: Paul S. Amidon and Associates; 1966 Benson Ave., St. Paul, MN 55116-9990
Age Level: 5-8

Designed to determine specific skill strengths and weaknesses of each learner as a basis for differentiated instruction. A sequential reading program applicable for learners from prekindergarten through adult level. Designed to measure achievement of functional literacy. The major goals of the program include multisensory readiness skills, alphabetic mastery skills, regular spelling patterns, variant spelling patterns, and phonic generalizations. Step 28 measures skills in phonic generalizations for diphthongs; plural forms; decodable word meanings; context; figurative phrase meanings; details; classification; sequence; inference; title page of book; and table of contents. Step 29 measures skills in phonic generalizations for silent letters in clusters or digraphs; abbreviations; decodable word meanings; context; homonyms; main idea; cause and effect; comparisons and contrasts; reliability and validity; dictionary skill; third letter and following directions. Step 30 measures skills in 3 letter consonant clusters; plurals; syllabication; decodable word meanings, context; synonyms; details; classification; inference; conclusions; library skill, card catalog; and following directions.

9335
Developmental Reading: Diagnostic/Prescriptive Tests, Fundamental Stage: Advanced, Steps 7-12.
Reading Task Force, Los Angeles Unified School District, CA 1975
Descriptors: *Adults; *Diagnostic Teaching; *Diagnostic Tests; *Elementary School Students; *Functional Literacy; Intermediate Grades; Letters (Alphabet); Phonics; Pretests Posttests; Reading Tests; Secondary Education; *Secondary School Students; Spelling
Identifiers: Test Batteries
Availability: Paul S. Amidon and Associates; 1966 Benson Ave., St. Paul, MN 55116-9990
Age Level: 9-64

Designed to determine specific skill strengths and weaknesses of each learner as a basis for differentiated instruction. A sequential reading program applicable for learners from prekindergarten through adult level. Designed to measure achievement of functional literacy. The major goals of the program include multisensory readiness skills, alphabetic mastery skills, regular spelling patterns, variant spelling patterns, and phonic generalizations. Step 7 measures skills in letter names and beginning consonant sounds and main idea. Step 8 assesses skills in letter names and beginning consonant sounds and sight words. Step 9 assesses skills in letter names and beginning consonant sounds; sight words; and objects classification. Step 10 measures skills in final consonant sounds; sight words; and relationships. Step 11 measures skills in letter names and short vowel sounds; phonograms; and sight words. Step 12 measures skills in CVC spelling patterns; sight words; singular or plural CVC label names; main idea; and sequence.

9336
Developmental Reading: Diagnostic/Prescriptive Tests, Fundamental Stage: Advanced, Steps 13-18.
Reading Task Force, Los Angeles Unified School District, CA 1975
Descriptors: *Adults; *Diagnostic Teaching; *Diagnostic Tests; *Elementary School Students; *Functional Literacy; Intermediate Grades; Letters (Alphabet); Phonics; Pretests Posttests; Reading Tests; Secondary Education; *Secondary School Students; Spelling
Identifiers: Test Batteries
Availability: Paul S. Amidon and Associates; 1966 Benson Ave., St. Paul, MN 55116-9990
Age Level: 9-64

Designed to determine specific skill strengths and weaknesses of each learner as a basis for differentiated instruction. A sequential reading program applicable for learners from prekindergarten through adult level. Designed to measure achievement of functional literacy. The major goals of the program include multisensory skills, alphabetic mastery skills, regular spelling patterns, variant spelling patterns, and phonic generalizations. Step 13 measures skills in long vowel sounds; initial consonant clusters; VCE phonograms; decodable label names; sight words; context; main idea; classification; and relationships. Step 14 measures skills in final consonant clusters; vowel digraphs; VCC phonograms; S-form verbs; sight words; decodable word meanings; antonyms; details; relationships, and inference. Step 15 measures skills in consonant digraphs; VCC phonogram; possessive; decodable word meanings; sight words; main idea; punctuation marks; sequence; and drawing conclusions. Step 16 measures skills in hard and soft sounds of [c] and [g]; final [y] sounds; [ar] vowel controller; long or short sound of diphthong [oo]; syllabication; sight words; decodable word meaning; context; cause and effect; and inference. Step 17 measures skills in [or] or [ar] vowel controller; compound words; syllabication; concrete and abstract abstract words; sight words; main idea; sequence; similes; and emotional reactions. Step 18 measures skills in vowel controllers [er], [ir], [ur]; diphthongs; plural possessive; sight words; meanings of decodable words; synonyms and antonyms; details, relationships; conclusions; compare and contrast; and dictionary skills.

9337
Developmental Reading: Diagnostic/Prescriptive Tests, Fundamental Stage: Advanced, Steps 19-24.
Reading Task Force, Los Angeles Unified School District, CA 1975
Descriptors: *Adults; *Diagnostic Teaching; *Diagnostic Tests; *Elementary School Students; *Functional Literacy; Intermediate Grades; Letters (Alphabet); Phonics; Pretests Posttests; Reading Tests; Secondary Education; *Secondary School Students; Spelling
Identifiers: Test Batteries
Availability: Paul S. Amidon and Associates; 1966 Benson Ave., St. Paul, MN 55116-9990
Age Level: 9-64

Designed to determine specific skill strengths and weaknesses of each learner as a basis for differentiated instruction. A sequential reading program applicable for learners from prekindergarten through adult level. Designed to measure achievement of functional literacy. The major goals of the program include multisensory skills, alphabetic mastery skills, regular spelling patterns, variant spelling patterns, and phonic generalizations. Step 19 assesses skills in controlled vowels; 3-letter consonant clusters; silent letters; variant spelling pattern; syllabication for V/CV patterns; sight words; main idea; classification; emotional reactions; dictionary skills, first letter. Step 20 assesses skills in consonant digraphs; variant vowel digraphs; contractions; syllabication; prefixes; sight words; decodable word meanings; details; sequence; similes; conclusions; dictionary skills, second letter. Step 21 assesses skills in final y sounds; plurals; contractions; syllabication; analogies; sight words; main idea; cause and effect; inference; comparison or contrast; table of contents; and following directions. Step 22 measures skills in schwa sound; variant vowel digraphs; reflexive compounds; plurals; words with prefixes; meanings of prefixed words; paragraph details; conclusions; reliability and validity; and following directions. Step 23 measures skills in silent letters; irregular plurals; contractions; syllabication and accenting of affixed words; words with suffixes; decodable word meanings; synonyms; main idea; inference; comparison or contrast; and following directions. Step 24 assesses contractions; words with suffixes; context; homonyms; meanings; cause and effect; emotional reactions; reliability and validity; and following directions.

9338
Developmental Reading: Diagnostic/Prescriptive Tests, Fundamental Stage: Advanced, Steps 25-30.
Reading Task Force, Los Angeles Unified School District, CA 1975
Descriptors: *Adults; *Diagnostic Teaching; *Diagnostic Tests; *Elementary School Students; *Functional Literacy; Intermediate Grades; Letters (Alphabet); Phonics; Pretests Posttests; Secondary Education; *Secondary School Students; Spelling
Identifiers: Test Batteries
Availability: Paul S. Amidon and Associates; 1966 Benson Ave., St. Paul, MN 55116-9990
Age Level: 9-64

Designed to determine specific skill strengths and weaknesses of each learner as a basis for differentiated instruction. A sequential reading program applicable for learners from prekindergarten through adult level. Designed to measure achievement of functional literacy. The major goals of the program include multisensory skills, alphabetic mastery skills, regular and variant spelling patterns, and phonic generalizations. Step 25 measures skills in phonic generalizations for consonant sound; inflectional ending; decodable word meanings; synonyms; main idea; sequence; similes; conclusions; and following directions. Step 26 measures skills in phonic generalizations for short vowels, long vowels, and controlled vowels; context; figurative phrase meanings; classification; emotional reactions; inference; dictionary skill, guide words. Step 28 measures skills in phonic generalizations for diphthongs; plural forms; decodable word meanings; details; classification; sequence; inference; title page of book; table of contents. Step 29 assesses skills in phonic generalizations for silent letters in clusters or digraphs; abbreviations; decodable word meanings; context; homonyms; main idea; cause and effect; comparisons and contrasts; reliability and validity; dictionary skill, third letter; and following directions. Step 30 assesses skills in 3-letter consonant clusters; plurals; syllabication; decodable word meanings; context; synonyms; details; classification; inference; conclusions; library skill, card catalog; and following directions.

9433
Country School Examinations. Austin, John J., Editor 1978
Descriptors: *Achievement Tests; Elementary Education; Elementary School Mathematics; *Elementary School Students; Primary Sources; Reading Tests; *State Programs
Identifiers: Michigan; Test Batteries
Availability: Research Concepts; 1368 Airport Rd., Muskegon, MI 49444
Grade Level: 1-8
A collection of historic educational achievement tests for grades 1-8 developed for the state of Michigan. Reprints of the 1913 Michigan Common Schools Winter Term Examination and 1914 Fall Term Examination are included. The State of Michigan Examination Questions for 1919, 1920, and 1921 are also included. Instruments were originally developed for use in country, or one-room, schools.

9697
Spanish Criterion Referenced Test. Austin Independent School District, TX Bilingual Program 1974
Descriptors: *Bilingual Students; *Criterion Referenced Tests; Elementary Education; Elementary School Students; *Mastery Tests; Phonetic Analysis; Reading Comprehension; *Reading Tests; *Spanish; *Spanish Speaking; Structural Analysis (Linguistics)
Identifiers: TIM(F)
Availability: Tests in Microfiche; Test Collection, Educational Testing Service, Princeton, NJ 08541
Grade Level: K-5
Designed to assess mastery level in a Spanish language reading program for bilingual students in grades K-5. Covers phonetic and structural analysis and comprehension.

9698
Tests of Word Awareness. Holden, Marjorie H. 1977
Subtests: Serial Lists (10); Sentences (10); Homaphones (10)
Descriptors: *Listening Comprehension Tests; Listening Skills; Primary Education; Sentence Structure; Word Study Skills
Identifiers: *Word Awareness
Availability: Marjorie H. Holden; School of Education; California State University, 1000 E. Victoria Pwy., Dominquez Hills, CA 90747
Grade Level: K-1
Notes: Items, 30
Designed to determine a child's ability to identify the lexical contents of a meaningful sentence. Child tells which word was added to a list or sentence or which group of new words containing a homophone was added.

9744
Dyadic Oral Tests. Findley, Charles A. 1977
Descriptors: *Communication Skills; *Daily Living Skills; Elementary Education; Elementary School Students; *English (Second Language); *Teaching Methods
Identifiers: *Oral Tests
Availability: ERIC Document Reproduction Service; 7420 Fullerton Rd., Ste. 110, Springfield, VA 22153-2852 (ED145692, 41 p.)
Grade Level: 1-6
Groups of tasks to provide experience in purposeful communication for students of English as a Second Language in the form of requests, manipulative instructions, and descriptions. May be used as a test of proficiency.

9762
Gates-MacGinitie Reading Tests. Second Edition, Basic R. MacGinitie, Walter H. 1978
Subtests: Letter Sounds; Vocabulary; Letter Recognition; Comprehension
Descriptors: *Beginning Reading; Elementary School Students; Grade 1; Norm Referenced Tests; Primary Education; *Reading Achievement; *Reading Comprehension; *Vocabulary
Availability: Riverside Publishing Co.; 8420 Bryn Mawr Ave., Chicago, IL 60631
Grade Level: 1

Notes: Time, 65 min.; Items, 61
Norm-referenced test series designed to determine instructional levels and to evaluate progress. Covers reading vocabulary, comprehension, letter recognition, and letter sounds for grades 1.0-1.9.

9763
Gates-MacGinitie Reading Tests. Second Edition, Level A. 1978
Subtests: Vocabulary; Comprehension
Descriptors: *Decoding (Reading); Elementary School Students; Grade 1; Norm Referenced Tests; Primary Education; *Reading Achievement; *Reading Comprehension; Vocabulary
Availability: Riverside Publishing Co.; 8420 Bryn Mawr Ave., Chicago, IL 60631
Grade Level: 1
Notes: Time, 35 min. approx.; Items, 85
Norm-referenced test series designed to determine instructional levels and evaluate progress. Covers vocabulary (decoding skills) and comprehension (understanding ideas) for grades 1.5-1.9.

9764
Gates-MacGinitie Reading Tests. Second Edition, Level B. MacGinitie, Walter H. 1978
Subtests: Vocabulary; Comprehension
Descriptors: *Decoding (Reading); Elementary School Students; Grade 2; Norm Referenced Tests; Primary Education; *Reading Achievement; *Reading Comprehension; Vocabulary
Availability: Riverside Publishing Co.; 8420 Bryn Mawr Ave., Chicago, IL 60631
Grade Level: 2
Notes: Time, 35 min. approx.; Items, 89
Norm-referenced test series designed to determine instructional levels and evaluate progress. Covers vocabulary (decoding) and comprehension (understanding ideas).

9765
Gates-MacGinitie Reading Tests. Second Edition, Level C. MacGinitie, Walter H. 1978
Subtests: Vocabulary; Comprehension
Descriptors: Elementary School Students; Grade 3; Norm Referenced Tests; Primary Education; *Reading Achievement; *Reading Comprehension; *Vocabulary
Availability: Riverside Publishing Co.; 8420 Bryn Mawr Ave., Chicago, IL 60631
Grade Level: 3
Notes: Time, 35 min. approx.; Items, 89
Norm-referenced test series designed to determine instructional levels and evaluate progress.

9766
Gates-MacGinitie Reading Tests. Second Edition, Level D. MacGinitie, Walter H. 1978
Subtests: Vocabulary; Comprehension
Descriptors: Elementary School Students; Intermediate Grades; Norm Referenced Tests; *Reading Achievement; *Reading Comprehension; *Vocabulary
Availability: Riverside Publishing Co.; 8420 Bryn Mawr Ave., Chicago, IL 60631
Grade Level: 4-6
Notes: Time, 35 min. approx.; Items, 88
Norm-referenced test series designed to determine instructional levels and evaluate progress. Covers vocabulary (word meanings) and comprehension of stated and implied information contained in reading passages.

9767
Gates-MacGinitie Reading Tests. Second Edition, Level E. MacGinitie, Walter H. 1978
Subtests: Vocabulary; Comprehension
Descriptors: Junior High Schools; Junior High School Students; Norm Referenced Tests; *Reading Achievement; *Reading Comprehension; Secondary School Students; *Vocabulary
Availability: Riverside Publishing Co.; 8420 Bryn Mawr Ave., Chicago, IL 60631
Grade Level: 7-9
Notes: Time, 35 min. approx.; Items, 88
Norm-referenced test series designed to determine instructional levels and evaluate progress. Covers vocabulary and comprehension of stated and implied information contained in reading passages.

9768
Gates-MacGinitie Reading Tests. Second Edition, Level F. MacGinitie, Walter H. 1978
Subtests: Vocabulary; Comprehension
Descriptors: Grade 10; Grade 11; Grade 12; High Schools; High School Students; Norm Referenced Tests; *Reading Achievement; *Reading Comprehension; Secondary School Students; *Vocabulary
Availability: Riverside Publishing Co.; 8420 Bryn Mawr Ave., Chicago, IL 60631
Grade Level: 10-12
Notes: Time, 35 min. approx.; Items, 88

Norm-referenced test series designed to determine instructional levels and evaluate progress. Covers vocabulary and comprehension of stated and implied information contained in reading passages.

9769
Diagnostic Word Patterns. Tests 1, 2, and 3. Buckley, Evelyn 1978
Descriptors: *Diagnostic Tests; Elementary Education; Elementary School Students; Group Testing; Individual Testing; Junior High Schools; *Phonics; Secondary School Students; *Spelling; *Word Lists
Identifiers: *Oral Tests; Written Tests
Availability: Educators Publishing Service; 75 Moulton St., Cambridge, MA 02138-9101
Grade Level: 3-9
Notes: Items, 300
Group or individually administered 100-word oral or written spelling tests designed to identify students' needs for further instruction in basic phonic and word analysis skills. May also be administered to remedial high school students or to adults.

9808
Nebraska—Assessment Battery of Essential Learning Skills. Nebraska State Dept. of Education, Lincoln 1977
Subtests: Reading Skill, Form A (1); Reading Skill, Form B (1); Reading Skill, Form C (1); Reading Skill, Form D (1); Writing Skill, Form A (1); Writing Skill, Form B (1); Writing Skill, Form C (1); Writing Skill, Form D (1); Writing Skill-Spelling, Form A (20); Writing Skill-Spelling, Form B (20); Writing Skill-Spelling, Form C (20); Writing Skill-Spelling, Form D (20); Math Skill 1, Form A (12); Math Skill 1, Form B (12); Math Skill 1, Form C (12); Math Skill 1, Form D (12); Math Skill 2, Form A (2); Math Skill 2, Form B (2); Math Skill 2, Form C (2); Math Skill 2, Form D (2); Math Skill 3 or 4, Form A (80); Math Skill 3 or 4, Form B (80); Math Skill 3 or 4, Form C (80); Math Skill 3 or 4, Form D (80); Math Skill 5, Form A (12); Math Skill 5, Form B (12); Math Skill 5, Form C (12); Math Skill 5, Form D (12); Reference Skill 1 (3); Reference Skill 2 (2); Reference Skill 3 (3); Reference Skill 4, Form B (10); Reference Skill, Form C (10); Reference Skill 4, Form D (10)
Descriptors: *Basic Skills; *Competency Based Education; Educational Assessment; Intermediate Grades; Junior High Schools; *Mastery Tests; Minimum Competency Testing; *State Programs; *Testing Programs
Identifiers: *Nebraska
Availability: ERIC Document Reproduction Service; 7420 Fullerton Rd., Ste. 110, Springfield, VA 22153-2852 (ED163027, ED163077, ED163078)
Grade Level: 5-7
Notes: Items, 560
Statewide assessment program to identify, to define precisely, and to establish performance standards for mastery in reading, writing, mathematics, and reference usage.

9846
Similes Test. Burt, Heather R. 1971
Descriptors: Achievement Tests; Elementary School Students; *Figurative Language; *Intermediate Grades; Language Arts; *Literature Appreciation; Multiple Choice Tests; *Reading Comprehension; *Reading Skills
Identifiers: *Similes; The Research Instruments Project; TRIP
Availability: ERIC Document Reproduction Service; 7420 Fullerton Rd., Ste. 110, Springfield, VA 22153-2852 (ED091754, 25 p.)
Grade Level: 4-6
Notes: Items, 30
This test is designed to measure children's reading understanding of similes found in literature books suitable for grades 4, 5, and 6. The simile is presented in context and questioned in multiple-choice format. This document is one of those reviewed in The Research Instruments Project (TRIP) monograph *Measures for Research and Evaluation in the English Language Arts.*

9851
Prueba de Lectura. Wisconsin State Dept. of Public Instruction, Madison Ozete, Oscar 1978
Descriptors: *Bilingual Students; *Cloze Procedure; Elementary Education; Grade 3; Grade 6; *Native Speakers; Reading Comprehension; *Reading Tests; *Spanish; *Spanish Speaking
Identifiers: TIM(F)
Availability: Tests in Microfiche; Test Collection, Educational Testing Service, Princeton, NJ 08541
Grade Level: 3; 6
Notes: Items, 40

Designed to assess reading comprehension in the child's native Spanish for bilingual children as part of a program for developing reading competence in the child's first language before attempting to instruct the child in reading in a second language. Uses cloze procedure and multiple-choice to measure literal comprehension and skill in making inferences and obtaining instruction. Has 2 parallel forms.

9854
Language Dominance Survey. San Bernardino City Unified School District, CA 1975
Subtests: Listening; Speaking; Reading; Writing; Home Language Usage
Descriptors: *Bilingual Education; Bilingualism; Bilingual Students; Elementary Secondary Education; *Language Dominance; *Language Tests; *Spanish Speaking
Identifiers: TIM(F)
Availability: Tests in Microfiche; Test Collection, Educational Testing Service, Princeton, NJ 08541
Grade Level: K-12
Notes: Items, 37

This 5-part survey was designed to identify students with problems in the development of English and/or Spanish language skills and to identify the dominant home language. Covers aural-oral skills in grades K-1 and listening, speaking, reading, writing and home language usage in the upper grades.

9870
Minimum Mathematics Competency Test. Kern Joint Union High School District, Bakersfield, CA 1976
Descriptors: *Computation; *Graduation Requirements; High Schools; *High School Students; Mathematical Applications; *Mathematical Concepts; *Mathematics; Mathematics Tests; Minimum Competencies; *Minimum Competency Testing
Identifiers: TIM(F)
Availability: Tests in Microfiche; Test Collection, Educational Testing Service, Princeton, NJ 08541
Grade Level: High Schools
Notes: Items, 45

Designed for use as a high school graduation requirement. Test content covers decimals, charts and graphs, measurement, mixed numbers, time, percentages, interest, and simple geometry. Minimum score was determined through testing of local employees in entry level positions to comply with the criterion of the test that graduated students should have the skills necessary to meet these job needs.

9871
Minimum Reading Competency Test. Kern Joint Union High School District, Bakersfield, CA 1976
Descriptors: *Functional Reading; *Graduation Requirements; High Schools; *High School Students; Minimum Competencies; *Minimum Competency Testing; Newspapers; *Reading Comprehension; Reading Tests
Identifiers: TIM(F)
Availability: Tests in Microfiche; Test Collection, Educational Testing Service, Princeton, NJ 08541
Grade Level: High Schools
Notes: Items, 30

Designed for use as a high school graduation requirement. Test content covers reading comprehension of material in the form of newspaper articles. Minimum score was determined through testing of local employees in entry level positions to comply with the criterion of the test that graduated students should have the skills necessary to meet these job needs.

9881
Traffic Safety Questionnaire. Form B. Schuster, Donald H. 1977
Descriptors: *Driver Education; High Schools; *High School Students; Multiple Choice Tests; *Traffic Accidents; *Traffic Control; *Traffic Safety
Identifiers: TIM(G)
Availability: Tests in Microfiche; Test Collection, Educational Testing Service, Princeton, NJ 08541
Grade Level: 9-12
Notes: Time, 30 min.; Items, 40

Two alternate forms of a multiple-choice test are used for pretesting and posttesting. Designed for both beginning and problem drivers. Measures 2 aspects of driving knowledge: accident avoidance and knowledge of rules of the road.

9903
Criterion Referenced Test: MGS/CRTest Eastern Navajo Agency, Level B. Dougherty, Don; And Others 1978
Subtests: Language Arts; Mathematics

Descriptors: *Academic Achievement; *American Indians; *Criterion Referenced Tests; Kindergarten; *Kindergarten Children; Language Arts; Mathematics; *Minimum Competencies; Primary Education
Identifiers: *Navajo (Nation); TIM(F)
Availability: Tests in Microfiche; Test Collection, Educational Testing Service, Princeton, NJ 08541
Grade Level: Kindergarten
Notes: Items, 34

Developed for use in instructional planning, diagnosis, and remediation, this series covers grades K-8 and is designed to measure Navajo student progress in the achievement of minimum grade standards (MGS) in basic skills. Level B, for grade K, covers language arts, listening (Navajo and English), visual skills, classification, and identification of objects; mathematics, counting, writing numbers, shapes, addition. Pictures and items reflect local living environment and culture. This test is untimed.

9904
Criterion-Referenced Test: MGS/CRTest Eastern Navajo Agency, Level C. Dougherty, Don; And Others 1978
Subtests: Language Arts; Mathematics
Descriptors: *Academic Achievement; *American Indians; *Criterion Referenced Tests; *Grade 1; Language Arts; Mathematics; *Minimum Competencies; Primary Education
Identifiers: *Navajo (Nation); TIM(F)
Availability: Tests in Microfiche; Test Collection, Educational Testing Service, Princeton, NJ 08541
Grade Level: 1
Notes: Items, 22

Developed for use in instructional planning, diagnosis, and remediation, this series covers grades K-8 and is designed to measure Navajo student progress in the achievement of minimum grade standards (MGS) in basic skills. Level C covers language arts, sounds, word and sentence recognition, reading comprehension, word skills; mathematics, shapes, time, more and less, numerals, addition, subtraction. Pictures, items reflect local environment and culture. This test is untimed.

9905
Criterion-Referenced Test: MGS/CRTest Eastern Navajo Agency, Level D. Dougherty, Don; And Others 1978
Subtests: Language Arts; Mathematics; Science
Descriptors: *Academic Achievement; *American Indians; *Criterion Referenced Tests; *Grade 2; Language Arts; Mathematics; *Minimum Competencies; Primary Education; Sciences
Identifiers: *Navajo (Nation); TIM(F)
Availability: Tests in Microfiche; Test Collection, Educational Testing Service, Princeton, NJ 08541
Grade Level: 2
Notes: Items, 26

Developed for use in instructional planning, diagnosis, and remediation, this series covers grades K-8 and is designed to measure Navajo student progress in the achievement of minimum grade standards (MGS) in basic skills. Level D covers language arts, punctuation, capitalization, comprehension, consonants, word usage; mathematics, place, equations, addition, time, problems, fractions, money; science, plants, animals, seasons, and energy. Pictures, items reflect local environmental and culture. This test is untimed.

9906
Criterion-Referenced Test: MGS/CRTest Eastern Navajo Agency, Level E. Dougherty, Don; And Others 1978
Subtests: Language Arts; Mathematics; Science; Social Studies
Descriptors: *Academic Achievement; *American Indians; *Criterion Referenced Tests; *Grade 3; Language Arts; Mathematics; *Minimum Competencies; Primary Education; Sciences; Social Studies
Identifiers: *Navajo (Nation); TIM(F)
Availability: Tests in Microfiche; Test Collection, Educational Testing Service, Princeton, NJ 08541
Grade Level: 3
Notes: Items, 30

Developed for use in instructional planning, diagnosis, and remediation, this series covers grades K-8 and is designed to measure Navajo student progress in the achievement of minimum grade standards (MGS) in basic skills. Level E covers language arts, parts of speech, punctuation, word usage, comprehension; mathematics, place value, operations, time, shape, money, fractions; science, plants, animals, machines; social studies, office holders, maps. This test is untimed.

9907
Criterion-Referenced Test: MGS/CRTest Eastern Navajo Agency, Level F. Dougherty, Don; And Others 1978
Subtests: Language Arts; Mathematics; Science; Social Studies; Health
Descriptors: *Academic Achievement; *American Indians; *Criterion Referenced Tests; *Grade 4; Health; Intermediate Grades; Language Arts; Mathematics; *Minimum Competencies; Sciences; Social Studies
Identifiers: *Navajo (Nation); TIM(F)
Availability: Tests in Microfiche; Test Collection, Educational Testing Service, Princeton, NJ 08541
Grade Level: 4
Notes: Items, 36

Developed for use in instructional planning, diagnosis, and remediation, this series covers grades K-8 and is designed to measure Navajo student progress in the achievement of minimum grade standards (MGS) in basic skills. Level F covers language arts, synonyms, reading comprehension, parts of speech, word skills, reference skills, sentences, punctuation, possessives, capitalization; mathematics, measuring, operations, time, fractions, perimeter, problems; science, habitats, weather, water cycle, man and environment; social studies, office holders, researching, map skills; health, safety, body systems, hygiene. This test is untimed.

9908
Criterion-Referenced Test: MGS/CRTest Eastern Navajo Agency, Level G. Dougherty, Don; And Others 1978
Subtests: Language Arts; Mathematics; Science; Social Studies; Health
Descriptors: *Academic Achievement; *American Indians; *Criterion Referenced Tests; *Grade 5; Health; Intermediate Grades; Language Arts; Mathematics; *Minimum Competencies; Sciences; Social Studies
Identifiers: *Navajo (Nation); TIM(F)
Availability: Tests in Microfiche; Test Collection, Educational Testing Service, Princeton, NJ 08541
Grade Level: 5
Notes: Items, 48

Developed for use in instructional planning, diagnosis, and remediation, this series covers grades K-8 and is designed to measure Navajo student progress in the achievement of minimum grade standards (MGS) in basic skills. Level G covers language arts, synonyms, affixes, reference skills, reading comprehension, sentences, mechanics, usage; mathematics, operations, time, shapes, measures, fractions, money, problems; science, animals, seasons, oxygen/carbon dioxide, oceans, minerals, friction, stars/planets; social studies, peoples, Navajo history, geography, topography; health, body systems, senses, exercises. This test is untimed.

9909
Criterion-Referenced Test: MGS/CRTest Eastern Navajo Agency, Level H. Dougherty, Don; And Others 1978
Subtests: Language Arts; Mathematics; Science; Social Studies; Health
Descriptors: *Academic Achievement; *American Indians; *Criterion Referenced Tests; *Grade 6; Health; Intermediate Grades; Language Arts; Mathematics; *Minimum Competencies; Sciences; Social Studies
Identifiers: *Navajo (Nation); TIM(F)
Availability: Tests in Microfiche; Test Collection, Educational Testing Service, Princeton, NJ 08541
Grade Level: 6
Notes: Items, 45

Developed for use in instructional planning, diagnosis, and remediation, this series covers grades K-8 and is designed to measure Navajo student progress in the achievement of minimum grade standards (MGS) in basic skills. Level H covers language arts, affixes, synonyms, comprehension, parts of speech, mechanics, usage, outlining; mathematics, operations, geometry, fractions, measurement, money, problems; science, earth and man, graph reading; social studies, people, countries, climate, consumer role; health, body systems, drugs, exercise, eating habits, first aid. This test is untimed.

9910
Criterion-Referenced Test: MGS/CRTest Eastern Navajo Agency, Level I. Dougherty, Don; And Others 1978
Subtests: Language Arts; Mathematics; Science; Social Studies
Descriptors: *Academic Achievement; *American Indians; *Criterion Referenced Tests; *Grade 7; Junior High Schools; Language Arts; Mathematics; *Minimum Competencies; Sciences; Social Studies
Identifiers: *Navajo (Nation); TIM(F)

Availability: Tests in Microfiche; Test Collection, Educational Testing Service, Princeton, NJ 08541
Grade Level: 7
Notes: Items, 45

Developed for use in instructional planning, diagnosis, and remediation, this series covers grades K-8 and is designed to measure Navajo student progress in the achievement of minimum grade standards (MGS) in basic skills. Level I covers language arts, vocabulary skills, parts of speech, comprehension, punctuation, directions, reference skills, business forms; mathematics, operations, geometry, operations with fractions, problems; science, animals, insects, plants, body systems, chemistry, space, physical forces; social studies, people, Navajo history, local geography, and economics. This test is untimed.

9911
Criterion-Referenced Test: MGS/CRTest Eastern Navajo Agency, Level J. Dougherty, Don; And Others 1978
Subtests: Language Arts; Mathematics; Science; Social Studies
Descriptors: *Academic Achievement; *American Indians; *Criterion Referenced Tests; *Grade 8; Junior High Schools; Language Arts; Mathematics; *Minimum Competencies; Sciences; Social Studies
Identifiers: *Navajo (Nation); TIM(F)
Availability: Tests in Microfiche; Test Collection, Educational Testing Service, Princeton, NJ 08541
Grade Level: 8
Notes: Items, 49

Developed for use in instructional planning, diagnosis, and remediation, this series covers grades K-8 and is designed to measure Navajo student progress in the achievement of minimum grade standards (MGS) in basic skills. Level J covers language arts, skimming, vocabulary, literary forms, comprehension, analysis, writing letters, job applications; mathematics, operations, geometry, operations with fractions, decimals, percent, metrics, problems; science, chemistry, machines, electricity, weather, pollution, first aid; social studies, tribal history and services, government, consumer education. This test is untimed.

9912
Appalachia Preschool Test of Cognitive Skills. Appalachian Educational Lab., Charleston, WV 1968
Descriptors: *Achievement Tests; Cognitive Development; Field Interviews; Individual Testing; Mathematical Concepts; Oral Reading; *Preschool Children; *Preschool Evaluation; Program Evaluation; Reading Readiness; *Rural Education; Visual Measures; Vocabulary Development; Young Children
Identifiers: *Appalachia; Appalachia Preschool Education Program; Home Oriented Preschool Education Program; HOPE; TIM(G)
Availability: Tests in Microfiche; Test Collection, Educational Testing Service, Princeton, NJ 08541
Age Level: 3-5
Notes: Items, 151

Designed for use as a curriculum specific test to measure performance of preschool children who participated in the Home-Oriented Preschool Education (HOPE) program. Questions are read to each child individually. Child responds by pointing to picture or object. Consists of a warm-up interview and 4 subject-related tests covering vocabulary, shapes, letter and sound recognition, a short reading selection, general information questions about time, weight, money, and counting. One point is given for each question answered correctly and one point for each word read in the reading selection.

9926
Test of Oral English Production. Luft, Max; And Others 1969
Descriptors: Audiotape Recorders; *Diagnostic Tests; *Elementary School Students; *English (Second Language); *Grammatical Acceptability; Individual Testing; *Language Proficiency; *Oral Language; Pretests Posttests; Primary Education; Program Evaluation
Availability: ERIC Document Reproduction Service; 7420 Fullerton Rd., Ste. 110, Springfield, VA 22153-2852 (ED042793, microfiche only)
Grade Level: K-3
Notes: Time, 15 min. approx.; Items, 83

Designed to elicit spontaneous responses to assess child's oral language proficiency. Responses are tape recorded for later scoring. Partial scores may be obtained for Vocabulary and Pronunciation and Use of English Grammatical Structures.

9933
Speaking Test in Spanish/English. Offenberg, Robert M. 1970
Subtests: Repetition; Questions; Spanish

Descriptors: *Achievement Tests; *Bilingual Education; *Communicative Competence (Languages); *Elementary School Students; *English (Second Language); Grade 1; Kindergarten; Language Tests; *Preschool Children; Preschool Education; Primary Education; Program Evaluation; Spanish Speaking
Availability: ERIC Document Reproduction Service; 7420 Fullerton Rd., Ste. 110, Springfield, VA 22153-2852 (ED046295, microfiche only)
Age Level: 2-6

Measures speaking skills in English and Spanish for bilingual students in nursery school through grade 1. Developed as part of "Let's Be Amigos" program in Philadelphia schools.

9996
Examen en Francais. Caribou Bilingual Project, ME
Subtests: Reading Comprehension; Vocabulary; Sentence Meaning; Scrambled Sentences; Vowel Sounds; Beginning Sounds; Rhymes
Descriptors: *Achievement Tests; Bilingual Students; *French; *Grade 3; *Language Proficiency; *Primary Education; Reading Comprehension; Sentences; Sentence Structure; Vocabulary; Word Recognition
Identifiers: Rhyming Words; TIM(G)
Availability: Tests in Microfiche; Test Collection, Educational Testing Service, Princeton, NJ 08541
Grade Level: 3
Notes: Items, 89

Group-administered test of facility in the French language for bilingual students.

10053
Sex Knowledge Test. Bloch, Doris 1970
Descriptors: Adults; *Information Sources; *Knowledge Level; Males; Physical Characteristics; Preadolescents; *Sex Education
Availability: ERIC Document Reproduction Service; 7420 Fullerton Rd., Ste. 110, Springfield, VA 22153-2852 (ED171763, 842 p.)
Age Level: 12-44
Notes: Items, 25

Designed to obtain a measure of the accuracy of a mother's estimate of her daughter's sex knowledge and sources of sexual information. Developed in 2 forms. Form A elicits information from mothers. Form B, designed for 12-year-old girls, elicits information and data on source of respondent's knowledge. Covers male anatomy and physiology; female anatomy, physiology, and menstruation; pregnancy and birth; father's role in reproduction and fertilization; and venereal disease.

10055
Sex Knowledge Questionnaire. Reichelt, P. A.; Werley, H. H. 1975
Descriptors: Abortions; Adolescents; *Attitude Measures; Contraception; *Information Sources; *Knowledge Level; *Sex Education; Sexuality; Venereal Diseases
Identifiers: *Sexual Attitudes
Availability: ERIC Document Reproduction Service; 7420 Fullerton Rd., Ste. 110, Springfield, VA 22153-2852 (ED171763, 842 p.)
Age Level: 13-17
Notes: Time, 10 min. approx.; Items, 44

Elicits information concerning the source of respondents knowledge of sexuality, attitudes, and general knowledge of human sexuality and knowledge of specific areas, such as venereal disease, menstruation, birth control pills, diaphragm, condom, intrauterine device, spermicides, and abortion. Designed to evaluate sex education program for teenagers at Youth Education on Sex (YES) Teen Center operated by Planned Parenthood League, Inc. of Detroit.

10162
Oral Language Proficiency Scale. Dade County Public Schools, Miami, FL Div. of Elementary and Secondary Education 1978
Subtests: Understanding of Spoken Language; Using Grammatical Structure; Pronunciation; Vocabulary
Descriptors: Bilingual Education; *Elementary School Students; Elementary Secondary Education; *English (Second Language); *Individual Testing; *Language Proficiency; Language Tests; *Secondary School Students; *Student Placement
Identifiers: Dade County Public Schools FL; *Oral Tests; TIM(E)
Availability: Tests in Microfiche; Test Collection, Educational Testing Service, Princeton, NJ 08541
Grade Level: K-12
Notes: Items, 20

Used in an oral interview for student placement in a program of English for Speakers of Other Languages (ESOL). Placement is based on proficiency in 4 areas:

understanding of spoken language, using grammatical structure, pronunciation and vocabulary. Two forms are available—elementary and secondary.

10163
Examen de Lectura en Espanol. Dade County Public Schools, Miami, FL. Div. of Elementary and Secondary Education 1975
Descriptors: Bilingual Education; Language Proficiency; Language Tests; Secondary Education; *Secondary School Students; *Spanish; *Student Placement
Identifiers: Dade County Public Schools FL; TIM(E)
Availability: Tests in Microfiche; Test Collection, Educational Testing Service, Princeton, NJ 08541
Grade Level: 7-12
Notes: Items, 30

A Spanish reading placement test for grades 7-12. The test consists of 30 multiple-choice questions, 2 of which are samples.

10164
Examen de Lenguaje en Espanol. Dade County Public Schools, Miami, FL Div. of Elementary and Secondary Education 1975
Subtests: Language Usage; Verbs; Vocabulary
Descriptors: Bilingual Education; *Elementary School Students; Grade 7; Intermediate Grades; Junior High School Students; Language Proficiency; Language Tests; *Spanish; *Student Placement
Identifiers: Dade County Public Schools FL; TIM(E)
Availability: Tests in Microfiche; Test Collection, Educational Testing Service, Princeton, NJ 08541
Grade Level: 5-7
Notes: Items, 48

A Spanish language placement test for grades 5-7. The multiple-choice test consists of 48 questions divided into 3 sections: language usage, verbs, and vocabulary.

10196
Bilingual Test Battery. Bilingual Education Service Center, Arlington Heights, IL 1974
Subtests: Mathematics; Social Studies; General Science; Attitude
Descriptors: *Achievement Tests; *Bilingual Students; *Elementary School Students; Elementary Secondary Education; Mathematics; Science Tests; *Secondary School Students; Social Studies; *Spanish; Student Attitudes
Identifiers: TIM(E)
Availability: Tests in Microfiche; Test Collection, Educational Testing Service, Princeton, NJ 08541
Grade Level: 3-10
Notes: Items, 40

Battery consists of English-Spanish bilingual tests in mathematics, social studies, science, and attitudes. Eighty multiple-choice questions are given in both languages. Students are instructed to choose the language they prefer. Three levels are available: Level I (grades 3-4), Level II (grades 5-6), and Level III (grades 7-10).

10201
Industrial Arts Test Development: Resource Items for Drawing, Electricity, Electronics, Power Mechanics, Woods. New York State Education Dept., Albany, Bureau of Industrial Arts Education 1973
Descriptors: *Drafting; *Electricity; *Electronics; Industrial Arts; *Item Banks; *Mechanics (Process); Motor Vehicles; Multiple Choice Tests; Secondary Education; *Secondary School Students; Visual Measures; *Woodworking
Availability: ERIC Document Reproduction Service; 7420 Fullerton Rd., Ste. 110, Springfield, VA 22153-2852 (ED109457, 192 p.)
Grade Level: 7-12
Notes: Items, 674

Designed to assist teachers in improvement of locally developed tests. Item bank from which secondary school teachers may choose selected questions for use as pretests; quizzes, or final examinations. Although most items are multiple-choice, some are completion (e.g., diagrams).

10269
Standard English Repetition Test. Kamehameha Schools, Honolulu, Hawaii. Kamehameha Early Education Project. 1974
Descriptors: *Hawaiians; *Imitation; *Language Tests; *Oral English; Pidgins; Primary Education; *Standard Spoken Usage; *Young Children
Identifiers: Hawaiian Pidgin; *Oral Tests; SERT; TIM(G)
Availability: Tests in Microfiche; Test Collection, Educational Testing Service, Princeton, NJ 08541

Grade Level: K-1
Notes: Items, 15
Measures standard English performance of young Hawaii Creole English-speaking children. Employs the technique of controlled, elicited imitation which requires the child to repeat standard English sentences spoken by an adult examiner. The 15 sentences measure 29 features of grammatical construction: past tense, present tense, copula, negation, yes-no question formation, passive, indefinite article, indirect question formation, and pronominalization.

10280
Job Knowledge Survey. Loesch, Larry C. 1973
Subtests: Realistic; Investigative; Artistic; Social; Enterprising; Conventional
Descriptors: Adults; Career Counseling; *Career Development; *College Students; Higher Education; High Schools; Knowledge Level; *Occupational Information; *Secondary School Students; Surveys; Two Year Colleges; *Vocational Maturity
Identifiers: TIM(G)
Availability: Tests in Microfiche; Test Collection, Educational Testing Service, Princeton, NJ 08541
Grade Level: 9-17
Notes: Time, 12 min.; Items, 48
Measures knowledge of occupations in terms of their content. Testee indicates whether each job has a high, medium, or low involvement with data, people or things. Job titles are grouped according to Holland's 6 occupational themes.

10311
Test of English for International Communication. Educational Testing Service, Princeton, NJ
Descriptors: Adults; *Business Communication; *Business English; *Communicative Competence (Languages); *English (Second Language); *Japanese; *Language Tests; Listening Comprehension; Multiple Choice Tests; Reading Comprehension
Identifiers: TOEIC
Availability: Educational Testing Service; International Office, Princeton, NJ 08541
Age Level: Adults
Notes: Items, 200
A secure testing program developed for non-English-speaking countries to measure English language skills outside of the traditional academic context. Used by foreign businesspeople to assess their knowledge and communicative abilities in English. Although currently in use in Japan, the program could be adapted for any other non-English-speaking country. Test is administered at designated centers only, not sold directly.

10323
Tests for Everyday Living. Halpern, Andrew; And Others 1979
Subtests: Purchasing Habits; Banking; Budgeting; Health Care; Home Management; Job Search Skills; Job Related Behavior
Descriptors: *Achievement Tests; Adolescents; *Adults; Consumer Education; *Daily Living Skills; Health; Home Management; Job Search Methods; Job Skills; *Learning Problems; *Minimum Competencies; Money Management; Multiple Choice Tests; *Secondary School Students; Verbal Tests
Identifiers: *Oral Tests; TEL
Availability: CTB/McMillan/McGraw Hill; Del Monte Research Park, 2500 Garden Rd., Monterey, CA 93940
Age Level: 12-64
Notes: Time, 140 min. approx.; Items, 245
Battery of 7 untimed tests that measure knowledge of life skills necessary to successfully perform everyday life tasks. Orally administered so that poor readers are not disadvantaged. Estimated time for each test is 20 minutes. Frequently used in grades 7 through 12 with average or low-achieving students or remedial and learning-disabled students. Does include some performance items, such as filling out an application form or writing a check where some reading is required.

10333
Test of Written English. Andersen, Velma R.; Thompson, Sheryl K. 1979
Subtests: Capitalization; Punctuation; Written Expression; Paragraph Writing
Descriptors: *Capitalization (Alphabetic); Criterion Referenced Tests; Diagnostic Tests; Elementary Education; *Elementary School Students; Individual Testing; *Paragraph Composition; *Punctuation; *Writing Skills
Identifiers: TWE
Availability: Academic Therapy Publications; 20 Commercial Blvd., Novato, CA 94947-6191
Grade Level: 2-6
Notes: Time, 20 min. approx.; Items, 29

Individually administered test designed to screen for student mastery of written language skills. May be used with learning-disabled children or students above grade 6 who are experiencing difficulty in school. Administration by regular or special education teachers is recommended.

10334
Basic Education Skills Test. Segel, Ruth; Golding, Sandra 1979
Subtests: Reading; Writing; Mathematics
Descriptors: *Aural Learning; Basic Skills; Diagnostic Tests; Elementary Education; *Elementary School Mathematics; Elementary School Students; *Learning Disabilities; Learning Modalities; *Reading Tests; *Screening Tests; *Speech Skills; *Tactual Perception; *Visual Learning; *Writing Skills
Identifiers: BEST
Availability: United Educational Services; P.O. Box 1099, Buffalo, NY 14224
Grade Level: 1-5
Notes: Time, 60 min.; Items, 75
Individually administered assessment of perceptual abilities and academic skills. May be administered by teacher, aide, or parent. Recording form correlates performance on each item with relevant perceptual modalities.

10390
Pre-School Screening Instrument. Cohen, Stephen Paul 1979
Subtests: Human Figure Drawing; Visual Fine Motor Perception; Visual Gross Motor Perception; Language Development; Speech; Behavior
Descriptors: *Behavior Development; Individual Testing; Language Acquisition; *Learning Problems; Observation; Performance Tests; *Preschool Children; *Psychomotor Skills; Questionnaires; *School Readiness; School Readiness Tests; *Screening Tests; Verbal Communication; *Verbal Development; Verbal Tests; Visual Perception; Young Children
Identifiers: Oral Tests; PSSI
Availability: Stoelting Co.; 620 Wheat Ln., Wood Dale, IL 60191
Age Level: 4-5
Notes: Time, 10 min. approx.; Items, 32
Individually administered screening test for prekindergarten children to identify those with potential learning problems. Includes observations by administrator, performance and some verbal responses by the testee, and a Parental Questionnaire on which the parent gives developmental, medical, behavioral, and general information about the child. Comes with the equipment needed to carry out the performance parts of the test.

10407
System FORE: Spanish Adaptation. Los Angeles Unified School District, CA 1975
Descriptors: *Children; Evaluation Methods; *Language Acquisition; Measures (Individuals); Morphology (Languages); Phonology; Preschool Children; Semantics; *Spanish; *Spanish Speaking; Syntax
Identifiers: TIM(F)
Availability: Tests in Microfiche; Test Collection, Educational Testing Service, Princeton, NJ 08541
Age Level: Children
Series of inventories designed to assess a child's linguistic development in the Spanish language for native speakers of developmental age 3-7 years. The inventories accompany instructional objectives arranged by developmental levels as an aid for individualizing and planning instruction. There are 10 developmental levels of this program. Each level is divided into strands to include the 4 aspects of language: phonology, morphology, syntax, and semantics. Level 3 has 34 items; level 4 has 34 items; level 5 has 24 items; level 6 has 22 items; level 7 has 27 items; level 8 has 25 items; level 9 has 14 items; and level 10 has 16 items.

10435
Louisiana Reading Assessment. Louisiana State Dept. of Education, Baton Rouge 1977
Descriptors: *Achievement Tests; Criterion Referenced Tests; Educational Objectives; Elementary Secondary Education; *Grade 4; *Grade 8; *Grade 11; Phonetic Analysis; *Reading Achievement; Reading Comprehension; Structural Analysis (Linguistics); Study Skills; Vocabulary
Identifiers: Louisiana
Availability: ERIC Document Reproduction Service; 7420 Fullerton Rd., Ste. 110, Springfield, VA 22153-2852 (ED171724, 13 p.)
Grade Level: 4; 8; 11
Notes: Time, 100 min. approx.
Designed to assess reading performance of students in grades 4, 8, and 11. Fourth grade test consists of 64 items measuring achievement in vocabulary, phonetic analysis, structural analysis, comprehension, and study skills. Eighth grade test consists of 80 items measuring achieve-

ment in vocabulary, phonetic analysis, structural analysis, comprehension, and study skills. Eleventh grade test consists of 80 items measuring achievement in vocabulary, word attack skills, comprehension, and study skills.

10462
Degrees of Reading Power. College Board, New York, NY 1981
Descriptors: Cloze Procedure; Context Clues; Culture Fair Tests; Elementary Secondary Education; Nonfiction; Postsecondary Education; Prose; *Reading Comprehension; *Reading Diagnosis; *Reading Tests; Student Placement
Identifiers: *Power Tests
Availability: Touchstone Applied Sciences Associates; Att: DRP Services, Field Ln., P.O. Box 382, Brewster, NY 10509
Grade Level: 3-14
Notes: Items, 21
Measures a student's ability to process and understand nonfiction prose written at different levels of difficulty. Test items are formed by deletion of words from each passage. For each deletion, 5 single-word options are provided. The DRP consists of a PA series, broad-band tests for use at the elementary-secondary grade levels, and a CP Series for use in student placement at the postsecondary level. Raw scores can be converted to identify independent, instructional, and frustration reading levels. See also New York State Preliminary Competency Test in Reading-Degrees of Reading Power (TC010959).

10487
Brigance Diagnostic Inventory of Basic Skills. Brigance, Albert H. 1977
Subtests: Readiness; Reading; Language Arts; Math
Descriptors: *Basic Skills; *Diagnostic Tests; Elementary Education; Elementary School Mathematics; *Elementary School Students; *Geometry; Grammar; *Handwriting; *Individualized Instruction; Individual Testing; *Language Arts; *Learning Readiness; *Mathematics; *Oral Reading; Reading Comprehension; *Reading Readiness Tests; Reading Skills; *Spelling; Vocabulary Skills; Word Recognition; Word Study Skills; Writing Skills
Availability: Curriculum Associates, Inc.; 5 Esquire Rd., N. Billerica, MA 01862-2589
Grade Level: K-6
Notes: Time, 20 min.; Items, 2890
Individually administered inventory designed to assess basic readiness and academic skills, to measure and record performance, and as an aid in individualizing instruction.

10499
Industrial Arts Test Development: Book 2: Resource Items for Ceramics, Graphic Arts, Metals, Plastics. New York State Education Dept., Albany, Bureau of Elementary and Secondary Educational Testing 1975
Descriptors: *Ceramics; *Graphic Arts; *Industrial Arts; *Item Banks; *Metal Working; Multiple Choice Tests; *Plastics; Secondary Education; *Secondary School Students
Availability: ERIC Document Reproduction Service; 7420 Fullerton Rd., Ste. 110, Springfield, VA 22153-2852 (ED114424, 183 p.)
Grade Level: 7-12
Notes: Items, 805
Item bank for secondary school teachers intended primarily for their use as pretests, quizzes, or final exams. Most of the items are multiple-choice; some are completion, such as completing diagrams.

10529
Revised Pre-Reading Screening Procedures to Identify First Grade Academic Needs. Slingerland, Beth H. 1977
Descriptors: *Academically Gifted; *Auditory Perception; *Grade 1; *Kindergarten Children; *Kinesthetic Perception; Language Handicaps; Learning Disabilities; Learning Modalities; Primary Education; *Screening Tests; *Visual Perception
Identifiers: PSP
Availability: Educators Publishing Service, Inc.; 75 Moulton St., Cambridge MA 02238-9101
Grade Level: K-1
Designed to screen groups of children to identify those for whom specific instruction can prevent failure in learning to read, write, spell, verbalize, and express language in writing. Designed for use at the end of kindergarten or the beginning of first grade with children who have not begun reading instruction. Useful for children of average or superior intelligence. Not meant to be used for diagnosis. There are 6 visual tasks and 6 auditory tasks.

10535
Life Skills. Riverside Publishing Co., Chicago, IL 1980
Subtests: Reading; Mathematics

Descriptors: *Achievement Tests; Adult Education; *Adults; Basic Skills; *Daily Living Skills; *Diagnostic Tests; High Schools; *High School Students; Mathematical Applications; Reading Achievement
Availability: Riverside Publishing; 8420 Bryn Mawr Ave., Chicago, IL 60631
Age Level: 15-64
Notes: Time, 80 min. approx.; Items, 98

Designed to measure ability to function in practical daily living. Reading test objectives include following directions, locating references, gaining information, and understanding forms. Mathematics test objectives include computing consumer problems; applying principles of percentages, interest, and fractional parts; identifying, estimating and converting time, currency, and measurements; and interpreting graphs, charts, and statistics. May be used with high school students or in adult education programs. Forms 1 and 2 are available.

10571
Knowledge of Handicapping Conditions Inventory.
Redick, Sharon 1974
Descriptors: *Achievement Tests; Adults; College Students; *Disabilities; Evaluative Thinking; Higher Education; Home Economics Education; Home Economics Teachers; Knowledge Level
Availability: Instruments for Assessing Selected Professional Competencies for Home Economics Teachers, Ames, IA: Iowa State University Press, 1978
Age Level: 18-65
Notes: Items, 66

This instrument measures a person's knowledge of handicapping conditions. It is multiple choice and concerns 5 areas of deviation: crippled, blind, mentally handicapped, emotionally handicapped, and speech defects. This device is adapted from an inventory by Haring.

10581
Iowa Tests of Basic Skills: Early Primary Battery, Form 7, Levels 5 and 6.
Hieronymus, A.N.; And Others 1979
Subtests: Listening; Vocabulary; Word Analysis; Language; Mathematics; Reading
Descriptors: Academic Achievement; *Achievement Tests; *Basic Skills; *Beginning Reading; Elementary School Mathematics; Elementary School Students; *Grade 1; *Kindergarten Children; Language Skills; Listening Skills; Primary Education
Identifiers: ITBS; Oral Testing
Availability: Riverside Publishing Co.; 3 O'Hare Towers, 8420 Bryn Mawr Ave., Chicago, IL 60631
Grade Level: K-1
Notes: Time, 160 min. approx.; Items, 225

Designed for comprehensive measurement of growth in fundamental skills: listening, vocabulary, word analysis, reading, use of language, and mathematics. Level 5 is designed for K.1-1.5 and does not include a reading subtest. The test has 157 items and requires 115 minutes to administer. It is suggested that Levels 5 and 6 be administered over a period of 5 days. The tests are power tests, and there is no emphasis on speed. All tests are administered orally except Reading subtest, Level 6.

10599
Examen Del Desarrolla Del Nino en Denver.
Frankenburg, William K.; And Others 1970
Descriptors: *Child Development; *Developmental Disabilities; *Language Acquisition; *Motor Development; Screening Tests; *Social Development; *Spanish Speaking; Young Children
Identifiers: Denver Development Screening Test
Availability: Denver Developmental Materials; P.O. Box 6919, Denver, CO 80206-0919
Age Level: 0-6
Notes: Items, 105

Spanish translation of the manual for the Denver Developmental Screening Test, 1970 edition, which was designed to provide a method of screening for evidence of slow development. Covers gross motor, language, fine-motor adaptive and personal-social functions.

10602
Bloomfield-Barnhart Developmental Reading Mastery Test.
Barnhart, Cynthia A.; Barnhart, Robert K. 1978
Subtests: Shape Discrimination; Letter Recognition; Short Vowel Monosyllables with a; Short Vowel Monosyllables with i, u; Short Vowel Monosyllables with e, o; Short Vowel Monosyllables with Simple Blends; Short Vowel Monosyllables with Consonant Clusters and Digraphs; Regular Long Vowels and Diphthongs; Commonest Irregular Words and Suffixes; Irregular Vowel Spelling Patterns; Irregular Consonant Spelling Patterns

Descriptors: Beginning Reading; Elementary Education; *Elementary School Students; Individual Testing; Mastery Tests; *Pretests Posttests; *Reading Achievement; Reading Readiness; *Reading Skills; *Reading Tests; Sequential Approach; Skill Development; Spelling
Availability: ERIC Document Reproduction Service; 7420 Fullerton Rd., Ste. 110, Springfield, VA 22153-2852 (ED177182, microfiche only)
Grade Level: 1-6
Notes: Time, 165 min. approx.

Designed to determine precisely which reading skills a student has developed. Tests are arranged in skill levels, rather than grade levels. Sequence of skills is based on *Let's Read* by Leonard Bloomfield, Clarence Barnhart, Robert Barnhart, and the masterbook, *Let's Read: A Linguistic Approach.* Student must also demonstrate accuracy in writing what can be read at any given level. Available from EDRS only in microfiche. Each subtest requires about 15 minutes to administer.

10632
Oral Placement Test.
Poczik, Robert
Descriptors: *Achievement Tests; *Adult Basic Education; Adults; Communicative Competence (Languages); Diagnostic Tests; *English (Second Language); Individual Testing; Oral English; Speech Communication; *Student Placement
Identifiers: English As A Second Language Tests; Oral Placement Test (Poczik)
Availability: ERIC Document Reproduction Service; 7420 Fullerton Rd., Ste. 110, Springfield, VA 22153-2852 (ED181036, 17 p.)
Age Level: 18-64
Notes: Time, 5 min. approx.

Designed to place adult students at various ESL levels solely on the basis of oral language abilities. May be used for diagnostic purposes if student's errors are noted on the test as it is scored. Developed to follow content and sequence of the "Orientation in American English" series.

10633
Oral Production Tests: Levels One-Three.
Poczik, Robert
Descriptors: *Achievement Tests; *Adult Basic Education; Adults; Communicative Competence (Languages); Diagnostic Tests; *English (Second Language); Individual Testing; *Listening Comprehension; Oral English; *Speech Skills
Identifiers: English As A Second Language Tests; Oral Production Tests (Poczik)
Availability: ERIC Document Reproduction Service; 7420 Fullerton Rd., Ste. 110, Springfield, VA 22153-2852 (ED181036, 17 p.)
Age Level: 18-64
Notes: Time, 10 min. approx.

Developed to assess oral English ability of adults. Three forms at each of 3 levels of difficulty are available. Assesses auditory comprehension and oral production. Tests are based on the "Orientation in American English" series.

10649
Secondary Level English Proficiency Test.
Educational Testing Service, Princeton, NJ 1981
Subtests: Listening Comprehension; Reading Comprehension
Descriptors: *Achievement Tests; *Audiotape Recordings; *English (Second Language); *Language Proficiency; Language Tests; *Listening Comprehension; *Reading Comprehension; Secondary Education; *Secondary School Students; Second Language Learning
Identifiers: SLEP
Availability: Secondary Level English Proficiency Test, School and Higher Education Programs; Princeton, NJ 08541
Grade Level: 7-11
Notes: Time, 85 min. approx.; Items, 150

Designed to measure ability of students whose native language is not English to understand spoken and written English. School Service Program enables school to purchase test, administer it and score locally. May be used in making some placement decisions. ETS sponsors SLEP test and administers it within the Test of English as a Foreign Language (TOEFL) program. May be administered in its entirety or in 2 sessions to individuals or groups.

10652
Advanced Placement Program: English Composition and Literature.
Educational Testing Service, Princeton, NJ 1981
Descriptors: *Advanced Placement Programs; *College English; *Equivalency Tests; Essay Tests; *Expository Writing; High Schools; *High School Students; *Literary Criticism; Multiple Choice Tests; Writing (Composition)
Identifiers: Advanced Placement Examinations (CEEB); APP
Availability: Advanced Placement Program; Box 977PD, Princeton, NJ 08541

Grade Level: 10-12
Notes: Time, 180 min.

Designed to assess achievement in English Literature and Composition. Questions are one-third objective and two-thirds essay. The number of items will vary from year to year. Candidates are to take only one English exam—either literature and composition or English language and composition. The Advanced Placement Program has been sponsored by the College Board since 1955.

10653
Advanced Placement Program: English Language and Composition.
Educational Testing Service, Princeton, NJ 1981
Descriptors: *Advanced Placement Programs; *College English; *Equivalency Tests; Essay Tests; High Schools; *High School Students; Multiple Choice Tests; Sentence Structure; Writing (Composition); Writing Skills
Identifiers: Advanced Placement Examinations (CEEB); APP
Availability: Advanced Placement Program; Box 977PD, Princeton, NJ 08541
Grade Level: 10-12
Notes: Time, 180 min.

Designed to assess achievement in English Language and Composition. Questions are one-third objective and two-thirds essay. The number of items will vary from year to year. Candidates are to take only one English exam—either literature and composition or English language and composition. The Advanced Placement Program has been sponsored by the College Board since 1955.

10654
System FORE: English.
Los Angeles Unified School District, CA 1975
Descriptors: *Children; Evaluation Methods; *Language Acquisition; Measures (Individuals); Morphology (Languages); Phonology; Preschool Children; Semantics; Syntax
Identifiers: TIM(F)
Availability: Tests in Microfiche; Test Collection, Educational Testing Service, Princeton, NJ 08541
Age Level: Children

Group of informal language inventories which utilize simple materials and paper and pencil to assess language development in children. Includes instructional objectives arranged by developmental levels 3-10. Level 3 has 34 items; level 4 has 34 items; level 5 has 24 items; level 6 has 25 items; level 7 has 27 items; level 8 has 25 items; level 9 has 14 items; level 10 has 15 items.

10686
Minimum Measurement Competencies for Classroom Teachers.
Allan, Salah M. 1980
Subtests: Formulating Behavioral Objectives; Planning Classroom Tests; Constructing and Scoring Test Items; Appraising Classroom Tests; Grading Classroom Tests
Descriptors: Adults; Behavioral Objectives; Diagnostic Tests; Knowledge Level; *Measurement; Multiple Choice Tests; Scoring; *Teacher Made Tests; Teachers; *Test Construction; *Testing; Test Interpretation
Identifiers: TIM(G)
Availability: Tests in Microfiche; Test Collection, Educational Testing Service, Princeton, NJ 08541
Age Level: Adults
Notes: Items, 91

Two sets of 91 parallel objective-referenced items are included. They cover formulation of behavioral objectives, planning classroom tests, constructing and scoring test items, appraising classroom tests, and grading classroom tests. For diagnostic use.

10693
Durrell Analysis of Reading Difficulty. Third Edition.
Durrell, Donald D.; Catterson, Jane H. 1980
Subtests: Oral Reading; Silent Reading; Listening Comprehension; Word Recognition-Word Analysis; Listening Vocabulary; Sounds in Isolation; Spelling; Phonic Spelling of Words; Visual Memory of Words; Identifying Sounds in Words; Prereading Phonics Abilities Inventories
Descriptors: Auditory Discrimination; *Diagnostic Tests; Elementary Education; *Elementary School Students; Individual Testing; Listening Comprehension; Listening Skills; Oral Reading; Phonics; *Reading Achievement; *Reading Difficulties; Silent Reading; Spelling; Visual Perception; Word Recognition
Identifiers: DARD
Availability: The Psychological Corp.; 555 Academic Ct., San Antonio, TX 78204-0952
Grade Level: 1-6
Notes: Time, 45 approx. min.

Individually administered diagnostic tests, consisting of a series of tests and situations in which the examiner can observe various aspects of the child's reading behavior. Primary purposes of tests are to estimate the general level of reading achievement and to discover weaknesses and faulty reading habits which may be corrected in a remedial program.

10700
Denver Prescreening Developmental Questionnaire.
Frankenburg, William K.; And Others 1975
Descriptors: *Developmental Tasks; Individual Testing; *Infants; Language Acquisition; Learning Disabilities; Motor Development; Parents; *Preschool Children; *Screening Tests; Social Development; Young Children
Identifiers: Denver Developmental Screening Test; Denver Screening Tests for Preschoolers; PDQ
Availability: Denver Developmental Materials; P.O. Box 6919, Denver, CO 80206-0919
Age Level: 0-6
Notes: Time, 5 min. approx.; Items, 97

Designed to be a "Prescreening" tool used to identify those children 3 months to 6 years of age who will require further screening with the Denver Developmental Screening Test (TC003628). Used to detect developmental lags and suggest more detailed screening required. Parents select the 10 age-appropriate questions for their children and answers these. Five color-coded forms arrange items by the chronological age at which most children can perform certain skills.

10701
Denver Prescreening Developmental Questionnaire (French Version). Frankenburg, William K.; And Others 1975
Descriptors: *Developmental Tasks; *French; Individual Testing; *Infants; Language Acquisition; Learning Disabilities; Motor Development; Parents; *Preschool Children; *Screening Tests; Social Development; Young Children
Identifiers: Denver Developmental Screening Test; Denver Screening Test for Preschoolers; PDQ
Availability: Denver Developmental Materials; P.O. Box 6919, Denver, CO 80206-0919
Age Level: 0-6
Notes: Time, 5 min. approx.; Items, 97

Designed to be a "prescreening" tool used to identify those children 3 months to 6 years of age who will require further screening with the Denver Developmental Screening Test (TC003628). Used to detect developmental lags and suggest more detailed screening is required. Parents select the 10 age-appropriate questions for their children and answers these. Five color-coded forms arrange items by the chronological age at which most children can perform certain skills.

10731
Compton Speech and Language Screening Evaluation. Compton, Arthur J. 1978
Descriptors: *Articulation (Speech); *Auditory Tests; Grade 1; Kindergarten; *Language Acquisition; *Screening Tests; Speech Evaluation; Speech Tests; *Vocabulary Development; Young Children
Availability: Carousel House; P.O. Box 4480; San Francisco, CA 94101
Age Level: 3-6
Notes: Time, 10 min. approx.; Items, 57

Designed to provide a quick estimate of the speech and language development of preschool, kindergarten, and first grade children. Intended to be used as a means of selecting out those children with potential speech and language handicaps. Toy objects are used.

10741
Consultant/Linker Knowledge and Skills Inventory.
Smink, Jay 1979
Descriptors: Adults; Change Agents; *Competence; *Consultants; Interpersonal Relationship; *Job Skills; Knowledge Level; Rating Scales; *Self Evaluation (Individuals)
Availability: ERIC Document Reproduction Service; 7420 Fullerton Rd., Ste. 110, Springfield, VA 22153-2852 (ED185080, 14 p.)
Age Level: Adults
Notes: Time, 30 min. approx.; Items, 72

Self-administered inventory, intended for educational consultants. Used to assess both existing and needed levels of knowledge and skills for consulting with school staff.

10743
Nutrition Knowledge Test. Byrd-Bredhenner, Carol 1980
Subtests: Basic Nutrition Principles; Sources of Nutrients; Functions of Nutrients
Descriptors: *Achievement Tests; Dietetics; Eating Habits; Elementary School Teachers; Food; Graduate Students; Higher Education; Knowledge Level; Multiple Choice Tests; Nurses; *Nutrition; Undergraduate Students

Identifiers: Home Economists; Nutritionists; TIM(G)
Availability: Tests in Microfiche; Test Collection, Educational Testing Service, Princeton, NJ 08541
Grade Level: 13-17
Notes: Items, 50

Designed to measure knowledge of basic nutrition principles, sources of nutrients, and functions of nutrients.

10746
English Reading Assessment. Bernard Cohen Research and Development Inc., New York, NY Barandiaran, Estela 1979
Subtests: Ready to Go (20); Easy to Start (40); Able to Read (40); Discovering (40); Imagining (40); Navigating (40); Galloping (40); Lickety Split (40)
Descriptors: Criterion Referenced Tests; *English (Second Language); Intermediate Grades; Primary Education; *Reading Comprehension; *Reading Readiness Tests; *Screening Tests; *Spanish Speaking; *Word Recognition
Availability: Santillana Publishing Co., Inc.; 901 W. Walnut St., Compton, CA 90220-5109
Grade Level: K-4
Notes: Time, 25 min. approx.; Items, 40

Designed for use with bilingual students. This group or individual test covers English oral language development, word recognition, and comprehension skills. Eight levels of difficulty including an oral comprehension assessment to determine general language readiness. Group administration requires approximately 45 minutes.

10747
Prueba de Lenguaje Santillana, Level G. Barandiaran, Estela 1980
Subtests: Reading Comprehension (25); Grammar (52); Study Skills (12)
Descriptors: *Bilingual Students; Criterion Referenced Tests; Grade 5; *Grammar; Intermediate Grades; *Reading Comprehension; *Screening Tests; Spanish; *Spanish Speaking; *Study Skills
Availability: Santillana Publishing Co., Inc.; 901 W. Walnut St., Compton, CA 90220-5109
Grade Level: 5
Notes: Items, 89

Designed for bilingual students who have an intermediate or advanced reading level in Spanish, this group or individual diagnostic placement test covers reading comprehension, grammar, and study skills. Levels G-J available.

10748
Prueba de Lenguaje Santillana, Level H. Barandiaran, Estela 1980
Subtests: Reading Comprehension (25); Grammar (52); Study Skills (10)
Descriptors: *Bilingual Students; Criterion Referenced Tests; Grade 6; *Grammar; Intermediate Grades; *Reading Comprehension; *Screening Tests; Spanish; *Spanish Speaking; *Study Skills
Availability: Santillana Publishing Co., Inc.; 901 W. Walnut St., Compton, CA 90220-5109
Grade Level: 6
Notes: Items, 87

Designed for bilingual students who have an intermediate or advanced reading level in Spanish, this group or individual diagnostic placement test covers reading comprehension, grammar, and study skills.

10749
Prueba de Lenguaje Santillana, Level I. Barandiaran, Estela 1980
Subtests: Reading Comprehension (25); Grammar (52); Study Skills (11)
Descriptors: *Bilingual Students; Criterion Referenced Tests; Grade 6; Grade 7; *Grammar; Intermediate Grades; Junior High Schools; *Reading Comprehension; *Screening Tests; Spanish; *Spanish Speaking; *Study Skills
Availability: Santillana Publishing Co., Inc.; 901 W. Walnut St., Compton, CA 90220-5109
Grade Level: 6-7
Notes: Items, 88

Designed for bilingual students who have an intermediate or advanced reading level in Spanish, this group or individual diagnostic placement test covers reading comprehension, grammar, and study skills. Levels G-J available.

10750
Prueba de Lenguaje Santillana, Level J. Barandiaran, Estela 1980
Subtests: Reading Comprehension (25); Grammar (52); Study Skills (11)
Descriptors: *Bilingual Students; Criterion Referenced Tests; Grade 8; *Grammar; Junior High Schools; *Reading Comprehension; *Screening Tests; Spanish; *Spanish Speaking; *Study Skills

Availability: Santillana Publishing Co., Inc.; 901 W. Walnut St., Compton, CA 90220-5109
Grade Level: 8
Notes: Items, 88

Designed for bilingual students who have an intermediate or advanced reading level in Spanish, this group or individual diagnostic placement test covers reading comprehension, grammar, and study skills. Levels G-J available.

10751
Language Assessment Umpire. Bernard Cohen Research and Development Inc., New York, NY Cohen, Bernard 1980
Subtests: Sentence Memory (25); Associations (27); Antonyms (27); Digits Reversed (15)
Descriptors: Adolescents; Associative Learning; *Cantonese; Children; *Chinese; *Creoles; *English; *French; *Italian; *Language Dominance; Language Tests; *Portuguese; Preschool Children; Sentences; *Spanish; *Tagalog
Identifiers: LAU
Availability: Santillana Publishing Co., Inc.; 901 W. Walnut St., Compton, CA 90220-5109
Age Level: 5-13
Notes: Time, 5-15 min. approx.; Items, 94

Designed for use with Bilingual Students. This individual diagnostic test identifies language dominance, based on cognitive criteria, from a choice of 8 languages: English, Spanish, French, Italian, Portuguese, Tagalog, Creole, and Chinese (Cantonese). All subtests are not used with all languages.

10790
Sample Safety Test Item S. New York State Education Dept., Albany, Bureau of Industrial Arts Education 1980
Descriptors: *Industrial Arts; *Item Banks; Multiple Choice Tests; *Safety; *School Shops; Secondary Education; *Secondary School Students; *Test Items
Identifiers: New York
Availability: ERIC Document Reproduction Service; 7420 Fullerton Rd., Ste. 110, Springfield, VA 22153-2852 (ED186493, 28 p.)
Grade Level: 7-12
Notes: Items, 149

A collection of sample test questions intended as a resource for developing teacher-made tests, based on course content.

10877
Peabody Picture Vocabulary Test—Revised, Form L. Dunn, Lloyd M.; Dunn, Leota M. 1981
Descriptors: *Academic Ability; Academic Aptitude; *Achievement Tests; Adolescents; Adults; Children; *Gifted; Job Placement; *Mental Retardation; *Non English Speaking; Preschool Children; *Screening Tests; *Verbal Ability; Vocabulary Skills
Identifiers: *Aural Vocabulary; PPVT
Availability: American Guidance Service; Publishers' Bldg., Circle Pines, MN 55014-1796
Age Level: 2-40
Notes: Time, 15 min.; Items, 175

Nationally standardized, individually administered measure of hearing vocabulary. Designed to measure verbal ability or scholastic aptitude. Used for screening special students, job candidates, and to assess vocabulary of non-English-speaking students, ranging in age from 2.5 to 40 years.

10878
Peabody Picture Vocabulary Test—Revised, Form M. Dunn, Lloyd M.; Dunn, Leota M. 1981
Descriptors: *Academic Ability; *Achievement Tests; Adolescents; Adults; Children; *Gifted; Job Placement; *Mental Retardation; *Non English Speaking; Preschool Children; *Screening Tests; *Verbal Ability; *Vocabulary Skills
Identifiers: *Aural Vocabulary; PPVT
Availability: American Guidance Service; Publishers' Bldg., Circle Pines, MN 55014-1796
Age Level: 2-40
Notes: Time, 15 min.; Items, 175

Nationally standardized, individually administered measure of hearing vocabulary. Designed to measure verbal ability or scholastic aptitude. Used for screening special students, job candidates, and to assess vocabulary of non-English-speaking students, ranging in age from 2.5 to 40 years.

10893
Brigance Diagnostic Inventory of Essential Skills.
Brigance, Albert H. 1981
Subtests: Reading (1155); Language Arts (361); Mathematics (949); Life Skills (1422)

Descriptors: Computation; *Daily Living Skills; Decimal Fractions; Diagnostic Tests; Elementary School Students; Elementary Secondary Education; Graphs; Handwriting; Writing Skills; Health; Home Economics; Individual Testing; Job Skills; *Language Arts; Library Skills; Mathematical Vocabulary; *Mathematics; Measurement; Metric System; Money Management; Number Concepts; Oral Reading; Percentage; Rating Scales; Reading Comprehension; *Reading Skills; Safety; Secondary Education; Secondary School Students; Spelling; Student Placement; Telephone Instruction; Travel; Verbal Communication; Word Recognition; Word Study Skills
Availability: Curriculum Associates, Inc.; 5 Esquire Rd., N. Billerica, MA 08162-2589
Grade Level: 4-12
Notes: Items, 3887

Criterion-referenced measure designed for use with special needs students in secondary programs for assessment, diagnosis, record keeping, and instructional planning. Covers basic academic and applied skills relevant to functioning as citizen, consumer, worker, and family member. Ten rating scales cover traits, behaviors, attitudes, and skills.

10923
AAHPERD Health Related Physical Fitness Test. American Alliance for Health, Physical Education, Recreation and Dance, Washington, DC 1980
Subtests: Distance Run; Skinfolds; Sit-Ups; Sit and Reach
Descriptors: Achievement Tests; *Adolescents; *Children; Elementary Secondary Education; *Performance Tests; *Physical Fitness; *Program Evaluation
Availability: American Alliance for Health, Physical Education, Recreation and Dance; 1900 Association Drive, Reston, VA 22091
Age Level: 6-17

Designed to assess physical fitness of students 6 to 17. Results may be used for diagnosis or to stimulate student interest in health-related topics. Group results may be used to evaluate school physical education program to determine whether desired goals are being achieved.

10930
Behavior Modification Achievement Test. MacNeil, Richard D. 1979
Descriptors: *Achievement Tests; *Behavior Modification; *College Students; Higher Education; *Pretests Posttests
Identifiers: BMTA; TIM(G)
Availability: Tests in Microfiche; Test Collection, Educational Testing Service, Princeton, NJ 08541
Grade Level: Higher Education
Notes: Items, 50

Pretest-posttest used to evaluate learning performance in a unit on behavior modification.

10951
Botel Reading Inventory. Botel, Morton 1978
Subtests: Decoding Test; Spelling Placement Test; Word Recognition Test; Word Opposites Test
Descriptors: *Achievement Tests; Decoding (Reading); Elementary Education; *Elementary School Students; Oral Reading; *Reading Achievement; Reading Comprehension; Spelling; *Student Placement; Word Recognition
Identifiers: Test Batteries
Availability: Modern Curriculum Press; 13900 Prospect Rd., Cleveland, OH 44136
Grade Level: 1-8

Designed to measure general comprehension and oral reading fluency to determine reading instructional level. Battery consists of 4 tests. Forms A and B are available for Word Recognition and Word Opposites Test.

10975
Screening Test for Auditory Perception. Revised Edition. Kimmell, Geraldine M.; Wahl, Jack 1981
Subtests: Vowel Sounds (12); Initial Single Consonant Sounds (12); Rhyming and Nonrhyming Words (12); Rhythmic Sound Patterns (6); Paired Words (12)
Descriptors: Adolescents; *Auditory Perception; Elementary Education; Norm Referenced Tests; Remedial Instruction; *Screening Tests
Availability: Academic Therapy Publications; 20 Commercial Blvd., Novato, CA 94947-6191
Grade Level: 1-6
Notes: Time, 45 min. approx.; Items, 54

Norm-referenced test for detection of weaknesses in auditory perception of elementary grade students and for older students in remedial classes. Total test scores may be converted to percentiles, grade equivalents, and age equivalents.

10977
Adult Basic Education/Learning Disabilities Screening Test. Vaillancourt, Beverly 1979
Subtests: Word Recognition; Arithmetic; Spelling; Writing Sample; Reading Comprehension
Descriptors: *Adult Basic Education; Adults; Arithmetic; Communication Skills; *Diagnostic Tests; *Learning Disabilities; Reading Tests; *Screening Tests; Spelling; Writing Skills
Availability: ERIC Document Reproduction Service; 7420 Fullerton Rd., Ste. 110, Springfield, VA 22153-2852 (ED193433, 233 p.)
Age Level: Adults
Notes: Items, 66

Designed to determine competencies in reading, written communication, and mathematics. For use with adults who cannot complete a reading placement test. Group or individually administered.

10994
Diagnostic Reading Scales. Spache, George D. 1981
Subtests: Word List 1 (50); Word List 2 (40); Word List 3 (40); Reading Selections-Set 1 (84); Reading Selections-Set 2 (84); Word Analysis and Phonics Tests (237)
Descriptors: Decoding (Reading); Elementary Education; Individual Testing; Nonstandard Dialects; Oral Reading; Phonics; Reading Comprehension; *Reading Diagnosis; *Reading Tests; Student Placement; Word Recognition
Availability: CTB/MacMillan/McGraw-Hill; Del Monte Research Park, 2500 Garden Road, Monterey, CA 93940
Grade Level: 1-7
Notes: Time, 60 min.; Items, 536

Individually administered series of graduated scales designed to identify strengths and weaknesses affecting reading proficiency. Used for placement and individualizing instruction. Identifies reading level. Covers word recognition, reading comprehension, phonics, word analysis. All responses are oral. Guidelines provided for speakers of nonstandard English.

11008
Emory Word Analysis Skill Inventory. Avant, Glen R.; O'Brien, Michael L. 1980
Subtests: Consonant Digraphs; Final Blends and Double Consonants; R Controls; Initial Blends; Land N, C, and G Patterns; Magic E; Vowel Combinations; Vowel Sounds; Compound Words; Inflectional Endings; Suffixes; Prefixes; Multisyllable Words
Descriptors: *Diagnostic Tests; Elementary Secondary Education; *Reading Difficulties; *Reading Skills; *Word Recognition; *Word Study Skills
Identifiers: EWASI
Availability: ERIC Document Reproduction Service; 7420 Fullerton Rd., Ste. 110, Springfield, VA 22153-2852 (ED193296, 46 p.)
Grade Level: 2-12
Age Level: 6-19
Notes: Items, 137

Diagnostic instrument to aid teachers in analyzing student performance in terms of specific objectives of knowledge, understanding, and skills in word analysis tasks as identified by the 13 subscales. Two parallel forms of the test are available.

11032
Diagnostic Analysis of Reading Errors. Gillespie, Jacquelyn; Shohet, Jacqueline 1979
Descriptors: Adolescents; Adults; Culture Fair Tests; *Diagnostic Tests; English (Second Language); *Language Handicaps; *Learning Disabilities; *Reading Difficulties; Secondary Education; *Sensory Integration; Spelling; Two Year Colleges
Identifiers: DARE; *Transcoding; Wide Range Achievement Test; WRAT
Availability: Jastak Associates; P.O. Box 3410, Wilmington, DE 19806
Age Level: 12-65
Notes: Time, 30 min. approx.; Items, 46

Designed to identify adults and adolescents with language-related learning disabilities; to provide indications of the nature of each identified individual's disability as it is reflected in reading and spelling; and to elicit diagnostic information for individual assessment as part of a battery of test procedures. DARE is a one-page test form which uses the 46-item word list of the Wide Range Achievement Test (Spelling, Level II) in a 4-alternative, multiple-choice format. Four scores are provided for each individual: number of correct responses; sound substitution; omissions; and reversals.

11038
Stanford Test of Academic Skills, Braille Edition, Level II. American Printing House for the Blind, Louisville, KY 1972
Subtests: Reading; English; Mathematics

Descriptors: *Achievement Tests; *Basic Skills; *Blindness; *Braille; High Schools; *High School Students; Language Skills; *Mathematics; Multiple Choice Tests; Reading Comprehension; Spelling; Two Year Colleges; *Two Year College Students; Vocabulary
Identifiers: TASK; Test Batteries
Availability: American Printing House for the Blind; 1839 Frankfort Ave., Louisville, KY 40206
Grade Level: 11-13
Notes: Time, 120 min.; Items, 195

Measures basic cognitive enabling skills: reading, English, and mathematics. Content assessed is usually taught before the end of Grade 8. TASK may be used to assess minimal competence in the basic skills for blind students. Each subtest requires 40 minutes of working time. Two equivalent forms, A and B, are available. Separate manual and forms for Junior/Community College, Grade 13.

11052
Criterion Referenced Inventory. Grade 7 Skill Clusters, Objectives, and Illustrations. Montgomery County Public Schools, Rockville, MD 1979
Subtests: Location of Resources; Understanding about Materials; Card Catalog; General Reference Skills; Dictionaries; Encyclopedias; Almanacs; Atlases; Newspapers, Magazines, and Periodical Indexes
Descriptors: *Achievement Tests; Atlases; Card Catalogs; Criterion Referenced Tests; Dictionaries; Encyclopedias; *Grade 7; Indexes; Junior High Schools; Junior High School Students; *Library Materials; *Library Skills; Multiple Choice Tests; Newspapers; Reference Materials
Availability: ERIC Document Reproduction Service; 7420 Fullerton Rd., Ste. 110, Springfield, VA 22153-2852 (ED192773, 61 p.)
Grade Level: 7
Notes: Items, 116

Part of a series of competency-based test materials for grades 6-10. Contains multiple-choice questions to aid in evaluation of students' library skills.

11053
Criterion Referenced Inventory. Grade 10 Skill Clusters, Objectives, and Illustrations. Montgomery County Public Schools, Rockville, MD 1979
Subtests: Understanding about Materials; Card Catalog; General Reference Skills; Dictionaries; Atlases; Newspapers; Periodical Indexes; Additional References; Production of Media
Descriptors: *Achievement Tests; Atlases; Card Catalogs; Criterion Referenced Tests; Dictionaries; *Grade 10; High Schools; High School Students; Indexes; *Library Materials; *Library Skills; Multiple Choice Tests; Newspapers; Reference Materials
Availability: ERIC Document Reproduction Service; 7420 Fullerton Rd., Ste. 110, Springfield, VA 22153-2852 (ED192774, 48 p.)
Grade Level: 10
Notes: Items, 82

Part of a series of competency-based test materials for grades 6-10. Contains multiple-choice questions to aid in the evaluation of students' library skills.

11054
Criterion Referenced Assessment Bank. Grade 9 Skill Clusters, Objectives, and Illustrations. Montgomery County Public Schools, Rockville, MD 1979
Subtests: Understanding about Materials; Card Catalog; General Reference Skills; Dictionaries; Atlases; Newspapers; Periodical Indexes; Additional References; Production of Media
Descriptors: *Achievement Tests; Atlases; Card Catalogs; Criterion Referenced Tests; Dictionaries; *Grade 9; High School Freshmen; High Schools; Indexes; *Library Materials; *Library Skills; Multiple Choice Tests; Newspapers; Reference Materials
Availability: ERIC Document Reproduction Service; 7420 Fullerton Rd., Ste. 110, Springfield, VA 22153-2852 (ED192772, 55 p.)
Grade Level: 9
Notes: Items, 93

Part of a series of competency-based test materials for grades 6-10. Contains multiple-choice questions to aid in evaluation of students' library skills.

11063
Environmental Language Intervention Program: Parent Administered Communication Inventory. 1978
Descriptors: *Child Language; Children; Communication Skills; *Disabilities; Informal Assessment; *Language Acquisition; *Language Handicaps; *Parent Participation

Identifiers: *Environmental Language Intervention Program
Availability: The Psychological Corp.; 555 Academic Ct., San Antonio, TX 78204-0952
Age Level: Children

Initial procedure in undertaking the Environmental Language Intervention Program. Used by parents and other caregivers to sample the child's range of communication-related behaviors in the natural living situation. Recommended for use before a professional assessment and parallels the content of the Environmental Prelanguage Battery (TC010985) and the Environmental Language Inventory (TC010986). Target population includes all who have yet to develop age-appropriate communication.

11080
Developmental Tasks for Kindergarten Readiness. Lesiak, Walter J. 1978
Subtests: Social Interaction; Name Printing; Body Concepts; Auditory Sequencing; Auditory Association; Visual Discrimination; Visual Memory; Visual Motor; Color Naming; Relational Concepts; Number Knowledge; Alphabet Knowledge
Descriptors: Cognitive Development; *Developmental Tasks; Diagnostic Tests; *Kindergarten Children; Oral Language; Perceptual Motor Learning; *Preschool Children; *School Readiness Tests; Screening Tests; Social Development
Identifiers: DTKR
Availability: Clinical Psychology Publishing Co.; 4 Conant Square, Brandon, VT 05733
Age Level: 4-6
Notes: Time, 30 min. approx.; Items, 177

Administered prior to a child's entrance into kindergarten or during first weeks of enrollment. Standardized for children ranging in age from 4 years, 6 months to 6 years, 2 months. Provides data about child's skills and abilities as they relate to successful performance in kindergarten. Instrument is multivariate in format, and subtests were selected from a child development model, instructional objectives in kindergarten curriculum guides, and research studies.

11087
Test of English as a Foreign Language. Understanding TOEFL: Test Kit 1. Educational Testing Service, Princeton, NJ
Subtests: Listening Comprehension; Structure and Written Expression; Reading Comprehension and Vocabulary
Descriptors: Adults; *English (Second Language); Foreign Students; *Graduate Students; Grammar; Higher Education; *High School Students; *Language Proficiency; *Language Tests; Listening Comprehension Tests; Multiple Choice Tests; Reading Comprehension; Secondary Education; Self Evaluation (Individuals); Sentence Structure; *Undergraduate Students; Vocabulary Skills; Workbooks; Writing Skills
Identifiers: Practice Tests; Self Scoring Tests; *TOEFL
Availability: TOEFL; Box 6155, Educational Testing Service, Princeton, NJ 08541
Grade Level: 11-18
Notes: Time, 120 min.; Items, 150

Practice materials containing an actual TOEFL test. Includes a cassette tape recording of the Listening Comprehension subtest. A workbook also supplies correct answers and explanations of each answer choice. TOEFL was designed to evaluate the English proficiency of nonnative speakers of English, primarily at the secondary level, who are preparing to study at North American colleges or universities.

11097
Environmental Language Intervention Program: Ready, Set, Go: Talk to Me. Horstmeier, DeAnna S.; MacDonald, James D. 1978
Descriptors: Adults; *Child Language; Children; Diagnostic Teaching; Diagnostic Tests; *Disabilities; Expressive Language; Informal Assessment; *Language Acquisition; *Language Handicaps; *Parent Participation
Identifiers: *Environmental Language Intervention Program; *Prelanguage
Availability: The Psychological Corp.; 555 Academic Ct., San Antonio, TX 78204-0952
Age Level: 1-30
Notes: Items, 13

Designed for and tested with a population ranging from totally immobile and unresponsive children to individuals with good receptive language but minimum social use of expressive language. Is basically a series of prescriptive training programs for establishing prelanguage skills and initial verbal communication in individuals whose language skills are developmentally delayed. Program is used primarily with 3 groups: parents, speech and language clinicians, and teachers.

11099
Gates-McKillop-Horowitz Reading Diagnostic Tests. Second Edition. Gates, Arthur I.; McKillop, Anne S.; Horowitz, Elizabeth Cliff 1981
Subtests: Oral Reading; Reading Sentences; Words: Flash; Words: Untimed; Syllabication; Recognizing and Blending Common Word Parts; Reading Words; Giving Letter Sounds; Naming Capital Letters; Naming Lower Case Letters; Vowels; Auditory Blending; Auditory Discrimination; Spelling; Writing Sample
Descriptors: *Diagnostic Tests; Elementary Education; *Elementary School Students; *Individual Testing; Oral Reading; *Reading Diagnosis; Reading Difficulties; Spelling; Writing Skills
Availability: Teachers College Press; P.O. Box 2032, Colchester, VT 05449
Grade Level: 1-6
Notes: Time, 60 min. approx.; Items, 338

Test battery consisting of 15 individually administered tests which provide profile of a student's ability to recognize words and their component sounds. Helps teacher and learning specialist assess student's strengths and weaknesses in areas of oral reading, spelling, and writing skills. By examining student's oral responses, weaknesses can be isolated in such areas as decoding skills, sight word recognition, auditory blending and discrimination, spelling and written expression.

11102
Test of English as a Foreign Language: Sample Test. Educational Testing Service, Princeton, NJ 1981
Subtests: Listening Comprehension; Structure and Written Expression; Reading Comprehension and Vocabulary
Descriptors: Adults; *English (Second Language); Foreign Students; Graduate Students; Grammar; Higher Education; *High School Students; *Language Proficiency; *Language Tests; Listening Comprehension Tests; Multiple Choice Tests; Reading Comprehension; Secondary Education; Sentence Structure; *Undergraduate Students; Vocabulary Skills; Writing Skills
Identifiers: Practice Tests; *TOEFL
Availability: TOEFL; Box 6155, Educational Testing Service, Princeton, NJ 08541
Grade Level: 11-18
Notes: Items, 70

Test booklet and answer key for use as practice materials for TOEFL. Half the length of an actual test. No percentile can be computed.

11103
English as a Second Language Assessment Battery. Rivera, Charlene; Lombardo, Maria 1979
Subtests: Oral Screening; Oral Competency; Aural Comprehension; Dictation Exercise; Structural Competency; Informal Reading Inventory; Writing Sample
Descriptors: *Bilingual Students; *Criterion Referenced Tests; *English (Second Language); Expressive Language; Informal Reading Inventories; Language Proficiency; Listening Comprehension; Oral Language; Reading Comprehension; Receptive Language; Secondary Education; *Secondary School Students; *Spanish Speaking; Student Placement; Writing Skills
Identifiers: ESLAB; TIM(G)
Availability: Tests in Microfiche; Test Collection, Educational Testing Service, Princeton, NJ 08541
Grade Level: 7-12
Notes: Time, 105 min.; Items, 208

Criterion-referenced measure designed to assess the English language proficiency of Spanish bilingual students. Covers receptive and expressive skills. For use in placing students at instructional levels in ESL classes.

11116
Language Proficiency Test. Gerard, Joan; Weinstock, Gloria 1981
Subtests: Commands; Short Answer Oral Production; Listening Comprehension; Vocabulary; Reading Comprehension; Grammar; Sentence Response; Paragraph Response; Translation
Descriptors: Adolescents; Adults; Audiolingual Skills; *Criterion Referenced Tests; Diagnostic Tests; *English (Second Language); *Language Proficiency; Learning Disabilities; Listening Comprehension; Older Adults; Oral Language; Paragraphs; Reading Skills; Sentences; Slow Learners; Translation; Vocabulary Skills; Writing Skills
Identifiers: LPT
Availability: Academic Therapy Publications; 20 Commercial Blvd., Novato, CA 94947-6191
Age Level: 13-65
Notes: Time, 90 min.; Items, 99

Criterion-referenced measure designed to assess language ability for students of English as a Second Language and native speakers with learning handicaps or low level skills. Measures aural/oral, reading, and writing skills. Utilizes multiple-choice and short answer questions. Includes an optional translation section to assess vocabulary and syntactical complexity. Two subtests measuring low level function must be individually administered.

11150
Spanish Reading Comprehension Test and English Reading Comprehension Test. Moreno, Steve 1978
Descriptors: *Achievement Tests; Bilingual Education; Elementary Education; *Elementary School Students; *English; *Reading Comprehension; *Spanish
Identifiers: *Mexico
Availability: Moreno Educational Co.; 7050 Belle Glade Ln., San Diego, CA 92119
Grade Level: 1-6
Notes: Time, 60 min.; Items, 146

The Spanish test was developed, standardized, and normed in Mexico. The English test was translated from the Spanish and used a smaller sample size for developing norms. The tests are designed to be used in the following ways: to determine levels of Spanish achievement compared with Mexican norms; to evaluate bilingual education programs; to measure growth of U.S. students who are studying Spanish; to determine degrees of bilingualism; to report progress to school boards; to include in research studies. Each test takes 30 minutes and consists of 73 items.

11151
Spanish Reading Comprehension Test and English Reading Comprehension Test. Moreno, Steve 1978
Descriptors: *Achievement Tests; *Adults; Bilingual Education; *English; *Reading Comprehension; Secondary Education; *Secondary School Students; *Spanish
Identifiers: *Mexico
Availability: Moreno Educational Co.; 7050 Belle Glade Ln., San Diego, CA 92119
Grade Level: 7-12
Notes: Time, 50 min.; Items, 162

The Spanish test was developed, standardized, and normed in Mexico. The English test was translated from the Spanish and used a smaller sample size for developing norms. The tests are designed to be used in the following ways: to determine levels of Spanish achievement compared with Mexican norms; to evaluate bilingual education programs; to measure growth of U.S. students who are studying Spanish; to determine degrees of bilingualism; to report progress to school boards; to include in research studies. Each test takes 25 minutes and consists of 81 items.

11156
Knowledge Test of Reading for Elementary School Teachers. Rude, Robert R. 1981
Descriptors: *Achievement Tests; Adults; *Elementary School Teachers; *Knowledge Level; *Reading; *Teaching Methods
Availability: *Journal of Educational Research;* v74 n6 p411-18, Jul-Aug 1981
Age Level: Adults
Notes: Items, 52

Used to assess elementary school teachers' knowledge of reading concepts. Twelve topical areas were identified which represented the content of several reading methods textbooks: stating objectives, reading theory, skills management systems, reading readiness, decoding, comprehension, study skills, basal reader approach, language experience approach, individualized reading approach, program evaluation, and program organization.

11163
Minimum Essential Test A. Scott, Foresman and Co., Glenview, IL 1980
Subtests: Reading; Language; Mathematics; Writing; Life Skills
Descriptors: Adults; *Basic Skills; Daily Living Skills; Language Usage; *Minimum Competency Testing; Reading Achievement; Secondary Education; Secondary School Mathematics; *Secondary School Students; Writing (Composition)
Availability: American Testronics; P.O. Box 2270, Iowa City, IA 52244-9990
Grade Level: 8-12
Notes: Time, 110 min. approx.; Items, 124

Part of the Comprehensive Assessment Program. Test is based on objectives considered basic for minimum competence. Test may be used alone or as part of the program and is suitable for adults as well as for secondary school students. Three forms of the test are available.

11191
Speech and Language Growth for the Mexican-American Student. Proul, Peter 1971

Subtests: Spanish Accent Sentence Completion Articulation Test; Spanish Accent Picture Stimulus Articulation Test; Spanish Accent Auditory Discrimination Test

Descriptors: *Articulation (Speech); *Auditory Discrimination; *Diagnostic Tests; Elementary Education; *Elementary School Students; *English (Second Language); Individual Testing; *Language Patterns; *Mexican Americans; *Nonstandard Dialects; Pictorial Stimuli; Remedial Instruction; *Spanish Speaking; *Speech Instruction

Identifiers: Sentence Completion Test; TIM (H)

Availability: Tests in Microfiche; Test Collection, Educational Testing Service, Princeton, NJ 08541

Grade Level: 1-6

Notes: Items, 35

Diagnostic tests of hearing and articulation and methods to aid in the diagnosis of language patterns, designed to measure deviations from standard English in those students speaking English with a Spanish accent. Hearing is tested by measuring auditory discrimination. Each subtest has between 30 and 40 items. Individually administered.

11196
ORBIT: Objectives Referenced Bank of Items and Tests—Reading and Communication Skills.
CTB/Macmillan/McGraw-Hill, Monterey, CA 1980

Subtests: Prereading; Phonic Analysis; Structural Analysis; Word Meaning; Literal Comprehension; Interpretive Comprehension; Critical Comprehension; Reading Applications; Study and Reference Skills; Language Mechanics; Language Expression

Descriptors: *Communication Skills; *Criterion Referenced Tests; Critical Reading; Early Childhood Education; Elementary Secondary Education; Form Classes (Languages); *Item Banks; Language Usage; Library Skills; Phonetic Analysis; Prereading Experience; Reading Comprehension; *Reading Skills; Semantics; Structural Analysis (Linguistics); Study Skills; Syntax

Identifiers: ORBIT

Availability: CTB/MacMillan/McGraw Hill; Del Monte Research Park, 2500 Garden Rd., Monterey, CA 93940

Grade Level: K-12

Notes: Items, 1428

Objectives with up to 4 accompanying test items designed for use in the development of multiple-choice criterion-referenced tests. Objectives are selected by the user. Tests are constructed by the publisher. To provide prescriptive information, objectives are keyed to basal reading texts in grades K-8. For information on mathematics and social studies items, see TC011197 and TC011198.

11197
ORBIT: Objectives Referenced Bank of Items and Tests—Mathematics. CTB/Macmillan/McGraw-Hill, Monterey, CA 1980

Subtests: Operations with Whole Numbers; Operations with Fractions; Operations with Rational Numbers (Fractions or Decimals); Operations with Decimals and Money; Operations with Integers; Number and Numeration; Number Theory; Number Sentences (Equalities and Inequalities); Number Properties; Set Theory; Geometry; Common Scales (Time, Money, Temperature; Measurement; Word Problems; Ratio, Proportion, Percent; Probability and Statistics; Algebra

Descriptors: Algebra; Computation; *Criterion Referenced Tests; Decimal Fractions; Early Childhood Education; Elementary Secondary Education; Fractions; Geometry; *Item Banks; *Mathematics; *Mathematics Tests; Measurement; Number Concepts; Percentage; Probability; Problem Solving; Ratios (Mathematics); Set Theory; Statistics; Time

Identifiers: Money; ORBIT

Availability: CTB/MacMillan/McGraw Hill; Del Monte Research Park, 2500 Garden Rd., Monterey, CA 93940

Grade Level: K-12

Notes: Items, 2324

Objectives with up to 4 accompanying test items designed for use in the development of multiple-choice criterion-referenced tests. Objectives are selected by the publisher. To provide prescriptive information, objectives are keyed to mathematics texts. For information on reading and communication and social studies items, see TC011196 and 011198.

11198
ORBIT: Objectives Referenced Bank of Items and Tests—Social Studies. CTB/Macmillan/McGraw-Hill, Monterey, CA 1980

Subtests: Banking; Purchasing; Insurance; Taxes; Budget; American Political System; National Government and the Constitution; State and Local Government; Citizenship; Law in American Society; Evaluating; Decision Making; Forecasting; Planning; Problems and Solutions

Descriptors: Banking; Budgets; Citizenship; Constitutional Law; *Criterion Referenced Tests; Decision Making; Early Childhood Education; Elementary Secondary Education; Evaluative Thinking; Federal Government; Insurance; *Item Banks; Laws; Planning; Politics; Prediction; Problem Solving; Purchasing; *Social Studies; State Government; Taxes

Identifiers: ORBIT

Availability: CTB/MacMillan/McGraw Hill; Del Monte Research Park, 2500 Garden Rd., Monterey, CA 93940

Grade Level: K-12

Notes: Items, 60

Objectives with up to 4 accompanying test items designed for use in the development of multiple-choice criterion-referenced tests. Objectives are selected by the user. Tests are constructed by the publisher, to provide prescriptive information; objectives are keyed to social studies texts. For information on reading and communication and mathematics items, see TC011196 and 011197.

11200
Blue Version Biology Pictorial Classroom Test.
Reese, Charles Dennis 1973

Descriptors: *Achievement Tests; Animals; Biochemistry; *Biology; Cytology; Evolution; High Schools; *High School Students; Individual Testing; Multiple Choice Tests; Pictorial Stimuli

Identifiers: Biological Sciences Curr Study Blue Version; BVBPCT

Availability: University Microfilms International; Dissertation Copies, P.O. Box 1764, Ann Arbor, MI 48106 (Order No. 73-28,899, 217 pp)

Grade Level: 10-11

Notes: Time, 33 min.; Items, 50

Multiple-choice test based on the first 12 chapters of the Biological Science Curriculum Study's Blue Version text, *Molecules and Man.* Each item relates to a picture. Administered individually or by passing the pictures around the class or through the use of slides. Covers evolution, biochemicals, cell theory, and multicellular organisms.

11215
Quickscreen. Kindergarten. Fudala, Janet B. 1980

Subtests: Name Writing; Figure Copying; Story; Sentence Repetition

Descriptors: Auditory Perception; *Handicap Identification; *Kindergarten Children; *Learning Disabilities; *Learning Problems; Listening Comprehension; Perceptual Motor Coordination; Primary Education; *Screening Tests

Availability: Western Psychological Services; 12031 Wilshire Blvd., Los Angeles, CA 90025

Grade Level: Kindergarten

Notes: Time, 25 min. approx.; Items, 4

Brief classroom procedure designed to screen for speech, language, and learning problems. The procedure can be administered to an average classroom at one time. The kindergarten level has 4 parallel forms. Designed as the first step to definitive diagnosis of students with learning problems.

11216
Quickscreen. First Grade. Fudala, Janet B. 1979

Subtests: Name Writing; Figures; Words; Story; Sentences

Descriptors: Auditory Perception; *Grade 1; *Handicap Identification; *Learning Disabilities; *Learning Problems; Listening Comprehension; Perceptual Motor Coordination; Primary Education; *Screening Tests

Availability: Western Psychological Services; 12031 Wilshire Blvd., Los Angeles, CA 90025

Grade Level: 1

Notes: Time, 25 min. approx.; Items, 8

Brief classroom procedure designed to screen for speech, language, and learning problems. The procedure can be administered to an average classroom at one time. The grade-1 level has 2 parallel forms. The subtests measure auditory comprehension, visual motor skills, and auditory vocal skills. Designed as the first step to definitive diagnosis of students with learning problems.

11217
Quickscreen. Second Grade. Fudala, Janet B. 1979

Subtests: Name Writing; Figures; Story; Cognitive; Sentences

Descriptors: Auditory Perception; Cognitive Development; *Grade 2; *Handicap Identification; *Learning Disabilities; *Learning Problems; Listening Comprehension; Perceptual Motor Coordination; Primary Education; *Screening Tests

Availability: Western Psychological Services; 12031 Wilshire Blvd., Los Angeles, CA 90025

Grade Level: 2

Notes: Time, 25 min. approx.; Items, 5

Brief classroom procedure designed to screen for speech language, and learning problems. The procedure can be administered to an average classroom at one time. The grade-2 level has 2 parallel forms. The subtests measure auditory comprehension, cognitive skills, visual motor, and auditory vocal development.

11244
Advanced Placement Program: Music Listening and Literature. Educational Testing Service, Princeton, NJ 1981

Subtests: Aural Perception; Music Listening and Literature

Descriptors: *Advanced Placement Programs; *Equivalency Tests; Essay Tests; High Schools; *High School Students; Multiple Choice Tests; *Music Appreciation

Identifiers: Advanced Placement Examinations (CEEB); APP

Availability: Advanced Placement Program; Box 977PD, Princeton, NJ 08541

Grade Level: 10-12

Notes: Time, 110 min.

Designed to measure achievement in college full-year introductory music course. Forty minutes of objective questions on aural perception, common to Music Listening and Literature and Music Theory Exams and 70 minutes of objective and essay questions on specified topic. Candidates take either or both examinations. The number of test items may vary from year to year. The Advanced Placement Program has been sponsored by the College Board since 1955.

11245
Advanced Placement Program: European History.
Educational Testing Service, Princeton, NJ 1981

Descriptors: *Advanced Placement Programs; *Equivalency Tests; Essay Tests; *European History; High Schools; *High School Students; Multiple Choice Tests

Identifiers: Advanced Placement Examinations (CEEB); APP

Availability: Advanced Placement Program; Box 977PD, Princeton, NJ 08541

Grade Level: 10-12

Notes: Time, 180 min.; Items, 92

Designed to measure achievement of information in college full-year introduction to European history from 1450 through early 1970s. The number of items will vary from year to year. The Advanced Placement Program has been sponsored by the College Board since 1955.

11246
Advanced Placement Program: French Literature.
Educational Testing Service, Princeton, NJ 1981

Descriptors: *Advanced Placement Programs; *Equivalency Tests; Essay Tests; *French; *French Literature; High Schools; *High School Students; Language Tests; Literary Criticism; Multiple Choice Tests; Second Language Learning

Identifiers: Advanced Placement Examinations (CEEB); APP

Availability: Advanced Placement Program; CN6670, Princeton, NJ 08541-6670

Grade Level: 10-12

Notes: Time, 180 min.

The examination tests students' ability to read and analyze representative works of French poetry, drama, and prose fiction. The writing section is based on a prescribed list of works and requires students to write 2 analytical essays on texts from the list. Both essays are written in French and scored for language proficiency as well as content. The multiple-choice questions test students' skill in understanding and analyzing passages from texts that, for the most part, have not been previously studied; some questions do test recall of required texts. Designed to assess achievement in French at the third-year college level. Number of test items may vary from year to year. The Advanced Placement Program has been sponsored by the College Board since 1955.

11248
Advanced Placement Program: Mathematics—Calculus BC. Educational Testing Service, Princeton, NJ 1981

Subtests: Multiple Choice Questions; Problem Solving

Descriptors: *Advanced Placement Programs; *Calculus; *Equivalency Tests; High Schools; *High School Students; *Mathematics Tests

Identifiers: Advanced Placement Examinations (CEEB); APP

Availability: Advanced Placement Program; Box 977PD, Princeton, NJ 08541

Grade Level: 10-12

Notes: Time, 180 min.; Items, 52

Designed to assess achievement in college level full-year mathematics course. Calculus BC measures elementary functions, introductory calculus, and one semester beyond AB. The number of items may vary from year to year. The Advanced Placement Program has been sponsored by the College Board since 1955. Candidates take only one of 2 calculus examinations.

11249
Advanced Placement Program: Spanish Literature. Educational Testing Service, Princeton, NJ 1981
Subtests: Aural Comprehension, Literary Analysis, and Reading Comprehension; Literary Appreciation, Interpretation, and Analysis and Skill in Writing Critical Expository Prose
Descriptors: *Advanced Placement Programs; Audiotape Recordings; *Equivalency Tests; Essay Tests; High Schools; *High School Students; Language Proficiency; Language Tests; *Literary Criticism; Multiple Choice Tests; *Second Language Learning; *Spanish
Identifiers: Advanced Placement Examinations (CEEB); APP
Availability: Advanced Placement Program; Box 977PD, Princeton, NJ 08541
Grade Level: 10-12
Notes: Time, 180 min.

Designed to assess achievement in college level third-year Spanish Objective questions on listening, reading and literary analysis; 2 essays in Spanish on required authors and one—in Spanish or English—on presented poems. The number of test items may vary from year to year. The Advanced Placement Program has been sponsored by the College Board since 1955. Candidates may take either or both Spanish examinations.

11250
Advanced Placement Program: Physics C. Educational Testing Service, Princeton, NJ 1981
Subtests: Mechanics; Electricity and Magnetism
Descriptors: *Advanced Placement Programs; Electricity; *Equivalency Tests; Essay Tests; High Schools; *High School Students; Mechanics (Physics); Multiple Choice Tests; *Physics
Identifiers: Advanced Placement Examinations (CEEB); APP
Availability: Advanced Placement Program; Box 977PD, Princeton, NJ 08541
Grade Level: 10-12
Notes: Time, 180 min.

Designed to assess achievement in a full-year college course of introductory physics with calculus. The number of items may vary from year to year. The Advanced Placement Program has been sponsored by the College Board since 1955. Candidates may take either Physics B or C examination.

11251
ACS Cooperative Examination: General Chemistry (Brief). American Chemical Society, Tampa, FL, Div. of Chemical Education
Subtests: Stoichiometry; Bonding-Periodicity-Geometry, States of Matter, Acid-Base Chemistry; Equilibria, Electrochemistry, Thermodynamics, Descriptive Chemistry, Carbon Chemistry; General Chemistry
Descriptors: *Achievement Tests; Chemical Bonding; Chemical Equilibrium; *Chemistry; Geometry; Higher Education; Matter; Multiple Choice Tests; Thermodynamics; *Undergraduate Students
Identifiers: Acid Base Chemistry; *American Chemical Society Cooperative Examinations; Carbon; Descriptive Chemistry; Electrochemistry; Periodic Law; Periodic Table; Stoichiometry
Availability: ACS DivCHED Examinations Institute; Oklahoma State University, 107 Physical Sciences, Stillwater, OK 74078-0447
Grade Level: 13-16
Notes: Time, 55 min.; Items, 50

Designed to measure achievement in a first-year college chemistry course. This is a brief version of another test (see TC011252). Test forms are updated periodically, and older forms may be retired from active use. Retired college-level forms may be released to high school teachers.

11252
ACS Cooperative Examination: General Chemistry. American Chemical Society, Tampa, FL, Div. of Chemical Education
Subtests: Stoichiometry; Bonding-Periodicity-Geometry, States of Matter, Acid-Base Chemistry; Equilibria, Electrochemistry, Thermodynamics, Descriptive Chemistry, Carbon Chemistry; General Chemistry
Descriptors: *Achievement Tests; Chemical Bonding; Chemical Equilibrium; *Chemistry; Geometry; Higher Education; Matter; Multiple Choice Tests; Thermodynamics; *Undergraduate Students
Identifiers: Acid Base Chemistry; *American Chemical Society Cooperative Examinations; Carbon; Descriptive Chemistry; Electrochemistry; Periodic Law; Periodic Table; Stoichiometry
Availability: ACS DivCHED Examinations Institute; Oklahoma State University, 107 Physical Sciences, Stillwater, OK 74078-0447
Grade Level: 13-16
Notes: Time, 110 min.; Items, 80

Designed to measure achievement in a first-year college chemistry course. Includes a complete periodic table. Test forms are updated periodically, and older forms may be retired from active use. Retired college-level forms may be released to high school teachers.

11255
ACS Cooperative Examination: Quantitative Analysis (Analytical Chemistry). American Chemical Society, Tampa, FL, Div. of Chemical Education
Descriptors: *Achievement Tests; Chemical Analysis; *Chemistry; Data Analysis; Higher Education; Multiple Choice Tests; *Undergraduate Students
Identifiers: Acid Base Chemistry; *American Chemical Society Cooperative Examinations; Analytical Methods; Oxides; *Quantitative Analysis; Solubility
Availability: ACS DivCHED Examinations Institute; Oklahoma State University, 107 Physical Sciences, Stillwater, OK 74078-0447
Grade Level: 13-16
Notes: Time, 50 min.; Items, 90

Appropriate for use in a one-semester course in analytical chemistry or quantitative analysis offered to second-, and third-year chemistry students. Also suitable for terminal courses for nonmajors. Covers gravimetric, volumetric, spectrophotometric, and electrometric analysis, and complexímetry, pH and buffers, solubility, analytical separations, data evaluation, oxidation-reduction, and indicators. Test forms are updated periodically, and older forms may be retired from active use. Retired college-level forms may be released to high school teachers.

11256
ACS Cooperative Examination: Instrumental Determinations (Analysis). American Chemical Society, Tampa, FL, Div. of Chemical Education
Descriptors: *Achievement Tests; Atomic Structure; Chemical Analysis; *Chemistry; Higher Education; Kinetics; Multiple Choice Tests; Spectroscopy; *Undergraduate Students; Chromatography
Identifiers: *American Chemical Society Cooperative Examinations; Electrochemistry; Electrons; Emission; Radiochemistry
Availability: ACS DivCHED Examinations Institute; Oklahoma State University, 107 Physical Sciences, Stillwater, OK 74078-0447
Grade Level: 13-16
Notes: Time, 110 min.; Items, 75

Intended for use with third or fourth year students who have taken a modern course dealing with instrumental methods. Covers electroanalytical chemistry, spectrophotometry, instrumentation, chromatography, choice of method for analytical situations, NMR, EDR, emission spectroscopy, atomic absorption spectroscopy, radiochemical methods, thermal methods, mass spectrometry, electron probe and kinetics. Test forms are updated periodically, and older forms may be retired from active use. Retired college-level forms may be released to high school teachers.

11258
ACS Cooperative Examination: Physical Chemistry—Chemical Dynamics. American Chemical Society, Tampa, FL, Div. of Chemical Education
Descriptors: *Achievement Tests; Chemical Equilibrium; *Chemistry; Higher Education; Matter; Multiple Choice Tests; *Undergraduate Students; *Physical Chemistry
Identifiers: *American Chemical Society Cooperative Examinations; *Chemical Dynamics; Electrochemistry
Availability: ACS DivCHED Examinations Institute; Oklahoma State University, 107 Physical Sciences, Stillwater, OK 74078-0447
Grade Level: 13-16
Notes: Time, 90 min.; Items, 45

Designed for use in quarter or semester courses. Covers equilibrium, electrochemistry, states of matter, phase equilibria. Can be combined with thermodynamics (TC011259). Test forms are updated periodically, and older forms may be retired from active use. Retired college-level forms may be released to high school teachers.

11259
ACS Cooperative Examination: Physical Chemistry Thermodynamics. American Chemical Society, Tampa, FL, Div. of Chemical Education
Descriptors: *Achievement Tests; Chemical Equilibrium; *Chemistry; Higher Education; Matter; Multiple Choice Tests; *Thermodynamics; *Undergraduate Students; *Physical Chemistry
Identifiers: *American Chemical Society; Cooperative Examinations; Electrochemistry
Availability: ACS DivCHED Examinations Institute; Oklahoma State University, 107 Physical Sciences, Stillwater, OK 74078-0447
Grade Level: 13-16
Notes: Time, 90 min.; Items, 45

Covers equilibrium, electrochemistry, states of matter, and phase equilibria. Used at the end of a quarter or semester course or combined with chemical dynamics (TC011258). Test forms are updated periodically, and older forms may be retired from active use. Retired college-level forms may be released to high school teachers.

11260
ACS Cooperative Examination: Physical Chemistry. American Chemical Society, Tampa, FL, Div. of Chemical Education
Descriptors: *Achievement Tests; Chemical Equilibrium; *Chemistry; Higher Education; Multiple Choice Tests; Spectroscopy; Thermodynamics; *Undergraduate Students; *Physical Chemistry
Identifiers: *American Chemical Society Cooperative Examinations; Quantum Chemistry
Availability: ACS DivCHED Examinations Institute; Oklahoma State University, 107 Physical Sciences, Stillwater, OK 74078-0447
Grade Level: 13-16
Notes: Time, 110 min.; Items, 49

An end-of-year test covering chemical thermodynamics and equilibrium, electrochemistry; states of matter and phase equilibria. Test forms are updated periodically, and older forms may be retired from active use. Retired college-level forms may be released to high school teachers.

11261
ACS Cooperative Examination: Physical Chemistry—Thermodynamics. American Chemical Society, Tampa, FL, Div. of Chemical Education
Descriptors: *Achievement Tests; Chemical Equilibrium; *Chemistry; Higher Education; Matter; Multiple Choice Tests; *Thermodynamics; *Undergraduate Students; *Physical Chemistry
Identifiers: *American Chemical Society Cooperative Examinations; Electrochemistry
Availability: ACS DivCHED Examinations Institute; Oklahoma State University, 107 Physical Sciences, Stillwater, OK 74078-0447
Grade Level: 13-16
Notes: Time, 90 min.; Items, 45

Used at the end of a quarter or semester course or combined with chemical dynamics (TC011262) and quantum chemistry (TC011263) for an end-of-year test. Covers equilibrium, electrochemistry, states of matter, phase equilibria. Test forms are updated periodically, and older forms may be retired from active use. Retired college-level forms may be released to high school teachers.

11262
ACS Cooperative Examination: Physical Chemistry—Chemical Dynamics. American Chemical Society, Tampa, FL, Div. of Chemical Education
Descriptors: *Achievement Tests; Chemical Reactions; *Chemistry; Higher Education; Kinetics; Multiple Choice Tests; *Undergraduate Students; *Physical Chemistry
Identifiers: *American Chemical Society Cooperative Examinations; *Chemical Dynamics; Gases; Transportability
Availability: ACS DivCHED Examinations Institute; Oklahoma State University, 107 Physical Sciences, Stillwater, OK 74078-0447
Grade Level: 13-16
Notes: Time, 90 min.; Items, 45

Used at the end of a quarter or semester course or combined with thermodynamics (TC011261) and quantum chemistry (TC011263) for an end-of-year test. Covers reaction rate theory, kinetic theory of gases, and transport phenomena. Test forms are updated periodically, and older forms may be retired from active use. Retired college-level forms may be released to high school teachers.

11263
ACS Cooperative Examination: Physical Chemistry—Quantum Chemistry. American Chemical Society, Tampa, FL, Div. of Chemical Education
Descriptors: *Achievement Tests; Atomic Structure; *Chemistry; Higher Education; Molecular Structure; Multiple Choice Tests; Quantum Mechanics; Spectroscopy; *Undergraduate Students; *Physical Chemistry

Identifiers: *American Chemical Society Cooperative Examinations; *Quantum Chemistry; Solid State Chemistry; Statistical Mechanics
Availability: ACS DivCHED Examinations Institute; Oklahoma State University, 107 Physical Sciences, Stillwater, OK 74078-0447
Grade Level: 13-16
Notes: Time, 90 min.; Items, 45
Used at the end of a quarter or semester course or combined with thermodynamics (TC011261) and chemical dynamics (TC011262) for an end-of-year test. Covers basic quantum mechanics, atomic structure, molecular structure, spectroscopy, statistical mechanics, solid state. Test forms are updated periodically, and older forms may be retired from active use. Retired college-level forms may be released to high school teachers.

11268
ACS Cooperative Examination: Polymer Chemistry. American Chemical Society, Tampa, FL, Div. of Chemical Education
Descriptors: *Achievement Tests; *Chemistry; *Graduate Students; Higher Education; Kinetics; Multiple Choice Tests; Organic Chemistry; *Undergraduate Students; Physical Chemistry
Identifiers: *American Chemical Society Cooperative Examinations; *Polymer Chemistry
Availability: ACS DivCHED Examinations Institute; Oklahoma State University, 107 Physical Sciences, Stillwater, OK 74078-0447
Grade Level: 13-16
Notes: Time, 110 min.; Items, 70
For use in introductory undergraduate polymer courses of 1 or 2 semesters. Suitable for admissions or placement of incoming graduate students. Covers organics, thermokinetics, characterization, physical behavior, and general questions. Test forms are updated periodically, and older forms may be retired from active use. Retired college-level forms may be released to high school teachers.

11269
National Assessment of Educational Progress: Released Items. Education Commission of the States, Denver, CO 1970
Subtests: Art; Career and Occupational Development; Citizenship/Social Studies; Math; Music; Reading/Literature; Science; Writing; Energy; Health; Literacy and Reading
Descriptors: *Achievement Tests; Adolescents; Adults; Art; Attitude Measures; Career Development; Children; Citizenship; Energy; Health; *Item Banks; Knowledge Level; Literacy; Literature; Mathematics; Music; National Surveys; Reading; Sciences; Social Studies; Test Construction; Writing (Composition)
Identifiers: NAEP; National Institute of Education
Availability: National Assessment of Educational Progress; Publication Order Services, Box 2923, Princeton, NJ 08541
Age Level: 9; 13; 17; 26-35
Items used in previous surveys of the knowledge, skills, attitudes, and understanding of young Americans. Sponsored by the National Institute of Education. Constructed to aid states or other education units in building their own tests. Many are available from the Educational Resources Information Center (ED186231; ED145201; ED187543; ED205588; ED205589; ED161686; ED205583; ED155-728).

11271
ACS Cooperative Examination: Inorganic Chemistry. American Chemical Society, Tampa, FL, Div. of Chemical Education
Descriptors: *Achievement Tests; Chemical Bonding; Chemical Nomenclature; Chemical Reactions; *Chemistry; Coordination Compounds; Higher Education; Molecular Structure; Multiple Choice Tests; Thermodynamics; *Undergraduate Students; *Inorganic Chemistry
Identifiers: *American Chemical Society Cooperative Examinations
Availability: ACS DivCHED Examinations Institute; Oklahoma State University, 107 Physical Sciences, Stillwater, OK 74078-0447
Grade Level: 13-16
Notes: Time, 60 min.; Items, 110
Covers theoretical and descriptive inorganic chemistry including nomenclature, bonding, structure, reaction mechanisms, coordination chemistry, and thermodynamics of inorganic elements and compounds. Used with a course that parallels or follows an elementary physical science course. Test forms are updated periodically, and older forms may be retired from active use. Retired college-level forms may be released to high school teachers.

11283
ACS Cooperative Examination: General-Organic-Biochemistry. American Chemical Society, Tampa, FL, Div. of Chemical Education
Subtests: General Chemistry; Organic Chemistry; Biological Chemistry

Descriptors: *Achievement Tests; *Biochemistry; *Chemistry; Higher Education; High Schools; *High School Students; Multiple Choice Tests; *Organic Chemistry; *Undergraduate Students
Identifiers: Allied Health Sciences Programs; *American Chemical Society Cooperative Examinations
Availability: ACS DivCHED Examinations Institute; Oklahoma State University, 107 Physical Sciences, Stillwater, OK 74078-0447
Grade Level: 9-16
Notes: Time, 165 min.; Items, 180
For use with courses covering basic material that are 3 months to 1 year in length. Each subtest consists of 2 parts that can be used separately as unit tests or combined as end-of-course tests. Test forms are updated periodically, and older forms may be retired from active use. Retired college-level forms may be released to high school teachers. This test has been retired from college use and has been released for use in high schools.

11284
ACS-NSTA Cooperative Examination: High School Chemistry, Advanced. American Chemical Society, Tampa, FL, Div. of Chemical Education
Descriptors: *Achievement Tests; Advanced Courses; Atomic Structure; Chemical Bonding; *Chemistry; *College Freshmen; Higher Education; High Schools; *High School Students; Honors Curriculum; Kinetics; Laboratory Procedures; Matter; Molecular Structure; Multiple Choice Tests; Student Placement; Thermodynamics
Identifiers: Acid Base Chemistry; *American Chemical Society Cooperative Examinations; Carbon; Descriptive Chemistry; Electrochemistry; *National Science Teachers Association; Periodic Law; Stoichiometry
Availability: ACS DivCHED Examinations Institute; Oklahoma State University, 107 Physical Sciences, Stillwater, OK 74078-0447
Grade Level: 9-13
Notes: Time, 100 min.; Items, 60
Designed for use in honors or advanced courses. Written at the first-year college level. May be used for placement in college. Uses general and quantitative questions covering 10 areas: atomic structure (including nuclear); chemical bonding; molecular geometry and carbon chemistry; thermodynamics; kinetics; solids, liquids, gases and solutions; acid-base chemistry; electrochemistry; chemical periodicity; descriptive chemistry and stoichiometry; laboratory procedures and techniques. Test forms are updated periodically, and older forms may be retired from active use. Retired college-level forms may be released to high school teachers.

11285
ACS-NSTA Cooperative Examination: High School Chemistry. American Chemical Society, Tampa, FL, Div. of Chemical Education
Subtests: Introductory Concepts; Physical Concepts; Atomic and Molecular Concepts; Solutions Concepts
Descriptors: *Achievement Tests; Atomic Structure; Chemical Bonding; *Chemistry; Environmental Research; High Schools; *High School Students; Kinetics; Laboratory Procedures; Matter; Molecular Structure; Multiple Choice Tests; Nuclear Energy; Organic Chemistry; Thermodynamics; Physical Chemistry
Identifiers: Acid Base Chemistry; *American Chemical Society Cooperative Examinations; Descriptive Chemistry; Electrochemistry; Gases; *National Science Teachers Association; Periodic Table; Solubility; Stoichiometry
Availability: ACS DivCHED Examinations Institute; Oklahoma State University, 107 Physical Sciences, Stillwater, OK 74078-0447
Grade Level: 9-12
Notes: Time, 80 min.; Items, 80
Designed for use in testing the average student. Covers fundamental concepts and the application of basic principles in areas such as structure and bonding; acid base chemistry; and periodic charts and similar concepts appearing in textbooks, including laboratory techniques, descriptive chemistry, stoichiometric calculations, states of matter, gas laws, thermochemistry, kinetics, equilibrium, electrochemistry, organic chemistry, environmental topics, and nuclear chemistry. Test forms are updated periodically, and older forms may be retired from active use. Retired college-level forms may be released to high school teachers.

11288
ACS Cooperative Examination: Brief Physical Chemistry (Life Sciences). American Chemical Society, Tampa, FL, Div. of Chemical Education
Descriptors: *Physical Chemistry; *Achievement Tests; *Biological Sciences; *Chemistry; Higher Education; Multiple Choice Tests; *Undergraduate Students

Identifiers: *American Chemical Society; Cooperative Examinations
Availability: ACS DivCHED Examinations Institute; Oklahoma State University, 107 Physical Sciences, Stillwater, OK 74078-0447
Grade Level: 13-16
Notes: Time, 90 min.; Items, 50
Designed for use in a one-semester terminal course in physical chemistry for which calculus is not a prerequisite. Test forms are updated periodically, and older forms may be retired from active use. Retired college-level forms may be released to high school teachers.

11289
ACS Cooperative Examination: Toledo Chemistry Placement Examination. American Chemical Society, Tampa, FL, Div. of Chemical Education
Descriptors: *Achievement Tests; Algebra; Arithmetic; Chemical Nomenclature; *Chemistry; *College Freshmen; Higher Education; Mathematical Formulas; Multiple Choice Tests; Problem Solving; Student Placement; Undergraduate Students
Identifiers: *American Chemical Society Cooperative Examinations; Formulaic Expressions
Availability: ACS DivCHED Examinations Institute; Oklahoma State University, 107 Physical Sciences, Stillwater, OK 74078-0447
Grade Level: 13
Notes: Time, 55 min.; Items, 67
Designed to assess the background of beginning first-year college students for the purpose of determining the appropriate level of chemistry course. Covers background in arithmetic and algebra, general knowledge, formulas and nomenclature, equations, algebraic formulations, and chemical problems. Test forms are updated periodically, and older forms may be retired from active use. Retired college-level forms may be released to high school teachers.

11290
ACS Cooperative Examination: Analytical Chemistry, Graduate Level. American Chemical Society, Tampa, FL, Div. of Chemical Education
Descriptors: *Achievement Tests; Biochemistry; Chemical Analysis; *Chemistry; *Graduate Students; Higher Education; Multiple Choice Tests; Student Placement; Chemical Engineering
Identifiers: *American Chemical Society Cooperative Examinations; Analytical Methods
Availability: ACS DivCHED Examinations Institute; Oklahoma State University, 107 Physical Sciences, Stillwater, OK 74078-0447
Grade Level: 17-20
Notes: Time, 110 min.; Items, 35
For use in departments of chemistry, chemical engineering, and biochemistry that give training leading to master's or doctoral degrees. Covers subject matter taught in modern undergraduate programs preparatory for graduate work in chemistry. May not be administered to undergraduates. Test forms are updated periodically, and older forms may be retired from active use. Retired college-level forms may be released to high school teachers.

11295
ACS Cooperative Examination: Organic Chemistry, Graduate Level. American Chemical Society, Tampa, FL, Div. of Chemical Education
Descriptors: *Achievement Tests; Chemical Engineering; Biochemistry; *Chemistry; *Graduate Students; Higher Education; Multiple Choice Tests; *Organic Chemistry; Student Placement
Identifiers: *American Chemical Society Cooperative Examinations
Availability: ACS DivCHED Examinations Institute; Oklahoma State University, 107 Physical Sciences, Stillwater, OK 74078-0447
Grade Level: 17
Notes: Time, 110 min.; Items, 75
For use in departments of chemistry, chemical engineering, and biochemistry that give training leading to master's or doctoral degrees. Covers subject matter taught in modern undergraduate programs preparatory for graduate work in chemistry. May not be administered to undergraduates. Test forms are updated periodically, and older forms may be retired from active use. Retired college-level forms may be released to high school teachers.

11297
ACS Cooperative Examination: Physical Chemistry, Graduate Level. American Chemical Society, Tampa, FL, Div. of Chemical Education
Descriptors: *Achievement Tests; *Physical Chemistry; Chemical Engineering; *Chemistry; *Graduate Students; Higher Education; Multiple Choice Tests; Student Placement
Identifiers: *American Chemical Society Cooperative Examinations
Availability: ACS DivCHED Examinations Institute; Oklahoma State University, 107 Physical Sciences, Stillwater, OK 74078-0447
Grade Level: 17-20

Notes: Time, 120 min.; Items, 60

For use in departments of chemistry, chemical engineering, and biochemistry that give training leading to master's or doctoral degrees. Covers subject matter taught in modern undergraduate programs preparatory for graduate work in chemistry. May not be administered to undergraduates. Test forms are updated periodically, and older forms may be retired from active use. Retired college-level forms may be released to high school teachers.

11301

Nelson Denny Reading Test. Form F. Brown, James I.; And Others 1981

Subtests: Vocabulary; Comprehension and Rate

Descriptors: Academic Aptitude; *Achievement Tests; Adults; *College Students; Higher Education; High Schools; *High School Students; *Reading Achievement; *Reading Comprehension; Reading Diagnosis; Reading Rate; *Reading Tests; Screening Tests; *Vocabulary Development

Availability: Riverside Publishing; 8420 Bryn Mawr Ave., Chicago, IL 60631

Grade Level: 9-16

Notes: Time, 35 min.; Items, 136

Used primarily to assess student ability in reading comprehension, vocabulary development, and reading rate. May also be used as a screening test, for predicting academic success, and as a diagnostic tool. Available in 2 forms.

11317

Comprehensive Tests of Basic Skills. Form U, Level A. CTB/Macmillan/McGraw-Hill, Monterey, CA 1981

Subtests: Visual Recognition; Sound Recognition; Vocabulary; Oral Comprehension; Mathematics Concepts and Applications

Descriptors: *Achievement Tests; Basic Skills; *Elementary School Mathematics; *Kindergarten Children; *Mathematics Achievement; Norm Referenced Tests; Primary Education; *Reading Achievement

Identifiers: CTBS(U); Oral Tests; Test Batteries

Availability: CTB/MacMillan/McGraw Hill; Del Monte Research Park, 2500 Garden Rd., Monterey, CA 93940

Grade Level: K

Notes: Time, 68 min.; Items, 81

One of a series of norm-referenced achievement tests designed to measure achievement in the basic skills commonly found in state and school district curricula. Cognitive processes assessed include recall, explicit information skills, inferential reasoning, and evaluation. Level A tests in 2 basic content areas: reading and mathematics. A practice test is also available and should be administered early on the day of testing or the day before testing. It consists of 10 items. A review of this test by L. M. Schell appears in the *Journal of Reading;* v27 p586-89, Apr 1984.

11318

Comprehensive Tests of Basic Skills. Form U, Level B. CTB/Macmillan/McGraw-Hill, Monterey, CA 1981

Subtests: Word Attack; Vocabulary; Oral Comprehension; Language Expression; Mathematics Concepts and Applications

Descriptors: *Achievement Tests; Basic Skills; *Elementary School Mathematics; Elementary School Students; *Grade 1; *Kindergarten Children; *Language Usage; Mathematics Achievement; Norm Referenced Tests; Primary Education; *Reading Achievement

Identifiers: CTBS(U); Oral Tests; Test Batteries

Availability: CTB/MacMillan/McGraw Hill; Del Monte Research Park, 2500 Garden Rd., Monterey, CA 93940

Grade Level: K-1

Notes: Time, 72 min.

One of a series of norm-referenced achievement tests designed to measure achievement in the basic skills commonly found in state and school district curricula. Cognitive processes assessed include recall, explicit information skills, inferential reasoning, and evaluation. Level B contains tests in 3 basic content areas: reading, language, and mathematics. A practice test, consisting of 11 items, can be administered early on the day of testing or on the day before testing. A review of this test by L. M. Schell appears in the *Journal of Reading;* v27 p586-89, Apr 1984.

11319

Comprehensive Tests of Basic Skills. Form U, Level C. CTB/Macmillan/McGraw-Hill, Monterey, CA 1981

Subtests: Word Attack; Vocabulary; Reading Comprehension; Language Expression; Mathematics Computation; Mathematics Concepts and Applications

Descriptors: *Achievement Tests; Basic Skills; Elementary School Mathematics; Elementary School Students; *Grade 1; *Language Usage; *Mathematics Achievement; Norm Referenced Tests; Primary Education; *Reading Achievement

Identifiers: CTBS(U); Test Batteries

Availability: CTB/MacMillan/McGraw Hill; Del Monte Research Park, 2500 Garden Rd., Monterey, CA 93940

Grade Level: 1

Notes: Time, 119 min.; Items, 145

One of a series of norm-referenced achievement tests designed to measure achievement in the basic skills commonly found in state and school district curricula. Cognitive processes assessed include recall, explicit information skills, inferential reasoning, and evaluation. Level C tests in 3 basic content areas: reading, language, and mathematics. A practice test, consisting of 11 items, can be administered early on the day of testing or the day before testing. A locator test, to determine the appropriate level of CTBS to administer, is optional. A review of this test by L. M. Schell appears in the *Journal of Reading;* v27 p586-89, Apr 1984.

11320

Comprehensive Tests of Basic Skills. Form U, Level D. CTB/Macmillan/McGraw-Hill, Monterey, CA 1981

Subtests: Word Attack; Vocabulary; Reading Comprehension; Spelling; Language Mechanics; Language Expression; Mathematics Computation; Mathematics Concepts and Applications; Science; Social Studies

Descriptors: *Achievement Tests; Basic Skills; Elementary School Mathematics; *Elementary School Science; Elementary School Students; *Grade 1; *Grade 2; Language Usage; *Mathematics Achievement; Norm Referenced Tests; Primary Education; *Reading Achievement; *Social Studies; Spelling

Identifiers: CTBS(U); Test Batteries

Availability: CTB/MacMillan/McGraw Hill; Del Monte Research Park, 2500 Garden Rd., Monterey, CA 93940

Grade Level: 1-2

Notes: Time, 204 min.; Items, 260

One of a series of norm-referenced achievement tests designed to measure achievement in the basic skills commonly found in state and school district curricula. Cognitive processes assessed include recall, explicit information skills, inferential reasoning, and evaluation. Level D contains tests in 6 basic content areas: reading, spelling, language, mathematics, science, and social studies. A practice test, consisting of 11 items, can be administered early on the day of testing or the day before testing. A locator test, to determine the appropriate level of CTBS to administer, is optional. A review of this test by L. M. Schell appears in the *Journal of Reading;* v27 p586-89, Apr 1984.

11321

Comprehensive Tests of Basic Skills. Form U, Level E. CTB/Macmillan/McGraw-Hill, Monterey, CA 1981

Subtests: Word Attack; Vocabulary; Reading Comprehension; Spelling; Language Mechanics; Language Expression; Mathematics Computation; Mathematics Concepts and Applications; Science; Social Studies

Descriptors: *Achievement Tests; Basic Skills; Elementary School Mathematics; *Elementary School Science; Elementary School Students; *Grade 2; *Grade 3; Language Usage; *Mathematics Achievement; Norm Referenced Tests; Primary Education; *Reading Achievement; *Social Studies; Spelling

Identifiers: CTBS(U); Test Batteries

Availability: CTB/MacMillan/McGraw Hill; Del Monte Research Park, 2500 Garden Rd., Monterey, CA 93940

Grade Level: 2-3

Notes: Time, 228 min.; Items, 301

One of a series of norm-referenced achievement tests designed to measure achievement in the basic skills commonly found in state and school district curricula. Cognitive processes assessed include recall, explicit information skills, inferential reasoning, and evaluation. Level E contains tests in 6 basic content areas: reading, spelling, language, mathematics, science, and social studies. A practice test, containing 11 items, can be administered early on the day of testing or the day before testing. A locator test, to determine the appropriate level of CTBS to administer, is optional. A review of this test by L. M. Schell appears in the *Journal of Reading;* v27 p586-89, Apr 1984.

11322

Comprehensive Tests of Basic Skills. Form U, Level F. CTB/Macmillan/McGraw-Hill, Monterey, CA 1981

Subtests: Vocabulary; Reading Comprehension; Spelling; Language Mechanics; Language Expression; Mathematics Computation; Mathematics Concepts and Applications; Reference Skills; Science; Social Studies

Descriptors: *Achievement Tests; Basic Skills; Elementary Education; Elementary School Mathematics; *Elementary School Science; Elementary School Students; *Grade 3; *Grade 4; Language Usage; *Mathematics Achievement; Norm Referenced Tests; *Reading Achievement; *Social Studies; Spelling; Study Skills

Identifiers: CTBS(U); Reference Skills; Test Batteries

Availability: CTB/MacMillan/McGraw Hill; Del Monte Research Park, 2500 Garden Rd., Monterey, CA 93940

Grade Level: 3-4

Notes: Time, 278 min.; Items, 380

One of a series of norm-referenced achievement tests designed to measure achievement in the basic skills commonly found in state and school district curricula. Cognitive processes assessed include recall, explicit information skills, inferential reasoning, and evaluation. The complete battery contains tests in 7 basic content areas: reading, spelling, language, mathematics, reference skills, science, and social studies. A practice test, containing 9 items, can be administered early on the day of testing or the day before testing. A locator test, to determine the appropriate level of the CTBS to administer, is optional. A review of this test by L. M. Schell appears in the *Journal of Reading;* v27 p586-89, Apr 1984.

11323

Comprehensive Tests of Basic Skills. Form U, Level G. CTB/Macmillan/McGraw-Hill, Monterey, CA 1981

Subtests: Vocabulary; Reading Comprehension; Spelling; Language Mechanics; Language Expression; Mathematics Computation; Mathematics Concepts and Applications; Reference Skills; Science; Social Studies

Descriptors: *Achievement Tests; Basic Skills; Elementary School Mathematics; *Elementary School Science; *Elementary School Students; Intermediate Grades; Language Usage; *Mathematics Achievement; Norm Referenced Tests; *Reading Achievement; *Social Studies; Spelling; Study Skills

Identifiers: CTBS(U); Reference Skills; Test Batteries

Availability: CTB/MacMillan/McGraw Hill; Del Monte Research Park, 2500 Garden Rd., Monterey, CA 93940

Grade Level: 4-6

Notes: Time, 278 min.; Items, 380

One of a series of norm-referenced achievement tests designed to measure achievement in the basic skills commonly found in state and school district curricula. Cognitive processes assessed include recall, explicit information skills, inferential reasoning, and evaluation. The complete battery contains tests in 7 basic content areas: reading, spelling, language, mathematics, reference skills, science, and social studies. A practice test, containing 9 items, can be administered early on the day of testing or the day before testing. A locator test, to determine the appropriate level of the CTBS to administer, is optional. A review of this test by L. M. Schell appears in the *Journal of Reading;* v27 p586-89, Apr 1984.

11324

Comprehensive Tests of Basic Skills. Form U, Level H. CTB/Macmillan/McGraw-Hill, Monterey, CA 1981

Subtests: Vocabulary; Reading Comprehension; Spelling; Language Mechanics; Language Expression; Mathematics Computation; Mathematics Concepts and Applications; Reference Skills; Science; Social Studies

Descriptors: *Achievement Tests; Basic Skills; Elementary Education; Elementary School Mathematics; *Elementary School Science; *Elementary School Students; Junior High Schools; *Junior High School Students; Language Usage; *Mathematics Achievement; Norm Referenced Tests; *Reading Achievement; *Social Studies; Spelling; Study Skills

Identifiers: CTBS(U); Reference Skills; Test Batteries

Availability: CTB/MacMillan/McGraw Hill; Del Monte Research Park, 2500 Garden Rd., Monterey, CA 93940

Grade Level: 6-8

Notes: Time, 278 min.; Items, 380

One of a series of norm-referenced achievement tests designed to measure achievement in the basic skills commonly found in state and school district curricula. Cognitive processes assessed include recall, explicit information skills, inferential reasoning, and evaluation. The complete battery contains tests in 7 basic content areas: reading, spelling, language, mathematics, reference skills, science, and social studies. A practice test, containing 9 items, can be administered early on the day of testing or the day before testing. A locator test, to determine the appropriate level of the CTBS to administer, is optional. A review of this test by L. M. Schell appears in the *Journal of Reading*; v27 p586-89, Apr 1984.

11325
Comprehensive Tests of Basic Skills. Form U, Level J. CTB/Macmillan/McGraw-Hill, Monterey, CA 1981
Subtests: Vocabulary; Reading Comprehension; Spelling; Language Mechanics; Language Expression; Mathematics Computation; Mathematics Concepts and Applications; Reference Skills; Science; Social Studies
Descriptors: *Achievement Tests; Basic Skills; Language Usage; *Mathematics Achievement; Norm Referenced Tests; *Reading Achievement; Secondary Education; Secondary School Mathematics; *Secondary School Science; *Secondary School Students; *Social Studies; Spelling; Study Skills
Identifiers: CTBS(U); Reference Skills; Test Batteries
Availability: CTB/Macmillan/McGraw Hill; Del Monte Research Park, 2500 Garden Rd., Monterey, CA 93940
Grade Level: 8-12
Notes: Time, 278 min.; Items, 380

One of a series of norm-referenced achievement tests designed to measure achievement in the basic skills commonly found in state and school district curricula. Cognitive processes assessed include recall, explicit information skills, inferential reasoning, and evaluation. The complete battery contains tests in 7 basic content areas: reading, spelling, language, mathematics, reference skills, science, and social studies. A practice test, containing 9 items, can be administered early on the day of testing or the day before testing. A locator test, to determine the appropriate level of the CTBS to administer, is optional. A review of this test by L. M. Schell appears in the *Journal of Reading*; v27 p586-89, Apr 1984.

11334
Language Assessment Scales. English Level II, Form A. Duncan, Sharon E.; DeAvila, Edward A. 1981
Subtests: Minimal Pairs; Lexical; Phonemes; Sentence Comprehension; Oral Production; Observations
Descriptors: Communicative Competence (Languages); English; *Grade 6; Individual Testing; *Language Proficiency; *Language Tests; Nouns; *Oral Language; Phonology; Secondary Education; *Secondary School Students; Syntax
Identifiers: LAS
Availability: Publishers Test Service; 2500 Garden Rd., Monterey, CA 93940
Grade Level: 6-12
Notes: Time, 20 min. approx.; Items, 101

Measures oral language proficiency in Spanish or English. This test of oral language proficiency samples from each of 4 linguistic aspects: phonology, the lexicon, syntax, and pragmatics. Individually administered.

11335
Language Assessment Scales. Spanish Level II, Form A. Duncan, Sharon E.; DeAvila, Edward A. 1981
Subtests: Minimal Pairs; Lexical; Phonemes; Sentence Comprehension; Oral Production; Observation
Descriptors: Communicative Competence (Languages); *Grade 6; Individual Testing; *Language Proficiency; *Language Tests; Nouns; *Oral Language; Phonology; Secondary Education; *Secondary School Students; *Spanish; Syntax
Identifiers: LAS
Availability: Publishers Test Service; 2500 Garden Rd., Monterey, CA 93940
Grade Level: 6-12
Notes: Time, 20 min. approx.; Items, 101

Measures oral language proficiency in Spanish or English. This test of oral language proficiency samples from each of 4 linguistic aspects: phonology, the lexicon, syntax, and pragmatics. Individually administered.

11336
Language Assessment Scales. Spanish Level I, Form A. DeAvila, Edward A.; Duncan, Sharon E. 1981
Subtests: Minimal Sound Pairs; Lexical; Phonemes; Comprehension; Oral Production
Descriptors: Communicative Competence (Languages); Elementary Education; *Elementary School Students; Individual Testing; *Language Proficiency; *Language Tests; Nouns; *Oral Language; Phonology; *Spanish; Syntax
Identifiers: LAS

Availability: Publishers Test Service; 2500 Garden Rd., Monterey, CA 93940
Grade Level: K-5
Notes: Time, 20 min. approx.; Items, 97

Measures oral language proficiency in English or Spanish. This test of oral language proficiency samples from each of 4 linguistic aspects: phonology, the lexicon, syntax, and pragmatics. Individually administered.

11341
Test on Responsibility for Middle School Students. Singh, Balwant; Gearhart, E.B. 1980
Descriptors: *Citizenship Responsibility; Curriculum; Junior High Schools; *Junior High School Students; Multiple Choice Tests; *Responsibility
Identifiers: California Bar Association; Law in a Free Society
Availability: ERIC Document Reproduction Service; 7420 Fullerton Rd., Ste. 110, Springfield, VA 22153-2852 (ED206711, 17 p.)
Grade Level: 7-9
Notes: Items, 50

Designed for the Responsibility Unit of the Law in a Free Society. Materials published by the California Bar Association.

11353
S-D Primary ESL Inventory. Sheety, John A. 1981
Subtests: Vocabulary-Nouns; Simple Comprehension and Understanding Directions; Verb Tense and Preposition Use; Spelling and Vocabulary; Sentence Structure; Reading Comprehension
Descriptors: *Achievement Tests; Elementary Education; *Elementary School Students; *English (Second Language); *Foreign Students; *Junior High School Students; *Language Skills; Language Tests; Reading Comprehension; *Second Language Learning; Student Placement
Availability: Stoelting Co.; 620 Wheat Ln., Wood Dale, IL 60191
Grade Level: 1-8
Notes: Time, 35 min. approx.; Items, 60

Designed to measure foreign student's achievement in the English language. Provides a primary level of achievement based on learned material and identifies improvement within the prescribed context of the English language. Can be used as a tool for class placement. Inventory is available in 2 forms. This is primarily a power test, but working time should not exceed 35 minutes.

11354
A Taxonomy of Selected High School Equivalency Materials. Reading Social Studies Materials, Supplementary Inventory. New York State Education Dept., Albany, Bureau of General Education Curriculum Development 1976
Descriptors: Adults; Classification; *Equivalency Tests; High School Equivalency Programs; *Reading Comprehension; *Reading Skills; *Social Studies; *Test Items
Identifiers: *General Educational Development Tests
Availability: ERIC Document Reproduction Service; 7420 Fullerton Rd., Ste. 110, Springfield, VA 22153-2852 (ED163064, microfiche only)
Age Level: Adults
Notes: Items, 50

Tailored to skills tested on the reading skills test of the new form of the General Educational Development Tests (GED) to provide high school equivalency instructors with a means of assessing these skills. Assesses only those skills required for reading social studies-related materials. Once students' responses are evaluated, instructor can analyze weaknesses and prescribe instruction, using the designated card from *A Taxonomy of Selected High School Equivalency Materials* (ED114766).

11355
Taxonomy of Selected High School Equivalency Materials. Reading Science Materials, Supplementary Inventory. New York State Education Dept., Albany, Bureau of General Education Curriculum Development 1976
Descriptors: Adults; Classification; *Equivalency Tests; High School Equivalency Programs; *Natural Sciences; *Reading Skills; *Science Tests; *Scientific Literacy; *Test Items
Identifiers: *General Educational Development Tests
Availability: ERIC Document Reproduction Service; 7420 Fullerton Rd., Ste. 110, Springfield, VA 22153-2852 (ED163065, microfiche only)
Age Level: Adults
Notes: Items, 52

Tailored to skills tested on the reading skills test of the new form of the General Educational Development Tests (GED) to provide high school equivalency instructors with a means of assessing these skills. Assesses only those skills required for reading science-related materials. Once student's responses are evaluated, instructor can analyze

weaknesses and prescribe instruction, using the designated card from *A Taxonomy of Selected High School Equivalency Materials (Reading)* (ED114766).

11361
Language Assessment Scales. English Level 1, Form A. DeAvila, Edward A.; Duncan, Sharon E. 1981
Subtests: Minimal Sound Pairs; Lexical; Phonemes; Comprehension; Oral Production
Descriptors: Communicative Competence (Languages); Elementary Education; *Elementary School Students; English; Individual Testing; *Language Proficiency; *Language Tests; Nouns; *Oral Language; Phonology; Syntax
Identifiers: LAS
Availability: Publishers Test Service; 2500 Garden Rd., Monterey, CA 93940
Grade Level: K-5
Notes: Time, 20 min. approx.; Items, 97

Measures oral language proficiency in Spanish or English. This test of oral language proficiency samples from each of 4 linguistic aspects: phonology, the lexicon, syntax, and pragmatics. Individually administered.

11378
Ohio Vocational Achievement Tests: Agricultural Education, Agricultural Mechanic. Ohio State Dept. of Education, Div. of Vocational Education, Columbus, OH 1981
Subtests: Service and Repair Engines; Carburetion Systems; Diesel Engines; Cooling Systems; Hydraulic Systems; Brakes and Steering; Equipment Assembly; Charging Systems and Accessories; Cranking Systems; Ignition Systems; Power Trains and Transmissions; Metal Fabrication and Refinishing; Heating, Ventilation and Air Conditioning; Personal Development
Descriptors: *Achievement Tests; *Agricultural Education; *Agricultural Engineering; *Agricultural Machinery Occupations; Auto Mechanics; Data Analysis; Diesel Engines; Grade 11; Grade 12; High Schools; *High School Students; Individual Development; Knowledge Level; Problem Solving; Repair; Synthesis; *Vocational Education
Availability: Ohio State University, Instructional Materials Laboratory; 1885 Neil Ave., Columbus, OH 43210
Grade Level: 11-12
Notes: Time, 240 min.; Items, 343

For use in the evaluation and diagnosis of vocational achievement. Developed to measure skills and understandings in specific vocational areas. Items measure ability to solve problems, analyze data, recall facts, have a knowledge of principles, react to generalizations, use abstractions in specific situations, and form parts into complete structures. Administered with the California Short Form Test of Academic Aptitude (TC005919-005923).

11379
Ohio Vocational Achievement Tests: Agricultural Education, Farm Management. Ohio State Dept. of Education, Div. of Vocational Education, Columbus, OH 1981
Subtests: Plan and Supervise Work; Analyze Farm Records; Buildings and Structures; Finance Farm Operations; Maintain Inventory of Supplies; Plan Crop Enterprise; Market Farm Products; Plan Livestock Enterprise; Equipment and Machinery; General Management Duties; Employment Procedures
Descriptors: *Achievement Tests; *Agricultural Education; Agricultural Machinery; Agricultural Production; Data Analysis; Employment Practices; Facility Inventory; *Farm Management; Financial Policy; Grade 11; Grade 12; High Schools; *High School Students; Knowledge Level; Merchandising; Problem Solving; Recordkeeping; Supervision; Synthesis; *Vocational Education
Availability: Ohio State University, Instructional Materials Laboratory; 1885 Neil Ave., Columbus, OH 43210
Grade Level: 11-12
Notes: Time, 240 min.; Items, 334

For use in the evaluation and diagnosis of vocational achievement. Developed to measure skills and understandings in specific vocational areas. Items measure ability to solve problems, analyze data, recall facts, have a knowledge of principles, react to generalizations, use abstractions in specific situations, and form parts into complete structures. Administered with the California Short Form Test of Academic Aptitude (TC005919-005923).

11382
Ohio Vocational Achievement Tests: Business and Office Education, Clerk-Stenographer. Ohio State Dept. of Education, Div. of Vocational Education, Columbus, OH 1981

Subtests: Dictation; Correspondence; Financial Records; Communications; Copy Reproduction; Record Management; Personal Development/ Employment
Descriptors: *Achievement Tests; *Dictation; Business Correspondence; *Business Education; Data Analysis; Grade 11; Grade 12; High Schools; *High School Students; Individual Development; Knowledge Level; Problem Solving; Recordkeeping; Reprography; *Shorthand; Synthesis; *Vocational Education
Identifiers: Finance
Availability: Ohio State University, Instructional Materials Laboratory; 1885 Neil Ave., Columbus, OH 43210
Grade Level: 11-12
Notes: Time, 240 min.; Items, 278

For use in the evaluation and diagnosis of vocational achievement. Developed to measure skills and understandings in specific vocational areas. Items measure ability to solve problems, analyze data, recall facts, have a knowledge of principles, react to generalizations, use abstractions in specific situations, and form parts into complete structures. Administered with the California Short Form Test of Academic Aptitude (TC005919-005923).

11383
Ohio Vocational Achievement Tests; Business and Office Education, Data Processing.   Ohio State Dept. of Education, Div. of Vocational Education, Columbus, OH 1981
Subtests: Computer Systems; Clerical Procedures; Programming Languages; Human Relations; Automated Electronic D.P. Equipment; Flow Charting; Data Entry; Operations; Business Math/Accounting; Employment Procedures
Descriptors: Accounting; *Achievement Tests; *Business Education; Data Analysis; *Data Processing; Employment Practices; Equipment; Flow Charts; Grade 11; Grade 12; High Schools; *High School Students; Human Relations; Knowledge Level; Mathematics; Office Practice; Problem Solving; Programing Languages; Synthesis; *Vocational Education
Identifiers: Computer Systems; Data Entry
Availability: Ohio State University, Instructional Materials Laboratory; 1885 Neil Ave., Columbus, OH 43210
Grade Level: 11-12
Notes: Time, 240 min.; Items, 383

For use in the evaluation and diagnosis of vocational achievement. Developed to measure skills and understandings in specific vocational areas. Items measure ability to solve problems, analyze data, recall facts, have a knowledge of principles, react to generalizations, use abstractions in specific situations, and form parts into complete structures. Administered with the California Short Form Test of Academic Aptitude (TC005919-005923).

11388
Ohio Vocational Achievement Tests: Construction Trades, Masonry.   Ohio State Dept. of Education, Div. of Vocational Education, Columbus, OH 1981
Subtests: Prepare Materials and Job Site; Lay Brick and Block to a Line; Lay Brick and Block with a Plumb Rule; Fireplaces and Chimneys; Arches; Miscellaneous Masonry Construction; Concrete Masonry; Surveying; Mathematics and Blueprint Reading; Personal Development
Descriptors: *Achievement Tests; Blueprints; Bricklaying; *Building Trades; Chimneys; Data Analysis; Grade 11; Grade 12; High Schools; *High School Students; Individual Development; Knowledge Level; *Masonry; Mathematical Applications; Problem Solving; Surveys; Synthesis; *Trade and Industrial Education; *Vocational Education
Identifiers: Arches; Concrete (Building); Fireplaces
Availability: Ohio State University, Instructional Materials Laboratory; 1885 Neil Ave., Columbus, OH 43210
Grade Level: 11-12
Notes: Time, 240 min.; Items, 319

For use in the evaluation and diagnosis of vocational achievement. Developed to measure skills and understandings in specific vocational areas. Items measure ability to solve problems, analyze data, recall facts, have a knowledge of principles, react to generalizations, use abstractions in specific situations, and form parts into complete structures. Administered with the California Short Form Test of Academic Aptitude (TC005919-005923).

11390
Ohio Vocational Achievement Tests: Distributive Education, Food Service Personnel.   Ohio State Dept. of Education, Div. of Vocational Education, Columbus, OH 1981

Subtests: Restaurant Management; Inventory and Purchasing Procedures; Business Principles; Waiter/Waitressing; Cashiering; Employment Procedures; Human Relations; Communications; Selling Principles; Advertising; Product-Service Information; Safety and Housekeeping
Descriptors: *Achievement Tests; Advertising; Business Communication; Data Analysis; *Distributive Education; Employment Practices; Facility Inventory; *Food Service; Grade 11; Grade 12; High Schools; *High School Students; Human Relations; Knowledge Level; Merchandise Information; Problem Solving; Purchasing; Safety; Synthesis; *Vocational Education
Identifiers: Business Principles; Cashier Checker Training; Selling Practices; Waiters Waitresses
Availability: Ohio State University, Instructional Materials Laboratory; 1885 Neil Ave., Columbus, OH 43210
Grade Level: 11-12
Notes: Time, 240 min.; Items, 383

For use in the evaluation and diagnosis of vocational achievement. Developed to measure skills and understandings in specific vocational areas. Items measure ability to solve problems, analyze data, recall facts, have a knowledge of principles, react to generalizations, use abstractions in specific situations, and form parts into complete structures. Administered with the California Short Form Test of Academic Aptitude (TC005919-005923).

11397
Ohio Vocational Achievement Tests: Health Occupations Education, Dental Assisting.   Ohio State Dept. of Education, Div. of Vocational Education, Columbus, OH 1981
Subtests: Anatomy; Microbiology and Sterilization; Dental Emergencies and Pharmacology; Dental Laboratory; Restorative and Impression Materials; Preventive Dentistry; Ethics and Personal Development; Radiology; Dental Office Management; Chairside Assisting-Basic; Chairside Assisting Prosthetics; Chairside Assisting-Oral Surgery and Pathology; Chairside Assisting-Other Specialities; Expanded Duties
Descriptors: *Achievement Tests; Anatomy; Data Analysis; *Dental Assistants; Ethics; Grade 11; Grade 12; *Health Occupations; High Schools; *High School Students; Knowledge Level; Microbiology; Office Management; Pharmacology; Problem Solving; Radiology; Synthesis; *Vocational Education
Identifiers: Chairside Assisting (Dental); Dental Emergencies; Dental Laboratory Methods; Dental Materials; Preventive Dentistry
Availability: Ohio State University, Instructional Materials Laboratory; 1885 Neil Ave., Columbus, OH 43210
Grade Level: 11-12
Notes: Time, 240 min.; Items, 396

For use in the evaluation and diagnosis of vocational achievement. Developed to measure skills and understandings in specific vocational areas. Items measure ability to solve problems, analyze data, recall facts, have a knowledge of principles, react to generalizations, use abstractions in specific situations, and form parts into complete structures. Administered with the California Short Form Test of Academic Aptitude (TC005919-005923).

11400
Ohio Vocational Achievement Tests: Home Economics Education, Community and Home Services. Ohio State Dept. of Education, Div. of Vocational Education, Columbus, OH 1981
Subtests: Personal Care for Patient; Vital Signs; Lift, Move and Transport Patients; Perform Special Care; Infant and Child Care; Provide Food Service; Care of Cleaning Equipment; Care of Furnishings; Care of Resilient and Masonry Floors; Care of Draperies and Upholstery and Carpeting; Provide Room Care; Care of Restrooms; Care of Public Areas; Provide Laundry Service; Careers and Employment
Descriptors: *Achievement Tests; Child Caregivers; Cleaning; Data Analysis; *Food Service; Grade 11; Grade 12; High Schools; *High School Students; *Home Economics; Knowledge Level; *Medical Services; Problem Solving; Synthesis; *Vocational Education
Identifiers: Vital Signs
Availability: Ohio State University, Instructional Materials Laboratory; 1885 Neil Ave., Columbus, OH 43210
Grade Level: 11-12
Notes: Time, 240 min.; Items, 380

For use in the evaluation and diagnosis of vocational achievement. Developed to measure skills and understandings in specific vocational areas. Items measure ability to solve problems, analyze data, recall facts, have a knowledge of principles, react to generalizations, use abstrac-

tions in specific situations, and form parts into complete structures. Administered with the California Short Form Test of Academic Aptitude (TC005919-005923).

11401
Ohio Vocational Achievement Tests: Home Economics Education, Fabric Services.   Ohio State Dept. of Education, Div. of Vocational Education, Columbus, OH 1981
Subtests: Alteration Specialist; Custom Dressmaker; Custom Tailor; Fabric Coordinator; Fashion Coordinator; Power Machine Operator; Dry Cleaner; Interior Design Specialist; Drapery Consultant; Drapery Maker; Drapery Installer; Slipcover Maker; Upholsterer; Refinisher; Careers and Employment
Descriptors: *Achievement Tests; Career Awareness; Clothing; Data Analysis; Grade 11; Grade 12; High Schools; *High School Students; *Home Economics; Interior Design; Knowledge Level; Laundry Drycleaning Occupations; Problem Solving; Sewing Machine Operators; Synthesis; *Vocational Education
Identifiers: Drapery Makers; *Fabric Services; Upholsterers
Availability: Ohio State University, Instructional Materials Laboratory; 1885 Neil Ave., Columbus, OH 43210
Grade Level: 11-12
Notes: Time, 240 min.; Items, 371

For use in the evaluation and diagnosis of vocational achievement. Developed to measure skills and understandings in specific vocational areas. Items measure ability to solve problems, analyze data, recall facts, have a knowledge of principles, react to generalizations, use abstractions in specific situations, and form parts into complete structures. Administered with the California Short Form Test of Academic Aptitude (TC005919-005923).

11402
Ohio Vocational Achievement Tests: Home Economics Education, Food Services.   Ohio State Dept. of Education, Div. of Vocational Education, Columbus, OH 1981
Subtests: Baker; Cook Chef; Pantry Worker; Caterer; Dietary Aide; Dining Room Service; Cafeteria Line; Sanitation and Safety; Storeroom Operations; Careers and Employment
Descriptors: *Achievement Tests; *Bakery Industry; Career Awareness; Cooks; Data Analysis; *Dietetics; Dining Facilities; *Food Service; Grade 11; Grade 12; High Schools; *High School Students; *Home Economics; Knowledge Level; Problem Solving; Synthesis; *Vocational Education
Identifiers: Catering
Availability: Ohio State University, Instructional Materials Laboratory; 1885 Neil Ave., Columbus, OH 43210
Grade Level: 11-12
Notes: Time, 240 min.; Items, 376

For use in the evaluation and diagnosis of vocational achievement. Developed to measure skills and understandings in specific vocational areas. Items measure ability to solve problems, analyze data, recall facts, have a knowledge of principles, react to generalizations, use abstractions in specific situations, and form parts into complete structures. Administered with the California Short Form Test of Academic Aptitude (TC005919-005923).

11411
College Level Examination Program: Subject Examination in Western Civilization I: Ancient Near East to 1648.   Educational Testing Service, Princeton, NJ
Descriptors: Achievement Tests; *Adults; *Equivalency Tests; Essay Tests; Higher Education; Multiple Choice Tests; Undergraduate Students; *Western Civilization
Identifiers: CLEP
Availability: College Board Publication Orders; Box 2815, Princeton, NJ 08541
Grade Level: 13-16
Age Level: 18-65
Notes: Time, 90 min.; Items, 120

CLEP enables both traditional and nontraditional students to earn college credit by examination. Tests are updated periodically. Subject matter is divided into broad historical periods including Ancient Near East, Ancient Greece and Hellinistic Civilization, Ancient Rome, Medieval History, Renaissance and Reformation, and Early Modern Europe 1560-1648. The 90-minute optional essay measures ability of students to present their ideas in an organized and logical manner. Candidates must choose 2 of 4 topics about which to write.

11412
College-Level Examination Program: Subject Examination in Western Civilization II: 1648 to the Present.   Educational Testing Service, Princeton, NJ

Descriptors: Achievement Tests; *Adults; *Equivalency Tests; Essay Tests; Higher Education; Multiple Choice Tests; Undergraduate Students; *Western Civilization
Identifiers: CLEP
Availability: College Board Publication Orders; Box 2815, Princeton, NJ 08541
Age Level: 18-65
Notes: Time, 90 min.; Items, 120

CLEP enables both traditional and nontraditional students to earn college credit by examination. Tests are updated periodically. Subject matter is divided into 12 broad historical periods. The 90-minute operational essay section measures ability of students to present their ideas in an organized and logical manner. Candidates must choose 2 of 4 topics about which to write.

11413
College Level Examination Program: Subject Examination in American History: Early Colonizations to 1877. Educational Testing Service, Princeton, NJ
Descriptors: Achievement Tests; *Adults; *Equivalency Tests; Essay Tests; Higher Education; Multiple Choice Tests; Undergraduate Students; *United States History
Identifiers: CLEP
Availability: College Board Publication Orders; Box 2815, Princeton, NJ 08541
Age Level: 18-65
Notes: Time, 90 min.; Items, 120

CLEP enables both traditional and nontraditional students to earn college credit by examination. Tests are updated periodically. Covers period in American history from Spanish and French colonizations to the end of Reconstruction era. Major emphasis on period from 1790-1877. An optional 90-minute essay section measures ability to select material and present it in an organized and logical manner.

11414
College-Level Examination Program: Subject Examination in American History II: 1865 to the Present. Educational Testing Service, Princeton, NJ
Descriptors: Achievement Tests; *Adults; *Equivalency Tests; Essay Tests; Higher Education; Multiple Choice Tests; Undergraduate Students; *United States History
Identifiers: CLEP
Availability: College Board Publication Orders; Box 2815, Princeton, NJ 08541
Grade Level: 13-16
Age Level: 18-65
Notes: Time, 90 min.; Items, 120

CLEP enables both traditional and nontraditional students to earn college credit by examination. Tests are updated periodically. Covers period in American history from the end of the Civil War to the present. Major emphasis is on the period from 1915 to the present. An optional 90-minute essay section measures ability to select material and present it in an organized and logical manner.

11429
Ohio Vocational Achievement Tests. Ohio State Dept. of Education, Div. of Vocational Education, Columbus, OH 1980
Descriptors: *Achievement Tests; *Agricultural Education; *Business Education; Data Analysis; *Distributive Education; Grade 11; Grade 12; *Health Occupations; High Schools; *High School Students; *Home Economics; Knowledge Level; Problem Solving; Synthesis; *Trade and Industrial Education; *Vocational Education
Availability: Ohio State University, Instructional Materials Laboratory; 1885 Neil Ave., Columbus, OH 43210
Grade Level: 11-12
Notes: Time, 240 min.; Items, 300

Thirty-four achievement tests for use in secondary schools offering vocational education. Tests cover Agricultural Education, Business and Office Education, Distributive Education, Health Occupations, Home Economics, Trade and Industrial Education. Each has approximately 300 items. Developed to measure skills and understandings in specific vocational areas. Items measure ability to solve problems, analyze data, recall facts, have a knowledge of principles, react to generalizations, use abstractions in specific situations and form parts into complete structures. Administered with the California Short Form Test of Academic Aptitude (TC005919-005923).

11436
Orleans-Hanna Algebra Prognosis Test (Revised). Hanna, Gerald S.; Orleans, Joseph B. 1982
Descriptors: *Algebra; Predictive Measurement; *Prognostic Tests; Secondary Education; *Secondary School Students
Availability: The Psychological Corp.; 555 Academic Ct., San Antonio, TX 78204-0952
Grade Level: 7-12
Notes: Time, 60 min. approx.; Items, 60

Designed to identify before instruction begins, those students who may achieve relative success in an algebra course and those most likely to encounter difficulties. Test is useful for counseling, selecting, and grouping algebra students. Test is structured to tap selected aspects of 3 important variables: aptitude, achievement, and interest and motivation.

11438
EDS Diagnostic Skill Level Inventory for Advanced Reading. Henney, R. Lee 1979
Subtests: Word Meaning; Paragraph Meaning; Spelling; Language
Descriptors: *Adult Basic Education; Adults; *Diagnostic Tests; Grammar; Paragraphs; Predictive Measurement; *Pretests Posttests; *Reading Skills; Reading Tests; Semantics; Spelling
Availability: Educational Diagnostic Services; 2370 County Rd. 13, Corunna, IL 46730
Age Level: Adults
Notes: Items, 133

Developed to diagnose the strengths and weaknesses of adult students at the advanced level. Each inventory allows diagnosis of functional weaknesses within that academic discipline to concentrate on specific problems between the 5 to 8 equivalent grade levels. Can be used for predictive assessments for passing the new General Educational Development Tests (GED).

11439
EDS Diagnostic Skill Level Inventory for Advanced Mathematics. Henney, R. Lee 1979
Subtests: Mathematics Computation; Mathematical Concepts; Mathematics Application
Descriptors: *Adult Basic Education; Adults; Computation; *Diagnostic Tests; *Elementary School Mathematics; Mathematical Applications; Mathematical Concepts; Mathematics Tests; Predictive Measurement; *Pretests Posttests; Problem Solving
Availability: Educational Diagnostic Services; 2370 County Rd. 13, Corunna, IL 46730
Age Level: Adults
Notes: Items, 90

Designed to diagnose the strengths and weaknesses of adult students at the advanced level. Each inventory allows diagnosis of functional weaknesses within that academic discipline to concentrate on specific problems between the 5 to 8 equivalent grade levels. Can be used for predictive assessments for passing the new General Educational Development Tests (GED).

11441
EDS Diagnostic Skill Level Inventory for Mathematics. Henney, R. Lee 1975
Subtests: Basic Functions; Algebra; Geometry; Applications
Descriptors: *Adult Basic Education; Adults; Algebra; *Diagnostic Tests; Geometry; Mathematical Applications; Predictive Measurement; *Pretests Posttests; Problem Solving; *Secondary School Mathematics
Availability: Educational Diagnostic Services; 2370 County Rd. 13, Corunna, IL 46730
Age Level: Adults
Notes: Time, 60 min.; Items, 40

Developed to diagnose the strengths and weaknesses of adult students at the high school level. Each inventory allows diagnosis of functional weaknesses within that academic discipline to concentrate on specific problems between the 9 to 12 equivalent grade levels. Can be used for predictive assessments for passing the new General Educational Development Tests (GED).

11442
EDS Diagnostic Skill Level Inventory for Science. Henney, R. Lee 1975
Subtests: Introduction; Physics; Chemistry; Geology; Astronomy; Biology; Physiology
Descriptors: *Adult Basic Education; Adults; Astronomy; *Biological Sciences; Biology; Chemistry; *Diagnostic Tests; Geology; *Physical Sciences; Physics; Physiology; Predictive Measurement; *Pretests Posttests; *Secondary School Science
Availability: Educational Diagnostic Services; 2370 County Rd. 13, Corunna, IL 46730
Age Level: Adults
Notes: Time, 60 min.; Items, 40

Developed to diagnose the strengths and weaknesses of adult students at the high school level. Each inventory allows diagnosis of functional weaknesses within that academic discipline to concentrate on specific problems between the 9 to 12 equivalent grade levels. Can be used for predictive assessments for passing the new General Educational Development Tests (GED).

11443
EDS Diagnostic Skill Level Inventory for Social Studies. Henney, R. Lee 1975
Subtests: Introduction; U.S. History; Government; Economics; Geography; Behavioral Sciences
Descriptors: *Adult Basic Education; Adults; Behavioral Sciences; *Diagnostic Tests; Economics; Geography; Political Science; Predictive Measurement; *Pretests Posttests; *Social Studies; United States History
Availability: Educational Diagnostic Services; 2370 County Rd. 13, Corunna, IL 46730
Age Level: Adults
Notes: Time, 60 min.; Items, 60

Developed to diagnose the strengths and weaknesses of adult students at the high school level. Each inventory allows diagnosis of functional weaknesses within that academic discipline to concentrate on specific problems between the 9 to 12 equivalent grade levels. Can be used for predictive assessments for passing the new General Educational Development Tests (GED).

11444
EDS Diagnostic Skill Level Inventory for Basic Mathematics. Henney, R. Lee 1979
Subtests: Mathematics Computation; Mathematics Concepts; Mathematics Application
Descriptors: *Adult Basic Education; Adults; Computation; *Diagnostic Tests; *Elementary School Mathematics; Mathematical Applications; Mathematical Concepts; Predictive Measurement; *Pretests Posttests; Problem Solving
Availability: Educational Diagnostic Services; 2370 County Rd. 13, Corunna, IL 46730
Age Level: Adults
Notes: Items, 90

Developed to diagnose the strengths and weaknesses of adult students at the basic level. Each inventory allows diagnosis of functional weaknesses within that academic discipline to concentrate on specific problems between the 0 to 4 equivalent grade levels. Can be used for predictive assessments for passing the new General Educational Development Tests (GED).

11445
EDS Diagnostic Skill Level Inventory for Basic Reading. Henney, R. Lee 1979
Subtests: Word Meaning; Paragraph Meaning; Spelling; Language
Descriptors: *Adult Basic Education; Adults; *Diagnostic Tests; Grammar; Paragraphs; Predictive Measurement; *Pretests Posttests; *Reading Skills; Reading Tests; Semantics; Spelling
Availability: Educational Diagnostic Services; 2370 County Rd. 13, Corunna, IL 46730
Age Level: Adults
Notes: Items, 88

Developed to diagnose the strengths and weaknesses of adult students at the basic level. Each inventory allows diagnosis of functional weaknesses within that academic discipline to concentrate on specific problems between the 0 to 4 equivalent grade levels. Can be used for predictive assessments for passing the new General Educational Development Tests (GED).

11446
EDS Diagnostic Skill Level Inventory for Pre-Reading. Henney, R. Lee 1980
Subtests: Pictures; Letters; Words
Descriptors: *Adult Basic Education; Adults; *Beginning Reading; *Diagnostic Tests; Letters (Alphabet); Pictorial Stimuli; Predictive Measurement; Prereading Experience; *Pretests Posttests; Word Recognition
Availability: Educational Diagnostic Services; 2370 County Rd. 13, Corunna, IL 46730
Age Level: Adults
Notes: Items, 72

Developed to diagnose the strengths and weaknesses of adult students at the prereading level. Each inventory allows diagnosis of functional weaknesses within that academic discipline to concentrate on specific problems at the equivalent grade levels. Can be used for predictive assessments for passing the new General Educational Development Tests (GED).

11452
ATP Achievement Test in Literature. Educational Testing Service, Princeton, NJ 1980
Descriptors: *Achievement Tests; *College Bound Students; *College Entrance Examinations; *English Literature; High Schools; *High School Seniors; High School Students; Multiple Choice Tests; Reading Comprehension
Identifiers: Admissions Testing Program Achievement Tests; MAPS; Multiple Assessment Programs and Services
Availability: The College Board; Box 2844, Princeton, NJ 08541
Grade Level: 9-12
Notes: Time, 60 min. approx.; Items, 60

Designed to measure student's ability to read literature carefully. Questions are based on passages of poetry, prose, and drama provided in the test. Material for test items is drawn from literature written in English from the Renaissance to the present. Part of the Admissions Testing Program (ATP) administered by the College Board to high school juniors and seniors. Many colleges require the tests for admission, and some use the results for placement. Test specifications are revised periodically.

11453
Caso Two Language Battery of Tests. Caso, Adolph 1981
Subtests: Phonetics; Comprehension Situations; Writing; Oral Proficiency
Descriptors: *Adults; Bilingualism; Cambodian; *Criterion Referenced Tests; Culture Fair Tests; *Elementary School Students; Elementary Secondary Education; French; German; Group Testing; Italian; Language Dominance; *Language Proficiency; *Language Tests; *Limited English Speaking; Portuguese; *Secondary School Students; Spanish Speaking; Student Placement; Tape Recordings; Vietnamese
Availability: Branden Press Publishers; 17 Station St., Box 843, Brookline Village, MA 02147
Grade Level: K-12
Notes: Time, 21 min.

Used with limited English-speaking or native language-proficient students and adults to assess oral proficiency; written comprehension; initial letters and spelling; and reading, listening, and writing skills. Goals include determining extent of native and English language skills and proficiency, to establish current language dominance, to determine point of bilinguality, to help determine LAU categories, to help diagnose weak and strong language points, to help discover motor and/or other handicaps or disabilities, to evaluate rate of language acquisition and/or loss, to make available quick visual comparison between levels of proficiency of native language and English, to help make placement decisions, to help make program exit decisions. The Oral Proficiency section is optional. Test is available in English-Spanish, English-Italian, English-Portuguese, English-Vietnamese, English-French, English-German, and English-Cambodian. Administrator does not need to be proficient in the language.

11469
Graduate Record Examinations: Subject Tests—Computer Science. Educational Testing Service, Princeton, NJ
Descriptors: Academic Achievement; College Admission; College Applicants; *College Entrance Examinations; *College Seniors; *Computer Science; Computer Science Education; Degree Requirements; Doctoral Programs; Educational Counseling; Fellowships; *Graduate Students; Graduate Study; Higher Education; Majors (Students); Masters Programs; *Mathematics; *National Competency Tests; Predictive Measurement; *Programing; Science Tests; Student Evaluation; Timed Tests
Identifiers: GRE; Number Operations; Power Tests
Availability: Graduate Records Examinations; Educational Testing Service, Box 955, Princeton, NJ 08541
Grade Level: 16-18
Age Level: 21-65
Notes: Time, 170 min.; Items, 80

Designed to measure knowledge and understanding of computer science basic to graduate study; designed to be a power rather than speed test. For reasons of fairness, several editions are available each year. Large print answer sheets are available though the test itself is in regular sized print. In developing each new edition, special effort is made to survey the entire academic field and to include material from widely differing curricula. Used for selection of applicants for graduate school, selection of fellowship applicants, guidance and counseling, evaluation of the effectiveness of an undergraduate or master's program, requirement for conferral of a degree, senior comprehensive examination at the undergraduate level, and comprehensive examination for advancement to a master's or doctoral program. Known as the Cooperative Graduate Testing Program until 1940.

11475
MKM Visual Letter Recognition Test. Wold, Robert M. 1970
Descriptors: Decoding (Reading); *Educational Diagnosis; Elementary Education; *Elementary School Students; Individual Testing; Learning Disabilities; Letters (Alphabet); *Phoneme Grapheme Correspondence; Phonemes; *Screening Tests; *Speech Tests
Availability: MKM, Inc.; 809 Kansas City St., Rapid City, SD 57701
Grade Level: 1-6

Designed to determine how child converts various symbols into their speech sounds. This ability is vital to the reading process. Letters of the alphabet should be presented to the child in random order. The following observations should be made during testing: posture, speed and accuracy, concentration and attention, and frustration level. The Phonic Mnemonic Method of Teaching Reading Manual of Instructions for use with this instrument is available from MKM, Inc.

11476
MKM Auditory Letter Recognition Test. Wold, Robert M. 1970
Subtests: Consonant Sounds; Consonant Blends; Consonant Digraphs; Long and Short Vowel Sounds; Vowel Combination Sounds
Descriptors: *Auditory Perception; Auditory Stimuli; Dictation; Educational Diagnosis; Elementary Education; *Elementary School Students; Individual Testing; Learning Disabilities; Phonemes; *Screening Tests; *Sensory Integration
Availability: MKM, Inc.; 809 Kansas City St., Rapid City, SD 57701
Grade Level: 1-6

Designed to determine how children relate the things they hear to those they see and write. The lack of development of an efficient auditory-visual-motor integrative pattern is one of the most detrimental to efficient academic performance. Observations to be made during testing include posture; speed; concentration, attention, and fatigue; vocalization or subvocalization; frustration level; and formation. The Phonic Mnemonic Method of Teaching Reading Manual of Instructions for use with this instrument is available from MKM, Inc.

11478
Language Inventory for Teachers. Cooper, Arlene; School, Beverly A. 1982
Subtests: Spoken Assessment; Written Assessment
Descriptors: Criterion Referenced Tests; *Diagnostic Tests; Elementary Education; *Elementary School Students; *Individualized Education Programs; Individual Testing; Language Patterns; *Language Tests; Remedial Instruction; Remedial Programs; *Speech Evaluation; *Writing Evaluation
Identifiers: IEP; LIT
Availability: Academic Therapy Publications; 20 Commercial Blvd., Novato, CA 94947-6191
Grade Level: 1-6
Notes: Time, 60 min. approx.

Provides series of language tasks that can be used by special education teacher to assess status of students' spoken and written language, to prepare individualized educational plans (IEP), and to initiate a remedial program. Purpose of the inventory is to uncover incompetence at a specific task or a lack of basic language concept development. The checklist summarizes all information under 13 specific goals—5 for spoken language and 8 for written language. Individually administered. A review of the test by B. A. Blachman and S. I. James can be found in *Reading Teacher;* v37 n2 p176-79, Nov 1983. A review by Cecil R. Reynolds can be found in *School Psychology Review;* v12 n4 p482-83, Fall 1983.

11479
Diagnostic Spelling Potential Test. Arena, John 1982
Subtests: Spelling; Word Recognition-Sight; Word Recognition-Phonetic Decoding; Visual Recognition; Auditory Visual Recognition
Descriptors: *Achievement Tests; Adolescents; Adults; Auditory Perception; Children; Elementary Secondary Education; Individual Testing; Phonetics; Pretests Posttests; Sight Vocabulary; *Spelling; Visual Stimuli; Word Recognition
Identifiers: DSPT
Availability: Academic Therapy Publications; 20 Commercial Blvd., Novato, CA 94947-6191
Age Level: 7-65
Notes: Time, 40 min. approx.; Items, 360

Comprehensive spelling test designed for use with students age 7 through adult. There are 2 parallel forms. Individually administered and can be used by diagnosticians, psychologists, and remedial specialists to compare spelling efficiency with necessary skills, such as decoding, utilization of phonetic generalizations, visual recall, and matching auditory with visual representations. Only items appropriate to individual's ability level are administered. A review by B. A. Blachman can be found in *Journal of Reading;* v27 p134-38, Nov 1983, and a review by Cecil R. Reynolds can be found in School Psychology Review; v12 n4 p481-82, Fall 1983.

11486
English Placement Test. Spaan, Mary; Strowe, Laura 1972
Descriptors: *College Students; *English (Second Language); Grammar; Higher Education; *Homogeneous Grouping; Listening Comprehension; Reading Comprehension; *Screening Tests; Second Language Learning; Sentences; *Student Placement; Vocabulary Skills
Identifiers: ELIUM
Availability: University of Michigan; English Language Institute, 2001 N. University Bldg., Ann Arbor, MI 48109
Grade Level: Higher Education
Notes: Time, 75 min. approx.; Items, 100

Nondiagnostic, objectively scored test designed to place English-as-a-Second-Language (ESL) students into homogeneous ability groups in intensive English language courses. Cutoff scores must be locally determined. Three parallel forms are available.

11495
Day School Hebrew Language Achievement Test, Gimel Level. Jewish Education Service of North America, New York, NY
Subtests: Listening Comprehension; Reading Comprehension; Vocabulary; Language Structure
Descriptors: *Achievement Tests; Elementary Education; *Elementary School Students; *Hebrew; Language Patterns; Listening Comprehension; Parochial Schools; Reading Comprehension; *Second Language Learning; Vocabulary
Availability: Jewish Education Service of N. America; 114 Fifth Ave., New York, NY 10011
Grade Level: 3-6
Notes: Time, 105 min. approx.; Items, 75

Used with students in Jewish day schools to measure growth in Hebrew language in the skill areas of listening comprehension, reading comprehension, vocabulary, and language structure. Questions are based on daily life experiences, holidays, Jewish personalities, values, and Biblical characters. The test is given in 2 separate sessions. Parts 1 and 2 take 45 minutes; parts 3 and 4 take 60 minutes.

11496
Day School Hebrew Language Achievement Test, Vav Level. Jewish Education Service of North America, New York, NY
Subtests: Listening Comprehension; Language Structure; Reading Comprehension; Vocabulary
Descriptors: *Achievement Tests; Elementary Education; *Elementary School Students; *Hebrew; Language Patterns; Listening Comprehension; Parochial Schools; Reading Comprehension; *Second Language Learning; Vocabulary
Availability: Jewish Education Service of N. America; 114 Fifth Ave., New York, NY 10011
Grade Level: 3-6
Notes: Time, 105 min. approx.; Items, 75

Used with students in Jewish day schools to measure growth in Hebrew language in the skill areas of listening comprehension, reading comprehension, vocabulary, and language structure. Questions are based on daily life experiences, holidays, Jewish personality, values, and Biblical characters. The test is given in 2 separate sessions. Parts 1 and 2 take 45 minutes; parts 3 and 4 take 60 minutes.

11502
3-R's Test. Levels 6-8, Forms A and B. Achievement Edition. Cole, Nancy S.; And Others 1982
Subtests: Reading; Mathematics
Descriptors: *Achievement Tests; Culture Fair Tests; *Elementary School Mathematics; *Elementary School Students; *Mathematics Achievement; Primary Education; *Reading Achievement
Availability: Riverside Publishing Co.; 3 O'Hare Towers, 8420 Bryn Mawr Ave., Chicago, IL 60631
Grade Level: K-2

Designed to measure children's proficiency in basic reading and mathematics skills. All items are based on objectives commonly used in kindergarten and grades 1 and 2. Tests are available in 2 forms, A and B. For the achievement edition, tests at levels 6 and 7 each consist of 59 items; test level 8 consists of 65 items. All levels are administered in 2 class periods. Total testing time for levels 6 and 7 is approximately 90 minutes; total testing time for level 8 is approximately 95 minutes. There is also a class period edition of the tests. These are designed to be administered during a single class period and are available in one form only.

11503
3-R's Test. Levels 9-12, Forms A and B. Achievement Edition. Cole, Nancy S.; And Others 1982
Subtests: Reading; Language; Mathematics
Descriptors: *Language Usage; *Achievement Tests ; *Aptitude Tests; Capitalization (Alphabetic); Cognitive Measurement; Culture Fair Tests; Elementary Education; *Elementary School Mathematics; *Elementary School Students; Grammar; *Language Proficiency; *Mathematics Achievement; Punctuation; *Reading Achievement; Spelling
Availability: Riverside Publishing Co.; 3 O'Hare Towers, 8420 Bryn Mawr Ave., Chicago, IL 60631
Grade Level: 3-6
Notes: Time, 130 min. approx.; Items, 125

Designed to measure students' proficiency in reading, language arts, and mathematics. All items are based on objectives commonly used at these grade levels. The achievement edition of the tests are available in 2 forms, A and B. The achievement and abilities edition combines Form A of the achievement test with a 95-item verbal and quantitative abilities test. The abilities portion can be administered in about 60 minutes. The abilities portion consists of a verbal part comprised of 2 subtests, verbal classification and verbal analogies, and a quantitative part, comprised of 2 subtests, quantitative relations and number series. Also at levels 9-12, a class period edition is available. This is an achievement test designed to be administered in a single class period. One form of the test is available at each grade level.

11504
3-R's Test. Levels 13-14, Forms A and B. Achievement Edition. Cole, Nancy S.; And Others 1982
Subtests: Reading; Language; Mathematics
Descriptors: *Achievement Tests; *Language Usage; *Aptitude Tests; Capitalization (Alphabetic); Cognitive Measurement; Culture Fair Tests; Grammar; Junior High Schools; *Junior High School Students; *Language Proficiency; *Mathematics Achievement; Punctuation; *Reading Achievement; *Secondary School Mathematics; Spelling
Availability: Riverside Publishing Co.; 3 O'Hare Towers, 8420 Bryn Mawr Ave., Chicago, IL 60631
Grade Level: 7-8
Notes: Time, 130 min. approx.; Items, 125

Designed to measure students' proficiency in reading, language arts, and mathematics. All items are based on objectives commonly used at these grade levels. The achievement and abilities edition combines Form A of the achievement edition with a 95-item verbal and quantitative abilities test. The abilities portion can be administered in approximately 60 minutes. The abilities portion consists of a verbal part comprised of 2 subtests, verbal classification and verbal analogies, and a quantitative part, comprised of 2 subtests, quantitative relations and number series. Also at levels 13-14, a class period edition is available. This is an achievement test designed to be administered in a single class period. One form of the test is available at each grade level.

11505
3-R's Test. Levels 15-18, Forms A and B. Achievement Edition. Cole, Nancy S.; And Others 1982
Subtests: Reading; Language; Mathematics
Descriptors: *Achievement Tests; *Language Usage; *Aptitude Tests; Capitalization (Alphabetic); Cognitive Measurement; Culture Fair Tests; Grammar; High Schools; *High School Students; *Language Proficiency; *Mathematics Achievement; Punctuation; *Reading Achievement; *Secondary School Mathematics; Spelling
Availability: Riverside Publishing Co.; 3 O'Hare Towers, 8420 Bryn Mawr Ave., Chicago, IL 60631
Grade Level: 9-12
Notes: Time, 130 min. approx.; Items, 125

Designed to measure students' proficiency in reading, language arts, and mathematics. All items are based on objectives commonly used at these grade levels. The achievement editions are available in Forms A and B. The achievement and abilities edition combines form A of the achievement edition with a 95-item verbal and quantitative abilities test. The abilities portion can be administered in approximately 60 minutes. The abilities portion consists of a verbal part comprised of 2 subtests, verbal classification and verbal analogies, and a quantitative part, comprised of 2 subtests, quantitative relations and number series. Also at levels 15-18, a class period edition is available. This is an achievement test designed to be administered in a single class period. One form of the test is available at each grade level.

11506
Comprehensive Testing Program II, Levels 1 and 2. Educational Testing Service, Princeton, NJ 1982
Subtests: Listening; Mathematics; Reading; Word Analysis; Writing Skills
Descriptors: *Achievement Tests; *Elementary School Mathematics; *Elementary School Students; *Listening Comprehension Tests; *Phonetic Analysis; Primary Education; Private Schools; *Reading Tests; Suburban Schools; *Writing Skills
Identifiers: CTPII; Educational Records Bureau NY
Availability: Educational Records Bureau; Box 619, Princeton, NJ 08541
Grade Level: 1-3
Notes: Time, 240 min.; Items, 170

Levels 1 and 2 consist of an achievement battery for testing listening, mathematics, reading, word analysis, and, in Level 2, writing skills. This subtest yields scores in spelling, punctuation, capitalization, and usage. Includes an 8-item practice test. Provides norms for use with independent schools and suburban schools as well as national norms. Level 2 contains more items and requires more administration time.

11507
Comprehensive Testing Program II, Levels 3, 4 and 5. Educational Testing Service, Princeton, NJ 1982
Subtests: Verbal Aptitude; Quantitative Aptitude; Mathematics Concepts; Mathematics Computation; Vocabulary; Reading Mechanics of Writing; English Expression; Algebra; Geometry; General Mathematics
Descriptors: *Academic Ability; *Achievement Tests; *Algebra; *Aptitude Tests; Computation; Elementary School Students; Elementary Secondary Education; *Geometry; Grammar; Intermediate Grades; *Language Arts; Mathematical Concepts; *Mathematics; Private Schools; *Reading Tests; Secondary Education; Secondary School Students; Suburban Schools; *Verbal Ability; *Vocabulary Skills; Writing Skills
Identifiers: CTPII; Educational Records Bureau NY; *Quantitative Aptitude
Availability: Educational Records Bureau; Box 619, Princeton, NJ 08541
Grade Level: 4-12
Notes: Time, 300 min.; Items, 440

Levels 3, 4, and 5 consist of an achievement and an aptitude test. The aptitude test is designed to predict academic performance and has a verbal and quantitative section. An accompanying achievement battery covers reading, mathematics concepts and computation (levels 3 and 4), Algebra (levels 4 and 5), geometry and general mathematics (level 5), vocabulary, mechanics of writing and English expression. Provides norms for use with independent schools and suburban schools as well as national norms.

11512
Reading Yardsticks, Level 6. Riverside Publishing Co., Chicago, IL 1981
Subtests: Auditory Discrimination; Visual Discrimination; Matching Letters and Words; Vocabulary; Literal Comprehension; Interpretive Comprehension
Descriptors: Auditory Discrimination; *Behavioral Objectives; *Criterion Referenced Tests; *Diagnostic Tests; *Kindergarten Children; Letters (Alphabet); Primary Education; Reading Comprehension; *Reading Diagnosis; *Reading Processes; Reading Tests; Visual Discrimination; Vocabulary; Word Recognition
Identifiers: Elementary Secondary Education Act Title I
Availability: Riverside Publishing Co.; 3 O'Hare Towers, 8420 Bryn Mawr Ave., Chicago, IL 60631
Grade Level: K
Notes: Time, 110 min.; Items, 70

Criterion-referenced test that measures the major components of the reading process. Designed to indicate whether a student has mastered specific skills. Primary purpose of test is to diagnose student strengths and weaknesses in reading. Test assesses student mastery of specific instructional objectives and contains features that meet federal and most state guidelines for tests used in Title I project evaluations.

11513
Reading Yardsticks, Level 7. Riverside Publishing Co., Chicago, IL 1981
Subtests: Auditory Discrimination; Visual Discrimination; Study Skills; Consonant Identification and Substitution; Vowels; Vocabulary; Literal Comprehension; Interpretive Comprehension
Descriptors: Auditory Discrimination; *Behavioral Objectives; Consonants; *Criterion Referenced Tests; *Diagnostic Tests; Elementary School Students; *Grade 1; Primary Education; Reading Comprehension; *Reading Diagnosis; *Reading Processes; Reading Tests; Study Skills; Visual Discrimination; Vocabulary; Vowels
Identifiers: Elen:entary Secondary Education Act Title I
Availability: Riverside Publishing Co.; 3 O'Hare Towers, 8420 Bryn Mawr Ave., Chicago, IL 60631
Grade Level: 1
Notes: Time, 150 min.; Items, 105

Criterion-referenced test that measures the major components of the reading process. Designed to indicate whether a student has mastered specific skills. Primary purpose of test is to diagnose student strengths and weaknesses in reading. Test assesses student mastery of specific instructional objectives and contains features that meet federal and most state guidelines for tests used in Title I project evaluations.

11514
Reading Yardsticks, Level 8. Riverside Publishing Co., Chicago, IL 1981
Subtests: Auditory Discrimination; Visual Discrimination; Study Skills; Consonant Identification; Consonant Substitution and Variants; Vowels; Vocabulary; Literal Comprehension; Interpretive Comprehension; Word Parts
Descriptors: Auditory Discrimination; *Behavioral Objectives; Consonants; *Criterion Referenced Tests; *Diagnostic Tests; Elementary School Students; *Grade 2; Primary Education; Reading Comprehension; *Reading Diagnosis; Reading Tests; Structural Analysis (Linguistics); Study Skills; Visual Discrimination; Vocabulary; Vowels
Identifiers: Elementary Secondary Education Act Title I
Availability: Riverside Publishing Co.; 3 O'Hare Towers, 8420 Bryn Mawr Ave., Chicago, IL 60631
Grade Level: 2
Notes: Time, 185 min.; Items, 135

Criterion-referenced test that measures the major components of the reading process. Designed to indicate whether a student has mastered specific skills. Primary purpose of test is to diagnose student strengths and weaknesses in reading. Test assesses student mastery of specific instructional objectives and contains features that meet federal and most state guidelines for tests used in Title I project evaluations.

11515
Reading Yardsticks, Level 9. Riverside Publishing Co., Chicago, IL 1981
Subtests: Vocabulary; Literal Comprehension; Interpretive Comprehension; Evaluative Comprehension; Language Comprehension; Consonants; Vowels; Word Parts; Reference Material; Organizational Study Skills
Descriptors: *Behavioral Objectives; Consonants; *Criterion Referenced Tests; *Diagnostic Tests; Elementary School Students; *Grade 3; Library Skills; Primary Education; Reading Comprehension; *Reading Diagnosis; *Reading Processes; Reading Tests; Structural Analysis (Linguistics); Study Skills; Vocabulary; Vowels
Identifiers: Elementary Secondary Education Act Title I
Availability: Riverside Publishing Co.; 3 O'Hare Towers, 8420 Bryn Mawr Ave., Chicago, IL 60631
Grade Level: 3
Notes: Time, 210 min.; Items, 210

Criterion-referenced test that measures the major components of the reading process. Designed to indicate whether a student has mastered specific skills. Primary purpose of test is to diagnose student strengths and weaknesses in reading. Test assesses student mastery of specific instructional objectives and contains features that meet federal and most state guidelines for tests used in Title I project evaluations.

11516
Reading Yardsticks, Level 10. Riverside Publishing Co., Chicago, IL 1981
Subtests: Vocabulary; Literal Comprehension; Interpretive Comprehension; Evaluative Comprehension; Language Comprehension; Word Parts; Reference Materials; Organizational Study Skills
Descriptors: *Behavioral Objectives; *Criterion Referenced Tests; *Diagnostic Tests; Elementary School Students; *Grade 4; Intermediate Grades; Library Skills; Reading Comprehension; *Reading Diagnosis; *Reading Processes; Reading Tests; Structural Analysis (Linguistics); Study Skills; Vision Tests; Vocabulary
Identifiers: Elementary Secondary Education Act Title I
Availability: Riverside Publishing Co.; 3 O'Hare Towers, 8420 Bryn Mawr Ave., Chicago, IL 60631
Grade Level: 4
Notes: Time, 210 min.; Items, 210

Criterion-referenced test that measures the major components of the reading process. Designed to indicate whether a student has mastered specific skills. Primary purpose of test is to diagnose student strengths and weaknesses in reading. Test assesses student mastery of specific instructional objectives and contains features that meet federal and most state guidelines for tests used in Title I project evaluations. There is an eyesight check at levels 10-14. The eyesight check is not intended as a substitute for a school's vision screening program.

11517
Reading Yardsticks, Level 11. Riverside Publishing Co., Chicago, IL 1981

Subtests: Vocabulary; Literal Comprehension; Interpretive Comprehension; Evaluative Comprehension; Language Comprehension; Reference Material; Organizational Study Skills; Pictorial Study Skills; Word Parts
Descriptors: *Behavioral Objectives; *Criterion Referenced Tests; *Diagnostic Tests; Elementary School Students; *Grade 5; Intermediate Grades; Library Skills; Reading Comprehension; *Reading Diagnosis; *Reading Processes; Reading Rate; Reading Tests; Structural Analysis (Linguistics); Study Skills; Vision Tests; Vocabulary
Identifiers: Elementary Secondary Education Act Title I
Availability: Riverside Publishing Co.; 3 O'Hare Towers, 8420 Bryn Mawr Ave., Chicago, IL 60631
Grade Level: 5
Notes: Time, 227 min.; Items, 210

Criterion-referenced test that measures the major components of the reading process. Designed to indicate whether a student has mastered specific skills. Primary purpose of test is to diagnose student strengths and weaknesses in reading. Test assesses student mastery of specific instructional objectives and contains features that meet federal and most state guidelines for tests used in Title I project evaluations. There is a reading rate test with the comprehension section of levels 11-14 as well as an eyesight check in levels 10-14. The eyesight check is not intended as a substitute for a school's vision screening program.

11518
Reading Yardsticks, Level 12. Riverside Publishing Co., Chicago, IL 1981
Subtests: Vocabulary; Literal Comprehension; Interpretive Comprehension; Evaluative Comprehension; Language Comprehension; Word Parts; Reference Material; Organizational Study Skills; Pictorial Study Skills
Descriptors: *Behavioral Objectives; *Criterion Referenced Tests; *Diagnostic Tests; Elementary School Students; *Grade 6; Intermediate Grades; Library Skills; Reading Comprehension; *Reading Diagnosis; *Reading Processes; Reading Rate; Reading Tests; Structural Analysis (Linguistics); Study Skills; Vision Tests; Vocabulary
Identifiers: Elementary Secondary Education Act Title I
Availability: Riverside Publishing Co.; 3 O'Hare Towers, 8420 Bryn Mawr Ave., Chicago, IL 60631
Grade Level: 6
Notes: Time, 227 min.; Items, 210

Criterion-referenced test that measures the major components of the reading process. Designed to indicate whether a student has mastered specific skills. Primary purpose of test is to diagnose student strengths and weaknesses in reading. Test assesses student mastery of specific instructional objectives and contains features that meet federal and most state guidelines for tests used in Title I project evaluations. There is a reading rate test within the comprehension section of levels 11-14 as well as an eyesight check in levels 10-14. The eyesight check is not intended as a substitute for a school's vision screening program.

11519
Reading Yardsticks, Level 13. Riverside Publishing Co., Chicago, IL 1981
Subtests: Vocabulary; Literal Comprehension; Interpretive Comprehension; Evaluative Comprehension; Language Comprehension; Word Parts; Reference Material; Organizational Study Skills; Pictorial Study Skills
Descriptors: *Behavioral Objectives; *Criterion Referenced Tests; *Diagnostic Tests; *Grade 7; Junior High Schools; Junior High School Students; Library Skills; Reading Comprehension; *Reading Diagnosis; *Reading Processes; Reading Rate; Reading Tests; Structural Analysis (Linguistics); Study Skills; Vision Tests; Vocabulary
Identifiers: Elementary Secondary Education Act Title I
Availability: Riverside Publishing Co.; 3 O'Hare Towers, 8420 Bryn Mawr Ave., Chicago, IL 60631
Grade Level: 7
Notes: Time, 227 min.; Items, 210

Criterion-referenced test that measures the major components of the reading process. Designed to indicate whether a student has mastered specific skills. Primary purpose of test is to diagnose student strengths and weaknesses in reading. Test assesses student mastery of specific instructional objectives and contains features that meet federal and most state guidelines for tests used in Title I project evaluations. There is a reading rate test within the comprehension section of levels 11-14 as well as an eyesight check in levels 10-14. The eyesight check is not intended as a substitute for a school's vision screening program.

11520
Reading Yardsticks, Level 14. Riverside Publishing Co., Chicago, IL 1981
Subtests: Vocabulary; Literal Comprehension; Interpretive Comprehension; Evaluative Comprehension; Language Comprehension; Word Parts; Reference Material; Organizational Study Skills; Pictorial Study Skills; Life Skills
Descriptors: *Behavioral Objectives; *Criterion Referenced Tests; *Diagnostic Tests; Functional Reading; *Grade 8; Junior High Schools; Junior High School Students; Library Skills; Reading Comprehension; *Reading Diagnosis; *Reading Processes; Reading Rate; Reading Tests; Structural Analysis (Linguistics); Study Skills; Vision Tests; Vocabulary
Identifiers: Elementary Secondary Education Act Title I
Availability: Riverside Publishing Co.; 3 O'Hare Towers, 8420 Bryn Mawr Ave., Chicago, IL 60631
Grade Level: 8
Notes: Time, 227 min.; Items, 210

Criterion-referenced test that measures the major components of the reading process. Designed to indicate whether a student has mastered specific skills. Primary purpose of test is to diagnose student strengths and weaknesses in reading. Test assesses student mastery of specific instructional objectives and contains features that meet federal and most state guidelines for tests used in Title I project evaluations. There is a reading rate test within the comprehension section of levels 11-14 as well as an eyesight check in levels 10-14. The eyesight check is not intended as a substitute for a school's vision screening program.

11570
McCall-Crabbs Standard Test Lessons in Reading, Revised. McCall, William A.; Schroeder, Lelah Crabbs 1979
Descriptors: *Elementary School Students; Elementary Secondary Education; Individual Instruction; *Informal Reading Inventories; *Instructional Materials; Listening Skills; *Oral Reading; Reading Improvement; *Reading Tests; *Secondary School Students
Availability: Slosson Educational Publications; P.O. Box 280, East Aurora, NY 14052
Grade Level: 3-12
Notes: Items, 480

Instructional materials based on an actual reading test format. Used as a supplemental activity and to provide a rough estimate of growth in reading over time. Each of the 6 booklets contains 60 3-minute reading selections followed by 8 questions about the content of the story.

11572
Tests of Achievement in Basic Skills: Reading Language. Level A. Educational and Industrial Testing Service, San Diego, CA 1976
Subtests: Word Analysis; Oral Language; Comprehension; Study Skills
Descriptors: *Achievement Tests; Criterion Referenced Tests; Educational Objectives; Elementary Education; *Elementary School Students; Language Acquisition; *Reading Achievement; Reading Skills; Study Skills
Identifiers: TABS
Availability: Educational and Industrial Testing Service; P.O. Box 7234, San Diego, CA 92107
Grade Level: 3-4
Notes: Items, 152

Designed to assess skill competencies in reading and language. Two parallel forms are available. Test items for objectives 32, 33, 34, and 35 are individually administered and included with the TELAR Reading Language program. Primary use is for assessing individual student achievement and for evaluation of the effectiveness of instruction.

11579
Screening Test of Adolescent Language, Revised Edition. Prather, Elizabeth M.; And Others 1980
Subtests: Vocabulary; Auditory Memory Span; Language Processing; Proverb Explanation
Descriptors: Auditory Stimuli; Comprehension; *Expressive Language; Individual Testing; *Language Handicaps; Language Processing; Memory; *Receptive Language; *Screening Tests; Secondary Education; *Secondary School Students; Vocabulary
Identifiers: STAL
Availability: University of Washington Press; P.O. Box C-50096, Seattle, WA 98145-5096
Grade Level: 7-12
Notes: Time, 7 min. approx.; Items, 23

Screening instrument for language disorders and linguistic development of junior and senior high school students. Test is individually administered to identify those students who may warrant further diagnostic evaluation. However, test results should not be interpreted as a comprehensive diagnostic evaluation of linguistic development. Instrument measures both receptive and expressive language through 4 subtests.

11586
Miller Assessment for Preschoolers. Miller, Lucy Jane 1982
Descriptors: *Child Development; *Cognitive Development; *Individual Testing; *Preschool Children; *Psychomotor Skills; *Screening Tests
Identifiers: MAP
Availability: Foundation for Knowledge in Development; 4857 So. Albion, Littleton, CO 80121
Age Level: 2-5
Notes: Time, 30 min. approx.; Items, 27

Individually administered screening tool for children from the ages of 2 years, 9 months to 5 years, 8 months. Provides a comprehensive overview of child's development status with respect to other children of the same age. Developed to provide short screening tool for educators and clinicians to identify children in need of further evaluation and to provide comprehensive structured clinical framework for evaluation and remediation. For the latter, there is a MAP Supplemental Observations which requires broad clinical knowledge and is a separate entity from the 27 core items. For MAP, there are 5 performance indices: foundations (basic motor and sensory abilities); coordination (complex fine and oral motor abilities); verbal (cognitive language abilities); nonverbal (cognitive abilities not requiring spoken language); and complex tasks (interaction of sensory, motor, and cognitive abilities).

11588
Wisconsin Tests of Reading Skill Development: Comprehension, Level A. Otto, Wayne 1977
Subtests: Central Thought-Topic: Pictures; Relationships; Sequence-First/Last Event
Descriptors: *Achievement Tests; *Comprehension; Criterion Referenced Tests; Educational Objectives; *Kindergarten Children; Mastery Learning; Primary Education; *Reading Skills
Identifiers: Test Batteries; WTRSD
Availability: Learning Multi-Systems, Inc.; 340 Coyier Ln., Madison, WI 53713
Grade Level: K
Notes: Time, 40 min. approx.; Items, 42

The written assessment component for the Comprehension area of the Wisconsin Design for Reading Skill Development. Designed to assess a range of skills useful in understanding written text. May be administered during late kindergarten or early first grade. Forms P and Q are equivalent. It is recommended that Level A be administered in 2 sessions.

11589
Wisconsin Tests of Reading Skill Development: Comprehension, Level B. Otto, Wayne 1977
Subtests: Detail; Central Thought-Topic: With Organizer; Relationships/Conclusions: Outcomes; Sequence-Before; Sequence-After
Descriptors: *Achievement Tests; *Comprehension; Criterion Referenced Tests; Educational Objectives; Elementary School Students; *Grade 1; Mastery Learning; Primary Education; *Reading Skills
Identifiers: Test Batteries; WTRSD
Availability: Learning Multi-Systems, Inc.; 340 Coyier Ln., Madison, WI 53713
Grade Level: 1
Notes: Time, 80 min. approx.; Items, 82

Ths is the written assessment component for the Comprehension area of the Wisconsin Design for Reading Skill Development. Designed to assess a range of skills useful in understanding written text. It is recommended that tests be administered in 3 sessions. Forms P and Q are available in consumable test booklets.

11590
Wisconsin Tests of Reading Skill Development: Comprehension, Level C. Otto, Wayne 1977
Subtests: Detail: Negatives; Paraphrase: Negatives; Central Thought-Topic: Without Organizer; Conclusions: One Relationship; Sequence-Before/After
Descriptors: Criterion Referenced Tests; Educational Objectives; Elementary School Students; *Grade 2; Mastery Learning; Primary Education; *Reading Comprehension; *Reading Skills
Identifiers: Test Batteries; WTRSD
Availability: Learning Multi-Systems, Inc.; 340 Coyier Ln., Madison, WI 53713
Grade Level: 2
Notes: Items, 90

This is the written assessment component for the Comprehension area of the Wisconsin Design for Reading Skill Development. Designed to assess a range of skills useful in understanding written text.

11591
Wisconsin Tests of Reading Skill Development: Comprehension, Level D. Otto, Wayne 1977

Subtests: Context-Direct Clues; Detail: Passives; Paraphrase: Passives; Central Thought-Topic: Relevant Information; Relationships/Conclusions: Cause-Effect; Sequence-Calendar Markers
Descriptors: *Achievement Tests; Criterion Referenced Tests; Educational Objectives; Elementary School Students; *Grade 3; Mastery Learning; Primary Education; *Reading Comprehension; *Reading Skills
Identifiers: Test Batteries; WTRSD
Availability: Learning Multi-Systems, Inc.; 340 Coyier Ln., Madison, WI 53713
Grade Level: 3
Notes: Time, 95 min. approx.; Items, 117

This is the written assessment component for the Comprehension area of the Wisconsin Design for Reading Skill Development. Designed to assess a range of skills useful in understanding written text. Tests should be administered in 3 sessions. Forms P and Q are available in consumable test booklets.

11592
Wisconsin Tests of Reading Skill Development: Comprehension, Level E. 1977
Subtests: Word Parts-Prefixes; Context-Direct Clues: Application; Detail: Clauses; Paraphrase: Complex Sentences; Central Thought: With Organizer; Conclusions: Direct Relationships; Sequence-Explicit Cues
Descriptors: *Achievement Tests; Criterion Referenced Tests; Educational Objectives; Elementary Education; Elementary School Students; *Grade 4; Intermediate Grades; Mastery Learning; *Reading Comprehension; *Reading Skills
Identifiers: Test Batteries; WTRSD
Availability: Learning Multi-Systems, Inc.; 340 Coyier Ln., Madison, WI 53713
Grade Level: 4
Notes: Time, 150 min. approx.; Items, 114

This is the written assessment component for the Comprehension area of the Wisconsin Design for Reading Skill Development. Designed to assess a range of skills useful in understanding written text. Forms P and Q are equivalent and available in a reusable test booklet. Tests should be administered in 4 class sessions.

11593
Wisconsin Tests of Reading Skill Development: Comprehension, Level F. Otto, Wayne 1977
Subtests: Word Parts: Suffixes; Context-Indirect Clues: Application; Paraphrase: Prepositions; Central Thought: Without Organizer; Conclusions: Indirect Relationships; Sequence-Implicit Cues
Descriptors: *Achievement Tests; Criterion Referenced Tests; Educational Objectives; Elementary Education; Elementary School Students; *Grade 5; Intermediate Grades; Mastery Learning; *Reading Comprehension; *Reading Skills
Identifiers: Test Batteries; WTRSD
Availability: Learning Multi-Systems, Inc.; 340 Coyier Ln., Madison, WI 53713
Grade Level: 5
Notes: Time, 130 min. approx.; Items, 90

This is the written assessment component for the Comprehension area of the Wisconsin Design for Reading Skill Development. Designed to assess a range of skills useful in understanding written text. Forms P and Q are equivalent and available in a reusable test booklet. Tests should be administered in 3 class sessions.

11594
Wisconsin Tests of Reading Skill Development: Comprehension, Level G. Otto, Wayne 1977
Subtests: Word Parts-Combining Forms; Word Parts-Word Roots; Context-Uncommon Meanings; Paraphrase: Restatements; Central Thought: Generation; Conclusions: Supported/ Unsupported; Conclusions: Modification; Sequence-Implied/Stated Events
Descriptors: *Achievement Tests; Criterion Referenced Tests; Educational Objectives; Elementary Education; Elementary School Students; *Grade 6; Intermediate Grades; Mastery Learning; *Reading Comprehension; *Reading Skills
Identifiers: Test Batteries; WTRSD
Availability: Learning Multi-Systems, Inc.; 340 Coyier Ln., Madison, WI 53713
Grade Level: 6
Notes: Time, 150 min. approx.; Items, 169

This is the written assessment component for the Comprehension area of the Wisconsin Design for Reading Skill Development. Designed to assess a range of skills useful in understanding written text. Forms P and Q are equivalent and available in a reusable test booklet. Tests should be administered in 4 class sessions.

11601
Lollipop Test: A Diagnostic Screening Test of School Readiness.   Chew, Alex L. 1981

Subtests: Identification of Colors and Shapes, and Copying Shapes; Picture Description, Position, and Spatial Recognition; Identification of Numbers, and Counting; Identification of Letters, and Writing
Descriptors: Culture Fair Tests; *Educational Diagnosis; *Individual Testing; *Kindergarten Children; Number Concepts; *School Readiness; *Screening Tests; Spatial Ability; Visual Discrimination; Visual Perception
Availability: Stoelting Co.; 620 Wheat Ln., Wood Dale, IL 60191
Grade Level: K
Notes: Time, 15 min. approx.; Items, 52

Used primarily as a screening test to identify children's deficits and strengths in readiness skills necessary to obtain maximum benefit from first grade experiences and to identify those children who may require additional psychoeducational evaluation. It is not intended as a device to exclude or postpone admission to school but as an aid in developing the most appropriate programs for children's individual needs. Individually administered test.

11614
Adston Mathematics Skills Series: Diagnostic Instrument in Pre-Algebra Concepts and Skills (Junior High Level).   Beeson, B. F.; Adams, Sam 1980
Descriptors: *Algebra; *Criterion Referenced Tests; *Diagnostic Tests; Fractions; *Grade 6; Junior High Schools; *Junior High School Students; *Mathematics Tests; Number Concepts; *Secondary School Mathematics; Whole Numbers
Identifiers: TIM(J)
Availability: Tests in Microfiche; Test Collection, Educational Testing Service, Princeton, NJ 08541
Grade Level: 6-8
Notes: Items, 58

One of a series of criterion-referenced tests designed to aid in the diagnosis of specific difficulties. This test covers basic operations with whole numbers, basic operations with common fractions, and basic operations with decimal fractions, basic concepts of measurement (conversions), basic concepts of measurement (perimeters and area), number structure, simplifying expressions, rewriting word statements as algebraic expressions, and solving simple algebraic equations. Prescription materials are also included.

11615
Adston Mathematics Skills Series: Diagnostic Instrument in Common Fractions.   Adams, Sam 1977
Descriptors: *Criterion Referenced Tests; *Diagnostic Tests; *Fractions; *Grade 6; Junior High Schools; *Junior High School Students; *Mathematics Tests
Identifiers: TIM(J)
Availability: Tests in Microfiche; Test Collection, Educational Testing Service, Princeton, NJ 08541
Grade Level: 6-8
Notes: Items, 60

One of a series of diagnostic tests designed to help the teacher and student locate specific difficulties. There are prescriptive materials as well as a diagnostic test. The test on fractions was developed around the following skills: fraction concepts, rewriting fractions, adding fractions, subtracting fractions, multiplying fractions, dividing fractions.

11616
Adston Mathematics Skills Series: Diagnostic Instrument in Basics of Operations.   Adams, Sam; Beeson, B.F. 1979
Descriptors: *Arithmetic; *Criterion Referenced Tests; *Diagnostic Tests; *Elementary School Mathematics; *Elementary School Students; *Mathematics Tests; Primary Education
Identifiers: TIM(J)
Availability: Tests in Microfiche; Test Collection, Educational Testing Service, Princeton, NJ 08541
Grade Level: 1-3
Notes: Items, 50

One of a series of diagnostic tests designed to help the teacher and student locate specific difficulties. There are prescriptive materials as well as a diagnostic test. The test was developed around the following structure: sequencing, associating numerals with sets, addition, subtraction, and multiplication.

11617
Adston Mathematics Skills Series: Diagnostic Instrument in Problem Solving.   Beeson, B. F.; Adams, Sam 1979

Descriptors: Computation; *Criterion Referenced Tests; *Diagnostic Tests; Elementary School Mathematics; *Grade 6; Junior High Schools; *Junior High School Students; *Mathematics Tests; *Problem Solving; *Secondary School Mathematics
Identifiers: TIM(J)
Availability: Tests in Microfiche; Test Collection, Educational Testing Service, Princeton, NJ 08541
Grade Level: 6-8
Notes: Items, 62

One of a series of diagnostic tests designed to help the teacher and student locate specific difficulties. There are prescriptive materials as well as a diagnostic test. The test was developed around the following structure: skills (overview of whole number operational skills), vocabulary (language of problem solving), preproblem (emphasis on decision-making process), and problems (decisions with computation).

11618
Adston Mathematics Skills Series: Diagnostic Instrument in Decimal Numbers.   Beeson, B. F.; Pellegrin, Lionel O. 1977
Descriptors: *Criterion Referenced Tests; *Decimal Fractions; *Diagnostic Tests; Elementary School Mathematics; *Grade 6; Junior High Schools; *Junior High School Students; *Mathematics Tests; *Secondary School Mathematics
Identifiers: TIM(J)
Availability: Tests in Microfiche; Test Collection, Educational Testing Service, Princeton, NJ 08541
Grade Level: 6-8
Notes: Items, 42

One of a series of diagnostic tests designed to help the teacher and student locate specific difficulties. There are prescriptive materials as well as a diagnostic test. The test was developed around the following structure: decimal number concepts, adding decimal numbers, subtracting decimal numbers, multiplying decimal numbers, dividing decimal numbers.

11625
Michigan Test of English Language Proficiency.
English Language Institute, Ann Arbor, MI 1968
Subtests: Grammar; Vocabulary; Reading Comprehension
Descriptors: *Achievement Tests; *English (Second Language); *Graduate Students; Grammar; Higher Education; *Language Proficiency; Language Tests; Reading Comprehension; *Undergraduate Students; Vocabulary
Identifiers: ELIUM; Test Batteries
Availability: English Language Institute; 2001 N. University Bldg., University of Michigan, Ann Arbor, MI 48109
Grade Level: 13-16
Notes: Time, 75 min. approx.; Items, 100

Designed as part of battery to predict academic success of nonnative speakers of English in an English language college or university. Michigan battery includes impromptu 30-minute written theme on assigned topic and a test of aural comprehension. Equivalent forms A,B,D,E,F,G, and H are available for Michigan Test of English Language Proficiency. Should not be used as a placement test.

11635
National German Examination for High School Students.   American Association of Teachers of German, Cherry Hill, NJ 1982
Subtests: Listening Comprehension; Reading
Descriptors: *Achievement Tests; Audiotape Cassettes; *German; Higher Education; High Schools; *High School Students; Listening Comprehension; Reading Skills; *Second Language Learning; *Student Placement; *Undergraduate Students
Identifiers: AATG National Standardized Testing Program
Availability: American Association of Teachers of German; 523 Bldg., Ste. 201, Rte. 38, Cherry Hill, NJ 08034
Grade Level: 10-16
Notes: Time, 60 min. approx.; Items, 100

Standardized testing program administered in January of each year. Three separate levels, 2, 3, and 4, may be tested. Tests are updated annually, and previous years' tests are available for purpose of diagnostic and practice tests. Listening comprehension section is available in audiotape cassettes with a printed tape script. This section requires 20 minutes to administer. Reading section requires 40 minutes to administer.

11636
New York State Native Language Writing Test.
New York State Education Dept., Albany, Bureau of Elementary and Secondary Educational Testing

Descriptors: *Achievement Tests; Grade 11; Grade 12; High Schools; *High School Students; State Programs; Testing Programs; *Writing Skills
Identifiers: *Native Language; *New York; *State Testing Programs
Availability: New York State Education Dept.; Bureau of Elementary and Secondary Testing, University of the State of New York, Albany, NY, 12234
Grade Level: 11-12

Test in 26 languages for use with pupils having limited English proficiency.

11638
New York State Statewide Achievement Examination. New York State Education Dept., Albany, Bureau of Elementary and Secondary Educational Testing
Descriptors: *Achievement Tests; Grade 11; Grade 12; High Schools; *High School Students; State Programs; Testing Programs; *United States History
Identifiers: *New York; *State Testing Programs
Availability: New York State Education Dept.; Bureau of Elementary and Secondary Testing, University of the State of New York, Albany, NY 12234
Grade Level: 11-12
Notes: Items, 60

Used by school districts in New York State that have developed their own adaptations of the American history curriculum for achievement testing.

11639
New York State Regents Examinations. New York State Education Dept., Albany, Bureau of Elementary and Secondary Educational Testing
Descriptors: *Achievement Tests; *Biology; *Bookkeeping; *Chemistry; *Earth Science; *English; *French; *German; *Hebrew; High Schools; *High School Students; *Italian; *Latin; *Mathematics; *Physics; *Scholarships; *Shorthand; *Social Studies; *Spanish; State Programs; Testing Programs
Identifiers: *Business Law; *Business Mathematics; *New York; *State Testing Programs
Availability: New York State Education Dept.; Bureau of Elementary and Secondary Testing, University of the State of New York, Albany, NY 12234
Grade Level: 9-12

Statewide testing program used to measure achievement and grant scholarships. Exams are available in English, mathematics, biology, social studies, chemistry, Spanish, French, German, Hebrew, Italian, Latin, earth science, physics, bookkeeping, business law, business mathematics, and shorthand. Most of the exams are used in grades 11-12.

11640
New York Regents Competency Tests. New York State Education Dept., Albany, Bureau of Elementary and Secondary Educational Testing
Descriptors: High Schools; *High School Students; *Minimum Competency Testing; *Reading Tests; *Secondary School Mathematics; State Programs; Testing Programs; *Writing Skills
Identifiers: *Cloze Procedure (Modified); Degrees of Reading Power; New York; *State Testing Programs
Availability: New York State Education Dept.; Bureau of Elementary and Secondary Testing, University of the State of New York, Albany, NY 12234
Grade Level: 9-12
Notes: Items, 143

Includes a mathematics test which covers the core of the state math curriculum. The reading test is the Degrees of Reading Power (TC010462), a modified cloze procedure. The writing test consists of 3 writing tasks: a business letter, a report, and a persuasive discourse. The reading and writing tests are administered in grades 11 and 12 only as requirements for receipt of a diploma. The math section has been translated into 26 different languages.

11641
New York State Pupil Evaluation Program. New York State Education Dept., Albany, Bureau of Elementary and Secondary Educational Testing
Descriptors: Elementary Education; *Elementary School Mathematics; *Elementary School Students; Grade 3; Grade 5; Grade 6; *Reading Tests; State Programs; Testing Programs; *Writing Skills
Identifiers: *Cloze Procedure (Modified); Degrees of Reading Power; New York State Reading and Readiness Tests; PEP; *State Testing Programs
Availability: New York State Education Dept.; Bureau of Elementary and Secondary Testing, University of the State of New York, Albany, NY 12234

Grade Level: 3-6

Testing program for spring administration in grades 3, 5, and 6. Includes the New York State Reading Test, Degrees of Reading Power (TC010462), a modified cloze procedure for grades 3 and 6. The New York State Mathematics Test is also given in grades 3 and 6. A New York State Writing Test, consisting of 2 writing tasks, scored holistically, is offered to grade 5.

11642
New York State Preliminary Competency Tests. New York State Education Dept., Albany, Bureau of Elementary and Secondary Educational Testing
Descriptors: Junior High Schools; *Junior High School Students; *Minimum Competency Testing; *Reading Tests; State Programs; Testing Programs; *Writing Skills
Identifiers: *Cloze Procedure (Modified); New York; PCT; *State Testing Programs
Availability: New York State Education Dept.; Bureau of Elementary and Secondary Testing, University of the State of New York, Albany NY 12234
Grade Level: 8-9

A modified cloze procedure, the PCT in reading and the PCT in writing, which consists of 3 tasks rated holistically, are intended to point out pupil deficiencies early in secondary school so that appropriate instruction can be given prior to the New York Regents Competency Tests (TC011640), a requirement for receiving a high school diploma.

11643
ACS Cooperative Examination: Organic Chemistry Tests. American Chemical Society, Tampa, FL, Div. of Chemical Education
Descriptors: *Achievement Tests; Chemistry; Higher Education; Multiple Choice Tests; *Organic Chemistry; *Undergraduate Students
Identifiers: *American Chemical Society Cooperative Examinations
Availability: ACS DivCHED Examinations Institute; Oklahoma State University, 107 Physical Sciences, Stillwater, OK 74078-0447
Grade Level: 13-16
Notes: Time, 115 min.; Items, 70

Measures achievement after a full-year course in modern organic chemistry. Areas assessed include theoretical concepts, acid and basic character of organic compounds, stereochemistry, reaction types associated with organic molecules, reaction mechanisms, spectroscopic identification of organic structures, and synthetic sequences. Test forms are updated periodically, and older forms may be retired from active use. Retired college-level forms may be released to high school teachers.

11644
ACS Cooperative Examination: Biochemistry Tests, Form 1982. American Chemical Society, Tampa, FL, Div. of Chemical Education 1982
Descriptors: *Achievement Tests; *Biochemistry; Chemistry; *Graduate Students; Higher Education; Multiple Choice Tests; Student Placement; *Undergraduate Students
Identifiers: *American Chemical Society Cooperative Examinations
Availability: ACS DivCHED Examinations Institute; Oklahoma State University, 107 Physical Sciences, Stillwater, OK 74078-0447
Grade Level: 15-17
Notes: Time, 120 min.; Items, 60

Designed as a comprehensive final examination appropriate for junior- and senior-level undergraduate course in general biochemistry. May serve as placement test for entering graduate students. Areas assessed include properties and structure-function relationships of biological molecules, including bioenergetics and enzyme activity; intermediary metabolism and its control; the biochemistry of informational macromolecules; and biochemical methods. Test forms are updated periodically, and older forms may be retired from active use. Retired college-level forms may be released to high school teachers.

11645
ACS-NSTA Cooperative Examination: Advanced High School Chemistry Test. American Chemical Society, Tampa, FL, Div. of Chemical Education 1982
Descriptors: *Achievement Tests; Atomic Structure; *Chemistry; High Schools; *High School Students; *Honors Curriculum; Kinetics; Multiple Choice Tests; Thermodynamics
Identifiers: *American Chemical Society Cooperative Examinations
Availability: ACS DivCHED Examinations Institute; Oklahoma State University, 107 Physical Sciences, Stillwater, OK 74078-0447
Grade Level: 9-12
Notes: Time, 110 min.; Items, 60

Written at a first-year college level, tests are designed for students taking advanced placement or honors high school course. Useful as college placement tests. Areas assessed

include atomic structure (including nuclear); chemical bonding, molecular geometry and carbon chemistry; thermodynamics; kinetics; solids, liquids, gases, and solutions; acid-base chemistry; electrochemistry; chemical periodicity; descriptive chemistry and stoichiometry; and laboratory procedures and techniques. Test forms are updated periodically, and older forms may be retired from active use. Retired college-level forms may be released to high school teachers.

11650
Nutrition Knowledge Test for Nursery and Kindergarten. Pennsylvania State Univ., University Park. Nutrition Information and Resource Ctr. 1978
Descriptors: *Achievement Tests; Elementary School Curriculum; *Kindergarten Children; Knowledge Level; Nursery Schools; *Nutrition; Nutrition Instruction; *Preschool Children; *Pretests Posttests
Identifiers: Oral Tests; School Nutrition Education Curriculum Study; TIM(H)
Availability: Tests in Microfiche; Test Collection, Educational Testing Service, Princeton, NJ 08541
Age Level: 3-5
Notes: Time, 40 min. approx.; Items, 29

Developed to assess the nutrition knowledge of kindergarten students before and after being taught nutrition, using Nutrition in a Changing World, A Curriculum for Preschool (Provo, Utah). Can also be used as a general nutrition test for children, ages 3, 4, and 5. Test should be administered in 2 or 3 sessions, depending on age of children, and preferably in a classroom setting. Should also be administered within the first month of school if used as a basis for planning an instructional program in nutrition.

11651
Knowledge Test in Nutrition for Early Childhood. Pennsylvania State Univ., University Park. Nutrition Information and Resource Ctr. 1979
Descriptors: *Achievement Tests; Elementary School Curriculum; *Kindergarten Children; Knowledge Level; *Nutrition; Nutrition Instruction; *Pretests Posttests; Primary Education
Identifiers: Oral Tests; School Nutrition Education Curriculum Study; TIM(H)
Availability: Tests in Microfiche; Test Collection, Educational Testing Service, Princeton, NJ 08541
Grade Level: K
Notes: Time, 15 min. approx.; Items, 12

Used to assess kindergarten children's knowledge of selected nutrition concepts before and after being taught nutrition, using Nutrition in a Changing World, and before and after completing various classroom and lunchroom activities relevant to the instructional materials. Test items are intended to assess knowledge of the following nutrition concepts: variety of foods, vegetables, dental health, and snacking.

11653
Nutrition Knowledge Test for the Primary Grades. Pennsylvania State Univ., University Park. Nutrition Information and Resource Ctr. 1978
Descriptors: *Achievement Tests; Elementary School Curriculum; *Elementary School Students; Knowledge Level; *Nutrition; Nutrition Instruction; *Pretests Posttests; Primary Education
Identifiers: Oral Tests; School Nutrition Educational Curriculum Study; TIM(H)
Availability: Tests in Microfiche; Test Collection, Educational Testing Service, Princeton, NJ 08541
Grade Level: 1-3
Notes: Items, 28

A knowledge test which can be administered as a general nutrition test or as a pretest/posttest to determine student performance after using the curriculum, Nutrition in a Changing World. Designed to be administered to a group of children at one sitting. Time for administering the test will depend on the number of children tested and their grade level.

11654
Knowledge Test in Nutrition for Grade 1. Pennsylvania State Univ., University Park. Nutrition Information and Resource Ctr. 1979
Descriptors: *Achievement Tests; Dental Health; Elementary School Curriculum; Elementary School Students; Food; *Grade 1; Knowledge Level; *Nutrition; Nutrition Instruction; *Pretests Posttests; Primary Education
Identifiers: Oral Tests; School Nutrition Education Curriculum Study; TIM(H)
Availability: Tests in Microfiche; Test Collection, Educational Testing Service, Princeton, NJ 08541
Grade Level: 1
Notes: Time, 15 min. approx.; Items, 20

Developed to assess first graders' knowledge of selected nutrition concepts before and after participating in a nutrition education study, using the curriculum Nutrition in a Changing World and completing classroom and lunchroom activities. The following nutrition concepts were assessed: variety of foods, vegetables, dental health, and snacking.

11655
Knowledge Test in Nutrition for Grade 2. Pennsylvania State Univ., University Park. Nutrition Information and Resource Ctr. 1979
Descriptors: *Achievement Tests; Dental Health; Elementary School Curriculum; Elementary School Students; Food; *Grade 2; Knowledge Level; *Nutrition; Nutrition Instruction; *Pretests Posttests; Primary Education
Identifiers: Oral Tests; School Nutrition Education Curriculum Study; TIM(H)
Availability: Tests in Microfiche; Test Collection, Educational Testing Service, Princeton, NJ 08541
Grade Level: 2
Notes: Time, 15 min. approx.; Items, 20
Developed to assess second grade students' knowledge of selected nutrition concepts before and after participating in a nutrition education study using the curriculum Nutrition in a Changing World and completing classroom and lunchroom activities. Concepts being assessed are variety of foods, vegetables, dental health, and snacking.

11656
Knowledge Test in Nutrition for Grade 3. Pennsylvania State Univ., University Park. Nutrition Information and Resource Ctr. 1979
Descriptors: *Achievement Tests; Dental Health; Elementary School Curriculum; Elementary School Students; Food; *Grade 3; Knowledge Level; *Nutrition; Nutrition Instruction; *Pretests Posttests; Primary Education
Identifiers: Oral Tests; School Nutrition Educational Curriculum Study; TIM(H)
Availability: Tests in Microfiche; Test Collection, Educational Testing Service, Princeton, NJ 08541
Grade Level: 3
Notes: Time, 15 min. approx.; Items, 20
Developed to assess third grade students' knowledge of selected nutrition concepts before and after participating in a nutrition education study using Nutrition in a Changing World and completing related classroom and lunchroom activities. Knowledge of the following concepts was assessed: variety of foods, vegetables, dental health, and snacking.

11658
Nutrition Test Item Bank for the Intermediate Grades. Pennsylvania State Univ., University Park. Nutrition Information and Resource Ctr. 1979
Descriptors: *Achievement Tests; *Elementary School Students; Intermediate Grades; *Item Banks; *Nutrition
Identifiers: School Nutrition Education Curriculum Study; TIM(H)
Availability: Tests in Microfiche; Test Collection, Educational Testing Service, Princeton, NJ 08541
Grade Level: 4-6
Notes: Items, 90
A 90-item test bank containing questions that correspond to nutrition concepts appropriate to introduce to students in grades 4-6. Items were reviewed by panel of nutrition faculty and advanced level graduate students for content accuracy. Items to be used to design an evaluation instrument to assess cognitive effect of a particular nutrition education program.

11659
Knowledge Test in Nutrition for Grade 4. Pennsylvania State Univ., University Park. Nutrition Information and Resource Ctr. 1979
Descriptors: *Achievement Tests; Dental Health; Elementary School Students; *Food; *Grade 4; Intermediate Grades; Knowledge Level; *Nutrition; Nutrition Instruction; *Pretests Posttests
Identifiers: School Nutrition Education Curriculum Study; TIM(H)
Availability: Tests in Microfiche; Test Collection, Educational Testing Service, Princeton, NJ 08541
Grade Level: 4
Notes: Items, 33
Developed to assess fourth grade students' knowledge of selected nutrition concepts before and after participating in a nutrition education study using Nutrition in a Changing World and completing classroom and lunchroom activities. The following concepts are assessed: variety of foods, vegetables, dental health, and snacking. Items were reviewed by nutrition faculty and advanced-level graduate students for content.

11660
Knowledge Test in Nutrition for Grade 5. Pennsylvania State Univ., University Park. Nutrition Information and Resource Ctr. 1979
Descriptors: *Achievement Tests; Dental Health; Elementary School Students; *Food; *Grade 5; Intermediate Grades; Knowledge Level; *Nutrition; Nutrition Instruction; *Pretests Posttests
Identifiers: School Nutrition Education Curriculum Study; TIM(H)
Availability: Tests in Microfiche; Test Collection, Educational Testing Service, Princeton, NJ 08541
Grade Level: 5
Notes: Items, 30
Developed to assess fifth grade students' knowledge of selected nutrition concepts before and after participating in a nutrition education study using Nutrition in a Changing World and completing classroom and lunchroom activities. Concepts assessed are variety of foods, vegetables, dental health, and snacking. Items were reviewed by a panel of nutrition faculty and advanced-level graduate students for content accuracy.

11661
Knowledge Test in Nutrition for Grade 6. Pennsylvania State Univ., University Park. Nutrition Information and Resource Ctr. 1979
Descriptors: *Achievement Tests; Dental Health; Elementary School Students; *Food; *Grade 6; Intermediate Grades; Knowledge Level; *Nutrition; Nutrition Instruction; *Pretests Posttests
Identifiers: School Nutrition Education Curriculum Study; TIM(H)
Availability: Tests in Microfiche; Test Collection, Educational Testing Service, Princeton, NJ 08541
Grade Level: 6
Notes: Items, 26
Developed to assess sixth graders' knowledge of selected nutrition concepts before and after participating in a nutrition education study using Nutrition in a Changing World and completing classroom and lunchroom activities. Concepts assessed are variety of foods, vegetables, dental health, and snacking. Items were reviewed by nutrition faculty and advanced level graduate students for content accuracy.

11663
Knowledge Test in Nutrition for Home Economics, Grades 7-9. Pennsylvania State Univ., University Park. Nutrition Information and Resource Ctr. 1980
Descriptors: *Achievement Tests; *Food; Home Economics; Junior High Schools; *Junior High School Students; Knowledge Level; *Nutrition; Nutrition Instruction; *Pretests Posttests
Identifiers: School Nutrition Education Curriculum Study; TIM(H)
Availability: Tests in Microfiche; Test Collection, Educational Testing Service, Princeton, NJ 08541
Grade Level: 7-9
Developed to assess junior high school students' knowledge of nutrition before and after being taught nutrition, using Nutrition in a Changing World for Home Economics, Grades 7-9. Items were reviewed by nutrition faculty and advanced-level graduate students for content accuracy. Test for grade 7 consists of 38 items; for grade 8, 36 items; and for grade 9, 34 items.

11664
Knowledge Test in Nutrition for Junior High Health. Pennsylvania State Univ., University Park. Nutrition Information and Resource Ctr. 1980
Descriptors: *Achievement Tests; *Food; Health Education; Junior High Schools; *Junior High School Students; Knowledge Level; *Nutrition; Nutrition Instruction; *Pretests Posttests
Identifiers: School Nutrition Education Curriculum Study; TIM(H)
Availability: Tests in Microfiche; Test Collection, Educational Testing Service, Princeton, NJ 08541
Grade Level: 7-9
Notes: Items, 48
Developed to assess junior high school students' knowledge of nutrition before and after studying nutrition, using Nutrition in a Changing World for Junior High Health. Items were reviewed by nutrition faculty and advanced-level graduate students for content accuracy.

11665
Knowledge Test in Nutrition for Senior High Health. Pennsylvania State Univ., University Park. Nutrition Information and Resource Ctr. 1980

Descriptors: *Achievement Tests; *Food; Health Education; High Schools; *High School Students; Knowledge Level; *Nutrition; Nutrition Instruction; *Pretests Posttests
Identifiers: School Nutrition Education Curriculum Study; TIM(H)
Availability: Tests in Microfiche; Test Collection, Educational Testing Service, Princeton, NJ 08541
Grade Level: 9-12
Notes: Items, 45
Developed to assess senior high students' knowledge of nutrition before and after being taught nutrition using Nutrition in a Changing World for Senior High Health. Items were reviewed by nutrition faculty and advanced-level graduate students for content.

11667
Nutrition Knowledge Test for Elementary Teachers. Pennsylvania State Univ., University Park. Nutrition Information and Resource Ctr. 1978
Descriptors: *Achievement Tests; Adults; Elementary Education; *Elementary School Teachers; *Food; Knowledge Level; *Nutrition; *Pretests Posttests
Identifiers: School Nutrition Education Curriculum Study; TIM(H)
Availability: Tests in Microfiche; Test Collection, Educational Testing Service, Princeton, NJ 08541
Grade Level: K-6
Age Level: Adults
Notes: Items, 40
Developed to assess nutrition knowledge of elementary school teachers before and after participating in a nutrition education study, using Nutrition in a Changing World. Items were reviewed by a panel of nutrition faculty and advanced-level graduate students for content accuracy.

11676
Regents College Examination. New York State Education Dept., Albany, Cultural Education Center 1963
Descriptors: Adults; *Anatomy; *Applied Music; *Black History; *College Credits; *College English; *Earth Science; *Equivalency Tests; *Nursing; *Teacher Education; *Typewriting; *United States History; *Writing (Composition)
Identifiers: CPE; Criminal Justice; *New York; Shakespeare (William)
Availability: College Proficiency Examination Program; State Education Dept., Cultural Education Center, Albany, NY 12230
Age Level: Adults
Notes: Time, 180 min.
A program which provides college credit by examination to residents of the state of New York for knowledge obtained through independent study or on-the-job training. There are 20 proficiency examinations. Many of these examinations are also available to those living outside the state of New York. See ACT Proficiency Examination Program (TC008121-008126, 008130-008145, 008149-008167, and 011277-011281). Areas covered by the examinations are Afro-American History, American History, Anatomy and Physiology, Applied Music, College Composition, Earth Science, Freshman English, Shakespeare, Criminal Justice, Education, Nursing, Typewriting. Testing times vary from 1-20 hours but most are 3-hour exams.

11677
Regents College Examination. New York State Education Dept., Albany, Cultural Education Center 1971
Descriptors: *Accounting; Adults; College Credits; *Equivalency Tests; *External Degree Programs; *Marketing; *Nursing
Identifiers: Finance; Management Science; New York State; REDE
Availability: Regents External Degrees; The University of the State of New York, Cultural Education Center, Albany, NY 12230
Age Level: Adults
Series of examinations developed for use with the Regents Degree Program, to provide college credit by examination. This credit applies toward the granting of associate or baccalaureate degrees. Areas covered are accounting, finance, management, marketing, and nursing. Examination times vary from 3 to 7 hours.

11689
Yeshiva High School Entrance Examination. Board of Jewish Education of Greater New York, NY 1982
Subtests: Memory and Knowledge of Torah; Comprehension of Torah; Comprehension of Rashi; Prophets and Writings; Laws; Hebrew Language; Essay in Hebrew without Vowels; Talmud; Vocabulary; Sentence Completion; Reading Comprehension; Mathematics

Descriptors: Academic Achievement; *Achievement Tests; Admission (School); Adolescents; *Elementary School Students; *Grade 8; *Hebrew; Mathematical Concepts; Mathematics; *Parochial Schools; Timed Tests; Verbal Ability
Identifiers: *Admission Tests (High Schools); *Entrance Examinations; General Examination In the Subjects Of Judaica; *Jewish Studies; Yeshiva High Schools
Availability: Board of Jewish Education of Greater New York; BJE Testing Service, 426 W. 58th St., New York, NY 10019
Age Level: 13-14
Notes: Time, 180 min.; Items, 260

Designed as an entrance exam for yeshiva high schools in the greater New York area, though it could be used in other Jewish parochial schools. Includes both a general studies examination (knowledge acquired in all schools) and the Judaic studies examination. The subtest, Talmud, is given only to boys. Usually given to eighth graders of Jewish day schools in the New York area.

11735
Official GED Practice Test, Form A. American Council on Education, Washington, DC, General Educational Development Testing Service 1979
Subtests: Writing Skills; Social Studies; Science; Reading Skills; Mathematics
Descriptors: Adults; *Equivalency Tests; High School Equivalency Programs; *Mathematics Achievement; Multiple Choice Tests; Reading Comprehension; *Reading Skills; Sciences; *Scientific Concepts; *Social Studies; *Writing Skills
Identifiers: *General Educational Development Tests; *Practice Tests; Self Scoring Tests; Test Batteries
Availability: Prentice Hall Regents; Order Dept., 200 Old Tappan Rd., Old Tappan, NJ 07675
Age Level: Adults
Notes: Time, 180 min. approx.; Items, 145

Designed to provide an opportunity to adults to earn a high school equivalency diploma or certificate. Purpose is to assess as accurately as possible the major and lasting outcomes generally associated with 4 years of general high school instruction. Areas tested correspond to general organization of most high school curricula. Candidates are tested on broad knowledge and concepts rather than on details, historical facts, or precise definitions. Test batteries are available in French and Spanish and, for handicapped, in braille, large print, or on audiotapes. Tests are administered only to adults who meet eligibility requirements established by their state, territorial, or provincial department of education. Practice tests are half the length of the full-length GED tests.

11748
A Test of Graphicacy. Wainer, Howard 1980
Descriptors: *Comprehension; Concept Formation; *Elementary School Students; *Graphs; Intermediate Grades; Multiple Choice Tests; Nonverbal Learning; *Teaching Methods; *Visual Measures; *Visual Stimuli
Availability: Applied Psychological Measurement; v4 n3 p331-40, Sum 1980
Grade Level: 3-5
Notes: Items, 8

Used in a study to investigate the extent to which children learn to use graphic displays and at what age this learning is complete. Study also examined other aspects: kinds of questions for which graphs can be used, what sorts of displays work best and for what kinds of questions, do all children become graphically literate.

11755
Multilevel Informal Language Inventory. Goldsworthy, Candace; Secord, Wayne 1982
Descriptors: Children; *Informal Assessment; Language Acquisition; *Language Handicaps; *Oral Language; Remedial Instruction; *Semantics; Speech Pathology; *Syntax
Identifiers: *Language Sampling; MILI
Availability: The Psychological Corp.; 555 Academic Ct., San Antonio, TX 78204-0952
Age Level: 4-12
Notes: Time, 45 min. approx.

Developed as an informal assessment tool to measure a child's level of oral language functioning, specifically in the production of critical semantic relations and syntactic constructions. To be used with children suspected of having oral language production problems. Intended users are practicing clinicians of speech-language pathology and specialists in learning disabilities. The assessment is designed to supplement data gathered from other assessment methods. Primary objective is to help direct the course of language intervention programs.

11776
The Gesell Preschool Test. Haines, Jacqueline; And Others 1980
Subtests: Motor; Adaptive; Language; Personal-Social
Descriptors: Adjustment (to Environment); *Child Development; Culture Fair Tests; Individual Testing; Language Skills; Motor Development; *Preschool Tests; School Readiness; Social Adjustment; *Young Children
Identifiers: Test Batteries
Availability: Programs for Education; Dept. 217CI, Rosemont, NJ 08556
Age Level: 2-6

Includes a series of individual test situations which, taken together, reveal a child's relative maturity ratings in 4 basic fields of behavior: motor, adaptive language, and personal-social. Tests may be used to determine the normality of a child's level of development, to give parent a clear picture of child's individuality, to indicate how a child adapts to a new situation, and for school readiness and placement purposes. The tests are designed for children from 2.5 to 6 years of age.

11777
School Readiness Test. Gesell Institute of Child Development 1978
Subtests: Visuals 1 and 3; Face Sheet; Initial Interview; Cube Tests; Pencil and Paper; Right and Left; Incomplete Man
Descriptors: Age Grade Placement; Attention Span; Child Development; Eye Hand Coordination; Grade 1; Grade 2; Grade 3; Kindergarten; Psychomotor Skills; School Readiness; *School Readiness Tests; Verbal Development; Visual Perception; *Young Children
Availability: Programs for Education; Dept. 217CI, Rosemont, NJ 08556
Age Level: 4-9
Notes: Time, 40 min.

Designed for use as a measure of school readiness based on developmental not chronological age. Tests include figure copying, completing a figure, and handedness. Tests measure eye-hand coordination, motor skill, attention span, level of functioning in a structured fine-motor task, visual perception, and verbal ability.

11788
Test of Spoken English. Educational Testing Service, Princeton, NJ
Subtests: Pronunciation; Control of Grammar; Fluency
Descriptors: Colleges; *College Students; Culture Fair Tests; Diagnostic Tests; *English (Second Language); *Health Personnel; Higher Education; Individual Testing; *Language Proficiency; *Language Tests; *Oral English; *Second Language Learning; Tape Recordings; *Teaching Assistants; Universities
Identifiers: TSE
Availability: Educational Testing Service; Test of Spoken English, Box 6157, Princeton, NJ 08541
Grade Level: 17-20
Notes: Time, 20 min. approx.

Primary purpose is to evaluate the English-speaking proficiency of persons whose native language is not English. The test is not targeted to a single academic discipline, field of employment, or other specialized language usage. Permits examinee to demonstrate general speaking proficiency. Test may also be used to diagnose strengths and weaknesses in Spoken English at the end of a course of study. Was developed chiefly for use by academic institutions and has been validated in this context at present. Test is appropriate for all examinees regardless of their native language or culture. Examinee listens to tape recording of test questions and answers each question by speaking into a microphone. May be used with college students and health personnel.

11792
Brigance K and 1 Screen. Brigance, Albert H. 1982
Descriptors: *Basic Skills; *Grade 1; Individualized Education Programs; *Kindergarten Children; Primary Education; *Screening Tests; *Spanish Speaking; Special Programs; Student Placement
Availability: Curriculum Associates; 5 Esquire Rd., North Billerica, MA 01862-2589
Grade Level: K-1

Evaluation tool that assesses pupils' basic skills to identify special service referrals, determine appropriate pupil placement, and assist in planning individual pupil programs. Basic skills evaluated include personal data response; color recognition; picture vocabulary; visual discrimination; visual motor skills; standing gross motor skills; draw a person (body image); rate counting; identification of body parts; recite alphabet; follow verbal directions; numeral comprehension; recognition of lower and upper case letters; auditory discrimination; print personal data; syntax and fluency; numerals in sequence. Included in this edition is a section that allows personnel to assess additional, more advanced skills. These assessments are optional, and their use is recommended upon need. Skills include responses to picture, basic preprimer vocabulary, reads orally at preprimer/primer level, basic number skills, articulation of sounds, and comprehension and language. Spanish direction lines for screening Spanish-speaking children are available.

11795
Zaner-Bloser Kindergarten Screening Inventory. Milone, Michael N.; Lucas, Virginia H. 1980
Subtests: Naming Objects; Matching Objects; Naming Money; Matching Money; Naming Colors; Matching Colors; Naming Shapes; Matching Shapes; Naming Sets; Matching Sets; Naming Numerals; Matching Numerals; Naming Letters; Matching Letters; Spatial Relationship Words; Sequence Words; Sequencing; Counting; Writing Name; Tracing Strokes; Copying Strokes; Tracing Letters; Copying Letters
Descriptors: *Cognitive Development; *Criterion Referenced Tests; *Individual Testing; *Kindergarten Children; Primary Education; *School Readiness; *Screening Tests
Identifiers: KSI; Zaner Bloser Kindergarten Program
Availability: Zaner-Bloser; 2200 West Fifth Ave., P.O. Box 16764, Columbus, OH 43216-6764
Grade Level: K

Developed to help teachers identify educationally relevant differences among kindergarten children to allow for appropriate curriculum planning. KSI comprises skills that appear on the Zaner-Bloser Kindergarten Program Foundations for Formal Learning and the Check Lists of Kindergarten Skills. KSI focuses on skills important to prereading, prewriting, and prearithmetic. One skill prominent in KSI is left-to-right progression. Individually administered. KSI also allows for teacher observation and comments.

11796
Barbe-Lucas Handwriting Skill—Guide Check List. Barbe, Walter B.; Lucas, Virginia H. 1979
Descriptors: *Check Lists; *Cursive Writing; *Elementary School Students; Elementary Secondary Education; *Handwriting; *Manuscript Writing (Handlettering); *Secondary School Students
Availability: Zaner-Bloser; 2200 West Fifth Ave., P.O. Box 16764, Columbus, OH 43216-6764
Grade Level: K-12

Checklists that constitute systematic compilation of skills needed for handwriting mastery include basic concepts and mechanical, functional, and creative skills.

11816
Denver Developmental Screening Test Revised. Frankenburg, William K.; And Others 1978
Subtests: Gross Motor; Language; Fine Motor-Adaptive; Personal-Social
Descriptors: *Developmental Tasks; Individual Testing; *Infants; *Language Acquisition; Learning Disabilities; Motor Development; *Preschool Children; *Psychomotor Skills; *Screening Tests; *Social Development; Young Children
Identifiers: DDST R; Denver Developmental Screening Test; *Denver Screening Test for Preschoolers
Availability: Denver Developmental Materials; P.O. Box 6919, Denver, CO 80206-0919
Age Level: 0-6
Notes: Time, 20 min. approx.; Items, 105

Designed as a screening device to identify infants and preschool children with serious developmental delays. The test is to be used only for screening purposes to alert professional child workers to the possibility of developmental delays so that appropriate diagnostic studies may be pursued. A child at any given age is administered only 20 or so simple items. DDST-R test items are arranged in a chronological step-wise order.

11818
Denver Prescreening Developmental Questionnaire (Spanish Edition). Frankenburg, William K.; And Others 1975
Descriptors: *Developmentai Tasks; Individual Testing; *Infants; Language Acquisition; Learning Disabilities; Motor Development; Parents; *Preschool Children; *Screening Tests; Social Development; *Spanish; Young Children
Identifiers: PDQ; PreInvestigacion del Desarrollo Infantil en Denver
Availability: Denver Developmental Materials; P.O. Box 6919, Denver, CO 80206-0919
Age Level: 0-6
Notes: Time, 5 min. approx.; Items, 97

Designed to be a "prescreening" tool used to identify those children 3 months to 6 years of age who will require further screening with the Denver Developmental Screening Test (TC003628). Used to detect developmental lags and suggest more detailed screening is required. Parents select the 10 age-appropriate questions for their children and answer these. Five color-coded forms arrange items by the chronological age at which most children can perform certain skills.

11863
Prueba del Desarrollo Inicial del Languaje.
Hresko, Wayne P.; And Others 1982
Descriptors: Expressive Language; *Individual Testing; *Oral Language; Receptive Language; *Screening Tests; *Young Children
Identifiers: PDIL
Availability: PRO-ED; 8700 Shoal Creek Blvd., Austin, TX 78758-6897
Age Level: 3-7
Notes: Time, 20 min. approx.; Items, 38

Individually administered test designed to measure spoken language abilities of young children. This is an untimed test but may be administered in 15 to 20 minutes. The 2 language dimensions, content and form, are the basis for the development of the test. Also assesses aspects of receptive and expressive language. Test results may be used for identifying children significantly behind their peers in language development; to document child's progress in language; to use in research projects; or to suggest instructional practices. Spanish-language version is based on Test of Early Language Development, 1981 (TC011223).

11864
Basic School Skills Inventory—Diagnostic.
Hammill, Donald D.; Leigh, James E. 1983
Subtests: Daily Living Skills; Spoken Language; Reading Readiness; Writing Readiness; Mathematics Readiness; Classroom Behavior
Descriptors: *Basic Skills; Criterion Referenced Tests; Daily Living Skills; *Diagnostic Tests; Elementary School Mathematics; Handwriting; Writing Readiness; Individual Testing; Norm Referenced Tests; *Preschool Children; Primary Education; Reading Readiness; *School Readiness Tests; Speech Communication; Student Behavior
Identifiers: BSSI D
Availability: PRO-ED; 8700 Shoal Creek Blvd., Austin, TX 78758-6897
Age Level: 4-6
Notes: Time, 30 min. approx.; Items, 110

Used to assist teachers and other educational personnel in assessing abilities of young children. Test has 4 main uses: to identify children performing significantly below their peers in the areas measured; to reveal specific strengths and weaknesses for instructional purposes; to document progress resulting from intervention programs; to use in research studies involving young children. Also suitable for use with older children who function within the developmental range of 4 to 6 years, such as retarded, underachievers, slow learners, learning disabled, educationally handicapped, or developmentally young. There are no time limits on test; time will vary but generally should not exceed 30 minutes.

11865
Prueba de Lectura y Lenguaje Escrito. Hammill, Donald D.; And Others 1982
Subtests: Vocabulario; Lectura de Parrafos; Vocabulario Escrito; Composicion; Ortografia; Estilo
Descriptors: *Diagnostic Tests; Elementary Education; *Elementary School Students; Grammar; Group Testing; Individual Testing; *Reading Ability; *Reading Comprehension; Secondary Education; *Secondary School Students; *Spanish; Spanish Speaking; Spelling; Vocabulary; Writing (Composition); *Writing Evaluation; *Writing Skills
Identifiers: PLLE
Availability: PRO-ED; 8700 Shoal Creek Blvd., Austin, TX 78758-6897
Grade Level: 3-10
Notes: Time, 120 min. approx.; Items, 75

Diagnostic test of written language proficiency. Used to identify students who have problems with written expression in comparison with their peers; to determine a student's strengths and weaknesses; to document student progress in a reading or writing program; and/or to conduct research in writing or reading. May be administered individually or to groups. Based on the Test of Reading Comprehension, 1978 (TC010394) and the Test of Written Language, 1978 (TC010392). However, Spanish version is not a translation. The subjects were specifically designed for Spanish-language version.

11881
ACT Proficiency Examination Program: Foundations of Gerontology. American College Testing Program, Iowa City, IA 1982
Subtests: Theories and Concepts; Demography of Aging; Minorities; Biology; Health; Economics, Work, and Retirement; Environment; Psychology; Mental Health and Illness; Politics, Policy, and Legal Rights; Sociology; Death and Dying
Descriptors: Adults; *Adult Students; Aging (Individuals); *Aging Education; Death; Educational Gerontology; *Equivalency Tests; Geriatrics; *Gerontology; Objective Tests; *Older Adults; Postsecondary Education; Retirement; *Special Degree Programs; *Study Guides
Identifiers: American College Testing Program; New York; PEP; Regents External Degree
Availability: American College Testing Program; P.O. Box 168, Iowa City, IA 52240
Age Level: 18-64
Notes: Time, 180 min. approx.

Developed as part of 1 of 2 New York programs, the College Proficiency Examination Program and the Regents External Degree Program. Designed to assist postsecondary institutions in granting credit by examination. Tests are updated periodically. Measures knowledge and understanding of biological, psychological, and social aspects of aging. Candidate is expected to have an awareness of needs and realities involved in the aging process. Administered by American College Testing Program in all states except New York.

11882
ACT Proficiency Examination Program: Health Restoration, Area I. American College Testing Program, Iowa City, IA 1982
Subtests: Using the Nursing Process with Client Systems in Health Restoration; Profile of Major Health Problems; Major Health Problems
Descriptors: Adults; *Adult Students; Bachelors Degrees; *Equivalency Tests; *Nursing; Objective Tests; Physical Disabilities; Postsecondary Education; *Rehabilitation; *Special Degree Programs; Stress Variables; *Study Guides
Identifiers: American College Testing Program; New York; PEP; Regents External Degree
Availability: American College Testing Program; P.O. Box 168, Iowa City, IA 52240
Age Level: 18-64
Notes: Time, 180 min. approx.

Developed as part of 1 of 2 New York programs, the College Proficiency Examination Program and the Regents External Degree Program. Designed to assist postsecondary institutions in granting credit by examination. Designed for and standardized at baccalaureate degree level. Tests are updated periodically. Designed to assess candidate's ability to synthesize knowledge from the humanities, social sciences, and natural sciences in the application of the nursing process. Questions are based on the interrelationship between the nursing process and changes in the client system. Candidate should be able to analyze effects of stressors related to major health problems and evaluate biopsychosocial changes in the client system. Administered by American College Testing Program in all states except New York.

11883
ACT Proficiency Examination Program: Health Restoration, Area II. American College Testing Program, Iowa City, IA 1982
Subtests: Using the Nursing Process with Client Systems in Health Restoration; Profile of Major Health Problems; Major Health Problems
Descriptors: Adults; *Adult Students; Bachelors Degrees; *Equivalency Tests; *Nursing; Objective Tests; Physical Disabilities; Postsecondary Education; *Rehabilitation; *Special Degree Programs; Stress Variables; *Study Guides
Identifiers: American College Testing Program; New York; PEP; Regents External Degree
Availability: American College Testing Program; P.O. Box 168, Iowa City, IA 52240
Age Level: 18-64
Notes: Time, 180 min. approx.

Developed as part of 1 of 2 New York Programs, the College Proficiency Examination Program and the Regents External Degree Program. Designed to assist postsecondary institutions in granting credit by examination. Tests are updated periodically. Designed for and standardized at the baccalaureate degree level. Assesses candidate's ability to synthesize knowledge from the humanities, social sciences, and natural sciences in the application of the nursing process. Questions are based on the interrelationship between the nursing process and changes in the client system. Candidate should be able to analyze effects of stressors related to major health problems and evaluate biopsychosocial changes in the client system. Administered by American College Testing Program in all states except New York.

11884
ACT Proficiency Examination Program: Health Support, Area I. American College Testing Program, Iowa City, IA 1982
Subtests: Patterns of Activity; Patterns of Sustenance-Life-Sustaining; Patterns of Development; Patterns of Life-Space
Descriptors: Adults; *Adult Students; *Equivalency Tests; *Nursing; Objective Tests; *Physical Health; Postsecondary Education; *Special Degree Programs; *Study Guides; Well Being
Identifiers: American College Testing Program; New York; PEP; Regents External Degree
Availability: American College Testing Program; P.O. Box 168, Iowa City, IA 52240
Age Level: 18-64
Notes: Time, 180 min. approx.

Developed as part of 1 of 2 New York programs, the College Proficiency Examination Program and the Regents External Degree Program. Designed to assist postsecondary institutions in granting credit by examination. Tests are updated periodically. Designed to assess knowledge of concepts basic to the support of wellness. Questions focus on patterns that influence wellness and their interrelationships and potential barriers to wellness. Use of nursing process to support health of client throughout the life cycle is emphasized. Administered by American College Testing Program in all states except New York.

11885
ACT Proficiency Examination Program: Health Support, Area II. American College Testing Program, Iowa City, IA 1982
Subtests: Mental Health Problems; Nutritional Disturbances; Problems of Childbearing; Cardiovascular/Respiratory Problems; Problems of Safety and Environmental Health; Problems of Cellular Growth (Neoplasms); Infections and Communicable Diseases; Neurological Problems; Endocrine Problems; Autoimmune Problems; Birth Defects and Genetic Problems
Descriptors: Adults; *Adult Students; Bachelors Degrees; *Equivalency Tests; *Nursing; Objective Tests; Physical Disabilities; *Physical Health; Postsecondary Education; *Preventive Medicine; *Special Degree Programs; Stress Variables; *Study Guides; Well Being
Identifiers: American College Testing Program; New York; PEP; Regents External Degree
Availability: American College Testing Program; P.O. Box 168, Iowa City, IA 52240
Age Level: 18-64
Notes: Time, 180 min. approx.

Developed as part of 1 of 2 New York programs, the College Proficiency Examination Program and the Regents External Degree Program. Designed to assist postsecondary institutions in granting credit by examination. Designed for and standardized at baccalaureate degree level. Tests are updated periodically. Questions focus on alterations of developmental, sustenal, activity, or life-space patterns that place client at high risk for major health problems, including mental health, nutrition, problems of pregnancy, cardiovascular pulmonary problems, accidents, neoplasms, infections and communicable diseases, neurological and endocrine problems, autoimmune diseases, birth defects, and genetic problems. Administered by American College Testing Program in all states except New York.

11886
ACT Proficiency Examination Program: Physical Geology. American College Testing Program, Iowa City, IA 1982
Subtests: Earth as a Planet; Plate Tectonics; Minerals and Rocks; Igneous Activity; Crustal Deformation; Weathering; Mass Wasting; Eolian Processes; Geologic Work of Water; Glaciation; Shorelines; Geologic Time; Maps-Interpretation
Descriptors: Adults; *Adult Students; *Equivalency Tests; *Geology; Objective Tests; Postsecondary Education; *Special Degree Programs; *Study Guides
Identifiers: American College Testing Program; New York; PEP; Regents External Degree
Availability: American College Testing Program; P.O. Box 168, Iowa City, IA 52240
Age Level: 18-64
Notes: Time, 180 min. approx.

Developed as part of 1 of 2 New York programs, the College Proficiency Examination Program and the Regents External Degree Program. Designed to assist postsecondary institutions in granting credit by examination. Tests are updated periodically. Designed to assess knowledge and understanding of following areas: processes which form the earth through geologic time; the structure, composition, and evolution of the earth; and the landforms created by the processes that form the earth. Administered by American College Testing Program in all states except New York.

11887
ACT Proficiency Examination Program: Professional Strategies, Nursing. American College Testing Program, Iowa City, IA 1981
Subtests: Development of the Profession; Organizations; Professional Practice in Nursing; The Health Care Delivery System; Professional Role within the Occupations of Nursing
Descriptors: Adults; *Adult Students; Bachelors Degrees; *Equivalency Tests; *Nursing; Nursing Education; Objective Tests; Postsecondary Education; *Special Degree Programs; *Study Guides

Identifiers: American College Testing Program; New York; PEP; Regents External Degree
Availability: American College Testing Program; P.O. Box 168, Iowa City, IA 52240
Age Level: 18-64
Notes: Time, 180 min. approx.

Developed as part of 1 of 2 New York programs, the College Proficiency Examination Program and the Regents External Degree Program. Designed to assist postsecondary institutions in granting credit by examination. Designed for and standardized at the baccalaureate degree level. Tests are updated periodically. Designed to test candidate's knowledge and understanding of the professional role within the occupation of nursing. Professional practice and health delivery system are major areas assessed. Administered by American College Testing Program in all states except New York.

11888
Basic School Skills Inventory—Screen. Hammill, Donald D.; Leigh, James E. 1983
Descriptors: *High Risk Students; *Kindergarten Children; *Preschool Children; Primary Education; School Readiness; *Screening Tests
Identifiers: BSSI S
Availability: PRO-ED; 8700 Shoal Creek Blvd., Austin, TX 78758-6897
Age Level: 4-6
Notes: Time, 8 min. approx.; Items, 20

Used to identify children who are high-risk candidates for school failure and who may need remedial work, more comprehensive evaluation, or referral for possible special services. Scores may also serve as indication of child's readiness ability. Items were selected from items on BSSI—Diagnostic (TC011864).

11890
Speaking Proficiency English Assessment Kit. Educational Testing Service, Princeton, NJ 1982
Subtests: Pronunciation; Grammar; Fluency
Descriptors: *College Students; *English (Second Language); *Graduate Students; Grammar; Higher Education; Language Fluency; *Language Proficiency; *Oral Language; Pronunciation; *Speech Tests; *Teaching Assistants
Identifiers: Oral Tests; SPEAK
Availability: Educational Testing Service; TOEFL Program Office, Princeton, NJ 08541
Grade Level: 13-18
Notes: Time, 20 min.

A standardized test of English-speaking proficiency for internal use by colleges and universities for evaluating nonnative English-speaking students and applicants for positions as teaching assistants. Examinees respond orally to printed and recorded stimuli. Locally scored. May be used for pre- and posttesting in English courses and to identify those requiring additional instruction in spoken English.

11896
National Spanish Examinations. American Association of Teachers of Spanish and Portuguese, Frederick, MD 1982
Descriptors: *Achievement Tests; Grammar; High Schools; *High School Students; Listening Comprehension; Multiple Choice Tests; Reading Skills; Second Languages; *Spanish; Vocabulary
Identifiers: AATSP
Availability: The American Association of Teachers of Spanish and Portuguese; P.O. Box 6349, Mississippi State, MS 39762
Grade Level: 9-12
Notes: Time, 60 min.; Items, 80

Standard, objective examinations with multiple-choice items to test aural comprehension, vocabulary mastery, grammatical control, and reading skills. Use of a tape recorder or cassette recorder or language laboratory is mandatory for test administration. Test is part of a national contest sponsored by the American Association of Teachers of Spanish and Portuguese (AATSP). Only students of teachers who are members of AATSP are eligible to participate in the contest. There are 4 levels of the test. The level of the test given to students depends on how many years they have studied the language.

11901
SIGNALS Listening Test, Grade 3. Project SIGNALS, Norton, MA 1982
Subtests: Listening for the Main Idea; Following Geographic Directions; Following Instructions
Descriptors: Elementary School Students; Grade 2; *Grade 3; Group Testing; Listening Comprehension; *Listening Comprehension Tests; *Listening Skills; Magnetic Tape Cassettes; *Minimum Competencies; Primary Education; *Screening Tests
Availability: Project SIGNALS; A Div. of Project SPOKE, 315 W. Main St., Norton, MA 02766
Grade Level: 3
Notes: Time, 35 min. approx.; Items, 15

Designed to screen third grade students for difficulties in the basic skills of listening. The test is not designed to differentiate among students whose listening skills are ade-

quate but to detect those who should be given special help to attain basic listening skills. Students who do not obtain a passing score should be examined further on an individual basis. The test is group administered by the teacher who plays an audio tape recording. Students record answers in a student booklet. This test should not be used as the only measure for students who fail the test. This test has also been piloted with second grade students.

11902
SIGNALS Listening Test, Grade 5. Project SIGNALS, Norton, MA 1982
Subtests: Listening for the Main Idea; Following Geographic Directions; Following Instructions
Descriptors: Elementary School Students; *Grade 5; Group Testing; Intermediate Grades; Listening Comprehension; *Listening Comprehension Tests; *Listening Skills; Magnetic Tape Cassettes; *Minimum Competencies; *Screening Tests
Availability: Project SIGNALS; A Div. of Project SPOKE, 315 W. Main St., Norton, MA 02766
Grade Level: 5
Notes: Time, 35 min. approx.; Items, 15

Designed to screen fifth grade students for difficulties in the basic skills of listening. The test is not designed to differentiate among students whose listening skills are adequate but to detect those who should be given special help to attain basic listening skills. Students who do not obtain a passing score should be examined further on an individual basis. Test is group administered by the teacher who plays an audio tape recording. Students record answers in a student booklet. The test should not be used as the only measure for students who fail the test.

11903
Revised Developmental Screening Inventory. Knobloch, Hilda; And Others 1980
Descriptors: Adjustment (to Environment); *Child Development; Language Acquisition; Observation; Rating Scales; *Screening Tests; Social Behavior; *Young Children
Identifiers: Fine Motor Skills; Gesell Developmental Schedules; Gross Motor Skills
Availability: Developmental Evaluation Materials, Inc.; P.O. Box 272391, Houston, TX 77277-2391
Age Level: 0-3
Notes: Items, 180

Screening inventory designed to determine whether the child is functioning at age level or whether further testing is needed. Covers adaptive, gross motor, fine motor, language, and personal-social behavior. Ratings are made based on direct observation of the child. Derived from the Revised Gesell and Amatruda Developmental Schedules.

11904
New Jersey College Basic Skills Placement Test. College Entrance Examination Board, New York, NY
Subtests: Essay; Reading Comprehension; Sentence Sense; Math Computation; Elementary Algebra
Descriptors: Algebra; *Basic Skills; *College Freshmen; Computation; Essay Tests; Higher Education; *Mathematics; Multiple Choice Tests; Postsecondary Education; *Reading Comprehension; *Student Placement; Writing Skills
Identifiers: *Writing Sample
Availability: New Jersey Dept. of Higher Education; Basic Skills Council, 225 W. State St., Trenton, NJ 08618
Grade Level: 13
Notes: Time, 200 min.; Items, 167

Measures basic skills in reading comprehension, writing, computation, and elementary algebra for the placement of students who have been admitted to colleges in appropriate courses or course sections. Consists of multiple-choice questions and a 20-minute essay. Administered at all New Jersey public and participating private colleges. For information on purchase and use of the test contact Program Director, NJCBST, College Board, 45 Columbus Ave., New York, NY 10023-6992.

11920
Test of Practical Knowledge. Wiederholt, J. Lee; Larsen, Stephen C. 1983
Subtests: Personal Knowledge; Social Knowledge; Occupational Knowledge
Descriptors: *Achievement Tests; *Adolescents; Community Services; *Daily Living Skills; Employment; *Interpersonal Competence; Knowledge Level; Leisure Time; Secondary Education; *Secondary School Students
Identifiers: *Functional Competence; *Occupational Knowledge; TPK
Availability: PRO-ED; 8700 Shoal Creek Blvd., Austin, TX 78758-6897
Grade Level: 8-12
Age Level: 13-18
Notes: Time, 40 min. approx.; Items, 100

Mainly limited to testing the dimension of knowledge believed to be necessary for daily functioning. Results can be used to identify those significantly below their peers in practical knowledge; to determine particular areas of practical knowledge where students may be weak or strong; to serve as a measurement device to ascertain growth in intervention programs; to document student progress; or to investigate the construct of functional competency itself. May be administered individually or to groups.

11924
Learning Accomplishment Profile: Diagnostic Screening Edition. Chapel Hill Training-Outreach Project, NC; Kentucky State Dept. of Education, Frankfort 1981
Subtests: Fine Motor; Cognitive; Language; Gross Motor
Descriptors: Cognitive Ability; *High Risk Students; *Individual Testing; *Kindergarten Children; Language Skills; Primary Education; Psychomotor Skills; *Screening Tests
Identifiers: LAP(D)
Availability: Kaplan School Supply Corp.; 1310 Lewisville-Clemmons Rd., Lewisville, NC 27023
Grade Level: K
Notes: Time, 15 min. approx.; Items, 17

Developed for early identification of children potentially at risk in learning and developmental areas. All items must be administered. Results obtained should be considered first or initial phase of the screening, referral, diagnostic, individualized programing and instructional process. Items were selected from the Learning Accomplishment Profile-Diagnostic and includes items from the following subscales: fine motor, cognitive, language, and gross motor.

11925
Brigance Diagnostic Comprehensive Inventory of Basic Skills. Brigance, Albert H. 1983
Subtests: Readiness; Speech; Word Recognition Grade Placement; Oral Reading; Reading Comprehension; Listening; Functional Word Recognition; Word Analysis; Reference Skills; Writing; Math Grade Placement; Numbers; Number Facts; Computation of Whole Numbers; Fractions and Mixed Numbers; Decimals; Percents; Word Problems; Graphs and Maps; Spelling; Metrics; Math Vocabulary
Descriptors: Arithmetic; *Basic Skills; *Criterion Referenced Tests; Diagnostic Tests; Elementary Education; *Elementary School Students; Individualized Education Programs; Junior High Schools; *Junior High School Students; *Language Arts; *Mathematics Achievement
Availability: Curriculum Associates; 5 Esquire Rd., N. Billerica, MA 01862-2589
Grade Level: K-9

Designed primarily for use in elementary and middle schools and is of value for those school programs that emphasize individualized instruction and serve students with special needs. Inventory contains 203 skill sequences to be assessed in the areas of reading, listening, research and study skills, spelling, language, and mathematics. Forms A and B are available for 51 of the skill sequences. Inventory may be used as an assessment instrument for screening and diagnostic purposes, as an instructional guide for educational objectives, a record-keeping and tracking system, a tool to develop and communicate individualized instructional plans, and as a resource for curriculum and staff development.

11931
Bateria Woodcock Psico-Educativa en Espanol. Woodcock, Richard W. 1982
Subtests: Vocabulario Sobre Dibujos; Relaciones Espaciales; Aprendizaje Visual-Auditivo; Conceptos Cuantitativos; Pareo Visual; Antonimos-Sinonimos; Analisis-Sintesis; Inversion de Numeros; Formacion de Conceptos; Analogias; Identificacion de Letras y Palabras; Analisis de Palabras; Comprension de Textos; Calculo; Problemas Aplicados; Dictado; Comprobacion; Puncuacion y Empleo de Letras Mayusculas
Descriptors: *Academic Achievement; *Academic Aptitude; Adolescents; Adults; Bilingualism; Children; Clinical Diagnosis; *Cognitive Ability; *Cognitive Measurement; Handicap Identification; Individualized Education Programs; Individual Testing; Older Adults; Screening Tests; *Spanish; Spanish Speaking
Identifiers: Test Batteries; Woodcock Johnson Psycho Educational Battery
Availability: DLM Teaching Resources; P.O. Box 4000, One DLM Park, Allen, TX 75002
Age Level: 3-80

Consists of 17 subtests that measure cognitive functions, expected scholastic achievement, and actual academic achievement. To determine whether to assess a subject's psychoeducational abilities in English or Spanish, examiner may administer Oral Language Cluster (vocabulario sobre dibujos, antonimos-sinonimos, analogras) in Spanish from Bateria or in English from the Woodcock Language

Proficiency Battery-English (1980). Battery may be used for clinical assessment, program evaluation or research purposes with individuals ranging from preschool age through the geriatric level. Within the school-age range, a primary application is for students having learning and/or adjustment problems. Uses of the battery include individual evaluation, selection and placement, individual program planning, guidance, recording individual growth, program evaluation, research studies, and psychometric training.

11953
Kaufman Assessment Battery for Children.
Kaufman, Alan S.; Kaufman, Nadeen L. 1983
Subtests: Hand Movements; Number Recall; Word Order; Magic Window; Face Recognition; Gestalt Closure; Triangles; Matrix Analogies; Spatial Memory; Photo Series; Expressive Vocabulary; Faces and Places; Arithmetic; Riddles; Reading Decoding; Reading Understanding
Descriptors: *Academic Achievement; *Achievement Tests; *Children; Elementary School Mathematics; *Individual Testing; *Intelligence; *Intelligence Tests; Knowledge Level; Problem Solving; Reading Skills; Recall (Psychology); Spatial Ability; Vocabulary
Identifiers: Analogies; KABC; Test Batteries
Availability: American Guidance Service; Publishers' Bldg., Circle Pines, MN 55014-1796
Age Level: 2-12
Notes: Time, 85 min. approx.

Individually administered intelligence and achievement battery for children aged 2.5 to 12.5 years. Time varies according to age of children: 35-50 minutes for preschool child; 50-70 minutes for 5-6 year olds; and 75-85 minutes for a child aged 7 or above. Although the battery includes 16 subtests, no child is given more than 13. The subtests fall into 3 areas: sequential processing with emphasis on the process used to produce correct solutions; simultaneous processing in which the problems are primarily spatial or analogic in nature; and achievement which focuses on acquired facts and applied skills. Intended for psychological and clinical assessment, psychoeducational evaluation of learning-disabled and other exceptional children, educational planning and placement, minority group assessment, preschool assessment, neuropsychological assessment, and research. A review of the K-ABC by C. M. Narrett can be found in *Reading Teacher;* v37 p626-31, Mar 1984.

11957
National Business Competency Tests: Typewriting.
National Business Education Association, Reston, VA 1979
Descriptors: *Achievement Tests; Clerical Occupations; Higher Education; High Schools; *High School Students; *National Competency Tests; Occupational Tests; *Typewriting; *Undergraduate Students
Availability: National Business Education Association; 1914 Association Drive, Reston, VA 22091
Grade Level: 9-16
Notes: Time, 60 min. approx.

Administered to students in advanced typing, preferably their last course. May be used with both high school and college students. Administered to students in a national project to help teachers and employers determine whether students (prospective employees) are ready for typing jobs. Test consists of 2 parts to be administered on 2 different days.

11958
National Business Competency Tests: Office Procedures. National Business Education Association, Reston, VA 1981
Descriptors: *Achievement Tests; Clerical Occupations; Higher Education; High Schools; *High School Students; *National Competency Tests; Occupational Tests; *Office Practice; *Undergraduate Students
Identifiers: *Clerical Skills
Availability: National Business Education Association; 1914 Association Drive, Reston, VA 22091
Grade Level: 9-16
Notes: Time, 110 min. approx.; Items, 21

Administered to students in office procedures, secretarial practice, or cooperative office education, preferably the final course. May be used with high school and college populations who are participating in a national project to help teachers and employers determine whether students as prospective employees are ready for entry-level office jobs, excluding typewriting. Test consists of 2 parts which can be administered on 2 different days. The first part, Office Services, consists of jobs typically found in the office and includes such things as checking, proofreading, telephoning, and mail services. Part 2 consists of 9 jobs involving computation and accounting services typically performed in offices.

12034
Test Lessons in Primary Reading, Second Enlarged and Revised Edition. McCall, William A.; Harby, Mary Lourita 1980
Descriptors: Critical Thinking; Elementary Education; *Elementary School Students; *Reading Ability; *Reading Comprehension; *Reading Tests
Availability: Teachers College Press; P.O. Box 2032, Colchester, VT 05449
Grade Level: 2-6
Notes: Items, 62

Consists of 62 short stories followed by questions designed to evaluate students' reading progress and thinking skills. Teacher's manual also contains 8 questions for each story. These questions are designed to encourage such thinking skills as inference, drawing conclusions, making comparisons, recognizing cause and effect, understanding emotional reactions, and criticizing aspects of the story.

12044
Inventory of Language Abilities, Level II. Minskoff, Esther H.; And Others 1981
Subtests: Auditory Reception; Visual Reception; Auditory Association; Visual Association; Verbal Expression; Manual Expression; Auditory Memory; Visual Memory; Grammatic Closure; Visual Closure; Auditory Closure and Sound Blending
Descriptors: Auditory Stimuli; Disabilities; Elementary Education; *Elementary School Students; *Expressive Language; Language Proficiency; *Learning Disabilities; Psychomotor Skills; *Receptive Language; *Screening Tests; Verbal Ability; Visual Stimuli
Availability: Educational Performance Associates; 600 Broad Ave., Ridgefield, NJ 07657
Grade Level: 3-5
Notes: Items, 132

Screening device for use by classroom teacher in identifying children with possible language learning difficulties. The inventory has a separate checklist for each of the language areas of the MWM Program for Developing Language Abilities, except for auditory closure and sound blending that are combined. Each checklist has 12 behaviors or items and contains examples of everyday social and academic behaviors common in the lives of most children in grades 3, 4, and 5. Inventory may also be used by teachers of handicapped children and with other children at junior and senior high school level suspected of having severe language disabilities.

12091
Spadafore Diagnostic Reading Test. Spadafore, Gerald J. 1983
Subtests: Word Recognition; Oral Reading and Comprehension; Silent Reading Comprehension; Listening Comprehension
Descriptors: Adults; *Criterion Referenced Tests; *Decoding (Reading); *Diagnostic Tests; *Elementary School Students; Elementary Secondary Education; *Individual Testing; Listening Comprehension; Oral Reading; *Reading Comprehension; *Reading Diagnosis; Reading Tests; *Secondary School Students; Silent Reading; Word Recognition
Identifiers: SDRT
Availability: Academic Therapy Publications; 20 Commercial Blvd., Novato, CA 94947-6191
Grade Level: 1-12
Age Level: 6-64
Notes: Time, 60 min. approx.

Individually administered, criterion-referenced test intended for use with students reading at the primer through grade 12 levels and with adults. Decoding and comprehension tasks are arranged according to difficulty level and designated as representative of tasks on which students of a given grade level would be expected to show adequate performance. Recommended for use by educational diagnosticians, language specialists, resource teachers, and others requiring a comprehensive evaluation of reading skills.

12092
Denver Handwriting Analysis. Anderson, Peggy L. 1983
Subtests: Near Point Copying; Writing the Alphabet; Far Point Copying; Manuscript Cursive Transition; Dictation
Descriptors: *Criterion Referenced Tests; Dictation; Cursive Writing; Elementary Education; *Elementary School Students; Eye Hand Coordination; *Handwriting; Letters (Alphabet); Manuscript Writing (Handlettering); Remedial Instruction; Visual Discrimination
Identifiers: Copying Ability; DHA
Availability: Academic Therapy Publications; 20 Commercial Blvd., Novato, CA 94947-6191
Grade Level: 3-8
Notes: Time, 60 min. approx.

An informal, criterion-referenced test that uses a task analysis approach to identification of specific handwriting difficulties for purposes of remedial intervention. Can be administered individually or to groups by classroom teachers, remedial specialists, and educational diagnosticians. May also be extended to evaluate cursive handwriting of younger or older students. Each subtest yields a mastery level score.

12113
Test Lessons in Reading Figurative Language.
McCall, William A.; And Others 1980
Descriptors: *Figurative Language; Higher Education; Imagery; Irony; Metaphors; *Reading Comprehension; *Reading Tests; Secondary Education; *Secondary School Students; *Undergraduate Students
Identifiers: Euphemism; Hyperbole; Personification; Similes; Spoonerisms
Availability: Teachers College Press; P.O. Box 2032, Colchester, VT 05449
Grade Level: 7-16

Consists of 86 exercises designed to develop the reader's ability to recognize and to interpret figurative language and to distinguish between the literal use of language and its figurative use. Useful as an instructional tool in secondary and college reading and English classes. Among the figures of speech presented are similes, metaphors, personifications, hyperboles, ironies, and synecdoches. Also present are spoonerisms, malapropisms, and euphemisms, as well as practice in creating tropes.

12132
Mathematical Problems Solving Tests. Schoenfield, Alan H. 1980
Descriptors: Algebra; *College Students; Geometry; Higher Education; *Mathematics; *Problem Solving
Identifiers: TIM(I)
Availability: Tests in Microfiche; Test Collection, Educational Testing Service, Princeton, NJ 08541
Grade Level: 13-14
Notes: Items, 51

A measure of a student's approach to solving mathematical problems involving geometric figures and algebra. Student's procedure for solution to problems is graded according to specific criteria. A brief questionnaire to determine student's perception of the problem follows each question.

12161
Brigance Diagnostic Assessment of Basic Skills—Spanish Edition. Brigance, Albert H. 1983
Subtests: Readiness; Speech; Functional Word Recognition; Oral Reading; Reading Comprehension; Word Analysis; Listening; Writing and Alphabetizing; Numbers and Computation; Measurement
Descriptors: *Bilingual Students; Criterion Referenced Tests; *Diagnostic Tests; Elementary Education; *Elementary School Mathematics; *Elementary School Students; Individual Testing; Language Dominance; *Reading Achievement; Screening Tests; *Spanish; Spanish Speaking; Student Placement
Availability: Curriculum Associates, Inc.; 5 Esquire Rd., N. Billerica, MA 01862-2589
Grade Level: K-6
Notes: Items, 102

A diagnostic assessment designed for use with Spanish-speaking, elementary-aged children. Designed to determine functioning level in Spanish; learning problems and language barriers; and basic skills. The items were translated into Spanish from the Brigance Diagnostic Comprehensive Inventory of Basic Skills (TC011925). Several items are provided in English and Spanish to aid in determining language dominance.

12204
Teste de Prontidao para a Pre-Primaria. National Portuguese Materials Development Center, Providence, RI 1980
Subtests: Linguistic; Visual; Visual Motor; Motor; Auditive
Descriptors: Behavior Patterns; Bilingual Education; Educational Diagnosis; Language Acquisition; Listening Comprehension; Portuguese; Preschool Children; Psychomotor Skills; School Readiness; School Readiness Tests; Visual Discrimination
Identifiers: Elementary Secondary Education Act Title VII; TPP
Availability: National Dissemination Center; 417 Rock St., Fall River, MA 02720
Age Level: 4-5

Used to identify kind of behavior and level of knowledge of preschool children. Standardized test for psychoeducational assessment and the first of its kind in Portuguese. Diagnostic in nature. Test is useful for providing the classroom teacher, psychologists, pupil personnel specialists, and special educators with a quick profile of a child's behavioral patterns, before entering school. Deals with 5 different behavioral areas: motor, visual motor, visual, auditory, and linguistic.

12212
Basic Achievement Skills Individual Screener. Psychological Corp., San Antonio, TX 1983
Subtests: Reading; Mathematics; Spelling; Writing
Descriptors: *Achievement Tests; *Adults; *American Indians; *Criterion Referenced Tests; Diagnostic Tests; Educational Planning; *Elementary School Students; Elementary Secondary Education; Emotional Disturbances; Gifted; Hearing Impairments; Individualized Education Programs; *Individual Testing; Learning Disabilities; *Mathematics; Mild Mental Retardation; Norm Referenced Tests; *Reading Tests; *Secondary School Students; *Spelling; Student Placement
Identifiers: BASIS; *Writing Sample
Availability: The Psychological Corp.; 555 Academic Ct., San Antonio, TX 78204-0952
Grade Level: 1-12
Notes: Time, 55 min.

Individually administered achievement test providing norm- and criterion-referenced score interpretation in reading, mathematics, and spelling. An optional writing sample is included. For use as part of diagnostic assessment of students prior to development of IEPs or in placing students in class or text. Norms available for Native American (grades 5-7), hearing-impaired (grades 4-6), emotionally handicapped (grades 6-8), educable mentally retarded (grades 7-9), gifted (grades 2-5), and learning disabled (grades 3-8) students. Said to be useful with a post-high school population. A review of this instrument by A. R. Fitzpatrick can be found in *Journal of Educational Measurement;* v21 p309-11, Fall 1984.

12213
Vermont Basic Competency Program. Vermont State Dept. of Education, Montpelier 1985
Subtests: Reading; Writing; Speaking; Listening; Mathematics; Reasoning
Descriptors: *Basic Skills; Educational Objectives; *Elementary School Students; Elementary Secondary Education; Listening Skills; Mastery Learning; *Mastery Tests; Mathematics Achievement; Minimum Competency Testing; Reading Skills; *Secondary School Students; Speech Skills; Writing Skills
Availability: Vermont State Dept. of Education; Montpelier, VT 05602
Grade Level: K-8
Notes: Items, 51

A manual of information and guidelines for assessment of basic competencies in reading, writing, speaking, listening, and mathematics. Not a test, only a set of objectives. Local schools determine assessment methods and materials.

12250
Test for Examining Expressive Morphology. Shipley, Kenneth G.; And Others 1983
Subtests: Present Progressive; Plurals; Possessives; Third Person Singulars; Past Tense; Derived Adjectives
Descriptors: *Expressive Language; *Individual Testing; *Language Tests; *Morphemes; *Young Children
Availability: Communication Skill Builders; 3830 E. Bellevue, Tucson, AZ 85733
Age Level: 3-7
Notes: Time, 6 min. approx.; Items, 54

Developed to help clinicians evaluate expressive morpheme development of children whose language skills range from 3 to 8 years of age. Test fulfills following functions: sample a variety of morphemes and allomorphic variations; use an expressive sentence completion model; detect differences between age levels; employ a lexical-stimuli test paradigm; and sample various morphologic abilities. The test items examine the allomorphic variations of 6 major morphemes. Students view stimulus pictures while completing a target stimulus phrase. Individually administered.

12251
Joilet 3-Minute Speech and Language Screen. Kinzler, Mary C.; Johnson, Constance Cowing 1983
Subtests: Vocabulary; Grammar; Articulation; Voice; Fluency
Descriptors: Elementary Education; Expressive Language; *Grade 2; *Grade 5; Individual Testing; *Kindergarten Children; *Language Tests; Receptive Language; *Screening Tests; Syntax; Vocabulary
Availability: Communication Skill Builders; 3830 E. Bellevue, Tucson, AZ 85733
Grade Level: K; 2; 5
Notes: Time, 3 min.; Items, 18

A pass or fail measure especially designed for mass screening. It is not intended for in-depth diagnostic evaluation, and scores obtained do not indicate at which level a child may be functioning. Scores predict either that student possesses adequate or better speech and language skills or that the student should be considered high risk for speech and language, and additional diagnostic work is needed. Test focuses on areas of receptive vocabulary and expressive syntax, as well as voice, fluency, and phonological competence. Individually administered by certified speech pathologist.

12265
Comprehensive Tests of Basic Skills, Form U, Level K. CTB/Macmillan/McGraw-Hill, Monterey, CA 1983
Subtests: Vocabulary; Reading comprehension; Spelling; Language Mechanics; Language Expression; Mathematics Computation; Mathematics Concepts and Applications; Reference Skills; Science; Social Studies
Descriptors: *Achievement Tests; Basic Skills; *High Achievement; High Schools; *High School Students; Language Usage; *Mathematics Achievement; Norm Referenced Tests; *Reading Achievement; *Secondary School Science; *Social Studies; Spelling; Study Skills; Vocabulary
Identifiers: CTBS(U); Reference Skills; Test Batteries
Availability: CTB/MacMillan/McGraw Hill; Del Monte Research Park, 2500 Garden Rd., Monterey, CA 93940
Grade Level: 11-12
Notes: Time, 278 min.; Items, 380

One of a series of norm-referenced, achievement tests designed to measure achievement in the basic skills commonly found in state and school district curricula. Level K is especially appropriate for high-achieving students in grades 11 and 12. Cognitive processes assessed include recall, explicit information skills, inferential reasoning; and evaluation. The complete battery contains tests in the following basic content areas: reading, spelling, language, mathematics, reference skills, science, and social studies.

12267
The WORD Test—Elementary. Jorgensen, Carol; And Others 1981
Subtests: Associations; Synonyms; Semantic Absurdities; Antonyms; Definitions; Multiple Definitions
Descriptors: Adults; Aphasia; Auditory Stimuli; *Children; *Diagnostic Tests; *Expressive Language; *Language Handicaps; *Language Tests; Learning Disabilities; *Semantics; *Vocabulary Skills
Availability: LinguiSystems; 3100 4th Ave., P.O. Box 747, E. Moline, IL 61244
Age Level: 7-12
Notes: Time, 30 min.; Items, 83

A diagnostic test to assess expressive vocabulary and semantic abilities of school-aged children whose language problems adversely effect their academic achievement and communication skills. The 6 subtests are constructed to yield information in the following areas of expressive language: categorizing, defining, verbal reasoning, and choosing appropriate words. This test is also appropriate for older children and adults whose functional language is within the performance range of the test. Test should be administered by a trained professional, such as speech-language pathologist, psychologist, teacher of learning-disabled students, or special education consultant.

12268
Diagnostic Test of Arithmetic Strategies. Ginsburg, Herbert P.; Mathews, Steven C. 1984
Subtests: Addition; Subtraction; Multiplication; Division
Descriptors: Addition; *Arithmetic; *Computation; *Diagnostic Tests; Division; Elementary Education; *Elementary School Mathematics; *Elementary School Students; *Individual Testing; Mathematics Tests; Multiplication; *Problem Solving; Subtraction
Identifiers: DTAS
Availability: PRO-ED; 8700 Shoal Creek Blvd., Austin, TX 78758-6897
Grade Level: 1-6
Notes: Time, 80 min. approx.

Purpose is to measure procedures elementary school students use to perform arithmetic calculations in addition, subtraction, multiplication, and division. Focuses on successful and unsuccessful strategies and identifies procedures that lead to incorrect responses that must be modified or eliminated. Each of the tests contains 4 sections that measure ability to set up the problem; number fact knowledge; use of algorithms, invented procedures, bugs, and slips; and the capacity to use informal procedures. Test is untimed; on the average, each of the 4 tests should take approximately 20 minutes. Tests are individually administered. Typically, child will only take one of the 4 tests in a testing period.

12272
Test of Mathematical Abilities. Brown, Virginia L.; McEntire, Elizabeth 1984
Subtests: Attitude toward Math; Vocabulary; Computation; General Information; Story Problems
Descriptors: Academic Aptitude; *Achievement Tests; *Attitude Measures; Computation; *Elementary School Students; Elementary Secondary Education; Mathematical Applications; *Mathematics Achievement; Problem Solving; *Secondary School Students; *Student Attitudes; Vocabulary
Identifiers: Story Problems (Mathematics); TOMA
Availability: PRO-ED; 8700 Shoal Creek Blvd., Austin, TX 78758-6897
Grade Level: 3-12
Notes: Items, 107

Provides standardized information about 2 major skill areas, story problems and computation, and related information about students' attitudes toward mathematics, vocabulary of mathematical terms, and general cultural application of mathematically oriented information. There are no time requirements for the test, time required varies according to age and abilities of students. The general information subtest is individually administered; for students under the age of 11, the vocabulary subtest is not given. The test results may be used for various purposes: to identify students significantly below or above their peers in mathematics or mathematically related abilities, for diagnostic or placement purposes; to determine student's particular strengths or weaknesses; to document progress resulting from intervention strategies; to provide data and measurement to those interested in research into mathematics instruction and learning.

12294
MKM Spelling Test. Michael, Leland D.; And Others 1978
Descriptors: Achievement Tests; Diagnostic Tests; Elementary Education; *Elementary School Students; *Spelling
Availability: MKM, Inc.; 809 Kansas City St., Rapid City, SD 57701
Grade Level: 2-8
Notes: Items, 35

Designed to assess spelling ability. Children who are good spellers are generally good readers. Two forms are available. The first is suitable for grades 2-4, the second for grades 5-8. The Phonic Mnemonic Method of Teaching Reading Manual of Instructions for use with this instrument is available from MKM, Inc., 809 Kansas City St., Rapid City, SD 57701.

12295
MKM Listening Comprehension Test. Michael, Leland D.; And Others 1978
Descriptors: Diagnostic Tests; Elementary Education; *Elementary School Students; Listening Comprehension; *Listening Comprehension Tests; Listening Skills
Availability: MKM, Inc.; 809 Kansas City St., Rapid City, SD 57701
Grade Level: 1-6
Notes: Items, 6

Designed to assess listening ability. A story is read to the student followed by 6 comprehension questions. Specific training in listening is recommended for students who miss more than 2 questions. The Phonic Mnemonic Method of Teaching Reading Manual of Instructions for use with this instrument is available from MKM, Inc., 809 Kansas City St., Rapid City, SD 57701.

12353
Multiple-Choice Cloze Exercises: Textual Domain, Reading/Literature Revised 1977. New York State Education Dept., Albany, Div. of Research 1977
Subtests: American People; Foreign People; Myth and Legend; Biography; Nonfiction
Descriptors: Achievement Tests; Cloze Procedure; Difficulty Level; *Elementary School Students; Elementary Secondary Education; *Item Banks; Multiple Choice Tests; *Reading Achievement; *Reading Comprehension; *Secondary School Students; Student Evaluation
Identifiers: SPPED Form 81R
Availability: ERIC Document Reproduction Service; 7420 Fullerton Rd., Ste. 110, Springfield, VA 22153-2852 (ED226029, 452 p.)
Grade Level: 1-12
Notes: Items, 425

The "Test Development Notebook" is a resource designed for the preparation of tests of literal comprehension of students in grades 1 through 12. There are a total of 1725 multiple-choice closure exercises in the collection. The exercises have a common multiple-choice cloze format; they use passages from domains or types of materials that students read, and the passages are graded by difficulty levels. The *Multiple-Choice Cloze Exercises: Handbook* is available from ERIC Document Reproduction Service; P.O. Box 190, Arlington, VA 22210 (ED 226 028). This instrument consists of 425 items divided into 26 levels of difficulty. The items were drawn from basal readers and literature texts used in grades 1-12.

12354
Multiple-Choice Cloze Exercises: Textual Domain, Language Arts, Revised 1977.   New York State Education Dept., Albany, Div. of Research 1977
Subtests: Grammar; Etymology; Composition; Speech; Reference
Descriptors: Achievement Tests; Cloze Procedure; *Elementary School Students; Elementary Secondary Education; Etymology; Grammar; *Item Banks; *Language Arts; Multiple Choice Tests; Reading Comprehension; *Secondary School Students; Writing Skills
Identifiers: SPPED Form 81 LA
Availability: ERIC Document Reproduction Service; 7420 Fullerton Rd., Ste. 110, Springfield, VA 22153-2852 (ED226030, 219 p.)
Grade Level: 3-12
Notes: Items, 200

The "Test Development Notebook" is a resource designed for the preparation of tests of literal comprehension of students in grades 1 through 12. There are a total of 1725 multiple-choice closure exercises in the collection. The exercises have a common multiple-choice cloze format; they use passages from domains or types of materials that students read, and the passages are graded by difficulty levels. The *Multiple-Choice Cloze Exercises: Handbook* is available from ERIC Document Reproduction Service; P.O. Box 190, Arlington, VA 22210 (ED 226 028). This instrument contains 200 items culled from language arts textbooks at 22 levels of difficulty.

12355
Multiple-Choice Cloze Exercises: Textual Domain, Social Studies, Revised 1977.   New York State Education Dept., Albany, Div. of Research 1977
Subtests: History; Geography; Cultural Studies; Sociology/Civics; Economics; Psychology
Descriptors: Civics; Cloze Procedure; Cultural Education; Difficulty Level; Economics; *Elementary School Students; Elementary Secondary Education; Geography; History; *Item Banks; Multiple Choice Tests; Psychology; *Reading Comprehension; *Secondary School Students; *Social Studies; Sociology
Identifiers: SPPED Form 81SS
Availability: ERIC Document Reproduction Service; 7420 Fullerton Rd., Ste. 110, Springfield, VA 22153-2852 (ED226031, 282 p.)
Grade Level: 1-12
Notes: Items, 260

The "Test Development Notebook" is a resource designed for the preparation of tests of literal comprehension of students in grades 1 through 12. There are a total of 1725 multiple-choice closure exercises in the collection. The exercises have a common multiple-choice cloze format; they use passages from domains or types of materials that students read, and the passages are graded by difficulty levels. The *Multiple-Choice Cloze Exercises: Handbook* is available from ERIC Document Reproduction Service; P.O. Box 190, Arlington, VA 22210 (ED 226 028). This instrument contains 260 items taken from social studies textbooks at 27 levels of difficulty from grades 1-12.

12356
Multiple-Choice Cloze Exercises: Textual Domain, Science, Revised 1977.   New York State Education Dept., Albany, Div. of Research 1977
Subtests: Physics; Chemistry; Earth Science; Biology; Applied Science
Descriptors: Biology; Chemistry; Cloze Procedure; Difficulty Level; Earth Science; *Elementary School Students; Elementary Secondary Education; *Item Banks; Multiple Choice Tests; *Physical Sciences; Physics; *Reading Comprehension; *Secondary School Students
Identifiers: SSPED Form 81S
Availability: ERIC Document Reproduction Service; 7420 Fullerton Rd., Ste. 110, Springfield, VA 22153-2852 (ED226032, 219 p.)
Grade Level: 3-12
Notes: Items, 200

The "Test Development Notebook" is a resource designed for the preparation of tests of literal comprehension of students in grades 1 through 12. There are a total of 1725 multiple-choice closure exercises in the collection. The exercises have a common multiple-choice cloze format; they use passages from domains or types of materials that students read, and the passages are graded by difficulty levels. The *Multiple-Choice Cloze Exercises: Handbook* is available from ERIC Document Reproduction Service; P.O. Box 190, Arlington, VA 22210 (ED 226 028). Instrument consists of 200 items based on material drawn from science texts for grades 3-12. Maximum difficulty level for this instrument is 32.

12357
Multiple-Choice Cloze Exercises: Textual Domain, Mathematics, Revised 1977.   New York State Education Dept., Albany, Div. of Research 1977

Subtests: Measurement; History and Numeration; Operations; Sets; Geometry; Advanced Algebra; Trigonometry; Graphing; Number Theory; Analytic Geometry; Linear Algebra; Probability
Descriptors: Algebra; Analytic Geometry; Cloze Procedure; *Difficulty Level; *Elementary School Mathematics; *Elementary School Students; Elementary Secondary Education; Geometry; Graphs; *Item Banks; Mathematical Concepts; Multiple Choice Tests; Probability; *Secondary School Mathematics; *Secondary School Students
Identifiers: SPPED Form 81M
Availability: ERIC Document Reproduction Service; 7420 Fullerton Rd., Ste. 110, Springfield, VA 22153-2852 (ED226033, 219 p.)
Grade Level: 3-12
Notes: Items, 200

The "Test Development Notebook" is a resource designed for the preparation of tests of literal comprehension of students in grades 1 through 12. There are a total of 1725 multiple-choice closure exercises in the collection. The exercises have a common multiple-choice cloze format; they use passages from domains or types of materials that students read, and the passages are graded by difficulty levels. The *Multiple-Choice Cloze Exercises: Handbook* is available from ERIC Document Reproduction Service; P.O. Box 190, Arlington, VA 22210 (ED 226 028). Instrument consists of 200 items based on material in mathematics texts for grades 3-12. Items are arranged in 24 levels of difficulty.

12358
Multiple-Choice Cloze Exercises: Citizen Domain, Newspapers, Revised 1977.   New York State Education Dept., Albany, Div. of Research 1977
Subtests: Front Page Stories; Feature Stories; Editorials
Descriptors: Cloze Procedure; Difficulty Level; Editorials; *Elementary School Students; Elementary Secondary Education; *Item Banks; Multiple Choice Tests; *Newspapers; *Reading Comprehension; *Secondary School Students
Identifiers: SPPED Form 81N
Availability: ERIC Document Reproduction Service; 7420 Fullerton Rd., Ste. 110, Springfield, VA 22153-2852 (ED226034, 137 p.)
Grade Level: 1-12
Notes: Items, 120

The "Test Development Notebook" is a resource designed for the preparation of tests of literal comprehension of students in grades 1 through 12. There are a total of 1725 multiple-choice closure exercises in the collection. The exercises have a common multiple-choice cloze format; they use passages from domains or types of materials that students read, and the passages are graded by difficulty levels. The *Multiple-Choice Cloze Exercises: Handbook* is available from ERIC Document Reproduction Service; P.O. Box 190, Arlington, VA 22210 (ED 226 028). This instrument consists of 120 items grouped in 20 levels of difficulty. Items were taken from front page stories, feature stories, and editorials of newspapers.

12359
Multiple-Choice Cloze Exercises: Citizen Domain, News Magazines, Revised 1977.   New York State Education Dept., Albany, Div. of Research 1977
Subtests: Editorials/Reviews; Feature Stories; National News; International News
Descriptors: Cloze Procedure; Difficulty Level; Editorials; *Elementary School Students; Elementary Secondary Education; *Item Banks; Multiple Choice Tests; News Media; *Periodicals; *Reading Comprehension; *Secondary School Students
Identifiers: Form 81NM; *Newsmagazines
Availability: ERIC Document Reproduction Service; 7420 Fullerton Rd., Ste. 110, Springfield, VA 22153-2852 (ED226035, 136 p.)
Grade Level: 1-12
Notes: Items, 120

The "Test Development Notebook" is a resource designed for the preparation of tests of literal comprehension of students in grades 1 through 12. There are a total of 1725 multiple-choice closure exercises in the collection. The exercises have a common multiple-choice cloze format; they use passages from domains or types of materials that students read, and the passages are graded by difficulty levels. The *Multiple-Choice Cloze Exercises: Handbook* is available from ERIC Document Reproduction Service; P.O. Box 190, Arlington, VA 22210 (ED 226 028). This instrument consists of 120 items grouped into 16 levels of difficulty. The items were drawn from news magazines.

12360
Multiple-Choice Cloze Exercises: Consumer Domain, Revised 1977.   New York State Education Dept., Albany, Div. of Research 1977

Descriptors: Advertising; Catalogs; Cloze Procedure; *Consumer Education; Contracts; Difficulty Level; *Elementary School Students; Elementary Secondary Education; *Item Banks; Multiple Choice Tests; Periodicals; *Reading Comprehension; *Secondary School Students
Identifiers: Instructions; SPPED Form 81C
Availability: ERIC Document Reproduction Service; 7420 Fullerton Rd., Ste. 110, Springfield, VA 22153-2852 (ED226036, 115 p.)
Grade Level: 1-12
Notes: Items, 100

The "Test Development Notebook" is a resource designed for the preparation of tests of literal comprehension of students in grades 1 through 12. There are a total of 1725 multiple-choice closure exercises in the collection. The exercises have a common multiple-choice cloze format; they use passages from domains or types of materials that students read, and the passages are graded by difficulty levels. The *Multiple-Choice Cloze Exercises: Handbook* is available from ERIC Document Reproduction Service; P.O. Box 190, Arlington, VA 22210 (ED 226 028). This instrument consists of 100 items grouped into eighteen levels of difficulty. Items were drawn from consumer magazines, catalogs, instructions, advertisements and contracts.

12361
Multiple-Choice Cloze Exercises: Reference Domain Revised 1977.   New York State Education Dept., Albany, Div. of Research 1977
Descriptors: Cloze Procedure; Difficulty Level; *Elementary School Students; Elementary Secondary Education; Encyclopedias; *Item Banks; Multiple Choice Tests; Periodicals; *Reading Comprehension; *Reference Materials; *Secondary School Students
Identifiers: SSPED Form 81 RF
Availability: ERIC Document Reproduction Service; 7420 Fullerton Rd., Ste. 110, Springfield, VA 22153-2852 (ED226037, 115 p.)
Grade Level: 1-12

The "Test Development Notebook" is a resource designed for the preparation of tests of literal comprehension of students in grades 1 through 12. There are a total of 1725 multiple-choice closure exercises in the collection. The exercises have a common multiple-choice cloze format; they use passages from domains or types of materials that students read, and the passages are graded by difficulty levels. The *Multiple-Choice Cloze Exercises: Handbook* is available from ERIC Document Reproduction Service; P.O. Box 190, Arlington, VA 22210 (ED 226 028). This instrument consists of 100 items grouped into 21 levels of difficulty. The items were drawn from test instructions, instructional magazines, encyclopedias, reference books, and children's magazines.

12364
Vocational Competency Measures; Electronic Technician.   American Institutes for Research, Palo Alto, CA 1983
Descriptors: *Achievement Tests; Adolescents; Adults; *Competence; *Electronic Technicians; Knowledge Level; Personnel Selection; *Postsecondary Education; Rating Scales; Screening Tests; Secondary Education; *Secondary School Students; *Student Evaluation; *Vocational Education; *Work Sample Tests
Identifiers: Test Batteries; *Work Habits
Availability: American Association for Vocational Instructional Materials; 120 Driftmier Engineering Center, Athens, GA 30602
Grade Level: 7-16
Age Level: 12-64

Used to help teachers and administrators at secondary and postsecondary levels assess and improve the competencies of vocational education students, identify program areas in need of improvement, and inform prospective employers of student competencies. May also be used by employers to screen and select new employees and to assess training needs of present employees. The test battery consists of 3 components. The Job Information Test is a multiple-choice test of job-relevant knowledge. It is divided into 2 parts, each of which takes about 45 minutes to complete. The performance test has 12 performance tasks which are similar to entry-level activities expected of an electronics technician. Examinees are not required to perform all 12 tasks. The Work Habits Inventory has 3 parts: one that students complete concerning their own traits, one in which students are asked to estimate the importance of job traits from the employer's point of view; and one completed by the teacher concerning students' work habits.

12369
New Jersey Statewide Writing Assessment Program.   New Jersey State Department of Education, Trenton, NJ 1983

Descriptors: Curriculum Development; Graduation Requirements; *High School Students; *Minimum Competency Testing; Multiple Choice Tests; Student Placement; Testing Programs; Writing (Composition); *Writing Evaluation; Writing Skills
Identifiers: New Jersey; State Testing Programs; *Writing Sample
Availability: New Jersey State Dept. of Education; Bureau of Educational Assessment; 225 W. State St., Trenton, NJ 08625
Grade Level: 9-12
Notes: Time, 90 min.; Items, 54

Designed to identify student strengths and weaknesses for placement in remedial programs and to provide information for curriculum planning. A passing grade is required for graduation in New Jersey. Measures students' ability to apply writing mechanics to written text and to communicate effectively in writing. Consists of a multiple-choice and an essay section. Items cover sentence structure, spelling, usage, capitalization, and punctuation.

12370
New Jersey Minimum Basic Skills Testing Program. New Jersey State Department of Education, Trenton, NJ 1977
Subtests: Word Recognition; Reading Comprehension; Study Skills; Computation; Number Concepts; Measurement and Geometry; Problem Solving
Descriptors: *Basic Skills; Curriculum Development; *Elementary School Students; Geometry; *Grade 9; High School Students; Mathematics; *Minimum Competency Testing; Needs Assessment; Problem Solving; Reading Skills; Student Placement; Study Skills; Testing Programs
Identifiers: New Jersey; NJMBS; State Testing Programs
Availability: New Jersey State Dept. of Education; Bureau of Assessment and Evaluation; 225 W. State St., Trenton, NJ 08625
Grade Level: 3; 6; 9
Notes: Items, 205

Designed to measure basic reading and mathematical skills. The test will be superseded in 1985. Items are multiple-choice. Results are used for placement of students, curriculum planning, and needs assessment.

12371
New Jersey Statewide Testing System. New Jersey State Department of Education, Trenton, NJ 1984
Subtests: Reading; Writing; Mathematics
Descriptors: *Basic Skills; *Elementary School Students; *Grade 09; Graduation Requirements; High School Students; Mathematics; *Minimum Competency Testing; Reading Skills; Testing Programs; Writing Skills
Identifiers: New Jersey; State Testing Programs
Availability: New Jersey State Dept. of Education; 225 W. State St., CN 500, Trenton, NJ 08625
Grade Level: 3; 6; 9

This replacement for the New Jersey Minimum Basic Skills program became operational in 1985. At grade 9, the test serves as a graduation requirement. For further information on the Writing Assessment, see New Jersey Statewide Writing Assessment Program (TC012369).

12388
Expressive One-Word Picture Vocabulary Test—Upper Extension. Gardner, Morrison F. 1983
Descriptors: *Adolescents; Bilingual Students; *Cognitive Processes; *Concept Formation; Diagnostic Tests; *Expressive Language; Group Testing; Individual Testing; Intelligence; *Language Tests; Norm Referenced Tests; Pictorial Stimuli; Spanish Speaking; *Vocabulary
Identifiers: EOWPVT; *Verbal Intelligence
Availability: Academic Therapy Publications; 20 Commercial Blvd., Novato, CA 94947-6191
Age Level: 12-16
Notes: Time, 15 min. approx.; Items, 70

Purpose is to obtain a basal estimate of a student's verbal intelligence by means of his or her acquired one-word expressive picture vocabulary. Can be valuable in obtaining a valid estimate of child's verbal intelligence through child's ability to form an idea or concept from a picture. This is an upward extension of the original Expressive One-Word Picture Vocabulary Test (TC010322), published in 1979. Can also yield information on possible speech defects, possible learning disorders, bilingual child's fluency in English, auditory processing, and auditory-visual association ability. Although normed on children whose primary language is English, may also be used with bilingual students to determine extent of their English vocabulary. A Spanish version is also available. The pictures are arranged in increasing order of difficulty and range from single concrete objects to collections of objects representing abstract concepts. Students respond to each item with a single word. May be administered individually or to small groups.

12425
IEP Educational Diagnostic Inventories. Sedlak, Joseph E. 1979
Descriptors: *Diagnostic Tests; *Educational Diagnosis; Elementary Education; *Elementary School Students; Emotional Disturbances; Exceptional Persons; Gifted; Individualized Education Programs; Individual Testing; Intelligence; Learning Disabilities; Learning Modalities; Learning Problems; Mathematics Achievement; Mild Mental Retardation; Preschool Children; Preschool Education; Reading Skills; Screening Tests; Student Behavior
Identifiers: IEP Educational Diagnostic Inventories
Availability: National Press Publishing Co.; P.O. Box 237, Belle Vernon, PA 15012
Grade Level: K-6
Age Level: 3-12

Developed to enable classroom teachers to screen and diagnose those students with potential learning problems. The teacher may administer the entire battery or only those sections deemed suitable for the problem objectives. The instruments are individually administered and may be used for normal, gifted, educable mentally retarded, emotionally disturbed, and learning-disabled students. The battery results will yield information useful in developing an Individual Education Program for each student. The battery includes Diagnostic History Form (TC012531), National Intelligence Test (TC012532), Behavior Reinforcement Inventory (TC012533), Near-Point Visual Screening Inventory (TC012534), Reading Inventory (TC012535-012540), Math Inventory (TC012541-012543), Spelling Inventory (TC012544-012545), Handwriting Inventory (TC012546), Psycholinguistic Inventory (TC012547), and Modality Inventory (TC012548).

12438
Measuring Student Achievement in Home Health Assisting Health Occupations Education. New York State Education Dept., Albany, Bureau of Elementary and Secondary Educational Testing 1982
Descriptors: *Achievement Tests; Adults; *Home Health Aides; *Item Banks; Knowledge Level; *Performance Tests; *Visiting Homemakers
Availability: ERIC Document Reproduction Service; 7420 Fullerton Rd., Ste. 110, Springfield, VA 22153-2852 (ED222541, 83 p.)
Age Level: Adults

Test items developed specifically for use by educational agencies which offer a program in Home Health Assisting upon approval of the New York State Education Department. Items may be useful to other agencies or institutions. Home Health Assisting Program is designed to prepare adults to work in the home under supervision of a health-care agency. Focus is on the role of homemaker-personal care services provider and home health aide as members of an agency team in the care of a patient. Items selected may be used as a pretest, or achievement test. Areas covered by items include concepts of the world of work; home health and personal care services; communications and interpersonal relationships; household housekeeping and management services; nutritional status of patient and family; personal care services; patient care services; specialized home health care services; recognition of special patient handicaps.

12457
HPI Texas Preschool Screening Inventory.
Haber, Julian S. 1981
Subtests: Auditory Memory for Numbers and Letters; Visual Memory for Objects; Auditory Sequencing; Articulation; Sound Discrimination; Rotations and Reversals of Numbers and Letters; Following Instructions
Descriptors: Articulation (Speech); Auditory Perception; Handicap Identification; *Kindergarten Children; Learning Problems; *Preschool Children; Primary Education; *Screening Tests; Visual Perception
Identifiers: TPSI
Availability: ERIC Document Reproduction Service; 7420 Fullerton Rd., Ste. 110, Springfield, VA 22153-2852 (ED226013, 13 p.)
Grade Level: K-1
Age Level: 4-6

Screening test to help determine children who may be at risk for learning problems as they enter kindergarten or first grade. Is not meant as a definitive test of learning problems but may be used to indicate a need for full evaluation by the local educational agency.

12473
The Second Language Oral Test of English.
Fathman, Ann K. 1983
Descriptors: Adolescents; Adults; Children; *English (Second Language); *Grammar; Student Placement; *Syntax
Identifiers: Oral Tests; SLOTE

Availability: The Alemany Press; c/o Prentice-Hall, 200 Old Tappen Rd., Old Tappen, NJ 07675
Age Level: 6-64

Measures the ability of nonnative English speakers to produce specific syntactic structures orally. Group or individually administered for placement of beginning or intermediate students.

12474
Test Lessons in Reading and Reasoning. 2nd Enlarged and Revised Edition. McCall, William A.; Smith, Edwin H. 1980
Descriptors: *Adult Education; *Critical Reading; *Higher Education; Objective Tests; Reading Tests; *Secondary Education
Identifiers: *Fallacies
Availability: Teachers College Press; P.O. Box 2032, Colchester, VT 05449
Grade Level: 7-16
Age Level: 12-64

Contains 90 test lessons and more than 1,000 items used to teach and assess subjects' critical reading and reasoning skills. All lessons and questions contain material dealing with current issues and concerns, such as the environment, conservation, social problems, politics, economics, advertising and education. Passages and questions cover fallacies in the following categories: shifty word, false authority, either-or, circular reasoning, false analogy, improper data, inadequate data, self-contradiction, loaded words, appealing to conformity, red herring, part-whole, stereotyping, opinion-fact, spurious, mean, conventional wisdom, sexism, rationalization. Also deals with fallacious reasoning and proverbs.

12516
Vocational Competency Measures: Dental Assistant. American Institutes for Research, Palo Alto, CA 1983
Descriptors: *Achievement Tests; Adolescents; Adults; Competence; *Dental Assistants; *Entry Workers; Knowledge Level; *Personnel Selection; *Postsecondary Education; Rating Scales; Screening Tests; Secondary Education; *Secondary School Students; Student Evaluation; *Vocational Education; *Work Sample Tests
Identifiers: Test Batteries; *Work Habits
Availability: American Association for Vocational Instructional Materials; 120 Driftmier Engineering Center, Athens, GA 30602
Age Level: 12-64

Designed to help teachers and administrators at secondary and postsecondary levels assess and improve competencies of their students in vocational education, identify areas of program improvement, and inform prospective employers of students' vocational competencies. Also useful for employers to screen and select new employees and to assess training needs of present employees. Test package consists of a 2-part, multiple-choice job information test, each part consisting of 56 items and taking 45 minutes to complete; a performance test consisting of 12 tests which represent tasks similar to those performed on the job; and a work habits inventory for assessing nontechnical, work-related attitudes and behavior. The job information test for dental assistants covers general tasks, chairside assisting, sterilization and disinfection, laboratory tasks and radiographs, and office management.

12517
Vocational Competency Measures: Farm Equipment Mechanics. American Institutes for Research, Palo Alto, CA 1983
Descriptors: *Achievement Tests; Adolescents; Adults; *Agricultural Machinery Occupations; *Competence; *Entry Workers; Knowledge Level; *Mechanical Skills; *Mechanics (Process); *Personnel Selection; *Postsecondary Education; Rating Scales; Screening Tests; Secondary Education; *Secondary School Students; Student Evaluation; *Vocational Education; *Work Sample Tests
Identifiers: Test Batteries; *Work Habits
Availability: American Association for Vocational Instructional Materials; 120 Driftmier Engineering, Center, Athens, GA 30602
Age Level: 12-64

Intended to assess those enrolled in or completing vocational or technical school programs in farm-equipment set-up or repair, usually those preparing to work in either dealers' service shops or on farms where equipment maintenance tasks are to be performed. Designed as a competency test in vocational programs, to assess gains in proficiency, to identify areas for program improvement or to advise prospective employers about job-related competencies of students, or to screen students for advanced standing. May also be used by employers to screen prospective employees or to compare competencies among applicants. Test package consists of a 2-part, multiple-choice job information test, each part consisting of 54 items and requiring 45 minutes to complete; a performance section of 13 tests representative of actual on-the-job tasks, and a work habits inventory for assessing nontechnical work-related attitudes and behavior. The job information test covers the following topics: engineers and electrical; hydraulics; welding; assembly, adjustment, and repair of equipment.

12601
The Ohio School Library/Media Test. Hyland, Anne M. 1978
Descriptors: *Achievement Tests; Diagnostic Tests; *Elementary School Students; Elementary Secondary Education; *Learning Resources Centers; *Library Instruction; *Library Skills; *School Libraries; *Secondary School Students
Availability: ERIC Document Reproduction Service; 7420 Fullerton Rd., Ste. 110, Springfield, VA 22153-2852 (ED200240, microfiche only)
Grade Level: 4-12
Notes: Items, 53

An instrument that can be used to measure the school library/media ability of students. The test covers 5 broad areas: (1) how things are organized, (2) the skills needed to select appropriate resources, (3) the skills needed to use each resource, (4) the skills needed to comprehend the information given, and (5) the skills needed to present the information in a meaningful way to others. The test can be used for diagnosing areas where students need library instruction, as a pre/posttest to determine effectiveness of library instruction, and to correlate studies between library/media skills and academic achievement. An alternate for the test is Dr. Anne M. Hyland, 236 E. Clearview, Worthington, OH 43085.

12617
Vocational Competency Measures: Fabric Sales. American Institutes for Research, Palo Alto, CA 1983
Descriptors: *Achievement Tests; Adolescents; Adults; Clothing; Competence; *Entry Workers; Fashion Industry; Knowledge Level; Merchandising; *Personnel Selection; *Postsecondary Education; Rating Scales; *Sales Occupations; Screening Tests; Secondary Education; *Secondary School Students; Student Evaluation; *Vocational Education; *Work Sample Tests
Identifiers: *Fabrics; Test Batteries; *Work Habits
Availability: American Association for Vocational Instructional Materials; 120 Driftmier Engineering Center, Athens, GA 30602
Age Level: 12-64

Designed to help teachers and administrators at secondary and postsecondary levels assess and improve competencies of their students in vocational education, to identify areas for program improvement, and to inform prospective employers of students' vocational competencies. Also useful for employers to screen and to select new employees and to assess training needs of present employees. Test package consists of a two-part multiple-choice job information test, each part taking about 45 minutes to complete; a performance test consisting of tests that represent tasks similar to those performed on the job; and a work habits inventory for assessing nontechnical, work-related attitudes and behavior. Test is specifically designed for individuals interested in fabric sales that combine knowledge of clothing construction with merchandising. Intended for those in retail merchandising programs at the secondary or postsecondary level rather than for those completing 4-year fashion or textile marketing programs. The job information tests assess knowledge of general fashion, sales, and sewing. The performance test requires examinee to carry out the following: take body measurements, determine figure type and size, construct a double-pointed dart, sew seams, adjust a blouse pattern to increase bustline, insert a front fly zipper, complete an exchange/return, close out a cash register, complete a sale, maintain a book inventory. The performance section takes approximately 245 minutes to complete.

12620
Vocational Competency Measures: Water Treatment Technician. American Institutes for Research, Palo Alto, CA 1983
Descriptors: *Achievement Tests; Adolescents; Adults; Competence; *Entry Workers; Knowledge Level; *Personnel Selection; *Postsecondary Education; Rating Scales; Screening Tests; Secondary Education; *Secondary School Students; Student Evaluation; *Technical Occupations; *Vocational Education; Water Quality; *Water Treatment; *Work Sample Tests
Identifiers: Test Batteries; *Work Habits
Availability: American Association for Vocational Instructional Materials; 120 Driftmier Engineering Center, Athens, GA 30602
Age Level: 12-64

Designed to help teachers and administrators at secondary and postsecondary levels assess and improve competencies of their students in vocational education, to identify areas for program improvement, and to inform prospective employers of students' vocational competencies. Also useful for employers to screen and to select new employees and to assess training needs of present employees. Test package consists of a 2-part multiple-choice job information test, each part taking about 45 minutes to complete; a performance test consisting of tests that represent tasks similar to those performed on the job; and a work habits inventory for assessing nontechnical, work-related attitudes and behavior. Test package is intended for those completing vocational programs in water treatment and who are preparing to work as technicians in water treatment laboratories or plants. The job information test assesses knowledge of plant and equipment operation, record keeping, sampling and testing, inspection and calibration, plant and equipment maintenance. The following activities are carried out for the performance tests: using an air mask, repairing a leaking chlorine cylinder, changing chart in flow recorder, checking dosage of fluoridator, performing a jar test to estimate optimum alum dosage, collecting grab sample of process control. It takes approximately 100 minutes to complete the performance tests.

12621
Vocational Competency Measures: Wastewater Treatment Technician. American Institutes for Research, Palo Alto, CA 1983
Descriptors: *Achievement Tests; Adolescents; Adults; Competence; *Entry Workers; Knowledge Level; *Personnel Selection; *Postsecondary Education; Rating Scales; Screening Tests; Secondary Education; *Secondary School Students; Student Evaluation; *Technical Occupations; *Vocational Education; *Waste Water; *Water Treatment; *Work Sample Tests
Identifiers: Test Batteries; *Work Habits
Availability: American Association for Vocational Instructional Materials; 120 Driftmier Engineering Center, Athens, GA 30602
Age Level: 12-64

Designed to help teachers and administrators at secondary and postsecondary levels assess and improve competencies of their students in vocational education, to identify areas for program improvement, and to inform prospective employers of students' vocational competencies. Also useful for employers to screen and to select new employees and to assess training needs of present employees. Test package consists of a 2-part multiple-choice job information test, each part taking about 45 minutes to complete; a performance test consisting of tests that represent tasks similar to those performed on the job; and a work habits inventory for assessing nontechnical, work-related attitudes and behavior. Test package is intended for those completing vocational programs in wastewater treatment and who are preparing to work as technicians in wastewater treatment laboratories or plants. The job information test assesses knowledge of plant and equipment operation, record keeping, sampling and testing, inspection and calibration, plant and equipment maintenance. The tasks to be carried out on the performance test include using an air pack, measuring pH of plant influent, aligning pump coupling, performing MPN test to measure coliform bacteria, measuring dissolved oxygen (DO) of a sample, reading and recording thermometers and pressure gauges, deragging primary sludge pump. It takes approximately 100 minutes to complete the performance tests.

12622
Vocational Competency Measures: Apparel Sales. American Institutes for Research, Palo Alto, CA 1983
Descriptors: *Achievement Tests; Adolescents; Adults; *Clothing; Competence; *Entry Workers; Fashion Industry; Knowledge Level; Merchandising; *Personnel Selection; *Postsecondary Education; Rating Scales; *Sales Occupations; Screening Tests; Secondary Education; *Secondary School Students; Student Evaluation; *Vocational Education; *Work Sample Tests
Identifiers: Test Batteries; *Work Habits
Availability: American Association for Vocational Instructional Materials; 120 Driftmier Engineering Center, Athens, GA 30602
Age Level: 12-64

Designed to help teachers and administrators at secondary and postsecondary levels assess and improve competencies of their students in vocational education, to identify areas for program improvement, and to inform prospective employers of students' vocational competencies. Also useful for employers to screen and to select new employees and to assess training needs of present employees. Test package consists of a 2-part multiple-choice job information test, each part taking about 45 minutes to complete; a performance test consisting of tests that represent tasks similar to those performed on the job; and a work habits inventory for assessing nontechnical, work-related attitudes and behavior. Test is intended for persons in fashion apparel merchandising at the secondary or postsecondary level. It is not intended for individuals completing 4-year fashion merchandising programs. The 2 parts of the job information test assess general fashion knowledge and sales knowledge. The performance test requires examinee to carry out following activities: take body measurements, determine figure type and size, complete layaway forms, close out a cash register, handle a customer complaint, complete an exchange or return, complete a sale, maintain a book inventory. It takes approximately 180 minutes to complete the performance test.

12644
Wisconsin Mathematics Test, Grade 7. Wisconsin State Dept. of Public Instruction, Madison, Div. of Instructional Services 1978
Descriptors: *Achievement Tests; *Criterion Referenced Tests; *Diagnostic Tests; *Grade 7; Junior High Schools; Junior High School Students; *Secondary School Mathematics
Availability: ERIC Document Reproduction Service; 7420 Fullerton Rd., Ste. 110, Springfield, VA 22153-2852 (ED171586, 67 p.)
Grade Level: 7
Notes: Items, 85

This achievement test is based on objectives identified in "Guidelines to Mathematics, 6-8." The test can be used as a criterion-referenced instrument, a diagnostic instrument, or an achievement instrument. Each test item is cross-referenced to the corresponding student behavioral objective in the above publication. This cross-referencing makes it possible to analyze strengths and weaknesses through item analysis comparison with objectives.

12645
Wisconsin Mathematics Test, Grade 8. Wisconsin State Dept. of Public Instruction, Madison, Div. of Instructional Services 1978
Descriptors: *Achievement Tests; *Criterion Referenced Tests; *Diagnostic Tests; *Grade 8; Junior High Schools; Junior High School Students; *Secondary School Mathematics
Availability: ERIC Document Reproduction Service; 7420 Fullerton Rd., Ste. 110, Springfield, VA 22153-2852 (ED171586, 67 p.)
Grade Level: 8
Notes: Items, 63

This achievement test is based on objectives identified in "Guidelines to Mathematics, 6-8." The test can be used as a criterion-referenced instrument, a diagnostic instrument, or an achievement instrument. Each test item is cross-referenced to the corresponding student behavioral objective in the above publication. This cross-referencing makes it possible to analyze strengths and weaknesses through item analysis comparison with objectives.

12681
Preschool Screening System. Hainsworth, Peter K.; Hainsworth, Marian L. 1980
Subtests: Movement Pattern; Clapping; Body Directions; Finger Patterns; Copy Shapes; Visual Integration; Spatial Directions; Draw-a-Person; Serial Counting; Phrases; Sentences; Verbal Reasoning; General Information; Quantity Recognition; Read Shapes
Descriptors: Human Body; *Individual Testing; *Kindergarten Children; Language Proficiency; *Learning Readiness; *Preschool Children; Preschool Education; Psychomotor Skills; *Screening Tests
Identifiers: PSS
Availability: Early Recognition Intervention Systems; Box 1635, Pawtucket, RI 02862
Age Level: 2-6
Notes: Time, 20 min. approx.

An individually administered screening test of learning efficiency combined with a parent questionnaire (TC012684) that is used as a first step toward recognizing special learning needs of preschool or kindergarten children. Primary use is to quickly survey learning skills of children entering nursery school or kindergarten so that curriculum can be adapted to their needs. Can also serve as part of a more detailed assessment of individual children. May also be group administered by having a team of several adults meet with 8 children at a time. Test assesses body awareness, visual-perceptual-motor skills, and language skills. Older children (ages 4-9) are administered only selected items of the subtest.

12682
Preschool Screening System, Short Form. Hainsworth, Peter K.; Hainsworth, Marian L. 1980
Subtests: Body Direction; Copy Shapes; Serial Counting; Sentences; Verbal Reasoning
Descriptors: Human Body; *Individual Testing; *Kindergarten Children; Language Proficiency; *Learning Readiness; *Preschool Children; Preschool Education; Psychomotor Skills; *Screening Tests
Identifiers: PSS
Availability: ERISys; Box 1635, Pawtucket, RI 02862
Age Level: 2-6
Notes: Time, 12 min. approx.

Used as a prescreen if there are large numbers of children entering school or only a few personnel to do the screening. Procedure is to prescreen children, using 5 of the subtests from the Preschool Screening System (TC012681): body directions, copy shapes, serial counting, sentences, verbal reasoning.

12683
Preschool Screening System, Non-Language Form. Hainsworth, Peter K.; Hainsworth, Marian L. 1980
Subtests: Movement Patterns; Clapping; Finger Patterns; Copy Shapes; Draw-a-Person
Descriptors: English (Second Language); Hearing Impairments; *Individual Testing; *Kindergarten Children; Language Handicaps; *Learning Readiness; *Nonverbal Tests; *Pantomime; *Preschool Children; Preschool Education; *Screening Tests
Identifiers: PSS
Availability: ERISys; Box 1635, Pawtucket, RI 02862
Age Level: 2-6

A nonlanguage version of the Preschool Screening System (TC012681) for use with children with a hearing language problem or with children whose first language is not English. Score is used as a rough indicator of whether child should be tested further. Subtests used are movement patterns, clapping, finger patterns, copy shapes, and draw-a-person. Should be followed by complete evaluation if score is low.

12698
Henderson-Moriarty ESL/Literacy Placement Test. Henderson, Cindy; Moriarty, Pia 1982
Subtests: Oral; Written
Descriptors: *Adults; *Adult Students; *English (Second Language); *Individual Testing; Limited English Speaking; Non English Speaking; Oral English; Reading Skills; *Screening Tests; *Student Placement; Writing Skills
Identifiers: HELP Test
Availability: The Alemany Press; c/o Prentice-Hall, Inc., 200 Old Tappen Rd., Old Tappen, NJ 07675
Age Level: 18-64

Individually administered test for adult learners of English as a Second Language (ESL) who have minimal or no oral English skills and who fall into one of the following categories: no reading or writing skills in any language, minimal reading or writing skills in their native language, or reading and writing skills in a language that does not use the Roman alphabet. The HELP test has 3 components: intake information (first language assessment), oral English assessment (including reading and manipulative skills), and written English assessment (including reading skills). Test helps with appropriate class placement and identifies literacy levels of students. Test is untimed.

12700
Criterion-Referenced Metrics Tests. North Carolina State Dept. of Public Instruction, Raleigh Div. of Development 1977
Descriptors: *Criterion Referenced Tests; Elementary Education; *Elementary School Mathematics; Elementary School Students; *Item Banks; Junior High Schools; Junior High School Students; *Metric System; *Secondary School Mathematics
Availability: ERIC Document Reproduction Service; 7420 Fullerton Rd., Ste. 110, Springfield, VA 22153-2852 (ED160387, 33 p.)
Grade Level: K-8

This is an extensive list of criterion-referenced metric test items for use by educators in levels K-8. The items are referenced to the goals and behavioral objectives in the Winston-Salem/Forsyth County School System. Each test item is labeled according to grade level, broad goal, and behavioral objective. Questions for the kindergarten level are designed for a one-to-one setting. There are 2 choices for each item. At levels 1 and 2, the teacher reads each item aloud; the students mark their own papers. Again there are 2 choices. For children who can read with average skill in levels 3 to 8, a written test is given with 3 choices at levels 3 and 4, and 4 choices at levels 5 though 8. If reading level warrants, the teacher may read aloud and/or use transparencies.

12716
Mathematics Test: Grade One. Florida State Univ., Tallahassee, Project for the Mathematical Development of Children 1975
Descriptors: *Achievement Tests; *Elementary School Mathematics; *Grade 1; Individual Testing; Mathematical Concepts; Primary Education
Identifiers: *Oral Tests; PMDC; Project for Mathematical Development of Children
Availability: ERIC Document Reproduction Service; 7420 Fullerton Rd., Ste. 110, Springfield, VA 22153-2852 (ED144813, 211 p.)
Grade Level: 1
Notes: Items, 53

The PMDC Test, Grade 1 is an individually administered test designed to assess students' attainment of concepts and skills related to the following topics: counting set equivalence, ordering of numbers, addition and subtraction, and class inclusion. This test does not include conventional paper-and-pencil items. Directions are given orally, and the student responds orally and/or by demonstrating the solution to a problem with manipulative aids. The items within the test are organized from easy to hard, and combine several content strands within each difficulty level.

12717
Mathematics Test: Grade Two. Florida State Univ., Tallahassee, Project for the Mathematical Development of Children 1975
Descriptors: *Achievement Tests; *Elementary School Mathematics; *Grade 2; Individual Testing; Mathematical Concepts; Primary Education
Identifiers: *Oral Tests; PMDC; Project for Mathematical Development of Children
Availability: ERIC Document Reproduction Service; 7420 Fullerton Rd., Ste. 110, Springfield, VA 22153-2852 (ED144813, 211 p.)
Grade Level: 2
Notes: Items, 52

The PMDC Mathematics Test, Grade 2 is an individually administered test designed to assess students' attainment of concepts and skills related to the following topics: counting, patterns, place value, equivalence, number names, ordering of numbers, addition and subtraction, missing addends, and class inclusion. This test does not include conventional paper-and-pencil items. Directions are given orally, and the student responds orally and/or by demonstrating the solution to a problem with manipulative aids. The items within the test are organized from easy to hard and combine several content strands within each difficulty level.

12736
Alemany English Second Language Placement Test, Revised. Ilyin, Donna; And Others 1977
Descriptors: *Achievement Tests; Adults; *Adult Students; *English (Second Language); *Student Placement
Availability: The Alemany Press; c/o Prentice-Hall, Inc., 200 Old Tappen Rd., Old Tappen, NJ 07675
Age Level: Adults

An English language placement test for adults who are learning English as a Second Language.

12738
The Maculaitis Assessment Program: Basic Concept Test. Maculaitis, Jean D'Arcy 1982
Subtests: Identification of Color; Identification of Shapes; Counting; Number Identification; Alphabet; Letter Identification; Identification of Relationships
Descriptors: *Achievement Tests; *Admission Criteria; Criterion Referenced Tests; *Diagnostic Tests; Elementary School Students; *English (Second Language); *Grade 1; Group Testing; Individual Testing; *Kindergarten Children; *Language Proficiency; Listening Comprehension; Norm Referenced Tests; *North American English; Oral Language; Primary Education; Reading Comprehension; *Screening Tests; *Standard Spoken Usage; *Student Placement; Vocabulary; Writing Skills
Identifiers: MAC; Test Batteries
Availability: The Alemany Press; c/o Prentice-Hall, Inc., 200 Old Tappen Rd., Old Tappen, NJ 07675
Grade Level: K-1
Notes: Time, 15 min.; Items, 46

A multipurpose test for nonnative speakers of English in kindergarten through grade 12. The MAC battery can be used to provide an indication of a student's global as well as specific language proficiency; provide an indication of student's academic achievement in English (i.e., student's second language); provide specific diagnostic information; determine whether nonnative student will be chosen for selection into the ESL/BE program provided by a school district; and assist in establishing exit criteria from the program. MAC focuses on the functional meaning of language and emphasizes the vocabulary and structures needed by the learner to respond appropriately in specific situations. Skills tested by the battery include oral expression, listening comprehension, vocabulary knowledge, reading comprehension, writing ability. In the battery, item difficulty increases gradually. All components are color-coded so that students can be given subtests from different levels. Many of the subtests must be individually administered; others may be group administered. The battery has both norm-referenced and criterion-referenced applications. Target language of MAC is standard American English.

12739
The Maculaitis Assessment Program: K-1. Maculaitis, Jean D'Arcy 1982
Subtests: Asking Questions; Connected Discourse; Comprehension of Commands; Situational Comprehension; Minimal Pairs; Identification of Consonants and Vowels
Descriptors: *Achievement Tests; *Admission Criteria; Criterion Referenced Tests; *Diagnostic Tests; Elementary School Students; *English (Second Language); *Grade 1; Group Testing; Individual Testing; *Kindergarten Children; *Language Proficiency; Listening Comprehension; Norm Referenced Tests; *North American English; Oral Language; Primary Education; Reading Comprehension; *Screening Tests; *Standard Spoken Usage; *Student Placement; Vocabulary; Writing Skills
Identifiers: MAC; Test Batteries
Availability: The Alemany Press; c/o Prentice-Hall, Inc., 200 Old Tappen Rd., Old Tappen, NJ 07675
Grade Level: K-1
Notes: Time, 25 min.; Items, 43

A multipurpose test for nonnative speakers of English in kindergarten through grade 12. The MAC battery can be used to provide an indication of a student's global as well as specific language proficiency; provide an indication of student's academic achievement in English (i.e., student's second language); provide specific diagnostic information; determine whether nonnative student will be chosen for selection into the ESL/BE program provided by a school district; and assist in establishing exit criteria from the program. MAC focuses on the functional meaning of language and emphasizes the vocabulary and structures needed by the learner to respond appropriately in specific situations. Skills tested by the battery include oral expression, listening comprehension, vocabulary knowledge, reading comprehension, writing ability. In the battery, item difficulty increases gradually. All components are color-coded so that students can be given subtests from different levels. Many of the subtests must be individually administered; others may be group administered. The battery has both norm-referenced and criterion-referenced applications. Target language of MAC is standard American English.

12740
The Maculaitis Assessment Program: 2-3. Maculaitis, Jean D'Arcy 1982
Subtests: Answering Questions; Connected Discourse; Identification of Consonants and Vowels; Definition of Nouns; Identifying Words; Counting Words; Answering Questions; Comprehending Statements; Alphabetizing; Recognizing Vowels and Consonants; Recognizing Long and Short Vowels; Using Word Families; Singular and Plural Forms; Recognizing Silent Letters; Reading Outcomes
Descriptors: *Achievement Tests; *Admission Criteria; Criterion Referenced Tests; *Diagnostic Tests; *Elementary School Students; *English (Second Language); *Grade 2; *Grade 3; Group Testing; Individual Testing; *Language Proficiency; Listening Comprehension; Norm Referenced Tests; *North American English; Oral Language; Primary Education; Reading Comprehension; *Screening Tests; *Standard Spoken Usage; *Student Placement; Vocabulary; Writing Skills
Identifiers: MAC; Test Batteries
Availability: The Alemany Press; c/o Prentice-Hall, Inc., 200 Old Tappen Rd., Old Tappen, NJ 07675
Grade Level: 2-3
Notes: Time, 79 min.; Items, 111

A multipurpose test for nonnative speakers of English in kindergarten through grade 12. The MAC battery can be used to provide an indication of a student's global as well as specific language proficiency; provide an indication of student's academic achievement in English (i.e., student's second language); provide specific diagnostic information; determine whether nonnative student will be chosen for selection into the ESL/BE program provided by a school district; and assist in establishing exit criteria from the program. MAC focuses on the functional meaning of language and emphasizes the vocabulary and structures needed by the learner to respond appropriately in specific situations. Skills tested by the battery include oral expression, listening comprehension, vocabulary knowledge, reading comprehension, writing ability. In the battery, item difficulty increases gradually. All components are color-coded so that students can be given subtests from different levels. Many of the subtests must be individually administered; others may be group administered. The battery has both norm-referenced and criterion-referenced applications. Target language of MAC is standard American English.

12741
The Maculaitis Assessment Program: 4-5. Maculaitis, Jean D'Arcy 1982
Subtests: Asking Questions; Connected Discourse; Vocabulary Knowledge; Positional Auditory Discrimination; Answering Questions; Comprehending Statements; Comprehending Dialogues; Recognizing Homonyms; Recognizing Antonyms; Recognizing Abbreviations; Reading Outcomes; Grammatical Structure; Paragraph Construction

Descriptors: *Achievement Tests; *Admission Criteria; Criterion Referenced Tests; *Diagnostic Tests; *Elementary School Students; *English (Second Language); *Grade 4; *Grade 5; Group Testing; Individual Testing; Intermediate Grades; *Language Proficiency; Listening Comprehension; Norm Referenced Tests; *North American English; Oral Language; Reading Comprehension; *Screening Tests; *Standard Spoken Usage; *Student Placement; Vocabulary; Writing Skills
Identifiers: MAC; Test Batteries
Availability: The Alemany Press; c/o Prentice-Hall, Inc., 200 Old Tappen Rd., Old Tappen, NJ 07675
Grade Level: 4-5
Notes: Time, 119 min.; Items, 126

A multipurpose test for nonnative speakers of English in kindergarten through grade 12. The MAC battery can be used to provide an indication of a student's global as well as specific language proficiency; provide an indication of student's academic achievement in English (i.e., student's second language); provide specific diagnostic information; determine whether nonnative student will be chosen for selection into the ESL/BE program provided by a school district; and assist in establishing exit criteria from the program. MAC focuses on the functional meaning of language and emphasizes the vocabulary and structures needed by the learner to respond appropriately in specific situations. Skills tested by the battery include oral expression, listening comprehension, vocabulary knowledge, reading comprehension, writing ability. In the battery, item difficulty increases gradually. All components are color-coded so that students can be given subtests from different levels. Many of the subtests must be individually administered; others may be group administered. The battery has both norm-referenced and criterion-referenced applications. Target language of MAC is standard American English.

12742

The Maculaitis Assessment Program: 6-8. Maculaitis, Jean D'Arcy 1982
Subtests: Answering Questions (Oral Expression); Asking Questions (Oral Expression); Connected Discourse; Answering Questions (Listening Comprehension); Comprehending Statements; Comprehending Dialogues; Vocabulary; Reading Outcomes; Grammatical Structure; Paragraph Construction
Descriptors: *Achievement Tests; *Admission Criteria; Criterion Referenced Tests; *Diagnostic Tests; *English (Second Language); *Grade 6; Group Testing; Individual Testing; Junior High Schools; *Junior High School Students; *Language Proficiency; Listening Comprehension; Norm Referenced Tests; *North American English; Oral Language; Reading Comprehension; Screening Tests; *Standard Spoken Usage; *Student Placement; Vocabulary; Writing Skills
Identifiers: MAC; Test Batteries
Availability: The Alemany Press; c/o Prentice-Hall, Inc., 200 Old Tappen Rd., Old Tappen, NJ 07675
Grade Level: 6-8
Notes: Time, 108 min.; Items, 112

A multipurpose test for nonnative speakers of English in kindergarten through grade 12. The MAC battery can be used to provide an indication of a student's global as well as specific language proficiency; provide an indication of student's academic achievement in English (i.e., student's second language); provide specific diagnostic information; determine whether nonnative student will be chosen for selection into the ESL/BE program provided by a school district; and assist in establishing exit criteria from the program. MAC focuses on the functional meaning of language and emphasizes the vocabulary and structures needed by the learner to respond appropriately in specific situations. Skills tested by the battery include oral expression, listening comprehension, vocabulary knowledge, reading comprehension, writing ability. In the battery, item difficulty increases gradually. All components are color-coded so that students can be given subtests from different levels. Many of the subtests must be individually administered; others may be group administered. The battery has both norm-referenced and criterion-referenced applications. Target language of MAC is standard American English.

12743

The Maculaitis Assessment Program: 9-12. Maculaitis, Jean D'Arcy 1982
Subtests: Answering Questions (Oral Expression); Asking Questions (Oral Expression); Connected Discourse; Answering Questions (Listening Comprehension); Comprehending Statements; Comprehending Dialogues; Vocabulary; Reading Outcomes; Grammatical Structure; Paragraph Construction

Descriptors: *Achievement Tests; *Admission Criteria; Criterion Referenced Tests; *Diagnostic Tests; *English (Second Language); Group Testing; High Schools; *High School Students; Individual Testing; *Language Proficiency; Listening Comprehension; Norm Referenced Tests; *North American English; Oral Language; Reading Comprehension; *Screening Tests; *Standard Spoken Usage; *Student Placement; Vocabulary; Writing Skills
Identifiers: MAC; Test Batteries
Availability: The Alemany Press; c/o Prentice-Hall, Inc., 200 Old Tappen Rd., Old Tappen, NJ 07675
Grade Level: 9-12
Notes: Time, 108 min.; Items, 112

A multipurpose test for nonnative speakers of English in kindergarten through grade 12. The MAC battery can be used to provide an indication of a student's global as well as specific language proficiency; provide an indication of student's academic achievement in English (i.e., student's second language); provide specific diagnostic information; determine whether nonnative student will be chosen for selection into the ESL/BE program provided by a school district; and assist in establishing exit criteria from the program. MAC focuses on the functional meaning of language and emphasizes the vocabulary and structures needed by the learner to respond appropriately in specific situations. Skills tested by the battery include oral expression, listening comprehension, vocabulary knowledge, reading comprehension, writing ability. In the battery, item difficulty increases gradually. All components are color-coded so that students can be given subtests from different levels. Many of the subtests must be individually administered; others may be group administered. The battery has both norm-referenced and criterion-referenced applications. Target language of MAC is standard American English.

12811

Bank of Items for H.S.C. Biology Level III and Division I. Tasmanian Education Dept. Hobart (Australia) 1975
Subtests: Diversity; Interrelationships; Change; Living World; Organs and Systems; Interaction and Maintenance; Cellular Level; Continuity; Evolution
Descriptors: *Biology; Foreign Countries; High School Students; *Item Banks; Junior High School Students; Multiple Choice Tests; Norm Referenced Tests; *Science Education; *Secondary Education; Test Items
Identifiers: Australia (Tasmania)
Availability: ERIC Document Reproduction Service; 7420 Fullerton Rd., Ste. 110, Springfield, VA 22153-2852 (ED137053, 145 p.)
Grade Level: 7-12
Notes: Items, 116

This item bank is an organized collection of biology questions designed for use in evaluation at the secondary level in Tasmania. Each item has been tried for quality and is accompanied by its difficulty percentage as well as by its content area and the mental processes required to answer it. The mental processes include knowledge, comprehension, application, and analysis.

12823

Composition Diagnostic Test—A. Baltimore County Board of Education, Towson, MD 1976
Descriptors: *Diagnostic Tests; Educational Assessment; *English Instruction; Grade 7; Grade 8; Junior High Schools; *Junior High School Students; Multiple Choice Tests; Sentence Combining; *Student Evaluation; Writing (Composition); *Writing Skills
Availability: ERIC Document Reproduction Service; 7420 Fullerton Rd., Ste. 110, Springfield, VA 22153-2852 (ED130329, 246 p.)
Grade Level: 7-8
Notes: Items, 19

These are 3 composition diagnostic tests for the 7-8 grades. One is a multiple-choice test with 12 items, the second is a sentence-combining test of syntactic maturity, and the third has 7 open-ended items about a writing sample. These tests are part of the English curriculum development cycle prepared by the Baltimore County Board of Education. The diagnostic procedure for written composition has 3 stages designed to take a minimum of 3 class periods. The first stage is a multiple-choice test, the second stage is a sentence-combining test of syntactic maturity, and stage 3 involves a diagnostic writing sample. Individually, none of the tests provides a satisfactory diagnosis; collectively, however, all 3 tests give a fairly complete picture of a student's knowledge and ability in composition.

12824

Composition Diagnostic Test—B. Baltimore County Board of Education, Towson, MD 1976

Descriptors: *Diagnostic Tests; Educational Assessment; *English Instruction; Grade 9; Grade 10; High Schools; *High School Students; Multiple Choice Tests; Sentence Combining; *Student Evaluation; *Writing Skills
Availability: ERIC Document Reproduction Service; 7420 Fullerton Rd., Ste. 110, Springfield, VA 22153-2852 (ED130329, 246 p.)
Grade Level: 9-10
Notes: Items, 18

These are 3 tests, 2 are writing samples with questions. One is a multiple-choice test with 14 items, the second is a sentence-combining test of syntactic maturity, and the third has 4 open-ended questions on the writing sample. These tests are part of the English curriculum development cycle prepared by the Baltimore County Board of Education. The diagnostic procedure for written composition has 3 stages designed to take a minimum of 3 class periods. The first stage is a multiple-choice test, the second stage is a sentence-combining test of syntactic maturity, and stage 3 involves a diagnostic writing sample. Individually, none of the tests provides a satisfactory diagnosis; collectively, however, all 3 tests give a fairly complete picture of a student's knowledge and ability in composition.

12825

Composition Diagnostic Test—C. Baltimore County Board of Education, Towson, MD 1976
Descriptors: *Diagnostic Tests; Educational Assessment; *English Instruction; Grade 11; Grade 12; High Schools; *High School Students; Multiple Choice Tests; Rating Scales; Sentence Combining; *Student Evaluation; *Writing Skills
Availability: ERIC Document Reproduction Service; 7420 Fullerton Rd., Ste. 110, Springfield, VA 22153-2852 (ED130329, 246 p.)
Grade Level: 11-12
Notes: Items, 41

These are 3 tests, 2 are writing samples with questions. One is a multiple-choice test with 16 items, the second is a sentence combining test of syntactic maturity, and the third is a rating scale of 25 items. The scale is 5 points and goes from most to least important. These tests are part of the English curriculum development cycle prepared by the Baltimore County Board of Education. The diagnostic procedure for written composition has 3 stages designed to take a minimum of 3 class periods. The first stage is a multiple-choice test, the second stage is a sentence-combining test of syntactic maturity, and stage 3 involves a diagnostic writing sample. Individually, none of the tests provides a satisfactory diagnosis; collectively, however, all 3 tests give a fairly complete picture of a student's knowledge and ability in composition.

12826

Language Diagnostic Test—A. Baltimore County Board of Education, Towson, MD 1976
Descriptors: *Diagnostic Tests; Educational Assessment; English Instruction; *Grade 7; *Grade 8; Grammar; Junior High Schools; *Junior High School Students; Language Processing; *Language Skills; Student Evaluation; Writing Skills
Availability: ERIC Document Reproduction Service; 7420 Fullerton Rd., Ste. 110, Springfield, VA 22153-2852 (ED130329, 246 p.)
Grade Level: 7-8
Notes: Time, 40 min.; Items, 100

This multiple-choice test is to test the student's understanding of the English language. It tries to find (1) how well the student understands the way English sentences are constructed, and (2) the knowledge of standard English usage and mechanics. To determine student proficiency in grammar, standard usage, and the conventions of written English (mechanics), 3 diagnostic tests have been developed. Separate instruments have been developed for 3 grade levels (7-8, 9-10, 11-12). The appropriate test should be used early in the year as a screening device for diagnostic purposes only. These tests will in no way give a reliable or valid end-of-year measure of student mastery. Because each language test is rather long, it may be wise to administer the test over a 2-day period. These tests are part of the English curriculum development cycle prepared by the Baltimore County Board of Education. The diagnostic procedure for written composition has 3 stages designed to take a minimum of 3 class periods. The first stage is a multiple-choice test, the second stage is a sentence-combining test of syntactic maturity, and stage 3 involves a diagnostic writing sample. Individually, none of the tests provides a satisfactory diagnosis; collectively, however, all 3 tests give a fairly complete picture of a student's knowledge and ability in composition.

12827

Language Diagnostic Test—B. Baltimore County Board of Education, Towson, MD 1976
Subtests: Mechanics; Usage; Grammar
Descriptors: *Diagnostic Tests; Educational Assessment; *English Instruction; Grade 9; Grade 10; Grammar; High Schools; *High School Students; Language Processing; *Language Skills; *Student Evaluation; Writing Skills

Availability: ERIC Document Reproduction Service; 7420 Fullerton Rd., Ste. 110, Springfield, VA 22153-2852 (ED130329, 246 p.)
Grade Level: 9-10
Notes: Time, 40 min.; Items, 100

This multiple-choice test is to test the student's understanding of the English language. It tries to find (1) how well the student understands the way English sentences are constructed, and (2) the knowledge of standard English usage and mechanics. To determine student proficiency in grammar, standard usage, and the conventions of written English (mechanics), 3 diagnostic tests have been developed. Separate instruments have been developed for 3 grade levels (7-8, 9-10, 11-12). The appropriate test should be used early in the year as a screening device for diagnostic purposes only. These tests will in no way give a reliable or valid end-of-year measure of student mastery. Because each language test is rather long, it may be wise to administer the test over a 2-day period.

12828
Language Diagnostic Test—C. Baltimore County Board of Education, Towson, MD 1976
Subtests: Mechanics; Usage; Grammar
Descriptors: *Diagnostic Tests; Educational Assessment; *English Instruction; Grade 11; Grade 12; High Schools; *High School Students; Language Processing; *Language Skills; *Student Evaluation; Writing Skills
Availability: ERIC Document Reproduction Service; 7420 Fullerton Rd., Ste. 110, Springfield, VA 22153-2852 (ED130329, 246 p.)
Grade Level: 11-12
Notes: Time, 40 min.; Items, 100

This multiple-choice test is to test the student's understanding of the English language. It tries to find (1) how well the student understands the way English sentences are constructed, and (2) the knowledge of standard English usage and mechanics. To determine student proficiency in grammar, standard usage, and the conventions of written English (mechanics), 3 diagnostic tests have been developed. Separate instruments have been developed for 3 grade levels (7-8, 9-10, 11-12). The appropriate test should be used early in the year as a screening device for diagnostic purposes only. These tests will in no way give a reliable or valid end-of-year measure of student mastery. Because each language test is rather long, it may be wise to administer the test over a 2-day period.

12829
Observation Checklist for Reading. Baltimore County Board of Education, Towson, MD 1976
Subtests: Oral Reading; Silent Reading; Listening; Physical Limitations
Descriptors: Check Lists; *Diagnostic Tests; Educational Assessment; *English Instruction; *Oral Reading; Reading Ability; *Reading Diagnosis; Secondary Education; *Secondary School Students; *Student Evaluation
Availability: ERIC Document Reproduction Service; 7420 Fullerton Rd., Ste. 110, Springfield, VA 22153-2852 (ED130329, 246 p.)
Grade Level: 7-12

Teachers can use this checklist to get specific information about a student's reading problems. Teachers should select 2 or 3 paragraphs that are typical of the vocabulary, syntax, and concept load of the reading matter being considered for use with the class. The checklist can be used by the teacher as an individual reads to make a detailed analysis of problems and use the checklist as a basis for diagnostic procedures. These tests are part of the English curriculum development cycle prepared by the Baltimore County Board of Education. The diagnostic procedure for written composition has 3 stages designed to take a minimum of 3 class periods. The first stage is a multiple-choice test, the second stage is a sentence-combining test of syntactic maturity, and stage 3 involves a diagnostic writing sample. Individually, none of the tests provides a satisfactory diagnosis; collectively, however, all 3 tests give a fairly complete picture of a student's knowledge and ability in composition.

12830
Comprehension Survey for Reading. Baltimore County Board of Education, Towson, MD 1976
Subtests: Literal Interpretation; Interpretation beyond the Literal Level
Descriptors: *Diagnostic Tests; Educational Assessment; *English Instruction; *Reading Ability; *Reading Comprehension; *Reading Diagnosis; Secondary Education; *Secondary School Students; *Student Evaluation; Surveys
Availability: ERIC Document Reproduction Service; 7420 Fullerton Rd., Ste. 110, Springfield, VA 22153-2852 (ED130329, 246 p.)
Grade Level: 7-12

This survey is used by teachers as an aid in diagnostic procedures for reading. To construct this survey, teachers must first select a sufficient number of excerpts from the material being considered for use to reflect the vocabulary, syntax, and concept load typical of the entire selection. Each excerpt should be restricted to a length necessary to provide an obvious beginning, middle, and conclusion. A

set of comprehension questions to be used with each excerpt must be developed. These questions should begin at the literal level and progress gradually to the more difficult and more abstract. The finished comprehension survey can be presented to students individually, in small groups, or as a class and their responses can be oral or written. The survey lists ways in which the student must demonstrate ability. These tests are part of the English curriculum development cycle prepared by the Baltimore County Board of Education. The diagnostic procedure for written composition has 3 stages designed to take a minimum of 3 class periods. The first stage is a multiple-choice test, the second stage is a sentence-combining test of syntactic maturity, and stage 3 involves a diagnostic writing sample. Individually, none of the tests provides a satisfactory diagnosis; collectively, however, all 3 tests give a fairly complete picture of a student's knowledge and ability in composition.

12831
The Nursery Rhyme Grammar Test. Baltimore County Board of Education, Towson, MD 1976
Descriptors: *Diagnostic Tests; Educational Assessment; *English Instruction; Grammar; Multiple Choice Tests; *Reading Diagnosis; Secondary Education; *Secondary School Students; Student Evaluation; *Writing Skills
Availability: ERIC Document Reproduction Service; 7420 Fullerton Rd., Ste. 110, Springfield, VA 22153-2852 (ED130329, 246 p.)
Grade Level: 7-12
Notes: Items, 28

This is an example of a simpler, one-period diagnostic instrument than the Language Diagnostic Tests. It can be used as is or as a model for an easier or more difficult original version. The test is a series of 28 multiple-choice items all based on a single sentence. The items primarily test recognition of various grammatical forms within the nursery rhyme although a few items focus on usage and mechanics. This test was modeled on a similar one by Paul B. Diederich. Similar tests could be developed using other nursery rhymes of a famous quotation. These tests are part of the English curriculum development cycle prepared by the Baltimore County Board of Education. The diagnostic procedure for written composition has 3 stages designed to take a minimum of 3 class periods. The first stage is a multiple-choice test, the second stage is a sentence-combining test of syntactic maturity, and stage 3 involves a diagnostic writing sample. Individually, none of the tests provides a satisfactory diagnosis; collectively, however, all 3 tests give a fairly complete picture of a student's knowledge and ability in composition.

12834
MathComp: Measuring Basic Competence in Mathematics, K-1. Santa Clara Unified School District, CA 1979
Descriptors: Achievement Tests; Criterion Referenced Tests; *Elementary School Mathematics; *Grade 1; *Kindergarten Children; Mastery Tests; *Mathematics Achievement; *Mathematics Tests; *Minimum Competency Testing; Primary Education
Availability: Fearon Education; Div. of Pitman Learning, Inc., 500 Harbor Blvd., Belmont, CA 94002
Grade Level: K-1

Measurement system designed for use with any mathematics curriculum and any basal textbook program. Competency-based testing program consisting of 7 binders containing tests for grades K-8. For each grade level, except kindergarten, there are survey tests containing problems for each objective. Survey tests should be administered as pretests early in the school year. Students can be pretested at-level, or one level above or below skills to be taught. On-level survey tests are indicators of basic competencies to be learned in that grade by the end of the school year. There is also one objective test for each of 146 objectives in the series, providing 14 to 20 tests per grade. Each objective test includes approximately 10 problems. To pass an objective test, a student must solve at least 80 percent of the problems correctly. In each binder, on-level objective tests as well as tests for one level above and one level below are provided.

12835
MathComp: Measuring Basic Competence in Mathematics, 2. Santa Clara Unified School District, CA 1979
Descriptors: Achievement Tests; Criterion Referenced Tests; *Elementary School Mathematics; Elementary School Students; *Grade 2; Mastery Tests; *Mathematics Achievement; *Mathematics Tests; *Minimum Competency Testing; Primary Education
Availability: Fearon Education; Div. of Pitman Learning, Inc., 500 Harbor Blvd., Belmont, CA 94002
Grade Level: 2

Measurement system designed for use with any mathematics curriculum and any basal textbook program. Competency-based testing program consisting of 7 binders containing tests for grades K-8. For each grade level, except kindergarten, there are survey tests containing

problems for each objective. Survey tests should be administered as pretests early in the school year. Students can be pretested at-level, or one level above or below skills to be taught. On-level survey tests are indicators of basic competencies to be learned in that grade by the end of the school year. There is also one objective test for each of 146 objectives in the series, providing 14 to 20 tests per grade. Each objective test includes approximately 10 problems. To pass an objective test, a student must solve at least 80 percent of the problems correctly. In each binder, on-level objective tests as well as tests for one level above and one level below are provided.

12836
MathComp: Measuring Basic Competence in Mathematics, 3. Santa Clara Unified School District, CA 1979
Descriptors: Achievement Tests; Criterion Referenced Tests; *Elementary School Mathematics; Elementary School Students; *Grade 3; Mastery Tests; *Mathematics Achievement; *Mathematics Tests; *Minimum Competency Testing; Primary Education
Availability: Fearon Education; Div. of Pitman Learning, Inc., 500 Harbor Blvd., Belmont, CA 94002
Grade Level: 3

Measurement system designed for use with any mathematics curriculum and any basal textbook program. Competency-based testing program consisting of 7 binders containing tests for grades K-8. For each grade level, except kindergarten, there are survey tests containing problems for each objective. Survey tests should be administered as pretests early in the school year. Students can be pretested at-level, or one level above or below skills to be taught. On-level survey tests are indicators of basic competencies to be learned in that grade by the end of the school year. There is also one objective test for each of 146 objectives in the series, providing 14 to 20 tests per grade. Each objective test includes approximately 10 problems. To pass an objective test, a student must solve at least 80 percent of the problems correctly. In each binder, on-level objective tests as well as tests for one level above and one level below are provided.

12837
MathComp: Measuring Basic Competence in Mathematics, 4. Santa Clara Unified School District, CA 1979
Descriptors: Achievement Tests; Criterion Referenced Tests; *Elementary School Mathematics; Elementary School Students; *Grade 4; Intermediate Grades; Mastery Tests; *Mathematics Achievement; *Mathematics Tests; *Minimum Competency Testing
Availability: Fearon Education; Div. of Pitman Learning, Inc., 500 Harbor Blvd., Belmont, CA 94002
Grade Level: 4

Measurement system designed for use with any mathematics curriculum and any basal textbook program. Competency-based testing program consisting of 7 binders containing tests for grades K-8. For each grade level, except kindergarten, there are survey tests containing problems for each objective. Survey tests should be administered as pretests early in the school year. Students can be pretested at-level, or one level above or below skills to be taught. On-level survey tests are indicators of basic competencies to be learned in that grade by the end of the school year. There is also one objective test for each of 146 objectives in the series, providing 14 to 20 tests per grade. Each objective test includes approximately 10 problems. To pass an objective test, a student must solve at least 80 percent of the problems correctly. In each binder, on-level objective tests as well as tests for one level above and one level below are provided.

12838
MathComp: Measuring Basic Competence in Mathematics, 5. Santa Clara Unified School District, CA 1979
Descriptors: Achievement Tests; Criterion Referenced Tests; *Elementary School Mathematics; Elementary School Students; *Grade 5; Intermediate Grades; Mastery Tests; *Mathematics Achievement; *Mathematics Tests; *Minimum Competency Testing
Availability: Fearon Education; Div. of Pitman Learning, Inc., 500 Harbor Blvd., Belmont, CA 94002
Grade Level: 5

Measurement system designed for use with any mathematics curriculum and any basal textbook program. Competency-based testing program consisting of 7 binders containing tests for grades K-8. For each grade level, except kindergarten, there are survey tests containing problems for each objective. Survey tests should be administered as pretests early in the school year. Students can be pretested at-level, or one level above or below skills to be taught. On-level survey tests are indicators of basic competencies to be learned in that grade by the end of the school year. There is also one objective test for each of 146 objectives in the series, providing 14 to 20 tests per grade. Each objective test includes approximately 10 problems. To pass an objective test, a student must solve at least 80 percent of the problems correctly. In each binder, on-level objective tests as well as tests for one level above and one level below are provided.

12839
MathComp: Measuring Basic Competence in Mathematics, 6.   Santa Clara Unified School District, CA 1979
Descriptors: Achievement Tests; Criterion Referenced Tests; *Elementary School Mathematics; Elementary School Students; *Grade 6; Intermediate Grades; Mastery Tests; *Mathematics Achievement; *Mathematics Tests; *Minimum Competency Testing
Availability: Fearon Education; Div. of Pitman Learning, Inc., 500 Harbor Blvd., Belmont, CA 94002
Grade Level: 6

Measurement system designed for use with any mathematics curriculum and any basal textbook program. Competency-based testing program consisting of 7 binders containing tests for grades K-8. For each grade level, except kindergarten, there are survey tests containing problems for each objective. Survey tests should be administered as pretests early in the school year. Students can be pretested at-level, or one level above or below skills to be taught. On-level survey tests are indicators of basic competencies to be learned in that grade by the end of the school year. There is also one objective test for each of 146 objectives in the series, providing 14 to 20 tests per grade. Each objective test includes approximately 10 problems. To pass an objective test, a student must solve at least 80 percent of the problems correctly. In each binder, on-level objective tests as well as tests for one level above and one level below are provided.

12840
MathComp: Measuring Basic Competence in Mathematics, 7-8.   Santa Clara Unified School District, CA 1979
Descriptors: Achievement Tests; Criterion Referenced Tests; Junior High Schools; *Junior High School Students; Mastery Tests; *Mathematics Achievement; *Mathematics Tests; *Minimum Competency Testing; *Secondary School Mathematics
Availability: Fearon Education; Div. of Pitman Learning, Inc., 500 Harbor Blvd., Belmont, CA 94002
Grade Level: 7-8

Measurement system designed for use with any mathematics curriculum and any basal textbook program. Competency-based testing program consisting of 7 binders containing tests for grades K-8. For each grade level, except kindergarten, there are survey tests containing problems for each objective. Survey tests should be administered as pretests early in the school year. Students can be pretested at-level, or one level above or below skills to be taught. On-level survey tests are indicators of basic competencies to be learned in that grade by the end of the school year. There is also one objective test for each of 146 objectives in the series, providing 14 to 20 tests per grade. Each objective test includes approximately 10 problems. To pass an objective test, a student must solve at least 80 percent of the problems correctly. In each binder, on-level objective tests as well as tests for one level above and one level below are provided.

12842
Energy Education/Conservation Examination.
Wert, Jonathan M. 1975
Descriptors: *Achievement Tests; Adults; Conservation Education; Energy; *Energy Conservation; *Environmental Education; High Schools; High School Students; Natural Resources; Objective Tests; Teachers
Availability: ERIC Document Reproduction Service; 7420 Fullerton Rd., Ste. 110, Springfield, VA 22153-2852 (ED125866, 12 p.)
Grade Level: 9-12
Age Level: 18-64
Notes: Items, 100

This examination is designed to measure the general awareness level of high school students, teachers, and citizens in the area of energy development and conservation. It is composed of 100 true-false statements concerning energy education concepts. An examinee information sheet is included.

12846
Jobs and Engines, Mastery Test: Political Issues.
American Political Science Association, Washington, DC; National Evaluation Systems, Inc., Amherst, MA; Social Studies Development Center, Bloomington, IN 1975
Descriptors: Achievement Tests; *Grade 12; High Schools; High School Seniors; *Mastery Tests; Multiple Choice Tests; Organizational Development; *Political Issues; *Political Science; Politics; Social Studies
Identifiers: Comparing Political Experiences; High School Political Science Curriculum Project

Availability: ERIC Document Reproduction Service; 7420 Fullerton Rd., Ste. 110, Springfield, VA 22153-2852 (ED121687, 21 p.)
Grade Level: 12
Notes: Items, 25

This mastery test is designed to accompany unit 5 of the second-semester twelfth grade course, "Comparing Political Experiences." The 25-item multiple-choice test was developed by the National Evaluation Systems, Inc., in conjunction with the project directors to determine whether the unit objectives have been achieved. The test measures student knowledge of the concept of political development and its application to different political environments. The test should be administered to the class as a group and then returned to the project headquarters for grading and analysis for possible revision of the student materials.

12847
Clean Air Now, Mastery Test: Political Issues.
American Political Science Association, Washington, DC; National Evaluation Systems, Inc., Amherst, MA; Social Studies Development Center, Bloomington, IN 1975
Descriptors: Achievement Tests; Change Strategies; Community Change; *Grade 12; High Schools; High School Seniors; *Mastery Tests; Multiple Choice Tests; Political Issues; *Political Science; Politics; Social Studies
Identifiers: Comparing Political Experiences; High School Political Science Curriculum Project
Availability: ERIC Document Reproduction Service; 7420 Fullerton Rd., Ste. 110, Springfield, VA 22153-2852 (ED121686, 19 p.)
Grade Level: 12
Notes: Items, 25

This mastery test is designed to accompany unit 4 of the second-semester twelfth grade course, "Comparing Political Experiences." The 25-item multiple-choice test was developed by the National Evaluation Systems, Inc., in conjunction with the project directors to determine whether the unit objectives have been achieved. The test measures student knowledge of the concept of political change and its application to different political environments. The test should be administered to the class as a group and then returned to the project headquarters for grading and analysis for possible revision of the student materials.

12848
Union Underground, Mastery Test: Political Issues.   American Political Science Association, Washington, DC; National Evaluation Systems, Inc., Amherst, MA; Social Studies Development Center, Bloomington, IN 1975
Descriptors: Achievement Tests; *Grade 12; High Schools; High School Seniors; Maintenance; *Mastery Tests; Multiple Choice Tests; Political Issues; *Political Science; Politics; Social Studies; Unions
Identifiers: Comparing Political Experiences; High School Political Science Curriculum Project
Availability: ERIC Document Reproduction Service; 7420 Fullerton Rd., Ste. 110, Springfield, VA 22153-2852 (ED121685, 20 p.)
Grade Level: 12
Notes: Items, 24

This mastery test is designed to accompany unit 3 of the second-semester twelfth grade course, "Comparing Political Experiences." The 24-item multiple-choice test was developed by the National Evaluation Systems, Inc., in conjunction with the project directors to determine whether the unit objectives have been achieved. The test measures student knowledge of the concept of political maintenance and the application of this concept to various political situations. The test should be administered to the class as a group and then returned to the project headquarters for grading and analysis for possible revision of the student materials.

12849
Busing in Boston, Mastery Test: Political Issues.
American Political Science Association, Washington, DC; National Evaluation Systems, Inc., Amherst, MA; Social Studies Development Center, Bloomington, IN 1975
Descriptors: Achievement Tests; *Busing; Conflict; Conflict Resolution; *Grade 12; High Schools; High School Seniors; *Mastery Tests; Multiple Choice Tests; Political Issues; *Political Science; Politics; School Desegregation; Social Studies
Identifiers: Comparing Political Experiences; High School Political Science Curriculum Project
Availability: ERIC Document Reproduction Service; 7420 Fullerton Rd., Ste. 110, Springfield, VA 22153-2852 (ED121684, 19 p.)
Grade Level: 12
Notes: Items, 24

This mastery test is designed to accompany the second-semester twelfth grade course, "Comparing Political Experiences." The 24-item multiple-choice test was developed by the National Evaluation Systems, Inc., in conjunction with the project directors to determine whether

the unit objectives have been achieved. The test measures student knowledge of the concept of political conflict and the application of this concept to various political situations. The test should be administered to the class as a group and then returned to the project headquarters for grading and analysis for possible revision of the student materials.

12850
Save the System, Mastery Test: Political Issues.
American Political Science Association, Washington, DC; National Evaluation Systems, Inc., Amherst, MA; Social Studies Development Center, Bloomington, IN 1975
Descriptors: Achievement Tests; Civics; *Grade 12; High Schools; High School Seniors; *Mastery Tests; Multiple Choice Tests; *Political Science; Politics; Secondary Education; Social Studies
Identifiers: Comparing Political Experiences; High School Political Science Curriculum Project
Availability: ERIC Document Reproduction Service; 7420 Fullerton Rd., Ste. 110, Springfield, VA 22153-2852 (ED121683, 17 p.)
Grade Level: 12
Notes: Items, 27

This mastery test is designed to accompany the introductory unit to the second-semester twelfth grade course, "Comparing Political Experiences" course. The 27-item multiple-choice test was developed by the National Evaluation Systems, Inc., in conjunction with the project directors to determine whether the unit objectives have been achieved. Because this unit is a summary of the political systems' concepts developed in the first-semester course, the test measures student knowledge of political system types, fundamental systems' concepts, political resources, and political activities. The test should be administered to the class as a group and then returned to the project headquarters for grading and analysis for possible revision of the student materials.

12851
Participating in Political Activities, Mastery Test. Political Systems.   American Political Science Association, Washington, DC; National Evaluation Systems, Inc., Amherst, MA; Social Studies Development Center, Bloomington, IN 1975
Descriptors: Achievement Tests; Civics; *Grade 12; High Schools; High School Seniors; *Mastery Tests; Multiple Choice Tests; *Political Science; *Politics; Secondary Education; Social Studies; United States Government (Course)
Identifiers: Comparing Political Experiences; High School Political Science Curriculum Project
Availability: ERIC Document Reproduction Service; 7420 Fullerton Rd., Ste. 110, Springfield, VA 22153-2852 (ED121682, 23 p.)
Grade Level: 12
Notes: Items, 26

This mastery test is designed to accompany unit 3 of the first-semester twelfth grade course, "Comparing Political Experiences." The 26-item multiple-choice test was developed by the National Evaluation Systems, Inc., in conjunction with the project directors to determine whether the unit objectives have been achieved. The test measures student knowledge of various kinds of political activities, such as decision making, leadership, communication, and participation. Emphasis is placed on testing how political activities affect political experiences in elite, bureaucratic, coalitional, and participant political systems. The test should be administered to the class as a group and then returned to the project headquarters for grading and analysis for possible revision of the student materials.

12852
Using Political Resources, Mastery Test: Political System.   American Political Science Association, Washington, DC; National Evaluation Systems, Inc., Amherst, MA; Social Studies Development Center, Bloomington, IN 1975
Descriptors: Achievement Tests; *Civics; *Grade 12; High Schools; High School Seniors; *Mastery Tests; Multiple Choice Tests; *Political Science; Politics; Social Studies; United States Government (Course)
Identifiers: Comparing Political Experiences; High School Political Science Curriculum Project
Availability: ERIC Document Reproduction Service; 7420 Fullerton Rd., Ste. 110, Springfield, VA 22153-2852 (ED121681, 20 p.)
Grade Level: 12
Notes: Items, 27

This mastery test is designed to accompany unit 2 of the first-semester twelfth grade course "Comparing Political Experiences." The 27-item multiple-choice test was developed by the National Evaluation Systems, Inc., in conjunction with the project directors to determine whether the unit objectives have been achieved. The test measures student knowledge of the alternative patterns of political resources found in different political systems. Emphasis is placed on testing how different resources affect political maintenance, change, development, and conflict in elite and coalitional political systems. The test should be administered to the class as a group and then returned to the project headquarters for grading and analysis for possible revision of the student materials.

12853
Observing Political Systems, Mastery Test: Political Systems. American Political Science Association, Washington, DC; National Evaluation Systems, Inc., Amherst, MA; Social Studies Development Center, Bloomington, IN 1975
Descriptors: Achievement Tests; *Civics; *Grade 12; High Schools; High School Seniors; *Mastery Tests; Multiple Choice Tests; *Political Science; *Politics; Social Studies; United States Government (Course)
Identifiers: Comparing Political Experiences; High School Political Science Curriculum Project
Availability: ERIC Document Reproduction Service; 7420 Fullerton Rd., Ste. 110, Springfield, VA 22153-2852 (ED121680, 15 p.)
Grade Level: 12
Notes: Items, 21

This mastery test is designed to accompany unit 1 of the first-semester twelfth grade course, "Comparing Political Experiences." The 21-item multiple-choice test was developed by the National Evaluation Systems, Inc., in conjunction with the project directors to determine whether the unit objectives have been achieved. The test measures student knowledge of political activities, political participant roles, political observer roles, and political system concepts including maintenance, change, and political development. It should be administered to the class as a group and then returned to the project headquarters for grading and analysis for possible improvement of the student material.

12854
Physics Achievement Test. Harvard University, Cambridge, MA, Harvard Project Physics 1966
Descriptors: *Achievement Tests; High Schools; High School Students; Multiple Choice Tests; *Physics; Science Course Improvement Projects; Science Curriculum; Science Education; *Secondary School Science
Identifiers: Harvard Project Physics; HPP; PAT
Availability: ERIC Document Reproduction Service; 7420 Fullerton Rd., Ste. 110, Springfield, VA 22153-2852 (ED120017, 15 p.)
Grade Level: 9-12
Notes: Time, 40 min.; Items, 36

This document is an evaluation instrument developed as a part of the Harvard Project Physics (HPP). It is not intended to be a measure of knowledge of Harvard Project Physics, but rather to know how much general physics the student understands before taking the course so that the student's progress may be tracked throughout the term. The test consists of a 36-item, multiple-choice (5 options) physics achievement test (PAT) designed to measure general knowledge of physics as well as the material emphasized in HPP.

12857
Selected Test Items in American History. Anderson, Howard R.; Lindquist, E.F. 1964
Subtests: Exploration and Discovery; Colonial Settlement and Life; Revolution and Constitution; Early National Period; Westward Movement; Social Economic, and Cultural Development (1824-1860); Sectionalism; Civil War and Reconstruction; Passing of the Frontier; The Political Scene (1876-1900); Rise of Big Business; The Progressive Era; World War I and Postwar Adjustments; The Great Depression; World War II and After; and Chronology.
Descriptors: Civil War (United States); High Schools; *High School Students; *History Instruction; *Item Banks; Multiple Choice Tests; *United States History
Availability: ERIC Document Reproduction Service; 7420 Fullerton Rd., Ste. 110, Springfield, VA 22153-2852 (ED118496, 131 p.)
Grade Level: 9-12
Notes: Items, 1062

These test items are designed for high school students and comprise an extensive file of multiple-choice questions in American history. Taken largely from the Iowa Every-Pupil Program and the Cooperative Test Service Standardized Examinations, the questions are chronologically divided into 16 topic areas. These items are from Bulletin Number 6, Fifth Edition, and also available from the National Council for the Social Studies, 1200 17th St., N.W., Ste 404, Washington, DC 20036.

12891
EDS Diagnostic Skill Level Inventory for Reading Skills, Revised. Henney, R. Lee 1978
Subtests: General Reading; Practical Reading; Prose Interpretation; Poetry Interpretation; Drama Interpretation
Descriptors: *Adult Education; Adults; *Diagnostic Tests; Drama; Multiple Choice Tests; Poetry; *Pretests Posttests; Prose; Reading Comprehension; *Reading Difficulties; Reading Skills
Availability: Educational Diagnostic Services; 2370 County Rd. 13, Corunna, IL 46730
Age Level: 18-64
Notes: Time, 60 min.; Items, 65

This instrument was developed so that teachers could quickly diagnose the strengths and weaknesses of students. The Pre-Instructional Test is to be used to diagnose the student's initial skills in the subject matter. The Post-Instructional Test is to be used following the instructional process to test the student's progress. The 5 categories covered are (1) general reading, (2) practical reading, (3) prose interpretation, (4) poetry interpretation, and (5) drama interpretation. Students must demonstrate their ability to read and correctly interpret each of these types of literary material. These categories provide the instructor with the opportunity of determining exactly which type of material causes difficulty in interpretation for the adult so that a productive instructional program can be developed. This test is 1 part of the 5 which are part of the Diagnostic Program. The test is used in the GED (General Education Development) preparation programs conducted by public schools, manpower training organizations, industrial training departments, and private schools; in first-year literature courses; for remediation in high school and college; in industrial instruction programs; and in self-study programs.

12919
Industrial Arts Test Development, Drawing. New York State Education Dept., Albany, Bureau of Industrial Arts Education 1973
Subtests: Developmental Drawing; Production Drawing
Descriptors: *Achievement Tests; High Schools; *High School Students; *Industrial Arts; Industrial Education; *Item Banks; Multiple Choice Tests; Secondary Education
Identifiers: *Drawing; New York State Education Department
Availability: ERIC Document Reproduction Service; 7420 Fullerton Rd., Ste. 110, Springfield, VA 22153-2852 (ED109457, 192 p.)
Grade Level: 9-12
Notes: Items, 187

This collection of sample questions is intended primarily for use by secondary level teachers. The items may be used for pretesting, quizzes, or for final examinations. They are organized around the drawing area of industrial arts curriculum. The questions are not meant to be complete examinations; rather, the items are offered as a resource, with selection and use to be determined by the teacher. The items cover preparation, sketching, working drawing, charts, graphs, maps, flat developments, construction, careers, jigs and fixtures, fasteners, machine parts, assemblies, power transmission, manufacturing, and production personnel.

12920
Industrial Arts Test Development, Electricity/Electronics. New York State Education Dept., Albany, Bureau of Industrial Arts Education 1973
Subtests: Electricity; Electronics
Descriptors: *Achievement Tests; *Electricity; *Electronics; High Schools; *High School Students; *Industrial Arts; Industrial Education; *Item Banks; Multiple Choice Tests; Secondary Education
Identifiers: New York State Education Department
Availability: ERIC Document Reproduction Service; 7420 Fullerton Rd., Ste. 110, Springfield, VA 22153-2852 (ED109457, 192 p.)
Grade Level: 9-12
Notes: Items, 159

This collection of sample questions is intended primarily for use by secondary level teachers. The items may be used for pretesting, quizzes, or for final examinations. They are organized around the electricity and electronics area of the industrial arts curriculum. The questions are not meant to be complete examinations; rather, the items are offered as a resource with selection and use to be determined by the teacher. The items cover theory, measurement, circuitry, motors, light-heat, batteries and generators, power generation and transmission, industrial organization, in the Electricity section. In the Electronics section, the areas covered are science review, meters and instruments, inductance and capacitance, tubes and semiconductors, amplifiers/oscillators, radio and television, controls and computers, and careers and industry.

12921
Industrial Arts Test Development, Power Mechanics. New York State Education Dept., Albany, Bureau of Industrial Arts Education 1973
Subtests: Small Engines; Vehicle Power
Descriptors: *Achievement Tests; *Engines; High Schools; *High School Students; *Industrial Arts; Industrial Education; *Item Banks; Multiple Choice Tests; *Power Technology; Secondary Education
Identifiers: New York State Education Department
Availability: ERIC Document Reproduction Service; 7420 Fullerton Rd., Ste. 110, Springfield, VA 22153-2852 (ED109457, 192 p.)
Grade Level: 9-12
Notes: Items, 152

This collection of sample questions is intended primarily for use by secondary level teachers. The items may be used for pretesting, quizzes, or for final examinations. They are organized around the power mechanics area of the industrial arts curriculum. The questions are not meant to be complete examinations; rather, the items are offered as a resource with selection and use to be determined by the teacher. The items covered in the Small Engines section are construction, fuel systems, lubrication, cooling systems, ignition systems, care and maintenance, power transmission, and industry and careers. In the Vehicle Power section, the areas covered are gasoline engines, diesel engines, rotary engines, maintenance, power transmission, and industrial organization.

12922
Industrial Arts Test Development, Woods. New York State Education Dept., Albany, Bureau of Industrial Arts Education 1973
Subtests: Wood Products; Housing
Descriptors: *Achievement Tests; High Schools; *High School Students; *Industrial Arts; Industrial Education; *Item Banks; Multiple Choice Tests; Secondary Education; Trade and Industrial Education; *Woodworking
Identifiers: New York State Education Department
Availability: ERIC Document Reproduction Service; 7420 Fullerton Rd., Ste. 110, Springfield, VA 22153-2852 (ED109457, 192 p.)
Grade Level: 9-12
Notes: Items, 176

This collection of sample questions is intended primarily for use by secondary level teachers. The items may be used for pretesting, quizzes, or for final examinations. The items are organized around the woods area of the industrial arts curriculum. The questions are not meant to be complete examinations; rather, the items are offered as a resource with selection and use to be determined by the teacher. The items in the Wood Products section cover design and planning, hand tools and fixed machines, forestry, joinery, fasteners, mass production, finishes, and industrial organization. In the Housing section, the areas covered are design and planning, hand tools and portable machines, lumber, panels and boards, millwork and hardware, reconstruction and maintenance, and careers and industry.

12930
Fabric Fact Sheet. Bell, Sharon 1974
Descriptors: *Achievement Tests; Clothing Instruction; High School Students; *Home Economics Education; Junior High School Students; Knowledge Level; Secondary Education; *Secondary School Students; *Sewing Instruction
Identifiers: Indiana Home Economics Association
Availability: ERIC Document Reproduction Service; 7420 Fullerton Rd., Ste. 110, Springfield, VA 22153-2852 (ED109334, 151 p.)
Grade Level: 7-12
Notes: Items, 5

This is a short fact sheet used to assess the understanding of factors involved in selecting a pattern and fabric. This is one instrument in Evaluation in Home Economics published by the Indiana Home Economics Association. Included in the publication are a variety of instruments appropriate for evaluating to some degree the progress toward attainment of objectives in the several areas of home economics for junior and senior high school students, adults, and out-of-school youth. Along with the evaluation form are suggestions for their use in the following areas of home economics: child development, clothing and textiles, consumer education, foods and nutrition, family relationships, housing and home decorating, health of the family and home care of the sick interpersonal relations, and occupational home economics. Another source is University Book Store, 360 State St., West Lafayette, IN 47906.

12931
Selection of Pattern Type and Size Problem. Rodgers, Patricia 1974
Descriptors: *Achievement Tests; Clothing Instruction; High School Students; *Home Economics Education; Junior High School Students; Knowledge Level; Questionnaires; Secondary Education; *Secondary School Students; *Sewing Instruction
Identifiers: Indiana Home Economics Association

Availability: ERIC Document Reproduction Service; 7420 Fullerton Rd., Ste. 110, Springfield, VA 22153-2852 (ED109334, 151 p.)
Grade Level: 7-12
Notes: Items, 5

This instrument is used to assess the understanding of the selection and pattern size and type. From the descriptions that are given, the student is to select the correct pattern size and type. This is one instrument in Evaluation in Home Economics published by the Indiana Home Economics Association. Included in the publication are a variety of instruments appropriate for evaluating to some degree the progress toward attainment of objectives in the several areas of home economics for junior and senior high school students, adults, and out-of-school youth. Along with the evaluation form are suggestions for their use in the following areas of home economics: child development, clothing and textiles, consumer education, foods and nutrition, family relationships, housing and home decorating, health of the family and home care of the sick interpersonal relations, and occupational home economics. Another source is University Book Store, 360 State St., West Lafayette, IN 47906.

12932
Performance Test for Four Methods of Marking Fabric.   Kramer, Phyllis 1974
Descriptors: *Achievement Tests; Clothing Instruction; High School Students; *Home Economics Education; Junior High School Students; Knowledge Level; *Performance Tests; Secondary Education; *Secondary School Students; *Sewing Instruction
Identifiers: Indiana Home Economics Association
Availability: ERIC Document Reproduction Service; 7420 Fullerton Rd., Ste. 110, Springfield, VA 22153-2852 (ED109334, 151 p.)
Grade Level: 7-12

This performance test assesses the student's understanding of the principles of marking fabric. The student is to cut out the pattern piece, trace the darts, mark the darts with tailor tacks and chalk, and use the clipping method which was demonstrated by the teacher. This is one instrument in Evaluation in Home Economics published by the Indiana Home Economics Association. Included in the publication are a variety of instruments appropriate for evaluating to some degree the progress toward attainment of objectives in the several areas of home economics for junior and senior high school students, adults, and out-of-school youth. Along with the evaluation form are suggestions for their use in the following areas of home economics: child development, clothing and textiles, consumer education, foods and nutrition, family relationships, housing and home decorating, health of the family and home care of the sick interpersonal relations, and occupational home economics. Another source is University Book Store, 360 State St., West Lafayette, IN 47906.

12933
Score Card for Four Methods of Marking Fabric.   Peck, Sherry 1974
Descriptors: *Achievement Tests; Check Lists; Clothing Instruction; High School Students; *Home Economics Education; Junior High School Students; Knowledge Level; Secondary Education; *Secondary School Students; *Sewing Instruction
Identifiers: Indiana Home Economics Association
Availability: ERIC Document Reproduction Service; 7420 Fullerton Rd., Ste. 110, Springfield, VA 22153-2852 (ED109334, 151 p.)
Grade Level: 7-12
Notes: Items, 4

There are 4 procedures on this checklist. The student checks a yes or no in the appropriate column for each procedure listed and the teacher does the same. This is one instrument in Evaluation in Home Economics published by the Indiana Home Economics Association. Included in the publication are a variety of instruments appropriate for evaluating to some degree the progress toward attainment of objectives in the several areas of home economics for junior and senior high school students, adults, and out-of-school youth. Along with the evaluation form are suggestions for their use in the following areas of home economics: child development, clothing and textiles, consumer education, foods and nutrition, family relationships, housing and home decorating, health of the family and home care of the sick interpersonal relations, and occupational home economics. Another source is University Book Store, 360 State St., West Lafayette, IN 47906.

12934
Fabric and Pattern Preparation, Layout, and Cutting Checklist.   Richardson, Ita 1974
Descriptors: *Achievement Tests; Check Lists; Clothing Instruction; High School Students; *Home Economics Education; Junior High School Students; Knowledge Level; Secondary Education; *Secondary School Students; *Sewing Instruction
Identifiers: Indiana Home Economics Association

Availability: ERIC Document Reproduction Service; 7420 Fullerton Rd., Ste. 110, Springfield, VA 22153-2852 (ED109334, 151 p.)
Grade Level: 7-12
Notes: Items, 19

This checklist is used to assess the knowledge of factors to complete before cutting fabric. This is one instrument in Evaluation in Home Economics published by the Indiana Home Economics Association. Included in the publication are a variety of instruments appropriate for evaluating to some degree the progress toward attainment of objectives in the several areas of home economics for junior and senior high school students, adults, and out-of-school youth. Along with the evaluation form are suggestions for their use in the following areas of home economics: child development, clothing and textiles, consumer education, foods and nutrition, family relationships, housing and home decorating, health of the family and home care of the sick interpersonal relations, and occupational home economics. Another source is University Book Store, 360 State St., West Lafayette, IN 47906.

12935
Steps in Construction and Setting in Sleeves Test.   Azpell, Diane 1974
Descriptors: *Achievement Tests; Clothing Instruction; High School Students; *Home Economics Education; Junior High School Students; Knowledge Level; Secondary Education; *Secondary School Students; *Sewing Instruction
Identifiers: Indiana Home Economics Association
Availability: ERIC Document Reproduction Service; 7420 Fullerton Rd., Ste. 110, Springfield, VA 22153-2852 (ED109334, 151 p.)
Grade Level: 7-12
Notes: Items, 12

This test may be used to assess a student's knowledge of the steps used in the construction and setting of sleeves. A list of steps used is included, and the student is to place them in the proper order. This is one instrument in Evaluation in Home Economics published by the Indiana Home Economics Association. Included in the publication are a variety of instruments appropriate for evaluating to some degree the progress toward attainment of objectives in the several areas of home economics for junior and senior high school students, adults, and out-of-school youth. Along with the evaluation form are suggestions for their use in the following areas of home economics: child development, clothing and textiles, consumer education, foods and nutrition, family relationships, housing and home decorating, health of the family and home care of the sick interpersonal relations, and occupational home economics. Another source is University Book Store, 360 State St., West Lafayette, IN 47906.

12936
Rating Scale on Sleeves.   Azpell, Diane 1974
Descriptors: *Achievement Tests; Clothing Instruction; High School Students; *Home Economics Education; Junior High School Students; Knowledge Level; Rating Scales; Secondary Education; *Secondary School Students; *Sewing Instruction; Student Evaluation
Identifiers: Indiana Home Economics Association
Availability: ERIC Document Reproduction Service; 7420 Fullerton Rd., Ste. 110, Springfield, VA 22153-2852 (ED109334, 151 p.)
Grade Level: 7-12
Notes: Items, 8

This rating scale is used to evaluate sleeve construction in home economics classes. Both the student and teacher may do an evaluation. This is one instrument in Evaluation in Home Economics published by the Indiana Home Economics Association. Included in the publication are a variety of instruments appropriate for evaluating to some degree the progress toward attainment of objectives in the several areas of home economics for junior and senior high school students, adults, and out-of-school youth. Along with the evaluation form are suggestions for their use in the following areas of home economics: child development, clothing and textiles, consumer education, foods and nutrition, family relationships, housing and home decorating, health of the family and home care of the sick interpersonal relations, and occupational home economics. Another source is University Book Store, 360 State St., West Lafayette, IN 47906.

12937
Performance Test. 1974
Descriptors: Clothing Instruction; High School Students; *Home Economics Education; Junior High School Students; *Performance Tests; Secondary Education; *Secondary School Students; *Sewing Instruction
Identifiers: Indiana Home Economics Association
Availability: ERIC Document Reproduction Service; 7420 Fullerton Rd., Ste. 110, Springfield, VA 22153-2852 (ED109334, 151 p.)
Grade Level: 7-12
Notes: Items, 8

This test is used to assess how well the student understands and applies the principles of threading and operating a sewing machine. There is also a sewing machine operator's license which may be issued to the student. This is one instrument in Evaluation in Home Economics published by the Indiana Home Economics Association. Included in the publication are a variety of instruments appropriate for evaluating to some degree the progress toward attainment of objectives in the several areas of home economics for junior and senior high school students, adults, and out-of-school youth. Along with the evaluation form are suggestions for their use in the following areas of home economics: child development, clothing and textiles, consumer education, foods and nutrition, family relationships, housing and home decorating, health of the family and home care of the sick interpersonal relations, and occupational home economics. Another source is University Book Store, 360 State St., West Lafayette, IN 47906.

12943
Meal Preparation Problem Test.   Lord, Eleanor 1974
Descriptors: Daily Living Skills; High School Students; *Home Economics Education; *Home Management; Junior High School Students; *Nutrition; Secondary Education; *Secondary School Students; Situational Tests
Identifiers: Indiana Home Economics Association
Availability: ERIC Document Reproduction Service; 7420 Fullerton Rd., Ste. 110, Springfield, VA 22153-2852 (ED109334, 151 p.)
Grade Level: 7-12
Notes: Items, 8

In this test, a student is given a situation and then is to plan a nutritional meal with the specified food items and within a given time frame. This is one instrument in Evaluation in Home Economics published by the Indiana Home Economics Association. Included in the publication are a variety of instruments appropriate for evaluating to some degree the progress toward attainment of objectives in the several areas of home economics for junior and senior high school students, adults, and out-of-school youth. Along with the evaluation form are suggestions for their use in the following areas of home economics: child development, clothing and textiles, consumer education, foods and nutrition, family relationships, housing and home decorating, health of the family and home care of the sick interpersonal relations, and occupational home economics. Another source is University Book Store, 360 State St., West Lafayette, IN 47906.

12944
Test on Food Laws, Inspection, and Grading. Lutkus, Alice 1974
Descriptors: *Achievement Tests; *Consumer Education; High School Students; *Home Economics Education; Home Management; Junior High School Students; Knowledge Level; Nutrition; Questionnaires; Secondary Education; *Secondary School Students
Identifiers: Indiana Home Economics Association
Availability: ERIC Document Reproduction Service; 7420 Fullerton Rd., Ste. 110, Springfield, VA 22153-2852 (ED109334, 151 p.)
Grade Level: 7-12
Notes: Items, 13

This questionnaire is to assess a student's knowledge of food laws, government stamps, and grading agencies and their functions. This is one instrument in Evaluation in Home Economics published by the Indiana Home Economics Association. Included in the publication are a variety of instruments appropriate for evaluating to some degree the progress toward attainment of objectives in the several areas of home economics for junior and senior high school students, adults, and out-of-school youth. Along with the evaluation form are suggestions for their use in the following areas of home economics: child development, clothing and textiles, consumer education, foods and nutrition, family relationships, housing and home decorating, health of the family and home care of the sick interpersonal relations, and occupational home economics. Another source is University Book Store, 360 State St., West Lafayette, IN 47906.

12954
Reading Assessment for Language Learning Youngsters.   Mineola Union Free School District, NY 1975
Descriptors: *Bilingual Students; *Criterion Referenced Tests; Elementary Education; *Elementary School Students; *English (Second Language); Portuguese; Reading Achievement; *Reading Tests
Identifiers: RALLY; TIM(K)
Availability: Tests in Microfiche; Test Collection, Educational Testing Service, Princeton, NJ 08541
Grade Level: K-6

Reading assessment consisting of 9 parts to evaluate reading attainment of bilingual students. Parts I and II are appropriate for students in kindergarten through grade 3. The 9 parts cover word association, picture word association, life situation questions, classification-categorization and basic numerical computation, analogies, sentence completion-basic conceptual knowledge, sentence completion-own words, and story comprehension.

13003
National Assessment of Educational Progress, Released Exercises; Health, Energy, and Reading. Education Commission of the States, Denver, CO 1979
Subtests: Health; Energy; Reading
Descriptors: Achievement Tests; Adolescents; Conservation Education; *Energy; Energy Conservation; *Health Education; *Item Banks; *National Surveys; *Reading; Young Adults
Identifiers: Customized Tests; NAEP; National Institute of Education
Availability: National Assessment of Educational Progress; Box 2923, Princeton, NJ 08541
Age Level: 17; 26-35
Notes: Time, 135 min.; Items, 108

Items used in the National Assessment of Educational Progress (NAEP), which conducts yearly surveys of the knowledges, skills, and attitudes of individuals aged 9, 13, 17, and 26-35. This three-part document contains test items, scoring data and results from young adults obtained during the year 1977. There are 47 health items, 48 related to energy, and 13 in reading. Separate data are available for males, females, blacks, whites, and for big and medium cities. All items are in the public domain and may be used to build customized tests.

13007
Vocational Competency Measures: Physical Therapist Assistant. American Institutes for Research, Palo Alto, CA 1983
Descriptors: *Achievement Tests; Adolescents; Adults; Competence; *Entry Workers; Knowledge Level; *Personnel Selection; *Physical Therapists; Physical Therapy; *Postsecondary Education; Rating Scales; Screening Tests; Secondary Education; *Secondary School Students; Student Evaluation; *Two Year Colleges; *Vocational Education; *Work Sample Tests
Identifiers: Test Batteries; *Work Habits
Availability: American Association for Vocational Instructional Materials; 120 Driftmier Engineering Center, Athens, GA 30602
Age Level: 12-64

Designed to help teachers and administrators at secondary and postsecondary levels assess and improve competencies of their students in vocational education, to identify areas for program improvement, and to inform prospective employers of students' vocational competencies. Also useful for employers to screen and to select new employees and to assess training needs of present employees. Test package consists of a 2-part multiple-choice job information test, each part taking about 45 minutes to complete; a performance test consisting of tests that represent tasks similar to those performed on the job; and a work habits inventory for assessing nontechnical, work-related attitudes and behavior. Intended for persons enrolled in or completing a 2-year, postsecondary level training program to become physical therapist assistants. In states requiring board certification or licensing, test is generally applicable for those preparing for state board examinations. Not intended for those in physical therapist programs or for those in physical therapy aide programs. Job information test has 108 items and covers general activities, massage and exercise, physical modalities, gait training, patient assistance and instruction. The 10 performance tests include administering ultrasound treatment, cervical traction, hot packs, tilt table treatment, range of motion exercise, whirlpool treatment, paraffin bath treatment, massage, instructing patient on Williams' flexion exercises, providing gait training.

13008
Vocational Competency Measures: Grocery Clerk. American Institutes for Research, Palo Alto, CA 1983
Descriptors: *Achievement Tests; Adolescents; Adults; Competence; *Entry Workers; *Food Stores; Knowledge Level; *Personnel Selection; *Postsecondary Education; Rating Scales; Screening Tests; Secondary Education; *Secondary School Students; Student Evaluation; *Vocational Education; *Work Sample Tests
Identifiers: Grocery Checkers; *Grocery Clerks; Test Batteries; *Work Habits
Availability: American Association for Vocational Instructional Materials; 120 Driftmier Engineering Center, Athens, GA 30602
Age Level: 12-64

Designed to help teachers and administrators at secondary and postsecondary levels assess and improve competencies of their students in vocational education, to identify areas for program improvement, and to inform prospective employers of students' vocational competencies. Also useful for employers to screen and to select new employees and to assess training needs of present employees. Test package consists of a 2-part multiple-choice job information test, each part taking about 45 minutes to complete; a performance test consisting of tests that represent tasks similar to those performed on the job; and a work habits inventory for assessing nontechnical, work-related attitudes and behavior. Intended for people completing programs in food marketing and distribution and who are preparing to work in grocery stores as clerks, checkers, baggers, stockers. Applies to both workers in small retail businesses or large supermarket chains. Job information test consists of 108 items and covers general policies and procedures, checking, stocking, customers and co-workers. Six performance tests require examinee to set up and closeout a checkstand, check and bag merchandise, stock and price merchandise, take inventory, process a delivery, and organize a stockroom.

13009
Vocational Competency Measures: Restaurant Service (Waiter, Waitress, Cashier). American Institutes for Research, Palo Alto, CA 1983
Descriptors: *Achievement Tests; Adolescents; Adults; Competence; *Dining Facilities; *Entry Workers; Food Service; Knowledge Level; *Personnel Selection; *Postsecondary Education; Rating Scales; Screening Tests; Secondary Education; *Secondary School Students; Student Evaluation; *Vocational Education; *Work Sample Tests
Identifiers: *Cashiers; Test Batteries; *Waiters Waitresses; *Work Habits
Availability: American Association for Vocational Instructional Materials; 120 Driftmier Engineering Center, Athens, GA 30602
Age Level: 12-64

Designed to help teachers and administrators at secondary and postsecondary levels assess and improve competencies of their students in vocational education, to identify areas for program improvement, and to inform prospective employers of students' vocational competencies. Also useful for employers to screen and to select new employees and to assess training needs of present employees. Test package consists of a 2-part multiple-choice job information test, each part taking about 45 minutes to complete; a performance test consisting of tests that represent tasks similar to those performed on the job; and a work habits inventory for assessing nontechnical, work-related attitudes and behavior. Intended to assess job readiness of those who have been trained for front-of-the-house positions in restaurants, hotel dining rooms, and other eating facilities. The job information tests consists of 122 items and covers routine dining room activities, nonroutine and problem situations, cashier activities, sanitation and safety, kitchen and sidestand activities, vocabulary, restaurant operation. The 8 performance activities require examinee to handle cashier duties, change tablecloth, carry loaded tray, set dinner table, seat customer, serve dinner to customer, handle difficult customers, handle waiter-customer dispute.

13010
Vocational Competency Measures: Custom Sewing. American Institutes for Research, Palo Alto, CA 1983
Descriptors: *Achievement Tests; Adolescents; Adults; Competence; *Entry Workers; Knowledge Level; *Needle Trades; *Personnel Selection; *Postsecondary Education; Rating Scales; Screening Tests; Secondary Education; *Secondary School Students; *Sewing Machine Operators; Student Evaluation; *Vocational Education; *Work Sample Tests
Identifiers: Test Batteries; *Work Habits
Availability: American Association for Vocational Instructional Materials; 120 Driftmier Engineering Center, Athens, GA 30602
Age Level: 12-64

Designed to help teachers and administrators at secondary and postsecondary levels assess and improve competencies of their students in vocational education, to identify areas for program improvement, and to inform prospective employers of students' vocational competencies. Also useful for employers to screen and to select new employees and to assess training needs of present employees. Test package consists of a 2-part multiple-choice job information test, each part taking about 45 minutes to complete; a performance test consisting of tests that represent tasks similar to those performed on the job; and a work habits inventory for assessing nontechnical, work-related attitudes and behavior. Intended for persons in nonindustrial sewing programs at secondary or postsecondary level. Test is not designed for those completing 4-year fashion design or industrial sewing programs. Job information test consists of 101 items and covers general fashion knowledge and sewing. The 6 performance tests require examinee to take body measurements, determine figure type and size, construct a double-pointed dart, sew seams, adjust a blouse pattern to increase bustline, insert a front fly zipper.

13011
Vocational Competency Measures: Agricultural Chemicals Applications Technician. American Institutes for Research, Palo Alto, CA 1983
Descriptors: *Achievement Tests; Adolescents; Adults; *Agricultural Chemical Occupations; Agricultural Occupations; Competence; *Entry Workers; Knowledge Level; *Personnel Selection; *Postsecondary Education; Rating Scales; Screening Tests; Secondary Education; *Secondary School Students; Student Evaluation; *Vocational Education; *Work Sample Tests
Identifiers: Test Batteries; *Work Habits
Availability: American Association for Vocational Instructional Materials; 120 Driftmier Engineering Center, Athens, GA 30602
Age Level: 12-64

Designed to help teachers and administrators at secondary and postsecondary levels assess and improve competencies of their students in vocational education, to identify areas for program improvement, and to inform prospective employers of students' vocational competencies. Also useful for employers to screen and to select new employees and to assess training needs of present employees. Test package consists of a 2-part multiple-choice job information test, each part taking about 45 minutes to complete; a performance test consisting of tests that represent tasks similar to those performed on the job; and a work habits inventory for assessing nontechnical, work-related attitudes and behavior. Intended for people completing vocational training in the field of agriculture and preparing to work in the more specialized area of agricultural chemicals, either in the marketing and distribution of such chemicals or in the actual application of the chemicals on the farm. The job information test consists of 106 items and covers safety, consulting and problem recognition, chemical mixing and disposal, equipment set up and operation, clerical-customer service. The 9 performance tests require examinee to select and use protective clothing, identify broadleaf and narrowleaf weeds, calculate amount of pesticide to apply, prepare a billing form, calibrate a liquid spray applicator, operate a liquid spray application, clean it for storage, store chemicals safely, and rinse and empty pesticide containers.

13012
National Assessment of Educational Progress, Released Exercises: Mathematics. Education Commission of the States, Denver, CO 1983
Subtests: Mathematics in School; Mathematics and Oneself; Mathematics and Society; Mathematics as a Discipline; Experiences in Mathematics; Mathematical Process; Content
Descriptors: Achievement Tests; Adolescents; Adults; Algebra; Attitude Measures; Children; Computers; Geometry; *Item Banks; *Mathematics; Mathematics Anxiety; Measurement; Metric System; Motivation; *National Surveys; Numbers; Probability; Self Concept; Statistics; Trigonometry
Identifiers: Customized Tests; NAEP; National Institute of Education
Availability: National Assessment of Educational Progress; Box 2923, Princeton, NJ 08541
Age Level: 9; 13; 17; 26-35
Notes: Items, 227

Contains items used in the National Assessment of Educational Progress (NAEP), which conducts yearly surveys of the knowledge, skills, and attitudes of individuals aged 9, 13, 17 and 26-35. All items are in the public domain and may be used to build customized tests. Areas covered are attitudes toward math; perceptions of self in relation to math, including math anxiety and motivation; attitudes toward the usefulness and importance of math; views of mathematics as a discipline and process; experience with metric system, calculators, computers. Content areas are numbers, numeration, algebra, trigonometry, geometry measurement, probability, and statistics, use of calculator, computer literacy. Not all exercises are used with all age groups.

13013
National Assessment of Educational Progress: Released Exercises: Citizenship and Social Studies. Education Commission of the States, Denver, CO 1983
Descriptors: Achievement Tests; Adolescents; Adults; Children; *Citizenship; Communication Skills; Economics; Information Seeking; *Item Banks; *National Surveys; Politics; Social Change; *Social Studies; Sociology
Identifiers: Customized Tests; Global Awareness; Judicial System; NAEP; National Institute of Education
Availability: National Assessment of Educational Progress; Box 2923, Princeton, NJ 08541
Grade Level: 5; 8; 11
Age Level: 9; 13; 17; 26-35
Notes: Items, 130

Contains items used in the National Assessment of Educational Progress (NAEP), which is a yearly survey of the knowledge skills and attitudes of individuals aged 9, 13, 17, and 26-35. All items are in the public domain and may be used to build customized tests. Items cover skills necessary to acquire information; skills necessary to use information; communication skills; understandings of human societies; rights and global concerns; understanding of politics, economics, social changes, and the judicial system in the U.S.

13050
IEA Six-Subject Survey Instruments: Civic Education Tests, Cognition, Population I. International Association for the Evaluation of Educational Achievement, Stockholm (Sweden) 1975
Descriptors: *Academic Achievement; *Achievement Tests; *Civics; Cognitive Tests; *Comparative Education; *Cross Cultural Studies; Elementary Education; *Elementary School Students; Foreign Countries; Multiple Choice Tests
Identifiers: International Evaluation Educational Achievement; Sweden
Availability: ERIC Document Reproduction Service; 7420 Fullerton Rd., Ste. 110, Springfield, VA 22153-2852 (ED102187, 55 p.)
Age Level: 10-11
Notes: Time, 35 min.; Items, 41

In 1965, the International Association for the Evaluation of Educational Achievement (IEA) inaugurated a cross-national survey of achievement in 6 subjects: science, reading comprehension, literature, English as a foreign language, French as a foreign language, and civic education. The overall aim of the project was to use international tests to relate student achievement and attitudes to instructional, social, and economic factors and, from the results, to establish generalizations of value to policymakers worldwide. This is 1 of 3 civics cognitive tests for Population I that consists of students aged 10 to 11 years. The other tests are for Population II, students 14 to 15 years, and Population IV, students enrolled in the final year of preuniversity training.

13051
IEA Six-Subject Survey Instruments: Civic Education Tests, Cognition, Population II. International Association for the Evaluation of Educational Achievement, Stockholm (Sweden) 1975
Descriptors: *Academic Achievement; *Achievement Tests; *Civics; Cognitive Tests; *Comparative Education; *Cross Cultural Studies; Foreign Countries; *Junior High School Students; Multiple Choice Tests; Secondary Education
Identifiers: International Evaluation Educational Achievement; Sweden
Availability: ERIC Document Reproduction Service; 7420 Fullerton Rd., Ste. 110, Springfield, VA 22153-2852 (ED102187, 55 p.)
Age Level: 14-15
Notes: Time, 35 min.; Items, 47

In 1965, the International Association for the Evaluation of Educational Achievement (IEA) inaugurated a cross-national survey of achievement in 6 subjects: science, reading comprehension, literature, English as a foreign language, French as a foreign language, and civic education. The overall aim of the project was to use international tests to relate student achievement and attitudes to instructional, social, and economic factors and, from the results, to establish generalizations of value to policymakers worldwide. This is 1 of 3 civics cognitive tests for Population II that consists of students aged 14 to 15 years. The other tests are for Population I, students aged 10 to 11, and Population IV, students enrolled in the final years of preuniversity training.

13052
IEA Six-Subject Survey Instruments: Civic Education Tests, Cognition, Population IV. International Association for the Evaluation of Educational Achievement, Stockholm (Sweden) 1975
Descriptors: *Academic Achievement; *Achievement Tests; *Civics; Cognitive Tests; College Bound Students; *Comparative Education; *Cross Cultural Studies; Foreign Countries; *Grade 12; High School Students; Multiple Choice Tests; Secondary Education
Identifiers: International Evaluation Educational Achievement; Sweden
Availability: ERIC Document Reproduction Service; 7420 Fullerton Rd., Ste. 110, Springfield, VA 22153-2852 (ED102187, 55 p.)
Grade Level: 12
Notes: Time, 35 min.; Items, 48

In 1965, the International Association for the Evaluation of Educational Achievement (IEA) inaugurated a cross-national survey of achievement in 6 subjects: science, reading comprehension, literature, English as a foreign language, French as a foreign language, and civic education. The overall aim of the project was to use international tests to relate student achievement and attitudes to instructional, social, and economic factors and, from the results, to establish generalizations of value to policymakers worldwide. This is 1 of 3 civics cognitive tests for Population IV that consists of students enrolled in the final year of preuniversity training. The other tests are for Population I, students aged 10 to 11, and Population II that consists of students aged 14 to 15 years.

13055
IEA Six-Subject Survey Instruments: French Listening Test, Population I. International Association for the Evaluation of Educational Achievement, Stockholm (Sweden) 1975
Descriptors: *Academic Achievement; *Comparative Education; *Cross Cultural Studies; Elementary Education; Elementary School Students; Foreign Countries; *French; *Listening Comprehension Tests; *Second Language Learning
Identifiers: International Evaluation Educational Achievement; Sweden
Availability: ERIC Document Reproduction Service; 7420 Fullerton Rd., Ste. 110, Springfield, VA 22153-2852 (ED102184,155 p.)
Age Level: 10-11
Notes: Items, 35

In 1965, the International Association for the Evaluation of Educational Achievement (IEA) inaugurated a cross-national survey of achievement in 6 subjects: science, reading comprehension, literature, English as a foreign language, French as a foreign language, and civic education. The overall aim of the project was to use international tests to relate student achievement and attitudes to instructional, social, and economic factors and, from the results, to establish generalizations of value to policymakers worldwide. This test is for Population I, students who are 10 to 11 years of age to see how well they understand French they hear spoken. A tape recorder will tell them the number of the set of pictures in the mother tongue and then they hear a sentence spoken in French. The sentence will be about 1 of the pictures in the set of 4. The letter on the picture is the answer.

13056
IEA Six-Subject Survey Instruments: French Listening Test, Population II. International Association for the Evaluation of Educational Achievement, Stockholm (Sweden) 1975
Descriptors: *Academic Achievement; *Comparative Education; *Cross Cultural Studies; Foreign Countries; *French; *Listening Comprehension Tests; Multiple Choice Tests; Secondary Education; *Secondary School Students; *Second Language Learning
Identifiers: International Evaluation Educational Achievement; Sweden
Availability: ERIC Document Reproduction Service; 7420 Fullerton Rd., Ste. 110, Springfield, VA 22153-2852 (ED102184,155 p.)
Age Level: 14-15
Notes: Items, 80

In 1965, the International Association for the Evaluation of Educational Achievement (IEA) inaugurated a cross-national survey of achievement in 6 subjects: science, reading comprehension, literature, English as a foreign language, French as a foreign language, and civic education. The overall aim of the project was to use international tests to relate student achievement and attitudes to instructional, social, and economic factors and, from the results, to establish generalizations of value to policymakers worldwide. Population II students age 14 to 15. There are 5 parts to the test. In the first part, the student hears a series of statements. Each statement describes 1 of 4 pictures in the booklet and the student describes the correct one. In the second part, the student hears a series of questions or remarks. After each remark or question has been spoken, the student selects from among 4 printed choices. In the third part, the student listens to a series of short conversations between 2 people. One will ask a question or make a statement and the other will reply. After each conversation, the student chooses from 4 printed choices in the test booklet. In the next part, the student listens to a series of short announcements or broadcasts. At the end of each broadcast or announcement, a question will be asked about what was said. In the last part, the student listens to rather long conversations or dramatic scenes and is asked several questions about what was heard.

13057
IEA Six-Subject Survey Instruments: French Listening Test, Population IV. International Association for the Evaluation of Educational Achievement, Stockholm (Sweden) 1975
Descriptors: *Academic Achievement; College Bound Students; *Comparative Education; *Cross Cultural Studies; Foreign Countries; *French; *Grade 12; High Schools; *Listening Comprehension Tests; Multiple Choice Tests; *Second Language Learning
Identifiers: International Evaluation Educational Achievement; Sweden
Availability: ERIC Document Reproduction Service; 7420 Fullerton Rd., Ste. 110, Springfield, VA 22153-2852 (ED102184,155 p.)
Grade Level: 12
Notes: Items, 80

In 1965, the International Association for the Evaluation of Educational Achievement (IEA) inaugurated a cross-national survey of achievement in 6 subjects: science, reading comprehension, literature, English as a foreign language, French as a foreign language, and civic education. The overall aim of the project was to use international tests to relate student achievement and attitudes to instructional, social, and economic factors and, from the results, to establish generalizations of value to policymakers worldwide. Population IV are students enrolled in the final year of preuniversity training. There are 5 parts to the test. In the first part, the student hears a series of statements. Each statement describes one of 4 pictures. The student is to describe which one is described. In the second part, the student hears a series of remarks or questions. After listening, the student must decide from 4 answers which response would likely have been made in response to the question/remark. In the third section, the student listens to a series of short conversations between 2 people. One will make a statement or ask a question, and the other will reply. The student then selects, from 4 choices, the correct account of what has been told. In the fourth part, the student will listen to a series of short broadcasts or announcement. At the end of the broadcast/announcement, a question will be asked, and the student selects the best answer from 4 choices. In the last part, the student listens to rather long conversations or dramatic scenes, after which several questions will be asked about what was heard. There are 4 choices for the correct answer.

13058
IEA Six-Subject Survey Instruments: French Listening Test, Population IVS. International Association for the Evaluation of Educational Achievement, Stockholm (Sweden) 1975
Descriptors: *Academic Achievement; College Bound Students; *Comparative Education; *Cross Cultural Studies; Foreign Countries; *French; *Grade 12; High Schools; *Listening Comprehension Tests; Multiple Choice Tests; *Second Language Learning
Identifiers: International Evaluation Educational Achievement; Sweden
Availability: ERIC Document Reproduction Service; 7420 Fullerton Rd., Ste. 110, Springfield, VA 22153-2852 (ED102184,155 p.)
Grade Level: 12
Notes: Items, 74

In 1965, the International Association for the Evaluation of Educational Achievement (IEA) inaugurated a cross-national survey of achievement in 6 subjects: science, reading comprehension, literature, English as a foreign language, French as a foreign language, and civic education. The overall aim of the project was to use international tests to relate student achievement and attitudes to instructional, social, and economic factors and, from the results, to establish generalizations of value to policymakers worldwide. Population IV are those in population IV specializing in French. There are 4 parts to this test. In the first part, the student hears a series of remarks or questions. After each remark or question, the student selects, from among 4 choices, the response which would most likely be made to the remark or question. In the second part, the student listens to a series of short broadcasts or announcements. At the end, a question will be asked and the student must select the answer from 4 choices. In the third part, the student listens to a series of short conversations between 2 people. One person will ask a question or make a statement, and the other will reply. The student is to select from among the 4 choices the best answer. In the last part, the student listens to rather long conversations or dramatic scenes. After each, the student will be asked several questions about what was heard.

13059
IEA Six-Subject Survey Instruments: Reading French, Population I. International Association for the Evaluation of Educational Achievement, Stockholm (Sweden) 1975
Descriptors: *Academic Achievement; *Achievement Tests; *Comparative Education; *Cross Cultural Studies; Elementary School Students; Foreign Countries; *French; Multiple Choice Tests; *Reading Comprehension; Reading Tests; *Second Language Learning
Identifiers: International Evaluation Educational Achievement; Sweden
Availability: ERIC Document Reproduction Service; 7420 Fullerton Rd., Ste. 110, Springfield, VA 22153-2852 (ED102184,155 p.)
Age Level: 10-11
Notes: Items, 32

In 1965, the International Association for the Evaluation of Educational Achievement (IEA) inaugurated a cross-national survey of achievement in 6 subjects: science, reading comprehension, literature, English as a foreign language, French as a foreign language, and civic education. The overall aim of the project was to use international tests to relate student achievement and attitudes to instructional, social, and economic factors and, from the results, to establish generalizations of value to policymakers worldwide. This test is for Population I, students aged 10 to 11. In this test, there are pictures arranged in sets of 4, and each set of pictures has a sentence written below it. The sentence is about one of the 4 pictures, and the student has to decide which picture.

13060
IEA Six-Subject Survey Instruments: Reading French, Population II. International Association for the Evaluation of Educational Achievement, Stockholm (Sweden) 1975
Descriptors: *Academic Achievement; *Achievement Tests; *Comparative Education; *Cross Cultural Studies; Foreign Countries; *French; High School Students; Junior High Schools; Junior High School Students; Multiple Choice Tests; *Reading Comprehension; Reading Tests
Identifiers: International Evaluation Educational Achievement; Sweden
Availability: ERIC Document Reproduction Service; 7420 Fullerton Rd., Ste. 110, Springfield, VA 22153-2852 (ED102184,155 p.)

In 1965, the International Association for the Evaluation of Educational Achievement (IEA) inaugurated a cross-national survey of achievement in 6 subjects: science, reading comprehension, literature, English as a foreign language, French as a foreign language, and civic education. The overall aim of the project was to use international tests to relate student achievement and attitudes to instructional, social, and economic factors and, from the results, to establish generalizations of value to policy-makers worldwide. This test is for Population II, students ages 14 to 15. It is a test of the student's ability to understand written French and is a multiple-choice test. In the second part, a passage is given in French, and several questions are then asked.

13061
IEA Six-Subject Survey Instruments: Reading French, Population IV. International Association for the Evaluation of Educational Achievement, Stockholm (Sweden) 1975
Descriptors: *Academic Achievement; *Achievement Tests; College Bound Students; *Comparative Education; *Cross Cultural Studies; Foreign Countries; *French; *Grade 12; Multiple Choice Tests; Reading Tests; *Second Language Learning
Identifiers: International Evaluation Educational Achievement; Sweden
Availability: ERIC Document Reproduction Service; 7420 Fullerton Rd., Ste. 110, Springfield, VA 22153-2852 (ED102184, 155 p.)
Grade Level: 12
Notes: Items, 35

In 1965, the International Association for the Evaluation of Educational Achievement (IEA) inaugurated a cross-national survey of achievement in 6 subjects: science, reading comprehension, literature, English as a foreign language, French as a foreign language, and civic education. The overall aim of the project was to use international tests to relate student achievement and attitudes to instructional, social, and economic factors and, from the results, to establish generalizations of value to policy-makers worldwide. This is a test of the student's ability to understand written French. There are 4 choices for each answer. This test is for Population IV, those students enrolled in the final year of preuniversity training.

13062
IEA Six-Subject Survey Instruments: Reading French, Population IVS. International Association for the Evaluation of Educational Achievement, Stockholm (Sweden) 1975
Descriptors: *Academic Achievement; *Achievement Tests; College Bound Students; *Comparative Education; *Cross Cultural Studies; Foreign Countries; *French; *Grade 12; Multiple Choice Tests; Reading Tests; *Second Language Learning
Identifiers: International Evaluation Educational Achievement; Sweden
Availability: ERIC Document Reproduction Service; 7420 Fullerton Rd., Ste. 110, Springfield, VA 22153-2852 (ED102184, 155 p.)
Grade Level: 12
Notes: Items, 36

In 1965, the International Association for the Evaluation of Educational Achievement (IEA) inaugurated a cross-national survey of achievement in 6 subjects: science, reading comprehension, literature, English as a foreign language, French as a foreign language, and civic education. The overall aim of the project was to use international tests to relate student achievement and attitudes to instructional, social, and economic factors and, from the results, to establish generalizations of value to policy-makers worldwide. This test is for Population IVS, students enrolled in the final year of preuniversity training and specializing in French. This is to test their ability to understand written French. Four choices are given for every question.

13063
IEA Six-Subject Survey Instruments: French Writing Test, Population II. International Association for the Evaluation of Educational Achievement, Stockholm (Sweden) 1975
Subtests: Sentence Completion; Composition
Descriptors: *Academic Achievement; *Achievement Tests; *Comparative Education; *Cross Cultural Studies; Foreign Countries; *French; *Junior High School Students; Secondary Education; *Second Language Learning; *Writing (Composition)
Identifiers: International Evaluation Educational Achievement; Sweden
Availability: ERIC Document Reproduction Service; 7420 Fullerton Rd., Ste. 110, Springfield, VA 22153-2852 (ED102184, 155 p.)
Age Level: 14-15

In 1965, the International Association for the Evaluation of Educational Achievement (IEA) inaugurated a cross-national survey of achievement in 6 subjects: science, reading comprehension, literature, English as a foreign language, French as a foreign language, and civic education. The overall aim of the project was to use international tests to relate student achievement and attitudes to instructional, social, and economic factors and, from the results, to establish generalizations of value to policy-makers worldwide. This test is for Population II which consists of students aged 14 to 15 years. There are 2 parts to this test, sentence completion and composition. There are 35 items in the first part, and the student has 10 minutes to complete the second section.

13064
IEA Six-Subject Survey Instruments: French Writing Test, Population IV. International Association for the Evaluation of Educational Achievement, Stockholm (Sweden) 1975
Subtests: Sentence Completion; Composition
Descriptors: *Academic Achievement; *Achievement Tests; College Bound Students; *Comparative Education; *Cross Cultural Studies; *Foreign Countries; *French; *Grade 12; High Schools; *Second Language Learning; *Writing (Composition)
Identifiers: International Evaluation Educational Achievement; Sweden
Availability: ERIC Document Reproduction Service; 7420 Fullerton Rd., Ste. 110, Springfield, VA 22153-2852 (ED102184, 155 p.)
Grade Level: 12

In 1965, the International Association for the Evaluation of Educational Achievement (IEA) inaugurated a cross-national survey of achievement in 6 subjects: science, reading comprehension, literature, English as a foreign language, French as a foreign language, and civic education. The overall aim of the project was to use international tests to relate student achievement and attitudes to instructional, social, and economic factors and, from the results, to establish generalizations of value to policy-makers worldwide. This writing test is for Population IV; students enrolled in the final year of preuniversity training. There are 2 parts to the test, the first part is sentence completion with 32 items, and the second is a 10-minute composition test.

13065
IEA Six-Subject Survey Instruments: French Speaking Test, Population I. International Association for the Evaluation of Educational Achievement, Stockholm (Sweden) 1975
Descriptors: *Academic Achievement; *Achievement Tests; *Comparative Education; *Cross Cultural Studies; Elementary Education; Elementary School Students; Foreign Countries; *French; *Language Fluency; *Pronunciation; *Second Language Learning; Tape Recordings
Identifiers: International Evaluation Educational Achievement; Sweden
Availability: ERIC Document Reproduction Service; 7420 Fullerton Rd., Ste. 110, Springfield, VA 22153-2852 (ED102184, 155 p.)
Age Level: 10-11

In 1965, the International Association for the Evaluation of Educational Achievement (IEA) inaugurated a cross-national survey of achievement in 6 subjects: science, reading comprehension, literature, English as a foreign language, French as a foreign language, and civic education. The overall aim of the project was to use international tests to relate student achievement and attitudes to instructional, social, and economic factors and, from the results, to establish generalizations of value to policy-makers worldwide. This test is entirely on tape so there is no instrument; the script of the tape is shown. This test is for Population I which consists of students 10 to 11 years of age. In the first section, students listen to sentences on the tape and then repeat them. In the second section, there are 10 pictures, and the student is asked a question about each of the pictures and then must reply. The Fluency section does not require a tape. The students is to choose 1 of 2 pictures and to describe it in French. The description is taped.

13066
IEA Six-Subject Survey Instruments: French Speaking Test, Populations II, IV. International Association for the Evaluation of Educational Achievement, Stockholm (Sweden) 1975
Subtests: Pronunciation; Structural Control; Oral Reading; Fluency 1; Fluency 2
Descriptors: *Academic Achievement; *Achievement Tests; *Comparative Education; *Cross Cultural Studies; Foreign Countries; *French; Grade 12; *High School Students; *Junior High School Students; *Language Fluency; *Oral Reading; *Pronunciation; Secondary Education; *Second Language Learning; Tape Recordings
Identifiers: International Evaluation Educational Achievement; Sweden
Availability: ERIC Document Reproduction Service; 7420 Fullerton Rd., Ste. 110, Springfield, VA 22153-2852 (ED102184, 155 p.)
Age Level: 14-15; 17-18

In 1965, the International Association for the Evaluation of Educational Achievement (IEA) inaugurated a cross-national survey of achievement in 6 subjects: science, reading comprehension, literature, English as a foreign language, French as a foreign language, and civic education. The overall aim of the project was to use international tests to relate student achievement and attitudes to instructional, social, and economic factors and, from the results, to establish generalizations of value to policy-makers worldwide. This test is for Population II, students age 14 to 15, and Population IV, students enrolled in the final year of preuniversity training. The test is on tape so there is no instrument; the script of the tape is shown. In the Pronunciation section, the student listens to some sentences and then repeats them. In the Structural section, the student is asked one question about each of 10 pictures and must reply to the question in French. The third section tests oral reading. The student has 3 minutes to look over a passage and then is required to read it aloud. The final section of the test, Fluency, is a free-response section. In the Fluency I section, the student chooses 1 of 2 pictures to describe in French; in the Fluency 2 section, there are 3 pictures from which to choose and then describe what is happening in the picture. All responses are taped.

13067
Consumer Skills Items. Education Commission of the States, Denver, CO 1978
Descriptors: Behavior Development; Citizenship Responsibility; Consumer Economics; *Consumer Education; Consumer Protection; Contracts; Decision Making; *Educational Assessment; Energy Conservation; High Schools; *High School Students; *Item Banks; Mathematics; Money Management; Purchasing; *Skill Development
Identifiers: National Assessment of Educational Progress
Availability: ERIC Document Reproduction Service; 7420 Fullerton Rd., Ste. 110, Springfield, VA 22153-2852 (ED163182, 239 p.)
Age Level: 17

This is a collection of consumer skills items for state and local education agencies to draw upon in composing consumer skills instruments. It provides items to assess 17 year olds' consumer skills. The items are classified under 8 major topics: behavior, contracts, economics, energy, finances, mathematics, projection, and purchases. Items classified as miscellaneous make up a ninth topic, and background questions constitute a tenth topic. There are also subtopics. For example, subtopics under behavior include advertising, decision making, and shopping. All items are assigned numbers which refer to the topic and subtopic. Most items are multiple-choice. The directions for answering the exercises and 2 exercise examples are included, but the answer key is found in ED163181.

13091
IEA Six-Subject Survey Instruments: English as a Foreign Language, Listening, Population II. International Association for the Evaluation of Educational Achievement, Stockholm (Sweden) 1975
Descriptors: *Academic Achievement; *Comparative Education; *Cross Cultural Studies; *English (Second Language); Foreign Countries; *Listening Comprehension Tests; Secondary Education; *Secondary School Students; Second Language Learning; Tape Recorders
Identifiers: International Evaluation Educational Achievement; Sweden
Availability: ERIC Document Reproduction Service; 7420 Fullerton Rd., Ste. 110, Springfield, VA 22153-2852 (ED102181, 123 p.)
Age Level: 14-15
Notes: Items, 24

In 1965, the International Association for the Evaluation of Educational Achievement (IEA) inaugurated a cross-national survey of achievement in 6 subjects: science, reading comprehension, literature, English as a foreign language, French as a foreign language, and civic education. The overall aim of the project was to use international tests to relate student achievement and attitudes to instructional, social, and economic factors and, from the results, to establish generalizations of value to policy-makers worldwide. This test is in 3 sections: discrimination of sounds, listening comprehension, and dictation. In the first section, students are given pictures and are asked to listen to 3 words and pick the one corresponding to the pictures. The second section is meant to discover whether the students understand what they hear. They listen to a tape asking questions, and the students are to choose the corresponding sentence in their native language. In the dictation section, a short piece of prose is read, and the students are to write it as they have heard it. This test is for Population II which consists of students aged 14 to 15 years.

13092

IEA Six-Subject Survey Instruments: English as a Foreign Language, Listening, Population IV. International Association for the Evaluation of Educational Achievement, Stockholm (Sweden) 1975
Descriptors: *Academic Achievement; *College Bound Students; *Comparative Education; *Cross Cultural Studies; *English (Second Language); Foreign Countries; *Grade 12; High Schools; *Listening Comprehension Tests; *Second Language Learning; Tape Recorders
Identifiers: International Evaluation Educational Achievement; Sweden
Availability: ERIC Document Reproduction Service; 7420 Fullerton Rd., Ste. 110, Springfield, VA 22153-2852 (ED102181, 123 p.)
Age Level: 12
Notes: Items, 36
In 1965, the International Association for the Evaluation of Educational Achievement (IEA) inaugurated a cross-national survey of achievement in 6 subjects: science, reading comprehension, literature, English as a foreign language, French as a foreign language, and civic education. The overall aim of the project was to use international tests to relate student achievement and attitudes to instructional, social, and economic factors and, from the results, to establish generalizations of value to policy-makers worldwide. Population IV consists of students enrolled in the final year of preuniversity training. The test is in 4 parts, and the students listen to the questions on a tape recorder and mark their answer on an answer sheet. The first section is discrimination of sounds and the students listen to 3 words on the tape and mark the picture which corresponds to the words. Section II is recognition of meaning though intonation. In this section, a question is asked in the students' native language, and they determine the answer to the question by listening to the way the voice rises and falls in the 3 sentences. In section III, listening comprehension, the students listen to a sentence or short paragraph and select from their book the one they heard. The last section is listening comprehension (conversation) in which the students listen to a conversation and then answer a question

13093

IEA Six-Subject Survey Instruments: English as a Foreign Language, Reading, Population II. International Association for the Evaluation of Educational Achievement, Stockholm (Sweden) 1975
Descriptors: *Academic Achievement; *Achievement Tests; *Comparative Education; *Cross Cultural Studies; *English (Second Language); Foreign Countries; Multiple Choice Tests; *Reading Comprehension; Reading Tests; Secondary Education; *Secondary School Students; *Second Language Learning
Identifiers: International Evaluation Educational Achievement; Sweden
Availability: ERIC Document Reproduction Service; 7420 Fullerton Rd., Ste. 110, Springfield, VA 22153-2852 (ED102181, 123 p.)
Age Level: 14-15
Notes: Items, 60
In 1965, the International Association for the Evaluation of Educational Achievement (IEA) inaugurated a cross-national survey of achievement in 6 subjects: science, reading comprehension, literature, English as a foreign language, French as a foreign language, and civic education. The overall aim of the project was to use international tests to relate student achievement and attitudes to instructional, social, and economic factors and, from the results, to establish generalizations of value to policy-makers worldwide. This test is for Population II that consists of students aged 14 to 15 years old. The test consists of 6 sections: recognition of antonyms, sound correspondences, recognition of structural features, vocabulary-recognition, reading comprehension (short sentences), and reading comprehension (continuous passages).

13094

IEA Six-Subject Survey Instruments: English as a Foreign Language, Reading, Population IV. International Association for the Evaluation of Educational Achievement, Stockholm (Sweden) 1975
Descriptors: *Academic Achievement; *Achievement Tests; *College Bound Students; *Comparative Education; *Cross Cultural Studies; *English (Second Language); *Grade 12; Multiple Choice Tests; *Reading Comprehension; Reading Tests; *Second Language Learning
Identifiers: International Evaluation Educational Achievement; Sweden

Availability: ERIC Document Reproduction Service; 7420 Fullerton Rd., Ste. 110, Springfield, VA 22153-2852 (ED102181, 123 p.)
Grade Level: 12
Notes: Items, 60
In 1965, the International Association for the Evaluation of Educational Achievement (IEA) inaugurated a cross-national survey of achievement in 6 subjects: science, reading comprehension, literature, English as a foreign language, French as a foreign language, and civic education. The overall aim of the project was to use international tests to relate student achievement and attitudes to instructional, social, and economic factors and, from the results, to establish generalizations of value to policy-makers worldwide. This test is for Population IV, students enrolled in the final year of preuniversity training. The test is divided into sections which are recognition of word stress, collocations, recognition of grammatical structures, reading comprehension (short sentences), reading comprehension (continuous passages).

13095

IEA Six-Subject Survey Instruments: English as a Foreign Language, Writing Populations II, IV. International Association for the Evaluation of Educational Achievement, Stockholm (Sweden) 1975
Descriptors: *Academic Achievement; *Achievement Tests; College Bound Students; *Comparative Education; *Cross Cultural Studies; *English (Second Language); Foreign Countries; Grade 12; Secondary Education; *Secondary School Students; *Second Language Learning; *Writing (Composition)
Identifiers: International Evaluation Educational Achievement; Sweden
Availability: ERIC Document Reproduction Service; 7420 Fullerton Rd., Ste. 110, Springfield, VA 22153-2852 (ED102181, 123 p.)
Age Level: 14-15; 17-18
Notes: Items, 31
In 1965, the International Association for the Evaluation of Educational Achievement (IEA) inaugurated a cross-national survey of achievement in 6 subjects: science, reading comprehension, literature, English as a foreign language, French as a foreign language, and civic education. The overall aim of the project was to use international tests to relate student achievement and attitudes to instructional, social, and economic factors and, from the results, to establish generalizations of value to policy-makers worldwide. Population II consists of students aged 14 to 15 years and Population IV, students enrolled in the final year of preuniversity training. This test is divided into 4 sections. The first 2 sections are sentence completion requiring one word, the third section requires the students to rearrange 3 words or phrases to complete the sentence, and the last section is composition. The student must use 12 words which are given and write no more than 200 words.

13096

IEA Six-Subject Survey Instruments: English as a Foreign Language, Speaking Populations II, IV. International Association for the Evaluation of Educational Achievement, Stockholm (Sweden) 1975
Descriptors: *Academic Achievement; *Achievement Tests; College Bound Students; *Comparative Education; *Cross Cultural Studies; *English (Second Language); Foreign Countries; Grade 12; *Language Fluency; Secondary Education; *Secondary School Students; *Second Language Learning; Tape Recordings
Identifiers: International Evaluation Educational Achievement; Sweden
Availability: ERIC Document Reproduction Service; 7420 Fullerton Rd., Ste. 110, Springfield, VA 22153-2852 (ED102181, 123 p.)
Age Level: 14-15; 17-18
In 1965, the International Association for the Evaluation of Educational Achievement (IEA) inaugurated a cross-national survey of achievement in 6 subjects: science, reading comprehension, literature, English as a foreign language, French as a foreign language, and civic education. The overall aim of the project was to use international tests to relate student achievement and attitudes to instructional, social, and economic factors and, from the results, to establish generalizations of value to policy-makers worldwide. Population II consists of students aged 14 to 15 years and Population IV, students enrolled in the final year of preuniversity training. This test is divided into sections on speaking, oral reading, and fluency. The students are asked questions and answer them on tape recorders.

13103

IEA Six-Subject Survey Instruments: Word Knowledge Test, Population I. International Association for the Evaluation of Educational Achievement, Stockholm (Sweden) 1975

Descriptors: *Academic Achievement; *Achievement Tests; *Comparative Education; *Cross Cultural Studies; Elementary Education; *Elementary School Students; Foreign Countries; Knowledge Level; *Vocabulary
Identifiers: International Evaluation Educational Achievement; Sweden
Availability: ERIC Document Reproduction Service; 7420 Fullerton Rd., Ste. 110, Springfield, VA 22153-2852 (ED102177, 17 p.)
Age Level: 10-11
Notes: Time, 10 min.; Items, 40
In 1965, the International Association for the Evaluation of Educational Achievement (IEA) inaugurated a cross-national survey of achievement in 6 subjects: science, reading comprehension, literature, English as a foreign language, French as a foreign language, and civic education. The overall aim of the project was to use international tests to relate student achievement and attitudes to instructional, social, and economic factors and, from the results, to establish generalizations of value to policy-makers worldwide. This test measures word knowledge for student population I. Population I consists of students aged 10 to 11 years old. The items contain 2 words, and the student is to decide whether they are alike or opposite in meaning.

13104

IEA Six-Subject Survey Instruments: Word Knowledge Test, Population II. International Association for the Evaluation of Educational Achievement, Stockholm (Sweden) 1975
Descriptors: *Academic Achievement; *Achievement Tests; *Comparative Education; *Cross Cultural Studies; Foreign Countries; Junior High Schools; Junior High School Students; Knowledge Level; Secondary Education; *Secondary School Students; *Vocabulary
Identifiers: International Evaluation Educational Achievement; Sweden
Availability: ERIC Document Reproduction Service; 7420 Fullerton Rd., Ste. 110, Springfield, VA 22153-2852 (ED102177, 17 p.)
Age Level: 14-15
Notes: Time, 10 min.; Items, 40
In 1965, the International Association for the Evaluation of Educational Achievement (IEA) inaugurated a cross-national survey of achievement in 6 subjects: science, reading comprehension, literature, English as a foreign language, French as a foreign language, and civic education. The overall aim of the project was to use international tests to relate student achievement and attitudes to instructional, social, and economic factors and, from the results, to establish generalizations of value to policy-makers worldwide. This test measures word knowledge for the student population II; students aged 14-15. Word pairs are listed, and the student marks whether the pairs are more alike or more opposite.

13105

IEA Six-Subject Survey Instruments: Word Knowledge Test, Population IV. International Association for the Evaluation of Educational Achievement, Stockholm (Sweden) 1975
Descriptors: *Academic Achievement; *Achievement Tests; *College Bound Students; *Comparative Education; *Cross Cultural Studies; Foreign Countries; *Grade 12; Knowledge Level; Secondary Education; *Vocabulary
Identifiers: International Evaluation Educational Achievement; Sweden
Availability: ERIC Document Reproduction Service; 7420 Fullerton Rd., Ste. 110, Springfield, VA 22153-2852 (ED102177, 17 p.)
Grade Level: 12
Notes: Items, 40
In 1965, the International Association for the Evaluation of Educational Achievement (IEA) inaugurated a cross-national survey of achievement in 6 subjects: science, reading comprehension, literature, English as a foreign language, French as a foreign language, and civic education. The overall aim of the project was to use international tests to relate student achievement and attitudes to instructional, social, and economic factors and, from the results, to establish generalizations of value to policy-makers worldwide. This test measures word knowledge for the student population IV: students enrolled in the final year of preuniversity training. Word pairs are listed, and the student must decide whether the words are more alike or more opposite.

13107

IEA Six-Subject Survey Instruments: Literature Tests. International Association for the Evaluation of Educational Achievement, Stockholm (Sweden) 1975
Subtests: The Use of Force; I See You Never; The Man by the Fountain; The Sea; The End of Something

Descriptors: *Academic Achievement; *Achievement Tests; College Bound Students; *Comparative Education; *Cross Cultural Studies; Foreign Countries; *Literature; Multiple Choice Tests; Secondary Education; *Secondary School Students; *Writing (Composition)
Identifiers: International Evaluation Educational Achievement; Sweden
Availability: ERIC Document Reproduction Service; 7420 Fullerton Rd., Ste. 110, Springfield, VA 22153-2852 (ED102175, 56 p.)
Age Level: 14-15; 17-18
Notes: Items, 153

In 1965, the International Association for the Evaluation of Educational Achievement (IEA) inaugurated a cross-national survey of achievement in 6 subjects: science, reading comprehension, literature, English as a foreign language, French as a foreign language and, civic education. The overall aim of the project was to use international tests to relate student achievement and attitudes to instructional, social, and economic factors and, from the results, to establish generalizations of value to policy-makers worldwide. The first 4 sections are multiple-choice tests and, for the last, "The End of Something," a composition must be written. This test is for Populations II and IV. Population II consists of students aged 14 to 15 years; population IV, students enrolled in the final year of preuniversity training. Answer keys can be found in ED085709.

13110
IEA Six-Subject Survey Instruments: Reading Comprehension, Section C, Population I. International Association for the Evaluation of Educational Achievement, Stockholm (Sweden) 1975
Descriptors: *Academic Achievement; *Achievement Tests; *Comparative Education; *Cross Cultural Studies; Elementary Education; *Elementary School Students; Foreign Countries; Multiple Choice Tests; *Reading Comprehension
Identifiers: International Evaluation Educational Achievement; Sweden
Availability: ERIC Document Reproduction Service; 7420 Fullerton Rd., Ste. 110, Springfield, VA 22153-2852 (ED102172, 72 p.)
Age Level: 10-11
Notes: Items, 21

In 1965, the International Association for the Evaluation of Educational Achievement (IEA) inaugurated a cross-national survey of achievement in 6 subjects: science, reading comprehension, literature, English as a foreign language, French as a foreign language, and civic education. The overall aim of the project was to use international tests to relate student achievement and attitudes to instructional, social, and economic factors and, from the results, to establish generalizations of value to policy-makers worldwide. This test measures reading comprehension for Population I, students aged 10 to 11 years. Some answer keys can be found in ED084503.

13111
IEA Six-Subject Survey Instruments: Reading Comprehension, Section D, Population I. International Association for the Evaluation of Educational Achievement, Stockholm (Sweden) 1975
Descriptors: *Academic Achievement; *Achievement Tests; *Comparative Education; *Cross Cultural Studies; Elementary Education; *Elementary School Students; Foreign Countries; Multiple Choice Tests; *Reading Comprehension
Identifiers: International Evaluation Educational Achievement; Sweden
Availability: ERIC Document Reproduction Service; 7420 Fullerton Rd., Ste. 110, Springfield, VA 22153-2852 (ED102172, 72 p.)
Age Level: 10-11
Notes: Time, 25 min.; Items, 24

In 1965, the International Association for the Evaluation of Educational Achievement (IEA) inaugurated a cross-national survey of achievement in 6 subjects: science, reading comprehension, literature, English as a foreign language, French as a foreign language, and civic education. The overall aim of the project was to use international tests to relate student achievement and attitudes to instructional, social, and economic factors and, from the results, to establish generalizations of value to policy-makers worldwide. This test measures reading comprehension for Population I, students aged 10 to 11 years. Some answer keys can be found in ED084503.

13112
IEA Six-Subject Survey Instruments: Reading Speed Test. International Association for the Evaluation of Educational Achievement, Stockholm (Sweden) 1975
Descriptors: *Academic Achievement; *Achievement Tests; *Comparative Education; *Cross Cultural Studies; *Elementary School Students; Elementary Secondary Education; Foreign Countries; Multiple Choice Tests; *Reading Comprehension; *Reading Rate; *Secondary School Students
Identifiers: International Evaluation Educational Achievement; Sweden
Availability: ERIC Document Reproduction Service; 7420 Fullerton Rd., Ste. 110, Springfield, VA 22153-2852 (ED102172, 72 p.)
Age Level: 10-11; 14-15
Notes: Time, 4 minutes min.; Items, 40

In 1965, the International Association for the Evaluation of Educational Achievement (IEA) inaugurated a cross-national survey of achievement in 6 subjects: science, reading comprehension, literature, English as a foreign language, French as a foreign language, and civic education. The overall aim of the project was to use international tests to relate student achievement and attitudes to instructional, social, and economic factors and, from the results, to establish generalizations of value to policy-makers worldwide. This test measures reading comprehension for Population I, students aged 10 to 11 years, and II, students 14 and 15 years. Some answer keys can be found in ED084503.

13113
IEA Six-Subject Survey Instruments: Reading Comprehension, Section C, Population II. International Association for the Evaluation of Educational Achievement, Stockholm (Sweden) 1975
Descriptors: *Academic Achievement; *Achievement Tests; *Comparative Education; *Cross Cultural Studies; Foreign Countries; Multiple Choice Tests; *Reading Comprehension; Secondary Education; *Secondary School Students
Identifiers: International Evaluation Educational Achievement; Sweden
Availability: ERIC Document Reproduction Service; 7420 Fullerton Rd., Ste. 110, Springfield, VA 22153-2852 (ED102172, 72 p.)
Age Level: 14-15
Notes: Items, 26

In 1965, the International Association for the Evaluation of Educational Achievement (IEA) inaugurated a cross-national survey of achievement in 6 subjects: science, reading comprehension, literature, English as a foreign language, French as a foreign language, and civic education. The overall aim of the project was to use international tests to relate student achievement and attitudes to instructional, social, and economic factors and, from the results, to establish generalizations of value to policy-makers worldwide. This test measures reading comprehension for Population II, students 14 to 15 years old. Some answer keys can be found in ED084503.

13114
IEA Six-Subject Survey Instruments: Reading Comprehension, Section D, Population II. International Association for the Evaluation of Educational Achievement, Stockholm (Sweden) 1975
Descriptors: *Academic Achievement; *Achievement Tests; *Comparative Education; *Cross Cultural Studies; Foreign Countries; Multiple Choice Tests; *Reading Comprehension; Secondary Education; *Secondary School Students
Identifiers: International Evaluation Educational Achievement; Sweden
Availability: ERIC Document Reproduction Service; 7420 Fullerton Rd., Ste. 110, Springfield, VA 22153-2852 (ED102172, 72 p.)
Age Level: 14-15
Notes: Items, 26

In 1965, the International Association for the Evaluation of Educational Achievement (IEA) inaugurated a cross-national survey of achievement in 6 subjects: science, reading comprehension, literature, English as a foreign language, French as a foreign language, and civic education. The overall aim of the project was to use international tests to relate student achievement and attitudes to instructional, social, and economic factors and, from the results, to establish generalizations of value to policy-makers worldwide. This test measures reading comprehension for Population II, students 14 to 15 years old. Some answer keys can be found in ED084503.

13115
IEA Six-Subject Survey Instruments: Reading Comprehension, Section C, Population IV. International Association for the Evaluation of Educational Achievement, Stockholm (Sweden) 1975
Descriptors: *Academic Achievement; *Achievement Tests; *College Bound Students; *Comparative Education; *Cross Cultural Studies; Foreign Countries; *Grade 12; Multiple Choice Tests; *Reading Comprehension; Secondary Education
Identifiers: International Evaluation Educational Achievement; Sweden
Availability: ERIC Document Reproduction Service; 7420 Fullerton Rd., Ste. 110, Springfield, VA 22153-2852 (ED102172, 72 p.)
Grade Level: 12
Notes: Items, 25

In 1965, the International Association for the Evaluation of Educational Achievement (IEA) inaugurated a cross-national survey of achievement in 6 subjects: science, reading comprehension, literature, English as a foreign language, French as a foreign language, and civic education. The overall aim of the project was to use international tests to relate student achievement and attitudes to instructional, social, and economic factors and, from the results, to establish generalizations of value to policy-makers worldwide. This is a test that measures reading comprehension for Population IV, students enrolled in the final year of preuniversity training. Some answer keys can be found in ED084503.

13116
IEA Six-Subject Survey Instruments: Reading Comprehension, Section D, Population IV. International Association for the Evaluation of Educational Achievement, Stockholm (Sweden) 1975
Descriptors: *Academic Achievement; *Achievement Tests; *College Bound Students; *Comparative Education; *Cross Cultural Studies; Foreign Countries; *Grade 12; Multiple Choice Tests; *Reading Comprehension; Secondary Education
Identifiers: International Evaluation Educational Achievement; Sweden
Availability: ERIC Document Reproduction Service; 7420 Fullerton Rd., Ste. 110, Springfield, VA 22153-2852 (ED102172, 72 p.)
Grade Level: 12
Notes: Items, 29

In 1965, the International Association for the Evaluation of Educational Achievement (IEA) inaugurated a cross-national survey of achievement in 6 subjects: science, reading comprehension, literature, English as a foreign language, French as a foreign language, and civic education. The overall aim of the project was to use international tests to relate student achievement and attitudes to instructional, social, and economic factors and, from the results, to establish generalizations of value to policy-makers worldwide. This is a test that measures reading comprehension for Population IV, students enrolled in the final year of preuniversity training. Some answer keys can be found in ED084503.

13128
Spanish 101 Unit Exam. Omaggio, Alice C.
Descriptors: *Achievement Tests; *College Students; Higher Education; *Language Proficiency; *Language Skills; Listening Comprehension; *Second Languages; *Spanish; Tape Recorders
Availability: ERIC Document Reproduction Service; 7420 Fullerton Rd., Ste. 110, Springfield, VA 22153-2852 (ED233589, 121 p.)
Grade Level: 13-16
Notes: Time, 60 min.

This test is an hour-long unit exam for a college Spanish class. The test covers listening comprehension, grammar/translation, communication/composition, culture. This test is part of a report on Proficiency-Oriented Classroom Testing also available from the Center for Applied Linguistics, Box 4866 Hampden Station, Baltimore, MD 21211.

13129
French 101 Unit Exam. Omaggio, Alice C.
Descriptors: *Achievement Tests; *College Students; *French; Higher Education; *Language Proficiency; *Language Skills; Reading Comprehension; *Second Languages
Availability: ERIC Document Reproduction Service; 7420 Fullerton Rd., Ste. 110, Springfield, VA 22153-2852 (ED233589, 121 p.)
Grade Level: 13-16
Notes: Time, 60 min.

This test is an hour-long unit exam for college students. This test is part of a report on Proficiency-Oriented Classroom Testing available from the Center for Applied Linguistics, Box 4866, Hampden Station, Baltimore, MD 21211.

13130
French 101 Final Exam. Omaggio, Alice C.
Descriptors: *Achievement Tests; *College Students; *French; Higher Education; *Language Proficiency; *Language Skills; Reading Comprehension; *Second Languages
Availability: ERIC Document Reproduction Service; 7420 Fullerton Rd., Ste. 110, Springfield, VA 22153-2852 (ED233589, 121 p.)
Grade Level: 13-16

This test is the final for French 101 for college students. The test covers reading comprehension, sentence completion, grammar, composition, cultural comprehension. This test is part of a report on Proficiency-Oriented Classroom Testing available from the Center for Applied Linguistics, Box 4866, Hampden Station, Baltimore, MD 21211.

13148
Intermediate Individual Reading Skills Checklist.
1978
Descriptors: Check Lists; *Elementary School Students; Intermediate Grades; Oral Reading; Reading Comprehension; *Reading Skills; *Student Evaluation; Study Skills; Word Recognition
Availability: Modern Curriculum Press; 13900 Prospect Rd., Cleveland, OH 44136
Grade Level: 4-6

The Reading Skills Checklist has been designed to provide teachers with a practical tool for assessing an individual's progress toward mastery of reading skills in any reading program. Each level provides the teacher with a comprehensive sequential checklist of skills to be learned at that level. Using this checklist can provide the basis for skill instruction, individual and/or small group instruction, for parent teacher conferences, and professional staff conferences. Skills assessed include word recognition, comprehension, study skills, oral reading, and/or oral expression.

13149
Junior High Individual Reading Skills Checklist.
1978
Descriptors: Check Lists; Independent Reading; Junior High Schools; *Junior High School Students; Listening Skills; Oral Reading; Reading Comprehension; *Reading Skills; *Student Evaluation; Study Skills; Word Recognition
Availability: Modern Curriculum Press; 13900 Prospect Rd., Cleveland, OH 44136
Grade Level: 7-9
Notes: Items, 77

The Reading Skills Checklist has been designed to provide teachers with a practical tool for assessing an individual's progress toward mastery of reading skills in any reading program. Each level provides the teacher with a comprehensive sequential checklist of skills to be learned at that level. Using this checklist can provide the basis for skill instruction, individual and/or small group instruction, for parent teacher conferences, and professional staff conferences. Areas covered include word recognition, comprehension, study skills, oral reading, listening, and interest.

13150
Primary Individual Reading Skills Checklist. 1978
Descriptors: Auditory Discrimination; Check Lists; Elementary School Students; Independent Reading; Kindergarten Children; Oral Reading; *Primary Education; Reading Comprehension; Reading Readiness; *Reading Skills; Silent Reading; *Student Evaluation; Study Skills; Visual Discrimination; Word Recognition
Availability: Modern Curriculum Press; 13900 Prospect Rd., Cleveland, OH 44136
Grade Level: K-3

The Reading Skills Checklist has been designed to provide teachers with a practical tool for assessing an individual's progress toward mastery of reading skills in any reading program. The checklist can be used to provide the basis for skill instruction, individual and/or small group instruction, for parent-teacher conferences, and professional staff conferences. Areas covered include word recognition, perception, comprehension, oral expression, word attack, silent reading, interest, and/or study skills.

13164
Assessment of Fluency in School-Age Children.
Thompson, Julia 1983
Descriptors: Articulation Impairments; *Criterion Referenced Tests; Elementary School Students; Elementary Secondary Education; Interviews; *Screening Tests; Secondary School Students; *Speech Evaluation; Speech Therapy; *Stuttering; Tape Recordings; Therapists
Identifiers: AFSC
Availability: PRO-ED; 8700 Shoal Creek Blvd., Austin, TX 78758-6897
Grade Level: K-12
Age Level: 5-18
Notes: Time, 45 min.

The Assessment of Fluency in School-Age Children (AFSC) is a criterion-referenced instrument to be used with children between the ages of 5 and 18. The assessment tool incorporates a multisourced, multifactored format. Parent/teacher/child interview forms are included with the differential evaluation, as well as sequenced tasks to determine speech, language, and physiological functioning. This tool assists in determining which young children would benefit from early intervention. There are complete directions for administration plus reference information describing management procedures in public school settings. The purpose is to direct speech therapists to appropriate procedures for children who stutter.

13172
Multiethnic Awareness Survey. Coffin, Gregory C.; And Others 1977
Descriptors: *Achievement Tests; Adults; American Indians; Black Achievement; Blacks; College Students; *Cultural Awareness; *Ethnic Groups; Higher Education; Jews; *Knowledge Level; Majority Attitudes; Secondary Education; Secondary School Students; Surveys; United States History
Identifiers: Asians; Irish Americans; Italians; Latinos; Native Americans; TIM(J)
Availability: Tests in Microfiche; Test Collection, Educational Testing Service, Princeton, NJ 08541
Grade Level: 7-16
Age Level: Adults
Notes: Time, 40 min. approx.; Items, 100

Measures factual knowledge about the contributions of minorities to the past and present growth of the U.S. and aims to create an awareness of these contributions. Items reflect awareness of deeds of Black, Irish, Italian, Jewish, Asian, Latin, and Native Americans.

13173
Black History Test: A Test to Create Awareness and Arouse Interest. Coffin, Gregory C.; And Others 1974
Descriptors: *Achievement Tests; Adults; *Black Achievement; *Black History; *Blacks; College Students; Higher Education; *Knowledge Level; Majority Attitudes; Secondary Education; Secondary School Students; United States History
Identifiers: TIM(J)
Availability: Tests in Microfiche; Test Collection, Educational Testing Service, Princeton, NJ 08541
Grade Level: 7-16
Age Level: Adults
Notes: Time, 40 min. approx.; Items, 100

Designed to measure knowledge of African American contributions to the U.S. and to create an awareness of the contributions of African Americans in the development of the U.S. Test covers the period from slavery to recent times.

13179
Computer Science Test for Grades Nine through Twelve. Northwest Regional Educational Lab., Portland, OR 1984
Subtests: Writing Programs; Hardware Operations; Problem Solving with Computers
Descriptors: *Achievement Tests; Computers; *Computer Science; High Schools; *High School Students; Knowledge Level; Problem Solving; Programing
Availability: Northwest Regional Educational Laboratory; 101 S.W. Main St., Ste. 500, Portland, OR 97204
Grade Level: 9-12
Notes: Time, 45 min. approx.; Items, 50

Group-administered survey developed to assess knowledge and skills related to computer education. Interpretation of results is most reliable at total test, rather than subtest, level. Subtests scores are useful for interpretation of strengths and weaknesses, especially at the group level. Items were field tested, but results of field testing are not offered as national norms to which a particular school or district should be compared. Norms are presented at item level to provide an indication of how easy or difficult each item was in the field testing and whether the item discriminates between various levels of computer knowledge appropriately. This test assesses knowledge based on the following broad program objectives: ability to write structured and documented computer software; ability to demonstrate knowledge of design and operation of computer hardware; ability to use the computer system in problem solving.

13180
Computer Literacy Test: Grade 4. Northwest Regional Educational Lab., Portland, OR 1984
Subtests: Interacting with Computers; Functions and Uses; Problem Solving; Impact on Society
Descriptors: *Achievement Tests; *Computer Literacy; Elementary School Students; *Grade 4; Intermediate Grades; *Knowledge Level; Problem Solving
Availability: Northwest Regional Educational Laboratory; 101 S.W. Main St., Ste. 500, Portland, OR 97204
Grade Level: 4
Notes: Time, 45 min. approx.; Items, 40

Group-administered survey developed to assess knowledge and skills related to computer education. Interpretation of results is most reliable at total test, rather than subtest level. Subtest scores are useful for interpretation of strengths and weaknesses, especially at the group level. Items were field tested, but results of field testing are not offered as national norms to which a school or district should be compared. Norms are presented at the item level to provide an indication of how easy or difficult each

item was in the field testing and whether the item discriminates between various levels of computer knowledge appropriately. The computer literacy test assesses knowledge based on the following broad program objectives: interacting with computers, functions and uses, problem solving, impact on society. The computer literacy test measure concepts related to understanding the capabilities, applications, and implications of computer technology. It includes an awareness of how computers are used in today's society but also requires knowledge of basic computer-related operations.

13181
Computer Literacy Test: Grade 7. Northwest Regional Educational Lab., Portland, OR 1984
Subtests: Interacting with Computers; Functions and Uses; Problem Solving; Impact on Society
Descriptors: *Achievement Tests; *Computer Literacy; *Grade 7; Junior High Schools; Junior High School Students; *Knowledge Level; Problem Solving
Availability: Northwest Regional Educational Laboratory; 101 S.W. Main St., Ste. 500, Portland, OR 97204
Grade Level: 7
Notes: Time, 45 min. approx.; Items, 50

Group-administered survey developed to assess knowledge and skills related to computer education. Interpretation of results is most reliable at total test, rather than subtest level. Subtest scores are useful for interpretation of strengths and weaknesses, especially at the group level. Items were field tested, but results of field testing are not offered as national norms to which a school or district should be compared. Norms are presented at the item level to provide an indication of how easy or difficult each item was in the field testing and whether the item discriminates between various levels of computer knowledge appropriately. The computer literacy test assesses knowledge based on the following broad program objectives: interacting with computers, functions and uses, problem solving, impact on society. The computer literacy test measures concepts related to understanding the capabilities, applications, and implications of computer technology. It includes an awareness of how computers are used in today's society but also requires knowledge of basic computer-related operations.

13182
Computer Literacy Test: Grade 11. Northwest Regional Educational Lab., Portland, OR 1984
Subtests: Interacting with Computers; Functions and Uses; Problem Solving; Impact on Society
Descriptors: *Achievement Tests; *Computer Literacy; *Grade 11; High Schools; High School Students; *Knowledge Level; Problem Solving
Availability: Northwest Regional Educational Laboratory; 101 S.W. Main St., Ste. 500, Portland, OR 97204
Grade Level: 11
Notes: Time, 45 min. approx.; Items, 50

Group-administered survey developed to assess knowledge and skills related to computer education. Interpretation of results is most reliable at total test, rather than subtest level. Subtest scores are useful for interpretation of strengths and weaknesses, especially at the group level. Items were field tested, but results of field testing are not offered as national norms to which a school or district should be compared. Norms are presented at the item level to provide an indication of how easy or difficult each item was in the field testing and whether the item discriminates between various levels of computer knowledge appropriately. The computer literacy test assesses knowledge based on the following broad program objectives: interacting with computers, functions and uses, problem solving, impact on society. The computer literacy test measures concepts related to understanding the capabilities, applications, and implications of computer technology. It includes an awareness of how computers are used in today's society but also requires knowledge of basic computer-related operations.

13190
Early Language Milestone Scale. Coplan, James 1983
Subtests: Auditory Expressive; Auditory Receptive; Visual
Descriptors: Expressive Language; Handicap Identification; *Infants; *Language Acquisition; Language Handicaps; Preschool Children; Receptive Language; *Screening Tests; Visual Stimuli
Identifiers: ELM Scale
Availability: PRO-ED; 8700 Shoal Creek Blvd., Austin, TX 78758-6897
Age Level: 0-3
Notes: Time, 3 min. approx.; Items, 41

Norm-referenced, validated language screening instrument covering the entire age range from birth to 36 months. Performance on most items may be ascertained by parental report. The scale is sensitive to various causes of speech or language delay, including mental retardation, hearing loss, dysarthria, and communicative disorders. It does not yield a specific developmental diagnosis. It is designed as a rapid, reliable screening test capable of detecting language-impaired children at the earliest possible age. Potential users of the scale include pediatricians, family practitioners, public health nurses, preschool teachers, speech pathologists, psychologists, and specialists in infant development.

13202
Electricity Test, Form A. South Carolina State Dept. of Education, Columbia, Office of Vocational Education 1983
Descriptors: *Achievement Tests; *Electricity; High Schools; *High School Students; Multiple Choice Tests; *Objective Tests; *Trade and Industrial Education
Identifiers: South Carolina
Availability: ERIC Document Reproduction Service; 7420 Fullerton Rd., Ste. 110, Springfield, VA 22153-2852 (ED234166, 68 p.)
Grade Level: 9-12
Notes: Items, 96
This achievement test was constructed by a research coordinating unit for the secondary school vocational electricity programs in South Carolina. Two other forms were prepared for the program.

13203
Electricity Test, Form B. South Carolina State Dept. of Education, Columbia, Office of Vocational Education 1983
Descriptors: *Achievement Tests; *Electricity; High Schools; *High School Students; Multiple Choice Tests; *Objective Tests; *Trade and Industrial Education
Identifiers: South Carolina
Availability: ERIC Document Reproduction Service; 7420 Fullerton Rd., Ste. 110, Springfield, VA 22153-2852 (ED234166, 68 p.)
Grade Level: 9-12
Notes: Items, 102
This achievement test was constructed by a research coordinating unit for the secondary school vocational electricity programs in South Carolina. Two other forms were prepared for the program.

13204
Electricity Test, Form C. South Carolina State Dept. of Education, Columbia, Office of Vocational Education 1983
Descriptors: *Achievement Tests; *Electricity; High Schools; *High School Students; Multiple Choice Tests; *Objective Tests; *Trade and Industrial Education
Identifiers: South Carolina
Availability: ERIC Document Reproduction Service; 7420 Fullerton Rd., Ste. 110, Springfield, VA 22153-2852 (ED234166, 68 p.)
Grade Level: 9-12
Notes: Items, 96
This achievement test was constructed by a research coordinating unit for the secondary school vocational electricity programs in South Carolina. Two other forms were prepared for the program.

13251
Grammar Test Packet. Stratton, Kenneth; Christian, George 1982
Descriptors: *Achievement Tests; Capitalization (Alphabetic); *Diagnostic Tests; *Grammar; High Schools; *High School Students; Punctuation; Sentence Structure; Syntax
Availability: Stratton-Christian Press; Box 1055, University Place Station, Des Moines, IA 50311-0055
Grade Level: 9-12
Consists of a series of diagnostic and achievement tests in grammar. Parallel diagnostic and achievement tests cover the following areas: parts of speech, parts of the sentence, joining parts of the sentence, capitalization and punctuation. There are also achievement tests on the following: nouns; pronouns; verbs; adjectives and adverbs; prepositions, conjunctions, and interjections; correct usage; variety in sentence arrangement; and a final examination on grammar and sentence construction.

13283
DANTES Subject Standardized Tests: General Anthropology. Educational Testing Service, Princeton, NJ
Descriptors: *Achievement Tests; Adults; *Adult Students; *Anthropology; Culture; *Equivalency Tests; Higher Education; Knowledge Level; Nontraditional Education; Nontraditional Students; Social Sciences; Standardized Tests
Identifiers: Defense Activity Non Traditional Education Support; DSST
Availability: Educational Testing Service; DANTES Program Office, Princeton, NJ 08540
Age Level: Adults
Notes: Time, 102 min.; Items, 66
The DANTES program is a series of secured tests administered by postsecondary institutions to grant credit by examination for education gained outside the classroom.

Examinations may be worth from 2 to 6 credit hours in a baccalaureate program, baccalaureate upper division program, or a technical program. A minimum score for credit has been established by the American Council on Education. Individual institutions administer examinations, as well as set the fees and schedules. These instruments complement the College Board's College Level Examination Program (CLEP) with several instruments in applied technology. They were originally developed for military personnel. Major areas of assessment include mathematics, social science, physical science, business, foreign language, and applied technology. For each test, a fact sheet containing the curriculum specifications of the course, a list of texts on which the test is based and statistical information are available. Qualified administrators and faculty may borrow sample tests for a period of 30 days. Tests are revised regularly, but generally the following topics commonly taught in courses on this subject are covered in this examination: anthropology as a discipline, various theoretical perspectives, physical anthropology, archaeology, nature of culture, social organization, economic organization, political organization, religion, modernization, and application of anthropology.

13284
DANTES Subject Standardized Tests: Introduction to Law Enforcement. Educational Testing Service, Princeton, NJ
Descriptors: *Achievement Tests; Adults; *Adult Students; Crime; Criminal Law; *Equivalency Tests; Higher Education; Knowledge Level; *Law Enforcement; Nontraditional Education; Nontraditional Students; Social Sciences; Standardized Tests
Identifiers: Defense Activity Non Traditional Education Support; DSST
Availability: Educational Testing Service; DANTES Program Office, Princeton, NJ 08540
Age Level: Adults
Notes: Time, 90 min. approx.; Items, 95
The DANTES program is a series of secured tests administered by postsecondary institutions to grant credit by examination for education gained outside the classroom. Examinations may be worth from 2 to 6 credit hours in a baccalaureate program, baccalaureate upper division program, or a technical program. A minimum score for credit has been established by the American Council on Education. Individual institutions administer examinations, as well as set the fees and schedules. These instruments complement the College Board's College Level Examination Program (CLEP) with several instruments in applied technology. They were originally developed for military personnel. Major areas of assessment include mathematics, social science, physical science, business, foreign language, and applied technology. For each test, a fact sheet containing the curriculum specifications of the course, a list of texts on which the test is based, and statistical information are available. Qualified administrators and faculty may borrow sample tests for a period of 30 days. Tests are revised regularly, but generally the following topics commonly taught in courses on this subject are covered in this examination: history and heritage of law enforcement, criminal justice in the U.S., contemporary police systems in the U.S., organization and management of police, police issues, constitutional law, and legal precedents.

13285
DANTES Subject Standardized Tests: Criminal Justice. Educational Testing Service, Princeton, NJ
Descriptors: *Achievement Tests; Adults; *Adult Students; Correctional Rehabilitation; *Crime; Crime Prevention; *Criminology; *Equivalency Tests; Higher Education; Knowledge Level; Nontraditional Education; Nontraditional Students; Social Sciences
Identifiers: Defense Activity Non Traditional Education Support; DSST
Availability: Educational Testing Service; DANTES Program Office, Princeton, NJ 08540
Age Level: Adults
Notes: Time, 90 min. approx.; Items, 88
The DANTES program is a series of secured tests administered by postsecondary institutions to grant credit by examination for education gained outside the classroom. Examinations may be worth from 2 to 6 credit hours in a baccalaureate program, baccalaureate upper division program, or a technical program. A minimum score for credit has been established by the American Council on Education. Individual institutions administer examinations, as well as set the fees and schedules. These instruments complement the College Board's College Level Examination Program (CLEP) with several instruments in applied technology. They were originally developed for military personnel. Major areas of assessment include mathematics, social science, physical science, business, foreign language, and applied technology. For each test, a fact sheet containing the curriculum specifications of the course, a list of texts on which the test is based, and statistical information are available. Qualified administrators and faculty may borrow sample tests for a period of 30 days. Tests are revised regularly, but generally the following topics

commonly taught in courses on this subject are covered in this examination: criminal behavior, criminal justice system, police, court system, corrections.

13286
DANTES Subject Standardized Tests: Astronomy. Educational Testing Service, Princeton, NJ
Descriptors: *Achievement Tests; Adults; *Adult Students; *Astronomy; College Science; *Equivalency Tests; Higher Education; Knowledge Level; Nontraditional Education; Nontraditional Students; Physical Sciences; Standardized Tests
Identifiers: Defense Activity Non Traditional Education Support; DSST
Availability: Educational Testing Service; DANTES Program Office, Princeton, NJ 08540
Age Level: Adults
Notes: Time, 90 min. approx.; Items, 87
The DANTES program is a series of secured tests administered by postsecondary institutions to grant credit by examination for education gained outside the classroom. Examinations may be worth from 2 to 6 credit hours in a baccalaureate program, baccalaureate upper division program, or a technical program. A minimum score for credit has been established by the American Council on Education. Individual institutions administer examinations, as well as set the fees and schedules. These instruments complement the College Board's College Level Examination Program (CLEP) with several instruments in applied technology. They were originally developed for military personnel. Major areas of assessment include mathematics, social science, physical science, business, foreign language, and applied technology. For each test, a fact sheet containing the curriculum specifications of the course, a list of texts on which the test is based, and statistical information are available. Qualified administrators and faculty may borrow sample tests for a period of 30 days. Tests are revised regularly, but generally the following topics commonly taught in courses on this subject are covered in this examination: history of astronomy; celestial mechanics, including gravitation and relativity; celestial systems; astronomical instruments; the solar system; the nature and evolution of the sun and stars; the galaxy; the universe; determining astronomical distances; life in the universe.

13288
DANTES: Principles of Physical Science I. Educational Testing Service, Princeton, NJ
Descriptors: *Achievement Tests; Adults; *Adult Students; Atomic Structure; College Science; *Equivalency Tests; Force; Higher Education; Knowledge Level; Motion; Nontraditional Education; Nontraditional Students; *Physical Sciences; Scientific Methodology
Identifiers: Defense Activity Non Traditional Education Support; DSST
Availability: Educational Testing Service; DANTES Program Office, Princeton, NJ 08540
Age Level: Adults
Notes: Time, 90 min. approx.; Items, 75
The DANTES program is a series of secured tests administered by postsecondary institutions to grant credit by examination for education gained outside the classroom. Examinations may be worth from 2 to 6 credit hours in a baccalaureate program, baccalaureate upper division program, or a technical program. A minimum score for credit has been established by the American Council on Education. Individual institutions administer examinations, as well as set the fees and schedules. These instruments complement the College Board's College Level Examination Program (CLEP) with several instruments in applied technology. They were originally developed for military personnel. Major areas of assessment include mathematics, social science, physical science, business, foreign language, and applied technology. For each test, a fact sheet containing the curriculum specifications of the course, a list of texts on which the test is based, and statistical information are available. Qualified administrators and faculty may borrow sample tests for a period of 30 days. Tests are revised regularly, but generally the following topics commonly taught in courses on this subject are covered in this examination: Newton's laws of motion, energy and momentum, thermodynamics, waves and optics, chemistry, general scientific principles or processes.

13294
DANTES Subject Standardized Tests: Principles of Financial Accounting. Educational Testing Service, Princeton, NJ
Descriptors: *Accounting; *Achievement Tests; Adults; *Adult Students; Business Administration Education; *Equivalency Tests; Higher Education; Knowledge Level; Nontraditional Education; Nontraditional Students; Standardized Tests
Identifiers: Defense Activity Non Traditional Education Support; DSST
Availability: Educational Testing Service; DANTES Program Office, Princeton, NJ 08540
Age Level: Adults
Notes: Time, 90 min. approx.; Items, 60

The DANTES program is a series of secured tests administered by postsecondary institutions to grant credit by examination for education gained outside the classroom. Examinations may be worth from 2 to 6 credit hours in a baccalaureate program, baccalaureate upper division program, or a technical program. A minimum score for credit has been established by the American Council on Education. Individual institutions administer examinations, as well as set the fees and schedules. These instruments complement the College Board's College Level Examination Program (CLEP) with several instruments in applied technology. They were originally developed for military personnel. Major areas of assessment include mathematics, social science, physical science, business, foreign language, and applied technology. For each test, a fact sheet containing the curriculum specifications of the course, a list of texts on which the test is based, and statistical information are available. Qualified administrators and faculty may borrow sample tests for a period of 30 days. Tests are revised regularly, but generally the following topics commonly taught in courses on this subject are covered in this examination: general concepts and principles; accounting cycle and account classification; transaction analysis and accounting equation; adjusting entries; merchandising transactions; internal control; current accounts; property, plant, equipment; long-term debt and interest; capital stock; retained earnings and dividends; financial statements.

13297

DANTES Subject Standardized Tests: Introduction to Business. Educational Testing Service, Princeton, NJ

Descriptors: *Achievement Tests; *Administrator Education; Adults; *Adult Students; *Business Administration Education; *Equivalency Tests; Higher Education; Introductory Courses; Knowledge Level; Nontraditional Education; Nontraditional Students; Standardized Tests

Identifiers: Defense Activity Non Traditional Education Support; DSST

Availability: Educational Testing Service; DANTES Program Office, Princeton, NJ 08540

Notes: Time, 90 min. approx.; Items, 76

The DANTES program is a series of secured tests administered by postsecondary institutions to grant credit by examination for education gained outside the classroom. Examinations may be worth from 2 to 6 credit hours in a baccalaureate program, baccalaureate upper division program, or a technical program. A minimum score for credit has been established by the American Council on Education. Individual institutions administer examinations, as well as set the fees and schedules. These instruments complement the College Board's College Level Examination Program (CLEP) with several instruments in applied technology. They were originally developed for military personnel. Major areas of assessment include mathematics, social science, physical science, business, foreign language, and applied technology. For each test, a fact sheet containing the curriculum specifications of the course, a list of texts on which the test is based, and statistical information are available. Qualified administrators and faculty may borrow sample tests for a period of 30 days. Tests are revised regularly, but generally the following topics commonly taught in courses on this subject are covered in this examination: economic issues affecting business, international business, government and business, forms of business ownership, small business ownership, entrepreneurship and franchise, management process, human resource management, production and operations, marketing management, financial management, risk management and insurance, management and information systems.

13298

DANTES Subject Standardized Tests: Risk and Insurance. Educational Testing Service, Princeton, NJ

Descriptors: *Achievement Tests; Adults; *Adult Students; *Business Administration Education; Education; *Equivalency Tests; Higher Education; *Insurance; Knowledge Level; Nontraditional Education; Nontraditional Students; Risk; Standardized Tests

Identifiers: Defense Activity Non Traditional Education Support; DSST

Availability: Educational Testing Service; DANTES Program Office, Princeton, NJ 08540

Age Level: Adults

Notes: Time, 90 min. approx.; Items, 91

The DANTES program is a series of secured tests administered by postsecondary institutions to grant credit by examination for education gained outside the classroom. Examinations may be worth from 2 to 6 credit hours in a baccalaureate program, baccalaureate upper division program, or a technical program. A minimum score for credit has been established by the American Council on Education. Individual institutions administer examinations, as well as set the fees and schedules. These instruments complement the College Board's College Level Examination Program (CLEP) with several instruments in applied technology. They were originally developed for military personnel. Major areas of assessment include mathematics, social science, physical science, business, foreign language, and applied technology. For each test, a fact sheet containing the curriculum specifications of the course, a list of

texts on which the test is based, and statistical information are available. Qualified administrators and faculty may borrow sample tests for a period of 30 days. Tests are revised regularly, but generally the following topics commonly taught in courses on this subject are covered in this examination: theory of risk, risk management, insurance concepts, the insurance industry, life insurance, health insurance, social insurance, automobile insurance, homeowners and tenants insurance, commerical lines.

13299

DANTES Subject Standardized Tests: Money and Banking. Educational Testing Service, Princeton, NJ

Descriptors: *Achievement Tests; Adults; *Adult Students; *Banking; *Business Administration Education; *Equivalency Tests; Financial Policy; Higher Education; Knowledge Level; *Monetary Systems; Nontraditional Education; Nontraditional Students; Standardized Tests

Identifiers: Defense Activity Non Traditional Education Support; DSST

Availability: Educational Testing Service; DANTES Program Office, Princeton, NJ 08540

Age Level: Adults

Notes: Time, 90 min. approx.; Items, 82

The DANTES program is a series of secured tests administered by postsecondary institutions to grant credit by examination for education gained outside the classroom. Examinations may be worth from 2 to 6 credit hours in a baccalaureate program, baccalaureate upper division program, or a technical program. A minimum score for credit has been established by the American Council on Education. Individual institutions administer examinations, as well as set the fees and schedules. These instruments complement the College Board's College Level Examination Program (CLEP) with several instruments in applied technology. They were originally developed for military personnel. Major areas of assessment include mathematics, social science, physical science, business, foreign language, and applied technology. For each test, a fact sheet containing the curriculum specifications of the course, a list of texts on which the test is based, and statistical information are available. Qualified administrators and faculty may borrow sample tests for a period of 30 days. Tests are revised regularly, but generally the following topics commonly taught in courses on this subject are covered in this examination: role and kinds of money, role of commercial banks and other intermediaries, central banking and the federal reserve system, money and macroeconomic activity, monetary policy in the U.S., the international monetary system.

13300

DANTES Subject Standardized Tests: Basic Marketing. Educational Testing Service, Princeton, NJ

Descriptors: *Achievement Tests; Adults; *Adult Students; *Business Administration Education; *Equivalency Tests; Higher Education; Knowledge Level; *Marketing; Nontraditional Education; Nontraditional Students; Public Policy; Standardized Tests

Identifiers: Defense Activity Non Traditional Education Support; DSST; Market Analysis; Market Research

Availability: Educational Testing Service; DANTES Program Office, Princeton, NJ 08540

Age Level: Adults

Notes: Time, 90 min. approx.; Items, 107

The DANTES program is a series of secured tests administered by postsecondary institutions to grant credit by examination for education gained outside the classroom. Examinations may be worth from 2 to 6 credit hours in a baccalaureate program, baccalaureate upper division program, or a technical program. A minimum score for credit has been established by the American Council on Education. Individual institutions administer examinations, as well as set the fees and schedules. These instruments complement the College Board's College Level Examination Program (CLEP) with several instruments in applied technology. They were originally developed for military personnel. Major areas of assessment include mathematics, social science, physical science, business, foreign language, and applied technology. For each test, a fact sheet containing the curriculum specifications of the course, a list of texts on which the test is based, and statistical information are available. Qualified administrators and faculty may borrow sample tests for a period of 30 days. Tests are revised regularly, but generally the following topics commonly taught in courses on this subject are covered in this examination: macro environment, planning and strategy, marketing mix, global marketing, service marketing, nonprofit marketing, marketing and public policy.

13303

DANTES Subject Standardized Tests: Fundamentals of Counseling. Educational Testing Service, Princeton, NJ

Descriptors: *Achievement Tests; Adults; *Adult Students; *Counseling Theories; *Equivalency Tests; Guidance; Higher Education; Knowledge Level; Nontraditional Education; Nontraditional Students; Standardized Tests

Identifiers: Defense Activity Non Traditional Education Support; DSST; *Guidance Education

Availability: Educational Testing Service; DANTES Program Office, Princeton, NJ 08540

Age Level: Adults

Notes: Time, 90 min. approx.; Items, 94

The DANTES program is a series of secured tests administered by postsecondary institutions to grant credit by examination for education gained outside the classroom. Examinations may be worth from 2 to 6 credit hours in a baccalaureate program, baccalaureate upper division program, or a technical program. A minimum score for credit has been established by the American Council on Education. Individual institutions administer examinations, as well as set the fees and schedules. These instruments complement the College Board's College Level Examination Program (CLEP) with several instruments in applied technology. They were originally developed for military personnel. Major areas of assessment include mathematics, social science, physical science, business, foreign language, and applied technology. For each test, a fact sheet containing the curriculum specifications of the course, a list of texts on which the test is based, and statistical information are available. Qualified administrators and faculty may borrow sample tests for a period of 30 days. Tests are revised regularly, but generally the following topics commonly taught in courses on this subject are covered in this examination: historical development, role and function of counseling, counseling relationship, theoretical approaches to counseling, counseling special populations, group approaches to counseling, career development and decision making, human development, appraisal techniques in counseling, legal and ethical issues, contemporary issues.

13310

DANTES Subject Standardized Tests: Beginning Italian I. Educational Testing Service, Princeton, NJ

Descriptors: *Achievement Tests; Adults; *Adult Students; *Equivalency Tests; Grammar; Higher Education; *Italian; Knowledge Level; Nontraditional Education; Nontraditional Students; Reading Comprehension; *Second Language Learning; Second Languages; Standardized Tests; Vocabulary

Identifiers: Defense Activity Non Traditional Education Support; DSST

Availability: Educational Testing Service; DANTES Program Office, Princeton, NJ 08540

Age Level: Adults

Notes: Time, 90 min. approx.; Items, 119

The DANTES program is a series of secured tests administered by postsecondary institutions to grant credit by examination for education gained outside the classroom. Examinations may be worth from 2 to 6 credit hours in a baccalaureate program, baccalaureate upper division program, or a technical program. A minimum score for credit has been established by the American Council on Education. Individual institutions administer examinations, as well as set the fees and schedules. These instruments complement the College Board's College Level Examination Program (CLEP) with several instruments in applied technology. They were originally developed for military personnel. Major areas of assessment include mathematics, social science, physical science, business, foreign language, and applied technology. For each test, a fact sheet containing the curriculum specifications of the course, a list of texts on which the test is based and statistical information are available. Qualified administrators and faculty may borrow sample tests for a period of 30 days. Tests are revised regularly, but generally the following topics commonly taught in courses on this subject are covered in this examination: vocabulary, grammar, listening comprehension, structure and vocabulary, reading comprehension.

13312

DANTES Subject Standardized Tests: Basic Automotive Service. Educational Testing Service, Princeton, NJ

Descriptors: *Achievement Tests; Adults; *Adult Students; *Auto Mechanics; Engines; *Equivalency Tests; Higher Education; Knowledge Level; *Mechanics (Process); Motor Vehicles; Nontraditional Education; Nontraditional Students; Standardized Tests; Technical Education

Identifiers: Defense Activity Non Traditional Education Support; DSST

Availability: Educational Testing Service; DANTES Program Office, Princeton, NJ 08540

Age Level: Adults

Notes: Time, 90 min. approx.; Items, 94

The DANTES program is a series of secured tests administered by postsecondary institutions to grant credit by examination for education gained outside the classroom. Examinations may be worth from 2 to 6 credit hours in a baccalaureate program, baccalaureate upper division program, or a technical program. A minimum score for credit has been established by the American Council on Education. Individual institutions administer examinations, as well as set the fees and schedules. These instruments complement the College Board's College Level Examination Program (CLEP) with several instruments in applied technology. They were originally developed for military personnel. Major areas of assessment include mathematics, social science, physical science, business, foreign language, and applied technology. For each test, a fact sheet containing the curriculum specifications of the course, a list of texts on which the test is based, and statistical information are available. Qualified administrators and faculty may borrow sample tests for a period of 30 days. Tests are revised regularly, but generally the following topics commonly taught in courses on this subject are covered in this examination: routine maintenance, engine lubrication, brakes, cooling system, fuel system, exhaust system, starting and charging systems, drive and suspension, emission control system, tires, engine fundamentals.

13313
DANTES Subject Standardized Tests: Automotive Electrical/Electronics. Educational Testing Service, Princeton, NJ
Descriptors: *Achievement Tests; Adults; *Adult Students; *Auto Mechanics; Engines; *Equivalency Tests; Higher Education; Knowledge Level; *Mechanics (Process); Nontraditional Education; Nontraditional Students; Power Technology; Standardized Tests; Technical Education
Identifiers: Defense Activity Non Traditional Education Support; DSST
Availability: Educational Testing Service; DANTES Program Office, Princeton, NJ 08540
Age Level: Adults
Notes: Time, 90 min. approx.; Items, 94

The DANTES program is a series of secured tests administered by postsecondary institutions to grant credit by examination for education gained outside the classroom. Examinations may be worth from 2 to 6 credit hours in a baccalaureate program, baccalaureate upper division program, or a technical program. A minimum score for credit has been established by the American Council on Education. Individual institutions administer examinations, as well as set the fees and schedules. These instruments complement the College Board's College Level Examination Program (CLEP) with several instruments in applied technology. They were originally developed for military personnel. Major areas of assessment include mathematics, social science, physical science, business, foreign language, and applied technology. For each test, a fact sheet containing the curriculum specifications of the course, a list of texts on which the test is based, and statistical information are available. Qualified administrators and faculty may borrow sample tests for a period of 30 days. Tests are revised regularly, but generally the following topics commonly taught in courses on this subject are covered in this examination: basic electricity and wiring diagrams, batteries, charging system, starting system, electric motor principles and accessories, ignition system, basic electronics.

13314
DANTES Subject Standardized Tests: Introduction to Carpentry. Educational Testing Service, Princeton, NJ
Descriptors: *Achievement Tests; Adults; *Adult Students; *Carpentry; Construction (Process); *Equivalency Tests; Higher Education; Knowledge Level; Nontraditional Education; Nontraditional Students; Standardized Tests; Technical Education
Identifiers: Defense Activity Non Traditional Education Support; DSST
Availability: Educational Testing Service; DANTES Program Office, Princeton, NJ 08540
Age Level: Adults
Notes: Time, 90 min. approx.; Items, 100

The DANTES program is a series of secured tests administered by postsecondary institutions to grant credit by examination for education gained outside the classroom. Examinations may be worth from 2 to 6 credit hours in a baccalaureate program, baccalaureate upper division program, or a technical program. A minimum score for credit has been established by the American Council on Education. Individual institutions administer examinations, as well as set the fees and schedules. These instruments complement the College Board's College Level Examination Program (CLEP) with several instruments in applied technology. They were originally developed for military personnel. Major areas of assessment include mathematics, social science, physical science, business, foreign language, and applied technology. For each test, a fact sheet containing the curriculum specifications of the course, a list of texts on which the test is based, and statistical information are available. Qualified administrators and faculty may borrow sample tests for a period of 30 days. Tests are revised regularly, but generally the following topics commonly taught in courses on this subject are covered in this examination: building materials; job site and equipment; building design and site planning; leveling instruments; foundations; framing methods, framing floors, walls, ceilings; roof framing; completing the exterior; energy conservation and moisture control; completing the interior; stairway construction.

13315
DANTES Subject Standardized Tests: Basic Technical Drafting. Educational Testing Service, Princeton, NJ
Descriptors: *Achievement Tests; Adults; *Adult Students; Drafting; *Equivalency Tests; *Graphic Arts; Higher Education; Knowledge Level; Nontraditional Education; Nontraditional Students; Standardized Tests; Technical Education; *Technical Illustration
Identifiers: Defense Activity Non Traditional Education Support; DSST
Availability: Educational Testing Service; DANTES Program Office, Princeton, NJ 08540
Age Level: Adults
Notes: Time, 90 min. approx.; Items, 35

The DANTES program is a series of secured tests administered by postsecondary institutions to grant credit by examination for education gained outside the classroom. Examinations may be worth from 2 to 6 credit hours in a baccalaureate program, baccalaureate upper division program, or a technical program. A minimum score for credit has been established by the American Council on Education. Individual institutions administer examinations, as well as set the fees and schedules. These instruments complement the College Board's College Level Examination Program (CLEP) with several instruments in applied technology. They were originally developed for military personnel. Major areas of assessment include mathematics, social science, physical science, business, foreign language, and applied technology. For each test, a fact sheet containing the curriculum specifications of the course, a list of texts on which the test is based, and statistical information are available. Qualified administrators and faculty may borrow sample tests for a period of 30 days. Tests are revised regularly, but generally the following topics commonly taught in courses on this subject are covered in this examination: freehand technical sketching, lettering, geometry in drafting, drawing with instruments, pictorial drawing, multi-view drawing, sectioning, auxiliaries, fasteners, dimensioning and tolerancing, reproductive processes.

13318
DANTES Subject Standardized Tests: Electric Circuits. Educational Testing Service, Princeton, NJ
Descriptors: *Achievement Tests; Adults; *Adult Students; *Electric Circuits; *Electronics; *Equivalency Tests; Higher Education; Knowledge Level; Nontraditional Education; Nontraditional Students; Standardized Tests; Technical Education
Identifiers: Defense Activity Non Traditional Education Support; DSST; *Magnetism
Availability: Educational Testing Service; DANTES Program Office, Princeton, NJ 08540
Age Level: Adults
Notes: Time, 90 min. approx.; Items, 66

The DANTES program is a series of secured tests administered by postsecondary institutions to grant credit by examination for education gained outside the classroom. Examinations may be worth from 2 to 6 credit hours in a baccalaureate program, baccalaureate upper division program, or a technical program. A minimum score for credit has been established by the American Council on Education. Individual institutions administer examinations, as well as set the fees and schedules. These instruments complement the College Board's College Level Examination Program (CLEP) with several instruments in applied technology. They were originally developed for military personnel. Major areas of assessment include mathematics, social science, physical science, business, foreign language, and applied technology. For each test, a fact sheet containing the curriculum specifications of the course, a list of texts on which the test is based, and statistical information are available. Qualified administrators and faculty may borrow sample tests for a period of 30 days. Tests are revised regularly, but generally the following topics commonly taught in courses on this subject are covered in this examination: electrical quantities and Ohm's Law, resistors, wires, sources, parallel and DC circuits, energy storing devices, alternating voltage and current, parallel and AC circuits, network analysis, resonance, DC and AC instruments.

13321
DANTES Subject Standardized Tests: Principles of Electronic Communication Systems. Educational Testing Service, Princeton, NJ
Descriptors: *Achievement Tests; Adults; *Adult Students; Electric Circuits; *Electricity; *Equivalency Tests; Higher Education; Knowledge Level; Nontraditional Education; Nontraditional Students; *Radio; Standardized Tests; Technical Education
Identifiers: Defense Activity Non Traditional Education Support; DSST; Magnetism
Availability: Educational Testing Service; DANTES Program Office, Princeton, NJ 08540
Age Level: Adults
Notes: Time, 90 min. approx.; Items, 67

The DANTES program is a series of secured tests administered by postsecondary institutions to grant credit by examination for education gained outside the classroom. Examinations may be worth from 2 to 6 credit hours in a baccalaureate program, baccalaureate upper division program, or a technical program. A minimum score for credit has been established by the American Council on Education. Individual institutions administer examinations, as well as set the fees and schedules. These instruments complement the College Board's College Level Examination Program (CLEP) with several instruments in applied technology. They were originally developed for military personnel. Major areas of assessment include mathematics, social science, physical science, business, foreign language, and applied technology. For each test, a fact sheet containing the curriculum specifications of the course, a list of texts on which the test is based, and statistical information are available. Qualified administrators and faculty may borrow sample tests for a period of 30 days. Tests are revised regularly, but generally the following topics commonly taught in courses on this subject are covered in this examination: concepts in electronics, information transmission, modulation theory and techniques, data transmission, and wave propagation.

13323
DANTES Subject Standardized Tests: Television Theory and Circuitry. Educational Testing Service, Princeton, NJ
Descriptors: *Achievement Tests; Adults; *Adult Students; Appliance Repair; *Equivalency Tests; Higher Education; Knowledge Level; Nontraditional Education; Nontraditional Students; Standardized Tests; Technical Education; *Television; *Television Radio Repairers
Identifiers: Defense Activity Non Traditional Education Support; DSST
Availability: Educational Testing Service; DANTES Program Office, Princeton, NJ 08540
Age Level: Adults
Notes: Time, 90 min. approx.; Items, 80

The DANTES program is a series of secured tests administered by postsecondary institutions to grant credit by examination for education gained outside the classroom. Examinations may be worth from 2 to 6 credit hours in a baccalaureate program, baccalaureate upper division program, or a technical program. A minimum score for credit has been established by the American Council on Education. Individual institutions administer examinations, as well as set the fees and schedules. These instruments complement the College Board's College Level Examination Program (CLEP) with several instruments in applied technology. They were originally developed for military personnel. Major areas of assessment include mathematics, social science, physical science, business, foreign language, and applied technology. For each test, a fact sheet containing the curriculum specifications of the course, a list of texts on which the test is based, and statistical information are available. Qualified administrators and faculty may borrow sample tests for a period of 30 days. Tests are revised regularly, but generally the following topics commonly taught in courses on this subject are covered in this examination: theory and practice, television receiver circuits, video tape recorders and disk players, cable and satellite television.

13327
Bader Reading and Language Inventory. Bader, Lois A. 1983
Subtests: Word Recognition Lists; Supplemental Word Lists; Graded Reading Passages; Phonics and Word Analysis Tests; Spelling Tests; Cloze Tests; Visual Discrimination Tests; Auditory Discrimination Test; Unfinished Sentences; Arithmetic Test, Oral Language; Written Language
Descriptors: Achievement Tests; *Adult Reading Programs; Arithmetic; Auditory Discrimination; Cloze Procedure; *Diagnostic Tests; *Elementary School Students; Elementary Secondary Education; Language Skills; Oral Language; Phonics; Reading Achievement; Reading Comprehension; *Reading Diagnosis; Reading Difficulties; *Secondary School Students; Spelling; Student Placement; Visual Discrimination; Word Recognition
Availability: Macmillan Publishing Co.; 866 Third Ave., New York, NY 10022
Grade Level: K-12

This inventory was constructed for use by reading specialists, resource teachers, and classroom teachers. The graded passages, the major section of the battery, were designed to determine appropriate placement of students in instructional materials. Because students experiencing difficulty in learning to read may have problems in other areas, several informal tests are provided to assess the reader's needs and level. Three sets of reading passages have been constructed for each level. The content of the first set has been adapted from the kinds of materials used in basals on the primary levels and content-area materials on the upper levels for children. Another set has been designed for use with children, adolescents, or adults, and the third set, written on a primary level, is intended for use with adults who are just beginning to read.

13341
Criterion Referenced Curriculum: Reading Assessment.   Stephens, Thomas M. 1982
Descriptors: *Achievement Tests; Auditory Discrimination; *Criterion Referenced Tests; Diagnostic Tests; *Elementary School Students; *Learning Disabilities; Oral Reading; Reading Comprehension; *Reading Diagnosis; Reading Improvement; *Remedial Programs; *Special Education; Structural Analysis (Linguistics)
Identifiers: CRC
Availability: The Psychological Corp.; 555 Academic Ct., San Antonio, TX 78204-0952
Grade Level: K-6
Notes: Items, 267

The Criterion-Referenced Curriculum is a comprehensive system of criterion-referenced tests and teaching strategies organized by objective sequences in reading. It is designed specifically for remedial and special education classes K-6 and includes virtually all of the basic reading objectives which normally achieving students are expected to master during the first 3 to 4 years of elementary school. Major categories in reading include auditory discrimination, sight words, phonic analysis, structural analysis, oral reading, and comprehension.

13342
Criterion Referenced Curriculum: Mathematics Assessment.   Stephens, Thomas M. 1982
Descriptors: *Achievement Tests; Arithmetic; *Criterion Referenced Tests; *Diagnostic Tests; Educational Strategies; *Elementary School Mathematics; *Elementary School Students; *Learning Disabilities; *Mastery Learning; Metric System; Numbers; *Remedial Programs; Sequential Approach; *Special Education
Identifiers: CRC
Availability: The Psychological Corp.; 555 Academic Ct., San Antonio, TX 78204-0952
Grade Level: K-6
Notes: Items, 378

The Criterion-Referenced Curriculum is a comprehensive system of criterion-referenced tests and teaching strategies organized by objective sequences in mathematics. It is designed specifically for remedial and special education classes K-6 and includes virtually all of the basic mathematics objectives which normally achieving students are expected to master during the first 3 to 4 years of elementary school. Major categories in mathematics include numbers, numerals and numeration systems, operations and their properties, sets, measurements, and metric skills and concepts.

13343
Educational Development Series, Revised. Level 10A.   Anderhalter, O. F.; And Others 1984
Descriptors: Abstract Reasoning; *Achievement Tests; Basic Skills; *Cognitive Tests; Elementary School Mathematics; *Kindergarten Children; Language Arts; Language Processing; Mathematics Achievement; Primary Education; Reading Achievement
Identifiers: EDSeries; Test Batteries
Availability: Scholastic Testing Service; 480 Meyer Rd., Bensenville, IL 60106
Grade Level: K
Notes: Time, 170 min.

Test battery comprises ability and achievement tests, as well as reports of school plans, career plans, and interests. Ability measures cover nonverbal and verbal cognitive skills. Achievement tests cover reading, language arts, mathematics, reference skills, science, and social studies. Provides a single report for all areas and permits teacher, counselor, or administrator to examine and evaluate each student from broadest possible perspective, while allowing for comparisons among students. Test results may be analyzed to identify students who may need counseling because of conflicts among achievement, ability, and school/career plans. Several battery formats are available: complete battery, core achievement battery, basic skills battery, or cognitive and basic skills battery. Level 10A test should be administered in 5 sessions over a one-week period.

13344
Educational Development Series, Revised. Level 11A.   Anderhalter, O. F.; And Others 1984
Descriptors: Abstract Reasoning; *Achievement Tests; Basic Skills; *Cognitive Tests; Elementary School Mathematics; *Elementary School Students; *Grade 1; *Grade 2; Language Arts; Language Processing; Mathematics Achievement; Primary Education; Reading Achievement; Sciences; Social Studies; Student Interests; Study Skills
Identifiers: EDSeries; Test Batteries
Availability: Scholastic Testing Service; 480 Meyer Rd., Bensenville, IL 60106
Grade Level: 1-2

Test battery comprises ability and achievement tests, as well as reports of school plans, career plans, and interests. Ability measures cover nonverbal and verbal cognitive

skills. Achievement tests cover reading, language arts, mathematics, reference skills, science, and social studies. Provides a single report for all areas and permits teacher, counselor, or administrator to examine and evaluate each student from broadest possible perspective, while allowing for comparisons among students. Test results may be analyzed to identify students who may need counseling because of conflicts among achievement, ability, and school/career plans. Several battery formats are available: complete battery, core achievement battery, basic skills battery, or cognitive and basic skills battery.

13345
Educational Development Series, Revised. Level 12A.   Anderhalter, O. F.; And Others 1984
Descriptors: Abstract Reasoning; *Achievement Tests; Basic Skills; *Cognitive Tests; Elementary School Mathematics; *Elementary School Students; *Grade 2; *Grade 3; Language Arts; Language Processing; Mathematics Achievement; Primary Education; Reading Achievement; Sciences; Social Studies; Student Interests; Study Skills
Identifiers: EDSeries; Test Batteries
Availability: Scholastic Testing Service; 480 Meyer Rd., Bensenville, IL 60106
Grade Level: 2-3
Notes: Items, 308

Test battery comprises ability and achievement tests, as well as reports of school plans, career plans, and interests. Ability measures cover nonverbal and verbal cognitive skills. Achievement tests cover reading, language arts, mathematics, reference skills, science, and social studies. Provides a single report for all areas and permits teacher, counselor, or administrator to examine and evaluate each student from broadest possible perspective, while allowing for comparisons among students. Test results may be analyzed to identify students who may need counseling because of conflicts among achievement, ability, and school/career plans. Several battery formats are available: complete battery, core achievement battery, basic skills battery, or cognitive and basic skills battery.

13346
Educational Development Series, Revised. Level 13A.   Anderhalter, O. F.; And Others 1984
Descriptors: Abstract Reasoning; *Achievement Tests; Basic Skills; *Cognitive Tests; Elementary Education; Elementary School Mathematics; *Elementary School Students; *Grade 3; *Grade 4; Language Arts; Language Processing; Mathematics Achievement; Reading Achievement; Sciences; Social Studies; Student Interests; Study Skills
Identifiers: EDSeries; Test Batteries
Availability: Scholastic Testing Service; 480 Meyer Rd., Bensenville, IL 60106
Grade Level: 3-4
Notes: Items, 388

Test battery comprises ability and achievement tests, as well as reports of school plans, career plans, and interests. Ability measures cover nonverbal and verbal cognitive skills. Achievement tests cover reading, language arts, mathematics, reference skills, science, and social studies. Provides a single report for all areas and permits teacher, counselor, or administrator to examine and evaluate each student from broadest possible perspective, while allowing for comparisons among students. Test results may be analyzed to identify students who may need counseling because of conflicts among achievement, ability, and school/career plans. Several battery formats are available: complete battery, core achievement battery, basic skills battery, or cognitive and basic skills battery.

13347
Educational Development Series, Revised. Level 14A.   Anderhalter, O. F.; And Others 1984
Descriptors: Abstract Reasoning; *Achievement Tests; Basic Skills; *Cognitive Tests; Educational Attainment; Elementary School Mathematics; *Elementary School Students; *Grade 4; *Grade 5; Interest Inventories; Intermediate Grades; Language Arts; Language Processing; Mathematics Achievement; Reading Achievement; Sciences; Social Studies; Student Interests; Study Skills; Vocational Interests
Identifiers: EDSeries; Test Batteries
Availability: Scholastic Testing Service; 480 Meyer Rd., Bensenville, IL 60106
Grade Level: 4-5
Notes: Time, 355 min.; Items, 503

Test battery comprises ability and achievement tests, as well as reports of school plans, career plans, and interests. Ability measures cover nonverbal and verbal cognitive skills. Achievement tests cover reading, language arts, mathematics, reference skills, science, and social studies. Provides a single report for all areas and permits teacher, counselor, or administrator to examine and evaluate each student from broadest possible perspective, while allowing for comparisons among students. Test results may be analyzed to identify students who may need counseling because of conflicts among achievement, ability, and school/career plans. Several battery formats are available: com-

plete battery, core achievement battery, basic skills battery, or cognitive and basic skills battery. Test battery should be administered over 3 sessions.

13348
Educational Development Series, Revised. Level 15A.   Anderhalter, O. F.; And Others 1984
Descriptors: Abstract Reasoning; *Achievement Tests; Basic Skills; *Cognitive Tests; Educational Attainment; Elementary School Mathematics; *Elementary School Students; *Grade 5; *Grade 6; Interest Inventories; Intermediate Grades; Language Arts; Language Processing; Mathematics Achievement; Reading Achievement; Sciences; Social Studies; Student Interests; Study Skills; Vocational Interests
Identifiers: EDSeries; Test Batteries
Availability: Scholastic Testing Service; 480 Meyer Rd., Bensenville, IL 60106
Grade Level: 5-6
Notes: Time, 355 min.; Items, 513

Test battery comprises ability and achievement tests, as well as reports of school plans, career plans, and interests. Ability measures cover nonverbal and verbal cognitive skills. Achievement tests cover reading, language arts, mathematics, reference skills, science, and social studies. Provides a single report for all areas and permits teacher, counselor, or administrator to examine and evaluate each student from broadest possible perspective, while allowing for comparisons among students. Test results may be analyzed to identify students who may need counseling because of conflicts among achievement, ability, and school/career plans. Several battery formats are available: complete battery, core achievement battery, basic skills battery, or cognitive and basic skills battery. Test battery should be administered in 3 sessions.

13349
Educational Development Series, Revised. Level 15B.   Anderhalter, O. F.; And Others 1984
Descriptors: Abstract Reasoning; *Achievement Tests; Basic Skills; *Cognitive Tests; Educational Attainment; Elementary School Mathematics; *Elementary School Students; *Grade 6; *Grade 7; Interest Inventories; Intermediate Grades; Junior High Schools; Language Arts; Language Processing; Mathematics Achievement; Reading Achievement; Sciences; Secondary School Mathematics; Social Studies; Student Interests; Study Skills; Vocational Interests
Identifiers: EDSeries; Test Batteries
Availability: Scholastic Testing Service; 480 Meyer Rd., Bensenville, IL 60106
Grade Level: 6-7
Notes: Time, 355 min.; Items, 513

Test battery comprises ability and achievement tests, as well as reports of school plans, career plans, and interests. Ability measures cover nonverbal and verbal cognitive skills. Achievement tests cover reading, language arts, mathematics, reference skills, science, and social studies. Provides a single report for all areas and permits teacher, counselor, or administrator to examine and evaluate each student from broadest possible perspective, while allowing for comparisons among students. Test results may be analyzed to identify students who may need counseling because of conflicts among achievement, ability, and school/career plans. Several battery formats are available: complete battery, core achievement battery, basic skills battery, or cognitive and basic skills battery. Test battery should be administrered in 3 sessions.

13350
Educational Development Series, Revised. Level 16A.   Anderhalter, O. F.; And Others 1984
Descriptors: Abstract Reasoning; *Achievement Tests; Basic Skills; *Cognitive Tests; Educational Attainment; *Grade 7; *Grade 8; Interest Inventories; Junior High Schools; *Junior High School Students; Language Arts; Language Processing; Mathematics Achievement; Reading Achievement; Sciences; Secondary School Mathematics; Social Studies; Student Interests; Study Skills; Vocational Interests
Identifiers: EDSeries; Test Batteries
Availability: Scholastic Testing Service; 480 Meyer Rd., Bensenville, IL 60106
Grade Level: 7-8
Notes: Items, 513

Test battery comprises ability and achievement tests, as well as reports of school plans, career plans, and interests. Ability measures cover nonverbal and verbal cognitive skills. Achievement tests cover reading, language arts, mathematics, reference skills, science, and social studies. Provides a single report for all areas and permits teacher, counselor, or administrator to examine and evaluate each student from broadest possible perspective, while allowing for comparisons among students. Test results may be analyzed to identify students who may need counseling because of conflicts among achievement, ability, and school/career plans. Several battery formats are available: complete battery, core achievement battery, basic skills battery, or cognitive and basic skills battery.

13351
Educational Development Series, Revised. Level 16B. Anderhalter, O. F.; And Others 1984
Descriptors: Abstract Reasoning; *Achievement Tests; Basic Skills; *Cognitive Tests; Educational Attainment; *Grade 8; *Grade 9; Interest Inventories; Junior High Schools; *Junior High School Students; Language Arts; Language Processing; Mathematics Achievement; Reading Achievement; Sciences; Secondary School Mathematics; Social Studies; Student Interests; Study Skills; Vocational Interests
Identifiers: EDSeries; Test Batteries
Availability: Scholastic Testing Service; 480 Meyer Rd., Bensenville, IL 60106
Grade Level: 8-9
Notes: Items, 513

Test battery comprises ability and achievement tests, as well as reports of school plans, career plans, and interests. Ability measures cover nonverbal and verbal cognitive skills. Achievement tests cover reading, language arts, mathematics, reference skills, science, and social studies. Provides a single report for all areas and permits teacher, counselor, or administrator to examine and evaluate each student from broadest possible perspective, while allowing for comparisons among students. Test results may be analyzed to identify students who may need counseling because of conflicts among achievement, ability, and school/career plans. Several battery formats are available: complete battery, core achievement battery, basic skills battery, or cognitive and basic skills battery.

13352
Educational Development Series, Revised. Level 17A. Anderhalter, O. F.; And Others 1984
Descriptors: Abstract Reasoning; *Achievement Tests; Basic Skills; *Cognitive Tests; Educational Attainment; *Grade 9; High Schools; *High School Students; Interest Inventories; Language Arts; Language Processing; Mathematics Achievement; Reading Achievement; Sciences; Secondary School Mathematics; Social Studies; Student Interests; Study Skills; Vocational Interests
Identifiers: EDSeries; Test Batteries
Availability: Scholastic Testing Service; 480 Meyer Rd., Bensenville, IL 60106
Grade Level: 9
Notes: Items, 523

Test battery comprises ability and achievement tests, as well as reports of school plans, career plans, and interests. Ability measures cover nonverbal and verbal cognitive skills. Achievement tests cover reading, language arts, mathematics, reference skills, science, and social studies. Provides a single report for all areas and permits teacher, counselor, or administrator to examine and evaluate each student from broadest possible perspective, while allowing for comparisons among students. Test results may be analyzed to identify students who may need counseling because of conflicts among achievement, ability, and school/career plans. Several battery formats are available: complete battery, core achievement battery, basic skills battery, or cognitive and basic skills battery.

13353
Educational Development Series, Revised. Level 17B. Anderhalter, O. F.; And Others 1984
Descriptors: Abstract Reasoning; *Achievement Tests; Basic Skills; *Cognitive Tests; Educational Attainment; *Grade 10; High Schools; *High School Students; Interest Inventories; Language Arts; Language Processing; Mathematics Achievement; Reading Achievement; Sciences; Secondary School Mathematics; Social Studies; Student Interests; Study Skills; Vocational Interests
Identifiers: EDSeries; Test Batteries
Availability: Scholastic Testing Service; 480 Meyer Rd., Bensenville, IL 60106
Grade Level: 10
Notes: Items, 523

Test battery comprises ability and achievement tests, as well as reports of school plans, career plans, and interests. Ability measures cover nonverbal and verbal cognitive skills. Achievement tests cover reading, language arts, mathematics, reference skills, science, and social studies. Provides a single report for all areas and permits teacher, counselor, or administrator to examine and evaluate each student from broadest possible perspective, while allowing for comparisons among students. Test results may be analyzed to identify students who may need counseling because of conflicts among achievement, ability, and school/career plans. Several battery formats are available: complete battery, core achievement battery, basic skills battery, or cognitive and basic skills battery.

13354
Educational Development Series, Revised. Level 18A. Anderhalter, O. F.; And Others 1984
Descriptors: Abstract Reasoning; *Achievement Tests; Basic Skills; *Cognitive Tests; Educational Attainment; *Grade 11; High Schools; *High School Students; Interest Inventories; Language Arts; Language Processing; Mathematics Achievement; Reading Achievement; Sciences; Secondary School Mathematics; Social Studies; Student Interests; Study Skills; Vocational Interests
Identifiers: EDSeries; Test Batteries
Availability: Scholastic Testing Service; 480 Meyer Rd., Bensenville, IL 60106
Grade Level: 11
Notes: Time, 360 min.; Items, 523

Test battery comprises ability and achievement tests, as well as reports of school plans, career plans, and interests. Ability measures cover nonverbal and verbal cognitive skills. Achievement tests cover reading, language arts, mathematics, reference skills, science, and social studies. Provides a single report for all areas and permits teacher, counselor, or administrator to examine and evaluate each student from broadest possible perspective, while allowing for comparisons among students. Test results may be analyzed to identify students who may need counseling because of conflicts among achievement, ability, and school/career plans. Several battery formats are available: complete battery, core achievement battery, basic skills battery, or cognitive and basic skills battery. Test battery should be administered over 3 sessions.

13355
Educational Development Series, Revised. Level 18B. Anderhalter, O. F.; And Others 1984
Descriptors: Abstract Reasoning; *Achievement Tests; Basic Skills; *Cognitive Tests; Educational Attainment; *Grade 12; High Schools; *High School Students; Interest Inventories; Language Arts; Language Processing; Mathematics Achievement; Reading Achievement; Sciences; Secondary School Mathematics; Social Studies; Student Interests; Study Skills; Vocational Interests
Identifiers: EDSeries; Test Batteries
Availability: Scholastic Testing Service; 480 Meyer Rd., Bensenville, IL 60106
Grade Level: 12
Notes: Time, 360 min.; Items, 523

Test battery comprises ability and achievement tests, as well as reports of school plans, career plans, and interests. Ability measures cover nonverbal and verbal cognitive skills. Achievement tests cover reading, language arts, mathematics, reference skills, science, and social studies. Provides a single report for all areas and permits teacher, counselor, or administrator to examine and evaluate each student from broadest possible perspective, while allowing for comparisons among students. Test results may be analyzed to identify students who may need counseling because of conflicts among achievement, ability, and school/career plans. Several battery formats are available: complete battery, core achievement battery, basic skills battery, or cognitive and basic skills battery. Test battery should be administered over 3 sessions.

13360
Screening Kit of Language Development. Bliss, Lynn S.; Allen, Doris V. 1983
Subtests: Vocabulary Comprehension; Story Completion; Sentence Comprehension; Paired Sentence Repetition with Pictures; Individual Sentence Repetition with Pictures; Individual Sentence Repetition without Pictures; Comprehension of Commands
Descriptors: *Black Dialects; Individual Testing; *Language Acquisition; *Language Handicaps; *Preschool Children; *Screening Tests; *Standard Spoken Usage
Identifiers: SKOLD
Availability: Slosson Educational Publications; P.O. Box 280, East Aurora, NY 14052
Age Level: 2-4
Notes: Time, 15 min.

Developed as a standardized test to meet the needs of speech-language pathologists and paraprofessionals as a screening test to identify children with language impairments. The manual contains normative data for preschool children who speak African-American English or Standard English so that test administrators can avoid misidentifying a nonstandard speaker as one with language impairments. The battery consists of 6 subtests to screen Standard-English-speaking children at 30 to 36 months, 37 to 42 months, and 43 to 48 months and equivalent subtests for the same age children whose responses are in African-American English. There are approximately 35 items in each subtest.

13372
Vocational Competency Measures: Hotel (Motel) Front Office. American Institutes for Research, Palo Alto, CA 1983
Descriptors: *Achievement Tests; Adolescents; Adults; Competence; *Entry Workers; *Hospitality Occupations; *Hotels; Knowledge Level; Office Occupations; *Personnel Selection; *Postsecondary Education; Rating Scales; Screening Tests; Secondary Education; *Secondary School Students; Student Evaluation; *Vocational Education; *Work Sample Tests
Identifiers: Test Batteries; *Work Habits
Availability: American Association for Vocational Instructional Materials; 120 Driftmier Engineering Center, Athens, GA 30602
Age Level: 12-64

Designed to help teachers and administrators at secondary and postsecondary levels assess and improve competencies of their students in vocational education, to identify areas for program improvement, and to inform prospective employers of student vocational competencies. Also useful for employers to screen and select new employees and to assess training needs of present employees. Test package consists of a 2-part multiple-choice job information test, each part taking about 45 minutes to complete; a performance test consisting of tests that represent tasks similar to those performed on the job; and a work habits inventory for assessing nontechnical, work-related attitudes and behavior. Intended for persons completing secondary or postsecondary level programs to train them for entry-level, front office jobs in motels or hotels. Not designed for those completing 4-year college programs for direct entry nto management positions. Job Information test section covers general front office duties, processing guests, cashier-accounting duties. The 4 tasks in the performance test include completing a hand transcript, checking guests in and out, completing an occupancy forecast sheet, collecting problem accounts.

13385
Preschool Screening System: Vietnamese Adaptation. Hainsworth, Peter K.; Hainsworth, Marian L. 1981
Subtests: Movement Patterns; Clapping; Body Directions; Finger Patterns; Copy Shapes; Visual Integration; Spatial Directions; Draw a Person; Serial Counting; Phrases; Sentences; Verbal Reasoning; General Information; Quantity Recognition; Read Shapes
Descriptors: Bilingual Education; Bilingual Teachers; Human Body; *Individual Testing; *Kindergarten Children; Language Proficiency; *Learning Readiness; *Preschool Children; Preschool Education; Psychomotor Skills; *Screening Tests; *Vietnamese
Identifiers: PSS
Availability: Early Recognition Intervention Systems; Box 1635, Pawtucket, RI 02862
Age Level: 2-6
Notes: Time, 20 min. approx.

This foreign language adaptation of the Preschool Screening System is an individually administered screening test of learning efficiency. It is used as an initial screening device for identifying the special learning needs of preschool or kindergarten children. Primary use is to quickly survey learning skills of children entering nursery school or kindergarten so that curriculum can be adapted to their needs. Can also serve as part of a more detailed assessment of individual children. May be group administered by having a team of several adults meet with 8 children at a time. Test assesses body awareness, visual-perceptual-motor skills, and language skills. Subtests may be combined to yield a short form or nonlanguage form. Several subtests may also be compiled to yield imitation and learned skills scores. English language manual is necessary for administration. This instrument is a Vietnamese adaptation of the Preschool Screening System (TC012681).

13386
Preschool Screening System: Spanish Adaptation. Hainsworth, Peter K.; Hainsworth, Marian L. 1981
Subtests: Movement Patterns; Clapping; Body Directions; Finger Patterns; Copy Shapes; Visual Integration; Spatial Directions; Draw a Person; Serial Counting; Phrases; Sentences; Verbal Reasoning; General Information; Quantity Recognition; Read Shapes
Descriptors: Bilingual Education; Bilingual Teachers; Human Body; *Individual Testing; *Kindergarten Children; Language Proficiency; *Learning Readiness; *Preschool Children; Preschool Education; Psychomotor Skills; *Screening Tests; *Spanish
Identifiers: PSS
Availability: Early Recognition Intervention Systems; Box 1635, Pawtucket, RI 02862
Age Level: 2-6
Notes: Time, 20 min. approx.

This foreign language adaptation of the Preschool Screening System is an individually administered screening test of learning efficiency. It is used as an initial screening device for identifying the special learning needs of preschool or kindergarten children. Primary use is to quickly survey learning skills of children entering nursery school or kindergarten so that curriculum can be adapted to their needs. Can also serve as part of a more detailed assessment of individual children. May be group administered by having a team of several adults meet with 8 children at a time. Test assesses body awareness, visual-perceptual-motor skills, and language skills. Subtests may be combined to yield a short form or nonlanguage form. Several subtests may also be compiled to yield imitation and learned skills scores. English language manual is necessary for administration. This instrument is a Spanish adaptation of the Preschool Screening System (TC012681).

13387
Preschool Screening System: Portuguese Adaptation. Hainsworth, Peter K.; Hainsworth, Marian L. 1981
Subtests: Movement Patterns; Clapping; Body Directions; Finger Patterns; Copy Shapes; Visual Integration; Spatial Directions; Draw a Person; Serial Counting; Phrases; Sentences; Verbal Reasoning; General Information; Quantity Recognition; Read Shapes
Descriptors: Bilingual Education; Bilingual Teachers; Human Body; *Individual Testing; *Kindergarten Children; Language Proficiency; *Learning Readiness; *Portuguese; *Preschool Children; Preschool Education; Psychomotor Skills; *Screening Tests
Identifiers: PSS
Availability: Early Recognition Intervention Systems; Box 1635, Pawtucket, RI 02862
Age Level: 2-6
Notes: Time, 20 min. approx.
This foreign language adaptation of the Preschool Screening System is an individually administered screening test of learning efficiency. It is used as an initial screening device for identifying the special learning needs of preschool or kindergarten children. Primary use is to quickly survey learning skills of children entering nursery school or kindergarten so that curriculum can be adapted to their needs. Can also serve as part of a more detailed assessment of individual children. May be group administered by having a team of several adults meet with 8 children at a time. Test assesses body awareness, visual-perceptual-motor skills, and language skills. Subtests may be combined to yield a short form or nonlanguage form. Several subtests may also be compiled to yield imitation and learned skills scores. English language manual is necessary for administration. This instrument is a Portuguese adaptation of the Preschool Screening System (TC012681).

13388
Preschool Screening System: Italian Adaptation. Hainsworth, Peter K.; Hainsworth, Marian L. 1981
Subtests: Movement Patterns; Clapping; Body Directions; Finger Patterns; Copy Shapes; Visual Integration; Spatial Directions; Draw a Person; Serial Counting; Phrases; Sentences; Verbal Reasoning; General Information; Quantity Recognition; Read Shapes
Descriptors: Bilingual Education; Bilingual Teachers; Human Body; *Individual Testing; *Italian; *Kindergarten Children; Language Proficiency; *Learning Readiness; *Preschool Children; Preschool Education; Psychomotor Skills; *Screening Tests
Identifiers: PSS
Availability: Early Recognition Intervention Systems; Box 1635, Pawtucket, RI 02862
Age Level: 2-6
Notes: Time, 20 min. approx.
This foreign language adaptation of the Preschool Screening System is an individually administered screening test of learning efficiency. It is used as an initial screening device for identifying the special learning needs of preschool or kindergarten children. Primary use is to quickly survey learning skills of children entering nursery school or kindergarten so that curriculum can be adapted to their needs. Can also serve as part of a more detailed assessment of individual children. May be group administered by having a team of several adults meet with 8 children at a time. Test assesses body awareness, visual-perceptual-motor skills, and language skills. Subtests may be combined to yield a short form or nonlanguage form. Several subtests may also be compiled to yield imitation and learned skills scores. English language manual is necessary for administration. This instrument is a Italian adaptation of the Preschool Screening System (TC012681).

13389
Preschool Screening System: Greek Adaptation. Hainsworth, Peter K.; Hainsworth, Marian L. 1981
Subtests: Movement Patterns; Clapping; Body Directions; Finger Patterns; Copy Shapes; Visual Integration; Spatial Directions; Draw a Person; Serial Counting; Phrases; Sentences; Verbal Reasoning; General Information; Quantity Recognition; Read Shapes

Descriptors: Bilingual Education; Bilingual Teachers; *Greek; Human Body; *Individual Testing; *Kindergarten Children; Language Proficiency; *Learning Readiness; *Preschool Children; Preschool Education; Psychomotor Skills; *Screening Tests
Identifiers: PSS
Availability: Early Recognition Intervention Systems; Box 1635, Pawtucket, RI 02862
Age Level: 2-6
Notes: Time, 20 min. approx.
This foreign language adaptation of the Preschool Screening System is an individually administered screening test of learning efficiency. It is used as an initial screening device for identifying the special learning needs of preschool or kindergarten children. Primary use is to quickly survey learning skills of children entering nursery school or kindergarten so that curriculum can be adapted to their needs. Can also serve as part of a more detailed assessment of individual children. May be group administered by having a team of several adults meet with 8 children at a time. Test assesses body awareness, visual-perceptual-motor skills, and language skills. Subtests may be combined to yield a short form or nonlanguage form. Several subtests may also be compiled to yield imitation and learned skills scores. English language manual is necessary for administration. This instrument is a Greek adaptation of the Preschool Screening System (TC012681).

13390
Preschool Screening System: French Adaptation. Hainsworth, Peter K.; Hainsworth, Marian L. 1981
Subtests: Movement Patterns; Clapping; Body Directions; Finger Patterns; Copy Shapes; Visual Integration; Spatial Directions; Draw a Person; Serial Counting; Phrases; Sentences; Verbal Reasoning; General Information; Quantity Recognition; Read Shapes
Descriptors: Bilingual Education; Bilingual Teachers; *French; Human Body; *Individual Testing; *Kindergarten Children; Language Proficiency; *Learning Readiness; *Preschool Children; Preschool Education; Psychomotor Skills; *Screening Tests
Identifiers: PSS
Availability: Early Recognition Intervention Systems; Box 1635, Pawtucket, RI 02862
Age Level: 2-6
Notes: Time, 20 min. approx.
This foreign language adaptation of the Preschool Screening System is an individually administered screening test of learning efficiency. It is used as an initial screening device for identifying the special learning needs of preschool or kindergarten children. Primary use is to quickly survey learning skills of children entering nursery school or kindergarten so that curriculum can be adapted to their needs. Can also serve as part of a more detailed assessment of individual children. May be group administered by having a team of several adults meet with 8 children at a time. Test assesses body awareness, visual-perceptual-motor skills, and language skills. Subtests may be combined to yield a short form or nonlanguage form. Several subtests may also be compiled to yield imitation and learned skills scores. English language manual is necessary for administration. This instrument is a French adaptation of the Preschool Screening System (TC012681).

13391
Preschool Screening System: Chinese Adaptation. Hainsworth, Peter K.; Hainsworth, Marian L. 1981
Subtests: Movement Patterns; Clapping; Body Directions; Finger Patterns; Copy Shapes; Visual Integration; Spatial Directions; Draw a Person; Serial Counting; Phrases; Sentences; Verbal Reasoning; General Information; Quantity Recognition; Read Shapes
Descriptors: Bilingual Education; Bilingual Teachers; *Chinese; Human Body; *Individual Testing; *Kindergarten Children; Language Proficiency; *Learning Readiness; *Preschool Children; Preschool Education; Psychomotor Skills; *Screening Tests
Identifiers: PSS
Availability: Early Recognition Intervention Systems; Box 1635, Pawtucket, RI 02862
Age Level: 2-6
Notes: Time, 20 min. approx.
This foreign language adaptation of the Preschool Screening System is an individually administered screening test of learning efficiency. It is used as an initial screening device for identifying the special learning needs of preschool or kindergarten children. Primary use is to quickly survey learning skills of children entering nursery school or kindergarten so that curriculum can be adapted to their needs. Can also serve as part of a more detailed assessment of individual children. May be group administered by having a team of several adults meet with 8 children at a time. Test assesses body awareness, visual-perceptual-motor skills, and language skills. Subtests may be combined to yield a short form or nonlanguage form. Several subtests may also be compiled to yield imitation and

learned skills scores. English language manual is necessary for administration. This instrument is a Chinese adaptation of the Preschool Screening System (TC012681).

13392
Preschool Screening System: Cape Verdean Adaptation. Hainsworth, Peter K.; Hainsworth, Marian L. 1981
Subtests: Movement Patterns; Clapping; Body Directions; Finger Patterns; Copy Shapes; Visual Integration; Spatial Directions; Draw a Person; Serial Counting; Phrases; Sentences; Verbal Reasoning; General Information; Quantity Recognition; Read Shapes
Descriptors: Bilingual Education; Bilingual Teachers; Human Body; *Individual Testing; *Kindergarten Children; Language Proficiency; *Learning Readiness; *Preschool Children; Preschool Education; Psychomotor Skills; *Screening Tests
Identifiers: *Cape Verdeans; PSS
Availability: Early Recognition Intervention Systems; Box 1635, Pawtucket, RI 02862
Age Level: 2-6
Notes: Time, 20 min. approx.
This foreign language adaptation of the Preschool Screening System is an individually administered screening test of learning efficiency. It is used as an initial screening device for identifying the special learning needs of preschool or kindergarten children. Primary use is to quickly survey learning skills of children entering nursery school or kindergarten so that curriculum can be adapted to their needs. Can also serve as part of a more detailed assessment of individual children. May be group administered by having a team of several adults meet with 8 children at a time. Test assesses body awareness, visual-perceptual-motor skills, and language skills. Subtests may be combined to yield a short form or nonlanguage form. Several subtests may also be compiled to yield imitation and learned skills scores. English language manual is necessary for administration. This instrument is a Cape Verdean adaptation of the Preschool Screening System (TC012681).

13393
Preschool Screening System: Armenian Adaptation. Hainsworth, Peter K.; Hainsworth, Marian L. 1981
Subtests: Movement Patterns; Clapping; Body Directions; Finger Patterns; Copy Shapes; Visual Integration; Spatial Directions; Draw a Person; Serial Counting; Phrases; Sentences; Verbal Reasoning; General Information; Quantity Recognition; Read Shapes
Descriptors: *Armenian; Bilingual Education; Bilingual Teachers; Human Body; *Individual Testing; *Kindergarten Children; Language Proficiency; *Learning Readiness; *Preschool Children; Preschool Education; Psychomotor Skills; *Screening Tests
Identifiers: PSS
Availability: Early Recognition Intervention Systems; Box 1635, Pawtucket, RI 02862
Age Level: 2-6
Notes: Time, 20 min. approx.
This foreign language adaptation of the Preschool Screening System is an individually administered screening test of learning efficiency. It is used as an initial screening device for identifying the special learning needs of preschool or kindergarten children. Primary use is to quickly survey learning skills of children entering nursery school or kindergarten so that curriculum can be adapted to their needs. Can also serve as part of a more detailed assessment of individual children. May be group administered by having a team of several adults meet with 8 children at a time. Test assesses body awareness, visual-perceptual-motor skills, and language skills. Subtests may be combined to yield a short form or nonlanguage form. Several subtests may also be compiled to yield imitation and learned skills scores. English language manual is necessary for administration. This instrument is an Armenian adaptation of the Preschool Screening System (TC012681).

13394
Preschool Screening System: Cambodian Adaptation. Hainsworth, Peter K.; Hainsworth, Marian L. 1981
Subtests: Movement Patterns; Clapping; Body Directions; Finger Patterns; Copy Shapes; Visual Integration; Spatial Directions; Draw a Person; Serial Counting; Phrases; Sentences; Verbal Reasoning; General Information; Quantity Recognition; Read Shapes
Descriptors: Bilingual Education; Bilingual Teachers; *Cambodian; Human Body; *Individual Testing; *Kindergarten Children; Language Proficiency; *Learning Readiness; *Preschool Children; Preschool Education; Psychomotor Skills; *Screening Tests
Identifiers: PSS
Availability: Early Recognition Intervention Systems; Box 1635, Pawtucket, RI 02862
Age Level: 2-6

Notes: Time, 20 min. approx.

This foreign language adaptation of the Preschool Screening System is an individually administered screening test of learning efficiency. It is used as an initial screening device for identifying the special learning needs of preschool or kindergarten children. Primary use is to quickly survey learning skills of children entering nursery school or kindergarten so that curriculum can be adapted to their needs. Can also serve as part of a more detailed assessment of individual children. May be group administered by having a team of several adults meet with 8 children at a time. Test assesses body awareness, visual-perceptual-motor skills, and language skills. Subtests may be combined to yield a short form or nonlanguage form. Several subtests may also be compiled to yield imitation and learned skills scores. English language manual is necessary for administration. This instrument is a Cambodian adaptation of the Preschool Screening System (TC012681).

13395

Preschool Screening System: Farsi Adaptation.
Hainsworth, Peter K.; Hainsworth, Marian L. 1981
Subtests: Movement Patterns; Clapping; Body Directions; Finger Patterns; Copy Shapes; Visual Integration; Spatial Directions; Draw a Person; Serial Counting; Phrases; Sentences; Verbal Reasoning; General Information; Quantity Recognition; Read Shapes
Descriptors: Bilingual Education; Bilingual Teachers; Human Body; *Individual Testing; *Kindergarten Children; Language Proficiency; *Learning Readiness; *Persian; *Preschool Children; Preschool Education; Psychomotor Skills; *Screening Tests
Identifiers: PSS
Availability: Early Recognition Intervention Systems; Box 1635, Pawtucket, RI 02862
Age Level: 2-6
Notes: Time, 20 min. approx.

This foreign language adaptation of the Preschool Screening System is an individually administered screening test of learning efficiency. It is used as an initial screening device for identifying the special learning needs of preschool or kindergarten children. Primary use is to quickly survey learning skills of children entering nursery school or kindergarten so that curriculum can be adapted to their needs. Can also serve as part of a more detailed assessment of individual children. May be group administered by having a team of several adults meet with 8 children at a time. Test assesses body awareness, visual-perceptual-motor skills, and language skills. Subtests may be combined to yield a short form or nonlanguage form. Several subtests may also be compiled to yield imitation and learned skills scores. English language manual is necessary for administration. This instrument is a Farsi or Persian adaptation of the Preschool Screening System (TC012681).

13396

Preschool Screening System: Japanese Adaptation.
Hainsworth, Peter K.; Hainsworth, Marian L. 1981
Subtests: Movement Patterns; Clapping; Body Directions; Finger Patterns; Copy Shapes; Visual Integration; Spatial Directions; Draw a Person; Serial Counting; Phrases; Sentences; Verbal Reasoning; General Information; Quantity Recognition; Read Shapes
Descriptors: Bilingual Education; Bilingual Teachers; Human Body; *Individual Testing; *Japanese; *Kindergarten Children; Language Proficiency; *Learning Readiness; *Preschool Children; Preschool Education; Psychomotor Skills; *Screening Tests
Identifiers: PSS
Availability: Early Recognition Intervention Systems; Box 1635, Pawtucket, RI 02862
Age Level: 2-6
Notes: Time, 20 min. approx.

This foreign language adaptation of the Preschool Screening System is an individually administered screening test of learning efficiency. It is used as an initial screening device for identifying the special learning needs of preschool or kindergarten children. Primary use is to quickly survey learning skills of children entering nursery school or kindergarten so that curriculum can be adapted to their needs. Can also serve as part of a more detailed assessment of individual children. May be group administered by having a team of several adults meet with 8 children at a time. Test assesses body awareness, visual-perceptual-motor skills, and language skills. Subtests may be combined to yield a short form or nonlanguage form. Several subtests may also be compiled to yield imitation and learned skills scores. English language manual is necessary for administration. This instrument is a Japanese adaptation of the Preschool Screening System (TC012681).

13397

Preschool Screening System: Laotian Adaptation.
Hainsworth, Peter K.; Hainsworth, Marian L. 1981

Subtests: Movement Patterns; Clapping; Body Directions; Finger Patterns; Copy Shapes; Visual Integration; Spatial Directions; Draw a Person; Serial Counting; Phrases; Sentences; Verbal Reasoning; General Information; Quantity Recognition; Read Shapes
Descriptors: Bilingual Education; Bilingual Teachers; Human Body; *Individual Testing; *Kindergarten Children; Language Proficiency; *Lao; Laotians; *Learning Readiness; *Preschool Children; Preschool Education; Psychomotor Skills; *Screening Tests
Identifiers: PSS
Availability: Early Recognition Intervention Systems; Box 1635, Pawtucket, RI 02862
Age Level: 2-6
Notes: Time, 20 min. approx.

This foreign language adaptation of the Preschool Screening System is an individually administered screening test of learning efficiency. It is used as an initial screening device for identifying the special learning needs of preschool or kindergarten children. Primary use is to quickly survey learning skills of children entering nursery school or kindergarten so that curriculum can be adapted to their needs. Can also serve as part of a more detailed assessment of individual children. May be group administered by having a team of several adults meet with 8 children at a time. Test assesses body awareness, visual-perceptual-motor skills, and language skills. Subtests may be combined to yield a short form or nonlanguage form. Several subtests may also be compiled to yield imitation and learned skills scores. English language manual is necessary for administration. This instrument is a Laotian adaptation of the Preschool Screening System (TC012681).

13398

Preschool Screening System: Samoan Adaptation.
Hainsworth, Peter K.; Hainsworth, Marian L. 1981
Subtests: Movement Patterns; Clapping; Body Directions; Finger Patterns; Copy Shapes; Visual Integration; Spatial Directions; Draw a Person; Serial Counting; Phrases; Sentences; Verbal Reasoning; General Information; Quantity Recognition; Read Shapes
Descriptors: Bilingual Education; Bilingual Teachers; Human Body; *Individual Testing; *Kindergarten Children; Language Proficiency; *Learning Readiness; *Preschool Children; Preschool Education; Psychomotor Skills; *Samoan; *Screening Tests
Identifiers: PSS
Availability: Early Recognition Intervention Systems; Box 1635, Pawtucket, RI 02862
Age Level: 2-6
Notes: Time, 20 min. approx.

This foreign language adaptation of the Preschool Screening System is an individually administered screening test of learning efficiency. It is used as an initial screening device for identifying the special learning needs of preschool or kindergarten children. Primary use is to quickly survey learning skills of children entering nursery school or kindergarten so that curriculum can be adapted to their needs. Can also serve as part of a more detailed assessment of individual children. May be group administered by having a team of several adults meet with 8 children at a time. Test assesses body awareness, visual-perceptual-motor skills, and language skills. Subtests may be combined to yield a short form or nonlanguage form. Several subtests may also be compiled to yield imitation and learned skills scores. English language manual is necessary for administration. This instrument is a Samoan adaptation of the Preschool Screening System (TC012681).

13399

Preschool Screening System: Tagalog Adaptation.
Hainsworth, Peter K.; Hainsworth, Marian L. 1981
Subtests: Movement Patterns; Clapping; Body Directions; Finger Patterns; Copy Shapes; Visual Integration; Spatial Directions; Draw a Person; Serial Counting; Phrases; Sentences; Verbal Reasoning; General Information; Quantity Recognition; Read Shapes
Descriptors: Bilingual Education; Bilingual Teachers; Human Body; *Individual Testing; *Kindergarten Children; Language Proficiency; *Learning Readiness; *Preschool Children; Preschool Education; Psychomotor Skills; *Screening Tests; *Tagalog
Identifiers: PSS
Availability: Early Recognition Intervention Systems; Box 1635, Pawtucket, RI 02862
Age Level: 2-6
Notes: Time, 20 min. approx.

This foreign language adaptation of the Preschool Screening System is an individually administered screening test of learning efficiency. It is used as an initial screening device for identifying the special learning needs of preschool or kindergarten children. Primary use is to quickly survey learning skills of children entering nursery school or kindergarten so that curriculum can be adapted to their

needs. Can also serve as part of a more detailed assessment of individual children. May be group administered by having a team of several adults meet with 8 children at a time. Test assesses body awareness, visual-perceptual-motor skills, and language skills. Subtests may be combined to yield a short form or nonlanguage form. Several subtests may also be compiled to yield imitation and learned skills scores. English language manual is necessary for administration. This instrument is a Tayalog adaptation of of the Preschool Screening System (TC012681).

13415

Computer Entry Level Skills Test. Project COFFEE, Oxford High School, Oxford, MA 1984
Descriptors: *Achievement Tests; *Computers; *Data Processing; High Schools; *High School Students; Problem Solving; Programing
Availability: French River Teacher Center; P.O. Box 476, N. Oxford, MA 01537
Grade Level: 9-12
Notes: Items, 60

Measures application skills including mastery of underlying processes, procedures, operation, computation, schematics, and entry-level programing skills. Item formats include fill-in blanks, data entry commands, program procedures, and applied problem solving. Has been field tested. For use in high schools to measure achievement.

13428

Preliminary Test of English as a Foreign Language. Educational Testing Service, Princeton, NJ
Subtests: Listening Comprehension; Structure and Written Expression; Reading Comprehension and Vocabulary
Descriptors: College Students; *English (Second Language); Foreign Students; Higher Education; High School Students; *Language Proficiency; *Language Tests; Listening Comprehension; Reading Comprehension; Secondary Education; Sentence Structure; Student Placement; Vocabulary Skills; Writing Skills
Identifiers: Nonnative Speakers; TOEFL
Availability: TOEFL; P.O. Box 6155, Educational Testing Service, Princeton, NJ 08541
Grade Level: 13-16
Notes: Time, 70 min.

Designed to measure the English proficiency of nonnative speakers of the language at the beginning and intermediate levels. For use by schools, colleges and universities to place students in ESL programs, to measure progress after instruction, or to determine whether student can function in an English-language instructional setting. Scored by publisher. Part and total scores are reported.

13458

Oral Reading and Recall Evaluation Scale. Taylor, Janet B. 1979
Descriptors: *Achievement Tests; *Elementary School Students; *Oral Reading; Primary Education; Rating Scales; *Reading Comprehension; *Recall (Psychology)
Identifiers: TIM(J)
Availability: Tests in Microfiche; Test Collection, Educational Testing Service, Princeton, NJ 08541
Grade Level: 1-3
Notes: Items, 20

A rating scale that allows teachers to rank students in the primary grades on a number of skills identified by primary school teachers as indicative of reading comprehension ability. It also allows teachers to make a more global assessment of students' oral reading and recall, using teachers' own criteria.

13460

National Achievement Test: Health and Safety Education Test. Crow, Lester D.; Ryan, Loretta C. 1959
Subtests: Good Health and Safety Habits; Cause and Effect in Relation to Health and Safety; Facts about Health and Safety; Application of Health and Safety Rules
Descriptors: *Achievement Tests; Elementary Education; *Elementary School Students; *Health Education; Knowledge Level; Safety; *Safety Education
Identifiers: Acorn National Achievement Tests
Availability: Psychometric Affiliates; P.O. Box 807, Murfreesboro, TN 37133
Grade Level: 3-6
Notes: Time, 40 min.; Items, 90

Designed to assess student's ability to select the best health and safety habits; to understand cause and effect in relation to health and safety; and to assess knowledge of facts about health and safety and to apply health and safety rules.

13464

Diagnostic Screening Test: Reading, Third Edition, Revised. Gnagey, Thomas D.; Gnagey, Patricia A. 1981

Descriptors: Diagnostic Teaching; *Diagnostic Tests; *Elementary School Students; Elementary Secondary Education; Phonics; Reading Achievement; Reading Comprehension; *Reading Tests; Screening Tests; *Secondary School Students; Word Recognition
Identifiers: DST (Reading); DSTR
Availability: Slosson Educational Publications; P.O. Box 280, East Aurora, NY 14052
Grade Level: 1-12
Notes: Time, 10 min. approx.

Designed to assess student's reading skills. Yields scores in word reading comfort level, word reading instructional level, word reading frustration level, and comprehension of passages level. Phonics and word attack proficiency skills are also assessed.

13465
Diagnostic Screening Test: Spelling, Third Edition, Revised. Gnagey, Thomas D. 1982
Descriptors: Diagnostic Teaching; *Diagnostic Tests; *Elementary School Students; Elementary Secondary Education; Individual Testing; Memory; Phonics; Screening Tests; *Secondary School Students; *Spelling
Identifiers: Auditory Memory; DST (Spelling); DSTS; *Sequential Memory; Visual Memory
Availability: Slosson Educational Publications; P.O. Box 280, East Aurora, NY 14052
Grade Level: 1-12
Notes: Time, 10 min. approx.; Items, 78

Designed to determine a differential diagnosis in 5 problem areas including sight vs. phonics orientation, verbal vs. written processing efficiency, sequential vs. gross visual memory, sequential vs. gross auditory memory, and good vs. poor spelling potential. Forms A and B are available.

13466
Diagnostic Screening Test: Math, Third Edition, Revised. Gnagey, Thomas D. 1980
Subtests: Money; Time; Percent; U.S. Measurement; Metric; Addition; Subtraction; Multiplication; Division
Descriptors: *Diagnostic Tests; *Elementary School Mathematics; *Elementary School Students; Elementary Secondary Education; *Mathematical Concepts; Mathematics Tests; Screening Tests; *Secondary School Mathematics; *Secondary School Students
Identifiers: DST (Math); DSTM
Availability: Slosson Educational Publications; P.O. Box 280, East Aurora, NY 14052
Grade Level: 1-10
Notes: Time, 20 min. approx.; Items, 73

Designed to assess basic computational skills as well as knowledge of percent metric measurement, money, and time. Yields a grade equivalent score. Forms A and B are available.

13470
Third Assessment of Writing, 1978-79 Released Exercise Set. Education Commission of the States, Denver, CO 1981
Descriptors: *Achievement Tests; *Educational Assessment; Elementary School Students; Elementary Secondary Education; Essay Tests; Language Tests; National Competency Tests; Secondary School Students; Student Writing Models; *Test Items; *Writing (Composition); *Writing Skills
Identifiers: National Assessment of Educational Progress
Availability: ERIC Document Reproduction Service; 7420 Fullerton Rd., Ste. 110, Springfield, VA 22153-2852 (ED205583, 514 p.)
Grade Level: 4; 8; 11
Age Level: 9; 13; 17

The National Assessment of Educational Progress (NAEP) third writing assessment was administered to 9-, 13-, and 17-year-old students in 1978-79. These are the released exercises from that assessment.

13483
Diagnosis of Language Competency Inventory (DLCI). Blake, Howard E.; Maull, Ethel M. 1977
Subtests: Motor Functions; Memory Functions; Visual Functions; Tactile-Kinesthetic Functions; Vocal Functions; Auditory Functions; Following Instructions; Language Concepts
Descriptors: Elementary School Students; *Expressive Language; *Individual Testing; *Language Acquisition; Language Aptitude; *Language Skills; *Language Tests; Primary Education; *Receptive Language
Identifiers: DLCI; *The Research Instruments Project
Availability: ERIC Document Reproduction Service; 7420 Fullerton Rd., Ste. 110, Springfield, VA 22153-2852 (ED236650, 12 p.)
Grade Level: K-3
Notes: Items, 57

This instrument is designed to measure children's receptive and expressive language competence in 8 language subareas. It is to be administered individually.

13487
Walmsley CVC Patterns Test. Walmsley, Sean A. 1975
Descriptors: *Consonants; *Criterion Referenced Tests; *Elementary School Students; Grammar; Measures (Individuals); Primary Education; *Reading Skills; Slides; *Vowels; *Word Recognition
Identifiers: *Consonant Vowel Consonant Combinations; CVC; *The Research Instruments Project
Availability: ERIC Document Reproduction Service; 7420 Fullerton Rd., Ste. 110, Springfield, VA 22153-2852 (ED236633, 21 p.)
Grade Level: K-3
Notes: Items, 152

Designed to provide a criterion-referenced measurement of CVC (consonant vowel consonant) word patterns, this test consists of 6 subtests of 152 items prepared as slides for projection. Items are to be presented to the subjects on 2 separate occasions separated by at least one day (76 slides per session).

13488
Smith/Palmer Figurative Language Interpretation Test. Smith, Edwin H.; Palmer, Barbara C. 1979
Descriptors: Adult Basic Education; Adult Students; Elementary School Students; Elementary Secondary Education; *Figurative Language; Higher Education; Measures (Individuals); Multiple Choice Tests; Postsecondary Education; *Reading Comprehension; *Reading Diagnosis; *Reading Skills; *Reading Tests; Secondary School Students
Identifiers: Personification; Similes; The Research Instruments Project
Availability: ERIC Document Reproduction Service; 7420 Fullerton Rd., Ste. 110, Springfield, VA 22153-2852 (ED236668, 23 p.)
Grade Level: 4-12
Notes: Items, 50

This test is designed to assess the ability to interpret the major types of figurative language or tropes such as similes, metaphors, proverbs, and personification. There are 2 forms of the test. Each form contains 50 items in a 2-part, multiple-choice format. Part I tests the meaning of figures of speech in isolation; Part II tests the meaning in the context of a sentence(s). In both parts, the reader is required to select which of 4 possible answer choices represents the most common meaning for each figure of speech. To aid the reader, figurative statements are underlined, no figurative statements are contained in the answer choices, the test is untimed, and the test items are written at or below the fifth grade readability level.

13489
Standard Test of Reading Effectiveness (STORE), Forms A, B, C. Pedersen, Elray L. 1980
Descriptors: Inferences; College Students; Elementary School Students; Elementary Secondary Education; Higher Education; Idioms; Measures (Individuals); Multiple Choice Tests; *Reading Achievement; *Reading Comprehension; *Reading Diagnosis; *Reading Skills; *Reading Tests; Secondary School Students; *Student Placement
Identifiers: STORE; The Research Instruments Project
Availability: ERIC Document Reproduction Service; 7420 Fullerton Rd., Ste. 110, Springfield, VA 22153-2852 (ED236669, 24 p.)
Grade Level: 7-16
Notes: Time, 25 min.; Items, 50

This instrument is used to assess a reader's achievement in various reading skills for instructional placement. There are 3 forms, A, B, and C; each contains 50 items. The items test comprehension of idioms and direct statements with emphasis on drawing inferences. Administration time for each test is 25 minutes. This test can be used for upper elementary, secondary, college, and continuing education students.

13490
Scale for Evaluating Expository Writing (SEEW). Quellmalz, Edys 1982
Descriptors: College Students; *Criterion Referenced Tests; Elementary Secondary Education; Evaluation Criteria; *Expository Writing; Higher Education; Junior High School Students; Mastery Tests; Measures (Individuals); Rating Scales; Secondary School Students; *Writing (Composition); *Writing Evaluation; Writing Skills
Identifiers: SEEW; The Research Instruments Project
Availability: ERIC Document Reproduction Service; 7420 Fullerton Rd., Ste. 110, Springfield, VA 22153-2852 (ED236670, 18 p.)
Grade Level: 7-16

Designed as a criterion-referenced scale to describe levels of writing skill development for basic essay elements, this instrument provides separate 6-point rating scales for general impression of the quality of an essay, general competence, coherence, paragraph organization, support for main ideas, and mechanics. SEEW defines score points 4-6 in terms of mastery or competence, and score points 1-3 in terms of nonmastery.

13492
IER Criterion-Referenced Mathematics Objective and Item Bank: A Bank of Mathematics Objectives and Test Items for Grades One through Eight. Cunningham, Sandra; And Others 1979
Descriptors: Achievement Tests; Arithmetic; Charts; *Criterion Referenced Tests; Decimal Fractions; Educational Objectives; Elementary Education; *Elementary School Mathematics; *Elementary School Students; Geometry; Graphs; Integers; *Item Banks; Mathematics Achievement; Multiple Choice Tests; Numbers; Problem Solving; Test Items
Identifiers: Institute for Educational Resarch
Availability: ERIC Document Reproduction Service; 7420 Fullerton Rd., Ste. 110, Springfield, VA 22153-2852 (ED237528, microfiche only)
Grade Level: 1-8
Notes: Items, 813

The mathematics objective-item bank contains 100 objectives each represented by 5 to 8 multiple-choice items and covers grade levels 1 through 8. The objectives deal with such topics as decimals, fractions, geometry, graphs and charts, integers, numeration, problem solving, and whole number operations. The bank can serve as a starting point for developing tests of mathematics achievement tailored to the local district curriculum. Such tests can be used for district program evaluation, student diagnosis, competency testing, and formative or mastery testing. An alternate source is Institute for Educational Research, 793 N. Main Street, Glen Ellyn, IL 60137.

13493
IER Criterion-Referenced Language Arts Objective and Item Bank: A Bank of Language Arts Objectives and Test Items for Grades One through Eight. Cunningham, Sandra; And Others 1979
Descriptors: Achievement Tests; *Criterion Referenced Tests; Educational Objectives; Elementary Education; *Elementary School Students; Grammar; *Item Banks; *Language Arts; *Language Tests; Literature; Multiple Choice Tests; Phonetic Analysis; Reading Comprehension; Structural Analysis (Linguistics); Study Skills; Test Items; Vocabulary Skills; Writing Skills
Identifiers: Institute for Educational Research
Availability: ERIC Document Reproduction Service; 7420 Fullerton Rd., Ste. 110, Springfield, VA 22153-2852 (ED237529, microfiche only)
Grade Level: 1-8
Notes: Items, 764

The language arts objective-item bank contains 100 objectives each represented by 5 to 8 multiple-choice items and covers grade levels 1 through 8. The objectives deal with such topics as composition, grammar, literature, phonetic analysis, reading comprehension, structural analysis, study and research skills, vocabulary, and writing mechanics. The bank can serve as a starting point for developing tests of language arts achievement tailored to the local district curriculum. Such tests can be used for district program evaluation, student diagnosis, competency testing, and formative or mastery testing. An alternate source is Institute for Educational Research, 793 N. Main St., Glen Ellyn, IL 60137.

13513
Criterion-Referenced Test for the Assessment of Reading and Writing Skills of Professional Educators. Dupuis, Mary M.; Snyder, Sandra L. 1980
Subtests: Comprehension; Vocabulary; Data Interpretation; Writing Sample
Descriptors: Achievement Tests; *Criterion Referenced Tests; Inservice Teacher Education; Measures (Individuals); Preservice Teacher Education; *Reading Comprehension; *Reading Skills; *Teacher Education; Teacher Qualifications; Teachers; *Writing Skills
Identifiers: The Research Instruments Project
Availability: ERIC Document Reproduction Service; 7420 Fullerton Rd., Ste. 110, Springfield, VA 22153-2852 (ED236643, 12 p.)
Age Level: 18-64
Notes: Items, 24

This instrument was designed to assess the reading and writing skills of preservice and inservice teachers and assesses 4 skills areas following the reading of a selected professional article. The skill areas assessed are the ability to (1) understand the professional vocabulary used in the selection, (2) answer literal level comprehension questions,

(3) answer inferential level comprehension questions, and (4) interpret information found in tables. The test includes a writing sample, a response to 1 of 2 evaluative questions related to the same reading selection.

13514
S-ESL Spoken English Test (the Standard English as a Second Language Spoken Test), Tests A, B, C. Pedersen, Elray L. 1978
Descriptors: Adult Education; *Communication Skills; Elementary School Students; Elementary Secondary Education; *English (Second Language); *Language Tests; *Oral Language; Secondary School Students; Tape Recorders; Vocabulary Skills
Identifiers: The Research Instruments Project
Availability: ERIC Document Reproduction Service; 7420 Fullerton Rd., Ste. 110, Springfield, VA 22153-2852 (ED236648, 67 p.)
Grade Level: K-12
Age Level: 18-64
Notes: Time, 20 min.; Items, 90

This is 1 of 3 tests designed to assess the oral communication, grammatical fluency, and vocabulary development of students for whom English is a second language. The spoken English test comes in 2 versions: one with 90 items on a cassette tape, the other with 90 items to be read aloud by the examiner. Each version is available in 3 forms that employ a multiple-choice format requiring the selection of the semantically and grammatically correct response. The test does not assume knowledge of grammatical terminology. Each test is of 20 minutes duration and may be machine or hand scored.

13515
S-ESL Spoken English Test (the Standard English as a Second Language Grammar Test), Forms O, A, B, C. Pedersen, Elray L. 1978
Descriptors: Adult Education; College Students; *Communication Skills; Elementary School Students; Elementary Secondary Education; *English (Second Language); *Grammar; Higher Education; *Language Tests; Secondary School Students
Identifiers: The Research Instruments Project
Availability: ERIC Document Reproduction Service; 7420 Fullerton Rd., Ste. 110, Springfield, VA 22153-2852 (ED236648, 67 p.)
Grade Level: K-16
Notes: Time, 15 min.; Items, 35

This is 1 of 3 tests designed to assess the oral communication, grammatical fluency, and vocabulary development of students for whom English is a second language. Two levels of the grammar test have been developed: Form O tests the grammatical fluency of primary graders; forms A, B, and C are similar tests for secondary or college and university students. The 35 questions on each form require no formal knowledge of grammatical terminology, require fifteen minutes to complete, and can be machine or hand scored.

13516
S-ESL Spoken English Test (the Standard English as a Second Language Vocabulary Tests) Forms O, A, B, C. Pedersen, Elray L. 1978
Descriptors: Adult Education; College Students; *Communication Skills; Elementary School Students; Elementary Secondary Education; *English (Second Language); Higher Education; Language Tests; Multiple Choice Tests; Secondary School Students; *Vocabulary Development; Vocabulary Skills
Identifiers: The Research Instruments Project
Availability: ERIC Document Reproduction Service; 7420 Fullerton Rd., Ste. 110, Springfield, VA 22153-2852 (ED236648, 67 p.)
Grade Level: K-16
Notes: Time, 15 min.; Items, 37

This is 1 of 3 tests designed to assess the oral communication, grammatical fluency, and vocabulary development of students for whom English is a second language. Two levels of the vocabulary test have been developed: Form O tests the vocabulary development of primary grades; forms A, B, and C are similar tests for secondary or college and university students. Each form of the test has 37 multiple-choice questions of 3 types: the student fills in a blank with a syntactically and semantically appropriate choice; the students respond to a question about the meaning, value, or usage of underlined words; the student matches a brief description with one of the choices provided. Administration of each form requires 15 minutes, and the tests can be machine or hand scored. Items come from survival and daily life contexts.

13517
Mastery Assessment of Basic Reading Concepts. Pavlik, Robert A. 1974
Descriptors: Adults; Elementary School Teachers; *Knowledge Level; Measures (Individuals); Multiple Choice Tests; *Outcomes of Education; Program Effectiveness; *Reading Teachers; *Teacher Attitudes; *Teacher Education
Identifiers: MABRC; The Research Instruments Project
Availability: ERIC Document Reproduction Service; 7420 Fullerton Rd., Ste. 110, Springfield, VA 22153-2852 (ED236649, 16 p.)
Age Level: 18-64
Notes: Items, 51

This instrument was designed to determine whether elementary school teachers have mastered the reading concepts most emphasized in undergraduate courses at the University of Northern Colorado, where they mastered these concepts, or why they have not mastered the concepts. The items cover basic reading concepts, defined to include nature of the reading process, the developmental reading program, reading readiness, and instructional practices in reading. This instrument is taken from the author's Ph.D. dissertation at the University of Northern Colorado.

13535
C.U.B.E. Math Mastery Tests. Monroe County Community Schools Corp., Bloomington, IN 1979
Descriptors: *Achievement Tests; *Adult Basic Education; Adults; Arithmetic; Fractions; Geometry; Mastery Tests; *Mathematics; Percentage
Identifiers: Continuity and Unity in Basic Education Program; CUBE
Availability: ERIC Document Reproduction Service; 7420 Fullerton Rd., Ste. 110, Springfield, VA 22153-2852 (ED211830, 467 pg)
Age Level: Adults
Notes: Items, 400

For use in measuring achievement in an adult basic education teaching/learning management system. Tests cover operations, graphs, algebra, fractions, decimals, percent measurements, formulas, geometry.

13536
C.U.B.E. Math Placement Inventory. Monroe County Community Schools Corp., Bloomington, IN 1979
Descriptors: Achievement Tests; *Adult Basic Education; Adults; Arithmetic; Fractions; Geometry; Mathematics; Mathematics Tests; Percentage; *Student Placement
Identifiers: Continuity and Unity in Basic Education Program; CUBE
Availability: ERIC Document Reproduction Service; 7420 Fullerton Rd., Ste. 110, Springfield, VA 22153-2852 (ED211830, 467 pg)
Age Level: Adults
Notes: Items, 80

For use as part of an adult basic education teaching/learning management system. Covers operations, fractions, percents, geometry, and money. Places adult students into a workbook series.

13560
Adolescent Language Screening Test. Morgan, Denise L.; And Others 1984
Subtests: Pragmatics; Receptive Vocabulary; Concepts; Expressive Vocabulary; Naming to Confrontation; Naming to Description; Use of Lexical Items; Sentence Formulation; Morphology; Phonology
Descriptors: *Adolescents; *Individual Testing; *Oral Language; *Screening Tests
Identifiers: ALST
Availability: PRO-ED; 8700 Shoal Creek Blvd., Austin, TX 78758-6897
Age Level: 11-17
Notes: Time, 15 min. approx.

Developed for use by speech and language pathologists and other professionals as a rapid screening tool of adolescent speech and language proficiency, specifically spoken language. The test consists of 7 subtests that evaluate in the language dimensions of use, form, and content. The test is based on the contemporary view of language advocated by Bloom and Lakey.

13566
Regional Resource Center Diagnostic Inventories in Reading and Math. Northwest Regional Resource Center, Eugene, OR 1971
Descriptors: *Computation; Criterion Referenced Tests; *Decoding (Reading); *Diagnostic Tests; Elementary Education; Elementary School Mathematics; *Elementary School Students; *Mathematics Tests; *Reading Tests
Identifiers: TIM(J)
Availability: Tests in Microfiche; Test Collection, Educational Testing Service, Princeton, NJ 08541
Grade Level: 1-6

Designed to allow the teacher to specify reading and math skills in which students may need remedial instruction and to identify the level at which instruction should be provided. The criterion-referenced tests cover basic math computation and reading decoding skills. The inventories are designed so that teachers can administer, score, and interpret the test so that educational planning can be done directly from the test.

13572
C.U.B.E. English/Vocabulary. Monroe County Community Schools Corp., Bloomington, IN 1979
Descriptors: Achievement Tests; *Adult Basic Education; Adults; English; *Grammar; Language Skills; *Vocabulary
Identifiers: Cambridge English (Examinations); Continuity and Unity in Basic Education Program; CUBE; Mott Basic Language Skills Program
Availability: ERIC Document Reproduction Service; 7420 Fullerton Rd., Ste. 110, Springfield, VA 22153-2852 (ED211832, 235 pg)
Age Level: Adults

A part of an adult basic education teaching/learning management system. Consists of a series of tests for use in teaching English and vocabulary skills to adult basic education students. Includes several tests from other sources: the "Mott Tests" and Cambridge language tests. Others cover recognition of parts of speech, tense, subject verb agreement, punctuation, capitalization, parts of a sentence, style and clarity, sentence structure, prefixes and suffixes.

13575
C.U.B.E. Reading. Vincennes University, IN 1979
Descriptors: Achievement Tests; *Adult Basic Education; Adult Reading Programs; Adults; Reading Difficulties; *Reading Tests
Identifiers: Continuity and Unity in Basic Education Program; CUBE
Availability: ERIC Document Reproduction Service; 7420 Fullerton Rd., Ste. 110, Springfield, VA 22153-2852 (ED211831, 767 p.)
Age Level: Adults

Part of the Continuity and Unity in Basic Education Program an adult basic education teaching/learning management system. Contains one group of inventories, answer sheets, and checklists geared to reading levels from primer to grade 6.9, and another covering grades 8-10. These measure skills commonly taught at those grade levels.

13584
Wide Range Achievement Test, Revised. Jastak, Sarah; Wilkinson, Gary S. 1984
Subtests: Reading; Spelling; Arithmetic
Descriptors: *Achievement Tests; Adolescents; Adults; *Arithmetic; Braille; Children; Diagnostic Tests; Large Type Materials; Older Adults; *Reading Skills; *Spelling; Visual Impairments
Identifiers: Test Batteries; WRAT(R)
Availability: Jastak Assessment Systems; P.O. Box 3410, Wilmington, DE 19806
Age Level: 5-74
Notes: Time, 30 min. approx.

A restandardization of the Wide Range Achievement Test available in 2 levels. Level 1 is designed for use with children from age 5 through age 11. Level 2 is designed for use for people from ages 12 through 74. The purpose of the WRAT is to measure the codes needed to learn the basic skills of reading, spelling, and arithmetic. It was intentionally designed to eliminate as much as possible the effects of comprehension. Can be used to determine whether and where individual is having difficulty and to prescribe remedial/educational programs to treat the deficit. Available in large-type print or Braille for the visually impaired from American Printing House for the Blind, 1839 Frankfort Ave., Louisville, KY 40206.

13608
Developmental Inventory of Learned Skills: General Version. Hainsworth, Peter K.; Hainsworth, Marian L. 1983
Descriptors: Check Lists; *Child Development; *Criterion Referenced Tests; Individual Needs; Interpersonal Competence; Language Skills; Perceptual Motor Coordination; *Young Children
Identifiers: DILS; ERIN
Availability: Early Recognition Intervention Systems; Box 1635, Pawtucket, RI 02862
Age Level: 0-8

Criterion-referenced checklists of the skills of children from 0 to 8 years of age. Provides a comprehensive picture of child's learning pattern and of strengths and weaknesses in the basic learning areas of participation, body awareness, and control, visual-perceptual-motor, and language. Also included are activities of daily living, basic developmental concepts, and academic concepts. These developmental inventories are designed to provide teacher with overall guide to teaching activities appropriate for children of different ages and are divided into 3 booklets by age. They are infant/toddler level covering birth to 3.5 years; preschool level covering 18 months to 5.5 years; and primary school level from 3.5 to 8.5 years. These inventories are used with young special needs children.

13609
Developmental Inventory of Learned Skills: Detailed Version.   Early Recognition Intervention Network, Dedham, MA 1981
Descriptors: Check Lists; *Child Development; *Criterion Referenced Tests; Expressive Language; Individual Needs; *Language Skills; *Perceptual Motor Coordination; Receptive Language; Special Education; *Young Children
Identifiers: DILS; ERIN
Availability: Early Recognition Intervention Systems; Box 1635, Pawtucket, RI 02862
Age Level: 0-8

Criterion-referenced checklists of skills of children from 0 to 8 years old. Created as part of the assessment component of the ERIN method of assessing young children with special needs in regular and special education settings. Assessment of visual-perceptual-motor skills includes visual attention, form discrimination, form sequences, understanding sequence/position, visual memory and association, planning with a tool, motor control of arms/hands/fingers, and formulating visual-motor ideas. Assessment of the language component includes auditory attention, sound discrimination, word sentence sequences, language memory and association, planning sentence construction, motor control of speech, and formulating language ideas. Should be used by highly trained special education teachers or teacher-therapist team.

13610
DMI Mathematics Systems: System 1, Level A.
Gessel, John 1983
Descriptors: *Achievement Tests; *Criterion Referenced Tests; *Diagnostic Tests; *Elementary School Mathematics; *Grade 01; *Kindergarten Children; Mathematics Achievement; Primary Education
Identifiers: DMI (MS)
Availability: CTB/MacMillan/McGraw Hill; Del Monte Research Park, 2500 Garden Rd., Monterey, CA 93940
Grade Level: K-1

A criterion-referenced approach to mathematics assessment and instruction for students in kindergarten through grade 8. Helps teachers to identify students' strengths and weaknesses. Designed to enable teachers to place students for assessment, diagnose students' instructional needs, prescribe activities; teach specific skills, monitor progress, and reinforce and enrich mastered skills. Assessment materials evaluate students' mastery of instructional objectives common to mathematics curricula in grades K-8 and above. Objectives are organized into 4 strands: whole numbers, fractions and decimals, measurement and geometry, and problem solving and special topics. Strands are divided into 29 categories of objectives, and these are subdivided into 82 instructional objectives.

13611
DMI Mathematics Systems: System 1, Level B.
Gessel, John 1983
Descriptors: *Achievement Tests; *Criterion Referenced Tests; *Diagnostic Tests; *Elementary School Mathematics; *Elementary School Students; Mathematics Achievement; Primary Education
Identifiers: DMI (MS)
Availability: CTB/MacMillan/McGraw Hill; Del Monte Research Park, 2500 Garden Rd., Monterey, CA 93940
Grade Level: 1-2

A criterion-referenced approach to mathematics assessment and instruction for students in kindergarten through grade 8. Helps teachers to identify students' strengths and weaknesses. Designed to enable teachers to place students for assessment, diagnose students' instructional needs, prescribe activities; teach specific skills, monitor progress, and reinforce and enrich mastered skills. Assessment materials evaluate students' mastery of instructional objectives common to mathematics curricula in grades K-8 and above. Objectives are organized into 4 strands: whole numbers, fractions and decimals, measurement and geometry, and problem solving and special topics. Strands are divided into 29 categories of objectives, and these are subdivided into 82 instructional objectives.

13612
DMI Mathematics Systems: System 1, Level C.
Gessel, John 1983
Descriptors: *Achievement Tests; *Criterion Referenced Tests; *Diagnostic Tests; *Elementary School Mathematics; *Elementary School Students; Mathematics Achievement; Primary Education
Identifiers: DMI (MS)
Availability: CTB/MacMillan/McGraw Hill; Del Monte Research Park, 2500 Garden Rd., Monterey, CA 93940
Grade Level: 2-3

A criterion-referenced approach to mathematics assessment and instruction for students in kindergarten through grade 8. Helps teachers to identify students' strengths and weaknesses. Designed to enable teachers to place students for assessment, diagnose students' instructional needs, pre-

scribe activities; teach specific skills, monitor progress, and reinforce and enrich mastered skills. Assessment materials evaluate students' mastery of instructional objectives common to mathematics curricula in grades K-8 and above. Objectives are organized into 4 strands: whole numbers, fractions and decimals, measurement and geometry, and problem solving and special topics. Strands are divided into 29 categories of objectives, and these are subdivided into 82 instructional objectives.

13613
DMI Mathematics Systems: System 1, Level D.
Gessel, John 1983
Descriptors: *Achievement Tests; *Criterion Referenced Tests; *Diagnostic Tests; Elementary Education; *Elementary School Mathematics; *Elementary School Students; Mathematics Achievement
Identifiers: DMI (MS)
Availability: CTB/MacMillan/McGraw Hill; Del Monte Research Park, 2500 Garden Rd., Monterey, CA 93940
Grade Level: 3-4

A criterion-referenced approach to mathematics assessment and instruction for students in kindergarten through grade 8. Helps teachers to identify students' strengths and weaknesses. Designed to enable teachers to place students for assessment, diagnose students' instructional needs, prescribe activities; teach specific skills, monitor progress, and reinforce and enrich mastered skills. Assessment materials evaluate students' mastery of instructional objectives common to mathematics curricula in grades K-8 and above. Objectives are organized into 4 strands: whole numbers, fractions and decimals, measurement and geometry, and problem solving and special topics. Strands are divided into 29 categories of objectives, and these are subdivided into 82 instructional objectives.

13614
DMI Mathematics Systems: System 1, Level E.
Gessel, John 1983
Descriptors: *Achievement Tests; *Criterion Referenced Tests; *Diagnostic Tests; *Elementary School Mathematics; *Elementary School Students; Intermediate Grades; Mathematics Achievement
Identifiers: DMI (MS)
Availability: CTB/MacMillan/McGraw Hill; Del Monte Research Park, 2500 Garden Rd., Monterey, CA 93940
Grade Level: 4-5

A criterion-referenced approach to mathematics assessment and instruction for students in kindergarten through grade 8. Helps teachers to identify students' strengths and weaknesses. Designed to enable teachers to place students for assessment, diagnose students' instructional needs, prescribe activities; teach specific skills, monitor progress, and reinforce and enrich mastered skills. Assessment materials evaluate students' mastery of instructional objectives common to mathematics curricula in grades K-8 and above. Objectives are organized into 4 strands: whole numbers, fractions and decimals, measurement and geometry, and problem solving and special topics. Strands are divided into 29 categories of objectives, and these are subdivided into 82 instructional objectives.

13615
DMI Mathematics Systems: System 1, Level F.
Gessel, John 1983
Descriptors: *Achievement Tests; *Criterion Referenced Tests; *Diagnostic Tests; *Elementary School Mathematics; *Elementary School Students; Intermediate Grades; Mathematics Achievement
Identifiers: DMI (MS)
Availability: CTB/MacMillan/McGraw Hill; Del Monte Research Park, 2500 Garden Rd., Monterey, CA 93940
Grade Level: 5-6

A criterion-referenced approach to mathematics assessment and instruction for students in kindergarten through grade 8. Helps teachers to identify students' strengths and weaknesses. Designed to enable teachers to place students for assessment, diagnose students' instructional needs, prescribe activities; teach specific skills, monitor progress, and reinforce and enrich mastered skills. Assessment materials evaluate students' mastery of instructional objectives common to mathematics curricula in grades K-8 and above. Objectives are organized into 4 strands: whole numbers, fractions and decimals, measurement and geometry, and problem solving and special topics. Strands are divided into 29 categories of objectives, and these are subdivided into 82 instructional objectives.

13616
DMI Mathematics Systems: System 1, Level G.
Gessel, John 1983
Descriptors: *Achievement Tests; *Criterion Referenced Tests; *Diagnostic Tests; *Elementary School Mathematics; *Grade 6; Intermediate Grades; Junior High Schools; Junior High School Students; Mathematics Achievement
Identifiers: DMI (MS)

Availability: CTB/MacMillan/McGraw Hill; Del Monte Research Park, 2500 Garden Rd., Monterey, CA 93940
Grade Level: 6-8

A criterion-referenced approach to mathematics assessment and instruction for students in kindergarten through grade 8. Helps teachers to identify students' strengths and weaknesses. Designed to enable teachers to place students for assessment, diagnose students' instructional needs, prescribe activities; teach specific skills, monitor progress, and reinforce and enrich mastered skills. Assessment materials evaluate students' mastery of instructional objectives common to mathematics curricula in grades K-8 and above. Objectives are organized into 4 strands: whole numbers, fractions and decimals, measurement and geometry, and problem solving and special topics. Strands are divided into 29 categories of objectives, and these are subdivided into 82 instructional objectives.

13636
Computer Literacy: Definition and Survey Items for Assessment in Schools.   Lockheed, Marlaine; And Others 1983
Descriptors: Computer Assisted Instruction; *Computer Literacy; *Computer Science Education; Computer Software; *Educational Resources; Elementary School Students; Elementary School Teachers; *Item Banks; Knowledge Level; *Needs Assessment; Principals; Questionnaires; School Policy; Secondary School Students; Secondary School Teachers; Social Problems; Superintendents; Surveys
Availability: ERIC Document Reproduction Service; 7420 Fullerton Rd., Ste. 110, Springfield, VA 22153-2852 (ED238895, 222 pg)
Grade Level: 6-12
Age Level: Adults

This item bank was designed for use with elementary and secondary school superintendents, principals, teachers, and students to assess the status of computer literacy in the educational system. Survey items elicit information on the respondent's computer-related knowledge, skills, experience with computers, and use of computers. Other items measure the validity of the respondents' answers by testing actual knowledge of parts of the computer, languages, etc. A third type of item collects information on computer resources in the district, school, and classroom. The validation items are not included on the document available from ERIC. They can be obtained by contacting 1983 Computer Literacy Validation Items, National Center for Educational Statistics, Attn: Brown Bldg., Rm. 600, 400 Maryland Ave., S.W., Washington, DC 20202. Over 350 items are included in the bank.

13651
Standardized Test of Computer Literacy.   Montag, Mary; And Others 1984
Descriptors: *Achievement Tests; Adults; *Anxiety; *Attitude Measures; College Students; *Computer Literacy; *Computers; Higher Education; High School Students; Programing; Screening Tests; Secondary Education
Identifiers: Computer Applications; Computer Systems; STCL
Availability: Michael Simonson; Professor, College of Education, Instructional Resources Center, Quadrangle Bldg., Iowa State University, Ames, IA 50011
Grade Level: 9-16
Age Level: Adults
Notes: Items, 96

Composed of 2 separate parts. Part 1 is an achievement test of student competence in computer systems, computer applications, and computer programing principles. Part 2 is a standardized measure of computer anxiety, the fear of using computers or the apprehension felt while using them. Part 1 has 70 items, and each of the subtests within it can be administered separately. Parts 1 and 2 can be purchased as separate tests. May be used with anyone who has taken a computer literacy course. Part 2 may be used to identify those who might have trouble succeeding in a computer literacy course.

13652
Ohio Vocational Achievement Tests: Production Agriculture.   Ohio State Dept. of Education, Div. of Vocational Education, Columbus, OH 1982
Subtests: Beef Production; Small Grain Production; Sheep Production; Soybean Production; Crop Chemical Application; Agricultural Construction; Operator Equipment Maintenance; Dairy Production; Corn Production; Swine Production; Forage Production; Employment Procedures
Descriptors: Abstract Reasoning; *Achievement Tests; *Agricultural Education; *Agricultural Occupations; *Agricultural Production; Data Analysis; Grade 11; Grade 12; High Schools; *High School Students; Knowledge Level; Problem Solving; *Vocational Education

Availability: Ohio State University, Instructional Materials Laboratory; 1885 Neil Ave., Columbus, OH 43210
Grade Level: 11-12
Notes: Time, 240 min. approx.; Items, 393

For use in the evaluation and diagnosis of vocational achievement. Developed to measure skills and understandings in specific vocational areas. Items measure ability to solve problems, analyze data, recall facts, have a knowledge of principles, react to generalizations, use abstractions in specific situations, and form parts into complete structures. Administered with the California Short Form Test of Academic Aptitude (TC005919-005923).

13653
Ohio Vocational Achievement Tests: Clerk-Typist.
Ohio State Dept. of Education, Div. of Vocational Education, Columbus, OH 1982
Subtests: Letters, Memos, and Envelopes; Filing; Proofreading and Editing; Mail Procedures; Employment Procedures-Human Relations; Reports; Manuscripts, and Forms; Counting-Calculating; Telephone and Receptionist Duties; Machine Transcription-Word Processing; Reprographics
Descriptors: *Achievement Tests; *Clerical Occupations; *Clerical Workers; Grade 11; Grade 12; High Schools; *High School Students; Office Occupations Education; *Typewriting; *Vocational Education
Identifiers: *Clerical Skills
Availability: Ohio State University, Instructional Materials Laboratory; 1885 Neil Ave., Columbus, OH 43210
Grade Level: 11-12
Notes: Time, 240 min. approx.; Items, 355

For use in the evaluation and diagnosis of vocational achievement. Developed to measure skills and understandings in specific vocational areas. Items measure ability to solve problems, analyze data, recall facts, have a knowledge of principles, react to generalizations, use abstractions in specific situations, and form parts into complete structures. Administered with the California Short Form Test of Academic Aptitude (TC005919-005923).

13654
Ohio Vocational Achievement Tests: Word Processing. Ohio State Dept. of Education, Div. of Vocational Education, Columbus, OH 1982
Subtests: Typing and Transcription; Reprographics; Word Processing Concepts and Procedures; Business Transactions; Proofreading and Editing; Automated Word Processing Equipment; Receptionist Duties; Composition and Dictation; Records Management; Employment Procedures
Descriptors: *Achievement Tests; *Clerical Occupations; Grade 11; Grade 12; High Schools; *High School Students; Office Occupations Education; *Vocational Education; *Word Processing
Identifiers: *Clerical Skills
Availability: Ohio State University, Instructional Materials Laboratory; 1885 Neil Ave., Columbus, OH 43210
Grade Level: 11-12
Notes: Time, 240 min. approx.; Items, 373

For use in the evaluation and diagnosis of vocational achievement. Developed to measure skills and understandings in specific vocational areas. Items measure ability to solve problems, analyze data, recall facts, have a knowledge of principles, react to generalizations, use abstractions in specific situations, and form parts into complete structures. Administered with the California Short Form Test of Academic Aptitude (TC005919 -005923).

13655
Ohio Vocational Achievement Tests: Apparel and Accessories. Ohio State Dept. of Education, Div. of Vocational Education, Columbus, OH 1982
Descriptors: *Achievement Tests; *Distributive Education; *Fashion Industry; Grade 11; Grade 12; High Schools; *High School Students; Retailing; *Vocational Education
Availability: Ohio State University, Instructional Materials Laboratory; 1885 Neil Ave., Columbus, OH 43210
Grade Level: 11-12
Notes: Time, 240 min. approx.; Items, 386

For use in the evaluation and diagnosis of vocational achievement. Developed to measure skills and understandings in specific vocational areas. Items measure ability to solve problems, analyze data, recall facts, have a knowledge of principles, react to generalizations, use abstractions in specific situations, and form parts into complete structures. Administered with the California Short Form Test of Academic Aptitude (TC005919-005923).

13656
Ohio Vocational Achievement Tests: Small Engine Repair. Ohio State Dept. of Education, Div. of Vocational Education, Columbus, OH 1983
Subtests: Tools and Fasteners; Fuel and Exhaust Systems; Cooling and Lubrication Systems; Short Block and Governor Systems; Charging and Electrical Systems; Starting Systems; Mechanics Mathematics; Ignition Systems; Valve Train Systems; Troubleshooting; Lawn and Garden Equipment; Motorcycle Equipment; Marine Equipment; Snowmobile Equipment; Business and Shop Operators
Descriptors: *Achievement Tests; Grade 11; Grade 12; High Schools; *High School Students; *Small Engine Mechanics; *Vocational Education
Availability: Ohio State University, Instructional Materials Laboratory; 1885 Neil Ave., Columbus, OH 43210
Grade Level: 11-12
Notes: Time, 240 min. approx.; Items, 369

For use in the evaluation and diagnosis of vocational achievement. Developed to measure skills and understandings in specific vocational areas. Items measure ability to solve problems, analyze data, recall facts, have a knowledge of principles, react to generalizations, use abstractions in specific situations, and form parts into complete structures. Administered with the California Short Form Test of Academic Aptitude (TC005919-005923).

13702
La Prueba Riverside de Realizacion en Espanol.
Cote, Nancy S. and Others 1984
Subtests: Reading Comprehension; Vocabulary; Study Skills; Grammar; Punctuation; Capitalization; Spelling; Math Computation; Math Problem Solving; Social Studies; Science
Descriptors: *Achievement Tests; Bilingual Students; Capitalization (Alphabetic); Elementary Secondary Education; Grammar; Language Skills; Literacy; Mathematics; Mathematics Tests; Punctuation; Reading; Reading Comprehension; Sciences; Social Studies; *Spanish; Spanish Speaking; Spelling; Study Skills; Vocabulary
Identifiers: 3 Rs Test; Test Batteries
Availability: Riverside Publishing Co.; 8420 Bryn Mawr Ave., Chicago, IL 60631
Grade Level: K-9
Notes: Time, 100 min. approx.

This Spanish-language edition of the 3-R's Test (TC011502-TC011505) is designed to assess the achievement of students whose primary language is Spanish and to determine the degree to which students are literate in Spanish. It is recommended that the school district select the level of the test that will be administered in each grade, according to the students' level of Spanish literacy. Results are reported in terms of local norms based on the use of a specific test level in a particular grade. Test times vary from 80 to 165 minutes by grade level.

13720
The Ber-Sil Spanish Test, Revised Edition. Beringer, Marjorie L. 1976
Descriptors: *Bilingual Students; Elementary Education; *Elementary School Students; English (Second Language); *Individual Testing; Language Dominance; *Language Proficiency; Magnetic Tape Cassettes; *Screening Tests; *Spanish Speaking
Availability: The Ber-Sil Co.; 3412 Seaglen Drive, Rancho Palos Verdes, CA 90274
Grade Level: K-6
Age Level: 5-11
Notes: Time, 30 min. approx.; Items, 118

Developed as an individual screening instrument to evaluate Spanish-speaking children in southern California. Non-Spanish-speaking examiner can observe the way the children respond to their native language. Test is divided into 3 sections: vocabulary, action responses to directions, and visual-motor activity involving writing and drawing. Directions and vocabulary are on tape. Test assists examiner in determining direction for further study of child. Test was developed in response to California legislation mandating that child be screened for language dominance before an approved intelligence test could be administered and before child can be placed in a special education program.

13721
The Ber-Sil Spanish Test, Secondary Level, Revised. Beringer, Marjorie L. 1984
Descriptors: *Bilingual Students; English (Second Language); *Individual Testing; Language Dominance; *Language Proficiency; Magnetic Tape Cassettes; *Screening Tests; Secondary Education; *Secondary School Students; *Spanish Speaking
Availability: The Ber-Sil Co.; 3412 Seaglen Drive, Rancho Palos Verdes, CA 90274
Grade Level: 7-12

Age Level: 13-17
Notes: Time, 45 min. approx.; Items, 175

Developed as a quick individual screening test to evaluate Spanish-speaking secondary students in southern California. Test was developed in response to state legislation mandating that child be screened for language dominance before an approved intelligence test can be administered and before child can be placed in a special education program. Test assesses knowledge and ability in 4 areas of Spanish: vocabulary, grammar, punctuation, and spelling. Also assesses knowledge of basic processes in mathematics. Can be administered by non-Spanish evaluators, using a cassette tape. Also translated into Phillipine languages of Tagalog and Ilokano.

13728
Bracken Basic Concept Scale. Bracken, Bruce A. 1984
Subtests: Color; Letter Identification; Numbers/Counting; Comparisons; Shapes; Direction/Position; Social/Emotional; Size; Texture/Material; Quantity; Time/Sequence
Descriptors: *Achievement Tests; *Concept Formation; Culture Fair Tests; *Diagnostic Tests; *Grade 1; *Kindergarten Children; Knowledge Level; *Preschool Children; Pretests Posttests; Primary Education; *Screening Tests
Identifiers: BBCS
Availability: The Psychological Corp.; 555 Academic Ct., San Antonio, TX 78204-0952
Grade Level: K-1
Age Level: 2-7

Divided into 2 separate instruments for quick identification or comprehensive diagnosis of basic concept development in children. The diagnostic full-scale instrument measures 258 concepts and is appropriate for use with children from ages 2.5 years through 7 years 11 months. The 30-item screening tests (forms A and B) are used to screen small groups of children to determine whether further diagnosis is necessary. The screening tests are intended for children in kindergarten and grade 1. The alternate forms allow for pretest/posttest design, program evaluation and/or reassessment. BBCS was designed to measure a subset of children's receptive vocabulary, namely basic concepts. The author's definition of a basic concept is a word that serves as a label for one of the basic colors, comparatives, directions, materials, positions, quantities, relationships, sequences, shapes, sizes, social or emotional states and characteristics, textures, and time.

13740
The Patterned Elicitation Syntax Test, Revised and Expanded Edition. Young, Edna Carter; Perachio, Joseph J. 1983
Descriptors: *Expressive Language; *Grammar; *Language Tests; *Young Children
Identifiers: PEST
Availability: Communication Skill Builders; 3830 E. Bellevue, Tucson, AZ 85733
Age Level: 3-7
Notes: Items, 44

Designed to determine whether a child's expressive grammatical skills are age appropriate. Is now an age-referenced measure that can be used to assess in the selection of subjects for treatment and as a means of gaining preliminary information on specific grammatical structures. May be used as a screening tool. Consists of 44 items of increasing complexity that range in sentence or phrase length from 3 to 8 words. Test is based on standard English and it is appropriate for speakers of standard English. Can be administered and interpreted by examinees without extensive experience in testing or in linguistic theory as well as by speech/language clinicians and hearing specialists.

13751
Evaluating Acquired Skills in Communication.
Riley, Anita Marcott 1984
Descriptors: Adolescents; *Autism; Children; *Communication Skills; Expressive Language; Informal Assessment; Language Handicaps; Mental Retardation; Preschool Children; Receptive Language; Young Adults; Young Children
Identifiers: EASIC; Prelanguage
Availability: Communication Skill Builders; 3830 E. Bellevue, Tucson, AZ 85733
Age Level: 2-26

Five-level informal communication skills inventory for the preschool, language-impaired, mentally impaired, and autistic student. The informal communication skills inventories include the areas of semantics, syntax, morphology, and pragmatics. Each assessment level is organized into skill clusters ordered from easy to difficult.

13765
Japanese Proficiency Test. Educational Testing Service, Princeton, NJ 1981
Subtests: Listening Comprehension; Reading Proficiency; Japanese Character Recognition

Descriptors: *Achievement Tests; College Students; Graduate Students; Higher Education; Ideography; *Japanese; Listening Comprehension; Reading Ability; *Second Language Learning
Identifiers: JPT
Availability: Educational Testing Service; Program Office P134, Princeton, NJ 08541
Grade Level: 13-20
Notes: Time, 120 min. approx.

Designed for use by American and other English-speaking learners of Japanese ranging from those who have completed at least one year of intensive Japanese instruction to those who have acquired greater proficiency usually associated with completing a college or graduate-level language program. Provides scores for listening comprehension and reading proficiency. Also provides a score for Japanese character recognition. Two equivalent forms of the test are available, permitting pre- and posttesting.

13766
Tests of Engineering Aptitude, Mathematics, and Science. JETS, Inc., Alexandria, VA
Descriptors: *Achievement Tests; Awards; Biology; *Chemistry; Competition; Computer Literacy; Computers; *Engineering; Engineering Graphics; *English; High Schools; *High School Students; Physics; *Secondary School Mathematics
Identifiers: TEAMS
Availability: JETS, Inc.; 1420 King St., Ste. 405, Alexandria, VA 22314-2715
Grade Level: 9-12

Two-level (state and national) competition program that encourages interest in engineering, technology, science, and mathematics. Student teams solve problems and answer questions related to engineering, science, technology, and mathematics. Problems are multidisciplinary in nature, so that students can see the relationships between subject areas in real-world applications.

13771
Brigance Preschool Screen for Three- and Four-Year Old Children. Brigance, Albert H. 1985
Descriptors: *Child Development; Criterion Referenced Tests; Developmental Tasks; *Preschool Children; School Readiness; *Screening Tests; *Spanish Speaking
Availability: Curriculum Associates; 5 Esquire Rd., N. Billerica, MA 08162-2589
Age Level: 3-4
Notes: Time, 12 min. approx.

A screening test for 3- and 4-year-old children used to obtain a sampling of a child's skills and behavior to identify those who may need more comprehensive evaluation. The skills that are assessed include personal data responses, identification of body parts, gross motor skills, object identification, sentence repetition, visual motor skills, number concepts, building a tower with blocks, matching colors, picture vocabulary, plurals and -ing, identifying use of objects, identifying colors, using prepositions and irregular plural nouns. Spanish direction lines for screening Spanish-speaking children are available.

13775
Informal Reading Comprehension Placement Test. Insel, Eunice; Edson, Ann
Subtests: Word Comprehension; Passage Comprehension
Descriptors: Achievement Tests; Computer Assisted Testing; *Elementary School Students; Elementary Secondary Education; *Junior High School Students; *Microcomputers; *Reading Comprehension; *Reading Tests; Remedial Reading; *Student Placement
Identifiers: Apple (Computer); TRS80
Availability: Educational Activities, Inc.; P.O. Box 392, Freeport, NY 11520
Grade Level: 1-8

Sequentially designed reading comprehension placement test for students in grades 1 through 8 and in remedial secondary programs. Administered, scored, and managed on either an Apple microcomputer (48K) or a TRS 80III or IV (32K). Word comprehension section has 60 items to measure students' knowledge of word meanings and uses an analogy format. Passage comprehension section consists of 8 graded selections and questions at varying degrees of difficulty.

13808
Illinois Inventory of Educational Progress, Grade 4. Illinois State Board of Education, Springfield 1984
Descriptors: *Achievement Tests; *Elementary School Mathematics; Elementary School Students; *Geometry; *Grade 4; Intermediate Grades; Mathematics Tests; *Reading Comprehension; Reading Tests; Science Tests; *State Programs; Student Attitudes
Identifiers: Illinois
Availability: ERIC Document Reproduction Service; 7420 Fullerton Rd., Ste. 110, Springfield, VA 22153-2852 (ED240160, 42p)

Grade Level: 4
Notes: Items, 143

A test of educational progress developed by the Illinois State Board of Education to assess student achievement in reading, mathematics, geometry, and science. The test booklet also contains a 27-item student questionnaire eliciting student attitudes toward science.

13809
Illinois Inventory of Educational Progress, Grade 8. Illinois State Board of Education, Springfield 1984
Descriptors: *Achievement Tests; *Geometry; *Grade 8; Junior High Schools; Junior High School Students; Mathematics Tests; *Reading Comprehension; Reading Tests; Science Tests; *Secondary School Mathematics; *Secondary School Science; *State Programs; Student Attitudes
Identifiers: Illinois
Availability: ERIC Document Reproduction Service; 7420 Fullerton Rd., Ste. 110, Springfield, VA 22153-2852 (ED240161, 50p)
Grade Level: 8
Notes: Items, 175

A test of educational progress developed by the Illinois State Board of Education to assess student achievement in reading, mathematics, geometry, and science. The test booklet also contains a 27-item student questionnaire eliciting student attitudes toward science.

13810
Illinois Inventory of Educational Progress, Grade 11. Illinois State Board of Education, Springfield 1984
Descriptors: *Achievement Tests; *Geometry; *Grade 11; High Schools; High School Students; Mathematics Tests; *Reading Comprehension; Reading Tests; Science Tests; *Secondary School Mathematics; *Secondary School Science; *State Programs; Student Attitudes
Identifiers: Illinois
Availability: ERIC Document Reproduction Service; 7420 Fullerton Rd., Ste. 110, Springfield, VA 22153-2852 (ED240162, 55 p.)
Grade Level: 11
Notes: Items, 183

A test of educational progress developed by the Illinois State Board of Education to assess student achievement in reading, mathematics, geometry, and science. Test booklet also contains a 27-item student questionnaire eliciting students' attitudes toward science.

13829
Computer Managed Screening Test. Fitch, James L. 1984
Descriptors: *Articulation (Speech); *Computer Assisted Testing; *Expressive Language; *Language Fluency; Microcomputers; *Receptive Language; *Screening Tests; *Voice Disorders; *Young Children
Availability: Communication Skill Builders; 3830 E. Bellevue, Tucson, AZ 85733
Age Level: 3-8
Notes: Time, 4 min. approx.; Items, 32

A screening test to evaluate child's articulation, expressive and receptive language, voice, and fluency. Administrator reads instructions from the screen, child responds, and administrator keys in whether the response was correct or incorrect. The test can be administered using the program that runs on the Apple II, IIe, or IIc.

13830
Receptive One-Word Picture Vocabulary Test. Gardner, Morrison F. 1985
Descriptors: *Vocabulary; Bilingual Students; Children; *Cognitive Development; Elementary School Students; Emotional Disturbances; *Individual Testing; *Norm Referenced Tests; Physical Disabilities; Pictorial Stimuli; Preschool Children; *Receptive Language; *Screening Tests; Spanish; Spanish Speaking; Speech Handicaps; Visual Measures; Basic Vocabulary
Identifiers: Oral Tests; ROWPVT
Availability: Academic Therapy Publications; 20 Commercial Blvd., Novato, CA 94947-6191
Age Level: 2-11
Notes: Time, 20 min. approx.

Individually administered, norm-referenced, untimed test developed to obtain an estimate of a child's one-word hearing vocabulary based on what child has learned from home and formal education. When used alone, provides a means for evaluating receptive vocabulary of those with expressive difficulties, such as bilingual, speech-impaired, immature and withdrawn, and emotionally or physically impaired children. Norms for the Receptive One-Word Picture Vocabulary Test and the Expressive One-Word Picture Vocabulary Test are equivalent. When both tests are used, comparison of results provides information about differences in these language skills that could be a result of specific language impairment, language delay,

bilingualism, nonstimulating home environment, cultural differences, learning difficulties, or other factors to be investigated. Spanish forms are also available to obtain an estimate of a child's Spanish vocabulary.

13844
Texas Preschool Screening Inventory, Revised. Haber, Julian S.; Norris, Marylee 1984
Subtests: Auditory Memory for Numbers and Letters; Visual Memory for Objects; Auditory Sequencing; Articulation; Sound Discrimination; Rotations and Reversals of Letters and Numbers; Following Instructions and Understanding Prepositions
Descriptors: Articulation (Speech); Auditory Perception; *Handicap Identification; *High Risk Students; Learning Problems; *Preschool Children; Preschool Education; Primary Education; *Screening Tests; Visual Perception
Identifiers: Coping Skills; Following Directions
Availability: ERIC Document Reproduction Service; 7420 Fullerton Rd., Ste. 110, Springfield, VA 22153-2852 (ED246057, 15 p.)
Age Level: 4-6

This instrument is a revision of the Texas Preschool Screening Inventory (TPSI). It is a screening test designed to identify children who may be at risk for learning problems as they enter kindergarten or first grade. The components include Auditory Memory for Numbers and Letters; Visual Memory for Objects; Auditory Sequencing; Articulation; Sound Discrimination; Rotations and Reversals of Letters and Numbers; and Following Instructions and Understanding Prepositions.

13866
Modular Examinations in Drug Abuse and Alcoholism. National Board of Medical Examiners, National Institute on Drug Abuse, Rockville, MD. 1983
Descriptors: *Achievement Tests; Adults; *Alcoholism; *Drug Abuse; Graduate Medical Students; *Health Personnel; Inservice Education; Knowledge Level; Medical Students
Availability: National Board of Medical Examiners; 3930 Chestnut St., Philadelphia, PA 19104
Age Level: Adults

Examinations offered through the National Board of Medical Examiners for use by medical schools, residency training programs, hospital in-house training programs, medical speciality, or allied health organizations interested in education and evaluation of health professionals in the areas of drug abuse and alcoholism. Each module consists of 2 books: a test book and a referenced answer book. The test book consists of one or more patient management programs (PMP) and multiple-choice questions generally related to the topic in the PMP. Eight modules are currently available and cover methadone maintenance, polydrug abuse, abuse of various individual drugs, and various clinical problems involving alcoholism.

13876
Metropolitan Achievement Test, Sixth Edition, Survey Battery, Preprimer. Prescott, George A.; And Others 1985
Subtests: Word Recognition; Mathematics Concepts; Mathematics Problem Solving; Language
Descriptors: *Achievement Tests; Elementary School Mathematics; Elementary School Students; Elementary Secondary Education; *Kindergarten Children; Language Skills; Primary Education; Reading; Student Placement; Word Recognition
Identifiers: Instructional Level; Reading Level; *Test Batteries
Availability: The Psychological Corp.; 555 Academic Ct., San Antonio, TX 78204-0952
Grade Level: K
Notes: Time, 98 min.; Items, 102

A measure of achievement in basic skill areas covering a broad range of objectives. The Word Recognition Skills subtest covers visual discrimination, single graphemes, grapheme combinations, letter recognition, auditory discrimination, and initial consonants. The Mathematics Concepts subtest covers numeration, basic concepts, units and tens, geometry and measurement, basic terms, shapes and figures, money. The Mathematics Problem Solving subtest covers addition and subtraction basic facts. The Language subtest covers listening comprehension. This test has empirical fall and spring norms and interpolated week of testing norms. Scores are scaled; national, nonpublic, and local percentile ranks; stanines, normal curve equivalents; grade equivalents. Reading and math tests provide an instructional level for pupil placement in texts and programs.

13877
Metropolitan Achievement Tests, Sixth Edition: Survey Battery, Primer. Prescott, George A.; And Others 1985
Subtests: Vocabulary; Word Recognition Skills; Reading comprehension; Mathematics; Language

Descriptors: *Achievement Tests; Elementary School Mathematics; Elementary School Students; Elementary Secondary Education; *Kindergarten Children; Language Skills; *Primary Education; Reading Comprehension; Student Placement; Vocabulary Skills; Word Recognition
Identifiers: Instructional Level; Reading Level; *Test Batteries
Availability: The Psychological Corp.; 555 Academic Ct., San Antonio, TX 78204-0952
Grade Level: K-1
Notes: Time, 134 min.; Items, 153

A measure of achievement in basic skill areas covering a broad range of objectives. The Vocabulary subtest covers meaning of words in context. The Word Recognition Skills subtest covers recognition, auditory discrimination; phoneme/grapheme consonants, rhyming words. The Reading Comprehension subtest covers words, rebus, sentences and passages, recognition of literal detail, inferring meaning, drawing conclusions. The Mathematics subtest covers numeration, geometry, measurement, problem solving, computation with whole numbers, number concepts through tens, money, dictated word problems involving arithmetic. The Language subtest covers listening comprehension, usage, spelling, selecting verb forms. This test has empirical fall and spring norms and interpolated week of testing norms. Scores are scaled; national, nonpublic, and local percentile ranks; stanines; normal curve equivalents; grade equivalents. Scores in higher order thinking skills and research skills can be derived from items embedded in content areas. Reading and math tests provide an instructional level for pupil placement in texts and programs.

13878
Metropolitan Achievement Tests, Sixth Edition: Survey Battery, Primary 1. Prescott, George A.; And Others 1985
Subtests: Vocabulary; Word Recognition Skills; Reading Comprehension; Math Concepts; Math Problem Solving; Math Computation; Spelling; Language; Science; Social Studies
Descriptors: *Achievement Tests; Arithmetic; Critical Thinking; *Elementary School Mathematics; Elementary School Students; Elementary Secondary Education; Language Skills; Mathematical Concepts; *Primary Education; Problem Solving; Reading Comprehension; Sciences; Social Sciences; Spelling; Student Placement; Vocabulary Skills; Word Recognition
Identifiers: Blooms Taxonomy; Instructional Level; Reading Level; *Test Batteries
Availability: The Psychological Corp.; 555 Academic Ct., San Antonio, TX 78204-0952
Grade Level: 1-2
Notes: Time, 215 min.; Items, 288

A measure of achievement in basic skill areas covering a broad range of objectives. The Vocabulary subtest covers words in context. The Word Recognition subtest covers phoneme/grapheme consonants and vowels, word part clues. The Reading Comprehension subtest covers rebus, sentences, passages, recognize detail and sequence, infer meaning, cause and effect, main idea, character analysis, drawing conclusions. The Math Concepts subtest covers numeration, geometry, measurement, counting, shapes, money, time. The Math Problem Solving subtest covers addition, subtraction, basic facts, regrouping; spelling; dictated words. The Language subtest covers listening comprehension, punctuation, capitalization, usage, written expression. The Science subtest covers physical, earth, space, and life sciences. The Social Studies subtest covers geography, economics, history, political science, human behaviors. Science and social studies subtests assess knowledge, comprehension, inquiry skills and critical analysis from Bloom's Taxonomy. This test has empirical fall and spring norms and interpolated week of testing norms. Scores are scaled; national, nonpublic, and local percentile ranks; stanines; normal curve equivalents; grade equivalents. Scores in higher order thinking skills can be derived from items embedded in content areas. Reading and Math tests provide an instructional level for pupil placement in texts and programs.

13879
Metropolitan Achievement Tests, Sixth Edition: Survey Battery, Primary 2. Prescott, George A.; And Others 1985
Subtests: Vocabulary; Word Recognition Skills; Reading Comprehension; Mathematics Concepts; Mathematics Problem Solving; Mathematics Computation; Spelling; Language; Science; Social Studies
Descriptors: *Achievement Tests; Arithmetic; Critical Thinking; Elementary School Mathematics; Elementary School Students; Elementary Secondary Education; Language Skills; Mathematical Concepts; *Primary Education; Problem Solving; Sciences; Social Sciences; Spelling; Student Placement; Vocabulary Skills
Identifiers: Blooms Taxonomy; Instructional Level; Reading Level; *Test Batteries
Availability: The Psychological Corp.; 555 Academic Ct., San Antonio, TX 78204-0952
Grade Level: 2-3
Notes: Time, 175 min.; Items, 245

A measure of achievement in basic skill areas covering a broad range of objectives. The Vocabulary subtest covers meaning of words in context. The Word Recognition subtest covers phoneme/grapheme consonants and vowels, word part clues. The Reading Comprehension subtest covers detail and sequence; inferring meaning; cause and effect, main idea, character analysis, drawing conclusions. The Mathematics Concepts subtest covers numeration, geometry, measurement, thousands, money, time. The Mathematics Problem Solving subtest covers word problems. The Mathematics Computation subtest covers addition and subtraction, basic facts, regrouping, multiplication, division. Spelling uses dictated words. Science covers physical, earth, space and life sciences. Social Studies covers geography, economics, history, political science, and human behavior. Science and Social Studies assess knowledge, comprehension, inquiry skills and critical analysis from Bloom's Taxonomy. There is a Language subtest. This test has empirical fall and spring norms and interpolated week of testing norms. Scores are scaled; national, nonpublic, and local percentile ranks; stanines; normal curve equivalents; grade equivalents. Scores in higher order thinking skills can be derived from items embedded in content areas. Reading and Math tests provide an instructional level for pupil placement in texts and programs.

13880
Metropolitan Achievement Tests, Sixth Edition: Survey Battery, Elementary. Prescott, George A.; And Others 1985
Subtests: Vocabulary; Word Recognition Skills; Reading Comprehension; Mathematics Concepts; Mathematics Problem Solving; Mathematics Computation; Spelling; Language; Science; Social Studies
Descriptors: *Achievement Tests; Arithmetic; Critical Thinking; *Elementary Education; Elementary School Mathematics; Elementary School Students; Elementary Secondary Education; Language Skills; Mathematical Concepts; Problem Solving; Research Skills; Sciences; Social Sciences; Spelling; Student Placement; Vocabulary Skills; Word Recognition
Identifiers: Blooms Taxonomy; Instructional Level; Reading Level; *Test Batteries
Availability: The Psychological Corp.; 555 Academic Ct., San Antonio, TX 78204-0952
Grade Level: 3-4
Notes: Time, 254 min.; Items, 359

A measure of achievement in basic skill areas covering a broad range of objectives. The Vocabulary subtest covers meaning of words in context. The Word Recognition subtest covers phoneme/grapheme consonants and vowels, word part clues. The Reading Comprehension subtest covers recognizing detail and sequence, inferring meaning; cause and effect, main idea, character analysis, drawing conclusions. The Mathematical Concepts subtest covers numeration, geometry, measurement, decimals and fractions, thousands, money, time. The Mathematics Problem Solving subtest covers word problems. The Mathematics Computation subtest covers computation with whole numbers requiring addition and subtraction, with or without regrouping, multiplication and division, computation with decimals and fractions requiring addition, subtraction, like denominators. The Spelling subtest requires correct spelling to be selected. The Language subtest covers rules for standard English including punctuation, capitalization, usage, written expression and study skills as alphabetizing and dictionary skills. The Science subtest covers physical, earth, space, and life sciences. The Social Studies subtest covers geography, economics, history, political science, and human behavior. The Science and Social Studies subtests assess knowledge, comprehension, inquiry skills and critical analysis from Bloom's Taxonomy. This test has empirical fall and spring norms and interpolated week of testing norms. Scores are scaled; national, nonpublic, and local percentile ranks; stanines; normal curve equivalents; grade equivalents. Scores in higher order thinking skills and research skills can be derived from items embedded in content areas. Reading and Math tests provide an instructional level for pupil placement in texts and programs.

13881
Metropolitan Achievement Tests, Sixth Edition: Survey Battery, Intermediate. Prescott, George A.; And Others 1985
Subtests: Vocabulary; Reading Comprehension; Mathematics Concepts; Mathematics Problem Solving; Mathematics Computation; Spelling; Language; Science; Social Studies
Descriptors: *Achievement Tests; Arithmetic; Critical Thinking; Elementary School Mathematics; Elementary School Students; Elementary Secondary Education; *Intermediate Grades; Language Skills; Mathematical Concepts; Problem Solving; Research Skills; Sciences; Social Studies; Spelling; Student Placement; Vocabulary Skills
Identifiers: Blooms Taxonomy; Instructional Level; Reading Level; *Test Batteries
Availability: The Psychological Corp.; 555 Academic Ct., San Antonio, TX 78204-0952
Grade Level: 5-6
Notes: Time, 244 min.; Items, 354

A measure of achievement in basic skill areas covering a broad range of objectives. The Vocabulary subtest covers meaning of words in context. The Reading Comprehension subtest covers recognizing detail and sequence, inferring meaning; cause and effect, main idea, character analysis, drawing conclusions, determining author's purpose, distinguishing fact from opinion. The Mathematical Concepts subtest covers numeration, geometry, measurement, decimals, numbers beyond thousands, fractions, advanced concepts, customary and metric measurement. The Mathematics Problem Solving subtest covers word problems, some including graphs and statistics. The Mathematics Computation subtest covers computation with whole numbers requiring addition and subtraction, multiplication, division; computation with decimals and fractions requires addition, subtraction, multiplication, like and unlike denominators. The Spelling subtest requires the selection of the correctly spelled word. The Language subtest covers rules for standard English including punctuation, capitalization, usage, written expression, and study skills as dictionary skills and use of reference sources. The Science subtest covers physical, earth, space, and life sciences. The Social Studies subtest covers geography, economics, history, political science, human behavior. Science and Social Studies subtests assess knowledge, comprehension, inquiry skills and critical analysis from Bloom's Taxonomy. This test has empirical fall and spring norms and interpolated week of testing norms. Scores are scaled; national, nonpublic, and local percentile ranks; stanines; normal curve equivalents; grade equivalents. Scores in higher order thinking skills and research skills can be derived from items embedded in content areas. Reading and Math tests provide an instructional level for pupil placement in texts and programs.

13882
Metropolitan Achievement Tests, Sixth Edition: Survey Battery, Advanced 1. Prescott, George A.; And Others 1985
Subtests: Vocabulary; Reading Comprehension; Mathematics Concepts; Mathematics Problem Solving; Mathematics Computation; Spelling; Language; Science; Social Studies
Descriptors: *Achievement Tests; Arithmetic; Computation; Critical Thinking; Elementary Secondary Education; *Junior High Schools; Junior High School Students; Language Skills; Mathematical Concepts; Problem Solving; Reading Comprehension; Research Skills; Sciences; Secondary Education; Secondary School Mathematics; Social Studies; Spelling; Student Placement; Vocabulary Skills
Identifiers: Blooms Taxonomy; Instructional Level; Reading Level; *Test Batteries
Availability: The Psychological Corp.; 555 Academic Ct., San Antonio, TX 78204-0952
Grade Level: 7-9
Notes: Time, 244 min.; Items, 354

A measure of achievement in basic skill areas covering a broad range of objectives. The Vocabulary subtest covers meaning of words in context. The Reading Comprehension subtest covers recognizing detail and sequence, inferring meaning; cause and effect, main idea, character analysis, drawing conclusions, determining author's purpose, distinguishing fact from opinion. The Mathematical Concepts subtest covers numeration, geometry, measurement, numbers beyond thousands, decimals, fractions, advanced concepts, functions and equations, customary and metric measurement. The Mathematics Problem Solving subtest covers word problems, some including graphs and statistics. The Mathematics Computation subtest covers computation with whole numbers requiring addition and subtraction, multiplication, division and estimation, addition, subtraction, multiplication and division with decimals, fractions and mixed numbers, percents and proportions. The Spelling subtest requires that correct spelling be selected. The Language subtest covers rules for standard English including punctuation, capitalization, usage, written expression and study skills as dictionary skills, use of reference source. The Science subtest covers physical, earth, space, and life sciences. The Social Studies subtest covers geography, economics, history, political science, human behavior. The Science and Social Studies subtests assess knowledge, comprehension, inquiry skills and critical analysis from Bloom's Taxonomy. This test has empirical fall and spring norms and interpolated week of testing norms. Scores are scaled; national, nonpublic, and local percentile ranks; stanines; normal curve equivalents; grade equivalents. Scores in higher order thinking skills and research skills can be derived from items embedded in content areas. Reading and Math tests provide an instructional level for pupil placement in texts and programs.

13883
Metropolitan Achievement Tests, Sixth Edition: Survey Battery, Advanced 2. Prescott, George A.; And Others 1985

Subtests: Vocabulary; Reading Comprehension; Mathematics; Spelling; Language; Science; Social Studies; Research Skills
Descriptors: *Achievement Tests; Critical Thinking; Elementary Secondary Education; *High School Students; Language Skills; Reading Comprehension; Research Skills; Sciences; Secondary Education; Secondary School Mathematics; Social Studies; Spelling; Student Placement; Vocabulary Skills
Identifiers: Blooms Taxonomy; Instructional Level; Reading Level; *Test Batteries
Availability: The Psychological Corp.; 555 Academic Ct., San Antonio, TX 78204-0952
Grade Level: 10-12
Notes: Time, 302 min.; Items, 190

A measure of achievement in basic skill areas covering a broad range of objectives. The Vocabulary subtest covers meaning of words in context. The Reading Comprehension subtest covers recognizing detail and sequence, inferring meaning; cause and effect, main idea, character analysis, drawing conclusions, determining author's purpose, distinguishing fact from opinion. The Mathematics subtest covers numeration, geometry, measurement, decimals, fractions, advanced concepts, functions and equations, customary and metric measurement, problem solving, graphs and statistics, computation with whole numbers requiring addition and subtraction, multiplication, division and estimation, addition, subtraction, multiplication and division with decimals, fractions and mixed numbers; percents and proportions. Spelling requires that the correct spelling be selected. The Language subtest covers rules for standard English including punctuation, capitalization, usage, written expression, study skills as dictionary skills, and use of reference sources. The Science subtest covers physical, earth, space, and life sciences. The Social Studies subtest covers geography, economics, history, political science, and human behavior. Science and Social Studies subtests assess knowledge, comprehension, inquiry skills and critical analysis from Bloom's Taxonomy. This test has empirical fall and spring nnorms and interpolated week of testing norms. Scores are scaled; national, nonpublic, and local percentile ranks; stanines; normal curve equivalents; grade equivalents. Scores in higher order thinking skills and research skills can be derived from items embedded in content areas. Reading and Math tests provide an instructional level for pupil placement in texts and programs.

13915
Computer Managed Articulation Diagnosis.
Fitch, James L. 1984
Descriptors: Adolescents; Adults; *Articulation (Speech); Children; *Computer Assisted Testing; *Diagnostic Tests; Individualized Education Programs; Language Tests; *Microcomputers
Availability: Communication Skill Builders, 3830 E. Bellevue, Tucson, AZ 85733
Age Level: 4-64
Notes: Items, 46

Articulation test given at a computer to assess students' and clients' articulation errors. Client produces single phonemes and blends for analysis. Each sound is presented in pre- and postvocalic position. Student data can be stored on a disk. Computer generates a 4-page analysis of error patterns. Program runs on Apple II IIe, and IIc.

13928
ACT Proficiency Examination Program: Microbiology. American College Testing Program, Iowa City, IA 1985
Descriptors: Adults; *Adult Students; *Equivalency Tests; *Microbiology; Objective Tests; Postsecondary Education; Study Guides
Identifiers: American College Testing Program; New York; PEP Regents External Degree
Availability: American College Testing Program; P.O. Box 168, Iowa City, IA 52240
Age Level: 18-64
Notes: Time, 180 min. approx.; Items, 150

Developed as part of one of 2 New York programs, the College Proficiency Examination Program and the Regents External Degree Program. Designed to assist postsecondary institutions in granting credit by examination. Tests are updated periodically. Administered by the American College Testing Program in all states except New York. Exam is based on material normally taught in a one-semester, introductory course at the undergraduate level. Tests for knowledge and understanding of bacteria, algea, fungi, protozoa, viruses and their relationships to humans. Covers areas such as history, morphology and ultrastructure, metabolism, growth and nutrition, genetics, physiological types, methods of control, and applied and environmental microbiology. Also covers major infectious agents, as well as specific and nonspecific resistance expressed by the host, humoral and cellular immunity, and disorders of the immune system. Exam will also test for comprehension of an ability to apply concepts of laboratory techniques and methods.

13929
ACT Proficiency Examination Program: Abnormal Psychology. American College Testing Program, Iowa City, IA 1985
Descriptors: Adults; *Adult Students; *Equivalency Tests; Objective Tests; Postsecondary Education; *Psychopathology; Study Guides
Identifiers: American College Testing Program; New York; PEP Regents External Degree
Availability: American College Testing Program; P.O. Box 168, Iowa City, IA 52240
Age Level: 18-64
Notes: Time, 180 min. approx.; Items, 150

Developed as part of 1 of 2 New York programs, the College Proficiency Examination Program and the Regents External Degree Program. Designed to assist postsecondary institutions in granting credit by examination. Tests are updated periodically. Administered by the American College Testing Program in all states except New York. Based on material normally taught in a one-semester course at the upper division level of an undergraduate program. Tests for knowledge and understanding of the historical background of abnormal psychology, major conceptualizations in the area, and the nature and description of abnormal disorders as well as their definitions, classification, etiology, and major treatments.

13930
ACT Proficiency Examination Program: Statistics. American College Testing Program, Iowa City, IA 1985
Descriptors: Adults; *Adult Students; *Equivalency Tests; Objective Tests; Postsecondary Education; *Statistics; Study Guides
Identifiers: American College Testing Program; New York; PEP Regents External Degree
Availability: American College Testing Program; P.O. Box 168, Iowa City, IA 52240
Age Level: 18-64
Notes: Time, 180 min. approx.; Items, 100

Developed as part of 1 of 2 New York programs, the College Proficiency Examination Program and the Regents External Degree Program. Designed to assist postsecondary institutions in granting credit by examination. Tests are updated periodically. Administered by the American College Testing Program in all states except New York. Based on material normally taught in a one-semester, introductory course in statistics at undergraduate level. Assumes a basic knowledge of algebra. Tests for knowledge and understanding of fundamental concepts of descriptive and inferential statistics.

13965
Test for Auditory Comprehension of Language, Revised Edition. Carrow-Woolfolk, Elizabeth 1985
Subtests: Word Classes and Relations; Grammatical Morphemes; Elaborated Sentence Constructions
Descriptors: Adolescents; Adults; *Children; *Individual Testing; Language Tests; *Listening Comprehension
Identifiers: TACL
Availability: DLM Teaching Resources; One DLM Park, Allen, TX 75002
Age Level: 3-64
Notes: Time, 10 min. approx.; Items, 120

Individually administered test of auditory comprehension covering the literal and most common meanings of word classes, meaning of grammatical morphemes, and the meaning of elaborated sentence constructions. Norms are available for children aged 3 through 10. Test may also be used with adults. No oral responses are required. Items are arranged according to difficulty within each of the 3 basic categories. May be used to help identify subjects with language problems, to plan intervention programs, to aid in predicting success in the early school years or as one indicator of school readiness, to measure improvement in language skills, or as a tool in research studies.

13994
Stanford Diagnostic Mathematics Test, Third Edition, Red Level. Beatty, Leslie S.; And Others 1984
Subtests: Number System and Numeration; Computation; Applications
Descriptors: Arithmetic; *Diagnostic Tests; Elementary Education; *Elementary School Mathematics; *Elementary School Students; Grouping (Instructional Purposes); Instructional Development; Measurement; Number Systems; Pretests Posttests; Primary Education; Problem Solving; Whole Numbers
Identifiers: Chapter One; SDMT
Availability: The Psychological Corp.; 555 Academic Ct., San Antonio, TX 78204-0952
Grade Level: 1-4
Notes: Time, 85 min.; Items, 90

Designed to measure progress in basic mathematics concepts and skills and to identify individual needs for developing instructional strategies. Said to contain more easy items to increase reliability for students scoring below the fiftieth percentile. Complies with Chapter 1 testing re-

quirements. Statistically linked with the Stanford Achievement Test (TC011695-011700) for pre- and posttesting use. Two forms are available. Covers whole numbers (addition, subtraction, multiplication, division), fractions, decimals, percent, equations, problem solving, tables and graphs, geometry and measurement.

13995
Stanford Diagnostic Mathematics Test, Third Edition, Green Level. Beatty, Leslie S.; And Others 1984
Subtests: Number System and Numeration; Computation; Applications
Descriptors: Arithmetic; *Diagnostic Tests; *Elementary School Mathematics; *Elementary School Students; Fractions; Geometry; Graphs; Grouping (Instructional Purposes); Instructional Development; Intermediate Grades; Measurement; Number Systems; Percentage; Pretests Posttests; Problem Solving; Tables (Data); Whole Numbers
Identifiers: SDMT
Availability: The Psychological Corp.; 555 Academic Ct., San Antonio, TX 78204-0952
Grade Level: 4-6
Notes: Time, 95 min.; Items, 108

Designed to measure progress in basic mathematics concepts and skills and to identify individual needs for developing instructional strategies. Said to contain more easy items to increase reliability for students scoring below the fiftieth percentile. Complies with Chapter 1 testing requirements. Statistically linked with the Stanford Achievement Test (TC011695-011700) for pre- and posttesting use. Two forms are available. Covers whole numbers (addition, subtraction, multiplication, division), fractions, decimals, percent, equations, problem solving, tables and graphs, geometry and measurement.

13996
Stanford Diagnostic Mathematics Test, Third Edition, Brown Level. Beatty, Leslie S.; And Others 1984
Subtests: Number System and Numeration; Computation; Applications
Descriptors: Arithmetic; Decimal Fractions; *Diagnostic Tests; Fractions; Geometry; *Grade 6; Graphs; Grouping (Instructional Purposes); Instructional Development; Intermediate Grades; Junior High Schools; *Junior High School Students; *Mathematics; Measurement; Number Systems; Percentage; Pretests Posttests; Problem Solving; Tables (Data); Whole Numbers
Identifiers: SDMT
Availability: The Psychological Corp.; 555 Academic Ct., San Antonio, TX 78204-0952
Grade Level: 6-8
Notes: Time, 114 min.; Items, 100

Designed to measure progress in basic mathematics concepts and skills and to identify individual needs for developing instructional strategies. Said to contain more easy items to increase reliability for students scoring below the fiftieth percentile. Complies with Chapter 1 testing requirements. Statistically linked with the Stanford Achievement Test (TC011695-011700) for pre- and posttesting use. Two forms are available. Covers whole numbers (addition, subtraction, multiplication, division), fractions, decimals, percent, equations, problem solving, tables and graphs, geometry and measurement.

13997
Stanford Diagnostic Mathematics Test, Third Edition, Blue Level. Beatty, Leslie S. 1984
Subtests: Number System and Numeration; Computation; Applications
Descriptors: Arithmetic; Diagnostic Tests; Fractions; Geometry; Graphs; Grouping (Instructional Purposes); Instructional Development; Measurement; Number Systems; Percentage; Pretests Posttests; Problem Solving; Secondary Education; *Secondary School Mathematics; *Secondary School Students; Tables (Data); Whole Numbers
Identifiers: SDMT
Availability: The Psychological Corp.; 555 Academic Ct., San Antonio, TX 78204-0952
Grade Level: 8-12
Notes: Time, 90 min.; Items, 114

Designed to measure progress in basic mathematics concepts and skills and to identify individual needs for developing instructional strategies. Said to contain more easy items to increase reliability for students scoring below the fiftieth percentile. Complies with Chapter 1 testing requirements. Statistically linked with the Stanford Achievement Test (TC011695-011700) for pre- and posttesting use. Two forms are available. Covers whole numbers (addition, subtraction, multiplication, division), fractions, decimals, percent, equations, problem solving, tables and graphs, geometry and measurement.

14001
Sequential Assessment of Mathematics Inventories. Reisman, Fredricka K. 1985
Subtests: Mathematical Language; Ordinality; Number and Notation; Computation; Measurement; Geometric Concepts; Mathematical Applications; Word Problems
Descriptors: *Achievement Tests; Diagnostic Tests; Elementary Education; *Elementary School Mathematics; *Elementary School Students; Individual Testing; Junior High Schools; *Junior High School Students; *Mathematics Tests; *Secondary School Mathematics; Special Education; Standardized Tests
Identifiers: SAMI
Availability: The Psychological Corp.; 555 Academic Ct., San Antonio, TX 78204-0952
Grade Level: K-8
Notes: Time, 60 min. approx.

Primarily intended for those educators who assess or instruct students who have difficulty in learning mathematics. May also be administered by teachers in regular classrooms to normally achieving students but is mainly intended for use by school personnel who normally assess student performance in mathematics, including school psychologists, educational diagnosticians, and special education teachers. Consists of 2 instruments to assess mathematics performance: the SAMI Standardized Inventory and a parallel program for classroom use, the SAMI Informal Inventory may be used independently or in combination to develop a comprehensive profile of a student's overall standing in the mathematics curriculum. Test is individually administered as takes from 20 to 60 minutes, depending on student's level.

14026
Stanford Diagnostic Reading Test, Third Edition, Red Level. Karlsen, Bjorn; And Others 1984
Subtests: Word Reading; Reading Comprehension; Auditory Discrimination; Phonetic Analysis; Auditory Vocabulary
Descriptors: Decoding (Reading); *Diagnostic Tests; Elementary Education; *Elementary School Students; Grouping (Instructional Purposes); Pretests Posttests; Primary Education; *Reading; Reading Comprehension; Vocabulary
Identifiers: SDRT
Availability: The Psychological Corp.; 555 Academic Ct., San Antonio, TX 78204-0952
Grade Level: 1-4
Notes: Time, 105 min.; Items, 184

Designed for the diagnosis of specific strengths and weaknesses in reading for grouping according to instructional needs. Said to contain more easy items to increase reliability for students scoring below the fiftieth percentile. The test covers comprehension, decoding, vocabulary, and reading rate. Separate scores are given for comprehension of textual, functional, and recreational reading passages. Complies with Chapter 1 testing requirements. Statistically linked with the Stanford Achievement Test (TC011695-011700) for pre- and posttesting use. Two forms are available. Subtests vary with levels. This level may be used from spring of grade 1 to spring of grade 3.

14027
Stanford Diagnostic Reading Test, Third Edition, Green Level. Karlsen, Bjorn; And Others 1984
Subtests: Reading Comprehension; Auditory Discrimination; Phonetic Analysis; Structural Analysis; Auditory Vocabulary
Descriptors: Auditory Discrimination; Decoding (Reading); *Diagnostic Tests; *Elementary School Students; Grouping (Instructional Purposes); Intermediate Grades; Phonetic Analysis; Pretests Posttests; *Reading; Structural Analysis (Linguistics); Vocabulary
Availability: The Psychological Corp.; 555 Academic Ct., San Antonio, TX 78204-0952
Grade Level: 4-6
Notes: Time, 114 min.; Items, 196

Designed for the diagnosis of specific strengths and weaknesses in reading for grouping according to instructional needs. Said to contain more easy items to increase reliability for students scoring below the fiftieth percentile. The test covers comprehension, decoding, vocabulary, and reading rate. Separate scores are given for comprehension of textual, functional, and recreational reading passages. Complies with Chapter 1 testing requirements. Statistically linked with the Stanford Achievement Test (TC011695-011700) for pre- and posttesting use. Two forms are available. Subtests vary with levels.

14028
Stanford Diagnostic Reading Test, Third Edition, Brown Level. Karlsen, Bjorn; And Others 1984
Subtests: Reading Comprehension; Phonetic Analysis; Structural Analysis; Auditory Vocabulary; Reading Rate
Descriptors: Decoding (Reading); *Diagnostic Tests; *Grade 6; Grouping (Instructional Purposes); Intermediate Grades; Junior High Schools; *Junior High School Students; Phonetic Analysis; Pretests Posttests; *Reading; Reading Comprehension; Reading Rate; Structural Analysis (Linguistics); Vocabulary
Identifiers: SDRT
Availability: The Psychological Corp.; 555 Academic Ct., San Antonio, TX 78204-0952
Grade Level: 6-8
Notes: Time, 108 min.; Items, 241

Designed for the diagnosis of specific strengths and weaknesses in reading for grouping according to instructional needs. Said to contain more easy items to increase reliability for students scoring below the fiftieth percentile. The test covers comprehension, decoding, vocabulary, and reading rate. Separate scores are given for comprehension of textual, functional and recreational reading passages. Complies with Chapter 1 testing requirements. Statistically linked with the Stanford Achievement Test (TC011695-011700) for pre- and posttesting use. Two forms are available. Subtests vary with levels.

14029
Stanford Diagnostic Reading Test, Third Edition, Blue Level. Karlsen, Bjorn; And Others 1984
Subtests: Reading Comprehension; Phonetic Analysis; Structural Analysis; Vocabulary; Word Parts; Reading Rate; Scanning and Skimming
Descriptors: College Students; Community Colleges; Decoding (Reading); *Diagnostic Tests; Grouping (Instructional Purposes); Higher Education; Phonetic Analysis; Pretests Posttests; Readability; *Reading; Reading Comprehension; Reading Rate; Recreational Reading; Secondary Education; *Secondary School Students; Speed Reading; Structural Analysis (Linguistics); Two Year Colleges; Vocabulary
Identifiers: SDRT
Availability: The Psychological Corp.; 555 Academic Ct., San Antonio, TX 78204-0952
Grade Level: 8-14
Notes: Time, 116 min.; Items, 484

Designed for the diagnosis of specific strengths and weaknesses in reading for grouping according to instructional needs. Said to contain more easy items to increase reliability for students scoring below the fiftieth percentile. The test covers comprehension, decoding, vocabulary, and reading rate. Separate scores are given for comprehension of textual, functional, and recreational reading passages. Complies with Chapter 1 testing requirements. Statistically linked with the Stanford Achievement Test (TC011695-011700) for pre- and posttesting use. Two forms are available. Subtests vary with levels. The Blue Level may be used for testing in community colleges.

14044
BCD Test: The Maryland/Baltimore County Design for Adult Basic Education. 1982
Subtests: Personal Data on Form; Calendar; Time; Money; Recognition of Printed Letters; Recognition of Cursive Letters; Reproduction of Printed Letters; Reproduction of Cursive Letters; Sequence of the Alphabet; Discrimination of Words; Recognition of Symbols for Beginning Sounds; Discrimination of Syllables; Directional/Spatial Information; Visual Perception of Symbols; Visual Discrimination among Symbols; Visual Perception of Words; Visual Discrimination among Words; Traffic Signs; Words in Isolation; Words in a Functional Setting; Sight Word Recognition in Context
Descriptors: *Adult Basic Education; *Adult Literacy; Adults; Criterion Referenced Tests; *Diagnostic Tests; Visual Discrimination; Word Recognition
Identifiers: Maryland
Availability: Prentice Hall Regents; Order Dept., 200 Old Tappan Rd., Old Tappan, NJ 07675
Age Level: Adults

A series of 5 diagnostic/prescriptive tests designed to identify prereading instructional needs of the adult basic education student. It is made up of 21 different criterion-referenced subtests in skill areas necessary for literacy. Used with adult nonreaders at the federal Level I grouping (levels 0-4 on standardized reading tests). No special training is necessary to administer or score the test. A chart of suggested remedial activities is included.

14056
Kaufman Test of Educational Achievement, Brief Form. Kaufman, Nadeen L.; Kaufman, Alan S. 1985
Subtests: Reading; Mathematics; Spelling
Descriptors: *Achievement Tests; Decoding (Reading); *Elementary School Students; Elementary Secondary Education; *Individual Testing; *Mathematics Achievement; Mental Retardation; Norm Referenced Tests; Pretests Posttests; *Reading Achievement; Reading Comprehension; Screening Tests; *Secondary School Students; *Spelling; Standardized Tests
Identifiers: KTEA; *Test Batteries
Availability: American Guidance Service; Publishers' Bldg., Circle Pines, MN 55014-1796
Grade Level: 1-12
Notes: Time, 30 min. approx.; Items, 144

Individually administered measure of school achievement. The Brief Form offers reliable standard scores in the global areas of reading, mathematics, and spelling. The mathematics subtest measures basic arithmetic concepts, applications of mathematical principles to lifelike situations, numerical reasoning, and simple and advanced computational skills. The reading subtest assesses both decoding skills and reading comprehension. The spelling subtest uses a steeply graded word list to assess spelling ability. The battery qualifies for Chapter 1 program evaluation with spring and fall norms. Applications of the brief form include part of a comprehensive psychological, psychoeducational, or neuropsychological battery; screening; program planning; research; pre- and posttesting; an aid in placement decisions; use by government agencies; personnel selection; measuring adaptive functioning.

14112
Language Assessment Battery, 1982. New York City Board of Education, Brooklyn 1982
Subtests: Reading; Writing; Listening; Speaking
Descriptors: *Achievement Tests; Cloze Procedure; *Elementary School Students; Elementary Secondary Education; *English (Second Language); Language Dominance; Language Proficiency; *Limited English Speaking; Listening; Reading; *Secondary School Students; *Spanish Speaking; Speech Skills; *Student Placement; Writing (Composition)
Identifiers: LAB
Availability: Dr. Muriel M. Abbott; Board of Education of the City of New York, 110 Livingston St., Rm. 738, Brooklyn, NY 11201
Grade Level: K-12
Notes: Time, 60 min.; Items, 130

A revised version of the Language Assessment Battery (1977, Riverside Publishing Company, Chicago) for use in the New York City Schools. It was designed to be of average difficulty for limited English speakers, and separate norms are available for them and the English proficient student so that comparisons can be made for placement purposes. The test is group administered and multiple-choice, except for the speaking subtest, which is individually administered and requires free-response from the student to each of a series of line drawings. The Reading and part of the Listening subtests use modified cloze procedure. The Writing subtest measures knowledge of language usage elements necessary for good writing. The Spanish version is not a translation but parallel in content and is used to measure language dominance. Parallel forms are available to measure gain in proficiency. Times and numbers of items vary with levels.

14118
Michigan English Language Assessment Battery. English Language Institute, Ann Arbor, MI
Subtests: Composition; Listening or Oral Rating; Objective Test
Descriptors: *Achievement Tests; Adults; Cloze Procedure; *English (Second Language); Grammar; Higher Education; Language Fluency; *Language Proficiency; Listening Skills; Rating Scales; Reading; Reading Comprehension; Vocabulary; Writing Skills
Identifiers: ELIUM; Oral Tests; Writing Samples
Availability: English Language Institute; Testing and Certification, University of Michigan, 3023 N. University Bldg., Ann Arbor, MI 48109-1057
Age Level: Adults
Notes: Time, 150 min. approx.

Designed to measure the English language proficiency of adult nonnative speakers who will use the language for academic purposes at the university level. The essay is judged on the clarity, fluency, and accuracy of the English. The Listening Test is tape-recorded. An oral rating is optional. The Objective Test is 100-items in multiple-choice format covering grammar, cloze reading, vocabulary, and reading passages. Administered at testing centers arranged by the publisher after registration by the test taker.

14123
Peace Corps Language Proficiency Interview. Foreign Service Institute, Washington, DC
Descriptors: Adults; Dialogs (Language); Expressive Language; Grammar; *Interviews; *Language Proficiency; *Language Tests; Listening Comprehension; Pronunciation; Receptive Language; *Second Languages; Vocabulary

Identifiers: Accents; *Peace Corps
Availability: Peace Corps; 806 Connecticut Ave.
N.W., Washington, DC 20526
Age Level: Adults
Notes: Time, 20 min.

An interview technique used by the Peace Corps to determine language proficiency of volunteers. It consists of a 15-20 minute conversation between the student and a qualified interviewer. Measures spoken mastery and understanding of the spoken language of the host country. Content of the interview is not fixed, topics will vary. Interviewee is evaluated on pronunciation and accent, grammatical accuracy, vocabulary, fluency and listening comprehension. Scored by assigning the interviewee to one of 6 proficiency categories (0-5).

14124
Student Occupational Competency Achievement Testing. National Occupational Competency Testing Institute, Big Rapids, MI
Descriptors: Accounting; *Achievement Tests; *Adults; Agricultural Engineering; Agricultural Production; Air Conditioning; Auto Body Repairers; Auto Mechanics; Banking; Bookkeeping; Bus Transportation; Cabinetmaking; Carpentry; Construction Industry; Credentials; Drafting; Electricity; Electronics; Food Service; Heating; High Schools; *High School Students; Horticulture; Industrial Arts; Machine Repairers; Machinists; Masonry; Medical Assistants; Merchandising; Multiple Choice Tests; Occupational Tests; Office Occupations Education; Performance Tests; Plumbing; *Postsecondary Education; Practical Nursing; Printing; Programing; Refrigeration; Secondary Education; Sewing Machine Operators; Television Radio Repairers; Two Year Colleges; *Vocational Education; Vocational Schools; Welding; *Work Sample Tests
Identifiers: Machine Trades; SOCAT; Trucks
Availability: National Occupational Competency Testing Institute; 318 Johnson Hall, Ferris State College, Big Rapids, MI 49307
Grade Level: 9-14
Notes: Time, 180 min.; Items, 150

A program for evaluating secondary and postsecondary vocational students with a standard, objective measure. Each test consists of a multiple-choice portion covering factual knowledge, technical information, understanding of principles, and problem-solving abilities related to the occupation. A performance component samples manipulative skills required. A mental ability test is also available. Currently, tests are available in Accounting/Bookkeeping, Agriculture Mechanics, Auto Body, Auto Mechanics, Carpentry, Commercial Foods, Computer Programming, Construction Electricity, Construction Masonry, Drafting, General Merchandising, General Office, Heating and Air Conditioning, Horticulture, Industrial Electricity, Industrial Electronics, Machine Trades, Plumbing, Practical Nursing, Printing, Radio and TV Repair, Refrigeration, Sewn Products, Small Engine Repair, Welding. Test results can be presented to employers as a credential, used by teachers for grading, used by vocational administrators for program evaluation. Currently, exams are being developed in Banking, Savings and Loan; Cabinetmaking; Medical Assistant; Production Agriculture; and Truck and Bus Mechanics.

14138
Pre-Professional Skills Test. Educational Testing Service, Princeton, NJ 1984
Subtests: Reading; Mathematics; Writing
Descriptors: *Achievement Tests; Admission (School); Adults; *Basic Skills; Certification; College Students; Higher Education; *Mathematics; Multiple Choice Tests; Personnel Selection; Professional Occupations; *Reading Tests; Teachers; *Writing Skills
Identifiers: PPST; *Writing Samples
Availability: PPST Program; Educational Testing Service, CN-6057 Princeton, NJ 08541-6057
Grade Level: 13-16
Age Level: Adults
Notes: Time, 150 min.; Items, 126

Three separate tests designed to measure basic proficiency of those preparing to be teachers. They may be used for selection, admissions, evaluation, and certification. Each test is multiple-choice except the writing test, which also has one essay item (30 minutes). Each test provides only a total score ranging from 150-190. For use by school districts, colleges, state agencies, licensing boards, and employers. The test is administered on a date specified by the user and scored by ETS.

14144
Word Processing Test. Psychological Corp., San Antonio, TX 1985
Descriptors: *Achievement Tests; Adults; *Clerical Workers; *Job Applicants; *Occupational Tests; *Vocational Education; *Word Processing; *Work Sample Tests
Identifiers: WPT

Availability: The Psychological Corp.; 555 Academic Ct., San Antonio, TX 78204-0952
Age Level: Adults

Designed to measure 2 of the most important word processing abilities: inputting and editing material. Both sections include material in text and tabular form. Includes 2 forms, each available for use with Wang OIS and VS systems, Wang PC, and selected IBM systems. Examinees should be tested with the type of word processor on which they claim competence. Form A will be available only to personnel departments of business and industrial firms for testing job applicants and employees. Form B will be available to schools, vocational training programs, and employment agencies, as well as to business and industrial firms.

14168
Decoding Skills Test. Richardson, Ellis; And Others 1979
Subtests: Basal Word Recognition; Phonic Decoding; Oral Passage Reading
Descriptors: *Criterion Referenced Tests; *Decoding (Reading); *Diagnostic Tests; *Dyslexia; Elementary Education; *Elementary School Students; Oral Reading; Phoneme Grapheme Correspondence; Remedial Reading; Word Recognition
Availability: ERIC Document Reproduction Service; 7420 Fullerton Rd., Ste. 110, Springfield, VA 22153-2852 (ED193304, microfiche only)
Grade Level: 1-5
Notes: Items, 180

Designed as a measure of decoding skills for use in research on developmental dyslexia. May be used as a diagnostic-prescriptive measure to evaluate children needing remedial reading. A brief reading comprehension test is included. This test is criterion referenced. Words used in subtest one are embedded in the oral passages.

14169
Teacher Occupational Competency Testing. National Occupational Competency Testing Institute, Big Rapids, MI
Descriptors: *Achievement Tests; Adults; *Certification; *Equivalency Tests; Industrial Arts; Multiple Choice Tests; *Occupational Tests; *Vocational Education Teachers; *Work Sample Tests
Identifiers: Machine Trade; NOCTI; TOCT; Trucks
Availability: National Occupational Competency Testing Institute; 318 Johnson Hall, Ferris State College, Big Rapids, MI 49307
Age Level: Adults

A series of tests designed to determine a level of occupational competence for vocational education teachers. A written test covers theoretical concepts of the occupation and a performance test examines selected manipulative skills. These tests do not measure instructional or teaching skills. The NOCTI tests were standardized by administration to workers in the specific fields. The tests are administered twice yearly at a testing site in each state participating. These tests may be used also for credit-by-examination and teacher certification. Currently, tests are available in Air Conditioning and Refrigeration, Airframe and Power Plant, Architectural Drafting, Audio-Visual Communications, Auto Body Repair, Automotive Body and Fender, Auto Mechanic, Baker, Brick Masonry, Building Construction Occupations, Building Trades Maintenance, Cabinet Making and Millwork, Carpentry, Civil Technology, Commercial Art, Commercial Photography, Computer Technology, Cosmetology, Diesel Engine Repair, Diesel Mechanic, Drafting Occupations, Electrical Installation, Electronics Communications, Electronics Technology, Heating, Industrial Electrician, Industrial Electronics, Machine Drafting, Machine Trades, Major Appliance Repair, Masonry, Masonry Occupations, Materials Handling, Mechanical Technology, Painting and Decorating, Plumbing, Power Sewing, Printing (Letterpress), Printing (Offset), Quantity Food Preparation, Quantity Foods, Radio and Television Repair, Refrigeration, Sheet Metal, Small Engine Repair, Textile Production and Fabrication, Tool and Die Making, Welding. For detailed information on each test, see TC014180-TC014229.

14180
Teacher Occupational Competency Testing: Air Conditioning and Refrigeration. National Occupational Competency Testing Institute, Big Rapids, MI
Descriptors: *Achievement Tests; Adults; *Air Conditioning; *Certification; College Credits; Credentials; *Equivalency Tests; *Heating; Multiple Choice Tests; *Occupational Tests; Performance Tests; *Refrigeration; *Vocational Education; *Vocational Education Teachers; *Work Sample Tests
Identifiers: NOCTI; TOCT
Availability: National Occupational Competency Testing Institute; 318 Johnson Hall, Ferris State College, Big Rapids, MI 49307
Age Level: Adults
Notes: Time, 480 min.; Items, 165

One of a series of tests designed to determine a level of occupational competence for vocational education teachers. A written test covers theoretical concepts of the occupation and a performance test examines selected manipulative skills. They may be used for credit by examination and also for teacher certification. The written test and the 5-hour performance test cover installation and servicing of domestic systems, commercial systems, residential air conditioning, heating, and industrial refrigeration.

14181
Teacher Occupational Competency Testing: Airframe and Power Plant. National Occupational Competency Testing Institute, Big Rapids, MI
Descriptors: *Achievement Tests; Adults; *Aviation Mechanics; *Certification; College Credits; Credentials; Electricity; *Equivalency Tests; Multiple Choice Tests; *Occupational Tests; Performance Tests; *Vocational Education; *Vocational Education Teachers; *Work Sample Tests
Identifiers: NOCTI; TOCT
Availability: National Occupational Competency Testing Institute; 318 Johnson Hall, Ferris State College, Big Rapids, MI 49307
Age Level: Adults
Notes: Time, 510 min.; Items, 183

One of a series of tests designed to determine a level of occupational competence for vocational education teachers. A written test covers theoretical concepts of the occupation and a performance test examines selected manipulative skills. They may be used for credit by examination and also for teacher certification. The written test covers general questions on electric circuits in aircraft, weight and balance principles and computation, types of fluid lines and fittings, specifications and requirements for ground operation and servicing, corrosion control, procedures and methods for aircraft inspection; airframe systems and components, including types of structures, principles of operation and methods of servicing; power plant operation and maintenance, systems, and components. The performance test covers hydraulic components and systems, sheet metal work, use of airworthiness directives, engine ignition timing, engine valve service, carburetor service, and generator service.

14182
Teacher Occupational Competency Testing: Architectural Drafting. National Occupational Competency Testing Institute, Big Rapids, MI
Descriptors: *Achievement Tests; Adults; *Architectural Education; *Certification; College Credits; Credentials; *Drafting; *Equivalency Tests; Multiple Choice Tests; Occupational Tests; Performance Tests; *Vocational Education; *Vocational Education Teachers; *Work Sample Tests
Identifiers: NOCTI; TOCT
Availability: National Occupational Competency Testing Institute; 318 Johnson Hall, Ferris State College, Big Rapids, MI 49307
Age Level: Adults
Notes: Time, 480 min.; Items, 150

One of a series of tests designed to determine a level of occupational competence for vocational education teachers. A written test covers theoretical concepts of the occupation and a performance test examines selected manipulative skills. They may be used for credit by examination and also for teacher certification. The written test covers basic architectural data, planning and design, materials and methods of construction, structural systems, legal and ethical considerations and professional relationships. The performance test requires the test taker to prepare sections for various items of construction from front elevations and partial floor plans of residence or commercial buildings; prepare working drawings from preliminary sketches of floor plans; include all required structural, electrical and heating information; make freehand perspective drawings and renderings.

14183
Teacher Occupational Competency Testing: Audio-Visual Communications. National Occupational Competency Testing Institute, Big Rapids, MI
Descriptors: *Achievement Tests; Adults; Audiovisual Aids; *Audiovisual Communications; *Certification; College Credits; Credentials; *Equivalency Tests; Multiple Choice Tests; *Occupational Tests; Performance Tests; *Photography; *Vocational Education; *Vocational Education Teachers; *Work Sample Tests
Identifiers: NOCTI; TOCT
Availability: National Occupational Competency Testing Institute; 318 Johnson Hall, Ferris State College, Big Rapids, MI 49307
Age Level: Adults
Notes: Time, 400 min.; Items, 180

One of a series of tests designed to determine a level of occupational competence for vocational education teachers. A written test covers theoretical concepts of the occupation and a performance test examines selected manipulative skills. They may be used for credit by examination and also for teacher certification. The written test covers general information and theory, including principles and concepts of communication types, methods and use of audiovisual aids, multimedia concepts, materials fabrication, instructional theory, transparencies, slides, film, photography, projection and sound systems; design and construction of visuals; catalog, storage and distribution of audiovisual materials; equipment identification and operation. The performance test covers photography, transparency design, motion picture operation, tape recorder operation.

14184
Teacher Occupational Competency Testing: Auto Body Repair.   National Occupational Competency Testing Institute, Big Rapids, MI
Descriptors: *Achievement Tests; Adults; *Auto Body Repairers; *Certification; College Credits; Credentials; *Equivalency Tests; Multiple Choice Tests; Occupational Tests; Performance Tests; *Vocational Education; *Vocational Education Teachers; *Work Sample Tests
Identifiers: NOCTI; TOCT
Availability: National Occupational Competency Testing Institute; 318 Johnson Hall, Ferris State College, Big Rapids, MI 49307
Age Level: Adults
Notes: Time, 540 min.; Items, 191
One of a series of tests designed to determine a level of occupational competence for vocational education teachers. A written test covers theoretical concepts of the occupation and a performance test examines selected manipulative skills. They may be used for credit by examination and also for teacher certification. The written test covers welding and brazing, filling operations and plastics, repairing sheet metal, refinishing, panel replacement, frame (unitized body repair), front end alignment, electrical and accessory systems, glass, trim and hardware, estimating, tools and equipment, safety. The performance test covers sheet metal repair, refinishing, solder application, glass trim repair, electrical work.

14185
Teacher Occupational Competency Testing: Automotive Body and Fender.   National Occupational Competency Testing Institute, Big Rapids, MI
Descriptors: *Achievement Tests; Adults; *Auto Body Repairers; *Certification; College Credits; Credentials; *Equivalency Tests; Multiple Choice Tests; Occupational Tests; Performance Tests; *Vocational Education; *Vocational Education Teachers; *Work Sample Tests
Identifiers: NOCTI; TOCT
Availability: National Occupational Competency Testing Institute; 318 Johnson Hall, Ferris State College, Big Rapids, MI 49307
Age Level: Adults
Notes: Time, 420 min.; Items, 191
One of a series of tests designed to determine a level of occupational competence for vocational education teachers. A written test covers theoretical concepts of the occupation and a performance test examines selected manipulative skills. They may be used for credit by examination and also for teacher certification. The written test covers metal forming, refinishing, welding, glass and trim, accessory systems, alignment, synthetics, estimating. The performance test covers metal bumping on panels, straightening, forming, shrinking, refinishing tasks, welding, including set-up and use of oxy-acetylene equipment.

14186
Teacher Occupational Competency Testing: Auto Mechanic.   National Occupational Competency Testing Institute, Big Rapids, MI
Descriptors: *Achievement Tests; Adults; *Auto Mechanics; *Certification; College Credits; Credentials; *Equivalency Tests; Multiple Choice Tests; Occupational Tests; Performance Tests; *Vocational Education; *Vocational Education Teachers; *Work Sample Tests
Identifiers: NOCTI; TOCT
Availability: National Occupational Competency Testing Institute; 318 Johnson Hall, Ferris State College, Big Rapids, MI 49307
Age Level: Adults
Notes: Time, 480 min.; Items, 200
One of a series of tests designed to determine a level of occupational competence for vocational education teachers. A written test covers theoretical concepts of the occupation and a performance test examines selected manipulative skills. They may be used for credit by examination and also for teacher certification. The written test covers basic shop practices, engines, suspensions and steering, brakes, engine electrical, drivelines, fuel and emission systems, accessories and chassic electrical, shop management and controls. The performance test covers engines, engine analysis and repair, air conditioning, brakes, fuel systems, electrical, charging system, emission systems, drive lines and components, suspension and steering, batteries, basic automotive practices.

14187
Teacher Occupational Competency Testing: Baker.   National Occupational Competency Testing Institute, Big Rapids, MI
Descriptors: *Achievement Tests; Adults; *Bakery Industry; *Certification; College Credits; Credentials; *Equivalency Tests; Food Service; Multiple Choice Tests; Occupational Tests; Performance Tests; *Vocational Education; *Vocational Education Teachers; *Work Sample Tests
Identifiers: NOCTI; TOCT
Availability: National Occupational Competency Testing Institute; 318 Johnson Hall, Ferris State College, Big Rapids, MI 49307
Age Level: Adults
Notes: Time, 420 min.; Items, 183
One of a series of tests designed to determine a level of occupational competence for vocational education teachers. A written test covers theoretical concepts of the occupation and a performance test examines selected manipulative skills. They may be used for credit by examination and also for teacher certification. The written test covers definition of terms, classifications of ingredients, substitutions, sanitation and safety, weights and measurements, interaction of ingredients, handling and storage of ingredients, general baking knowledge, equipment preparation, baking remedies. The performance test covers dough preparation, bread, rolls, cakes, pastries.

14188
Teacher Occupational Competency Testing: Brick Masonry.   National Occupational Competency Testing Institute, Big Rapids, MI
Descriptors: *Achievement Tests; Adults; *Certification; College Credits; *Construction Industry; Credentials; *Equivalency Tests; *Masonry; Multiple Choice Tests; Occupational Tests; Performance Tests; *Vocational Education; *Vocational Education Teachers; *Work Sample Tests
Identifiers: NOCTI; TOCT
Availability: National Occupational Competency Testing Institute; 318 Johnson Hall, Ferris State College, Big Rapids, MI 49307
Age Level: Adults
Notes: Time, 420 min.; Items, 200
One of a series of tests designed to determine a level of occupational competence for vocational education teachers. A written test covers theoretical concepts of the occupation and a performance test examines selected manipulative skills. They may be used for credit by examination and also for teacher certification. The written test covers types, sizes, composition, layout, estimating, tools, lay-up techniques and finishing work for brick, block, tile and stone. The performance test covers layout, dimensioning and cutting of brick, block, stone and tile.

14189
Teacher Occupational Competency Testing: Building Construction Occupations.   National Occupational Competency Testing Institute, Big Rapids, MI
Descriptors: *Achievement Tests; Adults; Carpentry; *Certification; College Credits; *Construction Industry; Credentials; Electricity; *Equivalency Tests; Masonry; Metal Working; Multiple Choice Tests; Occupational Tests; Painting (Industrial Arts); Performance Tests; Plumbing; *Vocational Education; *Vocational Education Teachers; *Work Sample Tests
Identifiers: NOCTI; TOCT
Availability: National Occupational Competency Testing Institute; 318 Johnson Hall, Ferris State College, Big Rapids, MI 49307
Age Level: Adults
Notes: Time, 540 min.; Items, 200
One of a series of tests designed to determine a level of occupational competence for vocational education teachers. A written test covers theoretical concepts of the occupation and a performance test examines selected manipulative skills. They may be used for credit by examination and also for teacher certification. The written test covers carpentry, masonry, electrical, plumbing, painting, building codes and safety, sheet metal. The performance test covers carpentry, masonry, electrical, plumbing, painting, sheet metal.

14190
Teacher Occupational Competency Testing: Building Trades Maintenance.   National Occupational Competency Testing Institute, Big Rapids, MI
Descriptors: *Achievement Tests; Adults; Carpentry; *Certification; College Credits; *Construction Industry; Credentials; Electricity; *Equivalency Tests; Masonry; Metal Working; Multiple Choice Tests; Occupational Tests; Painting (Industrial Arts); Performance Tests; Plumbing; *Vocational Education; *Vocational Education Teachers; *Work Sample Tests
Identifiers: NOCTI; TOCT

Availability: National Occupational Competency Testing Institute; 318 Johnson Hall, Ferris State College, Big Rapids, MI 49307
Age Level: Adults
Notes: Time, 510 min.; Items, 186
One of a series of tests designed to determine a level of occupational competence for vocational education teachers. A written test covers theoretical concepts of the occupation and a performance test examines selected manipulative skills. They may be used for credit by examination and also for teacher certification. The written test covers heating, air conditioning and refrigeration, carpentry, electrical, painting and wallpapering, plumbing, sheet metal, masonry, welding, custodial, management practices. The performance test covers plumbing, masonry, welding, electrical installation, carpentry, surface coating, custodial services, glass installation, door hardware.

14191
Teacher Occupational Competency Testing: Cabinet Making and Millwork.   National Occupational Competency Testing Institute, Big Rapids, MI
Descriptors: *Achievement Tests; Adults; *Cabinetmaking; Carpentry; *Certification; College Credits; Credentials; *Equivalency Tests; Multiple Choice Tests; Occupational Tests; *Vocational Education; *Vocational Education Teachers; *Work Sample Tests
Identifiers: NOCTI; TOCT
Availability: National Occupational Competency Testing Institute; 318 Johnson Hall, Ferris State College, Big Rapids, MI 49307
Age Level: Adults
Notes: Time, 480 min.; Items, 160
One of a series of tests designed to determine a level of occupational competence for vocational education teachers. A written test covers theoretical concepts of the occupation and a performance test examines selected manipulative skills. They may be used for credit by examination and also for teacher certification. The written test covers machines, hand tools, finishing, joinery, assembly, planning, wood/stock selection, safety. The performance test covers machines, hand tools, planning and layout, assembly, joinery, finish, safety, wood/stock selection.

14192
Teacher Occupational Competency Testing: Carpentry.   National Occupational Competency Testing Institute, Big Rapids, MI
Descriptors: *Achievement Tests; Adults; *Carpentry; *Certification; College Credits; Credentials; *Equivalency Tests; Multiple Choice Tests; Occupational Tests; Performance Tests; *Vocational Education; *Vocational Education Teachers; *Work Sample Tests
Identifiers: NOCTI; TOCT
Availability: National Occupational Competency Testing Institute; 318 Johnson Hall, Ferris State College, Big Rapids, MI 49307
Age Level: Adults
Notes: Time, 480 min.; Items, 159
One of a series of tests designed to determine a level of occupational competence for vocational education teachers. A written test covers theoretical concepts of the occupation and a performance test examines selected manipulative skills. They may be used for credit by examination and also for teacher certification. The written test covers exterior finish, interior finish, roof framing and roofing, wall and ceiling framing, floor framing, cabinetry, surveying, layout and blueprint reading, foundation work, concrete walks, floors, and step construction; stair construction, estimating, scaffolding. The performance test covers roof framing, exterior finish, wall framing, floor framing, roofing.

14193
Teacher Occupational Competency Testing: Civil Technology.   National Occupational Competency Testing Institute, Big Rapids, MI
Descriptors: *Achievement Tests; Adults; *Certification; *Civil Engineering; College Credits; Credentials; *Drafting; *Equivalency Tests; Multiple Choice Tests; Occupational Tests; Performance Tests; *Vocational Education; *Vocational Education Teachers; *Work Sample Tests
Identifiers: NOCTI; *Surveying (Engineering); Surveyors; TOCT
Availability: National Occupational Competency Testing Institute; 318 Johnson Hall, Ferris State College, Big Rapids, MI 49307
Age Level: Adults
Notes: Time, 480 min.; Items, 152
One of a series of tests designed to determine a level of occupational competence for vocational education teachers. A written test covers theoretical concepts of the occupation and a performance test examines selected manipulative skills. They may be used for credit by examination and also for teacher certification. The written test covers surveying, steel structures, drafting, soil, asphalt, concrete, instrumentation, general engineering information. The per-

formance test covers surveying, drafting, concrete, soils, asphalt, use of balances and sample splitters, Gilson-type mechanical screen, Ro-Tap or other standard sieve shaker.

14194
Teacher Occupational Competency Testing: Commercial Art.　National Occupational Competency Testing Institute, Big Rapids, MI
Descriptors: *Achievement Tests; Adults; *Certification; College Credits; *Commercial Art; Credentials; *Equivalency Tests; Multiple Choice Tests; Occupational Tests; Performance Tests; *Vocational Education; *Vocational Education Teachers; *Work Sample Tests
Identifiers: NOCTI; TOCT
Availability: National Occupational Competency Testing Institute; 318 Johnson Hall, Ferris State College, Big Rapids, MI 49307
Age Level: Adults
Notes: Time, 480 min.; Items, 125
One of a series of tests designed to determine a level of occupational competence for vocational education teachers. A written test covers theoretical concepts of the occupation and a performance test examines selected manipulative skills. They may be used for credit by examination and also for teacher certification. The written test covers design and typography, drawing and rendering, production, printing, general. The performance test covers black and white rendering, keyline/mechanical, magazine ad.

14195
Teacher Occupational Competency Testing: Commercial Photography.　National Occupational Competency Testing Institute, Big Rapids, MI
Descriptors: *Achievement Tests; Adults; *Certification; College Credits; Credentials; *Equivalency Tests; Multiple Choice Tests; *Occupational Tests; Performance Tests; *Photography; *Vocational Education; *Vocational Education Teachers; *Work Sample Tests
Identifiers: NOCTI; TOCT
Availability: National Occupational Competency Testing Institute; 318 Johnson Hall, Ferris State College, Big Rapids, MI 49307
Age Level: Adults
Notes: Time, 480 min.; Items, 150
One of a series of tests designed to determine a level of occupational competence for vocational education teachers. A written test covers theoretical concepts of the occupation and a performance test examines selected manipulative skills. They may be used for credit by examination and also for teacher certification. The written test covers 35mm camera operation, photo printing, film processing, film characteristics, lighting, print finishing, composition, filters, light meters, light and color. The performance test covers 35mm camera operation, film processing, printing/ enlarging, lighting.

14196
Teacher Occupational Competency Testing: Cosmetology.　National Occupational Competency Testing Institute, Big Rapids, MI
Descriptors: *Achievement Tests; Adults; *Certification; College Credits; *Cosmetology; Credentials; *Equivalency Tests; Multiple Choice Tests; Occupational Tests; Performance Tests; *Vocational Education; *Vocational Education Teachers; *Work Sample Tests
Identifiers: NOCTI; TOCT
Availability: National Occupational Competency Testing Institute; 318 Johnson Hall, Ferris State College, Big Rapids, MI 49307
Age Level: Adults
Notes: Time, 480 min.; Items, 150
One of a series of tests designed to determine a level of occupational competence for vocational education teachers. A written test covers theoretical concepts of the occupation and a performance test examines selected manipulative skills. They may be used for credit by examination and also for teacher certification. The written test covers chemical permanent waving, chemical hair straightening, hair and scalp characteristics, care of face and hands, hair styling, hair pieces, hair shaping, hair coloring, shop operation and management. The performance test covers hair coloring on a manikin, hair styling on a live model, haircutting on a live model, thermal waving on model or manikin, chemical permanent waving or chemical straightening on live model, manicuring or facial and makeup on live model.

14197
Teacher Occupational Competency Testing: Computer Technology.　National Occupational Competency Testing Institute, Big Rapids, MI
Descriptors: *Achievement Tests; Adults; *Certification; College Credits; *Computer Science; Credentials; *Equivalency Tests; Multiple Choice Tests; Occupational Tests; Performance Tests; *Programing; *Vocational Education; *Vocational Education Teachers; *Work Sample Tests

Identifiers: NOCTI; TOCT
Availability: National Occupational Competency Testing Institute; 318 Johnson Hall, Ferris State College, Big Rapids, MI 49307
Age Level: Adults
Notes: Time, 480 min.; Items, 180
One of a series of tests designed to determine a level of occupational competence for vocational education teachers. A written test covers theoretical concepts of the occupation and a performance test examines selected manipulative skills. They may be used for credit by examination and also for teacher certification. The written test covers general operations, programing and analysis information, key entry, unit record equipment operations, peripheral equipment operations, programing languages, systems analysis and design, flowcharting and documentation. The performance test requires the test taker to flowchart the logic to a problem, code the solution to the problem in ANSI COBOL or RPG II, design files for magnetic tape and/or disk on file layout forms using industry-standard file design techniques.

14198
Teacher Occupational Competency Testing: Diesel Engine Repair.　National Occupational Competency Testing Institute, Big Rapids, MI
Descriptors: *Achievement Tests; Adults; Auto Mechanics; *Certification; College Credits; Credentials; *Diesel Engines; *Equivalency Tests; Multiple Choice Tests; Occupational Tests; Performance Tests; *Vocational Education; *Vocational Education Teachers; *Work Sample Tests
Identifiers: NOCTI; TOCT
Availability: National Occupational Competency Testing Institute; 318 Johnson Hall, Ferris State College, Big Rapids, MI 49307
Age Level: Adults
Notes: Time, 420 min.; Items, 167
One of a series of tests designed to determine a level of occupational competence for vocational education teachers. A written test covers theoretical concepts of the occupation and a performance test examines selected manipulative skills. They may be used for credit by examination and also for teacher certification. The written test covers basic engine diagnosis and repair, fuel injection pumps and nozzle repair and adjustment, electrical systems diagnosis and repair, power train operation and repair, hydraulic systems troubleshooting and repair. The performance test covers basic engine diagnosis and repair, power train operation and repair, fuel injection pump and nozzle repair and adjustment, electrical systems diagnosis and repair, testing and calibrating pump systems.

14199
Teacher Occupational Competency Testing: Diesel Mechanic.　National Occupational Competency Testing Institute, Big Rapids, MI
Descriptors: *Achievement Tests; Adults; *Auto Mechanics; *Certification; College Credits; Credentials; *Diesel Engines; *Equivalency Tests; Multiple Choice Tests; Occupational Tests; Performance Tests; *Vocational Education; *Vocational Education Teachers; *Work Sample Tests
Identifiers: NOCTI; TOCT
Availability: National Occupational Competency Testing Institute; 318 Johnson Hall, Ferris State College, Big Rapids, MI 49307
Age Level: Adults
Notes: Time, 420 min.; Items, 184
One of a series of tests designed to determine a level of occupational competence for vocational education teachers. A written test covers theoretical concepts of the occupation and a performance test examines selected manipulative skills. They may be used for credit by examination and also for teacher certification. The written test covers engine service, diesel fuel systems service, lubrication systems service, electrical systems service, engine auxiliaries, cooling system service, internal and external systems service, dynamometer and testing. The performance test covers engine service, fuel systems, electrical systems, cooling systems, lubrication.

14200
Teacher Occupational Competency Testing: Drafting Occupations.　National Occupational Competency Testing Institute, Big Rapids, MI
Descriptors: *Achievement Tests; Adults; *Certification; College Credits; Credentials; *Drafting; *Equivalency Tests; Multiple Choice Tests; Occupational Tests; Performance Tests; *Vocational Education; *Vocational Education Teachers; *Work Sample Tests
Identifiers: NOCTI; TOCT
Availability: National Occupational Competency Testing Institute; 318 Johnson Hall, Ferris State College, Big Rapids, MI 49307
Age Level: Adults
Notes: Time, 480 min.; Items, 194

One of a series of tests designed to determine a level of occupational competence for vocational education teachers. A written test covers theoretical concepts of the occupation and a performance test examines selected manipulative skills. They may be used for credit by examination and also for teacher certification. The written test covers drafting fundamentals, including common drafting instruments, materials and techniques; orthographics, projections, pictorials, sections and conventions; machining practices, threads and fasteners, dimensioning and tolerancing terms and techniques; related trades, related science, related mathematics. The performance test covers drawing and dimensioning, isometric and oblique, development, orthographics, sectioning, auxiliary projection, revolutions, threads and fasteners, intersections.

14201
Teacher Occupational Competency Testing: Electrical Installation.　National Occupational Competency Testing Institute, Big Rapids, MI
Descriptors: *Achievement Tests; Adults; *Certification; College Credits; Construction Industry; Credentials; *Electricity; *Equivalency Tests; Multiple Choice Tests; Occupational Tests; Performance Tests; *Vocational Education; *Vocational Education Teachers; *Work Sample Tests
Identifiers: NOCTI; TOCT
Availability: National Occupational Competency Testing Institute; 318 Johnson Hall, Ferris State College, Big Rapids, MI 49307
Age Level: Adults
Notes: Time, 480 min.; Items, 179
One of a series of tests designed to determine a level of occupational competence for vocational education teachers. A written test covers theoretical concepts of the occupation and a performance test examines selected manipulative skills. They may be used for credit by examination and also for teacher certification. The written test covers basic principles of electricity and magnetism and their application in the trade, reading working instructions and trade calculations, wiring practices and procedures, lighting, motors and generators, transformers, general trade information. The performance test covers installation of residential and commercial wiring, installation, testing and operation of controls; testing and troubleshooting of installations, layout and print reading, code applications, safety.

14202
Teacher Occupational Competency Testing: Electronics Communications.　National Occupational Competency Testing Institute, Big Rapids, MI
Descriptors: *Achievement Tests; Adults; *Certification; College Credits; Credentials; Electricity; *Electronics; *Equivalency Tests; Multiple Choice Tests; Occupational Tests; Performance Tests; Television Radio Repairers; *Vocational Education; *Vocational Education Teachers; *Work Sample Tests
Identifiers: NOCTI; TOCT
Availability: National Occupational Competency Testing Institute; 318 Johnson Hall, Ferris State College, Big Rapids, MI 49307
Age Level: Adults
Notes: Time, 420 min.; Items, 130
One of a series of tests designed to determine a level of occupational competence for vocational education teachers. A written test covers theoretical concepts of the occupation and a performance test examines selected manipulative skills. They may be used for credit by examination and also for teacher certification. The written test covers basic electricity, including DC circuits—series, parallel and combinations; vacuum tube and solid state devices, methods and procedures, electronic circuits, single phase circuits, amplifiers in cascade for RF and AF, measurements, standards and tolerances, inductive devices, alternating current, conductors, insulators and semiconductors, batteries, source of voltage, and other electronics concepts. The performance test covers television service, radio equipment, and recording equipment.

14203
Teacher Occupational Competency Testing: Electronics Technology.　National Occupational Competency Testing Institute, Big Rapids, MI
Descriptors: *Achievement Tests; Adults; *Certification; College Credits; Credentials; *Electronics; *Equivalency Tests; Multiple Choice Tests; Occupational Tests; Performance Tests; *Vocational Education; *Vocational Education Teachers; *Work Sample Tests
Identifiers: NOCTI; TOCT
Availability: National Occupational Competency Testing Institute; 318 Johnson Hall, Ferris State College, Big Rapids, MI 49307
Age Level: Adults
Notes: Time, 420 min.; Items, 200
One of a series of tests designed to determine a level of occupational competence for vocational education teachers. A written test covers theoretical concepts of the occupation and a performance test examines selected manipulative skills. They may be used for credit by examination

and also for teacher certification. The written test covers DC circuits/basic electricity, AC circuits/basic electronics, semiconductors/basic circuits, basic digital electronics, electronic components, instrumentation, analysis, troubleshooting. The performance test covers instrumentation, analysis, fabrication and inspection, basic theory, electronic components, troubleshooting and repair.

14204
Teacher Occupational Competency Testing: Heating. National Occupational Competency Testing Institute, Big Rapids, MI
Descriptors: *Achievement Tests; Adults; *Certification; College Credits; Credentials; *Equivalency Tests; *Heating; Multiple Choice Tests; Occupational Tests; Performance Tests; *Vocational Education; *Vocational Education Teachers; *Work Sample Tests
Identifiers: NOCTI; TOCT
Availability: National Occupational Competency Testing Institute; 318 Johnson Hall, Ferris State College, Big Rapids, MI 49307
Age Level: Adults
Notes: Time, 420 min.; Items, 178
One of a series of tests designed to determine a level of occupational competence for vocational education teachers. A written test covers theoretical concepts of the occupation and a performance test examines selected manipulative skills. They may be used for credit by examination and also for teacher certification. The written test covers hot water, hot air, steam, gravity, forced air, and loop systems, different types of controls, service and testing of heating systems, heating plants. The performance test covers hot water, hot air, gravity, forced air, and loop systems; primary controls, thermostats; fan, limit, safety switches; stack controls; zone controls; circulators; ignition; heating plants; service and testing, including inspection, disassembly, repair and troubleshooting.

14205
Teacher Occupational Competency Testing: Industrial Electrician. National Occupational Competency Testing Institute, Big Rapids, MI
Descriptors: *Achievement Tests; Adults; *Certification; College Credits; Credentials; *Electricity; *Equivalency Tests; Multiple Choice Tests; Occupational Tests; Performance Tests; *Vocational Education; *Vocational Education Teachers; *Work Sample Tests
Identifiers: NOCTI; TOCT
Availability: National Occupational Competency Testing Institute; 318 Johnson Hall, Ferris State College, Big Rapids, MI 49307
Age Level: Adults
Notes: Time, 420 min.; Items, 200
One of a series of tests designed to determine a level of occupational competence for vocational education teachers. A written test covers theoretical concepts of the occupation and a performance test examines selected manipulative skills. They may be used for credit by examination and also for teacher certification. The written test covers basic theory, DC circuits/calculations, AC circuits/calculations, DC machines, A.C machines/polyphase circuits, N.E.C. Code, motor control/symbols, motor controls. The performance test covers installing and wiring magnetic motor control circuit system, which may include jog/run, pilot lights, limit switches, relays, timers, sequence control, etc.; cutting, bending, threading, and installing rigid metal conduit; cutting and bending electrical metallic tubing to various shapes and specific dimensions; troubleshooting problems in a motor control circuit; connecting, energizing, and testing digital circuit components according to a given diagram.

14206
Teacher Occupational Competency Testing: Industrial Electronics. National Occupational Competency Testing Institute, Big Rapids, MI
Descriptors: *Achievement Tests; Adults; *Certification; College Credits; Credentials; *Electronics; *Equivalency Tests; Multiple Choice Tests; Occupational Tests; Performance Tests; *Vocational Education; *Vocational Education Teachers; *Work Sample Tests
Identifiers: NOCTI; TOCT
Availability: National Occupational Competency Testing Institute; 318 Johnson Hall, Ferris State College, Big Rapids, MI 49307
Age Level: Adults
Notes: Time, 480 min.; Items, 200
One of a series of tests designed to determine a level of occupational competence for vocational education teachers. A written test covers theoretical concepts of the occupation and a performance test examines selected manipulative skills. They may be used for credit by examination and also for teacher certification. The written test covers basic electronic fundamentals, amplifiers, detectors and active circuits; digital circuits, components, use of instruments, troubleshooting, electronic control devices, network (passive), computer technology, energy conversion (servoloops), transducers, electronic assembly precautions.

The performance test requires use of measuring instruments; use of test equipment; measuring, observing; and recording; and the programing of simple problems.

14207
Teacher Occupational Competency Testing: Machine Drafting. National Occupational Competency Testing Institute, Big Rapids, MI
Descriptors: *Achievement Tests; Adults; *Certification; College Credits; Credentials; *Drafting; *Equivalency Tests; *Machine Tools; Multiple Choice Tests; Occupational Tests; Performance Tests; *Vocational Education; *Vocational Education Teachers; *Work Sample Tests
Identifiers: NOCTI; TOCT
Availability: National Occupational Competency Testing Institute; 318 Johnson Hall, Ferris State College, Big Rapids, MI 49307
Age Level: Adults
Notes: Time, 420 min.; Items, 195
One of a series of tests designed to determine a level of occupational competence for vocational education teachers. A written test covers theoretical concepts of the occupation and a performance test examines selected manipulative skills. They may be used for credit by examination and also for teacher certification. The written test covers trade computations, drafting room procedures, orthographic and pictorial drawings, dimensioning, tolerances and symbols, applied science, threads and fasteners, cams, gears and pulleys. The performance test covers drawing and dimensioning, revolutions, developments, isometric, intersections, orthographic projection, auxiliary projection, sectioning.

14208
Teacher Occupational Competency Testing: Machine Trades. National Occupational Competency Testing Institute, Big Rapids, MI
Descriptors: *Achievement Tests; Adults; *Certification; College Credits; Credentials; *Equivalency Tests; Machine Tools; *Machinists; Multiple Choice Tests; Occupational Tests; Performance Tests; *Vocational Education; *Vocational Education Teachers; *Work Sample Tests
Identifiers: NOCTI; TOCT
Availability: National Occupational Competency Testing Institute; 318 Johnson Hall, Ferris State College, Big Rapids, MI 49307
Age Level: Adults
Notes: Time, 480 min.; Items, 160
One of a series of tests designed to determine a level of occupational competence for vocational education teachers. A written test covers theoretical concepts of the occupation and a performance test examines selected manipulative skills. They may be used for credit by examination and also for teacher certification. The written test covers application of technical information, milling machines and shapers, lathes, grinders, layout and measurement, drill presses, interpretation of drawings, benchwork and assembly, power saws, electrical discharge machines. The performance test covers turning and processing, milling processes and machines, bench and assembly, layout and inspection, grinding and precision finishing, drilling, tapping, reaming—machines and attachments.

14209
Teacher Occupational Competency Testing: Major Appliance Repair. National Occupational Competency Testing Institute, Big Rapids, MI
Descriptors: *Achievement Tests; Adults; *Appliance Repair; *Certification; College Credits; Credentials; *Equivalency Tests; Multiple Choice Tests; Occupational Tests; Performance Tests; Refrigeration; Vocational Education; *Vocational Education Teachers; *Work Sample Tests
Identifiers: NOCTI; TOCT
Availability: National Occupational Competency Testing Institute; 318 Johnson Hall, Ferris State College, Big Rapids, MI 49307
Age Level: Adults
Notes: Time, 540 min.; Items, 180
One of a series of tests designed to determine a level of occupational competence for vocational education teachers. A written test covers theoretical concepts of the occupation and a performance test examines selected manipulative skills. They may be used for credit by examination and also for teacher certification. The written test covers refrigeration, fundamentals, kitchen equipment, major heating devices, laundry equipment, power tools and small appliances. The performance test covers disassembly and repair of refrigeration equipment, laundry equipment, and major heating devices such as an electric range.

14210
Teacher Occupational Competency Testing: Masonry. National Occupational Competency Testing Institute, Big Rapids, MI

Descriptors: *Achievement Tests; Adults; *Certification; College Credits; Credentials; *Equivalency Tests; *Masonry; Multiple Choice Tests; Occupational Tests; Performance Tests; *Vocational Education; *Vocational Education Teachers; *Work Sample Tests
Identifiers: NOCTI; TOCT
Availability: National Occupational Competency Testing Institute; 318 Johnson Hall, Ferris State College, Big Rapids, MI 49307
Age Level: Adults
Notes: Time, 300 min.; Items, 100
One of a series of tests designed to determine a level of occupational competence for vocational education teachers. A written test covers theoretical concepts of the occupation and a performance test examines selected manipulative skills. They may be used for credit by examination and also for teacher certification. The written test covers masonry practices using brick, stone, concrete, tile, plaster and stucco, brick veneer and combined masonry, trade tools, terminology, layout procedures, materials of the trade, estimating procedures, safety. The performance test covers skill with trowel, hammer, cutting chisel, level, and jointer; lack of waste motion; efficient location and use of materials; layout procedures, quality of completed work; observation of safe practices.

14211
Teacher Occupational Competency Testing: Masonry Occupations. National Occupational Competency Testing Institute, Big Rapids, MI
Descriptors: *Achievement Tests; Adults; *Certification; College Credits; Credentials; *Equivalency Tests; *Masonry; Multiple Choice Tests; Occupational Tests; Performance Tests; *Vocational Education; *Vocational Education Teachers; *Work Sample Tests
Identifiers: NOCTI; TOCT
Availability: National Occupational Competency Testing Institute; 318 Johnson Hall, Ferris State College, Big Rapids, MI 49307
Age Level: Adults
Notes: Time, 420 min.; Items, 200
One of a series of tests designed to determine a level of occupational competence for vocational education teachers. A written test covers theoretical concepts of the occupation and a performance test examines selected manipulative skills. They may be used for credit by examination and also for teacher certification. The written test covers blueprint reading, layout, bond cutting of brick and blocks, arch work, pointing; plaster, dry wall, tile, stone, concrete, estimating. The performance test covers cutting, fitting, pointing, patterning stone; layout of block, tile, flagstone; application of plaster, types and patterns of brick, including mortar, composition, facing.

14212
Teacher Occupational Competency Testing: Materials Handling. National Occupational Competency Testing Institute, Big Rapids, MI
Descriptors: *Achievement Tests; Adults; *Certification; College Credits; Credentials; *Equivalency Tests; *Facility Inventory; Multiple Choice Tests; Occupational Tests; Performance Tests; *Vocational Education; *Vocational Education Teachers; Warehouses; *Work Sample Tests
Identifiers: NOCTI; TOCT
Availability: National Occupational Competency Testing Institute; 318 Johnson Hall, Ferris State College, Big Rapids, MI 49307
Age Level: Adults
Notes: Time, 420 min.; Items, 199
One of a series of tests designed to determine a level of occupational competence for vocational education teachers. A written test covers theoretical concepts of the occupation and a performance test examines selected manipulative skills. They may be used for credit by examination and also for teacher certification. The written test covers receiving, inventory controls, warehousing, shipping and distribution, equipment for materials handling, transportation, purchasing, storage of material. The performance test covers equipment use and operation, shipping procedures, receiving procedures, warehouse proposal, inventory, storage, purchasing.

14213
Teacher Occupational Competency Testing: Mechanical Technology. National Occupational Competency Testing Institute, Big Rapids, MI
Descriptors: *Achievement Tests; Adults; *Certification; College Credits; Computer Oriented Programs; Credentials; Electricity; Engineering Drawing; *Equivalency Tests; Fluid Mechanics; Knowledge Level; Machine Tools; Mathematics; *Mechanics (Physics); *Mechanics (Process); Multiple Choice Tests; Occupational Tests; Performance Tests; *Vocational Education; *Vocational Education Teachers; *Work Sample Tests
Identifiers: NOCTI; TOCT

Availability: National Occupational Competency Testing Institute; 318 Johnson Hall, Ferris State College, Big Rapids, MI 49307
Age Level: Adults
Notes: Time, 540 min.; Items, 65

One of a series of tests designed to determine a level of occupational competence for vocational education teachers. A written test covers theoretical concepts of the occupation and a performance test examines selected manipulative skills. They may be used for credit by examination and also for teacher certification. The written test covers statics, strength of materials, mathematics, machine tool operations, metallurgy, electricity, physics, fluid mechanics, thermodynamics, applications of basic computer programing to engineering. The performance test requires the test taker to design a component part from data provided; prepare pertinent drawings from sketches and other information; conduct tests, using test instruments to determine, evaluate, and record data; report on data.

14214
Teacher Occupational Competency Testing: Painting and Decorating. National Occupational Competency Testing Institute, Big Rapids, MI
Descriptors: *Achievement Tests; Adults; *Certification; College Credits; Credentials; *Equivalency Tests; *Interior Design; Multiple Choice Tests; *Occupational Tests; *Painting (Industrial Arts); Performance Tests; *Vocational Education; *Vocational Education Teachers; *Work Sample Tests
Identifiers: NOCTI; TOCT
Availability: National Occupational Competency Testing Institute; 318 Johnson Hall, Ferris State College, Big Rapids, MI 49307
Age Level: Adults
Notes: Time, 420 min.; Items, 190

One of a series of tests designed to determine a level of occupational competence for vocational education teachers. A written test covers theoretical concepts of the occupation and a performance test examines selected manipulative skills. They may be used for credit by examination and also for teacher certification. The written test covers exterior and interior painting, wall covering, wood finishing, color and color harmony, estimating, special wall finishes. The performance test covers wood finishing, wall covering, exterior and interior painting, color and color harmony, clean up.

14215
Teacher Occupational Competency Testing: Plumbing. National Occupational Competency Testing Institute, Big Rapids, MI
Descriptors: *Achievement Tests; Adults; *Certification; College Credits; Credentials; *Equivalency Tests; Multiple Choice Tests; Occupational Tests; Performance Tests; *Plumbing; *Vocational Education; *Vocational Education Teachers; *Work Sample Tests
Identifiers: NOCTI; TOCT
Availability: National Occupational Competency Testing Institute; 318 Johnson Hall, Ferris State College, Big Rapids, MI 49307
Age Level: Adults
Notes: Time, 480 min.; Items, 167

One of a series of tests designed to determine a level of occupational competence for vocational education teachers. A written test covers theoretical concepts of the occupation and a performance test examines selected manipulative skills. They may be used for credit by examination and also for teacher certification. The written test covers physical properties and characteristics of commonly used materials and supplies; operating principles and installation of commonly used materials and supplies; installation and principles of building drains and sewers; installation and operation of storm water drains; water supply and distribution—fixture units; plumbing fixtures (water supply and soil, waste and venting); industrial and special wastes; inspection and tests; general trade information. The performance test requires the test taker to work from builder's or architect's drawings, rough-in standard installation, install fixtures and accessories on a variety of materials (toilets, wash basins, etc.); testing systems.

14216
Teacher Occupational Competency Testing: Power Sewing. National Occupational Competency Testing Institute, Big Rapids, MI
Descriptors: *Achievement Tests; Adults; *Certification; College Credits; Credentials; *Equivalency Tests; Multiple Choice Tests; Occupational Tests; Performance Tests; *Sewing Machine Operators; *Vocational Education; *Vocational Education Teachers; *Work Sample Tests
Identifiers: NOCTI; TOCT
Availability: National Occupational Competency Testing Institute; 318 Johnson Hall, Ferris State College, Big Rapids, MI 49307
Age Level: Adults
Notes: Time, 420 min.; Items, 200

One of a series of tests designed to determine a level of occupational competence for vocational education teachers. A written test covers theoretical concepts of the occupation and a performance test examines selected manipulative skills. They may be used for credit by examination and also for teacher certification. The written test covers power machine operation, apparel assembly, general knowledge of the needle trade, general knowledge of terminology in apparel assembly trade; tools and attachments. The performance test covers assembling techniques, sewing machines, tools and attachments, finishing techniques, materials, safety and clean up.

14217
Teacher Occupational Competency Testing: Printing (Offset). National Occupational Competency Testing Institute, Big Rapids, MI
Descriptors: *Achievement Tests; Adults; *Certification; College Credits; Credentials; *Equivalency Tests; Multiple Choice Tests; Occupational Tests; Performance Tests; *Printing; *Vocational Education; *Vocational Education Teachers; *Work Sample Tests
Identifiers: NOCTI; TOCT
Availability: National Occupational Competency Testing Institute; 318 Johnson Hall, Ferris State College, Big Rapids, MI 49307
Age Level: Adults
Notes: Time, 480 min.; Items, 183

One of a series of tests designed to determine a level of occupational competence for vocational education teachers. A written test covers theoretical concepts of the occupation and a performance test examines selected manipulative skills. They may be used for credit by examination and also for teacher certification. The written test covers typography, layout and composition, camera photo mechanical, presswork, stripping and platemaking, binding and finishing, trade information, job safety. The performance test covers design and composition, bindery/finishing, photo preparatory-image carriers, image transfer (presswork).

14218
Teacher Occupational Competency Testing: Printing (Letterpress). National Occupational Competency Testing Institute, Big Rapids, MI
Descriptors: *Achievement Tests; Adults; *Certification; College Credits; Credentials; *Equivalency Tests; Multiple Choice Tests; Occupational Tests; Performance Tests; *Printing; *Vocational Education; *Vocational Education Teachers; *Work Sample Tests
Identifiers: NOCTI; TOCT
Availability: National Occupational Competency Testing Institute; 318 Johnson Hall, Ferris State College, Big Rapids, MI 49307
Age Level: Adults
Notes: Time, 480 min.; Items, 183

One of a series of tests designed to determine a level of occupational competence for vocational education teachers. A written test covers theoretical concepts of the occupation and a performance test examines selected manipulative skills. They may be used for credit by examination and also for teacher certification. The written test covers typography, layout and composition, camera photo mechanical, presswork, stripping and platemaking, binding and finishing, trade information, job safety. The performance test covers design and composition, presswork, bindery/finishing.

14219
Teacher Occupational Competency Testing: Quantity Food Preparation. National Occupational Competency Testing Institute, Big Rapids, MI
Descriptors: *Achievement Tests; Adults; *Certification; College Credits; Credentials; *Equivalency Tests; *Food Service; Multiple Choice Tests; Occupational Tests; Performance Tests; *Vocational Education; *Vocational Education Teachers; *Work Sample Tests
Identifiers: NOCTI; TOCT
Availability: National Occupational Competency Testing Institute; 318 Johnson Hall, Ferris State College, Big Rapids, MI 49307
Age Level: Adults
Notes: Time, 360 min.; Items, 195

One of a series of tests designed to determine a level of occupational competence for vocational education teachers. A written test covers theoretical concepts of the occupation and a performance test examines selected manipulative skills. They may be used for credit by examination and also for teacher certification. The written test covers food groups, sanitation, purchasing, guest service, cost control; proper use, selection, and cleaning of equipment and tools; receiving/storage; menu planning; safety. The performance test covers methods of food preparation; assembling and portioning ingredients; use of equipment; general knowledge, including organization and timing of preparation; interpretation of recipes; cleaning procedures; use of utensils and hand tools; use of preparation areas; recipes and menus.

14220
Teacher Occupational Competency Testing: Quantity Foods. National Occupational Competency Testing Institute, Big Rapids, MI
Descriptors: *Achievement Tests; Adults; *Certification; College Credits; Credentials; *Equivalency Tests; *Food Service; Multiple Choice Tests; Occupational Tests; Performance Tests; *Vocational Education; *Vocational Education Teachers; *Work Sample Tests
Identifiers: NOCTI; TOCT
Availability: National Occupational Competency Testing Institute; 318 Johnson Hall, Ferris State College, Big Rapids, MI 49307
Age Level: Adults
Notes: Time, 420 min.; Items, 200

One of a series of tests designed to determine a level of occupational competence for vocational education teachers. A written test covers theoretical concepts of the occupation and a performance test examines selected manipulative skills. They may be used for credit by examination and also for teacher certification. The written test covers food preparation, food purchasing, food receiving and storage, nutrition, cost control and menu planning, waitressing and customer service, safety and cleanliness, food service occupations. The performance test covers food preparation and work organization.

14221
Teacher Occupational Competency Testing: Radio/TV Repair. National Occupational Competency Testing Institute, Big Rapids, MI
Descriptors: *Achievement Tests; Adults; *Certification; College Credits; Credentials; *Equivalency Tests; Multiple Choice Tests; Occupational Tests; Performance Tests; *Television Radio Repairers; *Vocational Education; *Vocational Education Teachers; *Work Sample Tests
Identifiers: NOCTI; TOCT
Availability: National Occupational Competency Testing Institute; 318 Johnson Hall, Ferris State College, Big Rapids, MI 49307
Age Level: Adults
Notes: Time, 420 min.; Items, 193

One of a series of tests designed to determine a level of occupational competence for vocational education teachers. A written test covers theoretical concepts of the occupation and a performance test examines selected manipulative skills. They may be used for credit by examination and also for teacher certification. The written test covers color and black and white receivers, solid state and tube circuitry, fundamental electronic theory, signal characteristics, TV & FM transmissions and reception, antenna and transmission lines, test equipment, servicing. The performance test covers television service and repair, radio equipment service and repair, recording equipment service and repair.

14222
Teacher Occupational Competency Testing: Refrigeration. National Occupational Competency Testing Institute, Big Rapids, MI
Descriptors: *Achievement Tests; Adults; *Certification; College Credits; Credentials; *Equivalency Tests; Multiple Choice Tests; Occupational Tests; Performance Tests; *Refrigeration; *Vocational Education; *Vocational Education Teachers; *Work Sample Tests
Identifiers: NOCTI; TOCT
Availability: National Occupational Competency Testing Institute; 318 Johnson Hall, Ferris State College, Big Rapids, MI 49307
Age Level: Adults
Notes: Time, 420 min.; Items, 180

One of a series of tests designed to determine a level of occupational competence for vocational education teachers. A written test covers theoretical concepts of the occupation and a performance test examines selected manipulative skills. They may be used for credit by examination and also for teacher certification. The written test covers commercial service and installation, domestic service, industrial service and installation. The performance test requires the test taker to assemble refrigeration system; cut, flare, swedge, solder tubing; wire components; charge system, set controls, troubleshoot, and correct faults made by candidate; operate system to specifications.

14223
Teacher Occupational Competency Testing: Sheet Metal. National Occupational Competency Testing Institute, Big Rapids, MI
Descriptors: *Achievement Tests; Adults; *Certification; College Credits; Credentials; *Equivalency Tests; *Metal Working; Multiple Choice Tests; Occupational Tests; Performance Tests; *Vocational Education; *Vocational Education Teachers; *Work Sample Tests
Identifiers: NOCTI; TOCT

Availability: National Occupational Competency Testing Institute; 318 Johnson Hall, Ferris State College, Big Rapids, MI 49307
Age Level: Adults
Notes: Time, 480 min.; Items, 112

One of a series of tests designed to determine a level of occupational competence for vocational education teachers. A written test covers theoretical concepts of the occupation and a performance test examines selected manipulative skills. They may be used for credit by examination and also for teacher certification. The written test covers layout and drafting, sheet metal machinery, bench and hand tools—processing, materials used in fabrication, assembly, erection and repairing of sheet metal; sheet metal fabrication, fluxes, application of trade science, computations, welding, building code and regulations, hazards. The performance test covers fabrication and assembly, pattern development, welding and fastening, identification and protection of materials, grinding and drilling.

14224
Teacher Occupational Competency Testing: Small Engine Repair. National Occupational Competency Testing Institute, Big Rapids, MI
Descriptors: *Achievement Tests; Adults; *Certification; College Credits; Credentials; *Equivalency Tests; *Machine Repairers; Multiple Choice Tests; Occupational Tests; Performance Tests; *Vocational Education; *Vocational Education Teachers; *Work Sample Tests
Identifiers: NOCTI; TOCT
Availability: National Occupational Competency Testing Institute; 318 Johnson Hall, Ferris State College, Big Rapids, MI 49307
Age Level: Adults
Notes: Time, 420 min.; Items, 165

One of a series of tests designed to determine a level of occupational competence for vocational education teachers. A written test covers theoretical concepts of the occupation and a performance test examines selected manipulative skills. They may be used for credit by examination and also for teacher certification. The written test covers fuel systems and carburetion, ignition and starting systems, troubleshooting, engine operation, cylinder block servicing and overhaul, benchwork, testing and inspection, trade applications of science, trade-related information, preventive maintenance, lubricating systems and lubrication, transmissions of power and drive units, trade computations, cooling and exhaust systems. The performance test covers engine analysis, cylinder block servicing and overhaul, fuel systems and carburetion, ignition and starting systems, troubleshooting, lubricating systems and lubrication, cooling and exhaust systems, preventive maintenance, benchwork, testing and inspection.

14225
Teacher Occupational Competency Testing: Textile Production/Fabrication. National Occupational Competency Testing Institute, Big Rapids, MI
Descriptors: *Achievement Tests; Adults; *Certification; College Credits; Credentials; *Equivalency Tests; *Finishing; Machine Tool Operators; Multiple Choice Tests; Occupational Tests; Performance Tests; *Textiles Instruction; *Vocational Education; *Vocational Education Teachers; *Work Sample Tests
Identifiers: NOCTI; TOCT
Availability: National Occupational Competency Testing Institute; 318 Johnson Hall, Ferris State College, Big Rapids, MI 49307
Age Level: Adults
Notes: Time, 420 min.; Items, 200

One of a series of tests designed to determine a level of occupational competence for vocational education teachers. A written test covers theoretical concepts of the occupation and a performance test examines selected manipulative skills. They may be used for credit by examination and also for teacher certification. The written test covers apparel assembly, power machine operations, textile terms, fabric finishes, fiber content, fabric structure, fiber content handling, alterations, pattern making. The performance test covers apparel assembly, power machine operations, textiles, alterations, pattern making.

14226
Teacher Occupational Competency Testing: Small Engine Repair. National Occupational Competency Testing Institute, Big Rapids, MI
Descriptors: *Achievement Tests; Adults; *Certification; College Credits; Credentials; *Equivalency Tests; *Machine Repairers; Multiple Choice Tests; Occupational Tests; Performance Tests; *Vocational Education; *Vocational Education Teachers; *Work Sample Tests
Identifiers: NOCTI; TOCT
Availability: National Occupational Competency Testing Institute; 318 Johnson Hall, Ferris State College, Big Rapids, MI 49307
Age Level: Adults
Notes: Time, 420 min.; Items, 180

One of a series of tests designed to determine a level of occupational competence for vocational education teachers. A written test covers theoretical concepts of the occupation and a performance test examines selected manipulative skills. They may be used for credit by examination and also for teacher certification. The written test covers engine servicing, knowledge of safety and safe use of tools, equipment, and measuring devices of the trade; theory of 2-cycle and 4-cycle engines; electrical system; fuel system; parts and inventory. The performance test covers electrical systems, engine service and repair, fuel systems, peripheral.

14227
Teacher Occupational Competency Testing: Tool and Die Making. National Occupational Competency Testing Institute, Big Rapids, MI
Descriptors: *Achievement Tests; Adults; *Certification; College Credits; Credentials; *Equivalency Tests; Multiple Choice Tests; Occupational Tests; Performance Tests; *Tool and Die Makers; *Vocational Education; *Vocational Education Teachers; *Work Sample Tests
Identifiers: NOCTI; TOCT
Availability: National Occupational Competency Testing Institute; 318 Johnson Hall, Ferris State College, Big Rapids, MI 49307
Age Level: Adults
Notes: Time, 480 min.; Items, 180

One of a series of tests designed to determine a level of occupational competence for vocational education teachers. A written test covers theoretical concepts of the occupation and a performance test examines selected manipulative skills. They may be used for credit by examination and also for teacher certification. The written test covers inspection, tool design and cost estimating, characteristics of metals, math (plane geometry and trigonometry), metallurgy/heat treat, physical mechanics (canes, levers, gearing), metal fabrication, profiling machines, surface finish pages, extruding and molding. The performance test covers tooling, die making (piercing, forming, diesinking and coining), jig and fixture work.

14228
Teacher Occupational Competency Testing: Welding (021). National Occupational Competency Testing Institute, Big Rapids, MI
Descriptors: *Achievement Tests; Adults; *Certification; College Credits; Credentials; *Equivalency Tests; Multiple Choice Tests; Occupational Tests; Performance Tests; *Vocational Education; *Vocational Education Teachers; *Welding; *Work Sample Tests
Identifiers: NOCTI; TOCT
Availability: National Occupational Competency Testing Institute; 318 Johnson Hall, Ferris State College, Big Rapids, MI 49307
Age Level: Adults
Notes: Time, 420 min.; Items, 174

One of a series of tests designed to determine a level of occupational competence for vocational education teachers. A written test covers theoretical concepts of the occupation and a performance test examines selected manipulative skills. They may be used for credit by examination and also for teacher certification. The written test covers shielded metal arc welding, gas tungsten arc welding, oxy-fuel welding, brazing, gas metal arc welding, basic metallurgy, testing, welding defects and causes, welding symbols, hard surfacing, electricity, joint design, general welder qualifications, other processes. The performance test covers gas metal arc welding, shielded metal arc welding, oxy-fuel welding, gas tungsten arc welding.

14229
Teacher Occupational Competency Testing: Welding (057). National Occupational Competency Testing Institute, Big Rapids, MI
Descriptors: *Achievement Tests; Adults; *Certification; College Credits; Credentials; *Equivalency Tests; Multiple Choice Tests; Occupational Tests; Performance Tests; *Vocational Education; Vocational Education Teachers; *Welding; *Work Sample Tests
Identifiers: NOCTI; TOCT
Availability: National Occupational Competency Testing Institute; 318 Johnson Hall, Ferris State College, Big Rapids, MI 49307
Age Level: Adults
Notes: Time, 430 min.; Items, 180

One of a series of tests designed to determine a level of occupational competence for vocational education teachers. A written test covers theoretical concepts of the occupation and a performance test examines selected manipulative skills. They may be used for credit by examination and also for teacher certification. The written test covers gas metal arc welding, shielded metal arc welding, oxy-fuel welding, torch brazing, basic metallurgy, general knowledge. The performance test covers shielded metal arc welding, oxy-fuel welding, gas metal arc welding, gas tungsten arc welding.

14231
Watson-Barker Listening Test, Short Form. Watson, Kittie W.; Barker, Larry L. 1984
Descriptors: Adults; College Students; Higher Education; Listening; *Listening Comprehension Tests; Multiple Choice Tests; Tape Recorders
Availability: Spectra Incorporated, Publishers; P.O. Box 13591, New Orleans, LA 70185-3591
Grade Level: 13-16
Age Level: Adults
Notes: Items, 20

A measure of listening abilities for adults in general, those involved in business and industry, and college students. Norms are available. A tape recorder is required.

14244
Student Occupational Competency Achievement Testing: Accounting/Bookkeeping. National Occupational Competency Testing Institute, Big Rapids, MI
Descriptors: *Accounting; *Achievement Tests; Adults; *Bookkeeping; Credentials; High Schools; *High School Students; Multiple Choice Tests; Occupational Tests; Performance Tests; *Postsecondary Education; Secondary Education; Two Year Colleges; *Vocational Education; Vocational Schools; *Work Sample Tests
Identifiers: NOCTI; SOCAT
Availability: National Occupational Competency Testing Institute; 318 Johnson Hall, Ferris State College, Big Rapids, MI 49307
Grade Level: 9-14
Notes: Time, 360 min.; Items, 189

This test is part of a program developed to evaluate secondary and postsecondary vocational students with a standardized, objective measure. Each test consists of a multiple-choice portion covering factual knowledge, technical information, understanding of principles and problem-solving abilities related to the occupation. A performance component samples manipulative skills required. A mental ability test is also available. The written test covers sales and receivables, processing payroll and related records, cash receipts and cash payments, processing purchases and payables, inventory, operating mechanical and electronic accounting devices, filing and records management, completing the accounting cycle, performing general office functions, obtaining employment as an accounting/computing clerk. The performance test covers journalizing business transactions, posting from specialized journals, payroll procedures, worksheet and statement preparation, locating source data, banking and banking procedures.

14245
Student Occupational Competency Achievement Testing: Agriculture Mechanics. National Occupational Competency Testing Institute, Big Rapids, MI
Descriptors: *Achievement Tests; Adults; *Agricultural Engineering; Credentials; High Schools; *High School Students; Multiple Choice Tests; Occupational Tests; Performance Tests; *Postsecondary Education; Secondary Education; Two Year Colleges; *Vocational Education; Vocational Schools; *Work Sample Tests
Identifiers: NOCTI; SOCAT
Availability: National Occupational Competency Testing Institute; 318 Johnson Hall, Ferris State College, Big Rapids, MI 49307
Grade Level: 9-14
Notes: Time, 360 min.; Items, 175

This test is part of a program developed to evaluate secondary and postsecondary vocational students with a standardized, objective measure. Each test consists of a multiple-choice portion covering factual knowledge, technical information, understanding of principles and problem-solving abilities related to the occupation. A performance component samples manipulative skills required. A mental ability test is also available. The written test covers agricultural power and machinery, agricultural mechanic skills, agricultural electrical power and processing, agricultural structures, soil and water management, orientation and safety. The performance test covers wheel bearings, electrical installation, oxyacetylene cutting, agricultural structures, farm level, shielded metal arc welding.

14246
Student Occupational Competency Achievement Testing: Auto Body. National Occupational Competency Testing Institute, Big Rapids, MI
Descriptors: *Achievement Tests; Adults; *Auto Body Repairers; Credentials; High Schools; *High School Students; Multiple Choice Tests; Occupational Tests; Performance Tests; *Postsecondary Education; Secondary Education; Two Year Colleges; *Vocational Education; Vocational Schools; *Work Sample Tests
Identifiers: NOCTI; SOCAT

Availability: National Occupational Competency Testing Institute; 318 Johnson Hall, Ferris State College, Big Rapids, MI 49307
Grade Level: 9-14
Notes: Time, 360 min.; Items, 160
This test is part of a program developed to evaluate secondary and postsecondary vocational students with a standardized, objective measure. Each test consists of a multiple-choice portion covering factual knowledge, technical information, understanding of principles and problem-solving abilities related to the occupation. A performance component samples manipulative skills required. A mental ability test is also available. The written test covers body preparation and painting, basic knowledge and terminology, math and science, hand tools and power tools, welding, safety, customer relations, soldering and brazing. The performance test covers sheet metal repair, painting, welding panel construction.

14247
Student Occupational Competency Achievement Testing: Auto Mechanics. National Occupational Competency Testing Institute, Big Rapids, MI
Descriptors: *Achievement Tests; Adults; *Auto Mechanics; Credentials; High Schools; *High School Students; Multiple Choice Tests; Occupational Tests; Performance Tests; *Postsecondary Education; Secondary Education; Two Year Colleges; *Vocational Education; Vocational Schools; *Work Sample Tests
Identifiers: NOCTI; SOCAT
Availability: National Occupational Competency Testing Institute; 318 Johnson Hall, Ferris State College, Big Rapids, MI 49307
Grade Level: 9-14
Notes: Time, 360 min.; Items, 177
This test is part of a program developed to evaluate secondary and postsecondary vocational students with a standardized, objective measure. Each test consists of a multiple-choice portion covering factual knowledge, technical information, understanding of principles and problem-solving abilities related to the occupation. A performance component samples manipulative skills required. A mental ability test is also available. The written test covers engine tune-up, engine repair, brakes, electrical systems, front end, manual transmission/rear axle, heating/air conditioning, automatic transmissions. The performance test requires the test taker to perform minor tune-up, maintain and repair electrical systems, maintain and repair brake system.

14248
Student Occupational Competency Achievement Testing: Carpentry. National Occupational Competency Testing Institute, Big Rapids, MI
Descriptors: *Achievement Tests; Adults; *Carpentry; Credentials; High Schools; *High School Students; Multiple Choice Tests; Occupational Tests; Performance Tests; *Postsecondary Education; Secondary Education; Two Year Colleges; *Vocational Education; Vocational Schools; *Work Sample Tests
Identifiers: NOCTI; SOCAT
Availability: National Occupational Competency Testing Institute; 318 Johnson Hall, Ferris State College, Big Rapids, MI 49307
Grade Level: 9-14
Notes: Time, 360 min.; Items, 171
This test is part of a program developed to evaluate secondary and postsecondary vocational students with a standardized, objective measure. Each test consists of a multiple-choice portion covering factual knowledge, technical information, understanding of principles and problem-solving abilities related to the occupation. A performance component samples manipulative skills required. A mental ability test is also available. The written test covers blueprint reading, preparation of specifications, building materials, hand and power tools, foundations, forms, rough framing, roof components, interior and exterior finish, stair construction. The performance test covers rafters, door frame construction, engineer's transit, batter board elevation, stairway stringer, partition walls.

14249
Student Occupational Competency Achievement Testing: Commercial Foods. National Occupational Competency Testing Institute, Big Rapids, MI
Descriptors: *Achievement Tests; Adults; Credentials; *Food Service; High Schools; *High School Students; Multiple Choice Tests; Occupational Tests; Performance Tests; *Postsecondary Education; Secondary Education; Two Year Colleges; *Vocational Education; Vocational Schools; *Work Sample Tests
Identifiers: NOCTI; SOCAT
Availability: National Occupational Competency Testing Institute; 318 Johnson Hall, Ferris State College, Big Rapids, MI 49307
Grade Level: 9-14
Notes: Time, 360 min.; Items, 184

This test is part of a program developed to evaluate secondary and postsecondary vocational students with a standardized, objective measure. Each test consists of a multiple-choice portion covering factual knowledge, technical information, understanding of principles and problem-solving abilities related to the occupation. A performance component samples manipulative skills required. A mental ability test is also available. The written test covers food preparation, food service occupations, sanitation, safety, equipment, service, purchasing, management skills, specialty service. The performance test covers preparation of cold salad, preparation of entree, preparation of quick bread, table service.

14250
Student Occupational Competency Achievement Testing: Computer Programming. National Occupational Competency Testing Institute, Big Rapids, MI
Descriptors: *Achievement Tests; Adults; Credentials; High Schools; *High School Students; Multiple Choice Tests; Occupational Tests; Performance Tests; *Postsecondary Education; *Programing; Programing Languages; Secondary Education; Two Year Colleges; *Vocational Education; Vocational Schools; *Work Sample Tests
Identifiers: BASIC; COBOL; NOCTI; RPG; SOCAT
Availability: National Occupational Competency Testing Institute; 318 Johnson Hall, Ferris State College, Big Rapids, MI 49307
Grade Level: 9-14
Notes: Time, 420 min.; Items, 150
This test is part of a program developed to evaluate secondary and postsecondary vocational students with a standardized, objective measure. Each test consists of a multiple-choice portion covering factual knowledge, technical information, understanding of principles and problem-solving abilities related to the occupation. A performance component samples manipulative skills required. A mental ability test is also available. The written test covers operational information, design, flowcharting, operations, BASIC COBOL, RPG, related math, problem solving. The performance test covers program design, coding, testing, output.

14251
Student Occupational Competency Achievement Testing: Construction Electricity. National Occupational Competency Testing Institute, Big Rapids, MI
Descriptors: *Achievement Tests; Adults; *Construction Industry; Credentials; *Electricity; Electronics; High Schools; *High School Students; Multiple Choice Tests; Occupational Tests; Performance Tests; *Postsecondary Education; Secondary Education; Two Year Colleges; *Vocational Education; Vocational Schools; *Work Sample Tests
Identifiers: NOCTI; SOCAT
Availability: National Occupational Competency Testing Institute; 318 Johnson Hall, Ferris State College, Big Rapids, MI 49307
Grade Level: 9-14
Notes: Time, 360 min.; Items, 195
This test is part of a program developed to evaluate secondary and postsecondary vocational students with a standardized, objective measure. Each test consists of a multiple-choice portion covering factual knowledge, technical information, understanding of principles and problem-solving abilities related to the occupation. A performance component samples manipulative skills required. A mental ability test is also available. The written test covers branch circuits, wiring methods, lighting, AC electricity, electronics, blueprints, planning, layout, transformers, AC motors and starters, heating and air conditioning, orientation, tools and equipment, low voltage. The performance test covers planning and layout, wiring methods, service installation.

14252
Student Occupational Competency Achievement Testing: Construction Masonry. National Occupational Competency Testing Institute, Big Rapids, MI
Descriptors: *Achievement Tests; Adults; *Construction Industry; Credentials; High Schools; *High School Students; *Masonry; Multiple Choice Tests; Occupational Tests; Performance Tests; *Postsecondary Education; Secondary Education; Two Year Colleges; *Vocational Education; Vocational Schools; *Work Sample Tests
Identifiers: NOCTI; SOCAT
Availability: National Occupational Competency Testing Institute; 318 Johnson Hall, Ferris State College, Big Rapids, MI 49307
Grade Level: 9-14
Notes: Time, 375 min.; Items, 145

This test is part of a program developed to evaluate secondary and postsecondary vocational students with a standardized, objective measure. Each test consists of a multiple-choice portion covering factual knowledge, technical information, understanding of principles and problem-solving abilities related to the occupation. A performance component samples manipulative skills required. A mental ability test is also available. The written test covers tools and equipment, masonry materials, fastening devices, blueprint reading, interpretation of measurements, building site layout, construction methods, fireplace construction, maintenance of masonry structures, specialty construction areas of bricklaying, blocklaying, or stone masonry, safety. The performance covers layout techniques, tools and equipment, building materials, construction techniques, safety.

14253
Student Occupational Competency Achievement Testing: Drafting. National Occupational Competency Testing Institute, Big Rapids, MI
Descriptors: *Achievement Tests; Adults; Credentials; *Drafting; High Schools; *High School Students; Multiple Choice Tests; Occupational Tests; Performance Tests; *Postsecondary Education; Secondary Education; Two Year Colleges; *Vocational Education; Vocational Schools; *Work Sample Tests
Identifiers: NOCTI; SOCAT
Availability: National Occupational Competency Testing Institute; 318 Johnson Hall, Ferris State College, Big Rapids, MI 49307
Grade Level: 9-14
Notes: Time, 360 min.; Items, 120
This test is part of a program developed to evaluate secondary and postsecondary vocational students with a standardized, objective measure. Each test consists of a multiple-choice portion covering factual knowledge, technical information, understanding of principles and problem-solving abilities related to the occupation. A performance component samples manipulative skills required. A mental ability test is also available. The written test covers interpretation of drawings, machine drawing, architectural drawing, mathematical calculations, electrical/electronic drawing, sheet metal drawing, mapping and cartography, computer-assisted drawing. The performance test covers production/detail, specialty areas of electrical, piping or architectural, orthographic projection, auxiliary, threads.

14254
Student Occupational Competency Achievement Testing: General Merchandising. National Occupational Competency Testing Institute, Big Rapids, MI
Descriptors: *Achievement Tests; Adults; Credentials; High Schools; *High School Students; *Merchandising; Multiple Choice Tests; Occupational Tests; Performance Tests; *Postsecondary Education; Secondary Education; Two Year Colleges; *Vocational Education; Vocational Schools; *Work Sample Tests
Identifiers: NOCTI; SOCAT
Availability: National Occupational Competency Testing Institute; 318 Johnson Hall, Ferris State College, Big Rapids, MI 49307
Grade Level: 9-14
Notes: Time, 220 min.; Items, 150
This test is part of a program developed to evaluate secondary and postsecondary vocational students with a standardized, objective measure. Each test consists of a multiple-choice portion covering factual knowledge, technical information, understanding of principles and problem-solving abilities related to the occupation. A performance component samples manipulative skills required. A mental ability test is also available. The written test covers operations, merchandising, management, communications, human relations, sales. The performance test covers product knowledge and selling, human relations and communications, mechanics of completing a sale and handling money.

14255
Student Occupational Competency Achievement Testing: General Office. National Occupational Competency Testing Institute, Big Rapids, MI
Descriptors: *Achievement Tests; Adults; Credentials; High Schools; *High School Students; Multiple Choice Tests; Occupational Tests; *Office Occupations; Performance Tests; *Postsecondary Education; Secondary Education; Two Year Colleges; *Vocational Education; Vocational Schools; *Work Sample Tests
Identifiers: NOCTI; SOCAT
Availability: National Occupational Competency Testing Institute; 318 Johnson Hall, Ferris State College, Big Rapids, MI 49307
Grade Level: 9-14
Notes: Time, 360 min.; Items, 165
This test is part of a program developed to evaluate secondary and postsecondary vocational students with a standardized, objective measure. Each test consists of a multiple-choice portion covering factual knowledge, tech-

nical information, understanding of principles and problem-solving abilities related to the occupation. A performance component samples manipulative skills required. A mental ability test is also available. The written test covers business communications, personal business management for the executive, business dynamics, filing and records management, job seeking and behavior on the job, machine transcription, office recordkeeping, production typing, modern office technology. The performance test covers office filing, machine calculation, tabulation, letter writing, forms preparation, envelope preparation.

14256
Student Occupational Competency Achievement Testing: Heating and Air Conditioning. National Occupational Competency Testing Institute, Big Rapids, MI
Descriptors: *Achievement Tests; Adults; *Air Conditioning; Credentials; *Heating; High Schools; *High School Students; Multiple Choice Tests; Occupational Tests; Performance Tests; *Postsecondary Education; Secondary Education; Two Year Colleges; *Vocational Education; Vocational Schools; *Work Sample Tests
Identifiers: NOCTI; SOCAT
Availability: National Occupational Competency Testing Institute; 318 Johnson Hall, Ferris State College, Big Rapids, MI 49307
Grade Level: 9-14
Notes: Time, 360 min.; Items, 170
This test is part of a program developed to evaluate secondary and postsecondary vocational students with a standardized, objective measure. Each test consists of a multiple-choice portion covering factual knowledge, technical information, understanding of principles and problem-solving abilities related to the occupation. A performance component samples manipulative skills required. A mental ability test is also available. The written test covers theory and fundamentals of air conditioning, oil heating and gas heating, installation and service of air conditioning, oil heating and gas heating equipment, electricity, heat pumps, solar heating, hydronic heating, psychometrics, air movement. The performance test requires the test taker to troubleshoot and repair a cooling and/or a heating system and fabricate a heat exchanger.

14257
Student Occupational Competency Achievement Testing: Horticulture. National Occupational Competency Testing Institute, Big Rapids, MI
Descriptors: *Achievement Tests; Adults; Credentials; High Schools; *High School Students; *Horticulture; Multiple Choice Tests; Occupational Tests; Performance Tests; *Postsecondary Education; Secondary Education; Two Year Colleges; *Vocational Education; Vocational Schools; *Work Sample Tests
Identifiers: NOCTI; SOCAT
Availability: National Occupational Competency Testing Institute; 318 Johnson Hall, Ferris State College, Big Rapids, MI 49307
Grade Level: 9-14
Notes: Time, 360 min.; Items, 158
This test is part of a program developed to evaluate secondary and postsecondary vocational students with a standardized, objective measure. Each test consists of a multiple-choice portion covering factural knowledge, technical information, understanding of principles and problem-solving abilities related to the occupation. A performance component samples manipulative skills required. A mental ability test is also available. The written test covers floriculture, floristry, greenhouse management, arboriculture, landscaping, nursery, turf, vegetables, small fruits, tree fruits. The performance test covers arboriculture, nursery, turf, small fruits, tree fruits, floriculture, greenhouse, special areas of landscaping, floristry, or olericulture.

14258
Student Occupational Competency Achievement Testing: Industrial Electricity. National Occupational Competency Testing Institute, Big Rapids, MI
Descriptors: *Achievement Tests; Adults; Credentials; *Electricity; High Schools; *High School Students; Industrial Arts; Multiple Choice Tests; Occupational Tests; Performance Tests; *Postsecondary Education; Secondary Education; Two Year Colleges; *Vocational Education; Vocational Schools; *Work Sample Tests
Identifiers: NOCTI; SOCAT
Availability: National Occupational Competency Testing Institute; 318 Johnson Hall, Ferris State College, Big Rapids, MI 49307
Grade Level: 9-14
Notes: Time, 360 min.; Items, 156
This test is part of a program developed to evaluate secondary and postsecondary vocational students with a standardized, objective measure. Each test consists of a multiple-choice portion covering factual knowledge, technical information, understanding of principles and problem-solving abilities related to the occupation. A per-

formance component samples manipulative skills required. A mental ability test is also available. The written test covers AC and DC current theory, test equipment, electrical drawings, general wiring, controls, generators, alternators, motors, transformers. The performance test covers diagrams, installation techniques, disconnect, control panel, raceway, circuit conductors, control circuit, motor circuit, safety, testing.

14259
Student Occupational Competency Achievement Testing: Industrial Electronics. National Occupational Competency Testing Institute, Big Rapids, MI
Descriptors: *Achievement Tests; Adults; Credentials; *Electronics; High Schools; *High School Students; Multiple Choice Tests; Occupational Tests; Performance Tests; *Postsecondary Education; Secondary Education; Two Year Colleges; *Vocational Education; Vocational Schools; Work Sample Tests
Identifiers: NOCTI; SOCAT
Availability: National Occupational Competency Testing Institute; 318 Johnson Hall, Ferris State College, Big Rapids, MI 49307
Grade Level: 9-14
Notes: Time, 360 min.; Items, 165
This test is part of a program developed to evaluate secondary and postsecondary vocational students with a standardized, objective measure. Each test consists of a multiple-choice portion covering factual knowledge, technical information, understanding of principles and problem-solving abilities related to the occupation. A performance component samples manipulative skills required. A mental ability test is also available. The written test covers AC and DC concepts, amplifier circuits and operation, solid state devices, power supplies, rectification, miscellaneous circuits and components, basic theory, digital electronics, test equipment, vacuum tubes. The performance test covers power supply, logic circuit, photosensitive transducer, computer testing, circuit timing, desolder PC board, oscilloscope.

14260
Student Occupational Competency Achievement Testing: Machine Trades. National Occupational Competency Testing Institute, Big Rapids, MI
Descriptors: *Achievement Tests; Adults; Credentials; High Schools; *High School Students; *Machine Repairers; *Machine Tools; Multiple Choice Tests; Occupational Tests; Performance Tests; *Postsecondary Education; Secondary Education; Two Year Colleges; *Vocational Education; Vocational Schools; *Work Sample Tests
Identifiers: *Machine Trades; NOCTI; SOCAT
Availability: National Occupational Competency Testing Institute; 318 Johnson Hall, Ferris State College, Big Rapids, MI 49307
Grade Level: 9-14
Notes: Time, 480 min.; Items, 180
This test is part of a program developed to evaluate secondary and postsecondary vocational students with a standardized, objective measure. Each test consists of a multiple-choice portion covering factual knowledge, technical information, understanding of principles and problem-solving abilities related to the occupation. A performance component samples manipulative skills required. A mental ability test is also available. The written test covers lathes, milling, grinding, benchwork, drilling, sawing, related theory. The performance test covers lathe operations, drilling and hole forming, milling machine operations, measurement, safety, layout, bench work.

14261
Student Occupational Competency Achievement Testing: Plumbing. National Occupational Competency Testing Institute, Big Rapids, MI
Descriptors: *Achievement Tests; Adults; Credentials; High Schools; *High School Students; Multiple Choice Tests; Occupational Tests; Performance Tests; *Plumbing; *Postsecondary Education; Secondary Education; Two Year Colleges; *Vocational Education; Vocational Schools; *Work Sample Tests
Identifiers: NOCTI; SOCAT
Availability: National Occupational Competency Testing Institute; 318 Johnson Hall, Ferris State College, Big Rapids, MI 49307
Grade Level: 9-14
Notes: Time, 360 min.; Items, 150
This test is part of a program developed to evaluate secondary and postsecondary vocational students with a standardized, objective measure. Each test consists of a multiple-choice portion covering factual knowledge, technical information, understanding of principles and problem-solving abilities related to the occupation. A performance component samples manipulative skills required. A mental ability test is also available. The written test covers assembly and layout, installation, planning, inspecting, evaluating, maintenance and repair. The performance test covers drawings, layout, rough installation, installation of fixtures.

14262
Student Occupational Competency Achievement Testing: Practical Nursing. National Occupational Competency Testing Institute, Big Rapids, MI
Descriptors: *Achievement Tests; Adults; Credentials; High Schools; *High School Students; Multiple Choice Tests; Occupational Tests; Performance Tests; *Postsecondary Education; *Practical Nursing; Secondary Education; Two Year Colleges; *Vocational Education; Vocational Schools; *Work Sample Tests
Identifiers: NOCTI; SOCAT
Availability: National Occupational Competency Testing Institute; 318 Johnson Hall, Ferris State College, Big Rapids, MI 49307
Grade Level: 9-14
Notes: Time, 360 min.; Items, 150
This test is part of a program developed to evaluate secondary and postsecondary vocational students with a standardized, objective measure. Each test consists of a multiple-choice portion covering factual knowledge, technical information, understanding of principles and problem-solving abilities related to the occupation. A performance component samples manipulative skills required. A mental ability test is also available. The written test covers medical/surgical nursing, anatomy and physiology, maternal and child health, basic nursing, personal/vocational relationships. The performance test covers tube feeding, collection of clean catch/midstream urine specimen, perineal care, demonstration of sterile technique/indwelling catheter, administration of oral medication, administration of an intramuscular injection, administration of subcutaneous medication, taking vital signs, making an occupied bed, transferring patient from bed to wheelchair.

14265
Student Occupational Competency Achievement Testing: Refrigeration. National Occupational Competency Testing Institute, Big Rapids, MI
Descriptors: *Achievement Tests; Adults; Credentials; High Schools; *High School Students; Multiple Choice Tests; Occupational Tests; Performance Tests; Postsecondary Education; *Refrigeration; Secondary Education; Two Year Colleges; *Vocational Education; Vocational Schools; Work Sample Tests
Identifiers: NOCTI; SOCAT
Availability: National Occupational Competency Testing Institute; 318 Johnson Hall, Ferris State College, Big Rapids, MI 49307
Grade Level: 9-14
Notes: Time, 360 min.; Items, 150
This test is part of a program developed to evaluate secondary and postsecondary vocational students with a standardized, objective measure. Each test consists of a multiple-choice portion covering factual knowledge, technical information, understanding of principles and problem-solving abilities related to the occupation. A performance component samples manipulative skills required. A mental ability test is also available. The written test covers installation and service, electricity, nomenclature, valves, gauges and controls, related math and science, safety. The performance test requires the test taker to troubleshoot and repair refrigeration systems, including setting up the system and installing the gauge and manifold, checking and monitoring the system, using proper tools, meters, and diagnostic equipment.

14266
Student Occupational Competency Achievement Testing: Sewn Products. National Occupational Competency Testing Institute, Big Rapids, MI
Descriptors: *Achievement Tests; Adults; Credentials; High Schools; *High School Students; Multiple Choice Tests; Occupational Tests; Performance Tests; Postsecondary Education; Secondary Education; *Sewing Machine Operators; *Textiles Instruction; Two Year Colleges; *Vocational Education; Vocational Schools; *Work Sample Tests
Identifiers: NOCTI; SOCAT
Availability: National Occupational Competency Testing Institute; 318 Johnson Hall, Ferris State College, Big Rapids, MI 49307
Grade Level: 9-14
Notes: Time, 180 min.; Items, 153
This test is part of a program developed to evaluate secondary and postsecondary vocational students with a standardized, objective measure. Each test consists of a multiple-choice portion covering factual knowledge, technical information, understanding of principles and problem-solving abilities related to the occupation. A performance component samples manipulative skills required. A mental ability test is also available. The written test covers construction, textiles, fitting garments, altering finished garments, operation of equipment, industrial sewing methods, pressing. The performance test covers industrial sewing methods, garment construction methods, alteration of finished garments, pattern alterations, taking body measurements, machine usage, industrial sewing machine maintenance.

14267
Student Occupational Competency Achievement Testing: Small Engine Repair. National Occupational Competency Testing Institute, Big Rapids, MI
Descriptors: *Achievement Tests; Adults; Credentials; High Schools; *High School Students; *Machine Repairers; Multiple Choice Tests; Occupational Tests; Performance Tests; *Postsecondary Education; Secondary Education; Two Year Colleges; *Vocational Education; Vocational Schools; *Work Sample Tests; Engines
Identifiers: NOCTI; SOCAT
Availability: National Occupational Competency Testing Institute; 318 Johnson Hall, Ferris State College, Big Rapids, MI 49307
Grade Level: 9-14
Notes: Time, 180 min.; Items, 188
This test is part of a program developed to evaluate secondary and postsecondary vocational students with a standardized, objective measure. Each test consists of a multiple-choice portion covering factual knowledge, technical information, understanding of principles and problem-solving abilities as related to the occupation. A performance component samples manipulative skills required. A mental ability test is also available. The written test covers theory and shop arithmetic, ignition, compression and lubrication, valves and ports, engine block components and cooling, fuel, shop procedures and safety, governors, starters, powered equipment mechanisms. The performance test requires the test taker to check engine and start disassembly, complete disassembly, check and measure parts, reassemble engine and operate; invoice parts, use of time.

14268
Student Occupational Competency Achievement Testing: Welding. National Occupational Competency Testing Institute, Big Rapids, MI
Descriptors: *Achievement Tests; Adults; Credentials; High Schools; *High School Students; Multiple Choice Tests; Occupational Tests; Performance Tests; *Postsecondary Education; Secondary Education; Two Year Colleges; *Vocational Education; Vocational Schools; *Welding; *Work Sample Tests
Identifiers: NOCTI; SOCAT
Availability: National Occupational Competency Testing Institute; 318 Johnson Hall, Ferris State College, Big Rapids, MI 49307
Grade Level: 9-14
Notes: Time, 180 min.; Items, 150
This test is part of a program developed to evaluate secondary and postsecondary vocational students with a standardized, objective measure. Each test consists of a multiple-choice portion covering factual knowledge, technical information, understanding of principles and problem-solving abilities related to the occupation. A performance component samples manipulative skills required. A mental ability test is also available. The written test covers shielded metal arc welding, oxyfuel welding, welding terms and symbols, safety, electricity, basic metallurgy, gas metal arc welding, gas tungsten arc welding. The performance test covers shielded metal arc welding, oxyacetylene welding and brazing, gas metal arc welding, gas tungsten arc welding.

14275
Test of Computational Processes. Kingston, Neldon D. 1985
Descriptors: *Achievement Tests; Addition; *Computation; Criterion Referenced Tests; Decimal Fractions; Division; Elementary Education; *Elementary School Students; Fractions; Multiplication; Norm Referenced Tests; Remedial Instruction; *Screening Tests; Subtraction; Whole Numbers
Identifiers: TCP
Availability: DLM Teaching Resources; One DLM Park, Allen, TX 75002
Grade Level: 1-8
Notes: Items, 122
Developed to measure students' ability to add, subtract, multiply, and divide with whole numbers, fractions, and decimals. Some measurement facts and calculations are also included. Contains computational processes most commonly found in grades 1 through 8. Untimed test independent of vocabulary and reading level. Appropriate for use with students in grades 1 through 8. Administration time can range from 20 to 80 minutes. Developed using criterion-referenced principles; also a norm-referenced test standardized on more than 6,000 subjects. Can be useful in identifying remedial and mathematically handicapped students.

14288
Formal Reading Inventory: A Method for Assessing Silent Reading Comprehension and Oral Reading Miscues. Wiederholt, J. Lee 1986
Descriptors: *Achievement Tests; *Elementary School Students; Elementary Secondary Education; *Individual Testing; Miscue Analysis; *Oral Reading; Pretests Posttests; Reading Comprehension; *Reading Tests; *Secondary School Students; *Silent Reading
Identifiers: FRI
Availability: PRO-ED; 8700 Shoal Creek Blvd., Austin, TX 78758-6897
Grade Level: 1-12
A measure of silent reading comprehension and oral reading miscues. There are 4 forms of the test that allow for pretesting and posttesting. Two forms are for silent reading and 2 forms for oral reading. Test is individually administered. Five types of miscues can be assessed: meaning similarity, function similarity, graphic/phoneme similarity, multiple miscue sources, and self-correction. FRI is meant to accomplish 4 purposes: help identify students performing below their peers, as an aid in determining particular strengths and weaknesses of individual students, to document student progress as a result of intervention, and as a tool in research projects. Test was standardized on children in 12 states.

14298
Fixing My Food. Iowa State University, Ames, IA; National Dairy Council, Rosemont, IL 1985
Descriptors: *Achievement Tests; Elementary Education; *Elementary School Students; *Food; *Nutrition Instruction; *Pictorial Stimuli
Availability: National Dairy Council; 6300 N. River Rd., Rosemont IL 60018-4233
Grade Level: 1-6
Notes: Items, 26
Practical and reliable instrument to evaluate elementary school students' application of nutrition behaviors of selecting, preparing, and serving foods. The behaviors relate to the major nutrition curriculum concept of food handling. Three concepts relating to food handling were identified: food quality, cleanliness, and personal safety. Inventory may be used to assess nutrition behaviors; evaluate the effectiveness of specific nutrition education programs; or measure individual test scores, group mean scores, or group gain scores.

14299
Nutrition Achievement Test 4. National Dairy Council, Rosemont, IL; University of Illinois, Chicago, IL 1985
Descriptors: *Achievement Tests; Adults; Multiple Choice Tests; *Nutrition; *Nutrition Instruction; Secondary Education; *Secondary School Students
Availability: National Dairy Council; 6300 N. River Rd., Rosemont IL 60018-4233
Grade Level: 7-12
Age Level: Adults
Notes: Items, 47
Nationally field tested, reliable, and valid measure of generalized nutrition knowledge. May be used with adults as well as junior high and high school students. Measures knowledge of broad nutrition concepts including nutrition, nutrients, food handling, life cycle, social and psychological needs, food technology, and nutrition and society. May be used to evaluate nutrition education needs in a particular school or to assess the effectiveness of a specific nutrition education program.

14301
Computer Literacy Examination: Cognitive Aspect. Cheng, Tina T.; And Others 1985
Descriptors: *Achievement Tests; *Computer Literacy; High Schools; *High School Students; Knowledge Level; Multiple Choice Tests
Availability: AEDS Journal; v18 n3 p139-52, Spr 1985
Grade Level: 9-12
Notes: Items, 32
Developed to test high school students' cognitive knowledge about computers. Emphasizes general knowledge about computers and BASIC programing skills. Developers used 7 cognitive-related computer literacy topics as basis for test construction; computer terminology, computer language commands, writing computer programs, parts of computers, writing algorithms, math concepts, and history of computers.

14314
Kaufman Test of Educational Achievement, Comprehensive Form. Kaufman, Alan S.; Kaufman, Nadeen L. 1985
Subtests: Mathematics Applications; Reading Decoding; Spelling; Reading Comprehension; Mathematics Computation
Descriptors: Achievement Tests; Computation; Decoding (Reading); Educational Diagnosis; *Elementary School Students; Elementary Secondary Education; *Individual Testing; Mathematical Applications; *Mathematics Achievement; Norm Referenced Tests; *Reading Achievement; Reading Comprehension; Remedial Instruction; *Secondary School Students; *Spelling; Standardized Tests
Identifiers: KTEA; *Test Batteries
Availability: American Guidance Service; Publishers' Bldg., Circle Pines, MN 55014-1796
Grade Level: 1-12
Notes: Time, 75 min. approx.; Items, 280
Individually administered test of school achievement. The comprehensive form offers reliable scores in the specific domains of reading decoding, reading comprehension, mathematics applications, mathematics computation, and spelling. In addition to offering norm-referenced measurement in selected achievement domains, this form offers criterion-referenced assessment in the analysis of students' errors in various content areas. Mathematics applications subtest covers arithmetic concepts and applications of mathematical principles and reasoning skills to real-life situations. Reading decoding assesses the ability to identify letters and pronounce words of increasing difficulty. The spelling section uses a word list of increasingly difficult words. Mathematics computation assesses skills in solving written computational problems using the 4 basic operations and also complex computational abilities in areas such as algebra. The comprehensive form may be used as part of a comprehensive psychological or psycho-educational battery, for analyzing strengths and weaknesses, analyzing errors, program planning, research, placement, and personnel selection.

14320
SRA Survey of Basic Skills, Level 20. Science Research Associates, Chicago, IL 1985
Subtests: Auditory Discrimination; Reading: Letters and Sounds; Reading: Decoding; Listening Comprehension; Mathematics: Concepts/Problem Solving
Descriptors: *Academic Achievement; Academic Aptitude; *Achievement Tests; Aptitude Tests; Auditory Discrimination; *Basic Skills; Decoding (Reading); Elementary School Mathematics; Elementary School Students; *Grade 1; *Kindergarten Children; Knowledge Level; Listening Comprehension; Norm Referenced Tests; *Primary Education; Reading Processes
Identifiers: EAS; Educational Ability Series; SBS; *Test Batteries
Availability: CTB/MacMillan/McGraw-Hill; Del Monte Research Park, 2500 Garden Rd., Monterey, CA 93940
Grade Level: K-1
Notes: Time, 100 min. approx.
A battery of norm-referenced, standardized tests in basic curriculum areas for grades K-12. Designed to survey students' general academic achievement. Contents of tests are based on learner objectives most commonly taught in the U.S. Two forms are available, forms P and Q. An optional test to include with the achievement battery is the Educational Ability Series (EAS), which provides an estimate of general learning ability for students in grades K-12. The EAS assesses those factors most closely associated with overall academic performance, such as verbal, numerical, and reasoning abilities. Test administrators may decide to do out-of-level testing with the Survey of Basic Skills for special groups of students, such as Chapter I, special education, gifted or high-achieving students. Level 20 test is designed for spring testing in kindergarten and fall testing in grade 1 at most schools.

14321
SRA Survey of Basic Skills, Level 21. Science Research Associates, Chicago, IL 1985
Subtests: Letters and Sounds; Listening Comprehension; Vocabulary; Reading Comprehension; Language Arts; Mechanics; Mathematics: Concepts/Problem Solving; Mathematics Computation
Descriptors: *Academic Achievement; Academic Aptitude; *Achievement Tests; Aptitude Tests; *Basic Skills; Elementary School Mathematics; Elementary School Students; *Grade 1; *Grade 2; Knowledge Level; Language Arts; Listening Comprehension; Norm Referenced Tests; *Primary Education; Reading Comprehension; Reading Processes; Vocabulary
Identifiers: EAS; Educational Ability Series; SBS; *Test Batteries
Availability: CTB/MacMillan/McGraw-Hill; Del Monte Research Park, 2500 Garden Rd., Monterey, CA 93940
Grade Level: 1-2
Notes: Time, 165 min. approx.
A battery of norm-referenced, standardized tests in basic curriculum areas for grades K-12. Designed to survey students' general academic achievement. Contents of tests are based on learner objectives most commonly taught in

the U.S. Two forms are available, forms P and Q. An optional test to include with the achievement battery is the Educational Ability Series (EAS), which provides an estimate of general learning ability for students in grades K-12. The EAS assesses those factors most closely associated with overall academic performance, such as verbal, numerical, and reasoning abilities. Test administrators may decide to do out-of-level testing with the Survey of Basic Skills for special groups of students, such as Chapter I, special education, gifted, or high-achieving students. Level 21 test is designed for spring testing in first grade and fall testing in second grade at most schools.

14322
SRA Survey of Basic Skills, Level 22. Science Research Associates, Chicago, IL 1985
Subtests: Letters and Sounds; Vocabulary; Reading Comprehension; Language Arts: Mechanics; Language Arts: Usage; Spelling; Mathematics: Concepts/Problem Solving; Mathematics Computation
Descriptors: *Academic Achievement; Academic Aptitude; *Achievement Tests; Aptitude Tests; *Basic Skills; Elementary School Mathematics; Elementary School Students; *Grade 2; *Grade 3; Knowledge Level; Language Arts; Norm Referenced Tests; *Primary Education; Reading Comprehension; Reading Processes; Spelling; Vocabulary
Identifiers: EAS; Educational Ability Series; SBS; *Test Batteries
Availability: CTB/MacMillan/McGraw-Hill; Del Monte Research Park, 2500 Garden Rd., Monterey, CA 93940
Grade Level: 2-3
Notes: Time, 165 min. approx.

A battery of norm-referenced, standardized tests in basic curriculum areas for grades K-12. Designed to survey students' general academic achievement. Contents of tests are based on learner objectives most commonly taught in the U.S. Two forms are available, forms P and Q. An optional test to include with the achievement battery is the Educational Ability Series (EAS), which provides an estimate of general learning ability for students in grades K-12. The EAS assesses those factors most closely associated with overall academic performance, such as verbal, numerical, and reasoning abilities. Test administrators may decide to do out-of-level testing with the Survey of Basic Skills for special groups of students, such as Chapter I, special education, gifted, or high-achieving students. The level 22 test is designed for spring testing in grade 2 and fall testing in grade 3 at most schools.

14323
SRA Survey of Basic Skills, Level 23. Science Research Associates, Chicago, IL 1985
Subtests: Vocabulary; Reading Comprehension; Language Mechanics; Language Usage; Spelling; Mathematics: Concepts/Problem Solving; Mathematics Computation; Reference Materials
Descriptors: *Academic Achievement; Academic Aptitude; *Achievement Tests; Aptitude Tests; *Basic Skills; *Elementary Education; Elementary School Mathematics; Elementary School Students; *Grade 3; *Grade 4; Knowledge Level; Language Arts; Norm Referenced Tests; Reading Comprehension; Reference Materials; Spelling; Vocabulary
Identifiers: EAS; Educational Ability Series; SBS; *Test Batteries
Availability: CTB/MacMillan/McGraw-Hill; Del Monte Research Park, 2500 Garden Rd., Monterey, CA 93940
Grade Level: 3-4
Notes: Time, 215 min. approx.

A battery of norm-referenced, standardized tests in basic curriculum areas for grades K-12. Designed to survey students' general academic achievement. Contents of tests are based on learner objectives most commonly taught in the U.S. Two forms are available, forms P and Q. An optional test to include with the achievement battery is the Educational Ability Series (EAS), which provides an estimate of general learning ability for students in grades K-12. The EAS assesses those factors most closely associated with overall academic performance, such as verbal, numerical, and reasoning abilities. Test administrators may decide to do out-of-level testing with the Survey of Basic Skills for special groups of students, such as Chapter I, special education, gifted, or high-achieving students. Level 23 test is designed for spring testing in grade 3 and fall testing in grade 4 in most schools. The reference materials subtest is optional.

14324
SRA Survey of Basic Skills, Level 34. Science Research Associates, Chicago, IL 1985
Subtests: Vocabulary; Reading Comprehension; Language Mechanics; Language Usage; Spelling; Mathematics Computation; Mathematics Concepts; Mathematics Problem Solving; Reference Materials; Social Studies; Science
Descriptors: *Academic Achievement; Academic Aptitude; *Achievement Tests; Aptitude Tests; *Basic Skills; Elementary School Mathematics; Elementary School Science; *Elementary School Students; *Intermediate Grades; Knowledge Level; Language Arts; Norm Referenced Tests; Reading Comprehension; Reference Materials; Social Studies; Spelling; Vocabulary
Identifiers: EAS; Educational Ability Series; SBS; *Test Batteries
Availability: CTB/MacMillan/McGraw-Hill; Del Monte Research Park, 2500 Garden Rd., Monterey, CA 93940
Grade Level: 4-6
Notes: Time, 280 min. approx.

A battery of norm-referenced, standardized tests in basic curriculum areas for grades K-12. Designed to survey students' general academic achievement. Contents of tests are based on learner objectives most commonly taught in the U.S. Two forms are available, forms P and Q. An optional test to include with the achievement battery is the Educational Ability Series (EAS), which provides an estimate of general learning ability for students in grades K-12. The EAS assesses those factors most closely associated with overall academic performance, such as verbal, numerical, and reasoning abilities. Test administrators may decide to do out-of-level testing with the Survey of Basic Skills for special groups of students, such as Chapter I, special education, gifted, or high-achieving students. Levels 34 through 37 are multilevel tests designed for use from the spring of grade 4 through high school. The reference materials, social studies, and science subtests are optional.

14325
SRA Survey of Basic Skills, Level 35. Science Research Associates, Chicago, IL 1985
Subtests: Vocabulary; Reading Comprehension; Language Mechanics; Language Usage; Spelling; Mathematics Computation; Mathematics Concepts; Mathematics Problem Solving; Reference Materials; Social Studies; Science
Descriptors: *Academic Achievement; Academic Aptitude; *Achievement Tests; Aptitude Tests; *Basic Skills; Elementary School Mathematics; Elementary School Science; *Grade 6; Intermediate Grades; Junior High Schools; Junior High School Students; Knowledge Level; Language Arts; Norm Referenced Tests; Reading Comprehension; Reference Materials; Secondary School Mathematics; Secondary School Science; Social Studies; Vocabulary
Identifiers: EAS; Educational Ability Series; SBS; *Test Batteries
Availability: CTB/MacMillan/McGraw-Hill; Del Monte Research Park, 2500 Garden Rd., Monterey, CA 93940
Grade Level: 6-8
Notes: Time, 280 min. approx.

A battery of norm-referenced, standardized tests in basic curriculum areas for grades K-12. Designed to survey students' general academic achievement. Contents of tests are based on learner objectives most commonly taught in the U.S. Two forms are available, forms P and Q. An optional test to include with the achievement battery is the Educational Ability Series (EAS), which provides an estimate of general learning ability for students in grades K-12. The EAS assesses those factors most closely associated with overall academic performance, such as verbal, numerical, and reasoning abilities. Test administrators may decide to do out-of-level testing with the Survey of Basic Skills for special groups of students, such as Chapter I, special education, gifted, or high-achieving students. Levels 34 through 37 are multilevel tests designed for use from the spring of grade 4 through high school. The reference materials, social studies, and science subtests are optional.

14326
SRA Survey of Basic Skills, Level 36. Science Research Associates, Chicago, IL 1985
Subtests: Vocabulary; Reading Comprehension; Language Mechanics; Language Usage; Spelling; Mathematics Computation; Mathematics Concepts; Mathematics Problem Solving; Reference Materials; Social Studies; Science
Descriptors: *Academic Achievement; Academic Aptitude; *Achievement Tests; Aptitude Tests; *Basic Skills; Knowledge Level; Language Arts; Norm Referenced Tests; Reading Comprehension; Reference Materials; Secondary Education; Secondary School Mathematics; Secondary School Science; *Secondary School Students; Social Studies; Spelling; Vocabulary
Identifiers: EAS; Educational Ability Series; SBS; *Test Batteries
Availability: CTB/MacMillan/McGraw-Hill; Del Monte Research Park, 2500 Garden Rd., Monterey, CA 93940
Grade Level: 8-10
Notes: Time, 280 min. approx.

A battery of norm-referenced, standardized tests in basic curriculum areas for grades K-12. Designed to survey students' general academic achievement. Contents of tests are based on learner objectives most commonly taught in the U.S. Two forms are available, forms P and Q. An optional test to include with the achievement battery is the Educational Ability Series (EAS), which provides an estimate of general learning ability for students in grades K-12. The EAS assesses those factors most closely associated with overall academic performance, such as verbal, numerical, and reasoning abilities. Test administrators may decide to do out-of-level testing with the Survey of Basic Skills for special groups of students, such as Chapter I, special education, gifted, or high-achieving students. Levels 34 through 37 are multilevel tests designed for use from the spring of grade 4 through high school. The reference materials, social studies, and science subtests are optional.

14327
SRA Survey of Basic Skills, Level 37. Science Research Associates, Chicago, IL 1985
Subtests: Vocabulary; Reading Comprehension; Language Mechanics; Language Usage; Spelling; Mathematics Computation; Mathematics Concepts; Mathematics Problem Solving; Reference Materials; Social Studies; Science
Descriptors: *Academic Achievement; Academic Aptitude; *Achievement Tests; Aptitude Tests; *Basic Skills; High Schools; *High School Students; Knowledge Level; Language Arts; Norm Referenced Tests; Reading Comprehension; Reference Materials; Secondary School Mathematics; Secondary School Science; Social Studies; Spelling; Vocabulary
Identifiers: EAS; Educational Ability Series; SBS; *Test Batteries
Availability: CTB/MacMillan/McGraw-Hill; Del Monte Research Park, 2500 Garden Rd., Monterey, CA 93940
Grade Level: 9-12
Notes: Time, 280 min. approx.

A battery of norm-referenced, standardized tests in basic curriculum areas for grades K-12. Designed to survey students' general academic achievement. Contents of tests are based on learner objectives most commonly taught in the U.S. Two forms are available, forms P and Q. An optional test to include with the achievement battery is the Educational Ability Series (EAS), which provides an estimate of general learning ability for students in grades K-12. The EAS assesses those factors most closely associated with overall academic performance, such as verbal, numerical, and reasoning abilities. Test administrators may decide to do out-of-level testing with the Survey of Basic Skills for special groups of students, such as Chapter I, special education, gifted, or high-achieving students. Levels 34 through 37 are multilevel tests designed for use from the spring of grade 4 through high school. The reference materials, social studies, and science subtests are optional.

14335
School Readiness Screening Test. Gesell Institute of Child Development 1978
Subtests: Visuals 1 and 3; Animals and Interests; Incomplete Man; Copying; Cube Test; Initial Interview; Interview
Descriptors: Age Grade Placement; Attention Span; Child Development; Eye Hand Coordination; Grade 1; Kindergarten; Psychomotor Skills; School Readiness; *School Readiness Tests; Verbal Development; Visual Perception; *Young Children
Availability: Programs for Education; Dept. 217CI, Rosemont, NJ 08556
Age Level: 4-5
Notes: Time, 20 min.

Designed for use as a measure of school readiness based on developmental not chronological age. Norms are included for preschool children for accuracy in diagnosing 5-year olds responding at a younger than 5-year level. Tests include figure copying, completing a figure, visual matching of figures, recalling names of animals. They measure eye-hand coordination, attention span, level of functioning in a structured motor task, visual perception, and verbal ability.

14336
Speech-Ease Screening Inventory. Speech-Ease 1985
Subtests: Articulation; Language Association; Auditory Recall; Expressive Vocabulary; Concept Development
Descriptors: *Articulation (Speech); Expressive Language; *Grade 1; Individual Testing; *Kindergarten Children; *Language Acquisition; Primary Education; Receptive Language; *Screening Tests
Availability: PRO-ED; 8700 Shoal Creek Blvd., Austin, TX 78758-6897
Grade Level: K-1
Notes: Time, 10 min. approx.

Designed to screen the articulation and language development of kindergarten and first grade children. Identifies those students needing professional speech-language services. Inventory is composed of 5 main tasks and 4 optional tasks. The optional tasks are additional auditory items, similarities and differences, language sample, and linguistic relationships. Can be used in many settings, including classrooms, halls, gymnasiums. Should be administered by a qualified speech-language pathologist.

14339
Test of Written Spelling—2.   Larsen, Stephen C.; Hammill, Donald D. 1986
Subtests: Predictable Words; Unpredictable Words
Descriptors: *Achievement Tests; *Elementary School Students; Elementary Secondary Education; Remedial Programs; *Secondary School Students; *Spelling
Identifiers: TWS2
Availability: PRO-ED; 8700 Shoal Creek Blvd., Austin, TX 78758-6897
Grade Level: 1-12
Notes: Items, 100
Revision of an earlier test. Is used to assess students' ability to spell words. Consists of 2 subtests, both employing a dictated word format. One subtest measures predictable words that conform to rules and generalizations. The second subtest measures unpredictable words. Normed on a large national sample of students in grades 1 through 12. Appropriate for use with remedial students as well as for regular students.

14343
California Achievement Tests, Form E, Level 10.
CTB/Macmillan/McGraw-Hill, Monterey, CA 1985
Subtests: Visual Recognition; Sound Recognition; Vocabulary; Comprehension; Language Expression; Mathematics Concepts and Applications
Descriptors: *Achievement Tests; *Basic Skills; Criterion Referenced Tests; Elementary School Mathematics; *Kindergarten Children; Language Arts; Mathematics Achievement; *Norm Referenced Tests; Primary Education; Reading Achievement; Reading Comprehension; Spelling; Vocabulary
Identifiers: CAT; Test Batteries
Availability: CTB/Macmillan/McGraw-Hill; Del Monte Research Park, 2500 Garden Rd., Monterey, CA 93940
Grade Level: K
Notes: Time, 154 min.; Items, 126
A series of norm-referenced, objectives-based tests for kindergarten through grade 12. Series is designed to measure achievement in the basic skills commonly found in state and district curricula. The tests combine the most useful characteristics of norm-referenced and criterion-referenced tests and therefore provide information about the relative ranking of students against a norm group as well as specific information about students' instructional needs. Subject areas measured are reading, spelling, language, mathematics, and study skills. Optional tests are available for science and social studies. The test battery also serves measurement needs of special programs, such as Chapter I, ECIA, etc. Available in Form E, only.

14344
California Achievement Tests, Form E, Level 11.
CTB/Macmillan/McGraw-Hill, Monterey, CA 1985
Subtests: Word Analysis; Vocabulary; Comprehension; Language Expression; Mathematics Computation; Mathematics Concepts and Applications
Descriptors: *Achievement Tests; *Basic Skills; Criterion Referenced Tests; Elementary School Mathematics; Grade 1; Grade 2; Kindergarten Children; Language Arts; Mathematics Achievement; *Norm Referenced Tests; *Primary Education; Reading Achievement; Reading Comprehension; Spelling; Vocabulary
Identifiers: CAT; Test Batteries
Availability: CTB/Macmillan/McGraw-Hill; Del Monte Research Park, 2500 Garden Rd., Monterey, CA 93940
Grade Level: K-2
Notes: Time, 175 min.; Items, 179
A series of norm-referenced, objectives-based tests for kindergarten through grade 12. Series is designed to measure achievement in the basic skills commonly found in state and district curricula. The tests combine the most useful characteristics of norm-referenced and criterion-referenced tests and therefore provide information about the relative ranking of students against a norm group as well as specific information about students' instructional needs. Subject areas measured are reading, spelling, language, mathematics, and study skills. Optional tests are available for science and social studies. The test battery also serves measurement needs of special programs, such as Chapter I, ECIA, etc. Available in form E, only.

14345
California Achievement Tests, Form E, Level 12.
CTB/Macmillan/McGraw-Hill, Monterey, CA 1985
Subtests: Word Analysis; Vocabulary; Comprehension; Spelling; Language Mechanics; Language Expression; Mathematics Computation; Mathematics Concepts and Applications; Science; Social Studies
Descriptors: *Achievement Tests; *Basic Skills; Criterion Referenced Tests; Elementary School Mathematics; Elementary School Science; Elementary School Students; Language Arts; Mathematics Achievement; *Norm Referenced Tests; *Primary Education; Reading Achievement; Reading Comprehension; Social Studies; Spelling; Vocabulary
Identifiers: CAT; Test Batteries
Availability: CTB/MacMillan/McGraw-Hill; Del Monte Research Park, 2500 Garden Rd., Monterey, CA 93940
Grade Level: 1-3
Notes: Time, 315 min.; Items, 305
A series of norm-referenced, objectives-based tests for kindergarten through grade 12. Series is designed to measure achievement in the basic skills commonly found in state and district curricula. The tests combine the most useful characteristics of norm-referenced and criterion-referenced tests and therefore provide information about the relative ranking of students against a norm group as well as specific information about students' instructional needs. Subject areas measured are reading, spelling, language, mathematics, and study skills. Optional tests are available for science and social studies. The test battery also serves measurement needs of special programs, such as Chapter I, ECIA, etc. Available in form E only.

14346
California Achievement Tests, Forms E and F, Level 13.   CTB/Macmillan/McGraw-Hill, Monterey, CA 1985
Subtests: Word Analysis; Vocabulary; Comprehension; Spelling; Language Mechanics; Language Expression; Mathematics Computation; Mathematics Concepts and Applications; Science; Social Studies
Descriptors: *Achievement Tests; *Basic Skills; Criterion Referenced Tests; Elementary School Mathematics; Elementary School Science; Elementary School Students; *Intermediate Grades; Language Arts; Mathematics Achievement; *Norm Referenced Tests; *Primary Education; Reading Achievement; Reading Comprehension; Social Studies; Spelling; Vocabulary
Identifiers: CAT; Test Batteries
Availability: CTB/MacMillan/McGraw-Hill; Del Monte Research Park, 2500 Garden Rd., Monterey, CA 93940
Grade Level: 2-4
Notes: Time, 317 min.; Items, 357
A series of norm-referenced, objectives-based tests for kindergarten through grade 12. Series is designed to measure achievement in the basic skills commonly found in state and district curricula. The tests combine the most useful characteristics of norm-referenced and criterion-referenced tests and therefore provide information about the relative ranking of students against a norm group as well as specific information about students' instructional needs. Subject areas measured are reading, spelling, language, mathematics, and study skills. Optional tests are available for science and social studies. The test battery also serves measurement needs of special programs, such as Chapter I, ECIA, etc.

14347
California Achievement Tests, Forms E and F, Level 14.   CTB/Macmillan/McGraw-Hill, Monterey, CA 1985
Subtests: Vocabulary; Comprehension; Spelling; Language Mechanics; Language Expression; Mathematics Computation; Mathematics Concepts and Applications; Study Skills; Science; Social Studies
Descriptors: *Achievement Tests; *Basic Skills; Criterion Referenced Tests; Elementary School Mathematics; Elementary School Science; Elementary School Students; *Intermediate Grades; Language Arts; Mathematics Achievement; *Norm Referenced Tests; *Primary Education; Reading Achievement; Reading Comprehension; Social Studies; Spelling; Study Skills; Vocabulary
Identifiers: CAT; Test Batteries
Availability: CTB/MacMillan/McGraw-Hill; Del Monte Research Park, 2500 Garden Rd., Monterey, CA 93940
Grade Level: 3-5
Notes: Time, 408 min.; Items, 469
A series of norm-referenced, objectives-based tests for kindergarten through grade 12. Series is designed to measure achievement in the basic skills commonly found in state

and district curricula. The tests combine the most useful characteristics of norm-referenced and criterion-referenced tests and therefore provide information about the relative ranking of students against a norm group as well as specific information about students' instructional needs. Subject areas measured are reading, spelling, language, mathematics, and study skills. Optional tests are available for science and social studies. The test battery also serves measurement needs of special programs, such as Chapter I, ECIA, etc.

14348
California Achievement Tests, Forms E and F, Level 15.   CTB/Macmillan/McGraw-Hill, Monterey, CA 1985
Subtests: Vocabulary; Comprehension; Spelling; Language Mechanics; Language Expression; Mathematics Computation; Mathematics Concepts and Applications; Study Skills; Science; Social Studies
Descriptors: *Achievement Tests; *Basic Skills; Criterion Referenced Tests; Elementary School Mathematics; Elementary School Science; Elementary School Students; *Intermediate Grades; Language Arts; Mathematics Achievement; *Norm Referenced Tests; Reading Achievement; Reading Comprehension; Social Studies; Spelling; Study Skills; Vocabulary
Identifiers: CAT; Test Batteries
Availability: CTB/MacMillan/McGraw-Hill; Del Monte Research Park, 2500 Garden Rd., Monterey, CA 93940
Grade Level: 4-6
Notes: Time, 408 min.; Items, 469
A series of norm-referenced, objectives-based tests for kindergarten through grade 12. Series is designed to measure achievement in the basic skills commonly found in state and district curricula. The tests combine the most useful characteristics of norm-referenced and criterion-referenced tests and therefore provide information about the relative ranking of students against a norm group as well as specific information about students' instructional needs. Subject areas measured are reading, spelling, language, mathematics, and study skills. Optional tests are available for science and social studies. The test battery also serves measurement needs of special programs, such as Chapter I, ECIA, etc.

14349
California Achievement Tests, Forms E and F, Level 16.   CTB/Macmillan/McGraw-Hill, Monterey, CA 1985
Subtests: Vocabulary; Comprehension; Spelling; Language Mechanics; Language Expression; Mathematics Computation; Mathematics Concepts and Applications; Study Skills; Science; Social Studies
Descriptors: *Achievement Tests; *Basic Skills; Criterion Referenced Tests; Elementary School Mathematics; Elementary School Science; Elementary School Students; *Grade 7; *Intermediate Grades; Language Arts; Mathematics Achievement; *Norm Referenced Tests; Reading Achievement; Reading Comprehension; Social Studies; Spelling; Study Skills; Vocabulary
Identifiers: CAT; Test Batteries
Availability: CTB/MacMillan/McGraw-Hill; Del Monte Research Park, 2500 Garden Rd., Monterey, CA 93940
Grade Level: 5-7
Notes: Time, 408 min.; Items, 469
A series of norm-referenced, objectives-based tests for kindergarten through grade 12. Series is designed to measure achievement in the basic skills commonly found in state and district curricula. The tests combine the most useful characteristics of norm-referenced and criterion-referenced tests and therefore provide information about the relative ranking of students against a norm group as well as specific information about students' instructional needs. Subject areas measured are reading, spelling, language, mathematics, and study skills. Optional tests are available for science and social studies. The test battery also serves measurement needs of special programs, such as Chapter I, ECIA, etc.

14350
California Achievement Tests, Forms E and F, Level 17.   CTB/Macmillan/McGraw-Hill, Monterey, CA 1985
Subtests: Vocabulary; Comprehension; Spelling; Language Mechanics; Language Expression; Mathematics Computation; Mathematics Concepts and Applications; Study Skills; Science; Social Studies

Descriptors: *Achievement Tests; *Basic Skills; Criterion Referenced Tests; Elementary School Mathematics; Elementary School Science; *Grade 06; Intermediate Grades; Junior High Schools; *Junior High School Students; Language Arts; Mathematics Achievement; *Norm Referenced Tests; Reading Achievement; Reading Comprehension; Secondary School Mathematics; Secondary School Science; Social Studies; Spelling; Study Skills; Vocabulary
Identifiers: CAT; Test Batteries
Availability: CTB/MacMillan/McGraw-Hill; Del Monte Research Park, 2500 Garden Rd., Monterey, CA 93940
Grade Level: 6-8
Notes: Time, 408 min.; Items, 469

A series of norm-referenced, objectives-based tests for kindergarten through grade 12. Series is designed to measure achievement in the basic skills commonly found in state and district curricula. The tests combine the most useful characteristics of norm-referenced and criterion-referenced tests and therefore provide information about the relative ranking of students against a norm group as well as specific information about students' instructional needs. Subject areas measured are reading, spelling, language, mathematics, and study skills. Optional tests are available for science and social studies. The test battery also serves measurement needs of special programs, such as Chapter I, ECIA, etc.

14351
California Achievement Tests, Forms E and F, Level 18. CTB/Macmillan/McGraw-Hill, Monterey, CA 1985
Subtests: Vocabulary; Comprehension; Spelling; Language Mechanics; Language Expression; Mathematics Computation; Mathematics Concepts and Applications; Study Skills; Science; Social Studies
Descriptors: *Achievement Tests; *Basic Skills; Criterion Referenced Tests; Junior High Schools; *Junior High School Students; Language Arts; Mathematics Achievement; *Norm Referenced Tests; Reading Achievement; Reading Comprehension; Secondary School Mathematics; Secondary School Science; Social Studies; Spelling; Study Skills; Vocabulary
Identifiers: CAT; Test Batteries
Availability: CTB/MacMillan/McGraw-Hill; Del Monte Research Park, 2500 Garden Rd., Monterey, CA 93940
Grade Level: 7-9
Notes: Time, 408 min.; Items, 469

A series of norm-referenced, objectives-based tests for kindergarten through grade 12. Series is designed to measure achievement in the basic skills commonly found in state and district curricula. The tests combine the most useful characteristics of norm-referenced and criterion-referenced tests and therefore provide information about the relative ranking of students against a norm group as well as specific information about students' instructional needs. Subject areas measured are reading, spelling, language, mathematics, and study skills. Optional tests are available for science and social studies. The test battery also serves measurement needs of special programs, such as Chapter I, ECIA, etc.

14352
California Achievement Tests, Forms E and F, Level 19. CTB/Macmillan/McGraw-Hill, Monterey, CA 1985
Subtests: Vocabulary; Comprehension; Spelling; Language Mechanics; Language Expression; Mathematics Computation; Mathematics Concepts and Applications; Study Skills; Science; Social Studies
Descriptors: *Achievement Tests; *Basic Skills; Criterion Referenced Tests; Language Arts; Mathematics Achievement; *Norm Referenced Tests; Reading Achievement; Reading Comprehension; Secondary Education; Secondary School Mathematics; Secondary School Science; *Secondary School Students; Social Studies; Spelling; Study Skills; Vocabulary
Identifiers: CAT; Test Batteries
Availability: CTB/MacMillan/McGraw-Hill; Del Monte Research Park, 2500 Garden Rd., Monterey, CA 93940
Grade Level: 8-11
Notes: Time, 408 min.; Items, 469

A series of norm-referenced, objectives-based tests for kindergarten through grade 12. Series is designed to measure achievement in the basic skills commonly found in state and district curricula. The tests combine the most useful characteristics of norm-referenced and criterion-referenced tests and therefore provide information about the relative ranking of students against a norm group as well as specific information about students' instructional needs. Subject areas measured are reading, spelling, language, mathematics, and study skills. Optional tests are available for

science and social studies. The test battery also serves measurement needs of special programs, such as Chapter I, ECIA, etc.

14353
California Achievement Tests, Forms E and F, Level 20. CTB/Macmillan/McGraw-Hill, Monterey, CA 1985
Subtests: Vocabulary; Comprehension; Spelling; Language Mechanics; Language Expression; Mathematics Computation; Mathematics Concepts and Applications; Study Skills; Science; Social Studies
Descriptors: *Achievement Tests; *Basic Skills; Criterion Referenced Tests; High Schools; *High School Students; Language Arts; Mathematics Achievement; *Norm Referenced Tests; Reading Achievement; Reading Comprehension; Secondary School Mathematics; Secondary School Science; Social Studies; Spelling; Study Skills; Vocabulary
Identifiers: CAT; Test Batteries
Availability: CTB/MacMillan/McGraw-Hill; Del Monte Research Park, 2500 Garden Rd., Monterey, CA 93940
Grade Level: 10-12
Notes: Time, 408 min.; Items, 469

A series of norm-referenced, objectives-based tests for kindergarten through grade 12. Series is designed to measure achievement in the basic skills commonly found in state and district curricula. The tests combine the most useful characteristics of norm-referenced and criterion-referenced tests and therefore provide information about the relative ranking of students against a norm group as well as specific information about students' instructional needs. Subject areas measured are reading, spelling, language, mathematics, and study skills. Optional tests are available for science and social studies. The test battery also serves measurement needs of special programs, such as Chapter I, ECIA, etc.

14369
Gray Oral Reading Tests, Revised. Wiederholt, J. Lee; Bryant, Brian R. 1986
Descriptors: *Achievement Tests; Diagnostic Tests; *Elementary School Students; Elementary Secondary Education; *Individual Testing; *Miscue Analysis; Norm Referenced Tests; *Oral Reading; *Reading Comprehension; *Reading Tests; *Secondary School Students
Identifiers: GORT
Availability: PRO-ED; 8700 Shoal Creek Blvd., Austin, TX 78758-6897
Grade Level: 1-12
Age Level: 6-17
Notes: Time, 30 min. approx.; Items, 65

A revision of the reading test created by William S. Gray and later edited by Helen M. Robinson. Purposes of the test are to help identify students significantly below their peers in oral reading proficiency, to help determine particular kinds of reading strengths and weaknesses of students, to document students' progress in reading as a result of intervention programs, and to use in research projects. Consists of 2 alternate, equivalent forms, each containing 13 increasingly difficult passages. There are 5 comprehension questions for each passage. Test yields information on oral reading speed and accuracy, oral reading comprehension, total oral reading ability, and oral reading miscues. Normative data on the revised edition are more extensive than on the earlier edition.

14370
Test of Reading Comprehension, Revised. Brown, Virginia L.; And Others 1986
Subtests: General Vocabulary; Syntactic Similarities; Paragraph Reading; Sentence Sequencing
Descriptors: *Achievement Tests; Diagnostic Tests; *Elementary School Students; Elementary Secondary Education; Norm Referenced Tests; *Reading Comprehension; *Reading Tests; *Secondary School Students; *Silent Reading
Identifiers: TORC
Availability: PRO-ED; 8700 Shoal Creek Blvd., Austin, TX 78758-6897
Grade Level: 2-12
Age Level: 7-17
Notes: Items, 85

Revised test of silent reading comprehension, which can be used to determine a student's relative reading comprehension status in relation to a normative group, to determine how well students comprehend written language when a program-independent measure is used, to examine results on various subtests for diagnostic purposes, to compare relative performance in reading comprehension with other conceptual abilities assessed by appropriate measures, to compare performance on TORC with other language behaviors, to investigate behaviors related to reading comprehension, and to study the construct of reading comprehension. The 4 subtests of syntactic abilities, paragraph reading, general vocabulary, and sentence sequencing constitute the Reading Comprehension Core. Diagnostic subtest supplements which are optional include content area vocabularies in mathematics, social studies,

and science, each consisting of 25 items: the subtests Reading the Directions of Schoolwork, consists of 25 items and is meant for younger and remedial readers to measure their understanding of written directions commonly found in schoolwork.

14424
Reading Evaluation and Diagnostic Screen. Shapiro, Alvin 1983
Subtests: Lower Case Alphabet; Printing Sounded-Out Letters; Letter Sequence Memory; Speech Articulation; Body Image
Descriptors: Articulation (Speech); *Diagnostic Tests; Elementary Secondary Education; Human Body; *Individual Testing; Letters (Alphabet); Phoneme Grapheme Correspondence; *Reading Diagnosis; Short Term Memory
Identifiers: READS
Availability: The Listening Corp.; 809 Dundas St. E., London, Ontario, Canada N5W 2Z8
Grade Level: K-10
Age Level: 4-15
Notes: Time, 20 min. approx.

Measures speech-language and perceptual processes necessary to blend words. Also has a direct nonverbal measure of body image related to letter reversals. Developed to help educators find out what is going wrong with a child or adolescent who either cannot sound through words, reverses letters, or mixes up letters in spelling. Scale scores assess accuracy of printed alphabet, letter sounds, letter sequence memory, natural phonic blending, and directionability. This is an experimental edition. Reliability and validity data are provided. Individually administered.

14427
Spelling Achievement Tests. Zaner-Bloser, Columbus, OH 1984
Descriptors: *Achievement Tests; Elementary Education; *Elementary School Students; *Spelling
Availability: Zaner-Bloser; 2200 West Fifth Ave., P.O. Box 16764, Columbus, OH 43216-6764
Grade Level: 2-8

Reproducible achievement tests to be used with the Zaner-Bloser series: Spelling, Basic Skills, and Applications. Each grade level has 30 tests, one for each instructional unit in the text.

14429
The Knowledge of Child Development Inventory. Larsen, John J.; Juhasz, Anne McCreary 1980
Descriptors: *Achievement Tests; Adolescents; Adults; *Child Development; Cognitive Development; Emotional Development; Knowledge Level; Multiple Choice Tests; Physical Development; Social Development; *Young Children
Identifiers: KCDI
Availability: ERIC Document Reproduction Service; 7420 Fullerton Rd., Ste. 110, Springfield, VA 22153-2852 (ED259025, 26 p.)
Age Level: 13-65
Notes: Items, 56

A multiple-choice test of the knowledge of child development in children ages 0-3. It was designed to test the knowledge of young adolescents and parent-education students. Norms are available for adolescent and adult females. Items cover knowledge of emotional, cognitive, physical, and social development.

14431
Khan-Lewis Phonological Analysis. Khan, Linda M.L.; Lewis, Nancy P. 1986
Descriptors: Articulation Impairments; Children; *Diagnostic Tests; *Phonetic Analysis; Remedial Instruction; *Young Children
Identifiers: Goldman Fristoe Test of Articulation; KLPA
Availability: American Guidance Service; Publishers' Bldg., Circle Pines, MN 55014-1796
Age Level: 2-5

Provides a means of assessing the use of 15 phonological processes in the speech of young children 2 through 5 years of age. Analysis may also be used with children 6 years and older who have articulation/phonological disorders. To perform the analysis, one must use the Sounds-in-Words subtest of the Goldman-Fristoe Test of Articulation. The Khan-Lewis Phonological Analysis is recommended for use in the diagnosis and description of articulation or phonological disorders in preschool children. Norms are provided for children between the ages of 2 years 0 months and 5 years 11 months. Of the 15 phonological processes assessed, 12 are characteristic of normal speech development and 3 are not.

14469
Structured Photographic Expressive Language Test—Preschool. Werner, Ellen O'Hara; Kresheck, Janet Dawson 1983
Descriptors: Articulation (Speech); Black Dialects; *Expressive Language; Grammar; Individual Testing; Morphology (Languages); Photographs; Preschool Education; *Screening Tests; Syntax; *Young Children

Identifiers: SPELT
Availability: Janelle Publications; P.O. Box 12, Sandwich, IL 60548
Age Level: 3-5
Notes: Time, 10 min.; Items, 50

Designed as a screening tool to identify children who may have difficulty in their expression of early morphological and syntactic features. Not for diagnosis, but indicates the need for further evaluation. Uses photographs of children in various activities. Contains a section on African-American English usage. The structures covered are plural and possessive nouns, present and past tense, auxiliary verbs, copulas, prepositions, and personal pronouns. Normed on Caucasian, monolingual children, from middle-class rural and urban families. An optional test of articulation is included.

14470
Structured Photographic Expressive Language Test—II.　Werner, Ellen O'Hara; Kresheck, Janet Dawson 1983
Descriptors: *Children; Elementary Education; *Expressive Language; Grammar; Individual Testing; Morphology (Languages); Photographs; Preschool Education; *Screening Tests; Syntax
Identifiers: SPELT
Availability: Janelle Publications; P.O. Box 12, Sandwich, IL 60548
Age Level: 4-8
Notes: Items, 50

Designed to assess a child's expressive formulation of critical syntactic structures and morphological structures through structured auditory stimuli and a series of photographs. This test is not for diagnosis but may be used to indicate the need for further evaluation. Covers nouns, pronouns, verbs, copulas, prepositions, contractions, negatives, conjunctions. Contains a section on African-American English usage. Identifies children performing below the level of their peers and suggests remedial work. Normed on Caucasian monolingual children from middle-class rural and urban families.

14524
Evaluating Communicative Competence, Revised Edition.　Simon, Charlann S. 1986
Descriptors: Adolescents; Children; *Communication Skills; Criterion Referenced Tests; *Elementary School Students; Elementary Secondary Education; *Expressive Language; Individual Testing; *Informal Assessment; Language Handicaps; Learning Disabilities; *Listening Skills; *Secondary School Students
Identifiers: ECC
Availability: Communication Skill Builders; 3830 E. Bellevue, Tucson, AZ 85733
Grade Level: 4-12
Age Level: 9-18
Notes: Items, 21

A series of 21 informal evaluation probes in 2 categories: auditory tasks and expressive tasks. It is useful for clinicians to use to aid in obtaining descriptive data, on metalinguistic and communication skills. Information from the probes allows clinician to decide whether a student should be included in the case load, to determine the frequency of remediation contacts, and to determine a realistic baseline upon which specific pragmatic individualized education program (IEP) objectives can be written. Cognitive level of the 21 tasks is appropriate for those who have reached or are entering Piaget's concrete operational stage and who have a mean length of utterance of at least 4.5 words.

14532
Conley-Vernon Idiom Test.　Conley, Janet; Vernon, McCay 1975
Descriptors: *Achievement Tests; *Context Clues; *Deafness; Elementary Education; *Elementary School Students; *Idioms; *Vocabulary Skills
Availability: Janet Conley; 1105 River Rd., Sykesville, MD 21784
Grade Level: 1-6
Notes: Items, 50

May be used with either deaf or hearing students to assess their skills in use of idiomatic English.

14550
Facts on Aging Quiz, Alternate Form.　Palmore, Erdman
Descriptors: Adults; *Aging (Individuals); Aging Education; Attitude Measures; *Knowledge Level; Older Adults; Social Bias
Identifiers: FAQ
Availability: The Gerontologist; v21 n4 p431-37, 1981
Age Level: Adults
Notes: Items, 25

Designed for use in assessing knowledge level about the aging process for use in stimulating discussion, for identifying misconceptions, and for measuring the effects of education in gerontology. Also measures bias toward the

aged. Also available in Palmore, Erdman B. *The Facts on Aging Quiz: A Handbook of Uses and Results.* New York: Springer Publishing Company, 1988.

14553
Reading Progress Scale, College Version, Forms 2C and 5C.　Carver, Ronald P. 1981
Descriptors: *College Students; Higher Education; *Reading Ability; *Reading Tests
Identifiers: RPS
Availability: Revrac Publications; 207 W. 116th St., Kansas City, MO 64114
Grade Level: 13-16
Notes: Time, 7 min.

Designed to measure levels of reading ability. Test is most useful for detecting college students with low reading ability. Provides immediate feedback to college students regarding which type of courses they should take. There are 4 paragraphs on the test, each representing a different level of difficulty.

14559
Basic Tests for General Business Classes.　Mintz, Herman 1985
Descriptors: *Achievement Tests; *Business Education; Criterion Referenced Tests; High Schools; *High School Students
Availability: J. Weston Walch, Publisher; P.O. Box 658, Portland, ME 04104-0658
Grade Level: 9-12

Complete set of tests that covers the major units in traditional general business programs. In addition to 8 unit tests, there are also midyear and end-of-year exams. Purpose of this test package is to provide comprehensive general business tests that all students can do and read. Questions use only the 1,000 words most commonly used in English plus 46 special business words. Most of the tests are divided into 5 basic parts: business word test, yes-no test, pick-an-answer test, completion test, and problem test. Meets the needs of almost all levels of general business students, including low achievers, average students, and high-achieving students. The 8 unit tests cover the world of business, the forming of business, money in our world, banks in our lives, becoming a good buyer, the land of work, knowing about credit, insurance against loss.

14560
Diagnostic Tests for Minimal Math Competencies.　Pyrczak, Fred; Longmire, John 1980
Descriptors: *Achievement Tests; *Diagnostic Tests; High Schools; *High School Students; Mathematical Applications; Mathematical Vocabulary; Minimum Competencies; Secondary Education; *Secondary School Mathematics
Availability: J. Weston Walch, Publisher; P.O. Box 658, Portland, ME 04104-0658
Grade Level: 9-12
Notes: Items, 15

A series of tests designed for diagnosing student strengths and weaknesses for guiding instruction in general math courses and in preparing them for minimum competency exams as a graduation requirement. Math problems have practical applications such as budgeting and taxes. Math vocabulary is tested to identify poor reading or conceptual skills. Each test also has a series of computational problems. A survey test is included to monitor overall progress. The tests are available as copy masters to be reproduced by the individual purchaser as necessary.

14561
Word Discrimination Exercises and Tests in a Multiple-Choice Format.　Black, John W. 1985
Descriptors: *Articulation (Speech); High Schools; *High School Students; *Speech Improvement; *Speech Tests
Identifiers: Multiple Choice Intelligibility Test; Oral Tests
Availability: Interstate Printers and Publishers; 19-27 N. Jackson St., Danville, IL 61832-0594
Grade Level: 9-12

Clusters of similar sounding words were developed to assess speaker intelligiblity. This is a revision of the Multiple-Choice Intelligibility Test to convince students they are not as understandable as they believe they are. Among other uses teachers have made of these exercises and tests are to assess aural discrimination, short-term memory, word discrimination among aphasics and right brain-damaged individuals, word discrimination among foreign students, and remedial reading.

14562
Language Processing Test.　Richard, Gail; Hanner, Mary Anne 1985
Subtests: Associations; Categorization; Similarities; Differences; Multiple Meanings; Attributes
Descriptors: Children; *Diagnostic Tests; *Individual Testing; Language Handicaps; *Language Processing; Remedial Instruction
Identifiers: LPT
Availability: Linguisystems; 3100 4th Ave., P.O. Box 747, E. Moline, IL 61244
Age Level: 5-12
Notes: Time, 30 min. approx.

Used to identify childrens' language processing strengths and weaknesses in a hierarchical framework so that professionals can determine special program placement, remedial placement, the point at which children's language processing breaks down, and which behaviors contribute to the processing disorders. These disorders may be caused by word retrieval difficulties, inappropriate word substitutions, nonspecific word usage, inability to correct recognized errors, avoidance of responding, rehearsal of responses, or unusual responses. Hierarchy of tasks used in test was based on A.R. Luria's model of brain organization.

14569
Slosson Articulation, Language Test with Phonology.　Tade, Wilma Jean 1986
Subtests: Articulation; Language; Phonology
Descriptors: *Articulation (Speech); *Communicative Competence (Languages); Individual Testing; *Language Skills; Language Tests; Norm Referenced Tests; *Phonology; Pictorial Stimuli; *Screening Tests; *Young Children
Identifiers: SALT(P)
Availability: Slosson Educational Publications; P.O. Box 280, East Aurora, NY 14052
Age Level: 3-5

A screening test that covers communicative competence in the areas of phonology, articulation, and language. A composite score serves as an index to communicative proficiency, with respect to age. This test alone should not be used for diagnosis or preferential placement. There are 8 screening probes that provide the examiner with information regarding the child's ability to respond in a conversational setting. The articulation portion allows for assessing 22 consonants in the initial word position and 18 in the final position, 10 consonant blends or clusters, and 8 vowels and/or diphthongs. The phonological processes covered by the test are initial consonant omission, final consonant omission, fronting of velars, fronting of consonants in words with back vowels, stopping and cluster reduction. The language section covers the child's performance on 31 language behaviors.

14570
Prueba Para El Diagnostico del Lenguaje Pre-Escolar.　Blank, Marion; And Others 1983
Descriptors: Abstract Reasoning; Classroom Communication; *Individual Testing; *Language Skills; Learning Readiness; Perceptual Development; Pictorial Stimuli; *Preschool Children; *Preschool Tests; *Screening Tests; *Spanish; *Spanish Speaking; Young Children
Identifiers: PDLP; Preschool Language Assessment Instrument
Availability: Grune and Stratton; 111 Fifth Ave., New York, NY 10003
Age Level: 3-6
Notes: Time, 20 min. approx.; Items, 60

Individually administered test designed to assess young children's skills in coping with the language demands of the teaching situation. In cases where children's language skills are questionable, the test may be administered to children up to 10 years of age. Test was developed to meet 2 major objectives: to offer a picture of a child's language skills so that teaching can be matched to the child's level of functioning and to allow for the early identification of children who may encounter severe difficulties in school. Based on a model of classroom discourse where teacher is seen as placing demands on the child that require varying levels of abstraction that can be viewed as being on a continuum: matching perception, selective analysis of perception, reordering perception, and reasoning about perception. This test has been adapted for Spanish-speaking children from the English version, Preschool Language Assessment Instrument.

14571
Slosson Oral Reading Test, Form A for Adults and Visually/Verbally Handicapped.　Slosson, Richard L. 1986
Descriptors: Achievement Tests; *Adult Literacy; Adults; Individual Testing; *Oral Reading; *Reading Tests; *Speech Handicaps; *Visual Impairments
Identifiers: SORT
Availability: Slosson Educational Publications; P.O. Box 280, East Aurora, NY 10452
Age Level: Adults
Notes: Items, 200

Word lists are identical to those in the Slosson Oral Reading Test (TC011187). Scoring instructions have been revised to accommodate adult literacy programs and visually and verbally or speech handicapped persons. For visually handicapped individuals, the reading lists have been enlarged and placed on separate cards for ease of presentation.

14572
Diagnostic Screening Test: Language, Second Edition.　Gnagey, Thomas D.; Gnagey, Patricia A. 1980

Descriptors: *Achievement Tests; Capitalization (Alphabetic); *Diagnostic Tests; *Elementary School Students; Elementary Secondary Education; Grammar; Postsecondary Education; Punctuation; *Secondary School Students; Sentence Structure; Spelling; *Two Year College Students; *Written Language
Identifiers: DST
Availability: Slosson Educational Publications; P.O. Box 280, East Aurora, NY 14052
Grade Level: 1-13
Notes: Time, 10 min. approx.

Tests are designed to assist teachers, psychologists, and counselors in quickly obtaining diagnostic information which can be translated into classroom learning activities appropriate to each student's needs. Tests were developed as a quick, valid method to estimate students' overall achievement level in written language, specifically skill mastery levels in grammar, punctuation, capitalization, sentence structure, and formal spelling rules. Students' overall achievement level is then divided into formal knowledge (rote rule knowledge) and applied knowledge (habitual correct usage). Wide-range test with items from early primary grades through junior college level. Items are arranged in developmental order from the most elementary concepts to those generally most difficult.

14573
Boehm Test of Basic Concepts, Revised. Boehm, Ann E. 1986
Descriptors: Abstract Reasoning; Achievement Tests; *Concept Formation; Elementary School Students; *Primary Education; *School Readiness; *Screening Tests; *Verbal Communication; Visual Measures
Availability: The Psychological Corp.; 555 Academic Ct., San Antonio, TX 78204-0952
Grade Level: K-2
Notes: Time, 40 min. approx.; Items, 50

Designed to assess children's mastery of basic concepts that are fundamental to understanding verbal instruction and necessary for early school achievement. Test is read aloud by the classroom teacher. Results of test may be used to identify children with basic concept deficiencies and to identify concept areas that should be targeted for further instruction. Basic concepts measured are relational concepts, a subset of concepts children use to make relational decisions about persons, objects, and situations. Concepts targeted in test also involve judgments that can be made across the contexts of space, quantity, and time, at increasingly complex levels of abstraction. There is also an applications booklet consisting of 26 items of basic concepts frequently used in combination with easier concepts, with each other, or with other concepts familiar to the child.

14574
World History Map Test Folios. Perfection Form Co., Logan, IA
Descriptors: *Achievement Tests; Criterion Referenced Tests; High Schools; *High School Students; *Maps; *World History
Availability: Perfection Form Co.; 1000 N. Second Ave., Logan, IA 51546
Grade Level: 9-12

A collection of outline maps with questions printed on them. Maps deal with some fragment of history, politics, religion, or other topic. Students respond by filling in answers on map.

14575
World History Tests, Revised. Perfection Form Co., Logan, IA
Descriptors: *Achievement Tests; Criterion Referenced Tests; High Schools; *High School Students; *World History
Availability: Perfection Form Co.; 1000 N. Second Ave., Logan, IA 51546
Grade Level: 9-12

A series of 16 objective tests covering the history of man's experience. Most of the tests consist of 100 items. Test series covers earliest civilizations, the Greeks, the Romans, Middle Ages, bridge to modern times, era of political revolution, revolution continues, new imperialism, between 2 great wars, the great global conflict, postwar world, Far Eastern history, Russian history, plus 2 semester tests and a final examination.

14576
American History Tests, Revised, Senior High. Perfection Form Co., Logan, IA
Descriptors: *Achievement Tests; High Schools; *High School Students; *United States History
Availability: Perfection Form Co.; 1000 N. Second Ave., Logan, IA 51546
Grade Level: 9-12

A series of American history tests covering 13 topics plus 2 semester tests and a final examination. The topics include America's heritage, background of the Revolution, U.S. Constitution, Washington's administration, the age of Jackson, expansion, war and reconstruction, emergence of modern America, U.S. becomes a world power, prosperity and depression, the U.S. and world leadership.

14585
Communication Competency Assessment Instrument. Rubin, Rebecca B. 1982
Descriptors: *College Students; Competence; *Higher Education; Interpersonal Communication; Listening Skills; Nonverbal Communication; Nonverbal Tests; *Rating Scales; *Speech Communication; Speech Skills; Videotape Recordings
Identifiers: CCAI; Oral Tests
Availability: Speech Communication Association; 5105 Backlick Rd., Ste. E, Annandale, VA 22003
Grade Level: 13-16
Notes: Time, 30 min.; Items, 19

A rating instrument designed to assess college students' communication skills, i.e., their ability to speak, listen, and relate to others within the college classroom and with advisors, peers, etc. Four main competence areas are Communication Codes, Oral Messages Evaluation, Basic Speech Communication Skills, and Human Relations. Nineteen skills are covered within these areas. All student responses to administrator's prompts, or to videotape, are oral or nonverbal.

14591
American History Tests: Junior High Series, Revised. Perfection Form Co., Logan, IA 1970
Descriptors: *Achievement Tests; Junior High Schools; *Junior High School Students; *United States History
Availability: Perfection Form Co.; 1000 N. Second Ave., Logan, IA 51546
Grade Level: 7-9
Notes: Items, 75

A series of U.S. history tests, covering the period from exploration and colonization to post-World War II. These are objective tests and use true-false, multiple-choice, and matching items. Besides the area tests, 2 semester tests and a final exam are included. The area tests cover exploration and colonization, revolutionary America, founding of government, development of democracy, westward expansion, division and reunion, U.S. as a world power, modern U.S., and post-World War II.

14592
American Government Tests. Perfection Form Co., Logan, IA 1970
Descriptors: *Achievement Tests; High Schools; *High School Students; Junior High Schools; *Junior High School Students; Secondary Education; *United States Government (Course)
Availability: Perfection Form Co.; 1000 N. Second Ave., Logan, IA 51546
Grade Level: 7-12
Notes: Items, 75

A series of tests covering state and local government, the judiciary system and civil liberties, the legislative branch, the executive branch including political parties and elections, fundamentals of government. These are objective tests and use true-false, multiple-choice, and matching items. Besides the area tests, 2 semester tests and a final exam are included.

14593
Economics Tests. Perfection Form Co., Logan, IA 1970
Descriptors: *Achievement Tests; *Economics; High Schools; *High School Students; Junior High Schools; *Junior High School Students; Secondary Education
Availability: Perfection Form Co.; 1000 N. Second Ave., Logan, IA 51546
Grade Level: 7-12
Notes: Items, 75

A series of tests covering concepts in economics; price, income, and personal growth; money, banking, and insurance; and international trade. These are objective tests and use true-false, multiple-choice, and matching items. Besides the area tests, a final exam is included.

14595
Multilevel Academic Survey Test. Howell, Kenneth W.; And Others 1985
Descriptors: *Achievement Tests; Criterion Referenced Tests; *Elementary School Students; Elementary Secondary Education; *Low Achievement; *Mathematics Achievement; Norm Referenced Tests; *Reading Achievement; *Secondary School Students
Identifiers: MAST
Availability: The Psychological Corp.; 555 Academic Ct., San Antonio, TX 78204-0952
Grade Level: K-12

Intended for use by school personnel who make decisions about student performance in reading or mathematics. Test is intended primarily for those students who have academic difficulties. There are 2 basic instruments: a grade level test and a curriculum level test. If the primary need is to rank students' performances versus that of their peers, the grade level test provides a short, wide-range measure of academic achievement. It is a norm-referenced

measure. If the primary goal is to collect criterion-referenced information on specific areas of curriculum performance, the curriculum level test surveys critical clusters of reading and math skills. The 2 basic instruments may be used independently or in combination.

14596
Content Inventories: English, Social Studies, Science. McWilliams, Lana; Rakes, Thomas A. 1979
Descriptors: Attitude Measures; Cloze Procedure; Cognitive Style; Content Area Reading; *Elementary Secondary Education; *English; Graphs; Informal Reading Inventories; Interest Inventories; Locational Skills (Social Studies); Reading Tests; *Sciences; *Screening Tests; *Social Studies; Speed Reading; Student Attitudes; *Student Interests; *Student Placement; Study Skills
Identifiers: Frustration Reading Level; Independent Reading Level; Instructional Reading Level; Scanning; Skimming
Availability: Kendall Hunt Publishing Co.; 2460 Kerper Blvd., Dubuque, IA 52001
Grade Level: 4-12

A series of placement tests, reading inventories, informal tests for assessing study skills, and inventories for assessing student attitudes, habits, and interests in general and in the 3 content areas. Used for screening groups of students prior to instruction, to determine general study skill abilities within content areas. Cloze reading inventories determine students' ability levels. Group reading inventories identify independent, instructional, and frustration levels. Study skills assessed are locational, organizing, use of graphs, skimming, and scanning. Other inventories measure study strategies, interests in English, science and social studies, content knowledge and learning style.

14597
Computer-Based Reading Assessment Instrument. Blanchard, Jay S. 1985
Descriptors: Achievement Tests; *Computer Assisted Testing; Elementary Education; *Elementary School Students; *Informal Reading Inventories; Microcomputers; Reading Comprehension; *Reading Tests; Spanish; Word Lists
Identifiers: CRAI
Availability: Kendall Hunt Publishing Co.; 2460 Kerper Blvd., Dubuque, IA 52001
Grade Level: 1-8

Informal reading instrument consisting of word lists, reading passages, and comprehension questions. There are 2 forms at each of 8 graded readability levels. Available in either English or Spanish versions. Some parts of the inventory may be computer administered. Either the computer-based version or the non-computer-based inventory may be used for individualized testing or for group testing. For computer-administered testing, software is available for Apple, IBM, Commodore, Texas Instrument, or Tandy microcomputers.

14599
Diagnostic Reading Inventory, Second Edition. Jacobs, H. Donald; Searfoss, Lyndon W. 1979
Descriptors: *Decoding (Reading); *Diagnostic Tests; Elementary Education; *Elementary School Students; Individual Testing; Listening Comprehension Tests; Oral Reading; *Reading Diagnosis; *Reading Difficulties; *Reading Tests; Silent Reading
Identifiers: Frustration Reading Level; Independent Reading Level; Instructional Reading Level
Availability: Kendall Hunt Publishing Co.; 2460 Kerper Blvd., Dubuque, IA 52001
Grade Level: 4-8

This test is designed for use with students who have already been identified as having reading problems. It is individually administered. It consists of 8 each of graded oral reading passages, word lists, phrase lists, silent reading passages, listening passages, and a decoding inventory. A profile is drawn for each child. Identifies independent, instructional, and frustration reading levels. Parts of the test are timed.

14628
Test of English Proficiency Level. Rathmell, George 1985
Subtests: Oral; Structure; Reading; Writing
Descriptors: *Adult Education; Adult Programs; Adults; *English (Second Language); Expressive Language; Individual Testing; *Language Tests; *Limited English Speaking; Reading Comprehension; Secondary Education; *Secondary School Students; *Student Placement; Writing Skills
Identifiers: TEPL
Availability: Prentice-Hall, Inc.; 200 Old Tappan Rd., Old Tappan, NJ 07675
Grade Level: 7-12
Age Level: 12-65

Notes: Time, 80 min. approx.

A multiskill placement test used with limited English proficient students in secondary and adult programs to determine their placement in English-as-a-Second-Language programs. It measures 4 distinct areas of language competence to provide a comprehensive sampling of a student's proficiency in English. The oral section assesses the ability to comprehend and to respond to 30 questions which move from simple to more complex grammatical forms, lexical items, and communicative functions. The structure section measures degree of mastery of lexical, morphological, and syntactic features of English through recognition of correct forms in the context of a sentence. The reading section uses a multiple-choice cloze format to assess reading comprehension. The writing section measures the ability to compose original expressions in English and is scored holistically. Results are used to indicate a student's appropriate placement in one of 7 instructional levels in each of the 4 skill areas.

14635
Technology Literacy Test. Smalley, Lee; Brady, Steve 1984
Descriptors: *Achievement Tests; Criterion Referenced Tests; *Grade 12; *High School Seniors; Knowledge Level; Secondary Education; Technical Education; *Technological Literacy
Availability: ERIC Document Reproduction Service; 7420 Fullerton Rd., Ste. 110, Springfield, VA 22153-2852 (ED255637, 24 p.)
Grade Level: 12
Notes: Items, 27

Two forms of a test were developed to measure knowledge of aspects of current technologies and technological change. Items were constructed based on literature review and expert opinion. Items concern such criteria as knowledge of existing and emerging technologies and ability to evaluate technology as to its appropriateness in our world. The short form contains 10 items.

14657
ACT ASSET Program. American College Testing Program, Iowa City, IA 1983
Descriptors: *Basic Skills; *Educational Counseling; Higher Education; Language Skills; Mathematics Skills; Reading Ability; School Holding Power; *Screening Tests; *Student Needs; Student Placement; Student Recruitment; Study Skills; *Two Year Colleges; *Two Year College Students
Availability: ACT ASSET Program; Operations Div., P.O. Box 168, Iowa City, IA 52243
Grade Level: 13-14

An assessment-advising program developed to identify basic skill levels of students as they enter 2-year postsecondary institutions. Primary goal of the program is to gather information about individual student's skills, needs, and plans to assist student in developing and implementing a sound program of study to meet student needs and goals. As part of the program, students complete educational planning forms, take tests in the areas of language usage, reading, and numerical skills, and participate in advising sessions.

14671
National Tests of Basic Skills, Level P. American Testronics, Iowa City, IA 1985
Subtests: Visual Matching; Auditory Attention; Auditory Picture Closure; Auditory Picture Rhymes; Combining Information; Auditory Comprehension; Silly Pictures; Visual Oddities; Generalizations; Developmental Mathematics
Descriptors: *Achievement Tests; *Basic Skills; *Kindergarten Children; Listening Skills; Mathematical Concepts; *Norm Referenced Tests; Prereading Experience; *Preschool Children; Primary Education; Visual Discrimination
Identifiers: Test Batteries
Availability: American Testronics; P.O. Box 2270, Iowa City, IA 52244-9990
Grade Level: K
Age Level: 4-6
Notes: Items, 96

Multiple-choice tests developed to measure students' achievement level in the basic skill areas commonly found in school curricula. Series consists of 14 overlapping test levels spanning prekindergarten to college. Each test level contains the content objectives and item characteristics appropriate for its corresponding grade level in school. Level P consists of 10 subtests designed to evaluate the development of learning processes and capabilities in children, ages 4 through 6. Subtests provide information on child's level of growth in the following areas: facility with language, ease in dealing with written symbols, and perception of quantity and its applications.

14672
National Tests of Basic Skills, Level A. American Testronics, Iowa City, IA 1985
Subtests: Listening Comprehension; Alphabet Knowledge; Letter Recognition; Sound Recognition; Word Matching; Mathematics

Descriptors: *Achievement Tests; *Basic Skills; Elementary School Mathematics; *Kindergarten Children; Language Skills; Mathematics Achievement; *Norm Referenced Tests; Primary Education; Reading Ability
Identifiers: Test Batteries
Availability: American Testronics; P.O. Box 2270, Iowa City, IA 52244-9990
Grade Level: K
Notes: Time, 109 min.; Items, 120

Multiple-choice tests developed to measure students' achievement level in the basic skill areas commonly found in school curricula. Series consists of 14 overlapping test levels spanning prekindergarten to college. Each test level contains the content objectives and item characteristics appropriate for its corresponding grade level in school. Level A consists of 6 tests that measure students' learning in reading, language, and mathematics. It is suggested that test sessions be spaced over 3 or 4 days.

14673
National Tests of Basic Skills, Level B. American Testronics, Iowa City, IA 1985
Subtests: Word Attack; Listening Comprehension; Vocabulary; Reading Comprehension; Language Expression; Mathematics
Descriptors: *Achievement Tests; *Basic Skills; Elementary School Mathematics; *Grade 1; *Kindergarten Children; Language Skills; Mathematics Achievement; *Norm Referenced Tests; Primary Education; Reading Ability
Identifiers: Test Batteries
Availability: American Testronics; P.O. Box 2270, Iowa City, IA 52244-9990
Grade Level: K-1
Notes: Time, 123 min.; Items, 150

Multiple-choice tests developed to measure students' achievement level in the basic skill areas commonly found in school curricula. Series consists of 14 overlapping test levels spanning prekindergarten to college. Each test level contains the content objectives and item characteristics appropriate for its corresponding grade level in school. Level B consists of 6 subtests that measure students' learning in reading, language, and mathematics. It is suggested that test sessions be spaced over 3 or 4 days.

14674
National Tests of Basic Skills, Level C. American Testronics, Iowa City, IA 1985
Subtests: Word Attack; Vocabulary; Reading Comprehension; Language Expression; Mathematics Computation; Mathematics Concepts and Applications; Social Studies; Science
Descriptors: *Achievement Tests; *Basic Skills; Elementary School Mathematics; Elementary School Science; *Grade 1; Language Skills; Mathematics Achievement; *Norm Referenced Tests; Primary Education; Reading Ability; Social Studies
Identifiers: Test Batteries
Availability: American Testronics; P.O. Box 2270, Iowa City, IA 52244-9990
Grade Level: 1
Notes: Time, 173 min.; Items, 200

Multiple-choice tests developed to measure students' achievement level in the basic skill areas commonly found in school curricula. Series consists of 14 overlapping test levels spanning prekindergarten to college. Each test level contains the content objectives and item characteristics appropriate for its corresponding grade level in school. Level C consists of 8 subtests that measure students' learning in reading, language, and mathematics, as well as science and social studies.

14675
National Tests of Basic Skills, Level D. American Testronics, Iowa City, IA 1985
Subtests: Word Attack; Vocabulary; Reading Comprehension; Spelling; Language Mechanics; Language Expression; Mathematics Computation; Mathematics Concepts and Applications; Social Studies; Science
Descriptors: *Achievement Tests; *Basic Skills; Elementary School Mathematics; Elementary School Science; Elementary School Students; *Grade 1; *Grade 2; Language Skills; Mathematics Achievement; *Norm Referenced Tests; Primary Education; Reading Ability; Social Studies
Identifiers: Test Batteries
Availability: American Testronics; P.O. Box 2270, Iowa City, IA 52244-9990
Grade Level: 1-2
Notes: Time, 193 min.; Items, 240

Multiple-choice tests developed to measure students' achievement level in the basic skill areas commonly found in school curricula. Series consists of 14 overlapping test levels spanning prekindergarten to college. Each test level contains the content objectives and item characteristics appropriate for its corresponding grade level in school.

Level D consists of 10 subtests that measure students' learning in reading, language, mathematics, social studies, and science.

14676
National Tests of Basic Skills, Level E. American Testronics, Iowa City, IA 1985
Subtests: Vocabulary; Reading Comprehension; Spelling; Language Mechanics; Language Expression; References; Mathematics Computation; Mathematics Concepts; Mathematics Applications; Social Studies; Science
Descriptors: *Achievement Tests; *Basic Skills; Elementary School Mathematics; Elementary School Science; Elementary School Students; *Grade 2; *Grade 3; Language Skills; Mathematics Achievement; *Norm Referenced Tests; Primary Education; Reading Comprehension; Social Studies; Spelling; Study Skills; Vocabulary
Identifiers: Test Batteries
Availability: American Testronics; P.O. Box 2270, Iowa City, IA 52244-9990
Grade Level: 2-3
Notes: Time, 228 min.; Items, 290

Multiple-choice tests developed to measure students' achievement level in the basic skill areas commonly found in school curricula. Series consists of 14 overlapping test levels spanning prekindergarten to college. Each test level contains the content objectives and item characteristics appropriate for its corresponding grade level in school. Level E consists of 11 subtests that measure students' learning in language arts, reading, mathematics, social studies, science, and reference skills.

14677
National Tests of Basic Skills, Level F. American Testronics, Iowa City, IA 1985
Subtests: Vocabulary; Reading Comprehension; Spelling; Language Mechanics; Language Expression; References; Mathematics Computation; Mathematics Concepts; Mathematics Applications; Social Studies; Science
Descriptors: *Achievement Tests; *Basic Skills; Elementary School Mathematics; Elementary School Science; Elementary School Students; *Grade 3; *Grade 4; Language Skills; Mathematics Achievement; *Norm Referenced Tests; Primary Education; Reading Comprehension; Social Studies; Spelling; Study Skills; Vocabulary
Identifiers: Test Batteries
Availability: American Testronics; P.O. Box 2270, Iowa City, IA 52244-9990
Grade Level: 3-4
Notes: Time, 261 min.; Items, 345

Multiple-choice tests developed to measure students' achievement level in the basic skill areas commonly found in school curricula. Series consists of 14 overlapping test levels spanning prekindergarten to college. Each test level contains the content objectives and item characteristics appropriate for its corresponding grade level in school. Level F consists of 11 subtests that measure students' learning in language arts, reading, mathematics, social studies, science, and reference skills.

14678
National Tests of Basic Skills, Level G. American Testronics, Iowa City, IA 1985
Subtests: Vocabulary; Reading Comprehension; Spelling; Language Mechanics; Language Expression; References; Mathematics Computation; Mathematics Concepts; Mathematics Applications; Social Studies; Science
Descriptors: *Achievement Tests; *Basic Skills; Elementary School Mathematics; Elementary School Science; Elementary School Students; *Grade 4; *Grade 5; Intermediate Grades; Language Skills; Mathematics Achievement; *Norm Referenced Tests; Reading Comprehension; Social Studies; Spelling; Study Skills; Vocabulary
Identifiers: Test Batteries
Availability: American Testronics; P.O. Box 2270, Iowa City, IA 52244-9990
Grade Level: 4-5
Notes: Time, 261 min.; Items, 345

Multiple-choice tests developed to measure students' achievement level in the basic skill areas commonly found in school curricula. Series consists of 14 overlapping test levels spanning prekindergarten to college. Each test level contains the content objectives and item characteristics appropriate for its corresponding grade level in school. Level G consists of 11 subtests that measure students' learning in language arts, reading, mathematics, social studies, science, and reference skills.

14679
National Tests of Basic Skills, Level H. American Testronics, Iowa City, IA 1985

Subtests: Vocabulary; Reading Comprehension; Spelling; Language Mechanics; Language Expression; References; Mathematics Computation; Mathematics Concepts; Mathematics Applications; Social Studies; Science
Descriptors: *Achievement Tests; *Basic Skills; Elementary School Mathematics; Elementary School Science; Elementary School Students; *Grade 5; *Grade 6; Intermediate Grades; Language Skills; Mathematics Achievement; *Norm Referenced Tests; Reading Comprehension; Social Studies; Spelling; Study Skills; Vocabulary
Identifiers: Test Batteries
Availability: American Testronics; P.O. Box 2270, Iowa City, IA 52244-9990
Grade Level: 5-6
Notes: Time, 261 min.; Items, 345
Multiple-choice tests developed to measure students' achievement level in the basic skill areas commonly found in school curricula. Series consists of 14 overlapping test levels spanning prekindergarten to college. Each test level contains the content objectives and item characteristics appropriate for its corresponding grade level in school. Level H consists of 11 subtests that measure students' learning in language arts, reading, mathematics, social studies, science, and reference skills.

14680
National Tests of Basic Skills, Level I. American Testronics, Iowa City, IA 1985
Subtests: Vocabulary; Reading Comprehension; Spelling; Language Mechanics; Language Expression; References; Mathematics Computation; Mathematics Concepts; Mathematics Applications; Social Studies; Science
Descriptors: *Achievement Tests; *Basic Skills; Elementary School Mathematics; Elementary School Science; Elementary School Students; *Grade 6; *Grade 7; Intermediate Grades; Language Skills; Mathematics Achievement; *Norm Referenced Tests; Reading Comprehension; Social Studies; Spelling; Study Skills; Vocabulary
Identifiers: Test Batteries
Availability: American Testronics; P.O. Box 2270, Iowa City, IA 52244-9990
Grade Level: 6-7
Notes: Time, 261 min.; Items, 345
Multiple-choice tests developed to measure students' achievement level in the basic skill areas commonly found in school curricula. Series consists of 14 overlapping test levels spanning prekindergarten to college. Each test level contains the content objectives and item characteristics appropriate for its corresponding grade level in school. Level I consists of 11 subtests that measure students' learning in language arts, reading, mathematics, social studies, science, and reference skills.

14681
National Tests of Basic Skills, Level J. American Testronics, Iowa City, IA 1985
Subtests: Vocabulary; Reading Comprehension; Spelling; Language Mechanics; Language Expression; References; Mathematics Computation; Mathematics Concepts; Mathematics Applications; Social Studies; Science
Descriptors: *Achievement Tests; *Basic Skills; *Grade 7; *Grade 8; Junior High Schools; *Junior High School Students; Language Skills; Mathematics Achievement; *Norm Referenced Tests; Reading Comprehension; Secondary School Mathematics; Secondary School Science; Social Studies; Spelling; Study Skills; Vocabulary
Identifiers: Test Batteries
Availability: American Testronics; P.O. Box 2270, Iowa City, IA 52244-9990
Grade Level: 7-8
Notes: Time, 261 min.; Items, 345
Multiple-choice tests developed to measure students' achievement level in the basic skill areas commonly found in school curricula. Series consists of 14 overlapping test levels spanning prekindergarten to college. Each test level contains the content objectives and item characteristics appropriate for its corresponding grade level in school. Level J consists of 11 subtests that measure students' learning in language arts, reading, mathematics, social studies, science, and reference skills.

14682
National Tests of Basic Skills, Level K. American Testronics, Iowa City, IA 1985
Subtests: Vocabulary; Reading Comprehension; Spelling; Language Mechanics; Language Expression; Written Expression; Mathematics Computation; Mathematics Concepts and Applications; Social Studies; Science

Descriptors: *Achievement Tests; *Basic Skills; Language Skills; Mathematics Achievement; *Norm Referenced Tests; Reading Comprehension; Secondary Education; Secondary School Mathematics; Secondary School Science; *Secondary School Students; Social Studies; Spelling; Vocabulary; Writing Skills
Identifiers: Test Batteries
Availability: American Testronics; P.O. Box 2270, Iowa City, IA 52244-9990
Grade Level: 8-10
Notes: Time, 177 min.; Items, 255
Multiple-choice tests developed to measure students' achievement level in the basic skill areas commonly found in school curricula. Series consists of 14 overlapping test levels spanning prekindergarten to college. Each test level contains the content objectives and item characteristics appropriate for its corresponding grade level in school. Level K consists of 10 subtests that measure students' learning in language arts, reading, mathematics, social studies, and science.

14683
National Tests of Basic Skills, Level L. American Testronics, Iowa City, IA 1985
Subtests: Vocabulary; Reading Comprehension; Spelling; Language Mechanics; Language Expression; Written Expression; Mathematics Computation; Mathematics Concepts and Applications; Social Studies; Science
Descriptors: *Achievement Tests; *Basic Skills; High Schools; *High School Students; Language Skills; Mathematics Achievement; *Norm Referenced Tests; Reading Comprehension; Secondary School Mathematics; Secondary School Science; Social Studies; Spelling; Vocabulary; Writing Skills
Identifiers: Test Batteries
Availability: American Testronics; P.O. Box 2270, Iowa City, IA 52244-9990
Grade Level: 10-12
Notes: Time, 177 min.; Items, 255
Multiple-choice tests developed to measure students' achievement level in the basic skill areas commonly found in school curricula. Series consists of 14 overlapping test levels spanning prekindergarten to college. Each test level contains the content objectives and item characteristics appropriate for its corresponding grade level in school. Level L consists of 10 subtests that measure students' learning in language arts, reading, mathematics, social studies, and science.

14684
National Tests of Basic Skills, Level M. American Testronics, Iowa City, IA 1985
Subtests: Vocabulary; Reading Comprehension; Spelling; Language Mechanics; Language Expression; References; Mathematics Computation; Mathematics Concepts and Applications; Social Studies; Science
Descriptors: *Achievement Tests; *Basic Skills; College Students; Higher Education; High Schools; *High School Students; Language Skills; Mathematics Achievement; *Norm Referenced Tests; Reading Comprehension; Secondary School Mathematics; Secondary School Science; Social Studies; Spelling; Vocabulary; Writing Skills
Identifiers: Test Batteries
Availability: American Testronics; P.O. Box 2270, Iowa City, IA 52244-9990
Grade Level: 11-16
Notes: Time, 177 min.; Items, 255
Multiple-choice tests developed to measure students' achievement level in the basic skill areas commonly found in school curricula. Series consists of 14 overlapping test levels spanning prekindergarten to college. Each test level contains the content objectives and item characteristics appropriate for its corresponding grade level in school. Level M consists of 10 subtests that measure students' learning in reading, language, mathematics, social studies, and science.

14685
Tests of Achievement and Proficiency, Level 15. Scannell, Dale P.; And Others 1986
Subtests: Reading Comprehension; Mathematics; Written Expression; Using Sources of Information; Social Studies; Science; Listening Test; Writing Test
Descriptors: *Achievement Tests; *Basic Skills; Daily Living Skills; *Grade 9; High Schools; *High School Students; Language Arts; Listening Skills; Reading Comprehension; Secondary School Mathematics; Secondary School Science; Social Studies; Study Skills; Writing (Composition); Writing Skills
Identifiers: Basic Skills Assessment Program; TAP; Test Batteries
Availability: Riverside Publishing Co.; 8420 Bryn Mawr Ave., Chicago, IL 60631

Grade Level: 9
One of 3 test batteries that comprise the Basic Skills Assessment Program, a comprehensive standardized testing program designed to assess student achievement and abilities. The Tests of Achievement and Proficiency (TAP), levels 15-18, comprise an assessment program for students in grades 9-12. Each test level provides comprehensive measurement of basic skills and basic curricular areas. TAP is available in a basic battery and a complete battery. Both batteries include 4 tests: reading comprehension, mathematics, written expression, and using sources of information. The complete battery also includes tests in social studies and science. The 4 tests common to both batteries include items that measure skills needed in adult life and assess how effectively students use the basic skills and respond to basic tasks they need to function in everyday society. There are also optional listening and writing tests. The complete battery takes 240 minutes, and the basic battery takes 160 minutes to complete. The complete battery has 344 items, and the basic battery has 229 items. The Iowa Tests of Basic Skills, the Cognitive Abilities Test, and the Tests of Achievement and Proficiency were normed concurrently.

14686
Tests of Achievement and Proficiency, Level 16. Scannell, Dale P.; And Others 1986
Subtests: Reading Comprehension; Mathematics; Written Expression; Using Sources of Information; Social Studies; Science; Listening Test; Writing Test
Descriptors: *Achievement Tests; *Basic Skills; Daily Living Skills; *Grade 10; High Schools; *High School Students; Language Arts; Listening Skills; Reading Comprehension; Secondary School Mathematics; Secondary School Science; Social Studies; Study Skills; Writing (Composition); Writing Skills
Identifiers: Basic Skills Assessment Program; TAP; Test Batteries
Availability: Riverside Publishing Co.; 8420 Bryn Mawr Ave., Chicago, IL 60631
Grade Level: 9-12
Notes: Time, 240 min.; Items, 351
One of 3 test batteries that comprise the Basic Skills Assessment Program, a comprehensive standardized testing program designed to assess student achievement and abilities. The Tests of Achievement and Proficiency (TAP), levels 15-18, comprise an assessment program for students in grades 9-12. Each test level provides comprehensive measurement of basic skills and basic curricular areas. TAP is available in a basic battery and a complete battery. Both batteries include 4 tests: reading comprehension, mathematics, written expression, and using sources of information. The complete battery also includes tests in social studies and science. The 4 tests common to both batteries include items that measure skills needed in adult life and assess how effectively students use the basic skills and respond to basic tasks they need to function in everyday society. There are also optional listening and writing tests. The complete battery takes 240 minutes, and the basic battery takes 160 minutes to complete. The complete battery has 351 items, and the basic battery has 235 items. The Iowa Tests of Basic Skills, the Cognitive Abilities Test, and the Tests of Achievement and Proficiency were normed concurrently.

14687
Tests of Achievement and Proficiency, Level 17. Scannell, Dale P.; And Others 1986
Subtests: Reading Comprehension; Mathematics; Written Expression; Using Sources of Information; Social Studies; Science; Listening Test; Writing Test
Descriptors: *Achievement Tests; *Basic Skills; Daily Living Skills; *Grade 11; High Schools; *High School Students; Language Arts; Listening Skills; Reading Comprehension; Secondary School Mathematics; Secondary School Science; Social Studies; Study Skills; Writing (Composition); Writing Skills
Identifiers: Basic Skills Assessment Program; TAP; Test Batteries
Availability: Riverside Publishing Co.; 8420 Bryn Mawr Ave., Chicago, IL 60631
Grade Level: 11
One of 3 test batteries that comprise the Basic Skills Assessment Program, a comprehensive standardized testing program designed to assess student achievement and abilities. The Tests of Achievement and Proficiency (TAP), levels 15-18, comprise an assessment program for students in grades 9-12. Each test level provides comprehensive measurement of basic skills and basic curricular areas. TAP is available in a basic battery and a complete battery. Both batteries include 4 tests: reading comprehension, mathematics, written expression, and using sources of information. The complete battery also includes tests in social studies and science. The 4 tests common to both batteries include items that measure skills needed in adult life and assess how effectively students use the basic skills and respond to basic tasks they need to function in everyday society. There are also optional listening and writing tests. The complete battery has 357 items, and the

basic battery has 241 items. The Iowa Tests of Basic Skills, the cognitive Abilities Test, and the Tests of Achievement and Proficiency were normed concurrently.

14688
Tests of Achievement and Proficiency, Level 18. Scannell, Dale P.; And Others 1986
Subtests: Reading Comprehension; Mathematics; Written Expression; Using Sources of Information; Social Studies; Science; Listening Test; Writing Test
Descriptors: *Achievement Tests; *Basic Skills; Daily Living Skills; *Grade 12; High Schools; *High School Seniors; High School Students; Language Arts; Listening Skills; Reading Comprehension; Secondary School Mathematics; Secondary School Science; Social Studies; Study Skills; Writing (Composition); Writing Skills
Identifiers: Basic Skills Assessment Program; TAP; Test Batteries
Availability: Riverside Publishing Co.; 8420 Bryn Mawr Ave., Chicago, IL 60631
Grade Level: 12

One of 3 test batteries that comprise the Basic Skills Assessment Program, a comprehensive standardized testing program designed to assess student achievement and abilities. The Tests of Achievement and Proficiency (TAP), levels 15-18, comprise an assessment program for students in grades 9-12. Each test level provides comprehensive measurement of basic skills and basic curricular areas. TAP is available in a basic battery and a complete battery. Both batteries include 4 tests: reading comprehension, mathematics, written expression, and using sources of information. The complete battery also includes tests in social studies and science. The 4 tests common to both batteries include items that measure skills needed in adult life and assess how effectively students use the basic skills and respond to basic tasks they need to function in everyday society. There are also optional listening and writing tests. The complete battery takes 240 minutes and the basic battery takes 160 minutes to complete. The complete battery has 361 items, and the basic battery has 245 items. The Iowa Tests of Basic Skills, the Cognitive Abilities Test, and the Tests of Achievement and Proficiency were normed concurrently.

14689
Tests of Achievement and Proficiency, Multilevel Test. Scannell, Dale P.; And Others 1986
Subtests: Reading Comprehension; Mathematics; Written Expression; Using Sources of Information; Social Studies; Science; Listening Test; Writing Test
Descriptors: *Achievement Tests; *Basic Skills; Daily Living Skills; High Schools; *High School Students; Language Arts; Listening Skills; Reading Comprehension; Secondary School Mathematics; Secondary School Science; Social Studies; Study Skills; Writing (Composition); Writing Skills
Identifiers: Basic Skills Assessment Program; TAP; Test Batteries
Availability: Riverside Publishing Co.; 8420 Bryn Mawr Ave., Chicago, IL 60631
Grade Level: 9-12

One of 3 test batteries that comprise the Basic Skills Assessment Program, a comprehensive standardized testing program designed to assess student achievement and abilities. The Tests of Achievement and Proficiency (TAP), levels 15-18, comprise an assessment program for students in grades 9-12. Each test level provides comprehensive measurement of basic skills and basic curricular areas. TAP is available in a basic battery and a complete battery. Both batteries include 4 tests: reading comprehension, mathematics, written expression, and using sources of information. The complete battery also includes tests in social studies and science. The 4 tests common to both batteries include items that measure skills needed in adult life and assess how effectively students use the basic skills and respond to basic tasks they need to function in everyday society. There are also optional listening and writing tests. The complete battery takes 240 minutes and the basic battery takes 160 minutes to complete. The Iowa Tests of Basic Skills, the Cognitive Abilities Test, and the Tests of Achievement and Proficiency were normed concurrently.

14690
Iowa Tests of Basic Skills, Forms G and H, Multilevel Battery, Levels 9-14, Complete Battery. Hieronymus, A.N.; And Others 1986
Subtests: Vocabulary; Reading Comprehension; Spelling; Mathematics Concepts; Mathematics Problem Solving; Mathematics Computation; Capitalization; Punctuation; Usage and Expression; Visual Materials; Reference Materials; Writing; Listening; Social Studies; Science
Descriptors: *Achievement Tests; *Basic Skills; Capitalization (Alphabetic); Elementary Education; Elementary School Mathematics; Elementary School Science; *Elementary School Students; Grammar; Junior High Schools; Listening Skills; Punctuation; Reading Comprehension; Social Studies; Spelling; Study Skills; Vocabulary; Writing Skills
Identifiers: Basic Skills Assessment Program; ITBS; Test Batteries
Availability: Riverside Publishing Co.; 8420 Bryn Mawr Ave., Chicago, IL 60631
Grade Level: 3-9

One of 3 test batteries that comprise the Basic Skills Assessment Program, a comprehensive, standardized testing program designed to assess student achievement and abilities. The Iowa Tests of Basic Skills (ITBS) were developed to assess student progress in the basic skills. Assesses readiness and achievement in the basic skills and content areas appropriate to the grade covered. Behavioral objectives to which test items at each level are written coordinate with those of state and local courses of study and instructional materials and methods. The early primary battery consists of 5 subtests at level 5 and 6 subtests at level 6. All level 5 and 6 tests, except reading, are untimed and are orally administered. Levels 7 and 8 of the primary battery and levels 9 through 14 of the multilevel edition are available in either a basic battery or a complete battery. The basic battery has fewer tests than the complete battery and is ideal for use when testing time is limited. For the multilevel edition, a supplementary social studies/science test booklet is also available. For levels 9-14, separate test booklets for each level are also available and each separate level booklet contains all 11 subtests of the complete battery plus the social studies and science tests. Optional writing and listening tests are also available for levels 9-14. The number of items for all subtests and time required to complete the batteries are level 5 (157 items, 125-170 minutes); level 6 (225 items, 125-170 minutes); level 7 (316 items basic, 204 minutes; 539 items complete, 297 minutes); level 8 (345 items basic, 204 minutes; 613 items complete, 297 minutes); level 9 (302 items basic, 285 minutes; 457 items complete, 406 minutes); level 10 (334 items basic, 285 minutes; 503 items complete, 406 minutes); level 11 (357 items basic, 285 minutes; 538 items complete, 406 minutes); level 12 (376 items basic, 285 minutes; 560 items complete, 406 minutes); level 13 (385 items basic, 285 minutes; 581 items complete, 406 minutes); level 14 (390 items basic, 285 minutes; 591 items complete, 406 minutes). The Iowa Tests of Basic Skills, the Cognitive Abilities Test, and the Tests of Achievement and Proficiency were normed concurrently.

14691
Iowa Tests of Basic Skills, Forms G, Multilevel Battery, Levels 9-14, Basic Battery. Hieronymus, A.N.; And Others 1986
Subtests: Vocabulary; Reading Comprehension; Spelling; Mathematics Concepts; Mathematics Problem Solving; Mathematics Computation
Descriptors: *Achievement Tests; *Basic Skills; Elementary Education; Elementary School Mathematics; *Elementary School Students; Junior High Schools; *Junior High School Students; Reading Comprehension; Spelling; Vocabulary
Identifiers: Basic Skills Assessment Program; ITBS; Oral Testing; Test Batteries
Availability: Riverside Publishing Co.; 8420 Bryn Mawr Ave., Chicago, IL 60631
Grade Level: 3-9

One of 3 test batteries that comprise the Basic Skills Assessment Program, a comprehensive, standardized testing program designed to assess student achievement and abilities. The Iowa Tests of Basic Skills (ITBS) were developed to assess student progress in the basic skills. Assesses readiness and achievement in the basic skills and content areas appropriate to the grade covered. Behavioral objectives to which test items at each level are written coordinate with those of state and local courses of study and instructional materials and methods. The early primary battery consists of 5 subtests at level 5 and 6 subtests at level 6. All level 5 and 6 tests, except reading, are untimed and are orally administered. Levels 7 and 8 of the primary battery and levels 9 through 14 of the multilevel edition are available in either a basic battery or a complete battery. The basic battery has fewer tests than the complete battery and is ideal for use when testing time is limited. For the multilevel edition, a supplementary social studies/science test booklet is also available. For levels 9-14, separate test booklets for each level are also available and each separate level booklet contains all 11 subtests of the complete battery plus the social studies and science tests. Optional writing and listening tests are also available for levels 9-14. The number of items for all subtests and time required to complete the batteries are level 5 (157 items, 125-170 minutes); level 6 (225 items, 125-170 minutes); level 7 (316 items basic, 204 minutes; 539 items complete, 297 minutes); level 8 (345 items basic, 204 minutes; 613 items complete, 297 minutes); level 9 (302 items basic, 285 minutes; 457 items complete, 406 minutes); level 10 (334 items basic, 285 minutes; 503 items complete, 406 minutes); level 11 (357 items basic, 285 minutes; 538 items complete, 406 minutes); level 12 (376 items basic, 285 minutes; 560 items complete, 406 minutes); level 13 (385 items basic, 285 minutes; 581 items complete, 406 minutes); level 14 (390 items basic, 285 minutes; 591 items complete, 406 minutes). The Iowa Tests of Basic Skills, the Cognitive Abilities Test, and the Tests of Achievement and Proficiency were normed concurrently.

14692
Iowa Tests of Basic Skills, Forms G and H, Level 14. Hieronymus, A.N.; And Others 1986
Subtests: Vocabulary; Reading Comprehension; Spelling; Mathematics Concepts; Mathematics Problem Solving; Mathematics Computation; Capitalization; Punctuation; Usage and Expression; Visual Materials; Reference Materials; Writing; Listening; Social Studies; Science
Descriptors: *Achievement Tests; *Basic Skills; Capitalization (Alphabetic); Elementary School Mathematics; Elementary School Science; *Grade 8; *Grade 9; Grammar; Junior High Schools; *Junior High School Students; Listening Skills; Punctuation; Reading Comprehension; Social Studies; Spelling; Study Skills; Vocabulary; Writing Skills
Identifiers: Basic Skills Assessment Program; ITBS; Test Batteries
Availability: Riverside Publishing Co.; 8420 Bryn Mawr Ave., Chicago, IL 60631
Grade Level: 8-9

One of 3 test batteries that comprise the Basic Skills Assessment Program, a comprehensive, standardized testing program designed to assess student achievement and abilities. The Iowa Tests of Basic Skills (ITBS) were developed to assess student progress in the basic skills. Assesses readiness and achievement in the basic skills and content areas appropriate to the grade covered. Behavioral objectives to which test items at each level are written coordinate with those of state and local courses of study and instructional materials and methods. The early primary battery consists of 5 subtests at level 5 and 6 subtests at level 6. All level 5 and 6 tests, except reading, are untimed and are orally administered. Levels 7 and 8 of the primary battery and levels 9 through 14 of the multilevel edition are available in either a basic battery or a complete battery. The basic battery has fewer tests than the complete battery and is ideal for use when testing time is limited. For the multilevel edition, a supplementary social studies/science test booklet is also available. For levels 9-14, separate test booklets for each level are also available and each separate level booklet contains all 11 subtests of the complete battery plus the social studies and science tests. Optional writing and listening tests are also available for levels 9-14. The number of items for all subtests and time required to complete the batteries are level 5 (157 items, 125-170 minutes); level 6 (225 items, 125-170 minutes); level 7 (316 items basic, 204 minutes; 539 items complete, 297 minutes); level 8 (345 items basic, 204 minutes; 613 items complete, 297 minutes); level 9 (302 items basic, 285 minutes; 457 items complete, 406 minutes); level 10 (334 items basic, 285 minutes; 503 items complete, 406 minutes); level 11 (357 items basic, 285 minutes; 538 items complete, 406 minutes); level 12 (376 items basic, 285 minutes; 560 items complete, 406 minutes); level 13 (385 items basic, 285 minutes; 581 items complete, 406 minutes); level 14 (390 items basic, 285 minutes; 591 items complete, 406 minutes). The Iowa Tests of Basic Skills, the Cognitive Abilities Test, and the Tests of Achievement and Proficiency were normed concurrently.

14693
Iowa Tests of Basic Skills, Forms G and H, Level 13. Hieronymus, A.N.; And Others 1986
Subtests: Vocabulary; Reading Comprehension; Spelling; Mathematics Concepts; Mathematics Problem Solving; Mathematics Computation; Capitalization; Punctuation; Usage and Expression; Visual Materials; Reference Materials; Writing; Listening; Social Studies; Science
Descriptors: *Achievement Tests; *Basic Skills; Capitalization (Alphabetic); Elementary School Mathematics; Elementary School Science; *Grade 7; Grammar; Junior High Schools; *Junior High School Students; Listening Skills; Punctuation; Reading Comprehension; Social Studies; Spelling; Study Skills; Vocabulary; Writing Skills
Identifiers: Basic Skills Assessment Program; ITBS; Test Batteries
Availability: Riverside Publishing Co.; 8420 Bryn Mawr Ave., Chicago, IL 60631
Grade Level: 7

One of 3 test batteries that comprise the Basic Skills Assessment Program, a comprehensive, standardized testing program designed to assess student achievement and abilities. The Iowa Tests of Basic Skills (ITBS) were developed to assess student progress in the basic skills. Assesses readiness and achievement in the basic skills and content areas appropriate to the grade covered. Behavioral objectives to which test items at each level are written coordinate with those of state and local courses of study and instructional materials and methods. The early primary battery consists of 5 subtests at level 5 and 6 subtests at level 6. All level 5 and 6 tests, except reading, are untimed and are orally administered. Levels 7 and 8 of the primary battery and levels 9 through 14 of the multilevel edition are available in either a basic battery or a complete battery. The basic battery has fewer tests than the complete battery and is ideal for use when testing time is limited. For the multilevel edition, a supplementary social studies/ science test booklet is also available. For levels 9-14, separate test booklets for each level are also available and each separate level booklet contains all 11 subtests of the complete battery plus the social studies and science tests. Optional writing and listening tests are also available for levels 9-14. The number of items for all subtests and time required to complete the batteries are level 5 (157 items, 125-170 minutes); level 6 (225 items, 125-170 minutes); level 7 (316 items basic, 204 minutes; 539 items complete, 297 minutes); level 8 (345 items basic, 204 minutes; 613 items complete, 297 minutes); level 9 (302 items basic, 285 minutes; 457 items complete, 406 minutes); level 10 (334 items basic, 285 minutes; 503 items complete, 406 minutes); level 11 (357 items basic, 285 minutes; 538 items complete, 406 minutes); level 12 (376 items basic, 285 minutes; 560 items complete, 406 minutes); level 13 (385 items basic, 285 minutes; 581 items complete, 406 minutes); level 14 (390 items basic, 285 minutes; 591 items complete, 406 minutes). The Iowa Tests of Basic Skills, the Cognitive Abilities Test, and the Tests of Achievement and Proficiency were normed concurrently.

14694

Iowa Tests of Basic Skills, Forms G and H, Level 12. Hieronymus, A.N.; And Others 1986
Subtests: Vocabulary; Reading Comprehension; Spelling; Mathematics Concepts; Mathematics Problem Solving; Mathematics Computation; Capitalization; Punctuation; Usage and Expression; Visual Materials; Reference Materials; Writing; Listening; Social Studies; Science
Descriptors: *Achievement Tests; *Basic Skills; Capitalization (Alphabetic); Elementary School Mathematics; Elementary School Science; *Elementary School Students; *Grade 6; Grammar; Intermediate Grades; Listening Skills; Punctuation; Reading Comprehension; Social Studies; Spelling; Study Skills; Vocabulary; Writing Skills
Identifiers: Basic Skills Assessment Program; ITBS; Test Batteries
Availability: Riverside Publishing Co.; 8420 Bryn Mawr Ave., Chicago, IL 60631
Grade Level: 6

One of 3 test batteries that comprise the Basic Skills Assessment Program, a comprehensive, standardized testing program designed to assess student achievement and abilities. The Iowa Tests of Basic Skills (ITBS) were developed to assess student progress in the basic skills. Assesses readiness and achievement in the basic skills and content areas appropriate to the grade covered. Behavioral objectives to which test items at each level are written coordinate with those of state and local courses of study and instructional materials and methods. The early primary battery consists of 5 subtests at level 5 and 6 subtests at level 6. All level 5 and 6 tests, except reading, are untimed and are orally administered. Levels 7 and 8 of the primary battery and levels 9 through 14 of the multilevel edition are available in either a basic battery or a complete battery. The basic battery has fewer tests than the complete battery and is ideal for use when testing time is limited. For the multilevel edition, a supplementary social studies/ science test booklet is also available. For levels 9-14, separate test booklets for each level are also available and each separate level booklet contains all 11 subtests of the complete battery plus the social studies and science tests. Optional writing and listening tests are also available for levels 9-14. The number of items for all subtests and time required to complete the batteries are level 5 (157 items, 125-170 minutes); level 6 (225 items, 125-170 minutes); level 7 (316 items basic, 204 minutes; 539 items complete, 297 minutes); level 8 (345 items basic, 204 minutes; 613 items complete, 297 minutes); level 9 (302 items basic, 285 minutes; 457 items complete, 406 minutes); level 10 (334 items basic, 285 minutes; 503 items complete, 406 minutes); level 11 (357 items basic, 285 minutes; 538 items complete, 406 minutes); level 12 (376 items basic, 285 minutes; 560 items complete, 406 minutes); level 13 (385 items basic, 285 minutes; 581 items complete, 406 minutes); level 14 (390 items basic, 285 minutes; 591 items complete, 406 minutes). The Iowa Tests of Basic Skills, the Cognitive Abilities Test, and the Tests of Achievement and Proficiency were normed concurrently.

14695

Iowa Tests of Basic Skills, Forms G and H, Level 11. Hieronymus, A.N.; And Others 1986
Subtests: Vocabulary; Reading Comprehension; Spelling; Mathematics Concepts; Mathematics Problem Solving; Mathematics Computation; Capitalization; Punctuation; Usage and Expression; Visual Materials; Reference Materials; Writing; Listening; Social Studies; Science

Descriptors: *Achievement Tests; *Basic Skills; Capitalization (Alphabetic); Elementary School Mathematics; Elementary School Science; *Elementary School Students; *Grade 5; Grammar; Intermediate Grades; Listening Skills; Punctuation; Reading Comprehension; Social Studies; Spelling; Study Skills; Vocabulary; Writing Skills
Identifiers: Basic Skills Assessment Program; ITBS; Test Batteries
Availability: Riverside Publishing Co.; 8420 Bryn Mawr Ave., Chicago, IL 60631
Grade Level: 5

One of 3 test batteries that comprise the Basic Skills Assessment Program, a comprehensive, standardized testing program designed to assess student achievement and abilities. The Iowa Tests of Basic Skills (ITBS) were developed to assess student progress in the basic skills. Assesses readiness and achievement in the basic skills and content areas appropriate to the grade covered. Behavioral objectives to which test items at each level are written coordinate with those of state and local courses of study and instructional materials and methods. The early primary battery consists of 5 subtests at level 5 and 6 subtests at level 6. All level 5 and 6 tests, except reading, are untimed and are orally administered. Levels 7 and 8 of the primary battery and levels 9 through 14 of the multilevel edition are available in either a basic battery or a complete battery. The basic battery has fewer tests than the complete battery and is ideal for use when testing time is limited. For the multilevel edition, a supplementary social studies/ science test booklet is also available. For levels 9-14, separate test booklets for each level are also available and each separate level booklet contains all 11 subtests of the complete battery plus the social studies and science tests. Optional writing and listening tests are also available for levels 9-14. The number of items for all subtests and time required to complete the batteries are level 5 (157 items, 125-170 minutes); level 6 (225 items, 125-170 minutes); level 7 (316 items basic, 204 minutes; 539 items complete, 297 minutes); level 8 (345 items basic, 204 minutes; 613 items complete, 297 minutes); level 9 (302 items basic, 285 minutes; 457 items complete, 406 minutes); level 10 (334 items basic, 285 minutes; 503 items complete, 406 minutes); level 11 (357 items basic, 285 minutes; 538 items complete, 406 minutes); level 12 (376 items basic, 285 minutes; 560 items complete, 406 minutes); level 13 (385 items basic, 285 minutes; 581 items complete, 406 minutes); level 14 (390 items basic, 285 minutes; 591 items complete, 406 minutes). The Iowa Tests of Basic Skills, the Cognitive Abilities Test, and the Tests of Achievement and Proficiency were normed concurrently.

14696

Iowa Tests of Basic Skills, Forms G and H, Level 10. Hieronymus, A.N.; And Others 1986
Subtests: Vocabulary; Reading Comprehension; Spelling; Mathematics Concepts; Mathematics Problem Solving; Mathematics Computation; Capitalization; Punctuation; Usage and Expression; Visual Materials; Reference Materials; Writing; Listening; Social Studies; Science
Descriptors: *Achievement Tests; *Basic Skills; Capitalization (Alphabetic); Elementary Education; Elementary School Mathematics; Elementary School Science; *Elementary School Students; *Grade 4; Grammar; Intermediate Grades; Listening Skills; Punctuation; Reading Comprehension; Social Studies; Spelling; Study Skills; Vocabulary; Writing Skills
Identifiers: Basic Skills Assessment Program; ITBS; Oral Testing; Test Batteries
Availability: Riverside Publishing Co.; 8420 Bryn Mawr Ave., Chicago, IL 60631
Grade Level: 4

One of 3 test batteries that comprise the Basic Skills Assessment Program, a comprehensive, standardized testing program designed to assess student achievement and abilities. The Iowa Tests of Basic Skills (ITBS) were developed to assess student progress in the basic skills. Assesses readiness and achievement in the basic skills and content areas appropriate to the grade covered. Behavioral objectives to which test items at each level are written coordinate with those of state and local courses of study and instructional materials and methods. The early primary battery consists of 5 subtests at level 5 and 6 subtests at level 6. All level 5 and 6 tests, except reading, are untimed and are orally administered. Levels 7 and 8 of the primary battery and levels 9 through 14 of the multilevel edition are available in either a basic battery or a complete battery. The basic battery has fewer tests than the complete battery and is ideal for use when testing time is limited. For the multilevel edition, a supplementary social studies/ science test booklet is also available. For levels 9-14, separate test booklets for each level are also available and each separate level booklet contains all 11 subtests of the complete battery plus the social studies and science tests. Optional writing and listening tests are also available for levels 9-14. The number of items for all subtests and time required to complete the batteries are level 5 (157 items, 125-170 minutes); level 6 (225 items, 125-170 minutes); level 7 (316 items basic, 204 minutes; 539 items complete, 297 minutes); level 8 (345 items basic, 204 minutes; 613 items complete, 297 minutes); level 9 (302 items basic,

285 minutes; 457 items complete, 406 minutes); level 10 (334 items basic, 285 minutes; 503 items complete, 406 minutes); level 11 (357 items basic, 285 minutes; 538 items complete, 406 minutes); level 12 (376 items basic, 285 minutes; 560 items complete, 406 minutes); level 13 (385 items basic, 285 minutes; 581 items complete, 406 minutes); level 14 (390 items basic, 285 minutes; 591 items complete, 406 minutes). The Iowa Tests of Basic Skills, the Cognitive Abilities Test, and the Tests of Achievement and Proficiency were normed concurrently.

14697

Iowa Tests of Basic Skills, Forms G and H, Level 9. Hieronymus, A.N.; And Others 1986
Subtests: Vocabulary; Reading Comprehension; Spelling; Mathematics Concepts; Mathematics Problem Solving; Mathematics Computation; Capitalization; Punctuation; Usage and Expression; Visual Materials; Reference Materials; Writing; Listening; Social Studies; Science
Descriptors: *Achievement Tests; *Basic Skills; Capitalization (Alphabetic); Elementary Education; Elementary School Mathematics; Elementary School Science; *Elementary School Students; *Grade 3; Grammar; Listening Skills; Primary Education; Punctuation; Reading Comprehension; Social Studies; Spelling; Study Skills; Vocabulary; Writing Skills
Identifiers: Basic Skills Assessment Program; ITBS; Oral Testing; Test Batteries
Availability: Riverside Publishing Co.; 8420 Bryn Mawr Ave., Chicago, IL 60631
Grade Level: 3

One of 3 test batteries that comprise the Basic Skills Assessment Program, a comprehensive, standardized testing program designed to assess student achievement and abilities. The Iowa Tests of Basic Skills (ITBS) were developed to assess student progress in the basic skills. Assesses readiness and achievement in the basic skills and content areas appropriate to the grade covered. Behavioral objectives to which test items at each level are written coordinate with those of state and local courses of study and instructional materials and methods. The early primary battery consists of 5 subtests at level 5 and 6 subtests at level 6. All level 5 and 6 tests, except reading, are untimed and are orally administered. Levels 7 and 8 of the primary battery and levels 9 through 14 of the multilevel edition are available in either a basic battery or a complete battery. The basic battery has fewer tests than the complete battery and is ideal for use when testing time is limited. For the multilevel edition, a supplementary social studies/ science test booklet is also available. For levels 9-14, separate test booklets for each level are also available and each separate level booklet contains all 11 subtests of the complete battery plus the social studies and science tests. Optional writing and listening tests are also available for levels 9-14. The number of items for all subtests and time required to complete the batteries are level 5 (157 items, 125-170 minutes); level 6 (225 items, 125-170 minutes); level 7 (316 items basic, 204 minutes; 539 items complete, 297 minutes); level 8 (345 items basic, 204 minutes; 613 items complete, 297 minutes); level 9 (302 items basic, 285 minutes; 457 items complete, 406 minutes); level 10 (334 items basic, 285 minutes; 503 items complete, 406 minutes); level 11 (357 items basic, 285 minutes; 538 items complete, 406 minutes); level 12 (376 items basic, 285 minutes; 560 items complete, 406 minutes); level 13 (385 items basic, 285 minutes; 581 items complete, 406 minutes); level 14 (390 items basic, 285 minutes; 591 items complete, 406 minutes). The Iowa Tests of Basic Skills, the Cognitive Abilities Test, and the Tests of Achievement and Proficiency were normed concurrently.

14698

Iowa Tests of Basic Skills, Forms G and H, Level 8. Hieronymus, A.N.; And Others 1986
Subtests: Vocabulary; Word Analysis; Reading Comprehension; Spelling; Mathematics Concepts; Mathematics Problem Solving; Mathematics Computation; Listening; Capitalization; Punctuation; Usage and Expression; Visual Materials; Reference Materials
Descriptors: *Achievement Tests; *Basic Skills; Capitalization (Alphabetic); Elementary School Mathematics; Elementary School Students; *Grade 2; *Grade 3; Grammar; Listening Skills; *Primary Education; Punctuation; Reading Comprehension; Spelling; Study Skills; Vocabulary
Identifiers: Basic Skills Assessment Program; ITBS; Test Batteries
Availability: Riverside Publishing Co.; 8420 Bryn Mawr Ave., Chicago, IL 60631
Grade Level: 2-3

One of 3 test batteries that comprise the Basic Skills Assessment Program, a comprehensive, standardized testing program designed to assess student achievement and abilities. The Iowa Tests of Basic Skills (ITBS) were developed to assess student progress in the basic skills. Assesses readiness and achievement in the basic skills and content areas appropriate to the grade covered. Behavioral objectives to which test items at each level are written coordinate with those of state and local courses of study and instructional materials and methods. The early primary battery consists of 5 subtests at level 5 and 6 subtests at level 6. All level 5 and 6 tests, except reading, are untimed and are orally administered. Levels 7 and 8 of the primary battery and levels 9 through 14 of the multilevel edition are available in either a basic battery or a complete battery. The basic battery has fewer tests than the complete battery and is ideal for use when testing time is limited. For the multilevel edition, a supplementary social studies/ science test booklet is also available. For levels 9-14, separate test booklets for each level are also available and each separate level booklet contains all 11 subtests of the complete battery plus the social studies and science tests. Optional writing and listening tests are also available for levels 9-14. The number of items for all subtests and time required to complete the batteries are level 5 (157 items, 125-170 minutes); level 6 (225 items, 125-170 minutes); level 7 (316 items basic, 204 minutes; 539 items complete, 297 minutes); level 8 (345 items basic, 204 minutes; 613 items complete, 297 minutes); level 9 (302 items basic, 285 minutes; 457 items complete, 406 minutes); level 10 (334 items basic, 285 minutes; 503 items complete, 406 minutes); level 11 (357 items basic, 285 minutes; 538 items complete, 406 minutes); level 12 (376 items basic, 285 minutes; 560 items complete, 406 minutes); level 13 (385 items basic, 285 minutes; 581 items complete, 406 minutes); level 14 (390 items basic, 285 minutes; 591 items complete, 406 minutes). The Iowa Tests of Basic Skills, the Cognitive Abilities Test, and the Tests of Achievement and Proficiency were normed concurrently.

14699

Iowa Tests of Basic Skills, Forms G and H, Level 7. Hieronymus, A.N.; And Others 1986
Subtests: Vocabulary; Word Analysis; Reading Comprehension; Spelling; Mathematics Concepts; Mathematics Problem Solving; Mathematics Computation; Listening; Capitalization; Punctuation; Usage and Expression; Visual Materials; Reference Materials
Descriptors: *Achievement Tests; *Basic Skills; Capitalization (Alphabetic); Elementary School Mathematics; Elementary School Students; *Grade 1; *Grade 2; Grammar; Listening Skills; *Primary Education; Punctuation; Reading Comprehension; Spelling; Study Skills; Vocabulary
Identifiers: Basic Skills Assessment Program; ITBS; Test Batteries
Availability: Riverside Publishing Co.; 8420 Bryn Mawr Ave., Chicago, IL 60631
Grade Level: 1-2

One of 3 test batteries that comprise the Basic Skills Assessment Program, a comprehensive, standardized testing program designed to assess student achievement and abilities. The Iowa Tests of Basic Skills (ITBS) were developed to assess student progress in the basic skills. Assesses readiness and achievement in the basic skills and content areas appropriate to the grade covered. Behavioral objectives to which test items at each level are written coordinate with those of state and local courses of study and instructional materials and methods. The early primary battery consists of 5 subtests at level 5 and 6 subtests at level 6. All level 5 and 6 tests, except reading, are untimed and are orally administered. Levels 7 and 8 of the primary battery and levels 9 through 14 of the multilevel edition are available in either a basic battery or a complete battery. The basic battery has fewer tests than the complete battery and is ideal for use when testing time is limited. For the multilevel edition, a supplementary social studies/ science test booklet is also available. For levels 9-14, separate test booklets for each level are also available and each separate level booklet contains all 11 subtests of the complete battery plus the social studies and science tests. Optional writing and listening tests are also available for levels 9-14. The number of items for all subtests and time required to complete the batteries are level 5 (157 items, 125-170 minutes); level 6 (225 items, 125-170 minutes); level 7 (316 items basic, 204 minutes; 539 items complete, 297 minutes); level 8 (345 items basic, 204 minutes; 613 items complete, 297 minutes); level 9 (302 items basic, 285 minutes; 457 items complete, 406 minutes); level 10 (334 items basic, 285 minutes; 503 items complete, 406 minutes); level 11 (357 items basic, 285 minutes; 538 items complete, 406 minutes); level 12 (376 items basic, 285 minutes; 560 items complete, 406 minutes); level 13 (385 items basic, 285 minutes; 581 items complete, 406 minutes); level 14 (390 items basic, 285 minutes; 591 items complete, 406 minutes). The Iowa Tests of Basic Skills, the Cognitive Abilities Test, and the Tests of Achievement and Proficiency were normed concurrently.

14700

Iowa Tests of Basic Skills, Forms G and H, Level 6. Hieronymus, A.N.; And Others 1986
Subtests: Listening; Word Analysis; Vocabulary; Reading; Language; Mathematics
Descriptors: *Achievement Tests; *Basic Skills; Elementary School Mathematics; *Grade 1; *Kindergarten Children; Language Arts; Listening Skills; *Primary Education; Reading Skills; Vocabulary
Identifiers: Basic Skills Assessment Program; ITBS; Oral Testing; Test Batteries
Availability: Riverside Publishing Co.; 8420 Bryn Mawr Ave., Chicago, IL 60631

Grade Level: K-1
Notes: Time, 170 min. approx.; Items, 225

One of 3 test batteries that comprise the Basic Skills Assessment Program, a comprehensive, standardized testing program designed to assess student achievement and abilities. The Iowa Tests of Basic Skills (ITBS) were developed to assess student progress in the basic skills. Assesses readiness and achievement in the basic skills and content areas appropriate to the grade covered. Behavioral objectives to which test items at each level are written coordinate with those of state and local courses of study and instructional materials and methods. The early primary battery consists of 5 subtests at level 5 and 6 subtests at level 6. All level 5 and 6 tests, except reading, are untimed and are orally administered. Levels 7 and 8 of the primary battery and levels 9 through 14 of the multilevel edition are available in either a basic battery or a complete battery. The basic battery has fewer tests than the complete battery and is ideal for use when testing time is limited. For the multilevel edition, a supplementary social studies/ science test booklet is also available. For levels 9-14, separate test booklets for each level are also available and each separate level booklet contains all 11 subtests of the complete battery plus the social studies and science tests. Optional writing and listening tests are also available for levels 9-14. The number of items for all subtests and time required to complete the batteries are level 5 (157 items, 125-170 minutes); level 6 (225 items, 125-170 minutes); level 7 (316 items basic, 204 minutes; 539 items complete, 297 minutes); level 8 (345 items basic, 204 minutes; 613 items complete, 297 minutes); level 9 (302 items basic, 285 minutes; 457 items complete, 406 minutes); level 10 (334 items basic, 285 minutes; 503 items complete, 406 minutes); level 11 (357 items basic, 285 minutes; 538 items complete, 406 minutes); level 12 (376 items basic, 285 minutes; 560 items complete, 406 minutes); level 13 (385 items basic, 285 minutes; 581 items complete, 406 minutes); level 14 (390 items basic, 285 minutes; 591 items complete, 406 minutes). The Iowa Tests of Basic Skills, the Cognitive Abilities Test, and the Tests of Achievement and Proficiency were normed concurrently.

14701

Iowa Tests of Basic Skills, Forms G and H, Level 5. Hieronymus, A.N.; And Others 1986
Subtests: Listening; Word Analysis; Vocabulary; Language; Mathematics
Descriptors: *Achievement Tests; *Basic Skills; Elementary School Mathematics; *Grade 1; *Kindergarten Children; Language Arts; Listening Skills; *Primary Education; Reading Skills; Vocabulary
Identifiers: Basic Skills Assessment Program; ITBS; Oral Testing; Test Batteries
Availability: Riverside Publishing Co.; 8420 Bryn Mawr Ave., Chicago, IL 60631
Grade Level: K-1
Notes: Time, 170 min. approx.; Items, 157

One of 3 test batteries that comprise the Basic Skills Assessment Program, a comprehensive, standardized testing program designed to assess student achievement and abilities. The Iowa Tests of Basic Skills (ITBS) were developed to assess student progress in the basic skills. Assesses readiness and achievement in the basic skills and content areas appropriate to the grade covered. Behavioral objectives to which test items at each level are written coordinate with those of state and local courses of study and instructional materials and methods. The early primary battery consists of 5 subtests at level 5 and 6 subtests at level 6. All level 5 and 6 tests, except reading, are untimed and are orally administered. Levels 7 and 8 of the primary battery and levels 9 through 14 of the multilevel edition are available in either a basic battery or a complete battery. The basic battery has fewer tests than the complete battery and is ideal for use when testing time is limited. For the multilevel edition, a supplementary social studies/ science test booklet is also available. For levels 9-14, separate test booklets for each level are also available and each separate level booklet contains all 11 subtests of the complete battery plus the social studies and science tests. Optional writing and listening tests are also available for levels 9-14. The number of items for all subtests and time required to complete the batteries are level 5 (157 items, 125-170 minutes); level 6 (225 items, 125-170 minutes); level 7 (316 items basic, 204 minutes; 539 items complete, 297 minutes); level 8 (345 items basic, 204 minutes; 613 items complete, 297 minutes); level 9 (302 items basic, 285 minutes; 457 items complete, 406 minutes); level 10 (334 items basic, 285 minutes; 503 items complete, 406 minutes); level 11 (357 items basic, 285 minutes; 538 items complete, 406 minutes); level 12 (376 items basic, 285 minutes; 560 items complete, 406 minutes); level 13 (385 items basic, 285 minutes; 581 items complete, 406 minutes); level 14 (390 items basic, 285 minutes; 591 items complete, 406 minutes). The Iowa Tests of Basic Skills, the Cognitive Abilities Test, and the Tests of Achievement and Proficiency were normed concurrently.

14713

Quick Tests. Seven Hills Software, Tallahassee, FL
Descriptors: *Computer Software; Elementary Secondary Education; Higher Education; Item Banks; Teacher Made Tests; *Test Construction; Test Items

Availability: Seven Hills Software; 2310 Oxford Rd., Tallahassee, FL 32304
Grade Level: K-16

A software package for producing and editing tests. Accepts questions from true-false to essay. Allows for use of special symbols for math, sciences, and languages. Descriptive terms can be assigned to each question for retrieval through searching. Currently, it may be used with Apple IIc and IIe and IBM-PC.

14714

Obesity Knowledge Quiz. Price, James H.; And Others 1985
Descriptors: *Achievement Tests; Adults; *Knowledge Level; *Obesity
Availability: *Journal of School Health;* v55 n9 p382-84, Nov 1985
Age Level: Adults
Notes: Items, 12

Test developed to measure individual's obesity knowledge. The test was developed around the 4 aspects of obesity: etiology of obesity, diseases related to obesity, weight loss techniques, and general information on obesity.

14715

Diagnostic Achievement Test for Adolescents. Newcomer, Phyllis L.; Bryant, Brian R. 1986
Subtests: Word Identification; Reading Comprehension; Math Calculations; Math Problem Solving; Spelling; Writing Composition; Science; Social Studies; Reference Skills
Descriptors: *Academic Achievement; *Achievement Tests; Knowledge Level; Library Skills; Norm Referenced Tests; Reading Comprehension; Secondary Education; Secondary School Mathematics; Secondary School Science; *Secondary School Students; Sight Vocabulary; Social Studies; Spelling; Word Problems (Mathematics); Writing (Composition)
Identifiers: DATA
Availability: PRO-ED; 8700 Shoal Creek Blvd., Austin, TX 78758-6897
Grade Level: 7-12
Age Level: 13-18
Notes: Time, 120 min. approx.

Provides examiners with an estimate of a student's knowledge of information commonly taught in the schools. The test has 4 purposes: to identify students below their peers in the content areas of reading, writing, mathematics, science, social studies and reference skills; to identify individual students' strengths and weaknesses; to document students' progress as a result of intervention programs; and to use as a measurement tool in research studies.

14720

Standardized Reading Inventory. Newcomer, Phyllis L.
Descriptors: Criterion Referenced Tests; Elementary Education; *Elementary School Students; Informal Reading Inventories; Norm Referenced Tests; Oral Reading; *Reading Ability; Reading Comprehension; *Reading Tests; Silent Reading; Standardized Tests
Identifiers: SRI
Availability: PRO-ED; 8700 Shoal Creek Blvd., Austin, TX 78758-6897
Grade Level: 1-8
Notes: Time, 45 min. approx.

Instrument for evaluating students' reading ability. Designed like an informal reading inventory. There are 2 forms, each consisting of 10 graded passages, ranging from the lowest level, preprimer, to the highest level, eighth grade. Each passage consists of vocabulary extracted from 5 basal reading series and combined with other words to form a new word list for primary, intermediate, and advanced readers. Students are assessed on oral and silent reading and on reading comprehension. SRI is designed as a criterion-referenced test. However, it has also been standardized on a representative group of typical readers at each designated level.

14757

Advanced Russian Listening/Reading Proficiency Test. Educational Testing Service, Princeton, NJ 1986
Descriptors: *Achievement Tests; Adults; College Students; Graduate Students; Higher Education; *Language Proficiency; Listening Comprehension Tests; Pretests Posttests; Reading Tests; *Russian; *Second Language Learning
Availability: Russian Proficiency Test; Program Office P107, Educational Testing Service, Princeton, NJ 08541
Grade Level: 13-16
Age Level: Adults
Notes: Time, 100 min. approx.

Intended for use by recognized academic institutions and other language teaching programs, including those of government agencies, within the U.S. and overseas. Tests will serve needs of institutions in the following ways: determine whether graduates of bachelors or masters Russian language programs and area studies programs are proficient; establish whether prospective teaching assistants and secondary school teachers have required Russian listening/reading skills; help employers fill certain jobs requiring a particular proficiency level; assist with admission and placement in undergraduate and graduate programs; assess proficiency of students before and after a significant linguistic experience, such as study abroad; and monitor and evaluate the success of language teaching programs.

14765
Classroom Reading Inventory, Fifth Edition. Silvaroli, Nicholas J. 1986
Descriptors: Adults; Diagnostic Tests; Elementary School Students; Elementary Secondary Education; Individual Testing; *Informal Reading Inventories; Instructional Program Divisions; Listening Skills; Oral Reading; Paragraphs; *Reading Ability; Reading Comprehension; Secondary School Students; Word Lists; Word Recognition
Identifiers: Reading Level
Availability: Wm. C. Brown Publishers; 2460 Kerper Blvd., Dubuque, IA 52001
Grade Level: 1-12
Notes: Time, 12 min.

This test is an informal reading inventory, for individual administration, designed to identify a student's specific word recognition and comprehension skills and determine the student's independent, instructional, frustration, and listening capacity levels. Separate forms are available for grades 1-6 (Forms A and B), grades 7-9 (Form C), grades 10 through Adult level (Form D). Story content for upper levels is more mature. Forms A and B contain graded word lists, graded paragraphs, and a spelling survey. Forms C and D contain graded word lists and graded oral paragraphs.

14787
IDEA Oral Language Proficiency Test I, Form A. Ballard, Wanda S.; And Others 1982
Descriptors: *Diagnostic Tests; Elementary Education; *English (Second Language); *Language Proficiency; *Language Tests; Listening Comprehension; Morphology (Languages); *Oral English; Phonology; Pictorial Stimuli; Syntax; Vocabulary
Identifiers: IPT; Oral Testing
Availability: Ballard and Tighe; 480 Atlas St., Brea, CA 92621
Grade Level: K-6
Notes: Items, 83

This test was developed for use in determining students' levels of oral language proficiency and also for use as a diagnostic tool. It covers syntax, morphology, lexicon and phonology. It is organized by developmental or sequential levels of difficulty. For use with students whose primary language is other than English to determine adequacy of English Skills (comprehending and responding) prior to the introduction of reading skills. Verbal and visual stimuli were used. Normed in California.

14788
IDEA Oral Language Proficiency Test II—English, Form A. Dalton, Enrique F.; Amori, Beverly A. 1983
Descriptors: Articulation (Speech); Bilingual Students; Comprehension; English (Second Language); Expressive Language; Individual Testing; Language Proficiency; *Language Tests; *Oral Language; Receptive Language; Secondary Education; Spanish Speaking; Syntax; Vocabulary
Identifiers: IPT
Availability: Ballard and Tighe; 480 Atlas St., Brea, CA 92621
Grade Level: 7-12
Notes: Time, 15 min.; Items, 83

This individually administered proficiency test in English for nonnative English-speaking children tests 4 basic areas of oral proficiency: vocabulary, comprehension, syntax, and verbal expression including articulation. There are 6 levels of difficulty. The test taker advances by levels until the test is completed or stops at a proficiency level indicated by a score. The examiner should be bilingual in English and the language of the test taker.

14789
IDEA Oral Language Proficiency Test, Spanish. Dalton, Enrique F. 1980
Descriptors: Articulation (Speech); Bilingual Students; Comprehension; Elementary Education; Expressive Language; Individual Testing; Language Proficiency; *Language Tests; *Oral Language; Receptive Language; *Spanish; *Spanish Speaking; Syntax; Vocabulary
Identifiers: IPT
Availability: Ballard and Tighe; 480 Atlas St., Brea, CA 92621
Grade Level: K-6
Notes: Time, 14 min.; Items, 83

This individually administered proficiency test in Spanish for Spanish-speaking children tests 4 basic areas of oral proficiency: vocabulary, comprehension, syntax, and verbal expression including articulation. There are 6 levels of difficulty. The test taker advances by levels until the test is completed or stops at a proficiency level indicated by a score. Level A indicates that the testeee has less than 50 percent of the proficiency of level 1. Level F indicates mastery of the test. The examiner must speak Spanish.

14793
MAPS: College Entry Level Assessment. Educational Testing Service, Princeton, NJ
Subtests: English; Mathematics; Reading; Written English Expression; Computation; Applied Arithmetic; Elementary Algebra; Intermediate Algebra; Test of Standard Written English; Scholastic Aptitude Test; Biology; Chemistry; English Composition; French Reading; German Reading; Mathematics Level 1; Physics; Spanish Reading; Mathematics Level 2; Conventions of Written English; Critical Reasoning
Descriptors: Academic Aptitude; Achievement Tests; Algebra; Arithmetic; Biology; Chemistry; *College Admission; *College Students; Computation; *Counseling; Diagnostic Tests; *Educational Diagnosis; English; Equivalency Tests; French; German; Higher Education; Mathematics; Physics; Reading; Second Language Learning; Social Studies; Spanish; *Student Placement; Tests; United States History; Writing (Composition); Writing Skills
Identifiers: MAPS; Self Scoring Tests; Writing Sample
Availability: Multiple Assessment Program and Services of the College Board; Box 2869, Princeton, NJ 08541
Grade Level: 13-14

This series of tests is for use by colleges, for admissions, placement of students, remedial or developmental studies, exemption, guidance and counseling. Some of the tests are drawn from the national Admissions Testing Program, including the Test of Standard Written English, Scholastic Aptitude Test and Achievement Tests. Some are self-scoring (English, Mathematics).

14799
Bilingual Vocational Oral Proficiency Test. Melton Peninsula, Dallas, TX 1981
Descriptors: Adults; *Bilingualism; Bilingual Students; *Criterion Referenced Tests; *English (Second Language); Expressive Language; Language Proficiency; Oral Language; Pictorial Stimuli; Pretests Posttests; Receptive Language; *Vocational Education
Identifiers: BVOPT; Oral Testing
Availability: Melton Peninsula; 111 Leslie St., Dallas, TX 75207
Age Level: Adults
Notes: Time, 30 min.

This test is designed to determine the language needs of limited English-speaking applicants to vocational training programs and to determine how much English a trainee has learned during the training program. The test is criterion referenced and based on a study of actual language in the vocational setting. There are 2 parallel forms for pre- and posttesting. The test measures oral proficiency and consists of: questions and answers; an open-ended interview; elicited imitation (repetition); and imperatives (receptive language).

14800
Comprehensive English Language Test. Harris, David P.; Palmer, Leslie A. 1986
Subtests: Listening; Structure; Vocabulary
Descriptors: *Achievement Tests; Adolescents; Adults; *College Students; *English (Second Language); Expressive Language; Grammar; Higher Education; *High School Students; *Language Proficiency; Listening; Oral Language; Receptive Language; Secondary Education; Student Placement; Vocabulary
Identifiers: CELT; Oral Testing
Availability: Delta Systems; 570 Rock Rd. Drive, Unit H, Dundee, IL 60118
Grade Level: 9-16
Notes: Time, 135 min.

This test is designed to measure the English language proficiency of nonnative speakers. It is used with students in high school, college, or adult programs of English as a second or foreign language, at the intermediate and advanced levels. May be used for placement or measuring achievement. Covers the ability to comprehend short statements, questions and dialogues spoken by native speakers; manipulate grammatical structures in spoken English; understand lexical items in advanced English reading.

14802
Design Entry Test. Kamm, Karlyn; Otto, Wayne 1983
Subtests: Word Attack; Study Skills; Comprehension
Descriptors: Dictionaries; Graphs; High Schools; Instructional Program Divisions; Junior High Schools; Map Skills; Placement; *Postsecondary Education; *Reading; Reading Comprehension; *Remedial Programs; *Screening Tests; *Secondary School Students; Study Skills; Word Study Skills
Identifiers: Design Tests; Wisconsin Design Tests
Availability: Learning Multi-Systems; 340 Coyier Ln., Madison, WI 53713
Grade Level: 7-14
Notes: Items, 9

This test is designed for use with students having a reading level of grades 5 to 6. It is used as a screening instrument and provides a general overview of reading ability. Based on their performance, students then take Design Test I, intermediate (TC014803) or Design Test CS for Reading Placement: Test A for advanced students (TC014804). The tests are objective based and appropriate for junior high, high school, or postsecondary remediation programs. They cover skill in understanding: initial consonants, initial blends, long vowels, compound words, contractions, prefixes, synonyms/antonyms, context, indexes, dictionary use, graphs, tables of contents, sources, outlining, maps, similes, author's purpose for writing, conclusions, cause and effect, main idea, detail.

14803
Design Test I. Kamm, Karlyn; Otto, Wayne 1983
Subtests: Word Attack; Study Skills; Comprehension
Descriptors: *Diagnostic Tests; Dictionaries; High Schools; Instructional Program Divisions; Junior High Schools; Map Skills; *Postsecondary Education; *Reading; Reading Comprehension; *Remedial Programs; *Secondary School Students; Study Skills; Word Study Skills
Identifiers: Design Tests
Availability: Learning Multi-Systems; 340 Coyier Ln., Madison, WI 53713
Grade Level: 7-14
Notes: Items, 81

This test is designed for use with students having a reading level of grade 3, 4, or 5. It provides information about reading ability that is useful for remedial programs. A screening test (TC014802) places students at this level or an advanced level (TC014804). The tests are objective based. They cover skill in understanding: initial consonants, initial blends, long vowels, compound words, contractions, prefixes, synonyms/antonyms, context, indexes, dictionary use, graphs, tables of contents, sources, outlining, maps, similes, author's purpose for writing, conclusions, cause and effect, main idea, detail.

14804
The Design Tests for Reading Placement: Test A. Kamm, Karlyn; Otto, Wayne 1983
Subtests: Word Attack; Study Skills; Comprehension
Descriptors: *Diagnostic Tests; Dictionaries; High Schools; Instructional Program Divisions; Junior High Schools; Map Skills; *Postsecondary Education; *Reading; Reading Comprehension; *Remedial Programs; *Secondary School Students; Study Skills; Word Study Skills
Identifiers: Design Tests; Wisconsin Design Tests
Availability: Learning Multi-Systems; 340 Coyier Ln., Madison, WI 53713
Grade Level: 7-14
Notes: Items, 78

This test is designed for use with students having a reading level of grade 6, 7, or 8. It provides information about reading ability that is useful for remedial programs. A screening test (TC014802) places students at this advanced level or an intermediate level (TC014803). The tests are objective based. They cover skill in understanding: initial consonants, initial blends, long vowels, compound words, contractions, prefixes, synonyms/antonyms, context, indexes, dictionary use, graphs, tables of contents, sources, outlining, maps, similes, author's purpose for writing, conclusions, cause and effect, main idea, detail.

14811
Test de Vocabulario en Imagenes Peabody: Adaptacion Hispanomerica. Dunn, Lloyd M.; And Others 1986
Descriptors: *Academic Aptitude; *Achievement Tests; Adolescents; Bilingual Students; Children; Individual Testing; Mexicans; Nonverbal Tests; Pictorial Stimuli; Puerto Ricans; *Screening Tests; Second Languages; *Spanish; *Spanish Speaking; *Vocabulary
Identifiers: Oral Tests; Peabody Picture Vocabulary Test; PPVT, TVIP
Availability: American Guidance Service; Publishers' Bldg., Circle Pines, MN 55014-1796
Age Level: 2-18
Notes: Time, 15 min.; Items, 125

This measure of Spanish-hearing vocabulary is a version of the Peabody Picture Vocabulary Test developed for use with Spanish-speaking children and adolescents. It was standardized in Puerto Rico and Mexico. The manual is available in both Spanish and English. When it is used as an achievement test, it may be used to show student progress when Spanish is the language of instruction or when assessing proficiency in Spanish as a second language. It may be used as a screening test of scholastic aptitude when Spanish is the language of the home and community and when Spanish is the language of instruction. It is individually administered and does not require reading, verbal, or written responses. Also said to be useful for screening at the kindergarten and first grade level for follow-up assessment, to determine language of instruction for bilingual children. The examinee points to one of a series of plates in response to an oral stimulus. Norms for Hispanic children and youth on the U.S. mainland will be developed if examiners volunteer to test a group of these students.

14843
Bicycle Skills Test Manual. Highway Safety Research Center, North Carolina University, Chapel Hill, NC 1979
Descriptors: *Bicycling; *Elementary School Students; Elementary Secondary Education; *Performance Tests; *Safety Education; *Secondary School Students; *Traffic Safety
Availability: ERIC Document Reproduction Service; 7420 Fullerton Rd., Ste. 110, Springfield, VA 22153-2852 (ED255628, 70 p.)
Age Level: 6-16
Notes: Items, 25

This test is designed for use in programs promoting safety awareness and the mastery of basic riding skills among bicyclists. A written test, an oral test, and a skills performance test are included. The performance test requires that a course be laid out that includes such equipment as stop signs, paint, nails, etc. The written test has 25 true-false items and covers safety skills for riding in the street.

14848
Decoding Skills Test. Richardson, Ellis; Di Benedetto, Barbara 1985
Subtests: Basal Vocabulary; Phonic Patterns; Contextual Decoding
Descriptors: *Criterion Referenced Tests; *Decoding (Reading); *Diagnostic Tests; *Dyslexia; Elementary Education; *Elementary School Students; Oral Reading; Phonics; Reading Difficulties; *Reading Skills
Identifiers: DST; National Institute Child Health Human Development; National Institutes of Health
Availability: York Press; 2712 Mt. Carmel Rd., Parkton, MD 21120
Grade Level: 1-5
Notes: Time, 30 min. approx.

A diagnostic, criterion-referenced instrument that measures the abilities and progress of readers on the first to fifth grade levels. Assesses phonic pattern knowledge, phonic decoding deficiencies, the effects of word context, and oral fluency. Can be used with an individual child or an entire classroom. Useful for dyslexia research. Designed under contract with the National Institute of Child Health and Human Development/National Institutes of Health. Can be used to form groups and make program decisions, for formative evaluation, as part of a battery of psychoeducational tests, for formative and summative evaluation of a class or entire school, and in research on reading disorders.

14859
Goldman-Fristoe Test of Articulation, 1986 Edition. Goldman, Ronald; Fristoe, Macalyne 1986
Subtests: Sounds in Words; Sounds in Sentences; Stimulability
Descriptors: Adolescents; *Articulation (Speech); Children; Expressive Language; Phonemes; *Speech Tests; Young Children
Availability: American Guidance Service; Publishers' Bldg., Circle Pines, MN 55014-1796
Age Level: 2-16

Provides a means of assessing an individual's articulation of all the necessary phonemes and consonant sounds. Can be used by speech-language pathologists, audiologists, and educational specialists as a basis for remedial planning. Allows examiner to obtain samples of subjects' speech production under several conditions ranging from imitative to conversational speech. In the Sounds-in-Words subtest, the subject names pictures and the examiner records the child's articulation of the major speech sounds in the initial, medial, and final positions. In the Sounds-in-Sentences subtest, the child retells 2 stories read by the examiner, and the examiner records information about the articulatory skills used in connected speech. The Stimulability subtest provides information on the relative ease with which the child correctly articulates the sounds most difficult for him or her. Norms are based on a stratified national sample of children in grades 1 through 12. Additional norms for the Sounds-in-Words subtest for children ages 2 through 5 are based on the Khan-Lewis Phonological Analysis standardization in 1984 (TC014431).

14860
Test of Adolescent Language—2. Hammill, Donald D.; And Others 1987
Subtests: Listening/Vocabulary; Listening/Grammar; Speaking/Vocabulary; Speaking/Grammar; Reading/Vocabulary; Reading/Grammar; Writing/Vocabulary; Writing/Grammar
Descriptors: *Adolescents; Expressive Language; Individual Testing; *Language Acquisition; *Language Tests; Norm Referenced Tests; Receptive Language
Identifiers: TOAL2
Availability: PRO-ED; 8700 Shoal Creek Blvd., Austin, TX 78758-6897
Age Level: 12-18
Notes: Time, 105 min. approx.; Items, 240

A norm-referenced assessment instrument to examine the language development of adolescents. Test is based on a model of language development that has 3 dimensions: form (spoken or written language); features (semantics and syntax), and systems (expressive or receptive). TOAL-2 may be used for 4 purposes: to identify students significantly below their peers and who may profit from interventions to improve language proficiency; to determine areas of strength and weakness in language abilities; to document progress in language development as a result of intervention; and to serve as an assessment instrument in research studies which investigate language development of adolescents.

14865
Test of Economic Literacy, Second Edition, Forms A and B. Soper, John C.; Walstad, William B. 1986
Descriptors: *Achievement Tests; *Economics; Grade 11; Grade 12; High Schools; *High School Students
Identifiers: Joint Council on Economic Education
Availability: Joint Council on Economic Education; 2 Park Ave., New York, NY 10016
Grade Level: 11-12
Notes: Items, 46

A multiple-choice test which measures how well one understands the principles of economics and the way our economy operates. It is not necessary for the test taker to have taken a formal course in economics; it is assumed that most people have learned something about the subject in school, or through reading, listening to the radio, or watching television. Targeted for students in grades 11-12. Two equivalent test forms (A and B) are available.

14894
Kindergarten Screening Inventory. Milone, Michael N.; Lucas, Virginia H. 1980
Subtests: Naming and Matching Familiar Objects; Naming and Matching Money; Naming and Matching Basic Colors; Naming and Matching Shapes; Naming and Matching Sets; Naming and Matching Numerals; Naming and Matching Letters; Naming and Matching Words; Sequence Words and Ordinal Numbers; Sequencing Counting; Child Writes Own Name; Tracing Basic Strokes; Copying Basic Strokes; Tracing, Letters and Numerals; Copying Letter and Numerals
Descriptors: Cognitive Development; *Criterion Referenced Tests; *Curriculum Development; *Individual Development; Individual Testing; *Kindergarten Children; Learning Readiness; *Preschool Tests; Primary Education; Reading Readiness; *School Readiness Tests; Writing Readiness
Identifiers: KSI
Availability: Zaner-Bloser; 2200 West Fifth Ave., P.O. Box 16764, Columbus, OH 43216-6764
Grade Level: K
Age Level: 5-6

The KSI is a curriculum planner for the kindergarten teacher. It is an individually administered criterion-referenced instrument designed to identify educationally relevant differences in children beginning kindergarten. The KSI comprises skills that appear in the Zaner-Bloser Kindergarten Program, but it can serve as a prelude to almost any kindergarten program. The 23 skills that are assessed are those important to prereading, prewriting, and prearithmetic. Some examples include naming and matching objects, sequencing, counting, copying, and tracing. Scoring for each skill is based on a 6-point scale and yields a Pupil Skill Profile.

14897
Fullerton Language Test for Adolescents, Revised Edition. Thorum, Arden R. 1986
Subtests: Auditory Synthesis; Morphology Competency; Oral Commands; Convergent Production; Divergent Production; Syllabication; Grammatic Competency; Idioms
Descriptors: *Adolescents; *Expressive Language; Grammar; Idioms; Individual Testing; Language Handicaps; Language Processing; Language Proficiency; *Language Tests; Morphemes; Norm Referenced Tests; Phonemes; *Preadolescents; *Receptive Language; Screening Tests; Syllables
Availability: Consulting Psychologists Press, Inc.; 3803 E. Bayshore Rd., Palo Alto, CA 94303
Age Level: 11-18
Notes: Time, 45 min. approx.; Items, 142

Developed as a valid language assessment instrument to differentiate non-language-impaired from language-impaired adolescents. Consists of 8 subtests, each assessing a specific function important to the acquisition and use of language skills. Two of the subtests, oral commands and syllabication, assess receptive processing skills. The other 6 subtests assess expressive language production skills. The subtests do not have to be administered in any order, and the test does not have to be given in one administration.

14899
Quick-Score Achievement Test. Hammill, Donald D.; And Others 1987
Subtests: Reading; Writing; Arithmetic; Facts
Descriptors: *Achievement Tests; Computation; *Elementary School Students; Elementary Secondary Education; Knowledge Level; Mathematics Achievement; Norm Referenced Tests; Reading Achievement; *Secondary School Students; Word Recognition; Writing Skills
Identifiers: QSAT
Availability: PRO-ED; 8700 Shoal Creek Blvd., Austin, TX 78758-6897
Grade Level: 2-12
Age Level: 7-17
Notes: Time, 60 min. approx.; Items, 122

Designed to be a quick, reliable, and valid measure of school achievement for use with students from ages 7 through 17. There are 2 forms available. Test yields scores for 4 subtests and one composite score. The writing subtest primary skill assessed is mechanics. Calculation is the primary mathematics skill assessed. Word recognition is emphasized in the reading subtest, and the facts subtest measures basic school-taught facts. Test has 4 main uses: to determine strengths and weaknesses among academic achievement abilities, to identify students below their peers in academic achievement, to use in periodic reevaluations, and to use in research studies dealing with achievement.

14908
A Musical Test of Prosody. Rickert, William E. 1986
Descriptors: Higher Education; High Schools; Multiple Choice Tests; *Music; *Poetry; Singing
Availability: Communication Education; v35 n2 p169-74 Apr 1986
Grade Level: 9-16
Notes: Items, 15

A multiple-choice test that aids students in understanding the metrical structure of poems. A verse of a poem is given along with the titles of popular, traditional songs. The student is to determine which melody best fits the lines of poetry. Test is to be used for questioning, exploration, and discovery. Can also be used for discussion of why answers are right or wrong.

14919
Reading Evaluation Adult Diagnosis. Colvin, Ruth J.; Root, Jane H. 1982
Subtests: Sight Words; Word Analysis Skills; Reading/Listening Inventory
Descriptors: Adult Literacy; Adults; *Adult Students; *Diagnostic Tests; *Reading Diagnosis
Availability: Literacy Volunteers of America, Inc.; Widewaters One Office Bldg., 5795 Widewaters Pwy., Syracuse, NY 13214
Age Level: Adults

A series of pre- and posttests designed to assess adult students' reading needs and reading progress. Used to measure students' current knowledge prior to instruction and then at the end of instruction to determine what has been learned.

14934
DANTES Subject Standardized Tests: Technical Writing. Educational Testing Service, Princeton, NJ
Descriptors: *Achievement Tests; Adults; *Adult Students; *Equivalency Tests; Higher Education; Nontraditional Education; Nontraditional Students; Norm Referenced Tests; *Technical Writing
Identifiers: Defense Activity Non Traditional Education Support; DSST
Availability: Educational Testing Service; DANTES Program Office, Princeton, NJ 08541
Age Level: Adults
Notes: Time, 90 min. approx.; Items, 92

The DANTES program is a series of secured tests administered by postsecondary institutions to grant credit by examination for education gained outside the classroom.

Examinations may be worth from 2 to 6 credit hours in a baccalaureate program, baccalaureate upper division program, or a technical program. A minimum score for credit has been established by the American Council on Education. Individual institutions administer the examinations, as well as set the fees and schedules. These instruments complement the College Board's College Level Examination Program (CLEP) with several instruments in applied technology. They were originally developed for military personnel. Major areas of assessment include mathematics, social science, physical science, business, foreign language, and applied technology. For each test, a fact sheet containing the curriculum specifications of the course, a list of texts on which the test is based, and statistical information is available. Qualified administrators and faculty may borrow sample tests for a period of 30 days. This instrument is one of a series assessing knowledge in technical writing. Topics covered include theory and practice of technical writing, modes of technical writing, technical documents, parts of formal documents, organizing technical information, and technical editing. This form was normed in the spring of 1985 and has not been equated to previous forms.

14935
DANTES Subject Standardized Tests: Introduction to Computers with BASIC Programming. Educational Testing Service, Princeton, NJ
Descriptors: *Achievement Tests; Adults; *Adult Students; *Computers; Computer Software; Data Processing; *Equivalency Tests; Higher Education; Nontraditional Education; Nontraditional Students; Norm Referenced Tests; *Programing Languages; Systems Analysis
Identifiers: *BASIC Programming Language; Defense Activity Non Traditional Education Support; DSST
Availability: Educational Testing Service; DANTES Program Office, Princeton, NJ 08541
Age Level: Adults
Notes: Time, 90 min. approx.; Items, 80
The DANTES program is a series of secured tests administered by postsecondary institutions to grant credit by examination for education gained outside the classroom. Examinations may be worth from 2 to 6 credit hours in a baccalaureate program, baccalaureate upper division program, or a technical program. A minimum score for credit has been established by the American Council on Education. Individual institutions administer the examinations, as well as set the fees and schedules. These instruments complement the College Board's College Level Examination Program (CLEP) with several instruments in applied technology. They were originally developed for military personnel. Major areas of assessment include mathematics, social science, physical science, business, foreign language, and applied technology. For each test, a fact sheet containing the curriculum specifications of the course, a list of texts on which the test is based, and statistical information is available. Qualified administrators and faculty may borrow sample tests for a period of 30 days. This instrument is one of a series assessing knowledge in computers. Topics covered include hardware, history of computers, software, data management, systems analysis, data processing organization and careers, data communications, applications of computers, and trends and concerns related to computer usage. There is only one form of this test. Topics in BASIC include input/output commands, expressions, loops, conditionals, nested structures, string manipulation, array operations, transfer of control.

14937
DANTES Subject Standardized Tests: Personnel/ Human Resource Management. Educational Testing Service, Princeton, NJ 1985
Descriptors: *Achievement Tests; Adults; *Adult Students; *Equivalency Tests; Higher Education; *Labor Force Development; Nontraditional Education; Nontraditional Students; Norm Referenced Tests; *Personnel Management
Identifiers: Defense Activity Non Traditional Education Support; DSST; *Human Resources Administration
Availability: Educational Testing Service; DANTES Program Office, Princeton, NJ 08541
Age Level: Adults
Notes: Time, 90 min. approx.; Items, 93
The DANTES program is a series of secured tests administered by postsecondary institutions to grant credit by examination for education gained outside the classroom. Examinations may be worth from 2 to 6 credit hours in a baccalaureate program, baccalaureate upper division program, or a technical program. A minimum score for credit has been established by the American Council on Education. Individual institutions administer the examinations, as well as set the fees and schedules. These instruments complement the College Board's College Level Examination Program (CLEP) with several instruments in applied technology. They were originally developed for military personnel. Major areas of assessment include mathematics, social science, physical science, business, foreign language, and applied technology. For each test, a fact sheet containing the curriculum specifications of the course, a list of texts on which the test is based, and statistical information is available. Qualified administrators and faculty may

borrow sample tests for a period of 30 days. This instrument is one of a series assessing knowledge in personnel and human resource management. Topics covered include an overview of the field of personnel; employment; job analysis; training and development; performance appraisal; motivation, communication, and leadership styles; compensation; security; personnel legislation; labor relations; and current issues. This test was normed in the spring 1985 and has not been equated to previous forms.

14950
Comprehensive Occupational Exams: Advertising and Display Services, Master Employee Level. Marketing Education Resource Center, Inc., Columbus, OH 1986
Descriptors: Adults; *Advertising; Criterion Referenced Tests; *Item Banks; *Marketing; Merchandising; *Occupational Tests
Identifiers: IDECC
Availability: Marketing Education Resource Center; 1375 King Ave., P.O. Box 12226, Columbus, OH 43212-0226
Age Level: Adults
Notes: Items, 100
Designed to assess the marketing skills of midlevel employees involved in advertising and display services. Examples include salespersons, copywriters, buyers, or manufacturers' representatives. One of a series of competency-based instruments based on the curriculum developed by the Marketing Education Resource Center. Each instrument tests a different level, facet, or industry-specific knowledge of marketing principles. Descriptive test keys included with the test provide a rationale for each answer and are useful for review and remediation. Items used in this test have been randomly selected from the Resource Center test item bank.

14951
Comprehensive Occupational Exams: Common "Core" Competencies. Marketing Education Resource Center, Inc., Columbus, OH 1986
Descriptors: Adults; Criterion Referenced Tests; *Item Banks; *Marketing; *Occupational Tests
Identifiers: IDECC
Availability: Marketing Education Resource Center; 1375 King Ave., P.O. Box 12226, Columbus, OH 43212-0226
Age Level: Adults
Notes: Items, 100
Designed to assess students' knowledge of foundation or "common core" concepts of marketing theory. One of a series of competency-based instruments keyed to the curriculum developed by the Marketing Education Resource Center. Each instrument tests a different level, facet, or industry-specific knowledge of marketing principles. Descriptive test keys included with the test provide a rationale for each answer and are useful for review and remediation. Items used in this test have been randomly selected from the Resource Center test item bank.

14952
Comprehensive Occupational Exams: Finance and Credit Services, Master Employee Level. Marketing Education Resource Center, Inc., Columbus, OH 1986
Descriptors: Adults; Criterion Referenced Tests; *Finance Occupations; *Item Banks; *Marketing; *Occupational Tests
Identifiers: IDECC
Availability: Marketing Education Resource Center; 1375 King Ave., P.O. Box 12226, Columbus, OH 43212-0226
Age Level: Adults
Notes: Items, 100
Designed to assess the marketing skills of midlevel employees involved in finance and credit services. Examples include salespersons, copywriters, buyers, or manufacturers' representatives. One of a series of competency-based instruments based on the curriculum developed by the Marketing Education Resource Center. Each instrument tests a different level, facet, or industry-specific knowledge of marketing principles. Descriptive test keys included with the test provide a rationale for each answer and are useful for review and remediation. Items used in this test have been randomly selected from the Resource Center test item bank.

14954
Comprehensive Occupational Exams: Food Marketing, Supervisory Level. Marketing Education Resource Center, Inc., Columbus, OH 1986
Descriptors: Adults; Criterion Referenced Tests; *Food Service; Food Stores; *Item Banks; *Marketing; *Occupational Tests; *Supervisors
Identifiers: IDECC
Availability: Marketing Education Resource Center; 1375 King Ave., P.O. Box 12226, Columbus, OH 43212-0226
Age Level: Adults
Notes: Items, 100
Designed to assess the skills of supervisors in food marketing whose responsibilities include planning, coordinating, and supervising people and/or marketing-related ac-

tivities. One of a series of competency-based instruments based on the curriculum developed by the Marketing Education Resource Center. Each instrument tests a different level, facet, or industry-specific knowledge of marketing principles. Descriptive test keys included with the test provide a rationale for each answer and are useful for review and remediation. Items used in this test have been randomly selected from the Resource Center test item bank.

14961
Comprehensive Occupational Exams: Restaurant Marketing and Management, Master Employee Level. Marketing Education Resource Center, Inc., Columbus, OH 1986
Descriptors: Adults; Criterion Referenced Tests; *Dining Facilities; *Item Banks; *Marketing; *Occupational Tests
Identifiers: IDECC
Availability: Marketing Education Resource Center; 1375 King Ave., P.O. Box 12226, Columbus, OH 43212-0226
Age Level: Adults
Notes: Items, 100
Designed to assess the marketing skills of midlevel marketing employees involved in the restaurant industry. Examples include salespersons, copywriters, buyers, or manufacturer's representatives. One of a series of competency-based instruments based on the curriculum developed by the Marketing Education Resource Center. Each instrument tests a different level, facet, or industry-specific knowledge of marketing principles. Descriptive test keys included with the test provide a rationale for each answer and are useful for review and remediation. Items used in this test have been randomly selected from the Resource Center test item bank.

14962
Comprehensive Occupational Exams: Restaurant Marketing and Management, Supervisory Level. Marketing Education Resource Center, Inc., Columbus, OH 1986
Descriptors: Adults; Criterion Referenced Tests; *Dining Facilities; *Food Service; *Item Banks; *Marketing; *Occupational Tests
Identifiers: IDECC
Availability: Marketing Education Resource Center; 1375 King Ave., P.O. Box 12226, Columbus, OH 43212-0226
Age Level: Adults
Notes: Items, 100
Designed to assess the skills of marketing supervisors in the restaurant industry. One of a series of competency-based instruments based on the curriculum developed by the Marketing Education Resource Center. Each instrument tests a different level, facet, or industry-specific knowledge of marketing principles. Descriptive test keys included with the test provide a rationale for each answer and are useful for review and remediation. Items used in this test have been randomly selected from the Resource Center test item bank.

14963
Comprehensive Occupational Exams: Service Station Retailing, Master Employee Level. Marketing Education Resource Center, Inc., Columbus, OH 1986
Descriptors: Adults; Criterion Referenced Tests; *Item Banks; *Marketing; *Occupational Tests; *Retailing; Supervisors
Identifiers: Gas Stations; IDECC
Availability: Marketing Education Resource Center; 1375 King Ave., P.O. Box 12226, Columbus, OH 43212-0226
Age Level: Adults
Notes: Items, 100
Designed to assess the marketing skills of midlevel employees involved in automotive service station retailing. Examples include salespersons or manufacturers' representatives. One of a series of competency-based instruments based on the curriculum developed by the Marketing Education Resource Center. Each instrument tests a different level, facet, or industry-specific knowledge of marketing principles. Descriptive test keys included with the test provide a rationale for each answer and are useful for review and remediation. Items used in this test have been randomly selected from the Resource Center test item bank.

14964
Comprehensive Occupational Exams: Service Station Retailing, Supervisory Level. Marketing Education Resource Center, Inc., Columbus, OH 1986
Descriptors: Adults; Criterion Referenced Tests; *Item Banks; *Marketing; *Occupational Tests; *Retailing; Supervisors
Identifiers: Gas Stations; IDECC
Availability: Marketing Education Resource Center; 1375 King Ave., P.O. Box 12226, Columbus, OH 43212-0226
Age Level: Adults
Notes: Items, 100

Designed to assess the skills of marketing supervisors in automotive service station retailing whose responsibilities include planning, coordinating, and supervising people and/or marketing-related activities. One of a series of competency-based instruments based on the curriculum developed by the Marketing Education Resource Center. Each instrument tests a different level, facet, or industry-specific knowledge of marketing principles. Descriptive test keys included with the test provide a rationale for each answer and are useful for review and remediation. Items used in this test have been randomly selected from the Resource Center test item bank.

14971
Ohio Vocational Achievement Tests: Accounting/ Computing Clerk.   Ohio State Dept. of Education, Div. of Vocational Education, Columbus, OH 1987
Subtests: Purchases and Payables; Receipts and Payments; Specialized Accounting; Payroll Records; Sales and Receivables; Maintaining Files and Inventory Records; General Office Duties; Electronic Accounting Functions; Personal Development and Employment
Descriptors: *Accounting; *Achievement Tests; *Business Education; Clerical Occupations; *Data Processing; Employment Practices; Grade 11; Grade 12; High Schools; *High School Students; Payroll Records; Recordkeeping; *Vocational Education
Identifiers: Accounts Receivable Clerks
Availability: Ohio State University, Instructional Materials Laboratory; 1885 Neil Ave, Columbus, OH 43210
Grade Level: 11-12
Notes: Time, 240 min.
This test is part of a series of achievement tests for use in secondary schools offering vocational education. The tests cover Agricultural Education, Business and Office Education, Distributive Education, Health Occupations, Home Economics, Trade and Industrial Education. Each has approximately 300 items. The tests were developed to measure skills and understandings in specific vocational areas. Individual items measure ability to solve problems, analyze data, recall facts, have a knowledge of principles, react to generalizations, use abstractions in specific situations, and form parts into complete structures. Included in the administration of each test is the test of cognitive skills.

14972
Ohio Vocational Achievement Tests: Agricultural Business.   Ohio State Dept. of Education, Div. of Vocational Education, Columbus, OH 1987
Subtests: Retail Sales; Maintain Stock; Storage and Distribution; Marketing; Office Functions; Establish and Manage an Agribusiness; Agricultural Skills; Personal Development
Descriptors: *Achievement Tests; *Agribusiness; *Agricultural Education; Agricultural Occupations; Data Analysis; Grade 11; Grade 12; High Schools; *High School Students; Individual Development; Merchandising; Office Practice; Problem Solving; *Vocational Education
Availability: Ohio State University, Instructional Materials Laboratory; 1885 Neil Ave., Columbus, OH 43210
Grade Level: 11-12
Notes: Time, 240 min.
This test is part of a series of achievement tests for use in secondary schools offering vocational education. The tests cover Agricultural Education, Business and Office Education, Distributive Education, Health Occupations, Home Economics, Trade and Industrial Education. Each has approximately 300 items. The tests were developed to measure skills and understandings in specific vocational areas. Individual items measure ability to solve problems, analyze data, recall facts, have a knowledge of principles, react to generalizations, use abstractions in specific situations, and form parts into complete structures. Included in the administration of each test is the California Short Form Test of Academic Aptitude (TC005919-005923).

14973
Ohio Vocational Achievement Tests: Auto Body Mechanic.   Ohio State Dept. of Education, Div. of Vocational Education, Columbus, OH 1986
Subtests: Welding; Repair and Straighten, Patch and Fill; Panel Replacement; Fiberglass and Plastic Repair; Refinishing; Reconditioning; Trim, Hardware, and Glass; Frame and Unit Body Repair; Suspension Systems; Electrical Systems; Engine Cooling Systems; Heating and Air Conditioning; Personal Development and Shop Management
Descriptors: *Achievement Tests; Air Conditioning Equipment; *Auto Body Repairers; *Auto Mechanics; Electrical Systems; Glaziers; Grade 11; Grade 12; High Schools; *High School Students; *Vocational Education

Availability: Ohio State University, Instructional Materials Laboratory; 1885 Neil Ave., Columbus, OH 43210
Grade Level: 11-12
Notes: Time, 240 min.; Items, 300
This test is part of a series of achievement tests for use in secondary schools offering vocational education. The tests cover Agricultural Education, Business and Office Education, Distributive Education, Health Occupations, Home Economics, Trade and Industrial Education. Each has approximately 300 items. The tests were developed to measure skills and understandings in specific vocational areas. Individual items measure ability to solve problems, analyze data, recall facts, have a knowledge of principles, react to generalizations, use abstractions in specific situations, and form parts into complete structures. Included in the administration of each test is the California Short Form Test of Academic Aptitude (TC005919-005923).

14974
Ohio Vocational Achievement Tests: Automotive Mechanics.   Ohio State Dept. of Education, Div. of Vocational Education, Columbus, OH 1986
Subtests: Lubrication, Preventive Maintenance, and Shop Management; Service and Repair Engine; Service and Repair Cooling Systems; Service and Repair Fuel and Exhaust Systems; Service and Repair Ignition Systems; Personal Development; Service and Repair Cranking and Charging Systems; Accessory System; Transmissions and Drive Lines; Emission Systems; Brake Systems; Steering and Suspension Systems; Heating, Ventilation and Air Conditions Systems
Descriptors: *Achievement Tests; Air Conditioning Equipment; Auto Body Repairers; *Auto Mechanics; Electrical Systems; Engineers; Grade 11; Grade 12; Heating; High Schools; *High School Students; *Vocational Education
Availability: Ohio State University, Instructional Materials Laboratory; 1885 Neil Ave., Columbus, OH 43210
Grade Level: 11-12
Notes: Time, 240 min.; Items, 300
This test is part of a series of achievement tests for use in secondary schools offering vocational education. The tests cover Agricultural Education, Business and Office Education, Distributive Education, Health Occupations, Home Economics, Trade and Industrial Education. Each has approximately 300 items. The tests were developed to measure skills and understandings in specific vocational areas. Individual items measure ability to solve problems, analyze data, recall facts, have a knowledge of principles, react to generalizations, use abstractions in specific situations, and form parts into complete structures. Included in the administration of each test is the California Short Form Test of Academic Aptitude (TC005919-005923).

14975
Ohio Vocational Achievement Tests: Building Maintenance.   Ohio State Dept. of Education, Div. of Vocational Education, Columbus, OH 1986
Subtests: Carpentry; Masonry; Electrical; Heating/ Air Conditioning; Painting/Decorating; Plumbing; Welding; Flooring; Custodial; Grounds and Landscape; Personal Development
Descriptors: *Achievement Tests; Air Conditioning Equipment; Carpentry; Electricity; Grade 11; Grade 12; Heating; High Schools; *High School Students; Individual Development; Painting (Industrial Arts); Plumbing; Trade and Industrial Education; *Vocational Education; Welding
Availability: Ohio State University, Instructional Materials Laboratory; 1885 Neil Ave., Columbus, OH 43210
Grade Level: 11-12
Notes: Time, 240 min.
This test is part of a series of achievement tests for use in secondary schools offering vocational education. The tests cover Agricultural Education, Business and Office Education, Distributive Education, Health Occupations, Home Economics, Trade and Industrial Education. Each has approximately 300 items. The tests were developed to measure skills and understandings in specific vocational areas. Individual items measure ability to solve problems, analyze data, recall facts, have a knowledge of principles, react to generalizations, use abstractions in specific situations, and form parts into complete structures. Included in the administration of each test is the California Short Form Test of Academic Aptitude (TC005919-005923).

14976
Ohio Vocational Achievement Tests: Carpentry.
Ohio State Dept. of Education, Div. of Vocational Education, Columbus, OH
Subtests: Blueprint Reading; Surveying; Footers and Foundations; Floor Framing; Stairs; Wall and Ceiling Framing; Roof Framing; Roofing; Exterior Finish; Insulation; Interior Finish; Special Applications; Energy Efficient Construction; Personal Development

Descriptors: *Achievement Tests; Blueprints; *Building Trades; *Carpentry; Energy Conservation; Estimation (Mathematics); Flooring; Grade 11; Grade 12; High Schools; *High School Students; Roofing; *Trade and Industrial Education; *Vocational Education
Availability: Ohio State University, Instructional Materials Laboratory; 1885 Neil Ave., Columbus, OH 43210
Grade Level: 11-12
Notes: Time, 240 min.
This test is part of a series of achievement tests for use in secondary schools offering vocational education. The tests cover Agricultural Education, Business and Office Education, Distributive Education, Health Occupations, Home Economics, Trade and Industrial Education. Each has approximately 300 items. The tests were developed to measure skills and understandings in specific vocational areas. Individual items measure ability to solve problems, analyze data, recall facts, have a knowledge of principles, react to generalizations, use abstractions in specific situations, and form parts into complete structures. Included in the administration of each test is the California Short Form Test of Academic Aptitude (TC005919-005923).

14977
Ohio Vocational Achievement Tests: Child Care Services.   Ohio State Dept. of Education, Div. of Vocational Education, Columbus, OH 1986
Subtests: Assist in Managing the Center; Assist in Maintaining Facilities and Supplies; Aid in Program Planning; Conduct Routine Activities; Assist Infant/Toddler Instruction; Assist Preschool Instruction; Assist Elementary School Instruction; Assist Exceptional Children Instruction; Personal Development
Descriptors: *Achievement Tests; Administration; *Day Care; Disabilities; Elementary Schools; Grade 11; Grade 12; High Schools; *High School Students; Nursery Schools; Preschool Education; *Teacher Aides; *Vocational Education
Availability: Ohio State University, Instructional Materials Laboratory; 1885 Neil Ave., Columbus, OH 43210
Grade Level: 11-12
Notes: Time, 240 min.; Items, 300
This test is part of a series of achievement tests for use in secondary schools offering vocational education. The tests cover Agricultural Education, Business and Office Education, Distributive Education, Health Occupations, Home Economics, Trade and Industrial Education. Each has approximately 300 items. The tests were developed to measure skills and understandings in specific vocational areas. Individual items measure ability to solve problems, analyze data, recall facts, have a knowledge of principles, react to generalizations, use abstractions in specific situations, and form parts into complete structures. Included in the administration of each test is the California Short Form Test of Academic Aptitude (TC005919-005923).

14978
Ohio Vocational Achievement Tests: Commercial Art.   Ohio State Dept. of Education, Div. of Vocational Education, Columbus, OH 1987
Subtests: Illustration; Lettering; Layout; Photography; Specialized Functions; Business Functions; Design; Mechanical; Typography; Reproduction; Personal Development
Descriptors: *Achievement Tests; *Commercial Art; Design; Drafting; Engineering Drawing; Freehand Drawing; Grade 11; Grade 12; *Graphic Arts; High Schools; *High School Students; Layout (Publications); Photography; *Vocational Education
Availability: Ohio State University, Instructional Materials Laboratory; 1885 Neil Ave, Columbus, OH 43210
Grade Level: 11-12
Notes: Time, 240 min.
This test is part of a series of achievement tests for use in secondary schools offering vocational education. The tests cover Agricultural Education, Business and Office Education, Distributive Education, Health Occupations, Home Economics, Trade and Industrial Education. Each has approximately 300 items. The tests were developed to measure skills and understandings in specific vocational areas. Individual items measure ability to solve problems, analyze data, recall facts, have a knowledge of principles, react to generalizations, use abstractions in specific situations, and form parts into complete structures. Included in the administration of each test is the test of cognitive skills.

14979
Ohio Vocational Achievement Tests: Communication Products Electronics.   Ohio State Dept. of Education, Div. of Vocational Education, Columbus, OH 1983

Subtests: Personal Development; D.C. Electronics; A.C. Electronics; Active Electronic Devices; Electronic Circuitry; Electronic Test Equipment; Audio Systems; Radio Receiver Systems; T.V. Receiver Systems; Digital Electronic Circuits; Troubleshooting and Analysis; Special Systems; Digital Logic Systems
Descriptors: *Achievement Tests; Broadcast Reception Equipment; Electricity; *Electronics; Grade 11; Grade 12; High Schools; *High School Students; Television; *Trade and Industrial Education; *Vocational Education
Availability: Ohio State University, Instructional Materials Laboratory; 1885 Neil Ave., Columbus, OH 43210
Grade Level: 11-12
Notes: Time, 240 min.

This test is part of a series of achievement tests for use in secondary schools offering vocational education. The tests cover Agricultural Education, Business and Office Education, Distributive Education, Health Occupations, Home Economics, Trade and Industrial Education. Each has approximately 300 items. The tests were developed to measure skills and understandings in specific vocational areas. Individual items measure ability to solve problems, analyze data, recall facts, have a knowledge of principles, react to generalizations, use abstractions in specific situations, and form parts into complete structures. Included in the administration of each test is the California Short Form Test of Academic Aptitude (TC005919-005923).

14980
Ohio Vocational Achievement Tests: Construction Electricity. Ohio State Dept. of Education, Div. of Vocational Education, Columbus, OH 1984
Subtests: Basic Electricity; National Electric Code; Planning and Layout; Rough-In Wiring; Finish Wiring; Safety; Service Entrance; Motors and Controls; Low-Voltage Systems; Electrician's Mathematics; Personal Development
Descriptors: *Achievement Tests; *Building Trades; *Electricity; Electric Motors; Grade 11; Grade 12; High Schools; *High School Students; Mathematics; *Trade and Industrial Education; *Vocational Education
Availability: Ohio State University, Instructional Materials Laboratory; 1885 Neil Ave., Columbus, OH 43210
Grade Level: 11-12
Notes: Time, 240 min.

This test is part of a series of achievement tests for use in secondary schools offering vocational education. The tests cover Agricultural Education, Business and Office Education, Distributive Education, Health Occupations, Home Economics, Trade and Industrial Education. Each has approximately 300 items. The tests were developed to measure skills and understandings in specific vocational areas. Individual items measure ability to solve problems, analyze data, recall facts, have a knowledge of principles, react to generalizations, use abstractions in specific situations, and form parts into complete structures. Included in the administration of each test is the California Short Form Test of Academic Aptitude (TC005919-005923).

14981
Ohio Vocational Achievement Tests: Cosmetology. Ohio State Dept. of Education, Div. of Vocational Education, Columbus, OH 1987
Subtests: Manicuring; Facials and Skin Care; Hair Shaping; Hairstyling; Hair Color; Sanitation and Safety; Scalp Care; Permanent Waving; Shop Management and Customer Relations; Personal Development
Descriptors: *Achievement Tests; *Cosmetology; Grade 11; Grade 12; High Schools; *High School Students; Individual Development; Sanitation; *Service Occupations; *Vocational Education
Identifiers: Hairstyles
Availability: Ohio State University, Instructional Materials Laboratory; 1885 Neil Ave., Columbus, OH 43210
Grade Level: 11-12
Notes: Time, 240 min.

This test is part of a series of achievement tests for use in secondary schools offering vocational education. The tests cover Agricultural Education, Business and Office Education, Distributive Education, Health Occupations, Home Economics, Trade and Industrial Education. Each has approximately 300 items. The tests were developed to measure skills and understandings in specific vocational areas. Individual items measure ability to solve problems, analyze data, recall facts, have a knowledge of principles, react to generalizations, use abstractions in specific situations, and form parts into complete structures. Included in the administration of each test is the California Short Form Test of Academic Aptitude (TC005919-005923).

14983
Ohio Vocational Achievement Tests: Diversified Health Occupations. Ohio State Dept. of Education, Div. of Vocational Education, Columbus, OH 1985
Subtests: Anatomy and Physiology; Asepsis and Sterilization; Vital Signs; Acute Care Nursing; Ward Clerk; Emergency First Aid; Long Term Care Nursing; Home Health Aide; Medical Assisting and Laboratory; Dental Assisting; Personal Development, Employment Skills, and Ethics
Descriptors: *Achievement Tests; *Dental Assistants; Grade 11; Grade 12; *Health Occupations; High Schools; *High School Students; Laboratory Procedures; *Medical Assistants; Medical Services; Office Practice
Availability: Ohio State University, Instructional Materials Laboratory; 1885 Neil Ave., Columbus, OH 43210
Grade Level: 11-12
Notes: Time, 240 min.; Items, 300

This test is part of a series of achievement tests for use in secondary schools offering vocational education. The tests cover Agricultural Education, Business and Office Education, Distributive Education, Health Occupations, Home Economics, Trade and Industrial Education. Each has approximately 300 items. The tests were developed to measure skills and understandings in specific vocational areas. Individual items measure ability to solve problems, analyze data, recall facts, have a knowledge of principles, react to generalizations, use abstractions in specific situations, and form parts into complete structures. Included in the administration of each test is the California Short Form Test of Academic Aptitude (TC005919-005923).

14984
Ohio Vocational Achievement Tests: Drafting. Ohio State Dept. of Education, Div. of Vocational Education, Columbus, OH
Subtests: Geometric Shapes and Construction; Orthographic and Auxiliary Projection; Pictorial Drawings; Sectional Views; Production/Working Drawings; Fastening Methods; Industrial Materials and Processes; Dimensions and Tolerancing; Intersections and Developments; Mechanics; Architectural Drawings; Structural and Civil Drawings; Electrical and Electronic Drawings; Personal Development
Descriptors: *Achievement Tests; Architectural Drafting; *Commercial Art; *Drafting; Engineering Drawing; Grade 11; Grade 12; High Schools; *High School Students; Orthographic Projection; *Vocational Education
Availability: Ohio State University, Instructional Materials Laboratory; 1885 Neil Ave, Columbus, OH 43210
Grade Level: 11-12
Notes: Time, 240 min.

This test is part of a series of achievement tests for use in secondary schools offering vocational education. The tests cover Agricultural Education, Business and Office Education, Distributive Education, Health Occupations, Home Economics, Trade and Industrial Education. Each has approximately 300 items. The tests were developed to measure skills and understandings in specific vocational areas. Individual items measure ability to solve problems, analyze data, recall facts, have a knowledge of principles, react to generalizations, use abstractions in specific situations, and form parts into complete structures. Included in the administration of each test is the test of cognitive skills.

14985
Ohio Vocational Achievement Tests: Food Marketing. Ohio State Dept. of Education, Div. of Vocational Education, Columbus, OH 1987
Subtests: Receiving and Storing; Operations; Front-End Operations; Product and Service Technology; Selling; Advertising; Display/Merchandising; Communications; Human Relations; Economics, Marketing, and Entrepreneurship; Personal Development
Descriptors: *Achievement Tests; Advertising; Business Communication; *Distributive Education; *Food Service; Grade 11; Grade 12; High Schools; *High School Students; Marketing; Public Relations; *Vocational Education
Availability: Ohio State University, Instructional Materials Laboratory; 1885 Neil Ave., Columbus, OH 43210
Grade Level: 11-12
Notes: Time, 240 min.

This test is part of a series of achievement tests for use in secondary schools offering vocational education. The tests cover Agricultural Education, Business and Office Education, Distributive Education, Health Occupations, Home Economics, Trade and Industrial Education. Each has approximately 300 items. The tests were developed to measure skills and understandings in specific vocational areas. Individual items measure ability to solve problems, analyze data, recall facts, have a knowledge of principles,

react to generalizations, use abstractions in specific situations, and form parts into complete structures. Included in the administration of each test is the California Short Form Test of Academic Aptitude (TC005919-005923).

14986
Ohio Vocational Achievement Tests: Food Services. Ohio State Dept. of Education, Div. of Vocational Education, Columbus, OH 1987
Subtests: Cook/Chef; Sanitation and Safety; Dietary Aide; Pantry Worker; Steward Worker; Baker; Front of the House; Caterer; Management and Supervision; Personal Development
Descriptors: *Achievement Tests; Administration; Bakery Industry; Dining Facilities; *Food Service; Grade 11; Grade 12; High Schools; *High School Students; *Vocational Education
Availability: Ohio State University, Instructional Materials Laboratory; 1885 Neil Ave., Columbus, OH 43210
Grade Level: 11-12
Notes: Time, 240 min.

This test is part of a series of achievement tests for use in secondary schools offering vocational education. The tests cover Agricultural Education, Business and Office Education, Distributive Education, Health Occupations, Home Economics, Trade and Industrial Education. Each has approximately 300 items. The tests were developed to measure skills and understandings in specific vocational areas. Individual items measure ability to solve problems, analyze data, recall facts, have a knowledge of principles, react to generalizations, use abstractions in specific situations, and form parts into complete structures. Included in the administration of each test is the California Short Form Test of Academic Aptitude (TC005919-005923).

14987
Ohio Vocational Achievement Tests: General Merchandise Retailing. Ohio State Dept. of Education, Div. of Vocational Education, Columbus, OH 1987
Subtests: Selling; Cashiering; Store Security; Housekeeping and Safety; Human Relations; Merchandise Display; Receiving, Stocking, Inventory Control; Marketing; Personal Development
Descriptors: *Achievement Tests; Grade 11; Grade 12; High Schools; *High School Students; Human Relations; Individual Development; Marketing; Merchandising; Safety; *Sales Occupations; *Vocational Education
Availability: Ohio State University, Instructional Materials Laboratory; 1885 Neil Ave., Columbus, OH 43210
Grade Level: 11-12
Notes: Time, 240 min.

This test is part of a series of achievement tests for use in secondary schools offering vocational education. The tests cover Agricultural Education, Business and Office Education, Distributive Education, Health Occupations, Home Economics, Trade and Industrial Education. Each has approximately 300 items. The tests were developed to measure skills and understandings in specific vocational areas. Individual items measure ability to solve problems, analyze data, recall facts, have a knowledge of principles, react to generalizations, use abstractions in specific situations, and form parts into complete structures. Included in the administration of each test is the California Short Form Test of Academic Aptitude (TC005919-005923).

14989
Ohio Vocational Achievement Tests: Heating, Air Conditioning, Refrigeration. Ohio State Dept. of Education, Div. of Vocational Education, Columbus, OH 1986
Subtests: Install Heating Systems; Install Refrigeration and Air Conditioning Equipment; Troubleshoot Refrigeration and Air Conditioning Equipment; Service and Repair Refrigeration and Air Conditioning Equipment-Electrical; Service and Repair Refrigeration and Air Conditioning Equipment-Mechanical; Troubleshoot, Service, and Repair Oil Heating Systems; Troubleshoot, Service, and Repair Gas Heating Systems; Troubleshoot, Service, and Repair Alternate Heating Systems; Personal Development
Descriptors: *Achievement Tests; *Air Conditioning; *Building Trades; Equipment Maintenance; Grade 11; Grade 12; *Heating; High Schools; *High School Students; Individual Development; *Refrigeration; Repair; *Trade and Industrial Education; *Vocational Education
Availability: Ohio State University, Instructional Materials Laboratory; 1885 Neil Ave., Columbus, OH 43210
Grade Level: 11-12
Notes: Time, 240 min.

This test is part of a series of achievement tests for use in secondary schools offering vocational education. The tests cover Agricultural Education, Business and Office Education, Distributive Education, Health Occupations, Home Economics, Trade and Industrial Education. Each has approximately 300 items. The tests were developed to measure skills and understandings in specific vocational areas. Individual items measure ability to solve problems, analyze data, recall facts, have a knowledge of principles, react to generalizations, use abstractions in specific situations, and form parts into complete structures. Included in the administration of each test is the California Short Form Test of Academic Aptitude (TC005919-005923).

14990
Ohio Vocational Achievement Tests: Horticulture.
Ohio State Dept. of Education, Div. of Vocational Education, Columbus, OH 1986
Subtests: Soil and Plant Science; Greenhouse Operations; Interior Plantscape Services; Landscape Services; Turf Services; Retail Floriculture; Nursery; Garden Center; Fruit and Vegetable Production; Equipment and Mechanics; Personal Development
Descriptors: *Achievement Tests; *Agricultural Education; Agricultural Machinery; Agricultural Production; Floriculture; Grade 11; Grade 12; High Schools; *High School Students; *Horticulture; Individual Development; Landscaping; Nurseries (Horticulture); Retailing; Soil Science; Turf Management; *Vocational Education
Availability: Ohio State University, Instructional Materials Laboratory; 1885 Neil Ave., Columbus, OH 43210
Grade Level: 11-12
Notes: Time, 240 min.
This test is part of a series of achievement tests for use in secondary schools offering vocational education. The tests cover Agricultural Education, Business and Office Education, Distributive Education, Health Occupations, Home Economics, Trade and Industrial Education. Each has approximately 300 items. The tests were developed to measure skills and understandings in specific vocational areas. Individual items measure ability to solve problems, analyze data, recall facts, have a knowledge of principles, react to generalizations, use abstractions in specific situations, and form parts into complete structures. Included in the administration of each test is the California Short Form Test of Academic Aptitude (TC005919-005923).

14991
Ohio Vocational Achievement Tests: Industrial Electronics. Ohio State Dept. of Education, Div. of Vocational Education, Columbus, OH 1983
Subtests: Personal Development; Selling, Installing, and Testing Equipment; Fabricate Circuits and Enclosures; DC Electronics; AC Electronics; Semiconductors; Test Equipment; Analog Electronic Circuits; Digital Logic; Digital Electronic Circuits; Troubleshooting and Analysis; Special Electronic Devices; Electromechanical Devices
Descriptors: *Achievement Tests; Electricity; *Electronics; Grade 11; Grade 12; High Schools; *High School Students; Semiconductor Devices; *Trade and Industrial Education; *Vocational Education; Welding
Availability: Ohio State University, Instructional Materials Laboratory; 1885 Neil Ave., Columbus, OH 43210
Grade Level: 11-12
Notes: Time, 240 min.
This test is part of a series of achievement tests for use in secondary schools offering vocational education. The tests cover Agricultural Education, Business and Office Education, Distributive Education, Health Occupations, Home Economics, Trade and Industrial Education. Each has approximately 300 items. The tests were developed to measure skills and understandings in specific vocational areas. Individual items measure ability to solve problems, analyze data, recall facts, have a knowledge of principles, react to generalizations, use abstractions in specific situations, and form parts into complete structures. Included in the administration of each test is the California Short Form Test of Academic Aptitude (TC005919-005923).

14992
Ohio Vocational Achievement Tests: Lithographic Printing. Ohio State Dept. of Education, Div. of Vocational Education, Columbus, OH 1985
Subtests: Layout and Design; Composing; Proofing; Paste-up; Camera and Film Processing; Personal Development; Stripping; Platemaking and Proofs; Offset Presses; Finishing Operations
Descriptors: *Achievement Tests; Design; Grade 11; Grade 12; *Graphic Arts; High Schools; *High School Students; Layout (Publications); Photographic Equipment; Printing; *Vocational Education
Availability: Ohio State University, Instructional Materials Laboratory; 1885 Neil Ave., Columbus, OH 43210
Grade Level: 11-12
Notes: Time, 240 min.; Items, 300

This test is part of a series of achievement tests for use in secondary schools offering vocational education. The tests cover Agricultural Education, Business and Office Education, Distributive Education, Health Occupations, Home Economics, Trade and Industrial Education. Each has approximately 300 items. The tests were developed to measure skills and understandings in specific vocational areas. Individual items measure ability to solve problems, analyze data, recall facts, have a knowledge of principles, react to generalizations, use abstractions in specific situations, and form parts into complete structures. Included in the administration of each test is the California Short Form Test of Academic Aptitude (TC005919-005923).

14993
Ohio Vocational Achievement Tests: Machine Trades. Ohio State Dept. of Education, Div. of Vocational Education, Columbus, OH 1986
Subtests: Benchwork; Inspection and Measuring Instruments; Drilling Machines; Turning Machines; Sawings and Special Operations; Layout and Blueprint; Milling; Abrasive Machining; Heat Treating and Applied Science; N.C./C.N.C; Personal Development
Descriptors: *Achievement Tests; Blueprints; Grade 11; Grade 12; High Schools; *High School Students; *Machine Tool Operators; Machine Tools; Mathematical Applications; *Metal Working; *Trade and Industrial Education; *Vocational Education
Availability: Ohio State University, Instructional Materials Laboratory; 1885 Neil Ave., Columbus, OH 43210
Grade Level: 11-12
Notes: Time, 240 min.
This test is part of a series of achievement tests for use in secondary schools offering vocational education. The tests cover Agricultural Education, Business and Office Education, Distributive Education, Health Occupations, Home Economics, Trade and Industrial Education. Each has approximately 300 items. The tests were developed to measure skills and understandings in specific vocational areas. Individual items measure ability to solve problems, analyze data, recall facts, have a knowledge of principles, react to generalizations, use abstractions in specific situations, and form parts into complete structures. Included in the administration of each test is the California Short Form Test of Academic Aptitude (TC005919-005923).

14994
Ohio Vocational Achievement Tests: Medical Assistant. Ohio State Dept. of Education, Div. of Vocational Education, Columbus, OH 1984
Subtests: Personal Development; Body Systems; Clinical Skills; Medications; Medical Office Skills; Sterilization; Laboratory Skills; E.K.G.; X-ray; Diet and Nutrition; First Aid; Medical Terminology; Medical Office Computations
Descriptors: *Achievement Tests; First Aid; Grade 11; Grade 12; *Health Occupations; High Schools; *High School Students; Laboratory Procedures; *Medical Assistants; Medical Vocabulary; Nutrition; Office Practice; *Vocational Education
Availability: Ohio State University, Instructional Materials Laboratory; 1885 Neil Ave., Columbus, OH 43210
Grade Level: 11-12
Notes: Time, 240 min.
This test is part of a series of achievement tests for use in secondary schools offering vocational education. The tests cover Agricultural Education, Business and Office Education, Distributive Education, Health Occupations, Home Economics, Trade and Industrial Education. Each has approximately 300 items. The tests were developed to measure skills and understandings in specific vocational areas. Individual items measure ability to solve problems, analyze data, recall facts, have a knowledge of principles, react to generalizations, use abstractions in specific situations, and form parts into complete structures. Included in the administration of each test is the California Short Form Test of Academic Aptitude (TC005919-005923).

14995
Ohio Vocational Achievement Tests: Welding.
Ohio State Dept. of Education, Div. of Vocational Education, Columbus, OH 1987
Subtests: Oxyfuel Welding; Shielded Metal Arc Welding; Fabrication and Assembly; Personal Development; Gas Tungsten Arc Welding; Gas Metal Arc Welding; Specialized Welding Process (Resistance, Plasma, and Submerged Arc)
Descriptors: *Achievement Tests; Blueprints; Grade 11; Grade 12; High Schools; *High School Students; Machine Tool Operators; *Metal Working; *Trade and Industrial Education; *Vocational Education; *Welding
Availability: Ohio State University, Instructional Materials Laboratory; 1885 Neil Ave., Columbus, OH 43210
Grade Level: 11-12
Notes: Time, 240 min.

This test is part of a series of achievement tests for use in secondary schools offering vocational education. The tests cover Agricultural Education, Business and Office Education, Distributive Education, Health Occupations, Home Economics, Trade and Industrial Education. Each has approximately 300 items. The tests were developed to measure skills and understandings in specific vocational areas. Individual items measure ability to solve problems, analyze data, recall facts, have a knowledge of principles, react to generalizations, use abstractions in specific situations, and form parts into complete structures. Included in the administration of each test is the California Short Form Test of Academic Aptitude (TC005919-005923).

14999
Advanced Placement Program: Computer Science.
Educational Testing Service, Princeton, NJ 1988
Descriptors: *Advanced Placement Programs; *Computer Science; *Equivalency Tests; Essay Tests; High Schools; *High School Students; Multiple Choice Tests; *Programing
Identifiers: Advanced Placement Examinations (CEEB); APP; *PASCAL
Availability: Advanced Placement Program; Box 977PD, Princeton, NJ 08541
Grade Level: 10-12
Notes: Time, 180 min.

Designed to assess achievement in computer science. It is a 2-part test designed to cover a full year's work in computer science. It covers content of 2 courses: computer science A, which assesses programing methodology, and computer science AB, which assesses programing methodology, data structures, and analysis of algorithms. The content based on course AB covers the equivalent of a full year's course in computer science; the content of course A covers about one semester's work in an introductory computer science course. Candidates who elect to take the full format will receive a second grade for the content of course AB. All candidates will receive a grade for the content covered by course A. Programing language used in the test is currently Pascal. The Advanced Placement Program has been sponsored by the College Board since 1955.

15000
Facts on Aging Quiz. Palmore, Erdman 1977
Descriptors: Adults; *Aging (Individuals); *Knowledge Level; *Older Adults; Social Bias
Identifiers: FAQ
Availability: The Gerontologist; v17 n4 p315-20, 1977
Age Level: Adults
Notes: Time, 5 min. approx.; Items, 25

Short test confined to factual statements on aging that can be documented by empirical research. It is designed to cover the basic physical, mental, and social facts and the most common misconceptions about aging. Quiz may be used to stimulate discussion, to compare different groups' levels of information about aging, to identify the most frequent misconceptions about aging, or as an indirect measure of bias toward the aged. Also available in Palmore, Erdman B. *The Facts on Aging Quiz: A Handbook of Uses and Results.* New York: Springer Publishing Company, 1988.

15007
American History Map Test Folio. 1970
Descriptors: *Achievement Tests; *Intermediate Grades; *Maps; *Secondary Education; *Secondary School Students; *United States History
Availability: Perfection Forum Co.; 1000 N. Second Ave., Logan, IA 51546
Grade Level: 4-12
Notes: Items, 21

A collection of American history map tests covering the time period of precolonization through the Korean War. Each map test has a slightly different format, but, generally, the student is requested to label or locate places or events.

15013
American Literature Test Series: 1800-1899.
Perfection Form Co., Logan, IA 1986
Subtests: The Adventures of Tom Sawyer; Billy Budd; The Courtship of Miles Standish; The House of the Seven Gables; The Last of the Mohicans; Moby Dick; The Prince and the Pauper; Pudd'nhead Wilson; The Red Badge of Courage; Uncle Tom's Cabin
Descriptors: *Achievement Tests; High Schools; *High School Students; Nineteenth Century Literature; *United States Literature
Availability: Perfection Form Co.; 1000 N. Second Ave., Logan, IA 51546
Grade Level: 9-12
Notes: Items, 50

The test series for 1800-1899 consists of 10, 50-question, reproducible tests. Each test contains matching-type questions on identification of characters, multiple-choice questions on story content, and true-false questions on story content. Other test series are available for years covering 1900-40 (TC015014), 1961-present (TC015015).

15014
American Literature Test Series: 1900-1940.
Perfection Form Co., Logan, IA 1986
Subtests: Babbitt; Ethan Frome; A Farewell to Arms; Gone with the Wind; The Grapes of Wrath; The Great Gatsby; My Antonia; of Mice and Men; The Sea Wolf; The Yearling
Descriptors: *Achievement Tests; High Schools; *High School Students; Twentieth Century Literature; *United States Literature
Availability: Perfection Form Co.; 1000 N. Second Ave., Logan, IA 51546
Grade Level: 9-12
Notes: Items, 50

The test series for 1900-40 consists of 10, 50-question, reproducible tests. Each test contains matching-type questions on identification of characters, multiple-choice questions on story content, and true-false questions on story content. Other test series are available for years covering 1800-99 (TC015013), 1961-present (TC015015).

15015
American Literature Test Series: 1961-Present.
Perfection Form Co., Logan, IA 1986
Subtests: Bless the Beasts and Children; The Chocolate War; A Day No Pigs Would Die; Durango Street; The Learning Tree; My Darling, My Hamburger; Ordinary People; The Outsiders; A Separate Peace; To Kill a Mockingbird
Descriptors: *Achievement Tests; High Schools; *High School Students; Twentieth Century Literature; *United States Literature
Availability: Perfection Form Co.; 1000 N. Second Ave., Logan, IA 51546
Grade Level: 9-12
Notes: Items, 50

The test series for 1961-present consists of 10, 50-question, reproducible tests. Each test contains matching-type questions on identification of characters, multiple-choice questions on story content, and true-false questions on story content. Other test series are available for years covering 1800-99 (TC015013), 1900-40 (TC015014).

15016
Adult Basic Learning Examination, Level 1, Second Edition. Karlsen, Bjorn; Gardner, Eric F. 1986
Subtests: Vocabulary; Reading Comprehension; Spelling; Number Operations; Problem Solving
Descriptors: *Achievement Tests; *Adult Basic Education; *Adult Education; *Adult Students; *Basic Skills; Language Arts; Mathematics Achievement; Reading Achievement
Identifiers: ABLE
Availability: Psychological Corp.; 555 Academic Ct., San Antonio, TX 78024-0952
Age Level: Adults
Notes: Time, 130 min.; Items, 142

Battery of tests measuring the level of educational achievement among adults. Determines general educational level of adults who have not completed 12 years of schooling and evaluates efforts to raise the educational level of these adults. Has adult-oriented content and a nonthreatening format. Covers basic skills in reading, mathematics, and the language arts. Easy to administer. No single subtest requires more than 35 minutes. Content of ABLE, second edition, is totally new. The 3 levels were developed to accommodate meaningful segments of 12 years of schooling. The grade designation of each level refers to the achievement level that can be assessed most readily. At each level, 2 forms are available, Form E and Form F, which are parallel in content and difficulty. Two forms are to be used when reevaluation or periodic testing is desired. SelectABLE is a screening device to determine which level is most suitable for a particular individual if prior educational information is not available. Level 1 is for adults who have had 1 to 4 years of formal education (the primary grades). Many subtests are dictated to allow assessment of adults who do not have the necessary reading skills.

15017
Adult Basic Learning Examination, Level 2, Second Edition. Karlsen, Bjorn; Gardner, Eric F. 1986
Subtests: Vocabulary; Reading Comprehension; Spelling; Number Operations; Problem Solving; Applied Grammar; Capitalization and Punctuation
Descriptors: *Achievement Tests; *Adult Basic Education; *Adult Education; *Adult Students; *Basic Skills; Language Arts; Mathematics Achievement; Reading Achievement
Identifiers: ABLE
Availability: Psychological Corp.; 555 Academic Ct., San Antonio, TX 78024-0952
Age Level: Adults
Notes: Time, 175 min.; Items, 206

Battery of tests measuring the level of educational achievement among adults. Determines general educational level of adults who have not completed 12 years of schooling and evaluates efforts to raise the educational level of these

adults. Has adult-oriented content and a nonthreatening format. Covers basic skills in reading, mathematics, and the language arts. Easy to administer. No single subtest requires more than 35 minutes. Content of ABLE, second edition, is totally new. The 3 levels were developed to accommodate meaningful segments of 12 years of schooling. The grade designation of each level refers to the achievement level that can be assessed most readily. At each level, 2 forms are available, Form E and Form F, which are parallel in content and difficulty. Two forms are to be used when reevaluation or periodic testing is desired. SelectABLE is a screening device to determine which level is most suitable for a particular individual if prior educational information is not available. Level 2 is for adults who have had 5 to 8 years of schooling (the intermediate grades).

15018
Adult Basic Learning Examination, Level 3, Second Edition. Karlsen, Bjorn; Gardner, Eric F. 1986
Subtests: Vocabulary; Reading Comprehension; Spelling; Number Operations; Problem Solving; Applied Grammar; Capitalization and Punctuation
Descriptors: *Achievement Tests; *Adult Education; *Adult Students; *Basic Skills; Language Arts; Mathematics Achievement; Reading Achievement
Identifiers: ABLE
Availability: Psychological Corp.; 555 Academic Ct., San Antonio, TX 78024-0952
Age Level: Adults
Notes: Time, 175 min.; Items, 210

Battery of tests measuring the level of educational achievement among adults. Determines general educational level of adults who have not completed 12 years of schooling and evaluates efforts to raise the educational level of these adults. Has adult-oriented content and a nonthreatening format. Covers basic skills in reading, mathematics, and the language arts. Easy to administer. No single subtest requires more than 35 minutes. Content of ABLE, second edition, is totally new. The 3 levels were developed to accommodate meaningful segments of 12 years of schooling. The grade designation of each level refers to the achievement level that can be assessed most readily. At each level, 2 forms are available, Form E and Form F, which are parallel in content and difficulty. Two forms are to be used when reevaluation or periodic testing is desired. SelectABLE is a screening device to determine which level is most suitable for a particular individual if prior educational information is not available. Level 3 is for adults who have had at least 8 years of schooling, but who have not graduated from high school (the high school grades).

15019
Metropolitan Readiness Tests, Level 1, Fifth Edition. Nurss, Joanne R.; McGauvran, Mary E. 1986
Subtests: Auditory Memory; Beginning Consonants; Letter Recognition; Visual Matching; School Language and Listening; Quantitative Language; Copying
Descriptors: Auditory Perception; Cognitive Development; Language Skills; *Learning Readiness; Listening Skills; *Preschool Education; Preschool Tests; *Reading Readiness; Reading Readiness Tests; *School Readiness; *School Readiness Tests
Identifiers: Metropolitan Readiness Assessment Program; MRT
Availability: Psychological Corp.; 555 Academic Ct., San Antonio, TX 78204-0952
Age Level: 4-5
Notes: Time, 90 min. approx.; Items, 77

Metropolitan Readiness Test (MRT) provides a skill-based assessment of the enabling skills that are important for early school learning, particularly, reading, mathematics, and language development. Specifically designed to determine the child's level of cognitive development as it relates to beginning reading and mathematics instruction. Identifies instructional needs of each child, allowing the teacher to group children according to their needs. Provides content-referenced information that helps instructional planning, facilitates small-group instruction, and determines a pupil's strengths and weaknesses. Test content is based on current theories related to early childhood education and is drawn from the auditory, visual, language, and quantitative concept areas. Two levels provide flexibility in assessing the diverse range of prereading skills present in prekindergarten, kindergarten, and beginning grade 1 students. Content of each level is different because of the different stages of development between 4, and 5, and 6 year olds. Level 1 is designed for use at the end of prekindergarten and at the beginning and middle of kindergarten. Level 1 concentrates on the more basic reading skills.

15020
Metropolitan Readiness Tests, Level 2, Fifth Edition. Nurss, Joanne R.; McGauvran, Mary E. 1986

Subtests: Beginning Consonants; Sound-Letter Correspondence; Visual Matching; Finding Patterns; School Language Listening; Quantitative Concepts; Quantitative Operations; Copying
Descriptors: Auditory Perception; *Beginning Reading; Cognitive Development; Elementary School Mathematics; *Grade 1; *Kindergarten Children; Language Skills; *Learning Readiness; Listening Skills; Primary Education; Reading Readiness; Reading Readiness Tests; *School Readiness; *School Readiness Tests
Identifiers: Metropolitan Readiness Assessment Program; MRT
Availability: Psychological Corp.; 555 Academic Ct., San Antonio, TX 78204-0952
Grade Level: K-1
Age Level: 5-6
Notes: Time, 90 min. approx.; Items, 97

Metropolitan Readiness Test (MRT) provides a skill-based assessment of the enabling skills that are important for early school learning, particularly, reading, mathematics, and language development. Specifically designed to determine the child's level of cognitive development as it relates to beginning reading and mathematics instruction. Identifies instructional needs of each child, allowing the teacher to group children according to their needs. Provides content-referenced information that helps instructional planning, facilitates small-group instruction, and determines a pupil's strengths and weaknesses. Test content is based on current theories related to early childhood education and is drawn from the auditory, visual, language, and quantitative concept areas. Two levels provide flexibility in assessing the diverse range of prereading skills present in prekindergarten, kindergarten, and beginning grade 1 students. Content of each level is different because of the different stages of development between 4, 5, and 6 year olds. Level 2 is designed for use at the middle and end of kindergarten and at the beginning of grade 1. Level 2 focuses on the more advanced skills that are important in beginning reading and mathematics.

15021
Metropolitan Achievement Tests, Sixth Edition, Language Diagnostic Tests, Primary 1. Barlow, Irving H.; And Others 1986
Subtests: Listening Comprehension; Punctuation and Capitalization and Usage; Written Expression; Spelling; Study Skills
Descriptors: Achievement Tests; Capitalization (Alphabetic); Criterion Referenced Tests; *Diagnostic Tests; *Elementary School Students; *Language Arts; *Language Skills; Language Tests; Listening Comprehension; Primary Education; Punctuation; Sentence Structure; Spelling; Standardized Tests; Study Skills; Writing (Composition)
Identifiers: MAT6
Availability: Psychological Corp.; 555 Academic Ct., San Antonio, TX 78024-0952
Grade Level: 1-2
Notes: Time, 115 min.; Items, 135

Provides detailed, criterion-referenced, prescriptive information in terms of specific learning objectives in language. Diagnoses strengths and weaknesses in language arts. Within each skill cluster, each objective is assessed at least 3 times. Designed as an instructional planning tool for classroom teachers and instructional specialists. Adheres to major instructional goals of language arts curriculum surveyed nationwide. Primary 1 is for students in grades 1 and 2. Provides both criterion- and norm-referenced scores. Norm-referenced scores can be used by administrators who require normative scores, especially federally funded programs.

15022
Metropolitan Achievement Tests, Sixth Edition, Language Diagnostic Tests, Primary 2. Barlow, Irving H.; And Others 1986
Subtests: Listening Comprehension; Punctuation and Capitalization; Usage; Written Expression; Spelling; Study Skills
Descriptors: Achievement Tests; Capitalization (Alphabetic); Criterion Referenced Tests; *Diagnostic Tests; *Elementary School Students; *Language Arts; *Language Skills; Language Tests; Listening Comprehension; Primary Education; Punctuation; Sentence Structure; Spelling; Standardized Tests; Study Skills; Writing (Composition)
Identifiers: MAT6
Availability: Psychological Corp.; 555 Academic Ct., San Antonio, TX 78024-0952
Grade Level: 2-3
Notes: Time, 130 min.; Items, 187

Provides detailed, criterion-referenced, prescriptive information in terms of specific learning objectives in language. Diagnoses strengths and weaknesses in language arts. Within each skill cluster, each objective is assessed at least 3 times. Designed as an instructional planning tool for classroom teachers and instructional specialists. Adheres to major instructional goals of language arts curriculum surveyed nationwide. Primary 2 is for students in grades 2 and 3. Provides both criterion- and norm-referenced scores. Norm-referenced scores can be used by administrators who require normative scores, especially for federally funded programs.

15023
Metropolitan Achievement Tests, Sixth Edition, Language Diagnostic Tests, Elementary. Barlow, Irving H.; And Others 1986
Subtests: Listening Comprehension; Punctuation and Capitalization; Usage; Written Expression; Spelling; Study Skills
Descriptors: Achievement Tests; Capitalization (Alphabetic); Criterion Referenced Tests; *Diagnostic Tests; Elementary Education; *Elementary School Students; *Language Arts; *Language Skills; Language Tests; Listening Comprehension; Punctuation; Sentence Structure; Spelling; Standardized Tests; Study Skills; Writing (Composition)
Identifiers: MAT6
Availability: Psychological Corp.; 555 Academic Ct., San Antonio, TX 78024-0952
Grade Level: 3-4
Notes: Time, 150 min.; Items, 211
Provides detailed, criterion-referenced, prescriptive information in terms of specific learning objectives in language. Diagnoses strengths and weaknesses in language arts. Within each skill cluster, each objective is assessed at least 3 times. Designed as an instructional planning tool for classroom teachers and instructional specialists. Adheres to major instructional goals of language arts curriculum surveyed nationwide. Elementary is for students in grades 3 and 4. Provides both criterion- and norm-referenced scores. Norm-referenced scores can be used by administrators who require normative scores, especially for federally funded programs.

15024
Metropolitan Achievement Tests, Sixth Edition, Language Diagnostic Tests, Intermediate. Barlow, Irving H.; And Others 1986
Subtests: Punctuation and Capitalization; Usage; Written Expression; Spelling; Study Skills
Descriptors: Achievement Tests; Capitalization (Alphabetic); Criterion Referenced Tests; *Diagnostic Tests; *Elementary School Students; Intermediate Grades; *Language Arts; *Language Skills; Language Tests; Punctuation; Sentence Structure; Spelling; Standardized Tests; Study Skills; Writing (Composition)
Identifiers: MAT6
Availability: Psychological Corp.; 555 Academic Ct., San Antonio, TX 78024-0952
Grade Level: 5-6
Notes: Time, 120 min.; Items, 202
Provides detailed, criterion-referenced, prescriptive information in terms of specific learning objectives in language. Diagnoses strengths and weaknesses in language arts. Within each skill cluster, each objective is assessed at least 3 times. Designed as an instructional planning tool for classroom teachers and instructional specialists. Adheres to major instructional goals of language arts curriculum surveyed nationwide. Intermediate is for students in grades 5 and 6. Provides both criterion- and norm-referenced scores. Norm-referenced scores can be used by administrators who require normative scores, especially for federally funded programs.

15025
Metropolitan Achievement Tests, Sixth Edition, Language Diagnostic Tests, Advanced. Barlow, Irving H.; And Others 1986
Subtests: Punctuation and Capitalization; Usage; Written Expression; Spelling; Study Skills
Descriptors: Achievement Tests; Capitalization (Alphabetic); Criterion Referenced Tests; *Diagnostic Tests; Junior High Schools; *Junior High School Students; *Language Arts; *Language Skills; Language Tests; *Punctuation; Sentence Structure; Spelling; Standardized Tests; Study Skills; Writing (Composition)
Identifiers: MAT6
Availability: Psychological Corp.; 555 Academic Ct., San Antonio, TX 78024-0952
Grade Level: 7-9
Notes: Time, 105 min.; Items, 192
Provides detailed, criterion-referenced, prescriptive information in terms of specific learning objectives in language. Diagnoses strengths and weaknesses in language arts. Within each skill cluster, each objective is assessed at least 3 times. Designed as an instructional planning tool for classroom teachers and instructional specialists. Adheres to major instructional goals of language arts curriculum surveyed nationwide. Advanced is for students in grades 7 through 9. Provides both criterion- and norm-referenced scores. Norm-referenced scores can be used by administrators who require normative scores, especially for federally funded programs.

15027
Early School Inventory—Preliteracy. Nurss, Joanne R.; McGauvran, Mary E. 1986

Subtests: Print Concepts; Writing Concepts; Story Structure
Descriptors: Individual Testing; Language Skills; *Literacy; Measures (Individuals); *Preschool Education; Preschool Tests; *Reading Readiness; *Writing Readiness
Identifiers: ESI(P)
Availability: Psychological Corp.; 555 Academic Ct., San Antonio, TX 78204-0952
Age Level: 4-5
Notes: Time, 20 min. approx.
Designed to assist in the interpretation of the child's performance on the Metropolitan Readiness Tests. Provides information about child's preliteracy concepts. An inventory that assesses a child's concept of print, writing and story. Provides teacher with information for planning reading and writing instruction. Is individually administered.

15029
Boehm Test of Basic Concepts—Preschool Version. Boehm, Ann E. 1986
Descriptors: *Cognitive Development; *Individual Testing; Language Acquisition; Language Skills; Learning Disabilities; *Preschool Children; Preschool Education; *Preschool Tests; *School Readiness Tests; Standardized Tests
Identifiers: BOEHM (Preschool)
Availability: Psychological Corp.; 555 Academic Ct., San Antonio, TX 78204-0952
Age Level: 3-5
Notes: Time, 15 min. approx.; Items, 52
An individually administered instrument designed to measure a child's knowledge of 26 relational concepts considered necessary for achievement in the first years of school. These concepts include characteristics of size, direction, position in space, quantity, and time. Can be used by a preschool teacher as an indicator of school readiness and as a guide for planning language instruction but should not be used as the sole determinant of school readiness. Also appropriate for older children who have special educational needs. Yields norm-referenced scores for children at 5 age levels between 3 and 5.

15030
Computer Competence Tests, Module 1: Development and Impact. Psychological Corp., San Antonio, TX 1986
Descriptors: *Achievement Tests; *Computer Literacy; Computers; *High School Students; *Junior High School Students; Secondary Education; *Secondary School Students; Standardized Tests; Student Placement
Identifiers: CCT
Availability: Psychological Corp.; 555 Academic Ct., San Antonio, TX 78204-0952
Grade Level: 7-12
Notes: Time, 35 min. approx.; Items, 25
A multiple-choice test that assesses student knowledge of the development and impact of computers. Based on a comprehensive analysis of computer curriculums across the U.S., the Computer Competence Tests, Module 1, is 1 of 5 independent modules, each measuring a different aspect of the development, operation, or applications of computers. This instrument evaluates knowledge of generic concepts and is, therefore, hardware and software independent. Can be used for student placement or student assessment.

15031
Computer Competence Tests, Module 2A; Computer Operations, Level 1. Psychological Corp., San Antonio, TX 1986
Descriptors: *Achievement Tests; *Computer Literacy; Computers; *High School Students; *Junior High School Students; Secondary Education; *Secondary School Students; Standardized Tests; Student Placement
Identifiers: CCT
Availability: Psychological Corp.; 555 Academic Ct., San Antonio, TX 78204-0952
Grade Level: 7-12
Notes: Time, 35 min. approx.; Items, 25
A multiple-choice test that assesses student knowledge of how computers work (computer operations) at the introductory level. Based on a comprehensive analysis of computer curriculums across the U.S., the Computer Competence Tests, Module 2A, Computer Operations, Level 1 is 1 of 5 independent modules, each measuring a different aspect of the development, operation, or applications of computers. This instrument evaluates knowledge of generic concepts and is, therefore, hardware and software independent. Can be used for student placement or assessment.

15032
Computer Competence Tests, Module 2B; Computer Operations, Level 2. Psychological Corp., San Antonio, TX 1986

Descriptors: *Achievement Tests; *Computer Literacy; Computers; *High School Students; *Junior High School Students; Secondary Education; *Secondary School Students; Standardized Tests; Student Placement
Identifiers: CCT
Availability: Psychological Corp.; 555 Academic Ct., San Antonio, TX 78204-0952
Grade Level: 7-12
Notes: Time, 35 min. approx.; Items, 20
A multiple-choice test that assesses secondary school students' knowledge of computer operations at an intermediate level. The concepts measured are primarily those of program design and procedures. Based on a comprehensive analysis of computer curriculums across the U.S., this is 1 of 5 independent modules, each measuring a different aspect of the development, operation, or applications of computers. Evaluates knowledge of generic concepts and is, therefore, hardware and software independent. Can be used for student placement or assessment.

15033
Computer Competence Tests, Module 3A: Applications Level 1. Psychological Corp., San Antonio, TX 1986
Descriptors: *Achievement Tests; *Computer Literacy; Computers; *High School Students; *Junior High School Students; Secondary Education; *Secondary School Students; Standardized Tests; Student Placement
Identifiers: CCT
Availability: Psychological Corp.; 555 Academic Ct., San Antonio, TX 78204-0952
Grade Level: 7-12
Notes: Time, 35 min. approx.; Items, 25
An introductory level, multiple-choice test that assesses secondary school students' knowledge of the basic uses or applications of computers. One of 5 independent modules, each measuring a different aspect of the development, operation or applications of computers. Evaluates knowledge of generic concepts and is, therefore, hardware and software independent. Can be used for student placement or assessment.

15034
Computer Competence Tests, Module 3B: Applications Level 2. Psychological Corp., San Antonio, TX 1986
Descriptors: *Achievement Tests; *Computer Literacy; Computers; *High School Students; Junior High School Students; Secondary Education; *Secondary School Students; Standardized Tests; Student Placement
Identifiers: CCT
Availability: Psychological Corp.; 555 Academic Ct., San Antonio, TX 78204-0952
Grade Level: 7-12
Notes: Time, 35 min. approx.; Items, 20
An intermediate level, multiple-choice test that assesses secondary school students' knowledge of the uses or applications of computers. The emphasis is on measuring the students' understanding of software and programing concepts. One of 5 independent modules, each measuring a different aspect of the development, operation or applications of computers. The instrument evaluates knowledge of generic concepts and is, therefore, hardware and software independent. Can be used for student placement or assessment.

15040
Woodcock Reading Mastery Tests—Revised, Forms G and H. Woodcock, Richard W. 1987
Subtests: Visual-Auditory Learning; Letter Identification; Word Identification; Word Attack; Word Comprehension; Passage Comprehension
Descriptors: *Achievement Tests; Adults; College Students; Elementary School Students; *Elementary Secondary Education; *Higher Education; High School Students; Individual Testing; Norm Referenced Tests; *Reading Achievement; Reading Skills; *Reading Tests
Availability: American Guidance Service; Publishers' Bldg., Circle Pines, MN 55014-1796
Age Level: 5-65
Notes: Time, 45 min. approx.
A battery of individually administered tests of reading. Norms are provided from the kindergarten to the adult level. Special college/university norms are also given. Similar to the original Woodcock Reading Mastery Tests, but changes enhance its diagnostic utility and extend its usefulness to college and adult populations. Two forms are provided. Basal and ceiling levels for each individual are established, and only the items falling within this range are administered.

15041
Tests of Adult Basic Education, Forms 5 and 6, Level E (Easy), Complete Battery. CTB/Macmillan/McGraw-Hill, Monterey, CA 1987

Subtests: Vocabulary; Comprehension; Mathematics Computation; Mathematics Concepts and Applications; Language Mechanics; Language Expression; Spelling
Descriptors: *Achievement Tests; *Adult Basic Education; Adults; *Adult Students; *Basic Skills; Language Skills; Mathematics Achievement; Norm Referenced Tests; Reading Achievement; Spelling
Identifiers: TABE
Availability: CTB/MacMillan/McGraw-Hill; Del Monte Research Park, 2500 Garden Rd., Monterey, CA 93940
Age Level: Adults
Notes: Time, 293 min.

Norm-referenced tests designed to measure achievement in reading, mathematics, language, and spelling, the subjects most commonly found in adult basic education curricula. Test focuses on the basic skills required for an individual to function in society. Tests combine the characteristics of norm-referenced and criterion-referenced tests and provide information about the relative ranking of examinees against a norm group and specific information about the instructional needs of the examinees. Results allow teachers and administrators to diagnose, evaluate, and place examinees in adult education programs. There is a correlation between scores on this test and the scores on the General Educational Development (GED) tests. Items on this test reflect language and content appropriate for adults and measure the understanding and application of conventions and principles. Test items are not intended to measure specific knowledge or recall of facts. There are 4 overlapping levels and 2 parallel forms for each level. The 4 levels and their estimated grade ranges are E (easy) with a grade range of 2.6-4.9; M (medium) with a grade range of 4.6-6.9; D (difficult) with a grade range of 6.6-8.9; and A (advanced) with a grade range of 8.6-12.9. There is also a survey form, which is a subset of the complete battery, that can be used to quickly screen examinees for appropriate placement in programs of instruction.

15042
Tests of Adult Basic Education, Forms 5 and 6, Level M (Medium), Complete Battery. CTB/MacMillan/McGraw-Hill, Monterey, CA 1987
Subtests: Vocabulary; Comprehension; Mathematics Computation; Mathematics Concepts and Applications; Language Mechanics; Language Expression; Spelling
Descriptors: *Achievement Tests; *Adult Basic Education; Adults; *Adult Students; *Basic Skills; Language Skills; Mathematics Achievement; Norm Referenced Tests; Reading Achievement; Spelling
Identifiers: TABE
Availability: CTB/MacMillan/McGraw-Hill; Del Monte Research Park, 2500 Garden Rd., Monterey, CA 93940
Age Level: Adults
Notes: Time, 293 min.; Items, 263

Norm-referenced tests designed to measure achievement in reading, mathematics, language, and spelling, the subjects most commonly found in adult basic education curricula. Test focuses on the basic skills required for an individual to function in society. Tests combine the characteristics of norm-referenced and criterion-referenced tests and provide information about the relative ranking of examinees against a norm group and specific information about the instructional needs of the examinees. Results allow teachers and administrators to diagnose, evaluate, and place examinees in adult education programs. There is a correlation between scores on this test and the scores on the General Educational Development (GED) tests. Items on this test reflect language and content appropriate for adults and measure the understanding and application of conventions and principles. Test items are not intended to measure specific knowledge or recall of facts. There are 4 overlapping levels and 2 parallel forms for each level. The 4 levels and their estimated grade ranges are E (easy) with a grade range of 2.6-4.9; M (medium) with a grade range of 4.6-6.9; D (difficult) with a grade range of 6.6-8.9; and A (advanced) with a grade range of 8.6-12.9. There is also a survey form, which is a subset of the complete battery, that can be used to quickly screen examinees for appropriate placement in programs of instruction.

15043
Tests of Adult Basic Education, Form 5, Level D (Difficult), Complete Battery. CTB/MacMillan/McGraw-Hill, Monterey, CA 1987
Subtests: Vocabulary; Comprehension; Mathematics Computation; Mathematics Concepts and Applications; Language Mechanics; Language Expression; Spelling
Descriptors: *Achievement Tests; *Adult Basic Education; Adults; *Adult Students; *Basic Skills; Language Skills; Mathematics Achievement; Norm Referenced Tests; Reading Achievement; Spelling
Identifiers: TABE
Availability: CTB/MacMillan/McGraw-Hill; Del Monte Research Park, 2500 Garden Rd., Monterey, CA 93940

Age Level: Adults
Notes: Time, 293 min.; Items, 263

Norm-referenced tests designed to measure achievement in reading, mathematics, language, and spelling, the subjects most commonly found in adult basic education curricula. Test focuses on the basic skills required for an individual to function in society. Tests combine the characteristics of norm-referenced and criterion-referenced tests and provide information about the relative ranking of examinees against a norm group and specific information about the instructional needs of the examinees. Results allow teachers and administrators to diagnose, evaluate, and place examinees in adult education programs. There is a correlation between scores on this test and the scores on the General Educational Development (GED) tests. Items on this test reflect language and content appropriate for adults and measure the understanding and application of conventions and principles. Test items are not intended to measure specific knowledge or recall of facts. There are 4 overlapping levels and 2 parallel forms for each level. The 4 levels and their estimated grade ranges are E (easy) with a grade range of 2.6-4.9; M (medium) with a grade range of 4.6-6.9; D (difficult) with a grade range of 6.6-8.9; and A (advanced) with a grade range of 8.6-12.9. There is also a survey form, which is a subset of the complete battery, that can be used to quickly screen examinees for appropriate placement in programs of instruction.

15044
Tests of Adult Basic Education, Form 5, Level A (Advanced), Complete Battery. CTB/MacMillan/McGraw-Hill, Monterey, CA 1987
Subtests: Vocabulary; Comprehension; Mathematics Computation; Mathematics Concepts and Applications; Language Mechanics; Language Expression; Spelling
Descriptors: *Achievement Tests; *Adult Basic Education; Adults; *Adult Students; *Basic Skills; Language Skills; Mathematics Achievement; Norm Referenced Tests; Reading Achievement; Spelling
Identifiers: TABE
Availability: CTB/MacMillan/McGraw-Hill; Del Monte Research Park, 2500 Garden Rd., Monterey, CA 93940
Age Level: Adults
Notes: Time, 293 min.; Items, 263

Norm-referenced tests designed to measure achievement in reading, mathematics, language, and spelling, the subjects most commonly found in adult basic education curricula. Test focuses on the basic skills required for an individual to function in society. Tests combine the characteristics of norm-referenced and criterion-referenced tests and provide information about the relative ranking of examinees against a norm group and specific information about the instructional needs of the examinees. Results allow teachers and administrators to diagnose, evaluate, and place examinees in adult education programs. There is a correlation between scores on this test and the scores on the General Educational Development (GED) tests. Items on this test reflect language and content appropriate for adults and measure the understanding and application of conventions and principles. Test items are not intended to measure specific knowledge or recall of facts. There are 4 overlapping levels and 2 parallel forms for each level. The 4 levels and their estimated grade ranges are E (easy) with a grade range of 2.6-4.9; M (medium) with a grade range of 4.6-6.9; D (difficult) with a grade range of 6.6-8.9; and A (advanced) with a grade range of 8.6-12.9. There is also a survey form, which is a subset of the complete battery, that can be used to quickly screen examinees for appropriate placement in programs of instruction.

15045
End-of-Course Tests: Geometry. Educational Testing Service, Princeton, NJ 1986
Descriptors: *Achievement Tests; *Geometry; *High School Students; *Junior High School Students; Secondary Education; *Secondary School Students
Availability: CTB/MacMillan/McGraw-Hill; Del Monte Research Park, 2500 Garden Rd., Monterey, CA 93940
Grade Level: 7-12
Notes: Time, 45 min.; Items, 42

Designed to measure the subject matter taught in certain junior and senior high school courses. Tests can be used to supplement or substitute for basic skills achievement testing at these levels. There are 9 different end-of-course tests, one in each of the following areas: algebra, geometry, physics, chemistry, biology, world history, American history, computer literacy, and consumer economics. Tests represent the most commonly taught curricula in a one-year course in each of these subject areas. Normative data were derived from national reference groups who had completed a course in the content area. Geometry test measures knowledge and understanding of such concepts as congruence, similarity, angle relationships, special properties of polygons, and determination of perimeters, areas, and volumes of the most common polygons and solids.

15046
End-of-Course Tests: Chemistry. Educational Testing Service, Princeton, NJ 1986

Descriptors: *Achievement Tests; *Chemistry; *High School Students; *Junior High School Students; Secondary Education; *Secondary School Students
Availability: CTB/MacMillan/McGraw-Hill; Del Monte Research Park, 2500 Garden Rd., Monterey, CA 93940
Grade Level: 7-12
Notes: Time, 45 min.; Items, 48

Designed to measure the subject matter taught in certain junior and senior high school courses. Tests can be used to supplement or substitute for basic skills achievement testing at these levels. There are 9 different end-of-course tests, one in each of the following areas: algebra, geometry, physics, chemistry, biology, world history, American history, computer literacy, and consumer economics. Tests represent the most commonly taught curricula in a one-year course in each of these subject areas. Normative data were derived from national reference groups who had completed a course in the content area. The chemistry items measure knowledge and understanding obtained in the classroom and laboratory. There is an emphasis on items that require students to apply their acquired knowledge. Item content relates to structure of matter, chemical formulas and equations, states of matter, properties and characteristics of matter, and chemical reactions.

15047
End-of-Course Tests: World History. Educational Testing Service, Princeton, NJ 1986
Descriptors: *Achievement Tests; *High School Students; *Junior High School Students; Secondary Education; *Secondary School Students; *World History
Availability: CTB/MacMillan/McGraw-Hill; Del Monte Research Park, 2500 Garden Rd., Monterey, CA 93940
Grade Level: 7-12
Notes: Time, 45 min.; Items, 50

Designed to measure the subject matter taught in certain junior and senior high school courses. Tests can be used to supplement or substitute for basic skills achievement testing at these levels. There are 9 different end-of-course tests, one in each of the following areas: algebra, geometry, physics, chemistry, biology, world history, American history, computer literacy, and consumer economics. Tests represent the most commonly taught curricula in a one-year course in each of these subject areas. Normative data were derived from national reference groups who had completed a course in the content area. The world history test measures the understanding and knowledge of the events, individuals, and political and religious ideas that formed Western, Asian, and African civilizations. Historical and political changes and trends of the twentieth century are also explored.

15048
End-of-Course Tests: Physics. Educational Testing Service, Princeton, NJ 1986
Descriptors: *Achievement Tests; *High School Students; *Junior High School Students; *Physics; Secondary Education; *Secondary School Students
Availability: CTB/MacMillan/McGraw-Hill; Del Monte Research Park, 2500 Garden Rd., Monterey, CA 93940
Grade Level: 7-12
Notes: Time, 45 min.; Items, 48

Designed to measure the subject matter taught in certain junior and senior high school courses. Tests can be used to supplement or substitute for basic skills achievement testing at these levels. There are 9 different end-of-course tests, one in each of the following areas: algebra, geometry, physics, chemistry, biology, world history, American history, computer literacy, and consumer economics. Tests represent the most commonly taught curricula in a one-year course in each of these subject areas. Normative data were derived from national reference groups who had completed a course in the content area. The physics test measures knowledge and understanding obtained in the classroom and laboratory and emphasizes items that require the students to apply what they have learned. Items relate to atomic structure and theory, kinetic theory and gases, heat, mechanics, waves, and electricity and magnetism.

15049
End-of-Course Tests: Consumer Economics. Educational Testing Service, Princeton, NJ 1986
Descriptors: *Achievement Tests; *Consumer Economics; *High School Students; *Junior High School Students; Secondary Education; *Secondary School Students
Availability: CTB/MacMillan/McGraw-Hill; Del Monte Research Park, 2500 Garden Rd., Monterey, CA 93940
Grade Level: 7-12
Notes: Time, 45 min.; Items, 45

Designed to measure the subject matter taught in certain junior and senior high school courses. Tests can be used to supplement or substitute for basic skills achievement testing at these levels. There are 9 different end-of-course tests, one in each of the following areas: algebra, geometry, physics, chemistry, biology, world history, American history, computer literacy, and consumer economics. Tests represent the most commonly taught curricula in a one-year course in each of these subject areas. Normative data were derived from national reference groups who had completed a course in the content area. Consumer economics items measure the ability to conceptualize basic economic principles and to make decisions based on this knowledge. The student is expected to understand sound financial management and appropriate consumer strategy and to respond as a participating citizen in the economic process.

15050
End-of-Course Tests: American History. Educational Testing Service, Princeton, NJ 1986
Descriptors: *Achievement Tests; *High School Students; *Junior High School Students; Secondary Education; *Secondary School Students; *United States History
Availability: CTB/MacMillan/McGraw-Hill; Del Monte Research Park, 2500 Garden Rd., Monterey, CA 93940
Grade Level: 7-12
Notes: Time, 45 min.; Items, 50
Designed to measure the subject matter taught in certain junior and senior high school courses. Tests can be used to supplement or substitute for basic skills achievement testing at these levels. There are 9 different end-of-course tests, one in each of the following areas: algebra, geometry, physics, chemistry, biology, world history, American history, computer literacy, and consumer economics. Tests represent the most commonly taught curricula in a one-year course in each of these subject areas. Normative data were derived from national reference groups who had completed a course in the content area. The American history test focuses on the cultural and economic forces that influenced the development of the U.S. Also included are political events and the role of U.S. foreign policy.

15051
End-of-Course Tests: Algebra. Educational Testing Service, Princeton, NJ 1986
Descriptors: *Achievement Tests; *Algebra; *High School Students; *Junior High School Students; Secondary Education; *Secondary School Students
Availability: CTB/MacMillan/McGraw-Hill; Del Monte Research Park, 2500 Garden Rd., Monterey, CA 93940
Grade Level: 7-12
Notes: Time, 45 min.; Items, 42
Designed to measure the subject matter taught in certain junior and senior high school courses. Tests can be used to supplement or substitute for basic skills achievement testing at these levels. There are 9 different end-of-course tests, one in each of the following areas: algebra, geometry, physics, chemistry, biology, world history, American history, computer literacy, and consumer economics. Tests represent the most commonly taught curricula in a one-year course in each of these subject areas. Normative data were derived from national reference groups who had completed a course in the content area. Algebra test includes items that measure the ability to perform fundamental operations of algebra, to solve linear equations and inequalities and simple quadratics, and to distinguish between real and imaginary numbers.

15052
End-of-Course Tests: Biology. Educational Testing Service, Princeton, NJ 1986
Descriptors: *Achievement Tests; *Biology; *High School Students; *Junior High School Students; Secondary Education; *Secondary School Students
Availability: CTB/MacMillan/McGraw-Hill; Del Monte Research Park, 2500 Garden Rd., Monterey, CA 93940
Grade Level: 7-12
Notes: Time, 45 min.; Items, 48
Designed to measure the subject matter taught in certain junior and senior high school courses. Tests can be used to supplement or substitute for basic skills achievement testing at these levels. There are 9 different end-of-course tests, one in each of the following areas: algebra, geometry, physics, chemistry, biology, world history, American history, computer literacy, and consumer economics. Tests represent the most commonly taught curricula in a one-year course in each of these subject areas. Normative data were derived from national reference groups who had completed a course in the content area. Biology test items measure knowledge of scientific methodology, and items have been included that require students to apply acquired knowledge. Content of the test covers cellular, molecular, and organismic biology, heredity, evolution, and ecology.

15053
End-of-Course Tests: Computer Literacy. Educational Testing Service, Princeton, NJ 1986
Descriptors: *Achievement Tests; *Computer Literacy; *High School Students; *Junior High School Students; Secondary Education; *Secondary School Students

Availability: CTB/MacMillan/McGraw-Hill; Del Monte Research Park, 2500 Garden Rd., Monterey, CA 93940
Grade Level: 7-12
Notes: Time, 45 min.; Items, 45
Designed to measure the subject matter taught in certain junior and senior high school courses. Tests can be used to supplement or substitute for basic skills achievement testing at these levels. There are 9 different end-of-course tests, one in each of the following areas: algebra, geometry, physics, chemistry, biology, world history, American history, computer literacy, and consumer economics. Tests represent the most commonly taught curricula in a one-year course in each of these subject areas. Normative data were derived from national reference groups who had completed a course in the content area. Measures understanding of how computers work, knowledge of computer applications, and the use of computers for various types of applications. Also includes items dealing with social issues in the age of computers. Programing skills are assessed by presenting programing code in 3 different languages: BASIC, Pascal, and Logo. Students use the language with which they are most familiar.

15084
CAT Writing Assessment System, Level 13.
CTB/Macmillan/McGraw-Hill, Monterey, CA 1987
Subtests: Descriptive; Narrative
Descriptors: *Achievement Tests; Descriptive Writing; *Elementary Education; *Elementary School Students; Grade 2; Grade 3; Grade 4; Holistic Evaluation; *Primary Education; *Writing Evaluation; *Writing Skills
Identifiers: CAT
Availability: CTB/MacMillan/McGraw-Hill; Del Monte Research Park, 2500 Garden Rd., Monterey, CA 93940
Grade Level: 2-4
Notes: Time, 50 min.
Measures students' writing skills. Provides survey information for evaluation of writing programs and diagnostic information for individual writing remediation. Provides opportunity to evaluate writing samples of students in grades 3 through 12. Each booklet contains a prompt (assignment) to elicit a particular type of writing—descriptive, narrative, expository, or persuasive—that is appropriate for students of that age. An Administration Scoring Manual that focuses on the prompt and the level for which it is appropriate is provided. Holistic scoring guidelines are provided for the prompts and analytic scoring guidelines are provided for the type of writing elicited. Scoring can be done at the local level or by CTB. Level 13 intended for grades 2-4.

15085
CAT Writing Assessment System, Level 14.
CTB/Macmillan/McGraw-Hill, Monterey, CA 1987
Subtests: Descriptive; Narrative
Descriptors: *Achievement Tests; Descriptive Writing; *Elementary Education; *Elementary School Students; Grade 3; Grade 4; Grade 5; Holistic Evaluation; Intermediate Grades; Primary Education; *Writing Evaluation; *Writing Skills
Identifiers: CAT
Availability: CTB/MacMillan/McGraw-Hill; Del Monte Research Park, 2500 Garden Rd., Monterey, CA 93940
Grade Level: 3-5
Notes: Time, 60 min.
Measures students' writing skills. Provides survey information for evaluation of writing programs and diagnostic information for individual writing remediation. Provides opportunity to evaluate writing samples of students in grades 3 through 12. Each booklet contains a prompt (assignment) to elicit a particular type of writing—descriptive, narrative, expository, or persuasive—that is appropriate for students of that age. An Administration Scoring Manual that focuses on the prompt and the level for which it is appropriate is provided. Holistic scoring guidelines are provided for the prompts and analytic scoring guidelines are provided for the type of writing elicited. Scoring can be done at the local level or by CTB. Level 14 intended for grades 3-5.

15086
CAT Writing Assessment System, Level 15.
CTB/Macmillan/McGraw-Hill, Monterey, CA 1987
Subtests: Descriptive; Narrative; Expository
Descriptors: *Achievement Tests; Descriptive Writing; *Elementary School Students; Grade 4; Grade 5; Grade 6; Holistic Evaluation; *Intermediate Grades; *Writing Evaluation; *Writing Skills
Identifiers: CAT
Availability: CTB/MacMillan/McGraw-Hill; Del Monte Research Park, 2500 Garden Rd., Monterey, CA 93940
Grade Level: 4-6
Notes: Time, 60 min.

Measures students' writing skills. Provides survey information for evaluation of writing programs and diagnostic information for individual writing remediation. Provides opportunity to evaluate writing samples of students in grades 3 through 12. Each booklet contains a prompt (assignment) to elicit a particular type of writing—descriptive, narrative, expository, or persuasive—that is appropriate for students of that age. An Administration Scoring Manual that focuses on the prompt and the level for which it is appropriate is provided. Holistic scoring guidelines are provided for the prompts and analytic scoring guidelines are provided for the type of writing elicited. Scoring can be done at the local level or by CTB. Level 15 intended for grades 4-6.

15087
CAT Writing Assessment System, Level 16.
CTB/Macmillan/McGraw-Hill, Monterey, CA 1987
Subtests: Descriptive; Narrative; Expository
Descriptors: *Achievement Tests; Descriptive Writing; *Elementary School Students; Grade 5; Grade 6; Grade 7; Holistic Evaluation; Intermediate Grades; Junior High Schools; Junior High School Students; *Writing Evaluation; *Writing Skills
Identifiers: CAT
Availability: CTB/MacMillan/McGraw-Hill; Del Monte Research Park, 2500 Garden Rd., Monterey, CA 93940
Grade Level: 5-7
Notes: Time, 90 min.

Measures students' writing skills. Provides survey information for evaluation of writing programs and diagnostic information for individual writing remediation. Provides opportunity to evaluate writing samples of students in grades 3 through 12. Each booklet contains a prompt (assignment) to elicit a particular type of writing—descriptive, narrative, expository, or persuasive—that is appropriate for students of that age. An Administration Scoring Manual that focuses on the prompt and the level for which it is appropriate is provided. Holistic scoring guidelines are provided for the prompts and analytic scoring guidelines are provided for the type of writing elicited. Scoring can be done at the local level or by CTB. Level 16 intended for grades 5-7.

15088
CAT Writing Assessment System, Level 17.
CTB/Macmillan/McGraw-Hill, Monterey, CA 1987
Subtests: Narrative; Expository; Persuasive
Descriptors: *Achievement Tests; Descriptive Writing; *Elementary School Students; Grade 6; Grade 7; Grade 8; Holistic Evaluation; *Intermediate Grades; Junior High Schools; *Junior High School Students; *Writing Evaluation; *Writing Skills
Identifiers: CAT
Availability: CTB/MacMillan/McGraw-Hill; Del Monte Research Park, 2500 Garden Rd., Monterey, CA 93940
Grade Level: 6-8
Notes: Time, 105 min.

Measures students' writing skills. Provides survey information for evaluation of writing programs and diagnostic information for individual writing remediation. Provides opportunity to evaluate writing samples of students in grades 3 through 12. Each booklet contains a prompt (assignment) to elicit a particular type of writing—descriptive, narrative, expository, or persuasive—that is appropriate for students of that age. An Administration Scoring Manual that focuses on the prompt and the level for which it is appropriate is provided. Holistic scoring guidelines are provided for the prompts and analytic scoring guidelines are provided for the type of writing elicited. Scoring can be done at the local level or by CTB. Level 17 intended for grades 6-8.

15089
CAT Writing Assessment System, Level 18.
CTB/Macmillan/McGraw-Hill, Monterey, CA 1987
Subtests: Narrative; Expository; Persuasive
Descriptors: *Achievement Tests; Grade 7; Grade 8; Grade 9; Holistic Evaluation; Junior High Schools; *Junior High School Students; *Writing Evaluation; *Writing Skills
Identifiers: CAT
Availability: CTB/MacMillan/McGraw-Hill; Del Monte Research Park, 2500 Garden Rd., Monterey, CA 93940
Grade Level: 7-9
Notes: Time, 105 min.

Measures students' writing skills. Provides survey information for evaluation of writing programs and diagnostic information for individual writing remediation. Provides opportunity to evaluate writing samples of students in grades 3 through 12. Each booklet contains a prompt (assignment) to elicit a particular type of writing—descriptive, narrative, expository, or persuasive—that is appropriate for students of that age. An Administration Scoring Manual that focuses on the prompt and the level for which it is appropriate is provided. Holistic scoring guidelines are provided for the prompts and analytic scoring guidelines are provided for the type of writing elicited. Scoring can be done at the local level or by CTB. Level 18 intended for grades 7-9.

15090
CAT Writing Assessment System, Level 19. CTB/Macmillan/McGraw-Hill, Monterey, CA 1987
Subtests: Narrative; Expository; Persuasive
Descriptors: *Achievement Tests; Grade 8; Grade 9; Grade 10; Grade 11; Holistic Evaluation; *Secondary Education; *Secondary School Students; *Writing Evaluation; *Writing Skills
Identifiers: CAT
Availability: CTB/MacMillan/McGraw-Hill; Del Monte Research Park, 2500 Garden Rd., Monterey, CA 93940
Grade Level: 8-11
Notes: Time, 120 min.

Measures students' writing skills. Provides survey information for evaluation of writing programs and diagnostic information for individual writing remediation. Provides opportunity to evaluate writing samples of students in grades 3 through 12. Each booklet contains a prompt (assignment) to elicit a particular type of writing—descriptive, narrative, expository, or persuasive—that is appropriate for students of that age. An Administration Scoring Manual that focuses on the prompt and the level for which it is appropriate is provided. Holistic scoring guidelines are provided for the prompts and analytic scoring guidelines are provided for the type of writing elicited. Scoring can be done at the local level or by CTB. Level 19 intended for grades 8-11

15091
CAT Writing Assessment System, Level 20. CTB/Macmillan/McGraw-Hill, Monterey, CA 1987
Subtests: Expository; Persuasive
Descriptors: *Achievement Tests; Grade 10; Grade 11; Grade 12; High Schools; *High School Students; Holistic Evaluation; *Writing Evaluation; *Writing Skills
Identifiers: CAT
Availability: CTB/MacMillan/McGraw-Hill; Del Monte Research Park, 2500 Garden Rd., Monterey, CA 93940
Grade Level: 10-12
Notes: Time, 80 min.

Measures students' writing skills. Provides survey information for evaluation of writing programs and diagnostic information for individual writing remediation. Provides opportunity to evaluate writing samples of students in grades 3 through 12. Each booklet contains a prompt (assignment) to elicit a particular type of writing—descriptive, narrative, expository, or persuasive—that is appropriate for students of that age. An Administration Scoring Manual that focuses on the prompt and the level for which it is appropriate is provided. Holistic scoring guidelines are provided for the prompts and analytic scoring guidelines are provided for the type of writing elicited. Scoring can be done at the local level or by CTB. Level 20 intended for grades 10-12.

15102
Stanford Listening Comprehension Test. Gardner, Eric F.; And Others 1982
Descriptors: Achievement Tests; *Elementary School Students; Elementary Secondary Education; *Junior High School Students; Listening Comprehension; *Listening Comprehension Tests; Listening Skills
Availability: Psychological Corp.; 555 Academic Ct., San Antonio, TX 78204-0952
Grade Level: 1-9
Notes: Time, 20 min.; Items, 28

This subtest of the Stanford Achievement Test (TC011695-011700) evaluates pupils' ability to process information that has been heard in terms of retention of specific details and organization of the material as a whole. It is also administered as part of the full achievement battery.

15124
Metropolitan Achievement Test, Sixth Edition, Writing Test. Hogan, Thomas P.; And Others 1986
Descriptors: *Achievement Tests; *Creative Writing; *Elementary School Students; Elementary Secondary Education; Grammar; Holistic Evaluation; Norm Referenced Tests; *Secondary School Students; Sentence Structure; *Writing (Composition); Writing Evaluation
Identifiers: Writing Sample
Availability: Psychological Corp.; 555 Academic Ct., San Antonio, TX 78204-0952
Grade Level: 2-12
Notes: Time, 20 min.

The MAT6 Writing Test is an optional subtest of the Metropolitan Achievement Test, Sixth Edition. It is a free-response writing sample in response to a pictorial stimulus. Norm-referenced information is provided for use in program evaluation, and measurement of achievement. Level 1 covers the grade range from 2.5-4.9. Level 2 covers the grade range from 5.0-8.9. Level 3 covers the grade range from 9.0-12.9. Each level has 2 forms, L and M. The sample can be holistically scored by 2 independent raters against 8 anchorpoints (previously scored papers assigned a rating of 1 through 8). It can also be scored analytically as to content development, sentence formation, word usage, and writing mechanics.

15125
National Business Competency Tests, Stenographic Test. National Business Education Association, Reston, VA 1972
Descriptors: Achievement Tests; Adults; *Clerical Occupations; *High School Students; Occupational Tests; *Postsecondary Education; *Secondary Education; *Secretaries; *Shorthand; *Vocational Education; *Work Sample Tests
Identifiers: Oral Testing
Availability: National Business Education Association; 1914 Association Drive, Reston, VA 22091
Grade Level: 9-12
Age Level: Adults
Notes: Time, 90 min.; Items, 13

Designed to measure the ability to take dictation and transcribe it under office conditions, as far as can be reproduced in a testing situation. Dictation is given at 80 words per minute. Test materials include dictation paragraphs, letterhead, and carbon paper.

15126
National Business Competency Tests, Secretarial Procedures Test. National Business Education Association, Reston, VA 1983
Descriptors: Achievement Tests; *Business Education; *Clerical Occupations; Editing; *High School Students; Multiple Choice Tests; Occupational Tests; *Postsecondary Education; *Secondary Education; *Secretaries; Typewriting; *Vocational Education; *Work Sample Tests
Availability: National Business Education Association; 1914 Association Drive, Reston, VA 22091
Grade Level: 9-12
Age Level: Adults
Notes: Items, 60

The test consists of 2 parts. Part 1 consists of 3 parts: a job application form, secretarial procedures information, and editing. Part 2 requires a typewriter and consists of the scheduling and performance of 6 tasks. These include updating a calendar, typing minutes of a meeting, typing a letter and envelope, typing an agenda, a memo, and a purchase order.

15127
National Business Competency Tests, Accounting Procedures Test, Trial Edition. National Business Education Association, Reston, VA 1984
Descriptors: *Accounting; Achievement Tests; *Business Education; *High School Students; Microcomputers; Multiple Choice Tests; Occupational Tests; *Postsecondary Education; Secondary Education; *Vocational Education; *Work Sample Tests
Availability: National Business Education Association; 1914 Association Drive, Reston, VA 22091
Grade Level: 9-12
Age Level: Adults
Notes: Items, 80

The test consists of 2 parts and a supplementary page on microcomputers in accounting. Part I is a series of multiple-choice questions based on payroll records, a bank reconciliation, and a worksheet for a merchandising business. Part II is a journalizing and posting project with source documents. Students with one year of accounting may not finish the test.

15128
Informal Evaluation of Oral Reading Grade Level. Edel, Deborah 1973
Subtests: Independent Reading Level; Instructional Reading Level; Frustration Reading Level; Oral Comprehension Level
Descriptors: Elementary Education; *Elementary School Students; *Informal Reading Inventories; *Instructional Program Divisions; *Oral Reading; Reading Comprehension; *Reading Tests
Identifiers: Frustration Reading Level; Independent Reading Level; Instructional Reading Level; Reading Level
Availability: Book-Lab, Inc.; 1449 Thirty-Seven St., Brooklyn, NY 11218
Grade Level: 1-8

Designed to determine the grade level at which the individual student is reading and the level at which the student has comprehension of orally presented material. Passages range in grade level from primer through grade 8. Number of errors made on a passage is an indication of the student's independent, instructional, or frustration reading level.

15131
MicroCAT Testing System, Second Edition. Assessment Systems Corp., St. Paul, MN 1987
Descriptors: *Adaptive Testing; Adolescents; Adults; Children; *Computer Assisted Testing; *Computer Software; Data Analysis; Elementary Secondary Education; Higher Education; *Item Banks; Microcomputers; Scoring; *Test Construction; Test Items; Item Response Theory
Identifiers: Rasch Model
Availability: Assessment Systems Corp.; 2233 University Ave., St. Paul, MN 55114
Grade Level: 1-16
Age Level: Adults

MicroCAT is a microcomputer-based system for developing, administering, scoring, and analyzing computerized tests. It also allows printing of paper-and-pencil tests. Graphics can be used with color monitors. Creates thousands of item banks holding up to 999 items each. Multiple-choice and free-response items can be used. Three programs allow development of conventional or adaptive testing strategies. Item analysis includes indication of which items and responses contribute to the reliability of the test and mean, variance, skewness, kurtosis, alpha reliability, standard error and intercorrelations among subtests. A Rasch Model Item Calibration Program (RASCAL) estimates difficulty parameters of the Rasch IRT model. The test preevaluation program evaluates the test's potential before it is given.

15135
Reading Comprehension Inventory. Giordano, Gerard 1987
Descriptors: Elementary Education; *Elementary School Students; Reading Achievement; *Reading Comprehension; *Reading Tests
Identifiers: RCI
Availability: Scholastic Testing Service; 480 Meyer Rd., Bensenville, IL 60106-8056
Grade Level: K-6
Notes: Items, 30

An assessment of reading ability that employs "mechanical" reading skills (syllabification, phonics, spelling, word derivation) in tandem with other less technical aspects of reading. Designed to create a functional reading situation which measures actual comprehension, not just the skills that correlate with it. Comprised of 6 graded passages. The student must answer 5 questions relating to the narrative elements, the sequencing of information, and the response level of each passage. There are 23 instructional exercises to help improve the identified reading characteristics.

15139
Spellmaster Revised. Greenbaum, Claire R. 1987
Subtests: Regular Word Test; Irregular Word Test; Homophone Test; Entry Level Test
Descriptors: *Adult Basic Education; Adults; *Criterion Referenced Tests; *Diagnostic Tests; *Elementary School Students; Elementary Secondary Education; Remedial Instruction; *Secondary School Students; *Spelling; Spelling Instruction
Availability: PRO-ED; 8700 Shoal Creek Blvd., Austin, TX 78758-6897
Grade Level: K-10
Age Level: 6-65
Notes: Time, 20 min. approx.

A criterion-referenced, self-contained assessment and teaching system used in both remedial and regular classroom spelling instruction. Allows for the identification of specific problem areas as tests are scored, and later yields a rapid analysis of an individual's progress or a whole class's ability. The manual contains teaching methods and strategies, learning activities, and supplemental word lists. Suitable for use with students of varying ability levels, and can be integrated with other spelling programs already is use. A revision of the Spellmaster system originally published in 1974.

15142
Career Programs Assessment. American College Testing Program, Iowa City, IA 1987
Subtests: Language Usage Test; Reading Skills Test; Numerical Skills Test
Descriptors: *Achievement Tests; *Basic Skills; *College Students; Language Tests; Mathematics Tests; *Postsecondary Education; Reading Tests; *Screening Tests; *Vocational Education
Identifiers: CPAt
Availability: CPAt Coordinator; ACT Operations Div., 2255 N. Dubuque Rd., Iowa City, IA 52243
Age Level: 18-65

Notes: Time, 60 min. approx.; Items, 110
An assessment program designed to measure basic skills (Language Usage, Reading and Numeric) of students planning to attend career schools and colleges and other post-secondary institutions offering specific, job-related educational programs. Information from this instrument can be used to determine remediation strategies; and, when used with specialized follow-up reports, can provide information on the effectiveness of these strategies. A Student Information Section gathers information on the student's background and goals, which can be used in advising and retention efforts, marketing activities, and institutional reporting.

15146
Metropolitan Achievement Tests, Sixth Edition, Reading Diagnostic Tests, Primer. Farr, Roger C.; And Others 1986
Subtests: Visual Discrimination; Letter Recognition; Auditory Discrimination; Sight Vocabulary; Phoneme/Grapheme Consonants; Vocabulary in Context; Reading Comprehension
Descriptors: Achievement Tests; Auditory Discrimination; Context Clues; Criterion Referenced Tests; *Diagnostic Tests; *Grade 1; *Kindergarten Children; Letters (Alphabet); Phoneme Grapheme Correspondence; Primary Education; Reading Comprehension; *Reading Diagnosis; *Reading Tests; Sight Vocabulary; Standardized Tests; Visual Discrimination
Identifiers: MAT6
Availability: Psychological Corp.; 555 Academic Ct., San Antonio, TX 78204-0952.
Grade Level: K-1
Notes: Time, 133 min.; Items, 187
This is the diagnostic component of the Metropolitan Achievement Tests, sixth edition (MAT6). When used with the survey component, provides a comprehensive assessment package to meet varied needs of schools. For each level of the test, instructional objectives were identified. Each objective is assessed by at least 3 items. Criterion-referenced information is provided for each objective so that students' competence in meeting the objectives can be assessed. Designed as an instructional planning tool for classroom teachers and instructional specialists. Provides detailed prescriptive information on educational performance of individual students in terms of specific instructional objectives. Aids in instructional planning for students needing remediation or for those performing at average or above average levels. Diagnostic batteries are statistically equated to scores in the same domain as the corresponding MAT6 survey batteries. Provides both norm-referenced and criterion-referenced scores.

15147
Metropolitan Achievement Tests, Sixth Edition, Reading Diagnostic Tests, Primary 1. Farr, Roger C.; And Others 1986
Subtests: Auditory Discrimination; Sight Vocabulary; Phoneme/Grapheme Consonants; Phoneme/Grapheme Vowels; Vocabulary in Context; Word Part Clues; Reading Comprehension
Descriptors: Achievement Tests; Auditory Discrimination; Context Clues; Criterion Referenced Tests; *Diagnostic Tests; *Grade 1; *Grade 2; Phoneme Grapheme Correspondence; Primary Education; Reading Comprehension; *Reading Diagnosis; *Reading Tests; Sight Vocabulary; Standardized Tests
Identifiers: MAT6
Availability: Psychological Corp.; 555 Academic Ct., San Antonio, TX 78204-0952.
Grade Level: 1-2
Notes: Time, 142 min.; Items, 203
This is the diagnostic component of the Metropolitan Achievement Tests, sixth edition (MAT6). When used with the survey component, provides a comprehensive assessment package to meet varied needs of schools. For each level of the test, instructional objectives were identified. Each objective is assessed by at least 3 items. Criterion-referenced information is provided for each objective so that students' competence in meeting the objectives can be assessed. Designed as an instructional planning tool for classroom teachers and instructional specialists. Provides detailed prescriptive information on educational performance of individual students in terms of specific instructional objectives. Aids in instructional planning for students needing remediation or for those performing at average or above average levels. Diagnostic batteries are statistically equated to scores in the same domain as the corresponding MAT6 survey batteries. Provides both norm-referenced and criterion-referenced scores.

15148
Metropolitan Achievement Tests, Sixth Edition, Reading Diagnostic Tests, Primary 2. Farr, Roger C.; And Others 1986

Subtests: Sight Vocabulary; Phoneme/Grapheme Consonants; Phoneme/Grapheme Vowels; Vocabulary in Context; Word Part Clues; Reading Comprehension
Descriptors: Achievement Tests; Context Clues; Criterion Referenced Tests; *Diagnostic Tests; *Grade 2; *Grade 3; Phoneme Grapheme Correspondence; Primary Education; Reading Comprehension; *Reading Diagnosis; *Reading Tests; Sight Vocabulary; Standardized Tests
Identifiers: MAT6
Availability: Psychological Corp.; 555 Academic Ct., San Antonio, TX 78204-0952.
Grade Level: 2-3
Notes: Time, 120 min.; Items, 194
This is the diagnostic component of the Metropolitan Achievement Tests, sixth edition (MAT6). When used with the survey component, provides a comprehensive assessment package to meet varied needs of schools. For each level of the test, instructional objectives were identified. Each objective is assessed by at least 3 items. Criterion-referenced information is provided for each objective so that students' competence in meeting the objectives can be assessed. Designed as an instructional planning tool for classroom teachers and instructional specialists. Provides detailed prescriptive information on educational performance of individual students in terms of specific instructional objectives. Aids in instructional planning for students needing remediation or for those performing at average or above average levels. Diagnostic batteries are statistically equated to scores in the same domain as the corresponding MAT6 survey batteries. Provides both norm-referenced and criterion-referenced scores.

15149
Metropolitan Achievement Tests, Sixth Edition, Reading Diagnostic Tests, Elementary. Farr, Roger C.; And Others 1986
Subtests: Phoneme/Grapheme Consonants; Phoneme Grapheme Vowels; Vocabulary in Context; Word Part Clues; Rate of Comprehension; Reading Comprehension
Descriptors: Achievement Tests; Context Clues; Criterion Referenced Tests; *Diagnostic Tests; Elementary Education; Elementary School Students; *Grade 3; *Grade 4; Phoneme Grapheme Correspondence; Reading Comprehension; *Reading Diagnosis; Reading Rate; *Reading Tests; Standardized Tests
Identifiers: MAT6
Availability: Psychological Corp.; 555 Academic Ct., San Antonio, TX 78204-0952.
Grade Level: 3-4
Notes: Time, 124 min.; Items, 205
This is the diagnostic component of the Metropolitan Achievement Tests, sixth edition (MAT6). When used with the survey component, provides a comprehensive assessment package to meet varied needs of schools. For each level of the test, instructional objectives were identified. Each objective is assessed by at least 3 items. Criterion-referenced information is provided for each objective so that students' competence in meeting the objectives can be assessed. Designed as an instructional planning tool for classroom teachers and instructional specialists. Provides detailed prescriptive information on educational performance of individual students in terms of specific instructional objectives. Aids in instructional planning for students needing remediation or for those performing at average or above average levels. Diagnostic batteries are statistically equated to scores in the same domain as the corresponding MAT6 survey batteries. Provides both norm-referenced and criterion-referenced scores.

15150
Metropolitan Achievement Tests, Sixth Edition, Reading Diagnostic Tests, Intermediate. Farr, Roger C.; And Others 1986
Subtests: Phoneme/Grapheme Consonants; Phoneme Grapheme Vowels; Vocabulary in Context; Word Part Clues; Rate of Comprehension; Skimming and Scanning; Reading Comprehension
Descriptors: Achievement Tests; Context Clues; Criterion Referenced Tests; *Diagnostic Tests; Elementary School Students; *Grade 5; *Grade 6; *Intermediate Grades; Phoneme Grapheme Correspondence; Reading Comprehension; *Reading Diagnosis; Reading Rate; *Reading Tests; Speed Reading; Standardized Tests
Identifiers: MAT6
Availability: Psychological Corp.; 555 Academic Ct., San Antonio, TX 78204-0952.
Grade Level: 5-6
Notes: Time, 134 min.; Items, 223
This is the diagnostic component of the Metropolitan Achievement Tests, sixth edition (MAT6). When used with the survey component, provides a comprehensive assessment package to meet varied needs of schools. For each level of the test, instructional objectives were identified. Each objective is assessed by at least 3 items.

Criterion-referenced information is provided for each objective so that students' competence in meeting the objectives can be assessed. Designed as an instructional planning tool for classroom teachers and instructional specialists. Provides detailed prescriptive information on educational performance of individual students in terms of specific instructional objectives. Aids in instructional planning for students needing remediation or for those performing at average or above average levels. Diagnostic batteries are statistically equated to scores in the same domain as the corresponding MAT6 survey batteries. Provides both norm-referenced and criterion-referenced scores.

15151
Metropolitan Achievement Tests, Sixth Edition, Reading Diagnostic Tests, Advanced 1. Farr, Roger C.; And Others 1986
Subtests: Vocabulary in Context; Rate of Comprehension; Skimming and Scanning; Reading Comprehension
Descriptors: Achievement Tests; Context Clues; Criterion Referenced Tests; *Diagnostic Tests; Junior High Schools; *Junior High School Students; Reading Comprehension; *Reading Diagnosis; Reading Rate; *Reading Tests; Speed Reading; Standardized Tests
Identifiers: MAT6
Availability: Psychological Corp.; 555 Academic Ct., San Antonio, TX 78204-0952.
Grade Level: 7-9
Notes: Time, 79 min.; Items, 135
This is the diagnostic component of the Metropolitan Achievement Tests, sixth edition (MAT6). When used with the survey component, provides a comprehensive assessment package to meet varied needs of schools. For each level of the test, instructional objectives were identified. Each objective is assessed by at least 3 items. Criterion-referenced information is provided for each objective so that students' competence in meeting the objectives can be assessed. Designed as an instructional planning tool for classroom teachers and instructional specialists. Provides detailed prescriptive information on educational performance of individual students in terms of specific instructional objectives. Aids in instructional planning for students needing remediation or for those performing at average or above average levels. Diagnostic batteries are statistically equated to scores in the same domain as the corresponding MAT6 survey batteries. Provides both norm-referenced and criterion-referenced scores.

15174
Metropolitan Achievement Tests, Sixth Edition, Mathematics Diagnostic Tests, Primary 1. Hogan, Thomas P.; And Others 1986
Subtests: Numeration; Geometry and Measurement; Problem Solving; Computation-Whole Numbers
Descriptors: Achievement Tests; Computation; Criterion Referenced Tests; *Diagnostic Tests; Geometric Concepts; *Grade 1; *Grade 2; *Mathematics Achievement; Mathematics Skills; *Mathematics Tests; Primary Education; Problem Solving; Standardized Tests; Whole Numbers
Identifiers: MAT6
Availability: The Psychological Corp.; 555 Academic Ct., San Antonio, TX 78204-0952
Grade Level: 1-2
Notes: Time, 130 min.; Items, 138
This is the diagnostic component of the Metropolitan Achievement Tests, sixth edition (MAT6). When used with the survey component, provides a comprehensive assessment package to meet varied needs of schools. For each level of the test, instructional objectives were identified. Each objective is assessed by at least 3 items. Criterion-referenced information is provided for each objective so that students' competence in meeting the objectives can be assessed. Designed as an instructional planning tool for classroom teachers and instructional specialists. Provides detailed prescriptive information on educational performance of individual students in terms of specific instructional objectives. Aids in instructional planning for students needing remediation or for those performing at average or above average levels. Diagnostic batteries are statistically equated to scores in the same domain as the corresponding MAT6 survey batteries. Provides both norm-referenced and criterion-referenced scores.

15175
Metropolitan Achievement Tests, Sixth Edition, Mathematics Diagnostic Tests, Primary 2. Hogan, Thomas P.; And Others 1986
Subtests: Numeration; Geometry and Measurement; Problem Solving; Computation-Whole Numbers

Descriptors: Achievement Tests; Computation; Criterion Referenced Tests; *Diagnostic Tests; Geometric Concepts; *Grade 2; *Grade 3; *Mathematics Achievement; *Mathematics Tests; Primary Education; Problem Solving; Standardized Tests; Whole Numbers
Identifiers: MAT6
Availability: The Psychological Corp.; 555 Academic Ct., San Antonio, TX 78204-0952
Grade Level: 2-3
Notes: Time, 117 min.; Items, 135

This is the diagnostic component of the Metropolitan Achievement Tests, sixth edition (MAT6). When used with the survey component, provides a comprehensive assessment package to meet varied needs of schools. For each level of the test, instructional objectives were identified. Each objective is assessed by at least 3 items. Criterion-referenced information is provided for each objective so that students' competence in meeting the objectives can be assessed. Designed as an instructional planning tool for classroom teachers and instructional specialists. Provides detailed prescriptive information on educational performance of individual students in terms of specific instructional objectives. Aids in instructional planning for students needing remediation or for those performing at average or above average levels. Diagnostic batteries are statistically equated to scores in the same domain as the corresponding MAT6 survey batteries. Provides both norm-referenced and criterion-referenced scores.

15176
Metropolitan Achievement Tests, Sixth Edition, Mathematics Diagnostic Tests, Elementary. Hogan, Thomas P.; And Others 1986
Subtests: Numeration; Geometry and Measurement; Problem Solving; Computation-Whole Numbers
Descriptors: Achievement Tests; Computation; Criterion Referenced Tests; *Diagnostic Tests; Elementary Education; Elementary School Students; Geometric Concepts; *Grade 3; *Grade 4; *Mathematics Achievement; *Mathematics Tests; Problem Solving; Standardized Tests; Whole Numbers
Identifiers: MAT6
Availability: The Psychological Corp.; 555 Academic Ct., San Antonio, TX 78204-0952
Grade Level: 3-4
Notes: Time, 127 min.; Items, 168

This is the diagnostic component of the Metropolitan Achievement Tests, sixth edition (MAT6). When used with the survey component, provides a comprehensive assessment package to meet varied needs of schools. For each level of the test, instructional objectives were identified. Each objective is assessed by at least 3 items. Criterion-referenced information is provided for each objective so that students' competence in meeting the objectives can be assessed. Designed as an instructional planning tool for classroom teachers and instructional specialists. Provides detailed prescriptive information on educational performance of individual students in terms of specific instructional objectives. Aids in instructional planning for students needing remediation or for those performing at average or above average levels. Diagnostic batteries are statistically equated to scores in the same domain as the corresponding MAT6 survey batteries. Provides both norm-referenced and criterion-referenced scores.

15177
Metropolitan Achievement Tests, Sixth Edition, Mathematics Diagnostic Tests, Intermediate. Hogan, Thomas P.; And Others 1986
Subtests: Numeration; Geometry and Measurement; Problem Solving; Computation-Whole Numbers; Computation-Decimals and Fractions; Graphs and Statistics
Descriptors: Achievement Tests; Criterion Referenced Tests; Decimal Fractions; *Diagnostic Tests; Elementary School Students; Fractions; Geometric Concepts; *Grade 5; *Grade 6; Graphs; Intermediate Grades; *Mathematics Achievement; Mathematics Tests; Problem Solving; Standardized Tests; Whole Numbers
Identifiers: MAT6
Availability: The Psychological Corp.; 555 Academic Ct., San Antonio, TX 78204-0952
Grade Level: 5-6
Notes: Time, 175 min.; Items, 210

This is the diagnostic component of the Metropolitan Achievement Tests, sixth edition (MAT6). When used with the survey component, provides a comprehensive assessment package to meet varied needs of schools. For each level of the test, instructional objectives were identified. Each objective is assessed by at least 3 items. Criterion-referenced information is provided for each objective so that students' competence in meeting the objectives can be assessed. Designed as an instructional planning tool for classroom teachers and instructional specialists. Provides detailed prescriptive information on educational performance of individual students in terms of specific instructional objectives. Aids in instructional planning for students needing remediation or for those performing at average or above average levels. Diagnostic batteries are statistically equated to scores in the same domain as the corresponding MAT6 survey batteries. Provides both norm-referenced and criterion-referenced scores.

15178
Metropolitan Achievement Tests, Sixth Edition, Mathematics Diagnostic Tests, Advanced 1. Hogan, Thomas P.; And Others 1986
Subtests: Numeration; Geometry and Measurement; Problem Solving; Computation-Whole Numbers; Computation-Decimals and Fractions; Graphs and Statistics
Descriptors: Achievement Tests; Criterion Referenced Tests; Decimal Fractions; *Diagnostic Tests; Geometric Concepts; Graphs; Junior High Schools; *Junior High School Students; *Mathematics Achievement; *Mathematics Tests; Problem Solving; Standardized Tests; Whole Numbers
Identifiers: MAT6
Availability: The Psychological Corp.; 555 Academic Ct., San Antonio, TX 78204-0952
Grade Level: 7-9
Notes: Time, 167 min.; Items, 213

This is the diagnostic component of the Metropolitan Achievement Tests, sixth edition (MAT6). When used with the survey component, provides a comprehensive assessment package to meet varied needs of schools. For each level of the test, instructional objectives were identified. Each objective is assessed by at least 3 items. Criterion-referenced information is provided for each objective so that students' competence in meeting the objectives can be assessed. Designed as an instructional planning tool for classroom teachers and instructional specialists. Provides detailed prescriptive information on educational performance of individual students in terms of specific instructional objectives. Aids in instructional planning for students needing remediation or for those performing at average or above average levels. Diagnostic batteries are statistically equated to scores in the same domain as the corresponding MAT6 survey batteries. Provides both norm-referenced and criterion-referenced scores.

15181
Holbrook Screening Battery and Parent Questionnaire, Revised. Holbrook Public Schools, Holbrook, MA 1986
Subtests: Information; Sentences; Similarities; Language Sample; Colors; Letters; Shapes; Arithmetic; Visual Matching; Name Writing; Copy Forms; Pencil Grasp; Draw-a-Person; Cutting; Gross Motor
Descriptors: *Child Development; *Kindergarten Children; *Language Skills; *Preschool Children; Primary Education; *Psychomotor Skills; *School Readiness; School Readiness Tests; *Screening Tests
Identifiers: Fine Motor Skills; Gross Motor Skills; HSB; *Test Batteries; TIM(M)
Availability: Tests in Microfiche; Test Collection, Educational Testing Service, Princeton, NJ 08541
Grade Level: K
Age Level: 4-5

Screening battery used by the Holbrook Public Schools in Massachusetts each spring to evaluate children about to enter kindergarten and who will be 5 years old by the end of the calendar year. Children are individually tested by each member of a team of 5 examiners. The battery consists of 15 subtests divided into 4 major groups: language, readiness, fine motor skills, and gross motor skills. Some of the subtests used are part of the Wechsler Preschool and Primary Scale of Intelligence (1963) (TC001424). There is also a developmental questionnaire to be filled out by the parents.

15189
Howell Prekindergarten Screening Test. Howell Township Public Schools, Howell, NJ 1984
Subtests: Shapes; Listening Comprehension; Auditory Memory; Color Words; Vocabulary; Classification; Letter Identification; Rhyming; Letter Writing; Directionality and Spatial Relation; Consonant Sounds; Visual Motor; Visual Discrimination; Name; Number Identification; Number Writing; Counting Sets; Math Concepts; Addition and Subtraction; Copying
Descriptors: Kindergarten; *Kindergarten Children; *School Readiness; *School Readiness Tests; *Screening Tests
Availability: Book-Lab; 500 74th St., N. Bergen, NJ 07047
Grade Level: K
Notes: Time, 120 min. approx.; Items, 73

A pencil-and-paper screening instrument that identifies students in need of appropriate supportive instructional programs. Students are classified into 3 general categories: those who may need special assistance, those with appropriate skills, and those with unusually well-developed skills. The abilities that are assessed represent a sampling of verbal, quantitative, perceptual, and general cognitive skills that are commonly recognized as necessary for adequate participation in kindergarten-level activities. Does not specifically test gross motor activities. Suggested that the test be administered in 4 sittings over a 2-day period.

15197
Teste de Matematica II. Gaio, Joaquim F.
Subtests: Numbers; Geometry and Measuring; Basic Operations; Problems
Descriptors: *Achievement Tests; Arithmetic; Computation; *Diagnostic Tests; Elementary School Students; Geometry; Grade 2; Grade 3; *Mathematics Tests; Number Concepts; *Portuguese; *Primary Education; *Student Placement
Availability: National Dissemination Center; 417 Rock St., Fall River, MA 02720
Grade Level: 2-3
Notes: Time, 45 min.; Items, 111

A measure in Portuguese, of the knowledge of the major concepts of elementary mathematics of Portuguese-speaking students. Can be used as a diagnostic tool to determine the strengths and weaknesses of its subjects. Also, aids educators in placement and grouping of students. Last, it helps monitor students' progress in mathematics. Primarily intended for the classroom teacher, but school psychologists and special educators will find it useful.

15198
Teste de Lingua Portuguesa II. Gaio, Joaquim F.
Subtests: Phonetics; Vocabulary; Comprehension
Descriptors: *Achievement Tests; *Diagnostic Tests; Elementary School Students; Grade 2; Grade 3; Phonetics; *Portuguese; *Primary Education; *Reading Achievement; Reading Comprehension; Reading Diagnosis; *Reading Tests; *Student Placement; Vocabulary Skills
Identifiers: TLP II
Availability: National Dissemination Center; 417 Rock St., Fall River, MA 02720
Grade Level: 2-3
Notes: Time, 45 min.; Items, 216

A measure in Portuguese, of the major components of the reading process mastered by Portuguese-speaking students. Can be used as a diagnostic tool, for placement purposes, or for monitoring progress in reading. Primarily intended for the classroom teacher, but school psychologists and special educators will also find it useful.

15200
Comprehensive Identification Process, Spanish Language Edition. Zehrbach, R. Reid 1985
Subtests: Cognitive-Verbal; Fine Motor; Gross Motor; Speech and Expressive Language; Hearing; Vision; Socio-affective Behavior; Medical History
Descriptors: Affective Measures; Auditory Tests; *Cognitive Development; Cognitive Measurement; Language Tests; Motor Development; *Preschool Children; *Preschool Tests; *Screening Tests; Social Development; Spanish; *Spanish Speaking; Speech Tests; Verbal Tests; Vision Tests
Identifiers: CIP
Availability: Scholastic Testing Service; 480 Meyer Rd., Bensenville, IL 60106
Age Level: 3-5

A total process of locating, screening, and evaluating preschool children. Provides data that will quickly screen these children and help identify those who appear to warrant further testing to determine eligibility for special programs. It accomplishes this task in such a manner that there is no labeling of children or arousal of anxiety in parents before all necessary information is available. Most test materials available in both Spanish and English language.

15204
Academic Profile. Educational Testing Service, Princeton, NJ; The College Board, New York, NY 1987
Subtests: College-Level Reading; College-Level Writing; Critical Thinking; Using Mathematical Data; Humanities; Social Sciences; Natural Sciences
Descriptors: *Achievement Tests; College Freshmen; *College Mathematics; College Seniors; *College Students; Core Curriculum; *Critical Thinking; Essay Tests; *General Education; Higher Education; *Humanities; Mathematics; *Natural Sciences; *Reading; *Social Sciences; Two Year Colleges; *Two Year College Students; *Writing (Composition); *Writing Skills
Identifiers: Outcomes Assessment; Sophomores; Writing Sample
Availability: Program Director; ETS College and University Programs; Educational Testing Service, Princeton, NJ 08541

Grade Level: 13-16

The Academic Profile is designed to assess student outcomes, academic achievement or growth, on the completion of general education requirements (introductory courses in major discipline areas) in higher education. It is for use by 2- and 4-year colleges and universities with entering first-year students, sophomores completing general education, and seniors. The profile measures academic skills (college-level reading, college-level writing, critical thinking, and using mathematical data) in the context of 3 major discipline groups (humanities, social sciences, natural sciences). An optional essay is available. Fifty questions can be written and added by the user college. A short form (48 items, one hour) provides group data. A long-form (3 hours, 144 items) provides scores for individuals. Eight scores are reported: one in each content area, one in each skill area, and a total score. Scores can be reported for subgroups based on student demographic data. Group scores can be compared to scores reported by other colleges. The program became operational beginning in fall of 1988.

15213
Sawyer's Test of Awareness of Language Segments. Sawyer, Diane J. 1987
Subtests: Segmenting Sentences into Word Units; Segmenting Words into Syllabic Units; Segmenting Words into Phonemic Units
Descriptors: Adults; Developmental Disabilities; Elementary School Students; Elementary Secondary Education; Exceptional Persons; *Kindergarten Children; Language Acquisition; *Language Tests; Learning Disabilities; Prereading Experience; Preschool Children; *Preschool Tests; *Primary Education; Reading Difficulties; *Reading Readiness Tests; *Screening Tests; Secondary School Students
Identifiers: TALS
Availability: Aspen Publishers; P.O. Box 990, 7201 McKinney Circle, Frederick, MD 21701
Grade Level: K-1
Age Level: 4-65
Notes: Items, 46

Assesses a child's ability to segment the stream of spoken language into words, syllables, and phonemes (sounds). A child's performance on this instrument helps the teacher to determine whether the child's language segmenting abilities are sufficiently developed to meet the instructional demands of typical eclectic or phonics-oriented beginning reading programs. In addition, the patterns of performance on the subtests may be helpful in choosing prereading experiences and beginning recoding experiences that are most likely to promote progress toward efficient recoding. Useful to reading and language specialists, learning disabilities specialists, early childhood specialists and special educators for identifying those individuals lacking the level of language awareness that is necessary for reading development. Reliability and validity data included. Has also been pilot tested with learning-disabled students, adult poor readers, developmentally delayed adults, and language-delayed and language-impaired children.

15214
Listening Test, Level 1. CTB/Macmillan/McGraw-Hill, Monterey, CA; Educational Testing Service, Princeton, NJ 1985
Descriptors: *Achievement Tests; Elementary Education; *Elementary School Students; *Grade 3; *Grade 4; Listening Comprehension; *Listening Comprehension Tests; Listening Skills; Norm Referenced Tests
Availability: CTB/MacMillan/McGraw-Hill; Del Monte Research Park, 2500 Garden Rd., Monterey, CA 93940
Grade Level: 3-4
Notes: Time, 40 min. approx.; Items, 20

Norm-referenced test designed to measure the ability to follow directions and interpret connected discourse. Among the specific skills measured are memory and the ability to follow sequences. Test may be used alone or in conjunction with the California Achievement Tests, Forms E and F (TC014343-014353) or the Comprehensive Tests of Basic Skills, Forms U and V (TC011317-011325, TC012265). There are 6 overlapping levels covering grades 3 through 12. The Listening Tests for Levels 1 - 4 measure students' skills in following directions and interpreting oral passages. For the level 5 and level 6 tests, all items are presented orally. There is no time limit to the test, but testing can probably be completed in 30 to 40 minutes.

15215
Listening Test, Level 2. CTB/Macmillan/McGraw-Hill, Monterey, CA; Educational Testing Service, Princeton, NJ 1985
Descriptors: *Achievement Tests; *Elementary School Students; *Grade 4; *Grade 5; Intermediate Grades; Listening Comprehension; *Listening Comprehension Tests; Listening Skills; Norm Referenced Tests
Availability: CTB/MacMillan/McGraw-Hill; Del Monte Research Park, 2500 Garden Rd., Monterey, CA 93940
Grade Level: 4-5
Notes: Time, 40 min. approx.; Items, 20

Norm-referenced test designed to measure the ability to follow directions and interpret connected discourse. Among the specific skills measured are memory and the ability to follow sequences. Test may be used alone or in conjunction with the California Achievement Tests, Forms E and F (TC014343-014353) or the Comprehensive Tests of Basic Skills, Forms U and V (TC011317-011325, TC012265). There are 6 overlapping levels covering grades 3 through 12. The Listening Tests for Levels 1 - 4 measure students' skills in following directions and interpreting oral passages. For the level 5 and level 6 tests, all items are presented orally. There is no time limit to the test, but testing can probably be completed in 30 to 40 minutes.

15216
Listening Test, Level 3. CTB/Macmillan/McGraw-Hill, Monterey, CA; Educational Testing Service, Princeton, NJ 1985
Descriptors: *Achievement Tests; *Elementary School Students; *Grade 5; *Grade 6; Intermediate Grades; Listening Comprehension; *Listening Comprehension Tests; Listening Skills; Norm Referenced Tests
Availability: CTB/MacMillan/McGraw-Hill; Del Monte Research Park, 2500 Garden Rd., Monterey, CA 93940
Grade Level: 5-6
Notes: Time, 40 min. approx.; Items, 20

Norm-referenced test designed to measure the ability to follow directions and interpret connected discourse. Among the specific skills measured are memory and the ability to follow sequences. Test may be used alone or in conjunction with the California Achievement Tests, Forms E and F (TC014343-014353) or the Comprehensive Tests of Basic Skills, Forms U and V (TC011317-011325, TC012265). There are 6 overlapping levels covering grades 3 through 12. The Listening Tests for Levels 1 - 4 measure students' skills in following directions and interpreting oral passages. For the level 5 and level 6 tests, all items are presented orally. There is no time limit to the test, but testing can probably be completed in 30 to 40 minutes.

15217
Listening Test, Level 4. CTB/Macmillan/McGraw-Hill, Monterey, CA; Educational Testing Service, Princeton, NJ 1985
Descriptors: *Achievement Tests; *Elementary School Students; *Grade 6; *Grade 7; Intermediate Grades; Junior High Schools; *Junior High School Students; Listening Comprehension; *Listening Comprehension Tests; Listening Skills; Norm Referenced Tests
Availability: CTB/MacMillan/McGraw-Hill; Del Monte Research Park, 2500 Garden Rd., Monterey, CA 93940
Grade Level: 6-7
Notes: Time, 40 min. approx.; Items, 20

Norm-referenced test designed to measure the ability to follow directions and interpret connected discourse. Among the specific skills measured are memory and the ability to follow sequences. Test may be used alone or in conjunction with the California Achievement Tests, Forms E and F (TC014343-014353) or the Comprehensive Tests of Basic Skills, Forms U and V (TC011317-011325, TC012265). There are 6 overlapping levels covering grades 3 through 12. The Listening Tests for Levels 1 - 4 measure students' skills in following directions and interpreting oral passages. For the level 5 and level 6 tests, all items are presented orally. There is no time limit to the test, but testing can probably be completed in 30 to 40 minutes.

15218
Listening Test, Level 5. CTB/Macmillan/McGraw-Hill, Monterey, CA; Educational Testing Service, Princeton, NJ 1985
Descriptors: *Achievement Tests; Listening Comprehension; *Listening Comprehension Tests; Listening Skills; Norm Referenced Tests; Secondary Education; *Secondary School Students
Availability: CTB/MacMillan/McGraw-Hill; Del Monte Research Park, 2500 Garden Rd., Monterey, CA 93940
Grade Level: 7-10
Notes: Time, 40 min. approx.; Items, 18

Norm-referenced test designed to measure the ability to follow directions and interpret connected discourse. Among the specific skills measured are memory and the ability to follow sequences. Test may be used alone or in conjunction with the California Achievement Tests, Forms E and F (TC014343-014353) or the Comprehensive Tests of Basic Skills, Forms U and V (TC011317-011325, TC012265). There are 6 overlapping levels covering grades 3 through 12. The Listening Tests for Levels 1 - 4 measure students' skills in following directions and interpreting oral passages. For the level 5 and level 6 tests, all items are presented orally. There is no time limit to the test, but testing can probably be completed in 30 to 40 minutes.

15219
Listening Test, Level 6. CTB/Macmillan/McGraw-Hill, Monterey, CA; Educational Testing Service, Princeton, NJ 1985
Descriptors: *Achievement Tests; High Schools; *High School Students; Listening Comprehension; *Listening Comprehension Tests; Listening Skills; Norm Referenced Tests
Availability: CTB/MacMillan/McGraw-Hill; Del Monte Research Park, 2500 Garden Rd., Monterey, CA 93940
Grade Level: 10-12
Notes: Time, 40 min. approx.; Items, 18

Norm-referenced test designed to measure the ability to follow directions and interpret connected discourse. Among the specific skills measured are memory and the ability to follow sequences. Test may be used alone or in conjunction with the California Achievement Tests, Forms E and F (TC014343-014353) or the Comprehensive Tests of Basic Skills, Forms U and V (TC011317-011325, TC012265). There are 6 overlapping levels covering grades 3 through 12. The Listening Tests for Levels 1 - 4 measure students' skills in following directions and interpreting oral passages. For the level 5 and level 6 tests, all items are presented orally. There is no time limit to the test, but testing can probably be completed in 30 to 40 minutes.

15223
The Connectives Reading Test and Written Connectives Test. Robertson, Jean E. 1966
Descriptors: *Achievement Tests; *Cloze Procedure; Elementary Education; *Elementary School Students; Grammar; Language Skills; Multiple Choice Tests
Identifiers: *Connectives; Modified Cloze Procedure; TIM(M)
Availability: Tests in Microfiche; Test Collection, Educational Testing Service, Princeton, NJ 08541
Grade Level: 5-8
Notes: Items, 170

These 2 instruments were designed to measure children's understanding of the connective, e.g., although, because, and, and 14 others. The reading test uses a modified cloze procedure with 4 multiple-choice responses. The Written Connectives Test uses actual cloze procedure with the test taker providing the response to complete the meaning of the sentence.

15224
Fitness Knowledge Test. Sander, Allan N.; Burton, Elsie C. 1987
Descriptors: Elementary Education; *Elementary School Students; *Knowledge Level; Multiple Choice Tests; Physical Education; *Physical Fitness
Availability: *Journal of Physical Education, Recreation and Dance;* v58 n6 p90-93 Aug 1987
Grade Level: 4-8
Notes: Items, 26

A multiple-choice test designed to measure elementary school students' knowledge about physical fitness. Items are written at the fourth grade reading level, and the content may be too difficult for children in lower grades. Information on reliability included.

15229
De Santi Cloze Reading Inventory. De Santi, Roger J. 1986
Descriptors: *Cloze Procedure; Diagnostic Tests; *Elementary School Students; Elementary Secondary Education; Instructional Materials; *Reading Comprehension; *Reading Tests; *Secondary School Students; Student Teachers; Teacher Education; Word Lists; Word Recognition
Identifiers: Reading Levels
Availability: De Santi, Roger J. The De Santi Cloze Reading Inventory. Boston: Allyn and Bacon, 1986
Grade Level: 1-12
Notes: Time, 45 min.; Items, 50

Designed to measure reading ability; determine independent, instructional, and frustration reading levels; diagnose strengths and weaknesses. May be used in the classroom for assessing students and for course material for training of preservice and inservice teachers. Measures comprehension through cloze passages. Word recognition and identification are measured through word lists. Group or individual administration is possible. Each passage has 50 cloze responses.

15231
Crane Oral Dominance Test: Spanish/English. Crane, Barbara J. 1978
Descriptors: *Elementary School Students; Elementary Secondary Education; *English (Second Language); Individual Testing; *Language Dominance; Language Usage; Oral Language; Preschool Education; *Secondary School Students; *Spanish Speaking; Verbal Tests

Availability: Crane Publishing; 1301 Hamilton Ave., P.O. Box 3713, Trenton, NJ 08629
Grade Level: K-12
Age Level: 4-18
Notes: Time, 20 min. approx.; Items, 8
Instrument used to determine the dominant language of elementary and high school pupils who speak both English and Spanish. Eight words are read to the pupil, each word being said twice. Four of the words are Spanish words, and 4 are English. The pupil then is asked to recall the words he or she has been presented. This procedure is repeated 8 times, using different words each time. Examines the number of words recalled which were Spanish and the number which were English. Also notes the number of times the pupil translates a Spanish word into English and vice versa. The results of these observations determine which language is dominant for the pupil. A list of questions concerning language use at home is also presented to the pupil. With modifications the test may be administered to preschool children.

15240
ASSURE Test Development Software System.
Armstrong, Robert J.; And Others 1984
Descriptors: *Computer Software; *Criterion Referenced Tests; Elementary Secondary Education; Grammar; *Item Banks; Mathematics; Reading; School Readiness; Sciences; Social Studies; *Test Construction
Availability: Assurance, Inc.; 2455 E. Speedway, Ste. 203, Tucson, AZ 85719
Grade Level: K-12
ASSURE is a software program controlling a database of test items for criterion-referenced test development. It allows the user to modify items and add new ones. The basic system (levels 1-8) contains 10,920 items in reading, grammar and mathematics (10 items per skill). Item banks for readiness skills and for levels 9-12 as well as item banks for science and social studies are available. The software operates on IBM, IBM Compatible, and Apple IIe computers.

15262
Test of Language Development—2, Primary.
Newcomer, Phyllis L.; Hammill, Donald D. 1988
Subtests: Picture Vocabulary; Grammatic Understanding; Sentence Imitation; Grammatic Completion; Word Discrimination; Word Articulation
Descriptors: *Individual Testing; *Language Handicaps; *Language Skills; *Language Tests; *Speech Skills; Standardized Tests; Visual Measures; *Young Children
Identifiers: TOLD2
Availability: PRO-ED; 8700 Shoal Creek Blvd., Austin, TX 78758-6897
Age Level: 4-8
Notes: Time, 45 min. approx.; Items, 190
Assesses spoken language. Identifies children, 4 through 8 years old, who have language disorders and isolates the particular types of disorders that they have. Profiles individual strengths and deficiencies in basic language abilities. Has 7 subtests that measure different components of spoken language. Picture Vocabulary and Oral Vocabulary assess the understanding and meaningful use of spoken words. Grammatic Understanding, Sentence Imitation, and Grammatic Completion assess differing aspects of grammar; Word Articulation, and Word Discrimination measure the abilities to say words correctly and distinguish between words that sound similar. Results reported as standard scores, percentiles, and age equivalents.

15263
Clinical Pharmacy Knowledge and Skill Inventory.
Pray, W. Steven; Popovich, Nicholas G. 1983
Descriptors: *Achievement Tests; *Doctoral Programs; Higher Education; *Pharmaceutical Education; *Pharmacists
Availability: W. Steven Pray; School of Pharmacy, Southwestern Oklahoma State University, Weatherford, OK 73096
Age Level: Adults
Notes: Time, 120 min.; Items, 125
This instrument measures knowledge in several areas of clinical pharmacy practice. It is the first such examination for Doctor of Pharmacy students.

15290
Bulimia Knowledge Test for the Significant Others of Bulimics. Kapoor, Sandy 1987
Descriptors: Achievement Tests; Adults; *Bulimia; *Knowledge Level; Multiple Choice Tests
Availability: Sandy Kapoor; Michigan State University, School of Hotel, Restaurant, and Institutional Management, Eppley Center, E. Lansing, MI 48824-1121
Age Level: Adults
Notes: Items, 50
A multiple-choice test for friends and family members of bulimics about their knowledge of bulimia.

15291
Test of Language Development—2, Intermediate.
Hammill, Donald D.; Newcomer, Phyllis L. 1988
Subtests: Sentence Combining; Vocabulary; Word Ordering; Generals; Grammatic Comprehension; Malapropisms
Descriptors: *Individual Testing; *Language Handicaps; *Language Skills; *Language Tests; *Preadolescents; *Speech Skills; Standardized Tests
Identifiers: TOLD2
Availability: PRO-ED; 8700 Shoal Creek Blvd., Austin, TX 78758-6897
Age Level: 8-12
Notes: Time, 45 min. approx.; Items, 180
Assesses spoken language. Identifies children, 8 to 12 years old, who have language disorders and isolates the particular types of disorders that they have. Profiles individual strengths and deficiencies in basic language abilities. Has 6 subtests that measure different components of spoken language. Generals, Malapropisms, and Vocabulary assess the understanding and meaningful use of spoken words. Sentence Combining, Word Ordering, and Grammar Comprehension assess differing aspects of grammar. Results are reported as standard scores, percentiles, and age equivalents.

15292
Elicited Articulatory System Evaluation. Steed, Susie Finn; Haynes, William O. 1988
Descriptors: Adolescents; Adults; *Articulation (Speech); *Articulation Impairments; Children; Consonants; *Individual Testing; Phonemes; Pictorial Stimuli; *Screening Tests; *Speech Tests; Vowels; Young Children
Identifiers: EASE
Availability: PRO-ED; 8700 Shoal Creek Blvd., Austin, TX 78758-6897
Age Level: 3-65
Notes: Time, 15 min. approx.
An imitative sentence articulation assessment instrument designed to provide a traditional and phonological analysis; to assess each vowel and consonant numerous times in multiple contexts in connected speech; to serve as an initial assessment tool and/or to assess therapy progress over a period of time; and to provide an articulation assessment instrument that can be administered in a short period of time. It is intended to be used as an adjunct to other procedures in the assessment of articulation. The instrument assesses 337 consonant and 187 vowel productions and provides an evaluation of 10 phonological processes.

15304
Student Occupational Competency Achievement Testing: Heating (Field Test). National Occupational Competency Testing Institute, Big Rapids, MI
Descriptors: *Achievement Tests; Adults; Credentials; *Heating; High Schools; *High School Students; Multiple Choice Tests; Occupational Tests; Performance Tests; *Postsecondary Education; Secondary Education; Two Year Colleges; *Vocational Education; *Work Sample Tests
Identifiers: NOCTI; SOCAT
Availability: National Occupational Competency Testing Institute; 409 Bishop Hall, Ferris State University, Big Rapids, MI 49307
Grade Level: 9-14
Notes: Time, 345 min.; Items, 158
This test is part of a program developed to evaluate secondary and postsecondary vocational students with a standardized, objective measure. Each test consists of a multiple-choice portion covering factual knowledge, technical information, understanding of principles and problem-solving abilities related to the occupation. A performance component samples manipulative skills required. A mental ability test is also available. The written test covers tools and equipment, fuels, general information, service and repair, heat pump, heat loss, components, controls, steam heat, gas and oil furnaces, welding and soldering, solar heating, electric furnaces, safety. The performance test covers gas or oil burner inspection and service, controls, installation/building section of a heating system.

15307
Test of Physical Fitness Knowledge. Mood, Dale 1970
Descriptors: *Achievement Tests; *College Seniors; Higher Education; Knowledge Level; *Majors (Students); Multiple Choice Tests; *Physical Education; *Physical Fitness
Identifiers: TIM(N)
Availability: Tests in Microfiche; Test Collection, Educational Testing Service, Princeton, NJ 08541
Grade Level: 16
Notes: Time, 27 min.; Items, 64

Multiple-choice test which measures the physical fitness knowledge of college senior physical education majors. Two parallel test forms are available. Normed on 4,000 students in the U.S. Topic areas include status and promotion of fitness; evaluation; kinesiological aspects; nutritional aspects; fitness programs; fitness versus disease; physiological aspects; psychological aspects; sociological aspects; and other miscellaneous concepts. Validity and reliability are discussed in *Research Quarterly;* v42 n4 p423-30, 1970.

15354
Texas Educational Assessment of Minimum Skills: Exit Level Reading Test. Texas Education Agency, Div. of Educational Assessment, Austin, TX 1985
Descriptors: *Grade 12; *Graduation Requirements; High Schools; *High School Seniors; Literary Criticism; *Minimum Competency Testing; Reading Achievement; Reading Processes; *Reading Skills; *Reading Tests; Research Skills; State Programs
Identifiers: TEAMS; Texas
Availability: ERIC Document Reproduction Service; 7420 Fullerton Rd., Ste. 110, Springfield, VA 22153-2852 (ED266162, 46 p.)
Grade Level: 12
This test must be completed in a satisfactory manner as a requirement for high school graduation in Texas. Six skill areas are covered: identifying the main idea; using context and word structure to identify word meanings; identifying specific details and sequences of events; drawing logical inferences; selecting and using reference sources; literary analysis and distinguishing fact from opinion.

15355
Texas Educational Assessment of Minimum Skills: Writing, Exit Level. Texas Education Agency, Div. of Educational Assessment, Austin, TX 1985
Descriptors: Essay Tests; *Graduation Requirements; High Schools; *High School Seniors; *Minimum Competency Testing; State Programs; Testing Programs; *Writing Evaluation; Writing Processes; *Writing Skills
Identifiers: TEAMS; Texas
Availability: ERIC Document Reproduction Service; 7420 Fullerton Rd., Ste. 110, Springfield, VA 22153-2852 (ED266161, 39 p.)
Grade Level: 12
This test is designed to cover 5 skill areas: mechanics-demonstrating knowledge of capitalization, punctuation, and spelling; demonstrating knowledge of correct English usage; recognizing correct and complete sentences; organizing a written communication; proofreading. Satisfactory performance on this test is required for high school graduation in Texas.

15407
College Level Examination Program Education Assessment Series, English Composition. College Board, New York, NY 1988
Descriptors: *Achievement Tests; *College English; *College Freshmen; *College Students; *Critical Reading; *Grammar; Higher Education; Pretests Posttests; Reading; Reading Comprehension; Sentence Structure; *Writing (Composition); *College Sophomores
Identifiers: EAS
Availability: The College Board; 45 Columbus Ave., New York, NY 10023-6992
Grade Level: 13-14
Notes: Time, 45 min.
The Education Assessment Series (EAS) examinations are designed to measure how much students are learning in general education areas in the first 2 years of college and how they compare with students at other institutions. Two equated forms of each test are available for use at college entry and at the end of sophomore year. English Composition requires students to identify wording that is unclear or wordy or that is not standard grammar or usage; select the best version of a sentence after following directions to reword it; make judgments from passages read about assumptions and implications, logic of argument, organization, coherence, suitability of language to audience, and purpose. May be scored locally or through publisher.

15408
College Level Examination Program Education Assessment Series, Mathematics. College Board, New York, NY 1988
Descriptors: *Achievement Tests; Algebra; Arithmetic; *College Freshmen; *College Mathematics; College Students; Data Interpretation; Functions (Mathematics); Geometry; Higher Education; Pretests Posttests; Probability; Set Theory; Statistics; *College Sophomores
Identifiers: EAS
Availability: The College Board; 45 Columbus Ave., New York, NY 10023-6992
Grade Level: 13-14
Notes: Time, 45 min.

The Education Assessment Series (EAS) examinations are designed to measure how much students are learning in general education areas in the first 2 years of college and how they compare with students at other institutions. Two equated forms of each test are available for use at college entry and at the end of sophomore year. The Mathematics test assesses students' ability in mathematical skills and elementary concepts that are normally included in a college mathematics course for nonmajors or others that do not require knowledge of advanced mathematics. Multiple-choice questions cover quantitative skill in arithmetic, elementary algebra, geometry, data interpretation, elementary concepts in sets, logic, real number system, functions and graphs, probability, and statistics.

15411
Revised (1986) Denver Prescreening Developmental Questionnaire.   Frankenburg, William K. 1986
Descriptors: *Child Development; *Developmental Tasks; Disabilities; High Risk Students; *Infants; Norm Referenced Tests; *Screening Tests; *Young Children
Identifiers: DDST; Denver Developmental Screening Test; RPDQ
Availability: Denver Developmental Materials; P.O. Box 20037, Denver, CO 80220-0037
Age Level: 0-6
Notes: Time, 5 min. approx.

Designed to screen out children likely to be suspect on the longer Denver Developmental Screening Test (DDST). This revised version of the Prescreening Developmental Questionnaire (PDQ) differs in 3 ways from the original: items on the revised form are more age appropriate; items may be answered beyond the chronological age so that parents can see how far their child has progressed; by using the item titles on the revised form, one can refer to the DDST scale to determine what percentage of children in the DDST standardization sample performed that particular task on the revised PDQ. The DDST consists of a series of developmental tasks used to determine whether a child's development is within the normal range and to identify children likely to have significant motor, social, and/or language delays or to fail in school.

15413
Advanced Placement Program United States Government and Politics.   Educational Testing Service, Princeton, NJ 1988
Descriptors: *Achievement Tests; *Advanced Placement Programs; Essay Tests; High Schools; *High School Students; Multiple Choice Tests; *United States Government (Course)
Identifiers: AP; *Comparative Government (Course)
Availability: Advanced Placement Program; Educational Testing Service, Princeton, NJ 08541-6670
Grade Level: 10-12
Notes: Time, 90 min. approx.

Designed to assess achievement in introductory college-level government and politics courses so that high school students taking the Advanced Placement course and test can expect colleges and universities to grant advanced placement when they have passed the test. The Advanced Placement Program has been sponsored by the College Board since 1955. Each test is divided between a multiple-choice section and a free-response or essay section. There are 2 examinations, one in U.S. government and politics and one in comparative government and politics. Students may take one or both examinations. The U.S. government and politics test covers constitutional underpinnings of democracy; political beliefs and behaviors of individuals; political parties and interest groups; Congress, the presidency, the bureaucracy, and the federal courts; and civil liberties and civil rights. The comparative government and politics test covers sources of public authority and political power; society and politics; citizen and state; political framework; political change; and introduction to comparative politics.

15415
Undergraduate Assessment Program: Business Test.   Educational Testing Service, Princeton, NJ
Descriptors: Accounting; *Achievement Tests; Administration; *Business Administration Education; *Diagnostic Tests; Economics; Higher Education; Marketing; *Outcomes of Education; *Undergraduate Students; *Undergraduate Study
Identifiers: UAP
Availability: Undergraduate Assessment Program; ETS School and Higher Education Programs, 01-P, Princeton, NJ 08541
Grade Level: 13-16
Notes: Time, 120 min.; Items, 125

Designed to measure students' knowledge of significant facts, concepts, theories, and methodology covered in the core business curriculum. Also evaluates the students' ability to apply this knowledge. Although it is recognized that the core may vary somewhat from one institution to another, it is assumed that most students will have in common the equivalent of introductory courses in Accounting,

Finance, Economics, Marketing, Business Law, Management, and Quantitative Business Analysis. Available for local scoring on a rental basis only. Can be used by colleges and universities to evaluate their academic outcomes and examine their strengths and weaknesses or to measure individual student achievement. This program was the successor to the Undergraduate Program for Counseling and Evaluation (UP).

15428
Sexual Knowledge Questionnaire (Gough Adaptation).   Miller, Warren; Fisk, Norman M. 1974
Descriptors: Achievement Tests; *Adults; *College Students; Contraception; Higher Education; *Knowledge Level; Physiology; Reproduction (Biology); *Sexuality; Menstruation
Identifiers: Fertility; Sex Drive
Availability: Journal of Psychology; v87 n2, p183-92, Jul 1974
Grade Level: 13-16
Age Level: Adults
Notes: Time, 10 min.; Items, 24

Developed from the original 49-item version to be brief and reliable and, therefore, useful in studies of family planning, population, and related issues. Twenty-five questions with weak or unacceptable statistical properties were deleted. This version was administered to new samples of 287 males and 246 females. Items cover reproductive physiology, effectiveness of different contraception methods, menstrual functioning, and factors influencing sex drive and fertility.

15430
Drugs and Alcohol Information Survey.   Gough, Harrison G. 1985
Subtests: Drugs; Alcohol; Tobacco
Descriptors: Achievement Tests; Adults; *Alcoholism; *College Students; *Drug Use; Higher Education; High Schools; High School Students; *Knowledge Level; Prisoners; Research Tools; Surveys; *Tobacco
Identifiers: DAIS
Availability: Harrison G. Gough; Institute of Personality Assessment and Research, University of California, Berkeley, CA 94720
Grade Level: 9-16
Age Level: Adults
Notes: Time, 10 min.; Items, 35

A standardized test of knowledge of drugs and alcohol designed for use in studies of substance use and abuse and also for work with individual clients. Normed on a sample of 132 males and 71 females who are graduate or undergraduate students or staff associated with the institute, high school students, or correctional inmates. A total score and 3 subscores are tallied: drugs (29 items), alcohol (13 items), tobacco (3 items). Items and some normative data can be found in *International Journal of the Addictions;* v20 n4, p519-26, 1985.

15474
Rosenthal Diagnostic Phonics Assessment.
Rosenthal, Nadine 1987
Descriptors: Children; *Diagnostic Tests; Elementary Education; *Elementary School Students; Instructional Program Divisions; *Phonics; Primary Education; *Reading; *Spelling; Word Lists
Availability: Pitman Learning; 6 Davis Drive, Belmont, CA 94002
Grade Level: 1-4
Notes: Items, 90

An informal test of a student's ability to read lists of progressively difficult but phonically regular words. The lists range from a grade 1 to grade 4 level. Each word missed by the student is recorded. Areas in which student needs work can be identified from the list. It can be used as a spelling test to identify error patterns. Covers beginning consonants blends and digraphs; end consonants blends and digraphs; 3-letter blends; short vowels; vowel combinations; vowel with r, l, w; vowel with silent e, prefixes, syllables, endings. This test is part of a booklet called "Teach Someone to Read."

15475
Rosenthal Diagnostic Comprehension Assessment.
Rosenthal, Nadine 1987
Descriptors: Children; *Diagnostic Tests; Elementary Education; *Elementary School Students; *Reading Comprehension; *Reading Tests
Availability: Pitman Learning; 6 Davis Drive, Belmont, CA 94002
Grade Level: 1-6
Notes: Items, 30

This informal test of a student's ability to read short selections consists of 6 paragraphs written at progressively higher grade levels from 1-6. Each is followed by a set of comprehension questions that measure ability to handle literal recall and interpretive and active questions. The test is part of a booklet called "Teach Someone to Read."

15477
High School Subject Tests: Advanced Algebra, Form B-1.   Wick, John W.; Gatta, Louis A. 1988

Descriptors: *Achievement Tests; *Algebra; Criterion Referenced Tests; High Schools; *High School Students; *Mathematics Tests; Norm Referenced Tests; Pretests Posttests; Secondary Education
Identifiers: HSST
Availability: American Testronics; P.O. Box 2270, Iowa City, IA 52244-9990
Grade Level: 9-12
Notes: Time, 40 min. approx.; Items, 40

Two equivalent forms A and B allow pre- and posttest analyses of individuals, classes, or specific groups for grades 9 through 12. Tests are both norm referenced and criterion referenced. Can be used as an end-of-course assessment to measure students' knowledge of Advanced Algebra or as preassessments to measure students' knowledge prior to formal course of study of Advanced Algebra.

15478
High School Subject Tests: Algebra, Form B.
Wick, John W.; Gatta, Louis A. 1988
Descriptors: *Achievement Tests; *Algebra; Criterion Referenced Tests; High Schools; *High School Students; *Mathematics Tests; Norm Referenced Tests; Pretests Posttests; Secondary Education
Availability: American Testronics; P.O. Box 2270, Iowa City, IA 52244-9990
Grade Level: 9-12
Notes: Time, 40 min. approx.; Items, 40

Two equivalent forms A and B allow pre- and posttest analyses of individuals, classes, or specific groups for grades 9 through 12. Tests are both norm referenced and criterion referenced. Can be used as an end-of-course assessment to measure students' knowledge of algebra or as preassessments to measure students' knowledge prior to formal course of study of algebra.

15479
High School Subject Tests: American Government, Form B.   Wick, John W.; Gatta, Louis A. 1988
Descriptors: *Achievement Tests; Criterion Referenced Tests; High Schools; *High School Students; Norm Referenced Tests; Pretests Posttests; Secondary Education; *United States Government (Course)
Identifiers: HSST
Availability: American Testronics; P.O. Box 2270, Iowa City, IA 52244-9990
Grade Level: 9-12
Notes: Time, 40 min. approx.; Items, 50

Two equivalent forms A and B allow pre- and posttest analyses of individuals, classes, or specific groups for grades 9 through 12. Tests are both norm referenced and criterion referenced. Can be used as an end-of-course assessment to measure students' knowledge of American government or as preassessments to measure students' knowledge prior to formal course of study of American government.

15480
High School Subject Tests: American History, Form B.   Wick, John W.; Gatta, Louis A. 1988
Descriptors: *Achievement Tests; Criterion Referenced Tests; High Schools; *High School Students; Norm Referenced Tests; Pretests Posttests; Secondary Education; *United States History
Identifiers: HSST
Availability: American Testronics; P.O. Box 2270, Iowa City, IA 52244-9990
Grade Level: 9-12
Notes: Time, 40 min. approx.; Items, 50

Two equivalent forms A and B allow pre- and posttest analyses of individuals, classes, or specific groups for grades 9 through 12. Tests are both norm referenced and criterion referenced. Can be used as an end-of-course assessment to measure students' knowledge of American history or as preassessments to measure students' knowledge prior to formal course of study of American history.

15481
High School Subject Tests: Biology, Form B.
Wick, John W.; Gatta, Louis A. 1988
Descriptors: *Achievement Tests; *Biology; Criterion Referenced Tests; High Schools; *High School Students; Norm Referenced Tests; Pretests Posttests; *Science Tests; Secondary Education
Identifiers: HSST
Availability: American Testronics; P.O. Box 2270, Iowa City, IA 52244-9990
Grade Level: 9-12
Notes: Time, 40 min. approx.; Items, 60

Two equivalent forms A and B allow pre- and posttest analyses of individuals, classes, or specific groups for grades 9 through 12. Tests are both norm referenced and criterion referenced. Can be used as an end-of-course assessment to measure students' knowledge of biology or as preassessments to measure students' knowledge prior to formal course of study of biology.

15482
High School Subject Tests: Chemistry, Form B-1.
Wick, John W.; Gatta, Louis A. 1988
Descriptors: *Achievement Tests; *Chemistry; Criterion Referenced Tests; High Schools; *High School Students; Norm Referenced Tests; Pretests Posttests; *Science Tests; Secondary Education
Identifiers: HSST
Availability: American Testronics; P.O. Box 2270, Iowa City, IA 52244-9990
Grade Level: 9-12
Notes: Time, 40 min. approx.; Items, 40
Two equivalent forms A and B allow pre- and posttest analyses of individuals, classes, or specific groups for grades 9 through 12. Tests are both norm referenced and criterion referenced. Can be used as an end-of-course assessment to measure students' knowledge of chemistry or as preassessments to measure students' knowledge prior to formal course of study of chemistry.

15483
High School Subject Tests: Computer Literacy, Form B. Wick, John W.; Gatta, Louis A. 1988
Descriptors: *Achievement Tests; *Computer Literacy; Criterion Referenced Tests; High Schools; *High School Students; Norm Referenced Tests; Pretests Posttests; Secondary Education
Identifiers: HSST
Availability: American Testronics; P.O. Box 2270, Iowa City, IA 52244-9990
Grade Level: 9-12
Notes: Time, 40 min. approx.; Items, 45
Two equivalent forms A and B allow pre- and posttest analyses of individuals, classes, or specific groups for grades 9 through 12. Tests are both norm referenced and criterion referenced. Can be used as an end-of-course assessment to measure students' knowledge of computer literacy or as a preassessment to measure students' knowledge prior to formal course of study of computer literacy.

15484
High School Subject Tests: Consumer Economics, Form B. Wick, John W.; Gatta, Louis A. 1988
Descriptors: *Achievement Tests; *Consumer Economics; Criterion Referenced Tests; High Schools; *High School Students; Norm Referenced Tests; Pretests Posttests; Secondary Education
Identifiers: HSST
Availability: American Testronics; P.O. Box 2270, Iowa City, IA 52244-9990
Grade Level: 9-12
Notes: Time, 40 min. approx.; Items, 55
Two equivalent forms A and B allow pre- and posttest analyses of individuals, classes, or specific groups for grades 9 through 12. Tests are both norm referenced and criterion referenced. Can be used as an end-of-course assessment to measure students' knowledge of consumer economics or as a preassessment to measure students' knowledge prior to formal course of study of consumer economics.

15485
High School Subject Tests: Language, Form B.
Wick, John W.; Gatta, Louis A. 1988
Descriptors: *Achievement Tests; Criterion Referenced Tests; High Schools; *High School Students; Language; *Language Tests; Norm Referenced Tests; Pretests Posttests; Secondary Education
Identifiers: HSST
Availability: American Testronics; P.O. Box 2270, Iowa City, IA 52244-9990
Grade Level: 9-12
Notes: Time, 40 min. approx.; Items, 70
Two equivalent forms A and B allow pre- and posttest analyses of individuals, classes, or specific groups for grades 9 through 12. Tests are both norm referenced and criterion referenced. Can be used as an end-of-course assessment to measure students' knowledge of language or as a preassessment to measure students' knowledge prior to formal course of study of language.

15486
High School Subject Tests: Literature and Vocabulary, Form B. Wick, John W.; Gatta, Louis A. 1988
Descriptors: *Achievement Tests; Criterion Referenced Tests; High Schools; *High School Students; *Literature; Norm Referenced Tests; Pretests Posttests; Secondary Education; *Vocabulary
Identifiers: HSST
Availability: American Testronics; P.O. Box 2270, Iowa City, IA 52244-9990
Grade Level: 9-12
Notes: Time, 40 min. approx.; Items, 50
Two equivalent forms A and B allow pre- and posttest analyses of individuals, classes, or specific groups for grades 9 through 12. Tests are both norm referenced and criterion referenced. Can be used as an end-of-course assessment to measure students' knowledge of literature and vocabulary or as a preassessment to measure students' knowledge prior to formal course of study of literature and vocabulary.

15487
High School Subject Tests: Physical Science, Form B. Wick, John W.; Gatta, Louis A. 1988
Descriptors: *Achievement Tests; Criterion Referenced Tests; High Schools; *High School Students; Norm Referenced Tests; *Physical Sciences; Pretests Posttests; Secondary Education
Identifiers: HSST
Availability: American Testronics; P.O. Box 2270, Iowa City, IA 52244-9990
Grade Level: 9-12
Notes: Time, 40 min. approx.; Items, 50
Two equivalent forms A and B allow pre- and posttest analyses of individuals, classes, or specific groups for grades 9 through 12. Tests are both norm referenced and criterion referenced. Can be used as an end-of-course assessment to measure students' knowledge of physical science or as a preassessment to measure students' knowledge prior to formal course of study of physical science.

15488
High School Subject Tests: Physics, Form B.
Wick, John W.; Gatta, Louis A. 1988
Descriptors: *Achievement Tests; Criterion Referenced Tests; High Schools; *High School Students; Norm Referenced Tests; *Physics; Pretests Posttests; Secondary Education
Identifiers: HSST
Availability: American Testronics; P.O. Box 2270, Iowa City, IA 52244-9990
Grade Level: 9-12
Notes: Time, 40 min. approx.; Items, 40
Two equivalent forms A and B allow pre- and posttest analyses of individuals, classes, or specific groups for grades 9 through 12. Tests are both norm referenced and criterion referenced. Can be used as an end-of-course assessment to measure students' knowledge of physics or as a preassessment to measure students' knowledge prior to formal course of study of physics.

15489
High School Subject Tests: Pre-Algebra, Form B-1. Wick, John W.; Gatta, Louis A. 1988
Descriptors: *Achievement Tests; Algebra; Criterion Referenced Tests; High Schools; *High School Students; *Mathematics Tests; Norm Referenced Tests; Pretests Posttests; Secondary Education
Identifiers: HSST; *Pre Algebra
Availability: American Testronics; P.O. Box 2270, Iowa City, IA 52244-9990
Grade Level: 9-12
Notes: Time, 40 min. approx.; Items, 40
Two equivalent forms A and B allow pre- and posttest analyses of individuals, classes, or specific groups for grades 9 through 12. Tests are both norm referenced and criterion referenced. Can be used as an end-of-course assessment to measure students' knowledge of prealgebra or as a preassessment to measure students' knowledge prior to formal course of study of prealgebra.

15490
High School Subject Tests: World History, Form B. Wick, John W.; Gatta, Louis A. 1988
Descriptors: *Achievement Tests; Criterion Referenced Tests; High Schools; *High School Students; Norm Referenced Tests; Pretests Posttests; Secondary Education; *World History
Identifiers: HSST
Availability: American Testronics; P.O. Box 2270, Iowa City, IA 52244-9990
Grade Level: 9-12
Notes: Time, 40 min. approx.; Items, 45
Two equivalent forms A and B allow pre- and posttest analyses of individuals, classes, or specific groups for grades 9 through 12. Tests are both norm referenced and criterion referenced. Can be used as an end-of-course assessment to measure students' knowledge of world history or as a preassessment to measure students' knowledge prior to formal course of study of world history.

15491
High School Subject Tests: Writing and Mechanics, Form B. Wick, John W.; Gatta, Louis A. 1988
Descriptors: *Achievement Tests; Criterion Referenced Tests; High Schools; *High School Students; Norm Referenced Tests; Pretests Posttests; Secondary Education; *Writing Skills
Identifiers: HSST
Availability: American Testronics; P.O. Box 2270, Iowa City, IA 52244-9990
Grade Level: 9-12
Notes: Time, 40 min. approx.; Items, 50
Two equivalent forms A and B allow pre- and posttest analyses of individuals, classes, or specific groups for grades 9 through 12. Tests are both norm referenced and criterion referenced. Can be used as an end-of-course assessment to measure students' knowledge of writing and mechanics or as a preassessment to measure students' knowledge prior to formal couse of study of writing and mechanics.

15494
Multiscore: Mathematics Objectives. Riverside Publishing Co., Chicago, IL 1984
Descriptors: *Achievement Tests; Addition; *Criterion Referenced Tests; Decimal Fractions; Division; *Elementary Education; *Elementary School Students; Fractions; Geometry; Graphs; *Item Banks; *Junior High Schools; *Junior High School Students; Logical Thinking; Mathematics; *Mathematics Tests; Measurement; *Minimum Competency Testing; Multiplication; Numbers; Pretests Posttests; Probability; Ratios (Mathematics); Statistics; Subtraction
Availability: Riverside Publishing Co.; 8420 Bryn Mawr Ave., Chicago, IL 60631
Grade Level: 1-8
A catalog of several hundred objectives in mathematics. By selecting the objectives most important to their respective schools, educators can design criterion-referenced test booklets from an item bank of several thousand items. Part of the MULTISCORE customized criterion-referenced test development service, which measures student proficiency in 6 basic skill areas. The tests may be used as minimum competency examinations, as exit tests for assessing specific end-of-year proficiencies, and as pretests or posttests for federal programs and other special projects. The system is multidimensional and multidirectional.

15495
Multiscore: Reading and Language Arts Objectives. Riverside Publishing Co., Chicago, IL 1984
Descriptors: *Achievement Tests; *Criterion Referenced Tests; *Elementary Education; *Elementary School Students; *Item Banks; Junior High Schools; *Junior High School Students; *Language Arts; *Minimum Competency Testing; Pretests Posttests; *Reading Ability; *Reading Achievement; Reading Comprehension; *Reading Tests
Availability: Riverside Publishing Co.; 8420 Bryn Mawr Ave., Chicago, IL 60631
Grade Level: 1-8
A catalog of several hundred objectives in the subject areas of reading and language arts. By selecting the objectives most important to their respective schools, educators can design criterion-referenced test booklets from an item bank of several thousand items. Part of the MULTISCORE customized criterion-referenced test development service, which measures student proficiency in 6 basic skill areas. The tests may be used as minimum competency examinations, as exit tests for assessing specific end-of-year proficiencies, and as pretests or posttests for federal programs and other special projects. The system is multidimensional and multidirectional.

15496
Multiscore: Science, Social Studies and Life Skills Objectives. Riverside Publishing Co., Chicago, IL 1984
Descriptors: *Achievement Tests; Computer Literacy; *Criterion Referenced Tests; *Daily Living Skills; Economics; *Elementary School Students; *Elementary Secondary Education; Geography; Government (Administrative Body); *Item Banks; *Minimum Competency Testing; Pretests Posttests; Science History; *Sciences; *Science Tests; Scientific Methodology; *Secondary School Students; *Social Studies; Sociology
Availability: Riverside Publishing Co.; 8420 Bryn Mawr Ave., Chicago, IL 60631
Grade Level: 1-12
A catalog of several hundred objectives in the subject areas of science, social studies and life skills. By selecting the objectives most important to their respective schools, educators can design criterion-referenced test booklets from an item bank of several thousand items. Part of the MULTISCORE customized criterion-referenced test development service, which measures student proficiency in 6 basic skill areas. The tests may be used as minimum competency examinations, as exit tests for assessing specific end-of-year proficiencies, and as pretests or posttests for federal programs and other special projects. The system is multidimensional and multidirectional.

15499
Informal Tests for Diagnosing Specific Reading Problems. Paulak, Stephen A. 1985
Subtests: Phonic Analysis; Structural Analysis; Comprehension Skills; Survival Reading Skills

Descriptors: *Diagnostic Tests; Elementary Education; *Elementary School Students; Functional Reading; *Informal Reading Inventories; Phonetic Analysis; Phonics; Reading Comprehension; *Reading Difficulties; *Reading Tests; Structural Analysis (Linguistics)
Availability: Prentice Hall; 200 Old Tappan Rd., Old Tappan, NJ 07675
Grade Level: 1-6

Contains over 60 informal tests to diagnose specific reading skill weaknesses of elementary school students in the areas of phonic analysis, structural analysis comprehension and survival reading. Provides reading specialists and classroom teachers with ready-to-use diagnostic aids that can be adapted to any program to prescribe corrective or remedial activities for each individual.

15502
Missouri Kindergarten Inventory of Developmental Skills, Alternate Form.   Missouri Department of Elementary and Secondary Education
Subtests: Number Concepts; Language; Verbal Concepts; Paper and Pencil Skills; Auditory and Visual Skills; Gross Motor Skills
Descriptors: Auditory Perception; Early Childhood Education; *Kindergarten Children; Language Skills; Mathematics; Number Concepts; Preschool Education; Psychomotor Skills; *School Readiness; *Screening Tests; Verbal Development; Visual Perception; Writing Readiness; *Young Children
Identifiers: KIDS
Availability: University of Missouri-Columbia; Center for Educational Assessment, 403 S. Sixth St., Columbia, MO 65211
Grade Level: K
Age Level: 4-6
Notes: Time, 35 min.

A version of the original test (see TC015501) designed for use at an earlier age level (48 to 72 months). It is also for screening children prior to entrance into kindergarten. Norms are based on a representative sample of children drawn from within the state. May be given in the spring or summer preceding kindergarten or at entrance. A parent questionnaire elicits information about the child at home.

15508
Analysis of the Language of Learning.   Blodgett, Elizabeth G.; Cooper, Eugene B. 1987
Subtests: Defining concepts; Giving Concrete Examples; Recognizing Concepts; Segmenting Sentences; Generating Words; Segmenting Words; Repairing Sentences
Descriptors: *Diagnostic Tests; Elementary Education; *Elementary School Students; *Expressive Language; Grammar; Language Arts; *Language Patterns; *Language Processing; *Linguistic Difficulty (Inherent); Primary Education; Reading Readiness; *Receptive Language; Semantics; Sentence Structure; *Structural Linguistics
Identifiers: ALL
Availability: LinguiSystems; 3100 4th Ave., P.O. Box 747, E. Moline, IL 61244
Age Level: 5-9
Notes: Time, 30 min. approx.; Items, 68

A receptive and expressive test designed to assess a child's level of awareness of the structural aspects of language. The specific tasks of the test are constructed to yield information regarding the following areas of language awareness: language concepts, sentences as sequences of words, words as sequences of phonemes, initial and final phonemes of words, and the ability to repair structurally incorrect utterances. The test provides standardized analyses of a subject's strengths and weaknesses, as well as an overall estimate of the individual child's metalinguistic ability as compared to other children his or her age. Test norms have been established on children from the ages of 5 years, 0 months through 9 years, 11 months. May also be appropriate for older subjects whose overall metalinguistic abilities are within the performance range of the test. Because metalinguistic skills are necessary for reading and language arts instruction, this instrument can be used to determine whether deficiencies in these skills have the potential to affect academic or clinical performance.

15509
Einstein Assessment of School-Related Skills, Level K.   Gottesman, Ruth L.; Cerullo, Frances M. 1988
Subtests: Language/Cognition; Letter Recognition; Auditory Memory; Arithmetic; Visual-Motor Integration
Descriptors: Arithmetic; *High Risk Students; *Individual Testing; Kindergarten; *Kindergarten Children; Language Tests; *Learning Disabilities; *Learning Problems; Mathematics Tests; Perceptual Motor Coordination; *Primary Education; *Screening Tests; Short Term Memory
Availability: Modern Curriculum Press; 13900 Prospect Rd., Cleveland, OH 44136

Grade Level: K
Age Level: 5
Notes: Time, 10 min. approx.; Items, 17

An individually administered screening instrument that measures the major skill areas underlying school achievement. Designed to identify kindergarten children who are at risk for, or are experiencing, learning difficulties and who therefore should be referred for a comprehensive evaluation. Easily administered without special training. There are 5 additional test levels to be used with grades 1-5 (See TC015510-TC015514).

15510
Einstein Assessment of School-Related Skills, Level 1.   Gottesman, Ruth L.; Cerullo, Frances M. 1988
Subtests: Language/Cognition; Word Recognition; Oral Reading; Reading Comprehension; Auditory Memory; Arithmetic; Visual-Motor Integration
Descriptors: Arithmetic; *Elementary School Students; *Grade 1; *High Risk Students; *Individual Testing; Language Tests; *Learning Disabilities; *Learning Problems; Mathematics Tests; Oral Reading; Perceptual Motor Coordination; Primary Education; Reading Comprehension; Reading Tests; *Screening Tests; Short Term Memory; Word Recognition
Availability: Modern Curriculum Press; 13900 Prospect Rd., Cleveland, OH 44136
Grade Level: 1
Notes: Time, 10 min. approx.; Items, 24

An individually administered screening instrument that measures the major skill areas underlying school achievement. Designed to identify first grade children who are at risk for, or are experiencing, learning difficulties and who, therefore, should be referred for a comprehensive evaluation. Easily administered without special training. There are 5 additional test levels to be used with grades kindergarten and 2-5 (See TC015509, TC015511-TC015514).

15511
Einstein Assessment of School-Related Skills, Level 2.   Gottesman, Ruth L.; Cerullo, Frances M. 1988
Subtests: Language/Cognition; Word Recognition; Oral Reading; Reading Comprehension; Auditory Memory; Arithmetic; Visual-Motor Integration
Descriptors: Arithmetic; *Elementary School Students; *Grade 2; *High Risk Students; *Individual Testing; Language Tests; *Learning Disabilities; *Learning Problems; Mathematics Tests; Oral Reading; Perceptual Motor Coordination; Primary Education; Reading Comprehension; Reading Tests; *Screening Tests; Short Term Memory; Word Recognition
Availability: Modern Curriculum Press; 13900 Prospect Rd., Cleveland, OH 44136
Grade Level: 2
Notes: Time, 10 min. approx.; Items, 25

An individually administered screening instrument that measures the major skill areas underlying school achievement. Designed to identify second grade children who are at risk for, or are experiencing, learning difficulties and who, therefore, should be referred for a comprehensive evaluation. Easily administered without special training. There are 5 additional test levels to be used with grades kindergarten-1, and 3-5 (see TC015509-TC015510, TC015513-TC015514).

15512
Einstein Assessment of School-Related Skills, Level 3.   Gottesman, Ruth L.; Cerullo, Frances M. 1988
Subtests: Language/Cognition; Word Recognition; Oral Reading; Reading Comprehension; Auditory Memory; Arithmetic; Visual Motor Integration
Descriptors: Arithmetic; Elementary School Students; *Grade 3; *High Risk Students; *Individual Testing; Language Tests; *Learning Disabilities; *Learning Problems; Mathematics Tests; Oral Reading; Perceptual Motor Coordination; *Primary Education; Reading Comprehension; Reading Tests; *Screening Tests; Short Term Memory; Word Recognition
Availability: Modern Curriculum Press; 13900 Prospect Rd., Cleveland, OH 44136
Grade Level: 3
Notes: Time, 10 min. approx.; Items, 21

An individually administered screening instrument that measures the major skill areas underlying school achievement. Designed to identify third grade children who are at risk for, or are experiencing, learning difficulties and who, therefore, should be referred for a comprehensive evaluation. Easily administered without special training. There are 5 additional test levels to be used with grades kindergarten-2, 4-5 (see TC015509-TC015511, TC015513-TC105514).

15513
Einstein Assessment of School-Related Skills, Level 4.   Gottesman, Ruth L.; Cerullo, Frances M. 1988
Subtests: Language/Cognition; Word Recognition; Oral Reading; Reading Comprehension; Auditory Memory; Arithmetic; Visual-Motor Integration
Descriptors: Arithmetic; Elementary Education; *Elementary School Students; *Grade 4; *High Risk Students; *Individual Testing; Language Tests; *Learning Disabilities; *Learning Problems; Mathematics Tests; Oral Reading; Perceptual Motor Coordination; Reading Comprehension; Reading Tests; *Screening Tests; Short Term Memory; Word Recognition
Availability: Modern Curriculum Press; 13900 Prospect Rd., Cleveland, OH 44136
Grade Level: 4
Notes: Time, 10 min. approx.; Items, 23

An individually administered screening instrument that measures the major skill areas underlying school achievement. Designed to identify fourth grade children who are at risk for, or are experiencing, learning difficulties and who should, therefore, be referred for a comprehensive evaluation. Easily administered without special training. There are 5 additional test levels to be used with grades K-3 and 5 (see TC015509-015512, TC015514).

15514
Einstein Assessment of School-Related Skills, Level 5.   Gottesman, Ruth L.; Cerullo, Frances M. 1988
Subtests: Language/Cognition; Word Recognition; Oral Reading; Reading Comprehension; Auditory Memory; Arithmetic; Visual-Motor Integration
Descriptors: Arithmetic; Elementary Education; *Elementary School Students; *Grade 5; *High Risk Students; *Individual Testing; Language Tests; *Learning Disabilities; *Learning Problems; Mathematics Tests; Oral Reading; Perceptual Motor Coordination; Reading Comprehension; Reading Tests; *Screening Tests; Short Term Memory; Word Recognition
Availability: Modern Curriculum Press; 13900 Prospect Rd., Cleveland, OH 44136
Grade Level: 5
Notes: Time, 10 min. approx.; Items, 25

An individually administered screening instrument that measures the major skill areas underlying school achievement. Designed to identify fifth grade children who are at risk for, or are experiencing, learning difficulties and who, therefore, should be referred for a comprehensive evaluation. Easily administered without special training. There are 5 additional test levels to be used with grades kindergarten-4, (see TC015509-TC015513).

15517
Clymer-Barrett Readiness Test, Revised Edition, Forms A and B.   Clymer, Theodore; Barrett, Thomas C. 1983
Subtests: Recognizing Letters; Matching Words; Beginning Sounds; Ending Sounds; Completing Shapes; Copy A Sentence
Descriptors: Auditory Discrimination; Early Childhood Education; Eye Hand Coordination; Perceptual Motor Coordination; Pretests Posttests; *Primary Education; *Reading Readiness; *Reading Readiness Tests; Reading Tests; Visual Discrimination
Availability: Chapman, Brook and Kent; 27775 Hwy. 189, Arrowhead, CA 92352
Grade Level: K-1
Notes: Time, 90 min.; Items, 110

A readiness for reading measure that considers visual and auditory discrimination and visual-motor coordination. Used at end of kindergarten to determine success of readiness program, and at beginning of first grade to group students and determine which skills need emphasis. Two forms are available as pre- and posttest. To create a short form, the first test of each discrimination subarea can be used as a quick readiness survey (Recognizing Letters; Beginning Sounds). Each section of the test is given in one separate half-hour sitting.

15541
High School Subject Tests: General Mathematics, Form B.   Wick, John W.; Gatta, Louis A. 1988
Descriptors: *Achievement Tests; Criterion Referenced Tests; High Schools; *High School Students; *Mathematics; *Mathematics Tests; Norm Referenced Tests; Secondary Education
Identifiers: General Mathematics; HSST
Availability: American Testronics; P.O. Box 2270, Iowa City, IA 52244-9990
Grade Level: 9-12
Notes: Time, 40 min. approx.; Items, 40

Two equivalent forms A and B allow pre- and posttest analyses of individuals, classes, or specific groups for grades 9 through 12. Tests are both norm-referenced and criterion-referenced. Can be used as an end-of-course assessment to measure students' knowledge of general mathematics or as preassessments to measure students' knowledge prior to formal course of study of general mathematics.

15542
High School Subject Tests: Geometry, Form B.
Wick, John W.; Gatta, Louis A. 1988
Descriptors: *Achievement Tests; Criterion Referenced Tests; *Geometry; High Schools; *High School Students; *Mathematics Tests; Norm Referenced Tests; Secondary Education
Identifiers: HHST
Availability: American Testronics; P.O. Box 2270, Iowa City, IA 52244-9990
Grade Level: 9-12
Notes: Time, 40 min. approx.; Items, 40

Two equivalent forms A and B allow pre- and posttest analyses of individuals, classes, or specific groups for grades 9 through 12. Tests are both norm-referenced and criterion-referenced. Can be used as an end-of-course assessment to measure students' knowledge of geometry or as preassessments to measure students' knowledge prior to formal course of study of geometry.

15547
EDS Power Language Tests: Basic Level. Henney, R. Lee 1984
Descriptors: *Achievement Tests; *Vocabulary; Definitions; *Elementary School Students; Elementary Secondary Education; *Junior High School Students; Multiple Choice Tests; Vocabulary Skills; Basic Vocabulary
Availability: Educational Diagnostic Services; 2370 County Rd. 13, Corunna, IL 46730
Grade Level: 4-8
Notes: Time, 30 min.; Items, 30

This series of 20 tests measures knowledge of vocabulary words. Each test is at a higher level of difficulty. Student selects one of 3 choices of definitions of a given word. Each test has 30 items. No technical information is available as of this writing. Approximately 30 minutes are allowed for each test. Time is decreased as student proficiency increases.

15548
EDS Power Language Tests: Advanced Level. 1984
Descriptors: *Achievement Tests; Definitions; Multiple Choice Tests; Secondary Education; *Secondary School Students; *Vocabulary Skills
Availability: Educational Diagnostic Services; 2370 County Rd. 13, Corunna, IL 46730
Grade Level: 8-12
Notes: Time, 12 min.; Items, 50

This series of vocabulary tests measures knowledge of the meanings of words. Each of the 20 tests is at a greater level of difficulty. Student selects one of 3 choices of definitions of a given word. Each test has 50 items. No technical information is available as of this writing. Approximately 12 minutes are allowed for each test. Time is decreased as student proficiency increases.

15549
EDS Power Mathematics Tests: Basic Level.
Henney, R. Lee 1984
Descriptors: *Achievement Tests; Addition; *Arithmetic; Division; *Elementary School Students; Elementary Secondary Education; *Junior High School Students; *Mathematics Tests; Multiplication; Subtraction
Availability: Educational Diagnostic Services; 2370 County Rd. 13, Corunna, IL 46730
Grade Level: 4-8
Notes: Time, 40 min.; Items, 30

This series of arithmetic operations tests requires the student to perform addition, subtraction, multiplication, and division on 30 items per test. Completion time is decreased as student proficiency increases. No technical information on the properties of the instrument or norms are available as of this writing.

15550
EDS Power Mathematics Tests: Advanced Level.
Henney, R. Lee 1984
Descriptors: *Achievement Tests; Addition; *Adult Basic Education; Adults; Division; *Elementary School Students; Elementary Secondary Education; Graphs; *Mathematics Tests; Multiplication; Subtraction; *Word Problems (Mathematics)
Availability: Educational Diagnostic Services; 2370 County Rd. 13, Corunna, IL 46730
Grade Level: 5-8
Age Level: 11-65
Notes: Items, 800

A series of word problems divided into 20 tests with 40 items per test. The student is required to demonstrate competency in addition, subtraction, multiplication, division, fractions, decimals, averages, and interpretation of graphs. Developed for use in adult education programs, it is also suitable for mathematics assessment in the appro-

priate grade level. No technical information on the properties of the instrument or norms are available at this writing. (See also EDS Power Mathematics Tests: Basic Level, TC015549).

15551
EDS-GED Series: English. Henney, R. Lee 1987
Descriptors: *Achievement Tests; *Adult Education; Adults; *English; Grammar; *High School Equivalency Programs; Punctuation; Sentence Structure; Spelling
Identifiers: GED; *General Educational Development Tests; Power Tests
Availability: Educational Diagnostic Services; 2370 County Rd. 13, Corunna, IL 46730
Age Level: Adults
Notes: Items, 480

These tests are part of a course of study taken by adult students who are preparing to take the General Educational Development Tests (GED) to qualify for a high school equivalency certificate or diploma. Each of the power tests is to be used following completion of designated lessons in the student textbook. The tests are divided into developmental sections and GED-type questions. The topics covered by the lessons and tests include parts of speech; structure; mechanics; spelling; putting it together; and communicating. Each test should be completed in 60 minutes or less; otherwise, the section should be restudied and the test readministered.

15552
EDS-GED Series: Literature. Henney, R. Lee 1984
Descriptors: *Achievement Tests; *Adult Education; Adults; Drama; *High School Equivalency Programs; *Literature; Poetry; Prose
Identifiers: GED; *General Educational Development Tests; Power Tests
Availability: Educational Diagnostic Services; 2370 County Rd. 13, Corunna, IL 46730
Age Level: Adults
Notes: Items, 320

These tests are part of a course of study taken by adult students who are preparing to take the General Educational Development Tests (GED) to qualify for a high school equivalency certificate or diploma. Each of the power tests is to be used following completion of designated lessons in the student textbook. The tests are divided into developmental sections and GED-type questions. The topics covered by the lessons and tests are prose, poetry, and drama.

15553
EDS-GED Series: Mathematics. Henney, R. Lee 1987
Descriptors: *Achievement Tests; *Adult Education; Adults; Algebra; Arithmetic; Geometry; *High School Equivalency Programs; *Mathematics; Word Problems (Mathematics)
Identifiers: GED; *General Educational Development Tests; Power Tests
Availability: Educational Diagnostic Services; 2370 County Rd. 13, Corunna, IL 46730
Age Level: Adults
Notes: Items, 400

These tests are part of a course of study taken by adult students who are preparing to take the General Educational Development Tests (GED) to qualify for a high school equivalency certificate or diploma. Each of the power tests is to be used following completion of designated lessons in the student textbook. The tests are divided into developmental sections and GED-type questions. The lessons and tests cover basic mathematics skills, algebra, geometry, and the use of mathematical skills to solve problems. Each test should be completed in 50 minutes or less or else the section should be restudied and the test readministered.

15554
EDS-GED Series: Social Studies. Henney, R. Lee 1984
Descriptors: *Achievement Tests; *Adult Education; Adults; Ancient History; Federal Government; *High School Equivalency Programs; Medieval History; Modern History; *Social Studies; United States History
Identifiers: GED; *General Educational Development Tests; Power Tests
Availability: Educational Diagnostic Services; 2370 County Rd. 13, Corunna, IL 46730
Age Level: Adults
Notes: Items, 480

These tests are part of a course of study taken by adult students who are preparing to take the General Educational Development Tests (GED) to qualify for a high school equivalency certificate or diploma. Each of the power tests is to be used following completion of designated lessons in the student textbook. The tests are divided into developmental sections and GED-type questions. Lessons and tests cover studying history, ancient history, medieval history, modern history, U.S. history,

and government of the U.S. Each test should be completed in 50 minutes or less; otherwise appropriate sections should be restudied and the tests readministered.

15555
EDS-GED Series: Science. Henney, R. Lee 1987
Descriptors: *Achievement Tests; *Adult Education; Adults; Astronomy; Biology; Chemistry; Earth Science; *High School Equivalency Programs; Physics; Physiology; *Sciences
Identifiers: GED; *General Educational Development Tests; Power Tests
Availability: Educational Diagnostic Services; 2370 County Rd. 13, Corunna, IL 46730
Age Level: Adults
Notes: Items, 320

These tests are part of a course of study taken by adult students who are preparing to take the General Educational Development Tests (GED) to qualify for a high school equivalency certificate or diploma. Each of the power tests is to be used following completion of designated lessons in the student textbook. The tests are divided into developmental sections and GED-type questions. The lessons and tests cover general science and the scientific methods, physics, chemistry, earth science, astronomy, biology, and physiology. Each test should be completed in 50 minutes or less; otherwise, appropriate sections should be restudied and the tests readministered.

15561
Ber-Sil Spanish Test: Elementary Level, 1987 Revision. Beringer, Marjorie L. 1987
Subtests: Vocabulary; Response to Directions; Visual/Motor Skills; Mathematics
Descriptors: Basic Vocabulary; Elementary Education; Elementary School Mathematics; *Elementary School Students; *Individual Testing; Psychomotor Skills; Receptive Language; *Screening Tests; *Spanish Speaking; *Student Placement
Availability: BER-SIL Co.; 3412 Seaglen Drive, Rancho Palos Verdes, CA 90274
Age Level: 4-12

Assists in placing Spanish-speaking students, ages 4-12. Provides information on learning style and present level of skills of each child. Samples 5 areas of learning: receptive vocabulary in Spanish, ability to follow verbal directions, visual motor skills, math skills, comprehension of basic English vocabulary. Translations are available in Chinese, Korean, Philippino, and Persian.

15565
Michigan Prescriptive Program: Mathematics.
Lockhart, William E. 1979
Descriptors: *Adults; *Equivalency Tests; *High School Equivalency Programs; Mathematics; *Mathematics Achievement; *Mathematics Tests
Identifiers: GED; General Educational Development Tests
Availability: Ann Arbor Publishers; P.O. Box 7249, Naples, FL 33941
Age Level: Adults
Notes: Items, 70

Indicates student ability or deficiency in mathematics skills—elementary to adult. Designed to help students obtain a tenth grade equivalency and pass the General Educational Development Tests (GED) in math. Results of test show the items the individual should study. Average math gain is 1.5 years in 24 hours of study.

15572
Major Field Achievement Tests. Educational Testing Service, Princeton, NJ 1988
Subtests: Biology; Chemistry; Computer Science; Economics; Education; Engineering; Geology; History; Literature in English; Mathematics; Music; Physics; Political Science; Psychology; Sociology; Business
Descriptors: *Achievement Tests; Biology; *Business Education; Chemistry; *College Students; Computer Science; Economics; Education Courses; Engineering; English Literature; Geology; Higher Education; History; Mathematics; Music; *Outcomes of Education; Physics; Political Science; Psychology; Sociology; *Undergraduate Students
Identifiers: *Outcomes Assessment
Availability: Program Director; Major Field Achievement Tests; GRE Programs; Educational Testing Service, Princeton, NJ 08541
Grade Level: 13-16
Notes: Time, 120 min.

Designed to assess the outcomes of higher education by measuring undergraduate learning in specific disciplines. These tests are based on subject area tests from the Graduate Record Examination but are less difficult and cover the undergraduate curriculum. Tests are administered by the institution at their convenience and scored by the publisher. Tests reflect basic knowledge and understanding gained from courses. Subscores are reported for areas within each field. Different departmental needs for information can be met by administering different subforms of the test. Departmental and individual scores can be provided.

15574
WICAT Test of Basic Skills.   WICAT Systems, Orem, UT 1987
Subtests: Mathematics; Reading; Language Arts
Descriptors: *Achievement Tests; Basic Skills; *Computer Assisted Testing; Criterion Referenced Tests; Diagnostic Teaching; Diagnostic Tests; Educational Objectives; Elementary Education; *Elementary School Students; *Language Arts; *Mathematics; Pretests Posttests; *Reading
Identifiers: Educational Prescriptions
Availability: WICAT Systems; 1875 S. State St., Orem, UT 84058
Grade Level: 2-8

A series of tests in reading, mathematics, and language arts designed to measure students' basic competencies. Each test covers specific educational objectives based on the learning objectives of 35 states. Provides educational prescriptions for remediation. Assesses knowledge and mastery of skills, determines strengths and weaknesses of particular students. May be used at the beginning of the year for curriculum development based on student needs and at year's end to describe performance. Fourteen tests each contain 80-150 objective-referenced items covering 20-35 objective clusters. Items are multiple-choice with graphics and audio. Online administrations are scored online. Paper-and-pencil testing requires a scanner and special software for scoring. All equipment for administration is purchased from WICAT. Also runs on IBM-PC and Apple IIe.

15575
WICAT Test Creation Package.   WICAT Systems, Orem, UT 1987
Subtests: Reading; Mathematics; Language Arts
Descriptors: *Achievement Tests; Adaptive Testing; *Computer Assisted Testing; Computer Software; *Criterion Referenced Tests; Diagnostic Teaching; Diagnostic Tests; Educational Objectives; *Elementary School Students; Elementary Secondary Education; Item Analysis; *Item Banks; *Language Arts; *Mathematics; *Reading; Scoring; *Secondary School Students; Test Construction; Test Items
Identifiers: Educational Prescriptions
Availability: WICAT Systems; 1875 S. State St., Orem, UT 84058
Grade Level: 2-12

This relational database software package is designed for use by testing specialists in preparing localized criterion-referenced tests. Tailored to school district objectives, in paper-and-pencil and online administration formats. Contains data-banks of 700 objectives, 5,000 test items and also teaching prescriptions. Said to be useful for both mainstream and special students. Online tests are scored automatically. Paper-and-pencil tests are scored via document scanner and scoring software. Report options include objectives-based, prescriptive student and class reports, and conventional item analysis. Preparation of parallel forms and adaptive test administration is also performed. WICAT supplies the necessary computer software. Also runs on IBM-PC and Apple IIe.

15576
WICAT Make a Test.   WICAT Systems, Orem, UT
Descriptors: Adults; *Computer Assisted Testing; Computer Software; *Elementary School Teachers; Elementary Secondary Education; Item Analysis; Scoring; *Secondary School Teachers; *Teacher Made Tests; Test Construction
Availability: WICAT Systems; 1875 S. State St., Orem, UT 84058
Grade Level: 1-12

A computer-based program that allows teachers to create, store, and score tests for classroom use. Allows a mix of multiple-choice, true-false, and short-answer items in the same test. Can be administered via computer or printed. Program will provide feedback if desired. Compiles results and prepares reports. Reports include group performance by raw-score; item responses by time and number of students; item statistics by number of responses, percent of correct responses, average total score, median split, number of students in upper- and lower-scoring half of class, and how they responded to the item, plus item correlation with whole test. WICAT supplies the computer systems. Also runs on IBM-PC and Apple IIe.

15577
WICAT Reading Abilities Profile.   WICAT Systems, Orem, UT 1987
Descriptors: *Computer Assisted Testing; Computer Software; *Diagnostic Tests; Elementary Education; *Elementary School Students; Profiles; *Reading; *Reading Diagnosis; Reading Difficulties
Identifiers: WRAP

Availability: WICAT Systems; 1875 S. State St., Orem, UT 84058
Grade Level: 1-6
Notes: Items, 400

A diagnostic measure for use with students who have specific reading problems, or who are suspected of having difficulty. It is designed for use through sixth grade level, but the content is said to be appropriate for adolescents and adults. Administered via computer. Covers 22 diagnostic reading subskills. Each subtest contains 15-20 items. Content focuses on cognitive skills of identification, discrimination, memory, analysis, classification, and learning, at 4 levels of language organization: segmental, lexical, syntactic, and discourse. A profile identifies student's reliance on sound patterns, letter shapes and word association. WICAT supplies the computer systems that run this software. Also runs on IBM-PC and Apple IIe.

15578
WICAT Early Childhood Profile.   WICAT Systems, Orem, UT 1987
Subtests: Alphabet Recognition; Number Recognition; Counting; Listening Comprehension; Concept Relations; Classification Skills; Sound/Symbol Identification
Descriptors: *Academic Ability; *Computer Assisted Testing; Concept Formation; Curriculum Development; *Early Childhood Education; Learning Readiness; Listening Comprehension; Multiple Choice Tests; Numbers; Preschool Education; Pretests Posttests; Reading Readiness; *School Readiness; Young Children
Availability: WICAT Systems; 1875 S. State St., Orem, UT 84058
Age Level: 3-6
Notes: Time, 30 min.; Items, 24

Consists of 2 levels of a computer-administered test designed to assess the academic abilities of young children. Level 1 is for ages 3.5 to 4.5, and level 2 is for ages 4.5 to 6.0. Items are read to the child who selects the answer from a multiple-choice format. Can be used to determine readiness for preschool or kindergarten, for curriculum planning and as a pretest/posttest measure of student progress. WICAT supplies the computer systems that run this software. Also runs on IBM-PC and Apple IIe.

15579
WICAT Comprehensive Assessment Test - Texas.
WICAT Systems, Orem, UT 1987
Subtests: Reading; Writing; Mathematics
Descriptors: *Achievement Tests; *Computer Assisted Testing; Computer Software; Diagnostic Teaching; Educational Objectives; *Elementary School Students; Elementary Secondary Education; Mathematics; *Minimum Competency Testing; Prognostic Tests; Reading; *Secondary School Students; *Testing Programs; Writing Skills
Identifiers: Test Batteries; Texas; Texas Educational Assessment of Minimum Skills
Availability: WICAT Systems; 1875 S. State St., Orem, UT 84058
Grade Level: 3; 5; 7; 9; 11
Notes: Items, 40

Designed to measure student performance in subject areas, against state-mandated minimum skill objectives, for curriculum and instructional decisions. Based on the 1986 Texas Educational Assessment of Minimum Skills (TEAMS). Individual student scores are said to be predictive of success on the TEAMS. Prescriptive reports refer to specific lessons in WICAT-developed curriculum materials. Tests can be administered online or via paper and pencil. One test is available for each subject area, for each grade level. Each test measures 10 objectives. Tests are administered via WICAT systems computer workstations when given online. Also runs on IBM-PC and Apple IIe.

15580
WICAT Skills Assessment Test—Florida.
WICAT Systems, Orem, UT 1987
Subtests: Mathematics; Reading; Writing
Descriptors: *Achievement Tests; *Computer Assisted Testing; Computer Software; Diagnostic Teaching; Educational Objectives; *Elementary School Students; Elementary Secondary Education; Mathematics; *Minimum Competency Testing; Prognostic Tests; Reading; *Secondary School Students; *Testing Programs; Writing Skills
Identifiers: Florida; Test Batteries
Availability: WICAT Systems; 1875 S. State St., Orem, UT 84058
Grade Level: 3; 5; 8; 11
Notes: Items, 46

Designed to measure student performance in subject areas against state-mandated minimum performance standards. Provides information for teachers to make individual curriculum and instructional decisions. Test results are said to be predictive of student performance on the state testing program and helpful in preparing students for the state tests. Prescriptive strategies for improving student performance are given. Tests can be administered online or via

paper and pencil. When given online, Wicat Systems Computer Workstations are used. Also runs on IBM-PC and Apple IIe.

15590
Receptive One-Word Picture Vocabulary Test—Upper Extension.   Brownell, Rick 1987
Descriptors: *Adolescents; Bilingual Students; Emotional Disturbances; *Individual Testing; *Norm Referenced Tests; Physical Disabilities; Pictorial Stimuli; *Receptive Language; *Screening Tests; Secondary Education; Secondary School Students; Spanish; Spanish Speaking; Speech Handicaps; Visual Measures
Identifiers: Oral Tests; ROWPVT
Availability: Academic Therapy Publications; 20 Commercial Blvd., Novato, CA 94949-6191
Age Level: 12-15
Notes: Time, 15 min. approx.; Items, 72

Individually administered, norm-referenced test designed for use with adolescents as a quick and reliable measure of an individual's hearing vocabulary. It is an extension of the original Receptive One-Word Picture Vocabulary Test. Administrator presents a word, and adolescent identifies picture that matches the word, from a group of 4 pictures, either orally or by pointing. Test can be used with speech-impaired, shy or withdrawn, and physically impaired students. Norms are equivalent to those of the Expressive One-Word Picture Vocabulary Test Upper Extension, so that an individual's scores on one test can be compared to his or her scores on the other. Designed to provide clinicians with information about an individual's knowledge of language. May be administered also to Spanish-speaking or bilingual subjects. Results of this test should not be used as the only basis of an evaluation of a subject's receptive language but should be used with other measures for a more complete understanding of an individual's profile of abilities.

15591
Kindergarten Readiness Test.   Larson, Sue L.; Vitali, Gary J. 1988
Descriptors: Developmental Tasks; *Kindergarten Children; Norm Referenced Tests; *School Readiness Tests; *Screening Tests
Identifiers: KRT
Availability: Slosson Educational Publications; P.O. Box 280, East Aurora, NY 14052
Grade Level: K
Age Level: 4-6
Notes: Time, 20 min. approx.

Developed to assess a child's functioning on various developmental tasks. Intended for use by early education teachers and other professionals to assess levels of maturity and development of typical later-4 to 6 year olds who are entering kindergarten. Is meant to be used in combination with other factors to provide additional information to help parents determine whether their children are developmentally ready to enter kindergarten. It is designed so that the majority of children will successfully complete between 78 and 90 percent of the measured tasks. Handicapped children and non-English-speaking children may have difficulties with some items. Although the test was intended to remove as many ethnic and socioeconomic biases as possible, consideration should be given to the child's social, family, and cultural environments if a significantly low score is obtained. The general assessed skill areas include understanding, awareness, and interaction with one's environment; judgment and reasoning in problem solving; numerical awareness; visual and fine-motor coordination; and auditory attention span and concentration.

15600
Sequenced Inventory of Communication Development, Revised Edition—1984, Spanish Language Edition (Cuban).   Hedrick, Dona Lea; And Others 1984
Subtests: Receptive; Expressive
Descriptors: *Communication Skills; *Cubans; *Diagnostic Tests; *Expressive Language; *Hispanic Americans; Language Acquisition; Language Handicaps; *Language Skills; Mental Retardation; *Receptive Language; Remedial Programs; *Spanish; *Spanish Speaking; *Young Children
Identifiers: Cuban Spanish; SICD
Availability: University of Washington Press; P.O. Box C-50096, Seattle, WA 98145-5096
Age Level: 0-4

This instrument is the Spanish (Cuban) language edition of an instrument designed to assist clinicians in development of remedial programs for atypical children. Receptive language scale measures awareness, discrimination, understanding. The expressive scale covers motor response, vocal response, verbal response, initiating behaviors, and responding behaviors. For a description of the English-language version, see TC013812. The SICD has also been modified and standardized for use with Yup'ik Eskimo, autistic, and other difficult-to-test children. This Cuban Spanish edition is not standardized. It is also available in the manual of the English version from Slosson Educational Publications; P.O. Box 280, East Aurora, NY 14052.

15609
Reading Skills Checklist; Primary. Horan, Theresa; And Others 1978
Subtests: Word Recognition Skills; Perception Skills; Comprehension Skills; Oral Expression Skills; Word-Attack Skills; Silent Reading Skills; Interest
Descriptors: Auditory Discrimination; *Check Lists; *Elementary School Students; *Kindergarten Children; Phonetic Analysis; Primary Education; Reading Comprehension; *Reading Skills; *Reading Tests; Silent Reading; Speech Communication; Structural Analysis (Linguistics); Visual Discrimination; Word Recognition
Availability: Modern Curriculum Press; 13900 Prospect Rd., Cleveland, OH 44136
Grade Level: K-3
Notes: Items, 160

A checklist of reading skills which allows a teacher to assess an individual student's progress toward mastery of reading skills in any reading program. Provides teacher with a comprehensive sequential checklist of skills to be learned at that level. Enables a teacher to see each student's skill level and plan reading instructions accordingly.

15610
Reading Skills Checklist; Intermediate. Horan, Theresa; And Others 1978
Subtests: Word Recognition Skills; Comprehension Skills; Study Skills; Oral Reading Skills; Oral Expression Skills
Descriptors: *Check Lists; *Elementary School Students; Intermediate Grades; Oral Reading; Reading Comprehension; *Reading Skills; *Reading Tests; Speech Communication; Study Skills; Word Recognition
Availability: Modern Curriculum Press; 13900 Prospect Rd., Cleveland, OH 44136
Grade Level: 4-6

A checklist of reading skills that allows a teacher to assess an individual student's progress toward mastery of reading skills in any reading program. Provides teacher with a comprehensive sequential checklist of skills to be learned at that level. Enables a teacher to see each student's skill level and plan reading instructions accordingly.

15611
Reading Skills Checklist; Junior High. Horan, Theresa; And Others 1978
Subtests: Word Recognition Skills; Comprehension Skills; Study Skills; Oral Reading Skills; Listening Skills; Interest
Descriptors: *Check Lists; Junior High Schools; *Junior High School Students; Listening Skills; Oral Reading; Reading Comprehension; *Reading Skills; *Reading Tests; Study Skills; Word Recognition
Availability: Modern Curriculum Press; 13900 Prospect Rd., Cleveland, OH 44136
Grade Level: 7-9

A checklist of reading skills that allows a teacher to assess an individual student's progress toward mastery of reading skills in any reading program. Provides teacher with a comprehensive sequential checklist of skills to be learned at that level. Enables a teacher to see each student's skill level and plan reading instructions accordingly.

15617
Journalism Test. Miller, Frances; Stratton, Kenneth
Descriptors: *Achievement Tests; Diagnostic Tests; High Schools; *High School Students; Journalism; *Journalism Education
Availability: Stratton-Christian Press; Box 1055, University Place Station, Des Moines, IA 50311-0095
Grade Level: 9-12
Notes: Items, 180

This measure is designed to assess journalism skills for diagnosis and achievement. No evidence of normative or other technical data is present. Uses multiple-choice, true-false, and open-ended format for items. Covers judgments of news values, arrangement of facts, news headlines, newspaper makeup, headlines, paragraphing, sentence variety, news sources, sports, judgment of feature values, speech-interview stories, editorials, terminology, copyreading.

15618
Test of Early Written Language. Hresko, Wayne P. 1988
Descriptors: Creative Writing; Dictation; Grammar; Norm Referenced Tests; *Screening Tests; *Writing Skills; *Young Children
Identifiers: TEWL
Availability: PRO-ED; 8700 Shoal Creek Blvd., Austin, TX 78758-6897
Age Level: 3-7
Notes: Time, 30 min. approx.; Items, 42

Measure of early writing ability developed to detect written language problems to develop educational interventions for young children. Used to measure several different aspects of writing: transcription, conventions of print, communication, creative expression, and record keeping. Transcription includes copying from a model. Convention requires identification of the uses of punctuation; knowledge of differences among words, sentences, and paragraphs; spelling; and proofing. Communication involves activities, such as writing notes, shopping lists, and titles of favorite books and television shows. Creative expression is assessed by requiring development of sentences from target words and the use of aspects of writing in composing a story. Record Keeping involves copying and dictation. This test does not contain any direct measure of handwriting or penmanship ability.

15629
Language Assessment Scales, Reading and Writing, Level 1. Duncan, Sharon E.; DeAvila, Edward A. 1988
Subtests: Vocabulary; Fluency; Reading for Information; Mechanics and Usage; Finishing Sentences; What's Happening
Descriptors: Elementary School Students; *English; *English (Second Language); Grammar; *Limited English Speaking; Multiple Choice Tests; Norm Referenced Tests; Pictorial Stimuli; Pretests Posttests; *Primary Education; Reading Comprehension; *Reading Skills; *Screening Tests; *Student Placement; Vocabulary; *Writing Skills
Identifiers: LAS(RW)
Availability: CTB/MacMillan/McGraw-Hill; Del Monte Research Park, 2500 Garden Rd., Monterey, CA 93940
Grade Level: 2-3
Notes: Time, 75 min. approx.; Items, 55

Intended as a screening test to produce placement and reclassification information for language-minority students. Designed for use with students who are minimally proficient in English, i.e., those who are at least able to produce a simple sentence orally. Measures those English language skills in reading and writing necessary to function in a mainstream academic environment. Is not an achievement test per se and does not measure achievement in course content. There are 2 parallel forms that can be used in a pretest-posttest situation. Design of test was guided by a review of state guidelines, district curriculum guides, expected learning outcomes and the scope and sequence of widely used English-as-a-Second-Language (ESL) instructional programs. May be administered as timed or untimed test. May be used in conjunction with the Language Assessment Scales, English Level 1, Form A (TC011361) to provide a complete assessment of listening, speaking, reading, and writing skills or an independent measure of reading and writing in English.

15630
Language Assessment Scales, Reading and Writing, Level 2. Duncan, Sharon E.; DeAvila, Edward A. 1988
Subtests: Vocabulary; Mechanics and Usage; Fluency; Reading for Information; Finishing Sentences; What's Happening, Let's Write
Descriptors: Elementary School Students; *English; *English (Second Language); Grammar; *Intermediate Grades; *Limited English Speaking; Multiple Choice Tests; Norm Referenced Tests; Pictorial Stimuli; Pretests Posttests; Reading Comprehension; *Reading Skills; *Screening Tests; *Student Placement; Vocabulary; *Writing Skills
Identifiers: LAS(RW)
Availability: CTB/MacMillan/McGraw-Hill; Del Monte Research Park, 2500 Garden Rd., Monterey, CA 93940
Grade Level: 4-6
Notes: Items, 55

Intended as a screening test to produce placement and reclassification information for language-minority students. Designed for use with students who are minimally proficient in English, i.e., those who are at least able to produce a simple sentence orally. Measures those English language skills in reading and writing necessary to function in a mainstream academic environment. Is not an achievement test per se and does not measure achievement in course content. There are 2 parallel forms that can be used in a pretest-posttest situation. Design of test was guided by a review of state guidelines, district curriculum guides, expected learning outcomes and the scope and sequence of widely used English-as-a-Second-Language (ESL) insructional programs. May be used in conjunction with the Language Assessment Scales, English Level 1, Form A (TC011361) to provide a complete assessment of listening, speaking, reading, and writing skills or as an independent measure of reading and writing in English. This level has a subtest which contains graphic prompts to elicit a story-writing sample.

15631
Language Assessment Scales, Reading and Writing, Level 3. Duncan, Sharon E.; DeAvila, Edward A. 1988
Descriptors: *English; *English (Second Language); Grammar; *Limited English Speaking; Multiple Choice Tests; Norm Referenced Tests; Pictorial Stimuli; Pretests Posttests; Reading Comprehension; *Reading Skills; *Screening Tests; Secondary Education; *Secondary School Students; *Student Placement; Vocabulary; *Writing Skills
Identifiers: LAS(RW)
Availability: CTB/MacMillan/McGraw-Hill; Del Monte Research Park, 2500 Garden Rd., Monterey, CA 93940
Grade Level: 7-11
Notes: Time, 85 min. approx.; Items, 60

Intended as a screening test to produce placement and reclassification information for language-minority students. Designed for use with students who are minimally proficient in English, i.e., those who are at least able to produce a simple sentence orally. Measures those English language skills in reading and writing necessary to function in a mainstream academic environment. Is not an achievement test per se and does not measure achievement in course content. There are 2 parallel forms that can be used in a pretest-posttest situation. Design of test was guided by a review of state guidelines, district curriculum guides, expected learning outcomes and the scope and sequence of widely used English-as-a-Second-Language (ESL) insructional programs. May be used in conjunction with the Language Assessment Scales, English Level 1, Form A (TC011361) to provide a complete assessment of listening, speaking, reading, and writing skills or as an independent measure of reading and writing in English. This level has a subtest which contains graphic prompts to elicit a story-writing sample.

15656
Test of Diabetes Knowledge Assessment Battery, Revised—2. Johnson, Suzanne Bennett 1984
Subtests: General Information; Problem Solving; Behavioral Skills
Descriptors: Adolescents; Children; *Diabetes; *Knowledge Level; *Measures (Individuals)
Identifiers: TDK
Availability: Suzanne Bennett Johnson; University of Florida, Children's Mental Health Unit, Box J-234, J. Hillis Miller Health Center, Gainesville, FL 32610-0234
Age Level: 6-18
Notes: Items, 148

Assesses 3 broad areas of diabetes knowledge in children or adolescents: general information, problem solving, and behavioral skills. The general information and problem-solving components include items dealing with diet, insulin, urine testing, insulin reactions, illness, exercise, anxiety/excitement, and miscellaneous. The behavioral skills assess the ability to perform serum glucose monitoring, urine glucose monitoring, and preparation for self-injection.

15688
Accuracy Level Test. Carver, Ronald P. 1987
Descriptors: *Achievement Tests; Adults; *College Students; *Elementary School Students; Elementary Secondary Education; Higher Education; Norm Referenced Tests; Reading Ability; *Reading Comprehension; *Secondary School Students; *Vocabulary
Identifiers: ALT; *Rauding Accuracy Level; Reading Efficiency Level Battery; RELB; Test Batteries
Availability: Revrac Publications; 207 W. 116th St., Kansas City, MO 64114
Grade Level: 2-16
Age Level: Adults
Notes: Time, 10 min.; Items, 100

Vocabulary test that measures the reading level of students in grade equivalent (GE) units from 0 to 15. Appropriate for group administration from grade 2 though college and adults. May also be appropriate for above average children in grade 1. There are 2 equivalent forms of the test. Raw score on test can be used to derive a grade equivalent (GE) score and a vocabulary score. Experimental data indicate that test provides a GE score that is valid for indicating the most difficult material at which students can comprehend 75 percent when reading at their typical rate. Reading at 75 percent comprehension is termed "rauding" by the author, a word formed by combining 2 words, "reading" and "auding." There is a companion test, Rate Level Test, which measures reading rate in GE units. These 2 tests form the Reading Efficiency Level Battery.

15689
Rate Level Test. Carver, Ronald P. 1987
Descriptors: *Achievement Tests; *College Students; *Elementary School Students; Elementary Secondary Education; Higher Education; Norm Referenced Tests; Reading Ability; Reading Comprehension; *Reading Rate; *Secondary School Students

Identifiers: *Rauding Accuracy Level; Reading Efficiency Level Battery; RELB; RLT; Test Batteries
Availability: Revrac Publications; 207 W. 116th St., Kansas City, MO 64114
Grade Level: 2-16
Age Level: Adults
Notes: Time, 2 min.

Measures how fast individuals can read in grade equivalent (GE) units from 0 to 18.9. Appropriate for group administration in grades 2 through college and for adults. May also be appropriate for use with above average children in grade 1. There are 2 equivalent forms of the test. Measures fastest reading rate at which individuals can accurately comprehend relatively easy material. This is called rauding rate by the author. The term "rauding" is a combination of the words "reading" and "auding." Raw scores can be converted into estimated rauding rates in words per minute. When used with the Accuracy Level Test, it constitutes the Reading Efficiency Level Battery. The average GE scores on the 2 tests provide an Efficiency Level Score which is valid as measure of general reading ability.

15690
Rauding Efficiency Level Test.　Carver, Ronald P. 1987
Descriptors: Adults; *College Students; *Computer Assisted Testing; *Elementary School Students; Elementary Secondary Education; Higher Education; *Individual Testing; *Microcomputers; *Reading Comprehension; *Reading Rate; *Reading Tests; *Secondary School Students
Identifiers: *Rauding Efficiency Level; RELT
Availability: Revrac Publications; 207 W. 116th St., Kansas City, MO 64114
Grade Level: 2-16
Age Level: Adults
Notes: Items, 90

Individually administered reading test that determines the most difficult material an individual can comprehend while reading at a rate appropriate for the difficulty level of the material. Rauding is a term that means comprehending more than 75 percent of the sentences in a passage while reading. Test consists of 18 passages, each of which has 5 test items, ranging in difficulty from grade 1 level to grade 18 level. Test is currently available only on a computer disk for use on an IMB-PC microcomputer.

15691
Bormuth's Reading Passages and Carver's Questions.　Bormuth, John R.; Carver, Ronald P. 1984
Descriptors: *College Students; *Elementary School Students; Elementary Secondary Education; *Reading Comprehension; *Reading Tests; *Secondary School Students
Availability: Revrac Publications; 207 W. 116th St., Kansas City, MO 64114
Grade Level: 2-14

Test questions are based on 330 100-word passages selected by Bormuth from instructional materials used in grades 1 through college. Carver has developed test items for the passages. The difficulty level of each passage has been measured by a number of techniques, including cloze, degree of reading power, and the Rauding Scale of Prose Difficulty. For 80 of the passages, there are multiple-choice tests. Paraphrase tests for 65 of the passages have been developed for good readers and paraphrase tests for 160 passages have been developed for children. Passages will be useful for reading research, and many of the questions will be useful for investigating reading comprehension.

15693
Screening Children for Related Early Educational Needs.　Hresko, Wayne P. 1988
Subtests: Language; Reading; Writing; Mathematics
Descriptors: *Achievement Tests; Elementary School Mathematics; Elementary School Students; *High Risk Students; Norm Referenced Tests; Oral Language; *Primary Education; Reading Ability; *Screening Tests; Writing Skills
Identifiers: SCREEN
Availability: PRO-ED; 8700 Shoal Creek Blvd., Austin, TX 78758-6897
Grade Level: K-2
Age Level: 3-7
Notes: Items, 70

Developed to provide for early detection of potential academic problems. Is a measure of the early development of educationally relevant abilities. Developed to focus on early academic-related behaviors in areas of oral language, reading, writing, and mathematics. As designed, should be considered an early achievement test. Items for SCREEN were the most discriminating items taken from the Test of Early Language Development (TC011223), Test of Early Reading Ability (TC011211), Test of Early Written Language (TC015618), and Test of Early Mathematics Ability (TC012363). Test has 4 purposes: to identify students significantly below their peers in the academic areas of language, reading, writing, and mathematics; to identify

strengths and weaknesses of individual students; to document students' progress as a result of intervention programs; and to use in research studies.

15701
Kindergarten Diagnostic Instrument.　Robinson, Robert W.; Miller, Daniel C. 1986
Subtests: Auditory Memory; Body Awareness; Concept Mastery; Form Perception; General Information; Gross Motor; Number Skills; Verbal Associations; Verbal Opposites; Visual Discrimination; Visual Memory; Visual-Motor Integration; Vocabulary
Descriptors: Academically Gifted; Diagnostic Tests; Enrichment; Individual Testing; *Kindergarten Children; Primary Education; School Readiness; *School Readiness Tests; Screening Tests; Student Placement
Identifiers: KDI
Availability: KIDS Inc.; 825 Sandpiper Drive, Denton, TX 76205
Grade Level: K
Notes: Time, 45 min. approx.

Screens children for kindergarten readiness skills. Can be used diagnostically for program placement for alternative kindergarten programs, Chapter 1 reading programs, and for enrichment/gifted programs and/or prescriptively to aid in educational programing. Can be administered individually but is designed to be used primarily in a screening team approach. Identifies children's kindergarten readiness skills from below average to above average. Consists of 13 subtests. Short form of the test, consisting of 9 subtests, takes approximately 25 minutes. Long form, consisting of all 13 subtests, takes approximately 45 minutes.

15711
Tests of General Educational Development, 1988 Revision.　American Council on Education, Washington, DC, General Educational Development Testing Service 1988
Subtests: Writing Skills; Social Studies; Science; Interpreting Literature and the Arts; Mathematics
Descriptors: *Academic Achievement; Achievement Tests; Adults; Braille; Dropouts; Educational Certificates; *Equivalency Tests; French; General Education; Grade Equivalent Scores; Large Type Materials; Older Adults; Reading; Sciences; *Secondary Education; Secondary School Mathematics; Secondary School Science; Social Studies; Spanish; Writing (Composition); Writing Skills
Identifiers: GED; General Certificate of Education; General Educational Development Tests; Test Batteries
Availability: GED Testing Service; American Council on Education, One Dupont Circle, Ste. 20, Washington, DC 20036
Age Level: 18-80

This test battery is used to determine an individual's eligibility to receive a high school equivalency certificate. It is designed for use by anyone who has not completed a 4-year high school education program. There are 5 subtests. The Writing Skills subtest includes an essay section and items concerning sentence structure, usage, mechanics. Social Studies content includes history, economics, political science, geography, and behavioral sciences (anthropology, psychology, sociology). Science covers life sciences and physical sciences. The language section covers popular literature, classical literature and a commentary section on film, art, theater, etc. Mathematics covers arithmetic, algebra, geometry. Information about computer literacy has been integrated into the context of questions in several of the subtest areas. The test items measure skills relevant to adult experiences. Items require understanding of broad concepts and generalizations and measure the general ability to evaluate, synthesize, and draw conclusions. The GED battery is available in French, Spanish, Braille, large print, and on audio cassettes. These tests were originally developed by the Examination Staff of the U.S. Armed Forces Institute (a committee of civilian educators) as a method of evaluating military personnel who lacked a high school diploma. After the Second World War, the use of the test battery was extended to civilians also. Generally, changes in the examination consist of requiring examinees to use high level thinking skills and problem-solving skills rather than merely supplying factual answers. The teacher's manual for the test can be purchased from Contemporary Books, 180 N. Michigan Ave., Chicago, IL 60601.

15717
Compton Phonological Assessment of Children.　Compton, Arthur J. 1986
Descriptors: *Articulation (Speech); *Error Analysis (Language); Phonetic Analysis; *Speech Tests; *Young Children
Availability: Carousel House; P.O. Box 4480, San Francisco, CA 94101
Age Level: 3-6
Notes: Time, 60 min. approx.

Developed to provide a structured, step-by-step approach to the linguistic analysis of children's misarticulations. There is a set of 51 pictorial stimuli used to elicit the production of consonants in initial and final-word position, consonant blends, and vowels. This is a revision of the Compton-Hutton Phonological Assessment (1978) (TC010732).

15740
Primary Education Program, Set 2.　Wang, Margaret C.; Resnick, Lauren B. 1978
Subtests: Counting and One to One Correspondence (0 to 5); Counting and One to One Correspondence (0 to 10); Numerals (0 to 5); Numerals (6-10); Comparison of Sets; Addition and Subtraction; Addition and Subtraction Equations
Descriptors: *Arithmetic; *Diagnostic Tests; Elementary School Mathematics; Mathematics Curriculum; *Mathematics Tests; *Preschool Children; Preschool Education
Identifiers: PEP
Availability: Media Materials; 2936 Remington Ave., Baltimore, MD 21211
Age Level: 3-6

Consists of a Quantification Skills Curriculum an introductory mathematics curriculum developed for children, ages 3 through 6. Intended to teach the fundamental concepts of math and the operations related to them. The diagnostic tests are designed to help teachers determine student learning needs upon entry into each unit of instruction of the curriculum and evaluate student learning progress through the units.

15750
Screening Test for Educational Prerequisite Skills, IBM Computer Format.　Smith, Frances 1987
Descriptors: Attention Span; *Child Development; Children; Computers; Grade 1; Motivation; Parent Attitudes; Persistence; Psychomotor Skills; *School Readiness; *Screening Tests; Speech Skills; Young Children
Identifiers: Fine Motor Skills; Gross Motor Skills; STEPS
Availability: Western Psychological Services; 12031 Wilshire Blvd., Los Angeles, CA 90025
Age Level: 5-6
Notes: Time, 10 min.

Designed for use with children eligible to enter first grade, within one year of the test date, to identify those who need structured help in preparing for first grade. Can be administered by volunteers and paraprofessionals. Evaluates first grade competency skills that are expected at the time of testing. A 20-item scale that allows for parent evaluation is also included, which measures general behavioral competence and motivation for school entry. Covers task persistence, attentional set, motivation, and developmental readiness in terms of fine motor skills, gross motor skills, speech skills and cognitive readiness. Computer program scores and produces a parent report.

15754
Academic Instructional Measurement System.　Psychological Corp., San Antonio, TX 1985
Subtests: Reading/Language Arts; Mathematics
Descriptors: *Achievement Tests; Computer Assisted Testing; *Criterion Referenced Tests; *Elementary School Students; Elementary Secondary Education; *High School Students; *Item Banks; *Language Tests; *Mathematics Tests; Microcomputers; *Reading Tests; Test Construction; *Test Items
Identifiers: AIMS
Availability: Psychological Corp.; 555 Academic Ct., San Antonio, TX 78204-0952
Grade Level: 1-12

A test development system for educators who wish to assess their students' skills and progress with locally developed tests comparable in quality to standardized tests. A large bank of achievement test items consisting of 7,000 items designed to test 985 curriculum-related, instructionally sequenced objectives in mathematics and language arts for grades 1-8 and grades 9-12. The entire test item bank is available in 2 formats, the Manual System and Microcomputer System.

15755
Parsky Inventory of Basic Math Skills.　Parsky, Larry M. 1988
Subtests: Basic Math Computational Problems; Writing Numbers; Rounding Numbers; Whole Numbers and Decimal Numbers; Understanding Decimals; Time Concepts; Figuring Interest; Interpreting Information on Graphs; Identifying Geometric Shapes; Recognizing Geometric Shapes; Measurement; Perimeter and Area; Word Problems; Writing Numbers and Numerical Amounts of Money; Reviewing Basic Multiplication Facts; Reviewing Basic Division Facts; Reviewing Decimals and Fractions; Reviewing Decimal Fractions; Using Zero as a Place Holder; Understanding Percentages

Descriptors: *Adult Basic Education; Adults; *Criterion Referenced Tests; Decimal Fractions; Fractions; High Schools; *High School Students; *Mathematics; *Mathematics Tests; Percentage; Statistics; Word Problems (Mathematics)
Availability: Media Materials; 2936 Remington Ave., Baltimore, MD 21211
Grade Level: 9-12
Age Level: Adults

A criterion-referenced measure designed for use by classroom teachers or clinicians in the diagnosis of the competency levels of secondary and adult basic education students who perform below grade level in mathematics. Content covers math skills from grades 3 through 9. Two forms are available. Covers basic computation, fractions, decimals, percentages, statistics. The 18 subtests should be completed over a period of 3 weeks. Six subtests consist of word problems. Each test has approximately 10 questions.

15765
Chinese Proficiency Test. Center for Applied Linguistics, Washington, DC 1983
Subtests: Reading Comprehension; Listening Comprehension
Descriptors: *Achievement Tests; *Chinese; *College Students; *Higher Education; *Language Proficiency; Listening Comprehension Tests; *Mandarin Chinese; Multiple Choice Tests; Reading Comprehension; *Second Language Learning; Sentence Structure
Identifiers: CPT
Availability: Center for Applied Linguistics; Div. of Foreign Language Education and Testing, 1118 22nd St., N.W., Washington, DC 20037
Grade Level: 13-16
Notes: Time, 120 min.; Items, 150

Designed to evaluate the proficiency in Chinese listening and reading comprehension attained by U.S. students and other English-speaking learners of Chinese. Uses situations typical of real life. Difficulty level ranges from one year of college-level instruction, equivalent high school instruction, up to all subsequent levels including graduate. Items are 4-option multiple choice. Listening comprehension requires responses to written questions after listening to dialogues and passages in Mandarin. Reading comprehension subsections are structure assessing ability to recognize correct written structural patterns; reading; assessing comprehension of various length passages.

15766
Grammatical Judgment Screening Test. Fujiki, Martin; And Others 1987
Subtests: Syntactic Omission; Word Order Reversal; Syntactic Agreement
Descriptors: Comparative Analysis; *Grammatical Acceptability; Handicap Identification; *Language Handicaps; Language Tests; *Primary Education; *Screening Tests; *Sentence Structure; Young Children
Availability: Language, Speech, and Hearing Services in the Schools; v18 n2 p131-43, Apr 1987
Grade Level: 1-3
Age Level: 6-9
Notes: Items, 36

Test used to separate first, second, and third grade level children with language-disorder problems from children who do not have such problems. Three types of incorrect sentences are presented: sentences with syntactic omission, sentences with word order rearrangement, and sentences with errors of syntactic agreement. Two correct sentences are included with each set as controls. Sentences are read to the child who indicates whether they sound right or wrong. If the child indicates that the sentence is wrong, he or she is asked to correct it. Test was found to be reliable and valid.

15767
Basic English Skills Test, Form B. Office of Refugee Resettlement, Dept. of Health and Human Services, Washington, DC 1984
Subtests: Oral Interview; Literacy Skills
Descriptors: *Adults; Basic Skills; *Criterion Referenced Tests; Diagnostic Tests; *English (Second Language); *Functional Literacy; Interviews; *Language Proficiency; *Language Tests; *Limited English Speaking; Listening Comprehension Tests; Literacy; Oral Language; Program Evaluation; Reading Skills; Screening Tests; *Second Language Learning; Speech Communication; Student Placement; Writing Skills
Identifiers: BEST
Availability: Center for Applied Linguistics; BEST Program, 1118 22nd St., N.W., Washington, DC 20037
Age Level: Adults
Notes: Time, 75 min.

A criterion-referenced measure designed to test listening comprehension, speaking, reading, and writing skills at an elementary level. It is intended for use with limited-English-speaking adults for whom information on the attainment of basic functional language skills is needed. The oral interview requires a series of real life listening and speaking tasks, a reading task, and a writing task. Those who screen successfully are given a literacy skills test, administered in a group or individually, that consists of a variety of everyday reading and writing tasks. May be used for placement in ESL classes, to measure proficiency in functional English and for student diagnoses and to assess readiness for subject matter instruction given in English. This is the 1984 version developed originally by the Office of Refugee Resettlement of the Department of Health and Human Services. The manual and scoring sheets have been revised extensively.

15768
College Level Academic Skills Test. Florida State Department of Education, Tallahassee 1984
Subtests: Reading; Writing; Essay; Computation
Descriptors: *Achievement Tests; Algebra; Arithmetic; *College Students; Communication Skills; Computation; Essays; Geometry; Higher Education; Listening Comprehension; *Mathematics; *Minimum Competency Testing; *Reading; Reading Comprehension; Statistics; *Writing (Composition); Writing Skills; College Sophomores
Identifiers: CLAST; Florida; Writing Sample
Availability: College Level Academic Skills Project; State of Florida, Dept. of Education, 116 Knott Bldg., Tallahassee, FL 32399
Grade Level: 14

Designed to measure college-level communication skills that students should have attained by the end of the sophomore year, and college-level computation skills. This achievement test consists of subtests in essay, writing, reading, and computation. Each subtest has one score. In the state of Florida, a passing score must be attained on all 4 subtests before an associate's degree is awarded. Content includes critical and literal comprehension in both reading and listening; multiple-choice writing skills and an essay; speaking skills; problem solving and concepts in arithmetic, geometry and measurement, algebra, statistics, including probability and logical reasoning. Not available for purchase. Special arrangements for use by others are at the discretion of CLAST officials.

15783
Math Management System, Criterion-Referenced Test. Clark County School District, Las Vegas, NV 1985
Descriptors: *Achievement Tests; *Criterion Referenced Tests; Elementary Education; *Elementary School Students; *Mathematics Tests
Identifiers: Nevada; *State Testing Programs
Availability: Clark County School District; 2832 E. Flamingo Rd., Las Vegas, NV 89121
Grade Level: 1-6

This series of tests was designed to fit the specific testing needs of the Clark County Schools, NV. They are used to evaluate student, group, school, and district performance and to assist in decision making concerning instruction and in establishing priorities. Tests are not timed. Each test is divided into 3 parts and administered in 3 sittings. Covers basic mathematics skills, graphs, problems, measurement, operations. Not available for distribution outside of Clark County.

15787
Assessing Linguistic Behaviors. Olswang, Lesley B. 1987
Descriptors: Child Development; Child Language; Cognitive Processes; Criterion Referenced Tests; *Infants; Interpersonal Communication; *Language Acquisition; *Language Handicaps; Language Skills; Learning Disabilities; Listening Comprehension; Multiple Disabilities; Norm Referenced Tests; Play; *Screening Tests
Identifiers: ALB
Availability: Olswang, Lesley B. and Others. *Assessing Prelinguistic and Early Linguistic Behaviors in Developmentally Young Children.* Seattle: University of Washington Press, 1987
Age Level: 1-2
Notes: Time, 150 min.

A series of exercises designed for the clinical assessment of pre- and early linguistic behaviors of developmentally young or low functioning children who are at risk for impaired language development. These children, functioning below age 2, may also be severely handicapped. Performance is measured regarding cognitive social prerequisites for language and early linguistic forms. The 5 scales should be used together but may be used separately. Both norm- and criterion-referenced interpretations are provided.

15788
Cognitive Antecedents to Word Meaning Scale. Olswang, Lesley B.; And Others 1987
Subtests: Nomination Task; Agent Tasks; Location Tasks
Descriptors: Child Development; *Cognitive Processes; Criterion Referenced Tests; *Infants; *Language Acquisition; *Language Handicaps; Language Skills; Learning Disabilities; Multiple Disabilities; Norm Referenced Tests; *Screening Tests; Semantics; Socialization
Identifiers: CAWM
Availability: Olswang, Lesley B. and Others. *Assessing Prelinguistic and Early Linguistic Behaviors in Developmentally Young Children.* Seattle: University of Washington Press, 1987
Age Level: 1-2
Notes: Time, 30 min.; Items, 6

Part of a series of exercises designed for the clinical assessment of pre- and early linguistic behaviors of developmentally young or low functioning children who are at risk for impaired language development. These children, functioning below age 2, may also be severely handicapped. Performance is measured regarding cognitive social prerequisites for language and early linguistic forms. The 5 scales should be used together but may be used separately. This exercise measures the child's ability to recognize or label an object; recognize that people and objects have a relationship that can require interaction; recognize that objects and people have a variety of spatial relationships. Uses a variety of common objects and tasks. For criterion-referenced use, but norms are available.

15789
Play Scale. Carpenter, Robert L.; And Others 1987
Descriptors: Child Development; Cognitive Processes; Criterion Referenced Tests; *Infants; *Language Acquisition; *Language Handicaps; Language Skills; Learning Disabilities; Multiple Disabilities; Norm Referenced Tests; *Play; *Screening Tests
Availability: Olswang, Lesley B. and Others. *Assessing Prelinguistic and Early Linguistic Behaviors in Developmentally Young Children.* Seattle: University of Washington Press, 1987
Age Level: 1-2
Notes: Time, 30 min.; Items, 4

Part of a series of exercises designed for the clinical assessment of pre- and early linguistic behaviors of developmentally young or low functioning children who are at risk for impaired language development. These children, functioning below age 2, may also be severely handicapped. Performance is measured regarding cognitive social prerequisites for language and early linguistic forms. The 5 scales should be used together but may be used separately. Toys are provided and a series of play episodes are encouraged, observed, and evaluated as a means of exploring language impairments in young children. Based on the knowledge that a child's play behavior shows an understanding of things and events.

15790
Communicative Intention Scale. Coggins, Truman E.; And Others 1987
Descriptors: Child Development; Criterion Referenced Tests; *Infants; *Interpersonal Communication; *Language Acquisition; *Language Handicaps; Language Skills; Learning Disabilities; Multiple Disabilities; Norm Referenced Tests; *Screening Tests
Availability: Olswang, Lesley B. and Others. *Assessing Prelinguistic and Early Linguistic Behaviors in Developmentally Young Children.* Seattle: University of Washington Press, 1987
Age Level: 1-2
Notes: Time, 30 min.; Items, 5

Part of a series of exercises designed for the clinical assessment of pre- and early linguistic behaviors of developmentally young or low functioning children who are at risk for impaired language development. These children, functioning below age 2, may also be severely handicapped. Performance is measured regarding cognitive social prerequisites for language and early linguistic forms. The 5 scales should be used together but may be used separately. This exercise is for use as a tool for observing and coding intentional behavior of children functioning in the latter stages of sensory motor development. It is a criterion-referenced measure of a child's intentional communication. May also be used to measure progress from intervention. Provides information about behaviors thought to be necessary for the acquisition of subsequent conversational skills. Norms are included.

15791
Language Comprehension Scale. Coggins, Truman E.; Kellogg, Susan E. 1987
Subtests: Action Games; Single Words; Comprehension of Word Combinations
Descriptors: Child Development; Criterion Referenced Tests; *Infants; *Language Acquisition; *Language Handicaps; Language Skills; Learning Disabilities; *Listening Comprehension; Multiple Disabilities; Norm Referenced Tests; *Screening Tests

Availability: Olswang, Lesley B. and Others. *Assessing Prelinguistic and Early Linguistic Behaviors in Developmentally Young Children.* Seattle: University of Washington Press, 1987
Age Level: 1-2

Part of a series of exercises designed for the clinical assessment of pre- and early linguistic behaviors of developmentally young or low functioning children who are at risk for impaired language development. These children, functioning below age 2, may also be severely handicapped. Performance is measured regarding cognitive social prerequisites for language and early linguistic forms. The 5 scales should be used together but may be used separately. A measure of a child's response given in a particular context that gives the appearance that the child is comprehending words, actions, and word combinations. For clinical use because judgment is required to determine whether comprehension has occurred.

15792
Language Production Scale. Stoel-Gammon, Carol; And Others 1987
Descriptors: Child Development; Child Language; Criterion Referenced Tests; *Expressive Language; *Infants; *Language Acquisition; *Language Handicaps; Language Skills; Norm Referenced Tests; Oral Language; *Screening Tests
Availability: Olswang, Lesley B. and Others. *Assessing Prelinguistic and Early Linguistic Behaviors in Developmentally Young Children.* Seattle: University of Washington Press, 1987
Age Level: 1-2
Notes: Time, 30 min.; Items, 50

Part of a series of exercises designed for the clinical assessment of pre- and early linguistic behaviors of developmentally young or low functioning children who are at risk for impaired language development. These children, functioning below age 2, may also be severely handicapped. Performance is measured regarding cognitive social prerequisites for language and early linguistic forms. The 5 scales should be used together but may be used separately. This scale was designed to examine the vocalizations and verbalizations of infants. Focuses on prelinguistic utterance (babble) and early meaningful speech (linguistic production). Phonetic complexity of babble is analyzed. Meaningful speech is analyzed for phonetic, phonological, syntactic, and semantic skills.

15797
Iowa Tests of Educational Development, Forms X-8 and Y-8, Levels I and II. Feldt, Leonard S.; And Others 1988
Subtests: Correctness and Appropriateness of Expression; Ability to Do Quantitative Thinking; Analysis of Social Studies Materials; Analysis of Natural Science Materials; Vocabulary; Use of Sources of Information
Descriptors: *Achievement Tests; High Schools; *High School Students; Inferences; Interpretive Skills; *Language Skills; *Library Skills; Logical Thinking; *Mathematics Skills; Norm Referenced Tests; Reference Materials; *Sciences; Secondary Education; *Social Studies; *Vocabulary; Thinking Skills
Identifiers: Analytical Thinking; ITED; *Test Batteries
Availability: Riverside Publishing Co.; 8420 Bryn Mawr Ave., Chicago, IL 60631
Grade Level: 9-12
Notes: Time, 250 min.

This achievement test for use at the high school level is designed to measure those broad skills considered fundamental to the goals of secondary education, regardless of course or curriculum content. Some skills measured are ability to recognize correct use of standard American English, mathematical reasoning in daily life, analytical thinking skills in social studies context, general scientific understanding and interpretation, interpretation of literary materials, knowledge of common words, competency in using sources of information. Scores are reported for each subtest. A total reading score is derived. Scores typically reported for major achievement batteries, such as stanines, percentiles, etc., are also available. Parallel forms are available.

15826
Student Occupational Competency Achievement Testing: Home Entertainment Equipment Repair. National Occupational Competency Testing Institute, Big Rapids, MI 1988
Descriptors: *Achievement Tests; Adults; *Audio Equipment; Credentials; *Equipment Maintenance; High Schools; *High School Students; Multiple Choice Tests; Occupational Tests; Performance Tests; Postsecondary Education; Secondary Education; Two Year Colleges; *Video Equipment; *Vocational Education; Vocational Schools; Work Sample Tests
Identifiers: SOCAT
Availability: National Occupational Competency Testing Institute; Ferris State College, 409 Bishop Hall, Big Rapids, MI 49307
Grade Level: 9-14
Notes: Time, 300 min. approx.

This test is part of a program developed to evaluate secondary and postsecondary vocational students with a standardized, objective measure. Each test consists of a multiple-choice portion covering factual knowledge, technical information, understanding of principles, and problem-solving abilities related to the occupation. A performance component samples manipulative skills required. A mental ability test is also available. The written test covers basic information, use of equipment, television/video circuits, radio/audio circuits, audio and video tape systems, antennae, audio disk players, and occupational safety. The performance test covers basic information, television/video circuits, radio/audio circuits, audio and video tape systems, troubleshooting, use of equipment, safety, and economy of time.

15827
Student Occupational Competency Achievement Testing: Graphic Arts. National Occupational Competency Testing Institute, Big Rapids, MI 1986
Descriptors: *Achievement Tests; Adults; Credentials; *Graphic Arts; High Schools; *High School Students; Multiple Choice Tests; Occupational Tests; Performance Tests; Postsecondary Education; Secondary Education; Two Year Colleges; *Vocational Education; Vocational Schools; Work Sample Tests
Identifiers: SOCAT
Availability: National Occupational Competency Testing Institute; Ferris State College, 409 Bishop Hall, Big Rapids, MI 49307
Grade Level: 9-14
Notes: Time, 330 min.; Items, 175

This test is part of a program developed to evaluate secondary and postsecondary vocational students with a standardized, objective measure. Each test consists of a multiple-choice portion covering factual knowledge, technical information, understanding of principles, and problem-solving abilities related to the occupation. A performance component samples manipulative skills required. A mental ability test is also available. The written test covers presswork, camera and darkroom, composition, stripping and platemaking, finishing/paper, copy preparation, layout and design. There is a choice of 1, 2, or 3 performance tests. Performance test 1 covers copy preparation; performance test 2 covers darkroom, stripping, and platemaking; performance test 3 covers presswork and finishing.

15828
Student Occupational Competency Achievement Testing: Electronics. National Occupational Competency Testing Institute, Big Rapids, MI 1988
Descriptors: *Achievement Tests; Adults; Credentials; *Electronics; High Schools; *High School Students; Multiple Choice Tests; Occupational Tests; Performance Tests; Postsecondary Education; Secondary Education; Two Year Colleges; *Vocational Education; Vocational Schools; Work Sample Tests
Identifiers: NOCTI; SOCAT
Availability: National Occupational Competency Testing Institute; Ferris State College, 409 Bishop Hall, Big Rapids, MI 49307
Grade Level: 9-14
Notes: Time, 360 min.; Items, 151

This test is part of a program developed to evaluate secondary and postsecondary vocational students with a standardized, objective measure. Each test consists of a multiple-choice portion covering factual knowledge, technical information, understanding of principles, and problem-solving abilities related to the occupation. A performance component samples manipulative skills required. A mental ability test is also available. The written test covers DC circuits, AC circuits, solid state circuits, digital circuits, and use of equipment. The performance test covers tests and measurements, selection of components, circuit construction, desoldering, soldering, use of time, and safety.

15831
IDEA Oral Language Proficiency Test II, Spanish. Dalton, Enrique F.; And Others 1987
Descriptors: Articulation (Speech); Bilingual Students; Comprehension; Expressive Language; *Individual Testing; *Language Proficiency; *Language Tests; *Oral Language; Receptive Language; Secondary Education; *Spanish; *Spanish Speaking; Syntax; Vocabulary
Identifiers: IPT
Availability: Ballard and Tighe; 480 Atlas St., Brea, CA 92621
Grade Level: 7-12
Notes: Time, 20 min.; Items, 83

This individually administered proficiency test in Spanish for native Spanish-speaking children, tests 4 basic areas of oral Spanish proficiency: vocabulary, comprehension, syntax, and verbal expression, including articulation. There are 6 levels of difficulty. The test taker advances by levels until the test is completed or stops at a proficiency level indicated by the test score. The examiner should be bilingual in English and Spanish.

15832
Tests of Adult Basic Education, Form 6, Level D (Difficult), Complete Battery. CTB/Macmillan/McGraw-Hill, Monterey, CA 1987
Subtests: Vocabulary; Comprehension; Mathematics Computation; Mathematics Concepts and Applications; Language Mechanics; Language Expression; Spelling
Descriptors: *Achievement Tests; *Adult Basic Education; Adults; *Adult Students; *Basic Skills; Language Skills; Mathematics Achievement; Norm Referenced Tests; Reading Achievement; Spelling
Identifiers: TABE
Availability: CTB/MacMillan/McGraw-Hill; Del Monte Research Park, 2500 Garden Rd., Monterey, CA 93940
Age Level: Adults
Notes: Time, 293 min.; Items, 263

Norm-referenced tests designed to measure achievement in reading, mathematics, language, and spelling, the subjects most commonly found in adult basic education curricula. Test focuses on the basic skills required for an individual to function in society. Tests combine the characteristics of norm-referenced and criterion-referenced tests and provide information about the relative ranking of examinees against a norm group and specific information about the instructional needs of the examinees. Results allow teachers and administrators to diagnose, evaluate, and place examinees in adult education programs. There is a correlation between scores on this test and the scores on the General Educational Development (GED) tests. Items on this test reflect language and content appropriate for adults and measure the understanding and application of conventions and principles. Test items are not intended to measure specific knowledge or recall of facts. There are 4 overlapping levels and 2 parallel forms for each level. The 4 levels and their estimated grade ranges are E (easy) with a grade range of 2.6-4.9; M (medium) with a grade range of 4.6-6.9; D (difficult) with a grade range of 6.6-8.9; and A (advanced) with a grade range of 8.6-12.9. There is also a survey form, which is a subset of the complete battery, that can be used to quickly screen examinees for appropriate placement in programs of instruction.

15833
Tests of Adult Basic Education, Form 6, Level A (Advanced), Complete Battery. CTB/Macmillan/McGraw-Hill, Monterey, CA 1987
Subtests: Vocabulary; Comprehension; Mathematics Computation; Mathematics Concepts and Applications; Language Mechanics; Language Expression; Spelling
Descriptors: *Achievement Tests; *Adult Basic Education; Adults; *Adult Students; *Basic Skills; Language Skills; Mathematics Achievement; Norm Referenced Tests; Reading Achievement; Spelling
Identifiers: TABE
Availability: CTB/MacMillan/McGraw-Hill; Del Monte Research Park, 2500 Garden Rd., Monterey, CA 93940
Age Level: Adults
Notes: Time, 293 min.; Items, 263

Norm-referenced tests designed to measure achievement in reading, mathematics, language, and spelling, the subjects most commonly found in adult basic education curricula. Test focuses on the basic skills required for an individual to function in society. Tests combine the characteristics of norm-referenced and criterion-referenced tests and provide information about the relative ranking of examinees against a norm group and specific information about the instructional needs of the examinees. Results allow teachers and administrators to diagnose, evaluate, and place examinees in adult education programs. There is a correlation between scores on this test and the scores on the General Educational Development (GED) tests. Items on this test reflect language and content appropriate for adults and measure the understanding and application of conventions and principles. Test items are not intended to measure specific knowledge or recall of facts. There are 4 overlapping levels and 2 parallel forms for each level. The 4 levels and their estimated grade ranges are E (easy) with a grade range of 2.6-4.9; M (medium) with a grade range of 4.6-6.9; D (difficult) with a grade range of 6.6-8.9; and A (advanced) with a grade range of 8.6-12.9. There is also a survey form, which is a subset of the complete battery, that can be used to quickly screen examinees for appropriate placement in programs of instruction.

15835
Functional Language Assessment. Chicago Public Schools, IL, Dept. of Multilingual Education and Department of Research and Evaluation 1985

Descriptors: *Elementary School Students; Elementary Secondary Education; *English (Second Language); *Individual Testing; Knowledge Level; *Limited English Speaking; *Oral English; *Secondary School Students; Speech Communication
Availability: Hamayan, Else V.; and Others. *Assessment of Language Minority Students: A Handbook for Educators,* Arlington Heights, IL; Resource Center, 1985
Age Level: 5-18
Notes: Items, 15

An individually administered instrument that assesses the ability of students to use the English language. The student is asked to perform simple tasks, correctly repeat sentences, and respond to open-ended questions.

15836
Boston Cloze Tests. Boston Public Schools, MA
Descriptors: *Cloze Procedure; *Elementary School Students; Elementary Secondary Education; *Reading Comprehension; *Reading Tests; *Secondary School Students
Availability: Hamayan, Else V. and Others. *Assessment of Language Minority Students: A Handbook for Educators,* Arlington Heights, IL: Resource Center, 1985
Grade Level: 4-12
Notes: Items, 33

A measure of reading comprehension using cloze format. Fourteen stories assess reading ability at several grade levels from grades 4-8 and 8-12.

15838
Portuguese Speaking Test. Stansfield, Charles; Kenyon, Dorry 1988
Subtests: Personal Conversation; Situations; Giving Directions; Detailed Description; Picture Sequences; Topical Discourse
Descriptors: *Achievement Tests; Adults; College Students; Higher Education; *Language Proficiency; *Oral Language; Personnel Selection; *Portuguese; Postsecondary Education; Program Evaluation; *Second Language Learning; Student Placement; Teacher Selection
Identifiers: PST
Availability: Center for Applied Linguistics; Div. of Foreign Language Education and Testing, 1118 22nd St., N.W., Washington, DC 20037
Grade Level: 13-16
Age Level: Adults
Notes: Time, 40 min.

Designed to measure oral language proficiency in Portuguese. This test was developed to be a secure, valid, and reliable test to be administered under standardized conditions. Testees receive an oral language proficiency rating using the scale developed by the American Council on the Teaching of Foreign Languages. Testing is requested by an institution and may be used for placement in instructional programs; to measure proficiency after instruction; for program evaluation; to demonstrate proficiency to an employer to select teaching assistants in Portuguese. Based on real-life language use situations. Administered via tape. Responses of testee are also recorded. For use with testees at intermediate and advanced levels.

15840
Murphy-Durrell Reading Readiness Screen. Murphy, Helen A.; Durrell, Donald D. 1988
Subtests: Lowercase Letter Names; Letter-Name Sounds in Spoken Words; Writing Letters from Dictation; Syntax Matching; Identifying Phonemes in Spoken Words
Descriptors: *Grade 1; *Kindergarten Children; *Phonics; Primary Education; *Reading Readiness; *Screening Tests
Availability: Curriculum Associates; 5 Esquire Rd., N. Billerica, MA 01862-2589
Grade Level: K-1
Notes: Time, 125 min. approx.; Items, 109

Screening instrument that provides information about children's phonics abilities before entering a formal reading program. Consists of 5 inventories administered in 5 sittings, usually over a 3-day period. Each sitting requires from 15 to 25 minutes. May be individually or group administered. The 5 inventories relate clusters of sounds in speech to clusters of letters in print. Intended for use with children in kindergarten or grade 1 who are being considered for placement in a formal reading program. Identifies those children who will be successful in a formal reading program and at-risk children, noting their reading readiness deficiencies.

15843
Teacher Occupational Competency Testing: Auto Body Repair (083). National Occupational Competency Testing Institute, Big Rapids, MI
Descriptors: *Achievement Tests; Adults; *Auto Body Repairers; *Certification; College Credits; Credentials; *Equivalency Tests; Multiple Choice Tests; Occupational Tests; Performance Tests; *Vocational Education Teachers; *Work Sample Tests
Identifiers: NOCTI; TOCT
Availability: National Occupational Competency Testing Institute; 409 Bishop Hall, Ferris State University, Big Rapids, MI 49307
Age Level: Adults
Notes: Time, 420 min.; Items, 190

One of a series of tests designed to determine a level of occupational competence for vocational education teachers. A written test covers theoretical concepts of the occupation and a performance test examines selected manipulative skills. The tests may be used for credit-by-examination and also for teacher certification. The written test covers welding; filling operations and plastics; repairing sheet metal; refinishing; panel replacement, frame (unitized body repair); front-end alignment; electrical and accessory systems; glass, trim, and hardware; estimating; tools and equipment; safety. The performance test covers metal forming, welding, diagnosing structural damage, refinishing, electrical troubleshooting.

15844
Teacher Occupational Competency Testing: Building and Home Maintenance Services (067). National Occupational Competency Testing Institute, Big Rapids, MI
Descriptors: *Achievement Tests; Adults; *Certification; College Credits; *Construction Industry; Credentials; *Equivalency Tests; *Maintenance; Multiple Choice Tests; Occupational Tests; Performance Tests; *Vocational Education Teachers; *Work Sample Tests
Identifiers: NOCTI; TOCT
Availability: National Occupational Competency Testing Institute; 409 Bishop Hall, Ferris State University, Big Rapids, MI 49307
Age Level: Adults
Notes: Time, 480 min.; Items, 162

One of a series of tests designed to determine a level of occupational competence for vocational education teachers. A written test covers theoretical concepts of the occupation. The performance test examines selected manipulative skills. The tests may be used for credit-by-examination and also for teacher certification. The written test covers floor stripping; refinishing and buffing; carpet care; general electricity and repair; building security; fire prevention; records; general cleaning; plumbing; employee/staff relations; heating; and painting. The performance test covers general cleaning of office or classroom and a restroom or shower/locker room area; floor stripping, refinishing and buffing; carpet care; welding or soldering; electrical repair; small hand/power tools; and interior/exterior painting.

15845
Teacher Occupational Competency Testing: Child Care and Guidance (081). National Occupational Competency Testing Institute, Big Rapids, MI 1988
Descriptors: *Achievement Tests; Adults; *Certification; *Child Care Occupations; College Credits; Credentials; *Day Care; *Equivalency Tests; Multiple Choice Tests; Occupational Tests; Performance Tests; *Vocational Education Teachers; *Work Sample Tests
Identifiers: NOCTI; TOCT
Availability: National Occupational Competency Testing Institute; 409 Bishop Hall, Ferris State University, Big Rapids, MI 49307
Age Level: Adults
Notes: Time, 480 min.; Items, 200

One of a series of tests designed to determine a level of occupational competence for vocational education teachers. A written test covers theoretical concepts of the occupation and a performance test examines selected manipulative skills. The tests may be used for credit-by-examination and also for teacher certification. The written test covers infant-toddler development and learning, preschool and young child development and learning, guiding behavior, health and safety, center management, special needs children. The performance test covers infant diapering, toddler observation, large group teaching, small group teaching, daily program plans, role play (parent/staff interaction), role play (child discipline situation).

15846
Teacher Occupational Competency Testing: Computer Science for Secondary Teachers (080). National Occupational Competency Testing Institute, Big Rapids, MI
Descriptors: *Achievement Tests; Adults; *Certification; College Credits; *Computer Science; Credentials; *Equivalency Tests; Multiple Choice Tests; Occupational Tests; Performance Tests; *Programing Languages; *Secondary School Teachers; *Vocational Education Teachers; *Work Sample Tests
Identifiers: NOCTI; TOCT
Availability: National Occupational Competency Testing Institute; 409 Bishop Hall, Ferris State University, Big Rapids, MI 49307
Age Level: Adults
Notes: Time, 540 min.; Items, 158

One of a series of tests designed to determine a level of occupational competence for vocational education teachers. A written test covers theoretical concepts of the occupation and a performance test examines selected manipulative skills. The tests may be used for credit-by-examination and also for teacher certification. The written test covers general concepts, program design, microcomputers, on-line communications including magnetic files and data communications. The performance test covers use of microcomputers for word processing and spreadsheets, systems analysis, program design, BASIC programing, PASCAL programing, FORTRAN programing, and COBOL programing.

15847
Teacher Occupational Competency Testing: Electrical Construction and Maintenance (061). National Occupational Competency Testing Institute, Big Rapids, MI
Descriptors: *Achievement Tests; Adults; *Certification; College Credits; Construction (Process); Credentials; *Electrical Occupations; Equipment Maintenance; *Equivalency Tests; Multiple Choice Tests; Occupational Tests; Performance Tests; *Vocational Education Teachers; *Work Sample Tests
Identifiers: NOCTI; TOCT
Availability: National Occupational Competency Testing Institute; 409 Bishop Hall, Ferris State University, Big Rapids, MI 49307
Age Level: Adults
Notes: Time, 420 min.; Items, 180

One of a series of tests designed to determine a level of occupational competence for vocational education teachers. A written test covers theoretical concepts of the occupation and a performance test examines selected manipulative skills. The tests may be used for credit-by-examination and also for teacher certification. The written test covers electron theory and basic circuit calculations, AC theory and conductors, motor control circuits and motors, wiring methods, transformers and lighting, basic electricity. The performance test covers motors and motor circuits, troubleshooting, transformer layout and connectors, component identification and testing, raceways and lighting.

15848
Teacher Occupational Competency Testing: Heavy Equipment Mechanics (069). National Occupational Competency Testing Institute, Big Rapids, MI
Descriptors: *Achievement Tests; Adults; *Certification; College Credits; Credentials; *Equipment; *Equivalency Tests; Mechanics (Process); Multiple Choice Tests; Occupational Tests; Performance Tests; *Vocational Education Teachers; *Work Sample Tests
Identifiers: NOCTI; TOCT
Availability: National Occupational Competency Testing Institute; 409 Bishop Hall, Ferris State University, Big Rapids, MI 49307
Age Level: Adults
Notes: Time, 480 min.; Items, 200

One of a series of tests designed to determine a level of occupational competence for vocational education teachers. A written test covers theoretical concepts of the occupation and a performance test examines selected manipulative skills. The tests may be used for credit-by-examination and also for teacher certification. The written test covers diesel fuel injection system and engine troubleshooting, diesel and gasoline engine tune-up and overhaul, power trains, steering and suspension, welding and cutting, brakes, cooling and exhaust systems, electrical system, hydraulic systems, general, including air conditioning. The performance test covers engine tune-up, hydraulic troubleshooting and repair, power trains (differentials), basic engine measurements, welding and cutting, gasoline engines, electrical system, undercarriage inspection, operation of tracked equipment, road grader, dump truck, or road tractor.

15849
Teacher Occupational Competency Testing: Scientific Data Processing (084). National Occupational Competency Testing Institute, Big Rapids, MI
Descriptors: *Achievement Tests; Adults; *Certification; College Credits; Credentials; *Data Processing; *Equivalency Tests; Multiple Choice Tests; Occupational Tests; Performance Tests; *Programing Languages; *Vocational Education Teachers; *Work Sample Tests
Identifiers: NOCTI; TOCT
Availability: National Occupational Competency Testing Institute; 409 Bishop Hall, Ferris State University, Big Rapids, MI 49307

Age Level: Adults
Notes: Time, 540 min.; Items, 167

One of a series of tests designed to determine a level of occupational competence for vocational education teachers. A written test covers theoretical concepts of the occupation and a performance test examines selected manipulative skills. The tests may be used for credit-by-examination and also for teacher certification. The written test covers understanding computer fundamentals, performance of equipment operations, using software packages, generating documentation, using programing languages (BASIC, FORTRAN, PASCAL, C), applying numerical analysis. The performance test covers understanding computer fundamentals by generating documentation that demonstrates an understanding of numerical analysis; performing equipment operations using operating systems and software packages with a programing language; developing program using a programing language to apply numerical analysis and generate a solution.

15850
Teacher Occupational Competency Testing: Welding (041).   National Occupational Competency Testing Institute, Big Rapids, MI
Descriptors: *Achievement Tests; Adults; *Certification; College Credits; Credentials; *Equivalency Tests; Multiple Choice Tests; Occupational Tests; Performance Tests; *Vocational Education Teachers; *Welding; *Work Sample Tests
Identifiers: NOCTI; TOCT
Availability: National Occupational Competency Testing Institute; 409 Bishop Hall, Ferris State University, Big Rapids, MI 49307
Age Level: Adults
Notes: Time, 420 min.; Items, 174

One of a series of tests designed to determine a level of occupational competence for vocational education teachers. A written test covers theoretical concepts of the occupation and a performance test examines selected manipulative skills. The tests may be used for credit-by-examination and also for teacher certification. The written test covers safety; oxyfuel welding; torch brazing and oxyfuel cutting; shielded metal arc welding; gas tungsten arc welding; welding symbols and joint design; gas metal arc welding; flux-cored arc welding; other industrial welding and cutting processes; inspection, testing, and welding codes; welding metallurgy. The performance test covers shielded metal arc welding, oxyfuel welding, oxyfuel torch brazing, flux-cored arc welding, gas metal arc welding, gas tungsten arc welding, air-arc cutting, oxyfuel cutting.

15851
Student Occupational Competency Achievement Testing: Appliance Repair.   National Occupational Competency Testing Institute, Big Rapids, MI 1988
Descriptors: *Achievement Tests; Adults; *Appliance Repair; Credentials; High Schools; *High School Students; Multiple Choice Tests; Occupational Tests; Performance Tests; *Postsecondary Education; Secondary Education; Two Year Colleges; *Vocational Education; *Work Sample Tests
Identifiers: NOCTI; SOCAT
Availability: National Occupational Competency Testing Institute; 409 Bishop Hall, Ferris State University, Big Rapids, MI 49307
Grade Level: 9-14
Notes: Time, 360 min.; Items, 169

This test is part of a program developed to evaluate secondary and postsecondary vocational students with a standardized, objective measure. Each test consists of a multiple-choice portion covering factual knowledge, technical information, understanding of principles, and problem-solving abilities related to the occupation. A performance component samples manipulative skills required. A mental ability test is also available. The written test covers laundry equipment, hot water heaters, dishwashers and garbage disposals, gas and electric ranges, radar ovens, refrigerators, freezers, air conditioners, vacuum cleaners, small appliances, basic electricity. The performance test covers identification of motor windings; troubleshooting and repair of small appliances, dishwashers, clothes washers and dryers, refrigerators and freezers, ranges.

15852
Student Occupational Competency Achievement Testing: Architectural Design.   National Occupational Competency Testing Institute, Big Rapids, MI 1988
Descriptors: *Achievement Tests; Adults; *Architectural Drafting; Credentials; High Schools; *High School Students; Multiple Choice Tests; Occupational Tests; Performance Tests; *Postsecondary Education; Secondary Education; Two Year Colleges; *Vocational Education; *Work Sample Tests
Identifiers: NOCTI; SOCAT
Availability: National Occupational Competency Testing Institute; 409 Bishop Hall, Ferris State University, Big Rapids, MI 49307
Grade Level: 9-14

Notes: Time, 330 min.; Items, 167

This test is part of a program developed to evaluate secondary and postsecondary vocational students with a standardized, objective measure. Each test consists of a multiple-choice portion covering factual knowledge, technical information, understanding of principles, and problem-solving abilities related to the occupation. A performance component samples manipulative skills required. A mental ability test is also available. The written test covers architectural drafting tools and techniques; site layout and plot plan; light framing; plumbing; heating, ventilating, and air conditioning; computer-aided drafting. The performance test covers development of plot plan, symbols, carpentry layouts, plumbing layouts.

15853
Student Occupational Competency Achievement Testing: Audio-Visual Communications.   National Occupational Competency Testing Institute, Big Rapids, MI 1988
Descriptors: *Achievement Tests; Adults; *Audiovisual Aids; Credentials; Films; High Schools; *High School Students; Multiple Choice Tests; Occupational Tests; Performance Tests; Photographic Equipment; Photography; *Postsecondary Education; Secondary Education; Slides; Two Year Colleges; Video Equipment; *Vocational Education; *Work Sample Tests
Identifiers: NOCTI; SOCAT
Availability: National Occupational Competency Testing Institute; 409 Bishop Hall, Ferris State University, Big Rapids, MI 49307
Grade Level: 9-14
Notes: Time, 360 min.; Items, 165

This test is part of a program developed to evaluate secondary and postsecondary vocational students with a standardized, objective measure. Each test consists of a multiple-choice portion covering factual knowledge, technical information, understanding of principles, and problem-solving abilities related to the occupation. A performance component samples manipulative skills required. A mental ability test is also available. The written test covers theory and history, broadcasting rules and regulations, a/v equipment and materials, technology, lighting, 35mm cameras and lenses, camera handling, film, darkroom procedures, "on-air" practices, finishing/professionalism, video. The performance test covers photography, video production, film repair, slide presentation, creation of commercial announcement.

15854
Student Occupational Competency Achievement Testing: Automotive Specialist (Field Test).   National Occupational Competency Testing Institute, Big Rapids, MI 1988
Descriptors: *Achievement Tests; Adults; *Auto Mechanics; Credentials; High Schools; *High School Students; Multiple Choice Tests; Occupational Tests; Performance Tests; *Postsecondary Education; Secondary Education; Two Year Colleges; *Vocational Education; *Work Sample Tests
Identifiers: NOCTI; SOCAT
Availability: National Occupational Competency Testing Institute; 409 Bishop Hall, Ferris State University, Big Rapids, MI 49307
Grade Level: 9-14
Notes: Time, 360 min.; Items, 166

This test is part of a program developed to evaluate secondary and postsecondary vocational students with a standardized, objective measure. Each test consists of a multiple-choice portion covering factual knowledge, technical information, understanding of principles, and problem-solving abilities related to the occupation. A performance component samples manipulative skills required. A mental ability test is also available. The written test covers fluids and lubes, tires, chassis, fuel systems, electrical systems, brakes, cooling systems, towing and road service, merchandising. The performance test covers vehicle inspection, lubrication, tire service, battery testing, headlamp service, inspection and testing of cooling system.

15855
Student Occupational Competency Achievement Testing: Baking.   National Occupational Competency Testing Institute, Big Rapids, MI 1988
Descriptors: *Achievement Tests; Adults; *Bakery Industry; Credentials; High Schools; *High School Students; Multiple Choice Tests; Occupational Tests; Performance Tests; *Postsecondary Education; Secondary Education; Two Year Colleges; *Vocational Education; *Work Sample Tests
Identifiers: NOCTI; SOCAT
Availability: National Occupational Competency Testing Institute; 409 Bishop Hall, Ferris State University, Big Rapids, MI 49307
Grade Level: 9-14
Notes: Time, 180 min.; Items, 167

This test is part of a program developed to evaluate secondary and postsecondary vocational students with a standardized, objective measure. Each test consists of a multiple-choice portion covering factual knowledge, technical information, understanding of principles, and problem-solving abilities related to the occupation. A performance component samples manipulative skills required. A mental ability test is also available. The written test covers general baking knowledge and terminology, cakes, cookies, breads and yeast doughs, donuts, pastry and pies, safety, sanitation, math. The performance test covers preparation of soft roll dough, formation of danish items, cake decorating, pie making, baking.

15856
Student Occupational Competency Achievement Testing: Building Construction Occupations.   National Occupational Competency Testing Institute, Big Rapids, MI
Descriptors: *Achievement Tests; Adults; *Building Trades; *Construction Industry; Credentials; High Schools; *High School Students; Multiple Choice Tests; Occupational Tests; Performance Tests; *Postsecondary Education; Secondary Education; Two Year Colleges; *Vocational Education; *Work Sample Tests
Identifiers: NOCTI; SOCAT
Availability: National Occupational Competency Testing Institute; 409 Bishop Hall, Ferris State University, Big Rapids, MI 49307
Grade Level: 9-14
Notes: Time, 330 min.; Items, 172

This test is part of a program developed to evaluate secondary and postsecondary vocational students with a standardized, objective measure. Each test consists of a multiple-choice portion covering factual knowledge, technical information, understanding of principles, and problem-solving abilities related to the occupation. A performance component samples manipulative skills required. A mental ability test is also available. The written test covers general building construction, blueprint reading, electrical, painting and decorating, plumbing and heating, general safety. The performance test covers plumbing, carpentry, electrical, and masonry.

15857
Student Occupational Competency Achievement Testing: Building Trades Maintenance.   National Occupational Competency Testing Institute, Big Rapids, MI 1988
Descriptors: *Achievement Tests; Adults; *Building Trades; Credentials; High Schools; *High School Students; *Maintenance; Multiple Choice Tests; Occupational Tests; Performance Tests; *Postsecondary Education; *Repair; Secondary Education; Two Year Colleges; *Vocational Education; *Work Sample Tests
Identifiers: NOCTI; SOCAT
Availability: National Occupational Competency Testing Institute; 409 Bishop Hall, Ferris State University, Big Rapids, MI 49307
Grade Level: 9-14
Notes: Time, 180 min.; Items, 176

This test is part of a program developed to evaluate secondary and postsecondary vocational students with a standardized, objective measure. Each test consists of a multiple-choice portion covering factual knowledge, technical information, understanding of principles, and problem-solving abilities related to the occupation. A performance component samples manipulative skills required. A mental ability test is also available. The written test covers general maintenance, tools, carpentry, grounds and equipment maintenance, masonry, plumbing, sheet metal and welding, painting, glazing, wall covering, hydraulics/pneumatics, electrical, heating, ventilation, air conditioning. The performance test covers plumbing repairs, rough and finish wiring, masonry repair, dry wall installation, carpentry, grounds maintenance.

15859
Student Occupational Competency Achievement Testing: Cabinetmaking.   National Occupational Competency Testing Institute, Big Rapids, MI 1987
Descriptors: *Achievement Tests; Adults; *Cabinetmaking; Credentials; High Schools; *High School Students; Multiple Choice Tests; Occupational Tests; Performance Tests; *Postsecondary Education; Secondary Education; Two Year Colleges; *Vocational Education; *Work Sample Tests
Identifiers: NOCTI; SOCAT
Availability: National Occupational Competency Testing Institute; 409 Bishop Hall, Ferris State University, Big Rapids, MI 49307
Grade Level: 9-14
Notes: Time, 480 min.; Items, 168

This test is part of a program developed to evaluate secondary and postsecondary vocational students with a standardized, objective measure. Each test consists of a multiple-choice portion covering factual knowledge, technical information, understanding of principles, and problem-solving abilities related to the occupation. A performance component samples manipulative skills required. A mental ability test is also available. The written test covers power sawing; drill and drill press; router, shaper, jointer, planer; safety; joint construction; casework design and layout; cutting, shaping, assembling, installing, finishing, transporting casework components; fastening; sanding; cylindrical work. The performance test covers selection of materials, use of hand tools, use of machines, planning, layout, preparation of joints, casework assembly, safety.

15860
Student Occupational Competency Achievement Testing: Child Care Services. National Occupational Competency Testing Institute, Big Rapids, MI 1988
Descriptors: *Achievement Tests; Adults; *Child Care Occupations; Credentials; High Schools; *High School Students; Multiple Choice Tests; Occupational Tests; Performance Tests; *Postsecondary Education; Secondary Education; Two Year Colleges; *Vocational Education; *Work Sample Tests
Identifiers: NOCTI; SOCAT
Availability: National Occupational Competency Testing Institute; 409 Bishop Hall, Ferris State University, Big Rapids, MI 49307
Grade Level: 9-14
Notes: Time, 180 min.; Items, 179
This test is part of a program developed to evaluate secondary and postsecondary vocational students with a standardized, objective measure. Each test consists of a multiple-choice portion covering factual knowledge, technical information, understanding of principles, and problem-solving abilities related to the occupation. A performance component samples manipulative skills required. A mental ability test is also available. The written test covers development of the young child, positive relationships with families, learning environment, advanced social and emotional development, intellectual competence, professionalism, positive guidance, program management. The performance test covers development of learning activity, development of lesson plan, employment application, self-evaluation.

15861
Student Occupational Competency Achievement Testing: Civil Technology (Field Test). National Occupational Competency Testing Institute, Big Rapids, MI 1988
Descriptors: *Achievement Tests; Adults; Credentials; *Engineering Technology; High Schools; *High School Students; Multiple Choice Tests; Occupational Tests; Performance Tests; *Postsecondary Education; Secondary Education; Two Year Colleges; *Vocational Education; *Work Sample Tests
Identifiers: *Civil Technology; NOCTI; SOCAT
Availability: National Occupational Competency Testing Institute; 409 Bishop Hall, Ferris State University, Big Rapids, MI 49307
Grade Level: 9-14
Notes: Time, 180 min.; Items, 179
This test is part of a program developed to evaluate secondary and postsecondary vocational students with a standardized, objective measure. Each test consists of a multiple-choice portion covering factual knowledge, technical information, understanding of principles, and problem-solving abilities related to the occupation. A performance component samples manipulative skills required. A mental ability test is also available. The written test covers foundations, general architectural technology, surveying and leveling, general drafting, framing and environmental, concrete and structural steel, sectional technology, engineering technology, cost analysis, construction technology. The performance test covers line drawing, data tables, profile level notes, contour lines, architectural drawing.

15862
Student Occupational Competency Achievement Testing: Clothing and Textiles Management and Production. National Occupational Competency Testing Institute, Big Rapids, MI 1988
Descriptors: *Achievement Tests; Adults; Clothing Design; Credentials; *Fashion Industry; Finishing; High Schools; *High School Students; Multiple Choice Tests; Occupational Tests; Performance Tests; *Postsecondary Education; Secondary Education; Two Year Colleges; *Vocational Education; *Work Sample Tests
Identifiers: NOCTI; SOCAT; *Textile Industry
Availability: National Occupational Competency Testing Institute; 409 Bishop Hall, Ferris State University, Big Rapids, MI 49307
Grade Level: 9-14
Notes: Time, 360 min.; Items, 156
This test is part of a program developed to evaluate secondary and postsecondary vocational students with a standardized, objective measure. Each test consists of a multiple-choice portion covering factual knowledge, technical information, understanding of principles, and problem-solving abilities related to the occupation. A performance component samples manipulative skills required.

A mental ability test is also available. The written test covers design and color, textiles, construction, sewing machine, patternmaking, alterations, fasteners, manufacturing, mathematics. The performance test covers zipper insertion, seam construction, alterations, garment construction.

15863
Student Occupational Competency Achievement Testing: Commercial Art. National Occupational Competency Testing Institute, Big Rapids, MI 1988
Descriptors: *Achievement Tests; Adults; *Commercial Art; Credentials; High Schools; *High School Students; Multiple Choice Tests; Occupational Tests; Performance Tests; *Postsecondary Education; Secondary Education; Two Year Colleges; *Vocational Education; *Work Sample Tests
Identifiers: NOCTI; SOCAT
Availability: National Occupational Competency Testing Institute; 409 Bishop Hall, Ferris State University, Big Rapids, MI 49307
Grade Level: 9-14
Notes: Time, 345 min.; Items, 154
This test is part of a program developed to evaluate secondary and postsecondary vocational students with a standardized, objective measure. Each test consists of a multiple-choice portion covering factual knowledge, technical information, understanding of principles, and problem-solving abilities related to the occupation. A performance component samples manipulative skills required. A mental ability test is also available. The written test covers graphic design, paper, photography, color, computer graphics, typography, product illustration/rendering, drawing, production. The performance test covers creation of graph, hand lettering, creation of mechanical, production of brochure, creation of geometric design.

15865
Student Occupational Competency Achievement Testing: Computer and Information Science. National Occupational Competency Testing Institute, Big Rapids, MI 1988
Descriptors: *Achievement Tests; Adults; Computer Literacy; *Computer Science; Computer Software; Credentials; High Schools; *High School Students; *Information Technology; Multiple Choice Tests; Occupational Tests; Performance Tests; *Postsecondary Education; Programing; Programing Languages; Secondary Education; Two Year Colleges; *Vocational Education; *Work Sample Tests
Identifiers: NOCTI; SOCAT
Availability: National Occupational Competency Testing Institute; 409 Bishop Hall, Ferris State University, Big Rapids, MI 49307
Grade Level: 9-14
Notes: Time, 420 min.; Items, 181
This test is part of a program developed to evaluate secondary and postsecondary vocational students with a standardized, objective measure. Each test consists of a multiple-choice portion covering factual knowledge, technical information, understanding of principles, and problem-solving abilities related to the occupation. A performance component samples manipulative skills required. A mental ability test is also available. The written test covers information technology uses, related mathematics, computer programing languages, applications software, computer literacy, computer user skills, computer programing concepts. The performance test covers spreadsheet application; word processing or text writer application; coding of program in BASIC, FORTRAN, or PASCAL; database application; diskette backup.

15866
Student Occupational Competency Achievement Testing: Dental Assisting. National Occupational Competency Testing Institute, Big Rapids, MI 1988
Descriptors: *Achievement Tests; Adults; Credentials; *Dental Assistants; High Schools; *High School Students; Multiple Choice Tests; Occupational Tests; Performance Tests; *Postsecondary Education; Secondary Education; Two Year Colleges; *Vocational Education; *Work Sample Tests
Identifiers: NOCTI; SOCAT
Availability: National Occupational Competency Testing Institute; 409 Bishop Hall, Ferris State University, Big Rapids, MI 49307
Grade Level: 9-14
Notes: Time, 285 min.; Items, 166
This test is part of a program developed to evaluate secondary and postsecondary vocational students with a standardized, objective measure. Each test consists of a multiple-choice portion covering factual knowledge, technical information, understanding of principles, and problem-solving abilities related to the occupation. A performance component samples manipulative skills required. A mental ability test is also available. The written test covers dental materials, laboratory skills, chairside skills, dental science/related skills, dental radiology, related the-

ory and skills. The performance test covers instruments, radiographs, handwashing, autoclave, insurance forms, syringes.

15867
Student Occupational Competency Achievement Testing: Diesel Engine Mechanic. National Occupational Competency Testing Institute, Big Rapids, MI 1988
Descriptors: *Achievement Tests; Adults; *Auto Mechanics; Credentials; *Diesel Engines; High Schools; *High School Students; Multiple Choice Tests; Occupational Tests; Performance Tests; *Postsecondary Education; Secondary Education; Two Year Colleges; *Vocational Education; *Work Sample Tests
Identifiers: NOCTI; SOCAT
Availability: National Occupational Competency Testing Institute; 409 Bishop Hall, Ferris State University, Big Rapids, MI 49307
Grade Level: 9-14
Notes: Time, 330 min.; Items, 179
This test is part of a program developed to evaluate secondary and postsecondary vocational students with a standardized, objective measure. Each test consists of a multiple-choice portion covering factual knowledge, technical information, understanding of principles, and problem-solving abilities related to the occupation. A performance component samples manipulative skills required. A mental ability test is also available. The written test covers servicing diesel fuel system; rebuilding engines; shop equipment; engine disassembly; maintaining and servicing cooling and lubrication systems; servicing intake and exhaust systems; testing and servicing electrical systems; maintenance testing and engine operation; maintaining and servicing cylinder heads; servicing flywheel, clutch, and transmission; safety. The performance test covers battery testing, clutch adjustment, drilling, tapping, engine repair.

15868
Student Occupational Competency Achievement Testing: Diversified Occupations. National Occupational Competency Testing Institute, Big Rapids, MI 1988
Descriptors: *Achievement Tests; Adults; Credentials; High Schools; *High School Students; *Job Skills; Multiple Choice Tests; Occupational Tests; *Occupations; *Postsecondary Education; Secondary Education; Two Year Colleges; *Vocational Education; *Vocational Evaluation
Identifiers: NOCTI; SOCAT
Availability: National Occupational Competency Testing Institute; 409 Bishop Hall, Ferris State University, Big Rapids, MI 49307
Grade Level: 9-14
Notes: Time, 180 min.; Items, 152
This test is part of a program developed to evaluate secondary and postsecondary vocational students with a standardized, objective measure. Each test consists of a multiple-choice portion covering factual knowledge, technical information, understanding of principles, and problem-solving abilities related to the occupation. A mental ability test is also available. The written test covers human relations, consumer skills, orientation, employment acquisition, employment retention, communications development, legal awareness, youth organizations, health, and safety. There is no performance test.

15869
Student Occupational Competency Achievement Testing: Electrical Construction/Maintenance. National Occupational Competency Testing Institute, Big Rapids, MI 1988
Descriptors: *Achievement Tests; Adults; Credentials; *Electrical Occupations; *Electrical Systems; High Schools; *High School Students; Multiple Choice Tests; Occupational Tests; Performance Tests; *Postsecondary Education; Secondary Education; Two Year Colleges; *Vocational Education; *Work Sample Tests
Identifiers: NOCTI; SOCAT
Availability: National Occupational Competency Testing Institute; 409 Bishop Hall, Ferris State University, Big Rapids, MI 49307
Grade Level: 9-14
Notes: Time, 345 min.; Items, 158
This test is part of a program developed to evaluate secondary and postsecondary vocational students with a standardized, objective measure. Each test consists of a multiple-choice portion covering factual knowledge, technical information, understanding of principles, and problem-solving abilities related to the occupation. A performance component samples manipulative skills required. A mental ability test is also available. The written test covers meters/measurements, symbols/architectural drawings, general information, materials, National Electrical Code, basic electricity, and installation. The performance test covers conduit bending, wiring diagram, motor control, and service installation.

15870
Student Occupational Competency Achievement Testing: Electrical Occupations. National Occupational Competency Testing Institute, Big Rapids, MI 1988
Descriptors: *Achievement Tests; Adults; Credentials; *Electrical Occupations; High Schools; *High School Students; Multiple Choice Tests; Occupational Tests; Performance Tests; *Postsecondary Education; Secondary Education; Two Year Colleges; *Vocational Education; *Work Sample Tests
Identifiers: NOCTI; SOCAT
Availability: National Occupational Competency Testing Institute; 409 Bishop Hall, Ferris State University, Big Rapids, MI 49307
Grade Level: 9-14
Notes: Time, 360 min.; Items, 183
This test is part of a program developed to evaluate secondary and postsecondary vocational students with a standardized, objective measure. Each test consists of a multiple-choice portion covering factual knowledge, technical information, understanding of principles, and problem-solving abilities related to the occupation. A performance component samples manipulative skills required. A mental ability test is also available. The written test covers motors and motor controls, National Electrical Code, materials, tools, blueprint reading and estimating, alternating current, direct current, safety. The performance test covers drawings/diagrams, wiring, use of tools, component mounting, and economy of time.

15871
Student Occupational Competency Achievement Testing: Electrical Technology. National Occupational Competency Testing Institute, Big Rapids, MI 1988
Descriptors: *Achievement Tests; Adults; Credentials; *Electrical Occupations; *Electrical Systems; High Schools; *High School Students; Multiple Choice Tests; Occupational Tests; Performance Tests; *Postsecondary Education; Secondary Education; Two Year Colleges; *Vocational Education; *Work Sample Tests
Identifiers: NOCTI; SOCAT
Availability: National Occupational Competency Testing Institute; 409 Bishop Hall, Ferris State University, Big Rapids, MI 49307
Grade Level: 9-14
Notes: Time, 360 min.; Items, 159
This test is part of a program developed to evaluate secondary and postsecondary vocational students with a standardized, objective measure. Each test consists of a multiple-choice portion covering factual knowledge, technical information, understanding of principles, and problem-solving abilities related to the occupation. A performance component samples manipulative skills required. A mental ability test is also available. The written test covers generators/alternators, meters, direct current, alternating current, motor controls, motors, transformers, general information, and National Electrical Code. The performance test covers materials, circuit design, installation, wiring, and testing.

15872
Student Occupational Competency Achievement Testing: Electromechanical Technology. National Occupational Competency Testing Institute, Big Rapids, MI 1988
Descriptors: *Achievement Tests; Adults; Credentials; *Electromechanical Technology; High Schools; *High School Students; Multiple Choice Tests; Occupational Tests; Performance Tests; *Postsecondary Education; Secondary Education; Two Year Colleges; *Vocational Education; *Work Sample Tests
Identifiers: NOCTI; SOCAT
Availability: National Occupational Competency Testing Institute; 409 Bishop Hall, Ferris State University, Big Rapids, MI 49307
Grade Level: 9-14
Notes: Time, 360 min.; Items, 185
This test is part of a program developed to evaluate secondary and postsecondary vocational students with a standardized, objective measure. Each test consists of a multiple-choice portion covering factual knowledge, technical information, understanding of principles, and problem-solving abilities related to the occupation. A performance component samples manipulative skills required. A mental ability test is also available. The written test covers fluid power, electrical power, general information, and control. The performance test covers motor rating, circuits, motor connection, and current power.

15873
Student Occupational Competency Achievement Testing: Electronic Technology. National Occupational Competency Testing Institute, Big Rapids, MI 1988

Descriptors: *Achievement Tests; Adults; Credentials; *Electronics; *Electronic Technicians; High Schools; *High School Students; Multiple Choice Tests; Occupational Tests; Performance Tests; *Postsecondary Education; Secondary Education; Two Year Colleges; *Vocational Education; *Work Sample Tests
Identifiers: NOCTI; SOCAT
Availability: National Occupational Competency Testing Institute; 409 Bishop Hall, Ferris State University, Big Rapids, MI 49307
Grade Level: 9-14
Notes: Time, 275 min.; Items, 160
This test is part of a program developed to evaluate secondary and postsecondary vocational students with a standardized, objective measure. Each test consists of a multiple-choice portion covering factual knowledge, technical information, understanding of principles, and problem-solving abilities related to the occupation. A performance component samples manipulative skills required. A mental ability test is also available. The written test covers soldering, schematic symbols, measurement, op amps, semiconductors and components, power supplies, alternating current, direct current, digital, logic, oscilloscopes, microprocessors, communications, safety. The performance test covers digital logic analysis, circuit construction, multimeter, use of oscilloscope.

15874
Student Occupational Competency Achievement Testing: Food Production, Management and Services. National Occupational Competency Testing Institute, Big Rapids, MI 1988
Descriptors: *Achievement Tests; Adults; Credentials; *Food Service; High Schools; *High School Students; Multiple Choice Tests; Occupational Tests; Performance Tests; *Postsecondary Education; Secondary Education; Two Year Colleges; *Vocational Education; *Work Sample Tests
Identifiers: NOCTI; SOCAT
Availability: National Occupational Competency Testing Institute; 409 Bishop Hall, Ferris State University, Big Rapids, MI 49307
Grade Level: 9-14
Notes: Time, 375 min.; Items, 160
This test is part of a program developed to evaluate secondary and postsecondary vocational students with a standardized, objective measure. Each test consists of a multiple-choice portion covering factual knowledge, technical information, understanding of principles, and problem-solving abilities related to the occupation. A performance component samples manipulative skills required. A mental ability test is also available. The written test covers large and small equipment, food preparation, baking, management and employment skills, customer service, sanitation, safety. The performance test covers food preparation, recipes, equipment/tools, food service, and safety/sanitation.

15875
Student Occupational Competency Achievement Testing: Forestry Products and Processing. National Occupational Competency Testing Institute, Big Rapids, MI 1988
Descriptors: *Achievement Tests; Adults; Credentials; *Forestry Occupations; High Schools; *High School Students; Multiple Choice Tests; Occupational Tests; Performance Tests; *Postsecondary Education; Secondary Education; Two Year Colleges; *Vocational Education; *Work Sample Tests
Identifiers: NOCTI; SOCAT
Availability: National Occupational Competency Testing Institute; 409 Bishop Hall, Ferris State University, Big Rapids, MI 49307
Grade Level: 9-14
Notes: Time, 180 min.; Items, 157
This test is part of a program developed to evaluate secondary and postsecondary vocational students with a standardized, objective measure. Each test consists of a multiple-choice portion covering factual knowledge, technical information, understanding of principles, and problem-solving abilities related to the occupation. A performance component samples manipulative skills required. A mental ability test is also available. The written test covers forest protection, silvaculture, tree identification, wildlife, sawmilling, forest ecology, forest management, diesel engines, hydraulics, logging/harvesting, timber cruising, surveying, chain saw, business management, employability skills, safety. The performance test covers tree felling, chain saw care, lumber grading, plot layout, calculation of load capacity, log scaling, leaf identification, calculation of acreage, employment application.

15876
Student Occupational Competency Achievement Testing: General Drafting and Design. National Occupational Competency Testing Institute, Big Rapids, MI 1988

Descriptors: *Achievement Tests; Adults; Credentials; *Drafting; High Schools; *High School Students; Multiple Choice Tests; Occupational Tests; Performance Tests; *Postsecondary Education; Secondary Education; Two Year Colleges; *Vocational Education; *Work Sample Tests
Identifiers: NOCTI; SOCAT
Availability: National Occupational Competency Testing Institute; 409 Bishop Hall, Ferris State University, Big Rapids, MI 49307
Grade Level: 9-14
Notes: Time, 360 min.; Items, 173
This test is part of a program developed to evaluate secondary and postsecondary vocational students with a standardized, objective measure. Each test consists of a multiple-choice portion covering factual knowledge, technical information, understanding of principles, and problem-solving abilities related to the occupation. A performance component samples manipulative skills required. A mental ability test is also available. The written test covers basic drawing skills, preparing to draw, introduction to drafting, calculations used in drawing, mechanical drafting, systems drafting, architectural drafting, drafting with machines. The performance test covers sheet metal development, section drawing, threaded assembly, constructions, architectural drawing, machined part, auxiliary view.

15877
Student Occupational Competency Achievement Testing: Health Assistant. National Occupational Competency Testing Institute, Big Rapids, MI 1988
Descriptors: *Achievement Tests; Adults; Credentials; *Health Personnel; High Schools; *High School Students; Multiple Choice Tests; Occupational Tests; Performance Tests; *Postsecondary Education; Secondary Education; Two Year Colleges; *Vocational Education; *Work Sample Tests
Identifiers: NOCTI; SOCAT
Availability: National Occupational Competency Testing Institute; 409 Bishop Hall, Ferris State University, Big Rapids, MI 49307
Grade Level: 9-14
Notes: Time, 270 min.; Items, 151
This test is part of a program developed to evaluate secondary and postsecondary vocational students with a standardized, objective measure. Each test consists of a multiple-choice portion covering factual knowledge, technical information, understanding of principles, and problem-solving abilities related to the occupation. A performance component samples manipulative skills required. A mental ability test is also available. The written test covers observation and communication, job responsibilities, health assistant skills, and medical terminology. The performance test covers patient medical records, vital signs, handwashing, patient transfer, patient preparation, and bed making.

15878
Student Occupational Competency Achievement Testing: Heavy Equipment Maintenance and Repair. National Occupational Competency Testing Institute, Big Rapids, MI 1988
Descriptors: *Achievement Tests; Adults; Credentials; Electrical Systems; *Equipment Maintenance; High Schools; *High School Students; Mechanical Equipment; Multiple Choice Tests; Occupational Tests; Performance Tests; *Postsecondary Education; Secondary Education; Two Year Colleges; *Vocational Education; *Work Sample Tests
Identifiers: NOCTI; SOCAT
Availability: National Occupational Competency Testing Institute; 409 Bishop Hall, Ferris State University, Big Rapids, MI 49307
Grade Level: 9-14
Notes: Time, 360 min.; Items, 180
This test is part of a program developed to evaluate secondary and postsecondary vocational students with a standardized, objective measure. Each test consists of a multiple-choice portion covering factual knowledge, technical information, understanding of principles, and problem-solving abilities related to the occupation. A performance component samples manipulative skills required. A mental ability test is also available. The written test covers electrical system, engines, power train, air system, hydraulic systems, welding, braking system, cooling system, preventive maintenance. The performance test covers valve grinding and adjustments, oil pressure measurement, cooling system testing, adjustments to clutch assembly, brake adjustments, setting of bearing preload, cutting/welding.

15879
Student Occupational Competency Achievement Testing: Home Health Aide. National Occupational Competency Testing Institute, Big Rapids, MI 1988

Descriptors: *Achievement Tests; Adults; Credentials; High Schools; *High School Students; *Home Health Aides; Multiple Choice Tests; Occupational Tests; Performance Tests; *Postsecondary Education; Secondary Education; Two Year Colleges; *Vocational Education; *Work Sample Tests
Identifiers: NOCTI; SOCAT
Availability: National Occupational Competency Testing Institute; 409 Bishop Hall, Ferris State University, Big Rapids, MI 49307
Grade Level: 9-14
Notes: Time, 300 min.; Items, 138

This test is part of a program developed to evaluate secondary and postsecondary vocational students with a standardized, objective measure. Each test consists of a multiple-choice portion covering factual knowledge, technical information, understanding of principles, and problem-solving abilities related to the occupation. A performance component samples manipulative skills required. A mental ability test is also available. The written test covers reporting, recording, abbreviations, vocabulary, first aid, vital signs, nutrition, elimination, basic emergency measures, patient care, positioning, employability skills, safety. The performance test covers vital signs, infant care, bed making, first aid, patient transfer, and measurement of fluids.

15880
Student Occupational Competency Achievement Testing: Marketing and Distributive Education. National Occupational Competency Testing Institute, Big Rapids, MI 1988
Descriptors: *Achievement Tests; Adults; Credentials; *Distributive Education; High Schools; *High School Students; *Marketing; Multiple Choice Tests; Occupational Tests; Performance Tests; *Postsecondary Education; Secondary Education; Two Year Colleges; *Vocational Education; *Work Sample Tests
Identifiers: NOCTI; SOCAT
Availability: National Occupational Competency Testing Institute; 409 Bishop Hall, Ferris State University, Big Rapids, MI 49307
Grade Level: 9-14
Notes: Time, 345 min.; Items, 170

This test is part of a program developed to evaluate secondary and postsecondary vocational students with a standardized, objective measure. Each test consists of a multiple-choice portion covering factual knowledge, technical information, understanding of principles, and problem-solving abilities related to the occupation. A performance component samples manipulative skills required. A mental ability test is also available. The written test covers advertising, economics, communications, general management, marketing, selling, electronic marketing, customer service, related mathematics, entrepreneurship, human relations, career development, employment preparation. The performance test covers design principles, sales presentation, human relations case study, job application, and interviews.

15881
Student Occupational Competency Achievement Testing: Mechanical Drafting. National Occupational Competency Testing Institute, Big Rapids, MI 1988
Descriptors: *Achievement Tests; Adults; Credentials; *Drafting; *Engineering Drawing; High Schools; *High School Students; Multiple Choice Tests; Occupational Tests; Performance Tests; *Postsecondary Education; Secondary Education; Two Year Colleges; *Vocational Education; *Work Sample Tests
Identifiers: NOCTI; SOCAT
Availability: National Occupational Competency Testing Institute; 409 Bishop Hall, Ferris State University, Big Rapids, MI 49307
Grade Level: 9-14
Notes: Time, 360 min.; Items, 167

This test is part of a program developed to evaluate secondary and postsecondary vocational students with a standardized, objective measure. Each test consists of a multiple-choice portion covering factual knowledge, technical information, understanding of principles, and problem-solving abilities related to the occupation. A performance component samples manipulative skills required. A mental ability test is also available. The written test covers drafting equipment and tools, pictorial and drawing skills, orthographic projections, sectioning, drawing preparation, drafting room practices, threads and fasteners, cams and gears, pulleys, machine assembly and casting, dimensioning, tolerance, symbols, computations. The performance test covers orthographic drawing, tolerances, dimensions, completion of missing views.

15882
Student Occupational Competency Achievement Testing: Medical Assisting. National Occupational Competency Testing Institute, Big Rapids, MI 1988
Descriptors: *Achievement Tests; Adults; Credentials; High Schools; *High School Students; *Medical Assistants; Multiple Choice Tests; Occupational Tests; Performance Tests; *Postsecondary Education; Secondary Education; Two Year Colleges; *Vocational Education; *Work Sample Tests
Identifiers: NOCTI; SOCAT
Availability: National Occupational Competency Testing Institute; 409 Bishop Hall, Ferris State University, Big Rapids, MI 49307
Grade Level: 9-14
Notes: Time, 180 min.; Items, 168

This test is part of a program developed to evaluate secondary and postsecondary vocational students with a standardized, objective measure. Each test consists of a multiple-choice portion covering factual knowledge, technical information, understanding of principles, and problem-solving abilities related to the occupation. A performance component samples manipulative skills required. A mental ability test is also available. The written test covers clinical assisting, laboratory procedures and equipment, medical terminology, anatomy and physiology, patient instruction, radiology, diagnostic procedures and equipment, electrocardiography, medical ethics, and law. The performance test covers laboratory procedures, diagnostic procedures, clinical procedures, and general office procedures.

15883
Student Occupational Competency Achievement Testing: Metalworking and Fabrication. National Occupational Competency Testing Institute, Big Rapids, MI 1988
Descriptors: *Achievement Tests; Adults; Credentials; High Schools; *High School Students; *Metal Working; Multiple Choice Tests; Occupational Tests; Performance Tests; *Postsecondary Education; Secondary Education; Two Year Colleges; *Vocational Education; *Work Sample Tests
Identifiers: NOCTI; SOCAT
Availability: National Occupational Competency Testing Institute; 409 Bishop Hall, Ferris State University, Big Rapids, MI 49307
Grade Level: 9-14
Notes: Time, 480 min.; Items, 160

This test is part of a program developed to evaluate secondary and postsecondary vocational students with a standardized, objective measure. Each test consists of a multiple-choice portion covering factual knowledge, technical information, understanding of principles, and problem-solving abilities related to the occupation. A performance component samples manipulative skills required. A mental ability test is also available. The written test covers welding terms and symbols, related theory, benchwork and layout, lathes, sawing, milling, drilling, grinding, shielded metal arc welding, oxyacetylene welding, gas tungsten arc welding, gas metal arc welding. The performance test covers oxyacetylene welding, machining, shielded metal arc welding.

15884
Student Occupational Competency Achievement Testing: Nursing Assisting. National Occupational Competency Testing Institute, Big Rapids, MI 1988
Descriptors: *Achievement Tests; Adults; Credentials; High Schools; *High School Students; Multiple Choice Tests; *Nurses Aides; Occupational Tests; Performance Tests; *Postsecondary Education; Secondary Education; Two Year Colleges; *Vocational Education; *Work Sample Tests
Identifiers: NOCTI; SOCAT
Availability: National Occupational Competency Testing Institute; 409 Bishop Hall, Ferris State University, Big Rapids, MI 49307
Grade Level: 9-14
Notes: Time, 270 min.; Items, 160

This test is part of a program developed to evaluate secondary and postsecondary vocational students with a standardized, objective measure. Each test consists of a multiple-choice portion covering factual knowledge, technical information, understanding of principles, and problem-solving abilities related to the occupation. A performance component samples manipulative skills required. A mental ability test is also available. The written test covers assisting with diagnostic studies; assisting with hydration, nutrition, and elimination; observing and communicating; assisting with mobility, positioning, range of motion; maintaining safety; assisting with personal hygiene; employability skills. The performance test covers vital signs, urine testing, patient transfer, making of occupied beds, and isolation garments.

15885
Student Occupational Competency Achievement Testing: Painting and Decorating. National Occupational Competency Testing Institute, Big Rapids, MI 1988
Descriptors: *Achievement Tests; Adults; Credentials; High Schools; *High School Students; Multiple Choice Tests; Occupational Tests; *Painting (Industrial Arts); Performance Tests; *Postsecondary Education; Secondary Education; Two Year Colleges; *Vocational Education; *Work Sample Tests
Identifiers: NOCTI; SOCAT
Availability: National Occupational Competency Testing Institute; 409 Bishop Hall, Ferris State University, Big Rapids, MI 49307
Grade Level: 9-14
Notes: Time, 300 min.; Items, 151

This test is part of a program developed to evaluate secondary and postsecondary vocational students with a standardized, objective measure. Each test consists of a multiple-choice portion covering factual knowledge, technical information, understanding of principles, and problem-solving abilities related to the occupation. A performance component samples manipulative skills required. A mental ability test is also available. The written test covers equipment, color, wall covering, wood finishing, interior and exterior painting, special wall finishes, and safety. The performance test covers interior or exterior wall painting, dry wall repair, and glass replacement.

15886
Student Occupational Competency Achievement Testing: Sheet Metal. National Occupational Competency Testing Institute, Big Rapids, MI 1988
Descriptors: *Achievement Tests; Adults; Credentials; High Schools; *High School Students; Multiple Choice Tests; Occupational Tests; Performance Tests; *Postsecondary Education; Secondary Education; *Sheet Metal Work; Two Year Colleges; *Vocational Education; *Work Sample Tests
Identifiers: NOCTI; SOCAT
Availability: National Occupational Competency Testing Institute; 409 Bishop Hall, Ferris State University, Big Rapids, MI 49307
Grade Level: 9-14
Notes: Time, 390 min.; Items, 153

This test is part of a program developed to evaluate secondary and postsecondary vocational students with a standardized, objective measure. Each test consists of a multiple-choice portion covering factual knowledge, technical information, understanding of principles, and problem-solving abilities related to the occupation. A performance component samples manipulative skills required. A mental ability test is also available. The written test covers ductwork, general shop practices, fiberglass, sheet metal layout, general information, and safety. The performance test covers center piece construction, end piece construction, round piece construction, and layout.

15887
Student Occupational Competency Achievement Testing: Upholstering. National Occupational Competency Testing Institute, Big Rapids, MI 1988
Descriptors: *Achievement Tests; Adults; Credentials; *Furniture Industry; High Schools; *High School Students; Multiple Choice Tests; Occupational Tests; Performance Tests; *Postsecondary Education; Secondary Education; Two Year Colleges; *Vocational Education; *Work Sample Tests
Identifiers: NOCTI; SOCAT; *Upholstery
Availability: National Occupational Competency Testing Institute; 409 Bishop Hall, Ferris State University, Big Rapids, MI 49307
Grade Level: 9-14
Notes: Time, 320 min.; Items, 176

This test is part of a program developed to evaluate secondary and postsecondary vocational students with a standardized, objective measure. Each test consists of a multiple-choice portion covering factual knowledge, technical information, understanding of principles, and problem-solving abilities related to the occupation. A performance component samples manipulative skills required. A mental ability test is also available. The written test covers frame preparation, tools and equipment, cushioning, covering, foundation and body work, finishing and trimming, general information, and estimating. The performance test covers handling fabric, mounting fabric, and working with coil springs.

15888
Student Occupational Competency Achievement Testing: Warehousing Services. National Occupational Competency Testing Institute, Big Rapids, MI 1988
Descriptors: *Achievement Tests; Adults; Credentials; High Schools; *High School Students; Multiple Choice Tests; Occupational Tests; Performance Tests; *Postsecondary Education; Secondary Education; Two Year Colleges; *Vocational Education; *Warehouses; *Work Sample Tests
Identifiers: NOCTI; SOCAT

Availability: National Occupational Competency Testing Institute; 409 Bishop Hall, Ferris State University, Big Rapids, MI 49307
Grade Level: 9-14
Notes: Time, 315 min.; Items, 167

This test is part of a program developed to evaluate secondary and postsecondary vocational students with a standardized, objective measure. Each test consists of a multiple-choice portion covering factual knowledge, technical information, understanding of principles, and problem-solving abilities related to the occupation. A performance component samples manipulative skills required. A mental ability test is also available. The written test covers inventory and control, equipment, purchasing, shipping and distribution, receiving, equipment safety, palleted skids, general information. The performance test covers inventory control, shipping procedures, and purchasing.

15911
Iowa Tests of Basic Skills, Forms G and H, Levels 9-11, Writing Supplement. Hieronymus, A.N.; Hoover, H.D. 1987
Subtests: Narrative; Explanation; Description; Informative Report; Persuasive Essay
Descriptors: *Achievement Tests; Elementary Education; *Elementary School Students; *Essay Tests; Holistic Evaluation; Writing (Composition); *Writing Evaluation; *Writing Skills
Identifiers: Basic Skills Assessment Program; ITBS
Availability: Riverside Publishing Co.; 8420 Bryn Mawr Ave., Chicago, IL 60631
Grade Level: 3-5
Notes: Time, 35 min.

Measures the productive writing skills of students. Assesses the students' ability to generate, to organize, and to express their ideas in a variety of written forms. Designed to complement the language tests in the regular battery of the Iowa Tests of Basic Skills. Measures the students' technical knowledge of written English and their ability to apply that knowledge to a specific writing situation. An essay topic was developed in each of 5 modes: narrative, explanation, description, informative report, and persuasive essay. Each essay requires 35 minutes of working time. Scored on a 4-point, focused holistic score scale. Level 9-11 is intended for use in grades 3 through 5.

15912
Iowa Tests of Basic Skills, Forms G and H, Levels 12-14, Writing Supplement. Hieronymus, A.N.; Hoover, H.D. 1987
Subtests: Narrative; Explanation; Description; Informative Report; Persuasive Essay
Descriptors: *Achievement Tests; Elementary Education; *Elementary School Students; *Essay Tests; Holistic Evaluation; Writing (Composition); *Writing Evaluation; *Writing Skills
Identifiers: Basic Skills Assessment Program; ITBS
Availability: Riverside Publishing Co.; 8420 Bryn Mawr Ave., Chicago, IL 60631
Grade Level: 6-8
Notes: Time, 35 min.

Measures the productive writing skills of students. Assesses the students' ability to generate, to organize, and to express their ideas in a variety of written forms. Designed to complement the language tests in the regular battery of the Iowa Tests of Basic Skills. Measures the students' technical knowledge of written English and their ability to apply that knowledge to a specific writing situation. An essay topic was developed in each of 5 modes: narrative, explanation, description, informative report, and persuasive essay. Each essay requires 35 minutes of working time. Scored on a 4-point, focused holistic score scale. Level 12-14 is intended for use in grades 6 through 8.

15913
California Diagnostic Reading Tests, Level A.
CTB/Macmillan/McGraw-Hill, Monterey, CA 1989
Subtests: Word Analysis; Vocabulary; Comprehension
Descriptors: Auditory Discrimination; Criterion Referenced Tests; *Diagnostic Tests; *Elementary School Students; *Grade 1; *Grade 2; *Low Achievement; Norm Referenced Tests; *Primary Education; *Reading Comprehension; *Reading Diagnosis; *Reading Processes; *Reading Skills; *Reading Tests; Visual Discrimination; *Vocabulary; Word Recognition
Identifiers: CDRT
Availability: CTB/MacMillan/McGraw-Hill; Del Monte Research Park, 2500 Garden Rd., Monterey, CA 93940
Grade Level: 1-2
Notes: Items, 170

Used to provide teachers with diagnostic information needed to plan remedial instruction for individual students or groups of students. Content and difficulty of various levels were developed with the special needs of lower-achieving students in mind. In addition to objectives-based diagnostic information, the test also pro-

vides norm-referenced information for evaluating individual and group progress and for fulfilling state and federal reporting requirements for compensatory education and other specially funded programs. Level A measures those skills that are prerequisite to reading: word analysis, vocabulary, and comprehension. CDRT is not a timed test. Most of the test is administered orally.

15914
California Diagnostic Reading Tests, Level B.
CTB/Macmillan/McGraw-Hill, Monterey, CA 1989
Subtests: Word Analysis; Vocabulary; Comprehension
Descriptors: Auditory Discrimination; Criterion Referenced Tests; *Diagnostic Tests; *Elementary School Students; *Grade 2; *Grade 3; *Low Achievement; Norm Referenced Tests; *Primary Education; *Reading Comprehension; *Reading Diagnosis; *Reading Processes; *Reading Skills; *Reading Tests; Structural Analysis (Linguistics); *Vocabulary; Word Recognition
Identifiers: CDRT
Availability: CTB/MacMillan/McGraw-Hill; Del Monte Research Park, 2500 Garden Rd., Monterey, CA 93940
Grade Level: 2-3
Notes: Items, 168

Used to provide teachers with diagnostic information needed to plan remedial instruction for individual students or groups of students. Content and difficulty of various levels were developed with the special needs of lower-achieving students in mind. In addition to objectives-based diagnostic information, the test also provides norm-referenced information for evaluating individual and group progress and for fulfilling state and federal reporting requirements for compensatory education and other specially funded programs. Level B measures those skills that students acquire as they progress through grades 2 and 3: word analysis, vocabulary, and comprehension. CDRT is not a timed test. Most of the test is administered orally.

15915
California Diagnostic Reading Tests, Level C.
CTB/Macmillan/McGraw-Hill, Monterey, CA 1989
Subtests: Word Analysis; Vocabulary; Comprehension
Descriptors: Auditory Discrimination; Criterion Referenced Tests; *Diagnostic Tests; Elementary Education; *Elementary School Students; *Grade 3; *Grade 4; *Low Achievement; Norm Referenced Tests; *Reading Comprehension; *Reading Diagnosis; *Reading Processes; *Reading Skills; *Reading Tests; Structural Analysis (Linguistics); *Vocabulary; Word Recognition
Identifiers: CDRT
Availability: CTB/MacMillan/McGraw-Hill; Del Monte Research Park, 2500 Garden Rd., Monterey, CA 93940
Grade Level: 3-4
Notes: Items, 164

Used to provide teachers with diagnostic information needed to plan remedial instruction for individual students or groups of students. Content and difficulty of various levels were developed with the special needs of lower-achieving students in mind. In addition to objectives-based diagnostic information, the test also provides norm-referenced information for evaluating individual and group progress and for fulfilling state and federal reporting requirements for compensatory education and other specially funded programs. Level C measures those skills that students acquire as they progress through grade 3 and grade 4: word analysis, vocabulary, and comprehension. CDRT is not a timed test.

15916
California Diagnostic Reading Tests, Level D.
CTB/Macmillan/McGraw-Hill, Monterey, CA 1989
Subtests: Word Analysis; Vocabulary; Comprehension; Applications
Descriptors: Auditory Discrimination; Criterion Referenced Tests; *Diagnostic Tests; *Elementary School Students; *Intermediate Grades; *Low Achievement; Norm Referenced Tests; *Reading Comprehension; *Reading Diagnosis; *Reading Processes; *Reading Skills; *Reading Tests; Structural Analysis (Linguistics); *Vocabulary; Word Recognition
Identifiers: CDRT
Availability: CTB/MacMillan/McGraw-Hill; Del Monte Research Park, 2500 Garden Rd., Monterey, CA 93940
Grade Level: 4-6
Notes: Items, 155

Used to provide teachers with diagnostic information needed to plan remedial instruction for individual students or groups of students. Content and difficulty of

various levels were developed with the special needs of lower-achieving students in mind. In addition to objectives-based diagnostic information, the test also provides norm-referenced information for evaluating individual and group progress and for fulfilling state and federal reporting requirements for compensatory education and other specially funded programs. Level D measures word analysis, vocabulary, comprehension, and applications. Most of CDRT is not timed.

15917
California Diagnostic Reading Tests, Level E.
CTB/Macmillan/McGraw-Hill, Monterey, CA 1989
Subtests: Word Analysis; Vocabulary; Comprehension; Applications
Descriptors: Auditory Discrimination; Criterion Referenced Tests; *Diagnostic Tests; *Grade 6; Intermediate Grades; Junior High Schools; *Junior High School Students; *Low Achievement; Norm Referenced Tests; *Reading Comprehension; *Reading Diagnosis; *Reading Processes; *Reading Skills; *Reading Tests; Structural Analysis (Linguistics); *Vocabulary; Word Recognition
Identifiers: CDRT
Availability: CTB/MacMillan/McGraw-Hill; Del Monte Research Park, 2500 Garden Rd., Monterey, CA 93940
Grade Level: 6-8
Notes: Items, 172

Used to provide teachers with diagnostic information needed to plan remedial instruction for individual students or groups of students. Content and difficulty of various levels were developed with the special needs of lower-achieving students in mind. In addition to objectives-based diagnostic information, the test also provides norm-referenced information for evaluating individual and group progress and for fulfilling state and federal reporting requirements for compensatory education and other specially funded programs. Level E measures word analysis, vocabulary, comprehension, and applications. Most of CDRT is not timed.

15918
California Diagnostic Reading Tests, Level F.
CTB/Macmillan/McGraw-Hill, Monterey, CA 1989
Subtests: Vocabulary; Comprehension; Applications
Descriptors: Criterion Referenced Tests; *Diagnostic Tests; *Low Achievement; Norm Referenced Tests; *Reading Comprehension; *Reading Diagnosis; *Reading Processes; *Reading Skills; *Reading Tests; Remedial Reading; Secondary Education; *Secondary School Students; *Vocabulary
Identifiers: CDRT
Availability: CTB/MacMillan/McGraw-Hill; Del Monte Research Park, 2500 Garden Rd., Monterey, CA 93940
Grade Level: 8-12
Notes: Items, 161

Used to provide teachers with diagnostic information needed to plan remedial instruction for individual students or groups of students. Content and difficulty of various levels were developed with the special needs of lower-achieving students in mind. In addition to objectives-based diagnostic information, the test also provides norm-referenced information for evaluating individual and group progress and for fulfilling state and federal reporting requirements for compensatory education and other specially funded programs. Assesses student performance in 4 critical areas of reading: word attack, vocabulary, reading comprehension, and reading applications.

15919
California Diagnostic Mathematics Tests, Level A.
CTB/Macmillan/McGraw-Hill, Monterey, CA 1989
Subtests: Number Concepts; Computation; Applications
Descriptors: *Computation; Criterion Referenced Tests; *Diagnostic Tests; Elementary School Students; *Grade 1; *Grade 2; *Low Achievement; *Mathematical Applications; *Mathematics Tests; Norm Referenced Tests; *Number Concepts; *Primary Education
Identifiers: CDMT
Availability: CTB/MacMillan/McGraw-Hill; Del Monte Research Park, 2500 Garden Rd., Monterey, CA 93940
Grade Level: 1-2
Notes: Items, 98

Used to provide teachers with diagnostic information needed to plan remedial instruction for individual students or groups of students. Content and difficulty of various levels were developed with the special needs of lower-achieving students in mind. In addition to objectives-based diagnostic information, test also provides norm-referenced information for evaluating individual and group progress and for fulfilling state and federal requirements for compensatory education and other specially funded programs. Assesses student performance in 3 areas: number concepts, computation, and mathematics applications. Level A measures skills that are prerequisite to mathematics. CDMT is not a timed test. Most of the test is administered orally.

15920
California Diagnostic Mathematics Tests, Level B.
CTB/Macmillan/McGraw-Hill, Monterey, CA 1989
Subtests: Number Concepts; Computation; Applications
Descriptors: *Computation; Criterion Referenced Tests; *Diagnostic Tests; Elementary School Students; *Grade 2; *Grade 3; *Low Achievement; *Mathematical Applications; *Mathematics Tests; Norm Referenced Tests; *Number Concepts; *Primary Education
Identifiers: CDMT
Availability: CTB/Macmillan/McGraw-Hill; Del Monte Research Park, 2500 Garden Rd., Monterey, CA 93940
Grade Level: 2-3
Notes: Items, 108

Used to provide teachers with diagnostic information needed to plan remedial instruction for individual students or groups of students. Content and difficulty of various levels were developed with the special needs of lower-achieving students in mind. In addition to objectives-based diagnostic information, test also provides norm-referenced information for evaluating individual and group progress and for fulfilling state and federal requirements for compensatory education and other specially funded programs. Assesses student performance in 3 areas: number concepts, computation, and mathematics applications. Level B measures those skills that are prerequisite to mathematics. CDMT is not a timed test.

15921
California Diagnostic Mathematics Tests, Level C.
CTB/Macmillan/McGraw-Hill, Monterey, CA 1989
Subtests: Number Concepts; Computation; Applications
Descriptors: *Computation; Criterion Referenced Tests; *Diagnostic Tests; Elementary Education; *Elementary School Students; *Grade 3; *Grade 4; *Low Achievement; *Mathematical Applications; *Mathematics Tests; Norm Referenced Tests; *Number Concepts
Identifiers: CDMT
Availability: CTB/Macmillan/McGraw-Hill; Del Monte Research Park, 2500 Garden Rd., Monterey, CA 93940
Grade Level: 3-4
Notes: Items, 127

Used to provide teachers with diagnostic information needed to plan remedial instruction for individual students or groups of students. Content and difficulty of various levels were developed with the special needs of lower-achieving students in mind. In addition to objectives-based diagnostic information, test also provides norm-referenced information for evaluating individual and group progress and for fulfilling state and federal requirements for compensatory education and other specially funded programs. Assesses student performance in 3 areas: number concepts, computation, and mathematics applications. Level C measures those skills that are prerequisite to mathematics. CDMT is not a timed test.

15922
California Diagnostic Mathematics Tests, Level D.
CTB/Macmillan/McGraw-Hill, Monterey, CA 1989
Subtests: Number Concepts; Computation; Applications
Descriptors: *Computation; Criterion Referenced Tests; *Diagnostic Tests; *Elementary School Students; *Intermediate Grades; *Low Achievement; *Mathematical Applications; *Mathematics Tests; Norm Referenced Tests; *Number Concepts
Identifiers: CDMT
Availability: CTB/Macmillan/McGraw-Hill; Del Monte Research Park, 2500 Garden Rd., Monterey, CA 93940
Grade Level: 4-6
Notes: Items, 125

Used to provide teachers with diagnostic information needed to plan remedial instruction for individual students or groups of students. Content and difficulty of various levels were developed with the special needs of lower-achieving students in mind. In addition to objectives-based diagnostic information, test also provides norm-referenced information for evaluating individual and group progress and for fulfilling state and federal requirements for compensatory education and other specially funded programs. Assesses student performance in 3 areas: number concepts, computation, and mathematics applications. Level D measures the skills that students acquire as they progress through grades 4, 5, and 6. CDMT is not a timed test.

15923
California Diagnostic Mathematics Tests, Level E.
CTB/Macmillan/McGraw-Hill, Monterey, CA 1989
Subtests: Number Concepts; Computation; Applications
Descriptors: *Computation; Criterion Referenced Tests; *Diagnostic Tests; *Grade 6; Intermediate Grades; Junior High Schools; *Junior High School Students; *Low Achievement; *Mathematical Applications; *Mathematics Tests; Norm Referenced Tests; *Number Concepts
Identifiers: CDMT
Availability: CTB/Macmillan/McGraw-Hill; Del Monte Research Park, 2500 Garden Rd., Monterey, CA 93940
Grade Level: 6-8
Notes: Items, 127

Used to provide teachers with diagnostic information needed to plan remedial instruction for individual students or groups of students. Content and difficulty of various levels were developed with the special needs of lower-achieving students in mind. In addition to objectives-based diagnostic information, test also provides norm-referenced information for evaluating individual and group progress and for fulfilling state and federal requirements for compensatory education and other specially funded programs. Assesses student performance in 3 areas: number concepts, computation, and mathematics applications. CDMT is not a timed test.

15924
California Diagnostic Mathematics Tests, Level F.
CTB/Macmillan/McGraw-Hill, Monterey, CA 1989
Subtests: Number Concepts; Computation; Mathematics Applications; Life Skills
Descriptors: *Computation; Criterion Referenced Tests; *Diagnostic Tests; *Low Achievement; *Mathematical Applications; *Mathematics Tests; Norm Referenced Tests; *Number Concepts; Secondary Education; *Secondary School Students; *Word Problems (Mathematics)
Identifiers: CDMT
Availability: CTB/Macmillan/McGraw-Hill; Del Monte Research Park, 2500 Garden Rd., Monterey, CA 93940
Grade Level: 8-12
Notes: Items, 157

Used to provide teachers with diagnostic information needed to plan remedial instruction for individual students or groups of students. Content and difficulty of various levels were developed with the special needs of lower-achieving students in mind. In addition to objectives-based diagnostic information, test also provides norm-referenced information for evaluating individual and group progress and for fulfilling state and federal requirements for compensatory education and other specially funded programs. Assesses student performance in 3 areas: number concepts, computation, and mathematics applications. CDMT is not a timed test.

15931
MAA Placement Test Program, Advanced Algebra Test, AA. Mathematical Association of America, Washington, DC 1982
Descriptors: *Algebra; *College Freshmen; *College Mathematics; Higher Education; Mathematics; *Mathematics Tests; *Student Placement
Identifiers: MAA; PTP
Availability: Mathematical Association of America; 1529 Eighteenth St., NW, Washington, DC 20077-6240
Grade Level: 13
Notes: Time, 30 min.; Items, 25

Placement test for entering college students into entry-level mathematics courses. Consists of 25 questions from intermediate and college algebra. Two parallel forms are available. Placement Test Program was established to assist 2- and 4-year colleges and universities with the development of on-campus placement programs to assess the mathematical skills of new students objectively.

15932
MAA Placement Test Program, Basic and Advanced Algebra Test, A. Mathematical Association of America, Washington, DC 1982
Descriptors: *Algebra; *College Freshmen; *College Mathematics; Higher Education; Mathematics; *Mathematics Tests; *Student Placement
Identifiers: MAA; PTP
Availability: Mathematical Association of America; 1529 Eighteenth St., NW, Washington, DC 20077-6240
Grade Level: 13
Notes: Time, 45 min.; Items, 32

Placement test for entering college students into entry-level mathematics courses. Consists of 32 questions from elementary, intermediate, and college algebra. Two parallel

forms are available. Placement Test Program was established to assist 2- and 4-year colleges and universities with the development of on-campus placement programs to assess the mathematical skills of new students objectively.

15933
MAA Placement Test Program, Basic Algebra Test, BA. Mathematical Association of America, Washington, DC 1982
Descriptors: *Algebra; *College Freshmen; *College Mathematics; Higher Education; Mathematics; *Mathematics Tests; *Student Placement
Identifiers: MAA; PTP
Availability: Mathematical Association of America; 1529 Eighteenth St., NW, Washington, DC 20077-6240
Grade Level: 13
Notes: Time, 30 min.; Items, 25

Placement test for entering college students into entry-level mathematics courses. Consists of 25 questions from elementary and intermediate algebra. Two parallel forms are available. Placement Test Program was established to assist 2- and 4-year colleges and universities with the development of on-campus placement programs to assess the mathematical skills of new students objectively.

15934
MAA Placement Test Program Basic Skills Test, A-SK. Mathematical Association of America, Washington, DC 1982
Descriptors: *Arithmetic; *College Freshmen; College Mathematics; Higher Education; *Mathematics; *Mathematics Skills; *Mathematics Tests; *Student Placement
Identifiers: MAA; PTP
Availability: Mathematical Association of America; 1529 Eighteenth St., NW, Washington, DC 20077-6240
Grade Level: 13
Notes: Time, 40 min.; Items, 32

Placement test for entering college students into entry-level mathematics courses. There are 2 versions of the Basic Skills Test, SK (25 questions) and A-SK (32 questions). Questions 8-32 in A-SK are parallel to questions 1-25 in SK. Part I contains 20 questions on arithmetic. Part II contains 12 questions on prealgebra, word problems, graphs and figures. Placement Test Program was established to assist 2- and 4-year colleges and universities with the development of on-campus placement programs to assess the mathematical skills of new students objectively.

15936
MAA Placement Test Program, Calculus Readiness Test, CR. Mathematical Association of America, Washington, DC 1982
Descriptors: *Calculus; *College Freshmen; College Mathematics; Higher Education; *Mathematics; *Mathematics Tests; *Student Placement
Identifiers: MAA; PTP
Availability: Mathematical Association of America; 1529 Eighteenth St., NW, Washington, DC 20077-6240
Grade Level: 13
Notes: Time, 30 min. approx.; Items, 25

Placement test for entering college students into entry-level mathematics courses. Designed to show a student's potential for handling calculus, either business calculus or the engineering-physical science type of calculus. Does not cover the content of a typical precalculus course. Concentrates on material related to the content of calculus. Two parallel forms of the test are available. Placement Test Program was established to assist 2- and 4-year colleges and universities with the development of on-campus placement programs to assess the mathematical skills of new students objectively.

15937
MAA Placement Test Program, High School—Elementary, HS-E. Mathematical Association of America, Washington, DC 1983
Descriptors: *Algebra; *College Bound Students; *High School Students; *Mathematics; *Mathematics Tests; *Prognostic Tests; Secondary Education; *Secondary School Mathematics
Identifiers: HS(E); MAA; PTP
Availability: Mathematical Association of America; 1529 Eighteenth St., NW, Washington, DC 20077-6240
Grade Level: 11
Notes: Time, 45 min.; Items, 32

Placement test for entering college students into entry-level mathematics courses. Prognostic mathematics test. Designed to test high school juniors and give projected placement in college mathematics. Purpose is to make students aware of any weaknesses in their mathematical skills while there is still time to take corrective action before entering college. Test is constructed around the Basic Algebra Test, BA, by adding 7 items in arithmetic and basic skills. The additional items in High School-

Intermediate (HS-I) are more difficult than those in High School-Elementary (HS-E). HS-E is more appropriate for the less advanced students.

15938
MAA Placement Test Program, High School—Intermediate, HS-I.   Mathematical Association of America, Washington, DC 1983
Descriptors: *Algebra; *College Bound Students; *High School Students; *Mathematics; *Mathematics Tests; *Prognostic Tests; Secondary Education; *Secondary School Mathematics
Identifiers: HS(I); MAA; PTP
Availability: Mathematical Association of America; 1529 Eighteenth St., NW, Washington, DC 20077-6240
Grade Level: 11
Notes: Time, 45 min.; Items, 32

Prognostic mathematics test. Designed to test high school juniors and give projected placement in college mathematics. Purpose is to make students aware of any weaknesses in their mathematical skills while there is still time to take corrective action before entering college. Test is constructed around the Basic Algebra Test, BA, by adding 7 items in arithmetic and basic skills. The additional items in High School-Intermediate (HS-I) are more difficult than those in High School-Elementary (HS-E). HS-I should be given to students who have completed or are taking Algebra II.

15939
MAA Placement Test Program, Trigonometry/Elementary Functions Test T.   Mathematical Association of America, Washington, DC 1982
Descriptors: *College Freshmen; College Mathematics; *Functions (Mathematics); Higher Education; *Mathematics; *Mathematics Tests; *Student Placement; *Trigonometry
Identifiers: MAA; PTP
Availability: Mathematical Association of America; 1529 Eighteenth St., NW, Washington, DC 20077-6240
Grade Level: 13
Notes: Time, 45 min.; Items, 30

Placement test for entering college students into entry-level mathematics courses. Covers basic skills from trigonometry and elementary functions. Test consists of 2 parts. Part I contains 15 questions from plane trigonometry. Part II contains 15 questions on elementary functions and analytic geometry. Each part may be administered separately. There are 2 parallel forms of the test available. Placement Test Program was established to assist 2- and 4-year colleges and universities with the development of on-campus placement programs to assess the mathematical skills of new students objectively.

15940
Tests of Achievement and Proficiency, Level 15, Writing Supplement.   Haugh, Oscar M.; Scannell, Dale P. 1987
Subtests: Narration; Explanation; Analysis; Argumentation
Descriptors: *Achievement Tests; *Essay Tests; *High School Students; *Holistic Evaluation; Secondary Education; Writing (Composition); *Writing Evaluation; Writing Skills
Identifiers: TAP
Availability: Riverside Publishing Co.; 8420 Bryn Mawr Ave., Chicago, IL 60631
Grade Level: 9
Notes: Time, 40 min.

Assesses students' ability to develop, organize, and express their ideas in a variety of written modes. Each level evaluates a particular mode. The 4 modes in ascending order of difficulty are narration, explanation, analysis, and argumentation. Level 15 is intended for use in grade 9. Measured by the focused holistic scoring method. May be used in conjunction with the Tests of Achievement and Proficiency Written Expression Test.

15941
Tests of Achievement and Proficiency, Level 16, Writing Supplement.   Haugh, Oscar M.; Scannell, Dale P. 1987
Subtests: Narration; Explanation; Analysis; Argumentation
Descriptors: *Achievement Tests; *Essay Tests; *High School Students; *Holistic Evaluation; Secondary Education; Writing (Composition); *Writing Evaluation; Writing Skills
Identifiers: TAP
Availability: Riverside Publishing Co.; 8420 Bryn Mawr Ave., Chicago, IL 60631
Grade Level: 10
Notes: Time, 40 min.

Assesses students' ability to develop, organize, and express their ideas in a variety of written modes. Each level evaluates a particular mode. The 4 modes in ascending order of difficulty are narration, explanation, analysis, and argumentation. Level 16 is intended for use in grade 10.

Measured by the focused holistic scoring method. May be used in conjunction with the Tests of Achievement and Proficiency Written Expression Test.

15942
Tests of Achievement and Proficiency, Level 17, Writing Supplement.   Haugh, Oscar M.; Scannell, Dale P. 1987
Subtests: Narration; Explanation; Analysis; Argumentation
Descriptors: *Achievement Tests; *Essay Tests; *High School Students; *Holistic Evaluation; Secondary Education; Writing (Composition); *Writing Evaluation; Writing Skills
Identifiers: TAP
Availability: Riverside Publishing Co.; 8420 Bryn Mawr Ave., Chicago, IL 60631
Grade Level: 11
Notes: Time, 40 min.

Assesses students' ability to develop, organize, and express their ideas in a variety of written modes. Each level evaluates a particular mode. The 4 modes in ascending order of difficulty are narration, explanation, analysis, and argumentation. Level 17 is intended for use in grade 11. Measured by the focused holistic scoring method. May be used in conjunction with the Tests of Achievement and Proficiency Written Expression Test.

15943
Tests of Achievement and Proficiency, Level 18, Writing Supplement.   Haugh, Oscar M.; Scannell, Dale P. 1987
Subtests: Narration; Explanation; Analysis; Argumentation
Descriptors: *Achievement Tests; *Essay Tests; *High School Students; *Holistic Evaluation; Secondary Education; Writing (Composition); *Writing Evaluation; Writing Skills
Identifiers: TAP
Availability: Riverside Publishing Co.; 8420 Bryn Mawr Ave., Chicago, IL 60631
Grade Level: 12
Notes: Time, 40 min.

Assesses students' ability to develop, organize, and express their ideas in a variety of written modes. Each level evaluates a particular mode. The 4 modes in ascending order of difficulty are narration, explanation, analysis, and argumentation. Level 18 is intended for use in grade 12. Measured by the focused holistic scoring method. May be used in conjunction with the Tests of Achievement and Proficiency Written Expression Test.

15989
English as a Second Language Oral Assessment, Revised.   Coy, Joy Jenkins; And Others 1980
Descriptors: Adults; *Diagnostic Tests; *English (Second Language); Expressive Language; Language Proficiency; Listening Comprehension; Oral Language; Receptive Language; Second Language Learning; Student Placement; Visual Measures
Identifiers: ESLOA
Availability: Literacy Volunteers of America; 5795 Widewaters Pwy., Syracuse, NY 13214
Age Level: Adults

Diagnostic instrument designed for use with adult students who are speakers of languages other than English. May be used by tutors to determine students' entry level, progress level, ability to follow directions, ability to follow English patterns, and ability to use specific basic vocabulary. Assesses students' auditory comprehension and oral levels of English proficiency. Divided into 4 levels of proficiency. Students must answer a required number of items correctly before they may progress to the next level. Tutor records students' responses on an answer sheet and follows scoring instructions to tally the number of correct responses. Makes use of drawings of objects to which students may either point or respond verbally to indicate that they know the English word for that object.

16005
Religious Education Outcomes Inventory of Knowledge, Attitudes and Practices.   National Catholic Educational Association, Washington, DC 1978
Descriptors: Adults; *Attitude Measures; *Catholics; *College Students; *Knowledge Level; Outcomes of Education; Postsecondary Education; Questionnaires; *Religious Education; Secondary Education; *Secondary School Students; *Surveys
Identifiers: REKAP
Availability: National Forum of Religious Educators; NCEA, 1077 30th St. N.W., Ste. 100, Washington, DC 20007
Age Level: 14-65
Notes: Items, 110

A survey of the religious knowledge, attitudes, and practices of Catholic senior high school students and of adults. This inventory includes 3 components: a 60-item religious knowledge survey, a 30-item religious belief and attitude survey, and a 20-item religious practices survey. Can be used to evaluate programs in Catholic high schools, col-

leges, and parish adult groups; to identify needs for program planning or individual study; and to provide group data and confidential feedback to teachers and members of parish adult education groups. Item-by-item, individual score, and group average score reports available.

16015
Literature Tests.   Perfection Form Co., Logan, IA 1988
Descriptors: *Achievement Tests; Essay Tests; *High School Students; *Junior High School Students; *Literature; Objective Tests; Reading Comprehension; Reading Tests; Secondary Education
Availability: Perfection Form Co.; 1000 N. Second Ave., Logan, IA 51546
Grade Level: 6-12

Reproducible literature tests for 263 titles. Essay and objective test formats. There is an essay test for every title. Each essay test includes 6 to 10 questions to develop critical thinking skills. The essay questions are written on 2 levels of comprehension. Half of the questions are on the literal level and half are on the interpretive level. Each title has either a 50- or 100-objective question test. Some have both. Measures students' literal comprehension. Questions are true-false, multiple choice, and matching. Covers plot, setting, and characters.

16038
College Board Achievement Tests: Modern Hebrew.   College Board, New York, NY 1989
Descriptors: *Achievement Tests; *College Entrance Examinations; *Hebrew; High Schools; *High School Students; Modern Languages; Reading Comprehension; Sentence Structure; Student Placement; Vocabulary
Availability: Admissions Testing Program; Educational Testing Service, Princeton, NJ 08541
Grade Level: 11-12
Notes: Time, 60 min.; Items, 85

This test is designed to measure proficiency in the Hebrew language as it is spoken today. It is expected that the test taker will have participated in from 2 to 4 years of study of the language. It replaces the existing measure of classical and Biblical Hebrew. The multiple-choice questions cover vocabulary, sentence structure, reading comprehension. The test is offered at testing centers nationwide. For this test only, one Sunday administration will be held each year in June. The College Board Achievement test scores are used by colleges as part of their admissions procedures and to place students within programs of instruction.

16041
Test of Conferencing Ability.   DeGroff, Linda-Jo Caple 1987
Descriptors: Conferences; *Discussion; Elementary Education; *Elementary School Students; Listening; Objective Tests; *Peer Evaluation; *Writing (Composition)
Availability: Elementary School Journal; v88 n2 p105-18, Nov 1987
Grade Level: 3-8
Notes: Items, 20

Designed to reflect elementary school students' understanding of proper conferencing behavior during discussions of classmates' essays. When examiners are interested in how the results of these conferences affect students' writing, this instrument may be used to weed out of the sample those students who are not familiar with proper conferencing behavior.

16064
Surveys of Problem Solving and Educational Skills: Survey of Educational Skills.   Meltzer, Lynn J. 1987
Subtests: Reading: Sight Vocabulary; Decoding Isolated Words; Decoding Text; Comprehension, Free Recall/Reformulation; Comprehension, Structured Questions; Writing: Automatized Alphabet Production; Motor Planning; Spatial Organization; Symbol Production; Language Usage; Overall Productivity; Spelling: Recognition; Retrieval; In-Context Spelling; Mathematics: Automatized Operations; Computation; Concepts; Application; Efficiency of Approaching Tasks; Flexibility in Applying Strategies; Style of Approaching Tasks; Attention; Responsiveness during Assessment
Descriptors: *Academic Ability; Adolescents; *Basic Skills; Children; *Cognitive Style; *Criterion Referenced Tests; *Diagnostic Tests; Elementary Secondary Education; Intermediate Grades; *Learning Processes; Mathematics; *Outcomes of Education; *Problem Solving; Rating Scales; Reading; Spelling; Writing (Composition); Writing Skills
Identifiers: SEDS; SPES
Availability: Educators Publishing Service; 75 Moulton St., Cambridge, MA 02138-9101
Age Level: 9-15
Notes: Time, 45 min. approx.; Items, 112

This test, with its companion instrument the Survey of Problem-Solving Skills, evaluates the connection between problem-solving strategies, learning processes, and educational outcomes. The SEDS is designed to identify processes and strategies used to perform reading, writing, spelling, and mathematical tasks. The test administrator records results and rates student performance during the examination. A summary profile provides a synopsis of findings. Included are measures of reading comprehension, vocabulary, decoding; writing in terms of organization, alphabet production, language usage, overall productivity; spelling recognition and retrieval; mathematics operations, computation, concepts, application. These are criterion-referenced measures.

16066
Descriptive Tests of Language Skills, Revised.
College Board, New York, NY 1988
Subtests: Reading Comprehension; Critical Reasoning; Conventions of Written English; Sentence Structure
Descriptors: Achievement Tests; *College Freshmen; College Students; Critical Thinking; Diagnostic Tests; *Grammar; Higher Education; *Language Skills; Microcomputers; Pretests Posttests; *Reading Comprehension; Remedial Instruction; Scoring; *Screening Tests; *Sentence Structure; *Student Placement; Two Year Colleges; *Two Year College Students
Identifiers: DTLS; Reasoning
Availability: Multiple Assessment Programs and Services; Educational Testing Service, P.O. Box 6725, Princeton, NJ 08541-6725
Grade Level: 13
Notes: Time, 120 min.; Items, 130
The DTLS is designed for use by 2- and 4-year colleges for both large scale and individual screening of entry-level students in basic academic competencies. Provides information for decisions regarding student placement and remediation, determination of effects of instructional programs, identification of students needing further testing, counseling for course selection. Support materials include instructor's guide with follow-up activities for remediation. Parallel forms for posttesting to assess mastery and outcomes are available. Self-scoring answer sheets are available. Microcomputer scoring will be available in spring 1989.

16067
Descriptive Tests of Mathematics Skills, Revised.
College Board, New York, NY 1988
Subtests: Arithmetic Skills; Elementary Algebra Skills; Intermediate Algebra Skills; Functions and Graphs (Calculus Readiness)
Descriptors: Achievement Tests; *Algebra; *Arithmetic; Calculus; *College Freshmen; College Students; Diagnostic Tests; *Functions (Mathematics); Higher Education; *Mathematics; Microcomputers; Pretests Posttests; Readiness; Remedial Instruction; Scoring; *Screening Tests; *Student Placement; Two Year Colleges; *Two Year College Students
Identifiers: DTMS; Self-scoring
Availability: Multiple Assessment Programs and Services; Educational Testing Service, P.O. Box 6725, Princeton, NJ 08541-6725
Grade Level: 13
Notes: Time, 120 min.; Items, 130
The DTMS is designed for use by 2- and 4-year colleges for both large scale and individual screening of entry-level students in basic academic competencies. Provides information for decisions regarding student placement and remediation, determination of effects of instructional programs, identification of students needing further testing, counseling for course selection. Support materials include instructor's guide with follow-up activities for remediation. Parallel forms for posttesting to assess mastery and outcomes are available. Self-scoring answer sheets are available. Microcomputer scoring will be available in spring 1989.

16085
Diagnostic Tests for Computer Literacy. Pyrczak, Fred 1988
Subtests: General Procedures; How Computers Work; Computer Applications; Knowledge of Programming Languages; Computer History; Computers and Society; Computer Vocabulary
Descriptors: Achievement Tests; *College Students; *Computer Literacy; Computers; *Diagnostic Tests; *Elementary School Students; Elementary Secondary Education; Higher Education; Microcomputers; Programing Languages; *Secondary School Students
Identifiers: TIM(O)
Availability: Tests in Microfiche; Test Collection, Educational Testing Service, Princeton, NJ 08541
Grade Level: 5-16
Notes: Items, 10

This series of diagnostic tests was designed to pinpoint the strengths and weaknesses of students in minimal computer literacy skills. Administered via paper and pencil or disk (Apple) available from the author at California State University, School of Education in Los Angeles. Sixteen tests consist of 10 questions each. Items were based on curriculum guides acquired from schools with computer education courses.

16086
Prereading Assessment for Perceptual Reading Readiness. Faber, Nathan 1980
Descriptors: *Auditory Perception; Diagnostic Teaching; *Grade 1; *High Risk Students; Memory; *Perceptual Motor Learning; *Prereading Experience; Primary Education; *Reading Readiness; *Reading Readiness Tests; Sequential Approach; *Visual Perception; Young Children
Identifiers: Dade County (Florida); Early Childhood Preventive Curriculum
Availability: Early Childhood Preventive Curriculum; 9240 S.W. 124 St., Miami, FL 33176
Grade Level: 1
Primarily intended for high-risk first grade students, prereading assessment is made up of a test series based on a set of priority objectives. These are perceptual readiness objectives, related to ability to respond to instruction in decoding skills. It is designed to give information on student levels of perceptual reading readiness. The domain map of prereading perceptual skills summarizes the organization and sequence of perceptual objectives assessed. The assessment battery is organized into 3 booklets representing 3 achievement levels in increasing order of difficulty. Each 4-page booklet contains items in the following perceptual areas: (1) visual perception skills; (2) auditory perception skills; (3) visual-auditory sequencing and memory; and (4) perceptual motor. An entire class may be tested at one time. High-risk children have a normal capacity to learn but start first grade without prereading perceptual skills and have poor concept and/or oral-language development.

16087
Hudson Education Skills Inventory—Reading.
Hudson, Floyd G.; And Others 1989
Subtests: Readiness; Vocabulary; Phonic Analysis; Structural Analysis; Comprehension
Descriptors: *Achievement Tests; *Criterion Referenced Tests; *Elementary School Students; Elementary Secondary Education; *Learning Problems; *Reading Achievement; *Secondary School Students
Identifiers: HESI(R)
Availability: PRO-ED; 8700 Shoal Creek Blvd., Austin, TX 78758-6897
Grade Level: K-12
Designed for use with students in grades K-12 who have dysfunctional learning patterns. Used to assess students' present level of performance in basic educational skills from a representative curriculum. Is a curriculum-based assessment tool using criterion-referenced principles and was developed to assist teachers, diagnosticians, and other educational specialists in assessing the academic performance of the targeted group. Assesses students' performance in specific curriculum skills, subskills, and objectives that are commonly taught in a continuous-progress K-6 curriculum. The K-6 structure is appropriate for assessing basic skill level of dysfunctional students in elementary, junior high, and high school grades. Provides the kinds of information needed to develop an individualized education program (IEP).

16089
Hudson Education Skills Inventory—Mathematics.
Hudson, Floyd G.; Colson, Steven E. 1989
Subtests: Numeration; Addition of Whole Numbers; Subtraction of Whole Numbers; Multiplication of Whole Numbers; Division of Whole Numbers; Fractions; Decimals; Percentages; Time; Money; Measurement; Statistics, Graphs, and Tables; Geometry; Word Problems
Descriptors: *Achievement Tests; *Criterion Referenced Tests; *Elementary School Mathematics; *Elementary School Students; Elementary Secondary Education; *Learning Problems; *Secondary School Students
Identifiers: HESI(M)
Availability: PRO-ED; 8700 Shoal Creek Blvd., Austin, TX 78758-6897
Grade Level: K-12
Designed for use with students in grades K-12 who have dysfunctional learning patterns. Used to assess students' present level of performance in basic educational skills from a representative curriculum. Is a curriculum-based assessment tool using criterion-referenced principles and was developed to assist teachers, diagnosticians, and other educational specialists in assessing the academic performance of the targeted group. Assesses performance in specific curriculum skills, subskills, and objectives that are commonly taught in a continuous-progress K-6 curriculum. The K-6 structure is appropriate for assessing basic skill level of dysfunctional students in elementary, junior

high, and senior high school grades. Provides the kinds of information needed for proper individualized education program (IEP) development.

16090
Ann Arbor Learning Inventory, Revised 1986. Skill Level B. Bullock, Waneta B.; Vitale, Barbara Meister 1986
Subtests: Visual Discrimination Skills; Visual Motor Coordination Skills; Sequential Memory Skills; Auditory Discrimination Skills; Comprehension Skills
Descriptors: Auditory Discrimination; Auditory Perception; Comprehension; *Diagnostic Tests; *Elementary Education; *Elementary School Students; *Learning Modalities; *Learning Problems; Listening Comprehension; Memory; Primary Education; *Psychomotor Skills; Remedial Programs; Visual Discrimination
Availability: Ann Arbor Publishers; P.O. Box 7249, Naples, FL 33941
Grade Level: 2-4
This test series is designed for use with various learner groups: early, regular, special. It is designed to determine why students may not be meeting basic achievement levels for their grade so that remediation can begin. Identifies strengths and weaknesses in central processing areas. Identifies specific visual and auditory perceptual problems such as difficulty with rotations, closure, omissions, directionality, and sequencing. Identifies strongest learning modality so teacher can present data in a manner that can be processed by the child for individual education plans. Remediation materials are available.

16097
Test Questions for Physical Education Activities.
McGee, Rosemary; Farrow, Andrea 1987
Subtests: Badminton; Basketball; Bowling; Field Hockey; Golf; Gymnastics; Racquetball; Recreational Dance; Soccer; Softball; Swimming and Diving; Tennis; Track and Field; Volleyball; Weight Training
Descriptors: *Achievement Tests; *Athletics; Badminton; Basketball; Bowling; College Students; Dance; Diving; Field Hockey; Golf; Gymnastics; Higher Education; High Schools; *High School Students; *Item Banks; Knowledge Level; Racquetball; Soccer; Softball; Swimming; Tennis; Track and Field; Volleyball; Weightlifting
Availability: Human Kinetics; Box 5076, Champaign, IL 61820
Grade Level: 9-16
This volume was designed to assist teachers in the creation of knowledge tests for physical education activity classes. Serves as an item bank by presenting 250 to 400 questions for each of the 15 activities. Can be used to construct short quizzes, to measure competencies for testing programs. All questions use a 4-choice multiple-choice format. Content validity is discussed. Directions are given for computing test reliability and performing an item analysis.

16099
Learning Inventory of Kindergarten Experiences.
Owings, Nathaniel O.; And Others 1988
Descriptors: Academic Ability; Cognitive Ability; *Early Childhood Education; *Kindergarten Children; Language Skills; Psychomotor Skills; *School Readiness Tests; *Screening Tests
Identifiers: Fine Motor Skills; Gross Motor Skills; LIKE
Availability: University of Washington Press; P.O. Box C-50096, Seattle, WA 98145-5096
Age Level: 5
This kindergarten screening procedure is designed to detect children who are not developmentally old enough for admission. Identifies preoperational and academic skills necessary for school success. Also identifies handicapping conditions in children of age 4 or 5 in speech, language and cognitive areas based on observations during the screening and test item analysis. May be used prior to preparation of individualized education programs (IEPs). Percentile norms were collected locally (Bozeman, MT) in small, middle class, urban and rural settings. Item selection is based on national norms. May be administered by classroom teachers.

16100
Spanish Computer Adaptive Placement Exam.
Brigham Young University, Provo, UT 1986
Descriptors: *Adaptive Testing; *College Students; *Computer Assisted Testing; Computer Software; Higher Education; Multiple Choice Tests; *Second Language Programs; *Spanish; *Student Placement
Identifiers: CALT; Computer Assisted Language Testing; SCAPE
Availability: CALI, Inc.; 526 E. Quail Rd., Orem, UT 84057
Grade Level: 13-16
Notes: Time, 30 min.

This computer-assisted language test is designed to place incoming students, at the college level, into appropriate lower-division Spanish courses. Uses adaptive testing methodology in which students' responses generate the selection, by the computer software, of other test questions at an appropriate level of difficulty for the student taking the test. Uses multiple-choice item format.

16101
French Computer Adaptive Placement Exam.
Brigham Young University, Provo, UT 1988
Descriptors: *Adaptive Testing; *College Students; *Computer Assisted Testing; Computer Software; *French; Higher Education; Multiple Choice Tests; *Second Language Programs; *Student Placement
Identifiers: CALT; Computer Assisted Language Testing; FCAPE
Availability: CALI, Inc.; 526 E. Quail Rd., Orem, UT 84057
Grade Level: 13-16
Notes: Time, 30 min.

This computer-assisted language test is designed to place incoming students, at the college level, into appropriate lower-division French courses. Uses adaptive testing methodology in which students' responses generate the selection, by the computer software, of other test questions at an appropriate level of difficulty for the student taking the test. Uses multiple-choice item format.

16110
Assessing Semantic Skills through Everyday Themes. Barrett, Mark; And Others 1988
Subtests: Identifying Labels; Identifying Categories; Identifying Attributes; Identifying Functions; Identifying Definitions; Stating Labels; Stating Categories; Stating Attributes; Stating Functions; Stating Definitions
Descriptors: Children; *Diagnostic Tests; *Early Childhood Education; *Expressive Language; *Individual Testing; *Language Skills; Pictorial Stimuli; *Preschool Children; *Receptive Language; Test Norms
Identifiers: ASSET
Availability: Lingui Systems; 716 17th St., Moline, IL 61265
Grade Level: K-3
Age Level: 3-9
Notes: Items, 150

ASSET is a diagnostic measure of receptive and expressive language, designed to assess a young child's semantic abilities and vocabulary. It consists of a series of questions pertaining to 20 large realistic line-drawings of scenes common to a young child's environment, such as preschool, a playground, a gas station. Norms are included for students age 3 through 9 years, 11 months. Total expressive and receptive language scores are converted to age equivalents, standard scores, and percentiles. The examiner interprets test performance through specific tasks, overall receptive performance, overall expressive performance, and total test result.

16112
Pretest for Introductory Crops Students. Southern Illinois University, Carbondale, School of Agriculture 1986
Descriptors: *Agricultural Education; *Agronomy; Course Organization; Higher Education; *Knowledge Level; Objective Tests; *Pretests Posttests; *Undergraduate Students
Availability: Journal of Agronomic Education; v16 n1 p36-38, Spr 1987
Grade Level: 13-16
Notes: Items, 48

A test to be administered to introductory crops students in the agricultural departments of colleges or universities. Used to determine level of students' knowledge so that teaching methods may be adjusted accordingly. Also used to give students a preview of the course, stimulate student curiosity and interests, and motivate students. Consists of 3 sections: 25 term definitions, 17 true-false and multiple-choice questions, and 6 short answer questions.

16117
Hudson Education Skills Inventory—Writing.
Hudson, Floyd G.; And Others 1989
Subtests: Capitalization; Punctuation; Grammar; Vocabulary; Sentences; Paragraphs
Descriptors: *Achievement Tests; *Criterion Referenced Tests; *Elementary School Students; Elementary Secondary Education; *Learning Problems; *Secondary School Students; *Writing Skills
Identifiers: HESI(W)
Availability: PRO-ED; 8700 Shoal Creek Blvd., Austin, TX 78758-6897
Grade Level: K-12

Designed for use with students in grades K-12 who have dysfunctional learning patterns. Used to assess students' present level of performance in basic educational skills from a representative curriculum. Is a curriculum-based assessment tool using criterion-referenced principles and

was developed to assist teachers, diagnosticians, and other educational specialists in assessing the academic performance of the targeted group. Assesses performance in specific curriculum skills, subskills, and objectives that are commonly taught in a continuous-progress K-6 curriculum. The K-6 structure is appropriate for assessing basic skill level of dysfunctional students in elementary, junior high, and senior high school grades. Provides the kinds of information needed to develop an individualized education program (IEP).

16127
AAPT/NSTA High School Physics Exam. National Science Teachers Association, Washington, DC 1988
Descriptors: *Achievement Tests; Electricity; Heat; High Schools; *High School Students; Kinetic Molecular Theory; Mechanics (Physics); Optics; Physical Sciences; *Physics; *Science Tests
Identifiers: NSTA
Availability: National Science Teachers Association; 1742 Connecticut Ave., N.W., Washington, DC 20009
Grade Level: 9-12
Notes: Time, 90 min.; Items, 80

The National Science Teachers Association (NSTA) examinations are designed to assess content and process skills in the science disciplines. They offer the advantage of a nationally normed, nationally developed exam to evaluate schools' science programs and students' achievement. The purpose of this test is to help students and their teachers evaluate the students' understanding of basic physics concepts. This examination is divided into sections on mechanics; waves, optics, and sound; heat and kinetic theory; electricity and magnetism; and modern physics. Each section can be administered separately or in combination with any other section. Two forms of the examination are available.

16128
NABT/NSTA High School Biology Exam. National Science Teachers Association, Washington, DC 1987
Descriptors: *Achievement Tests; *Biology; Classification; Cytology; Ecology; Evolution; Genetics; High Schools; *High School Students; *Science Tests
Identifiers: NABT; NSTA
Availability: National Science Teachers Association; 1742 Connecticut Ave., N.W., Washington, DC 20009
Grade Level: 9-12
Notes: Time, 110 min.; Items, 80

The National Science Teachers Association (NSTA) examinations are designed to assess content and process skills in the science disciplines. They offer the advantage of a nationally normed, nationally developed exam to evaluate schools' science programs and students' achievement. The purpose of this test is to help students and their teachers evaluate the students' understanding of basic biological concepts. This examination consists of multiple-choice questions on genetics, ecology, taxonomy, cell structure, evolution, animal morphology and behavior, and other topics. Two forms of the examination are available.

16129
AGI/NSTA Earth Science Exam. National Science Teachers Association, Washington, DC
Descriptors: *Achievement Tests; Astronomy; *Earth Science; Geology; High Schools; *High School Students; Meteorology; Oceanography; *Science Tests
Identifiers: NSTA
Availability: National Science Teachers Association; 1742 Connecticut Ave., N.W., Washington, DC 20009
Grade Level: 9-12
Notes: Time, 110 min.; Items, 120

The National Science Teachers Association (NSTA) examinations are designed to assess content and process skills in the science disciplines. They offer the advantage of a nationally normed, nationally developed exam to evaluate schools' science programs and students' achievement. The purpose of this test is to help students and their teachers evaluate the students' understanding of basic earth science concepts. The exam consists of 2 parts. Part I contains 60 items reflecting the concepts that should be included in all earth science courses. Part II has 4 in-depth areas of 15 items each in geology, astronomy, oceanography, meteorology. There are also 2 forms of the examination.

16151
ACS-NSTA Cooperative Examination: High School Chemistry, Form 1983 or 1983-S. Examinations Institute-ACS, Tampa, FL 1983
Descriptors: *Achievement Tests; *Chemistry; High Schools; *High School Students; Multiple Choice Tests; Science Tests
Availability: Examinations Institute-ACS; Oklahoma State University, 107 Physical Sciences, Stillwater, OK 74078-0447

Grade Level: 9-12
Notes: Time, 80 min.; Items, 80

End-of-year multiple-choice achievement tests in high school chemistry. Designed for first-year high school chemistry student in a modern concepts course. Measures degree to which student has mastered significant concepts. "S" form indicates a scrambled version of test with identical items. Covers the following topics: laboratory techniques; descriptive chemistry; stoichiometric calculations; states of matter, including gas laws; thermochemistry; kinetics; equilibrium; acids and bases; electrochemistry; bonding; introductory organic; trends in the periodic system; atomic structure; environmental topics; and nuclear chemistry.

16152
ACS-NSTA Cooperative Examination: High School Chemistry, Form 1985 or 1985-S. Examinations Institute-ACS, Tampa, FL 1985
Descriptors: *Achievement Tests; *Chemistry; High Schools; *High School Students; Multiple Choice Tests; Science Tests
Identifiers: ACS
Availability: Examinations Institute-ACS; Oklahoma State University, 107 Physical Sciences, Stillwater, OK 74078-0447
Grade Level: 9-12
Notes: Time, 80 min.; Items, 80

End-of-year multiple-choice achievement tests in high school chemistry. Designed for first-year high school chemistry student in a modern concepts course. Measures degree to which student has mastered significant concepts. "S" form indicates a scrambled version of test with identical items. Covers the following topics: laboratory techniques; descriptive chemistry; stoichiometric calculations; states of matter, including gas laws; thermochemistry; kinetics; equilibrium; acids and bases; electrochemistry; bonding; introductory organic; trends in the periodic system; atomic structure; environmental topics; and nuclear chemistry.

16153
ACS-NSTA Cooperative Examination: High School Chemistry, Form 1987. Examinations Institute-ACS, Tampa, FL
Descriptors: *Achievement Tests; *Chemistry; High Schools; *High School Students; Multiple Choice Tests; Science Tests
Identifiers: ACS
Availability: Examinations Institute-ACS; Oklahoma State University, 107 Physical Sciences, Stillwater, OK 74078-0447
Grade Level: 9-12
Notes: Time, 80 min.; Items, 80

End-of-year multiple-choice achievement test in high school chemistry. Designed for first-year high school chemistry student in a modern concepts course. Measures degree to which student has mastered significant concepts. Covers the following topics: laboratory techniques; descriptive chemistry; stoichiometric calculations; states of matter, including gas laws; thermochemistry; kinetics; equilibrium; acids and bases; electrochemistry; bonding; introductory organic; trends in the periodic system; atomic structure; environmental topics; and nuclear chemistry.

16154
ACS-NSTA Cooperative Examination: High School Chemistry, Advanced Form 1984 ADV. Examinations Institute-ACS, Tampa, FL 1984
Descriptors: *Achievement Tests; *Chemistry; High Schools; *High School Students; *Honors Curriculum; Multiple Choice Tests; Science Tests
Availability: Examinations Institute-ACS; Oklahoma State University, 107 Physical Sciences, Stillwater, OK 74078-0447
Grade Level: 9-12
Notes: Time, 110 min.; Items, 60

End-of-year multiple-choice achievement tests constructed for advanced or honors courses in high school chemistry. Written on approximately first-year college level. General and quantitative questions. Covers the following topics: atomic structure, including nuclear, chemical bonding, molecular geometry, and carbon chemistry; thermodynamics; kinetics; solids, liquids gases and solutions; acid-base chemistry; electrochemistry; chemical periodicity; descriptive chemistry and stoichiometry, and laboratory procedures and techniques.

16155
ACS-NSTA Cooperative Examination: High School Chemistry, Advanced Form 1986 ADV. Examinations Institute-ACS, Tampa, FL 1986
Descriptors: *Achievement Tests; *Chemistry; High Schools; *High School Students; *Honors Curriculum; Multiple Choice Tests; Science Tests
Availability: Examinations Institute-ACS; Oklahoma State University, 107 Physical Sciences, Stillwater, OK 74078-0447
Grade Level: 9-12
Notes: Time, 110 min.; Items, 60

End-of-year multiple-choice achievement tests constructed for advanced or honors courses in high school chemistry. Written on approximately first-year college level. General and quantitative questions. Covers the following topics: atomic structure, including nuclear, chemical bonding, molecular geometry, and carbon chemistry; thermodynamics; kinetics; solids, liquids gases and solutions; acid-base chemistry; electrochemistry; chemical periodicity; descriptive chemistry and stoichiometry, and laboratory procedures and techniques.

16162
Write A Sentence Test. Smith, Helen C. 1987
Descriptors: *Achievement Tests; Capitalization (Alphabetic); *Elementary School Students; Elementary Secondary Education; English Instruction; Grammar; Punctuation; *Secondary School Students; *Sentences; Sentence Structure; Syntax; *Writing Evaluation; *Writing Skills
Identifiers: *Write a Sentence Test
Availability: ERIC Document Reproduction Service; 7420 Fullerton Rd., Ste. 110, Springfield, VA 22153-2852 (ED291758, 20 p.)
Age Level: 5-17

This test was developed for use in the evaluation of student writing abilities. It consists of an elementary form with 6 items and a secondary form with 6 items. The test provides scores for capitalization, punctuation, grammar, and syntax. Respondents are asked to write one sentence on the lines next to the picture on the left-hand side of the test, describing that picture. No grade levels for use of the test are indicated.

16168
Test of Legible Handwriting. Larsen, Stephen C.; Hammill, Donald D. 1989
Descriptors: *Achievement Tests; Cursive Writing; *Elementary School Students; Elementary Secondary Education; *Handwriting; *Holistic Evaluation; Manuscript Writing (Handlettering); *Secondary School Students
Identifiers: TOLH
Availability: PRO-ED; 8700 Shoal Creek Blvd., Austin, TX 78758-6897
Grade Level: 2-12

Developed to help determine the legibility of students' handwriting. Examiner elicits and examines from 1 to 5 handwriting samples. To evaluate, each sample is matched as closely as possible with 1 of 3 scoring guides which serve as different writing styles: cursive style with a slant to the right; cursive style with a slant to the left; manuscript or modified manuscript style. Evaluation can serve to identify students below their peers in handwriting, identify strengths and weaknesses of individual students, document progress as a result of intervention and conduct research studies.

16181
Key Math, Form A: A Diagnostic Inventory of Essential Mathematics. Connolly, Austin J. 1988
Subtests: Numeration; Rational Numbers; Geometry; Addition; Subtraction; Multiplication; Division; Mental Computation; Measurement; Time and Money; Estimation; Interpreting Data; Problem Solving
Descriptors: Arithmetic; Computation; Computer Software; Data Interpretation; *Diagnostic Tests; *Elementary School Students; Elementary Secondary Education; Estimation (Mathematics); Geometry; *Individual Testing; Junior High Schools; *Junior High School Students; Item Response Theory; *Mathematics; Measurement; Norms; Problem Solving; Scoring; Test Reliability; Test Validity; Time
Identifiers: Rasch Model
Availability: American Guidance Service; Publishers' Bldg., Circle Pines, MN 55014-1796
Grade Level: K-9
Notes: Time, 40 min.

This revision of the Key Math Diagnostic Arithmetic Test measures a student's knowledge of basic concepts, operations and applications. It is individually administered. Two parallel forms are available. Each subtest allows analysis of its 3 or 4 domains to determine strengths and weaknesses. Has spring and fall norms. Scores available are percentile ranks, stanines, normal curve equivalents, grade equivalents, and age equivalents. Software is available to complete scoring. Several of the previous edition's subtests were expanded and 3 new subtests were added on estimation, data interpretation, and problem solving. Extensive information on validity, reliability and other technical considerations is provided.

16182
Key Math, Form B: A Diagnostic Inventory of Essential Mathematics. Connolly, Austin J. 1988
Subtests: Numeration; Rational Numbers; Geometry; Addition; Subtraction; Multiplication; Division; Mental Computation; Measurement; Time and Money; Estimation; Interpreting Data; Problem Solving
Descriptors: Arithmetic; Computation; Computer Software; Data Interpretation; *Diagnostic Tests; *Elementary School Students; Elementary Secondary Education; Estimation (Mathematics); Geometry; *Individual Testing; Junior High Schools; *Junior High School Students; Item Response Theory; *Mathematics; Measurement; Norms; Problem Solving; Scoring; Test Reliability; Test Validity; Time
Identifiers: Rasch Model
Availability: American Guidance Service; Publishers' Bldg., Circle Pines, MN 55014-1796
Grade Level: K-9
Notes: Time, 40 min.

This revision of the Key Math Diagnostic Arithmetic Test measures a student's knowledge of basic concepts, operations and applications. It is individually administered. Two parallel forms are available. Each subtest allows analysis of its 3 or 4 domains to determine strengths and weaknesses. Has spring and fall norms. Scores available are percentile ranks, stanines, normal curve equivalents, grade equivalents, and age equivalents. Software is available to complete scoring. Several of the previous edition's subtests were expanded and 3 new subtests were added on estimation, data interpretation, and problem solving. Extensive information on validity, reliability and other technical considerations is provided.

16183
Western Michigan University English Usage Skills Test, Forms A and B. Carlson, Bernadine P. 1986
Subtests: Recognition of Grammatical Errors; Punctuation for Meaning; Sentence Structure; Spelling Recognition; Word Usage Discrimination; Reading Comprehension
Descriptors: Administrators; Clerical Occupations; College Students; *Diagnostic Tests; *Graduate Students; Grammar; Higher Education; *Language Skills; *Occupational Tests; Punctuation; *Reading Comprehension; Semantics; Sentence Structure; Spelling; *Student Placement; *Undergraduate Students; Writing Skills
Availability: Western Michigan University; English Dept., Kalamazoo, MI 49008
Grade Level: 13-17
Age Level: Adults
Notes: Time, 100 min.; Items, 195

Designed to measure students' knowledge of the writing essentials relevant to their communication needs and their evaluation of the writings of others in their field. Used as a diagnostic and placement exam. Four forms are available. Norms were assembled from 1972-79 and consist of percentiles. Used to test graduate students for candidacy, upper undergraduate level students enrolled in writing or journalism programs. Has been used in business to test managers, state employees, corporate leadership groups, secretarial groups, and health care personnel.

16184
Western Michigan University English Usage Skills Test, Forms A and B. Carlson, Bernadine P. 1988
Subtests: Grammar, Word Usage and Spelling; Sentence Structure and Punctuation; Reading for Meaning
Descriptors: Administrators; Clerical Occupations; College Students; *Diagnostic Tests; *Graduate Students; Grammar; Higher Education; *Language Skills; Occupational Tests; Punctuation; *Reading Comprehension; Semantics; Sentence Structure; Spelling; *Student Placement; *Undergraduate Students; Writing Skills
Availability: Western Michigan University; English Dept., Kalamazoo, MI 49008
Grade Level: 13-16
Notes: Time, 100 min.; Items, 195

This test was designed to measure students' knowledge of the writing essentials they will need to communicate with others and evaluate the writings of others in their field. It is used both as a diagnostic and a placement examination. Four forms are available. Norms were assembled from 1972 through 1979 and consist of percentiles. Has been used to test graduate students for candidacy and upper undergraduate level students enrolled in writing or journalism programs. Has been used in business to test managers, state employees, corporate leadership groups, secretarial groups, and health care personnel. Norms for these groups are not provided.

16213
Santa Clara County Basic Skills Test: Mathematics, Grade 8. Santa Clara County Office of Education, San Jose, CA 1981
Descriptors: *Achievement Tests; *Basic Skills; Elementary Education; *Elementary School Mathematics; *Elementary School Students; *Grade 8; *Item Banks; Junior High Schools; *Mathematics Achievement; *Mathematics Tests
Availability: Santa Clara County Office of Education; 100 Skyport Drive, San Jose, CA 95115
Grade Level: 8
Notes: Time, 50 min. approx.

Basic skills tests developed from the Santa Clara County Office of Education's item bank to meet state-mandated requirements for school districts to assess periodically student proficiency in reading comprehension, writing, and computation in grades 4-11.

16214
Santa Clara County Basic Skills Test: Reading, Grade 8. Santa Clara County Office of Education, San Jose, CA 1981
Descriptors: *Achievement Tests; *Basic Skills; Elementary Education; *Elementary School Students; *Grade 8; *Item Banks; Junior High Schools; *Reading Achievement; Reading Comprehension; *Reading Tests
Availability: Santa Clara County Office of Education; 100 Skyport Drive, San Jose, CA 95115
Grade Level: 8
Notes: Time, 50 min. approx.

Basic skills tests developed from the Santa Clara County Office of Education's item bank to meet state-mandated requirements for school districts to assess periodically student proficiency in reading comprehension, writing, and computation in grades 4-11.

16215
Santa Clara County Basic Skills Test: Writing, Grade 8. Santa Clara County Office of Education, San Jose, CA 1981
Descriptors: *Achievement Tests; *Basic Skills; Elementary Education; *Elementary School Students; *Grade 8; *Grammar; *Item Banks; Junior High Schools; *Writing (Composition)
Availability: Santa Clara County Office of Education; 100 Skyport Drive, San Jose, CA 95115
Grade Level: 8
Notes: Time, 50 min. approx.

Basic skills tests developed from the Santa Clara County Office of Education's item bank to meet state-mandated requirements for school districts to assess periodically student proficiency in reading comprehension, writing, and computation in grades 4-11.

16216
Santa Clara County Basic Skills Test: Mathematics, Grade 7. Santa Clara County Office of Education, San Jose, CA 1982
Descriptors: *Achievement Tests; *Basic Skills; Elementary Education; *Elementary School Mathematics; *Elementary School Students; *Grade 7; *Item Banks; Junior High Schools; *Mathematics Achievement; *Mathematics Tests
Availability: Santa Clara County Office of Education; 100 Skyport Drive, San Jose, CA 95115
Grade Level: 7
Notes: Time, 50 min. approx.

Basic skills tests developed from the Santa Clara County Office of Education's item bank to meet state-mandated requirements for school districts to assess periodically student proficiency in reading comprehension, writing, and computation in grades 4-11.

16217
Santa Clara County Basic Skills Test: Reading, Grade 7. Santa Clara County Office of Education, San Jose, CA 1982
Descriptors: *Achievement Tests; *Basic Skills; Elementary Education; *Elementary School Students; *Grade 7; *Item Banks; Junior High Schools; *Reading Achievement; Reading Comprehension; *Reading Tests
Availability: Santa Clara County Office of Education; 100 Skyport Drive, San Jose, CA 95115
Grade Level: 7
Notes: Time, 50 min. approx.

Basic skills tests developed from the Santa Clara County Office of Education's item bank to meet state-mandated requirements for school districts to assess periodically student proficiency in reading comprehension, writing, and computation in grades 4-11.

16218
Santa Clara County Basic Skills Test: Writing, Grade 7. Santa Clara County Office of Education, San Jose, CA 1982
Descriptors: *Achievement Tests; *Basic Skills; Elementary Education; *Elementary School Students; *Grade 7; *Grammar; *Item Banks; Junior High Schools; *Writing (Composition)
Availability: Santa Clara County Office of Education; 100 Skyport Drive, San Jose, CA 95115
Grade Level: 7
Notes: Time, 50 min. approx.

Basic skills tests developed from the Santa Clara County Office of Education's item bank to meet state-mandated requirements for school districts to assess periodically student proficiency in reading comprehension, writing, and computation in grades 4-11.

16219
Santa Clara County Basic Skills Test: Mathematics, Grade 4. Santa Clara County Office of Education, San Jose, CA 1981
Descriptors: *Achievement Tests; *Basic Skills; Elementary Education; *Elementary School Mathematics; *Elementary School Students; *Grade 4; Intermediate Grades; *Item Banks; *Mathematics Achievement; *Mathematics Tests
Availability: Santa Clara County Office of Education; 100 Skyport Drive, San Jose, CA 95115
Grade Level: 4
Notes: Time, 50 min. approx.
Basic skills tests developed from the Santa Clara County Office of Education's item bank to meet state-mandated requirements for school districts to assess periodically student proficiency in reading comprehension, writing, and computation in grades 4-11.

16220
Santa Clara County Basic Skills Test: Reading, Grade 4. Santa Clara County Office of Education, San Jose, CA 1981
Descriptors: *Achievement Tests; *Basic Skills; Elementary Education; *Elementary School Students; *Grade 4; Intermediate Grades; *Item Banks; *Reading Achievement; Reading Comprehension; *Reading Tests
Availability: Santa Clara County Office of Education; 100 Skyport Drive, San Jose, CA 95115
Grade Level: 4
Notes: Time, 50 min. approx.
Basic skills tests developed from the Santa Clara County Office of Education's item bank to meet state-mandated requirements for school districts to assess periodically student proficiency in reading comprehension, writing, and computation in grades 4-11.

16221
Santa Clara County Basic Skills Test: Writing, Grade 4. Santa Clara County Office of Education, San Jose, CA 1981
Descriptors: *Achievement Tests; *Basic Skills; Elementary Education; *Elementary School Students; *Grade 4; *Grammar; Intermediate Grades; *Item Banks; *Writing (Composition)
Availability: Santa Clara County Office of Education; 100 Skyport Drive, San Jose, CA 95115
Grade Level: 4
Notes: Time, 50 min. approx.
Basic skills tests developed from the Santa Clara County Office of Education's item bank to meet state-mandated requirements for school districts to assess periodically student proficiency in reading comprehension, writing, and computation in grades 4-11.

16222
Santa Clara County Basic Skills Test: Mathematics, Grade 5. Santa Clara County Office of Education, San Jose, CA 1981
Descriptors: *Achievement Tests; *Basic Skills; Elementary Education; *Elementary School Mathematics; *Elementary School Students; *Grade 5; Intermediate Grades; *Item Banks; *Mathematics Achievement; *Mathematics Tests
Availability: Santa Clara County Office of Education; 100 Skyport Drive, San Jose, CA 95115
Grade Level: 5
Notes: Time, 50 min. approx.
Basic skills tests developed from the Santa Clara County Office of Education's item bank to meet state-mandated requirements for school districts to assess periodically student proficiency in reading comprehension, writing, and computation in grades 4-11.

16223
Santa Clara County Basic Skills Test: Reading, Grade 5. Santa Clara County Office of Education, San Jose, CA 1981
Descriptors: *Achievement Tests; *Basic Skills; Elementary Education; *Elementary School Students; *Grade 5; Intermediate Grades; *Item Banks; *Reading Achievement; Reading Comprehension; *Reading Tests
Availability: Santa Clara County Office of Education; 100 Skyport Drive, San Jose, CA 95115
Grade Level: 5
Notes: Time, 50 min. approx.
Basic skills tests developed from the Santa Clara County Office of Education's item bank to meet state-mandated requirements for school districts to assess periodically student proficiency in reading comprehension, writing, and computation in grades 4-11.

16224
Santa Clara County Basic Skills Test: Writing, Grade 5. Santa Clara County Office of Education, San Jose, CA 1981
Descriptors: *Achievement Tests; *Basic Skills; Elementary Education; *Elementary School Students; *Grade 5; *Grammar; Intermediate Grades; *Item Banks; *Writing (Composition)
Availability: Santa Clara County Office of Education; 100 Skyport Drive, San Jose, CA 95115
Grade Level: 5
Notes: Time, 50 min. approx.
Basic skills tests developed from the Santa Clara County Office of Education's item bank to meet state-mandated requirements for school districts to assess periodically student proficiency in reading comprehension, writing, and computation in grades 4-11.

16225
Santa Clara County Basic Skills Test: Mathematics, Grade 12, Revised. Santa Clara County Office of Education, San Jose, CA 1982
Descriptors: *Achievement Tests; *Basic Skills; *Grade 12; High Schools; *High School Seniors; *Item Banks; *Mathematics Achievement; *Mathematics Tests; *Minimum Competency Testing; *Secondary School Mathematics
Availability: Santa Clara County Office of Education; 100 Skyport Drive, San Jose, CA 95115
Grade Level: 12
Notes: Time, 50 min. approx.
Basic skills tests developed from the Santa Clara County Office of Education's item bank to meet state-mandated requirements for school districts to assess periodically student proficiency in reading comprehension, writing, and computation in grades 4-11. The grade 12 test is designed as a minimum competency test for about-to-graduate high school seniors.

16226
Santa Clara County Basic Skills Test: Reading, Grade 12, Revised. Santa Clara County Office of Education, San Jose, CA 1982
Descriptors: *Achievement Tests; *Basic Skills; *Grade 12; High Schools; *High School Seniors; *Item Banks; *Minimum Competency Testing; *Reading Achievement; Reading Comprehension; *Reading Tests
Availability: Santa Clara County Office of Education; 100 Skyport Drive, San Jose, CA 95115
Grade Level: 12
Notes: Time, 50 min. approx.
Basic skills tests developed from the Santa Clara County Office of Education's item bank to meet state-mandated requirements for school districts to assess periodically student proficiency in reading comprehension, writing, and computation in grades 4-11. The grade 12 test is designed as a minimum competency test for about-to-graduate high school seniors.

16227
Santa Clara County Basic Skills Test: Writing, Grade 12. Santa Clara County Office of Education, San Jose, CA 1982
Descriptors: *Achievement Tests; *Basic Skills; *Grade 12; *Grammar; High Schools; *High School Seniors; *Item Banks; *Minimum Competency Testing; *Writing (Composition)
Availability: Santa Clara County Office of Education; 100 Skyport Drive, San Jose, CA 95115
Grade Level: 12
Notes: Time, 50 min. approx.
Basic skills tests developed from the Santa Clara County Office of Education's item bank to meet state-mandated requirements for school districts to assess periodically student proficiency in reading comprehension, writing, and computation in grades 4-11. The grade 12 test is designed as a minimum competency test for about-to-graduate high school seniors.

16244
Pre-IPT: English. Williams, Constance O.; And Others 1988
Descriptors: *English (Second Language); *Individual Testing; *Language Proficiency; *Language Tests; Oral Language; *Preschool Children
Identifiers: IDEA Oral Language Proficiency Test
Availability: Ballard and Tighe; 480 Atlas St., Brea, CA 92621
Age Level: 3-5
Developed to assess the level of English oral language proficiency of English-as-a-Second-Language preschool children. Assists in the classification of children as non-English speaking (NES), limited English speaking (LES), or fluent English speaking (FES). Children are tested individually. Four basic areas of English oral language proficiency are assessed: vocabulary, comprehension, syntax, and verbal expression. There are 5 levels (A-E) of difficulty tested. The child advances by levels until the test is completed or stops at a level as indicated by information provided in the score box found at the end of each level. The test has been normed and technical data are available.

16246
Test of Written Language—2. Hammill, Donald D.; Larsen, Stephen C. 1988
Subtests: Vocabulary; Spelling; Style; Logical Sentences; Sentence Combining; Thematic Maturity; Contextual Vocabulary; Syntactic Maturity; Contextual Spelling; Contextual Style
Descriptors: Content Analysis; Creative Writing; Descriptive Writing; *Diagnostic Tests; *Elementary School Students; Elementary Secondary Education; Handwriting; *Secondary School Students; Sentence Structure; Spelling; Vocabulary; *Writing (Composition); *Writing Evaluation; *Writing Skills
Identifiers: TOWL2
Availability: Pro-Ed; 8700 Shoal Creek Blvd., Austin, TX 78758
Grade Level: 2-12
Age Level: 7-17
This extensive revision still uses essay analysis and traditional test formats. New subtests have been substituted. It remains a norm-referenced measure of written language. Two parallel forms are available. In addition to the above scores, 2 composite scores are derived. A contrived writing score focuses on the spelling and word usage aspects of the sample whereas a spontaneous score measures the ability to write meaningfully. An overall written language score is also calculated. Functions of the test are identifying remediation needs of students, documenting student progress in writing programs, conducting research in writing. Proficiency in English language usage is required for the hand scoring process.

16247
Sucher-Allred Group Reading Placement Test. Sucher, Floyd; Allred, Ruel A. 1986
Descriptors: Ability Grouping; *Elementary School Students; Elementary Secondary Education; Group Testing; *Reading; Reading Ability; Reading Comprehension; *Reading Tests; *Secondary School Students; *Student Placement; Vocabulary
Identifiers: *Instructional Reading Level
Availability: McGraw Hill Book Co.; School Div., 1200 N.W. 63rd St., Oklahoma City, OK 73125
Grade Level: 2-12
Notes: Items, 130
This test is designed for screening students for placement in reading. It is group administered and provides an approximate instructional reading level. Both forms have 13 subtests that measure either reading comprehension or vocabulary, that require the student to choose an opposite word. The reading comprehension items cover main idea or title, facts, sequence, inference, and critical thinking.

16250
PSB-Reading Comprehension Examination. Psychological Services Bureau, St. Thomas, PA 1987
Descriptors: *Achievement Tests; Adults; *Allied Health Occupations Education; Critical Reading; Postsecondary Education; *Reading; *Reading Comprehension; *Reading Tests; Secondary Education; *Secondary School Students; *Two Year College Students
Availability: Psychological Services Bureau; P.O. Box 4, St. Thomas, PA 17252
Grade Level: 9-14
Age Level: Adults
Notes: Time, 30 min.
Designed to determine the student's comprehension of material read. Designed for use at secondary and postsecondary levels and with students entering health-related occupational and professional programs. Measures comprehension as "thinking" or "critical" reading. Measures ability to understand direct statements, interpret passages, see intent of authors, detect organization of ideas, and use knowledge obtained from reading passages.

16252
Fast Health Knowledge Test, 1986 Revision. Fast, Charles G. 1986
Subtests: Personal Health; Exercise, Relaxation, Sleep; Nutrition and Diet; Consumer Health; Contemporary Health Problems; Tobacco, Alcohol, Drugs, Narcotics; Safety and First Aid; Communicable and Noncommunicable Diseases; Mental Health; Sex and Family Life
Descriptors: *Achievement Tests; Alcohol Education; *College Students; Diseases; Drug Use; *Health; *Health Education; Higher Education; Knowledge Level; Mental Health; Nutrition; Physical Health; Pretests Posttests; Safety; Secondary Education; *Secondary School Students; Sexuality; Smoking
Availability: Charles G. Fast; Professor Emeritus, Dept. of Health Education, Northeast Missouri State, Rte. 1, Novingar, MO 63559
Grade Level: 9-16
Notes: Time, 50 min.; Items, 100

This test was designed to measure the student's knowledge and understanding of health factors for use in testing prior to instruction and as a posttest for basic health courses. Questions are multiple-choice and measure discrimination and judgment in health matters. Validity and reliability information is available from the publisher. The test is secure and sample copies are available of older versions only.

16253
Collegiate Assessment of Academic Proficiency; Science Reasoning. American College Testing Program, Iowa City, IA 1988
Subtests: Reading; Writing; Mathematics; Critical Thinking
Descriptors: *Achievement Tests; *College Sophomores; College Students; *Critical Thinking; Higher Education; Instructional Effectiveness; *Mathematics; *Outcomes of Education; *Postsecondary Education; Program Evaluation; *Reading; *Sciences; *Thinking Skills; *Writing (Composition)
Identifiers: CAAP
Availability: American College Testing Program; P.O. Box 168, Iowa City, IA 52240
Grade Level: 13-14
This college-level assessment program is designed to measure students' academic skills at the end of the sophomore year of undergraduate study. Can be used for analyzing institutional effectiveness, documenting and guiding student learning, program evaluation, individual student evaluation. For use by 2- and 4-year institutions. User institutions will be able to evaluate with all subtests or modules or use them separately.

16255
Independent School Entrance Examination: Middle Level. Educational Records Bureau, Wellesley, MA 1989
Subtests: Verbal Aptitude-Synonyms, Sentence Completion; Quantitative Aptitude-Concepts/Understanding, Application; Reading Comprehension-Science Passages, Social Studies Passages; Mathematics Achievement-Computation, Applications; Essay
Descriptors: Academic Ability; *Admission (School); *Aptitude Tests; Content Area Reading; Elementary Education; *Elementary School Students; Essays; Mathematics; *Private Schools; Reading; Sciences; Social Studies; Student Placement; Verbal Ability; Writing (Composition)
Identifiers: ISEE; Writing Sample
Availability: Educational Records Bureau; Bardwell Hall, 37 Cameron St., Wellesley, MA 02181-6599
Grade Level: 5-7
Notes: Time, 180 min.; Items, 210
The ISEE is a secure, standardized admissions test for use by schools who are members of the Educational Records Bureau (ERB) consortium. An upper-level test for grades 8-11 (TC016266) is available also. The ISEE is also used for student placement in course levels and identifying areas in which the student needs help. Provides a writing sample. Norms represent students currently enrolled in independent boarding or day schools. The test is administered at ERB sites nationwide, by consortia of schools, and by individual schools using the test to evaluate prospective students.

16257
P-ACT. American College Testing Program, Iowa City, IA 1987
Subtests: Writing Skills Test; Mathematics Test; Reading Test; Science Reasoning Test; Interest Inventory; Study Skills Assessment; Student Information Section
Descriptors: *Achievement Tests; Biographical Inventories; Career Planning; *College Bound Students; College Preparation; *Grade 10; High Schools; *High School Students; Mathematics; Reading; Sciences; Student Needs; Study Skills; Vocational Interests; Writing Skills
Identifiers: Reasoning; Science Reasoning
Availability: American College Testing Program; P.O. Box 168, Iowa City, IA 52240
Grade Level: 10
Notes: Time, 165 min.; Items, 145
This program was developed to measure student achievement in skills developed early in high school and to encourage academic planning and decision making early in high school. The writing skills test covers punctuation, grammar, and usage. The math test requires application of algebra and geometry to problem solving. The reading test measures comprehension. The science reasoning test requires students to reason, generalize, and critically examine scientific information. The interest inventory measures interest in 60 work-related activities involving data, people, or things. The student information section elicits basic demographic data and students' perceived need for assistance.

16258
Enhanced ACT Assessment. American College Testing Program, Iowa City, IA 1989
Subtests: English Test; Mathematics Test; Reading Test; Science Reasoning Test
Descriptors: Academic Ability; Achievement Tests; Algebra; *College Admission; *College Bound Students; *College Entrance Examinations; Geometry; High Schools; *High School Students; Language Skills; Literature; Mathematics; Reading; Sciences; Social Studies; Student Interests; Trigonometry
Identifiers: Reasoning; Science Reasoning
Availability: American College Testing Program; P.O. Box 168, Iowa City, IA 52240
Grade Level: 11-12
Notes: Time, 175 min.
This is a revision of the ACT Assessment, a testing program designed to help colleges and students make decisions about college admission. Changes in the content of the cognitive tests are said to reflect changes in high school curriculum. The following subscores will be reported: English Usage/Mechanics; *Rhetorical Skills; *Pre-Algebra/Elementary Algebra; *Intermediate Algebra/Coordinate Geometry; *Plane Geometry/Trigonometry; *Arts/Literature (Reading); Social Studies/Sciences (Reading); *Science Reasoning; Composite Score. Asterisked subscores are new. The program includes an educational/biographical and an interest inventory.

16259
Bilingual Two-Language Battery of Tests. Caso, Adolph 1983
Descriptors: Adolescents; Adults; *Bilingualism; Bilingual Students; Children; *Criterion Referenced Tests; *English; *English (Second Language); *French; *Italian; *Language Proficiency; *Language Tests; *Portuguese; *Spanish; *Vietnamese; Young Adults
Availability: Branden Press; 21 Station St., P.O. Box 843, Brookline Village, MA 02147
Age Level: 5-65
Notes: Time, 40 min. approx.
The Bilingual-Two Language Battery of Tests (BTLBT) is criterion referenced. It can be given to any pupil who has any proficiency in his or her native language, in English, or in one language only. It can be used to determine LAU categories, and point of bilinguality. Instruction is given by tape; therefore administrator needs no language proficiency. Scoring is standardized. Can also be used to determine extent of native and/or English language skills and proficiency, to establish current language dominance, to diagnose language strengths and weaknesses, to screen for motor and/or other handicaps or disabilities, to evaluate rate of language acquisition or loss, to make quick comparisons between levels of native language and English language proficiency, to aid in program placement decisions and program exit decisions.

16266
Independent School Entrance Examination: Upper Level. Educational Records Bureau, Wellesley, MA 1989
Subtests: Verbal Aptitude-Synonyms, Sentence Completion; Quantitative Aptitude-Concepts/Understanding, Application; Reading Comprehension-Science Passages, Social Studies Passages; Mathematics Achievement-Arithmetic Concepts, Algebraic Concepts, Geometric Concepts, Logic Proof by Computer, Essay
Descriptors: Academic Ability; *Admission (School); *Aptitude Tests; Content Area Reading; Essays; Mathematics; *Private Schools; Reading; Sciences; Secondary Education; *Secondary School Students; Social Studies; Student Placement; Verbal Ability; Writing (Composition)
Identifiers: ISEE; Writing Sample
Availability: Educational Records Bureau; Bardwell Hall, 37 Cameron St., Wellesley, MA 02181-6599
Grade Level: 8-11
Notes: Time, 180 min.; Items, 210
The ISEE is a secure, standardized admissions test for use by schools who are members of the Educational Records Bureau (ERB) consortium. A middle-level test for grades 5-7 (TC016255) is available also. The ISEE is also used to facilitate student placement in course levels and for identifying areas in which the student needs help. Also provides a sample of the prospective student's writing.

16267
Basic Academic Skills for Employment. Educational Technologies, Trenton, NJ 1987
Subtests: Reading; Writing; Mathematics; Language Arts
Descriptors: Adults; *Basic Skills; *Computer Assisted Testing; Computer Software; Diagnostic Teaching; *Diagnostic Tests; *Disadvantaged Youth; *Item Banks; *Job Training; Language Skills; Mathematics; *Occupational Tests; Pretests Posttests; Reading; Writing Skills

Identifiers: BASE
Availability: Educational Technologies Inc.; 1007 Whitehead Rd. Extension, Trenton, NJ 08638
Age Level: 18-64
Notes: Items, 3000
BASE is a computerized diagnostic and remediation system designed to measure and teach the reading, writing, language, and mathematics skills needed to get and hold a job. Relates basic skills to the requirements of jobs. Contains a bank of 3,000 test items measuring 250 basic skill competencies. Said to automatically create diagnostic tests of skills needed for 12,000 jobs. Said to be useful in youth job training programs. Supplies computer-assisted instruction for all prescriptions. Supplies posttesting to show gains in job-specific basic skills knowledge.

16292
Computer Historical Evolution and Vocabulary. Cassel, Russel N.; Cassel, Susie
Descriptors: Adolescents; Adults; Children; *Computers; History; *Knowledge Level; Vocabulary; Workshops
Identifiers: COMHist
Availability: Project Innovation; 1362 Santa Cruz Ct., Chula Vista, CA 92010
Age Level: 10-64
Notes: Items, 110
This 3-part matching test is designed for use in computer workshops. The first section covers critical individuals in the evolutionary history of the computer. Other sections cover significant events and developments and specialized computer vocabulary. Column 1 is matched to column 2. Items appear in an article in the *Journal of Instructional Psychology*; v11 n1 p3-8 (not dated).

16294
English Language Institute Listening Comprehension Test. English Language Institute, Ann Arbor, MI 1986
Descriptors: *Admission Criteria; Adults; Audiotape Recordings; Auditory Stimuli; *College Admission; *English (Second Language); Higher Education; *Listening Comprehension Tests
Identifiers: LCT; Michigan English Language Assessment Battery; University of Michigan
Availability: English Language Institute; Test Publications, University of Michigan, 2001 N. University Bldg., Ann Arbor, MI 48109-1057
Age Level: Adults
Notes: Time, 15 min.; Items, 45
The English Language Institute Listening Comprehension Test (LCT) is a 45-item, 15-minute tape-recorded listening test. It is used to estimate ability to understand basic English structures presented orally. It can be considered an aural grammar test. One of the component tests of the Michigan English Language Assessment Battery. The LCT is used to assess the English language proficiency of nonnative speakers of English who would like to pursue academic work at colleges and universities where courses are taught in English. May also be given to secondary school students, although there are no norms for that population.

16328
Decoding Inventory, Second Edition. Jacobs, H. Donald; Searfoss, Lyndon W. 1986
Descriptors: Auditory Discrimination; *Decoding (Reading); Elementary Education; *Elementary School Students; *Individual Testing; *Phonics; *Reading Difficulties; Reading Skills; *Reading Tests; Syllables; Visual Discrimination
Availability: Kendall Hunt Publishing Co.; 2460 Kerper Blvd., Dubuque, IA 52001
Grade Level: 4-8
The Decoding Inventory (DI) is a "controlled observation instrument" for helping to determine proficiencies in visual and auditory discrimination, syllabication, structural analysis, and the use of context cues for decoding words. It is to be used by teachers and reading clinicians with students who have decoding problems. The 19 assessments have been organized into 3 levels—level R is readiness; level 1, basic decoding skills; and level 2, advanced decoding skills.

16330
CAP Writing Assessment. Wick, John W.; Gatta, Louis A. 1988
Descriptors: *Holistic Evaluation; *Curriculum Evaluation; Diagnostic Tests; Secondary Education; *Secondary School Students; *Student Placement; *Writing (Composition); Writing Skills
Identifiers: Writing Samples
Availability: American Testronics; P.O. Box 2270, Iowa City, IA 52244-9990
Grade Level: 7-12
This instrument uses an actual writing sample and holistic scoring to assess writing. Three levels are available and are designated for grades 7-8, 9-10, and 11-12. Provides scores for individuals and profiles for groups of students for curriculum evaluation and student placement. The topic and method of discourse are selected by the user. Local

scoring can be used or scoring by the publisher can produce a computerized analysis. Holistic scoring provides a rating on a 6 point-scale from excellent to seriously deficient. Diagnostic scoring option evaluates content, organization, usage/sentence structure, and mechanics. A videotape for training local scorers is available.

16347
Student Occupational Competency Achievement Testing: Production Agriculture. National Occupational Competency Testing Institute, Big Rapids, MI
Descriptors: *Achievement Tests; Adults; *Agricultural Occupations; *Agricultural Production; Credentials; Farm Management; High Schools; *High School Students; Multiple Choice Tests; Occupational Tests; Performance Tests; *Postsecondary Education; Secondary Education; Two Year Colleges; *Vocational Education; *Work Sample Tests
Identifiers: NOCTI; SOCAT
Availability: National Occupational Competency Testing Institute; 409 Bishop Hall, Ferris State University, Big Rapids, MI 49307
Grade Level: 9-14
This test is part of a program developed to evaluate secondary and postsecondary vocational students with a standardized, objective measure. Each test consists of a multiple-choice portion covering factual knowledge, technical information, understanding of principles, and problem-solving abilities related to the occupation. A performance component samples manipulative skills required. A mental ability test is also available. The written test covers farm management and recordkeeping, animal science, plant science, leadership and employability, agricultural mechanics. The performance test covers animal science, agricultural mechanics, farm management, recordkeeping, and plant science.

16423
Reading/Learning Assessment. Cramer, Ronald L.; And Others 1980
Descriptors: Adults; College Students; *Reading Comprehension; Reading Skills; *Reading Tests
Availability: Learn Inc.; Mount Laurel Plaza, 113 Gaither Drive, Mount Laurel, NJ 08054
Age Level: Adults
Notes: Time, 20 min. approx.; Items, 30
Three-part instrument to measure reading comprehension skills. Measures a person's ability to use important information to preview a nonfiction book, to find factual, literal information, to make decisions about authors' opinions and attitudes in editorialized articles. Two equivalent forms.

16431
Knowledge of Infant Development Inventory and Catalog of Previous Experience with Infants. MacPhee, David 1981
Descriptors: Adults; Background; *Child Development; *Child Rearing; College Students; Experience; *Infants; *Knowledge Level; Mothers; Parenting Skills; Parents; Pediatrics; Physicians
Identifiers: KIDI, COPE; TIM(O)
Availability: Tests in Microfiche; Test Collection, Educational Testing Service, Princeton, NJ 08541
Age Level: Adults
Notes: Items, 100
The Knowledge of Infant Development Inventory (KIDI) was designed to assess one's knowledge of parental practices, developmental processes, and infant norms of behavior. Has been used in research on what determines parent behavior. Also used to evaluate parent education programs. Accompanied by a questionnaire assessing previous experience with infants to correlate with knowledge level assessed by KIDI. Subscores (not factor analysed) are norms and milestones, principles, parenting, health and safety. Norms, reliability coefficients .50-.92, and a discussion of validity (preliminary) are included.

16439
Stanford Early School Achievement Test, Third Edition, Level 1. Psychological Corp., San Antonio, TX 1989
Subtests: Sounds and Letters; Word Reading; Listening to Words and Stories; Mathematics; Environment
Descriptors: *Achievement Tests; Auditory Discrimination; Auditory Perception; *Cognitive Ability; *Cognitive Measurement; Kindergarten; *Kindergarten Children; Listening Comprehension; Number Concepts; Physical Environment; Primary Education; Social Environment; *Standardized Tests; Visual Discrimination; Visual Perception; Word Recognition
Identifiers: SESAT; Stanford Achievement Test Series; Test Batteries
Availability: Psychological Corp.; 555 Academic Ct., San Antonio, TX 78204-0952
Grade Level: K
Age Level: 5

Notes: Time, 130 min. approx.; Items, 205
Component of the Stanford Achievement Tests, Eighth Edition. Purpose of this test is to assess the cognitive development of children as they enter school to establish a baseline for initial instructional experiences. Assesses the learning that children have acquired upon beginning school and gain as they progress to the middle of kindergarten.

16440
Stanford Early School Achievement Test, Third Edition, Level 2. Psychological Corp., San Antonio, TX 1989
Subtests: Sounds and Letters; Word Reading; Sentence Reading; Listening to Words and Stories; Mathematics; Environment
Descriptors: *Achievement Tests; Auditory Discrimination; Auditory Perception; *Cognitive Ability; *Cognitive Measurement; *Grade 1; *Kindergarten Children; Listening Comprehension; Number Concepts; Physical Environment; Primary Education; Reading Comprehension; Sentences; Social Environment; *Standardized Tests; Visual Discrimination; Visual Perception; Word Recognition
Identifiers: SESAT; Stanford Achievement Test Series; Test Batteries
Availability: Psychological Corp.; 555 Academic Ct., San Antonio, TX 78204-0952
Grade Level: K-1
Age Level: 5-7
Notes: Time, 145 min. approx.; Items, 239
Component of the Stanford Achievement Tests, Eighth Edition. Designed to measure a segment of the cognitive learning of children ages 5, 6, and 7. Assesses learning that children gain as they progress through kindergarten and the first of grade 1. Knowledge of their cognitive development can serve as a baseline from which to begin instruction.

16441
Stanford Achievement Test, Eighth Edition, Primary 1. Psychological Corp., San Antonio, TX 1989
Subtests: Word Study Skills; Word Reading; Reading Comprehension; Language; Spelling; Listening; Concepts of Number; Mathematics Computation; Mathematics Application; Environment
Descriptors: *Academic Achievement; *Achievement Tests; Computation; Culture Fair Tests; Elementary School Students; *Grade 1; *Grade 2; Listening Comprehension; Mathematical Applications; Number Concepts; Physical Environment; *Primary Education; Reading Comprehension; Social Environment; Spelling; *Standardized Tests; Word Recognition; Word Study Skills; Writing Skills
Identifiers: Stanford Achievement Test Series; Test Batteries
Availability: Psychological Corp.; 555 Academic Ct., San Antonio, TX 78204-0952
Grade Level: 1-2
Notes: Time, 280 min. approx.; Items, 355
Comprehensive, standardized battery of tests designed to measure school achievement at each grade from K-12. Tests were developed to measure important learning outcomes of the school curriculum for use in improving instruction and evaluating progress. Was developed to have the highest possible degree of curricular validity for the concepts and skills taught throughout the nation. The Stanford Achievement Tests were standardized with the Otis-Lennon School Ability Tests (TC016432-TC016438) to allow for generation of achievement/ability comparisons when the 2 tests are administered together. Concepts and skills assessed in the Primary 1 level test are those ordinarily taught during the second half of grade 1 and the first half of grade 2. Each subtest may be administered at a separate sitting. No more than 2 subtests should be given at one sitting.

16442
Stanford Achievement Test, Eighth Edition, Primary 2. Psychological Corp., San Antonio, TX 1989
Subtests: Word Study Skills; Reading Vocabulary; Reading Comprehension; Language; Spelling; Listening; Concepts of Numbers; Mathematics Computation; Mathematics Application; Environment
Descriptors: *Academic Achievement; *Achievement Tests; Computation; Culture Fair Tests; *Elementary School Students; *Grade 2; *Grade 3; Listening Comprehension; Mathematical Applications; Number Concepts; Physical Environment; *Primary Education; Reading Comprehension; Social Environment; Spelling; *Standardized Tests; Vocabulary; Word Study Skills; Writing Skills
Identifiers: Stanford Achievement Test Series; Test Batteries

Availability: Psychological Corp.; 555 Academic Ct., San Antonio, TX 78204-0952
Grade Level: 2-3
Notes: Time, 285 min. approx.; Items, 392
Comprehensive, standardized battery of tests designed to measure school achievement at each grade from K-12. Tests were developed to measure important learning outcomes of the school curriculum for use in improving instruction and evaluating progress. Was developed to have the highest possible degree of curricular validity for the concepts and skills taught throughout the nation. The Stanford Achievement Tests were standardized with the Otis-Lennon School Ability Tests (TC016432-TC016438) to allow for generation of achievement/ability comparisons when the 2 tests are administered together. Concepts and skills assessed in the Primary 2 level test are those ordinarily taught during the second half of grade 2 and the first half of grade 3. Each subtest can be administered at a separate sitting. No more than 2 subtests should be given at one sitting.

16443
Stanford Achievement Test, Eighth Edition, Primary 3. Psychological Corp., San Antonio, TX 1989
Subtests: Word Study Skills; Reading Vocabulary; Reading Comprehension; Language Mechanics; Language Expression; Study Skills; Spelling; Listening; Concepts of Number; Mathematics Computation; Mathematics Application; Science; Social Science
Descriptors: *Academic Achievement; *Achievement Tests; Computation; Culture Fair Tests; Elementary Education; *Elementary School Students; *Grade 3; *Grade 4; Language Skills; Listening Comprehension; Mathematical Applications; Number Concepts; Reading Comprehension; Sciences; Social Studies; Spelling; *Standardized Tests; Study Skills; Vocabulary; Word Study Skills; Writing Skills
Identifiers: Stanford Achievement Test Series; Test Batteries
Availability: Psychological Corp.; 555 Academic Ct., San Antonio, TX 78204-0952
Grade Level: 3-4
Notes: Time, 370 min. approx.; Items, 529
Comprehensive, standardized battery of tests designed to measure school achievement at each grade from K-12. Tests were developed to measure important learning outcomes of the school curriculum for use in improving instruction and evaluating progress. Was developed to have the highest possible degree of curricular validity for the concepts and skills taught throughout the nation. The Stanford Achievement Tests were standardized with the Otis-Lennon School Ability Tests (TC016432-TC016438) to allow for generation of achievement/ability comparisons when the 2 tests are administered together. Concepts and skills assessed in the Primary 3 test are those ordinarily taught during the second half of grade 3 and the first half of grade 4. Each subtest may be administered at a separate sitting. No more than 2 subtests should be given at one time. The Stanford Writing Assessment Program, available in a separate booklet, provides for the assessment of written expression in 4 modes: descriptive, narrative, expository, and persuasive.

16444
Stanford Achievement Test, Eighth Edition, Intermediate 1. Psychological Corp., San Antonio, TX 1989
Subtests: Reading Vocabulary; Reading Comprehension; Language Mechanics; Language Expression; Study Skills; Spelling; Listening; Concepts of Number; Mathematics Computation; Mathematics Applications; Science; Social Science; Using Information; Thinking Skills
Descriptors: *Academic Achievement; *Achievement Tests; Cognitive Processes; Computation; Critical Thinking; Culture Fair Tests; Data Interpretation; *Elementary School Students; *Grade 4; *Grade 5; *Intermediate Grades; Language Skills; Listening Comprehension; Mathematical Applications; Number Concepts; Reading Comprehension; Sciences; Social Studies; Spelling; *Standardized Tests; Study Skills; Vocabulary; Writing Skills
Identifiers: Stanford Achievement Test Series; Test Batteries
Availability: Psychological Corp.; 555 Academic Ct., San Antonio, TX 78204-0952
Grade Level: 4-5
Notes: Time, 355 min. approx.; Items, 487
Comprehensive, standardized battery of tests designed to measure school achievement at each grade from K-12. Tests were developed to measure important learning outcomes of the school curriculum for use in improving instruction and evaluating progress. Was developed to have the highest possible degree of curricular validity for the concepts and skills taught throughout the nation. The Stanford Achievement Tests were standardized with the Otis-Lennon School Ability Tests (TC016432-TC016438) to allow for generation of achievement/ability comparisons

when the 2 tests are administered together. Concepts and skills assessed in each content area are those ordinarily taught during the second half of grade 4 and the first half of grade 5. Each subtest may be administered at a separate sitting. No more than 2 subtests should be administered at one time. The Stanford Writing Assessment Program, available in a separate booklet, provides for the assessment of written expression in 4 modes: descriptive, narrative, expository, and persuasive.

16445
Stanford Achievement Test, Eighth Edition, Intermediate 2. Psychological Corp., San Antonio, TX 1989
Subtests: Reading Vocabulary; Reading Comprehension; Language Mechanics; Language Expression; Study Skills; Spelling; Listening; Concepts of Number; Mathematics Computation; Mathematics Application; Sciences; Social Science; Using Information; Thinking Skills
Descriptors: *Academic Achievement; *Achievement Tests; Cognitive Processes; Computation; Critical Thinking; Culture Fair Tests; Data Interpretation; *Elementary School Students; *Grade 5; *Grade 6; *Intermediate Grades; Language Skills; Listening Comprehension; Mathematical Applications; Number Concepts; Reading Comprehension; Sciences; Social Studies; Spelling; *Standardized Tests; Study Skills; Vocabulary; Writing Skills
Identifiers: Stanford Achievement Test Series; Test Batteries
Availability: Psychological Corp.; 555 Academic Ct., San Antonio, TX 78204-0952
Grade Level: 5-6
Notes: Time, 355 min. approx.; Items, 497

Comprehensive, standardized battery of tests designed to measure school achievement at each grade from K-12. Tests were developed to measure important learning outcomes of the school curriculum for use in improving instruction and evaluating progress. Was developed to have the highest possible degree of curricular validity for the concepts and skills taught throughout the nation. The Stanford Achievement Tests were standardized with the Otis-Lennon School Ability Tests (TC016432-TC016438) to allow for generation of achievement/ability comparisons when the 2 tests are administered together. Concepts and skills assessed in each content area are those ordinarily taught during the second half of grade 5 and the first half of grade 6. Each subtest may be administered at a separate sitting. No more than 2 subtests should be administered at one time. The Stanford Writing Assessment Program, available in a separate booklet, provides for the assessment of written expression in 4 modes: descriptive, narrative, expository, and persuasive.

16446
Stanford Achievement Test, Eighth Edition, Intermediate 3. Psychological Corp., San Antonio, TX 1989
Subtests: Reading Vocabulary; Reading Comprehension; Language Mechanics; Language Expression; Study Skills; Spelling; Listening; Concepts of Number; Mathematics Computation; Mathematics Application; Sciences; Social Science; Using Information; Thinking Skills
Descriptors: *Academic Achievement; *Achievement Tests; Cognitive Processes; Computation; Critical Thinking; Culture Fair Tests; Data Interpretation; Elementary Education; *Elementary School Students; *Grade 6; *Grade 7; Language Skills; Listening Comprehension; Mathematical Applications; Number Concepts; Reading Comprehension; Sciences; Social Studies; Spelling; *Standardized Tests; Study Skills; Vocabulary; Writing Skills
Identifiers: Stanford Achievement Test Series; Test Batteries
Availability: Psychological Corp.; 555 Academic Ct., San Antonio, TX 78204-0952
Grade Level: 6-7
Notes: Time, 355 min. approx.; Items, 499

Comprehensive, standardized battery of tests designed to measure school achievement at each grade from K-12. Tests were developed to measure important learning outcomes of the school curriculum for use in improving instruction and evaluating progress. Was developed to have the highest possible degree of curricular validity for the concepts and skills taught throughout the nation. The Stanford Achievement Tests were standardized with the Otis-Lennon School Ability Tests (TC016432-TC016438) to allow for generation of achievement/ability comparisons when the 2 tests are administered together. Concepts and skills assessed in each content area are those ordinarily taught during the second half of grade 6 and the first half of grade 7. Each subtest may be administered at a separate sitting. No more than 2 subtests should be administered at one time. The Stanford Writing Assessment Program, available in a separate booklet, provides for the assessment of written expression in 4 modes: descriptive, narrative, expository, and persuasive.

16447
Stanford Achievement Test, Eighth Edition, Advanced 1. Psychological Corp., San Antonio, TX 1989
Subtests: Reading Vocabulary; Reading Comprehension; Language Mechanics; Study Skills; Spelling; Listening; Concepts of Number; Mathematics Computation; Mathematics Applications; Science; Social Science; Using Information; Thinking Skills
Descriptors: *Academic Achievement; *Achievement Tests; Cognitive Processes; Computation; Critical Thinking; Culture Fair Tests; Data Interpretation; Junior High Schools; *Junior High School Students; Language Skills; Listening Comprehension; Mathematical Applications; Number Concepts; Reading Comprehension; Sciences; Social Studies; Spelling; *Standardized Tests; Study Skills; Vocabulary; Writing Skills
Identifiers: Stanford Achievement Test Series; Test Batteries
Availability: Psychological Corp.; 555 Academic Ct., San Antonio, TX 78204-0952
Grade Level: 7-8
Notes: Time, 355 min. approx.; Items, 499

Comprehensive, standardized battery of tests designed to measure school achievement at each grade from K-12. Tests were developed to measure important learning outcomes of the school curriculum for use in improving instruction and evaluating progress. Was developed to have the highest possible degree of curricular validity for the concepts and skills taught throughout the nation. The Stanford Achievement Tests were standardized with the Otis-Lennon School Ability Tests (TC016432-TC016438) to allow for generation of achievement/ability comparisons when the 2 tests are administered together. Concepts and skills assessed are those ordinarily taught during the second half of grade 7 and the first half of grade 8. Each subtest may be administered at a separate sitting. No more than 2 subtests should be administered at one time. The Stanford Writing Assessment Program, available in a separate booklet, provides for the assessment of written expression in 4 modes: descriptive, narrative, expository, and persuasive.

16448
Stanford Achievement Test, Eighth Edition, Advanced 2. Psychological Corp., San Antonio, TX 1989
Subtests: Reading Vocabulary; Reading Comprehension; Language Mechanics; Language Expression; Study Skills; Spelling; Listening; Concepts of Number; Mathematics Computation; Mathematics Applications; Science; Social Science; Using Information; Thinking Skills
Descriptors: *Academic Achievement; *Achievement Tests; Cognitive Processes; Computation; Critical Thinking; Culture Fair Tests; Data Interpretation; Junior High Schools; *Junior High School Students; Language Skills; Listening Comprehension; Mathematical Applications; Number Concepts; Reading Comprehension; Sciences; Social Studies; Spelling; *Standardized Tests; Study Skills; Vocabulary; Writing Skills
Identifiers: Stanford Achievement Test Series; Test Batteries
Availability: Psychological Corp.; 555 Academic Ct., San Antonio, TX 78204-0952
Grade Level: 8-9
Notes: Time, 355 min. approx.; Items, 499

Comprehensive, standardized battery of tests designed to measure school achievement at each grade from K-12. Tests were developed to measure important learning outcomes of the school curriculum for use in improving instruction and evaluating progress. Was developed to have the highest possible degree of curricular validity for the concepts and skills taught throughout the nation. The Stanford Achievement Tests were standardized with the Otis-Lennon School Ability Tests (TC016432-TC016438) to allow for generation of achievement/ability comparisons when the 2 tests are administered together. Concepts and skills assessed in each content area are those ordinarily taught during the second half of grade 8 and the first half of grade 9. Each subtest may be administered at a separate sitting. No more than 2 subtests should be administered at one time. The Stanford Writing Assessment Program, available in a separate booklet, provides for the assessment of written expression in 4 modes: descriptive, narrative, expository, and persuasive.

16449
Stanford Test of Academic Skills, Third Edition, Level 1. Psychological Corp., San Antonio, TX 1989
Subtests: Reading Vocabulary; Reading Comprehension; English; Study Skills; Spelling; Mathematics; Science; Social Science; Using Information; Thinking Skills
Descriptors: *Academic Achievement; *Achievement Tests; Cognitive Processes; Critical Thinking; Culture Fair Tests; Data Interpretation; *Grade 9; Junior High Schools; *Junior High School Students; Reading Comprehension; Sciences; Secondary School Mathematics; Social Studies; Spelling; *Standardized Tests; Study Skills; Vocabulary; Writing Skills
Identifiers: Stanford Achievement Test Series; TASK1; Test Batteries
Availability: Psychological Corp.; 555 Academic Ct., San Antonio, TX 78204-0952
Grade Level: 9
Notes: Time, 225 min. approx.; Items, 370

Comprehensive, standardized battery of tests designed to measure school achievement at each grade from K-12. Tests were developed to measure important learning outcomes of the school curriculum for use in improving instruction and evaluating progress. Was developed to have the highest possible degree of curricular validity for the concepts and skills taught throughout the nation. The Stanford Achievement Tests were standardized with the Otis-Lennon School Ability Tests (TC016432-TC016438) to allow for generation of achievement/ability comparisons when the 2 tests are administered together. The 3 levels of Stanford Test of Academic Skills are intended for use as measures of basic skills in grades 9 through 12 and for entering college students. Level 1 is designed primarily for students in grade 9. All 3 levels of TASK, which are linked in terms of content and score information to the rest of the Stanford series, assess those skills that are requisite to continued academic training. Each subtest may be administered at a separate sitting. No more than 2 subtests should be administered at one time. The Stanford Writing Assessment Program, available in a separate booklet, provides for the assessment of written expression in 4 modes: descriptive, narrative, expository, and persuasive.

16450
Stanford Test of Academic Skills, Third Edition, Level 2. Psychological Corp., San Antonio, TX 1989
Subtests: Reading Vocabulary; Reading Comprehension; English; Study Skills; Spelling; Mathematics; Science; Social Science; Using Information; Thinking Skills
Descriptors: *Academic Achievement; *Achievement Tests; Cognitive Processes; Critical Thinking; Culture Fair Tests; Data Interpretation; *Grade 10; High Schools; *High School Students; Reading Comprehension; Sciences; Secondary School Mathematics; Social Studies; Spelling; *Standardized Tests; Study Skills; Vocabulary; Writing Skills
Identifiers: Stanford Achievement Test Series; TASK2; Test Batteries
Availability: Psychological Corp.; 555 Academic Ct., San Antonio, TX 78204-0952
Grade Level: 10
Notes: Time, 235 min. approx.; Items, 370

Comprehensive, standardized battery of tests designed to measure school achievement at each grade from K-12. Tests were developed to measure important learning outcomes of the school curriculum for use in improving instruction and evaluating progress. Was developed to have the highest possible degree of curricular validity for the concepts and skills taught throughout the nation. The Stanford Achievement Tests were standardized with the Otis-Lennon School Ability Tests (TC016432-TC016438) to allow for generation of achievement/ability comparisons when the 2 tests are administered together. The 3 levels of Stanford Test of Academic Skills are intended for use as measures of basic skills in grades 9 through 12 and for entering college students. Level 2 is intended for students in grade 10. All 3 levels of TASK, which are linked in terms of content and score information to the rest of the Stanford series, assess those skills that are requisite to continued academic training. Each subtest may be administered at a separate sitting. No more than 2 subtests should be administered at one time. The Stanford Writing Assessment Program, available in a separate booklet, provides for the assessment of written expression in 4 modes: descriptive, narrative, expository, and persuasive.

16451
Stanford Test of Academic Skills, Third Edition, Level 3. Psychological Corp., San Antonio, TX 1989
Subtests: Reading Vocabulary; Reading Comprehension; English; Study Skills; Spelling; Mathematics; Science; Social Science; Using Information; Thinking Skills
Descriptors: *Academic Achievement; *Achievement Tests; Cognitive Processes; *College Freshmen; Critical Thinking; Culture Fair Tests; Data Interpretation; *Grade 11; *Grade 12; Higher Education; High Schools; *High School Students; Reading Comprehension; Sciences; Secondary School Mathematics; Social Studies; Spelling; *Standardized Tests; Study Skills; Vocabulary; Writing Skills
Identifiers: Stanford Achievement Test Series; TASK3; Test Batteries

Availability: Psychological Corp.; 555 Academic
Ct., San Antonio, TX 78204-0952
Grade Level: 11-13
Notes: Time, 235 min. approx.; Items, 370

Comprehensive, standardized battery of tests designed to measure school achievement at each grade from K-12. Tests were developed to measure important learning outcomes of the school curriculum for use in improving instruction and evaluating progress. Was developed to have the highest possible degree of curricular validity for the concepts and skills taught throughout the nation. The Stanford Achievement Tests were standardized with the Otis-Lennon School Ability Tests (TC016432-TC016438) to allow for generation of achievement/ability comparisons when the 2 tests are administered together. The 3 levels of Stanford Test of Academic Skills are intended for use as measures of basic skills in grades 9 through 12 and for entering college students. Level 3 is designed for grades 11 and 12 and entering first-year college students. All 3 levels of TASK, which are linked in terms of content and score information to the rest of the Stanford series, assess those skills that are requisite to continued academic training. Each subtest may be administered at a separate sitting. No more than 2 subtests should be administered at one time. The Stanford Writing Assessment Program, available in a separate booklet, provides for the assessment of written expression in 4 modes: descriptive, narrative, expository, and persuasive.

16464
Stanford Writing Assessment Program, Second Edition, Level P3. Psychological Corp., San Antonio, TX 1989
Descriptors: *Descriptive Writing; *Diagnostic Tests; Elementary Education; *Elementary School Students; *Expository Writing; *Grade 3; *Grade 4; *Writing (Composition)
Identifiers: *Narrative Writing; *Persuasive Writing; Stanford Achievement Test Series
Availability: Psychological Corp.; 555 Academic Ct., San Antonio, TX 78204-0952
Grade Level: 3-4
Notes: Time, 35 min. approx.

Can be used to diagnose strengths and weaknesses of individual students or in conducting a school or district survey of students' writing ability through holistically and analytically scored writing samples. Can be used in conjunction with other subtests in the Stanford Achievement Test, Eighth Edition, such as spelling, language mechanics, and language expression. Four modes of writing assessed in this program are descriptive, narrative, expository, and persuasive. Students are presented with a prompt designed to elicit a writing sample in the intended mode. Prompts are dictated by the teacher.

16465
Stanford Writing Assessment Program, Second Edition, Level I1. Psychological Corp., San Antonio, TX 1989
Descriptors: *Descriptive Writing; *Diagnostic Tests; *Elementary School Students; *Expository Writing; *Grade 4; *Grade 5; *Intermediate Grades; *Writing (Composition)
Identifiers: *Narrative Writing; *Persuasive Writing; Stanford Achievement Test Series
Availability: Psychological Corp.; 555 Academic Ct., San Antonio, TX 78204-0952
Grade Level: 4-5
Notes: Time, 35 min. approx.

Can be used to diagnose strengths and weaknesses of individual students or in conducting a school or district survey of students' writing ability through holistically and analytically scored writing samples. Can be used in conjunction with other subtests in the Stanford Achievement Test, Eighth Edition, such as spelling, language mechanics, and language expression. Four modes of writing assessed in this program are descriptive, narrative, expository, and persuasive. Students are presented with a prompt designed to elicit a writing sample in the intended mode. Prompts are dictated by the teacher.

16466
Stanford Writing Assessment Program, Second Edition, Level I2. Psychological Corp., San Antonio, TX 1989
Descriptors: *Descriptive Writing; *Diagnostic Tests; *Elementary School Students; *Expository Writing; *Grade 5; *Grade 6; *Intermediate Grades; *Writing (Composition)
Identifiers: *Narrative Writing; *Persuasive Writing; Stanford Achievement Test Series
Availability: Psychological Corp.; 555 Academic Ct., San Antonio, TX 78204-0952
Grade Level: 5-6
Notes: Time, 35 min. approx.

Can be used to diagnose strengths and weaknesses of individual students or in conducting a school or district survey of students' writing ability through holistically and analytically scored writing samples. Can be used in conjunction with other subtests in the Stanford Achievement Test, Eighth Edition, such as spelling, language mechanics, and language expression. Four modes of writing assessed in this program are descriptive, narrative, expository, and

persuasive. Students are presented with a prompt designed to elicit a writing sample in the intended mode. Prompts are dictated by the teacher.

16467
Stanford Writing Assessment Program, Second Edition, Level I3. Psychological Corp., San Antonio, TX 1989
Descriptors: *Descriptive Writing; *Diagnostic Tests; Elementary Education; *Elementary School Students; *Expository Writing; *Grade 6; *Grade 7; *Writing (Composition)
Identifiers: *Narrative Writing; *Persuasive Writing; Stanford Achievement Test Series
Availability: Psychological Corp.; 555 Academic Ct., San Antonio, TX 78204-0952
Grade Level: 6-7
Notes: Time, 35 min. approx.

Can be used to diagnose strengths and weaknesses of individual students or in conducting a school or district survey of students' writing ability through holistically and analytically scored writing samples. Can be used in conjunction with other subtests in the Stanford Achievement Test, Eighth Edition, such as spelling, language mechanics, and language expression. Four modes of writing assessed in this program are descriptive, narrative, expository, and persuasive. Students are presented with a prompt designed to elicit a writing sample in the intended mode. Prompts are dictated by the teacher.

16468
Stanford Writing Assessment Program, Second Edition, Level A1. Psychological Corp., San Antonio, TX 1989
Descriptors: *Descriptive Writing; *Diagnostic Tests; *Expository Writing; Junior High Schools; *Junior High School Students; *Writing (Composition)
Identifiers: *Narrative Writing; *Persuasive Writing; Stanford Achievement Test Series
Availability: Psychological Corp.; 555 Academic Ct., San Antonio, TX 78204-0952
Grade Level: 7-8
Notes: Time, 35 min. approx.

Can be used to diagnose strengths and weaknesses of individual students or in conducting a school or district survey of students' writing ability through holistically and analytically scored writing samples. Can be used in conjunction with other subtests in the Stanford Achievement Test, Eighth Edition, such as spelling, language mechanics, and language expression. Four modes of writing assessed in this program are descriptive, narrative, expository, and persuasive. Students are presented with a prompt designed to elicit a writing sample in the intended mode. Prompts are dictated by the teacher.

16469
Stanford Writing Assessment Program, Second Edition, Level A2. Psychological Corp., San Antonio, TX 1989
Descriptors: *Descriptive Writing; *Diagnostic Tests; *Expository Writing; Junior High Schools; *Junior High School Students; *Writing (Composition)
Identifiers: *Narrative Writing; *Persuasive Writing; Stanford Achievement Test Series
Availability: Psychological Corp.; 555 Academic Ct., San Antonio, TX 78204-0952
Grade Level: 8-9
Notes: Time, 35 min. approx.

Can be used to diagnose strengths and weaknesses of individual students or in conducting a school or district survey of students' writing ability through holistically and analytically scored writing samples. Can be used in conjunction with other subtests in the Stanford Achievement Test, Eighth Edition, such as spelling, language mechanics, and language expression. Four modes of writing assessed in this program are descriptive, narrative, expository, and persuasive. Students are presented with a prompt designed to elicit a writing sample in the intended mode. Prompts are dictated by the teacher.

16470
Stanford Writing Assessment Program, Second Edition, Level T1. Psychological Corp., San Antonio, TX 1989
Descriptors: *Descriptive Writing; *Diagnostic Tests; *Expository Writing; *Grade 9; Junior High Schools; *Junior High School Students; *Writing (Composition)
Identifiers: *Narrative Writing; *Persuasive Writing; Stanford Achievement Test Series
Availability: Psychological Corp.; 555 Academic Ct., San Antonio, TX 78204-0952
Grade Level: 9
Notes: Time, 35 min. approx.

Can be used to diagnose strengths and weaknesses of individual students or in conducting a school or district survey of students' writing ability through holistically and analytically scored writing samples. Can be used in conjunction with other subtests in the Stanford Test of Academic Skills, Third Edition, such as spelling. Four modes

of writing assessed in this program are descriptive, narrative, expository, and persuasive. Students are presented with a prompt designed to elicit a writing sample in the intended mode. Prompts are dictated by the teacher.

16471
Stanford Writing Assessment Program, Second Edition, Level T2. Psychological Corp., San Antonio, TX 1989
Descriptors: *Descriptive Writing; *Diagnostic Tests; *Expository Writing; *Grade 10; High Schools; *High School Students; *Writing (Composition)
Identifiers: *Narrative Writing; *Persuasive Writing; Stanford Achievement Test Series
Availability: Psychological Corp.; 555 Academic Ct., San Antonio, TX 78204-0952
Grade Level: 10
Notes: Time, 35 min. approx.

Can be used to diagnose strengths and weaknesses of individual students or in conducting a school or district survey of students' writing ability through holistically and analytically scored writing samples. Can be used in conjunction with other subtests in the Stanford Test of Academic Skills, Third Edition, such as spelling. Four modes of writing assessed in this program are descriptive, narrative, expository, and persuasive. Students are presented with a prompt designed to elicit a writing sample in the intended mode. Prompts are dictated by the teacher.

16472
Stanford Writing Assessment Program, Second Edition, Level T3. Psychological Corp., San Antonio, TX 1989
Descriptors: *College Freshmen; *Descriptive Writing; *Diagnostic Tests; *Expository Writing; *Grade 11; *Grade 12; Higher Education; High Schools; *High School Students; *Writing (Composition)
Identifiers: *Narrative Writing; *Persuasive Writing; Stanford Achievement Test Series
Availability: Psychological Corp.; 555 Academic Ct., San Antonio, TX 78204-0952
Grade Level: 11-13
Notes: Time, 35 min. approx.

Can be used to diagnose strengths and weaknesses of individual students or in conducting a school or district survey of students' writing ability through holistically and analytically scored writing samples. Can be used in conjunction with other subtests in the Stanford Test of Academic Skills, Third Edition, such as spelling. Four modes of writing assessed in this program are descriptive, narrative, expository, and persuasive. Students are presented with a prompt designed to elicit a writing sample in the intended mode. Prompts are dictated by the teacher.

16491
Facts on Aging and Mental Health Quiz. Palmore, Erdman 1988
Descriptors: Adults; *Aging (Individuals); Aging Education; Attitude Measures; *Knowledge Level; *Mental Health; *Older Adults; Questionnaires; Social Bias
Identifiers: FAMHQ
Availability: Palmore, Erdman B. The Facts on Aging Quiz: A Handbook of Uses and Results. New York: Springer Publishing Co., 1988
Age Level: Adults
Notes: Items, 25

Designed to assess knowledge level about the mental health of aging individuals. Quiz may be used to educate, measure learning, test knowledge, and measure attitudes. May also be used to stimulate discussion, compare level of knowledge among groups, and target misconceptions which are most frequent. Useful to health care workers and relatives of older people. Related instruments are Facts on Aging Quiz (TC015000), Facts on Aging Quiz, Alternative Form (TC014550), and Psychological Facts on Aging Quiz (TC016492), which also assess knowledge about aging.

16492
Psychological Facts on Aging Quiz.
McCutcheon, Lynn E. 1986
Descriptors: Adults; *Aging (Individuals); Aging Education; Attitude Measures; Knowledge Level; *Older Adults; Questionnaires
Identifiers: PFAQ
Availability: Palmore, Erdman B. The Facts on Aging Quiz: A Handbook of Uses and Results. New York: Springer Publishing Co., 1988
Age Level: Adults
Notes: Items, 22

Uses 10 items from Facts on Aging Quiz (TC015000) and 10 items from the Facts on Aging Quiz, Alternate Form (TC014550), along with 2 original items to create a quiz dealing solely with psychological and sociological facts about aging. May be used to educate or to measure knowledge or attitudes.

16494
Mental Health and Aging: A Short Quiz.
Pruchno, Rachel; Smyer, Michael A. 1983

Descriptors: Adults; *Aging (Individuals); *Knowledge Level; *Mental Health; *Older Adults; Questionnaires
Availability: *International Journal of Aging and Human Development;* v17 n2 p123-40, 1983
Age Level: Adults
Notes: Items, 16

A true-false test designed to assess individuals' knowledge on the facts about aging. Does not assess attitudes about aging. Items represent an overview of empirical and theoretical issues on mental health and aging and are designed to promote discussion on the topic. Detailed information on the reasons each answer is correct are included. Average scores, item difficulties, and item-to-total correlations, based on the results of individuals who completed the quiz, are presented.

16496
Brigance Early Preschool Screen for Two-Year-Old and Two-and-a-Half-Year-Old Children. Brigance, Albert H. 1990
Descriptors: *Criterion Referenced Tests; *Developmental Tasks; Knowledge Level; Language Acquisition; Psychomotor Skills; *Screening Tests; *Spanish Speaking; *Toddlers; *Young Children
Identifiers: Body Awareness
Availability: Curriculum Associates; 5 Esquire Rd., N. Billerica, MA 01862-2589
Age Level: 2
Notes: Time, 20 min. approx.

Screening instrument to provide a sampling of a child's learning development, and skills in a broad range of areas such as fine-motor skills, body awareness, general knowledge, language development, and gross-motor skills. The assessment is criterion referenced and curriculum referenced to provide data, that in combination with other information, may be useful in establishing instructional objectives. If a problem or disability is indicated during the screening, it should be confirmed or dismissed only after a diagnostic assessment has been completed. The screening test may be used to provide supplementary skills assessment, and to assist teachers with program planning, appropriate classroom grouping, special service referrals, and mandated screening compliance. The skills included in this assessment are at a skill level that normative data indicate children develop between the ages of 1 year, 9 months to 2 years, 6 months (for the 2-year level) and 2 years, 3 months to 3 years (for the 2.5 year level). Spanish direction lines for screening Spanish-speaking children are available.

16497
Microcomputer Managed Information for Criterion Referenced Objectives in Language Arts 1-8. Educational Development Corp., Tulsa, OK 1988
Descriptors: Computer Uses in Education; *Criterion Referenced Tests; *Diagnostic Tests; *Educational Diagnosis; Elementary Education; *Elementary School Students; *Grammar; *Knowledge Level; *Language Arts; Objective Tests
Identifiers: MMICRO
Availability: Educational Development Corp.; P.O. Box 470663, Tulsa, OK 74145
Grade Level: 1-8

A series of diagnostic single objective, language arts tests for use with students in grades one through 8. Consists of 8 forms of the test, one for each grade level. Assesses students' spelling, grammar, and writing skills at each grade level. Items cover skills students should have mastery of to determine whether they actually do. Results are used to determine teachers' next instructional steps, progress being made, and accomplishments. Instrument may be administered to individuals or groups. This is a paper-and-pencil test which makes use of microcomputer software for scoring, printing reports, and keeping records of students' test performance. Documentation notes that validity has been confirmed, empirically, through extensive use, but there are no accompanying statistics.

16498
Microcomputer Managed Information for Criterion Referenced Objectives in Mathematics, Developmental Edition. Educational Development Corp., Tulsa, OK 1982
Descriptors: Classroom Environment; *Computation; *Criterion Referenced Tests; Decimal Fractions; Elementary Education; *Elementary School Students; Fractions; Geometry; Junior High Schools; *Junior High School Students; *Mathematical Applications; *Mathematics Tests; *Microcomputers; Percentage; Whole Numbers
Identifiers: MMICRO
Availability: Educational Development Corp.; P.O. Box 470663, Tulsa, OK 74145
Grade Level: 1-9

This microcomputer-based management system is designed to deliver instructional information for classroom use, measure and monitor student progress, test skills being taught, tailor instruction to individual needs, group and regroup students for instruction, and select materials for the skills needed. It is programed to produce instructional information that describes the basic skills a student must acquire to be able to compute and problem solve. The statements correspond to the skills of the leading basal texts. Questions are divided into diagnostic and single-objective tests that are grouped by grade level. The scope and sequence of objectives are whole numbers, fractions, measurement, geometry, decimals-percent, and special topics, such as graphs-tables, money, time, roman numerals, and others. This is not a timed test and may be administered to individual students or in groups.

16499
Microcomputer Managed Information for Criterion Referenced Objectives in Reading K-8. Educational Development Corp., Tulsa, OK 1986
Descriptors: *Criterion Referenced Tests; *Diagnostic Tests; Elementary Education; *Elementary School Students; *Microcomputers; *Phonetic Analysis; *Reading Comprehension; *Reading Diagnosis; Reading Skills; *Reading Tests; *Structural Analysis (Linguistics)
Identifiers: MMICRO
Availability: Educational Development Corp.; P.O. Box 470663, Tulsa, OK 74145
Grade Level: K-8
Notes: Items, 304

These computerized management system and tests are built around a collection of criterion-referenced objectives. The diagnostic and single-objective tests are used to determine whether a student has mastered the basic skills required to read with comprehension. The system is designed to deliver instructional information for day-to-day use, using a questioning method. This tool collects, analyzes, stores, and retrieves information for teachers, students, parents, and administrative use. The scope and sequence of objectives include phonetic analysis, structural analysis/word functions; comprehension. Slower students should be allowed to work on their tests each day until completed.

16500
Test of Language Competence, Expanded Edition, Level 1. Wiig, Elisabeth E.; Secord, Wayne 1989
Subtests: Ambiguous Sentences; Listening Comprehension: Making Inferences; Oral Expression: Recreating Speech Acts; Figurative Language
Descriptors: Children; *Individual Testing; *Language Handicaps; *Language Tests; Norm Referenced Tests; *Screening Tests
Identifiers: TLC(E)
Availability: Psychological Corp.; 555 Academic Ct., San Antonio, TX 78204-0952
Age Level: 5-9
Notes: Time, 60 min. approx.

Downward extension of Test of Language Competence, Expanded Edition, Level 2 (TC016501). Designed to aid speech-language pathologists, psychologists, and special educators to identify children ages 5 through 9 with language disabilities. Used to identify those who have not attained expected levels of competence in semantics, syntax, and/or pragmatics. May be used with individuals beyond age 9 who have been administered Test of Language Competence, Expanded Edition, Level 2 and have shown significant language delays. Test is norm referenced and helps determine students' need for language intervention. Test is individually administered.

16501
Test of Language Competence, Expanded Edition, Level 2. Wiig, Elisabeth E.; Secord, Wayne 1989
Subtests: Ambiguous Sentences; Listening Comprehension: Making Inferences; Oral Expression: Recreating Sentences; Figurative Language
Descriptors: Adolescents; Adults; Children; *Individual Testing; *Language Handicaps; *Language Tests; Norm Referenced Tests; *Screening Tests
Identifiers: TLC(E)
Availability: Psychological Corp.; 555 Academic Ct., San Antonio, TX 78204-0952
Age Level: 9-64
Notes: Time, 60 min. approx.

Designed to aid speech-language pathologists, psychologists, and special educators to identify children ages 9 and above and adults with language disabilities. Expected to identify those who have not attained the expected levels of competence in semantics, syntax and pragmatics. The test is not designed to provide in-depth assessment at the level of phonology. Test is individually administered. Test replaces Test of Language Competence. Test of Language Competence, Expanded Edition, Level 1, (TC016500) is for use with children ages 5 through 9.

16502
National Educational Development Tests. Science Research Associates, Chicago, IL 1984
Subtests: English Usage; Mathematics Usage; Natural Sciences Reading; Social Studies Reading; Educational Ability
Descriptors: *Academic Aptitude; *Achievement Tests; Adolescents; *Aptitude Tests; *College Bound Students; High Schools; *High School Students; *Language Usage; *Mathematics Skills; *Natural Sciences; *Reading Comprehension; *Social Sciences
Identifiers: NEDT
Availability: CTB/MacMillan/McGraw Hill; Del Monte Research Park, 2500 Garden Rd., Monterey, CA 93940
Grade Level: 9-10

The National Educational Development Test (NEDT) were set up to give ninth and tenth grade students information about educational development. The NEDT helps them to relate this information to plans for remaining high school studies and beyond. The student's educational development is tested in 4 areas: (1) English usage; (2) mathematics uage; (3) natural sciences reading; and (4) social studies reading. The English usage test measures ability to use capitalization, punctuation, diction, and sentence reconstruction. The mathematics usage test measures the ability to apply mathematics rules in formal exercises and practical quantitative problems. The pupil's ability to interpret and evaluate reading materials in the natural sciences (physical, earth, and life) is measured in the natural sciences reading test. The ability to evaluate and interpret reading passages from history, anthropology, geography, economics, sociology, psychology, and politics is measured in the social sciences reading test. The test also assesses the developed abilities most closely associated with academic performance. These abilities include verbal, numerical, reasoning, and spatial skills.

16541
ACT Proficiency Examination Program: Introductory Accounting. American College Testing Program, Iowa City, IA 1989
Descriptors: *Accounting; Adults; Adult Students; *Equivalency Tests; *External Degree Programs; Higher Education; *Special Degree Programs
Identifiers: ACT; American College Testing Program; PEP
Availability: ACT Proficiency Examination Program; P.O. Box 168, Iowa City, IA 52240
Grade Level: 13-16
Age Level: Adults
Notes: Time, 180 min.

The ACT PEP program is designed to grant credit in college-level coursework for learning taking place outside the college as through advanced high school courses, service experience, correspondence courses, or home study. Based on exams, colleges may grant credit. The exams originated in the State of New York Regents College Degree program. They cover material similar to one- or 2-semester courses. This exam covers material taught in a 2-semester, 6-credit undergraduate course. Covers basic accounting concepts; accounting recording process; financial statements and analysis; accounting for assets, liabilities, owner's equity revenues, and expenses; manufacturing accounting; analysis for managerial decision making.

16542
ACT Proficiency Examination Program: Labor Relations. American College Testing Program, Iowa City, IA 1989
Descriptors: Adults; Adult Students; *Equivalency Tests; *External Degree Programs; Higher Education; *Labor Relations; *Special Degree Programs
Identifiers: ACT; American College Testing Program; PEP
Availability: ACT Proficiency Examination Program; P.O. Box 168, Iowa City, IA 52240
Grade Level: 13-16
Age Level: Adults
Notes: Time, 180 min.

The ACT PEP program is designed to grant credit in college-level coursework for learning taking place outside the college, as through advanced high school courses, service experience, correspondence courses, or home study. Based on exams, colleges may grant credit. The exams originated in the State of New York Regents College Degree program. They cover material similar to 1- or 2-semester courses. This exam covers knowledge of material from a 3-credit, 1-semester course, similar to those taken by business management majors. Covers U.S. labor relations, U.S. labor law, collective bargaining, contract administration, and miscellaneous topics.

16543
ACT Proficiency Examination Program: Organizational Behavior. American College Testing Program, Iowa City, IA 1989
Descriptors: Adults; Adult Students; Behavior Patterns; *Equivalency Tests; *External Degree Programs; *Group Behavior; Higher Education; Interpersonal Relationship; *Organizations (Groups); *Special Degree Programs
Identifiers: ACT; American College Testing Program; PEP
Availability: ACT Proficiency Examination Program; P.O. Box 168, Iowa City, IA 52240
Grade Level: 13-16

Age Level: Adults
Notes: Time, 180 min.

The ACT PEP program is designed to grant credit in college-level coursework for learning taking place outside the college, as through advanced high school courses, service experience, correspondence courses, or home study. Based on exams, colleges may grant credit. The exams originated in the State of New York Regents College Degree program. They cover material similar to 1- or 2-semester courses. This exam covers knowledge of materials from a 1-semester, 3-credit, undergraduate course. A knowledge of management principles is assumed. Covers individual behavior, group and interpersonal behavior, and organizational and intergroup behavior.

16544
ACT Proficiency Examination Program: Personal Management. American College Testing Program, Iowa City, IA 1989
Descriptors: Administrator Education; Adults; Adult Students; *Equivalency Tests; *External Degree Programs; Higher Education; Human Resources; Job Performance; Labor Relations; Managerial Occupations; *Personnel Management; *Special Degree Programs
Identifiers: ACT; American College Testing Program; PEP
Availability: ACT Proficiency Examination Program; P.O. Box 168, Iowa City, IA 52240
Grade Level: 13-16
Age Level: Adults
Notes: Time, 180 min.

The ACT PEP program is designed to grant credit in college-level coursework for learning taking place outside the college, as through advanced high school courses, service experience, correspondence courses, or home study. Based on exams, colleges may grant credit. The exams originated in the State of New York Regents College Degree program. They cover material similar to 1- or 2-semester courses. This exam covers material taught in a 1-semester, 3-credit, undergraduate course for management majors. Covers the role and context of personnel management, human resources planning and staffing, performance and the individual, compensation, and labor-management relations.

16545
ACT Proficiency Examination Program: Principles of Management. American College Testing Program, Iowa City, IA 1989
Descriptors: Administration; *Administrator Education; Adults; Adult Students; *Equivalency Tests; *External Degree Programs; Higher Education; Leadership; Management Development; Managerial Occupations; *Special Degree Programs
Identifiers: ACT; American College Testing Program; PEP
Availability: ACT Proficiency Examination Program; P.O. Box 168, Iowa City, IA 52240
Grade Level: 13-16
Age Level: Adults
Notes: Time, 180 min.

The ACT PEP program is designed to grant credit in college-level coursework for learning taking place outside the college, as through advanced high school courses, service experience, correspondence courses, or home study. Based on exams, colleges may grant credit. The exams originated in the State of New York Regents College Degree program. They cover material similar to 1- or 2-semester courses. This exam covers content taught in a 1-semester introductory course. Covers background of management thought, planning function, organizing, leading and influencing, controlling, special issues in management. Questions cover knowledge, comprehension, and application.

16546
ACT Proficiency Examination Program: Principles of Marketing. American College Testing Program, Iowa City, IA 1989
Descriptors: Adults; Adult Students; *Equivalency Tests; *External Degree Programs; Higher Education; *Marketing; *Special Degree Programs
Identifiers: ACT; American College Testing Program; PEP
Availability: ACT Proficiency Examination Program; P.O. Box 168, Iowa City, IA 52240
Grade Level: 13-16
Age Level: Adults
Notes: Time, 180 min.

The ACT PEP program is designed to grant credit in college-level coursework for learning taking place outside the college, as through advanced high school courses, service experience, correspondence courses, or home study. Based on exams, colleges may grant credit. The exams originated in the State of New York Regents College Degree program. They cover material similar to 1- or 2-semester courses. This exam covers knowledge of material taught in a 1-semester, 3-credit introductory course for business majors. Covers the role of marketing in the organization and society, analysis of markets, functional areas of marketing, and special topics.

16549
Advanced Placement Program; Economics, Microeconomics. College Entrance Examination Board, New York, NY 1989
Descriptors: *Advanced Placement Programs; *Economics; *Equivalency Tests; Higher Education; *High School Students; Secondary Education; *Student Placement
Identifiers: *Microeconomics
Availability: Advanced Placement Program; Educational Testing Service, Princeton, NJ 08541-6670
Grade Level: 11-12
Notes: Time, 90 min.

This test is part of a program to grant college credit or advanced placement into college level courses. These tests are intended for qualified students who are taking courses in secondary school similar to a 1-semester college course. Both multiple-choice questions and free-response items are included. This test covers basic economic concepts; nature and function of product markets; factor markets; efficiency, equity, and the role of government. Tests are administered at participating schools or at multischool test centers.

16550
Advanced Placement Program; Economics, Macroeconomics. College Entrance Examination Board, New York, NY 1989
Descriptors: *Advanced Placement Programs; *Economics; *Equivalency Tests; Higher Education; *High School Students; Secondary Education; *Student Placement
Identifiers: *Macroeconomics
Availability: Advanced Placement Program; Educational Testing Service, Princeton, NJ 08541-6670
Grade Level: 11-12
Notes: Time, 90 min.

This test is part of a program to grant college credit or advanced placement into college level courses. These tests are intended for qualified students who are taking courses in secondary school similar to a 1-semester college course. Both multiple-choice questions and free-response items are included. This test covers basic economic concepts; measurement of economic performance; national income and price determination; international economics and growth. Tests are administered at participating schools or at multischool test centers.

16551
Survey of AIDS Information. Goodwin, Megan P.; Roscoe, Bruce 1988
Descriptors: *Acquired Immune Deficiency Syndrome; Adults; *Attitude Measures; *College Students; Fear; Higher Education; *Homosexuality; *Knowledge Level; Objective Tests
Availability: *Journal of American College Health;* v36 p214-21, Jan 1988
Grade Level: 13-16
Age Level: Adults
Notes: Items, 49

True-false instrument to measure college students' knowledge and attitudes concerning Acquired Immunodeficiency Syndrome (AIDS). Consists of 3 sections: Knowledge of AIDS (32 items); fear of contracting AIDS (9 items); and attitudes toward homosexuality (8 items). Used to study if relationships exist between or among the 3 issues focused upon. Results may be used to assist educators in setting up programs concerning AIDS and programs educating about homosexuality.

16577
San Diego State University AIDS Survey. Winslow, Robert W. 1986
Descriptors: *Acquired Immune Deficiency Syndrome; Adults; *College Students; *Communicable Diseases; Higher Education; *Knowledge Level; Questionnaires
Identifiers: AIDS
Availability: Sociology and Social Research; v72 n2 p110-13, Jan 1988
Grade Level: 13-16
Notes: Items, 13

A 13-item questionnaire designed to measure college students' knowledge of how the Acquired Immunodeficiency Syndrome (AIDS) virus is transmitted. Items focus on perceived transmission of AIDS through casual contact, oral ingestion, saliva transmission, and sexual intercourse. Does not contain items concerning blood transfusions, shared needles, or homosexual contact. Information on factor analysis included.

16589
Ann Arbor Learning Inventory, Skill Level C. Vitale, Barbara Meister; Bullock, Waneta B. 1989
Subtests: Visual Discrimination Skills; Visual Motor Coordination Skills; Sequential Memory Skills; Auditory Discrimination Skills; Auditory Sequential Memory Skills; Comprehension Skills
Descriptors: Auditory Discrimination; Auditory Perception; Comprehension; *Diagnostic Tests; Elementary Education; Elementary School Students; *Learning Modalities; *Learning Problems; Listening Comprehension; Memory; Psychomotor Skills; Remedial Programs; Visual Discrimination
Availability: Academic Therapy Publications; 20 Commercial Blvd., Novato, CA 94949-6191
Grade Level: 5-8

This inventory is designed to determine an exact level of remediation for students who are not meeting basic requirements at their grade level. Measures student competencies, deficiencies, nature of deficiencies and allows instructor to select appropriate texts and remediation materials. Identifies strengths and weaknesses in the central processing areas. Contains 15 brief tests in one booklet. Also useful in indicating students' preferred learning modality. Additional levels are available for grades K-1 (Level A) and 2-4 (Level B).

16590
National Proficiency Survey Series, Algebra 1. Scannell, Dale P. 1989
Subtests: Basic Concepts; Exponents and Variables; Perform Operations with Real Numbers; Solve Equations; Algebraic Expressions/World Problems; Solve Inequalities and Graph Solution Sets; Computations with Polynominals; Factor Algebraic Expressions; Fractional/Proportional Ratio Equations; Graph and Solve Linear Equations; Function Values and Line Equations; Rational Expressions; Problems with Fractional Numbers; Quadratic Equations/Rational Square Roots; Central Tendency; Probability, and Graphs
Descriptors: *Achievement Tests; *Algebra; High Schools; *High School Students; *Mathematics Tests; Pretests Posttests
Identifiers: NPSS
Availability: Riverside Publishing Co.; 8420 Bryn Mawr Ave., Chicago, IL 60631
Grade Level: 9-12
Notes: Time, 40 min. approx.; Items, 39

Comprehensive evaluation of student proficiency in high school courses. Designed to meet normative and criterion-referenced testing requirements of selected departments of an individual school. Emphasizes current high school curriculum and measures what is taught. May be administered at beginning or end of course or both. Algebra I measures understanding of real numbers and variables and their operations in equations and inequalities.

16591
National Proficiency Survey Series, Algebra 2. Scannell, Dale P. 1989
Subtests: Basic Concepts; Real Number System; Inequalities/Graphing; Solution Sets; Lines and Linear Equations; Factor Polynomial Equations; Quadratic Equations/Functions; Linear and Quadratic Systems; Rational Equations; Irrational Expressions; Conic Sections; Number Series; Logarithms and Exponential Equations; Central Tendency
Descriptors: *Achievement Tests; *Algebra; High Schools; *High School Students; *Mathematics Tests; Pretests Posttests
Identifiers: NPSS
Availability: Riverside Publishing Co.; 8420 Bryn Mawr Ave., Chicago, IL 60631
Grade Level: 9-12
Notes: Time, 40 min. approx.; Items, 39

Comprehensive evaluation of student proficiency in high school courses. Designed to meet normative and criterion-referenced testing requirements of selected departments of an individual school. Emphasizes current high school curriculum and measures what is taught. May be administered at beginning or end of course or both. Algebra 2 measures an understanding of real numbers and polynomials, the solving of linear, quadratic, and trigonometric equations; and the graphing of functions.

16592
National Proficiency Survey Series, American Government. Scannell, Dale P. 1989
Subtests: Basic Concepts; Origins of American Government; Documents of American Government; Constitutional Amendments; Structure of Federal Government; Executive Powers; Cabinet Offices/Government Agencies; Congress; Judiciary Powers and Functions; How a Bill Becomes a Law; State and Local Governments; Function of Political Parties; Elections and Voting Requirements; Foreign Policy; Civil Rights and Liberties
Descriptors: *Achievement Tests; Governmental Structure; Government Role; High Schools; *High School Students; Pretests Posttests; *Social Studies; *United States Government (Course)
Identifiers: NPSS

Availability: Riverside Publishing Co.; 8420 Bryn Mawr Ave., Chicago, IL 60631
Grade Level: 9-12
Notes: Time, 40 min. approx.; Items, 45
Comprehensive evaluation of student proficiency in high school courses. Designed to meet normative and criterion-referenced testing requirements of selected departments of an individual school. Emphasizes current high school curriculum and measures what is taught. May be administered at beginning or end of course or both. American Government Survey measures information about state and federal governments, elections, and the Constitution.

16593
National Proficiency Survey Series, Biology.
Scannell, Dale P. 1989
Subtests: Basic Concepts; Cell Structure; Cell Function; Life Processes; Nucleic Acids/Protein Synthesis; Genetic Expression; Development/ Adaptation/Selection; Classification; Microorganisms; Plants; Invertebrates; Vertebrates; Human Biology; Experiments and Lab Equipment; Ecological Relationships
Descriptors: *Achievement Tests; *Biology; High Schools; *High School Students; Pretests Posttests; *Science Tests
Identifiers: NPSS
Availability: Riverside Publishing Co.; 8420 Bryn Mawr Ave., Chicago, IL 60631
Grade Level: 9-12
Notes: Time, 40 min. approx.; Items, 45
Comprehensive evaluation of student proficiency in high school courses. Designed to meet normative and criterion-referenced testing requirements of selected departments of an individual school. Emphasizes current high school curriculum and measures what is taught. May be administered at beginning or end of course or both. Biology Survey measures knowledge about the living world ranging from single-celled organisms to the human body.

16594
National Proficiency Survey Series, Chemistry.
Scannell, Dale P. 1989
Subtests: Basic Concepts; Measurement; Matter and Its Changes; Atomic Structure; Periodic Table; Chemical Bonding and Formulas; Equations and Mass Relationships; Gas Laws and Properties; Solutions/Mixtures/Ionizations; Acids and Bases; Carbon and Carbon Compounds; Chemical Reactions and Rates; Metals and Nonmetals; Chemical Equilibrium/Oxidation
Descriptors: *Achievement Tests; *Chemistry; High Schools; *High School Students; Pretests Posttests; *Science Tests
Identifiers: NPSS
Availability: Riverside Publishing Co.; 8420 Bryn Mawr Ave., Chicago, IL 60631
Grade Level: 9-12
Notes: Time, 40 min. approx.; Items, 42
Comprehensive evaluation of student proficiency in high school courses. Designed to meet normative and criterion-referenced testing requirements of selected departments of an individual school. Emphasizes current high school curriculum and measures what is taught. May be administered at beginning or end of course or both. Chemistry Survey measures understanding of atomic theory, the nature of matter, and its states.

16595
National Proficiency Survey Series, English IV.
Scannell, Dale P. 1989
Subtests: Coordination of Sentence Elements; Subordination of Sentence Elements; Combination of Sentences; Appropriateness of Style; Details/ Examples/Specific Language; Editing/Revising (Diction); Editing/Revising (Clarity); Organization/Structure (Controlling Idea); Organization/Structure (Support); Organization/ Structure (Arrangement); Organization/Structure (Relevancy); Analysis of Exposition (Purpose); Analysis of Exposition (Adequacy); Analysis of Exposition (Language)
Descriptors: *Achievement Tests; *English; High Schools; *High School Students; Language Skills; *Language Tests; Pretests Posttests
Identifiers: NPSS
Availability: Riverside Publishing Co.; 8420 Bryn Mawr Ave., Chicago, IL 60631
Grade Level: 9-12
Notes: Time, 40 min. approx.; Items, 42
Comprehensive evaluation of student proficiency in high school courses. Designed to meet normative and criterion-referenced testing requirements of selected departments of an individual school. Emphasizes current high school curriculum and measures what is taught. May be administered at beginning or end of course or both. The English IV Survey evaluates a student's ability to use language effectively to organize and support ideas.

16596
National Proficiency Survey Series, General Math.
Scannell, Dale P. 1989

Subtests: Basic Concepts; Operations with Fractions; Decimals and Percents; Equivalent Forms; Ratios and Proportions; Consumer Mathematics; Central Tendency and Probability; Calculations with Signed Numbers; Exponents and Variables; Graphs and Charts; Basic Geometry; Units of Measure; Perimeter of Polygons; Word Problems
Descriptors: *Achievement Tests; High Schools; *High School Students; *Mathematics Tests; Pretests Posttests; *Secondary School Mathematics
Identifiers: NPSS
Availability: Riverside Publishing Co.; 8420 Bryn Mawr Ave., Chicago, IL 60631
Grade Level: 9-12
Notes: Time, 40 min. approx.; Items, 42
Comprehensive evaluation of student proficiency in high school courses. Designed to meet normative and criterion-referenced testing requirements of selected departments of an individual school. Emphasizes current high school curriculum and measures what is taught. May be administered at beginning or end of course or both. General Mathematics measures computation skills with integers and the knowledge of basic geometric concepts.

16597
National Proficiency Survey Series, Geometry.
Scannell, Dale P. 1989
Subtests: Basic Concepts; Line Segment and Rays; Parallel Lines; Right Angles; Supplemental Angles; Similarity; Ratio and Proportion; Congruent Angles; Congruent Triangles; Polygons; Circles; Area; Volume
Descriptors: *Achievement Tests; *Geometry; High Schools; *High School Students; *Mathematics Tests; Pretests Posttests
Identifiers: NPSS
Availability: Riverside Publishing Co.; 8420 Bryn Mawr Ave., Chicago, IL 60631
Grade Level: 9-12
Notes: Time, 40 min. approx.; Items, 39
Comprehensive evaluation of student proficiency in high school courses. Designed to meet normative and criterion-referenced testing requirements of selected departments of an individual school. Emphasizes current high school curriculum and measures what is taught. May be administered at beginning or end of course or both. Geometry measures an understanding of the nature and relationship of points, lines, angles, planes, circles, polygons, and solids.

16598
National Proficiency Survey Series, Literature.
Scannell, Dale P. 1989
Subtests: Basic Concepts; Explicit Information; Implicit Information; Sequence of Events; Author's Purpose or Main Idea; Generalizations from Specific Details; Literary Techniques; Cause and Effect Relationships; Comparisons and Contrasts; Conclusions; Characterization; Paraphrasing Author's Words; Meaning of a Word from Context
Descriptors: *Achievement Tests; High Schools; *High School Students; *Literature; Pretests Posttests; Reading Comprehension
Identifiers: NPSS
Availability: Riverside Publishing Co.; 8420 Bryn Mawr Ave., Chicago, IL 60631
Grade Level: 9-12
Notes: Time, 40 min. approx.; Items, 39
Comprehensive evaluation of student proficiency in high school courses. Designed to meet normative and criterion-referenced testing requirements of selected departments of an individual school. Emphasizes current high school curriculum and measures what is taught. May be administered at beginning or end of course or both. Literature Survey draws from the works of a wide variety of authors and from different types of literature. This test evaluates literal and inferential comprehension.

16599
National Proficiency Survey Series, Physics.
Scannell, Dale P. 1989
Subtests: Basic Concepts; Measurement and Problem Solving; Nature/Type/Causes of Motion; Resolution/Composition of Forces; Conservation of Energy and Momentum; Types and States of Matter; Heat and Thermal Effects; Work and Energy; Nature of Sound; Nature of Light; Refraction and Diffraction; Magnetism; Electricity; Electromagnetic Waves; Atomic Structure/Nuclear Reactions
Descriptors: *Achievement Tests; High Schools; *High School Students; *Physics; Pretests Posttests; *Science Tests
Identifiers: NPSS
Availability: Riverside Publishing Co.; 8420 Bryn Mawr Ave., Chicago, IL 60631
Grade Level: 9-12
Notes: Time, 40 min. approx.; Items, 45

Comprehensive evaluation of student proficiency in high school courses. Designed to meet normative and criterion-referenced testing requirements of selected departments of an individual school. Emphasizes current high school curriculum and measures what is taught. May be administered at beginning or end of course or both. Physics Survey examines the nature of energy and the relationship between energy and matter from mechanics through nuclear reactions.

16600
National Proficiency Survey Series, U.S. History.
Scannell, Dale P. 1989
Subtests: Exploration of America; Colonization of America; Revolutionary War; Basic Tenets of the Constitution; Foreign Policy of the Early Republic; Westward Expansion; America from Jefferson to Jackson; Civil War; Industrialization of America; World War I; The 1920s and 1930s; World War II, Post War Year (1945-1960); Contemporary America
Descriptors: *Achievement Tests; High Schools; *High School Students; Pretests Posttests; *United States History
Identifiers: NPSS
Availability: Riverside Publishing Co.; 8420 Bryn Mawr Ave., Chicago, IL 60631
Grade Level: 9-12
Notes: Time, 40 min. approx.; Items, 42
Comprehensive evaluation of student proficiency in high school courses. Designed to meet normative and criterion-referenced testing requirements of selected departments of an individual school. Emphasizes current high school curriculum and measures what is taught. May be administered at beginning or end of course or both. U.S. history spans the period from early exploration to the present.

16601
National Proficiency Survey Series, World History.
Scannell, Dale P. 1989
Subtests: Basic Concepts; Beginnings of Civilization; Ancient Near East Civilizations; Ancient Greece; Roman Life; Middle Ages; Civilizations beyond Europe; Renaissance and Reformation; Ages of Exploration; Age of Enlightenment; World Geography; Industrial Age; Age of Imperialism; World Wars I and II; Contemporary Age
Descriptors: *Achievement Tests; Geography; High Schools; *High School Students; Pretests Posttests; *World History
Identifiers: NPSS
Availability: Riverside Publishing Co.; 8420 Bryn Mawr Ave., Chicago, IL 60631
Grade Level: 9-12
Notes: Time, 40 min. approx.; Items, 45
Comprehensive evaluation of student proficiency in high school courses. Designed to meet normative and criterion-referenced testing requirements of selected departments of an individual school. Emphasizes current high school curriculum and measures what is taught. May be administered at beginning or end of course or both. World history measures knowledge of world geography and historical information from early civilizations to the current age.

16602
National Proficiency Survey Series, Writing Fundamentals. Scannell, Dale P. 1989
Subtests: Meaning of Words in Context; Verb Tense; Diction; Sentence Clarity; Modification; Transition Words/Conjunctions; Punctuation Errors; Comma Usage; Capitalization; Vocabulary Development Skills
Descriptors: *Achievement Tests; Grammar; High Schools; *High School Students; Pretests Posttests; Vocabulary Skills; *Writing Skills
Identifiers: NPSS
Availability: Riverside Publishing Co.; 8420 Bryn Mawr Ave., Chicago, IL 60631
Grade Level: 9-12
Notes: Time, 40 min. approx.; Items, 66
Comprehensive evaluation of student proficiency in high school courses. Designed to meet normative and criterion-referenced testing requirements of selected departments of an individual school. Emphasizes current high school curriculum and measures what is taught. May be administered at beginning or end of course or both. Writing Fundamental Survey includes spelling and vocabulary in addition to grammar, usage, and mechanics. Two objectives measure the meaning of words and vocabulary development in specific academic subject areas.

16606
Utah Test of Language Development—3.
Mecham, Merlin J. 1989
Subtests: Language Comprehension; Language Expression

Descriptors: Children; Disabilities; Elementary Education; *Elementary School Students; English (Second Language); *Expressive Language; *Language Acquisition; *Language Skills; *Language Tests; *Receptive Language
Identifiers: Nonnative Speakers; UTLD 3
Availability: Pro-Ed; 8700 Shoal Creek Blvd., Austin, TX 78758
Age Level: 3-11
Notes: Time, 45 min.

This test is designed to measure receptive and expressive language skills in handicapped and nonhandicapped children. Used by speech pathologists, audiologists, and psychologists in clinical and educational settings. The UTLD-3 is norm-referenced and uses a developmental approach in that it assesses language milestones that emerge in a similar order across child populations. Can be used in research contexts to measure change from maturation or intervention. For use with English-speaking children where English or another language may be the primary language.

16607
Hausa Speaking Test. Center for Applied Linguistics, Washington, DC 1989
Subtests: Personal Conversation; Giving Directions; Picture Sequence Narration; Topical Discourse; Situational Discourse
Descriptors: *Achievement Tests; Adults; *Chad Languages; *Hausa; *Language Fluency; Language Skills; Language Tests; Oral Language; *Postsecondary Education; *Second Languages; *Speech Communication
Identifiers: HaST; Oral Tests
Availability: Center for Applied Linguistics; 1118 22nd St., N.W., Washington, DC 20037
Age Level: Adults
Notes: Time, 40 min.

This test was designed to evaluate the level of oral proficiency attained by English-speaking learners of the African language, Hausa. It is intended for use with postsecondary students and adults at intermediate and advanced levels. The test has 5 parts and is administered by a master test tape on a tape recorder. Responses to questions are recorded on a separate tape. Some of the questions are in English; others are given in Hausa. Pictures and text in a test booklet are used as test questions. The test is administered to students by institutions who acquire it from the Center for Applied Linguistics, or to individuals who contact the center to take the test. The HaST may be used for admission to an Hausa study program; placement within an Hausa study program; exemption from an Hausa language requirement; application for scholarship or appointment; competency testing on exit from an Hausa program; certification of language proficiency for occupational purposes; evaluation of an Hausa instructional program.

16608
Indonesian Speaking Test. Center for Applied Linguistics, Washington, DC 1989
Subtests: Personal Conversation; Giving Directions; Picture Sequence Narration; Topical Discourse; Situational Discourse
Descriptors: *Achievement Tests; Adults; *Indonesian; *Indonesian Languages; *Language Fluency; Language Skills; Language Tests; Malayo Polynesian Languages; Oral Language; *Postsecondary Education; *Second Languages; *Speech Communication
Identifiers: IST; Oral Tests
Availability: Center for Applied Linguistics; 1118 22nd St., N.W., Washington, DC 20037
Age Level: Adults
Notes: Time, 40 min.

This test was designed to evaluate the level of oral proficiency attained by English-speaking learners of Indonesian. It is intended for use with postsecondary students and adults at intermediate and advanced levels. The test has 5 parts and is administered by a master test tape on a tape recorder. Responses to questions are recorded on a separate tape. Some of the questions are in English; others are given in Indonesian. Pictures and text in a test booklet are used as test questions. The test is administered to students by institutions who acquire it from the Center for Applied Linguistics, or to individuals who contact the center to take the test. The Indonesian Speaking Test may be used for admission to an Indonesian study program; placement within an Indonesian study program; exemption from an Indonesian language requirement; application for scholarship or appointment; competency testing on exit from an Indonesian study program; certification of language proficiency for occupational purposes; evaluation of an Indonesian instructional program.

16609
Hebrew Speaking Test. Center for Applied Linguistics, Washington, DC 1989
Subtests: Personal Conversation; Giving Directions; Picture Sequence Narration; Topical Discourse; Situational Discourse
Descriptors: *Achievement Tests; Adults; *Hebrew; *Language Fluency; Language Skills; Language Tests; Oral Language; *Postsecondary Education; *Second Languages; Semitic Languages; *Speech Communication
Identifiers: HeST
Availability: Center for Applied Linguistics; 1118 22nd St., N.W., Washington, DC 20037
Age Level: Adults
Notes: Time, 40 min.

This test was designed to evaluate the level of oral proficiency attained by English-speaking learners of Hebrew. It is intended for use with postsecondary students and adults at intermediate and advanced levels. The test has 5 parts and is administered by a master test tape on a tape recorder. Responses to questions are recorded on a separate tape. Some of the questions are in English; others are given in Hebrew. Pictures and text in a test booklet are used as test questions. The test is administered to students by institutions who acquire it from the Center for Applied Linguistics, or to individuals who contact the center to take the test. The Hebrew Speaking Test may be used for admission to a Hebrew study program; placement within a Hebrew study program; exemption from a Hebrew language requirement; application for scholarship or appointment; competency testing on exit from a Hebrew study program; certification of language proficiency for occupational purposes; evaluation of a Hebrew instructional program.

16625
Test of Kindergarten/First Grade Readiness Skills. Codding, Karen Gardner 1987
Subtests: Reading; Spelling; Arithmetic
Descriptors: *Arithmetic; *Grade 1; *Kindergarten Children; Preschool Education; *Reading; *School Readiness Tests; *Spelling; *Young Children
Identifiers: SECA; TKFGRS
Availability: Children's Hospital of San Francisco; Publications Dept. OPR-714, P.O. Box 3805, San Francisco, CA 94119
Grade Level: K-1
Notes: Items, 96

Part of the Survey of Early Childhood Abilities developed to provide educational personnel and other professionals with a criterion to aid in determining a child's readiness for kindergarten and first grade. The survey also helps to determine areas of a child's low functioning. This tool assesses children's readiness skills in reading, spelling, and arithmetic. Remediation can be determined and implemented with the use of this instrument, if it is determined that a child has difficulty in one or more areas of readiness skills.

16633
Iowa Tests of Basic Skills, Form J, Level 5, Early Primary Battery. Hieronymus, A.N.; And Others 1989
Subtests: Listening; Word Analysis; Vocabulary; Language; Mathematics
Descriptors: *Achievement Tests; *Basic Skills; Elementary School Mathematics; *Elementary School Students; *Grade 1; *Individual Testing; Kindergarten; *Kindergarten Children; *Learning Readiness; Listening Skills; Norm Referenced Tests; *Primary Education; Vocabulary
Identifiers: ITBS; Test Batteries
Availability: Riverside Publishing Co.; 8420 Bryn Mawr Ave., Chicago, IL 60631
Grade Level: K-1
Age Level: 5
Notes: Time, 115 min. approx.; Items, 157

Assesses the development of early educational experiences in the basic skills: listening, prereading, vocabulary, language, and mathematics. Useful in determining readiness for learning and for diagnosing strengths and weaknesses in skill performance. All items are in multiple-choice format. All tests are administered orally and are untimed. Form J is a parallel form to Form G and H of the Iowa Test of Basic Skills.

16634
Iowa Tests of Basic Skills, Form J, Level 6, Early Primary Battery. Hieronymus, A.N.; And Others 1989
Subtests: Listening; Word Analysis; Vocabulary; Language; Mathematics; Reading
Descriptors: *Achievement Tests; *Basic Skills; Elementary School Mathematics; *Elementary School Students; *Grade 1; *Individual Testing; *Kindergarten Children; Language Arts; *Learning Readiness; Listening Skills; Norm Referenced Tests; *Primary Education; Reading Skills; Vocabulary
Identifiers: ITBS
Availability: Riverside Publishing; 8420 Bryn Mawr Ave., Chicago, IL 60631
Grade Level: K-1
Age Level: 6
Notes: Time, 160 min. approx.; Items, 216

Assesses the development of early educational experiences in the basic skills: listening, prereading, vocabulary, language, mathematics, and reading. Useful in determining readiness for learning and for diagnosing strengths and weaknesses in skill performance. All items are in multiple-choice format. All tests are administered orally and are untimed. Form J is a parallel form to Form G of the Iowa Tests of Basic Skills.

16635
Iowa Tests of Basic Skills, Primary Battery, Form J, Level 7. Hieronymus, A.N.; And Others
Subtests: Listening; Word Analysis; Vocabulary; Reading Comprehension (Pictures, Sentences, Stories); Spelling; Capitalization; Punctuation; Usage and Expression; Work Study Skills (Visual Materials, Reference Materials); Mathematics Concepts; Mathematics Problems; Mathematics Computation; Social Studies; Science
Descriptors: *Achievement Tests; *Basic Skills; Capitalization (Alphabetic); Elementary Education; Elementary School Mathematics; *Elementary School Students; *Grade 1; *Grade 2; Grammar; Listening Skills; Norm Referenced Tests; Punctuation; Reading Comprehension; Spelling; Study Skills; Vocabulary
Identifiers: ITBS
Availability: Riverside Publishing; 8420 Bryn Mawr Ave., Chicago, IL 60631
Grade Level: 1-2
Age Level: 7

Assesses student progress in the basic skills. Provides information about strengths and weaknesses in the instructional program and about skills performance. Published in 3 forms: Complete Battery (13 tests, 465 items, 227 minutes; approximately), Complete Battery Plus Social Studies and Science (15 tests, 539 items, 267 minutes; approximately), and Basic Battery (7 tests, 242 items, 134 minutes; approximately). Tests are in multiple-choice format and are untimed. Many of the tests are administered orally. Form J is a parallel form to Forms G and H of the Iowa Tests of Basic Skills.

16636
Iowa Tests of Basic Skills, Primary Battery, Form J, Level 8. Hieronymus, A.N.; And Others 1989
Subtests: Listening; Word Analysis; Vocabulary; Reading Comprehension (Pictures, Sentences, Stories); Spelling; Capitalization; Punctuation; Usage and Expression; Work Study Skills (Visual Materials, Reference Materials); Mathematics Concepts; Mathematics Problems; Mathematics Computation; Social Studies; Science
Descriptors: *Achievement Tests; *Basic Skills; Capitalization (Alphabetic); Elementary Education; Elementary School Mathematics; *Elementary School Students; *Grade 2; *Grade 3; Grammar; Listening Skills; Norm Referenced Tests; Punctuation; Reading Comprehension; Spelling; Study Skills; Vocabulary
Identifiers: ITBS
Availability: Riverside Publishing; 8420 Bryn Mawr Ave., Chicago, IL 60631
Grade Level: 2-3
Age Level: 8

Assesses student progress in the basic skills. Provides information about strengths and weaknesses in the instructional program and about skills performance. Published in 3 forms: Complete Battery (13 tests, 513 items, 227 minutes; approximately), Complete Battery Plus Social Studies and Science (15 tests, 587 items, 267 minutes; approximately), and Basic Battery (7 tests, 266 items, 134 minutes; approximately). Tests are in multiple-choice format and are untimed. Many of the tests are administered orally. Form J is a parallel form to Forms G and H of the Iowa Tests of Basic Skills.

16637
Iowa Tests of Basic Skills, Form J, Multilevel Battery, Level 9-14. Hieronymus, A.N.; And Others 1989
Subtests: Vocabulary; Reading; Spelling; Capitalization; Punctuation; Usage and Expression; Visual Materials; Reference Materials; Math Concepts; Math Problems; Math Computation; Social Studies; Science
Descriptors: *Achievement Tests; *Basic Skills; Capitalization (Alphabetic); *Elementary School Students; Elementary Secondary Education; Grammar; *Junior High School Students; Mathematics; Punctuation; Reading Comprehension; Sciences; Social Studies; Spelling; Study Skills; Vocabulary
Identifiers: ITBS
Availability: Riverside Publishing; 8420 Bryn Mawr Ave., Chicago, IL 60631
Grade Level: 3-9

Assesses student progress in the basic skills. Provides information about strengths and weaknesses in the instructional program and about skills performance. Published in

3 forms: Complete Battery (13 tests, 256 minutes), Basic Battery (6 tests, 135 minutes), Complete Battery Plus Social Studies and Science (15 tests, 326 minutes). Tests are multiple-choice. Form J is a parallel for to Forms G and H of the Iowa Tests of Basic Skills.

16648
Children's Handwriting Evaluation Scale for Manuscript Writing. Phelps, Joanne; Stempel, Lynn 1987
Descriptors: Children; *Diagnostic Tests; *Grade 1; *Grade 2; *Handwriting; *Manuscript Writing (Handlettering); *Primary Education
Identifiers: CHESM
Availability: Texas Scottish Rite Hospital for Crippled Children; 2222 Welborn St., Dallas, TX 75219
Grade Level: 1-2

Children's Handwriting Evaluation Scale-Manuscript (CHES-M) scoring standards are based on 643 students in grades one and 2 in Dallas (Texas) County Schools. These are rate scales to identify those children whose copying rates reflect blockage. Quality standards are defined and delineated. The reliability of objective scoring is based on a comparison of judgments of 3 independent raters. The CHES-M consists of 2 sentences, widely separated on a page of unlined paper. The test can be given to a group or an individual. The CHES-M has 57 letters. It includes all the letters of the alphabet except i, q, v, x, and z. Children are read the passage and told to copy it, writing as they usually do and as well as they can. If they finish before 2 minutes are up, they are asked to start again. At the end of 2 minutes, the test is stopped.

16654
Test of Academic Performance. Adams, Wayne; And Others 1989
Subtests: Mathematics; Spelling; Reading; Word Recognition; Reading Comprehension; Written Composition; Copying Rate
Descriptors: *Achievement Tests; *Clinical Diagnosis; *Elementary School Students; Elementary Secondary Education; Language Skills; *Learning Disabilities; Mathematics; Reading; Reading Comprehension; *Screening Tests; *Secondary School Students; Spelling; Word Recognition; Writing (Composition)
Identifiers: TAP; Writing Speed
Availability: Psychological Corp.; 555 Academic Ct., San Antonio, TX 78204-0952
Grade Level: K-12
Notes: Time, 40 min.

Designed for use by educators and psychologists who work with children in a clinical setting, to quickly estimate a student's level of academic achievement. Measures achievement in ways used in the classroom, including spelling dictation, mathematics computation, and reading decoding and comprehension. Includes 2 optional measures of written language. All tests except Reading Recognition and Reading Comprehension are group administered. These subtests are administered orally. Standardized on a representative sample of students aged 5.5 to 18. Scores are converted to scaled scores, NCEs, grade equivalents, percentiles, standard scores, and stanines.

16655
AIDS Information and Opinion Survey. Rhodes, Fen; Wolitslci, Richard J.
Subtests: Personal Vulnerability; Perception of Social Norms; Desire for AIDS Information; Severity of Disease; Prevention Effectiveness
Descriptors: *Acquired Immune Deficiency Syndrome; Adolescents; Adults; *Attitude Measures; College Students; High School Students; *Knowledge Level; Likert Scales; Spanish; Surveys
Identifiers: TIM(P)
Availability: Tests in Microfiche; Test Collection, Educational Testing Service, Princeton, NJ 08541
Age Level: 13-65

This scale is designed to measure attitudes toward and knowledge about AIDS. Uses Likert-type agree/disagree scale for attitude survey and 5-point true-false scales for knowledge portion. A Spanish language version is included. Norms in the form of mean scores can be located in the *Journal of American College Health;* v37, p266-71, May 1989. Reliabilities for attitude subscales range from .54 to .77. For the Knowledge test, reliability was .85.

16692
Basic English Skills Test, Form C. Center for Applied Linguistics, Washington, DC 1989
Subtests: Listening Comprehension; Communication; Fluency; Pronunciation; Reading; Writing
Descriptors: Adults; *English (Second Language); *Knowledge Level; *Language Proficiency; Limited English Speaking; Listening Comprehension; Oral English; Reading Tests; Speech Communication; *Standardized Tests; *Vocational English (Second Language); Writing Evaluation
Identifiers: BEST

Availability: Basic English Skills Test; Center for Applied Linguistics, 1118 22nd St. NW, Washington, DC 20037
Age Level: Adults
Notes: Time, 75 min. approx.

A measurement tool designed for adult English-as-a-Second-Language (ESL) learners at the survival and preemployment skills level. Uses real life materials and tasks to measure student performance of basic language competencies. Can be used for placement, progress monitoring, diagnosis, screening, and progress evaluation. Contains 2 separate components: an Oral Interview Section and a Literacy Skills Section, which together provide 6 separate language skills scores.

16696
Test of Achievement and Proficiency, Level 15, Form J. Scannell, Dale P.; And Others 1990
Subtests: Reading Comprehension; Mathematics; Written Expression; Using Sources of Information; Social Studies; Science; Applied Proficiency Skills
Descriptors: *Achievement Tests; *Basic Skills; *Grade 9; High Schools; *High School Students; Reading Comprehension; Sciences; Secondary Education; Secondary School Mathematics; Social Studies
Identifiers: TAP
Availability: Riverside Publishing; 8420 Bryn Mawr Ave., Chicago, IL 60631
Grade Level: 9
Notes: Time, 240 min. approx.; Items, 344

Assesses high school students' progress in the basic skill and basic curricular areas. Form J is a parallel form to the TAP, Forms G and H. The Basic Battery includes Reading Comprehension, Mathematics, Written Expression, and Using Sources of Information. The Complete Battery also includes Social Studies and Science. Optional Writing and Listening Tests are also available with Form J. Norms are available. Level 15 was developed for grade 9. The Complete Battery consists of 344 items. The Basic Battery consists of 229 items.

16697
Test of Achievement and Proficiency, Level 16, Form J. Scannell, Dale P.; And Others 1990
Subtests: Reading Comprehension; Mathematics; Written Expression; Using Sources of Information; Social Studies; Science; Writing; Listening; Applied Proficiency Skills
Descriptors: *Achievement Tests; *Basic Skills; *Grade 10; High Schools; *High School Students; Listening Comprehension; Reading Comprehension; Sciences; Secondary Education; Secondary School Mathematics; Social Studies; Writing (Composition)
Identifiers: TAP
Availability: Riverside Publishing; 8420 Bryn Mawr Ave., Chicago, IL 60631
Grade Level: 10
Notes: Time, 240 min. approx.; Items, 351

Assesses high school students' progress in the basic skill and basic curricular areas. Form J is a parallel form to the TAP, Forms G and H. The Basic Battery includes Reading Comprehension, Mathematics, Written Expression, and Using Sources of Information. The Complete Battery also includes Social Studies and Science. Optional Writing and Listening Tests are also available with Form J. Norms are available. Level 16 was developed for grade 10. The Complete Battery consists of 351 items. The Basic Battery consists of 235 items.

16698
Test of Achievement and Proficiency, Level 17, Form J. Scannell, Dale P.; And Others 1990
Subtests: Reading Comprehension; Mathematics; Written Expression; Using Sources of Information; Social Studies; Science; Writing; Listening; Applied Proficiency Skills
Descriptors: *Achievement Tests; *Basic Skills; *Grade 11; High Schools; *High School Students; Listening Comprehension; Reading Comprehension; Sciences; Secondary Education; Secondary School Mathematics; Social Studies; Writing (Composition)
Identifiers: TAP
Availability: Riverside Publishing; 8420 Bryn Mawr Ave., Chicago, IL 60631
Grade Level: 11
Notes: Time, 240 min. approx.; Items, 357

Assesses high school students' progress in the basic skill and basic curricular areas. Form J is a parallel form to the TAP, Forms G and H. The Basic Battery includes Reading Comprehension, Mathematics, Written Expression, and Using Sources of Information. The Complete Battery also includes Social Studies and Science. Optional Writing and Listening Tests are also available with Form J. Norms are available. Level 17 was developed for grade 11. The Complete Battery consists of 357 items. The Basic Battery consists of 241 items.

16699
Test of Achievement and Proficiency, Level 18, Form J. Scannell, Dale P.; And Others 1990
Subtests: Reading Comprehension; Mathematics; Written Expression; Using Sources of Information; Social Studies; Science; Writing; Listening; Applied Proficiency Skills
Descriptors: *Achievement Tests; *Basic Skills; *Grade 12; High Schools; *High School Seniors; *High School Students; Listening Comprehension; Reading Comprehension; Sciences; Secondary Education; Secondary School Mathematics; Social Studies; Writing (Composition)
Identifiers: TAP
Availability: Riverside Publishing; 8420 Bryn Mawr Ave., Chicago, IL 60631
Grade Level: 12
Notes: Time, 240 min. approx.; Items, 361

Assesses high school students' progress in the basic skill and basic curricular areas. Form J is a parallel form to the TAP, Forms G and H. The Basic Battery includes Reading Comprehension, Mathematics, Written Expression, and Using Sources of Information. The Complete Battery also includes Social Studies and Science. Optional Writing and Listening Tests are also available with Form J. Norms are available. Level 18 was developed for grade 12. The Complete Battery consists of 361 items. The Basic Battery consists of 245 items.

16705
Bankson Language Test—2. Bankson, Nicholas W. 1990
Subtests: Semantic Knowledge; Morphological and Syntactical Rules
Descriptors: Diagnostic Tests; *Expressive Language; *Individual Testing; *Language Tests; Norm Referenced Tests; *Young Children
Identifiers: BLT
Availability: PRO-ED; 8700 Shoal Creek Blvd., Austin, TX 78758-6897
Age Level: 3-9
Notes: Time, 30 min. approx.; Items, 120

Norm-referenced measure primarily designed to assess children's expressive language. Individually administered measure. There are 20 sections, each with 6 items. Test has 2 subtests (semantic knowledge and morphological and syntactic rules) plus one optional subtest (pragmatic knowledge). Semantic knowledge subtest assesses vocabulary knowledge in its expressive form and also provides the opportunity to observe receptive behavior, which is not scored. The Morphological and Syntactic Rules subtest assesses language form. The optional subtest reflects language usage and assesses whether content and form are employed in appropriate social contexts. Test has 3 major uses: as a norm-referenced survey of language skills, as a brief diagnostic inventory of the three areas, and in research studies involving young children.

16707
Pre-IPT: Spanish. Williams, Constance O.; Dalton, Enrique F. 1989
Descriptors: Comprehension; Expressive Language; *Individual Testing; *Language Proficiency; *Language Tests; Norm Referenced Tests; *Oral Language; *Preschool Children; Receptive Language; *Spanish; *Spanish Speaking; Syntax; Vocabulary
Availability: Ballard and Tighe, Inc.; 480 Atlas St., Brea, CA 92621
Age Level: 3-5

Used to assess 4 basic areas of Spanish oral language proficiency: vocabulary, comprehension, syntax, and verbal expression. Is individually administered. Children advance by levels (A-E) until the test is completed or stop at a proficiency level as indicated by information provided by scores at the end of each level. Assesses language in a holistic and natural way. Can be used in bilingual education as well as English-as-a-Second-Language classes for children whose primary language is Spanish.

16709
Comprehensive Tests of Basic Skills, Fourth Edition, Level K. CTB/Macmillan/McGraw-Hill, Monterey, CA 1989
Subtests: Reading; Mathematics
Descriptors: *Achievement Tests; *Basic Skills; Criterion Referenced Tests; *Kindergarten Children; Mathematics; Norm Referenced Tests; Primary Education; Reading
Identifiers: CTBS
Availability: CTB/MacMillan/McGraw-Hill; Del Monte Research Park, 2500 Garden Rd., Monterey, CA 93940
Grade Level: K
Notes: Time, 80 min.; Items, 123

Achievement tests which measure the basic skills of reading, language, spelling, mathematics, study skills, science, and social studies. Eleven levels cover kindergarten through grade 12. Three separate formats, Complete Battery, Survey, and Benchmark, are available. All formats place achievement on the same normative scale and results can be directly compared. Complete Battery has 2 forms at each of the levels and includes all areas. A Basic Skills Battery, consisting only of the areas of Reading, Spelling, Language, Mathematics, and Study Skills, is available at Level 12 and above. Survey Tests are for those test users who need only a quick survey of achievement levels, have no need for curriculum-referenced information, and for whom testing time is the major consideration. Survey Tests have the same basic content as the Complete Battery, are about half as long, and take about half the time to administer. Benchmark Tests are for users who want only norm-referenced scores of the highest degree of accuracy and have no need for curricular-referenced information. Benchmark Tests have the same basic content structures as the Complete Battery and are about the same length. Level K covers kindergarten.

16710
Comprehensive Tests of Basic Skills, Fourth Edition, Level 10. CTB/Macmillan/McGraw-Hill, Monterey, CA 1989
Subtests: Reading; Mathematics
Descriptors: *Achievement Tests; *Basic Skills; Criterion Referenced Tests; *Grade 1; *Kindergarten Children; Mathematics; Norm Referenced Tests; Primary Education; Reading
Identifiers: CTBS
Availability: CTB/Macmillan/McGraw-Hill; Del Monte Research Park, 2500 Garden Rd., Monterey, CA 93940
Grade Level: K-1
Notes: Time, 82 min. approx.; Items, 114
Achievement tests that measure the basic skills of reading, language, spelling, mathematics, study skills, science, and social studies. Eleven levels cover kindergarten through grade 12. Three separate formats, Complete Battery, Survey, and Benchmark, are available. All formats place achievement on the same normative scale and results can be directly compared. Complete Battery has 2 forms at each of the levels and includes all areas. A Basic Skills Battery, consisting only of the areas of Reading, Spelling, Language, Mathematics, and Study Skills, is available at Level 12 and above. Survey Tests are for those test users who need only a quick survey of achievement levels, have no need for curriculum-referenced information, and for whom testing time is the major consideration. Survey Tests have the same basic content as the Complete Battery, are about half as long, and take about half the time to administer. Benchmark Tests are for users who want only norm-referenced scores of the highest degree of accuracy and have no need for curricular-referenced information. Benchmark Tests have the same basic content structures as the Complete Battery and are about the same length. Level 10 covers kindergarten and grade one.

16711
Comprehensive Tests of Basic Skills, Fourth Edition, Level 11. CTB/Macmillan/McGraw-Hill, Monterey, CA 1989
Subtests: Reading; Mathematics; Language; Science; Social Studies
Descriptors: *Achievement Tests; *Basic Skills; Criterion Referenced Tests; *Elementary School Students; *Grade 1; *Grade 2; Language; Mathematics; Norm Referenced Tests; Primary Education; Reading; Sciences; Social Studies
Identifiers: CTBS
Availability: CTB/Macmillan/McGraw-Hill; Del Monte Research Park, 2500 Garden Rd., Monterey, CA 93940
Grade Level: 1-2
Notes: Time, 215 min. approx.; Items, 261
Achievement tests that measure the basic skills of reading, language, spelling, mathematics, study skills, science, and social studies. Eleven levels cover kindergarten through grade 12. Three separate formats, Complete Battery, Survey, and Benchmark, are available. All formats place achievement on the same normative scale and results can be directly compared. Complete Battery has 2 forms at each of the levels and includes all areas. A Basic Skills Battery, consisting only of the areas of Reading, Spelling, Language, Mathematics, and Study Skills, is available at Level 12 and above. Survey Tests are for those test users who need only a quick survey of achievement levels, have no need for curriculum-referenced information, and for whom testing time is the major consideration. Survey Tests have the same basic content as the Complete Battery, are about half as long, and take about half the time to administer. Benchmark Tests are for users who want only norm-referenced scores of the highest degree of accuracy and have no need for curricular-referenced information. Benchmark Tests have the same basic content structures as the Complete Battery and are about the same length. Level 11 covers grades one and 2.

16712
Comprehensive Tests of Basic Skills, Fourth Edition, Level 12. CTB/Macmillan/McGraw-Hill, Monterey, CA 1989
Subtests: Reading; Mathematics; Spelling; Language; Science; Social Studies

Descriptors: *Achievement Tests; *Basic Skills; Criterion Referenced Tests; *Elementary School Students; *Grade 1; *Grade 2; *Grade 3; Language; Mathematics; Norm Referenced Tests; Primary Education; Reading; Sciences; Social Studies; Spelling
Identifiers: CTBS
Availability: CTB/MacMillan/McGraw-Hill; Del Monte Research Park, 2500 Garden Rd., Monterey, CA 93940
Grade Level: 1-3
Notes: Time, 255 min. approx.; Items, 310
Achievement tests that measure the basic skills of reading, language, spelling, mathematics, study skills, science, and social studies. Eleven levels cover kindergarten through grade 12. Three separate formats, Complete Battery, Survey, and Benchmark, are available. All formats place achievement on the same normative scale and results can be directly compared. Complete Battery has 2 forms at each of the levels and includes all areas. A Basic Skills Battery, consisting only of the areas of Reading, Spelling, Language, Mathematics, and Study Skills, is available at Level 12 and above. Survey Tests are for those test users who need only a quick survey of achievement levels, have no need for curriculum-referenced information, and for whom testing time is the major consideration. Survey Tests have the same basic content as the Complete Battery, are about half as long, and take about half the time to administer. Benchmark Tests are for users who want only norm-referenced scores of the highest degree of accuracy and have no need for curricular-referenced information. Benchmark Tests have the same basic content structures as the Complete Battery and are about the same length. Level 12 covers grades 1, 2, and 3.

16713
Comprehensive Tests of Basic Skills, Fourth Edition, Level 13. CTB/Macmillan/McGraw-Hill, Monterey, CA 1989
Subtests: Reading; Mathematics; Spelling; Language; Science; Social Studies
Descriptors: *Achievement Tests; *Basic Skills; Criterion Referenced Tests; Elementary Education; *Elementary School Students; Grade 2; Grade 3; Grade 4; Language; Mathematics; Norm Referenced Tests; Reading; Sciences; Social Studies; Spelling
Identifiers: CTBS
Availability: CTB/MacMillan/McGraw-Hill; Del Monte Research Park, 2500 Garden Rd., Monterey, CA 93940
Grade Level: 2-4
Notes: Time, 291 min. approx.; Items, 349
Achievement tests that measure the basic skills of reading, language, spelling, mathematics, study skills, science, and social studies. Eleven levels cover kindergarten through grade 12. Three separate formats, Complete Battery, Survey, and Benchmark, are available. All formats place achievement on the same normative scale and results can be directly compared. Complete Battery has 2 forms at each of the levels and includes all areas. A Basic Skills Battery, consisting only of the areas of Reading, Spelling, Language, Mathematics, and Study Skills, is available at Level 12 and above. Survey Tests are for those test users who need only a quick survey of achievement levels, have no need for curriculum-referenced information, and for whom testing time is the major consideration. Survey Tests have the same basic content as the Complete Battery, are about half as long, and take about half the time to administer. Benchmark Tests are for users who want only norm-referenced scores of the highest degree of accuracy and have no need for curricular-referenced information. Benchmark Tests have the same basic content structures as the Complete Battery and are about the same length. Level 13 covers grades 2, 3, and 4.

16714
Comprehensive Tests of Basic Skills, Fourth Edition, Level 14. CTB/Macmillan/McGraw-Hill, Monterey, CA 1989
Subtests: Reading; Mathematics; Spelling; Language; Study Skills; Science; Social Studies
Descriptors: *Achievement Tests; *Basic Skills; Criterion Referenced Tests; Elementary Education; *Elementary School Students; Grade 3; Grade 4; Grade 5; Language; Mathematics; Norm Referenced Tests; Reading; Sciences; Social Studies; Spelling; Study Skills
Identifiers: CTBS
Availability: CTB/MacMillan/McGraw-Hill; Del Monte Research Park, 2500 Garden Rd., Monterey, CA 93940
Grade Level: 3-5
Notes: Time, 314 min. approx.; Items, 410
Achievement tests that measure the basic skills of reading, language, spelling, mathematics, study skills, science, and social studies. Eleven levels cover kindergarten through grade 12. Three separate formats, Complete Battery, Survey, and Benchmark, are available. All formats place achievement on the same normative scale and results can be directly compared. Complete Battery has 2 forms at each of the levels and includes all areas. A Basic Skills Battery, consisting only of the areas of Reading, Spelling,

Language, Mathematics, and Study Skills, is available at Level 12 and above. Survey Tests are for those test users who need only a quick survey of achievement levels, have no need for curriculum-referenced information, and for whom testing time is the major consideration. Survey Tests have the same basic content as the Complete Battery, are about half as long, and take about half the time to administer. Benchmark Tests are for users who want only norm-referenced scores of the highest degree of accuracy and have no need for curricular-referenced information. Benchmark Tests have the same basic content structures as the Complete Battery and are about the same length. Level 14 covers grades 3, 4, and 5.

16715
Comprehensive Tests of Basic Skills, Fourth Edition, Level 15. CTB/Macmillan/McGraw-Hill, Monterey, CA 1989
Subtests: Reading; Mathematics; Spelling; Language; Study Skills; Science; Social Studies
Descriptors: *Achievement Tests; *Basic Skills; Criterion Referenced Tests; Elementary Education; *Elementary School Students; Grade 4; Grade 5; Grade 6; *Intermediate Grades; Language; Mathematics; Norm Referenced Tests; Reading; Sciences; Social Studies; Spelling; Study Skills
Identifiers: CTBS
Availability: CTB/MacMillan/McGraw-Hill; Del Monte Research Park, 2500 Garden Rd., Monterey, CA 93940
Grade Level: 4-6
Notes: Time, 314 min. approx.; Items, 410
Achievement tests that measure the basic skills of reading, language, spelling, mathematics, study skills, science, and social studies. Eleven levels cover kindergarten through grade 12. Three separate formats, Complete Battery, Survey, and Benchmark, are available. All formats place achievement on the same normative scale and results can be directly compared. Complete Battery has 2 forms at each of the levels and includes all areas. A Basic Skills Battery, consisting only of the areas of Reading, Spelling, Language, Mathematics, and Study Skills, is available at Level 12 and above. Survey Tests are for those test users who need only a quick survey of achievement levels, have no need for curriculum-referenced information, and for whom testing time is the major consideration. Survey Tests have the same basic content as the Complete Battery, are about half as long, and take about half the time to administer. Benchmark Tests are for users who want only norm-referenced scores of the highest degree of accuracy and have no need for curricular referenced-information. Benchmark Tests have the same basic content structures as the Complete Battery and are about the same length. Level 15 covers grades 4, 5, and 6.

16716
Comprehensive Tests of Basic Skills, Fourth Edition, Level 16. CTB/Macmillan/McGraw-Hill, Monterey, CA 1989
Subtests: Reading; Mathematics; Spelling; Language; Study Skills; Science; Social Studies
Descriptors: *Achievement Tests; *Basic Skills; Criterion Referenced Tests; *Elementary School Students; Elementary Secondary Education; Grade 5; Grade 6; Grade 7; *Intermediate Grades; Language; Mathematics; Norm Referenced Tests; Reading; Sciences; Social Studies; Spelling; Study Skills
Identifiers: CTBS
Availability: CTB/MacMillan/McGraw-Hill; Del Monte Research Park, 2500 Garden Rd., Monterey, CA 93940
Grade Level: 5-7
Notes: Time, 314 min. approx.; Items, 410
Achievement tests that measure the basic skills of reading, language, spelling, mathematics, study skills, science, and social studies. Eleven levels cover kindergarten through grade 12. Three separate formats, Complete Battery, Survey, and Benchmark, are available. All formats place achievement on the same normative scale and results can be directly compared. Complete Battery has 2 forms at each of the levels and includes all areas. A Basic Skills Battery, consisting only of the areas of Reading, Spelling, Language, Mathematics, and Study Skills, is available at Level 12 and above. Survey Tests are for those test users who need only a quick survey of achievement levels, have no need for curriculum-referenced information, and for whom testing time is the major consideration. Survey Tests have the same basic content as the Complete Battery, are about half as long, and take about half the time to administer. Benchmark Tests are for users who want only norm-referenced scores of the highest degree of accuracy and have no need for curricular-referenced information. Benchmark Tests have the same basic content structures as the Complete Battery and are about the same length. Level 16 covers grades 5, 6, and 7.

16717
Comprehensive Tests of Basic Skills, Fourth Edition, Level 17/18. CTB/Macmillan/McGraw-Hill, Monterey, CA 1989
Subtests: Reading; Mathematics; Spelling; Language; Study Skills; Science; Social Studies

Descriptors: *Achievement Tests; *Basic Skills; Criterion Referenced Tests; *Elementary School Students; Elementary Secondary Education; Grade 6; Grade 7; Grade 8; Grade 9; *Junior High School Students; Language; Mathematics; Norm Referenced Tests; Reading; Sciences; Social Studies; Spelling; Study Skills
Identifiers: CTBS
Availability: CTB/MacMillan/McGraw-Hill; Del Monte Research Park, 2500 Garden Rd., Monterey, CA 93940
Grade Level: 6-9
Notes: Time, 314 min. approx.; Items, 410

Achievement tests that measure the basic skills of reading, language, spelling, mathematics, study skills, science, and social studies. Eleven levels cover kindergarten through grade 12. Three separate formats, Complete Battery, Survey, and Benchmark, are available. All formats place achievement on the same normative scale and results can be directly compared. Complete Battery has 2 forms at each of the levels and includes all areas. A Basic Skills Battery, consisting only of the areas of Reading, Spelling, Language, Mathematics, and Study Skills, is available at Level 12 and above. Survey Tests are for those test users who need only a quick survey of achievement levels, have no need for curriculum-referenced information, and for whom testing time is the major consideration. Survey Tests have the same basic content as the Complete Battery, are about half as long, and take about half the time to administer. Benchmark Tests are for users who want only norm-referenced scores of the highest degree of accuracy and have no need for curricular-referenced information. Benchmark Tests have the same basic content structures as the Complete Battery and are about the same length. Level 17/18 covers grades 6, 7, 8, and 9.

16718
Comprehensive Tests of Basic Skills, Fourth Edition, Level 19/20. CTB/MacMillan/McGraw-Hill, Monterey, CA 1989
Subtests: Reading; Mathematics; Spelling; Language; Study Skills; Science; Social Studies
Descriptors: *Achievement Tests; *Basic Skills; Criterion Referenced Tests; Grade 8; Grade 9; Grade 10; Grade 11; *High School Students; Language; Mathematics; Norm Referenced Tests; Reading; Sciences; Secondary Education; *Secondary School Students; Social Studies; Spelling; Study Skills
Identifiers: CTBS
Availability: CTB/MacMillan/McGraw-Hill; Del Monte Research Park, 2500 Garden Rd., Monterey, CA 93940
Grade Level: 8-11
Notes: Time, 314 min. approx.; Items, 410

Achievement tests that measure the basic skills of reading, language, spelling, mathematics, study skills, science, and social studies. Eleven levels cover kindergarten through grade 12. Three separate formats, Complete Battery, Survey, and Benchmark, are available. All formats place achievement on the same normative scale and results can be directly compared. Complete Battery has 2 forms at each of the levels and includes all areas. A Basic Skills Battery, consisting only of the areas of Reading, Spelling, Language, Mathematics, and Study Skills, is available at Level 12 and above. Survey Tests are for those test users who need only a quick survey of achievement levels, have no need for curriculum-referenced information, and for whom testing time is the major consideration. Survey Tests have the same basic content as the Complete Battery, are about half as long, and take about half the time to administer. Benchmark Tests are for users who want only norm-referenced scores of the highest degree of accuracy and have no need for curricular-referenced information. Benchmark Tests have the same basic content structures as the Complete Battery and are about the same length. Level 19/20 covers grades 8, 9, 10, and 11.

16719
Comprehensive Tests of Basic Skills, Fourth Edition, Level 21/22. CTB/MacMillan/McGraw-Hill, Monterey, CA 1989
Subtests: Reading; Mathematics; Spelling; Language; Study Skills; Science; Social Studies
Descriptors: *Achievement Tests; *Basic Skills; Criterion Referenced Tests; Grade 10; Grade 11; Grade 12; High Schools; *High School Students; Language; Mathematics; Norm Referenced Tests; Reading; Sciences; Secondary Education; Social Studies; Spelling; Study Skills
Identifiers: CTBS
Availability: CTB/MacMillan/McGraw-Hill; Del Monte Research Park, 2500 Garden Rd., Monterey, CA 93940
Grade Level: 10-12
Notes: Time, 314 min. approx.; Items, 410

Achievement tests that measure the basic skills of reading, language, spelling, mathematics, study skills, science, and social studies. Eleven levels cover kindergarten through grade 12. Three separate formats, Complete Battery, Survey, and Benchmark, are available. All formats place achievement on the same normative scale and results can be directly compared. Complete Battery has 2 forms at

each of the levels and includes all areas. A Basic Skills Battery, consisting only of the areas of Reading, Spelling, Language, Mathematics, and Study Skills, is available at Level 12 and above. Survey Tests are for those test users who need only a quick survey of achievement levels, have no need for curriculum-referenced information, and for whom testing time is the major consideration. Survey Tests have the same basic content as the Complete Battery, are about half as long, and take about half the time to administer. Benchmark Tests are for users who want only norm-referenced scores of the highest degree of accuracy and have no need for curricular-referenced information. Benchmark Tests have the same basic content structures as the Complete Battery and are about the same length. Level 21/22 covers grades 10, 11, and 12.

16722
ESL/Adult Literacy Scale. Roddy, Michael 1989
Subtests: Listening; Grammar; Life Skills; Reading; Composition
Descriptors: Adolescents; *Adult Literacy; Adults; Daily Living Skills; *English (Second Language); Grammar; Individual Testing; Listening Skills; *Literacy Education; Multiple Choice Tests; Placement; Reading Skills; *Screening Tests; *Second Language Instruction; Writing (Composition)
Availability: Academic Therapy Publications; 20 Commercial Blvd., Novato, CA 94949-6191
Age Level: 16-99
Notes: Time, 20 min. approx.

Assessment instrument used to determine the appropriate level at which individuals should begin English as a Second Language (ESL) or adult literacy instruction. After a brief oral, individual screening, the remainder of the test may be group administered. Answers are multiple-choice. Consists of 5 subtests: Listening, Grammar, Life Skills, Reading, and Composition. No technical data included.

16727
Children's Articulation Test. Haspiel, George S. 1989
Descriptors: Articulation (Speech); Children; Consonants; *Individual Testing; Pictorial Stimuli; *Speech Evaluation; *Speech Tests; Speech Therapy; Vowels
Identifiers: CAT
Availability: Academic Therapy Publications; 20 Commercial Blvd., Novato, CA 94949-6191
Age Level: 3-11

An articulation test administered to 3 to 11 year olds to assess their ability to produce consonants, vowels and diphthongs in an in-depth relationship to other consonants and vowels. On an individual basis, children are presented with pictures and are asked to name each. Examiners record errors on a scoring sheet. Results provide an analysis of sound production adequacy; observation of voice quality, loudness rate, repetition, and inflection; a description of children's vocabulary, language content, sentence length, and syntax; and a sample of children's familiarity with size, shape, family relationships, and alphabet and number recognition. May be used as a guideline for therapy. Retesting may be administered throughout therapy to assess changes.

16729
Written Language Assessment. Grill, J. Jeffrey; Kirwin, Margaret M. 1989
Subtests: General Writing Ability; Productivity; Word Complexity; Readability
Descriptors: *Elementary School Students; Elementary Secondary Education; Handwriting; *Norm Referenced Tests; Readability; Rhetorical Invention; *Secondary School Students; *Student Placement; *Writing Evaluation; *Writing Skills
Identifiers: WLA
Availability: Academic Therapy Publications; 20 Commercial Blvd.; Novato, CA 94949-6191
Age Level: 8-18
Notes: Time, 15 min. approx.

A norm-referenced test used to assess the writing ability of students ages 8 through 18 and above through the evaluation of writing samples. Instrument includes 3 writing tasks. Writing samples are scored for general writing ability, productivity, word complexity, and readability. General writing ability is measured according to each writing sample's rhetoric, legibility, and overall quality. Productivity, word complexity, and readability are measured according to counts of words, syllables, and sentences in the writing sample. Test may be used to help make placement decisions about students in regular classrooms, as well as in special education settings. May also be used to help make instructional decisions. Technical data are included.

16739
Early School Assessment. CTB/MacMillan/McGraw-Hill, Monterey, CA 1990
Subtests: Visual Discrimination; Auditory Discrimination; Language Concepts; Number Concepts; Memory; Logical Operations

Descriptors: *Aptitude Tests; Early Childhood Education; Educational Needs; *Grade 1; *Kindergarten Children; *Mathematics Skills; *Preschool Children; Primary Education; *Reading Skills; *Screening Tests; *Young Children
Identifiers: Early Childhood System; ECS; ESA
Availability: CTB/MacMillan/McGraw-Hill; Del Monte Research Park, 2500 Garden Rd., Monterey, CA 93940
Grade Level: K-1

CTB Early Childhood System is a program to assist with screening, diagnosing, and instructional planning for young children. The components of the system are the Primary Test of Cognitive Skills, the Early School Assessment, and the Development Skills Checklist. The Early School Assessment (ESA) is a group-administered test to determine the educational needs of children in their early school years (end of prekindergarten through the beginning of first grade). Test measures prereading and premathematical skills. Useful in determining appropriate instructional programs for young children and identifying children who qualify for Chapter 1 programs. There are 2 levels: Level 1 is used from end of prekindergarten through the middle of kindergarten and through the end of kindergarten for those who are not mastering basic kindergarten skills; Level 2 is used from the middle of kindergarten through the beginning of first grade.

16740
Developing Skills Checklist. CTB/Macmillan/McGraw-Hill, Monterey, CA 1990
Subtests: Language; Visual Auditory; Mathematical Concepts and Operations; Memory; Social and Emotional; Fine and Gross Motor; Print and Writing
Descriptors: Check Lists; Early Childhood Education; Emotional Development; *Grade 1; *Individual Testing; Interpersonal Competence; *Kindergarten Children; Mathematics Skills; *Preschool Children; Psychomotor Skills; Reading Skills; *Screening Tests; Skill Analysis; *Skill Development; *Young Children
Identifiers: DSC; Early Childhood System; ECS
Availability: CTB/MacMillan/McGraw-Hill; Del Monte Research Park, 2500 Garden Rd., Monterey, CA 93940
Grade Level: K-1
Notes: Time, 90 min. approx.

CTB Early Childhood System is a program to assist with screening, diagnosing, and instructional planning for young children. The components of the system are the Primary Test of Cognitive Skills, the Early School Assessment, and the Developing Skills Checklist. The Developing Skills Checklist (DSC) measures skills that children typically develop between prekindergarten and beginning first grade. Individually administered. Measures prereading and premathematics skills, social and emotional skills, fine and gross motor development, and print and writing concepts. Useful in determining appropriate instructional programs and identifying children for Chapter 1 programs.

16741
Peabody Individual Achievement Test—Revised. American Guidance Service, Circle Pines, MN 1989
Subtests: General Information; Reading Recognition; Reading Comprehension; Mathematics; Spelling; Written Expression
Descriptors: *Achievement Tests; *Elementary School Students; Elementary Secondary Education; *Individual Testing; Knowledge Level; Mathematics Achievement; Reading Comprehension; *Secondary School Students; Spelling; *Standardized Tests; Word Recognition; Writing Skills
Identifiers: PIAT(R)
Availability: American Guidance Service; Publishers' Bldg., Circle Pines, MN 55014-1796
Grade Level: K-12
Age Level: 5-18
Notes: Time, 60 min. approx.

Individually administered achievement test providing wide-range assessment in 6 content areas. This is a revision of the 1970 test and has updated norms, more items, and more contemporary item content. Each subtest covers a wide range of achievement levels, from preschool through post-high school, but only the appropriate subset, or critical range, of items is administered to each subject. Items measure functional knowledge and abilities that are generally expected educational outcomes and are not tied to a specific curriculum. Items are arranged in ascending order of difficulty. Test is untimed but should typically take about one hour to administer. May be used for individual evaluation, program planning, guidance and counseling, admissions and transfers, grouping students, follow-up evaluation, personnel selection, and training. Research uses include longitudinal studies, demographic studies, program evaluation studies, basic research studies, validation studies. The test is not designed as a diagnostic test nor is it meant to provide highly precise assessment of achievement nor to sample the curriculum of a specific school system. Standardization was conducted in 33 communities nationwide.

16742

DANTES: Principles of Public Speaking. Educational Testing Service, Princeton, NJ 1989
Descriptors: *Achievement Tests; Adults; College Students; *Equivalency Tests; Higher Education; *Public Speaking; Speech Communication; Two Year Colleges
Identifiers: Defense Activity Non Traditional Education Support
Availability: DANTES Program Office; Educational Testing Service, Princeton, NJ 08541
Grade Level: 13-16
Age Level: Adults
Notes: Time, 90 min. approx.; Items, 84

The DANTES program is a series of secure tests administered by postsecondary institutions to grant credit by examination for education gained outside the classroom. Examinations may be worth from 2 to 6 credit hours in a baccalaureate program, baccalaureate upper division program, or a technical program. A minimum score for credit has been established by the American Council on Education. Individual institutions administer the examinations, as well as set the fees and schedules. These instruments complement the College Board's College Level Examination Program (CLEP) with several instruments in applied technology. They were originally developed for military personnel. Major areas of assessment include mathematics, social science, physical science, business, foreign language, and applied technology. For each test, a fact sheet containing the curriculum specifications of the course, a list of texts on which the test is based, and statistical information is available. Qualified administrators and faculty may borrow sample tests for a period of 30 days. This test covers ethical, historical, and social considerations of public speaking; audience analysis and adaptation, topics and purposes of speeches; organization; supporting materials; research; language and style; delivery; communication apprehension; listening and feedback; criticism and evaluation. Requires the recording of an impromptu speech.

16748

Test of Academic Achievement Skills—Reading, Arithmetic, Spelling. Gardner, Morrison F. 1989
Subtests: Reading; Arithmetic; Spelling
Descriptors: *Achievement Tests; *Arithmetic; Elementary Education; *Elementary School Students; Learning Disabilities; Mathematics; Preschool Education; *Reading; Reading Difficulties; School Readiness; *Spelling
Identifiers: TASS RAS
Availability: Health Publishing Co.; P.O. Box 3805, San Francisco, CA 94119
Age Level: 4-12
Notes: Time, 20 min.

This test is designed to measure overall abilities, or problems, in reading, arithmetic, and spelling for a population of normally functioning students attending public, private, and parochial schools. There are 2 levels of testing. One, for ages 4-6, has approximately 50 questions. For ages 6-12, there are 100 questions, approximately. For use by psychologists, therapists, and consultants who need a relatively brief and accessible achievement test. Covers letter and word recognition, pronunciation, comprehension, number identification, computation, number concepts, written spelling. Scores convert to age equivalents, scaled scores, percentiles.

16749

DANTES: Principles of Real Estate. Educational Testing Service, Princeton, NJ 1989
Descriptors: *Achievement Tests; Adults; Calculators; College Students; *Equivalency Tests; Higher Education; *Real Estate
Identifiers: Defense Activity Non Traditional Education Support
Availability: DANTES Program Office; Educational Testing Service, Princeton, NJ 08541
Grade Level: 13-16
Age Level: Adults
Notes: Time, 90 min. approx.; Items, 93

The DANTES program is a series of secure tests administered by postsecondary institutions to grant credit by examination for education gained outside the classroom. Examinations may be worth from 2 to 6 credit hours in a baccalaureate program, baccalaureate upper division program, or a technical program. A minimum score for credit has been established by the American Council on Education. Individual institutions administer the examinations, as well as set the fees and schedules. These instruments complement the College Board's College Level Examination Program (CLEP) with several instruments in applied technology. They were originally developed for military personnel. Major areas of assessment include mathematics, social science, physical science, business, foreign language, and applied technology. For each test, a fact sheet containing the curriculum specifications of the course, a list of texts on which the test is based, and statistical information is available. Qualified administrators and faculty may borrow sample tests for a period of 30 days. A hand-held

calculator is allowed for this test. Multiple-choice items cover methods and instruments of financing, valuation of real estate, real estate investment, legal aspects, economic characteristics, building and development, working with real estate brokers, property management.

16750

DANTES: Organizational Behavior. Educational Testing Service, Princeton, NJ 1985
Descriptors: *Achievement Tests; Adults; *Behavior Patterns; College Students; *Equivalency Tests; Higher Education; Organizational Change; Organizational Climate; *Organizations (Groups)
Identifiers: Defense Activity Non Traditional Education Support
Availability: DANTES Program Office; Educational Testing Service, Princeton, NJ 08541
Grade Level: 13-16
Age Level: Adults
Notes: Time, 90 min. approx.; Items, 92

The DANTES program is a series of secure tests administered by postsecondary institutions to grant credit by examination for education gained outside the classroom. Examinations may be worth from 2 to 6 credit hours in a baccalaureate program, baccalaureate upper division program, or a technical program. A minimum score for credit has been established by the American Council on Education. Individual institutions administer the examinations, as well as set the fees and schedules. These instruments complement the College Board's College Level Examination Program (CLEP) with several instruments in applied technology. They were originally developed for military personnel. Major areas of assessment include mathematics, social science, physical science, business, foreign language, and applied technology. For each test, a fact sheet containing the curriculum specifications of the course, a list of texts on which the test is based, and statistical information is available. Qualified administrators and faculty may borrow sample tests for a period of 30 days. Questions are multiple-choice and cover organizational behavior, individual processes and characteristics, interpersonal and group process, organizational process and characteristics, change and development processes.

16751

DANTES: Principles of Finance. Educational Testing Service, Princeton, NJ 1985
Descriptors: Accounting; *Achievement Tests; Adults; Bookkeeping; Budgeting; Calculators; College Students; *Equivalency Tests; *Finance Occupations; *Financial Services; Higher Education
Identifiers: Defense Activity Non Traditional Education Support; Finance
Availability: DANTES Program Office; Educational Testing Service, Princeton, NJ 08541
Grade Level: 13-16
Age Level: Adults
Notes: Time, 90 min. approx.; Items, 86

The DANTES program is a series of secure tests administered by postsecondary institutions to grant credit by examination for education gained outside the classroom. Examinations may be worth from 2 to 6 credit hours in a baccalaureate program, baccalaureate upper division program, or a technical program. A minimum score for credit has been established by the American Council on Education. Individual institutions administer the examinations, as well as set the fees and schedules. These instruments complement the College Board's College Level Examination Program (CLEP) with several instruments in applied technology. They were originally developed for military personnel. Major areas of assessment include mathematics, social science, physical science, business, foreign language, and applied technology. For each test, a fact sheet containing the curriculum specifications of the course, a list of texts on which the test is based, and statistical information is available. Qualified administrators and faculty may borrow sample tests for a period of 30 days. A nonprogrammable calculator may be used to respond to this multiple-choice test that covers financial statements, time value of money, forecasting, break-even analysis, leverage, budgeting, debt, common stock, financial management.

16752

DANTES: War and Peace in the Nuclear Age. Educational Testing Service, Princeton, NJ 1989
Descriptors: *Achievement Tests; Adults; College Students; Current Events; *Disarmament; *Equivalency Tests; Higher Education; *International Relations; *Nuclear Warfare; Social Studies; World History
Identifiers: Defense Activity Non Traditional Education Support
Availability: DANTES Program Office; Educational Testing Service, Princeton, NJ 08541
Grade Level: 13-16
Age Level: Adults
Notes: Time, 90 min. approx.; Items, 100

The DANTES program is a series of secure tests administered by postsecondary institutions to grant credit by examination for education gained outside the classroom. Examinations may be worth from 2 to 6 credit hours in a

baccalaureate program, baccalaureate upper division program, or a technical program. A minimum score for credit has been established by the American Council on Education. Individual institutions administer the examinations, as well as set the fees and schedules. These instruments complement the College Board's College Level Examination Program (CLEP) with several instruments in applied technology. They were originally developed for military personnel. Major areas of assessment include mathematics, social science, physical science, business, foreign language, and applied technology. For each test, a fact sheet containing the curriculum specifications of the course, a list of texts on which the test is based, and statistical information is available. Qualified administrators and faculty may borrow sample tests for a period of 30 days. This test is multiple-choice and covers such topics as arms control, strategic doctrine, domestic politics, international negotiations, domestic politics, nuclear proliferation, technology, terminology, personalities. Tests are revised regularly, but generally the above topics that are taught in courses on the subject will be tested.

16753

DANTES: Lifespan Developmental Psychology. Educational Testing Service, Princeton, NJ 1987
Descriptors: *Achievement Tests; Adults; College Students; *Developmental Psychology; *Equivalency Tests; Higher Education
Identifiers: Defense Activity Non Traditional Education Support
Availability: DANTES Program Office; Educational Testing Service, Princeton, NJ 08541
Grade Level: 13-16
Age Level: Adults
Notes: Time, 90 min. approx.; Items, 100

The DANTES program is a series of secure tests administered by postsecondary institutions to grant credit by examination for education gained outside the classroom. Examinations may be worth from 2 to 6 credit hours in a baccalaureate program, baccalaureate upper division program, or a technical program. A minimum score for credit has been established by the American Council on Education. Individual institutions administer the examinations, as well as set the fees and schedules. These instruments complement the College Board's College Level Examination Program (CLEP) with several instruments in applied technology. They were originally developed for military personnel. Major areas of assessment include mathematics, social science, physical science, business, foreign language, and applied technology. For each test, a fact sheet containing the curriculum specifications of the course, a list of texts on which the test is based, and statistical information is available. Qualified administrators and faculty may borrow sample tests for a period of 30 days. Covers study of lifespan development; biological development; perception, learning, memory; cognition and language; social, emotional, and personality development.

16754

DANTES: Geography. Educational Testing Service, Princeton, NJ
Descriptors: *Achievement Tests; Adults; College Students; *Equivalency Tests; Higher Education; *Human Geography; *Physical Geography
Identifiers: Defense Activity Non Traditional Education Support
Availability: DANTES Program Office; Educational Testing Service, Princeton, NJ 08541
Grade Level: 13-16
Age Level: Adults
Notes: Time, 90 min. approx.; Items, 100

The DANTES program is a series of secure tests administered by postsecondary institutions to grant credit by examination for education gained outside the classroom. Examinations may be worth from 2 to 6 credit hours in a baccalaureate program, baccalaureate upper division program, or a technical program. A minimum score for credit has been established by the American Council on Education. Individual institutions administer the examinations, as well as set the fees and schedules. These instruments complement the College Board's College Level Examination Program (CLEP) with several instruments in applied technology. They were originally developed for military personnel. Major areas of assessment include mathematics, social science, physical science, business, foreign language, and applied technology. For each test, a fact sheet containing the curriculum specifications of the course, a list of texts on which the test is based, and statistical information is available. Qualified administrators and faculty may borrow sample tests for a period of 30 days. Contains 90 multiple-choice items and covers physical geography, culture and environment, spatial processes, regional geography.

16755

DANTES: Physical Geology. Educational Testing Service, Princeton, NJ 1988
Descriptors: *Achievement Tests; Adults; College Students; *Equivalency Tests; *Geology; Higher Education
Identifiers: Defense Activity Non Traditional Education Support
Availability: DANTES Program Office; Educational Testing Service, Princeton, NJ 08541

Grade Level: 13-16
Age Level: Adults
Notes: Time, 90 min. approx.; Items, 108
The DANTES program is a series of secure tests administered by postsecondary institutions to grant credit by examination for education gained outside the classroom. Examinations may be worth from 2 to 6 credit hours in a baccalaureate program, baccalaureate upper division program, or a technical program. A minimum score for credit has been established by the American Council on Education. Individual institutions administer the examinations, as well as set the fees and schedules. These instruments complement the College Board's College Level Examination Program (CLEP) with several instruments in applied technology. They were originally developed for military personnel. Major areas of assessment include mathematics, social science, physical science, business, foreign language, and applied technology. For each test, a fact sheet containing the curriculum specifications of the course, a list of texts on which the test is based, and statistical information is available. Qualified administrators and faculty may borrow sample tests for a period of 30 days. All items are multiple-choice. Covers earth materials, surface processes, internal earth processes, applications of geology.

16759
DANTES: Principles of Statistics.   Educational Testing Service, Princeton, NJ 1989
Descriptors: *Achievement Tests; Adults; College Students; *Equivalency Tests; Higher Education; *Statistics
Identifiers: Defense Activity Non Traditional Education Support
Availability: DANTES Program Office; Educational Testing Service, Princeton, NJ 08541
Grade Level: 13-16
Age Level: Adults
Notes: Time, 90 min. approx.; Items, 93
The DANTES program is a series of secure tests administered by postsecondary institutions to grant credit by examination for education gained outside the classroom. Examinations may be worth from 2 to 6 credit hours in a baccalaureate program, baccalaureate upper division program, or a technical program. A minimum score for credit has been established by the American Council on Education. Individual institutions administer the examinations, as well as set the fees and schedules. These instruments complement the College Board's College Level Examination Program (CLEP) with several instruments in applied technology. They were originally developed for military personnel. Major areas of assessment include mathematics, social science, physical science, business, foreign language, and applied technology. For each test, a fact sheet containing the curriculum specifications of the course, a list of texts on which the test is based, and statistical information is available. Qualified administrators and faculty may borrow sample tests for a period of 30 days. This test covers descriptive statistics, correlation and regression, probability.

16760
DANTES: Ethics in America.   Educational Testing Service, Princeton, NJ 1989
Descriptors: *Achievement Tests; Adults; *Codes of Ethics; College Students; *Equivalency Tests; Essay Tests; *Ethics; Higher Education
Identifiers: Defense Activity Non Traditional Education Support
Availability: DANTES Program Office; Educational Testing Service, Princeton, NJ 08541
Grade Level: 13-16
Age Level: Adults
Notes: Time, 90 min. approx.; Items, 120
The DANTES program is a series of secure tests administered by postsecondary institutions to grant credit by examination for education gained outside the classroom. Examinations may be worth from 2 to 6 credit hours in a baccalaureate program, baccalaureate upper division program, or a technical program. A minimum score for credit has been established by the American Council on Education. Individual institutions administer the examinations, as well as set the fees and schedules. These instruments complement the College Board's College Level Examination Program (CLEP) with several instruments in applied technology. They were originally developed for military personnel. Major areas of assessment include mathematics, social science, physical science, business, foreign language, and applied technology. For each test, a fact sheet containing the curriculum specifications of the course, a list of texts on which the test is based, and statistical information is available. Qualified administrators and faculty may borrow sample tests for a period of 30 days. This test is multiple choice with an essay. Covers ethical traditions, biblical traditions, moral law, consequentialist ethics, ethical analysis of issues in interpersonal and personal-societal relationships and in professional and occupational roles, relationships between ethical traditions and the ethical analysis of situations.

16777
Screening Instrument for Targeting Educational Risk.   Anderson, Karen L. 1989
Subtests: Academics; Attention; Communication; Class Participation; School Behavior

Descriptors: Academic Achievement; Attention Span; Communication Skills; Elementary Education; *Elementary School Students; *Hearing Impairments; *High Risk Students; Rating Scales; *Screening Tests; Student Behavior; Student Participation; *White Students
Identifiers: SIFTER
Availability: Interstate Printers & Publishers; P.O. Box 50, Danville, IL 61834-0050
Grade Level: K-5
Notes: Items, 15
Developed to provide a valid method by which children with known or suspected hearing problems can be screened for educational purposes. Those identified as being at risk for educational difficulties can be considered for formal assessment procedures. Based on field testing, the instrument is felt to be most representative when used with white children in kindergarten through grade 5 who have a known hearing loss ranging from faint to moderate and who are educated in regular classrooms only.

16786
Prekindergarten Saginaw Objective Referenced Test.   Quimper, Barry E.; Claus, Richard N. 1978
Descriptors: *Academic Achievement; *Achievement Tests; *Cognitive Development; *Criterion Referenced Tests; *Individual Testing; *Preschool Children; Preschool Education; *Pretests Posttests; *Psychomotor Skills; *School Readiness
Identifiers: PK(SORT); Saginaw(MI); TIM(P)
Availability: Tests in Microfiche; Test Collection, Educational Testing Service, Princeton, NJ 08541
Age Level: 4
Notes: Items, 31
Used as a pretest posttest to determine whether children enrolled in the Saginaw, MI prekindergarten program met the program's behavioral objectives. Children in this program, whose purpose is to prepare inner-city children for entry into kindergarten, should be at least on a par with other children as they enter kindergarten. The test is individually administered and measures children's achievement in both cognitive and psychomotor skills.

16795
DANTES: Business Mathematics.   Educational Testing Service, Princeton, NJ 1988
Descriptors: *Achievement Tests; Adults; *Business Education; Business Skills; College Students; *Equivalency Tests; Higher Education; *Mathematics
Identifiers: Defense Activity Non Traditional Education Support
Availability: DANTES Program Office; Educational Testing Service, Princeton, NJ 08541
Age Level: Adults
Notes: Time, 90 min. approx.; Items, 76
The DANTES program is a series of secure tests administered by postsecondary institutions to grant credit by examination for education gained outside the classroom. Examinations may be worth from 2 to 6 credit hours in a baccalaureate program, baccalaureate upper division program, or a technical program. A minimum score for credit has been established by the American Council on Education. Individual institutions administer the examinations, as well as set the fees and schedules. These instruments complement the College Board's College Level Examination Program (CLEP) with several instruments in applied technology. They were originally developed for military personnel. Major areas of assessment include mathematics, social science, physical science, business, foreign language, and applied technology. For each test, a fact sheet containing the curriculum specifications of the course, a list of texts on which the test is based, and statistical information is available. Qualified administrators and faculty may borrow sample tests for a period of 30 days. This multiple-choice test covers basic concepts and computation, business applications, ratios, lending costs, depreciation, net worth, etc. Content is related to the mathematics text *Essential Business Mathematics,* 7th Ed., 1979, McGraw-Hill Book Company (Snyder and Jackson).

16796
DANTES: Electronic Devices.   Educational Testing Service, Princeton, NJ 1987
Descriptors: *Achievement Tests; Adults; College Students; *Electronics; *Equivalency Tests; Higher Education
Identifiers: Defense Activity Non Traditional Education Support
Availability: DANTES Program Office; Educational Testing Service, Princeton, NJ 08541
Age Level: Adults
Notes: Time, 90 min. approx.; Items, 74
The DANTES program is a series of secure tests administered by postsecondary institutions to grant credit by examination for education gained outside the classroom. Examinations may be worth from 2 to 6 credit hours in a baccalaureate program, baccalaureate upper division program, or a technical program. A minimum score for credit has been established by the American Council on Educa-

tion. Individual institutions administer the examinations, as well as set the fees and schedules. These instruments complement the College Board's College Level Examination Program (CLEP) with several instruments in applied technology. They were originally developed for military personnel. Major areas of assessment include mathematics, social science, physical science, business, foreign language, and applied technology. For each test, a fact sheet containing the curriculum specifications of the course, a list of texts on which the test is based, and statistical information is available. Qualified administrators and faculty may borrow sample tests for a period of 30 days. This multiple-choice test covers semiconductor diode characteristics and applications, bipolar junction transistors, BJT amplifiers, field effect transistors, operational amplifiers, special semiconductor devices.

16797
DANTES: Fundamentals of Electronics (Revised).
Educational Testing Service, Princeton, NJ 1987
Descriptors: *Achievement Tests; Adults; Calculators; College Students; *Electronics; *Equivalency Tests; Higher Education
Identifiers: Defense Activity Non Traditional Education Support
Availability: DANTES Program Office; Educational Testing Service, Princeton, NJ 08541
Age Level: Adults
Notes: Time, 90 min. approx.; Items, 81
The DANTES program is a series of secure tests administered by postsecondary institutions to grant credit by examination for education gained outside the classroom. Examinations may be worth from 2 to 6 credit hours in a baccalaureate program, baccalaureate upper division program, or a technical program. A minimum score for credit has been established by the American Council on Education. Individual institutions administer the examinations, as well as set the fees and schedules. These instruments complement the College Board's College Level Examination Program (CLEP) with several instruments in applied technology. They were originally developed for military personnel. Major areas of assessment include mathematics, social science, physical science, business, foreign language, and applied technology. For each test, a fact sheet containing the curriculum specifications of the course, a list of texts on which the test is based, and statistical information is available. Qualified administrators and faculty may borrow sample tests for a period of 30 days. This multiple-choice test covers direct current circuits, alternating current circuits, electronic devices, electronic circuit applications, digital electronic circuits, electromagnetic devices, measurements and instrumentation.

16798
DANTES: Principles of Refrigeration Technology.
Educational Testing Service, Princeton, NJ 1989
Descriptors: *Achievement Tests; Adults; College Students; *Equivalency Tests; Higher Education; *Refrigeration
Identifiers: Defense Activity Non Traditional Education Support
Availability: DANTES Program Office; Educational Testing Service, Princeton, NJ 08541
Age Level: Adults
Notes: Time, 90 min. approx.; Items, 104
The DANTES program is a series of secure tests administered by postsecondary institutions to grant credit by examination for education gained outside the classroom. Examinations may be worth from 2 to 6 credit hours in a baccalaureate program, baccalaureate upper division program, or a technical program. A minimum score for credit has been established by the American Council on Education. Individual institutions administer the examinations, as well as set the fees and schedules. These instruments complement the College Board's College Level Examination Program (CLEP) with several instruments in applied technology. They were originally developed for military personnel. Major areas of assessment include mathematics, social science, physical science, business, foreign language, and applied technology. For each test, a fact sheet containing the curriculum specifications of the course, a list of texts on which the test is based, and statistical information is available. Qualified administrators and faculty may borrow sample tests for a period of 30 days. This multiple-choice test covers component identification and functions, physical laws.

16799
Diagnostic Test of Library Skills (Computerized Version).   Feldstein, Barbara; Rawdon, Janet 1990
Descriptors: Achievement Tests; *Computer Assisted Testing; Computers; *Diagnostic Tests; *Elementary School Students; Intermediate Grades; Junior High Schools; *Junior High School Students; Knowledge Level; *Library Skills; Pretests Posttests
Availability: Learnco, Inc.; Box L, Exeter, NH 03833
Grade Level: 5-9
Notes: Time, 30 min.; Items, 50
The test is designed to evaluate students' current knowledge of library skills in the areas of use of title page; table of contents; card catalog; library arrangement; reference

books. Two forms are available for pre- and posttesting. Apple and Macintosh versions are available. In addition to testing, the program keeps track of scores, performs error analysis to determine individual student instructional needs. All items are multiple-choice. Student receives immediate feedback on correctness of response.

16809
Concepts of Print and Writing. CTB/Macmillan/ McGraw-Hill, Monterey, CA 1990
Subtests: Print Concepts; Writing and Drawing Concepts
Descriptors: *Grade 1; *Kindergarten Children; *Literacy; Preschool Children; Preschool Education; Primary Education; Reading Readiness; *Reading Writing Relationship; Writing Processes; *Young Children
Identifiers: Developing Skills Checklist; DSC; Early Childhood System; ECS
Availability: CTB/MacMillan/McGraw-Hill; Del Monte Research Park, 2500 Garden Rd., Monterey, CA 93940
Grade Level: K-1

Designed to measure "eminent literacy" in young children from prekindergarten through beginning first-grade students. Assesses a prereading child's understanding of the function of print (that print carries messages), and the conventions of print (what people do when they read). Measures writing and drawing concepts that have been validated in predicting reading readiness. The Concepts of Printing and Writing components are also included in the Developing Skills Checklist, which is one component of the CTB Early Childhood System.

16814
Monitoring Basic Skills Progress, Basic Reading. Fuchs, Lynn S.; And Others 1990
Descriptors: *Achievement Tests; Computer Assisted Instruction; *Computer Assisted Testing; *Computer Software; Elementary Education; *Elementary School Students; *Reading Achievement; *Reading Tests; Special Education
Identifiers: MBSP
Availability: PRO-ED; 8700 Shoal Creek Blvd., Austin, TX 78758-6897
Grade Level: 1-7

One of 3 software programs in the Monitoring Basic Skills Progress Measurement series. All programs run on Apple II microcomputers. Designed to monitor students' acquisition of reading proficiency. Computer automatically administers a reading test to the student at a grade level designated by the teacher. Every week students take an alternate form of the test, once for regular education students and twice for special education students. The test is based on the cloze procedure, referred to as a maze. Computer automatically scores tests, provides feedback, and saves test scores. Uses of test include documenting student progress, describing students' basic rates of progress, identifying students for whom program changes are necessary, comparing effectiveness of different programs, or determining how to improve substance of students' programs.

16815
Monitoring Basic Skills Progress, Basic Spelling. Fuchs, Lynn S.; And Others 1990
Descriptors: *Achievement Tests; Computer Assisted Instruction; *Computer Assisted Testing; *Computer Software; Elementary Education; *Elementary School Students; Microcomputers; *Spelling
Identifiers: MBSP
Availability: PRO-ED; 8700 Shoal Creek Blvd., Austin, TX 78758-6897
Grade Level: 1-6
Notes: Time, 3 min.; Items, 20

One of 3 software programs in the Monitoring Basic Skills Progress Measurement series, which run on Apple II microcomputers. The series is designed to monitor students' acquisition of basic skills. This test is used to track the development of students' spelling proficiency. The basic spelling measurement relies on a dictation format and should be administered at least twice each week. It is a set of standardized methods for selecting test stimuli from a student's curriculum, administering and scoring tests, summarizing the assessment information and using the information to formulate instructional decisions in the basic skills area.

16816
Monitoring Basic Skills Progress, Basic Math. Fuchs, Lynn S.; And Others 1990
Descriptors: *Achievement Tests; *Computation; Computer Assisted Instruction; *Computer Assisted Testing; *Computer Software; Elementary Education; *Elementary School Students; *Mathematics Achievement; *Mathematics Tests; Microcomputers
Identifiers: MBSP
Availability: PRO-ED; 8700 Shoal Creek Blvd., Austin, TX 78758-6897
Grade Level: 1-6
Notes: Time, 3 min.; Items, 25

One of 3 software programs in the Monitoring Basic Skills Progress Measurement series, which run on Apple II microcomputers. The series is designed to monitor students' acquisition of basic skills. This test assesses students' computation skills in mathematics. It is used to document student progress, describe student rate of progress on basic skills in math, formulate appropriate goals for individual students, identify students whose progress is inadequate and whose programs need changing, compare the effectiveness of different programs, and determine how to improve the substance of students' programs.

16830
Temple University Short Syntax Inventory, Revised. Gerber, Adele; And Others 1988
Descriptors: *Diagnostic Tests; Disabilities; *Language Handicaps; *Language Proficiency; Mental Retardation; *Preschool Children; *Screening Tests; *Syntax; *Verbal Ability; Verbal Development
Identifiers: *Language Delayed; TUSSI
Availability: Slosson Educational Publications; P.O. Box 280, East Aurora, NY 14052
Age Level: 3-4

Designed for early detection of preschool children at risk for language delay/disorder. This revised edition was changed for the purpose of brevity of administration from a game format used in the original diagnostic test to a more rapid process of securing responses to picture stimuli. The options for the screening test may be used for large-scale screening of preschoolers enrolled in programs for children without identified handicapping conditioning; and as a means of assessing the degree of mastery. The options for the diagnostic test may be used for assessment of children identified as at risk for analysis of abnormal patterns; and for comparison of pre- and posttreatment performance. Useful for mentally retarded or disabled children.

16831
Slosson Oral Reading Test, Revised. Nicholson, Charles L. 1990
Descriptors: *Elementary School Students; Elementary Secondary Education; *Individual Testing; *Oral Reading; *Reading Tests; *Screening Tests; *Secondary School Students; *Word Recognition
Identifiers: SORT(R)
Availability: Slosson Educational Publications; P.O. Box 280, East Aurora, NY 14052
Grade Level: K-12
Notes: Items, 200

Designed as a quick screening test to obtain an estimate of a person's level of oral word recognition. Has been nationally standardized with the Slosson-Intelligence Test. Contains 200 words arranged in ascending order of difficulty in groups of 20 words. The word groups approximate grade reading levels.

16833
The Primary Language Screen for Kindergarten and First Grade. Eger, Diane L.; And Others 1990
Subtests: Receptive; Expressive
Descriptors: *Expressive Language; *Grade 1; Individual Testing; *Kindergarten Children; Language Skills; *Language Tests; *Primary Education; *Receptive Language; *Screening Tests
Identifiers: TPLS
Availability: United Educational Services; P.O. Box 605, East Aurora, NY 14052
Grade Level: K-1
Notes: Time, 35 min. approx.; Items, 33

A language screening instrument designed for use with children in kindergarten and first grade. Assesses receptive areas of language by measuring various semantic, syntactic, and grammatic structures. Assesses expressive areas of language by measuring opposites and analogies, sentence repetition, and grammatic closure. Receptive portion of instrument may be administered to a group. Expressive portion should be administered individually. Was found to distinguish students with normal language skills from those with disordered language skills. Several tables charting various statistical analyses of data compiled as a result of instrument are included.

16835
Spanish Structured Photographic Expressive Language Test–Preschool. Werner, Ellen O'Hara; Kresheck, Janet Dawson 1989
Descriptors: Auditory Stimuli; *Bilingual Education; Criterion Referenced Tests; *Expressive Language; *Hispanic Americans; *Individual Testing; *Language Tests; Morphology (Languages); Pictorial Stimuli; *Preschool Education; *Screening Tests; *Spanish; *Spanish Speaking; Syntax; Visual Stimuli; *Young Children
Identifiers: SPELT(P)
Availability: Janelle Publications; P.O. Box 15, Sandwich, IL 60548
Age Level: 3-5
Notes: Items, 25

Designed to examine expressive language abilities and to provide a developmentally appropriate assessment of Spanish language development of Hispanic American young children. May also be used with older children who appear to have language deficits or deprivation. May also be used as part of a preschool battery. To be used by professionals working in bilingual education. Primary purposes of test are to help identify children in need of language intervention and to help plan an effective remedial program. Intended as part of a criterion-referenced assessment process. Test focuses on early developing morphological and syntactic structures and uses photographs of children in contexts conducive to using linguistic markers, particularly those related to noun, adjective, and verb morphology.

16836
Spanish Structured Photographic Expressive Language Test—II. Werner, Ellen O'Hara; Kresheck, Janet Dawson 1989
Descriptors: Auditory Stimuli; *Bilingual Education; *Bilingual Students; Criterion Referenced Tests; *Elementary School Students; *Expressive Language; *Hispanic Americans; *Individual Testing; *Language Tests; Morphology (Languages); Pictorial Stimuli; *Primary Education; *Screening Tests; *Spanish; *Spanish Speaking; Syntax; Visual Stimuli
Identifiers: SPELTII
Availability: Janelle Publications; P.O. Box 15, Sandwich, IL 60548
Age Level: 4-9
Notes: Time, 25 min. approx.; Items, 50

Designed to assess expressive language abilities of monolingual or bilingual children and their use of specific morphological and syntactical structures. May be used as part of a battery for language assessment for Hispanic Americans. To be used by professionals working in bilingual education. Primary purposes of test are to help identify children in need of language intervention and to help plan an effective remedial program. Intended as part of a criterion-referenced assessment process. Test focuses on early developing morphological and syntactic structures and uses photographs of children in contexts conducive to using linguistic markers, particularly those related to noun, adjective, and verb morphology.

16837
Structured Photographic Articulation Test. Kresheck, Janet Dawson; Werner, Ellen O'Hara 1989
Descriptors: *Articulation (Speech); Children; *Consonants; *Diagnostic Tests; Performance Tests; Phonetics; Photographs; Pictorial Stimuli; *Screening Tests
Identifiers: SPAT(D)
Availability: Janelle Publications; P.O. Box 15, Sandwich, IL 60548
Age Level: 3-9
Notes: Time, 15 min. approx.; Items, 48

Forty-eight photographs of an appealing dog are used to elicit a child's production of 59 consonant sounds. Also identifies errors on 21 consonant blends, /s/, /r/, and /l/ and allows for analysis of their production in complex phonetic contexts. Elicits more than one sound per word allowing for reduction of the number of stimuli and administration time, alleviating loss of interest. Consonants are assessed according to syllabic function in initial, medial, and final position. The test is administered by persons trained in articulation who have a basic knowledge of phonetics. Technical data on reliability and validity are included.

16839
The Pennsylvania Assessment System: Testing for Essential Learning and Literacy Skills. Pennsylvania Dept. of Education, Harrisburg 1990
Descriptors: Elementary Education; *Elementary School Students; *Grade 3; *Grade 5; *Grade 8; *Mathematics Achievement; *Public Schools; *Reading Achievement; *Screening Tests; *State Departments of Education; *Testing Programs
Identifiers: Pennsylvania
Availability: Pennsylvania Dept. of Education; Div. of Educational Testing and Evaluation, 333 Market St., Harrisburg, PA 17126-0333
Grade Level: 3; 5; 8

The Testing for Essential Learning and Literacy Skills is part of the Pennsylvania Assessment System designed to screen and identify students with reading and mathematics problems to make help available to them. The State Board of Education requires testing to be done in all public schools in grades 3, 5, and 8. Nonpublic schools may participate on a voluntary basis.

16862
National Achievement Test, Level A. Wick, John W.; And Others 1989
Subtests: Letter Identification; Word Sounds; Word Recognition; Book Concepts; Listening Vocabulary; Listening Comprehension; Mathematics

Descriptors: *Achievement Tests; *Kindergarten Children; Language Arts; Listening Comprehension; Mathematics; Primary Education; Reading
Identifiers: CAP; Comprehensive Assessment Program; NAT
Availability: American Testronics; P.O. Box 2270, Iowa City, IA 52244-9990
Grade Level: K
Notes: Time, 134 min. approx.; Items, 184
Measures student achievement in the skill areas commonly found in school curricula. Available in 12 levels that correspond to grades kindergarten through grade 12. Level A corresponds to grade kindergarten. One of the elements of the Comprehensive Assessment Program along with the Developing Cognitive Abilities Test and the School Attitude Measure. Can be used alone or in combination with the other instruments. Level A is teacher dictated.

16863
National Achievement Test, Level B. Wick, John W.; And Others 1989
Subtests: Word Recognition; Word Analysis; Book Concepts; Listening Vocabulary; Listening Comprehension; Mathematics
Descriptors: *Achievement Tests; *Elementary School Students; *Grade 1; *Kindergarten Children; Language Arts; Mathematics; Primary Education; Reading
Identifiers: CAP; Comprehensive Assessment Program; NAT
Availability: American Testronics; P.O. Box 2270, Iowa City, IA 52244-9990
Grade Level: K-1
Notes: Time, 144 min. approx.; Items, 192
Measures student achievement in the skill areas commonly found in school curricula. Available in 12 levels that correspond to grades kindergarten through grade 12. Level B corresponds to grades K and 1. One of the elements of the Comprehensive Assessment Program along with the Developing Cognitive Abilities Test and the School Attitude Measure. Can be used alone or in combination with the other instruments. Level B is teacher dictated.

16864
National Achievement Test, Level C. Wick, John W.; And Others 1989
Subtests: Reading; Language; Mathematics; Social Studies; Science
Descriptors: *Achievement Tests; *Elementary School Students; *Grade 1; *Grade 2; Language Arts; Mathematics; Primary Education; Reading; Sciences; Social Sciences
Identifiers: CAP; Comprehensive Assessment Program; NAT
Availability: American Testronics; P.O. Box 2270, Iowa City, IA 52244-9990
Grade Level: 1-2
Notes: Time, 195 min. approx.; Items, 299
Measures student achievement in the skill areas commonly found in school curricula. Available in 12 levels that correspond to grades kindergarten through grade 12. Level C corresponds to grades 1 and 2. One of the elements of the Comprehensive Assessment Program along with the Developing Cognitive Abilities Test and the School Attitude Measure. Can be used alone or in combination with the other instruments. Level C is mostly teacher dictated.

16865
National Achievement Test, Level D. Wick, John W.; And Others 1989
Subtests: Reading; Language; Mathematics; Reference Skills; Social Studies; Science
Descriptors: *Achievement Tests; *Elementary School Students; *Grade 2; *Grade 3; Language Arts; Mathematics; Primary Education; Reading; Research Skills; Sciences; Social Sciences
Identifiers: CAP; Comprehensive Assessment Program; NAT
Availability: American Testronics; P.O. Box 2270, Iowa City, IA 52244-9990
Grade Level: 2-3
Notes: Time, 291 min. approx.; Items, 390
Measures student achievement in the skill areas commonly found in school curricula. Available in 12 levels that correspond to grades kindergarten through grade 12. Level D corresponds to grades 2 and 3. One of the elements of the Comprehensive Assessment Program along with the Developing Cognitive Abilities Test and the School Attitude Measure. Can be used alone or in combination with the other instruments. Some subtests in Level D are teacher dictated.

16866
National Achievement Test, Level E. Wick, John W.; And Others 1989
Subtests: Reading; Language; Mathematics; Reference Skills; Social Studies; Science
Descriptors: *Achievement Tests; Elementary Education; *Elementary School Students; *Grade 3; *Grade 4; Language Arts; Mathematics; Reading; Research Skills; Sciences; Social Sciences

Identifiers: CAP; Comprehensive Assessment Program; NAT
Availability: American Testronics; P.O. Box 2270, Iowa City, IA 52244-9990
Grade Level: 3-4
Notes: Time, 321 min.; Items, 412
Measures student achievement in the skill areas commonly found in school curricula. Available in 12 levels that correspond to grades kindergarten through grade 12. Level E corresponds to grades 3 and 4. One of the elements of the Comprehensive Assessment Program along with the Developing Cognitive Abilities Test and the School Attitude Measure. Can be used alone or in combination with the other instruments.

16867
National Achievement Test, Level F. Wick, John W.; And Others 1989
Subtests: Reading; Language; Mathematics; Reference Skills; Social Studies; Science
Descriptors: *Achievement Tests; Elementary Education; *Elementary School Students; *Grade 4; *Grade 5; Intermediate Grades; Language Arts; Mathematics; Reading; Research Skills; Sciences; Social Sciences
Identifiers: CAP; Comprehensive Assessment Program; NAT
Availability: American Testronics; P.O. Box 2270, Iowa City, IA 52244-9990
Grade Level: 4-5
Notes: Time, 319 min.; Items, 431
Measures student achievement in the skill areas commonly found in school curricula. Available in 12 levels that correspond to grades kindergarten through grade 12. Level F corresponds to grades 4 and 5. One of the elements of the Comprehensive Assessment Program along with the Developing Cognitive Abilities Test and the School Attitude Measure. Can be used alone or in combination with the other instruments.

16868
National Achievement Test, Level G. Wick, John W.; And Others 1989
Subtests: Reading; Language; Mathematics; Reference Skills; Social Studies; Science
Descriptors: *Achievement Tests; Elementary Education; *Elementary School Students; *Grade 5; *Grade 6; Intermediate Grades; Language Arts; Mathematics; Reading; Research Skills; Sciences; Social Sciences
Identifiers: CAP; Comprehensive Assessment Program; NAT
Availability: American Testronics; P.O. Box 2270, Iowa City, IA 52244-9990
Grade Level: 5-6
Notes: Time, 319 min.; Items, 431
Measures student achievement in the skill areas commonly found in school curricula. Available in 12 levels that correspond to grades kindergarten through grade 12. Level G corresponds to grades 5 and 6. One of the elements of the Comprehensive Assessment Program along with the Developing Cognitive Abilities Test and the School Attitude Measure. Can be used alone or in combination with the other instruments.

16869
National Achievement Test, Level H. Wick, John W.; And Others 1989
Subtests: Reading; Language; Mathematics; Reference Skills; Social Studies; Science
Descriptors: *Achievement Tests; Elementary Education; *Elementary School Students; *Grade 6; *Grade 7; Language Arts; Mathematics; Reading; Research Skills; Sciences; Social Sciences
Identifiers: CAP; Comprehensive Assessment Program; NAT
Availability: American Testronics; P.O. Box 2270, Iowa City, IA 52244-9990
Grade Level: 6-7
Notes: Time, 319 min.; Items, 431
Measures student achievement in the skill areas commonly found in school curricula. Available in 12 levels that correspond to grades kindergarten through grade 12. Level H corresponds to grades 6 and 7. One of the elements of the Comprehensive Assessment Program along with the Developing Cognitive Abilities Test and the School Attitude Measure. Can be used alone or in combination with the other instruments.

16870
National Achievement Test, Level I. Wick, John W.; And Others 1989
Subtests: Reading; Language; Mathematics; Reference Skills; Social Studies; Science
Descriptors: *Achievement Tests; *Grade 7; *Grade 8; Junior High Schools; *Junior High School Students; Language Arts; Mathematics; Reading; Research Skills; Sciences; Secondary Education; Social Sciences
Identifiers: CAP; Comprehensive Assessment Program; NAT

Availability: American Testronics; P.O. Box 2270, Iowa City, IA 52244-9990
Grade Level: 7-8
Notes: Time, 319 min.; Items, 431
Measures student achievement in the skill areas commonly found in school curricula. Available in 12 levels that correspond to grades kindergarten through grade 12. Level I corresponds to grades 7 and 8. One of the elements of the Comprehensive Assessment Program along with the Developing Cognitive Abilities Test and the School Attitude Measure. Can be used alone or in combination with the other instruments.

16871
National Achievement Test, Level J. Wick, John W.; And Others 1989
Subtests: Reading; Language; Mathematics; Reference Skills; Social Studies; Science
Descriptors: *Achievement Tests; *Grade 8; *Grade 9; Junior High Schools; *Junior High School Students; Language Arts; Mathematics; Reading; Research Skills; Sciences; Secondary Education; Social Sciences
Identifiers: CAP; Comprehensive Assessment Program; NAT
Availability: American Testronics; P.O. Box 2270, Iowa City, IA 52244-9990
Grade Level: 8-9
Notes: Time, 319 min.; Items, 431
Measures student achievement in the skill areas commonly found in school curricula. Available in 12 levels that correspond to grades kindergarten through grade 12. Level J corresponds to grades 8 and 9. One of the elements of the Comprehensive Assessment Program along with the Developing Cognitive Abilities Test and the School Attitude Measure. Can be used alone or in combination with the other instruments.

16872
National Achievement Test, Level K. Wick, John W.; And Others 1989
Subtests: Reading; Language; Mathematics; Reference Skills; Social Studies; Science
Descriptors: *Achievement Tests; *Grade 9; *Grade 10; *Grade 11; High Schools; *High School Students; Language Arts; Mathematics; Reading; Research Skills; Sciences; Social Sciences
Identifiers: CAP; Comprehensive Assessment Program; NAT
Availability: American Testronics; P.O. Box 2270, Iowa City, IA 52244-9990
Grade Level: 9-11
Notes: Time, 255 min.; Items, 356
Measures student achievement in the skill areas commonly found in school curricula. Available in 12 levels that correspond to grades kindergarten through grade 12. Level K corresponds to grades 9 to 11. One of the elements of the Comprehensive Assessment Program along with the Developing Cognitive Abilities Test and the School Attitude Measure. Can be used alone or in combination with the other instruments.

16873
National Achievement Test, Level L. Wick, John W.; And Others 1989
Subtests: Reading; Language; Mathematics; Reference Skills; Social Studies; Science
Descriptors: *Achievement Tests; *Grade 11; *Grade 12; High Schools; *High School Students; Language Arts; Mathematics; Reading; Research Skills; Sciences; Secondary Education; Social Sciences
Identifiers: CAP; Comprehensive Assessment Program; NAT
Availability: American Testronics; P.O. Box 2270, Iowa City, IA 52244-9990
Grade Level: 11-12
Notes: Time, 255 min.; Items, 356
Measures student achievement in the skill areas commonly found in school curricula. Available in 12 levels that correspond to grades kindergarten through grade 12. Level L corresponds to grades 11 and 12. One of the elements of the Comprehensive Assessment Program along with the Developing Cognitive Abilities Test and the School Attitude Measure. Can be used alone or in combination with the other instruments.

16889
Test of Early Reading Ability—2. Reid, D. Kim; And Others 1989
Descriptors: Elementary Education; *Elementary School Students; *Individual Testing; *Preschool Children; Primary Education; *Reading Ability; *Reading Tests; *Young Children
Identifiers: TERA2
Availability: PRO-ED; 8700 Shoal Creek Blvd., Austin, TX 78758-6897
Age Level: 3-9
Notes: Time, 30 min. approx.; Items, 46

Measures early reading in children. Unique in that it assesses reading behaviors that emerge spontaneously during the preschool years. This test is a revision and an expansion of the Test of Early Reading Ability (TC011211) but now contains 2 equivalent forms, covers ages up to 9, and uses standardized logos using regional examples. Item selection has also been improved. Can be used to identify gifted or delayed students, to document progress, to serve as a research instrument, and to suggest instructional practices. Data on norms, validity, and reliability are available. Test is individually administered.

16890
Test of Early Mathematics Ability, Second Edition. Ginsburg, Herbert P.; Baroody, Arthur J. 1990
Descriptors: Diagnostic Tests; Elementary Education; *Elementary School Students; *Individual Testing; Kindergarten Children; Knowledge Level; Mathematics Achievement; *Mathematics Skills; *Mathematics Tests; *Preschool Children; Primary Education; *Young Children
Identifiers: TEMA2
Availability: PRO-ED; 8700 Shoal Creek Blvd., Austin, TX 78758-6897
Age Level: 3-8
Notes: Time, 20 min. approx.; Items, 65

A test of young children's mathematical thinking skills. Measures informal mathematics awareness in the areas of relative magnitude concepts, counting skills, and calculational skills. Also assesses competence in formal mathematics thinking with respect to knowledge of conventions, number facts, calculational skill, and base 10 concepts. Can be used to identify gifted or delayed students, to identify strengths and weaknesses in mathematical thinking, to suggest instructional practices, to document progress, and for research projects. An update of the original Test of Early Mathematics Ability (TC012363). Data on norms, reliability and validity are available. Test is individually administered. Is not a timed test but children should be able to finish relevant portion of test in approximately 20 minutes.

16895
SCAN-TRON Reading Test, Level 8. Wick, John W.; And Others 1985
Subtests: Vocabulary; Reading Comprehension; Word Attack
Descriptors: Elementary Education; Elementary School Students; *Grade 3; *Reading Comprehension; *Reading Tests; *Vocabulary
Identifiers: SCAN TRON
Availability: SCAN-TRON Corp.; Reading Test Div., 2021 E. Del Amo Blvd., Rancho Dominguez, CA 90220
Grade Level: 3
Notes: Time, 85 min. approx.; Items, 95

Measures 2 areas of reading: vocabulary and reading comprehension. Tests are scored using the Scan-Tron Optical Mark Reader at the testing site to provide immediate results. All items are 4-option multiple-choice items. Available in 5 levels that correspond to grades 3 through 8. Level 8 corresponds to grade 3.

16896
SCAN-TRON Reading Test, Level 9. Wick, John W.; And Others 1985
Subtests: Vocabulary; Reading Comprehension
Descriptors: Elementary Education; Elementary School Students; *Grade 4; Intermediate Grades; *Reading Comprehension; *Reading Tests; *Vocabulary
Identifiers: SCAN TRON
Availability: SCAN-TRON Corp.; Reading Test Div., 2021 E. Del Amo Blvd., Rancho Dominguez, CA 90220
Grade Level: 4
Notes: Time, 80 min. approx.; Items, 80

Measures 2 areas of reading: vocabulary and reading comprehension. Tests are scored using the Scan-Tron Optical Mark Reader at the testing site to provide immediate results. All items are 4-option multiple-choice items. Available in 5 levels that correspond to grades 3 through 8. Level 9 corresponds to grade 4.

16897
SCAN-TRON Reading Test, Level 10. Wick, John W.; And Others 1985
Subtests: Vocabulary; Reading Comprehension
Descriptors: Elementary Education; *Elementary School Students; *Grade 5; Intermediate Grades; *Reading Comprehension; *Reading Tests; *Vocabulary
Identifiers: SCAN TRON
Availability: SCAN-TRON Corp.; Reading Test Div., 2021 E. Del Amo Blvd., Rancho Dominguez, CA 90220
Grade Level: 5
Notes: Time, 80 min. approx.; Items, 80

Measures 2 areas of reading: vocabulary and reading comprehension. Tests are scored using the Scan-Tron Optical Mark Reader at the testing site to provide immediate results. All items are 4-option multiple-choice items. Available in 5 levels that correspond to grades 3 through 8. Level 10 corresponds to grade 5.

16898
SCAN-TRON Reading Test, Level 11. Wick, John W.; And Others 1985
Subtests: Vocabulary; Reading Comprehension
Descriptors: Elementary Education; Elementary School Students; *Grade 6; Intermediate Grades; *Reading Comprehension; *Reading Tests; *Vocabulary
Identifiers: SCAN TRON
Availability: SCAN-TRON Corp.; Reading Test Div., 2021 E. Del Amo Blvd., Rancho Dominguez, CA 90220
Grade Level: 6
Notes: Time, 80 min. approx.; Items, 80

Measures 2 areas of reading: vocabulary and reading comprehension. Tests are scored using the Scan-Tron Optical Mark Reader at the testing site to provide immediate results. All items are 4-option, multiple-choice items. Available in 5 levels that correspond to grades 3 through 8. Level 11 corresponds to grade 6.

16899
SCAN-TRON Reading Test, Level 12. Wick, John W.; And Others 1985
Subtests: Vocabulary; Reading Comprehension
Descriptors: Junior High Schools; *Junior High School Students; *Reading Comprehension; *Reading Tests; *Vocabulary
Identifiers: SCAN TRON
Availability: SCAN-TRON Corp.; Reading Test Div., 2021 E. Del Amo Blvd., Rancho Dominguez, CA 90220
Grade Level: 7-8
Notes: Time, 80 min. approx.; Items, 80

Measures 2 areas of reading: vocabulary and reading comprehension. Tests are scored using the Scan-Tron Optical Mark Reader at the testing site to provide immediate results. All items are 4-option multiple-choice items. Available in 5 levels that correspond to grades 3 through 8. Level 12 corresponds to grades 7 and 8.

16900
Comprehensive Tests of Basic Skills, Fourth Edition, Level K, Benchmark Tests. CTB/ Macmillan/McGraw-Hill, Monterey, CA 1989
Subtests: Reading; Mathematics;
Descriptors: *Achievement Tests; *Basic Skills; *Kindergarten Children; Mathematics; *Norm Referenced Tests; Primary Education; Reading
Identifiers: CTBS
Availability: CTB/MacMillan/McGraw-Hill; Del Monte Research Park, 2500 Garden Rd., Monterey, CA 93940
Grade Level: K
Notes: Time, 95 min.; Items, 150

Achievement tests that measure the basic skills of reading, language, spelling, mathematics, study skills, science, and social studies. Eleven levels cover kindergarten through grade 12. Three separate formats, Complete Battery, Survey, and Benchmark are available. All formats place achievement on the same normative scale and results can be directly compared. Complete Battery has 2 forms at each of the levels and includes all areas. A Basic Skills Battery, consisting only of the areas of Reading, Spelling, Language, Mathematics, and Study Skills, is available at Level 12 and above. Survey Tests are for those test users who need only a quick survey of achievement levels, have no need for curriculum-referenced information and for whom testing time is the major consideration. Survey Tests have the same basic content as the Complete Battery, are about half as long, and take about half the time to administer. Benchmark Tests are for users who want only norm-referenced scores of the highest degree of accuracy and have no need for curricular-referenced information. Benchmark Tests have the same basic content structures as the Complete Battery and are about the same length. Level K covers kindergarten.

16901
Comprehensive Tests of Basic Skills, Fourth Edition, Level 10, Benchmark Tests. CTB/ Macmillan/McGraw-Hill, Monterey, CA 1989
Subtests: Reading; Mathematics
Descriptors: *Achievement Tests; *Basic Skills; *Grade 1; *Kindergarten Children; Mathematics; *Norm Referenced Tests; Primary Education; Reading
Identifiers: CTBS
Availability: CTB/MacMillan/McGraw-Hill; Del Monte Research Park, 2500 Garden Rd., Monterey, CA 93940
Grade Level: K-1
Notes: Time, 85 min.; Items, 120

Achievement tests that measure the basic skills of reading, language, spelling, mathematics, study skills, science, and social studies. Eleven levels cover kindergarten through grade 12. Three separate formats, Complete Battery, Survey, and Benchmark are available. All formats place achievement on the same normative scale and results can be directly compared. Complete Battery has 2 forms at each of the levels and includes all areas. A Basic Skills Battery, consisting only of the areas of Reading, Spelling, Language, Mathematics, and Study Skills, is available at Level 12 and above. Survey Tests are for those test users who need only a quick survey of achievement levels, have no need for curriculum-referenced information and for whom testing time is the major consideration. Survey Tests have the same basic content as the Complete Battery, are about half as long, and take about half the time to administer. Benchmark Tests are for users who want only norm-referenced scores of the highest degree of accuracy and have no need for curricular-referenced information. Benchmark Tests have the same basic content structures as the Complete Battery and are about the same length. Level 10 covers kindergarten and grade 1.

16902
Comprehensive Tests of Basic Skills, Fourth Edition, Level 11, Benchmark Tests. CTB/ Macmillan/McGraw-Hill, Monterey, CA 1989
Subtests: Reading; Mathematics; Language; Science; Social Studies
Descriptors: *Achievement Tests; *Basic Skills; *Grade 1; *Grade 2; Language Arts; Mathematics; *Norm Referenced Tests; Reading; Sciences; Social Studies
Identifiers: CTBS
Availability: CTB/MacMillan/McGraw-Hill; Del Monte Research Park, 2500 Garden Rd., Monterey, CA 93940
Grade Level: 1-2
Notes: Time, 233 min.; Items, 290

Achievement tests that measure the basic skills of reading, language, spelling, mathematics, study skills, science, and social studies. Eleven levels cover kindergarten through grade 12. Three separate formats, Complete Battery, Survey, and Benchmark are available. All formats place achievement on the same normative scale and results can be directly compared. Complete Battery has 2 forms at each of the levels and includes all areas. A Basic Skills Battery, consisting only of the areas of Reading, Spelling, Language, Mathematics, and Study Skills, is available at Level 12 and above. Survey Tests are for those test users who need only a quick survey of achievement levels, have no need for curriculum-referenced information and for whom testing time is the major consideration. Survey Tests have the same basic content as the Complete Battery, are about half as long, and take about half the time to administer. Benchmark Tests are for users who want only norm-referenced scores of the highest degree of accuracy and have no need for curricular-referenced information. Benchmark Tests have the same basic content structures as the Complete Battery and are about the same length. Level 11 covers grades 1 and 2.

16903
Comprehensive Tests of Basic Skills, Fourth Edition, Level 12, Benchmark Tests. CTB/ Macmillan/McGraw-Hill, Monterey, CA 1989
Subtests: Reading; Mathematics; Spelling; Language; Science; Social Studies
Descriptors: *Achievement Tests; *Basic Skills; *Elementary School Students; *Grade 1; *Grade 2; *Grade 3; Language Arts; Mathematics; *Norm Referenced Tests; Primary Education; Reading; Sciences; Social Studies; Spelling
Identifiers: CTBS
Availability: CTB/MacMillan/McGraw-Hill; Del Monte Research Park, 2500 Garden Rd., Monterey, CA 93940
Grade Level: 1-3
Notes: Time, 273 min.; Items, 338

Achievement tests that measure the basic skills of reading, language, spelling, mathematics, study skills, science, and social studies. Eleven levels cover kindergarten through grade 12. Three separate formats, Complete Battery, Survey, and Benchmark are available. All formats place achievement on the same normative scale and results can be directly compared. Complete Battery has 2 forms at each of the levels and includes all areas. A Basic Skills Battery, consisting only of the areas of Reading, Spelling, Language, Mathematics, and Study Skills, is available at Level 12 and above. Surey Tests are for those test users who need only a quick survey of achievement levels, have no need for curriculum-referenced information, and for whom testing time is the major consideration. Survey Tests have the same basic content as the Complete Battery, are about half as long, and take about half the time to administer. Benchmark Tests are for users who want only norm-referenced scores of the highest degree of accuracy and have no need for curriculum-referenced information. Benchmark Tests have the same basic content structures as the Complete Battery and are about the same length. Level 12 covers grades 1, 2, and 3.

16904
Comprehensive Tests of Basic Skills, Fourth Edition, Level 13, Benchmark Tests. CTB/ Macmillan/McGraw-Hill, Monterey, CA 1989
Subtests: Reading; Mathematics; Spelling; Language; Sciences; Social Sciences

Descriptors: *Achievement Tests; *Basic Skills; Elementary Education; *Elementary School Students; *Grade 2; *Grade 3; *Grade 4; Language Arts; Mathematics; *Norm Referenced Tests; Reading; Sciences; Social Studies; Spelling
Identifiers: CTBS
Availability: CTB/MacMillan/McGraw-Hill; Del Monte Research Park, 2500 Garden Rd., Monterey, CA 93940
Grade Level: 2-4
Notes: Time, 297 min.; Items, 356

Achievement tests that measure the basic skills of reading, language, spelling, mathematics, study skills, science, and social studies. Eleven levels cover kindergarten through grade 12. Three separate formats, Complete Battery, Survey, and Benchmark are available. All formats place achievement on the same normative scale and results can be directly compared. Complete Battery has 2 forms at each of the levels and includes all areas. A Basic Skills Battery, consisting only of the areas of Reading, Spelling, Language, Mathematics, and Study Skills, is available at Level 12 and above. Survey Tests are for those test users who need only a quick survey of achievement levels, have no need for curriculum-referenced information and for whom testing time is the major consideration. Survey Tests have the same basic content as the Complete Battery, are about half as long, and take about half the time to administer. Benchmark Tests are for users who want only norm-referenced scores of the highest degree of accuracy and have no need for curricular-referenced information. Benchmark Tests have the same basic content structures as the Complete Battery and are about the same length. Level 13 covers grades 2, 3, and 4.

16905
Comprehensive Tests of Basic Skills, Fourth Edition, Level 14, Benchmark Tests. CTB/Macmillan/McGraw-Hill, Monterey, CA 1989
Subtests: Reading; Mathematics; Spelling; Language; Study Skills; Science; Social Studies
Descriptors: *Achievement Tests; *Basic Skills; Elementary Education; *Elementary School Students; *Grade 3; *Grade 4; *Grade 5; Language Arts; Mathematics; *Norm Referenced Tests; Reading; Sciences; Social Studies; Spelling
Identifiers: CTBS
Availability: CTB/MacMillan/McGraw-Hill; Del Monte Research Park, 2500 Garden Rd., Monterey, CA 93940
Grade Level: 3-5
Notes: Time, 300 min.; Items, 400

Achievement tests that measure the basic skills of reading, language, spelling, mathematics, study skills, science, and social studies. Eleven levels cover kindergarten through grade 12. Three separate formats, Complete Battery, Survey, and Benchmark are available. All formats place achievement on the same normative scale and results can be directly compared. Complete Battery has 2 forms at each of the levels and includes all areas. A Basic Skills Battery, consisting only of the areas of Reading, Spelling, Language, Mathematics, and Study Skills, is available at Level 12 and above. Survey Tests are for those test users who need only a quick survey of achievement levels, have no need for curriculum-referenced information and for whom testing time is the major consideration. Survey Tests have the same basic content as the Complete Battery, are about half as long, and take about half the time to administer. Benchmark Tests are for users who want only norm-referenced scores of the highest degree of accuracy and have no need for curricular-referenced information. Benchmark Tests have the same basic content structures as the Complete Battery and are about the same length. Level 14 covers grades 3-5.

16906
Comprehensive Tests of Basic Skills, Fourth Edition, Level 15, Benchmark Tests. CTB/Macmillan/McGraw-Hill, Monterey, CA 1989
Subtests: Reading; Mathematics; Spelling; Language; Study Skills; Science; Social Studies
Descriptors: *Achievement Tests; *Basic Skills; Elementary Education; *Elementary School Students; *Grade 4; *Grade 5; *Grade 6; *Intermediate Grades; Language Arts; Mathematics; *Norm Referenced Tests; Reading; Sciences; Social Studies; Spelling; Study Skills
Identifiers: CTBS
Availability: CTB/MacMillan/McGraw-Hill; Del Monte Research Park, 2500 Garden Rd., Monterey, CA 93940
Grade Level: 4-6
Notes: Time, 300 min.; Items, 400

Achievement tests that measure the basic skills of reading, language, spelling, mathematics, study skills, science, and social studies. Eleven levels cover kindergarten through grade 12. Three separate formats, Complete Battery, Survey, and Benchmark are available. All formats place achievement on the same normative scale and results can be directly compared. Complete Battery has 2 forms at each of the levels and includes all areas. A Basic Skills Battery, consisting only of the areas of Reading, Spelling, Language, Mathematics, and Study Skills, is available at Level 12 and above. Survey Tests are for those test users who need only a quick survey of achievement levels, have no need for curriculum-referenced information and for whom testing time is the major consideration. Survey Tests have the same basic content as the Complete Battery, are about half as long, and take about half the time to administer. Benchmark Tests are for users who want only norm-referenced scores of the highest degree of accuracy and have no need for curricular-referenced information. Benchmark Tests have the same basic content structures as the Complete Battery and are about the same length. Level 15 covers grades 4, 5, and 6.

16907
Comprehensive Tests of Basic Skills, Fourth Edition, Level 16, Benchmark Tests. CTB/Macmillan/McGraw-Hill, Monterey, CA 1989
Subtests: Reading; Mathematics; Spelling; Language; Study Skills; Science; Social Studies
Descriptors: *Achievement Tests; *Basic Skills; Elementary Education; *Elementary School Students; *Grade 5; *Grade 6; *Grade 7; Language Arts; Mathematics; *Norm Referenced Tests; Reading; Sciences; Social Studies; Spelling; Study Skills
Identifiers: CTBS
Availability: CTB/MacMillan/McGraw-Hill; Del Monte Research Park, 2500 Garden Rd., Monterey, CA 93940
Grade Level: 5-7
Notes: Time, 300 min.; Items, 400

Achievement tests that measure the basic skills of reading, language, spelling, mathematics, study skills, science, and social studies. Eleven levels cover kindergarten through grade 12. Three separate formats, Complete Battery, Survey, and Benchmark are available. All formats place achievement on the same normative scale and results can be directly compared. Complete Battery has 2 forms at each of the levels and includes all areas. A Basic Skills Battery, consisting only of the areas of Reading, Spelling, Language, Mathematics, and Study Skills, is available at Level 12 and above. Survey Tests are for those test users who need only a quick survey of achievement levels, have no need for curriculum-referenced information and for whom testing time is the major consideration. Survey Tests have the same basic content as the Complete Battery, are about half as long, and take about half the time to administer. Benchmark Tests are for users who want only norm-referenced scores of the highest degree of accuracy and have no need for curricular-referenced information. Benchmark Tests have the same basic content structures as the Complete Battery and are about the same length. Level 16 covers grades 5, 6, and 7.

16908
Comprehensive Tests of Basic Skills, Fourth Edition, Level 17/18, Benchmark Tests. CTB/Macmillan/McGraw-Hill, Monterey, CA 1989
Subtests: Reading; Mathematics; Spelling; Language; Sciences; Social Studies; Study Skills
Descriptors: *Achievement Tests; *Basic Skills; *Elementary School Students; Elementary Secondary Education; Grade 6; Grade 7; Grade 8; Grade 9; *Junior High School Students; Language Arts; Mathematics; *Norm Referenced Tests; Reading; Sciences; Social Studies; Spelling; Study Skills
Identifiers: CTBS
Availability: CTB/MacMillan/McGraw-Hill; Del Monte Research Park, 2500 Garden Rd., Monterey, CA 93940
Grade Level: 6-9
Notes: Time, 300 min.; Items, 400

Achievement tests that measure the basic skills of reading, language, spelling, mathematics, study skills, science, and social studies. Eleven levels cover kindergarten through grade 12. Three separate formats, Complete Battery, Survey, and Benchmark are available. All formats place achievement on the same normative scale and results can be directly compared. Complete Battery has 2 forms at each of the levels and includes all areas. A Basic Skills Battery, consisting only of the areas of Reading, Spelling, Language, Mathematics, and Study Skills, is available at Level 12 and above. Survey Tests are for those test users who need only a quick survey of achievement levels, have no need for curriculum-referenced information and for whom testing time is the major consideration. Survey Tests have the same basic content as the Complete Battery, are about half as long, and take about half the time to administer. Benchmark Tests are for users who want only norm-referenced scores of the highest degree of accuracy and have no need for curricular-referenced information. Benchmark Tests have the same basic content structures as the Complete Battery and are about the same length. Level 17/18 covers grades 6 through 9.

16909
Comprehensive Tests of Basic Skills, Fourth Edition, Level 19/20, Benchmark Tests. CTB/Macmillan/McGraw-Hill, Monterey, CA 1989
Subtests: Reading; Mathematics; Spelling; Language; Study Skills; Science; Social Studies
Descriptors: *Achievement Tests; *Basic Skills; Grade 8; Grade 9; Grade 10; Grade 11; *High School Students; *Junior High School Students; Language Arts; Mathematics; *Norm Referenced Tests; Reading; Sciences; Secondary Education; Social Studies; Spelling; Study Skills
Identifiers: CTBS
Availability: CTB/MacMillan/McGraw-Hill; Del Monte Research Park, 2500 Garden Rd., Monterey, CA 93940
Grade Level: 8-11
Notes: Time, 300 min.; Items, 400

Achievement tests that measure the basic skills of reading, language, spelling, mathematics, study skills, science, and social studies. Eleven levels cover kindergarten through grade 12. Three separate formats, Complete Battery, Survey, and Benchmark are available. All formats place achievement on the same normative scale and results can be directly compared. Complete Battery has 2 forms at each of the levels and includes all areas. A Basic Skills Battery, consisting only of the areas of Reading, Spelling, Language, Mathematics, and Study Skills, is available at Level 12 and above. Survey Tests are for those test users who need only a quick survey of achievement levels, have no need for curriculum-referenced information and for whom testing time is the major consideration. Survey Tests have the same basic content as the Complete Battery, are about half as long, and take about half the time to administer. Benchmark Tests are for users who want only norm-referenced scores of the highest degree of accuracy and have no need for curricular-referenced information. Benchmark Tests have the same basic content structures as the Complete Battery and are about the same length. Level 19/20 covers grades 8 through 11.

16910
Comprehensive Tests of Basic Skills, Fourth Edition, Level 21/22, Benchmark Tests. CTB/Macmillan/McGraw-Hill, Monterey, CA 1989
Subtests: Reading; Mathematics; Spelling; Language; Study Skills; Science; Social Studies
Descriptors: *Achievement Tests; *Basic Skills; Grade 10; Grade 11; Grade 12; High Schools; *High School Students; Language Arts; Mathematics; *Norm Referenced Tests; Reading; Sciences; Social Studies; Spelling; Study Skills
Identifiers: CTBS
Availability: CTB/MacMillan/McGraw-Hill; Del Monte Research Park, 2500 Garden Rd., Monterey, CA 93940
Grade Level: 10-12
Notes: Time, 300 min.; Items, 400

Achievement tests that measure the basic skills of reading, language, spelling, mathematics, study skills, science, and social studies. Eleven levels cover kindergarten through grade 12. Three separate formats, Complete Battery, Survey, and Benchmark are available. All formats place achievement on the same normative scale and results can be directly compared. Complete Battery has 2 forms at each of the levels and includes all areas. A Basic Skills Battery, consisting only of the areas of Reading, Spelling, Language, Mathematics, and Study Skills, is available at Level 12 and above. Survey Tests are for those test users who need only a quick survey of achievement levels, have no need for curriculum-referenced information and for whom testing time is the major consideration. Survey Tests have the same basic content as the Complete Battery, are about half as long, and take about half the time to administer. Benchmark Tests are for users who want only norm-referenced scores of the highest degree of accuracy and have no need for curricular-referenced information. Benchmark Tests have the same basic content structures as the Complete Battery and are about the same length. Level 21/22 covers grades 10 through 12.

16911
Comprehensive Tests of Basic Skills, Fourth Edition, Level K, Survey Tests. CTB/Macmillan/McGraw-Hill, Monterey, CA 1989
Subtests: Reading; Mathematics
Descriptors: *Achievement Tests; *Basic Skills; *Kindergarten Children; Mathematics; *Norm Referenced Tests; Primary Education; Reading
Identifiers: CTBS
Availability: CTB/MacMillan/McGraw-Hill; Del Monte Research Park, 2500 Garden Rd., Monterey, CA 93940
Grade Level: K
Notes: Time, 64 min.; Items, 100

Achievement tests that measure the basic skills of reading, language, spelling, mathematics, study skills, science, and social studies. Eleven levels cover kindergarten through grade 12. Three separate formats, Complete Battery, Survey, and Benchmark are available. All formats place achievement on the same normative scale and results can be directly compared. Complete Battery has 2 forms at each of the levels and includes all areas. A Basic Skills Battery, consisting only of the areas of Reading, Spelling, Language, Mathematics, and Study Skills, is available at Level 12 and above. Survey Tests are for those test users who need only a quick survey of achievement levels, have no need for curriculum-referenced information and for whom testing time is the major consideration. Survey

Tests have the same basic content as the Complete Battery, are about half as long, and take about half the time to administer. Benchmark Tests are for users who want only norm-referenced scores of the highest degree of accuracy and have no need for curricular-referenced information. Benchmark Tests have the same basic content structures as the Complete Battery and are about the same length. Level K covers kindergarten.

16912

Comprehensive Tests of Basic Skills, Fourth Edition, Level 10, Survey Tests. CTB/Macmillan/McGraw-Hill, Monterey, CA 1989
Subtests: Reading; Mathematics
Descriptors: *Achievement Tests; *Basic Skills; *Grade 1; *Kindergarten Children; Mathematics; *Norm Referenced Tests; Primary Education; Reading
Identifiers: CTBS
Availability: CTB/Macmillan/McGraw-Hill; Del Monte Research Park, 2500 Garden Rd., Monterey, CA 93940
Grade Level: K-1
Notes: Time, 59 min.; Items, 80

Achievement tests that measure the basic skills of reading, language, spelling, mathematics, study skills, science, and social studies. Eleven levels cover kindergarten through grade 12. Three separate formats, Complete Battery, Survey, and Benchmark are available. All formats place achievement on the same normative scale and results can be directly compared. Complete Battery has 2 forms at each of the levels and includes all areas. A Basic Skills Battery, consisting only of the areas of Reading, Spelling, Language, Mathematics, and Study Skills, is available at Level 12 and above. Survey Tests are for those test users who need only a quick survey of achievement levels, have no need for curriculum-referenced information and for whom testing time is the major consideration. Survey Tests have the same basic content as the Complete Battery, are about half as long, and take about half the time to administer. Benchmark Tests are for users who want only norm-referenced scores of the highest degree of accuracy and have no need for curricular-referenced information. Benchmark Tests have the same basic content structures as the Complete Battery and are about the same length. Level 10 covers kindergarten and grade 1.

16913

Comprehensive Tests of Basic Skills, Fourth Edition, Level 11, Survey Tests. CTB/Macmillan/McGraw-Hill, Monterey, CA 1989
Subtests: Reading; Mathematics; Science; Social Studies; Language
Descriptors: *Achievement Tests; *Basic Skills; *Grade 1; *Grade 2; Language Arts; Mathematics; *Norm Referenced Tests; Primary Education; Reading; Sciences; Social Studies
Identifiers: CTBS
Availability: CTB/Macmillan/McGraw-Hill; Del Monte Research Park, 2500 Garden Rd., Monterey, CA 93940
Grade Level: 1-2
Notes: Time, 147 min.; Items, 180

Achievement tests that measure the basic skills of reading, language, spelling, mathematics, study skills, science, and social studies. Eleven levels cover kindergarten through grade 12. Three separate formats, Complete Battery, Survey, and Benchmark are available. All formats place achievement on the same normative scale and results can be directly compared. Complete Battery has 2 forms at each of the levels and includes all areas. A Basic Skills Battery, consisting only of the areas of Reading, Spelling, Language, Mathematics, and Study Skills is available at Level 12 and above. Survey Tests are for those test users who need only a quick survey of achievement levels, have no need for curriculum-referenced information and for whom testing time is the major consideration. Survey Tests have the same basic content as the Complete Battery, are about half as long, and take about half the time to administer. Benchmark Tests are for users who want only norm-referenced scores of the highest degree of accuracy and have no need for curricular-referenced information. Benchmark Tests have the same basic content structures as the Complete Battery and are about the same length. Level 11 covers grades 1 and 2.

16914

Comprehensive Tests of Basic Skills, Fourth Edition, Level 12, Survey Tests. CTB/Macmillan/McGraw-Hill, Monterey, CA 1989
Subtests: Reading; Mathematics; Spelling; Language; Science; Social Studies
Descriptors: *Achievement Tests; *Basic Skills; *Elementary School Students; *Grade 1; *Grade 2; *Grade 3; Language Arts; Mathematics; *Norm Referenced Tests; Primary Education; Reading; Sciences; Social Studies; Spelling
Identifiers: CTBS
Availability: CTB/Macmillan/McGraw-Hill; Del Monte Research Park, 2500 Garden Rd., Monterey, CA 93940
Grade Level: 1-3
Notes: Time, 164 min.; Items, 200

Achievement tests that measure the basic skills of reading, language, spelling, mathematics, study skills, science, and social studies. Eleven levels cover kindergarten through grade 12. Three separate formats, Complete Battery, Survey, and Benchmark are available. All formats place achievement on the same normative scale and results can be directly compared. Complete Battery has 2 forms at each of the levels and includes all areas. A Basic Skills Battery, consisting only of the areas of Reading, Spelling, Language, Mathematics, and Study Skills, is available at Level 12 and above. Survey Tests are for those test users who need only a quick survey of achievement levels, have no need for curriculum-referenced information and for whom testing time is the major consideration. Survey Tests have the same basic content as the Complete Battery, are about half as long, and take about half the time to administer. Benchmark Tests are for users who want only norm-referenced scores of the highest degree of accuracy and have no need for curricular-referenced information. Benchmark Tests have the same basic content structures as the Complete Battery and are about the same length. Level 12 covers grades 1, 2, and 3.

16915

Comprehensive Tests of Basic Skills, Fourth Edition, Level 13, Survey Tests. CTB/Macmillan/McGraw-Hill, Monterey, CA 1989
Subtests: Reading; Mathematics; Spelling; Language; Science; Social Studies
Descriptors: *Achievement Tests; *Basic Skills; Elementary Education; *Elementary School Students; *Grade 2; *Grade 3; *Grade 4; Language Arts; Mathematics; *Norm Referenced Tests; Reading; Sciences; Social Studies; Spelling
Identifiers: CTBS
Availability: CTB/Macmillan/McGraw-Hill; Del Monte Research Park, 2500 Garden Rd., Monterey, CA 93940
Grade Level: 2-4
Notes: Time, 167 min.; Items, 200

Achievement tests that measure the basic skills of reading, language, spelling, mathematics, study skills, science, and social studies. Eleven levels cover kindergarten through grade 12. Three separate formats, Complete Battery, Survey, and Benchmark are available. All formats place achievement on the same normative scale and results can be directly compared. Complete Battery has 2 forms at each of the levels and includes all areas. A Basic Skills Battery, consisting only of the areas of Reading, Spelling, Language, Mathematics, and Study Skills, is available at Level 12 and above. Survey Tests are for those test users who need only a quick survey of achievement levels, have no need for curriculum-referenced information and for whom testing time is the major consideration. Survey Tests have the same basic content as the Complete Battery, are about half as long, and take about half the time to administer. Benchmark Tests are for users who want only norm-referenced scores of the highest degree of accuracy and have no need for curricular-referenced information. Benchmark Tests have the same basic content structures as the Complete Battery and are about the same length. Level 13 covers grades 2 through 4.

16916

Comprehensive Tests of Basic Skills, Fourth Edition, Level 14, Survey Tests. CTB/Macmillan/McGraw-Hill, Monterey, CA 1989
Subtests: Reading; Mathematics; Spelling; Language; Science; Social Studies; Study Skills
Descriptors: *Achievement Tests; *Basic Skills; Elementary Education; *Elementary School Students; *Grade 3; *Grade 4; *Grade 5; Language Arts; Mathematics; *Norm Referenced Tests; Reading; Sciences; Social Studies; Spelling; Study Skills
Identifiers: CTBS
Availability: CTB/Macmillan/McGraw-Hill; Del Monte Research Park, 2500 Garden Rd., Monterey, CA 93940
Grade Level: 3-5
Notes: Time, 151 min.; Items, 200

Achievement tests that measure the basic skills of reading, language, spelling, mathematics, study skills, science, and social studies. Eleven levels cover kindergarten through grade 12. Three separate formats, Complete Battery, Survey, and Benchmark are available. All formats place achievement on the same normative scale and results can be directly compared. Complete Battery has 2 forms at each of the levels and includes all areas. A Basic Skills Battery, consisting only of the areas of Reading, Spelling, Language, Mathematics, and Study Skills, is available at Level 12 and above. Survey Tests are for those test users who need only a quick survey of achievement levels, have no need for curriculum-referenced information and for whom testing time is the major consideration. Survey Tests have the same basic content as the Complete Battery, are about half as long, and take about half the time to administer. Benchmark Tests are for users who want only norm-referenced scores of the highest degree of accuracy and have no need for curricular-referenced information. Benchmark Tests have the same basic content structures as the Complete Battery and are about the same length. Level 14 covers grades 3, 4, and 5.

16917

Comprehensive Tests of Basic Skills, Fourth Edition, Level 15, Survey Tests. CTB/Macmillan/McGraw-Hill, Monterey, CA 1989
Subtests: Reading; Mathematics; Spelling; Language; Science; Social Studies; Study Skills
Descriptors: *Achievement Tests; *Basic Skills; Elementary Education; *Elementary School Students; *Grade 4; *Grade 5; *Grade 6; Intermediate Grades; Language Arts; Mathematics; *Norm Referenced Tests; Reading; Sciences; Social Studies; Spelling; Study Skills
Identifiers: CTBS
Availability: CTB/Macmillan/McGraw-Hill; Del Monte Research Park, 2500 Garden Rd., Monterey, CA 93940
Grade Level: 4-6
Notes: Time, 151 min.; Items, 200

Achievement tests that measure the basic skills of reading, language, spelling, mathematics, study skills, science, and social studies. Eleven levels cover kindergarten through grade 12. Three separate formats, Complete Battery, Survey, and Benchmark are available. All formats place achievement on the same normative scale and results can be directly compared. Complete Battery has 2 forms at each of the levels and includes all areas. A Basic Skills Battery, consisting only of the areas of Reading, Spelling, Language, Mathematics, and Study Skills, is available at Level 12 and above. Survey Tests are for those test users who need only a quick survey of achievement levels, have no need for curriculum-referenced information and for whom testing time is the major consideration. Survey Tests have the same basic content as the Complete Battery, are about half as long, and take about half the time to administer. Benchmark Tests are for users who want only norm-referenced scores of the highest degree of accuracy and have no need for curricular-referenced information. Benchmark Tests have the same basic content structures as the Complete Battery and are about the same length. Level 15 covers grades 4, 5, and 6.

16918

Comprehensive Tests of Basic Skills, Fourth Edition, Level 16, Survey Tests. CTB/Macmillan/McGraw-Hill, Monterey, CA 1989
Subtests: Reading; Mathematics; Spelling; Language; Science; Social Studies; Study Skills
Descriptors: *Achievement Tests; *Basic Skills; Elementary Education; *Elementary School Students; *Grade 5; *Grade 6; *Grade 7; Language Arts; Mathematics; *Norm Referenced Tests; Reading; Sciences; Social Studies; Spelling; Study Skills
Identifiers: CTBS
Availability: CTB/Macmillan/McGraw-Hill; Del Monte Research Park, 2500 Garden Rd., Monterey, CA 93940
Grade Level: 5-7
Notes: Time, 151 min.; Items, 200

Achievement tests that measure the basic skills of reading, language, spelling, mathematics, study skills, science, and social studies. Eleven levels cover kindergarten through grade 12. Three separate formats, Complete Battery, Survey, and Benchmark are available. All formats place achievement on the same normative scale and results can be directly compared. Complete Battery has 2 forms at each of the levels and includes all areas. A Basic Skills Battery, consisting only of the areas of Reading, Spelling, Language, Mathematics, and Study Skills, is available at Level 12 and above. Survey Tests are for those test users who need only a quick survey of achievement levels, have no need for curriculum-referenced information and for whom testing time is the major consideration. Survey Tests have the same basic content as the Complete Battery, are about half as long, and take about half the time to administer. Benchmark Tests are for users who want only norm-referenced scores of the highest degree of accuracy and have no need for curricular-referenced information. Benchmark Tests have the same basic content structures as the Complete Battery and are about the same length. Level 16 covers grades 5, 6, and 7.

16919

Comprehensive Tests of Basic Skills, Fourth Edition, Level 17/18, Survey Tests. CTB/Macmillan/McGraw-Hill, Monterey, CA 1989
Subtests: Reading; Mathematics; Spelling; Language; Sciences; Social Studies; Study Skills
Descriptors: *Achievement Tests; *Basic Skills; *Elementary School Students; Elementary Secondary Education; Grade 6; Grade 7; Grade 8; Grade 9; *Junior High School Students; Language Arts; Mathematics; *Norm Referenced Tests; Reading; Sciences; Social Studies; Spelling; Study Skills
Identifiers: CTBS
Availability: CTB/Macmillan/McGraw-Hill; Del Monte Research Park, 2500 Garden Rd., Monterey, CA 93940
Grade Level: 6-9
Notes: Time, 151 min.; Items, 200

Achievement tests that measure the basic skills of reading, language, spelling, mathematics, study skills, science, and social studies. Eleven levels cover kindergarten through grade 12. Three separate formats, Complete Battery, Survey, and Benchmark are available. All formats place achievement on the same normative scale and results can be directly compared. Complete Battery has 2 forms at each of the levels and includes all areas. A Basic Skills Battery, consisting only of the areas of Reading, Spelling, Language, Mathematics, and Study Skills, is available at Level 12 and above. Survey Tests are for those test users who need only a quick survey of achievement levels, have no need for curriculum-referenced information and for whom testing time is the major consideration. Survey Tests have the same basic content as the Complete Battery, are about half as long, and take about half the time to administer. Benchmark Tests are for users who want only norm-referenced scores of the highest degree of accuracy and have no need for curricular-referenced information. Benchmark Tests have the same basic content structures as the Complete Battery and are about the same length. Level 17/18 covers grades 6 through 9.

16920
Comprehensive Tests of Basic Skills, Fourth Edition, Level 19/20, Survey Tests. CTB/ Macmillan/McGraw-Hill, Monterey, CA 1989
Subtests: Reading; Mathematics; Spelling; Language; Science; Social Studies; Study Skills
Descriptors: *Achievement Tests; *Basic Skills; Grade 8; Grade 9; Grade 10; Grade 11; *High School Students; *Junior High School Students; Language Arts; Mathematics; *Norm Referenced Tests; Reading; Sciences; Secondary Education; Social Studies; Spelling; Study Skills
Identifiers: CTBS
Availability: CTB/MacMillan/McGraw-Hill; Del Monte Research Park, 2500 Garden Rd., Monterey, CA 93940
Grade Level: 8-11
Notes: Time, 151 min.; Items, 200

Achievement tests that measure the basic skills of reading, language, spelling, mathematics, study skills, science, and social studies. Eleven levels cover kindergarten through grade 12. Three separate formats, Complete Battery, Survey, and Benchmark are available. All formats place achievement on the same normative scale and results can be directly compared. Complete Battery has 2 forms at each of the levels and includes all areas. A Basic Skills Battery, consisting only of the areas of Reading, Spelling, Language, Mathematics, and Study Skills is available at Level 12 and above. Survey Tests are for those test users who need only a quick survey of achievement levels, have no need for curriculum-referenced information and for whom testing time is the major consideration. Survey Tests have the same basic content as the Complete Battery, are about half as long, and take about half the time to administer. Benchmark Tests are for users who want only norm-referenced scores of the highest degree of accuracy and have no need for curricular-referenced information. Benchmark Tests have the same basic content structures as the Complete Battery and are about the same length. Level 19/20 covers grades 8 through 11.

16921
Comprehensive Tests of Basic Skills, Fourth Edition, Level 21/22, Survey Tests. CTB/ Macmillan/McGraw-Hill, Monterey, CA 1989
Subtests: Reading; Mathematics; Spelling; Language; Study Skills; Social Studies; Science
Descriptors: *Achievement Tests; *Basic Skills; Grade 10; Grade 11; Grade 12; High Schools; *High School Students; Language Arts; Mathematics; *Norm Referenced Tests; Reading; Sciences; Social Studies; Spelling; Study Skills
Identifiers: CTBS
Availability: CTB/MacMillan/McGraw-Hill; Del Monte Research Park, 2500 Garden Rd., Monterey, CA 93940
Grade Level: 10-12
Notes: Time, 151 min.; Items, 200

Achievement tests that measure the basic skills of reading, language, spelling, mathematics, study skills, science, and social studies. Eleven levels cover kindergarten through grade 12. Three separate formats, Complete Battery, Survey, and Benchmark are available. All formats place achievement on the same normative scale and results can be directly compared. Complete Battery has 2 forms at each of the levels and includes all areas. A Basic Skills Battery, consisting only of the areas of Reading, Spelling, Language, Mathematics, and Study Skills, is available at Level 12 and above. Survey Tests are for those test users who need only a quick survey of achievement levels, have no need for curriculum-referenced information and for whom testing time is the major consideration. Survey Tests have the same basic content as the Complete Battery, are about half as long, and take about half the time to administer. Benchmark Tests are for users who want only norm-referenced scores of the highest degree of accuracy and have no need for curricular-referenced information. Benchmark Tests have the same basic content structures as the Complete Battery and are about the same length. Level 21/22 covers grades 10 through 12.

16927
Alzheimer's Disease Knowledge Test. Dieckmann, Lisa 1988
Descriptors: Adults; *Alzheimers Disease; Criterion Referenced Tests; *Family Caregivers; *Health Personnel; *Knowledge Level; Multiple Choice Tests
Identifiers: ADK
Availability: *Gerontologist,* v28 n3 p402-07, Jun 1988
Age Level: Adults
Notes: Items, 20

A multiple-choice test designed to measure individuals' level of knowledge about Alzheimer's Disease. Intended for use of caregivers (including the families of individuals with Alzheimer's Disease), mental health professionals, and nursing home staff members. May be used to evaluate programs, introduce topics in educational settings, stimulate group discussion, clarify common misconceptions, establish educational objectives, and evaluate support groups. Multiple-choice format is such that it allows test administrators to analyze the direction of incorrect answers to determine whether respondents have a positive or negative bias: contains an "I don't know" option to help differentiate between lack of knowledge and misinformation. Technical data included.

16929
Rating Inventory for Screening Kindergartners. Coleman, J. Michael; Dover, G. Michael 1990
Descriptors: *At Risk Persons; *Computer Assisted Testing; Educational Diagnosis; *Kindergarten Children; Mainstreaming; *Software; Preschool Education; Rating Scales; *Screening Tests; Special Education
Identifiers: RISK
Availability: PRO-ED; 8700 Shoal Creek Blvd., Austin, TX 78758-6897
Grade Level: K
Age Level: 5-6
Notes: Items, 42

This screening instrument is used to assess kindergarten children who are likely to encounter difficulties in the educational mainstream. It is a computer program that uses the teachers' ratings from each kindergarten classroom to provide local norms against which to contrast the performance of each child being screened. This program is menu driven and is designed to be used by teachers who do not have extensive computer knowledge. It is organized by modules that control the 6 basic functions: general instructions; rating students; printing results; selecting active teacher; end-of-year processing; and utilities. This tool cannot be used solely as the basis for placement in special education.

16934
Spanish Language Assessment Procedures, Revised Edition. Mattes, Larry J. 1989
Descriptors: Children; *Communication Skills; *Criterion Referenced Tests; *Elementary School Students; *Individual Testing; Language Skills; *Listening Skills; Primary Education; *Spanish Speaking; *Speech Skills; Verbal Ability
Identifiers: SLAP
Availability: United Educational Services, Inc.; P.O. Box 1099, Buffalo, NY 14224
Grade Level: K-3
Age Level: 5-8

Designed to be used by bilingual education teachers, speech and language pathologists in determining children's learning needs and in developing instructional programs. Used to assess the structural and functional aspects of communication, and a variety of listening and speaking skills. A management system is included to maintain an ongoing record of performance as children progress from kindergarten through the third grade. The inventory is organized into 3 components: criterion-referenced assessment of Spanish communication; assessment of Spanish speech sound production; and communication sampling and the identification of communicative disorders. Older children who demonstrate significant delays in language development may be assessed with the use of this instrument.

16937
Aprenda: La Prueba de Logros en Espanol, Intermediate 2. Psychological Corp., San Antonio, TX 1990
Subtests: Vocabulary (Vocabulario); Language Expression (Lenguaje: Expression); Reading Comprehension (Comprehension de Lectura); Study Skills (Destrezas de estudio); Concepts of Numbers (Conceptos de Numero); Listening Comprehension (comprension auditiva); Mathematics Computation (calculos matematicos); Spelling (Ortografia); Thinking Skills (Destrezas de Pensamiento); Language Mechanics (Lengvje: Mecanica); Mathematics Application (Aplicaciones matematicos)
Descriptors: *Achievement Tests; Computation; *Elementary School Students; *Grade 05; *Grade 06; Intermediate Grades; Language Skills; *Limited English Speaking; Listening Comprehension; Mathematical Applications; Mathematics Skills; Non English Speaking; Number Concepts; Reading Comprehension; *Spanish Speaking; Spelling; Study Skills; Thinking Skills; Vocabulary
Identifiers: Stanford Achievement Test Series
Availability: The Psychological Corp.; 555 Academic Ct., San Antonio, TX 78204-0952
Grade Level: 5-6
Notes: Time, 285 min. approx.; Items, 357

Aprenda: La Prueba de Logros en Espanol was designed for students whose primary language of instruction is Spanish. This instrument measures Spanish-speaking students' grasp of content and was developed in the Spanish language. It has been constructed to match those objectives of the Stanford Achievement Test Series, Eighth Edition, and assesses the primary educational objectives at each grade from kindergarten through grade 8. The Intermediate 2 level includes measures of reading, mathematics, spelling, language, study skills, and listening. It assesses both vocabulary knowledge and skills and reading for meaning with various types of texts. The concepts and skills that are assessed in each content area are those ordinarily taught during the second half of grade 5 and the first half of grade 6.

16938
Aprenda: La Prueba de Logros en Espanol, Preprimer Level. Psychological Corp., San Antonio, TX 1990
Subtests: Sounds and Letters (Sonidos y letras); Mathematics (Matematicas); Word Reading (Lectura de Palabras); Sentence Reading (Lectura de Oraciones); Listening to Words and Stories (Palabras y Cuentos)
Descriptors: *Achievement Tests; Elementary School Students; *Grade 01; *Kindergarten Children; *Limited English Speaking; Listening Comprehension; Mathematics Skills; Non English Speaking; Phonetics; Primary Education; Reading Skills; *Spanish Speaking
Identifiers: Stanford Achievement Test Series
Availability: The Psychological Corp.; 555 Academic Ct., San Antonio, TX 78204-0952
Grade Level: K-1
Age Level: 5-7
Notes: Time, 155 min. approx.; Items, 200

Aprenda: La Prueba de Logros en Espanol was designed for students whose primary language of instruction is Spanish. It measures Spanish-speaking students' grasp of content and was developed in the Spanish language. This instrument has been constructed to match those objectives of the Stanford Achievement Test Series, Eighth Edition, and assesses the primary educational objectives at each grade from kindergarten through grade 8. The PrePrimer Level is designed to measure a segment of the cognitive learning of 5-, 6-, and 7-year-old children, assessing the learning that children gain as they progress through kindergarten and the first half of grade 1.

16939
Aprenda: La Prueba de Logros en Espanol, Primary 1 Level. Psychological Corp., San Antonio, TX 1990
Subtests: Word Reading (Lectura de Palabros); Language (Lenguaje); Reading Comprehension (comprension); Listening Comprehension (comprension auditiva); Concepts of Numbers (conceptos de numero); Mathematics Computation (calculos matematicos); Mathematics Applications (Applicacionas matematicos); Spelling (Ortografia)
Descriptors: *Achievement Tests; Computation; Elementary School Students; *Grade 01; *Grade 02; Language Skills; *Limited English Speaking; Listening Comprehension; Mathematical Applications; Mathematics Skills; Non English Speaking; Number Concepts; Primary Education; Reading Comprehension; *Spanish Speaking; Spelling
Identifiers: Stanford Achievement Test Series
Availability: The Psychological Corp.; 555 Academic Ct., San Antonio, TX 78204-0952
Grade Level: 1-2
Notes: Time, 235 min. approx.; Items, 275

Aprenda: La Prueba de Logros en Espanol was designed for students whose primary language of instruction is Spanish. It measures Spanish-speaking students' grasp of content and was developed in the Spanish language. This instrument has been constructed to match those objectives of the Stanford Achievement Test Series, Eighth Edition, and assesses the primary educational objectives at each grade from kindergarten through grade 8. The Primary 1 level includes measures of reading, mathematics, spelling, language, and listening. The concepts and skills that are assessed in each content area are those ordinarily taught during the second half of grade 1 and the first half of grade 2.

16940
Aprenda: La Prueba de Logros en Espanol, Primary 2 Level. Psychological Corp., San Antonio, TX 1990
Subtests: Vocabulary (Vocabulario); Spelling (Ortografia); Reading Comprehension (comprehension de lectura); Language (Lenguaje); Concepts of Numbers (conceptos de Numero); Listening Comprehension (comprension auditiva); Mathematics Computation (calculos Matematicos); Mathematics Applications (Applicaciones Matematicos)
Descriptors: *Achievement Tests; Computation; Elementary School Students; *Grade 2; *Grade 3; Language Skills; *Limited English Speaking; Listening Comprehension; Mathematical Applications; Mathematics Skills; Non English Speaking; Number Concepts; Primary Education; Reading Comprehension; *Spanish Speaking; Spelling; Vocabulary
Identifiers: Stanford Achievement Test Series
Availability: The Psychological Corp.; 555 Academic Ct., San Antonio, TX 78204-0952
Grade Level: 2-3
Notes: Time, 230 min. approx.; Items, 284

Aprenda: La Prueba de Logros en Espanol was designed for students whose primary language of instruction is Spanish. This instrument measures Spanish-speaking students' grasp of content and was developed in the Spanish language. It has been constructed to match those objectives of the Stanford Achievement Test Series, Eighth Edition, and assesses the primary educational objectives at each grade from kindergarten through grade 8. The Primary 2 level includes measures of reading, mathematics, spelling, language, and listening. The concepts and skills that are assessed in each content area are those ordinarily taught during the second half of grade 2 and the first half of grade 3.

16941
Aprenda: La Prueba de Logros en Espanol, Primary 3 Level. Psychological Corp., San Antonio, TX 1990
Subtests: Vocabulary (Vocabulario); Language Mechanics (Lenguaje: Mecanica); Reading Comprehension (comprehension de lectura); Language Expression (Lenguaje: Expression); Concept of Numbers (conceptos de Numero); Study Skills (Destrezas de estudio); Mathematics Computation (calculos matematicos); Listening Comprehension (comprehension auditiva); Mathematics Applications (Aplicaciones Matematicos); Spelling (Ortografia); Thinking Skills (Destrezas de Pensamiento Critico)
Descriptors: *Achievement Tests; Computation; Elementary Education; Elementary School Students; *Grade 3; *Grade 4; Language Skills; *Limited English Speaking; Listening Comprehension; Mathematical Applications; Mathematics Skills; Non English Speaking; Number Concepts; Reading Comprehension; *Spanish Speaking; Spelling; Study Skills; Thinking Skills; Vocabulary
Identifiers: Stanford Achievement Test Series
Availability: The Psychological Corp.; 555 Academic Ct., San Antonio, TX 78204-0952
Grade Level: 3-4
Notes: Time, 275 min. approx.; Items, 335

Aprenda: La Prueba de Logros en Espanol was designed for students whose primary language of instruction is Spanish. It measures Spanish-speaking students' grasp of content and was developed in the Spanish language. This instrument has been constructed to match those objectives of the Stanford Achievement Test Series, Eighth Edition, and assesses the primary educational objectives at each grade from kindergarten through grade 8. The Primary 3 level includes measures of reading, mathematics, language, spelling, study skills, and listening. The concepts and skills that are assessed in each content area are those ordinarily taught during the second half of grade 3 and the first half of grade 4.

16948
Diagnostic Achievement Battery, Second Edition. Newcomer, Phyllis L.; Curtis, Dolores 1990
Subtests: Story Comprehension; Characteristics; Synonyms; Grammatic Completion; Alphabet/Word Knowledge; Reading Comprehension; Capitalization; Punctuation; Spelling; Writing Composition; Mathematics Reasoning; Mathematics Calculation
Descriptors: *Academic Achievement; *Achievement Tests; Children; Elementary Education; *Elementary School Students; *Individual Testing; Language Arts; Mathematics Tests; Reading Tests; *Standardized Tests; Writing Tests
Identifiers: DAB2
Availability: PRO-ED; 8700 Shoal Creek Blvd., Austin, TX 78758-6897
Age Level: 6-14
Notes: Time, 120 min. approx.

A nationally standardized individual achievement test that can be used to assess children's abilities in listening, speaking, reading, writing, and mathematics. This instrument is intended to identify those students who are significantly below their peers and may profit from supplemental or remedial help; to determine the particular kinds of component strengths and weaknesses that individual students possess; to document students' progress in specific areas as a consequence of special intervention programs; and to serve as a measurement device in research studies of the academic achievement of elementary school children. Norming procedures were based on demographic characteristics and the types of normative statistics in terms of subtest standard scores, composite scores, percentile ranks, and grade equivalents.

16953
Preschool Health Knowledge Instrument. Andrews, Richard; Hendricks, Charlotte M. 1987
Descriptors: Early Childhood Education; *Health; *Individual Testing; *Knowledge Level; *Pictorial Stimuli; *Preschool Children; Preschool Education; Questionnaires
Identifiers: TIM(P)
Availability: Tests in Microfiche; Test Collection, Educational Testing Service, Princeton, NJ 08541
Age Level: 2-5
Notes: Time, 10 min. approx.; Items, 27

A set of 27 pictures depicting various healthy and unhealthy objects and situations. Teacher gives directions orally, and child points to correct picture.

16956
Gates-MacGinitie Reading Tests, Third Edition. MacGinitie, Walter H.; MacGinitie, Ruth K. 1989
Descriptors: *Achievement Tests; *Elementary School Students; Elementary Secondary Education; *High School Students; Reading Comprehension; *Reading Tests; *Secondary School Students; Vocabulary
Availability: Riverside Publishing Co.; 8420 Bryn Mawr Ave., Chicago, IL 60631
Grade Level: K-12
Notes: Time, 55 min. approx.

Assesses student achievement in reading skills for students from the end of kindergarten through grade 12. The third edition contains 9 test levels. Level PRE is a readiness test which assesses concepts on which reading development is built. Level R—Beginning Reading Skills—measures beginning reading achievement in grade 1 and allows evaluation of reading achievement between the beginning and end of grade 1. Test levels 1 through 10/12 are for grades 1-12. Each includes 2 tests, vocabulary, and comprehension.

16975
Diagnostic Pre-Tests for GED Instruction. Frechette, Ellen Carley 1987
Subtests: Writing Skills; Writing Assignment; Social Studies; Science; Literature and the Arts; Mathematics
Descriptors: *Achievement Tests; Adults; *Diagnostic Tests; *Equivalency Tests; *High School Equivalency Programs; *Humanities; *Mathematics Skills; *Pretesting; *Social Sciences; *Writing Skills
Identifiers: *General Educational Development Tests
Availability: Contemporary Books, Inc.; 180 N. Michigan Ave., Chicago, IL 60601
Age Level: Adults
Notes: Items, 183

Designed for the purpose of diagnosing students' strengths and weaknesses and for placement of students at the appropriate level of pre-GED or GED instruction. The format used will provide accurate and effective diagnosis of student performance in writing skills, social studies, science, literature and the arts, and mathematics. The test questions are organized according to the level of critical thinking they require.

16976
Evaluative Post-Tests for GED Readiness. Frechette, Ellen Carley 1987
Subtests: Writing Skills Parts 1 and 2; Social Studies; Science; Literature and the Arts; Mathematics
Descriptors: *Achievement Tests; Administrators; Adults; Answer Keys; *Equivalency Tests; *High School Equivalency Programs; *Humanities; *Mathematics Skills; *Pretests Posttests; *Sciences; *Social Sciences; Students; *Writing Skills
Identifiers: *General Educational Development Tests
Availability: Contemporary Books, Inc.; 180 N. Michigan Ave., Chicago, IL 60601
Age Level: Adults
Notes: Time, 455 min. approx.; Items, 287

The purpose of this evaluative tool is to give students the experience of taking a test that is comparable to a full-length GED test. These tests provide an opportunity for students to become adjusted to the item formats, the variety of stimulus materials, and the complexity of some of the more challenging questions while permitting the estimation of scores on the GED Tests. The scoring guide provides an overview of the GED assessment program. It contains all of the information needed to administer and evaluate student performance on both the diagnostic pretests and the evaluative posttests. This answer key provides interpretations of the pre- and posttest scores and offers a readiness worksheet to determine whether the student is ready to take the actual GED tests.

16977
Learning and Study Strategies Inventory—High School Version. Weinstein, Claire E.; Palmer, David R. 1990
Descriptors: *Anxiety; Educational Diagnosis; High Schools; *High School Students; *Learning Strategies; Low Achievement; Pretests Posttests; Rating Scales; *Student Attitudes; *Student Motivation; Study Habits; *Study Skills; Test Wiseness; *Time Management; Underachievement
Identifiers: LASSI(HS)
Availability: H&H Publishing Co.; 2165 Sunnydale Blvd., Ste. N, Clearwater, FL 35575
Grade Level: 9-12
Notes: Time, 25 min. approx.; Items, 76

This self-report assessment tool is designed to measure students' use of learning and study strategies, and methods at the secondary school level. It is also instrumental for making a successful transition into a college setting. This tool is designed to be used as a diagnostic measure, a counseling tool, planning individual prescriptions, a pre-post achievement measure, and an evaluation tool that assesses students' thought processes and behaviors that impact studying and learning. Students entering grade 9, 10, 11, or 12 who have a history of low achievement, those who are experiencing academic difficulty, and those who are preparing for college work can benefit from completing this study strategies inventory. The focus of this instrument relating to school achievement is on personal and metacognitive factors which are attitude, motivation, time management, anxiety, concentration, information processing, selecting main ideas, study aids, self-testing, and test strategies. This tool can be administered on an individual basis or on a group basis.

16984
Aprenda: La Prueba de Logros en Espanol, Intermediate 3. Psychological Corp., San Antonio, TX 1990
Subtests: Vocabulary (Vocabulario); Language Expression (Lenguaje: Expression); Reading Comprehension (comprehension de lectura); Study Skills (Destrezas de estudio); Concept of Numbers (conceptos de Numero); Mathematics Computation (Calculo Matematicos); Listening Comprehension (comprension auditiva); Spelling (Ortografia); Thinking Skills (Destrezas de Pensamiento Critico); Language Mechanics (lenguaje: mecanica)
Descriptors: *Achievement Tests; Computation; *Elementary School Students; *Grade 6; *Grade 7; Intermediate Grades; Language Skills; *Limited English Speaking; Listening Comprehension; Mathematical Applications; Mathematics Skills; Non English Speaking; Number Concepts; Reading Comprehension; *Spanish Speaking; Spelling; Study Skills; Thinking Skills; Vocabulary
Identifiers: Stanford Achievement Test Series
Availability: The Psychological Corp.; 555 Academic Ct., San Antonio, TX 78204-0952
Grade Level: 6-7
Notes: Time, 285 min.; Items, 357

Aprenda: La Prueba de Logros en Espanol was designed for students whose primary language of instruction is Spanish. It measures Spanish-speaking students' grasp of content and was developed in the Spanish language. This instrument has been constructed to match those objectives of the Stanford Achievement Test Series, Eighth Edition, and assesses the primary educational objectives at each grade from kindergarten through grade 8. The Intermediate 3 level includes measures of reading, mathematics, spelling, language, study skills, and listening. The concepts and skills that are assessed in each content area are those ordinarily taught in the second half of grade 6 and the first half of grade 7.

16985
Aprenda: La Prueba de Logros en Espanol, Intermediate 1. The Psychological Corp., San Antonio, TX 1990

Subtests: Vocabulario (Vocabulary); Comprension de lectura (Reading Comprehension); Lenguaje: mecanica (Language Mechanics); Lenguaje: Expresion (Language Expression); Destrezas de estudio (Study Skills); Ortografia (Spelling); Comprension Auditiva (Listening Comprehension); Conceptos de numero (Concepts of Numbers); Calculos Mathematicos (Mathematics Computation); Applicaciones Mathematicas (Mathematics Applications); Destrezas de pensamiento critico (Thinking Skills)
Descriptors: *Achievement Tests; Computation; *Elementary School Students; *Grade 4; *Grade 5; *Intermediate Grades; Language Skills; *Limited English Speaking; Listening Comprehension; Mathematical Applications; Mathematics Skills; Non English Speaking; Number Concepts; Reading Comprehension; *Spanish Speaking; Spelling; Study Skills; Thinking Skills; Vocabulary
Identifiers: Stanford Achievement Test Series
Availability: The Psychological Corp.; 555 Academic Ct., San Antonio, TX 78204-0952
Grade Level: 4-5
Notes: Time, 75 min. approx.

Aprenda: La Prueba de Logros en Espanol was designed for students whose primary language of instruction is Spanish. It measures Spanish-speaking students' grasp of content and was developed in the Spanish language. This instrument has been constructed to match those objectives of the Stanford Achievement Test Series, Eighth Edition, and assesses the primary educational objectives at each grade from kindergarten through grade 8. The Intermediate 1 level includes measures of reading, mathematics, spelling, language, study skills, and listening.

16987
Criterion-Referenced Articulation Profile. Mattes, Larry J. 1986
Descriptors: *Articulation (Speech); Children; *Communication Disorders; *Criterion Referenced Tests; Elementary Education; Elementary School Students; *Language Handicaps; *Phonemes; Phonology; *Speech Improvement
Availability: United Educational Services, Inc.; P.O. Box 1099, Buffalo, NY 14224
Grade Level: 1-6

This comprehensive inventory of informal measures was developed to facilitate program planning for individual students. It can be administered to assess communicatively handicapped children's production of individual phonemes and their use of basic phonological processes. The information obtained from these tasks can be used to identify children's specific learning needs, to develop instructional objectives, and to measure progress following intervention. This assessment tool is divided into 3 sections. Section one includes 5 tasks: spontaneous word production task; word repetition articulation task; sentence repetition articulation task; sound stimulability in syllables; and articulation in conversational speech. Section 2 includes tasks designed to measure production of 18 individual consonants in words, sentences, and in connected speech. Section 3 involves tasks designed for use in assessing 10 basic phonological processes often observed in speech of children with poor speech intelligibility. This instrument is not standardized.

16997
COMPUTEST: S CAPE. CALI, Inc., Orem, UT 1988
Descriptors: *Achievement Tests; Adaptive Testing; *College Students; *Computer Assisted Testing; Grammar; Higher Education; Knowledge Level; *Language Proficiency; *Language Tests; Listening Skills; Reading Achievement; *Second Languages; *Spanish; *Student Placement; Vocabulary Skills
Availability: CALI, Inc.; 526 E. Quail Rd., Orem, UT 84057
Grade Level: 13-16

The Computerized Adaptive Language Tests are intended for use as placement exams or as measures of general language proficiency. Each test administration is individually tailored to match the ability level of the examinee, is self-paced, reduces testing time, eliminates cheating, and will operate in monochrome. Results are available immediately. The Spanish exam (S-CAPE) is designed to indicate achievement levels corresponding to the first 4 semesters of college Spanish. The test evaluates 4 areas of language proficiency: listening, reading, grammar, and vocabulary.

16998
COMPUTEST: G-CAPE. CALI, Inc., Orem, UT 1990
Descriptors: *Achievement Tests; Adaptive Testing; *College Students; *Computer Assisted Testing; *German; Higher Education; Knowledge Level; *Language Proficiency; *Language Tests; Reading Achievement; *Second Languages; *Student Placement; Vocabulary Skills
Availability: CALI, Inc.; 526 E. Quail Rd., Orem, UT 84057
Grade Level: 13-16

The Computerized Adaptive Language Tests are intended for use as placement exams or as measures of general language proficiency. Each test administration is individually tailored to match the ability level of the examinee, is self-paced, reduces testing time, provides immediate results, eliminates cheating, and will operate in monochrome. The German exam (G-CAPE) is designed to indicate achievement levels corresponding to the first 4 semesters of college German. The test evaluates some areas of language proficiency: which include reading, grammar, and vocabulary.

16999
COMPUTEST: F CAPE. CALI, Inc., Orem, UT 1988
Descriptors: *Achievement Tests; Adaptive Testing; *College Students; *Computer Assisted Testing; *French; Grammar; Higher Education; Knowledge Level; *Language Proficiency; *Language Tests; Listening Skills; Reading Achievement; *Second Languages; *Student Placement; Vocabulary Skills
Availability: CALI, Inc.; 526 E. Quail Rd., Orem, UT 84057
Grade Level: 13-16

The Computerized Adaptive Language Tests are intended for use as placement exams or as measures of general language proficiency. Each test administration is individually tailored to match the ability level of the examinee, is self-paced, reduces testing time, eliminates cheating, and will operate in monochrome. Results are available immediately. The French exam (F-CAPE) is designed to indicate achievement levels corresponding to the first 4 semesters of college French. The test evaluates 4 areas of language proficiency: listening, grammar, reading, and vocabularly.

17000
COMPUTEST: ESL Version 2.5. CALI, Inc., Orem, UT 1986
Descriptors: *Achievement Tests; Adaptive Testing; *College Students; *Computer Assisted Testing; *English (Second Language); Grammar; Higher Education; Knowledge Level; Language Proficiency; *Language Tests; Listening Skills; Reading Achievement; *Student Placement; Vocabulary Skills
Identifiers: ESL
Availability: CALI, Inc.; 526 E. Quail Rd., Orem, UT 84057
Grade Level: 13-16

The Computerized Adaptive Language Tests are intended for use as placement exams or as measures of general language proficiency. Each test administration is individually tailored to match the ability level of the examinee, is self-paced, reduces testing time, eliminates cheating, and will operate in monochrome. Results are available immediately. The ESL Version 2.5 provides an aural dimension. Listening skills are evaluated along with other language proficiency skills: reading, grammar, and vocabulary. The test format can be modified by evaluating separate language skills, integrating skills, evaluating both separate and integrated listening skills, determining the amount of time given for answering questions, and adjusting the accuracy level.

17014
AGS Early Screening Profiles. Harrison, Patti L.; And Others 1990
Subtests: Cognitive/Language Profile; Motor Profile; Self-Help/Social Profile
Descriptors: Articulation (Speech); *At Risk Persons; Behavior Patterns; Child Health; Cognitive Development; Family Environment; *Gifted; *Individual Testing; Language Skills; Learning Problems; *Norm Referenced Tests; *Preschool Children; Preschool Education; Psychomotor Skills; *Screening Tests; Social Development
Identifiers: ESP
Availability: American Guidance Service; Publishers' Bldg., P.O. Box 99, Circle Pines, MN 55014-1796
Age Level: 2-6
Notes: Time, 40 min. approx.

Nationally normed assessment battery that measures cognitive, language, motor, self-help/social, articulation, health development, and the home environment of children aged 2 through 6. Useful for identifying children who are at risk for later learning problems and for identifying potentially gifted children. Individually administered. Consists of 3 profiles supplemented by 4 surveys.

17016
DIAL-R, AGS Edition. Mardell-Czudnowski, Carol; Goldenberg, Dorothea S. 1990
Subtests: Motor; Concepts; Language
Descriptors: Concept Formation; *Early Intervention; Educational Diagnosis; *Individual Testing; Language Skills; *Norm Referenced Tests; *Preschool Children; Preschool Education; Psychomotor Skills; *Screening Tests
Identifiers: DIAL R
Availability: American Guidance Service; Publishers' Bldg., P.O. Box 99, Circle Pines, MN 55014-1796
Age Level: 2-5
Notes: Time, 30 min. approx.

Identifies children aged 2 through 5 who may benefit from early intervention or diagnostic assessment. Screens motor skills, concepts, language skills, and indicates social/emotional development. Individually administered in a station to station format. This AGS edition is a modification of the 1983 DIAL-R. The norms have been reanalyzed and are different. This AGS edition also includes material for training examiners, wider range of cut-off scores, more complete explanation of standardization and norm samples, and expanded reliability and validity data.

17017
Differential Ability Scales. Elliott, Colin D. 1990
Subtests: Block Building; Verbal Comprehension; Picture Similarities; Naming Vocabulary; Early Number Concepts; Copying; Pattern Construction; Recall of Designs; Word Definitions; Matrices; Similarities; Sequential and Quantitative Reasoning; Matching Letter-Like Forms; Recall of Objects; Recognition of Pictures; Speed of Information Processing; Basic Number Skills; Spelling; Word Reading
Descriptors: *Achievement Tests; Adolescents; Children; *Cognitive Tests; *Elementary School Students; *Individual Testing; *Learning Disabilities; Learning Problems; Preschool Children; *Secondary School Students; *Standardized Tests
Identifiers: DAS
Availability: The Psychological Corp.; 555 Academic Ct., San Antonio, TX 78204-0952
Age Level: 2-17
Notes: Time, 150 min. approx.

Contains cognitive and achievement batteries for children aged 2.5 through 17 years. Diagnoses and analyzes children's learning disabilities and learning difficulties. Profiles a child's strengths and weaknesses. Cognitive Battery consists of 2 levels, preschool and school-age. Subtests are appropriate to the developmental level of the child. The Achievement Battery portion provides a standardized screening of literacy and numeracy skills. The 2 batteries combined provide a comprehensive picture of a child's current cognitive and intellectual functioning. Individually administered. For use by school and clinical psychologists and other trained professionals.

17035
IDEA Oral Language Proficiency Test, Pre-IPT: Spanish. Ballard & Tighe, Inc, Brea, CA 1989
Descriptors: *Age Grade Placement; Bilingualism; *Individual Testing; *Language Proficiency; *Language Tests; Limited English Speaking; Non English Speaking; Norm Referenced Tests; *Oral Language; *Spanish Speaking; *Young Children
Availability: Ballard & Tighe, Inc., Language Arts Programs; 480 Atlas St., Brea, CA 92621-3117
Age Level: 3-5
Notes: Time, 10 min. approx.; Items, 40

This is an individually administered, normed oral language proficiency test in Spanish for Spanish-speaking children. It provided non-, limited, and fluent English-speaking classifications for 3, 4, and 5 year olds, and assesses the level of oral language proficiency. This instrument assesses both basic interpersonal communication skills and cognitive academic language proficiency skills. It offers optional scoring on diagnostic score cards that display needed skills in a graphic manner for prescriptive instruction. Children at this level (Pre-IPT) are in the preproduction stage of language. Other than giving their name, verbal expression is not required of them. This instrument is a placement designation only.

17048
Essential Skills Reading Test, 5th Edition. Michigan Educational Assessment Program, Lansing, MI 1989
Descriptors: *Elementary School Students; Elementary Secondary Education; *High School Students; *Junior High School Students; Prior Learning; *Reading Attitudes; *Reading Comprehension; *Reading Interests; *Reading Skills; *Reading Tests
Identifiers: MEAP
Availability: Michigan Dept. of Education; Michigan Educational Assessment Program, P.O. Box 30008, Lansing, MI 48909
Grade Level: 4; 7; 10
Notes: Time, 150 min. approx.; Items, 46

This reading test is designed to measure how well students are able to construct meaning for different texts under a variety of reading conditions; knowledge about reading; and attitudes and self-perceptions toward reading texts. Topic familiarity items are included in the test that will assess a student's prior knowledge of the topics/ideas contained within the reading selections. Items are either multiple-choice or yes-no questions. The results of the tests will provide information that is useful to the individual classroom teacher, principal, and administrators for purposes of instructional planning and curriculum development.

17079
Progressive Reading Evaluation Portfolio, 2nd Edition. Joels, Rosie Webb; And Others 1983
Descriptors: *Diagnostic Teaching; *Elementary School Students; Elementary Secondary Education; Informal Reading Inventories; *Junior High School Students; Pretests Posttests; *Reading Achievement; Reading Readiness; *Reading Skills; *Reading Tests; Sight Vocabulary; Word Recognition
Identifiers: JAT; PREP
Availability: Education Services, Inc.; 8604 Baylor Circle, Orlando, FL 32817
Grade Level: 1-8

This reading resource for elementary school teachers contains a series of diagnostic devices designed to assist teachers in pinpointing individual student reading levels and skill levels. It also suggests remediation strategies to enhance the individual student's reading development. This tool is divided into 3 functional sections. Section 1 is the Joals-Anderson-Thompson (JAT) Reading Inventory, which is an informal reading assessment device. Section 2 is the Prereading Skills Assessment, which assesses major reading readiness, word recognition, and word attack skills. Section 3 is the Primary Reading Skills Assessment, which reveals the subject's knowledge of key sight words and a variety of word analysis skills.

17082
Test for Non-Native Comprehension of Intonation in English. Cruz-Ferreira, Madalena 1989
Descriptors: Adults; *English (Second Language); Forced Choice Technique; *Intonation; Language Patterns; *Language Tests; *Listening Comprehension Tests; Multiple Choice Tests; *Oral Language; Second Language Learning; Semantics; *Stress (Phonology)
Availability: IRAL; v27 n1 p23-29 Feb 1989
Age Level: Adults
Notes: Items, 24

An instrument designed to assess how well nonnative speakers of English comprehend the meanings of English sentences with intonation patterns of tonality, tonacity, and tone. Respondents either listen to sentences on a tape recorder or have the sentences read to them by an examiner. They then choose the meaning of the sentences from 3 alternatives. The 3 choices may be in the native language of the respondents or in English. Instrument is both diagnostic and predictive. Results may be used to analyze the difficulties individuals have with intonation in sentences, where difficulties lie, why they have those difficulties and what methods can be used to counteract the difficulties. Instrument consists of 24 sentences. There is also a 24-item supplement that consists of the same sentences with the stress in different places. No technical data included.

17124
Rossetti Infant Toddler Language Scale. Rossetti, Louis 1990
Subtests: Interaction Attachment; Pragmatics; Gesture; Play; Language Comprehension; Language Expression
Descriptors: Attachment Behavior; Body Language; Child Language; *Criterion Referenced Tests; *Infants; Interaction; *Nonverbal Communication; Play; *Toddlers; *Verbal Communication
Identifiers: *Baby Talk
Availability: LinguiSystems, Inc.; 3100 4th Ave., E. Moline, IL 61244
Age Level: 0-3

This criterion-referenced instrument is designed to provide the clinician with a comprehensive tool that assesses the preverbal and verbal aspects of communication and interaction in the young child. It measures interaction-attachment, pragmatics, gesture, play, language comprehension, and language expression. The results from this assessment tool reflect the child's mastery of skills in each of the areas assessed at 3-month intervals. Items are included only when they are considered chronologically appropriate and developmentally discriminating. This scale promotes the family's role as a full partner and may be administered in the home, diagnostic center, school, clinic, or hospital setting.

17127
Speech and Language Evaluation Scale. Fressola, Dianne; Hoerchler, Cipponeri 1989
Subtests: Speech: Articulation; Speech: Voice; Speech: Fluency; Language: Form; Language: Context; Language: Pragmatics
Descriptors: *Articulation (Speech); *Elementary School Students; Elementary Secondary Education; *Language Handicaps; *Language Proficiency; Rating Scales; *Screening Tests; *Secondary School Students; *Speech Handicaps
Identifiers: SLES
Availability: Hawthorne Educational Services; P.O. Box 7570, Columbia, MO 65205
Age Level: 4-18
Notes: Time, 20 min. approx.; Items, 68

This instrument is designed for in-school screening and referral of students with speech and language problems. It also serves a role in diagnosis, classification, development of goals and objectives, and intervention strategies for those students in need of speech and language success. This assessment tool includes the most commonly recognized subscales of speech: articulation, voice, and fluency; and language form, content, and pragmatics. It should provide the clinician with comprehensive professional input from classroom teachers without requiring lengthy and difficult anecdotal reporting. The prereferral checklist provides a means of calling attention to the communication difficulties for the purpose of early intervention before formal assessment of the student. Available with a quick score computerized version.

17128
ETS Tests of Applied Literacy Skills. Educational Testing Service, Princeton, NJ 1990
Subtests: Prose Literacy; Document Literacy; Quantitative Literacy
Descriptors: *Adult Basic Education; *Adult Education; *Adult Literacy; Adults; Basic Skills; *Functional Literacy; Functional Reading; Literacy; *Literacy Education; Mathematical Applications; Minimum Competencies; Vocational Education
Availability: Prentice Hall; Order Dept., 200 Old Tappan Rd., Old Tappan, NJ 07675
Age Level: Adults
Notes: Time, 40 min.

This test of applied literacy skills covers the broad range of skills used in work, home, community, and educational settings. It is comprised of simulation tasks. These tasks require the use of printed materials encountered in real life, e.g., advertisements, maps, news stories. Respondents are given several questions about each stimulus material and then read or perform arithmetic calculations. There are 2 parallel forms. Test may be group administered by nonprofessional staff. Scoring determines whether the test taker is above, below, or at literacy level. For use in vocational and basic skills education.

17134
Knowledge Master. Academic Hallmarks, Durango, CO 1981
Descriptors: Achievement Tests; Astronomy; Athletics; Biological Sciences; Biology; Building Trades; Chemistry; Civil Law; Competition; *Computer Assisted Testing; Computer Software; Criminal Law; Current Events; Earth Science; Economics; Educational Games; English; Fine Arts; Geography; Geology; Geometry; Grade 6; Health Education; High Schools; *High School Students; *Item Banks; Junior High Schools; *Junior High School Students; Literature; Mathematics; Mythology; North American History; Oceanography; Physical Sciences; Physics; Psychology; *Secondary School Curriculum; Social Studies; Spelling; United States Government (Course); Vocabulary; Word Problems (Mathematics); World History
Identifiers: Shakespeare (William)
Availability: Academic Hallmarks; P.O. Box 998, Durango, CO 81302
Grade Level: 6-12

This item pool or library of test items is contained on 47 Apple II compatible disks. It was designed for use in testing or quizzing students on screen or in print or as flash cards for academic competition. Items are arranged in difficulty levels based on Bloom's Taxonomy. Includes over 18,000 questions covering high school curriculum areas. A similar series is available for junior high and middle schools. Covers U.S. history, government, world history, geography, economics, law, current events, mathematics, geometry, word problems, biology, health, psychology, physics, chemistry, astronomy, meteorology, geology, oceanography, building trades, sports, fine arts, English, spelling, vocabulary, literature, mythology, Shakespeare, social studies, life science, earth science, physical science. A separate short-answer series is produced for "Knowledge Bowl" type competitions. New sets of secure questions for local, regional or state competitions are produced yearly.

17142
Cultural Literacy Test. Cultural Literacy Foundation, Charlottesville, VA 1989
Subtests: Humanities; Social Sciences; Sciences
Descriptors: *Achievement Tests; *Criterion Referenced Tests; *Culture; Grade 11; Grade 12; *High School Students; *Humanities; *Intellectual Disciplines; *Knowledge Level; *Sciences; *Social Sciences
Identifiers: *Cultural Literacy
Availability: Riverside Publishing; 8420 Bryn Mawr Ave., Chicago, IL 60631
Grade Level: 11-12
Notes: Time, 50 min.; Items, 115

Assesses students' progress in attaining general knowledge in the humanities, social sciences, and sciences. A criterion-referenced test for students in grades 11 and 12. Available in parallel forms A and B. Machine scored only by publisher. This is the "official" test of cultural literacy, developed by the Cultural Literacy Foundation. Test items are keyed to foundation's index to the core knowledge of functional literacy. Data on reliability, validity, and norms is available.

17148
Boehm Test of Basic Concept—Revised, Spanish Edition. Boehm, Ann E. 1987
Descriptors: Abstract Reasoning; *Basic Skills; *Concept Formation; Elementary School Students; Individual Testing; *Primary Education; *School Readiness; *Screening Tests; *Spanish Speaking; *Verbal Communication; Visual Measures
Identifiers: Boehm(R)
Availability: The Psychological Corp.; 555 Academic Ct., San Antonio, TX 78204-0952
Grade Level: K-2
Notes: Time, 30 min. approx.; Items, 26

This instrument measures mastery of basic concepts that are fundamental to understanding verbal instruction and necessary for early school achievement among children whose first language is Spanish. It was designed to help teachers of Spanish-speaking students, both in the U.S. and in Spanish-speaking countries, to identify students with basic concept deficiencies and target specific concept areas for futher instruction. Basic concepts measured are relational concepts, a subset of concepts children use to make relational decisions about persons, objects, and situations. Concepts targeted in test also involve judgments that can be made across the contexts of space, quality, and time, at increasingly complex levels of abstraction. This tool can be used by special education teachers, speech and language pathologists, school psychologists, and early childhood specialists. Test is administered orally to individual students or small groups. Spanish norms are not available for this test.

17156
Chinese Speaking Test. Center for Applied Linguistics, Washington, DC 1988
Descriptors: Adults; Audiotape Recordings; *Communicative Competence (Languages); Language Proficiency; *Language Tests; *Mandarin Chinese; *Oral Language; Pictorial Stimuli; Postsecondary Education; *Second Language Learning
Identifiers: ACTFL; ACTFL Proficiency Guidelines; American Council on the Teaching of Foreign Langs; Oral Proficiency Interview; Oral Tests
Availability: Center for Applied Linguistics; 1118 22nd St., N.W., Washington, DC 20037
Age Level: Adults
Notes: Time, 45 min.

This test was designed for use in evaluating the level of oral proficiency in Chinese, of English-speaking postsecondary and adult students of Mandarin Chinese, who are at intermediate and advanced levels of learning the language. It is based on the kinds of language-use situations that may be encountered in everyday life. It is designed to emulate the direct, face-to-face Oral Proficiency Interview used by U.S. government agencies and the American Council on the Teaching of Foreign Languages (ACTFL). There are 6 parts: Personal Conversation, Giving Directions, Detailed Description, Picture Sequences, Topical Discourse, and Situations. Twenty minutes of actual speaking is required. A master audio tape supplies the directions and questions, which are in English for 5 parts of the test and in Chinese for part one. Additional test items refer to pictures and text. Responses are recorded on a separate tape. An overall proficiency rating, based on the ACTFL Proficiency Guidelines, is given. The rating ranges from "Novice" to "High-Superior." Both individuals and institutions can register for testing by contacting the availability source.

17162
Student Occupational Competency Achievement Test: Business Data Processing. National Occupational Competency Testing Institute, Big Rapids, MI 1990
Subtests: Computer Literacy; Business Related Computer Functions; Computer Operations; General Software Applications; Systems; Computer Programming; Microcomputer Operations; Spreadsheets; Word Processing; Database File and Report

Descriptors: *Achievement Tests; Adults; Business; *Computer Literacy; *Computer Software; Credentials; Databases; Data Processing Occupations; High Schools; *High School Students; Knowledge Level; *Microcomputers; Multiple Choice Tests; Occupational Tests; Performance Tests; *Postsecondary Education; Problem Solving; Programing; Secondary Education; Spreadsheets; Two Year Colleges; *Vocational Education; Word Processing; *Work Sample Tests
Identifiers: NOCTI; SOCAT
Availability: National Occupational Competency Institute; 409 Bishop Hall, Ferris State University, Big Rapids, MI 49307
Grade Level: 9-14
Notes: Time, 195 min.

This test is part of a program developed to evaluate secondary and postsecondary vocational students with a standardized, objective measure. Each test consists of a multiple-choice portion covering factual knowledge, technical information, understanding of principles, and problem-solving abilities related to the occupation. A performance component samples manipulative skills required. A mental ability test is also available. The written test covers computer literacy, business related computer functions, computer operations, general software applications, systems/computer programing. The performance test requires the testee to backup a diskette, use a spreadsheet application, use a word processing package, use a database application. Test retest reliability coefficients range from .91 to .99.

17182
WORD Test—R (Elementary). Huisingh, Rosemary; And Others 1990
Subtests: Associations; Synonyms; Semantic Absurdities; Antonyms; Definitions; Multiple Definitions
Descriptors: *Diagnostic Tests; Elementary Education; *Elementary School Students; *Expressive Language; *Norm Referenced Tests; *Semantics; *Vocabulary
Availability: LinguiSystems; 3100 4th Ave., P.O. Box 747, E. Moline, IL 61244
Grade Level: 2-6
Age Level: 7-11
Notes: Items, 90

Diagnostic test of expressive vocabulary and semantics. Assesses subject's ability to recognize and express critical semantic attributes of the language. Constructed to yield information about categorizing, defining, verbal reasoning, and choosing appropriate words. Assists in identifying areas of strength and weakness in a child's language. Revised version retains only items that have remained contemporary and relevant. These have been supplemented by new items. Subject responds verbally to spoken questions. Scoring standards and all normative and statistical analyses have been newly developed.

17183
WORD Test (Adolescent). Zachman, Linda; And Others 1989
Subtests: Brand Names; Synonyms; Signs of the Times; Definitions
Descriptors: *Diagnostic Tests; *Expressive Language; *Norm Referenced Tests; Secondary Education; *Secondary School Students; *Semantics; *Vocabulary
Availability: LinguiSystems; 3100 4th Ave., P.O. Box 747, E. Moline, IL 61244
Grade Level: 7-12
Age Level: 12-17
Notes: Items, 60

Diagnostic test of expressive vocabulary and semantics for secondary students. Assesses a subject's facility with language and word meaning. Subject responds verbally to spoken questions. Tables are provided on standardization, reliability and validity.

17187
Gray Oral Reading Tests—Diagnostic. Bryant, Brian R.; Wiederholt, J. Lee 1991
Subtests: Paragraph Reading; Word Identification; Morphemic Analysis; Contextual Analysis; Decoding; Word Ordering; Word Attack
Descriptors: Context Clues; Decoding (Reading); *Diagnostic Tests; Elementary Education; *Elementary School Students; Morphology (Languages); *Oral Reading; *Reading Difficulties; *Reading Tests; Word Recognition
Identifiers: GORT(D)
Availability: PRO-ED; 8700 Shoal Creek Blvd., Austin, TX 78758-6897
Grade Level: K-6
Notes: Time, 90 min. approx.

This diagnostic instrument is appropriate for individuals who have difficulty with paragraph reading. It is designed to identify readers who are significantly below their peers in oral reading proficiency, to aid in determining the kinds of reading strengths and weaknesses that individuals possess, to document progress in reading, and to serve as a measurement device. This test is divided into 7 subtests. Two subtests assess the reader's ability to gain meaning from print; 3 subtests assess the reader's ability to use function or grammar cues; and the remaining 2 subtests assess the abilities of individuals in their use of graphic/phonemic cues.

17206
Quick Screen of Phonology. Bankson, Nicholas W.; Bernthal, John E. 1990
Descriptors: *Elementary School Students; Expressive Language; *Language Acquisition; *Phonology; *Preschool Children; Preschool Education; Primary Education; *Screening Tests
Identifiers: QSP
Availability: Communication Skill Builders; 3830 E. Bellevue, Tucson, AZ 85733
Age Level: 3-7
Notes: Time, 5 min. approx.; Items, 28

Provides a quick estimate of a young child's phonological development based on the number of words produced without consonant errors. Determines the need for further assessment. Norms are provided for 3-month intervals from age 3 to 6. Data on reliability, validity and standardization are provided.

17209
Woodcock-Johnson Psycho-Educational Battery, Revised—Tests of Achievement, Standard Battery and Supplemental Battery. Woodcock, Richard W.; Johnson, W. Bonner 1990
Subtests: Standard: Letter Word Identification, Passage Comprehension, Calculation, Applied Problems, Dictation, Writing Samples, Science, Social Studies, Humanities; Supplemental: Word Attack, Reading Vocabulary, Quantitative Concepts, Proofing, Writing Fluency, Punctuation and Capitalization, Spelling, Usage, Handwriting
Descriptors: *Academic Achievement; *Achievement Tests; Adults; College Students; Elementary School Students; Elementary Secondary Education; High School Students; *Knowledge Level; *Mathematics Achievement; Older Adults; Postsecondary Education; Preschool Children; Preschool Education; *Reading Ability; *Standardized Tests; *Written Language
Identifiers: WJR
Availability: DLM Teaching Resources; One DLM Park, Allen, TX 75002-1302
Age Level: 2-90
Notes: Time, 50 min. approx.

Woodcock-Johnson-Revised is a battery of standardized tests measuring cognitive abilities, scholastic aptitudes, and achievement. Cognitive and achievement batteries are each organized in standard and supplemental test books. The standard batteries provide in-depth testing when more information is desired. Covers age range 2-90. Common norms are provided for cognitive and achievement batteries along with derived scores and profiles. With this revision, 10 new tests have been added to the cognitive abilities battery and 4 new tests to the achievement battery. The achievement battery now has alternate forms, A and B. The achievement standard battery consists of 9 tests. The supplemental battery also has 9 tests. Both batteries can be used to assess 4 curricular areas: reading, mathematics, written language, and knowledge.

17213
Business Quiz for Marketing Education. Marketing Education Resource Center, Inc., Columbus, OH 1988
Descriptors: *Computer Assisted Testing; Computer Software; High Schools; *High School Students; *Item Banks; *Marketing; Teacher Made Tests; Test Construction
Availability: Marketing Education Resource Center, Inc.; 1375 King Ave., P.O. Box 12226, Columbus, OH 43212-0226
Age Level: 9-12
Notes: Items, 200

This test item bank is used by classroom teachers for designing drills and practice tests and actual classroom exams. For use by marketing students concerned with markets, market segmentation, marketing strategies, promotional mix, channels of distribution, business cycles, marketing basic concepts and fundamentals, topics concerning products, and prices. Software is both Apple and IBM compatible.

17214
Quiz Writer Plus. Marketing Education Resource Center, Inc., Columbus, OH 1988
Descriptors: *College Students; *Computer Assisted Testing; Computer Software; High Schools; *High School Students; *Marketing; Postsecondary Education; Teacher Made Tests; Test Construction
Availability: Marketing Education Resource Center, Inc.; 1375 King Ave., P.O. Box 12226, Columbus, OH 43212-0226
Age Level: 9-16

This test creation package permits a teacher to develop, edit, and modify test questions. Supports true-false, fill-in, matching, fill-in-the-blank, alternate choice, essay, and multiple-choice items. Generates printed tests or can be used for "on-line" practice or quizzes. Compatible with Apple and IBM computers.

17215
MarkeTest. Marketing Education Resource Center, Inc., Columbus, OH 1988
Subtests: Selling; Economics
Descriptors: Business Education; *Computer Assisted Testing; Computer Software; *Economics; High Schools; *High School Students; *Item Banks; *Merchandising; *Sales Occupations; Teacher Made Tests
Availability: Marketing Education Resource Center, Inc.; 1375 King Ave., P.O. Box 12226, Columbus, OH 43212-0226
Age Level: 9-12

This test generation software contains multiple-choice test items that measure specific competencies. Test may be printed or administered or scored on-line. The Selling item bank contains questions on marketing, apparel, food, restaurant, hotel-motel, and vehicle-related retailing. The Economics item bank contains questions also related to the industries identified above. Software is Apple and IBM compatible.

17216
Business Quiz for Other Classroom Needs. Marketing Education Resource Center, Inc., Columbus, OH 1988
Subtests: Banking; Business English; Business Knowledge I and II; Business Law; Business Math; Computer Concepts; Insurance; Parliamentary Procedures I and II; Typing; Food Service; World of Work; Word Usage; Spell Check
Descriptors: Banking; *Business Education; Business English; *Computer Assisted Testing; Computer Literacy; Computer Software; Food Service; High Schools; *High School Students; Insurance; *Item Banks; Teacher Made Tests; Typewriting
Availability: Marketing Education Resource Center, Inc.; 1375 King Ave., P.O. Box 12226, Columbus, OH 43212-0226
Age Level: 9-12

These computerized item banks are used by classroom teachers for designing drills and practice tests and other actual classroom exams. For use with students in business-related currricula. The Software is available in both Apple and IBM compatible formats.

17219
Processes of Biological Investigations Test. Germann, Paul J. 1989
Subtests: Hypothesis; Prediction; Assumption; Data and Hypotheses; Interpretation; Supporting Data; Evaluation
Descriptors: *Biology; *High School Students; Hypothesis Testing; *Inquiry; *Learning Processes; Multiple Choice Tests; *Science Tests; Scientific Methodology; Secondary Education; *Secondary School Science
Identifiers: PBIT; *Process Skills
Availability: *Journal of Research in Science Teaching;* v26 n7 p609-25, Oct 1989
Grade Level: 9-10

A multiple-choice test designed to measure the science process skills of high school biology students. Measures students' ability to formulate hypotheses, make predictions, identify assumptions, distinguish data from hypotheses, interpret data, evaluate supporting data, and evaluate causes. Instrument was found to be a valid and reliable method for biology teachers to assess the effectiveness of inquiry instruction on improving students' science process skills. Technical data are included.

17224
Northwest Evaluation Association Computerized Item Banks in Science. Northwest Evaluation Association, Lake Oswego, OR 1989
Subtests: Science Concepts and Processes; General Science; Biology; Chemistry; Physics; Earth/Space Sciences
Descriptors: Biology; Chemistry; *Computer Assisted Testing; Computer Software; Earth Science; *Elementary School Students; Elementary Secondary Education; General Science; *Item Banks; Physics; *Sciences; Scientific Concepts; Scientific Methodology; *Secondary School Students
Availability: Northwest Evaluation Association; 5 Centerpointe Drive, Ste. 100, Lake Oswego, OR 97035
Grade Level: K-12

This item bank is available as 10 different subsets or as a complete collection of 6,700 items. Subareas are available as sets of items covering specific grade ranges, such as K-9, 7-12, or K-12. For use by curriculum specialists, test developers, and science teachers to develop curriculum-referenced classroom tests. Measurement goals are specified and items selected to match goals and grade levels. A key is generated for computerized scoring later. Software is IBM compatible only, as of this writing.

17232
College BASE. Osterlind, Steven J. 1989
Subtests: English; Science; Mathematics; Social Studies; Interpretive Reasoning; Strategic Reasoning; Adaptive Reasoning
Descriptors: *Achievement Tests; *College Curriculum; College Sophomores; *College Students; *Criterion Referenced Tests; Higher Education; Language Tests; Mathematics Tests; Science Tests; Social Studies; *Thinking Skills; Writing Tests
Identifiers: College Basic Academic Subjects Examination
Availability: Riverside Publishing Co.; 8420 Bryn Mawr Ave., Chicago, IL 60631
Grade Level: 13-16
Notes: Time, 210 min.; Items, 180
A criterion-referenced achievement test developed to test college students' mastery of the college core curriculum. Assesses students' proficiency in English, mathematics, science, and social studies as well as their interpretive reasoning, strategic reasoning, and adaptive reasoning skills. Instrument yields several scores, including individual, institutional, composite, subject, cluster, skill, and competency scores. Instrument is available in 3 forms. The long form includes the complete test plus a writing sample, the short form includes only the mathematics and English sections with an optional writing sample, and the institutional matrix includes all subject areas and a writing sample. The most appropriate time for administration is the end of sophomore year.

17233
Lamme Green Scale of Children's Development in Composition. Green, Connie 1990
Descriptors: Diagnostic Tests; *Kindergarten Children; Primary Education; Rating Scales; *Spelling; *Writing (Composition); *Writing Evaluation; *Writing Skills
Availability: Dimensions; v18 n2 p14-18, Jan 1990
Grade Level: K
Notes: Items, 6
A scale developed to evaluate kindergarten children's levels of development in writing, spelling, and composition. Instrument describes characteristics of writing at 6 levels. Teachers or parents examine samples of children's writing and determine the level of writing. Results may be used to determine the types of intervention children need to improve their writing skills.

17236
Computerized Placement Tests—Reading Comprehension. College Board, New York, NY 1990
Descriptors: *Achievement Tests; Adaptive Testing; *Basic Skills; *College Freshmen; Computer Assisted Testing; Higher Education; Norm Referenced Tests; *Reading Comprehension; *Student Placement
Availability: The College Board; Computerized Placement Tests, Box 6800, Princeton, NJ 08541-6800
Grade Level: 13
Notes: Time, 20 min. approx.
This computerized testing program uses adaptive testing methods to provide a basic skills assessment useful in placing incoming first-year students in entry-level courses. The adaptive testing procedures move the test taker directly to test items that are at the correct level, thereby eliminating time consuming testing with questions that are too easy or too difficult. Items on the Reading Comprehension test consist of short passages with questions about the passages and others based on the relationships between 2 sentences. Content of passages and items include art, human relationships, practical affairs, social and physical sciences. Items involve statements relating to main or secondary ideas in passages, inferences, and applications. Scoring is completed by the computer as soon as the student has finished the untimed testing. Additional questions about students' background can be added by the user college.

17237
Computerized Placement Tests—Sentence Skills. College Board, New York, NY 1990
Descriptors: *Achievement Tests; Adaptive Testing; *Basic Skills; *College Freshmen; Computer Assisted Testing; Higher Education; Language Skills; Norm Referenced Tests; *Sentence Structure; *Student Placement; *Writing Skills
Availability: The College Board; Computerized Placement Tests, Box 6800, Princeton, NJ 08541-6800
Grade Level: 13
Notes: Time, 20 min. approx.
This computerized testing program uses adaptive testing methods to provide a basic skills assessment useful in placing incoming first-year students in entry-level courses. The adaptive testing procedures move the test taker di-

rectly to test items that are at the correct level, thereby eliminating time consuming testing with questions that are too easy or too difficult. Items on the Sentence Skills test consist of sentence corrections that test understanding of sentence structure and "construction shift" items that ask the test taker to select the most appropriate construction for a given sentence from several options to improve the sentence without changing meaning. Content of passages and items includes art, human relationships, practical affairs, social and physical sciences. Scoring is completed by the computer as soon as the student has finished the untimed testing. Additional questions about students' background can be added by the user college.

17238
Computerized Placement Tests—Arithmetic. College Board, New York, NY 1990
Descriptors: *Achievement Tests; Adaptive Testing; *Arithmetic; *Basic Skills; *College Freshmen; Computer Assisted Testing; Fractions; Higher Education; Mathematical Applications; Mathematics Tests; Norm Referenced Tests; Percentage; Problem Solving; *Student Placement; Thinking Skills
Availability: The College Board; Computerized Placement Tests, Box 6800, Princeton, NJ 08541-6800
Grade Level: 13
Notes: Time, 20 min. approx.
This computerized testing program uses adaptive testing methods to provide a basic skills assessment useful in placing incoming first-year students in entry-level courses. The adaptive testing procedures move the test taker directly to test items that are at the correct level, thereby eliminating time consuming testing with questions that are too easy or too difficult. Items on the arithmetic test consist of questions from 3 broad categories: whole numbers and fractions, decimals and percents, and applications and problem solving. Items concerning the applications of knowledge tend to test higher-level thinking skills and do not appear if the student is testing at a low level. Scoring is completed by the computer as soon as the student has finished the untimed testing. Additional questions about students' background can be added by the user college.

17239
Computerized Placement Tests—Algebra. College Board, New York, NY 1990
Descriptors: *Achievement Tests; Adaptive Testing; *Algebra; Basic Skills; *College Freshmen; Computer Assisted Testing; Higher Education; Mathematics Tests; Norm Referenced Tests; Problem Solving; *Student Placement
Availability: The College Board; Computerized Placement Tests, Box 6800, Princeton, NJ 08541-6800
Grade Level: 13
Notes: Time, 20 min. approx.
This computerized testing program uses adaptive testing methods to provide a basic skills assessment useful in placing incoming first-year students in entry-level courses. The adaptive testing procedures move the test taker directly to test items that are at the correct level, thereby eliminating time consuming testing with questions that are too easy or too difficult. Items on the algebra test consist of questions from 3 broad categories: operations with integers and rationals; operations with algebraic expressions; and solutions of equations, inequalities, and word problems (contains more challenging items). Scoring is completed by the computer as soon as the student has finished the untimed testing. Additional questions about students' background can be added by the user college.

17240
Computerized Placement Tests—College Level Mathematics. College Board, New York, NY 1990
Descriptors: *Achievement Tests; Adaptive Testing; Algebra; *Basic Skills; *College Freshmen; Computer Assisted Testing; Higher Education; *Mathematics Tests; Norm Referenced Tests; Problem Solving; *Student Placement
Availability: The College Board; Computerized Placement Tests, Box 6800, Princeton, NJ 08541-6800
Grade Level: 13
Notes: Time, 20 min. approx.
This computerized testing program uses adaptive testing methods to provide a basic skills assessment useful in placing incoming first-year students in entry-level courses. The adaptive testing procedures move the test taker directly to test items that are at the correct level, thereby eliminating time consuming testing with questions that are too easy or too difficult. Items on the College Level Mathematics test are designed to measure student mastery of intermediate algebra, college algebra, precalculus. This test may be administered separately or with other tests in the series. Scoring is completed by the computer as soon as the student has finished the untimed testing. Additional questions about students' background can be added by the user college.

17256
Daberon 2: Screening for School Readiness. Danzer, Virginia A.; And Others 1991
Descriptors: *Language Skills; *Norm Referenced Tests; Number Concepts; Plurals; Prepositions; *Preschool Children; Psychomotor Skills; *School Readiness Tests; *Screening Tests; Visual Perception; *Young Children
Availability: PRO-ED; 8700 Shoal Creek Blvd., Austin, TX 78758-6897
Age Level: 4-6
Notes: Time, 40 min. approx.; Items, 122
A screening tool developed for 4 purposes: to identify children who may not be ready to enter formal education; to identify strengths and weaknesses; to document students' progress in specific areas; and to serve as a measurement device in research studies. A large portion of this instrument is devoted to language skills to sample a variety of knowledge and skills of children as they begin school. Other skills assessed include body parts, color and number concepts, functional use of prepositions, plurals, ability to follow directions, general knowledge, visual perception, gross motor development, and the ability to categorize. Testing time varies from 20 to 40 minutes depending on the child's age and ability. Interpretative information is available.

17286
Communication Abilities Diagnostic Test. Johnston, Elizabeth; Johnston, Andrew V. 1990
Subtests: Semantics; Syntax; Pragmatics
Descriptors: *Communication Skills; *Diagnostic Tests; *Early Childhood Education; *Language Patterns; *Language Skills; *Language Tests; Pragmatics; Semantics; Standardized Tests; Syntax; Young Children
Identifiers: CADeT
Availability: Special Press; 11230 W. Ave., Ste. 3205, San Antonio, TX 78213
Age Level: 3-9
Notes: Time, 45 min. approx.
Standardized measure of language development for ages 3 to 9. Most sensitive for language growth in children ages 3 to 5. Useful in identifying language delays or deficits in children ages 6 to 9. Measures 3 components of language—semantics, syntax, and pragmatics—with separate scores for each. A total score can be computed for use in classification. Norms and technical data are provided.

17295
Classroom Assessment of Developmental Skills. Oelwein, Patricia L.; Fewell, Rebecca R. 1991
Subtests: Gross Motor; Fine Motor; Cognitive; Social/Self Help; Communication; Expressive; Communication; Receptive
Descriptors: *Child Development; *Developmental Disabilities; Early Childhood Education; *Norm Referenced Tests; *Young Children
Identifiers: CADS
Availability: Patricia L. Oelwein; 13110 N.E. 25th Place, Bellevue, WA 98005
Age Level: 0-8
Notes: Time, 60 min. approx.; Items, 288
Provides educational teams working with infant, preschool, and primary programs with a norm-referenced assessment that is easy to administer and score. Developed for children from birth to 8 years of age. Designed to assist staff in establishing goals and objectives to measure pupil progress and to provide a longitudinal record of the child's development. Includes 5 domains of development: gross motor, fine motor, cognitive, communication, and social self-help. Not a standardized instrument to be used for diagnostic and placement purposes. Technical data are provided.

17307
Expressive One-Word Picture Vocabulary Test—Revised. Gardner, Morrison F. 1990
Descriptors: Bilingual Students; Children; Elementary Education; *Elementary School Students; *Expressive Language; *Language Tests; Norm Referenced Tests; *Preschool Children; Preschool Education; Screening Tests; Visual Measures; *Vocabulary
Identifiers: EOWPVT(R)
Availability: Academic Therapy Publications; 20 Commercial Blvd., Novato, CA 94949-6191
Age Level: 2-11
Notes: Time, 10 min. approx.; Items, 100
Assesses a child's speaking vocabulary. Measures a child's verbal expression by means of a child's ability to make word-picture associations based on what the child has learned from home and from formal education. Can be used to screen for possible speech defects, or learning disorders, to estimate a bilingual student's fluency in English or to screen for school readiness or placement. The 1990 revision features new norms and standardization, larger test plates with improved illustrations and a revised format of the Individual Record Form.

17308
New Gap. McLeod, John; McLeod, Rita 1990

Descriptors: *Cloze Procedure; Elementary Education; *Elementary School Students; Norm Referenced Tests; *Reading Comprehension; *Reading Tests; *Screening Tests
Availability: Academic Therapy Publications; 20 Commercial Blvd., Novato, CA 94949-6191
Grade Level: 2-5
Notes: Time, 20 min. approx.

Assesses reading comprehension by means of the cloze technique. Suitable for students in grades 2 through 5 and for older students of any age who have difficulty comprehending what they read. Two equivalent forms available. Information pertaining to standardization, reliability and validity is included.

17314
General Chemistry Test. Wainwright, Camille L. 1989
Descriptors: *Achievement Tests; *Chemistry; Computer Assisted Instruction; High Schools; *High School Students; Knowledge Level; Multiple Choice Tests; *Science Instruction; *Science Tests; Teaching Methods
Availability: Journal of Research in Science Teaching; v26 n4 p275-90, Apr 1989
Grade Level: 9-12
Notes: Items, 25

An achievement test in general chemistry designed as part of a research study on the differences in knowledge attainment of students using computer-assisted instruction versus traditional instruction in chemistry. Test is a paper-and-pencil test in the multiple-choice format and includes items which measure knowledge of chemical formulas and writing chemical equations. Test is to be administered after completion of comparable units of study by students using one or the other instructional format. Statistical data on the differences between the performance of the 2 groups are included.

17315
ACS Chemistry in the Community (ChemCom) Curriculum, High School Chemistry. American Chemical Society, Div. of Chemical Education, Stillwater, OK 1991
Descriptors: *Achievement Tests; *Chemistry; *Decision Making; High Schools; *High School Students; Secondary Education; Secondary School Curriculum
Identifiers: ChemCom
Availability: ACS DivCHED Examinations Institute; Oklahoma State University, 107 Physical Sciences, Stillwater, OK 74078
Grade Level: 9-12
Notes: Time, 80 min.; Items, 60

This test series was designed to accompany the new Chemistry in the Community (ChemCom) curriculum developed by the American Chemical Society. Coursework, and the examination, emphasize both the acquisition of knowledge of chemistry and the development of high level decision-making skills. Special item formats are used to evaluate students' success in developing decision-making skills.

17316
Major Field Achievement Tests: Biology. Educational Testing Service, Princeton, NJ 1988
Subtests: Cellular and Subcellular Biology: Organismal Biology; Population Biology: Ecology and Evolution
Descriptors: *Achievement Tests; *Biology; *College Seniors; College Students; Cytology; Higher Education; Majors (Students); *Outcomes of Education; Undergraduate Study
Availability: Educational Testing Service; Higher Education Assessment, Princeton, NJ 08541
Grade Level: 16
Notes: Time, 120 min.; Items, 150

The entire series consists of 16 objective, end-of-program tests designed to measure student outcomes of undergraduate education. These are based on the Graduate Record Examinations (GRE) Subject Tests and a portion of the Undergraduate Assessment Program. National comparative data are available. The test can be administered by an institution in-house at any time. Additional locally written questions can be added. May be administered to college seniors majoring in a field. Total scores are reported on a scale from 100-120. Group means and standard deviations are reported. For the Biology test, subscores are reported. Additional part scores are reported for a group of more than 5 students. These are Cellular Structure and Organization, Molecular Biology and Molecular Genetics, Organismal Biology-Animal, Organismal Biology-Plant, Mendelian Genetics-Population Genetics, Populations, Communities and Ecosystems, Evolution. The test is scored by the publisher. The Biology test items are based on descriptions of laboratory and field situations, diagrams, or, experimental results.

17317
Major Field Achievement Tests: Business. Educational Testing Service, Princeton, NJ 1988

Descriptors: *Achievement Tests; Administration; *Business Education; *College Seniors; College Students; Economics; Finance Occupations; Higher Education; Laws; Majors (Students); Marketing; *Outcomes of Education; Statistical Analysis; Undergraduate Study
Availability: Educational Testing Service; Higher Education Assessment, Princeton, NJ 08541
Grade Level: 16
Notes: Time, 120 min.; Items, 120

The entire series consists of 16 objective, end-of-program tests designed to measure student outcomes of undergraduate education. These are based on the Graduate Record Examinations (GRE) Subject Tests and a portion of the Undergraduate Assessment Program. National comparative data are available. The test can be administered by an institution in-house at any time. Additional locally written questions can be added. May be administered to college seniors majoring in a field. Total scores are reported on a scale from 100-120. Group means and standard deviations are reported. For the business test, no subscores are reported for individual students. The test is scored by the publisher. The business test items are based on diagrams, charts and tables of data. They measure students' knowledge and ability to apply facts, concepts, theories, and analytical methods. Based on a common core of undergraduate business education courses. Group scores are reported for groups consisting of more than 5 students in accounting, economics, finance, law, management, marketing, and quantitative analysis.

17318
Major Field Achievement Tests: Chemistry. Educational Testing Service, Princeton, NJ 1988
Descriptors: *Achievement Tests; Chemical Analysis; *Chemistry; *College Seniors; College Students; Higher Education; Inorganic Chemistry; Majors (Students); Organic Chemistry; *Outcomes of Education; Physical Chemistry; Undergraduate Study
Availability: Educational Testing Service; Higher Education Assessment, Princeton, NJ 08541
Grade Level: 16
Notes: Time, 120 min.; Items, 106

The entire series consists of 16 objective, end-of-program tests designed to measure student outcomes of undergraduate education. These are based on the Graduate Record Examinations (GRE) Subject Tests and a portion of the Undergraduate Assessment Program. National comparative data are available. The test can be administered by an institution in-house at any time. Additional locally written questions can be added. May be administered to college seniors majoring in a field. Total scores are reported on a scale from 100-120. Group means and standard deviations are reported. The test is scored by the publisher. The tests measure students' knowledge and ability to apply facts, concepts, theories, and analytical methods. For the chemistry test, no subscores are reported. Based on the 4 fields into which chemistry has traditionally been divided and the interrelationships among those fields. Additional scores can be derived for groups of more than 5 students in the areas of analytical chemistry, inorganic chemistry, organic chemistry, physical chemistry. The chemistry test items are based on a descriptive paragraph or experimental result so calculations and logarithm tables are not needed.

17319
Major Field Achievement Tests: Computer Science. Educational Testing Service, Princeton, NJ 1988
Descriptors: *Achievement Tests; Algebra; *College Seniors; College Students; Computer Graphics; Computers; *Computer Science; Computer Software; Higher Education; Majors (Students); Mathematics; *Outcomes of Education; Programing; Undergraduate Study
Availability: Educational Testing Service; Higher Education Assessment, Princeton, NJ 08541
Grade Level: 16
Notes: Time, 120 min.; Items, 56

The entire series consists of 16 objective, end-of-program tests designed to measure student outcomes of undergraduate education. These are based on the Graduate Record Examinations (GRE) Subject Tests and a portion of the Undergraduate Assessment Program. National comparative data are available. The test can be administered by an institution in-house at any time. Additional locally written questions can be added. May be administered to college seniors majoring in a field. Total scores are reported on a scale from 100-120. Group means and standard deviations are reported. For the computer science test, no subscores are reported for individual students. The test is scored by the publisher. The computer science test items are based on diagrams, graphs and program fragments. They measure students' knowledge and ability to apply facts, concepts, theories, and analytical methods. Group scores are reported for groups consisting of more than 5 students in Software Systems and Methodology, Computer Organization and Architecture, Theory, Computational Mathematics and Special Topics (modeling and simulation, information retrieval, artificial intelligence, computer graphics, data communications, data bases and VLSI).

17320
Major Field Achievement Tests: Economics. Educational Testing Service, Princeton, NJ 1988
Subtests: Microeconomics; Macroeconomics
Descriptors: *Achievement Tests; *College Seniors; College Students; *Economics; Higher Education; Majors (Students); *Outcomes of Education; Statistics; Undergraduate Study
Identifiers: Macroeconomics; Microeconomics
Availability: Educational Testing Service; Higher Education Assessment, Princeton, NJ 08541
Grade Level: 16
Notes: Time, 120 min.; Items, 90

The entire series consists of 16 objective, end-of-program tests designed to measure student outcomes of undergraduate education. These are based on the Graduate Record Examinations (GRE) Subject Tests and a portion of the Undergraduate Assessment Program. National comparative data are available. The test can be administered by an institution in-house at any time. Additional locally written questions can be added. May be administered to college seniors majoring in a field. Total scores are reported on a scale from 100-120. Group means and standard deviations are reported. For the economics test, subscores are reported for individual students in microeconomics and macroeconomics. The test is scored by the publisher. The economics test items are based on diagrams, expository paragraphs, sets of equations and tables of data. They measure students' knowledge and ability to apply facts, concepts, theories, and analytical methods. The test reflects the general undergraduate economic curriculum. Items cover introductory economics and microeconomics, macroeconomics, statistics, and other areas, such as international trade, public economics, history of economic thought, and economic history.

17321
Major Field Achievement Tests: Education. Educational Testing Service, Princeton, NJ 1988
Descriptors: *Achievement Tests; Administration; *College Seniors; College Students; Curriculum Development; Educational Objectives; Educational Research; Evaluation Methods; Higher Education; Learning Theories; Majors (Students); *Outcomes of Education; *Teacher Education; Teaching Methods; Undergraduate Study
Availability: Educational Testing Service; Higher Education Assessment, Princeton, NJ 08541
Grade Level: 16
Notes: Time, 120 min.; Items, 142

The entire series consists of 16 objective, end-of-program tests designed to measure student outcomes of undergraduate education. These are based on the Graduate Record Examinations (GRE) Subject Tests and a portion of the Undergraduate Assessment Program. National comparative data are available. The test can be administered by an institution in-house at any time. Additional locally written questions can be added. May be administered to college seniors majoring in a field. Total scores are reported on a scale from 100-120. Group means and standard deviations are reported. For the education test, no subscores are reported for individual students. The test is scored by the publisher. The education test items are derived from courses covering basic material needed by any prospective teacher. These items measure students' knowledge and ability to apply facts, concepts, understandings and abilities. Group scores are reported for groups consisting of more than 5 students in Educational Goals, Administration and Supervision, Curriculum Development and Organization, Teaching-Learning, Evaluation and Research Appraisal.

17322
Major Field Achievement Tests: Engineering. Educational Testing Service, Princeton, NJ 1988
Subtests: Engineering; Mathematics
Descriptors: *Achievement Tests; Algebra; Calculus; *College Seniors; College Students; *Engineering; Higher Education; Majors (Students); Mathematics; *Outcomes of Education; Undergraduate Study
Availability: Educational Testing Service; Higher Education Assessment, Princeton, NJ 08541
Grade Level: 16
Notes: Time, 120 min.; Items, 94

The entire series consists of 16 objective, end-of-program tests designed to measure student outcomes of undergraduate education. These are based on the Graduate Record Examinations (GRE) Subject Tests and a portion of the Undergraduate Assessment Program. National comparative data are available. The test can be administered by an institution in-house at any time. Additional locally written questions can be added. May be administered to college seniors majoring in a field. Total scores are reported on a scale from 100-120. Group means and standard deviations are reported. For the engineering test, subscores are reported for individual students. The test is scored by the publisher. The engineering test items are based on material common to several branches of engineering usually studied during the first 3 college years, including circuits, mechanics, transfer and rate mechanisms, thermodynamics, chemistry, nature and properties of matter, fluid mechanics, engineering judgment, light and sound, mathematical facts, intuitive calculus. Two courses in calculus are needed and some knowledge of equations, linear algebra, probability and statistics, and numerical analysis. Items measure the ability to apply facts, concepts, understandings and abilities. Group scores are reported for groups consisting of more than 5 students in Mathematical Usage.

17323
Major Field Achievement Tests: Geology. Educational Testing Service, Princeton, NJ 1988
Subtests: Stratigraphy; Sedimentology; Paleontology; Geomorphology; Structural Geology and Geophysics; Mineralogy, Petrology; Geochemistry
Descriptors: *Achievement Tests; *College Seniors; College Students; *Geology; Higher Education; Majors (Students); Mineralogy; *Outcomes of Education; Paleontology; Seismology; Undergraduate Study
Availability: Educational Testing Service; Higher Education Assessment, Princeton, NJ 08541
Grade Level: 16
Notes: Time, 120 min.; Items, 140
The entire series consists of 16 objective, end-of-program tests designed to measure student outcomes of undergraduate education. These are based on the Graduate Record Examinations (GRE) Subject Tests and a portion of the Undergraduate Assessment Program. National comparative data are available. The test can be administered by an institution in-house at any time. Additional locally written questions can be added. May be administered to college seniors majoring in a field. Total scores are reported on a scale from 100-120. Group means and standard deviations are reported. For the geology test, subscores are reported for individual students. The test is scored by the publisher. The geology test items are based on diagrams, maps and graphs and are derived from curricular areas of stratigraphy, sedimentology, paleontology, geomorphology, structural geology and geophysics, mineralogy, petrology and geochemistry. Items measure the ability to apply facts, concepts, understandings and abilities. Group scores are reported for groups consisting of more than 5 students in Stratigraphy and Paleontology; Sedimentology; Structure-Field Relations; Structure-Dynamics; Isostasy, Gravity, Magnetism, Earthquakes and Seismology; Mineralogy; Petrology; Geochemistry.

17324
Major Field Achievement Tests: History. Educational Testing Service, Princeton, NJ 1988
Subtests: European History; United States History
Descriptors: *Achievement Tests; *College Seniors; College Students; *European History; Higher Education; Majors (Students); *Outcomes of Education; Undergraduate Study; *United States History
Availability: Educational Testing Service; Higher Education Assessment, Princeton, NJ 08541
Grade Level: 16
Notes: Time, 120 min.; Items, 160
The entire series consists of 16 objective, end-of-program tests designed to measure student outcomes of undergraduate education. These are based on the Graduate Record Examinations (GRE) Subject Tests and a portion of the Undergraduate Assessment Program. National comparative data are available. The test can be administered by an institution in-house at any time. Additional locally written questions can be added. May be administered to college seniors majoring in a field. Total scores are reported on a scale from 100-120. Group means and standard deviations are reported. For the history test, subscores are reported for individual students. The test is scored by the publisher. The history test items are based on historical documents, cartoons, graphs, and tables, and deal with political, diplomatic, economic, social, cultural, and intellectual history. Items measure the ability to apply facts, concepts, understandings and abilities. Group scores are reported for groups consisting of more than 5 students in Medieval-Renaissance; Early Modern; Industrialism to 1850; Late Nineteenth Century; Twentieth Century; Colonial; Pre-Civil War; Post Civil War; Twentieth Century.

17325
Major Field Achievement Tests: Literature in English. Educational Testing Service, Princeton, NJ 1988
Descriptors: *Achievement Tests; *College Seniors; College Students; *English Literature; Higher Education; Majors (Students); *Outcomes of Education; Undergraduate Study; *United States Literature
Availability: Educational Testing Service; Higher Education Assessment, Princeton, NJ 08541
Grade Level: 16
Notes: Time, 120 min.; Items, 150
The entire series consists of 16 objective, end-of-program tests designed to measure student outcomes of undergraduate education. These are based on the Graduate Record Examinations (GRE) Subject Tests and a portion of the Undergraduate Assessment Program. National comparative data are available. The test can be administered by an institution in-house at any time. Additional locally written

questions can be added. May be administered to college seniors majoring in a field. Total scores are reported on a scale from 100-120. Group means and standard deviations are reported. For the literature test no subscores are reported for individual students. The test is scored by the publisher. The Literature in English test items cover poetry, drama, biography, the essay, criticism, the short story, the novel, history of the language. Based on English and American literature of all periods, major authors, works, genres, and movements. Items measure the ability to apply facts, concepts, understandings and abilities. Group scores are reported for groups consisting of more than 5 students in English literature to 1660; English Literature 1660-1925; English Literature since 1925; and American Literature. Items cover literary analysis, identification of some information about the work, factual questions, literary criticism.

17326
Major Field Achievement Tests: Mathematics. Educational Testing Service, Princeton, NJ 1988
Descriptors: *Achievement Tests; Algebra; Calculus; *College Seniors; College Students; Graphs; Higher Education; Majors (Students); *Mathematics; *Outcomes of Education; Topology; Undergraduate Study
Availability: Educational Testing Service; Higher Education Assessment, Princeton, NJ 08541
Grade Level: 16
Notes: Time, 120 min.; Items, 50
The entire series consists of 16 objective, end-of-program tests designed to measure student outcomes of undergraduate education. These are based on the Graduate Record Examinations (GRE) Subject Tests and a portion of the Undergraduate Assessment Program. National comparative data are available. The test can be administered by an institution in-house at any time. Additional locally written questions can be added. May be administered to college seniors majoring in a field. Total scores are reported on a scale from 100-120. Group means and standard deviations are reported. For the mathematics test, no subscores are reported for individual students. The test is scored by the publisher. The mathematics test items are based on areas of mathematics currently offered in undergraduate programs, including logic, differential equations, topology, probability, combinatorics, complex variables, algorithmic processes, statistics, and graph theory. Group scores are reported for groups consisting of more than 5 students in calculus, and linear and abstract algebra.

17327
Major Field Achievement Tests: Music. Educational Testing Service, Princeton, NJ 1988
Subtests: Theory; History and Literature
Descriptors: *Achievement Tests; *College Seniors; College Students; Higher Education; History; Literature; Majors (Students); *Music; Music Theory; *Outcomes of Education; Undergraduate Study
Availability: Educational Testing Service; Higher Education Assessment, Princeton, NJ 08541
Grade Level: 16
Notes: Time, 120 min.; Items, 140
The entire series consists of 16 objective, end-of-program tests designed to measure student outcomes of undergraduate education. These are based on the Graduate Record Examinations (GRE) Subject Tests and a portion of the Undergraduate Assessment Program. National comparative data are available. The test can be administered by an institution in-house at any time. Additional locally written questions can be added. May be administered to college seniors majoring in a field. Total scores are reported on a scale from 100-120. Group means and standard deviations are reported. The test is scored by the publisher. The tests measure students' knowledge and ability to apply facts, concepts, theories, and analytical methods. For the music test, subscores are reported in music theory and music history and literature. Additional scores can be derived for groups of more than 5 students in the areas of music fundamentals and specialities. The music test items are based on undergraduate courses of study most commonly offered in schools or departments of music. Approximately one-third of the questions cover style analysis. Others cover terminology, reading and interpreting notation, identifying musical elements from written notation.

17328
Major Field Achievement Tests: Physics. Educational Testing Service, Princeton, NJ 1988
Descriptors: *Achievement Tests; Atomic Theory; *College Seniors; College Students; Higher Education; Laboratory Procedures; Majors (Students); Mechanics (Physics); Nuclear Physics; Optics; *Outcomes of Education; *Physics; Quantum Mechanics; Relativity; Thermodynamics; Undergraduate Study
Identifiers: Electromagnetism; Particle Physics
Availability: Educational Testing Service; Higher Education Assessment, Princeton, NJ 08541
Grade Level: 16
Notes: Time, 120 min.; Items, 70
The entire series consists of 16 objective, end-of-program tests designed to measure student outcomes of undergraduate education. These are based on the Graduate Record

Examinations (GRE) Subject Tests and a portion of the Undergraduate Assessment Program. National comparative data are available. The test can be administered by an institution in-house at any time. Additional locally written questions can be added. May be administered to college seniors majoring in a field. Total scores are reported on a scale from 100-120. Group means and standard deviations are reported. For the physics test, no subscores are reported for individual students. The test is scored by the publisher. The physics test items are based on diagrams, graphs, experimental data, and descriptions of physical situations. They measure students' grasp of fundamental principles and ability to apply them in the solution of problems. Presumes the mastery of the first 3 years of an undergraduate physics program. Group scores are reported for groups consisting of more than 5 students in Classical Mechanics; Fundamentals of Electromagnetism; Atomic Physics and Quantum Mechanics; Thermodynamics, Statistical Mechanics, Physical Optics, and Wave Phenomena; Special Relativity, Laboratory Methods, Solid State Physics, Nuclear and Particle Physics.

17329
Major Field Achievement Tests: Political Science. Educational Testing Service, Princeton, NJ 1988
Descriptors: *Achievement Tests; *College Seniors; College Students; Higher Education; International Relations; Majors (Students); *Outcomes of Education; *Political Science; Politics; Undergraduate Study; United States Government (Course)
Availability: Educational Testing Service; Higher Education Assessment, Princeton, NJ 08541
Grade Level: 16
Notes: Time, 120 min.; Items, 118
The entire series consists of 16 objective, end-of-program tests designed to measure student outcomes of undergraduate education. These are based on the Graduate Record Examinations (GRE) Subject Tests and a portion of the Undergraduate Assessment Program. National comparative data are available. The test can be administered by an institution in-house at any time. Additional locally written questions can be added. May be administered to college seniors majoring in a field. Total scores are reported on a scale from 100-120. Group means and standard deviations are reported. For the political science test, no subscores are reported for individual students. The test is scored by the publisher. The political science test items are based on theory passages, statistical tables, matrics, and sets of ungrouped data. Measures students' ability to apply facts, concepts, theories, and analytical methods. Items are based on courses of study commonly offered in undergraduate programs. Group scores are reported for groups consisting of more than 5 students in U.S. Government and Politics, Comparative Political Systems, International Relations, Political Theory and History of Political Thought, Methodology.

17331
Major Field Achievement Tests: Sociology. Educational Testing Service, Princeton, NJ 1988
Descriptors: *Achievement Tests; *College Seniors; College Students; Demography; Higher Education; Majors (Students); *Outcomes of Education; Racial Relations; Social Control; Social Psychology; Social Stratification; *Sociology; Statistical Analysis; Statistics; Undergraduate Study
Availability: Educational Testing Service; Higher Education Assessment, Princeton, NJ 08541
Grade Level: 16
Notes: Time, 120 min.; Items, 140
The entire series consists of 16 objective, end-of-program tests designed to measure student outcomes of undergraduate education. These are based on the Graduate Record Examinations (GRE) Subject Tests and a portion of the Undergraduate Assessment Program. National comparative data are available. The test can be administered by an institution in-house at any time. Additional locally written questions can be added. May be administered to college seniors majoring in a field. Total scores are reported on a scale from 100-120. Group means and standard deviations are reported. For the sociology test, no subscores are reported for individual students. The test is scored by the publisher. The sociology test items are based on diagrams, graphs and statistical data. They measure students' ability to interpret data, to apply concepts and ideas, and to analyze sociological data, theories and relationships, deductively and inductively. The test covers the major fields included in most undergraduate programs. Group scores are reported for groups consisting of more than 5 students in Methodology and Statistics, General Theory, Demography and Urban/Rural Sociology, Social Psychology, Social Stratification; Race and Ethnic Relations; Deviance and Social Control, and other areas, including complex organizations, family and gender, social institutions and social change.

17340
Figurative Language Interpretation Test. Palmer, Barbara C. 1991
Descriptors: *Diagnostic Tests; *Elementary School Students; *Elementary Secondary Education; *Figurative Language; Norm Referenced Tests; *Secondary School Students

Identifiers: FLIT
Availability: Academic Therapy Publications; 20 Commercial Blvd., Novato, CA 94949-6191
Grade Level: 4-10
Notes: Time, 60 min. approx.; Items, 50

Designed as a diagnostic test to assess the ability of students in grades 4 through 10 to comprehend frequently used types of figurative language, such as simile, metaphor, hyperbole, and personification. Instrument focuses specifically on this ability in order to determine the level of instruction needed. Consists of 2 equivalent 50-item forms that can be used for pre- and posttesting. Multiple-choice format. Information on norms, reliability, and standardizations is provided.

17356
Bankson-Bernthal Test of Phonology. Bankson, Nicholas W.; Bernthal, John E. 1990
Descriptors: Articulation Impairments; *Diagnostic Tests; *Early Childhood Education; *Elementary School Students; *Phonology; *Preschool Children; Preschool Education; Speech Handicaps; *Speech Tests
Identifiers: BBTOP
Availability: Special Press; 11230 W. Ave., Ste. 3205, San Antonio, TX 78213
Grade Level: K-3
Age Level: 3-9
Notes: Time, 15 min. approx.; Items, 80

Designed for use by speech-language clinicians to assess the phonology of preschool and school-age children. Consists of a consonant inventory, a phonological process inventory, and a word inventory. Useful particularly with children who demonstrate intelligibility problems and as a means of comparing a child's phonological behavior to that of other children of comparable age.

17362
Standardized Bible Content Tests, Forms A-F. Standardized Bible Content Test Committee 1976
Descriptors: *Biblical Literature; *College Students; Higher Education; *Knowledge Level; *Standardized Tests
Identifiers: New Testament; Old Testament
Availability: American Association of Bible Colleges; P.O. Box 1523, Fayetteville, AR 72702
Grade Level: 13-16
Notes: Time, 45 min.; Items, 150

Designed to assess general knowledge of biblical content at the college level. Covers areas of history, geography, facts about people, doctrine, identification of Bible quotes, and general book content. Each test covers both Old and New Testament.

17363
Standardized Bible Content Tests, Form SP. Standardized Bible Content Test Committee 1975
Descriptors: Adults; *Biblical Literature; High School Seniors; *Knowledge Level; *Standardized Tests
Identifiers: New Testament; Old Testament
Availability: American Association of Bible Colleges; P.O. Box 1523, Fayetteville, AR 72702
Grade Level: 12
Age Level: 18-65
Notes: Time, 45 min.; Items, 150

Developed for use by organizations, such as churches, mission boards, and Christian high schools, for determining the general Bible knowledge of missionary candidates, analyzing the Bible knowledge of a church congregation, or assessing the Bible knowledge of high school seniors. Covers areas of history, geography, facts about people, doctrine, identification of Bible quotes, and general book content.

17364
Diagnostic Test of the New Testament. Johnson, Fred R. 1986
Subtests: New Testament World and New Testament Records; Beginning of the Church; Establishment and Expansion of the Church A.D. 29-60; Doctrines and Duties for Church Members from the Epistles A.D. 40-100; Expectant Church
Descriptors: *Achievement Tests; *Biblical Literature; *College Students; *Diagnostic Tests; Higher Education; *Knowledge Level
Identifiers: *New Testament
Availability: American Association of Bible Colleges; P.O. Box 1523, Fayetteville, AR 72702
Grade Level: 13-16
Notes: Items, 150

Designed to assess general knowledge of biblical content at the college level. Covers only the New Testament. Covers areas of history, geography, facts about people, doctrine, identification of Bible quotes, and general book content.

17375
Metropolitan Readiness Tests, Spanish Edition, Level 1. Nurss, Joanne R.; McGauvran, Mary E. 1990
Subtests: Auditory Memory (Memoria auditiva); Beginning Consonants Sonidos indicales); Letter Recognition (Reconocimiento de letras); Visual Matching (semejanzas visuales); School Language and Listening (Lenguaje escolar y Comprension auditiva); Quantitative Language (Lenguaje Cuantitativo)
Descriptors: *Beginning Reading; Early Childhood Education; Early Reading; *Grade 1; *Kindergarten Children; Language Acquisition; *Language Skills; Language Tests; *Mathematics Skills; Mathematics Tests; *Preschool Education; *Reading Readiness; Reading Skills; Reading Tests; *School Readiness Tests; *Spanish Speaking
Identifiers: MRT Espanol
Availability: The Psychological Corp.; 555 Academic Ct., San Antonio, TX 78204-0952
Grade Level: K-1
Age Level: 4-6
Notes: Time, 95 min. approx.

The Spanish addition to the Metropolitan Readiness Assessment program provides a skill-based assessment of reading, mathematics, and language development. It is an enabling skills tool that is most likely to influence early school success. This instrument has 2 levels. Level 1 includes 6 different tests measuring prereading skill development, and level 2 has 8 different tests that measure the skills needed in beginning reading and mathematics.

17376
Metropolitan Readiness Tests, Spanish Edition, Level 2. Nurss, Joanne R.; McGauvran, Mary E. 1990
Subtests: Beginning Consonants (Silabas iniciales); Sound-Letter Correspondence (Correspondencia entre sonido y silaba); Visual Matching (Semejanzas visuales); Finding Patterns (Encontrar Modelos); School Language (Lenguaje escolar); Listening (Comprension auditiva); Quantitative Concepts (Conceptos Cuantitativos); Quantitative Operations (Operaciones cuantitativas)
Descriptors: *Beginning Reading; Early Childhood Education; Early Reading; *Grade 1; *Kindergarten Children; Language Acquisition; *Language Skills; Language Tests; *Mathematics Skills; Mathematics Tests; *Preschool Education; *Reading Readiness; Reading Skills; Reading Tests; *School Readiness Tests; *Spanish Speaking
Identifiers: MRT Espanol
Availability: The Psychological Corp.; 555 Academic Ct., San Antonio, TX 78204-0952
Grade Level: K-1
Age Level: 4-6
Notes: Time, 105 min. approx.

The Spanish addition to the Metropolitan Readiness Assessment Program provides a skill-based assessment of reading, mathematics, and language development. It is an enabling skills tool that is most likely to influence early school success. This instrument has 2 levels. Level 1 includes 6 different tests measuring prereading skill development; and level 2 has 8 different tests that measure the skills needed in beginning reading and mathematics.

17378
Screening Test for Educational Prerequisite Skills. Smith, Frances 1990
Descriptors: Childhood Attitudes; Criterion Referenced Tests; *Individual Testing; *Kindergarten Children; Knowledge Level; *Prerequisites; Primary Education; Psychomotor Skills; *School Readiness; *Screening Tests
Identifiers: STEPS
Availability: Western Psychological Services; 12031 Wilshire Blvd., Los Angeles, CA 90025
Age Level: 4-5
Notes: Time, 10 min. approx.

This individually administered screening test is for children who are preparing to enter kindergarten. It assesses whether each child has mastered specific skills expected of beginning kindergarteners, measuring behaviors that correspond with successful classroom functioning. It also identifies those children who may need to be monitored in certain areas, and reveals those children who demonstrate weaknesses and require further evaluation. This criterion-referenced assessment screens the child in 5 areas: intellectual skills, verbal information skills, cognitive strategies, motor skills, and attitudes in learning situations. It also provides an optional 23-item Home Questionnaire that can be completed by the parents.

17381
Adult Basic Learning Examination, Spanish Edition. Karlsen, Bjorn; Gardner, Eric F. 1990
Subtests: Comprehension de lectura (Reading Comprehension); Resolucion de problemas (Problem Solving)
Descriptors: *Academic Achievement; *Adult Basic Education; Adults; *Adult Students; *Basic Skills; *Reading Comprehension; *Screening Tests; *Spanish Speaking; *Word Problems (Mathematics)
Identifiers: ABLE
Availability: The Psychological Corp.; 555 Academic Ct., San Antonio, TX 78204-0952
Age Level: Adults
Notes: Time, 35 min. approx.; Items, 78

This screening battery measures the level of educational achievement among adults to determine the general educational level of those who may not have completed 12 years of schooling. The purpose of this Spanish edition of the ABLE Screening Battery is to get an estimate of performance in reading and mathematics of the Spanish-speaking subjects. This includes the subtests: reading comprehension, and problem solving. This instrument is not recommended for adults who do not read.

17382
Developmental Sentence Scoring. Lee, Laura L.; Koenigsknecht, R.A. 1988
Descriptors: Elementary Education; *Elementary School Students; Grammar; *Individual Testing; *Language Proficiency; *Sentence Structure
Identifiers: DSS
Availability: Northwestern University Press; 625 Colfax, Evanston, IL 60201
Age Level: 2-7
Notes: Time, 60 min. approx.; Items, 50

The purpose of this instrument is to provide a systematic procedure for analyzing a student's grammatical structure and for estimating the extent to which the student has learned generalized grammatical rules enough to use them in conversation. This tool should be given individually by speech and language clinicians.

17386
Quick Inventory of Competency in Mathematics, Forms A&B. Scholastic Testing Service, Bensenville, IL 1989
Descriptors: *Achievement Tests; *Elementary School Students; Elementary Secondary Education; *Mathematics Achievement; *Secondary School Students; Student Placement
Identifiers: QUIC
Availability: Scholastic Testing Service, Inc.; 480 Meyer Rd., Bensenville, IL 60106-8056
Grade Level: 2-12
Notes: Time, 30 min. approx.

This instrument can be used to establish and verify the functional level of student competency in mathematics. It may be used with classes or for screening and placement of new students for whom little information is available. Scores include a competency-based grade equivalent and a raw score, which is converted to a standard score indicating the student's general performance at, above, or below grade level. This tool will provide an alternative assessment option when time, cost, and convenience are important.

17387
Quick Inventory of Competency in Communications, Forms A&B. Scholastic Testing Service, Bensenville, IL 1989
Descriptors: *Achievement Tests; *Elementary School Students; Elementary Secondary Education; *Language Skills; Screening Tests; *Secondary School Students; Student Placement
Identifiers: QUIC
Availability: Scholastic Testing Service, Inc.; 480 Meyer Rd., Bensenville, IL 60106-8056
Grade Level: 2-12
Notes: Time, 30 min. approx.

This instrument can be used to establish and verify the functional level of student competency in Communicative Arts. It may be used with classes or for screening and placement of new students for whom little information is available. Scores include a competency-based grade equivalent and a raw score, which is converted to a standard score indicating the student's general performance at, above, or below grade level. This tool will provide an alternative assessment option when time, cost, and convenience are important.

17444
Payan INREAL Child Language Screening Test. Payan, Rose M. 1979
Subtests: Vocabulary; Receptive Language Skills; Articulation; Expressive Language Skills
Descriptors: *Articulation (Speech); *Vocabulary; *Expressive Language; Language Handicaps; *Language Skills; *Language Tests; *Phonemes; *Preschool Children; *Receptive Language; *Spanish Speaking; Basic Vocabulary
Identifiers: INREAL; PICLS
Availability: Latino Institute; Research Div., Town Center Office Bldg.; 1760 Reston Ave., Ste. 101, Reston, VA 22090
Age Level: 4-5
Notes: Time, 15 min. approx.

This instrument was developed to measure the Spanish-speaking child's ability to identify objects, to articulate phonemes, to understand language, and to express language through repetition techniques. It assists speech clinicians in determining possible language disorders among Spanish-speaking preschool children. In addition, it seeks to facilitate language-maturation and to remediate language impairment in young children by performing language enrichment and language therapy within the classroom without removing the children to clinical rooms. The test employs the use of real objects that can be handled by the child and are commonly found in a household. Total numerical rating of each subtest ranges from one, indicating severe, to 4 indicating normal.

17450
Graduate Record Examinations: Subject Tests—Computer Science Test. Graduate Record Examinations Board, Princeton, NJ 1987
Descriptors: *Achievement Tests; *College Admission; *College Seniors; College Students; *Computers; *Computer Science; Computer Software; *Graduate Students; *Graduate Study; Higher Education; Mathematics; Multiple Choice Tests; Programing Languages; Standardized Tests; Theories
Identifiers: Computer Architecture
Availability: Educational Testing Service; Graduate Record Examinations, P.O. Box 6000, Princeton, NJ 08541-6000
Grade Level: 16
Notes: Time, 170 min.; Items, 80
The GRE Subject Tests are standardized multiple-choice tests designed to assist graduate schools and fellowship sponsors in assessing the qualifications of applicants to graduate schools in specific fields of study. Scores are intended to show students' knowledge of subject matter that is taught in undergraduate programs as preparation for graduate study. These scores are said to be helpful in predicting students' academic success in graduate study. The tests are standardized, making it possible to compare students from different institutions with dissimilar undergraduate programs. For some subject tests, subscores are provided in addition to the total score. The Computer Science Test covers software systems and methodology, computer organization and architecture, theory, mathematical background, advanced topics. A total scaled score with a maximum value of 900 is reported.

17458
Survey of Early Childhood Abilities. Codding, Karen Gardner 1987
Subtests: Test of Visual Motor Skills; Test of Auditory Perceptual Skills; Test of Visual Perceptual Skills
Descriptors: Auditory Perception; *Grade 1; *Individual Development; *Kindergarten Children; Primary Education; Psychomotor Skills; *School Readiness Tests; *Standardized Tests; Visual Perception
Identifiers: SECA
Availability: Children's Hospital of San Francisco; Publication Dept., P.O. Box 3805, San Francisco, CA 94119
Grade Level: K-1
Age Level: 4-7
Notes: Items, 423
This assessment tool provides comprehensive evaluation to assist in determining a child's readiness in kindergarten and first grade. It also helps in determining areas of low functioning in children at those grade levels. This instrument is comprised of the lower levels of 3 standardized tests: Test of Visual-Motor Skills (TVMS) (TC015598); Test of Auditory-Perceptual Skills (TAPS) (TC014900); and Test of Visual Perceptual Skills (TVPS) (TC012229). TVMS measures how well the children translate with their hands what they visually perceive. TAPS measures children functioning in various areas of auditory perception and measures children's ability to understand various types of directions, accurate pronounciation of words, acuity of pronounced words, keenness of thought, and questionable hearing acuity. TVPS requires no verbal responses and is comprised of 7 visual factors measuring discrimination; memory; spatial relationships; form constancy; sequential memory; figure-ground; and closure. All tests are untimed.

17459
Tennis Skills Test. Hensley, Larry 1990
Descriptors: *College Students; Higher Education; *High School Students; *Junior High School Students; *Performance Tests; Physical Education; Psychomotor Skills; Secondary Education; *Tennis
Availability: American Alliance for Health, Physical Education, Recreation and Dance; 1900 Association Drive, Reston, VA 22091
Grade Level: 7-16
This test battery was developed to identify the essential skills of the sport of tennis. Two of the skill requirements measured for playing tennis are ground strokes (forehand and backhand drive) and the serve. The volley is an optional skill measured, because it is generally thought to

be more appropriate for intermediate or advanced players. Normative data were collected on over 7,000 students representing 42 states. This data provided information relative to the range of performance scores that can be expected for students of both sexes and different academic levels.

17481
Curriculum Frameworks Assessment System, Level 1. CTB/Macmillan/McGraw-Hill, Monterey, CA 1990
Subtests: System: (Reading; Language; Integrated Curriculum; Mathematics; Mathematics Technology; Science); Supplement: (Integrated Curriculum; Mathematics; Science)
Descriptors: *Achievement Tests; Curriculum; *Educational Objectives; *Elementary School Students; Elementary Secondary Education; *Grade 1; History; Integrated Curriculum; Language Arts; Mathematics; *Outcomes of Education; Reading; Sciences; Social Sciences; State Curriculum Guides; *State Standards
Identifiers: California; CFAS; *Performance Based Evaluation
Availability: CTB Macmillan/McGraw Hill; Del Monte Research Park, 2500 Garden Rd., Monterey, CA 93940
Grade Level: 1
Notes: Time, 123 min.; Items, 159
Designed to support the schools' need for national normative information, statewide normative information, and frameworks outcome information. Measures how well students in grades 1 through 12 meet the educational goals of their state and local curriculum. Directly measures outcomes that can be assessed using multiple-choice test items and helps integrate performance assessment data for other outcomes to give a more complete picture of student attainment. Series of tests based on outcomes and Model Curricula of 4 basic categories: English-Language Arts, History-Social Science, Science, and Mathematics. Curriculum Frameworks Assessment has 2 modules: System or the shorter Supplement. The Curriculum Frameworks Assessment System consists of 6 tests: Reading, Language, Integrated Curriculum, Mathematics, Mathematics Technology, and Science of 180-250 items that measure the frameworks educational outcomes. Provides statewide normative information and framework outcome information. When administered with the CTBS/4 Survey Test, national norms are provided. Curriculum Frameworks Assessment Supplement consists of 3 tests: Integrated Curriculum, Mathematics, and Science of 80-125 items that measure frameworks educational outcomes. When the supplement is administered in conjunction with the CTBS/4 Complete Battery, schools can receive national norms, objective scores, state norms, and framework outcome scores. Each level corresponds to the grade level. These tests are derived from work done by the California State Department of Education and are based on the 4 California Frameworks of English-Language Arts, History-Social Science, Science, and Mathematics.

17482
Curriculum Frameworks Assessment System, Level 2. CTB/Macmillan/McGraw-Hill, Monterey, CA 1990
Subtests: System: (Reading; Language; Integrated Curriculum; Mathematics; Mathematics Technology; Science); Supplement: (Integrated Curriculum; Mathematics; Science)
Descriptors: *Achievement Tests; Curriculum; *Educational Objectives; *Elementary School Students; Elementary Secondary Education; *Grade 2; History; Integrated Curriculum; Language Arts; Mathematics; *Outcomes of Education; Reading; Sciences; Social Sciences; State Curriculum Guides; *State Standards
Identifiers: California; CFAS; *Performance Based Evaluation
Availability: CTB Macmillan/McGraw Hill; Del Monte Research Park, 2500 Garden Rd., Monterey, CA 93940
Grade Level: 2
Notes: Time, 138 min.; Items, 182
Designed to support the schools' need for national normative information, statewide normative information, and frameworks outcome information. Measures how well students in grades 1 through 12 meet the educational goals of their state and local curriculum. Directly measures outcomes that can be assessed using multiple-choice test items and helps integrate performance assessment data for other outcomes to give a more complete picture of student attainment. Series of tests based on outcomes and Model Curricula of 4 basic categories: English-Language Arts, History-Social Science, Science, and Mathematics. Curriculum Frameworks Assessment has 2 modules: System or the shorter Supplement. The Curriculum Frameworks Assessment System consists of 6 tests: Reading, Language, Integrated Curriculum, Mathematics, Mathematics Technology, and Science of 180-250 items that measure the frameworks educational outcomes. Provides statewide normative information and framework outcome information. When administered with the CTBS/4 Survey Test, national norms are provided. Curriculum Frameworks Assessment Supplement consists of 3 tests: Integrated Cur-

riculum, Mathematics, and Science of 80-125 items that measure frameworks educational outcomes. When the supplement is administered in conjunction with the CTBS/4 Complete Battery, schools can receive national norms, objective scores, state norms, and framework outcome scores. Each level corresponds to the grade level. These tests are derived from work done by the California State Department of Education and are based on the 4 California Frameworks of English-Language Arts, History-Social Science, Science, and Mathematics.

17483
Curriculum Frameworks Assessment System, Level 3. CTB/Macmillan/McGraw-Hill, Monterey, CA 1990
Subtests: System: (Reading; Language; Integrated Curriculum; Mathematics; Mathematics Technology; Science); Supplement: (Integrated Curriculum; Mathematics; Science)
Descriptors: *Achievement Tests; Curriculum; *Educational Objectives; *Elementary School Students; Elementary Secondary Education; *Grade 3; History; Integrated Curriculum; Language Arts; Mathematics; *Outcomes of Education; Reading; Sciences; Social Sciences; State Curriculum Guides; *State Standards
Identifiers: California; CFAS; *Performance Based Evaluation
Availability: CTB Macmillan/McGraw Hill; Del Monte Research Park, 2500 Garden Rd., Monterey, CA 93940
Grade Level: 3
Notes: Time, 142 min.; Items, 195
Designed to support the schools' need for national normative information, statewide normative information, and frameworks outcome information. Measures how well students in grades 1 through 12 meet the educational goals of their state and local curriculum. Directly measures outcomes that can be assessed using multiple-choice test items and helps integrate performance assessment data for other outcomes to give a more complete picture of student attainment. Series of tests based on outcomes and Model Curricula of 4 basic categories: English-Language Arts, History-Social Science, Science, and Mathematics. Curriculum Frameworks Assessment has 2 modules: System or the shorter Supplement. The Curriculum Frameworks Assessment System consists of 6 tests: Reading, Language, Integrated Curriculum, Mathematics, Mathematics Technology, and Science of 180-250 items that measure the frameworks educational outcomes. Provides statewide normative information and framework outcome information. When administered with the CTBS/4 Survey Test, national norms are provided. Curriculum Frameworks Assessment Supplement consists of 3 tests: Integrated Curriculum, Mathematics, and Science of 80-125 items that measure frameworks educational outcomes. When the supplement is administered in conjunction with the CTBS/4 Complete Battery, schools can receive national norms, objective scores, state norms, and framework outcome scores. Each level corresponds to the grade level. These tests are derived from work done by the California State Department of Education and are based on the 4 California Frameworks of English-Language Arts, History-Social Science, Science, and Mathematics.

17484
Curriculum Frameworks Assessment System, Level 4. CTB/Macmillan/McGraw-Hill, Monterey, CA 1990
Subtests: System: (Reading; Language; Integrated Curriculum; Mathematics; Mathematics Technology; Science); Supplement: (Integrated Curriculum; Mathematics; Science)
Descriptors: *Achievement Tests; Curriculum; *Educational Objectives; *Elementary School Students; Elementary Secondary Education; *Grade 4; History; Integrated Curriculum; Language Arts; Mathematics; *Outcomes of Education; Reading; Sciences; Social Sciences; State Curriculum Guides; *State Standards
Identifiers: California; CFAS; *Performance Based Evaluation
Availability: CTB Macmillan/McGraw Hill; Del Monte Research Park, 2500 Garden Rd., Monterey, CA 93940
Grade Level: 4
Notes: Time, 154 min.; Items, 203
Designed to support the schools' need for national normative information, statewide normative information, and frameworks outcome information. Measures how well students in grades 1 through 12 meet the educational goals of their state and local curriculum. Directly measures outcomes that can be assessed using multiple-choice test items and helps integrate performance assessment data for other outcomes to give a more complete picture of student attainment. Series of tests based on outcomes and Model Curricula of 4 basic categories: English-Language Arts, History-Social Science, Science, and Mathematics. Curriculum Frameworks Assessment has 2 modules: System or the shorter Supplement. The Curriculum Frameworks Assessment System consists of 6 tests: Reading, Language, Integrated Curriculum, Mathematics, Mathematics Technology, and Science of 180-250 items that measure the frameworks educational outcomes. Provides statewide nor-

mative information and framework outcome information. When administered with the CTBS/4 Survey Test, national norms are provided. Curriculum Frameworks Assessment Supplement consists of 3 tests: Integrated Curriculum, Mathematics, and Science of 80-125 items that measure frameworks educational outcomes. When the supplement is administered in conjunction with the CTBS/4 Complete Battery, schools can receive national norms, objective scores, state norms, and framework outcome scores. Each level corresponds to the grade level. These tests are derived from work done by the California State Department of Education and are based on the 4 California Frameworks of English-Language Arts, History-Social Science, Science, and Mathematics.

17485
Curriculum Frameworks Assessment System, Level 5. CTB/Macmillan/McGraw-Hill, Monterey, CA 1990
Subtests: System: (Reading; Language; Integrated Curriculum; Mathematics; Mathematics Technology; Science); Supplement: (Integrated Curriculum; Mathematics; Science)
Descriptors: *Achievement Tests; Curriculum; *Educational Objectives; *Elementary School Students; Elementary Secondary Education; *Grade 5; History; Integrated Curriculum; Language Arts; Mathematics; *Outcomes of Education; Reading; Sciences; Social Sciences; State Curriculum Guides; *State Standards
Identifiers: California; CFAS; *Performance Based Evaluation
Availability: CTB Macmillan/McGraw Hill; Del Monte Research Park, 2500 Garden Rd., Monterey, CA 93940
Grade Level: 5
Notes: Time, 156 min.; Items, 203

Designed to support the schools' need for national normative information, statewide normative information, and frameworks outcome information. Measures how well students in grades 1 through 12 meet the educational goals of their state and local curriculum. Directly measures outcomes that can be assessed using multiple-choice test items and helps integrate performance assessment data for other outcomes to give a more complete picture of student attainment. Series of tests based on outcomes and Model Curricula of 4 basic categories: English-Language Arts, History-Social Science, Science, and Mathematics. Curriculum Frameworks Assessment has 2 modules: System or the shorter Supplement. The Curriculum Frameworks Assessment System consists of 6 tests: Reading, Language, Integrated Curriculum, Mathematics, Mathematics Technology, and Science of 180-250 items that measure the frameworks educational outcomes. Provides statewide normative information and framework outcome information. When administered with the CTBS/4 Survey Test, national norms are provided. Curriculum Frameworks Assessment Supplement consists of 3 tests: Integrated Curriculum, Mathematics, and Science of 80-125 items that measure frameworks educational outcomes. When the supplement is administered in conjunction with the CTBS/4 Complete Battery, schools can receive national norms, objective scores, state norms, and framework outcome scores. Each level corresponds to the grade level. These tests are derived from work done by the California State Department of Education and are based on the 4 California Frameworks of English-Language Arts, History-Social Science, Science, and Mathematics.

17486
Curriculum Frameworks Assessment System, Level 6. CTB/Macmillan/McGraw-Hill, Monterey, CA 1990
Subtests: System: (Reading; Language; Integrated Curriculum; Mathematics; Mathematics Technology; Science); Supplement: (Integrated Curriculum; Mathematics; Science)
Descriptors: *Achievement Tests; Curriculum; *Educational Objectives; *Elementary School Students; Elementary Secondary Education; *Grade 6; History; Integrated Curriculum; Language Arts; Mathematics; *Outcomes of Education; Reading; Sciences; Social Sciences; State Curriculum Guides; *State Standards
Identifiers: California; CFAS; *Performance Based Evaluation
Availability: CTB Macmillan/McGraw Hill; Del Monte Research Park, 2500 Garden Rd., Monterey, CA 93940
Grade Level: 6
Notes: Time, 147 min.; Items, 194

Designed to support the schools' need for national normative information, statewide normative information, and frameworks outcome information. Measures how well students in grades 1 through 12 meet the educational goals of their state and local curriculum. Directly measures outcomes that can be assessed using multiple-choice test items and helps integrate performance assessment data for other outcomes to give a more complete picture of student attainment. Series of tests based on outcomes and Model Curricula of 4 basic categories: English-Language Arts, History-Social Science, Science, and Mathematics. Curriculum Frameworks Assessment has 2 modules: System or the shorter Supplement. The Curriculum Frameworks Assessment System consists of 6 tests: Reading, Language, Integrated Curriculum, Mathematics, Mathematics Technology, and Science of 180-250 items that measure the frameworks educational outcomes. Provides statewide normative information and framework outcome information. When administered with the CTBS/4 Survey Test, national norms are provided. Curriculum Frameworks Assessment Supplement consists of 3 tests: Integrated Curriculum, Mathematics, and Science of 80-125 items that measure frameworks educational outcomes. When the supplement is administered in conjunction with the CTBS/4 Complete Battery, schools can receive national norms, objective scores, state norms, and framework outcome scores. Each level corresponds to the grade level. These tests are derived from work done by the California State Department of Education and are based on the 4 California Frameworks of English-Language Arts, History-Social Science, Science, and Mathematics.

17487
Curriculum Frameworks Assessment System, Level 7. CTB/Macmillan/McGraw-Hill, Monterey, CA 1990
Subtests: System: (Reading; Language; Integrated Curriculum; Mathematics; Mathematics Technology; Science); Supplement: (Integrated Curriculum; Mathematics; Science)
Descriptors: *Achievement Tests; Curriculum; *Educational Objectives; Elementary Secondary Education; *Grade 7; History; Integrated Curriculum; *Junior High School Students; Language Arts; Mathematics; *Outcomes of Education; Reading; Sciences; Social Sciences; State Curriculum Guides; *State Standards
Identifiers: California; CFAS; *Performance Based Evaluation
Availability: CTB Macmillan/McGraw Hill; Del Monte Research Park, 2500 Garden Rd., Monterey, CA 93940
Grade Level: 7
Notes: Time, 154 min.; Items, 200

Designed to support the schools' need for national normative information, statewide normative information, and frameworks outcome information. Measures how well students in grades 1 through 12 meet the educational goals of their state and local curriculum. Directly measures outcomes that can be assessed using multiple-choice test items and helps integrate performance assessment data for other outcomes to give a more complete picture of student attainment. Series of tests based on outcomes and Model Curricula of 4 basic categories: English-Language Arts, History-Social Science, Science, and Mathematics. Curriculum Frameworks Assessment has 2 modules: System or the shorter Supplement. The Curriculum Frameworks Assessment System consists of 6 tests: Reading, Language, Integrated Curriculum, Mathematics, Mathematics Technology, and Science of 180-250 items that measure the frameworks educational outcomes. Provides statewide normative information and framework outcome information. When administered with the CTBS/4 Survey Test, national norms are provided. Curriculum Frameworks Assessment Supplement consists of 3 tests: Integrated Curriculum, Mathematics, and Science of 80-125 items that measure frameworks educational outcomes. When the supplement is administered in conjunction with the CTBS/4 Complete Battery, schools can receive national norms, objective scores, state norms, and framework outcome scores. Each level corresponds to the grade level. These tests are derived from work done by the California State Department of Education and are based on the 4 California Frameworks of English-Language Arts, History-Social Science, Science, and Mathematics.

17488
Curriculum Frameworks Assessment System, Level 8. CTB/Macmillan/McGraw-Hill, Monterey, CA 1990
Subtests: System: (Reading; Language; Integrated Curriculum; Mathematics; Mathematics Technology; Science); Supplement: (Integrated Curriculum; Mathematics; Science)
Descriptors: *Achievement Tests; Curriculum; *Educational Objectives; Elementary Secondary Education; *Grade 8; History; Integrated Curriculum; *Junior High School Students; Language Arts; Mathematics; *Outcomes of Education; Reading; Sciences; Social Sciences; State Curriculum Guides; *State Standards
Identifiers: California; CFAS; *Performance Based Evaluation
Availability: CTB Macmillan/McGraw Hill; Del Monte Research Park, 2500 Garden Rd., Monterey, CA 93940
Grade Level: 8
Notes: Time, 162 min.; Items, 214

Designed to support the schools' need for national normative information, statewide normative information, and frameworks outcome information. Measures how well students in grades 1 through 12 meet the educational goals of their state and local curriculum. Directly measures outcomes that can be assessed using multiple-choice test items and helps integrate performance assessment data for other outcomes to give a more complete picture of student attainment. Series of tests based on outcomes and Model Curricula of 4 basic categories: English-Language Arts, History-Social Science, Science, and Mathematics. Curriculum Frameworks Assessment has 2 modules: System or the shorter Supplement. The Curriculum Frameworks Assessment System consists of 6 tests: Reading, Language, Integrated Curriculum, Mathematics, Mathematics Technology, and Science of 180-250 items that measure the frameworks educational outcomes. Provides statewide normative information and framework outcome information. When administered with the CTBS/4 Survey Test, national norms are provided. Curriculum Frameworks Assessment Supplement consists of 3 tests: Integrated Curriculum, Mathematics, and Science of 80-125 items that measure frameworks educational outcomes. When the supplement is administered in conjunction with the CTBS/4 Complete Battery, schools can receive national norms, objective scores, state norms, and framework outcome scores. Each level corresponds to the grade level. These tests are derived from work done by the California State Department of Education and are based on the 4 California Frameworks of English-Language Arts, History-Social Science, Science, and Mathematics.

17489
Curriculum Frameworks Assessment System, Level 9/10. CTB/Macmillan/McGraw-Hill, Monterey, CA 1990
Subtests: System: (Reading; Language; Integrated Curriculum; Mathematics; Mathematics Technology; Science); Supplement: (Integrated Curriculum; Mathematics; Science)
Descriptors: *Achievement Tests; Curriculum; *Educational Objectives; Elementary Secondary Education; *Grade 9; *Grade 10; *High School Students; History; Integrated Curriculum; Language Arts; Mathematics; *Outcomes of Education; Reading; Sciences; Social Sciences; State Curriculum Guides; *State Standards
Identifiers: California; CFAS; *Performance Based Evaluation
Availability: CTB Macmillan/McGraw Hill; Del Monte Research Park, 2500 Garden Rd., Monterey, CA 93940
Grade Level: 9-10

Designed to support the schools' need for national normative information, statewide normative information, and frameworks outcome information. Measures how well students in grades 1 through 12 meet the educational goals of their state and local curriculum. Directly measures outcomes that can be assessed using multiple-choice test items and helps integrate performance assessment data for other outcomes to give a more complete picture of student attainment. Series of tests based on outcomes and Model Curricula of 4 basic categories: English-Language Arts, History-Social Science, Science, and Mathematics. Curriculum Frameworks Assessment has 2 modules: System or the shorter Supplement. The Curriculum Frameworks Assessment System consists of 6 tests: Reading, Language, Integrated Curriculum, Mathematics, Mathematics Technology, and Science of 180-250 items that measure the frameworks educational outcomes. Provides statewide normative information and framework outcome information. When administered with the CTBS/4 Survey Test, national norms are provided. Curriculum Frameworks Assessment Supplement consists of 3 tests: Integrated Curriculum, Mathematics, and Science of 80-125 items that measure frameworks educational outcomes. When the supplement is administered in conjunction with the CTBS/4 Complete Battery, schools can receive national norms, objective scores, state norms, and framework outcome scores. Each level corresponds to the grade level. These tests are derived from work done by the California State Department of Education and are based on the 4 California Frameworks of English-Language Arts, History-Social Science, Science, and Mathematics.

17490
Curriculum Frameworks Assessment System, Level 11/12. CTB/Macmillan/McGraw-Hill, Monterey, CA 1990
Subtests: System: (Reading; Language; Integrated Curriculum; Mathematics; Mathematics Technology; Science); Supplement: (Integrated Curriculum; Mathematics; Science)
Descriptors: *Achievement Tests; Curriculum; *Educational Objectives; Elementary Secondary Education; *Grade 11; *Grade 12; *High School Students; History; Integrated Curriculum; Language Arts; Mathematics; *Outcomes of Education; Reading; Sciences; Social Sciences; State Curriculum Guides; *State Standards
Identifiers: California; CFAS; *Performance Based Evaluation
Availability: CTB Macmillan/McGraw Hill; Del Monte Research Park, 2500 Garden Rd., Monterey, CA 93940
Grade Level: 11-12

Designed to support the schools' need for national normative information, statewide normative information, and frameworks outcome information. Measures how well students in grades 1 through 12 meet the educational goals of their state and local curriculum. Directly measures outcomes that can be assessed using multiple-choice test items and helps integrate performance assessment data for other outcomes to give a more complete picture of student attainment. Series of tests based on outcomes and Model Curricula of 4 basic categories: English-Language Arts, History-Social Science, Science, and Mathematics. Curriculum Frameworks Assessment has 2 modules: System or the shorter Supplement. The Curriculum Frameworks Assessment System consists of 6 tests: Reading, Language, Integrated Curriculum, Mathematics, Mathematics Technology, and Science of 180-250 items that measure the frameworks educational outcomes. Provides statewide normative information and framework outcome information. When administered with the CTBS/4 Survey Test, national norms are provided. Curriculum Frameworks Assessment Supplement consists of 3 tests: Integrated Curriculum, Mathematics, and Science of 80-125 items that measure frameworks educational outcomes. When the supplement is administered in conjunction with the CTBS/4 Complete Battery, schools can receive national norms, objective scores, state norms, and framework outcome scores. Each level corresponds to the grade level. These tests are derived from work done by the California State Department of Education and are based on the 4 California Frameworks of English-Language Arts, History-Social Science, Science, and Mathematics.

17499
Slosson Test of Reading Readiness. Perry, Leslie Anne; Vitali, Gary J. 1991
Subtests: Recognition of Capital Letters; Recognition of Lower Case Letters; Matching Capital and Lower Case Letters; Visual Discrimination-Matching Word Forms; Auditory Discrimination-Rhyming Words; Auditory Discrimination and Memory-Recognition of Beginning Sounds; Sequencing; Opposites
Descriptors: Auditory Discrimination; Cognitive Ability; *Grade 1; *Individual Testing; *Kindergarten Children; Letters (Alphabet); *Norm Referenced Tests; Primary Education; *Reading Readiness; *Reading Readiness Tests; *Screening Tests; Visual Discrimination
Identifiers: STRR
Availability: Slosson Educational Publications; P.O. Box 280, East Aurora, NY 14052
Grade Level: K-1
Notes: Time, 15 min. approx.

Developed for use with children at the end of kindergarten or the beginning of grade 1 as a screening test to identify those children ready to begin formal reading instruction and those children who are at risk or likely to fail if placed in a formal reading program. The test is individually administered. The test is untimed but can usually be administered and scored in about 15 minutes. The subtest scores are grouped to reflect a visual skills total, a cognitive skills total, an auditory skills total, and a total score. Information on the norming sample, validity, and reliability is available.

17513
Curriculum Frameworks Assessment Supplement, Level 1. CTB/Macmillan/McGraw-Hill, Monterey, CA 1990
Subtests: System: (Reading; Language; Integrated Curriculum; Mathematics; Mathematics Technology; Science); Supplement: (Integrated Curriculum; Mathematics; Science)
Descriptors: *Achievement Tests; Curriculum; *Educational Objectives; *Elementary School Students; Elementary Secondary Education; *Grade 1; History; Integrated Curriculum; Language Arts; Mathematics; *Outcomes of Education; Reading; Sciences; Social Sciences; State Curriculum Guides; *State Standards
Identifiers: California; CFAS; *Performance Based Evaluation
Availability: CTB Macmillan/McGraw Hill; Del Monte Research Park, 2500 Garden Rd., Monterey, CA 93940
Grade Level: 1
Notes: Time, 66 min.; Items, 87

Designed to support the schools' need for national normative information, statewide normative information, and frameworks outcome information. Measures how well students in grades 1 through 12 meet the educational goals of their state and local curriculum. Directly measures outcomes that can be assessed using multiple-choice test items and helps integrate performance assessment data for other outcomes to give a more complete picture of student attainment. Series of tests based on outcomes and Model Curricula of 4 basic categories: English-Language Arts, History-Social Science, Science, and Mathematics. Curriculum Frameworks Assessment has 2 modules: System or the shorter Supplement. The Curriculum Frameworks Assessment System consists of 6 tests: Reading, Language, Integrated Curriculum, Mathematics, Mathematics Technology, and Science of 180-250 items that measure the frameworks educational outcomes. Provides statewide normative information and framework outcome information. When administered with the CTBS/4 Survey Test, national norms are provided. Curriculum Frameworks Assessment Supplement consists of 3 tests: Integrated Curriculum, Mathematics, and Science of 80-125 items that measure frameworks educational outcomes. When the supplement is administered in conjunction with the CTBS/4

Complete Battery, schools can receive national norms, objective scores, state norms, and framework outcome scores. Each level corresponds to the grade level. These tests are derived from work done by the California State Department of Education and are based on the 4 California Frameworks of English-Language Arts, History-Social Science, Science, and Mathematics.

17514
Curriculum Frameworks Assessment Supplement, Level 2. CTB/Macmillan/McGraw-Hill, Monterey, CA 1990
Subtests: System: (Reading; Language; Integrated Curriculum; Mathematics; Mathematics Technology; Science); Supplement: (Integrated Curriculum; Mathematics; Science)
Descriptors: *Achievement Tests; Curriculum; *Educational Objectives; *Elementary School Students; Elementary Secondary Education; *Grade 2; History; Integrated Curriculum; Language Arts; Mathematics; *Outcomes of Education; Reading; Sciences; Social Sciences; State Curriculum Guides; *State Standards
Identifiers: California; CFAS; *Performance Based Evaluation
Availability: CTB Macmillan/McGraw Hill; Del Monte Research Park, 2500 Garden Rd., Monterey, CA 93940
Grade Level: 2
Notes: Time, 75 min.; Items, 99

Designed to support the schools' need for national normative information, statewide normative information, and frameworks outcome information. Measures how well students in grades 1 through 12 meet the educational goals of their state and local curriculum. Directly measures outcomes that can be assessed using multiple-choice test items and helps integrate performance assessment data for other outcomes to give a more complete picture of student attainment. Series of tests based on outcomes and Model Curricula of 4 basic categories: English-Language Arts, History-Social Science, Science, and Mathematics. Curriculum Frameworks Assessment has 2 modules: System or the shorter Supplement. The Curriculum Frameworks Assessment System consists of 6 tests: Reading, Language, Integrated Curriculum, Mathematics, Mathematics Technology, and Science of 180-250 items that measure the frameworks educational outcomes. Provides statewide normative information and framework outcome information. When administered with the CTBS/4 Survey Test, national norms are provided. Curriculum Frameworks Assessment Supplement consists of 3 tests: Integrated Curriculum, Mathematics, and Science of 80-125 items that measure frameworks educational outcomes. When the supplement is administered in conjunction with the CTBS/4 Complete Battery, schools can receive national norms, objective scores, state norms, and framework outcome scores. Each level corresponds to the grade level. These tests are derived from work done by the California State Department of Education and are based on the 4 California Frameworks of English-Language Arts, History-Social Science, Science, and Mathematics.

17515
Curriculum Frameworks Assessment Supplement, Level 3. CTB/Macmillan/McGraw-Hill, Monterey, CA 1990
Subtests: System: (Reading; Language; Integrated Curriculum; Mathematics; Mathematics Technology; Science); Supplement: (Integrated Curriculum; Mathematics; Science)
Descriptors: *Achievement Tests; Curriculum; *Educational Objectives; *Elementary School Students; Elementary Secondary Education; *Grade 3; History; Integrated Curriculum; Language Arts; Mathematics; *Outcomes of Education; Reading; Sciences; Social Sciences; State Curriculum Guides; *State Standards
Identifiers: California; CFAS; *Performance Based Evaluation
Availability: CTB Macmillan/McGraw Hill; Del Monte Research Park, 2500 Garden Rd., Monterey, CA 93940
Grade Level: 3
Notes: Time, 73 min.; Items, 95

Designed to support the schools' need for national normative information, statewide normative information, and frameworks outcome information. Measures how well students in grades 1 through 12 meet the educational goals of their state and local curriculum. Directly measures outcomes that can be assessed using multiple-choice test items and helps integrate performance assessment data for other outcomes to give a more complete picture of student attainment. Series of tests based on outcomes and Model Curricula of 4 basic categories: English-Language Arts, History-Social Science, Science, and Mathematics. Curriculum Frameworks Assessment has 2 modules: System or the shorter Supplement. The Curriculum Frameworks Assessment System consists of 6 tests: Reading, Language, Integrated Curriculum, Mathematics, Mathematics Technology, and Science of 180-250 items that measure the frameworks educational outcomes. Provides statewide normative information and framework outcome information. When administered with the CTBS/4 Survey Test, national norms are provided. Curriculum Frameworks As-

sessment Supplement consists of 3 tests: Integrated Curriculum, Mathematics, and Science of 80-125 items that measure frameworks educational outcomes. When the supplement is administered in conjunction with the CTBS/4 Complete Battery, schools can receive national norms, objective scores, state norms, and framework outcome scores. Each level corresponds to the grade level. These tests are derived from work done by the California State Department of Education and are based on the 4 California Frameworks of English-Language Arts, History-Social Science, Science, and Mathematics.

17516
Curriculum Frameworks Assessment Supplement, Level 4. CTB/Macmillan/McGraw-Hill, Monterey, CA 1990
Subtests: System: (Reading; Language; Integrated Curriculum; Mathematics; Mathematics Technology; Science); Supplement: (Integrated Curriculum; Mathematics; Science)
Descriptors: *Achievement Tests; Curriculum; *Educational Objectives; *Elementary School Students; Elementary Secondary Education; *Grade 4; History; Integrated Curriculum; Language Arts; Mathematics; *Outcomes of Education; Reading; Sciences; Social Sciences; State Curriculum Guides; *State Standards
Identifiers: California; CFAS; *Performance Based Evaluation
Availability: CTB Macmillan/McGraw Hill; Del Monte Research Park, 2500 Garden Rd., Monterey, CA 93940
Grade Level: 4
Notes: Time, 106 min.; Items, 83

Designed to support the schools' need for national normative information, statewide normative information, and frameworks outcome information. Measures how well students in grades 1 through 12 meet the educational goals of their state and local curriculum. Directly measures outcomes that can be assessed using multiple-choice test items and helps integrate performance assessment data for other outcomes to give a more complete picture of student attainment. Series of tests based on outcomes and Model Curricula of 4 basic categories: English-Language Arts, History-Social Science, Science, and Mathematics. Curriculum Frameworks Assessment has 2 modules: System or the shorter Supplement. The Curriculum Frameworks Assessment System consists of 6 tests: Reading, Language, Integrated Curriculum, Mathematics, Mathematics Technology, and Science of 180-250 items that measure the frameworks educational outcomes. Provides statewide normative information and framework outcome information. When administered with the CTBS/4 Survey Test, national norms are provided. Curriculum Frameworks Assessment Supplement consists of three tests, Integrated Curriculum, Mathematics, and Science of 80-125 items that measure frameworks educational outcomes. When the supplement is administered in conjunction with the CTBS/4 Complete Battery, schools can receive national norms, objective scores, state norms, and framework outcome scores. Each level corresponds to the grade level. These tests are derived from work done by the California State Department of Education and are based on the 4 California Frameworks of English-Language Arts, History-Social Science, Science, and Mathematics.

17517
Curriculum Frameworks Assessment Supplement, Level 5. CTB/Macmillan/McGraw-Hill, Monterey, CA 1990
Subtests: System: (Reading; Language; Integrated Curriculum; Mathematics; Mathematics Technology; Science); Supplement: (Integrated Curriculum; Mathematics; Science)
Descriptors: *Achievement Tests; Curriculum; *Educational Objectives; *Elementary School Students; Elementary Secondary Education; *Grade 5; History; Integrated Curriculum; Language Arts; Mathematics; *Outcomes of Education; Reading; Sciences; Social Sciences; State Curriculum Guides; *State Standards
Identifiers: California; CFAS; *Performance Based Evaluation
Availability: CTB Macmillan/McGraw Hill; Del Monte Research Park, 2500 Garden Rd., Monterey, CA 93940
Grade Level: 5
Notes: Time, 86 min.; Items, 115

Designed to support the schools' need for national normative information, statewide normative information, and frameworks outcome information. Measures how well students in grades 1 through 12 meet the educational goals of their state and local curriculum. Directly measures outcomes that can be assessed using multiple-choice test items and helps integrate performance assessment data for other outcomes to give a more complete picture of student attainment. Series of tests based on outcomes and Model Curricula of 4 basic categories: English-Language Arts, History-Social Science, Science, and Mathematics. Curriculum Frameworks Assessment has 2 modules: System or the shorter Supplement. The Curriculum Frameworks Assessment System consists of 6 tests: Reading, Language, Integrated Curriculum, Mathematics, Mathematics Technology, and Science of 180-250 items that measure the frameworks educational outcomes. Provides statewide normative information and framework outcome information. When administered with the CTBS/4 Survey Test, national norms are provided. Curriculum Frameworks Assessment Supplement consists of 3 tests: Integrated Curriculum, Mathematics, and Science of 80-125 items that measure frameworks educational outcomes. When the supplement is administered in conjunction with the CTBS/4 Complete Battery, schools can receive national norms, objective scores, state norms, and framework outcome scores. Each level corresponds to the grade level. These tests are derived from work done by the California State Department of Education and are based on the 4 California Frameworks of English-Language Arts, History-Social Science, Science, and Mathematics.

17518
Curriculum Frameworks Assessment Supplement, Level 6. CTB/Macmillan/McGraw-Hill, Monterey, CA 1990
Subtests: System: (Reading; Language; Integrated Curriculum; Mathematics; Mathematics Technology; Science); Supplement: (Integrated Curriculum; Mathematics; Science)
Descriptors: *Achievement Tests; Curriculum; *Educational Objectives; *Elementary School Students; Elementary Secondary Education; *Grade 6; History; Integrated Curriculum; Language Arts; Mathematics; *Outcomes of Education; Reading; Sciences; Social Sciences; State Curriculum Guides; *State Standards
Identifiers: California; CFAS; *Performance Based Evaluation
Availability: CTB Macmillan/McGraw Hill; Del Monte Research Park, 2500 Garden Rd., Monterey, CA 93940
Grade Level: 6
Notes: Time, 90 min.; Items, 117

Designed to support the schools' need for national normative information, statewide normative information, and frameworks outcome information. Measures how well students in grades 1 through 12 meet the educational goals of their state and local curriculum. Directly measures outcomes that can be assessed using multiple-choice test items and helps integrate performance assessment data for other outcomes to give a more complete picture of student attainment. Series of tests based on outcomes and Model Curricula of 4 basic categories: English-Language Arts, History-Social Science, Science, and Mathematics. Curriculum Frameworks Assessment has 2 modules: System or the shorter Supplement. The Curriculum Frameworks Assessment System consists of 6 tests: Reading, Language, Integrated Curriculum, Mathematics, Mathematics Technology, and Science of 180-250 items that measure the frameworks educational outcomes. Provides statewide normative information and framework outcome information. When administered with the CTBS/4 Survey Test, national norms are provided. Curriculum Frameworks Assessment Supplement consists of 3 tests: Integrated Curriculum, Mathematics, and Science of 80-125 items that measure frameworks educational outcomes. When the supplement is administered in conjunction with the CTBS/4 Complete Battery, schools can receive national norms, objective scores, state norms, and framework outcome scores. Each level corresponds to the grade level. These tests are derived from work done by the California State Department of Education and are based on the 4 California Frameworks of English-Language Arts, History-Social Science, Science, and Mathematics.

17519
Curriculum Frameworks Assessment Supplement, Level 7. CTB/Macmillan/McGraw-Hill, Monterey, CA 1990
Subtests: System: (Reading; Language; Integrated Curriculum; Mathematics; Mathematics Technology; Science); Supplement: (Integrated Curriculum; Mathematics; Science)
Descriptors: *Achievement Tests; Curriculum; *Educational Objectives; Elementary Secondary Education; Grade 7; History; Integrated Curriculum; *Junior High School Students; Language Arts; Mathematics; *Outcomes of Education; Reading; Sciences; Social Sciences; State Curriculum Guides; *State Standards
Identifiers: California; CFAS; *Performance Based Evaluation
Availability: CTB Macmillan/McGraw Hill; Del Monte Research Park, 2500 Garden Rd., Monterey, CA 93940
Grade Level: 7
Notes: Time, 93 min.; Items, 122

Designed to support the schools' need for national normative information, statewide normative information, and frameworks outcome information. Measures how well students in grades 1 through 12 meet the educational goals of their state and local curriculum. Directly measures outcomes that can be assessed using multiple-choice test items and helps integrate performance assessment data for other outcomes to give a more complete picture of student attainment. Series of tests based on outcomes and Model Curricula of 4 basic categories: English-Language Arts, History-Social Science, Science, and Mathematics. Curriculum Frameworks Assessment has 2 modules: System

or the shorter Supplement. The Curriculum Frameworks Assessment System consists of 6 tests: Reading, Language, Integrated Curriculum, Mathematics, Mathematics Technology, and Science of 180-250 items that measure the frameworks educational outcomes. Provides statewide normative information and framework outcome information. When administered with the CTBS/4 Survey Test, national norms are provided. Curriculum Frameworks Assessment Supplement consists of 3 tests: Integrated Curriculum, Mathematics, and Science of 80-125 items that measure frameworks educational outcomes. When the supplement is administered in conjunction with the CTBS/4 Complete Battery, schools can receive national norms, objective scores, state norms, and framework outcome scores. Each level corresponds to the grade level. These tests are derived from work done by the California State Department of Education and are based on the 4 California Frameworks of English-Language Arts, History-Social Science, Science, and Mathematics.

17520
Curriculum Frameworks Assessment Supplement, Level 8. CTB/Macmillan/McGraw-Hill, Monterey, CA 1990
Subtests: System: (Reading; Language; Integrated Curriculum; Mathematics; Mathematics Technology; Science); Supplement: (Integrated Curriculum; Mathematics; Science)
Descriptors: *Achievement Tests; Curriculum; *Educational Objectives; Elementary Secondary Education; *Grade 8; History; Integrated Curriculum; *Junior High School Students; Language Arts; Mathematics; *Outcomes of Education; Reading; Sciences; Social Sciences; State Curriculum Guides; *State Standards
Identifiers: California; CFAS; *Performance Based Evaluation
Availability: CTB Macmillan/McGraw Hill; Del Monte Research Park, 2500 Garden Rd., Monterey, CA 93940
Grade Level: 8
Notes: Time, 84 min.; Items, 111

Designed to support the schools' need for national normative information, statewide normative information, and frameworks outcome information. Measures how well students in grades 1 through 12 meet the educational goals of their state and local curriculum. Directly measures outcomes that can be assessed using multiple-choice test items and helps integrate performance assessment data for other outcomes to give a more complete picture of student attainment. Series of tests based on outcomes and Model Curricula of 4 basic categories: English-Language Arts, History-Social Science, Science, and Mathematics. Curriculum Frameworks Assessment has 2 modules: System or the shorter Supplement. The Curriculum Frameworks Assessment System consists of 6 tests: Reading, Language, Integrated Curriculum, Mathematics, Mathematics Technology, and Science of 180-250 items that measure the frameworks educational outcomes. Provides statewide normative information and framework outcome information. When administered with the CTBS/4 Survey Test, national norms are provided. Curriculum Frameworks Assessment Supplement consists of 3 tests: Integrated Curriculum, Mathematics, and Science of 80-125 items that measure frameworks educational outcomes. When the supplement is administered in conjunction with the CTBS/4 Complete Battery, schools can receive national norms, objective scores, state norms, and framework outcome scores. Each level corresponds to the grade level. These tests are derived from work done by the California State Department of Education and are based on the 4 California Frameworks of English-Language Arts, History-Social Science, Science, and Mathematics.

17521
Curriculum Frameworks Assessment Supplement, Level 9/10. CTB/Macmillan/McGraw-Hill, Monterey, CA 1990
Subtests: System: (Reading; Language; Integrated Curriculum; Mathematics; Mathematics Technology; Science); Supplement: (Integrated Curriculum; Mathematics; Science)
Descriptors: *Achievement Tests; Curriculum; *Educational Objectives; Elementary Secondary Education; *Grade 9; *Grade 10; *High School Students; History; Integrated Curriculum; Language Arts; Mathematics; *Outcomes of Education; Reading; Sciences; Social Sciences; State Curriculum Guides; *State Standards
Identifiers: California; CFAS; *Performance Based Evaluation
Availability: CTB Macmillan/McGraw Hill; Del Monte Research Park, 2500 Garden Rd., Monterey, CA 93940
Grade Level: 9-10

Designed to support the schools' need for national normative information, statewide normative information, and frameworks outcome information. Measures how well students in grades 1 through 12 meet the educational goals of their state and local curriculum. Directly measures outcomes that can be assessed using multiple-choice test items and helps integrate performance assessment data for other outcomes to give a more complete picture of student attainment. Series of tests based on outcomes and Model

Curricula of 4 basic categories: English-Language Arts, History-Social Science, Science, and Mathematics. Curriculum Frameworks Assessment has 2 modules: System or the shorter Supplement. The Curriculum Frameworks Assessment System consists of 6 tests: Reading, Language, Integrated Curriculum, Mathematics, Mathematics Technology, and Science of 180-250 items that measure the frameworks educational outcomes. Provides statewide normative information and framework outcome information. When administered with the CTBS/4 Survey Test, national norms are provided. Curriculum Frameworks Assessment Supplement consists of 3 tests: Integrated Curriculum, Mathematics, and Science of 80-125 items that measure frameworks educational outcomes. When the supplement is administered in conjunction with the CTBS/4 Complete Battery, schools can receive national norms, objective scores, state norms, and framework outcome scores. Each level corresponds to the grade level. These tests are derived from work done by the California State Department of Education and are based on the 4 California Frameworks of English-Language Arts, History-Social Science, Science, and Mathematics.

17522
Curriculum Frameworks Assessment Supplement, Level 11/12. CTB/Macmillan/McGraw-Hill, Monterey, CA 1990
Subtests: System: (Reading; Language; Integrated Curriculum; Mathematics; Mathematics Technology; Science); Supplement: (Integrated Curriculum; Mathematics; Science)
Descriptors: *Achievement Tests; Curriculum; *Educational Objectives; Elementary Secondary Education; *Grade 11; *Grade 12; *High School Students; History; Integrated Curriculum; Language Arts; Mathematics; *Outcomes of Education; Reading; Sciences; Social Sciences; State Curriculum Guides; *State Standards
Identifiers: California; CFAS; *Performance Based Evaluation
Availability: CTB Macmillan/McGraw Hill; Del Monte Research Park, 2500 Garden Rd., Monterey, CA 93940
Grade Level: 11-12

Designed to support the schools' need for national normative information, statewide normative information, and frameworks outcome information. Measures how well students in grades 1 through 12 meet the educational goals of their state and local curriculum. Directly measures outcomes that can be assessed using multiple-choice test items and helps integrate performance assessment data for other outcomes to give a more complete picture of student attainment. Series of tests based on outcomes and Model Curricula of 4 basic categories: English-Language Arts, History-Social Science, Science, and Mathematics. Curriculum Frameworks Assessment has 2 modules: System or the shorter Supplement. The Curriculum Frameworks Assessment System consists of 6 tests: Reading, Language, Integrated Curriculum, Mathematics, Mathematics Technology, and Science of 180-250 items that measure the frameworks educational outcomes. Provides statewide normative information and framework outcome information. When administered with the CTBS/4 Survey Test, national norms are provided. Curriculum Frameworks Assessment Supplement consists of 3 tests: Integrated Curriculum, Mathematics, and Science of 80-125 items that measure frameworks educational outcomes. When the supplement is administered in conjunction with the CTBS/4 Complete Battery, schools can receive national norms, objective scores, state norms, and framework outcome scores. Each level corresponds to the grade level. These tests are derived from work done by the California State Department of Education and are based on the 4 California Frameworks of English-Language Arts, History-Social Science, Science, and Mathematics.

17541
Test of Early Language Development, 2nd Edition. Hresko, Wayne P.; And Others 1991
Descriptors: Early Intervention; *Expressive Language; *Individual Testing; *Language Acquisition; Language Skills; *Language Tests; *Oral Language; *Receptive Language; *Screening Tests; *Semantics; *Syntax; *Young Children
Identifiers: TELD(2)
Availability: PRO-ED; 8700 Shoal Creek Blvd., Austin, TX 78758-6897
Age Level: 2-7
Notes: Time, 40 min. approx.; Items, 68

A measure of the early development of oral language in the areas of receptive and expressive language, syntax, and semantics. The purpose of this tool is to identify those students who are between the ages of 2 through 7 years, 11 months, and those who are significantly below their peers in early language development; to identify strengths and weaknesses of individual students; to document students' progress as a consequence of special early intervention programs; to aid in directing instruction; and to serve as a measurement device in research studies pertaining to academic achievement of young children.

17558
Brigance Diagnostic Inventory of Early Development—Revised. Brigance, Albert H. 1991
Subtests: Preambulatory Motor Skills and Behaviors; Gross-Motor Skills and Behaviors; Fine-Motor Skills and Behaviors; Self-Help Skills; Speech and Language Skills; General Knowledge and Comprehension; Social and Emotional Development; Readiness; Basic Reading Skills; Manuscript Writing; Basic Math
Descriptors: At Risk Persons; Behavior Development; *Child Development; *Criterion Referenced Tests; Developmental Stages; *Diagnostic Tests; *Early Experience; Early Intervention; *Emotional Development; *Infants; *Language Acquisition; Numbers; Preschool Children; *Psychomotor Skills; *Reading Readiness; *Self Care Skills; *Young Children
Availability: Curriculum Associates, Inc.; 5 Esquire Rd.; N. Billerica, MA 01862-2589
Age Level: 0-7

With the use of a direct approach to assessment, this criterion-referenced instrument was designed to be used in programs for infants and children below the developmental level of 7 years. Serves as an assessment instrument, an instructional guide, a recordkeeping tracking system, a tool for developing and communicating an individualized education program, and as a resource for training parents and professionals. Different assessment methods may be used to accommodate different situations. The inventory offers a variety of possibilities: parent interview, teacher observation, group administration, informal appraisal of the child's performance in the school setting. The goal of the assessment is to identify those segments of the curriculum objectives that have been mastered.

800104
ACER Primary Reading Survey Tests: Level AA and BB. Australian Council for Educational Research, Hawthorn 1972
Subtests: Word Knowledge; Comprehension
Descriptors: *Achievement Tests; Educational Diagnosis; *Elementary School Students; Foreign Countries; *Language Skills; Multiple Choice Tests; Pictorial Stimuli; *Primary Education; *Reading Comprehension; Timed Tests; Verbal Ability; Verbal Development
Identifiers: Australia
Availability: Australian Council for Educational Research; P.O. Box 210, Hawthorn, Victoria, Australia 3122
Grade Level: 1-2
Notes: Time, 36 min.; Items, 43

To evaluate Australian first and second graders in their knowledge and comprehension of words, i.e., their language skills. Contains 2 forms: R and S. The Test for grade 1 (AA) has only one part, entitled Word Recognition. Level BB for grade 2 contains 2 subtests: Word Knowledge and Comprehension. May be used (1) to identify variations in the stages of development in basic reading skills; (2) to identify those students who need special diagnostic and remedial treatment; (3) to group students of comparable ability; and (4) to assist in the choice of instructional materials. Level BB also measures a student's ability to comprehend words both in and out of context. Level AA has 16 questions; and Level BB has 43. Level AA is a 16-item picture stimulus in which the students choose the appropriate word to fit the picture; the time limit is 16 minutes. Level BB has 43 multiple-choice items and a time limit of 36 minutes.

800105
ACER Primary Reading Survey Tests; Level D. Australian Council for Educational Research, Hawthorn 1972
Subtests: Word Discrimination; Word Formation; Dictionary Skills
Descriptors: *Achievement Tests; Cloze Procedure; Educational Diagnosis; Elementary Education; *Elementary School Students; Foreign Countries; *Form Classes (Languages); *Grade 6; *Language Skills; Multiple Choice Tests; Reading Skills; Timed Tests; Verbal Ability; *Verbal Tests; *Word Study Skills
Identifiers: ACER Primary Reading Special Skills Tests; Australia; Special Skills Test Level D
Availability: Australian Council for Educational Research; P.O. Box 210, Hawthorn, Victoria, Australia 3122
Grade Level: 6
Notes: Time, 75 min.; Items, 105

Level D supplements the ACER Primary Survey Reading Tests (TC800132). Part 1A, Word Discrimination, includes meanings of near synonyms, nouns that accompany a particular stem adjective, and words that are stronger in meaning. Part 1B, Word Formation, tests the formation of parts of speech by the addition of affixes to root words and uses the students' skill to recognize word forms of imaginary words. Part 1C presents a miniature dictionary, the use of which tests skills associated with abbreviations, word formation and recognition, definitions, pronunciation, accented syllables, and spelling. Used to identify reading problems as well as identify strengths or weaknesses in the student's word skills. It also enables the teacher to identify student's understanding of words both in and out of context. This is form R.

800132
ACER Primary Reading Survey Tests: Level A, B, C, and D. Australian Council for Educational Research, Hawthorn 1971
Subtests: Word Knowledge; Comprehension
Descriptors: *Achievement Tests; Elementary Education; *Elementary School Students; Foreign Countries; *Reading Ability; *Reading Achievement; *Reading Comprehension; Reading Diagnosis; Reading Tests; Timed Tests; *Vocabulary Development
Identifiers: ACER Primary Reading Survey Comprehension Test; ACER Primary Reading Survey Word Knowledge; Australia; *Synonyms
Availability: Australian Council for Educational Research; P.O. Box 210, Hawthorn, Victoria, Australia 3122
Grade Level: 3-6
Notes: Time, 50 min.; Items, 84

To assess reading comprehension and to aid teachers in their judgments concerning the students' strengths and weaknesses. May be used (1) to determine the students' development in basic reading skills, (2) to identify those students who need special diagnostic and remedial treatment, (3) to compare a student's ability to understand words both in and out of context, and (4) to group students according to reading ability. The number of items vary: Level A (Grade 3) has 75 items; Level B (Grade 4), 83; Level C (Grade 5), 84; and Level D (Grade 6), 74. Includes Forms R and S for most levels.

800150
GAPADOL Reading Comprehension Test. McLeod, J.; Anderson, J. 1972
Descriptors: *Achievement Tests; *Adolescents; *Cloze Procedure; Foreign Countries; Intermediate Grades; *Reading Comprehension; Reading Tests; Secondary Education
Identifiers: Australia
Availability: Australian Council for Educational Research; P.O. Box 210, Hawthorn, Victoria, Australia 3122
Age Level: 10-17
Notes: Time, 30 min. approx.

Designed for adolescent children to identify their retarded and superior reading ability. Designed to discriminate at higher ability and age levels than GAP Reading Comprehension Tests. Suitable for students in Australian school years 5-10. Two alternate forms may be given. If reading ages on 2 tests are averaged, greater reliability may be achieved.

800172
ACER Mathematics Profile Series: Measurement Test. Cornish, Greg; Wines, Robin 1979
Descriptors: *Achievement Tests; Cognitive Development; Criterion Referenced Tests; Educational Diagnosis; *Elementary School Students; Elementary Secondary Education; Foreign Countries; *Mathematical Concepts; Mathematics; *Mathematics Tests; Multiple Choice Tests; *Secondary School Students; Timed Tests
Identifiers: Australia; MAPS Scale; *Measurement (Mathematics); Piagetian Stages; Rasch Model
Availability: Australian Council for Educational Research; P.O. Box 210, Hawthorn, Victoria, Australia 3122
Grade Level: 2-12
Notes: Time, 30 min.; Items, 30

Designed to provide teachers with a flexible testing system by which the teacher can identify and monitor the students' mathematical ability and development throughout the students' schooling. Measures mathematical development pertaining to measurement and mensuration. Can be used as an achievement, diagnostic or criterion-referenced test. Used a Rasch Model to develop the MAPS scale in relationship to Piagetian cognitive stages of development. Consists of Units I, II, and III. Teachers decide which unit is appropriate for their students. The authors suggest that the unit chosen be the one in which most of the students will probably respond correctly to one-half or more of the items. Called an experimental edition.

800205
English Skills Assessment. Australian Council for Educational Research, Hawthorn 1982
Subtests: Comprehension I; Comprehension II
Descriptors: *Diagnostic Tests; Foreign Countries; High Schools; *High School Students; Language Tests; Postsecondary Education; Punctuation; *Reading Comprehension; *Reading Skills; Sentence Structure; Spelling; Timed Tests; Vocabulary
Identifiers: Australia; *English Usage; ESA; Test Batteries
Availability: Australian Council for Educational Research; P.O. Box 210, Hawthorn, Victoria 3122, Australia
Grade Level: 11-13
Notes: Time, 110 min.; Items, 188

A combination of 2 test batteries designed to identify student's strengths and weaknesses in areas of English and Reading Skills. Part I consists of 3 subtests consisting of a total of 95 items that require 50 minutes to complete. The subtests are Spelling, Punctuation and Capitalization, and Comprehension I. Part II consists of 5 subtests comprising a total of 93 items that require 60 minutes to complete. The subtests are Comprehension II, Usage, Vocabulary, Sentence Structure, and Logical Relationships.

800206
Science Library of Test Items. Mastery Testing Programme. Introduction and Manual. New South Wales Dept. of Education, Sydney (Australia) 1979
Descriptors: *Criterion Referenced Tests; Foreign Countries; *Item Banks; *Mastery Tests; Secondary Education; *Secondary School Science; *Secondary School Students; Teaching Guides; Testing Programs
Identifiers: Australia (New South Wales)
Availability: ERIC Document Reproduction Service; 7420 Fullerton Rd., Ste. 110, Springfield, VA 22153-2852 (ED223615, 103 p.)
Grade Level: 7-10
Age Level: 12-16

The Science Library of Test Items is a series of instruments developed for use in the New South Wales Australia junior secondary systems. Material is designed for students aged 12-16 in grades 7-10. The grade levels are roughly equivalent to those in the U.S. Criterion-referenced mastery tests may be compiled for specific course requirements from items in the program. This manual consists of series 3 and 4 supplements to the Science Mastery Testing Program. Includes sample tests and manual of directions. Manual for series 1 and 2 illustrates range of tests and explains educational rationale for their development.

800207
Science Library of Test Items. Practical Testing Guide. New South Wales Dept. of Education, Sydney (Australia) 1979
Descriptors: *Criterion Referenced Tests; Foreign Countries; *Item Banks; *Laboratory Equipment; *Mastery Tests; Performance Tests; Secondary Education; *Secondary School Science; *Secondary School Students; Testing Programs
Identifiers: Australia (New South Wales)
Availability: ERIC Document Reproduction Service; 7420 Fullerton Rd., Ste. 110, Springfield, VA 22153-2852 (ED223616, 106 p.)
Grade Level: 7-10
Age Level: 12-16

The Science Library of Test Items is a series of instruments developed for use in the New South Wales Australia junior secondary systems. Material is designed for students aged 12-16 in grades 7-10. The grade levels are roughly equivalent to those in the U.S. Criterion-referenced mastery tests may be compiled for specific course requirements from items in the program. Instruments in this guide are designed to assess student's practical skills by their manipulation of laboratory equipment. Measures science laboratory skills.

800208
Science Library of Test Items. Volume 7: Comprehension Testing Programme. Part 2: Print Masters for Reproduction (Exercises 1-63). New South Wales Dept. of Education, Sydney (Australia) 1980
Descriptors: *Criterion Referenced Tests; Foreign Countries; *Item Banks; *Mastery Tests; *Reading Comprehension; *Scientific Literacy; Secondary Education; *Secondary School Science; *Secondary School Students; Testing Programs
Identifiers: Australia (New South Wales)
Availability: ERIC Document Reproduction Service; 7420 Fullerton Rd., Ste. 110, Springfield, VA 22153-2852 (ED223619, 105 p.)
Grade Level: 7-10
Age Level: 12-16

The Science Library of Test Items is a series of instruments developed for use in the New South Wales Australia junior secondary systems. Material is designed for students aged 12-16 in grades 7-10. The grade levels are roughly equivalent to those in the U.S. Criterion-referenced mastery tests may be compiled for specific course requirements from items in the program. A manual for teachers to accompany this series of print masters is available from ERIC Document Reproduction Service, ED223618. Instruments in this collection were designed to assess reading comprehension and communication skills in science.

800209
Science Library of Test Items. Volume 18: A Collection of Multiple-Choice Test Items Relating Mainly to Chemistry. New South Wales Dept. of Education, Sydney (Australia) 1981
Descriptors: *Chemistry; *Criterion Referenced Tests; Foreign Countries; *Item Banks; *Mastery Tests; Multiple Choice Tests; Secondary Education; *Secondary School Science; *Secondary School Students; Testing Programs
Identifiers: Australia (New South Wales)
Availability: ERIC Document Reproduction Service; 7420 Fullerton Rd., Ste. 110, Springfield, VA 22153-2852 (ED223629, 99 p.)
Grade Level: 7-10
Age Level: 12-16
The Science Library of Test Items is a series of instruments developed for use in the New South Wales Australia junior secondary systems. Material is designed for students aged 12-16 in grades 7-10. The grade levels are roughly equivalent to those in the U.S. Criterion-referenced mastery tests may be compiled for specific course requirements from items in the program. A collection of all multiple-choice items in the Science Library relating to Chemistry.

800210
Science Library of Test Items. Volume 19: A Collection of Multiple-Choice Test Items Relating Mainly to Geology. New South Wales Dept. of Education, Sydney (Australia) 1981
Descriptors: *Criterion Referenced Tests; Foreign Countries; *Geology; *Item Banks; *Mastery Tests; Multiple Choice Tests; Secondary Education; *Secondary School Science; *Secondary School Students; Testing Programs
Identifiers: Australia (New South Wales)
Availability: ERIC Document Reproduction Service; 7420 Fullerton Rd., Ste. 110, Springfield, VA 22153-2852 (ED223630, 92 p.)
Grade Level: 7-10
Age Level: 12-16
The Science Library of Test Items is a series of instruments developed for use in the New South Wales Australia junior secondary systems. Material is designed for students aged 12-16 in grades 7-10. The grade levels are roughly equivalent to those in the U.S. Criterion-referenced mastery tests may be compiled for specific course requirements from items in the program. A collection of multiple-choice items relating to geology in the areas of soils, weathering, erosion, minerals, rocks, structures, mapping, history, fossils, and resources.

800211
Science Library of Test Items. Volume 21: A Collection of Multiple-Choice Test Items Relating Mainly to Physics–2. New South Wales Dept. of Education, Sydney (Australia) 1981
Descriptors: Astronomy; *Criterion Referenced Tests; Electronics; Foreign Countries; *Item Banks; *Mastery Tests; Multiple Choice Tests; *Physics; Secondary Education; *Secondary School Science; *Secondary School Students; Testing Programs
Identifiers: Australia (New South Wales)
Availability: ERIC Document Reproduction Service; 7420 Fullerton Rd., Ste. 110, Springfield, VA 22153-2852 (ED223632, 127 p.)
Grade Level: 7-10
Age Level: 12-16
The Science Library of Test Items is a series of instruments developed for use in the New South Wales Australia junior secondary systems. Material is designed for students aged 12-16 in grades 7-10. The grade levels are roughly equivalent to those in the U.S. Criterion-referenced mastery tests may be compiled for specific course requirements from items in the program. One of 2 volumes containing the collection of multiple-choice items relating to Physics. Volume 21 assesses electrostatics, electrodynamics, electronics, magnetism, mass and density, pressure, moving bodies, radioactivity, and astronomy.

800212
Science Library of Test Items. Volume 20: A Collection of Multiple-Choice Test Items Relating Mainly to Physics–1. New South Wales Dept. of Education, Sydney (Australia) 1981
Descriptors: *Criterion Referenced Tests; Energy; Foreign Countries; *Item Banks; *Mastery Tests; Meteorology; Multiple Choice Tests; Optics; *Physics; Secondary Education; *Secondary School Science; *Secondary School Students; Testing Programs
Identifiers: Australia (New South Wales)
Availability: ERIC Document Reproduction Service; 7420 Fullerton Rd., Ste. 110, Springfield, VA 22153-2852 (ED223631, 105 p.)
Grade Level: 7-10
Age Level: 12-16

The Science Library of Test Items is a series of instruments developed for use in the New South Wales Australia junior secondary systems. Material is designed for students aged 12-16 in grades 7-10. The grade levels are roughly equivalent to those in the U.S. Criterion-referenced mastery tests may be compiled for specific course requirements from items in the program. The first of 2 volumes containing the collection of multiple-choice items relating to Physics. Volume 20 contains items that assess measurement and scales, simple machines, properties of matter, energy, electromagnetic radiation, heat, light and optics, sound, communications, and meteorology.

800213
Science Library of Test Items. Volume 22: A Collection of Multiple-Choice Test Items Relating Mainly to Skills. New South Wales Dept. of Education, Sydney (Australia) 1981
Descriptors: *Criterion Referenced Tests; Foreign Countries; *Item Banks; *Mastery Tests; Multiple Choice Tests; Reading Comprehension; *Scientific Methodology; Secondary Education; *Secondary School Science; *Secondary School Students; Testing Programs
Identifiers: Australia (New South Wales)
Availability: ERIC Document Reproduction Service; 7420 Fullerton Rd., Ste. 110, Springfield, VA 22153-2852 (ED223633, 104 p.)
Grade Level: 7-10
Age Level: 12-16
The Science Library of Test Items is a series of instruments developed for use in the New South Wales Australia junior secondary systems. Material is designed for students aged 12-16 in grades 7-10. The grade levels are roughly equivalent to those in the U.S. Criterion-referenced mastery tests may be compiled for specific course requirements from items in the program. A collection of multiple-choice items that relate to methods by which scientific information is collected and analyzed.

800214
Science Library of Test Items. Volume 15: Comprehension Testing Programme 2. Part 4: Print Masters for Reproduction (Exercises 64-150). New South Wales Dept. of Education, Sydney (Australia) 1981
Descriptors: *Criterion Referenced Tests; *Diagnostic Tests; Foreign Countries; *Item Banks; *Mastery Tests; *Reading Comprehension; Scientific Literacy; Secondary Education; *Secondary School Science; *Secondary School Students; Teaching Guides; Testing Programs
Identifiers: Australia (New South Wales)
Availability: ERIC Document Reproduction Service; 7420 Fullerton Rd., Ste. 110, Springfield, VA 22153-2852 (ED223627, 121 p.)
Grade Level: 7-10
Age Level: 12-16
The Science Library of Test Items is a series of instruments developed for use in the New South Wales Australia junior secondary systems. Material is designed for students aged 12-16 in grades 7-10. The grade levels are roughly equivalent to those in the U.S. Criterion-referenced mastery tests may be compiled for specific course requirements from items in the program. Instruments in this collection were designed to assess reading comprehension and communication skills in science. A manual for teachers designed to accompany this series of print masters is available from ERIC Document Reproduction Service, ED223626.

800215
Science Library of Test Items. Volume 17: A Collection of Multiple-Choice Test Items Relating Mainly to Biology. New South Wales Dept. of Education, Sydney (Australia) 1981
Descriptors: *Biology; *Criterion Referenced Tests; Ecology; Evolution; Foreign Countries; Genetics; *Item Banks; *Mastery Tests; Multiple Choice Tests; Secondary Education; *Secondary School Science; *Secondary School Students; Testing Programs
Identifiers: Australia (New South Wales)
Availability: ERIC Document Reproduction Service; 7420 Fullerton Rd., Ste. 110, Springfield, VA 22153-2852 (ED223628, 140 p.)
Grade Level: 7-10
Age Level: 12-16
The Science Library of Test Items is a series of instruments developed for use in the New South Wales Australia junior secondary systems. Material is designed for students aged 12-16 in grades 7-10. The grade levels are roughly equivalent to those in the U.S. Criterion-referenced mastery tests may be compiled for specific course requirements from items in the program. A collection of multiple-choice items relating to biology. Topics assessed include cells; circulation; health; senses; muscles; hormones; digestion; foods; excretion; plants; reproduction; genetics; classification; ecology; adaptations; and evolution.

800216
Science Library of Test Items. Volume 12: Mastery Tests M39-M50. New South Wales Dept. of Education, Sydney (Australia) 1980
Descriptors: *Criterion Referenced Tests; Foreign Countries; *Item Banks; *Mastery Tests; *Natural Sciences; Secondary Education; *Secondary School Science; *Secondary School Students; Skills; Testing Programs
Identifiers: Australia (New South Wales)
Availability: ERIC Document Reproduction Service; 7420 Fullerton Rd., Ste. 110, Springfield, VA 22153-2852 (ED223624, 49 p.)
Grade Level: 7-10
Age Level: 12-16
The Science Library of Test Items is a series of instruments developed for use in the New South Wales Australia junior secondary systems. Material is designed for students aged 12-16 in grades 7-10. The grade levels are roughly equivalent to those in the U.S. Criterion-referenced mastery tests may be compiled for specific course requirements from items in the program. Designed to assess mastery of specific skills in the natural sciences.

800217
Science Library of Test Items. Volume 13: Mastery Tests M51-M65. New South Wales Dept. of Education, Sydney (Australia) 1980
Descriptors: *Criterion Referenced Tests; Foreign Countries; *Item Banks; *Mastery Tests; *Natural Sciences; Secondary Education; *Secondary School Science; *Secondary School Students; Skills; Testing Programs
Identifiers: Australia (New South Wales)
Availability: ERIC Document Reproduction Service; 7420 Fullerton Rd., Ste. 110, Springfield, VA 22153-2852 (ED223625, 64 p.)
Grade Level: 7-10
Age Level: 12-16
The Science Library of Test Items is a series of instruments developed for use in the New South Wales Australia junior secondary systems. Material is designed for students aged 12-16 in grades 7-10. The grade levels are roughly equivalent to those in the U.S. Criterion-referenced mastery tests may be compiled for specific course requirements from items in the program. Designed to assess mastery of specific skills in the natural sciences.

800218
Science Library of Test Items. Volume 10: Mastery Tests M14-M26. New South Wales Dept. of Education, Sydney (Australia) 1978
Descriptors: *Criterion Referenced Tests; Foreign Countries; *Item Banks; *Mastery Tests; *Natural Sciences; Secondary Education; *Secondary School Science; *Secondary School Students; Skills; Testing Programs
Identifiers: Australia (New South Wales)
Availability: ERIC Document Reproduction Service; 7420 Fullerton Rd., Ste. 110, Springfield, VA 22153-2852 (ED223622, 53 p.)
Grade Level: 7-10
Age Level: 12-16
The Science Library of Test Items is a series of instruments developed for use in the New South Wales Australia junior secondary systems. Material is designed for students aged 12-16 in grades 7-10. The grade levels are roughly equivalent to those in the U.S. Criterion-referenced mastery tests may be compiled for specific course requirements from items in the program. Designed to assess mastery of specific skills in the natural sciences.

800219
Science Library of Test Items. Volume 9: Mastery Tests M1-M13. New South Wales Dept. of Education, Sydney (Australia) 1978
Descriptors: *Criterion Referenced Tests; Foreign Countries; *Item Banks; *Mastery Tests; *Natural Sciences; Secondary Education; *Secondary School Science; *Secondary School Students; Skills; Testing Programs
Identifiers: Australia (New South Wales)
Availability: ERIC Document Reproduction Service; 7420 Fullerton Rd., Ste. 110, Springfield, VA 22153-2852 (ED223621, 55 p.)
Grade Level: 7-10
Age Level: 12-16
The Science Library of Test Items is a series of instruments developed for use in the New South Wales Australia junior secondary systems. Material is designed for students aged 12-16 in grades 7-10. The grade levels are roughly equivalent to those in the U.S. Criterion-referenced mastery tests may be compiled for specific course requirements from items in the program. Designed to assess specific skills mastery in the natural sciences.

800220
Science Library of Test Items. Volume 11: Mastery Tests M27-M38. New South Wales Dept. of Education, Sydney (Australia) 1979

Descriptors: *Criterion Referenced Tests; Foreign Countries; *Item Banks; *Mastery Tests; *Natural Sciences; Secondary Education; *Secondary School Science; *Secondary School Students; Skills; Testing Programs
Identifiers: Australia (New South Wales)
Availability: ERIC Document Reproduction Service; 7420 Fullerton Rd., Ste. 110, Springfield, VA 22153-2852 (ED223623, 49 p.)
Grade Level: 7-10
Age Level: 12-16

The Science Library of Test Items is a series of instruments developed for use in the New South Wales Australia junior secondary systems. Material is designed for students aged 12-16 in grades 7-10. The grade levels are roughly equivalent to those in the U.S. Criterion-referenced mastery tests may be compiled for specific course requirements from items in the program. Designed to assess mastery of specific skills in the natural sciences.

800225
Library of Test Items: Geography, Volume 2.
New South Wales Dept. of Education, Sydney (Australia) 1980
Subtests: Mountain Landscape: Coniferous Forest Landscape; Tundra Landscape; Mapping; Weather and Climate
Descriptors: Achievement Rating; Climate; Criterion Referenced Tests; Foreign Countries; *Geography; *Item Banks; Map Skills; Mastery Tests; Multiple Choice Tests; Secondary Education; *Secondary School Students; Student Evaluation; Test Construction; Weather
Identifiers: Assessment Instruments; Australia (New South Wales)
Availability: ERIC Document Reproduction Service; 7420 Fullerton Rd., Ste. 110, Springfield, VA 22153-2852 (ED218292, 90 p.)
Grade Level: 7-10

One of a series of test-item collections developed by the Assessment and Evaluation Unit of the Directorate of Studies. Designed for use by secondary school teachers for the construction of tests or as the basis for classroom discussions. Items in this second volume measure knowledge in areas including mountain, coniferous forest, and tundra landscapes; mapping; and weather and climate.

800226
Library of Test Items: Mathematics, Volume I.
New South Wales Dept. of Education, Sydney (Australia) 1978
Subtests: Number Theory; Fractions, Decimals; Percentages; Ratio, Rates; Surds, Indices, Logarithms; Basic Algebra
Descriptors: Achievement Rating; Algebra; Criterion Referenced Tests; Foreign Countries; *Item Banks; Mastery Tests; *Mathematical Concepts; Mathematics Tests; Multiple Choice Tests; Ratios (Mathematics); Secondary Education; *Secondary School Mathematics; *Secondary School Students; Student Evaluation; Test Construction
Identifiers: Assessment Instruments; Australia (New South Wales)
Availability: ERIC Document Reproduction Service; 7420 Fullerton Rd., Ste. 110, Springfield, VA 22153-2852 (ED218299, 94 p.)
Grade Level: 7-10

One of a series of test-item collections developed by the Assessment and Evaluation Unit of the Directorate of Studies. Designed for use by secondary school teachers for the construction of tests or as the basis for classroom discussions. Volume One in the Mathematics Library of Test Items includes items related to the areas of number theory; fractions and decimals; percentages; ratio and rates; surds, indices, and logarithms; and basic algebra

800227
Library of Test Items: Geography, Years 7-10, Volume 8. New South Wales Dept. of Education, Sydney (Australia) 1980
Descriptors: Achievement Rating; Criterion Referenced Tests; Foreign Countries; Geographic Concepts; *Geography; *Item Banks; Mastery Tests; Multiple Choice Tests; Secondary Education; *Secondary School Students; Student Evaluation; Test Construction
Identifiers: Assessment Instruments; Australia (New South Wales)
Availability: ERIC Document Reproduction Service; 7420 Fullerton Rd., Ste. 110, Springfield, VA 22153-2852 (ED218298, 172 p.)
Grade Level: 7-10

One of a series of test-item collections developed by the Assessment and Evaluation Unit of the Directorate of Studies. Designed for use by secondary school teachers for the construction of tests or as the basis for classroom discussions. The items in Volume 8 of the Geography Library of Test Items are drawn from the Higher School Certificate (HSC) broadsheets. Items are referenced to the source from which they were drawn.

800228
Library of Test Items: Geography, Volume 7.
New South Wales Dept. of Education, Sydney (Australia) 1980
Descriptors: Achievement Rating; Agricultural Production; *Agriculture; Criterion Referenced Tests; Foreign Countries; *Geography; Grains (Food); *Item Banks; Knowledge Level; Mastery Tests; Multiple Choice Tests; Secondary Education; *Secondary School Students; Student Evaluation; Test Construction; Units of Study
Identifiers: Assessment Instruments; Australia (New South Wales)
Availability: ERIC Document Reproduction Service; 7420 Fullerton Rd., Ste. 110, Springfield, VA 22153-2852 (ED218297, 49 p.)
Grade Level: 7-10

One of a series of test-item collections developed by the Assessment and Evaluation Unit of the Directorate of Studies. Designed for use by secondary school teachers for the construction of tests or as the basis for classroom discussions. The items in Volume 7 were developed for use with the resource kit "Rice Growing and Rice Milling in South-Western New South Wales."

800229
Library of Test Items: Geography, Volume 6.
New South Wales Dept. of Education, Sydney (Australia) 1980
Descriptors: *Minerals; Achievement Rating; Criterion Referenced Tests; Energy Conservation; Foreign Countries; *Geography; *Item Banks; Mastery Tests; Multiple Choice Tests; *Natural Resources; Secondary Education; *Secondary School Students; Student Evaluation; Test Construction
Identifiers: Assessment Instruments; Australia (New South Wales); *Energy Sources
Availability: ERIC Document Reproduction Service; 7420 Fullerton Rd., Ste. 110, Springfield, VA 22153-2852 (ED218296, 78 p.)
Grade Level: 7-10

One of a series of test-item collections developed by the Assessment and Evaluation Unit of the Directorate of Studies. Designed for use by secondary school teachers for the construction of tests or as the basis for classroom discussions. Designed by the School Certificate Development Unit to provide test items for geographical teaching units based on theme of Energy and Minerals.

800230
Library of Test Items: Geography, Volume 5.
New South Wales Dept. of Education, Sydney (Australia) 1979
Subtests: World Development; Population
Descriptors: Achievement Rating; Criterion Referenced Tests; Developed Nations; Developing Nations; Foreign Countries; *Geography; *Item Banks; Mastery Tests; Multiple Choice Tests; Population Distribution; Secondary Education; *Secondary School Students; Student Evaluation; Test Construction; *World Geography
Identifiers: Assessment Instruments; Australia (New South Wales)
Availability: ERIC Document Reproduction Service; 7420 Fullerton Rd., Ste. 110, Springfield, VA 22153-2852 (ED218295, 61 p.)
Grade Level: 7-10

One of a series of test-item collections developed by the Assessment and Evaluation Unit of the Directorate of Studies. Designed for use by secondary school teachers for the construction of tests or as the basis for classroom discussions. The items in Volume 5 measure knowledge in the areas of world development and population for developed nations, as well as third world countries.

800231
Library of Test Items: Geography, Volume 4.
New South Wales Dept. of Education, Sydney (Australia) 1979
Subtests: Industrial Landscape; Urban Landscape
Descriptors: Achievement Rating; Criterion Referenced Tests; Foreign Countries; *Geography; Industrialization; *Item Banks; Mastery Tests; Multiple Choice Tests; Secondary Education; *Secondary School Students; Student Evaluation; Test Construction; Urbanization
Identifiers: Assessment Instruments; Australia (New South Wales)
Availability: ERIC Document Reproduction Service; 7420 Fullerton Rd., Ste. 110, Springfield, VA 22153-2852 (ED218294, 96 p.)
Grade Level: 7-10

One of a series of test-item collections developed by the Assessment and Evaluation Unit of the Directorate of Studies. Designed for use by secondary school teachers for the construction of tests or as the basis for classroom discussions. Volume 4 is the second of 2 volumes assessing knowledge of cultural landscapes. Industrial and urban

landscapes are the topics of items in this volume. Volume 3 (TC800232) assesses knowledge in the areas of general features and other cultural landscapes.

800232
Library of Test Items: Geography, Volume 3.
New South Wales Dept. of Education, Sydney (Australia) 1979
Subtests: General Features; Monsoon Asian Landscapes; Mediterranean Rural Landscapes; Mid Latitude Commercial Farming
Descriptors: Achievement Rating; Agricultural Production; Agriculture; Asian Studies; Criterion Referenced Tests; Foreign Countries; *Geography; *Item Banks; Mastery Tests; Multiple Choice Tests; Secondary Education; *Secondary School Students; Student Evaluation; Test Construction
Identifiers: Assessment Instruments; Australia (New South Wales)
Availability: ERIC Document Reproduction Service; 7420 Fullerton Rd., Ste. 110, Springfield, VA 22153-2852 (ED218293, 124 p.)
Grade Level: 7-10

One of a series of test-item collections developed by the Assessment and Evaluation Unit of the Directorate of Studies. Designed for use by secondary school teachers for the construction of tests or as the basis for classroom discussions. Volume 3 is the first of 2 volumes that assess knowledge of cultural landscapes. The topics in this volume include general features, monsoon Asian landscapes, Mediterranean rural landscapes, and midlatitude commercial farming. Volume 4 (TC800231) assesses knowledge of industrial and urban landscapes.

800233
Library of Test Items: Agriculture, Volume 1.
New South Wales Dept. of Education, Sydney (Australia) 1979
Subtests: Plants; Animals; Soils; Miscellaneous; Items from the Science Collection; Items from the Geography Collection
Descriptors: Achievement Rating; Agricultural Education; *Agriculture; Animals; Criterion Referenced Tests; Foreign Countries; *Item Banks; Mastery Tests; Multiple Choice Tests; Plant Growth; Secondary Education; *Secondary School Students; Soil Science; Student Evaluation; Test Construction
Identifiers: Assessment Instruments; Australia (New South Wales)
Availability: ERIC Document Reproduction Service; 7420 Fullerton Rd., Ste. 110, Springfield, VA 22153-2852 (ED218284, 100 p.)
Grade Level: 7-10

One of a series of test-item collections developed by the Assessment and Evaluation Unit of the Directorate of Studies. Designed for use by secondary school teachers for the construction of tests or as the basis for classroom discussions. Items in this volume assess knowledge in areas of plants, animals, and soils as they relate to agriculture. Some items used in this volume were drawn from the Science and Geography item banks.

800234
Library of Test Items: Home Science, Volume 1.
New South Wales Dept. of Education, Sydney (Australia) 1980
Descriptors: Achievement Rating; Consumer Education; Criterion Referenced Tests; Foods Instruction; Foreign Countries; *Geography; *Home Economics; *Item Banks; Mastery Tests; Multiple Choice Tests; Nutrition Instruction; Secondary Education; *Secondary School Students; Student Evaluation; Test Construction; Values
Identifiers: Assessment Instruments; Australia (New South Wales)
Availability: ERIC Document Reproduction Service; 7420 Fullerton Rd., Ste. 110, Springfield, VA 22153-2852 (ED218285, 111 p.)
Grade Level: 7-10

One of a series of test-item collections developed by the Assessment and Evaluation Unit of the Directorate of Studies. Designed for use by secondary school teachers for the construction of tests or as the basis for classroom discussions. Items in this volume measure attitudes and values, knowledge of consumer economics, nutrition, and foods.

800235
Library of Test Items: Textiles and Design, Volume 1. New South Wales Dept. of Education, Sydney (Australia) 1980
Descriptors: Achievement Rating; Clothing Design; Criterion Referenced Tests; Fashion Industry; Foreign Countries; Home Economics; *Item Banks; Mastery Tests; Multiple Choice Tests; Secondary Education; *Secondary School Students; Student Evaluation; Test Construction; *Textiles Instruction

Identifiers: Assessment Instruments; Australia (New South Wales); *Fabrics
Availability: ERIC Document Reproduction Service; 7420 Fullerton Rd., Ste. 110, Springfield, VA 22153-2852 (ED218286, 120 p.)
Grade Level: 7-10

One of a series of test-item collections developed by the Assessment and Evaluation Unit of the Directorate of Studies. Designed for use by secondary school teachers for the construction of tests or as the basis for classroom discussions. Items in this collection assess knowledge of fabrics and their properties, textile design, and history of textile industry.

800236
Library of Test Items: Commerce, Volume 1.
New South Wales Dept. of Education, Sydney (Australia) 1978
Subtests: Business; Consumers; Finance
Descriptors: Achievement Rating; Banking; *Business Administration; *Consumer Education; Consumer Protection; Criterion Referenced Tests; Foreign Countries; *Item Banks; Mastery Tests; Money Management; Multiple Choice Tests; Secondary Education; *Secondary School Students; Student Evaluation; Test Construction
Identifiers: Assessment Instruments; Australia (New South Wales); *Commerce; *Finance
Availability: ERIC Document Reproduction Service; 7420 Fullerton Rd., Ste. 110, Springfield, VA 22153-2852 (ED218287, 155 p.)
Grade Level: 7-10

One of a series of test-item collections developed by the Assessment and Evaluation Unit of the Directorate of Studies. Designed for use by secondary school teachers for the construction of tests or as the basis for classroom discussions. Items in this volume assess knowledge of business activity, expansion, growth, modern business methods, as well as types of business organizations. The items in the second section measure knowledge of areas important to consumers, including buying goods and services, earning and budgeting an income, and consumer protection. The items in the final section of the volume measure knowledge related to personal, company, and government finance and banking.

800237
Library of Test Items: Commerce, Volume 2.
New South Wales Dept. of Education, Sydney (Australia) 1978
Subtests: Government; Labor; Records; Trade
Descriptors: *Accounting; Achievement Rating; Criterion Referenced Tests; Foreign Countries; *Government (Administrative Body); Governmental Structure; *International Trade; *Item Banks; *Labor Economics; Mastery Tests; Multiple Choice Tests; Secondary Education; *Secondary School Students; Student Evaluation; Test Construction; Unions
Identifiers: Assessment Instruments; Australia (New South Wales); *Commerce
Availability: ERIC Document Reproduction Service; 7420 Fullerton Rd., Ste. 110, Springfield, VA 22153-2852 (ED218288, 115 p.)
Grade Level: 7-10

One of a series of test-item collections developed by the Assessment and Evaluation Unit of the Directorate of Studies. Designed for use by secondary school teachers for the construction of tests or as the basis for classroom discussions. Items in this volume assess knowledge in areas of government, labor, financial records, and international trade.

800238
Library of Test Items: Geography, Volume 1.
New South Wales Dept. of Education, Sydney (Australia) 1980
Descriptors: Achievement Rating; Agriculture; Criterion Referenced Tests; Foreign Countries; *Geography; *Item Banks; Mastery Tests; Multiple Choice Tests; Secondary Education; *Secondary School Students; Student Evaluation; Test Construction
Identifiers: Assessment Instruments; Australia (New South Wales)
Availability: ERIC Document Reproduction Service; 7420 Fullerton Rd., Ste. 110, Springfield, VA 22153-2852 (ED218291, 111 p.)
Grade Level: 7-10

One of a series of test-item collections developed by the Assessment and Evaluation Unit of the Directorate of Studies. Designed for use by secondary school teachers for the construction of tests or as the basis for classroom discussions. This volume contains an introduction and suggestions for use of library of test items. Items in this volume measure knowledge of natural landscapes including rainforests, deserts, and tropical savannas.

800239
Library of Test Items: Languages, Volume 1. French, Indonesian. New South Wales Dept. of Education, Sydney (Australia) 1980
Descriptors: Achievement Rating; Criterion Referenced Tests; Foreign Countries; *French; *Indonesian; *Item Banks; Mastery Tests; Multiple Choice Tests; Secondary Education; *Secondary School Students; *Second Languages; Student Evaluation; Test Construction
Identifiers: Assessment Instruments; Australia (New South Wales)
Availability: ERIC Document Reproduction Service; 7420 Fullerton Rd., Ste. 110, Springfield, VA 22153-2852 (ED218289, 183 p.)
Grade Level: 7-10

One of a series of test-item collections developed by the Assessment and Evaluation Unit of the Directorate of Studies. Designed for use by secondary school teachers for the construction of tests or as the basis for classroom discussions. The items in this volume assess knowledge of language structure, vocabulary and comprehension in French and Indonesian.

800240
Library of Test Items: Languages, Volume 2. German, Latin. New South Wales Dept. of Education, Sydney (Australia) 1980
Descriptors: Achievement Rating; Criterion Referenced Tests; Foreign Countries; *German; *Item Banks; *Latin; Mastery Tests; Multiple Choice Tests; Secondary Education; *Secondary School Students; *Second Languages; Student Evaluation; Test Construction
Identifiers: Assessment Instruments; Australia (New South Wales)
Availability: ERIC Document Reproduction Service; 7420 Fullerton Rd., Ste. 110, Springfield, VA 22153-2852 (ED218290, 185 p.)
Grade Level: 7-10

One of a series of test-item collections developed by the Assessment and Evaluation Unit of the Directorate of Studies. Designed for use by secondary school teachers for the construction of tests or as the basis for classroom discussions. The items in this volume assess knowledge of language structure, vocabulary, and comprehension in German and Latin.

800265
Australian Biology Test Item Bank; Volume I: Year 11. Australian Council For Educational Research, Hawthorn 1985
Descriptors: *Achievement Tests; *Biology; Foreign Countries; High Schools; *High School Students; *Item Banks
Identifiers: Australia
Availability: Australian Council for Educational Research; P.O. Box 210, Hawthorn, Victoria 3122, Australia
Grade Level: 11

Developed to assist teachers in assessing students' knowledge of biology. Items were designed to be relevant to current biological concepts, assess key concepts within the biological curriculum, assess a wide range of cognitive processes, and be applicable to biology courses throughout Australia. Items in this volume deal with the living world and cover investigating the living world; variety of life; organisms and environments; reproduction; nutrition, development, and growth; populations; interaction and change in the natural world; and the living world.

800266
Australian Biology Test Item Bank; Volume II: Year 12. Australian Council For Educational Research, Hawthorn 1984
Descriptors: *Achievement Tests; *Biology; Foreign Countries; High Schools; *High School Students; *Item Banks
Identifiers: Australia
Availability: Australian Council for Educational Research; P.O. Box 210, Hawthorn, Victoria 3122, Australia
Grade Level: 12

Developed to assist teachers in assessing students' knowledge of biology. Objectives of the project are that items should be relevant to current biological concepts, assess key concepts within the biology curriculum, assess a wide range of cognitive processes, and be applicable to biology courses throughout Australia. Items in this volume deal with the functioning organism and cover the organism, function and structure in plants, function and structure in animals, integration and regulation in multicellular organisms, cellular processes, heredity, life—its continuity and change, the human species, and science and the scientific process.

800267
ACER Primary Reading Survey Tests, Revised Edition. Australian Council for Educational Research, Hawthorn 1976

Descriptors: *Achievement Tests; Elementary Education; *Elementary School Students; Foreign Countries; Reading Achievement; *Reading Comprehension; *Reading Tests; *Vocabulary Skills
Identifiers: Australia
Availability: Australian Council for Educational Research; P.O. Box 210, Hawthorn, Victoria 3122, Australia
Grade Level: 3-6
Notes: Time, 50 min. approx.

A multichoice instrument which is comprised of 2 separate tests: word knowledge and reading comprehension. Provides a source of information about the range of skills and levels of achievement in reading within a class for curriculum planning. Can also be used to measure the performance of individual students.

800269
The Early Detection of Reading Difficulties: A Diagnostic Survey with Recovery Procedures, Second Edition. Clay, Marie M. 1979
Subtests: Record of Reading Behavior; Letter Identification; Concepts About Print; Word Tests; Writing
Descriptors: *Diagnostic Tests; Foreign Countries; *Primary Education; *Reading Diagnosis; Reading Difficulties; Reading Instruction; Young Children
Identifiers: Australia
Availability: Australian Council for Educational Research; P.O. Box 210, Hawthorn, Victoria 3122, Australia
Age Level: 6-7
Notes: Time, 15-30 min.

An instrument used to identify children who by age 6 or 7 are having difficulty learning to read. It is contained in, and an integral part of, a text of the same name, which also contains a set of procedures for teaching these children in an individual reading program. The survey is divided into the following diagnostic areas: Record of Reading Behavior on Books, Letter Identification, Concepts about Print, Word Tests, and Writing.

800279
Progressive Achievement Tests: Reading Comprehension—2nd Edition. Australian Council for Educational Research, Hawthorn
Descriptors: *Achievement Tests; *Elementary School Students; Elementary Secondary Education; Foreign Countries; Multiple Choice Tests; *Reading Comprehension; *Reading Tests; *Secondary School Students
Identifiers: Australia; PAT
Availability: Australian Council for Educational Research; P.O. Box 210, Hawthorn, Victoria 3122, Australia
Grade Level: 3-9
Notes: Time, 40 min.; Items, 97

Multiple-choice survey test of reading comprehension for grades 3 through 9. Designed to measure 2 major aspects of reading skill: factual and inferential comprehension of prose material. Intended primarily to assist teachers in determining the level of development attained by their students in basic skills of reading comprehension. Two alternative tests (Form A and B) are available. Either test can be given alone but assessment with both is recommended.

800280
Progressive Achievement Tests: Reading Vocabulary—2nd Edition. Australian Council for Educational Research, Hawthorn 1986
Descriptors: *Achievement Tests; *Elementary School Students; Elementary Secondary Education; Foreign Countries; Multiple Choice Tests; *Reading Tests; *Secondary School Students; *Vocabulary Skills
Identifiers: Australia; PAT
Availability: Australian Council for Educational Research; P.O. Box 210, Hawthorn, Victoria 3122, Australia
Grade Level: 3-9
Notes: Time, 30 min.; Items, 125

Multiple-choice survey test of vocabulary knowledge for grades 3 through 9. Measures word knowledge. Intended primarily to assist teachers in determining the level of development attained by their students in word knowledge. Two alternative tests (Form A and B) are available. Either test can be given alone but assessment with both is recommended.

800284
Tests of Reading Comprehension. Mossenson, Leila and Others 1987
Descriptors: *Achievement Tests; Cloze Procedure; Criterion Referenced Tests; *Elementary School Students; Elementary Secondary Education; Foreign Countries; Individual Testing; Norm Referenced Tests; *Reading Comprehension; Reading Tests; *Secondary School Students
Identifiers: Australia; TORCH

Availability: Australian Council for Educational Research; P.O. Box 210, Hawthorn, Victoria, Australia 3122
Grade Level: 3-10

The tests consist of 14 graded passages designed to measure the extent to which students comprehend what they have read. Two test booklets are available, one for years 3-7, another for years 6-10. Students read passages, then fill in gaps in a retelling of the story on an answer sheet, using their own words. The tests are untimed. Both norm- and criterion-referenced interpretations are possible. Normative data are for students in Western Australia.

800287
Progressive Achievement Tests in Mathematics.
Australian Council for Educational Research, Hawthorn 1984
Descriptors: *Achievement Tests; Elementary Education; *Elementary School Mathematics; *Elementary School Students; Foreign Countries; *Mathematics Tests; Multiple Choice Tests; Norm Referenced Tests
Identifiers: Australia; PAT MATHS
Availability: Australian Council for Educational Research; P.O. Box 210, Hawthorn, Victoria 3122, Australia
Grade Level: 3-8
Notes: Time, 45 min. approx.; Items, 55

Assists teachers in determining the level of achievement attained by their students in the basic skills and understandings of mathematics. Series consists of 3 tests at different levels of difficulty. Multiple choice. Two equivalent forms of each test.

800291
Neale Analysis of Reading Ability, Revised.
Neale, Marie D. 1988
Descriptors: *Diagnostic Tests; Elementary Education; *Elementary School Students; Foreign Countries; *Individual Testing; *Oral Reading; *Reading Achievement; *Reading Diagnosis; *Reading Tests
Identifiers: Australia
Availability: Australian Council for Educational Research; P.O. Box 210, Hawthorn, Victoria 3122, Australia
Grade Level: 1-6
Age Level: 6-12
Notes: Time, 20 min. approx.

Reading test that consists of a set of graded passages to assess rate, accuracy, and comprehension of oral reading and a set of supplementary tests for diagnosis. Used to assess reading achievement in the elementary grades and for diagnostic or clinical observations at both the elementary level and above. Individually administered. Students beyond age 12 and some adults can be tested on appropriate passages for a general level of reading ability and for diagnostic purposes.

800299
ACER Word Knowledge Test.   de Lemos, Marion M. 1990
Descriptors: Foreign Countries; *Language Tests; Prior Learning; *Screening Tests; Secondary Education; *Secondary School Students; *Semantics; Verbal Ability; *Vocabulary Skills
Identifiers: Australia
Availability: Australian Council for Educational Research; P.O. Box 210, Hawthorn, Victoria 3122, Australia
Grade Level: 9-11
Notes: Time, 10 min.; Items, 72

This instrument is a test to measure knowledge of word meanings. However, exposure to relevant language background is a prerequisite to the acquisition of vocabulary. This tool was developed to replace the ACER Adult Form B Test. It is intended for use by psychologists, personal officers, training officers, and vocational or guidance counselors. It may also be used by teachers or other professionals as a screening test to assess vocabulary knowledge or verbal skills. Forms E and F included in this instrument are comprised of 72 items each. This test is group administered. Normed on students in grades 9, 10, and 11.

800301
Diagnostic Mathematics Profile.   Dolg, Brian 1990
Descriptors: Addition; *Arithmetic; Computation; *Diagnostic Tests; Division; Elementary Education; *Elementary School Students; Foreign Countries; *Mathematics Tests; Multiplication; Subtraction; Whole Numbers
Identifiers: Australia; DIAMAP; DMP
Availability: Australian Council for Educational Research; P.O. Box 210, Hawthorn, Victoria 3122, Australia
Grade Level: 3-6
Notes: Items, 80

These mathematics profiles are designed to provide diagnostic information about a student in addition, subtraction, multiplication, and division. They are made up of 2 parts. Part one assesses students from third to sixth grades in whole number computation. Part 2 is the diagnostic profile which is a visual map of a student's performance on the profile. This links students' responses on a diagnostic mathematics profile to specific objectives that determine which objectives have and have not been mastered by the students. These objectives provide a guide to further planning of learning for that student, establishing strengths and weaknesses in the 4 arithmetic processes.

800305
ACER Tests of Basic Skills, Blue Series, Year 3.
Lokan, Jan; Jones, Suzanne 1991
Subtests: Literacy; Numeracy
Descriptors: *Achievement Tests; *Basic Skills; Elementary Education; *Elementary School Students; Foreign Countries; *Grade 3; *Language Skills; Literacy; *Mathematics Skills
Identifiers: Australia
Availability: Australian Council for Educational Research; P.O. Box 210, Hawthorn, Victoria 3122, Australia
Grade Level: 3
Notes: Time, 67 min.; Items, 57

Assesses literacy and numeracy skills in major areas of school curriculum. Assesses basic skills in reading, language, and numbers. For each skill, a set of skill levels or "bands" are defined. These skill levels show the level of achievement. Can be used by the teacher to diagnose the individual's strengths and weaknesses. Year 3 test material is in a highly illustrated format. Includes questions to assess early reading skills by matching words to pictures and completing sentences.

800306
ACER Tests of Basic Skills, Blue Series, Year 6.
Lokan, Jan 1991
Subtests: Literacy; Numeracy
Descriptors: *Achievement Tests; *Basic Skills; Elementary Education; *Elementary School Students; Foreign Countries; *Grade 6; *Language Skills; Literacy; *Mathematics Skills
Identifiers: Australia
Availability: Australian Council for Educational Research; P.O. Box 210, Hawthorn, Victoria 3122, Australia
Grade Level: 6
Notes: Time, 103 min.; Items, 86

Assesses literacy and numeracy skills in major areas of school curriculum. Assesses 5 basic skills: reading, language, numbers, measurement, and space. For each skill, a set of skill levels or "bands" are defined. These skill levels show the level of achievement. Teachers can diagnose the individuals' strengths and weaknesses. Year 6 emphasizes the relevance of mathematics and language learning to everyday activities. Measurement and space items are covered in Year 6 only.

810158
Mathematics Attainment Test B (Oral).   National Foundation for Educational Research in England and Wales, London 1972
Descriptors: Academic Achievement; *Achievement Tests; Children; Computation; *Elementary School Mathematics; *Elementary School Students; Foreign Countries; *Mathematical Concepts; Mathematics; *Mathematics Achievement; *Mathematics Tests
Identifiers: England; Great Britain; Junior Mathematics Test B1 (Oral); *Oral Tests
Availability: NFER-Nelson Publishing Co.; Darville House, 2 Oxford Rd. E., Windsor SL4 1DF, Berkshire, England
Age Level: 8-10
Notes: Time, 60 min. approx.; Items, 42

Designed to measure a student's understanding of mathematical concepts and has almost no mechanical computation. Formerly Junior Mathematics Test B1 (oral).

810159
Mathematics Attainment Test C1.   National Foundation for Educational Research in England and Wales, London 1972
Descriptors: Academic Achievement; *Achievement Tests; Children; *Elementary School Mathematics; *Elementary School Students; Foreign Countries; *Intermediate Grades; *Mathematical Concepts; Mathematics; *Mathematics Achievement; Mathematics Tests
Identifiers: England; Great Britain; Junior Mathematics Test C1
Availability: NFER-Nelson Publishing Co.; Darville House, 2 Oxford Rd. E., Windsor SL4 1DF, Berkshire, England
Age Level: 9-12
Notes: Time, 50 min. approx; Items, 50

Designed to measure a student's understanding of mathematical concepts and has almost no mechanical computation. Though not timed, most students complete it in 50 minutes. Formerly Junior Mathematics Test C1.

810203
English Progress Test A2.   Barnard, Betsy 1972
Descriptors: *Achievement Tests; *Elementary School Students; Foreign Countries; *Language Proficiency; *Language Tests; Primary Education; *Reading Comprehension; Vocabulary
Identifiers: England; English Progress Tests Series; Great Britain
Availability: NFER-Nelson Publishing Co., Ltd.; Darville House, 2 Oxford Rd. E., Windsor SL4 1DF, Berkshire, England
Age Level: 7-8
Notes: Time, 50 min. approx.; Items, 42

Part of a series of tests designed to provide a continuous assessment of skill in English for children 8 to 14 years of age. Areas assessed in this test include rhymes, plurals, spelling, vocabulary, pronouns, tenses, and reading comprehension.

810204
English Progress Test B2.   Land, Valerie C. 1972
Descriptors: *Achievement Tests; Elementary Education; *Elementary School Students; Foreign Countries; *Language Proficiency; *Language Tests; *Reading Comprehension; Spelling; Writing Skills
Identifiers: England; English Progress Tests Series; Great Britain
Availability: NFER-Nelson Publishing Co., Ltd.; Darville House, 2 Oxford Rd. E., Windsor SL4 1DF, Berkshire, England
Age Level: 8-10
Notes: Time, 40 min. approx.; Items, 45

Part of a series of tests designed to provide a continuous assessment of skill in English for children 8 to 14 years of age. Areas assessed include ability to provide rhymes and opposites, change nouns into plural and verbs into past tense, spell and punctuate, write sentences, read passages and comprehend.

810205
English Progress Test C2.   Land, Valerie C. 1972
Descriptors: *Achievement Tests; Elementary Education; *Elementary School Students; Foreign Countries; *Language Proficiency; *Language Tests; Punctuation; *Reading Comprehension; Spelling; Vocabulary; *Writing Skills
Identifiers: England; English Progress Tests Series; Great Britain
Availability: NFER-Nelson Publishing Co., Ltd.; Darville House, 2 Oxford Rd. E., Windsor SL4 1DF, Berkshire, England
Age Level: 9-11
Notes: Time, 45 min. approx.; Items, 54

Part of a series of tests designed to provide a continuous assessment of skill in English for children 8 to 14 years of age. Areas assessed include spelling, punctuation, vocabulary, reading comprehension, and composition of sentences. Designed for students from ages 9.5 to 11.

810206
English Progress Test D2.   Henchman, Jennifer 1967
Descriptors: *Achievement Tests; Elementary Education; *Elementary School Students; Foreign Countries; *Language Proficiency; *Language Tests; Punctuation; *Reading Comprehension; Spelling; Vocabulary
Identifiers: England; English Progress Tests Series; Great Britain
Availability: NFER-Nelson Publishing Co., Ltd.; Darville House, 2 Oxford Rd. E., Windsor SL4 1DF, Berkshire, England
Age Level: 10-12
Notes: Time, 45 min. approx.; Items, 75

Part of a series of tests designed to provide a continuous assessment of skill in English for children 8 to 14 years of age. Skills assessed include spelling, punctuation, vocabulary, and reading comprehension. Several questions involve construction of acceptable sentences using given words and phrases. Designed for children ages 10.5 to 12.

810219
English Progress Test E2.   Unwin, S.M. 1971
Descriptors: *Achievement Tests; Elementary Education; *Elementary School Students; Foreign Countries; *Language Proficiency; *Language Tests; Punctuation; Vocabulary; Writing Skills
Identifiers: England; English Progress Tests Series; English Usage; Great Britain
Availability: NFER-Nelson Publishing Co., Ltd.; Darville House, 2 Oxford Rd. E., Windsor SL4 1DF, Berkshire, England
Age Level: 11-13
Notes: Time, 40 min. approx.; Items, 70

Part of a series of tests designed to provide a continuous assessment of skill in English for children 8 to 14 years of age. Topics assessed include use of pronouns; synonyms and homonyms; proverbs; punctuation; and construction of sentences from given phrases.

810224
English Progress Test F2. Henchman, Jennifer; Hendry, Elsa 1963
Descriptors: *Achievement Tests; Foreign Countries; Junior High Schools; *Junior High School Students; *Language Proficiency; *Language Tests; Punctuation; Vocabulary; Writing Skills
Identifiers: England; English Progress Tests Series; English Usage; Great Britain
Availability: NFER-Nelson Publishing Co., Ltd.; Darville House, 2 Oxford Rd. E., Windsor SL4 1DF, Berkshire, England
Age Level: 12-13
Notes: Time, 40 min. approx.; Items, 60
Part of a series of tests designed to provide a continuous assessment of skill in English for children 8 to 14 years of age. Items are of creative response type and assess areas of grammatical usage, written expression, vocabulary, comprehension, and punctuation.

810228
Reading Test EH 2. Bate, S.M. 1967
Descriptors: *Achievement Tests; Adolescents; Children; Foreign Countries; *Reading Achievement; *Reading Comprehension; *Reading Tests; Secondary Education; *Secondary School Students; Silent Reading
Identifiers: England; Great Britain; Secondary Reading Test 2; Wales
Availability: NFER-Nelson Publishing Co., Ltd.; Darville House, 2 Oxford Rd. E., Windsor SL4 1DF, Berkshire, England
Age Level: 11-15
Notes: Time, 45 min. approx.; Items, 35
Untimed comprehension test based upon reading passages. Measures the achievement level of reading comprehension.

810335
Reading Test BD. National Foundation for Educational Research in England and Wales, London 1971
Descriptors: *Achievement Tests; Children; Cloze Procedure; *Elementary School Students; Foreign Countries; Multiple Choice Tests; *Reading Achievement; *Reading Comprehension; *Reading Tests; *Vocabulary
Identifiers: England; Great Britain; Primary Reading Test 2; Wales
Availability: NFER-Nelson Publishing Co., Ltd.; Darville House, 2 Oxford Rd. E., Windsor SL4 1DF, Berkshire, England
Grade Level: 1-3
Age Level: 7-10
Notes: Time, 30 min. approx.; Items, 44
To determine achievement level of basic reading skills. Formerly called Primary Reading Test 2. Similar to Reading Test A but for use with slightly older students.

810336
Reading Test AD. Watts, A.F. 1971
Descriptors: *Achievement Tests; Children; Cloze Procedure; *Elementary School Students; Foreign Countries; Multiple Choice Tests; *Reading Achievement; *Reading Comprehension; *Reading Tests; *Vocabulary
Identifiers: England; Great Britain; Sentence Reading Test 1; Wales
Availability: NFER-Nelson Publishing Co.; Darville House, 2 Oxford Rd. E., Windsor, Berkshire SL4 1DF, England
Age Level: 8-10
Notes: Time, 30 min. approx.; Items, 35
To determine level of reading ability and comprehension. Formerly called Sentence Reading Test 1.

810337
Reading Test A. National Foundation For Educational Research In England and Wales, London 1971
Descriptors: *Achievement Tests; *Cloze Procedure; *Elementary School Students; Foreign Countries; Multiple Choice Tests; *Primary Education; *Reading Achievement; Reading Comprehension; *Reading Tests; Vocabulary; Young Children
Identifiers: England; Great Britain; Primary Reading Test 1; Wales
Availability: NFER-Nelson Publishing Co., Ltd.; Darville House, 2 Oxford Rd. E., Windsor SL4 1DF, Berkshire, England
Age Level: 6-8
Notes: Time, 30 min. approx.; Items, 38
To determine achievement level of basic reading skills. Formerly called Primary Reading Test 1.

810338
Reading Comprehension Test DE. Barnard, E.L. 1967
Subtests: Global Understanding; Drawing Conclusions; Understanding Individual Words and Phrases; Reading for Detail
Descriptors: *Achievement Tests; Children; *Critical Reading; Elementary Education; *Elementary School Students; Foreign Countries; *Logical Thinking; Reading Achievement; *Reading Comprehension; Reading Diagnosis; Reading Tests; Vocabulary
Identifiers: England; Great Britain; Reading Comprehension Test I; Wales
Availability: NFER-Nelson Publishing Co., Ltd.; Darville House, 2 Oxford Rd. E., Windsor SL4 1DF, Berkshire, England
Age Level: 10-12
Notes: Time, 45 min. approx.; Items, 50
To measure understanding of whole and sometimes quite complex passages rather than single sentences. May be used diagnostically. Previously called Reading Comprehension Test I.

810342
English Progress Test C3. National Foundation for Educational Research in England and Wales, London 1970
Descriptors: Achievement Tests; Elementary Education; *Elementary School Students; Foreign Countries; *Language Proficiency; *Language Tests; Punctuation; *Reading Comprehension
Identifiers: England; English Progress Tests Series; Great Britain
Availability: NFER-Nelson Publishing Co., Ltd.; Darville House, 2 Oxford Rd. E., Windsor SL4 1DF, Berkshire, England
Age Level: 9-10
Notes: Time, 45 min. approx.; Items, 50
Part of a series of tests designed to provide a continuous assessment of skill in English for children 8 to 14 years of age. Assesses knowledge of punctuation, ability to arrange phrases in meaningful order, and reading comprehension.

810343
English Progress Test D3. National Foundation for Educational Research in England and Wales, London 1970
Descriptors: Achievement Tests; Elementary Education; *Elementary School Students; Foreign Countries; *Language Proficiency; *Language Tests; Punctuation; Reading Comprehension
Identifiers: England; English Progress Tests Series; Great Britain
Availability: NFER-Nelson Publishing Co., Ltd.; Darville House, 2 Oxford Rd. E., Windsor SL4 1DF, Berkshire, England
Age Level: 10-11
Notes: Time, 45 min. approx.; Items, 50
Part of a series of tests designed to provide a continuous assessment of skill in English for children 8 to 14 years of age. Designed to measure knowledge of elementary punctuation, homonyms, vocabulary comprehension, and reading comprehension.

810346
Mathematics Attainment Test EF. National Foundation for Educational Research in England and Wales, London 1972
Descriptors: Academic Achievement; *Achievement Tests; Children; Computation; *Elementary School Mathematics; Foreign Countries; *Junior High School Students; *Mathematical Concepts; Mathematics; *Mathematics Achievement; *Mathematics Tests; Multiple Choice Tests; Timed Tests
Identifiers: England; Great Britain
Availability: NFER-Nelson Publishing Co.; Darville House, 2 Oxford Rd. E., Windsor SL4 1DF, Berkshire, England
Age Level: 11-13
Notes: Time, 50 min. approx.; Items, 60
Designed to measure a student's understanding of mathematical concepts and has almost no mechanical computation. It differs from the older Mathematics Attainment Tests in that this form is timed and uses multiple-choice type answers.

810347
Basic Mathematics Test A. National Foundation for Educational Research in England and Wales, London 1971
Descriptors: Academic Achievement; *Achievement Tests; *Diagnostic Tests; Educational Diagnosis; Elementary School Mathematics; *Elementary School Students; Foreign Countries; *Mathematical Concepts; Mathematics; *Mathematics Achievement; *Mathematics Tests; Primary Education
Identifiers: England; Great Britain; Oral Tests

Availability: NFER-Nelson Publishing Co.; Darville House, 2 Oxford Rd. E., Windsor SL4 1DF, Berkshire, England
Age Level: 6-8
Notes: Time, 60 min. approx.; Items, 40
Measures the students' knowledge of operations, relationships, and skills in the field of mathematics. The questions are read aloud by the test administrator and the student writes the answers on the test paper. By reading each question aloud, the poor readers are not unnecessarily discriminated against. The results may be used to determine the student's level of attainment, to compare students with each other, and to provide diagnostic information concerning the student's strengths and weaknesses.

810348
Basic Mathematics Test B. National Foundation for Educational Research in England and Wales, London 1971
Descriptors: Academic Achievement; *Achievement Tests; Children; *Diagnostic Tests; Educational Diagnosis; Elementary School Mathematics; *Elementary School Students; Foreign Countries; *Mathematical Concepts; Mathematics; *Mathematics Achievement; *Mathematics Tests; *Primary Education
Identifiers: England; Great Britain; Oral Tests
Availability: NFER-Nelson Publishing Co.; Darville House, 2 Oxford Rd. E., Windsor SL4 1DF, Berkshire, England
Age Level: 8-9
Notes: Time, 60 min. approx.; Items, 40
Measures the student's knowledge of mathematical relationships and handling of mathematical units. The questions are read aloud by the test administrator and the student writes the answers on the test paper. By administering the test orally the results are not influenced by a lack of reading ability but more accurately measure attainment in mathematics. The results may be used to determine the student's level of attainment, to compare students with each other, and to provide diagnostic information concerning the student's strengths and weaknesses.

810349
Basic Mathematics Test C. National Foundation for Educational Research in England and Wales, London 1970
Descriptors: Academic Achievement; *Achievement Tests; Children; *Diagnostic Tests; Educational Diagnosis; Elementary School Mathematics; *Elementary School Students; Foreign Countries; *Intermediate Grades; *Mathematical Concepts; Mathematics; Mathematics Achievement; *Mathematics Tests; Spatial Ability
Identifiers: England; Great Britain
Availability: NFER-Nelson Publishing Co.; Darville House, 2 Oxford Rd. E., Windsor SL4 1DF, Berkshire, England
Age Level: 9-10
Notes: Time, 60 min. approx.; Items, 50
Measures the student's understanding of relationship and processes which lay the foundation for understanding mathematics. Includes questions on area, graphical representation, inequality, elementary knowledge of sets, decimals, fractions, and symmetry. Although not timed, most students should finish in 50 minutes. The results may be used to determine the student's level of attainment, to compare students with each other, and to provide diagnostic information concerning the student's strengths and weaknesses.

810350
Basic Mathematics Test FG. National Foundation for Educational Research in England and Wales, London 1972
Descriptors: Academic Achievement; *Achievement Tests; Adolescents; Diagnostic Tests; Educational Diagnosis; Foreign Countries; *Junior High School Students; *Mathematical Concepts; *Mathematics; *Mathematics Achievement; *Mathematics Tests; Secondary School Mathematics; *Spatial Ability
Identifiers: England; Great Britain
Availability: NFER-Nelson Publishing Co.; Darville House, 2 Oxford Rd. E., Windsor SL4 1DF, Berkshire, England
Age Level: 12-14
Notes: Time, 50 min. approx.; Items, 55
Designed to measure a wide range of mathematical concepts and thinking. Although not timed, most students should finish in 50 minutes. The results may be used to determine the student's level of attainment, to compare students with each other, and to provide diagnostic information concerning the student's strengths and weaknesses.

810351
Basic Mathematics Test DE. National Foundation for Educational Research in England and Wales, London 1971

Subtests: Sets; Relations; Representation; Operations
Descriptors: Academic Achievement; *Achievement Tests; Children; *Diagnostic Tests; Educational Diagnosis; Elementary School Mathematics; *Elementary School Students; Foreign Countries; *Mathematical Concepts; Mathematics; Mathematics Achievement; *Mathematics Tests; *Middle Schools; *Spatial Ability
Identifiers: England; Great Britain
Availability: NFER-Nelson Publishing Co.; Darville House, 2 Oxford Rd. E., Windsor SL4 1DF, Berkshire, England
Age Level: 10-12
Notes: Time, 50 min. approx.; Items, 55

Designed to measure student's knowledge of various mathematical ideas and skills—symmetry, tabulation, fractions, elementary algebra, basic spatial ability, inequalities, graphical representation, area, etc. Although not timed, most students should finish in 50 minutes. The results may be used to determine the student's level of attainment, to compare students with each other, and to provide diagnostic information concerning the student's strengths and weaknesses.

810366
Nottingham Number Test. Gillham, W.E.C.; Hesse, K.A. 1973
Subtests: Number Concepts; Number Skills
Descriptors: Computation; *Diagnostic Tests; *Elementary School Mathematics; *Elementary School Students; Foreign Countries; Intermediate Grades; Mathematics Tests; Number Concepts
Identifiers: England; Great Britain
Availability: Hodder & Stoughton Educational; Mill Rd., Dunton Green, Sevenoaks, Kent TN13 2YA, England
Age Level: 9-11
Notes: Time, 55 min. approx.; Items, 88

A diagnostic test designed as a followup to the Leicester Number Test (TC810466). Assesses basic number concepts and basic calculation skills. Useful for discriminating among abilities of least able students.

810370
Graded Arithmetic-Mathematics Test: Metric Edition (Junior). Vernon, P.E.; Miller, K.M. 1976
Descriptors: *Achievement Tests; Children; Computation; *Elementary School Students; Foreign Countries; *Mathematical Concepts; *Mathematics; Mathematics Achievement; Mathematics Tests; *Metric System
Identifiers: *Competence Tests; England; Great Britain; Number Operations
Availability: Hodder & Stoughton Educational; Mill Rd., Dunton Green, Sevenoaks, Kent TN13 2YA, England
Age Level: 6-12
Notes: Time, 30 min. approx.; Items, 70

Developed to measure competency in mathematics. An oral version exists for students with limited reading ability. Frequently used for assessing the attainment of individual retarded or problem students by educational psychologists and for grading the mathematical competence of English social dropouts on entry to technical courses. A senior form (TC810371) is also available for ages 11-18.

810371
Graded Arithmetic-Mathematics Test: Metric Edition (Senior). Vernon, P.E.; Miller, K.M. 1976
Descriptors: *Achievement Tests; Adolescents; Adults; Children; *College Freshmen; Computation; Foreign Countries; *Mathematical Concepts; *Mathematics; Mathematics Achievement; Mathematics Tests; *Metric System; *Secondary School Students
Identifiers: *Competence Tests; England; Great Britain; Number Operations
Availability: Hodder & Stoughton Educational; Mill Rd., Dunton Green, Sevenoaks, Kent TN13 2YA, England
Age Level: 11-18
Notes: Time, 30 min. approx.; Items, 65

To measure achievement level of mathematics. An oral version exists for students with limited reading ability. Frequently used for assessing the attainment of individual retarded or problem students by educational psychologists and for grading the mathematical competence of English school dropouts on entry to technical courses. It could also be used as a screening device for first-year college students. A junior form for ages 6-12 is also available (TC810370).

810374
SPAR Spelling and Reading Tests. Young, D. 1976
Subtests: Spelling; Reading: Pictures; Reading: Sentences
Descriptors: Academic Ability; Adolescents; Basic Skills; Children; *Elementary School Students; Foreign Countries; Language Skills; Learning Problems; *Literacy; *Low Achievement; Multiple Choice Tests; Pictorial Stimuli; Reading Difficulties; *Reading Tests; *Screening Tests; *Secondary School Students; *Spelling; Student Evaluation; Verbal Ability; Verbal Development; Visual Measures
Identifiers: England; Great Britain; Group Reading Test; SPAR Reading Test; SPAR Spelling Test
Availability: Hodder & Stoughton Educational; Mill Rd., Dunton Green, Sevenoaks, Kent TN13 2YA, England
Age Level: 7-16
Notes: Time, 30 min. approx.; Items, 75

Designed to provide a complementary approach to the testing of literacy at a simple level; to alert the teacher to the need for remedial measures; and to be used as a means of following the literacy progress of primary school students and/or older, less able students in the secondary schools, this instrument is designed to discriminate particularly among the lower ability levels. The author emphasizes that (1) this instrument is not a diagnostic test, but a screening test; and (2) the reading and spelling tests may be used independently of each other even though this separation would prevent the comparison and contrasting of the results. The spelling items are divided into 2 banks, Bank A and Bank B, so that the administrator may select 10 matched tests without any overlap or a much larger number of words with only a partial overlap. Thus, the author feels that these spelling banks give a distinct advantage, especially in charting the student's progress over a number of years. Forms A and B of the reading test follow the same formula as that of the author's Group Reading Test (GRT) and the marking templates for the GRT can be used for this reading test. Spelling test is not timed but usually takes about 10 minutes; the 2 sections of the reading test are timed separately.

810387
Wide-Span Reading Test. Brimer, Alan; Gross, Herbert 1972
Descriptors: *Achievement Tests; Adolescents; Children; *Context Clues; *Decoding (Reading); *Elementary School Students; Elementary Secondary Education; Foreign Countries; *High School Students; Reading Achievement; *Reading Comprehension; Reading Diagnosis; Reading Difficulties; Reading Tests; Silent Reading; Timed Tests
Identifiers: England; Great Britain
Availability: NFER-Nelson Publishing Co.; Darville House, 2 Oxford Rd. E., Windsor Berks SL4 1DF, England
Age Level: 7-15
Notes: Time, 30 min.; Items, 80

Measures the level of reading comprehension within the range defined by the beginning of competent silent reading and the full development of reading comprehension effectiveness. Measures the student's skills in decoding printed symbols into meaningful sounds of language; in fitting meanings to groups of sounds; and in construing the structural relationship of meanings within the context of a sentence. Also includes diagnostic indications of the areas in which low-scoring students may have difficulty. Comes in Forms A and B.

810388
Neale Analysis of Reading Ability, Braille Adaptation. Neale, Marie D.; Lorimer, J. 1977
Descriptors: *Blindness; *Braille; Children; *Diagnostic Tests; Elementary Education; *Elementary School Students; Foreign Countries; Individual Testing; Oral Reading; *Reading Achievement; Reading Diagnosis; *Reading Difficulties; Reading Tests
Identifiers: England; Great Britain; Oral Tests
Availability: NFER-Nelson Publishing Co.; Darville House, 2 Oxford Rd. E., Windsor, Berkshire SL4 1DF, England
Age Level: 6-12
Notes: Time, 45 min. approx.

Adaptation by J. Lorimer of Neale Analysis of Reading Ability (TC830315) for use with blind children. Individually administered test designed to provide diagnostic information which can be used to help remedy reading difficulties. Comes in Forms A, B, and C. Pictures used in print edition are replaced by introductory sentences, also used to arouse interest in the story. M. Lorimer strongly recommends that the test be administered only by experienced teachers of blind children who have a sound knowledge of grade II Braille, who have taught Braille, and, thus, understand the problems of reading by touch.

810402
Mathematics Attainment Test A (Oral). National Foundation for Educational Research in England and Wales, London 1972
Descriptors: Academic Achievement; *Achievement Tests; Children; *Elementary School Mathematics; *Elementary School Students; Foreign Countries; *Mathematical Concepts; Mathematics; *Mathematics Achievement; *Mathematics Tests; *Primary Education
Identifiers: England; Great Britain; Junior Mathematics Test Al (Oral); Oral Tests
Availability: NFER-Nelson Publishing Co.; Darville House, 2 Oxford Rd. E., Windsor SL4 1DF, Berkshire, England
Age Level: 7-8
Notes: Time, 45 min. approx.; Items, 42

Designed to measure a student's understanding of mathematical concepts and has almost no mechanical computation. Formerly Junior Mathematics Test A1 (Oral).

810403
Mathematics Attainment Test DE2. National Foundation for Educational Research in England and Wales, London 1972
Descriptors: Academic Achievement; *Achievement Tests; Children; Elementary School Mathematics; *Elementary School Students; Foreign Countries; *Mathematical Concepts; *Mathematics; *Mathematics Achievement; *Mathematics Tests; *Middle Schools
Identifiers: England; Great Britain; Intermediate Mathematics Test 1
Availability: NFER-Nelson Publishing Co.; Darville House, 2 Oxford Rd. E., Windsor SL4 1DF, Berkshire, England
Age Level: 10-12
Notes: Time, 50 min. approx.; Items, 46

Designed to measure a student's understanding of mathematical concepts and has almost no mechanical computation. Though not timed, the authors feel that a student should complete it in 50 minutes or less. Test formerly Intermediate Mathematics Test 1.

810418
Oral Intonation Test. Cruttenden, A. 1974
Descriptors: Children; Foreign Countries; *Intonation; *Language Acquisition; Language Tests
Identifiers: *English (British); Foreign Tests; Great Britain
Availability: *Journal of Child Language;* v1 p221-31, Nov 1974
Age Level: 7-10

A procedure designed to measure the development of intonation in language learning. Children are required to report the winner of a game played by 2 teams, after only the first team's score is read, by interpreting the intonation placed on the first team's score. Used with an English population. The testing depends on the peculiarities of intonation of British sports announcers.

810465
Group Mathematics Test. Young, D. 1970
Subtests: Oral; Computation
Descriptors: *Achievement Tests; *Computation; Elementary Education; *Elementary School Mathematics; *Elementary School Students; Foreign Countries; Mathematics Tests
Identifiers: England; Great Britain
Availability: Hodder & Stoughton Educational; Mill Rd., Dunton Green, Sevenoaks, Kent TN13 2YA, England
Age Level: 6-12
Notes: Time, 50 min. approx.; Items, 60

Designed to assess simple mathematical understandings of elementary age students. Should be administered in 2 sessions, each approximately 25 minutes in duration. Alternate Forms A and B are available.

810466
The Leicester Number Test. Gillham, W.E.C.; Hesse, K.A. 1970
Descriptors: *Arithmetic; *Elementary School Students; Foreign Countries; *Mathematics Tests; *Number Concepts; Primary Education
Identifiers: England; Great Britain
Availability: Hodder & Stoughton Educational; Mill Rd., Dunton Green, Sevenoaks, Kent TN13 2YA, England
Age Level: 7-9
Notes: Items, 54

Designed to assess a child's understanding of basic concepts of the number system and basic methods of calculation. Areas covered include counting, number equivalence, number relativeness, number sequence, grouping, simple fractions (proportion), addition, subtraction, multiplication and division. Test is untimed, but experimental administrations took from 42 to 56 minutes.

810467
Thackray Reading Readiness Profiles. Thackray, Derek; Thackray, Lucy 1974

Subtests: Vocabulary and Concept Development; Auditory Discrimination; Visual Discrimination; General Ability
Descriptors: *Auditory Discrimination; Diagnostic Teaching; Diagnostic Tests; *Elementary School Students; Foreign Countries; *Grade 1; Primary Education; *Reading Readiness; *Reading Readiness Tests; Reading Skills; Visual Discrimination; *Vocabulary
Identifiers: England; Great Britain
Availability: Hodder & Stoughton Educational; Mill Rd., Dunton Green, Sevenoaks, Kent TN13 2YA, England
Grade Level: 1
Notes: Time, 70 min. approx.; Items, 67

The first original British reading readiness tests to be published are a measure of 4 important reading readiness indicators. Each of 4 subtests should be administrered separately. Children should be given an opportunity to rest between sessions. Total administration may be completed in 2 days. Designed for use with children at the beginning of grade 1. May also be used diagnostically with older nonreaders.

810469
London Reading Test.   Inner London Education Authority (England) 1980
Descriptors: Ability Grouping; Achievement Tests; Children; Cloze Procedure; *Elementary School Students; Foreign Countries; *Reading Achievement; *Reading Habits; *Reading Skills; Reading Tests; *Screening Tests; Silent Reading; Transfer Students
Identifiers: Biscoe (Margaret); England; Great Britain
Availability: NFER-Nelson Publishing Co.; Darville House, 2 Oxford Rd. E., Windsor, Berkshire SL4 1DF, England
Age Level: 10-12
Notes: Time, 60 min. approx,; Items, 56

Untimed test that measures a student's reading attainment and patterns of reading ability. Consists of 3 reading passages. The first 2 passages are tested by the cloze technique; the third requires short, written answers covering a whole range of comprehension skills. Includes the use of a practice test given the same day or the preceding day. Used as a survey or screening device for students transferring from English primary to secondary schools. Available in Forms B and A.

810470
Basic Number Screening Test, Forms A and B.
Gillham, W.E.C.; Hesse, K.A. 1976
Descriptors: Elementary Education; *Elementary School Mathematics; *Elementary School Students; Foreign Countries; Mathematics Tests; *Number Concepts; *Screening Tests
Identifiers: England; Great Britain
Availability: Hodder & Stoughton Educational; Mill Rd., Dunton Green, Sevenoaks, Kent TN13 2YA, England
Age Level: 7-12
Notes: Time, 30 min. approx.

Designed to provide a rapid assessment of number proficiency and understanding of number concepts. Screening test may be used with groups or individuals. Instructions are given verbally thus student is not required to read. Instrument is useful in identifying students whose attainments are lower than expected, or who are not progressing adequately. Alternate forms A and B are available.

810472
Diagnostic Spelling Test.   Vincent, Denis; Claydon, Jenny 1981
Subtests: Homophones; Common Words; Proofreading; Letter Strings; Nonsense Words; Dictionary Use; Self Concept
Descriptors: Proofreading; Children; *Dictation; *Diagnostic Tests; Foreign Countries; Learning Problems; *Self Concept; *Spelling
Identifiers: Dictionary Skills; England; Great Britain; Homophones
Availability: NFER-Nelson Publishing; Darville House, 2 Oxford Rd. E., Windsor, Berkshire SL4 1DF, England
Age Level: 7-11
Notes: Items, 110

Designed for the identification and diagnosis of spelling difficulties. Includes a measure of self-concept as a speller and a dictation section.

810479
Reading Tests SR-A and SR-B.   National Foundation for Educational Research in England and Wales, London 1970
Descriptors: *Achievement Tests; Children; *Cloze Procedure; *Elementary School Students; Foreign Countries; Multiple Choice Tests; Reading Ability; *Reading Achievement; *Reading Comprehension; *Reading Tests; *Screening Tests; Timed Tests

Identifiers: England; Great Britain; SR A; SR B
Availability: NFER-Nelson Publishing Co.; Darville House, 2 Oxford Rd. E., Windsor, Berkshire SL4 1DF, England
Age Level: 7-12
Notes: Time, 20 min.; Items, 48

Sentence completion instrument designed to measure reading achievement of students. Not designed to measure all reading skills; used as screening or survey tests.

810484
The Primary Reading Test.   France, Norman 1981
Descriptors: *Achievement Tests; Children; *Cloze Procedure; *Elementary School Students; Foreign Countries; Multiple Choice Tests; *Reading Achievement; Reading Comprehension; *Reading Skills; *Reading Tests; Word Recognition
Identifiers: Great Britain; PRT
Availability: NFER-Nelson Publishing Co.; Darville House, 2 Oxford Rd. E., Windsor, Berkshire SL4 1DF, England
Age Level: 6-12
Notes: Time, 30 min. approx.; Items, 48

Assesses the students' ability to apply their learned reading skills to a comprehension of words and simple sentences. When orally administered may be used as an assessment for word recognition. Comes in 4 forms: Level 1 and 1A for younger children and Level 2 and 2A for older or more advanced students. 1A and 2A (alternate forms) are copyrighted 1981; other forms copyrighted 1978. Untimed.

810486
Profile of Mathematical Skills, Levels 1 and 2.
France, Norman 1979
Subtests: Addition; Subtraction; Multiplication; Division; Operations Measurement and Money; Fractions; Decimal Fractions and Percentages; Diagrams; Extensions
Descriptors: Achievement Tests; Adolescents; Children; Computation; *Criterion Referenced Tests; *Diagnostic Tests; *Elementary School Mathematics; Elementary School Students; Foreign Countries; *Junior High School Students; Mathematical Applications; *Mathematical Concepts; *Mathematics; *Mathematics Achievement; *Mathematics Tests
Identifiers: England; Great Britain; PMS
Availability: NFER-Nelson Publishing Co.; Darville House, 2 Oxford Rd. E., Windsor, Berkshire SL4 1DF, England
Age Level: 8-14
Notes: Items, 232

A criterion referenced instrument used to measure a student's mathematical achievement and to diagnose strengths and weaknesses in the various math areas. To be administered at the rate of one subtest per class period over one to 2 weeks. Level 1, for younger children, has 47 4-part items and lacks the subtests for fractions, etc., and for diagrams; level 2 has 58 4-part items.

810490
British Picture Vocabulary Scales.   Dunn, Lloyd M.; And Others 1982
Descriptors: *Achievement Tests; Adolescents; Children; Foreign Countries; *Individual Testing; *Language Tests; Pictorial Stimuli; *Receptive Language; Screening Tests; *Standard Spoken Usage; *Vocabulary Skills
Identifiers: BPVS; England; Great Britain; Peabody Picture Vocabulary Test (Revised)
Availability: NFER-Nelson Publishing Co.; Darville House, 2 Oxford Rd. E., Windsor, Berkshire SL4 1DF, England
Age Level: 3-18
Notes: Items, 150

Designed to measure a subject's receptive vocabulary for standard English. The short form contains 32 items and is useful in rapid screening of large numbers of children. The long form contains 150 items and is useful for a more detailed investigation of receptive language. This is the British adaptation of the Peabody Picture Vocabulary Test, Revised Edition (TC010877 and TC010878). An individually administered test designed for use by teachers, speech therapists, and clinical and educational psychologists for the assessment and guidance of subjects ranging in age from preschool to young adult.

810517
Bristol Achievement Tests, Level 1. Second Edition.   Brimer, Alan; And Others 1982
Subtests: Word Meaning; Paragraph Meaning; Sentence Organisation; Organisation of Ideas; Spelling and Punctuation; Number; Reasoning; Measurement; Space; Arithmetic Laws and Processes; Properties; Structures; Processes; Explanations; Interpretations

Descriptors: *Achievement Tests; Arithmetic; Elementary Education; *Elementary School Students; Foreign Countries; *Language Arts; *Mathematics Achievement; Reading Comprehension; Spelling; *Study Skills; Timed Tests
Identifiers: England; Great Britain; Test Batteries
Availability: NFER-Nelson Publishing Co.; Darville House, 2 Oxford Rd. E., Windsor, Berkshire SL4 1DF, England
Age Level: 8-9
Notes: Time, 155 min.; Items, 259

Designed to measure achievement in basic areas of curriculum. Individual booklets are available for English Language, Mathematics, and Study Skills. Each booklet contains 5 subtests. The English Language test consists of 85 items requiring 50 minutes. The Mathematics test consists of 95 items requiring 55 minutes. The Study Skills test consists of 68 items requiring 50 minutes. Parallel forms A and B are available. A "length of schooling" variable, as well as chronological age, may be used to select the appropriate level of test for each child. Level 1 was developed for second year junior students in the English school system. Suitable for students ages 8.0 to 9.11.

810518
Bristol Achievement Tests, Level 2. Second Edition.   Brimer, Alan; And Others 1982
Subtests: Word Meaning; Paragraph Meaning; Sentence Organisation; Organisation of Ideas; Spelling and Punctuation; Number; Reasoning; Measurement; Space; Arithmetic Laws and Processes; Properties; Structures; Processes; Explanations; Interpretations
Descriptors: *Achievement Tests; Elementary Education; *Elementary School Students; Foreign Countries; Intermediate Grades; *Language Arts; *Mathematics Achievement; Reading Comprehension; Spelling; *Study Skills; Timed Tests
Identifiers: England; Great Britain; Test Batteries
Availability: NFER-Nelson Publishing Co.; Darville House, 2 Oxford Rd. E., Windsor, Berkshire SL4 1DF, England
Age Level: 9-10
Notes: Time, 155 min.; Items, 266

Designed to measure achievement in basic areas of curriculum. Individual booklets are available for English Language, Mathematics, and Study Skills. Each booklet contains 5 subtests. The English Language test consists of 100 items requiring 50 minutes. The Mathematics test consists of 100 items requiring 55 minutes. The Study Skills test consists of 66 items requiring 50 minutes. Parallel forms A and B are available. A "length of schooling" variable, as well as chronological age, may be used to select the appropriate level of test for each child. Level 2 was developed for third year junior students in the English school system. Suitable for students aged 9.0 to 10.11.

810519
Bristol Achievement Tests, Level 3. Second Edition.   Brimer, Alan; And Others 1982
Subtests: Word Meaning; Paragraph Meaning; Sentence Organisation; Organisation of Ideas; Spelling and Punctuation; Number; Reasoning; Measurement; Space; Arithmetic Laws and Processes; Properties; Structures; Processes; Explanations; Interpretations
Descriptors: *Achievement Tests; *Elementary School Students; Foreign Countries; Intermediate Grades; *Language Arts; *Mathematics Achievement; Reading Comprehension; Spelling; *Study Skills; Timed Tests
Identifiers: England; Great Britain; Test Batteries
Availability: NFER-Nelson Publishing Co.; Darville House, 2 Oxford Rd. E., Windsor, Berkshire SL4 1DF, England
Age Level: 10-11
Notes: Time, 155 min.; Items, 265

Designed to measure achievement in basic areas of curriculum. Individual booklets are available for English Language, Mathematics, and Study Skills. Each booklet contains 5 subtests. The English Language test consists of 100 items requiring 50 minutes. The Mathematics test consists of 100 items requiring 55 minutes. The Study Skills test consists of 65 items requiring 50 minutes. Parallel forms A and B are available. A "length of schooling" variable, as well as chronological age, may be used to select the appropriate level of test for each child. Level 3 was developed for fourth year junior students in the English school system. Suitable for students aged 10.0 to 11.11.

810522
Roy Hollands Progress Tests in Math, Levels 5-6.
Hollands, Roy 1983
Descriptors: *Achievement Tests; *Criterion Referenced Tests; Elementary Education; *Elementary School Mathematics; *Elementary School Students; Foreign Countries; Intermediate Grades
Identifiers: Great Britain

Availability: Macmillan Education Ltd.; Houndmills Basingstoke, Hampshire R621 2XS, England
Grade Level: 5-6

This test series (see also levels 3-4, TC810523) is designed to measure achievement and concept development in the classroom so that a teacher can develop an individual teaching strategy. It covers numbers, measurement, shapes, graphs and tables, operations.

810523
Roy Hollands Progress Tests in Math, Levels 3-4. Hollands, Roy 1983
Descriptors: *Achievement Tests; *Criterion Referenced Tests; Elementary Education; *Elementary School Mathematics; Foreign Countries
Identifiers: Great Britain
Availability: Macmillan Education Ltd.; Houndmills Basingstoke, Hampshire R621 2XS, England
Grade Level: 3-4

This test series (see also levels 5-6 TC810522) is designed to measure achievement and concept development in the classroom so that a teacher can develop an individual teaching strategy. It covers numbers, fractions, decimals, number operations, word problems.

810544
Group Literacy Assessment. Spooncer, Frank A. 1982
Descriptors: Achievement Tests; Cloze Procedure; Context Clues; Foreign Countries; Grammar; *Group Testing; Literacy; Logical Thinking; Perceptual Development; *Reading Achievement; *Reading Tests; Screening Tests; Secondary Education; *Secondary School Students; Short Term Memory; *Slow Learners; *Spelling
Identifiers: England; GLA; Great Britain
Availability: Hodder and Stoughton; P.O. Box 702, Mill Rd., Dunton Green, Sevenoaks, Kent TN13 2YD, England
Grade Level: 7-12
Notes: Time, 30 min. approx.

Used to indicate what students in intermediate grades have achieved, not only in reading, but in overall efficiency with written materials. Also used as students enter secondary level as a screening test. Test has 2 sections. The first contains a story with misspellings that students must correct. The second part is a modified cloze procedure with words or parts of words missing that students must fill in. A major aim of test is to provide information on slow learners. Test requires students to use and combine perceptual, contextual, and grammatical clues. It tests their ability to note particular details, to carry information in short-term memory and to make judgments about plausible inferences. Also provides useful information about their spelling.

810561
Mathematics 9. National Foundation for Educational Research in England and Wales, London 1983
Descriptors: *Achievement Tests; Computation; Elementary Education; *Elementary School Mathematics; *Elementary School Students; Foreign Countries; Mathematical Applications; Mathematical Concepts; *Mathematics Tests; Recall (Psychology)
Identifiers: England; Great Britain
Availability: NFER-Nelson Publishing Co.; Darville House, 2 Oxford Rd. E., Windsor, Berks SL4 1DF, England
Grade Level: 3-4
Age Level: 9
Notes: Time, 50 min. approx.; Items, 50

Group-administered test designed to assess the mathematics attainment of children toward the end of the academic year when it is likely that they will have covered most of the work for the year. Items have been compiled from the NFER Mathematics Item Bank and reflect educational guidelines and content of mathematics textbooks. The test covers number, measures, shape, and pictorial representation and assesses skills in understanding of basic concepts, computational skills, application of concepts and skills, and recall of basic facts. Test is not timed but can probably be completed by students within 45 to 50 minutes.

810562
Mathematics 10. National Foundation for Educational Research in England and Wales, London 1983
Descriptors: *Achievement Tests; Computation; Elementary Education; *Elementary School Mathematics; *Elementary School Students; Foreign Countries; Mathematical Applications; Mathematical Concepts; *Mathematics Tests; Recall (Psychology)
Identifiers: England; Great Britain
Availability: NFER-Nelson Publishing Co.; Darville House, 2 Oxford Rd. E., Windsor, Berks SL4 1DF, England

Grade Level: 4-5
Age Level: 10
Notes: Time, 50 min. approx.; Items, 50

Group-administered test designed to assess the mathematics attainment of children toward the end of the academic year when it is likely that they will have covered most of the work for the year. Items have been compiled from the NFER Mathematics Item Bank and reflect educational guidelines and content of mathematics textbooks. The test covers number, measures, shape, and pictorial representation and assesses skills in understanding of basic concepts, computational skills, application of concepts and skills, and recall of basic facts. Test is not timed but can probably be completed by students within 45 to 50 minutes.

810563
Mathematics 11. National Foundation for Educational Research in England and Wales, London 1983
Descriptors: *Achievement Tests; Computation; Elementary Education; *Elementary School Mathematics; *Elementary School Students; Foreign Countries; Mathematical Applications; Mathematical Concepts; *Mathematics Tests; Recall (Psychology)
Identifiers: England; Great Britain
Availability: NFER-Nelson Publishing Co.; Darville House, 2 Oxford Rd. E., Windsor, Berks SL4 1DF, England
Grade Level: 5-6
Notes: Time, 50 min. approx.; Items, 50

Group-administered test designed to assess the mathematics attainment of children toward the end of the academic year when it is likely that they will have covered most of the work for the year. Items have been compiled from the NFER Mathematics Item Bank and reflect educational guidelines and content of mathematics textbooks. The test covers number, measures, shape, and pictorial representation and assesses skills in understanding of basic concepts, computational skills, application of concepts and skills, and recall of basic facts. Test is not timed but can probably be completed by students within 45 to 50 minutes.

810564
Mathematics 12. National Foundation for Educational Research in England and Wales, London 1983
Descriptors: *Achievement Tests; Computation; Elementary Education; *Elementary School Mathematics; *Elementary School Students; Foreign Countries; Matnematical Applications; Mathematical Concepts; *Mathematics Tests; Recall (Psychology)
Identifiers: England; Great Britain
Availability: NFER-Nelson Publishing Co.; Darville House, 2 Oxford Rd. E., Windsor, Berks SL4 1DF, England
Grade Level: 6-7
Age Level: 12
Notes: Time, 50 min. approx.; Items, 50

Group-administered test designed to assess the mathematics attainment of children toward the end of the academic year when it is likely that they will have covered most of the work for the year. Items have been compiled from the NFER Mathematics Item Bank and reflect educational guidelines and content of mathematics textbooks. The test covers number, measures, shape, and pictorial representation and assesses skills in understanding of basic concepts, computational skills, application of concepts and skills, and recall of basic facts. Test is not timed but can probably be completed by students within 45 to 50 minutes.

810581
Mathematics 8. National Foundation for Educational Research in England and Wales, London 1984
Descriptors: *Achievement Tests; Computation; *Elementary School Mathematics; *Elementary School Students; Foreign Countries; Mathematical Applications; Mathematical Concepts; *Mathematics Tests; Primary Education; Recall (Psychology)
Identifiers: England; Great Britain
Availability: NFER-Nelson Publishing Co.; Darville House, 2 Oxford Read E., Windsor, Berks SL4 1DF, England
Grade Level: 2-3
Age Level: 8
Notes: Time, 50 min. approx.; Items, 36

Group-administered test designed to assess the mathematics attainment of children toward the end of the academic year when it is likely that they will have covered most of the work for the year. Items have been compiled from the NFER Mathematics Item Bank and reflect educational guidelines and content of mathematics textbooks. The test covers number, measures, shape, and pictorial representation and assesses skills in understanding of basic concepts, computational skills, application of concepts and skills, and recall of basic facts. Test is not timed but can probably be completed by students within 45 to 50 minutes.

810588
Parallel Spelling Tests, A and B. Young, D. 1983
Descriptors: *Achievement Tests; *Elementary School Students; Elementary Secondary Education; Foreign Countries; *Item Banks; *Secondary School Students; *Spelling
Identifiers: England; Great Britain
Availability: Hodder and Stoughton Educational; Mill Rd., Dunton Green, Sevenoaks, Kent TN13 2XX, England
Grade Level: 1-12
Age Level: 6-15
Notes: Time, 20 min. approx.

Spelling words presented in 2 item banks. From each bank, parallel tests can be formed. One item bank is suitable for lower grades and the other for the upper grades. The spelling words are presented in complete sentences. One pair of sentences is selected from each group of 6 pairs to form a test of the prescribed length for each group.

810590
Edinburgh Reading Tests, Stage 3B. Moray House College of Education, Edinburgh, Scotland 1982
Subtests: Reading for Facts; Comprehension of Sequences; Retention of Main Ideas; Comprehension of Points of View; Vocabulary
Descriptors: Diagnostic Tests; *Elementary School Students; Foreign Countries; Intermediate Grades; *Reading Skills; *Reading Tests
Identifiers: England; Great Britain
Availability: Hodder and Stoughton Educational; Mill Rd., Dunton Green, Sevenoaks, Kent TN13 2XX, England
Age Level: 10-12
Notes: Time, 105 min. approx.

Assesses skills that make up reading competence for children ages 10 to 12.5. Helps ascertain general attainment and strengths and weaknesses of each child. Two parallel booklets, A and B.

810605
Tests in Life Skills. Associated Examining Board, England 1985
Descriptors: *Achievement Tests; *Adolescents; Adults; *Daily Living Skills; Foreign Countries; *Job Applicants; Personnel Selection
Identifiers: England; Great Britain
Availability: Associated Examining Board; Stag Hill House, Guildford, Surrey GU2 5XJ, England
Age Level: 16-64
Notes: Time, 90 min.

Designed to assess transferable skills that enable individuals to get the best out of further training or education and to be more successful in their early years of employment. This test has been developed to enable teachers to design their own social and life skills teaching around a core content. Topics covered on the test include life-style, money management, looking after oneself, rights and responsibilities. The test assesses individuals' knowledge and ability to apply that knowledge, understand information, and make informed decisions.

810606
Basic Test in Computer Awareness. Associated Examining Board, England 1985
Descriptors: *Achievement Tests; *Adolescents; Adults; *Computer Literacy; Foreign Countries; *Job Applicants; Personnel Selection
Identifiers: England; Great Britain
Availability: Associated Examining Board; Stag Hill House, Guildford, Surrey GU2 5XJ, England
Age Level: 16-64
Notes: Time, 90 min.

Designed to assess transferable skills which will enable individuals to get the best out of further education or training and to be more successful in the early years of employment. Some practical work with computers is necessary in order to take the test that covers the ability to demonstrate knowledge of the uses and limitations of computers, to understand current trends in information technology and its economic and social implications; to understand what computer systems are; and to understand what a simple program is and why it works.

810618
Discourse Co-Operation Test. Friel, Michael 1985
Descriptors: *Communicative Competence (Languages); Foreign Countries; Multiple Choice Tests; *Second Language Learning
Identifiers: DisCoTest; Ireland; *Oral Tests
Availability: Michael Friel; c/o Rockall, Torquay Rd., Foxrock, County Dublin, Ireland
Notes: Items, 15

Test of certain conversational skills that reconciles need for test to be scorable with an approach based more on the process of language learning than on its product.

Based on a feature of conversation, Grice's Cooperative Principle. Test is aimed at students working or studying in a foreign country and wishing to be able to converse with native speakers. Also available in the journal *Systems;* v12 n3 p251-62, 1984.

810621
Test in English for Educational Purposes. Associated Examining Board, England 1984
Descriptors: *Academic Education; *College Students; *English (Second Language); *English for Academic Purposes; Foreign Countries; Foreign Students; Higher Education; *Language Proficiency; *Language Tests; Second Languages
Identifiers: England; English Proficiency Test; Great Britain; TEEP
Availability: Associated Examining Board; Wellington House, Aldershot, Hampshire GU11 1BQ, England
Grade Level: 13-16
Age Level: 18-65

Provides a profile of proficiency in reading, listening, writing, and speaking English for individuals whose native language is other than English. The profile is intended to show receiving higher education institutions how well students might be expected to cope with the language demands made on them in an educational environment and to show those responsible for English language teaching those areas in which a student might need help. The test assesses students' ability to produce adequate written English for formal academic writing tasks, to understand spoken English for listening to lectures; to understand written English for reading textbooks and other sources of information both intensively and extensively; and to produce adequate spoken English for taking part in academic discussions and presenting papers.

810634
Mathematics 7. National Foundation for Educational Research in England and Wales, London 1987
Subtests: Number; Money; Measures; Shape; Date Representation
Descriptors: Ability Grouping; Academic Achievement; Children; Diagnostic Tests; Elementary Education; *Elementary School Mathematics; *Elementary School Students; Foreign Countries; Primary Education; *Screening Tests; Student Placement
Identifiers: England; Great Britain
Availability: NFER-NELSON Publishing Co.; Darville House, 2 Oxford Rd. E., Windsor, Berks SL4 1DF, England
Age Level: 7
Notes: Time, 40 min.; Items, 28

Designed for use in the British school system with children who are nearing the end of the school year in which they become age 7. Determines whether a child is performing at or below the appropriate level. Questions cover understanding, computation, applications, and factual recall. All of the questions are read by the teacher. Percentiles are available based on a sample of British children.

810635
Suffolk Reading Scale. Hagley, Fred 1987
Descriptors: *Achievement Tests; Adolescents; Children; *Cloze Procedure; *Elementary School Students; Foreign Countries; Individual Testing; Multiple Choice Tests; *Reading Tests; Student Placement
Identifiers: England; Great Britain
Availability: NFER-Nelson Publishing Co.; Darville House, 2 Oxford Rd. E., Windsor, Berkshire SL4 1DF, England
Age Level: 6-13
Notes: Time, 40 min.; Items, 65

This scale may be group or individually administered. Uses a multiple-choice cloze procedure to measure reading ability. Used for comparison of child's score to a national sample to determine appropriate level, monitor progress, evaluate approaches to reading instruction, and place transferring students.

810636
Pergamon (Oxford) English Tests; General Test. Pergamon Press, Oxford, England 1984
Subtests: Reading; Writing; Interview
Descriptors: *Achievement Tests; Adults; *English; *English (Second Language); Foreign Countries; Interviews; *Language Proficiency; Oral English; Reading Tests; Student Placement; Writing (Composition)
Identifiers: England; Great Britain; *Nonnative Speakers; Writing Sample
Availability: Pergamon Press, Inc.; Maxwell House, Fairview Park, Elmsford, NY 10523
Age Level: Adults
Notes: Time, 60 min.; Items, 30

Part of test system for nonnative speakers of English consisting of elementary and advanced general tests and tests to measure knowledge of specifics, such as business or science. The general tests are used for measuring learners' performance for placement purposes and to determine progress in learning the English language. The elementary level test is for beginning-to-intermediate English speakers. The reading subtest is multiple-choice. An essay section requires a letter to be written and the interview is about a topic used in the writing test. English usage and speaking are evaluated on a 9-point scale ranging from expert to non-user in the areas of general English language usage, speaking, and writing.

810644
Sentence Comprehension Test, Revised Edition. Wheldall, Kevin; And Others 1987
Subtests: Simple Intransitive; Simple Transitive; Intransitive with Adjective; Plural; Past; Future; Negative; Prepositions; Embedded Phrase; Passive
Descriptors: Foreign Countries; *Interpretive Skills; *Language Acquisition; *Language Skills; *Language Tests; *Preschool Children; *Receptive Language; *Screening Tests
Identifiers: England; Great Britain; SCT
Availability: NFER-Nelson; Darville House, 2 Oxford Rd. E., Windsor, Berkshire, SL4 1DF, England
Age Level: 3-5
Notes: Time, 15 min. approx.; Items, 40

Measures a child's ability to comprehend sentences of varying length and grammatical complexity by requiring him or her to select appropriately from sets of pictures, following the presentation of stimulus sentences. No speech is required of the child. Useful to a wide range of childcare professionals who might be interested in assessing the receptive language development in young children. Differs from the previous edition (TC810450) in the following ways: shortened from 60 to 40 items, with the range of structures assessed reduced as well; each victoral item redrawn in a more modern style, avoiding sexist assumptions and attempting to reflect contemporary multicultural society where possible.

810645
Sentence Comprehension Test, Revised Edition: Panjabi Bilingual Version. Wheldall, Kevin; And Others 1987
Subtests: Simple Intransitive; Simple Transitive; Intransitive with Adjective; Plural; Past; Future; Negative; Prepositions/Postpositions; Embedded Phrase
Descriptors: Bilingual Students; Foreign Countries; *Language Acquisition; *Language Skills; *Language Tests; *Panjabi; *Preschool Children; *Receptive Language; *Screening Tests
Identifiers: England; Great Britain; SCT
Availability: NFER-Nelson Publishing Co.; Darville House, 2 Oxford Rd. E., Windsor, Berks, England SL4 1DF
Age Level: 3-5
Notes: Time, 15 min. approx.; Items, 36

Measures a child's ability to comprehend sentences of varying length and grammatical complexity in both Panjabi and English. Requires the subject to select appropriately from sets of pictures, following the presentation of stimulus sentences. No speech is required of the child. Useful to a wide range of childcare professionals who might be interested in assessing the receptive language development in young children.

810660
Bury Infant Check. Pearson, Lea; Quinn, John 1986
Subtests: Language Skills; Learning Style; Memory Skills; Number Skills; Perceptual Motor Skills
Descriptors: Cognitive Style; Foreign Countries; *Individual Needs; *Individual Testing; Language Skills; Memory; Numbers; Perceptual Motor Learning; *Preschool Children; Preschool Education; *Screening Tests
Identifiers: England; Great Britain
Availability: NFER-Nelson Publishing Co.; Darville House, 2 Oxford Rd. E., Windsor, Berks, England SL4 1DF
Age Level: 4-5
Notes: Items, 60

Screening device designed to identify children with problems during the first months of school. Individually administered with no time limits. A Quick Check comprising 13 teacher-rated items can be done for the whole class. The Full Check can then be administered to those children who score below the suggested intervention point.

810662
Practical/Oral Test. Vincent, Peter 1987
Descriptors: Foreign Countries; *Mathematical Concepts; Mathematical Vocabulary; Secondary Education; *Secondary School Mathematics; *Secondary School Students; *Verbal Tests
Identifiers: England; Great Britain
Availability: *Mathematics in School;* v16 n1 p14-16, Jan 1987
Grade Level: 7-12

Designed to assess students' abilities to carry out practical tasks and to express themselves verbally about carrying out those tasks, as well as about other areas involving mathematics. In the practical tasks section, students are presented with 3 containers of the same height but varying circumferences. They are asked to carry out tasks and to respond to questions pertaining to pouring liquid into the containers. In the second section, students are presented with a pair of solids, one person and one pyramid, and are asked to respond to questions about their properties. Examiners note responses on a response sheet, in most cases noting whether response was inadequate, adequate or fluent.

810663
English Language Skills Profile. University of Edinburgh, Scotland, Godfrey Thomson Unit Hutchinson, Carolyn; And Others 1987
Subtests: Study Skills; Reading; Listening; Oral Communication; Writing
Descriptors: Adolescents; *English; *Expressive Language; Foreign Countries; *Formative Evaluation; High Schools; *High School Students; *Language Tests; Listening Skills; Reading Ability; *Receptive Language; Speech Communication; Study Skills; Writing Skills
Identifiers: England; Great Britain; TELS
Availability: Macmillan Education; Houndmills, Basingstoke, Hampshire, RG21 2XS, England
Age Level: 14-16

Formative assessment package designed to develop and to measure students' competence in language. Uses a total language approach in which the emphasis is on assessing and developing receptive and expressive skills. TELS Profile consists of a number of integrative tests of communicative competence. Each subtest is designed as an activity that can be adapted for teaching, as well as assessment purposes. The receptive skills areas covered include study skills, reading, and listening. The expressive, or productive, skills areas include oral communication and writing.

810664
Effective Reading Tests. Vincent, Denis; de la Mare, Michael 1986
Descriptors: *Achievement Tests; Elementary Education; *Elementary School Students; Foreign Countries; *Reading Achievement; *Reading Diagnosis
Identifiers: England; ERT; Great Britain
Availability: Macmillan Education; Houndmills, Basingstoke, Hampshire, RG21 2XS, England
Grade Level: 2-6

This series of group reading tests covers the British grade ranges from junior to first year secondary (ages 7-12.8) school. Children read one of 4 brief readers containing one story and then answer questions related to the story content. Questions are multiple-choice and cover word meaning, or the meaning of sentences or larger units of text. Tests are divided into 2 parts; one contains easier items for children of lower ability. Another series of skills tests is used to check student's reading ability for curriculum planning.

810665
Macmillan Graded Word Reading Test. Macmillan Education, England 1985
Descriptors: *Achievement Tests; Adolescents; Age; Children; Elementary Education; *Elementary School Students; Foreign Countries; Individual Testing; *Informal Reading Inventories; *Reading Achievement; Sight Vocabulary; *Word Lists
Identifiers: England; Great Britain
Availability: Macmillan Education; Houndmills, Basingstoke, Hampshire, RG21 2XS, England
Age Level: 6-14
Notes: Time, 10 min.; Items, 50

This type of reading test is designed for use by teachers as a quick method of confirming their own judgments of a child's reading ability. Two parallel forms are available. It is not suitable for use in the U.S. because it contains words not found in typical U.S. vocabulary tests. Words are scored as sight vocabulary, requiring analysis, omitted, or incorrect. Scores are converted to age levels.

810666
Macmillan Group Reading Test. Macmillan Education, England 1985
Descriptors: *Achievement Tests; Adolescents; Children; *Cloze Procedure; Elementary Education; *Elementary School Students; Foreign Countries; Group Testing; Pretests Posttests; *Reading Achievement; Screening Tests
Identifiers: England; Great Britain
Availability: Macmillan Education; Houndmills, Basingstoke, Hampshire, RG21 2XS, England
Age Level: 6-13
Notes: Time, 30 min.; Items, 48

This multiple-choice cloze test measures reading achievement. Raw scores can be converted to a reading age level. Two parallel forms are available so it may be used as a pre- and posttest to monitor individual student progress. Also used for screening students with special needs.

810667
Staffordshire Mathematics Test. Barcham, Clive W.; And Others 1986
Subtests: Addition; Subtraction; Sets: Place Value; Multiplication; Division; Fractions; Time; Area; Length; Angles; Pictorial Representation; Sequences; Shape; Matching; Money
Descriptors: Arithmetic; Children; *Elementary School Mathematics; *Elementary School Students; Foreign Countries; Geometry; Primary Education; *Screening Tests; Time
Identifiers: England; Great Britain
Availability: Macmillan Education; Houndmills, Basingstoke, Hampshire, RG21 2XS, England
Age Level: 6-8
Notes: Items, 64

This standardized screening test was designed to identify children working below the level of their peers so that their difficulties can be remediated.

810672
Sandwell Bilingual Screening Assessment; Scales for Expressive Panjabi and English. Duncan, Deirdre M.; And Others 1988
Descriptors: *Bilingualism; *Bilingual Students; Elementary Education; *Elementary School Students; *English (Second Language); *Expressive Language; Foreign Countries; Language Handicaps; *Language Tests; *Panjabi; *Screening Tests
Identifiers: England; Great Britain
Availability: NFER-Nelson Publishing; Darville House, 2 Oxford Rd. E., Windsor, Berks, England SL4 1DF
Age Level: 6-9
Notes: Items, 114

Expressive language assessment for children ages 6 to 9 to yield grammatical profiles in Panjabi and English. Screening assessment in both languages provides checklists of grammatical language features to use in the diagnosis of bilingual children's language difficulties. Pupils' scores can be compared with norms tables to see whether there are language problems.

810692
Neale Analysis of Reading Ability, Revised British Edition. Neale, Marie D. 1989
Subtests: Rate; Accuracy; Comprehension;
Descriptors: *Diagnostic Tests; Elementary Education; *Elementary School Students; Foreign Countries; *Individual Testing; *Oral Reading; *Reading Ability; *Reading Comprehension; *Reading Diagnosis; Reading Difficulties; *Reading Rate; *Reading Tests
Identifiers: England; Great Britain
Availability: Nfer-Nelson; Darville House, 2 Oxford Rd. E., Windsor, Berks SL4 1DF, England
Age Level: 6-12
Notes: Time, 20 min. approx.; Items, 100

Individually administered test that measures oral reading ability, based on short narratives. It provides measures of reading accuracy, comprehension, and rate and detailed diagnostic information about children's reading difficulties. This instrument is designed to set up a dialogue between teacher and student to explore ways of facilitating acquisition of literacy in its broadest sense. Students beyond the age of 12 years and some adults can be tested on appropriate passages to obtain a general level of reading ability and for diagnostic purposes. Data are available on standardized scores, validity, norms, and reliability.

810696
Touchstones: Cross-Curricular Group Assessments. Jones, Gillian; And Others 1989
Subtests: English; Mathematics; Science; Design and Technology
Descriptors: *Achievement Tests; Content Area Reading; *Elementary School Students; English; Foreign Countries; Mathematics; Primary Education; Sciences
Identifiers: Cross Cultural Assessment; England; Great Britain
Availability: Nfer-Nelson; Darville House, 2 Oxford Rd. E., Windsor, Berks, SL4 1DF, England
Age Level: 6-8

This test is in response to the National Curriculum established in 1988 in Great Britain. It consists of a series of test items given as part of an activity booklet that assesses knowledge across curriculum areas. An activity booklet may be based on a story about a trip. The story may involve the child in map reading, reasoning, arithmetic, verbal responses made to questions, and a science experiment.

810705
Maths Microprobe. Hagues, Neil 1989
Descriptors: *Addition; *Arithmetic; *Computer Assisted Testing; *Diagnostic Tests; Elementary Education; *Elementary School Students; Foreign Countries; Mathematics; *Subtraction
Identifiers: England; Great Britain
Availability: NFER-Nelson Publishing Co.; Darville House, 2 Oxford Rd. E., Windsor, Berks SL4 1DF, England
Grade Level: 4-8

This computer-administered diagnostic test of addition and subtraction is designed to identify areas in which students need instruction. Can diagnose wrong responses made by the child in any of 32 different ways. Problems use 3-figure computation. For use by classroom teachers, educational psychologists, and other professionals. Used with a BBC Micro 40 Track computer.

810712
Living Language: A Picture Resource. Locke, Ann
Descriptors: Check Lists; *Elementary School Students; English (Second Language); Foreign Countries; *Informal Assessment; *Language Processing; *Language Skills; Primary Education; Visual Measures
Identifiers: England; Great Britain; LL
Availability: Nfer-Nelson Publishing Co., Ltd.; Darville House, 2 Oxford Rd. E., Windsor, Berks SL4 1DF, England
Grade Level: K-3
Notes: Items, 300

Designed to monitor children's ongoing language learning. This program includes a checking system that shows whether particular words or grammatical constructions have been learned and retained. It shows whether a child's general rate of learning is accelerating, remaining static, or slowing down and provides a means of evaluating their ongoing learning. A separate list of terms is included to help teachers select the appropriate pictures for checking target words. This resource tool can be used by speech therapists, teachers working in language units, special education teachers, and teachers who work with children learning English as a Second Language.

810716
Practical Math Assessments. Foxman, Derek; And Others 1990
Descriptors: *Diagnostic Tests; Elementary Education; *Elementary School Students; Foreign Countries; *Mathematical Applications; Mathematical Concepts; Mathematics Skills; *Mathematics Tests
Identifiers: England; Great Britain
Availability: NFER-Nelson Publishing Co.; Darville House, 2 Oxford Rd. E., Windsor, Berkshire SL4 1DF, England
Age Level: 9-12

This assessment tool is a series of 3 tests. It is intended primarily to diagnose students' needs with respect to the concepts and skills that support the achievement of the next level of attainment in the tests. It also measures the ways in which inexpensive equipment, such as counters, dice, and calculators, can be used to illuminate various areas of mathematical thinking and measurement. These tests are not timed and can be administered to a small group or to an entire class. Test A is orally administered for the youngest students.

830382
Gates-MacGinitie Reading Tests, Basic R, Forms 1 and 2. Canadian Edition. MacGinitie, Walter H. 1979
Subtests: Letter Sounds; Vocabulary; Letter Recognition; Comprehension
Descriptors: *Achievement Tests; Elementary School Students; Foreign Countries; *Grade 1; Letters (Alphabet); Primary Education; Reading Comprehension; *Reading Tests; Vocabulary
Identifiers: Canada
Availability: Nelson Canada Ltd.; 1120 Birchmount Rd., Scarborough, Ontario M1K 5G4, Canada
Grade Level: 1
Notes: Time, 60 min. approx.; Items, 61

Test is a measure of general level of reading achievement and can also be used to identify particular reading skills that individual children or groups need to learn. Tests can aid in determining appropriate instructional levels of individual students, in identifying those with need for added or special instruction, in making decisions about instructional groupings, in counseling and in reporting to parents.

830385
Canadian Tests of Basic Skills, Primary Battery, Levels 5-8, Form 5. Hieronymus, A.N.; And Others 1981
Subtests: Listening; Vocabulary; Word Analysis; Words; Pictures; Sentences; Word Attack; Picture Stories; Stories; Spelling; Capitalization; Punctuation; Usage; Visual Materials; Reference Materials; Mathematics Concepts; Mathematics Problems, Computation
Descriptors: *Achievement Tests; *Basic Skills; *Elementary School Students; Foreign Countries; *Language Arts; Library Skills; *Mathematics Achievement; *Primary Education; School Readiness; Study Skills
Identifiers: Canada; CTBS; Power Tests; Test Batteries
Availability: Nelson Canada, Ltd.; 1120 Birchmount Rd., Scarborough, Ontario M1K 5G4, Canada
Grade Level: K-3

Primary battery is the beginning of a series of tests providing for continuous measurement of achievement from kindergarten through high school. Measures growth in fundamental skills necessary for learning activities. In levels 5 and 6, emphasis is on reading skills. The number of subtests for levels 5-8 varies from 5 to 13, depending on level being used. Test battery is given in 5 sessions and takes from 115 to 235 minutes, depending on level being administered. Four levels in primary battery allow choice of test appropriate for students' developmental levels. Tests were normed concurrently with Canadian Cognitive Abilities Tests. Tests assess following skills: listening, word analysis, vocabulary, reading, oral language, written language, work study skills; mathematics.

830386
Canadian Tests of Basic Skills, Multilevel Edition, Levels 9-14, Forms 5 and 6. Hieronymus, A.N.; And Others 1981
Subtests: Vocabulary; Reading; Spelling; Capitalization; Punctuation; Usage; Visual Materials; Reference Materials; Mathematics Concepts; Mathematics Problems; Mathematics Computation
Descriptors: *Achievement Tests; *Basic Skills; Capitalization (Alphabetic); Elementary Education; *Elementary School Students; Foreign Countries; Grammar; *Junior High School Students; *Language Arts; Mathematical Concepts; *Mathematics Achievement; Punctuation; Reading Achievement; Spelling; Study Skills; Vocabulary
Identifiers: Canada; CTBS; Test Batteries
Availability: Nelson Canada, Ltd.; 1120 Birchmount Rd., Scarborough, Ontario M1K 5G4, Canada
Grade Level: 3-8
Notes: Time, 244 min.

Part of a series providing for comprehensive and continuous assessment in the fundamental skills of vocabulary, reading, mechanics of writing, study skills, and mathematics. Each of the 11 subtests is organized into 6 overlapping levels of skill development. Students take items appropriate in content and difficulty level for their level of skill development. Number of items in battery range from 350 to 465, depending on level of the battery being used.

830387
Canadian Tests of Basic Skills, High School, Multilevel Edition, Levels 15-18, Form 5. Scannell, Dale P.; And Others 1981
Subtests: Reading Comprehension; Mathematics; Written Expression; Using Sources of Information; Applied Proficiency Skills
Descriptors: *Achievement Tests; *Basic Skills; Foreign Countries; High Schools; *High School Students; Information Sources; Library Skills; Mathematics Achievement; Reading Comprehension; Secondary School Mathematics; Writing Skills
Identifiers: Canada; CTBS; Test Batteries
Availability: Nelson Canada, Ltd.; 1120 Birchmount Rd., Scarborough, Ontario M1K 5G4, Canada
Grade Level: 9-12
Notes: Time, 160 min.

Part of a series providing for comprehensive and continuous assessment of student progress in widely accepted secondary school goals in basic skills and basic curricular areas. Tests emphasize skills and ability to use information rather than being content specific. In addition to the 4 subtest scores, there is an applied proficiency skills score, based on test items which reflect types of out-of-school tasks necessary for functioning in society. Score on these items reflects how effectively students can apply practical skills in reading, mathematics, written expression, and finding and interpreting information.

830388
Gates-MacGinitie Reading Tests, Canadian Edition, Level A. MacGinitie, Walter H. 1979
Subtests: Vocabulary; Comprehension
Descriptors: *Achievement Tests; Decoding (Reading); *Elementary School Students; Foreign Countries; *Grade 1; Pictorial Stimuli; Pretests Posttests; Primary Education; *Reading Achievement; *Reading Comprehension; *Reading Tests; Timed Tests; *Vocabulary
Identifiers: Canada
Availability: Nelson Canada; 1120 Birchmount Rd., Scarborough, Ontario M1K 5G4, Canada
Grade Level: 1
Notes: Time, 55 min.; Items, 85

Designed to measure reading achievement in the areas of vocabulary and comprehension of students in grade 1.5-1.9. May also be used in early grade 2 for students of average or below average ability. Parallel forms 1 and 2 are available for pretesting and posttesting.

830389
Gates-MacGinitie Reading Tests, Canadian Edition, Level B. MacGinitie, Walter H. 1979
Subtests: Vocabulary; Comprehension
Descriptors: *Achievement Tests; Decoding (Reading); *Elementary School Students; Foreign Countries; *Grade 2; Pictorial Stimuli; Pretests Posttests; Primary Education; *Reading Achievement; *Reading Comprehension; *Reading Tests; Timed Tests; *Vocabulary
Identifiers: Canada
Availability: Nelson Canada; 1120 Birchmount Rd., Scarborough, Ontario M1K 5G4, Canada
Grade Level: 2
Notes: Time, 55 min.; Items, 85

Designed to measure reading comprehension and vocabulary of students in grade 2 and early grade 3. Parallel forms 1 and 2 are available for pretesting and posttesting.

830390
Gates-MacGinitie Reading Tests, Canadian Edition, Level C. MacGinitie, Walter H. 1979
Subtests: Vocabulary; Comprehension
Descriptors: *Achievement Tests; *Elementary School Students; Foreign Countries; *Grade 3; Pretests Posttests; Primary Education; *Reading Achievement; *Reading Comprehension; *Reading Tests; Timed Tests; *Vocabulary
Identifiers: Canada
Availability: Nelson Canada; 1120 Birchmount Rd., Scarborough, Ontario M1K 5G4, Canada
Grade Level: 3
Notes: Time, 55 min.; Items, 89

Designed to measure reading comprehension and vocabulary skills for students in grade 3 and early grade 4. Parallel forms 1 and 2 are available for pretesting and posttesting.

830391
Gates-MacGinitie Reading Tests, Canadian Edition, Level D. MacGinitie, Walter H. 1979
Subtests: Vocabulary; Comprehension
Descriptors: *Achievement Tests; *Elementary School Students; Foreign Countries; Intermediate Grades; Pretests Posttests; *Reading Achievement; *Reading Comprehension; *Reading Tests; Timed Tests; *Vocabulary
Identifiers: Canada
Availability: Nelson Canada; 1120 Birchmount Rd., Scarborough, Ontario M1K 5G4, Canada
Grade Level: 4-6
Notes: Time, 55 min.; Items, 88

Designed to assess reading comprehension and vocabulary skills for students in grades 4-6. Parallel forms 1 and 2 are available for pretesting and posttesting.

830392
Gates-MacGinitie Reading Tests, Canadian Edition, Level E. MacGinitie, Walter H. 1979
Subtests: Vocabulary; Comprehension
Descriptors: *Achievement Tests; Foreign Countries; Junior High Schools; *Junior High School Students; Pretests Posttests; *Reading Achievement; *Reading Comprehension; *Reading Tests; Timed Tests; *Vocabulary
Identifiers: Canada
Availability: Nelson Canada; 1120 Birchmount Rd., Scarborough, Ontario M1K 5G4, Canada
Grade Level: 7-9
Notes: Time, 55 min.; Items, 88

Designed to assess reading comprehension and vocabulary skills of students in grades 7-9. Parallel forms 1 and 2 are available for pretesting and posttesting.

830393
Gates-MacGinitie Reading Tests, Canadian Edition, Level F. MacGinitie, Walter H. 1979
Subtests: Vocabulary; Comprehension
Descriptors: *Achievement Tests; Foreign Countries; High Schools; *High School Students; Pretests Posttests; *Reading Achievement; *Reading Comprehension; *Reading Tests; Timed Tests; *Vocabulary
Identifiers: Canada
Availability: Nelson Canada; 1120 Birchmount Rd., Scarborough, Ontario M1K 5G4, Canada
Grade Level: 10-12
Notes: Time, 55 min.; Items, 88

Designed to assess reading comprehension and vocabulary skills in students in grades 10-12. Parallel forms 1 and 2 are available for pretesting and posttesting.

830438
Test de Comprehension de L'Ecrit, Revised, Levels A and B. Ontario Institute for Studies in Education, Canada, Modern Language Centre 1979
Descriptors: *Achievement Tests; *Elementary School Students; Elementary Secondary Education; Foreign Countries; *French; *Functional Reading; *Immersion Programs; Language Proficiency; *Secondary School Students; *Second Language Programs
Identifiers: Canada
Availability: Ontario Institute for Studies in Education; Modern Language Centre, 252 Bloor St. W., Toronto, Ontario, Canada M5S 1V6
Grade Level: 5-11

These tests were developed by the Bilingual Education Project for the evaluation of a French immersion program at the upper elementary and secondary school levels. Includes a measure of reading comprehension using articles from newspapers, advertisements, and other materials.

830440
Test de Mots a Trouver, Levels C and D. Ontario Institute for Studies in Education, Canada, Modern Language Centre 1978
Descriptors: *Cloze Procedure; *Elementary School Students; Elementary Secondary Education; Foreign Countries; *French; *Immersion Programs; *Secondary School Students; *Second Language Learning
Identifiers: Canada
Availability: Ontario Institute for Studies in Education; Modern Language Centre, 252 Bloor St. W., Toronto, Ontario, Canada M5S 1V6
Grade Level: 5-11
Notes: Items, 49

This cloze procedure is designed to provide a measure of second-language proficiency for students in immersion programs in the French language. The test consists of a prose passage from which every seventh word has been removed. Two forms are available.

830441
Test de Comprehension en Lecture pour Classes d'Immersion Precoce, Sixieme Annee. Forget, Solange 1981
Descriptors: *Achievement Tests; Elementary School Students; Foreign Countries; *French; *Grade 6; *Immersion Programs; Intermediate Grades; *Listening Comprehension; *Second Language Learning
Identifiers: Canada
Availability: Centre Franco-Ontarien de Ressources Pedagogiques; 339 Rue Wilbrod, Ottawa, Ontario K1N 6M4, Canada
Grade Level: 6
Notes: Items, 70

This series of readings in French is designed to measure the auditory comprehension of the language. The respondent listens to each reading and answers questions about the reading. Used in classes of advanced students who are taking part in an immersion program. No technical information is included. Uses a multiple-choice format with 4 response choices.

830442
Test de Comprehension en Lecture pour Classes d'Immersion Precoce, Cinquieme Annee. Forget, Solange 1981
Descriptors: *Achievement Tests; Elementary School Students; Foreign Countries; *French; *Grade 5; *Immersion Programs; Intermediate Grades; *Listening Comprehension; *Second Language Learning
Identifiers: Canada
Availability: Centre Franco-Ontarien de Ressources Pedagogiques; 339 Rue Wilbrod, Ottawa, Ontario K1N 6M4, Canada
Grade Level: 5

This series of readings in French is designed to measure the auditory comprehension of the language. The student listens to each reading and answers questions about the reading. Used in classes of advanced students who are taking part in an immersion program. No technical information is included. Uses a multiple-choice format with 4 response choices.

830443
Test de Comprehension en Lecture pour Classes d'Immersion Precoce, Quatrieme Annee. Forget, Solange 1981
Descriptors: *Achievement Tests; Elementary School Students; Foreign Countries; *French; *Grade 4; *Immersion Programs; Intermediate Grades; *Listening Comprehension; *Second Language Learning
Identifiers: Canada
Availability: Centre Franco-Ontarien de Ressources Pedagogiques; 339 Rue Wilbrod, Ottawa, Ontario K1N 6M4, Canada
Grade Level: 4

Notes: Items, 40

This series of readings in French is designed to measure the auditory comprehension of the language. The student listens to each reading and answers questions about the reading. Used in classes of advanced students who are taking part in an immersion program. No technical information is included. Uses a multiple-choice format with 4 response choices.

830447
Tests de Francais, Measure Normative de 6e, 9e et 12e Annees. New Brunswick Dept. of Education, Canada 1984
Descriptors: *Achievement Tests; Foreign Countries; *French; *Grade 6; *Grade 9; *Grade 12; Intermediate Grades; Secondary Education; Standardized Tests
Identifiers: Canada; New Brunswick
Availability: New Brunswick Dept. of Education; P.O. Box 6000, Fredericton, New Brunswick, Canada E3B 5H1
Grade Level: 6; 9; 12

Three standardized tests to measure student achievement in French at grades 6, 9, and 12. Grade 6 test has 50 items and takes 60 minutes to complete. Grade 9 test has 60 questions and takes up to 60 minutes. Grade 12 test consists of 55 questions and takes 50 minutes to complete. Tests are administered every 3 years and are developed provincially.

830448
Printing Performance School Readiness Test. Simner, Marvin L. 1985
Descriptors: High Risk Students; *Individual Testing; *Kindergarten Children; *Manuscript Writing (Handlettering); *Preschool Children; *School Readiness Tests; Screening Tests
Identifiers: Canada; PPSRT
Availability: Phylmar Associates; 191 Iroquois Ave., London, Ontario, Canada N6C 2K9
Age Level: 4-5
Notes: Time, 15 min. approx.; Items, 41

Designed to identify those preschool children who exhibit an excessive number of form errors when they begin to print. Based on research by the author, which shows that an excessive number of form errors in a child's printing can be important warning sign of later school failure. Individually administered test in which child is required to print a series of letters and numbers from pictures presented one at a time on cards in a spiral binder. Child's reproductions are scored for presence of form errors.

830449
Social Studies Assessment Program, Grade 9. Manitoba Department of Education, Winnipeg, Canada 1984
Descriptors: Achievement Tests; Attitude Measures; *Curriculum Evaluation; Elementary Secondary Education; Foreign Countries; *Grade 9; Knowledge Level; Research Skills; *Social Studies
Identifiers: Canada
Availability: ERIC Document Reproduction Service; 7420 Fullerton Rd., Ste. 110, Springfield, VA 22153-2852 (ED257866, 60 p.)
Grade Level: 9
Notes: Time, 75 min.; Items, 123

This program was used in the province of Manitoba, Canada, to develop a profile of student performance as part of a provincewide assessment of social studies concepts, skills, and attitudes in grades 3, 6, 9 and 12. This ninth grade version covers knowledge, values and attitudes, thinking and research skills, and social participation. Some items require a written response. Most are multiple-choice. This test has primarily Canadian content.

830450
Social Studies Assessment Program, Grade 6. Manitoba Department of Education, Winnipeg, Canada 1984
Descriptors: Achievement Tests; Attitude Measures; *Curriculum Evaluation; Elementary Secondary Education; Foreign Countries; *Grade 6; Knowledge Level; Research Skills; *Social Studies
Identifiers: Canada
Availability: ERIC Document Reproduction Service; 7420 Fullerton Rd., Ste. 110, Springfield, VA 22153-2852 (ED257865, 75 p.)
Grade Level: 6
Notes: Time, 100 min.; Items, 182

This program was used in the province of Manitoba, Canada, to develop a profile of student performance as part of a provincewide assessment of social studies concepts, skills, and attitudes in grades 3, 6, 9 and 12. This sixth grade version covers knowledge, values and attitudes, thinking and research skills, and social participation. Some items require a written response; most are multiple-choice. This test has primarily Canadian content.

830451
Social Studies Assessment Program, Grade 3.
Manitoba Department of Education, Winnipeg, Canada 1984
Subtests: Community Situation; Community History; Meeting Needs and Wants; Cooperation and Conflict; General Information; Comparing One Community to Another; Map and Graph Skills
Descriptors: Achievement Tests; Attitude Measures; *Curriculum Evaluation; Elementary Secondary Education; Foreign Countries; *Grade 3; Knowledge Level; Research Skills; *Social Studies
Identifiers: Canada
Availability: ERIC Document Reproduction Service; 7420 Fullerton Rd., Ste. 110, Springfield, VA 22153-2852 (ED257864, 49 p.)
Grade Level: 3
Notes: Time, 70 min.; Items, 90
This program was used in the province of Manitoba, Canada, to develop a profile of student performance as part of a provincewide assessment of social studies concepts, skills, and attitudes in grades 3, 6, 9 and 12. This third grade version covers knowledge, values, attitudes, thinking and research skills, and social participation. This test has primarily Canadian content.

830452
Social Studies Assessment Program, Year 12.
Manitoba Department of Education, Winnipeg, Canada 1984
Descriptors: Achievement Tests; Attitude Measures; *Curriculum Evaluation; Elementary Secondary Education; Foreign Countries; *Grade 12; Knowledge Level; Research Skills; *Social Studies
Identifiers: Canada
Availability: ERIC Document Reproduction Service; 7420 Fullerton Rd., Ste. 110, Springfield, VA 22153-2852 (ED257867, 62 p.)
Grade Level: 12
Notes: Items, 188
This program was used in the province of Manitoba, Canada, to develop a profile of student performance as part of a provincewide assessment of social studies concepts, and attitudes in grades 3, 6, 9 and 12. This grade 12 version covers knowledge, values and attitudes, thinking and research skills, and social participation. Much of the test has Canadian content.

830454
Teacher's School Readiness Inventory, Revised Edition. Simner, Marvin L. 1987
Descriptors: *Classroom Observation Techniques; Foreign Countries; High Risk Students; *Learning Problems; Norm Referenced Tests; *Preschool Children; Preschool Education; *School Readiness; *Screening Tests
Identifiers: Canada; TSRI
Availability: Phylmar Associates; 191 Iroquois Ave., London, Ontario, Canada N6C 2K9
Age Level: 4-6
Notes: Time, 3 min. approx.; Items, 5
A quick screening test to use with preschool children as the first stage in a 2-stage early program to identify children with potential learning problems. Requires no formal testing and allows the teacher to rate each child on 5 key items using everyday observations. The author recommends that the test should not be the sole means of identifying at-risk children. Those who are identified as having potential learning problems can be referred for assistance. Cutoff points were set at values that allowed correct identification of approximately 85 percent of the children in the sample study.

830455
Grade 6 Social Studies Achievement Test. Alberta Department of Education, Edmonton, Canada 1985
Descriptors: *Achievement Tests; Cognitive Processes; Elementary Education; Essays; Essay Tests; Foreign Countries; *Grade 6; Intermediate Grades; *Social Studies; Testing Programs
Identifiers: Alberta (Calgary); Canada
Availability: ERIC Document Reproduction Service; 7420 Fullerton Rd., Ste. 110, Springfield, VA 22153-2852 (ED267074, 32 p. and ED 267075, 11 pages)
Grade Level: 6
Notes: Time, 50 min.; Items, 50
This test is composed of 2 separate sections. One contains a series of multiple-choice items requiring reasoning and thinking skills in the context of the following social studies topics: early civilizations, Southeast Asia, application of government regulations. The second section requires a written essay and response to open-ended questions about senior citizens in the environment.

830456
Grade 12 Diploma Examination, Social Studies 30. Alberta Department of Education, Edmonton, Canada 1985
Descriptors: *Achievement Tests; Foreign Countries; *Grade 12; *Graduation Requirements; High Schools; *High School Seniors; Political Science; *Social Studies; State Programs; Testing Programs
Identifiers: Alberta (Calgary); Canada
Availability: ERIC Document Reproduction Service; 7420 Fullerton Rd., Ste. 110, Springfield, VA 22153-2852 (ED267073, 35 p. and ED26702, 34 pages)
Grade Level: 12
Notes: Time, 70 min. approx.; Items, 150
This examination is used as a twelfth grade diploma requirement in Alberta, Canada. There are multiple-choice questions and an essay section. Two forms are available. Most items cover political science issues from a Canadian perspective. Some deal with U.S. issues.

830463
Mount Saint Vincent University's English Writing Competency Test. 1986
Descriptors: Adults; *College Students; *Essay Tests; Foreign Countries; Higher Education; *Writing Evaluation
Identifiers: Canada
Availability: English Quarterly; v19 n4 p267-81, Win 1986
Grade Level: 13-16
Notes: Time, 90 min.; Items, 1
Assesses the writing ability of college students. Students are given the option of writing an essay of 300 to 500 words on one of 2 predetermined topics. Instructions to the students include the reason, purpose, audience, and subject of the essay. Instructions also provide a summary of the qualities of a good paper, which students may use as a guideline. Validity studies were made by comparing scores on the test to grades in a first-year composition course and to students' single semester grade point averages. Reliability was measured by having pairs of graders read and grade each paper and comparing the scores.

830479
Printing Performance School Readiness Test—Abbreviated Version. Simner, Marvin L. 1989
Descriptors: Diagnostic Tests; Individual Testing; *Manuscript Writing (Handlettering); *Preschool Children; Preschool Education; *Preschool Tests; *School Readiness Tests; Screening Tests
Identifiers: APPSRT
Availability: Journal of School Psychology; v27 p189-95, 1989
Age Level: 2-5
Notes: Time, 3 min. approx.; Items, 18
A shorter version of the Printing Performance School Readiness Test (TC830448) for use with prekindergarten children. Instrument was designed to evaluate errors of forms in children's printing. Children are presented with a response sheet of preprinted letters and numbers and are asked to copy those letters and numbers in blank boxes below each one. Excessive errors in form have been shown to predict school failure. May be used to help make decisions as to whether children may require special academic assistance before entering school.

865017
Proof-Reading Test of Spelling. Croft, Cedric; And Others 1981
Descriptors: *Proofreading; *Achievement Tests; Diagnostic Tests; Elementary Education; Elementary School Students; *Spelling; Student Placement
Identifiers: New Zealand; PRETOS
Availability: Australian Council for Educational Research; P.O. Box 210, Hawthorn, Victoria, Australia 3122
Age Level: 8-13
Notes: Items, 48
Measures a child's ability to distinguish between correctly and incorrectly spelled words within paragraphs. Mistakes are also corrected and passages with no errors are identified. Scores can indicate instructional groups and need for remedial work as well as achievement. Test is in 5 levels. Lowest level test contains only 36 items.

865027
Progressive Achievement Tests of Reading (Revised). Reid, Neil A.; Elley, Warwick B. 1991
Subtests: Reading Comprehension; Vocabulary
Descriptors: *Achievement Tests; Elementary Education; *Elementary School Students; Foreign Countries; *Reading Comprehension; *Reading Tests; *Standardized Tests; *Vocabulary
Identifiers: New Zealand; PAT
Availability: New Zealand Council for Educational Research; P.O. Box 3237, Wellington, New Zealand
Age Level: 8-14
Notes: Time, 95 min.; Items, 232
Standardized tests developed for use in New Zealand schools. Assists classroom teachers in determining student attainment in reading comprehension and use of vocabulary. Three test booklets cover all the class levels. Primary for Standards 2, 3, and 4, Intermediate for Forms 1 and 2, Secondary for Forms 3 and 4. There are 2 equivalent forms, A and B, for each level. Technical information and norms are provided.

870060
Mathematics Topics Pre-Test: Percentages, Integers. New Zealand Council for Educational Research, Wellington 1990
Descriptors: Foreign Countries; *High School Students; *Integers; *Junior High School Students; *Mathematics Tests; *Percentage; Pretests Posttests; Prior Learning; *Screening Tests; Secondary Education
Identifiers: New Zealand
Availability: New Zealand Council for Educational Research; Education House, 178-182 Willis St., Box 3237, Wellington, New Zealand
Grade Level: 7-12
Notes: Time, 35 min. approx.; Items, 60
These pretests are designed as screening devices to help teachers find the gaps in their students' prior knowledge of percentages and integers. Once common deficiencies are identified, teachers should be better able to provide a program suited to individual needs. Posttests, ordered by objectives, are provided and should be given when all students have either been taught the pretest percentages and integers material or have remediated their difficulties by completing worksheet exercises.

SUBJECT INDEX

Basketball

Beginning Reading

Behavior Development

Behavior Modification

Behavior Patterns

Behavioral Objectives

Biblical Literature

Bicycling

Bilingual Education

Bilingual Education Programs

Bilingual Students

Bilingual Teachers

Bilingualism

Biochemistry

Biographical Inventories

Biological Sciences

Dictation

Diesel Engines

Dietetics

Difficulty Level

Dining Facilities

Disabilities

Disadvantaged

Disadvantaged Youth

Disarmament

Discussion

Distributive Education

Doctoral Programs

Elementary School Teachers

Elementary Secondary Education

Emotional Development

Employees

Employment Potential

Energy

Energy Conservation

Energy Sources

Engineering

Engineering Drawing

Engineering Education

Engineering Technology

Engines

English

English (British)

English for Academic Purposes

English Instruction

English Literature

English (Second Language)

English Usage

Entrance Examinations

Entry Workers

Environmental Education

Environmental Language Intervention Program

Equipment

Equipment Maintenance

Equivalency Tests

DANTES Subject Standardized Tests: Personnel/Human Resource Management 14937
DANTES Subject Standardized Tests: Principles of Electronic Communication Systems 13321
DANTES Subject Standardized Tests: Principles of Financial Accounting 13294
DANTES Subject Standardized Tests: Risk and Insurance 13298
DANTES Subject Standardized Tests: Technical Writing 14934
DANTES Subject Standardized Tests: Television Theory and Circuitry 13323
DANTES: War and Peace in the Nuclear Age 16752
Diagnostic Pre-Tests for GED Instruction 16975
Evaluative Post-Tests for GED Readiness 16976
Michigan Prescriptive Program: Mathematics 15565
Official GED Practice Test, Form A 11735
Regents College Examination 11676
Regents College Examination 11677
Taxonomy of Selected High School Equivalency Materials. Reading Science Materials, Supplementary Inventory 11355
A Taxonomy of Selected High School Equivalency Materials. Reading Social Studies Materials, Supplementary Inventory 11354
Teacher Occupational Competency Testing 14169
Teacher Occupational Competency Testing: Air Conditioning and Refrigeration 14180
Teacher Occupational Competency Testing: Airframe and Power Plant 14181
Teacher Occupational Competency Testing: Architectural Drafting 14182
Teacher Occupational Competency Testing: Audio-Visual Communications 14183
Teacher Occupational Competency Testing: Auto Body Repair 14184
Teacher Occupational Competency Testing: Auto Body Repair (083) 15843
Teacher Occupational Competency Testing: Auto Mechanic 14186
Teacher Occupational Competency Testing: Automotive Body and Fender 14185
Teacher Occupational Competency Testing: Baker 14187
Teacher Occupational Competency Testing: Brick Masonry 14188
Teacher Occupational Competency Testing: Building and Home Maintenance Services (067) 15844
Teacher Occupational Competency Testing: Building Construction Occupations 14189
Teacher Occupational Competency Testing: Building Trades Maintenance 14190
Teacher Occupational Competency Testing: Cabinet Making and Millwork 14191
Teacher Occupational Competency Testing: Carpentry 14192
Teacher Occupational Competency Testing: Child Care and Guidance (081) 15845
Teacher Occupational Competency Testing: Civil Technology 14193
Teacher Occupational Competency Testing: Commercial Art 14194
Teacher Occupational Competency Testing: Commercial Photography 14195
Teacher Occupational Competency Testing: Computer Science for Secondary Teachers (080) 15846
Teacher Occupational Competency Testing: Computer Technology 14197
Teacher Occupational Competency Testing: Cosmetology 14196
Teacher Occupational Competency Testing: Diesel Engine Repair 14198
Teacher Occupational Competency Testing: Diesel Mechanic 14199
Teacher Occupational Competency Testing: Drafting Occupations 14200
Teacher Occupational Competency Testing: Electrical Construction and Maintenance (061) 15847
Teacher Occupational Competency Testing: Electrical Installation 14201
Teacher Occupational Competency Testing: Electronics Communications 14202
Teacher Occupational Competency Testing: Electronics Technology 14203
Teacher Occupational Competency Testing: Heating 14204
Teacher Occupational Competency Testing: Heavy Equipment Mechanics (069) 15848
Teacher Occupational Competency Testing: Industrial Electrician 14205
Teacher Occupational Competency Testing: Industrial Electronics 14206
Teacher Occupational Competency Testing: Machine Drafting 14207
Teacher Occupational Competency Testing: Machine Trades 14208
Teacher Occupational Competency Testing: Major Appliance Repair 14209
Teacher Occupational Competency Testing: Masonry 14210
Teacher Occupational Competency Testing: Masonry Occupations 14211
Teacher Occupational Competency Testing: Materials Handling 14212
Teacher Occupational Competency Testing: Mechanical Technology 14213
Teacher Occupational Competency Testing: Painting and Decorating 14214
Teacher Occupational Competency Testing: Plumbing 14215
Teacher Occupational Competency Testing: Power Sewing 14216
Teacher Occupational Competency Testing: Printing (Letterpress) 14218
Teacher Occupational Competency Testing: Printing (Offset) 14217
Teacher Occupational Competency Testing: Quantity Food Preparation 14219
Teacher Occupational Competency Testing: Quantity Foods 14220
Teacher Occupational Competency Testing: Radio/TV Repair 14221
Teacher Occupational Competency Testing: Refrigeration 14222
Teacher Occupational Competency Testing: Scientific Data Processing (084) 15849
Teacher Occupational Competency Testing: Sheet Metal 14223
Teacher Occupational Competency Testing: Small Engine Repair 14224
Teacher Occupational Competency Testing: Small Engine Repair 14226
Teacher Occupational Competency Testing: Textile Production/Fabrication 14225
Teacher Occupational Competency Testing: Tool and Die Making 14227
Teacher Occupational Competency Testing: Welding (021) 14228
Teacher Occupational Competency Testing: Welding (041) 15850
Teacher Occupational Competency Testing: Welding (057) 14229
Tests of General Educational Development, 1988 Revision 15711

Error Analysis (Language)
Compton Phonological Assessment of Children 15717

Essay Tests
Global Essay Test 6050
Iowa Tests of Basic Skills, Forms G and H, Levels 09-11, Writing Supplement 15911
Iowa Tests of Basic Skills, Forms G and H, Levels 12-14, Writing Supplement 15912
Mount Saint Vincent University's English Writing Competency Test 830463
Tests of Achievement and Proficiency, Level 15, Writing Supplement 15940
Tests of Achievement and Proficiency, Level 16, Writing Supplement 15941
Tests of Achievement and Proficiency, Level 17, Writing Supplement 15942
Tests of Achievement and Proficiency, Level 18, Writing Supplement 15943

Essays
Criteria for the Evaluation of Free-Response Interpretive Essays 8317

Ethics
DANTES: Ethics in America 16760

Ethnic Groups
Multiethnic Awareness Survey 13172

European History
Advanced Placement Program: European History 11245
ATP Achievement Test in European History and World Cultures 3297
Graduate Record Examinations: Subject Tests—History 3710
Major Field Achievement Tests: History 17324

Experimental Psychology
Graduate Record Examinations: Subject Tests—Psychology 3718

Expository Writing
Advanced Placement Program: English Composition and Literature 10652
College-Level Examination Program: General Examination in English Composition 2718
Scale for Evaluating Expository Writing (SEEW) 13490
Stanford Writing Assessment Program, Second Edition, Level A1 16468
Stanford Writing Assessment Program, Second Edition, Level A2 16469
Stanford Writing Assessment Program, Second Edition, Level I1 16465
Stanford Writing Assessment Program, Second Edition, Level I2 16466
Stanford Writing Assessment Program, Second Edition, Level I3 16467
Stanford Writing Assessment Program, Second Edition, Level P3 16464
Stanford Writing Assessment Program, Second Edition, Level T1 16470
Stanford Writing Assessment Program, Second Edition, Level T2 16471
Stanford Writing Assessment Program, Second Edition, Level T3 16472

Expressive Language
Analysis of the Language of Learning 15508
Assessing Semantic Skills through Everyday Themes 16110
Bankson Language Test—2 16705
Computer Managed Screening Test 13829
Diagnosis of Language Competency Inventory (DLCI) 13483
English Language Skills Profile 810663
Evaluating Communicative Competence, Revised Edition 14524
Expressive One-Word Picture Vocabulary Test—Revised 17307
Expressive One-Word Picture Vocabulary Test—Upper Extension 12388
Fullerton Language Test for Adolescents, Revised Edition 14897
Inventory of Language Abilities, Level II 12044
Language Production Scale 15792
The Patterned Elicitation Syntax Test, Revised and Expanded Edition 13740
Payan INREAL Child Language Screening Test 17444
The Primary Language Screen for Kindergarten and First Grade 16833
Sandwell Bilingual Screening Assessment; Scales for Expressive Panjabi and English 810672
Screening Test of Adolescent Language, Revised Edition 11579
Sequenced Inventory of Communication Development, Revised Edition—1984, Spanish Language Edition (Cuban) 15600
Spanish Structured Photographic Expressive Language Test—II 16836
Spanish Structured Photographic Expressive Language Test—Preschool 16835
Structured Photographic Expressive Language Test—II 14470
Structured Photographic Expressive Language Test—Preschool 14469
Test for Examining Expressive Morphology 12250
Test of Early Language Development, 2nd Edition 17541
Utah Test of Language Development—3 16606
WORD Test (Adolescent) 17183
The WORD Test—Elementary 12267
WORD Test—R (Elementary) 17182

External Degree Programs
ACT Proficiency Examination Program: Introductory Accounting 16541
ACT Proficiency Examination Program: Labor Relations 16542
ACT Proficiency Examination Program: Organizational Behavior 16543
ACT Proficiency Examination Program: Personal Management 16544
ACT Proficiency Examination Program: Principles of Management 16545
ACT Proficiency Examination Program: Principles of Marketing 16546
Regents College Examination 11677

Fabric Services
Ohio Vocational Achievement Tests: Home Economics Education, Fabric Services 11401

Fabrics
Library of Test Items: Textiles and Design, Volume 1 800235
Vocational Competency Measures: Fabric Sales 12617

Facility Inventory
Teacher Occupational Competency Testing: Materials Handling 14212

Fallacies
Test Lessons in Reading and Reasoning. 2nd Enlarged and Revised Edition 12474

Family Caregivers
Alzheimer's Disease Knowledge Test 16927

Farm Management
Ohio Vocational Achievement Tests: Agricultural Education, Farm Management 11379

Fashion Industry
Ohio Vocational Achievement Tests: Apparel and Accessories 13655
Student Occupational Competency Achievement Testing: Clothing and Textiles Management and Production 15862

Field Hockey
Belmont Measures of Athletic Performance: Field Hockey 2335

Figurative Language
Figurative Language Interpretation Test 17340
Similes Test 9846
Smith/Palmer Figurative Language Interpretation Test 13488
Test Lessons in Reading Figurative Language 12113

Finance
Library of Test Items: Commerce, Volume 1 800236

Grade 4

Aprenda: La Prueba de Logros en Espanol, Intermediate 1
16985
Aprenda: La Prueba de Logros en Espanol, Primary 3
Level 16941
California Diagnostic Mathematics Tests, Level C 15921
California Diagnostic Reading Tests, Level C 15915
Comprehensive Tests of Basic Skills. Form U, Level F
11322
Comprehensive Tests of Basic Skills, Fourth Edition, Level 13, Benchmark Tests 16904
Comprehensive Tests of Basic Skills, Fourth Edition, Level 13, Survey Tests 16915
Comprehensive Tests of Basic Skills, Fourth Edition, Level 14, Benchmark Tests 16905
Comprehensive Tests of Basic Skills, Fourth Edition, Level 14, Survey Tests 16916
Comprehensive Tests of Basic Skills, Fourth Edition, Level 15, Benchmark Tests 16906
Comprehensive Tests of Basic Skills, Fourth Edition, Level 15, Survey Tests 16917
Computer Literacy Test: Grade 04 13180
Criterion-Referenced Test: MGS/CRTest Eastern Navajo Agency, Level F 9907
Curriculum Frameworks Assessment Supplement, Level 04
17516
Curriculum Frameworks Assessment System, Level 04
17484
Educational Development Series, Revised. Level 13A
13346
Educational Development Series, Revised. Level 14A
13347
Einstein Assessment of School-Related Skills, Level 4
15513
French Achievement Test: Language Arts, Grade 4 7851
French Achievement Test: Mathematics, Grade 4 7857
Illinois Inventory of Educational Progress, Grade 04
13808
Iowa Tests of Basic Skills, Forms G and H, Level 10
14696
Knowledge Test in Nutrition for Grade 4 11659
Listening Test, Level 1 15214
Listening Test, Level 2 15215
Louisiana Reading Assessment 10435
The Maculaitis Assessment Program: 4-5 12741
MathComp: Measuring Basic Competence in Mathematics, 4 12837
Metropolitan Achievement Tests, Sixth Edition, Mathematics Diagnostic Tests, Elementary 15176
Metropolitan Achievement Tests, Sixth Edition, Reading Diagnostic Tests, Elementary 15149
National Achievement Test, Level E 16866
National Achievement Test, Level F 16867
National Achievement Tests: English Test, Grades 3-4
3580
National Tests of Basic Skills, Level F 14677
National Tests of Basic Skills, Level G 14678
Reading Yardsticks, Level 10 11516
Santa Clara County Basic Skills Test: Mathematics, Grade 04 16219
Santa Clara County Basic Skills Test: Reading, Grade 04
16220
Santa Clara County Basic Skills Test: Writing, Grade 04
16221
SCAN-TRON Reading Test, Level 09 16896
SRA Survey of Basic Skills, Level 23 14323
Stanford Achievement Test, Eighth Edition, Intermediate 1 16444
Stanford Achievement Test, Eighth Edition, Primary 3
16443
Stanford Writing Assessment Program, Second Edition, Level I1 16465
Stanford Writing Assessment Program, Second Edition, Level P3 16464
Test de Comprehension en Lecture pour Classes d'Immersion Precoce, Quatrieme Annee 830443
Tests of Achievement in Basic Skills: Mathematics—Level A 8062
Wisconsin Tests of Reading Skill Development: Comprehension, Level E 11592

Grade 5

Aprenda: La Prueba de Logros en Espanol, Intermediate 1
16985
Aprenda: La Prueba de Logros en Espanol, Intermediate 2
16937
Comprehensive Tests of Basic Skills, Fourth Edition, Level 14, Benchmark Tests 16905
Comprehensive Tests of Basic Skills, Fourth Edition, Level 14, Survey Tests 16916
Comprehensive Tests of Basic Skills, Fourth Edition, Level 15, Benchmark Tests 16906
Comprehensive Tests of Basic Skills, Fourth Edition, Level 15, Survey Tests 16917
Comprehensive Tests of Basic Skills, Fourth Edition, Level 16, Benchmark Tests 16907
Comprehensive Tests of Basic Skills, Fourth Edition, Level 16, Survey Tests 16918
Criterion-Referenced Test: MGS/CRTest Eastern Navajo Agency, Level G 9908
Curriculum Frameworks Assessment Supplement, Level 05
17517
Curriculum Frameworks Assessment System, Level 05
17485
Educational Development Series, Revised. Level 14A
13347

Educational Development Series, Revised. Level 15A
13348
Einstein Assessment of School-Related Skills, Level 5
15514
French Achievement Test: Language Arts, Grade 5 7852
French Achievement Test: Mathematics, Grade 5 7858
Iowa Tests of Basic Skills, Forms G and H, Level 11
14695
Joilet 3-Minute Speech and Language Screen 12251
Knowledge Test in Nutrition for Grade 5 11660
Listening Test, Level 2 15215
Listening Test, Level 3 15216
The Maculaitis Assessment Program: 4-5 12741
MathComp: Measuring Basic Competence in Mathematics, 5 12838
Metropolitan Achievement Tests, Sixth Edition, Mathematics Diagnostic Tests, Intermediate 15177
Metropolitan Achievement Tests, Sixth Edition, Reading Diagnostic Tests, Intermediate 15150
National Achievement Test, Level F 16867
National Achievement Test, Level G 16868
National Tests of Basic Skills, Level G 14678
National Tests of Basic Skills, Level H 14679
The Pennsylvania Assessment System: Testing for Essential Learning and Literacy Skills 16839
Reading Yardsticks, Level 11 11517
Santa Clara County Basic Skills Test: Mathematics, Grade 05 16222
Santa Clara County Basic Skills Test: Reading, Grade 05
16223
Santa Clara County Basic Skills Test: Writing, Grade 05
16224
SCAN-TRON Reading Test, Level 10 16897
SIGNALS Listening Test, Grade 05 11902
Stanford Achievement Test, Eighth Edition, Intermediate 1 16444
Stanford Achievement Test, Eighth Edition, Intermediate 2 16445
Stanford Writing Assessment Program, Second Edition, Level I1 16465
Stanford Writing Assessment Program, Second Edition, Level I2 16466
Test de Comprehension en Lecture pour Classes d'Immersion Precoce, Cinquieme Annee 830442
Wisconsin Tests of Reading Skill Development: Comprehension, Level F 11593
Wisconsin Tests of Reading Skill Development: Study Skills, Level F 7366

Grade 6

ACER Primary Reading Survey Tests; Level D 800105
ACER Tests of Basic Skills, Blue Series, Year 6 800306
Adston Mathematics Skills Series: Diagnostic Instrument in Common Fractions 11615
Adston Mathematics Skills Series: Diagnostic Instrument in Decimal Numbers 11618
Adston Mathematics Skills Series: Diagnostic Instrument in Pre-Algebra Concepts and Skills (Junior High Level)
11614
Adston Mathematics Skills Series: Diagnostic Instrument in Problem Solving 11617
Aprenda: La Prueba de Logros en Espanol, Intermediate 2
16937
Aprenda: La Prueba de Logros en Espanol, Intermediate 3
16984
California Achievement Tests, Forms E and F, Level 17
14350
California Diagnostic Mathematics Tests, Level E 15923
California Diagnostic Reading Tests, Level E 15917
Comprehensive Tests of Basic Skills, Fourth Edition, Level 15, Benchmark Tests 16906
Comprehensive Tests of Basic Skills, Fourth Edition, Level 15, Survey Tests 16917
Comprehensive Tests of Basic Skills, Fourth Edition, Level 16, Benchmark Tests 16907
Comprehensive Tests of Basic Skills, Fourth Edition, Level 16, Survey Tests 16918
Criterion-Referenced Test: MGS/CRTest Eastern Navajo Agency, Level H 9909
Curriculum Frameworks Assessment Supplement, Level 06
17518
Curriculum Frameworks Assessment System, Level 06
17486
DMI Mathematics Systems: System 1, Level G 13616
Educational Development Series, Revised. Level 15A
13348
Educational Development Series, Revised. Level 15B
13349
Grade 6 Social Studies Achievement Test 830455
Iowa Tests of Basic Skills, Forms G and H, Level 12
14694
Knowledge Test in Nutrition for Grade 6 11661
Language Assessment Scales. English Level II, Form A
11334
Language Assessment Scales. Spanish Level II, Form A
11335
Listening Test, Level 3 15216
Listening Test, Level 4 15217
The Maculaitis Assessment Program: 6-8 12742
MathComp: Measuring Basic Competence in Mathematics, 6 12839
Metropolitan Achievement Tests, Sixth Edition, Mathematics Diagnostic Tests, Intermediate 15177
Metropolitan Achievement Tests, Sixth Edition, Reading Diagnostic Tests, Intermediate 15150
National Achievement Test, Level G 16868
National Achievement Test, Level H 16869

National Achievement Tests: Geography, Grades 6-8
1153
National Achievement Tests: History and Civics Test, Grades 6-8, Short Form 1148
National Achievement Tests: Reading Test (Comprehension and Speed), Grades 6-8 3572
National Tests of Basic Skills, Level H 14679
National Tests of Basic Skills, Level I 14680
Portland Prognostic Test for Mathematics, Grade 7 4752
Reading Yardsticks, Level 12 11518
SCAN-TRON Reading Test, Level 11 16898
Social Studies Assessment Program, Grade 6 830450
SRA Survey of Basic Skills, Level 35 14325
Stanford Achievement Test, Eighth Edition, Intermediate 2 16445
Stanford Achievement Test, Eighth Edition, Intermediate 3 16446
Stanford Diagnostic Mathematics Test, Third Edition, Brown Level 13996
Stanford Diagnostic Reading Test, Third Edition, Brown Level 14028
Stanford Writing Assessment Program, Second Edition, Level I2 16466
Stanford Writing Assessment Program, Second Edition, Level I3 16467
Test de Comprehension en Lecture pour Classes d'Immersion Precoce, Sixieme Annee 830441
Test of Ability to Explain 8796
Tests de Francais, Measure Normative de 6e, 9e et 12e Annees 830447
Wisconsin Tests of Reading Skill Development: Comprehension, Level G 11594
Wisconsin Tests of Reading Skill Development: Study Skills, Level F 7366
Wisconsin Tests of Reading Skill Development: Study Skills, Level G 7367

Grade 7

Aprenda: La Prueba de Logros en Espanol, Intermediate 3
16984
California Achievement Tests, Forms E and F, Level 16
14349
Comprehensive Tests of Basic Skills, Fourth Edition, Level 16, Benchmark Tests 16907
Comprehensive Tests of Basic Skills, Fourth Edition, Level 16, Survey Tests 16918
Computer Literacy Test: Grade 07 13181
Criterion Referenced Inventory. Grade 07 Skill Clusters, Objectives, and Illustrations 11052
Criterion-Referenced Test: MGS/CRTest Eastern Navajo Agency, Level I 9910
Curriculum Frameworks Assessment System, Level 07
17487
Educational Development Series, Revised. Level 15B
13349
Educational Development Series, Revised. Level 16A
13350
Iowa Tests of Basic Skills, Forms G and H, Level 13
14693
Language Diagnostic Test—A 12826
Listening Test, Level 4 15217
National Achievement Test, Level H 16869
National Achievement Test, Level I 16870
National Tests of Basic Skills, Level I 14680
National Tests of Basic Skills, Level J 14681
Reading Yardsticks, Level 13 11519
Santa Clara County Basic Skills Test: Mathematics, Grade 07 16216
Santa Clara County Basic Skills Test: Reading, Grade 07
16217
Santa Clara County Basic Skills Test: Writing, Grade 07
16218
Stanford Achievement Test, Eighth Edition, Intermediate 3 16446
Stanford Writing Assessment Program, Second Edition, Level I3 16467
Wisconsin Mathematics Test, Grade 7 12644
Wisconsin Tests of Reading Skill Development: Study Skills, Level G 7367

Grade 8

Criterion-Referenced Test: MGS/CRTest Eastern Navajo Agency, Level J 9911
Curriculum Frameworks Assessment Supplement, Level 08
17520
Curriculum Frameworks Assessment System, Level 08
17488
Educational Development Series, Revised. Level 16A
13350
Educational Development Series, Revised. Level 16B
13351
Illinois Inventory of Educational Progress, Grade 08
13809
Iowa Tests of Basic Skills, Forms G and H, Level 14
14692
Language Diagnostic Test—A 12826
Louisiana Reading Assessment 10435
National Achievement Test, Level I 16870
National Achievement Test, Level J 16871
National Tests of Basic Skills, Level J 14681
The Pennsylvania Assessment System: Testing for Essential Learning and Literacy Skills 16839
Reading Yardsticks, Level 14 11520
Santa Clara County Basic Skills Test: Mathematics, Grade 08 16213
Santa Clara County Basic Skills Test: Reading, Grade 08
16214

Kinesthetic Perception

Knowledge Level

Labor Economics

Labor Force Development

Labor Relations

Laboratory Equipment

Language Acquisition

Language Arts

236 / Standard Spoken Usage SUBJECT INDEX

Wide Range Achievement Test, Revised 13584

Standard Spoken Usage
British Picture Vocabulary Scales 810490
The Maculaitis Assessment Program: 2-3 12740
The Maculaitis Assessment Program: 4-5 12741
The Maculaitis Assessment Program: 6-8 12742
The Maculaitis Assessment Program: 9-12 12743
The Maculaitis Assessment Program: Basic Concept Test 12738
The Maculaitis Assessment Program: K-1 12739
Screening Kit of Language Development 13360
Standard English Repetition Test 10269

Standardized Tests
Basic English Skills Test, Form C 16692
Diagnostic Achievement Battery, Second Edition 16948
Differential Ability Scales 17017
Peabody Individual Achievement Test—Revised 16741
Progressive Achievement Tests of Reading (Revised) 865027
Standardized Bible Content Tests, Form SP 17363
Standardized Bible Content Tests, Forms A-F 17362
Stanford Achievement Test, Eighth Edition, Advanced 1 16447
Stanford Achievement Test, Eighth Edition, Advanced 2 16448
Stanford Achievement Test, Eighth Edition, Intermediate 1 16444
Stanford Achievement Test, Eighth Edition, Intermediate 2 16445
Stanford Achievement Test, Eighth Edition, Intermediate 3 16446
Stanford Achievement Test, Eighth Edition, Primary 1 16441
Stanford Achievement Test, Eighth Edition, Primary 2 16442
Stanford Achievement Test, Eighth Edition, Primary 3 16443
Stanford Early School Achievement Test, Third Edition, Level 1 16439
Stanford Early School Achievement Test, Third Edition, Level 2 16440
Stanford Test of Academic Skills, Third Edition, Level 1 16449
Stanford Test of Academic Skills, Third Edition, Level 2 16450
Stanford Test of Academic Skills, Third Edition, Level 3 16451
Survey of Early Childhood Abilities 17458
Woodcock-Johnson Psycho-Educational Battery, Revised—Tests of Achievement, Standard Battery and Supplemental Battery 17209

State Departments of Education
The Pennsylvania Assessment System: Testing for Essential Learning and Literacy Skills 16839

State Programs
Country School Examinations 9433
Illinois Inventory of Educational Progress, Grade 04 13808
Illinois Inventory of Educational Progress, Grade 08 13809
Illinois Inventory of Educational Progress, Grade 11 13810
Nebraska—Assessment Battery of Essential Learning Skills 9808

State Standards
Curriculum Frameworks Assessment Supplement, Level 01 17513
Curriculum Frameworks Assessment Supplement, Level 02 17514
Curriculum Frameworks Assessment Supplement, Level 03 17515
Curriculum Frameworks Assessment Supplement, Level 04 17516
Curriculum Frameworks Assessment Supplement, Level 05 17517
Curriculum Frameworks Assessment Supplement, Level 06 17518
Curriculum Frameworks Assessment Supplement, Level 07 17519
Curriculum Frameworks Assessment Supplement, Level 08 17520
Curriculum Frameworks Assessment Supplement, Level 09/10 17521
Curriculum Frameworks Assessment Supplement, Level 11/12 17522
Curriculum Frameworks Assessment System, Level 01 17481
Curriculum Frameworks Assessment System, Level 02 17482
Curriculum Frameworks Assessment System, Level 03 17483
Curriculum Frameworks Assessment System, Level 04 17484
Curriculum Frameworks Assessment System, Level 05 17485
Curriculum Frameworks Assessment System, Level 06 17486
Curriculum Frameworks Assessment System, Level 07 17487
Curriculum Frameworks Assessment System, Level 08 17488
Curriculum Frameworks Assessment System, Level 09/10 17489
Curriculum Frameworks Assessment System, Level 11/12 17490

State Testing Programs
Math Management System, Criterion-Referenced Test 15783
New York Regents Competency Tests 11640
New York State Native Language Writing Test 11636
New York State Preliminary Competency Tests 11642
New York State Pupil Evaluation Program 11641
New York State Regents Examinations 11639
New York State Statewide Achievement Examination 11638

Statistics
ACT Proficiency Examination Program: Statistics 13930
DANTES: Principles of Statistics 16759
Graduate Record Examinations: Subject Tests—Sociology 3720

Stress (Phonology)
Test for Non-Native Comprehension of Intonation in English 17082

Stringed Instruments
Farnum String Scale 4134

Structural Analysis (Linguistics)
Microcomputer Managed Information for Criterion Referenced Objectives in Reading K-8 16499

Structural Grammar
Test of Grammatical Structure 8330

Structural Linguistics
Analysis of the Language of Learning 15508

Student Attitudes
The Knowledge about Psychology Test 7281
Learning and Study Strategies Inventory—High School Version 16977
Test of Mathematical Abilities 12272

Student Evaluation
Composition Diagnostic Test—A 12823
Composition Diagnostic Test—B 12824
Composition Diagnostic Test—C 12825
Comprehension Survey for Reading 12830
Intermediate Individual Reading Skills Checklist 13148
Junior High Individual Reading Skills Checklist 13149
Language Diagnostic Test—B 12827
Language Diagnostic Test—C 12828
Observation Checklist for Reading 12829
Primary Individual Reading Skills Checklist 13150
Vocational Competency Measures; Electronic Technician 12364

Student Improvement
Gillingham-Childs Phonics Proficiency Scales: Series I Basic Reading and Spelling 4032

Student Interests
Content Inventories: English, Social Studies, Science 14596

Student Motivation
Learning and Study Strategies Inventory—High School Version 16977

Student Needs
ACT ASSET Program 14657

Student Placement
Advanced Placement Program; Economics, Macroeconomics 16550
Advanced Placement Program; Economics, Microeconomics 16549
Alemany English Second Language Placement Test, Revised 12736
Ber-Sil Spanish Test: Elementary Level, 1987 Revision 15561
Botel Reading Inventory 10951
CAP Writing Assessment 16330
Computerized Placement Tests—Algebra 17239
Computerized Placement Tests—Arithmetic 17238
Computerized Placement Tests—College Level Mathematics 17240
Computerized Placement Tests—Reading Comprehension 17236
Computerized Placement Tests—Sentence Skills 17237
COMPUTEST: ESL Version 2.5 17000
COMPUTEST: F CAPE 16999
COMPUTEST: G-CAPE 16998
COMPUTEST: S CAPE 16997
Content Inventories: English, Social Studies, Science 14596
C.U.B.E. Math Placement Inventory 13536
Descriptive Tests of Language Skills, Revised 16066
Descriptive Tests of Mathematics Skills, Revised 16067
Developmental Reading: Orientation and Placement Tests, Fundamental Stage: Advanced, Steps 07-30 9324
Developmental Reading: Orientation and Placement Tests, Fundamental Stage: Primary, Steps 04-30 9323
English Placement Test 11486
Examen de Lectura en Espanol 10163
Examen de Lenguaje en Espanol 10164
French Computer Adaptive Placement Exam 16101
Henderson-Moriarty ESL/Literacy Placement Test 12698
Informal Reading Comprehension Placement Test 13775
Language Assessment Battery, 1982 14112
Language Assessment Scales, Reading and Writing, Level 1 15629
Language Assessment Scales, Reading and Writing, Level 2 15630
Language Assessment Scales, Reading and Writing, Level 3 15631
Leamos: Orientation and Placement Tests, Fundamental Stage: Primary, Steps 04-15 9250
MAA Placement Test Program, Advanced Algebra Test, AA 15931
MAA Placement Test Program, Basic Algebra Test, BA 15933
MAA Placement Test Program, Basic and Advanced Algebra Test, A 15932
MAA Placement Test Program Basic Skills Test, A-SK 15934
MAA Placement Test Program, Calculus Readiness Test, CR 15936
MAA Placement Test Program, Trigonometry/Elementary Functions Test T 15939
The Maculaitis Assessment Program: 2-3 12740
The Maculaitis Assessment Program: 4-5 12741
The Maculaitis Assessment Program: 6-8 12742
The Maculaitis Assessment Program: 9-12 12743
The Maculaitis Assessment Program: Basic Concept Test 12738
The Maculaitis Assessment Program: K-1 12739
MAPS: College Entry Level Assessment 14793
National German Examination for High School Students 11635
New Jersey College Basic Skills Placement Test 11904
Oral English/Spanish Proficiency Placement Test 6113
Oral Language Proficiency Scale 10162
Oral Placement Test 10632
Reading Management System: Elementary Reading Placement Test, Revised Edition, January 1976 8692
Spanish Computer Adaptive Placement Exam 16100
Standard Test of Reading Effectiveness (STORE), Forms A, B, C 13489
Standardized Bible Content Tests 69
STS High School Placement Test 1841
Sucher-Allred Group Reading Placement Test 16247
Test of English Proficiency Level 14628
Teste de Lingua Portuguesa II 15198
Teste de Matematica II 15197
Western Michigan University English Usage Skills Test, Forms A and B 16183
Western Michigan University English Usage Skills Test, Forms A and B 16184
Written Language Assessment 16729
Zip Test 4948

Study Guides
ACT Proficiency Examination Program: Educational Psychology 8140
ACT Proficiency Examination Program: Foundations of Gerontology 11881
ACT Proficiency Examination Program: Fundamentals of Nursing 8145
ACT Proficiency Examination Program: Health Restoration, Area I 11882
ACT Proficiency Examination Program: Health Restoration, Area II 11883
ACT Proficiency Examination Program: Health Support, Area I 11884
ACT Proficiency Examination Program: Health Support, Area II 11885
ACT Proficiency Examination Program: Maternal and Child Nursing: Associate Degree 8157
ACT Proficiency Examination Program: Maternal and Child Nursing: Baccalaureate Degree 8158
ACT Proficiency Examination Program: Occupational Strategy, Nursing 8160
ACT Proficiency Examination Program: Physical Geology 11886
ACT Proficiency Examination Program: Professional Strategies, Nursing 11887
ACT Proficiency Examination Program: Psychiatric/Mental Health Nursing 8165
ACT Proficiency Examination Program: Reading Instruction in the Elementary School 8166

Study Skills
Bristol Achievement Tests, Level 1. Second Edition 810517
Bristol Achievement Tests, Level 2. Second Edition 810518
Bristol Achievement Tests, Level 3. Second Edition 810519
Learning and Study Strategies Inventory—High School Version 16977
Prueba de Lenguaje Santillana, Level G 10747
Prueba de Lenguaje Santillana, Level H 10748
Prueba de Lenguaje Santillana, Level I 10749
Prueba de Lenguaje Santillana, Level J 10750
Wisconsin Tests of Reading Skill Development: Study Skills, Level A 7361
Wisconsin Tests of Reading Skill Development: Study Skills, Level B 7362
Wisconsin Tests of Reading Skill Development: Study Skills, Level C 7363
Wisconsin Tests of Reading Skill Development: Study Skills, Level D 7364
Wisconsin Tests of Reading Skill Development: Study Skills, Level E 7365

AUTHOR INDEX

TITLE INDEX